CASES, MATERIALS AND PROBLEMS ON
SPORTS AND THE LAW

By

Paul C. Weiler
Henry J. Friendly Professor of Law
Harvard Law School

Gary R. Roberts
Vice Dean and Professor of Law
Tulane Law School

AMERICAN CASEBOOK SERIES®

WEST PUBLISHING CO.
ST. PAUL, MINN., 1993

COPYRIGHT © 1993 By WEST PUBLISHING CO.
610 Opperman Drive
P.O. Box 64526
St. Paul, MN 55164–0526
1–800–328–9352

Library of Congress Cataloging-in-Publication Data
Weiler, Paul C.
    Cases, materials and problems on sports and the law / by Paul C.
Weiler, Gary R. Roberts.
        p.   cm. — (American casebook series)
    Includes index.
    ISBN 0–314–02162–0
    1. Sports—Law and legislation—United States—Cases.
I. Roberts, Gary R., 1948–   . II. Title. III. Series.
KF3989.A7W42 1993
344.73′099—dc20
[347.30499]   93–15363
                                                              CIP

ISBN 0–314–02162–0

TEXT IS PRINTED ON 10% POST CONSUMER RECYCLED PAPER   PRINTED WITH SOY INK

(W. & R.) Sports Law ACB
1st Reprint—1994

Preface

Over the last several years, more and more of the nation's sports pages have been devoted to news about lawsuits. In 1992, for example, we read about litigation regarding free agency in football, restrictions on superstation broadcasts in basketball, realignment of National League teams in baseball, and the NCAA's treatment of Jerry Tarkanian and the University of Nevada at Las Vegas in college basketball. Undoubtedly most sports fans deplore spending their time learning about the thrill of victory and agony of defeat in the courtroom, rather than on the playing field.

We hope our readers will suspend judgment until the end of this book about whether that initial reaction is wholly justified. But keep in mind this parallel phenomenon. Until the resignation of Fay Vincent in September 1992, the commissioners in all the major team sports were lawyers. So also were the heads of two of the players' associations (in baseball and hockey), while the other two associations (in football and basketball) were first turned into unions by their lawyer-leaders at the time. Law is not an external phenomenon that only occasionally comes into contact with the world of sports. Law is built right into the very structure of the game.

In this book we present a systematic picture of how the law influences the shape of sports. We emphasize here the title of this book—Sports *and* the Law. The common phrase "Sports Law" is a misnomer. Sports is a form of human activity and an increasingly lucrative enterprise; it is not a field of law. The conduct of sports is governed by the entire legal system—often in surprising ways. The bodies of law most often invoked are the common law of contracts and torts and the statutory law of labor and antitrust. But as we worked through the content of this book, we were struck by how significant were constitutional and civil rights law, for example, or workers' compensation and disability law, or taxation, communications, and eminent domain law.

Not all of the litigation that happens to involve a sports figure or sports franchise belongs in a book like this. For example, there is nothing special about the criminal law of rape that was used in the trial and conviction of a sports figure such as Mike Tyson. The principle that guided us in the design of this book was to present distinctive challenges that the world of sport poses to the legal system and intriguing lessons one could draw for the broader legal system from the way the law grapples with peculiar problems posed by sports. For example, how should the law of assault and battery apply to what happens in a hockey rink or on a football field?

v

The central feature of sports is its distinctive blend of competition and cooperation. The essence of sports is fierce competition for victory that inspires each participant to new heights of athletic accomplishment. But to make sporting contests available to, let alone enjoyable for, both participants and spectators, there must be an agreed-upon structure of rules by which the games are conducted and, just as important, a reasonable balance in playing strength that gives each side a fair chance of winning. Devising the rules that will promote balance on the playing field requires a considerable measure of cooperation off the field. To facilitate such cooperation, professional sports have evolved into leagues headed by commissioners, individual sports into tours or associations run by executive directors, and intercollegiate sports into a National Collegiate Athletic Association (NCAA) whose 400-page manual is as technical and detailed as the Internal Revenue Code.

Historically, the private law of each sport has been fashioned by the owners in professional team sports, university officials in intercollegiate sports, and federations in individual sports. Much of the time these parties share a common vision of the best interests of the game with players trying to win a championship and fans cheering for their favorite teams. Unsurprisingly, though, those in charge occasionally exhibit the all-too-human tendency to favor their own interests when these conflict with the interests of other constituencies—of fans who want more teams in new cities and more games on free television and players who want a larger share of the financial pie produced by fan enthusiasm.

This book tells the story of what happens when the private law of owners (or universities or athletic associations) is challenged by players, broadcasters, and local communities (and occasionally even by disgruntled owners) who try to win a better outcome in court. The two of us who collaborated on this work came to this field from different legal specialties and often with different points of view about whether the public law elaborated by judges has done a better job in serving the "best interests" of the game than the sport's private law elaborated by commissioners. But we found ourselves in remarkably close agreement about what are the key questions and the relevant arguments in understanding and appraising the role of law in sports.

Perhaps even more important than what participants in sports gain from law are the lessons that the use of law in sports provides for the broader legal and political community. If "Sports and the Law" is to be considered a worthwhile field of study in a university law school, it must provide both provocative examples and illuminating lessons about important topics such as drug policies for the nation's workplaces, racial and gender equality, the value and limits of competitive markets fostered by antitrust law and collective bargaining fostered by labor law, and methods of compensating and preventing personal injury. Indeed, the study of sports and the law provides interesting insights into the very definition of law and the many-sided role the legal system plays in shaping society's institutions. A growing body of scholarly work—not just in law, but also in philosophy, economics, and other social sciences—is now exploring precisely these kinds of questions about the world of sports. This book is our effort to distill the scholarly as well as judicial analysis of the legal issues into a format that will provide a valuable educational experience for students—and, we hope, their teachers.[1]

———

While working on this project over the last four years, we have had the advice of a good many colleagues, too numerous to list by name here. We do want to mention and thank Ken Shropshire and Lee Goldman who read a draft of the entire manuscript in the summer of 1992 and made a number of valuable suggestions for improving the final version.

The most important contribution to the success of this project, though, came from students and staff at our respective law schools. Gary Roberts' research assistants at Tulane, David Boyle, Pamela Jones, and Martin Hoffman, gathered many of the cases for us, and Roberts' administrative assistant, Michele Saunders, coordinated compilation of the statutory and documentary materials that are incorporated in the Supplement. Paul Weiler's Harvard Law students in his Sports and the Law seminar over the last several years wrote detailed comments about the successive drafts of this book. Weiler also had the benefit of in-depth research assistance from the following students: Jonathan Miller on Chapter 1; George Kokkines on Chapters 3, 5, 8 and 9; Ed Rippey on Chapters 4 and 8; James Garland on Chapters 6 and 10; Alex Laats on Chapter 7; Mitch Rubin on Chapter 8; Jackie Scott on Chapter 9; Gary Mitchell on Chapter 10; Whitney Fox on Chapter 11 and Vikki Wulf on Chapter 11. Pamela Jones, Martin Hoffman, Ed Rippey and James Garland proofread the manuscript and Florrie Darwin, Ed Rippey and James Garland compiled the Index.

Our most important debts are owed to Eric Reifschneider and Sylvia Baldwin. Eric took the skills he had honed as Executive Editor of the Harvard Law Review, and worked throughout all 1992—before and after he graduated from Law School—to edit painstakingly the entire manuscript and contribute a host of valuable insights to the text. Sylvia Baldwin, Weiler's secretary at Harvard, brought the manuscript through its four different versions, each longer than its predecessor, and was invaluable in ensuring that the contributions coming from all these sources fitted properly together.

To everyone who helped us bring this project to fruition, and especially to Sylvia and Eric, we offer our heart-felt gratitude.

*

———

1. In footnotes throughout the book, we have attempted to provide reasonably comprehensive references to the relevant scholarly literature, both legal and non-legal. To distinguish our footnote references from the footnotes we have reproduced from judicial opinion, we used this format: our footnotes are in two columns and judicial footnotes are in single columns across the page.

Summary of Contents

Table of Contents

*

Table of Cases

The principal cases are in bold type. Cases cited or discussed in the text are roman type. References are to pages. Cases cited in principal cases and within other quoted materials are not included.

xix

CASES, MATERIALS AND PROBLEMS ON
SPORTS AND THE LAW

*

Chapter One

THE OFFICE OF THE COMMISSIONER AND THE BEST INTERESTS OF THE SPORT

One of the unique features of sports as a social, economic, and legal institution is the office of commissioner of the league.[1] In addition to performing the duties of the league's chief executive officer—establishing schedules, supervising officials, negotiating network television contracts, and organizing the league championships—the commissioner, from the origins of this role in baseball in the early 1920s, has functioned as supreme voice of the "best interests" of the sport, empowered to resolve all disputes on this score among clubs, players, managers, and other participants in the game.

The commissioner's office and its aspiration towards the sport's "best interests" were at the center of a number of *causes celebres* that have recently dominated the sports pages over the last several years—for example, George Steinbrenner's removal as managing partner of the New York Yankees and the notorious locker room incident involving Lisa Olson, a Boston Herald sports writer, and several New England Patriots football players. More and more of these disputes have filtered into the courts as aggrieved parties challenge the source and scope of the commissioner's authority, the procedures followed, and the penalties meted out. The cases and materials in this chapter not only

1. Though there is no systematic scholarly treatment of this subject, several popular biographies and histories provide illuminating glimpses of the history and the issues covered in this chapter: e.g., J.G. Taylor Spink, *Judge Landis and 25 Years of Baseball* (St. Louis, Mo.: Sporting News Press, 1974); Harold Seymour, *Baseball: The Golden Age* (New York: Oxford, 1971); Red Barber, *1947: When All Hell Broke Loose in Baseball* (New York: DaCapo, 1982); Bowie Kuhn, *Hardball: The Education of a Baseball Commissioner* (New York: Time Books, 1987); and David Harris, *The League: The Rise and Decline of the NFL* (New York: Bantam Books, 1986). A detailed and valuable account of the evolution of the structure of baseball up to 1950, including the creation and definition of the office of the commissioner, can be found in the Report of the Subcommittee on Study of Monopoly Power of the Committee of the Judiciary, 82nd Congress, *Organized Baseball* (Washington D.C., 1952) (Celler Report).

explore the possible grounds for and likely success of such legal challenges, but also pose the fundamental question of what is the appropriate division between private and public authority in addressing gambling, drug use, women in the locker room, AIDS, and other controversies that have bedeviled modern sports.

A. PETE ROSE v. BART GIAMATTI [2]

No case raised these issues concerning the integrity of the game so dramatically as the "collision at home plate" between baseball Commissioner Bartlett Giamatti and baseball superstar Pete Rose.[3] The human dimensions of this tragic affair have been the subject of several books and countless articles. Only the key legal events will be recounted here. In the early winter of 1989, rumors began to filter into the Commissioner's Office that Rose, then manager of the Cincinnati Reds, had been betting on baseball games, even on games involving his own team. If true, that action would have violated a sixty-year-old Major League Rule that required a one-year suspension for anyone betting on baseball and a lifetime ban for betting on a game involving one's own team. Accordingly, on February 23, newly-selected Commissioner Giamatti hired John Dowd, a Washington lawyer, to investigate this allegation. The Commissioner was acting under the authority granted him by Article I of the "Major League Agreement" between all the clubs making up major league baseball—baseball's "constitution" that now has its equivalents in the National Football League, the National Basketball Association, and the National Hockey League.

Article I, § 2, reads:

The functions of the Commissioner shall be as follows:

(a) To investigate, either upon complaint or upon his own initiative, any act, transaction or practice charged, alleged or suspected to be not in the best interests of the national game of Baseball, with authority to summon persons and to order the production of documents and, in cases of refusal to appear or produce, to impose such penalties as are hereinafter provided;

(b) To determine, after investigation, what preventive, remedial or punitive action is appropriate in the premises, and to take such action either against Major Leagues, Major League Clubs, or individuals, as the case may be;

2. The key judicial decision quoted in the text is *Rose v. Giamatti*, 721 F.Supp. 906 (S.D.Ohio 1989). See also Matthew Pachman, *Limits on the Discretionary Powers of Professional Sports Commissioners: A Historical and Legal Analysis of Issues Raised by the Pete Rose Controversy*, 76 Virginia L. Rev. 1409 (1990).

3. See James Reston Jr., *Collision at Home Plate: The Lives of Pete Rose and Bart Giamatti*, (New York: Burlingame Books, 1991). Another useful account of this case is Michael Y. Sokolove, *Hustle: The Myth, Life, and Lies of Pete Rose* (New York: Simon and Schuster, 2d. ed. 1992).

(c) To hear, and determine finally, any dispute between the Major Leagues which may be certified to him for determination by the President of either Major League;

(d) To formulate, and from time to time announce, the rules of procedure to be observed by the Commissioner and all other parties in connection with the discharge of his duties. Such rules shall always recognize the right of any party and interest to appear before the Commissioner and be heard and the right of the Presidents of the two Major Leagues to be heard upon any matter affecting interests of the Major Leagues, or either of them.

After three months of investigating and interviewing some 40 witnesses, including taking sworn statements from Rose and the two key informants against him, Ron Peters and Paul Janszen, in early May Dowd delivered to Giamatti a 225–page report (with seven volumes of evidence and exhibits) that concluded with Dowd's judgment that Rose had regularly bet on Reds' games (although apparently Rose always bet on his Reds to win). Giamatti immediately sent this report to Rose and his lawyers and scheduled Rose's hearing before him for late June.

On April 18, however, Giamatti had sent a letter to U.S. District Judge Carl Rubin, who was preparing to sentence Peters for federal drug and income tax offenses. Giamatti stated in his letter that Peters had been "candid, forthright and truthful" in providing "critical sworn testimony" about Rose. The Cincinnati-based Judge Rubin, an avowed Reds fan and highly exercised by what he termed the Commissioner's "vendetta against Pete Rose," sent a copy of the letter to Reuven Katz, Rose's principal lawyer. Armed with this letter, Katz filed suit in state court to prohibit Giamatti from going any further with the disciplinary proceeding. The contention was that Giamatti had prejudged the facts of the case and thus had denied Rose his right to a proceeding conducted with "due regard for all the principles of natural justice and fair play," as the Commissioner's own rules required. After Rose won a controversial 10–day restraining order from state court Judge Norbert Nadel, Giamatti sought to remove the case to federal district court on diversity of citizenship grounds.

In arguing for removal, the Commissioner's counsel asserted that this case should be heard only by a "national tribunal":

In the state court in Cincinnati, I need not describe Mr. Rose's standing. He is a local hero, perhaps the first citizen of Cincinnati. And Commissioner Giamatti is viewed suspiciously as a foreigner from New York, trapped in an ivory tower, and accused of bias by Mr. Rose. Your Honor, this is a textbook example of why diversity jurisdiction was created in the Federal Courts and why it exists to this very day.

But that removal could be obtained only if this case were deemed to be a dispute just between Rose, a citizen of Ohio, and Giamatti, a citizen of New York. If the Cincinnati Reds, also a citizen of Ohio in the eyes of the law, were considered a real party to this conflict, then the complete diversity of citizenship required for federal jurisdiction would be lacking. In applying the arcane rules of federal versus state court jurisdiction, the judicial opinion in *Rose v. Giamatti*, 721 F.Supp. 906, 917 laid bare "the reality ... that Major League Baseball is a unique organization ... [with] extraordinary power invested in the Commissioner."

Rose's argument was quite simple. Rose was the manager of the Reds, under a contract paying him $500,000 a year, a contract whose benefits from the Reds he was in grave danger of losing because of Giamatti's violation of procedural fairness towards him. Clearly, then, the Reds were an appropriate party in Rose's lawsuit to prevent that happening.

The commissioner's answer, which the federal court accepted, was that the contract between Rose and the Reds provided that "the Major League and Professional Baseball Agreements and Rules and all amendments thereto hereafter adopted, are hereby made a part of this contract." This feature of Rose's personal employment contract stemmed from the following provision of the Major League Agreement:

> The form of players' contract to be used by the Major Leagues, and all contracts between Major Leagues or Clubs and their officers and employees, shall contain a clause by which the parties agree to submit themselves to the discipline of the Commissioner, and to accept his decisions rendered in accordance with this Agreement.

The commissioner's disciplinary authority was reinforced by the constituent members' further agreement to "be finally and unappealably bound" by all the disciplinary decisions of the commissioner, and to "waive such right of recourse to the courts as would otherwise have existed in their favor." The judge read this network of contractual relationships as establishing a commissioner's office wielding judicial power totally independent of control by either the Reds individually or the 26 clubs collectively. (As the judge observed, the constitution ordained that "neither the Commissioner's powers nor his compensation may be diminished during his term of office.") That meant that only Rose and Giamatti were real parties to this case, which hence was properly removable to the federal judicial arena.

This procedural ruling came down on July 31. The district judge granted Rose leave to file an interlocutory appeal, but his motion was denied by the Sixth Circuit on August 17. Perhaps because he was then facing even more pressing legal problems with the Internal Revenue Service, Rose agreed on August 23 to settle the case on the terms that Rose withdraw his suit, accept the Commissioner's jurisdiction and penalty, but neither admit nor deny having bet on baseball. As penalty, Giamatti declared Rose permanently ineligible to associate with any major or minor league baseball club. (After a year, however, Rose would be entitled to apply to the commissioner for termination of this lifetime ban.) A few days later, Giamatti was dead of a heart attack, succeeded in office by his counsel and close friend, Francis

"Fay" Vincent. A few months later, Rose went to jail for income tax fraud—in particular, for concealing large cash payments from baseball autograph shows (money that Rose had used to cover his large gambling losses).

The Rose affair presents in stark relief baseball's (and other team sports') historic abhorrence of gambling. The case thus poses the question whether it is truly in the best interests of the sport to ban the all-time hit leader from the game (and the Hall of Fame) for betting on his own team to win. How does this conduct compare in legal and moral turpitude with other offenses committed by professional athletes—for example, Rose's own income tax evasion (let alone Mike Tyson's rape)?

An underlying institutional question is why authority over this issue is reserved to the league speaking through its commissioner, rather than left for direct dealings between individual clubs and their managers and players. As we will see in the next several chapters, one of the characteristics that distinguishes sports from other industries is that the clubs make up a league that speaks through a commissioner, and that the league pursues objectives that are not necessarily the same as those of individual clubs and their players and fans. A crucial question, then, is whether, when they act collectively as a league, the owners should be treated as a single entity for purposes of contract, antitrust, labor, and other substantive areas of the law.

This legal question brings us to the most fundamental issue posed by *Rose v. Giamatti*—the constitutional theme that runs through the entire field of sports and the law. To what extent should public law, speaking through judges, venture to overturn decisions made by private leagues, speaking through their commissioners? The challenge to the law is captured by this passage from George Will's review of *Collision at Home Plate*:[4]

> Reston does not do justice to how close the Rose case came to becoming another case of a familiar political pathology. Yet another functioning American institution—the commissioner's office—almost became a victim of judicial overreaching. Today's courts have an unhealthy itch to supervise and fine-tune virtually every equity judgment in American life. Rose's legal strategy was to find a judge willing to insinuate himself into baseball's disciplinary procedures. If Rose had succeeded, the commissioner's office would have been irreparably damaged. Its core function, which is disciplinary, would permanently have been put in question. Another of civil society's intermediary associations—those that stand between the individual and the state—would have been broken to the saddle of government. A nanny-like judiciary would henceforth have made the commissioner's office negligible—another hitherto private institution permeated by state power.

4. George Will, *Foul Ball*, N.Y. Rev. of Books, June 27, 1991, at 31, 34.

Keep this journalistic version of the "public-private" distinction [5] in mind as you read the entire record presented in this book of the law's involvement in the world of sports.

B. THE LEGAL SCOPE OF THE COMMISSIONER'S AUTHORITY

In fact, Commissioner Giamatti did not assert quite the sweeping insulation from judicial control proclaimed by George Will.   In oral argument, Giamatti's counsel stated that the commissioner "has to answer in court as to whether his conduct comported with whatever is required by a court respecting due process."   (Was counsel correct to concede that the commissioner of a private sports league must observe judicial "due process" in his deliberations and decision?)   As we have seen, the reason given why the commissioner had to answer to a federal, rather than a state, court is that the commissioner did not have to answer to the Reds.   The source and scope of any such judicial scrutiny can be traced in the following cases.   As you read each of the decisions reproduced in this chapter, look for and reflect upon the answers to the following questions:

1.   What is the source of the commissioner's legal authority to act in the given case?   Why is this authority given to the commissioner rather than to an individual club, to an outside arbitrator, or to a public official or judge?

2.   What is the scope of the commissioner's power—that is, under the asserted source of authority, in what situations is the commissioner empowered to take action in cases of this type?

3.   What procedures should the commissioner follow in deciding on the course of action?   What is the source of these procedural requirements?

4.   If there are factual doubts or disputes, what standard of proof should the commissioner employ in the given case—reasonable suspicion, preponderance of the evidence, clear and convincing evidence, or proof beyond a reasonable doubt?

5.   What remedy or penalty may the commissioner employ in the specific case?

6.   Finally, and most importantly, what is (what should be) the jurisdiction of a court (or an arbitrator) to review the commissioner's action—i.e., the commissioner's answers to questions 2 through 5.   What legal theories can legitimately be employed to challenge the action?   What standard of review will a court use in these legal challenges?

---

5. This distinction is, of course, one of the principal targets of the entire Critical Legal Studies movement. See Mark Kel- man, *A Guide to Critical Legal Studies* 102–09, 253–57, 271–73 (Cambridge, Mass.: Harvard University Press, 1987).

The legal starting point is *American League Baseball Club of New York (Yankees) v. Johnson*, 109 Misc. 138, 179 N.Y.S. 498 (N.Y.1919). This litigation occurred near the end of the National Commission era in major league governance, during which A.L. President Byron "Ban" Johnson was acknowledged as the strongest figure in the game.[6] Carl Mays, a pitcher for the Boston Red Sox, walked off the field in the middle of a game, and went fishing the next day. While Johnson waited for the Red Sox to take disciplinary action, Sox owner Harry Frazee instead sold Mays to the Yankees (this being a rehearsal for the next such transaction between the two clubs, involving Babe Ruth that winter). When he learned of the sale, Johnson himself suspended Mays for "deserting his club and breaking contract." Furious at losing Mays' services in the midst of the pennant race, the Yankees sued Johnson, calling him an "unmolested despot." The case was heard by then Judge, later Senator, Robert Wagner of New York, who eventually authored the National Labor Relations Act of 1935 which was used by Players Association leader, Marvin Miller, to transform baseball in the 1970s.

Judge Wagner's decision began by stating:

It is undisputed, and, indeed, a matter of common knowledge, that the commercialization of baseball is a highly profitable undertaking, rendering lucrative returns to the member clubs, to their stockholders, and to their employees. Large capital is invested in the enterprise, and the property representative of this capital consists principally of contracts with individual players, together with the reputation of the club for skill and ability in playing the game. Suspension of a player, therefore, not only interferes with his individual contract, but may also interfere with the reputation and collective ability of the club. Inasmuch as the leading clubs of the league and their players are entitled at the end of the season to certain rights and privileges which are unquestionably to be deemed property rights, this interference with an individual player would confuse and possibly destroy the rights of the respective clubs and their players, for the validity of the games in which Mays participated might be questioned.

Johnson had asserted that the following language of section 20 of the league constitution gave him authority for his action:

The president, in the performance of his duties, shall have the power to impose fines or penalties, in the way of suspension or otherwise, upon any manager or player who, in his opinion, has been guilty of conduct detrimental to the general welfare of the game.

The Yankees responded, and Judge Wagner agreed, that the wording of section 24 assigned responsibility for these questions to the individual team:

---

6. See Seymour, *Baseball: The Golden Age*, note 1 above, at 264–68.

> Each club belonging to this league shall have the right to regulate its own affairs, to establish its own rules, and to discipline, punish, suspend or expel its manager, players or other employees, and these powers shall not be limited to cases of dishonest play or open insubordination, but shall include all questions of carelessness, indifference, or other conduct of the player that may be regarded by the club as prejudicial to its interest, but not in conflict with any provision of the National Agreement or this constitution.

In addition, the President had the authority to exercise disciplinary authority only "in the performance of his duties," which the judge characterized as follows:

> Under these rules it is the right and duty of the president to regulate the actual playing of the game on the field and to enforce the rules instituted for the governing of the game. Doubtless his powers would extend to the discipline of players for any infringement of these rules upon the field, or for an overt act committed by a player on the field in violation of the rules. Beyond that power, however, it does not seem that the president may proceed, for under the constitution he is given power to discipline only in the performance of his duties, and his duties are only such as are set forth in the constitution and playing rules.
>
> The offense of which Mays was accused was obviously not one of those embraced within the prohibition of these rules. It was not an overt act committed on the field.

Although that literal reading of the constitution did not square with historical practice, the judge stated:

> On behalf of the defendant, contention is made that many times in the past the defendant Johnson had exercised power similar to that which he claims the right to exercise under the present circumstances, that his jurisdiction to make orders similar to the one now in dispute has never been questioned, and that the parties to a contract will be bound by the construction which their conduct and acquiescence have placed upon it. Although courts have placed great weight on the construction which parties have put upon contracts existing between them, such considerations must never violate the fundamental concepts of justice. If the original act was unauthorized, repetition does not invest the act with authority. If the construction did not convey power to the president, he cannot prescriptively acquire power by continual usurpation. If the opposite were true he would, in effect, effectuate an amendment of the constitution by usurpation. In his immortal and always useful Farewell Address, Washington said:
>
>> "If in the opinion of the people the distribution or modification of the constitutional powers be in any particular wrong, let it be corrected by an amendment in the way which the Constitution designates, but let there be no change by usurpation."

So in this case there can be no change by usurpation. The structure of precedents must fall, unless laid on the foundation of authority.

Accordingly, Judge Wagner granted a permanent injunction against Mays' suspension. The Yankees' celebratory press release stated that "our fight has not been for Mays alone, but to safeguard the vested property rights of the individual club-owners against the continual encroachments on club rights by the president, who has never been clothed with the powers that he has taken unto himself."

Ironically, though, the *Johnson* decision was handed down just after completion of the infamous 1919 World Series, in which gamblers had bribed White Sox players to fix the games. When word of the "Black Sox" scandal emerged a year later, both fan and club owners felt that the source of the problem was the lax disciplinary approach of the National Commission (composed of the two league presidents and a chairman selected by the two of them). The owners decided to dismantle the tripartite commission and replace it with a single, powerful commissioner. The man tagged for that position was Kenesaw Mountain Landis, a 38–year–old federal judge in Chicago who had initially caught the owners' eye with his favorable handling of the Federal League antitrust suit a few years earlier (see Chapter 2). Landis agreed to take this new $50,000 per year position only if the Major League Agreement was rewritten to give the commissioner the sweeping powers described in *Rose v. Giamatti*.

There was one reported legal challenge to Landis' authority. Apparently a player named Fred Bennett had been transferred several times between the St. Louis Browns and several minor league teams, but all the clubs were secretly controlled by Browns' owner Phil Ball. When Landis learned of the inter-club relationship, he refused to approve this latest Browns' transaction with the Milwaukee club, and declared Bennett a free agent. The resulting lawsuit revealed a very different judicial attitude to commissioner authority than we saw in the *Johnson* case.

MILWAUKEE AM. ASS'N. v. LANDIS

United States District Court, Northern District of Illinois, 1931.

49 F.2d 298.

LINDLEY, DISTRICT JUDGE.

* * *

Under the Major League agreement the office of commissioner was created, and his functions were defined.... He was given jurisdiction to hear and determine finally any disputes between leagues and clubs or to which a player might be a party, certified to him, and authorized, in case of "conduct detrimental to baseball," to impose punishment and pursue appropriate legal remedies; to determine finally a disagreement over any proposed amendment to the rules; and "to take such other steps as he might deem necessary and proper in the interest and morale of the players and the honor of the game." Optional agreements with players were defined and assignments thereof required to be filed with, and approved by, the commissioner. The parties agreed to abide by the decisions of the latter and the discipline imposed by him under the agreement and severally waived right of recourse to the courts. Similar covenants appear in the Major–Minor agreement, the National Association agreement and the uniform contracts with players.

The Major–Minor League agreement recognizes the office of commissioner and the jurisdiction aforesaid and provides that, in case of any dispute between any Major club and any Minor club, the disputants may certify the dispute to the commissioner for decision, and that his determination shall be final.

The various agreements and rules constituting a complete code for, or charter and by-laws of, organized baseball in America, disclose a clear intent upon the part of the parties to endow the commissioner with all the attributes of a benevolent but absolute despot and all the disciplinary powers of the proverbial *pater familias*.

* * *

The parties endowed the commissioner with wide powers and discretion to hear controversies that might be submitted to him and of his own initiative to observe, investigate and take such action as necessary to secure observance of the provisions of the agreements and rules, promotion of the expressed ideals of, and prevention of conduct detrimental to, baseball. The code is expressly designed and intended to foster keen, clean competition in the sport of baseball, to preserve discipline and a high standard of morale, to produce an equality of conditions necessary to the promotion of keen competition and to protect players against clubs, clubs against players, and clubs against clubs.

* * *

Certain acts are specified as detrimental to baseball, but it is expressly provided that nothing contained in the code shall be construed as exclusively defining or otherwise limiting acts, practices or conduct detrimental to baseball. It is contended that this phrase should be so construed as to include only such conduct as is similar to that expressly mentioned. However, the provisions are so unlimited in character that we can conclude only that the parties did not intend so to limit the meaning of conduct detrimental to baseball, but intended to vest in the commissioner jurisdiction to prevent any conduct destructive of the aims of the code. Apparently it was the intent of the parties to make the commissioner an arbiter, whose decisions made in good faith, upon evidence, upon all questions relating to the purpose of the organization and all conduct detrimental thereto, should be absolutely binding. So great was the parties' confidence in the man selected for

Note

the position and so great the trust placed in him that certain of the
agreements were to continue only so long as he should remain commissioner.

Plaintiffs contend that the commissioner has no power to declare a
player a free agent. In his answer, the commissioner states that it is
his view that, by reason of the alleged breach of the code by plaintiffs
and their denial of Bennett's rights, plaintiffs have made it his duty to
declare Bennett absolved from any contractual obligations which he
may have had with either plaintiff and to declare him a free agent.
Obviously declaring Bennett a free agent is a mere declaration of legal
effect, that is, the result of finding that the St. Louis Club has forfeited
its rights by violating the spirit and intent of the code. Whether there
is given to the commissioner the power in so many words to declare
Bennett a free agent is immaterial, since the agreements and rules
grant to the commissioner jurisdiction to refuse to approve Bennett's
assignment by St. Louis to Milwaukee, and to declare him absolved
from the burdens of the same and of his contract with St. Louis.

* * *

It is asserted that this wide grant of jurisdiction of the commissioner is an attempt to deprive the court of its jurisdiction and that such a
provision as is contained in these agreements, rules, and uniform
contract is contrary to public policy. No doubt the decision of any
arbiter, umpire, engineer, or similar person endowed with the power to
decide may not be exercised in an illegal manner, that is fraudulently,
arbitrarily, without legal basis for the same or without any evidence to
justify action. The many cases cited upon the power and jurisdiction of
such officials are not in serious conflict. An agreement to arbitrate a
controverted question and to deprive all courts of jurisdiction, so long as
in executory form, is quite commonly held void, but an actual submission to an arbiter or umpire in good faith is proper, and decision under
same is binding, unless it is unsupported by evidence, or unless the
decision is upon some basis without legal foundation or beyond legal
recognition.

Plaintiffs submitted to the defendant as commissioner an optional
contract, which under the code could not be effective unless approved
by him. After ascertaining the facts, he refused to approve the same.
This, if we look at it from the point of arbitration, was an executed
agreement for arbitration, and called for more than ministerial action.
As we have seen, the commissioner is given almost unlimited discretion
in the determination of whether or not a certain state of facts creates a
situation detrimental to the national game of baseball. The commissioner rightfully found that the common control of St. Louis and the
named Minor Clubs by one person made it possible to create a situation
whereby the clear intent of the adopted code that the players under the
control of a Major club should not be kept with a Minor club more than
two successive seasons without giving other Major clubs the right to
claim him was clearly violated, and a result achieved highly detrimen-

tal to the national game of baseball. The facts negative any assertion that this decision was made arbitrarily or fraudulently. It was made in pursuance of jurisdiction granted to the commissioner with the expressed desire to achieve certain ends, that is, to keep the game of baseball clean, to promote clean competition, to prevent collusive or fraudulent contracts, to protect players' rights, to furnish them full opportunity to advance in accord with their abilities and to prevent their deprival of such opportunities by subterfuge, covering or other unfair conduct.

<u>Suit dismissed.</u>

RES
△ won

————

Beneath the surface of this technical dispute between Commissioner Landis and the owner of the Browns was a fundamental transformation taking place within organized baseball. Despite his formal constitutional authority, Landis fought a losing struggle against the emergence of the farm system pioneered by Branch Rickey of the St. Louis Cardinals. The *Milwaukee* case had enforced the letter of baseball's rules restricting multiple optioning of players to minor league teams. Just two years after this judicial ruling, though, the "farm bloc" owners used their majority position to push through a revision of the major league rules and baseball's reserve system to facilitate stockpiling of players on a minor league team owned or controlled by the major league club.[7] Who wins and who loses under the farm system arrangement? Keep this question in mind for succeeding chapters when we explore the broader parameters of the owners' reserve system for players.

The last two decades have witnessed much more active use of commissioner authority in a fast-changing sports environment. In his autobiography, *Hardball*,[8] former baseball commissioner Bowie Kuhn recounts many such cases: two of the most controversial involved maverick club owners Charlie Finley of the Oakland Athletics and Ted Turner of the Atlanta Braves. Both of these cases grew out of a legal ruling reproduced in Chapter 4—the 1976 arbitration decision in the *Andy Messersmith: Dave McNally* grievance. This ruling eviscerated the "reserve clause" that had tied baseball players for life to their original team, and gave players the freedom to move to a new team upon expiration of their current contracts. Collective bargaining that summer confirmed the concept of "free agency" in baseball, though limiting such status to players with six years of big league service. The

7. See the Celler Report, *Organized Baseball*, note 1 above, at 63–74, 177–89, for the historical details of, and the arguments for and against, the farm system.

8. See Kuhn, *Hardball: The Education of a Baseball Commissioner*, note 1 above, at 173–87 and 259–64. A revealing counterpoint to Kuhn's account of these times and these cases can be found in the memoirs of the leader of the Major League Baseball Players Association, which had just won free agency for its members. See Marvin Miller, *A Whole Different Ball*

prospect of free agency, while not unwelcome to wealthy owners like the Yankees' George Steinbrenner, yearning to win a pennant, frightened other owners.

Charles Finley was the most concerned. Despite an ill-advised move of his Kansas City Athletics to Oakland where they had to compete with the San Francisco Giants for support in the Bay Area, Finley had successfully used the draft system instituted by baseball in 1965, to build the most powerful team of the early 1970s: five straight divisional titles and three straight World Series championships. Unfortunately, Finley tended to treat his players like "plantation hands" (as Kuhn observed), including such Oakland stars as Reggie Jackson, Vida Blue, and Jim "Catfish" Hunter. With free agency pending, the A's appeared to be in dire straits. Thus, Finley devised the following strategy: he would sell off his current assets, the veteran stars of his three-time World Series champion A's, and invest the proceeds in development via the farm system of future assets—young stars who could not command high salaries through free agency. There was only one impediment to his plan—Commissioner Kuhn.

CHARLES O. FINLEY v. BOWIE KUHN

United States Court of Appeals, Seventh Circuit, 1978.

569 F.2d 527.

SPRECHER, CIRCUIT JUDGE.

[Just before baseball's trading deadline of June 15, 1976, Finley and the Athletics sold the contract rights to the services of Joe Rudi and Rollie Fingers to the Boston Red Sox for $2 million and of Vida Blue to the New York Yankees for $1.5 million. Rudi and Fingers were to become free agents upon the expiration of their contracts at the end of the 1976 season. Just before the Athletics' transaction with the Yankees, Blue signed a three-year contract extension, the benefit of which was transferred to the Yankees in this sale. The day after a quickly scheduled hearing on June 17, Commissioner Kuhn disapproved the assignments of the contracts of Rudi, Fingers, and Blue to the Red Sox and Yankees "as inconsistent with the best interests of baseball, the integrity of the game and the maintenance of public confidence in it." The Commissioner expressed his concern for (1) the debilitation of the Oakland club, (2) the loss of competitive balance in professional baseball through the buying of success by the wealthier clubs, and (3) "the present unsettled circumstances of baseball's reserve system." A week later, Finley brought this suit challenging Kuhn's authority to take such action.]

II

Basic to the underlying suit brought by Oakland and to this appeal is whether the Commissioner of baseball is vested by contract with the

Game: The Sport and Business of Baseball
(New York: Birch Lane Press, 1991).

authority to disapprove player assignments which he finds to be "not in the best interests of baseball." In assessing the measure and extent of the Commissioner's power and authority, consideration must be given to the circumstances attending the creation of the office of Commissioner, the language employed by the parties in drafting their contractual understanding, changes and amendments adopted from time to time, and the interpretation given by the parties to their contractual language throughout the period of its existence.

* * *

On September 28, 1920, an indictment issued charging that an effort had been made to "fix" the 1919 World Series by several Chicago White Sox players. Popularly known as the "Black Sox Scandal," this event rocked the game of professional baseball and proved the catalyst that brought about the establishment of a single, neutral Commissioner of baseball.

In November, 1920, the major league club owners unanimously elected federal Judge Kenesaw Mountain Landis as the sole Commissioner of baseball and appointed a committee of owners to draft a charter setting forth the Commissioner's authority. In one of the drafting sessions an attempt was made to place limitations on the Commissioner's authority. Judge Landis responded by refusing to accept the office of Commissioner.

On January 12, 1921, Landis told a meeting of club owners that he had agreed to accept the position upon the clear understanding that the owners had sought "an authority ... outside of your own business, and that a part of that authority would be a control over whatever and whoever had to do with baseball." Thereupon, the owners voted unanimously to reject the proposed limitation upon the Commissioner's authority, they all signed what they called the Major League Agreement, and Judge Landis assumed the position of Commissioner. Oakland has been a signatory to the Major League Agreement continuously since 1960. The agreement, a contract between the constituent clubs of the National and American Leagues, is the basic charter under which major league baseball operates.

* * *

The Major Leagues and their constituent clubs severally agreed to be bound by the decisions of the Commissioner and by the discipline imposed by him. They further agreed to "waive such right of recourse to the courts as would otherwise have existed in their favor." Major League Agreement, Art. VII, Sec. 2.[14]

14. ... Also, on the same day, January 12, 1921, that the Major League Agreement was signed on behalf of the two major leagues and sixteen baseball clubs, the league presidents and club presidents individually signed the following "Pledge to Support the Commissioner":

We, the undersigned, earnestly desirous of insuring to the public wholesome and high-class baseball, and believing that we ourselves should set for the players an example of

Upon Judge Landis' death in 1944, the Major League Agreement was amended in two respects to limit the Commissioner's authority. First, the parties deleted the provision by which they had agreed to waive their right of recourse to the courts to challenge actions of the Commissioner. Second the parties added the following language to Article I, Section 3:

> No Major League Rule or other joint action of the two Major Leagues, and no action or procedure taken in compliance with any such Major League Rule or joint action of the two Major Leagues shall be considered or construed to be detrimental to Baseball.

The district court found that this addition had the effect of precluding the Commissioner from finding an act that complied with the Major League Rules to be detrimental to the best interests of baseball.

The two 1944 amendments to the Major League Agreement remained in effect during the terms of the next two Commissioners, A. B. "Happy" Chandler and Ford Frick. Upon Frick's retirement in 1964 and in accordance with his recommendation, the parties adopted three amendments to the Major League Agreement: (1) the language added in 1944 preventing the Commissioner from finding any act or practice "taken in compliance" with a Major League Rule to be "detrimental to baseball" was removed; (2) the provision deleted in 1944 waiving any rights of recourse to the courts to challenge a Commissioner's decision was restored; and (3) in places where the language "detrimental to the best interests of the national game of baseball" or "detrimental to baseball" appeared those words were changed to "not in the best interests of the national game of Baseball" or "not in the best interests of Baseball."

* * *

III

Despite the Commissioner's broad authority to prevent any act, transaction or practice not in the best interests of baseball, Oakland has attacked the Commissioner's disapproval of the Rudi–Fingers–Blue transactions on a variety of theories which seem to express a similar thrust in differing language.

The complaint alleged that the "action of Kuhn was arbitrary, capricious, unreasonable, discriminatory, directly contrary to historical precedent, baseball tradition, and prior rulings and actions of the Commissioner." In pre-trial answers to interrogatories, Oakland acknowledged that the Commissioner could set aside a proposed assignment of a player's contract "in an appropriate case of violation of (Major League) Rules or immoral or unethical conduct."

the sportsmanship which accepts the umpire's decision without complaint, hereby pledge ourselves loyally to support the Commissioner in his important and difficult task; And we assure him that each of us will acquiesce in his decisions even when we believe them mistaken, and that we will not discredit the sport by public criticism of him or of one another.

* * *

The plaintiff has argued that it is a fundamental rule of law that the decisions of the head of a private association must be procedurally fair. Plaintiff then argued that it was "procedurally unfair" for the Commissioner to fail to warn the plaintiff that he would "disapprove large cash assignments of star players even if they complied with the Major League Rules."

In the first place it must be recalled that prior to the assignments involved here drastic changes had commenced to occur in the reserve system and in the creation of free agents. In his opinion disapproving the Rudi, Fingers and Blue assignments, the Commissioner said that "while I am of course aware that there have been cash sales of player contracts in the past, there has been no instance in my judgment which had the potential for harm to our game as do these assignments, particularly in the present unsettled circumstances of baseball's reserve system and in the highly competitive circumstances we find in today's sports and entertainment world."

Absent the radical changes in the reserve system, the Commissioner's action would have postponed Oakland's realization of value for these players.[27] Given those changes, the relative fortunes of all major league clubs became subject to a host of intangible speculations. No one could predict then or now with certainty that Oakland would fare better or worse relative to other clubs through the vagaries of the revised reserve system occurring entirely apart from any action by the Commissioner.

In the second place, baseball cannot be analogized to any other business or even to any other sport or entertainment. Baseball's relation to the federal antitrust laws has been characterized by the Supreme Court as an "exception," an "anomaly" and an "aberration." Baseball's management through a commissioner is equally an exception, anomaly and aberration.... In no other sport or business is there quite the same system, created for quite the same reasons and with quite the same underlying policies. Standards such as the best interests of baseball, the interests of the morale of the players and the honor of the game, or "sportsmanship which accepts the umpire's decision without complaint," are not necessarily familiar to courts and obviously require some expertise in their application. While it is true that professional baseball selected as its first Commissioner a federal judge, it intended only him and not the judiciary as a whole to be its umpire and governor.

As we have seen in Part II, the Commissioner was vested with broad authority and that authority was not to be limited in its exercise to situations where Major League Rules or moral turpitude was in-

---

27. This realization of value could come in the form of subsequent player transactions involving less cash but some returning-player value, or in box office profits attributable to these players, or possibly in the aggregate value of the club if and when eventually sold as a franchise and team.

volved. When professional baseball intended to place limitations upon the Commissioner's powers, it knew how to do so. In fact, it did so during the 20–year period from 1944 to 1964.

The district court found and concluded that the Rudi–Fingers–Blue transactions were not, as Oakland had alleged in its complaint, "directly contrary to historical precedent, baseball tradition, and prior rulings." During his almost 25 years as Commissioner, Judge Landis found many acts, transactions and practices to be detrimental to the best interests of baseball in situations where neither moral turpitude nor a Major League Rule violation was involved, and he disapproved several player assignments.

On numerous occasions since he became Commissioner of baseball in February 1969, Kuhn has exercised broad authority under the best interests clause of the Major League Agreement. Many of the actions taken by him have been in response to acts, transactions or practices that involved neither the violation of a Major League Rule nor any gambling, game-throwing or other conduct associated with moral turpitude. Moreover, on several occasions Commissioner Kuhn has taken broad preventive or remedial action with respect to assignments of player contracts.

On several occasions Charles O. Finley, the principal owner of the plaintiff corporation and the general manager of the Oakland baseball club, has himself espoused that the Commissioner has the authority to exercise broad powers pursuant to the best interests clause, even where there is no violation of the Major League Rules and no moral turpitude is involved.

Twenty-one of the 25 parties to the current Major League Agreement who appeared as witnesses in the district court testified that they intended and they presently understand that the Commissioner of baseball can review and disapprove an assignment of a player contract which he finds to be not in the best interests of baseball, even if the assignment does not violate the Major League Rules and does not involve moral turpitude.

* * *

We conclude that the evidence fully supports, and we agree with, the district court's finding that "[t]he history of the adoption of the Major League Agreement in 1921 and the operation of baseball for more than 50 years under it [strongly indicate] that the Commissioner has the authority to determine whether any act, transaction or practice is "not in the best interests of baseball," and upon such determination, to take whatever preventive or remedial action he deems appropriate, whether or not the act, transaction or practice complies with the Major League Rules or involves moral turpitude." Any other conclusion would involve the courts in not only interpreting often complex rules of baseball to determine if they were violated but also, as noted in the

Landis case, the "intent of the [baseball] code," an even more complicated and subjective task.

The Rudi–Fingers–Blue transactions had been negotiated on June 14 and 15, 1976. On June 16, the Commissioner sent a teletype to the Oakland, Boston and New York clubs and to the Players' Association expressing his "concern for possible consequences to the integrity of baseball and public confidence in the game" and setting a hearing for June 17. Present at the hearing were 17 persons representing those notified. At the outset of the hearing the Commissioner stated that he was concerned that the assignments would be harmful to the competitive capacity of Oakland; that they reflected an effort by Boston and New York to purchase star players and "bypass the usual methods of player development and acquisition which have been traditionally used in professional baseball"; and that the question to be resolved was whether the transactions "are consistent with the best interests of baseball's integrity and maintenance of public confidence in the game." He warned that it was possible that he might determine that the assignments not be approved. . . .

[In his decision] the Commissioner recognized "that there have been cash sales of player contracts in the past," but concluded that "these transactions were unparalleled in the history of the game" because there was "never anything on this scale or falling at this time of the year, or which threatened so seriously to unbalance the competitive balance of baseball." The district court concluded that the attempted assignments of Rudi, Fingers and Blue "were at a time and under circumstances making them unique in the history of baseball."

We conclude that the evidence fully supports, and we agree with, the district court's finding and conclusion that the Commissioner "acted in good faith, after investigation, consultation and deliberation, in a manner which he determined to be in the best interests of baseball" and that "[w]hether he was right or wrong is beyond the competence and the jurisdiction of this court to decide." [44]

* * *

V

Following the bench trial, the district court reached its decision in favor of the Commissioner without considering the impact of Article VII, Section 2 of the Major League Agreement, wherein the major league baseball clubs agreed to be bound by the Commissioner's decisions and discipline and to waive recourse to the courts.

---

44. It is beyond the province of this court to consider the wisdom of the Commissioner's reasons for disapproving the assignments of Rudi, Blue and Fingers. There is insufficient evidence, however, to support plaintiff's allegation that the Commissioner's action was arbitrary or capricious, or motivated by malice, ill will or anything other than the Commissioner's good faith judgment that these attempted assignments were not in the best interests of baseball. The great majority of persons involved in baseball who testified on this point shared Commissioner Kuhn's view.

* * *

Oakland has urged us to apply the substantive law dealing with the "policies and rules of a private association" to the Major League Agreement and actions taken thereunder. Illinois has developed a considerable body of law dealing with the activities of private voluntary organizations and we agree that the validity and effect of the waiver of recourse clause should initially be tested under these decisions.

Even in the absence of a waiver of recourse provision in an association charter, "[i]t is generally held that courts . . . will not intervene in questions involving the enforcement of bylaws and matters of discipline in voluntary associations."

* * *

Viewed in light of these decisions, the waiver of recourse clause contested here seems to add little if anything to the common law nonreviewability of private association actions. This clause can be upheld as coinciding with the common law standard disallowing court interference. We view its inclusion in the Major League Agreement merely as a manifestation of the intent of the contracting parties to insulate from review decisions made by the Commissioner concerning the subject matter of actions taken in accordance with his grant of powers.

* * *

Even if the waiver of recourse clause is divorced from its setting in the charter of a private, voluntary association and even if its relationship with the arbitration clause in the agreement is ignored, we think that it is valid under the circumstances here involved. Oakland claims that such clauses are invalid as against public policy. This is true, however, only under circumstances where the waiver of rights is not voluntary, knowing or intelligent, or was not freely negotiated by parties occupying equal bargaining positions. The trend of cases in many states and in the federal courts supports the conclusion of the district court under the circumstances presented here that "informed parties, freely contracting, may waive their recourse to the court."

Although the waiver of recourse clause is generally valid for the reasons discussed above, we do not believe that it forecloses access to the courts under all circumstances. Thus, the general rule of nonreviewability which governs the actions of private associations is subject to exceptions 1) where the rules, regulations or judgments of the association are in contravention to the laws of the land or in disregard of the charter or bylaws of the association, or 2) where the association has failed to follow the basic rudiments of due process of law. Similar exceptions exist for avoiding the requirements of arbitration under the United States Arbitration Act. We therefore hold that, absent the applicability of one of these narrow exceptions, the waiver of recourse clause contained in the Major League Agreement is valid and binding on the parties and the courts.

* * *

Suit dismissed.

Questions for Discussion

1. Ignoring for the moment the appropriate scope of judicial scrutiny of commissioner decisions, consider the merits of Commissioner Kuhn's ruling? Is there anything wrong with one owner selling a player's services to another? Remember the 1989 blockbuster hockey deal that sent Wayne Gretzky from the Edmonton Oilers to the Los Angeles Kings for $15 million plus players, a deal replicated in 1992 by the Quebec Nordiques who sent Eric Lindros to the Philadelphia Flyers for $15 million and players. Would it have been in the best interests of hockey for NHL President John Ziegler to have disallowed either of these transactions because of the huge sums of money involved?

2. Would the standard of review articulated in *Finley v. Kuhn* have been any different if the waiver of legal recourse clause had not been included in the Major League Agreement? If the court was simply adopting the same "hands off" judicial attitude exhibited towards the actions of private associations or the decisions of private arbitrators, was the validity of the waiver of recourse clause an important issue in the case?

Finley v. Kuhn accepted a broad authority of the commissioner to nullify club transactions. The next decision, which was issued between the dates of the district and appellate court rulings in *Finley v. Kuhn*, deals with the commissioner's authority to discipline owners and employees of the member teams and thus raises many issues similar to those posed in Pete Rose's case.

ATLANTA NATIONAL LEAGUE BASEBALL CLUB & TED TURNER v. BOWIE KUHN

United States District Court, Northern District of Georgia, 1977.

432 F.Supp. 1213.

EDENFIELD, DISTRICT JUDGE.

[In July 1976, following the events described in the *Finley* case above, Major League Baseball and its Players Association negotiated a new collective agreement with an elaborate free agency system. Players with six years of service in the major leagues could declare their intention to become free agents before the end of October. In early November a draft would be conducted for those declared free agents, under which up to twelve teams could elect to bid for any one player. Before the draft, though, only his prior club had the right to negotiate with that player.

In August 1976, Commissioner Kuhn issued a series of directives to owners that warned them against any dealings with potential free agents prior to the "reentry draft." In September 1976, the Commissioner found that the Atlanta Braves' General Manager had made improper contact with Gary Matthews of the San Francisco Giants. For this "tampering" offense the Commissioner fined the Braves $5,000 and took away their first pick in the winter amateur draft. Subsequently, at a cocktail party in October 1976, Braves' owner Ted Turner, told Bob Lurie, owner of the Giants, that the Braves would go as high as necessary to get Matthews. Members of the media present at this exchange published the story.

The free agent draft was conducted on November 4 and the Braves succeeded in signing Matthews on November 17. Subsequently, December 30, Commissioner Kuhn upheld Lurie's complaint against Turner. Kuhn decided not to disapprove Matthews contract. Instead, the Commissioner suspended Turner from baseball for one year and deprived Atlanta of its first round pick in the next summer's amateur draft. Turner and the Braves sued and this is the district judge's decision.]

* * *

To the extent this case involves a violation of the Major League Agreement, the court has no hesitation in saying that the defendant Commissioner had ample authority to punish plaintiffs in this case for acts considered not in the best interests of baseball....

The question which makes the case confusing and difficult, however, is to what extent the Major League Agreement applies here. This doubt arises for two reasons: First, when the current Major League Agreement was made in 1975 there did not exist in baseball any "free agencies" created solely by expiration of the player's contract, and certainly there was no "free-agent draft." Conceding that the Major League Agreement might be sufficiently broad to apply ordinarily to future developments, there is a still bigger obstacle: When such "free-agencies" came into being in 1976 ... the parties entered into a new, separate and independent contract to deal with the new situation thus created. This new agreement, in the form of a collective bargaining agreement between the clubs and the Players Association, is complete within itself. It provides for the creation of free agencies upon the expiration of player contracts (Art. XVII, B); spells out reentry procedures (Art. XVII, C); forbids clubs from contracting or negotiating terms with free agents in the interim between the end of the season and the reentry draft (Art. XVII C.(2)); and provides for three-party arbitration "as the exclusive remedy of the parties." (Art. X, prelim. par.).

Obviously this new agreement modified the Major League Agreement at least as to such subject matter as is covered by the later agreement. The two agreements must now be read together as forming the framework for the government of Major League baseball. The powers of the Commissioner under the Major League Agreement are therefore modified only so as to avoid infringing upon the rights secured by the parties to the collective bargaining agreement.

THE DIRECTIVES

* * *

[T]he court must hold in check a close scrutiny of the reasons given for the Commissioner's decision to discipline Turner. The Commissioner has general authority, without rules or directives, to punish both clubs and/or personnel for any act or conduct which, in his judgment, is "not in the best interests of baseball" within the meaning of the Major League Agreement. What conduct is "not in the best interests of baseball" is, of course, a question which addresses itself to the Commissioner, not this court. He has made his finding that Turner's conduct was of this character. The court knows of no authority which prevented him from making it, and cannot say his decision was either arbitrary or wrong. There is no evidence that the Commissioner's decision was the result of bias or ill will, although, during the same period, one other tampering violation was dealt with much less severely. The court therefore concludes, with some misgivings, that under this provision, the Commissioner did have authority to punish plaintiffs.

THE SANCTIONS

Viewing the evidence concerning punishment here, a casual, nonlegalistic observer might say that this case represents a comedy of strange tactical errors on both sides. Both at the hearing before the Commissioner and afterward, but before decision, Turner asked for "suspension" as his punishment in lieu of cancellation of the Matthews contract, which he feared. The Commissioner also did some inexplicable things: He approved Atlanta's signing of Matthews, apparently the only tangible mischief resulting from Turner's remarks, but having approved the act of signing he then punished Turner for publicly suggesting in advance he intended to do it. He also forbade Turner the right to manage his business or to even go on his own property except as a paying customer. The Atlanta Baseball Club is called the "Atlanta Braves"; and considering the severity of this punishment, the same casual observer might call this an Indian massacre in reverse. In their encounter with the Commissioner the Braves took "nary" a scalp, but lived to see their own dangling from the lodgepole of the Commissioner, apparently only as a grisly warning to others. At about the same time and for an identical offense, though perhaps not as flagrant, the venerable owner of the St. Louis Cardinals was fined $5,000. All of which adds nothing to the legal power of this court to extricate plaintiffs from a suspension which they invited and to which they assented, both orally and contractually.

* * *

Here the Commissioner could properly conclude that this was the second instance of improper conduct with respect to one player. He could also consider that Turner's comments were made after six warning directives had been issued, one of which cautioned that suspensions would follow from tampering violations. None of these aggravating circumstances were present in the St. Louis case. With these differences present, honest minds could, and indeed do, disagree as to what is an appropriate punishment. The court, therefore, simply cannot say the Commissioner abused his discretion. In Article VII, § 2, of the Major League Agreement the clubs explicitly agreed to be bound by the discipline imposed by the Commissioner and obviously intended to give him a certain amount of leeway to choose the appropriate sanction. Judicial review of every sanction imposed by the Commissioner would produce an unworkable system that the Major League Agreement endeavors to prevent. Here, Turner was warned of the suspension, he asked for the suspension, the contract specifically authorized it, and he got it.

The denial of the June draft choice, however, stands on a somewhat different legal footing. Under the best interests of baseball clause, Article I, § 2, the Commissioner is given the authority to "determine, after investigation, what preventive, remedial or punitive action is appropriate in the premises." Those punitive measures which the Commissioner may take are explicitly enumerated in Article I, § 3. . . . Denial of a draft choice is simply not among the penalties authorized for this offense.

Defendant argues, however, that the list of sanctions enumerated in this section is intended to be only illustrative rather than definitive, as indicated by use of the language that penalties "may include any one or more of the following." Thus he says that the listing of specific sanctions in § 3 does not preclude the Commissioner from imposing other sanctions that he deems appropriate.

* * *

[T]he language of the Major League Agreement and Major League Rules seems to imply that the list of sanctions in § 3 is exclusive, and basic rules of contract construction support this conclusion. Prior to the original Major League Agreement, there were no presumed powers vested in a Commissioner. The 1921 agreement created the office of the Commissioner and defined his powers out of whole cloth. In such a situation, the maxim "Expressio unius est exclusio alterius " is particularly applicable. Moreover, in light of the fact that this contract purports to authorize the imposition of a penalty or forfeiture, it must be strictly construed.

Set against this background are numerous instances where the Commissioner has taken action that was not listed in § 3, and testimony on the part of certain parties to the Major League Agreement which indicates that the intention of § 3 was to provide an illustrative list of sanctions available to the Commissioner.

* * *

[T]he court need not decide whether the Commissioner acted within his authority in those instances which are not now before the court. That the Commissioner's authority in those cases went unchallenged does not persuade this court of the Commissioner's unlimited punitive powers in light of contractual language and established rules of construction to the contrary. If the Commissioner is to have the unlimited punitive authority as he says is needed to deal with new and changing situations, the agreement should be changed to expressly grant the Commissioner that power. The deprivation of a draft choice was first and foremost a punitive sanction, and a sanction that is not specifically enumerated under § 3. Accordingly, the court concludes that the Commissioner was without the authority to impose that sanction, and its imposition is therefore void.

Petition upheld in part.

The legal scope of the commissioner's authority surfaced once more in the summer of 1992 in a case that was the most visible of a number of baseball *causes celebres* that summer. The dispute that reached the courts was a challenge by the Chicago Cubs to Commissioner Francis "Fay" Vincent's directive realigning the Eastern and Western Divisions of the National League.

CHICAGO NATIONAL LEAGUE BALL CLUB INC. v. FRANCIS VINCENT, JR.

United States District Court, Northern District of Illinois, 1992.

Unreported

CONLON, DISTRICT JUDGE.

[Given the need in the spring of 1992 to assign each of the two National League expansion clubs to a division, the league members decided to review their overall divisional alignment. The vast majority of clubs favored a realignment that would shift the Chicago Cubs and St. Louis Cardinals to the western division and the Cincinnati Reds and Atlanta Braves to the eastern division—partly to ease travel times, partly to enhance geographic rivalries, and partly to keep as many telecasts in local prime time as possible. The Cubs, however, were strongly opposed. Their stated reason was the loss of long-standing rivalries with teams such as the New York Mets. The unstated, but widely-assumed, reason was that under the National League's unbalanced divisional schedule the Cubs would now play many more games in western time zones, which would impair the television ratings of the Cub's corporate sibling within the Chicago Tribune empire—the superstation WGN. Thus, the Cubs (supported by the New York Mets) exercised their right under the National League constitution to veto their transfer to another division, thereby blocking the overall proposal.

A number of National League teams decided to pursue the matter further and ask Commissioner Fay Vincent to order realignment through his authority under Article I, § 2 of the Major League Agreement (MLA):

> to investigate ... any act, transaction or practice ... not in the best interests of the national game of Baseball ... [and] to determine ... what preventive, remedial or punitive action is appropriate ... and to take such action....

The Cubs (now supported by several National League teams and National League President Bill White) argued to the Commissioner that his authority in this case was limited to and by Article VII of the MLA, which empowers the Commissioner to decide:

> all disputes and controversies related in any way to professional baseball between clubs ... other than those whose resolution is expressly provided for by another means in this Agreement ... in the constitution of either Major League or the Basic Agreement between the Major Leagues and the Major League Baseball Players Association.

Commissioner Vincent rejected the Cubs' argument, concluded that he did have authority to act under Article I of the MLA, and decided that the best interests of Baseball were not served by the National League's stringent constraints upon realignment decisions. When Vincent ordered that the Cubs (and the Cardinals) be shifted to the National League's Western Division, the Cubs sued for an injunction to block that move.]

*   *   *

In challenging the Commissioner's decision, the Chicago Cubs contend that Sections 9.4 and 16.1 of the National League Constitution expressly provide for resolution of realignment disputes. Both of these provisions flatly bar a divisional transfer if the affected club does not consent.

Section 9.4 of the National League Constitution provides that the composition of the Eastern and Western Divisions

> shall not be changed except by a three-fourths vote of all the clubs of the League: provided, however, that no member club may be transferred to a different division without its consent.

Section 9.4 places the Chicago Cubs in the Eastern Division.

Section 16.1 of the National League Constitution governs amendment procedures. A provision of the National League Constitution may be amended by a three-fourths vote of all member clubs. One of only two exceptions provides that:

> [N]o club may be transferred to a division different from that provided in Section 9.4 of Article 9 without its consent.

The parties' dispute centers on whether the broad "best interests of baseball" authority in the Major League Agreement empowers the Commissioner to abrogate the Chicago Cubs' right to veto their transfer to the Western Division. Implicit in this dispute is the question whether the Commissioner is empowered to unilaterally amend the National League Constitution simply because he finds that a constitutional provision or procedure is "not in the best interests of baseball."

(Sub-issue)

* * *

Under Illinois rules for construing contracts, it is clear that the broad authority granted the Commissioner by Article I of the Major League Agreement is not as boundless as he suggests. Giving the language of Article I its common sense and ordinary meaning, the Commissioner's authority to investigate "acts," "transactions" and "practices" and to determine and take "preventive, remedial or punitive action" does not encompass restructuring the divisions of the National League. There has been no conduct for the Commissioner to investigate, punish or remedy under Article I. The veto exercised by the Chicago Cubs as a matter of contractual right merely resulted in the maintenance of long-standing divisional assignments reflected in the National League Constitution.

The Commissioner relies on the Seventh Circuit's decision in *Finley v. Kuhn*, 569 F.2d 527 (7th Cir.1978), to support his expansive view of Article I.... *Finley* is distinguishable because there the Commissioner was responding to affirmative conduct. The underlying purpose for Oakland's maneuvering was to avoid an upcoming deadline after which it could not sell the players' contracts without first offering them to all other teams at a stipulated waiver price of $20,000. Unlike the Chicago Cubs, Oakland was not acting pursuant to any contractual right authorized by the American League Constitution.

D's Def

More on point is *Atlanta National League Baseball Club Inc. v. Kuhn*, 432 F.Supp. 1213 (N.D.Ga.1977). There, the Atlanta Braves and their owner Ted Turner sued the Commissioner. Turner and the Braves challenged the Commissioner's authority to sanction Turner for violating a major league rule against tampering with potential free agents.... The court upheld Turner's suspension, but found that the Commissioner exceeded his authority in eliminating the Braves' first round draft choice. Because the latter sanction is not enumerated in the Major League Agreement, the court stated:

> If the Commissioner is to have the unlimited punitive authority as he says is needed to deal with new and changing situations, the [Major League] agreement should be changed to expressly grant the Commissioner that power.

Note
(Atl. v. Kuhn)

The Commissioner also cites two prior actions to support his position: Commissioner Kuhn's 1976 reversal of the National League's rejection of an expansion plan and Commissioner Ueberroth's 1985 approval of a new minority owner of the Texas Rangers. In both of these actions, the Commissioner overrode voting requirements of a league constitution. The Commissioner contends that these actions constitute "strong precedent" for his realignment decision. These incidents did not arise under comparable factual circumstances and implicated different constitutional provisions. More importantly, the fact that these actions did not result in a court challenge is neither probative nor persuasive evidence that the Commissioner in fact acted within his authority on those occasions.

Even if the terms "act," "transaction" or "practice" were construed to apply to the Chicago Cubs' exercise of its veto right against divisional transfer, the Commissioner's Article I authority must be considered in light of Article VII. Article VII expressly limits the Commissioner's jurisdiction to resolution of disputes "other than those whose resolution is expressly provided for by another means in ... the [Major League] constitution."

Sections 9.4 and 16.1 explicitly provide the means for resolving disputes among clubs concerning divisional realignment; any decision is conditioned on the consent of a transferred club. These provisions manifest a clear intention to protect the substantial interest of an individual club in its divisional assignment from adverse action by the majority.

Reading Article I in light of Article VII, the Commissioner lacked authority to unilaterally abrogate the Chicago Cubs' rights under Sections 9.4 and 16.1 of the National League Constitution.

* * *

Temporary injunction granted.

———

A series of controversial decisions in 1992 by Commissioner Vincent had gradually alienated a growing number of owners. Eventually, at a late August meeting, the owners voted (18 to 9 with one abstention) no confidence in Vincent and asked him to resign. Before the meeting Vincent had asserted that the owners had no power to fire him and that he would not quit his post. However, after reflecting over the Labor Day weekend about the owners' verdict, Vincent decided to leave office—saying that his resignation, not litigation, was in the best interests of baseball. With Vincent gone and a new Executive Committee in charge headed by Milwaukee Brewers' owner Allan "Bud" Selig, baseball dropped its appeal of the *Cubs* decision and put realignment on hold pending further study.

Questions for Discussion

1. Had the appeal of the District Court ruling in *Chicago Cubs* been pursued to the Seventh Circuit, how should it have ruled in light of its *Finley v. Kuhn* precedent? Which of the two arguably relevant provisions of the Major League Agreement (MLA) should take precedence—Article I regarding the "best interests" of baseball, or Article VII regarding "disputes and controversies" in baseball?

2. Before acquiescing in the owners' insurgency, Vincent and his lawyers had said that Article IX of the MLA protected him from being fired:

> Each of the parties hereto subscribes this Agreement in consideration of the promises of all the others that no diminution of the compensation or powers of the present or any succeeding Commissioner shall be made during his term of office.

(a) Does this clause block the owners from changing the occupant—as opposed to the prerogatives—of the commissioner's office? *N*

(b) Even if a court found that dismissal of the commissioner violated this provision of the MLA (which was incorporated in the commissioner's personal contract), what remedies would be available—specific performance, negative injunction, or monetary damages? (Keep this question in mind for Chapter 2.)

(c) Could dissident owners, the players association, or even disgruntled fans, have brought suit based on a violation of Article IX? *N* If so, for what relief?

3. Taking account of all three of these legal precedents, what advice would you have given to the Yankees' George Steinbrenner about his chances of overturning the two-year suspension that Commissioner Vincent was prepared to impose on Steinbrenner in July 1990 for paying Howard Spira (a gambler) $40,000 for information about Yankees' star Dave Winfield? Do the above judicial rulings help explain why Steinbrenner "plea bargained" Vincent's proposed two-year suspension into a lifetime ban, which Vincent lifted in July 1992 (effective March 1993)?

4. From a doctrinal perspective, what is the legal foothold upon which judges can scrutinize and overturn any aspect of the decisions made by a private association such as a sports league? From an institutional perspective, should courts be more or less ready to review the decisions of a baseball commissioner than those of a union official?[9] Does your answer depend upon whether the person challenging the commissioner is an owner, a manager, or a player? On whether the commissioner's decision infringes on specially favored public policies? For example, suppose a team executive is disciplined for speaking out against the commissioner's drug policy?

The basic structure of league governance in the other major team sports is similar, but not identical to, baseball's. Later in this chapter we will encounter the provisions of the National Football League constitution regarding the commissioner's disciplinary authority to

9. A classic article on the general common law in this area is Zechariah Chafee Jr., *The Internal Affairs of Associations Not for Profit*, 43 Harvard L. Rev. 993 (1930). In-depth analysis of the common law treatment of union-member conflicts (prior to enactment of the federal Landrum–Griffin Act of 1959) can be found in Clyde W. Summers, *Legal Limitations on Union Discipline*, 64 Harvard L. Rev. 1049 (1951) and Clyde W. Summers, *The Law of Union Discipline: What the Courts Do in Fact*, 70 Yale L.J. 175 (1960).

protect the "integrity of the sport," provisions that were at issue in the struggle with the NFL Players Association over drug use and drug testing. The NBA (under section 35 of its constitution), like the National Hockey League (NHL) (under section 17 of its by-laws), gives its commissioner (in the NHL, its president) the authority to expel, suspend, or fine any club official, employee, or player for conduct "detrimental or prejudicial to the Association" (in the NHL, conduct "dishonorable, prejudicial to or against the welfare of the League"). In both leagues, though, such chief executive decisions can be appealed to the Board of Governors, which consists of all the owners.[10] We note here another legal ruling, *Riko Enterprises (Philadelphia 76ers) v. Seattle Supersonics*, 357 F.Supp. 521 (S.D.N.Y.1973), which held that only the NBA Board of Governors, not Commissioner Walter Kennedy, had the power to award the 76ers the Supersonics' first-round draft pick to the 76ers when Seattle had signed a player, John Brisker, who had remained on the 76ers' reserve player list while playing in the American Basketball Association.

In the aftermath of the *Chicago Cubs* litigation and Fay Vincent's ouster, baseball owners are now studying ways of amending the Major League Agreement. Several owners, including Jerry Reinsdorf of the Chicago White Sox, have advocated making the commissioner into a chief executive officer responsible for the business of baseball, accountable in this regard to all the owners serving as a board of directors. The commissioner's disciplinary authority might well be retained in its current form (but perhaps these decisions would also be appealable to the owners collectively). Would such a development be in the best interests of baseball? What implications should such a change in the internal balance of power have for judicial scrutiny of rulings by the commissioner or by baseball's new board of owners?

C. CHALLENGES TO THE BEST INTERESTS OF THE SPORT

Armed with the legal authority described in the previous section, how should the commissioner address the host of issues raised in contemporary life about the "best interests" of the sport? Most league discipline responds to conduct on the field in violation of the rules of the game. The more difficult challenges arise from actions that take place off the field of play, but supposedly threaten the welfare of the game. Besides illustrating the human conflicts in this area, the following cases also display alternative lines of legal attack upon the commissioner's prerogatives.

---

10. Of related interest, both basketball and hockey draw a distinction between betting on a game and being involved in the "fix" of a game. While the former is explicitly made a disciplinary offense, only the latter is singled out for immediate expulsion from the sport. The NFL constitution does not explicitly address gambling.

1. GAMBLING

The perennial problem has been gambling. Shortly after his appointment, Judge Landis banned all White Sox players involved in (indeed, one player who merely had knowledge of) the "fixing" of the 1919 World Series, even though a Chicago jury acquitted all the players of criminal charges.[11] In 1942, Landis forced Philadelphia Phillies owner William Cox to sell his team when it was discovered he had placed about a dozen small bets on the Phillies to win. In 1963, NFL Commissioner Pete Rozelle suspended for a year All–Pros Paul Hornung of the Green Bay Packers and Alex Karras of the Detroit Lions for betting on their own teams to win.

Commissioners have also penalized mere association with gambling, even when no personal betting was involved. For example, Landis' successor, Albert "Happy" Chandler, suspended Dodgers' manager Leo Durocher for the 1947 season merely for associating with gamblers. This was a precedent for George Steinbrenner's 1990 removal from the baseball (though not the financial) affairs of the Yankees for paying a gambler, Howard Spira, to produce unsavory information about Dave Winfield. Finally, in 1979 Bowie Kuhn went so far as to ban Willie Mays and Mickey Mantle from any official connections with professional baseball because they took public relations jobs with gambling casinos. (To Kuhn's regret, his successor, Peter Ueberroth, rescinded that ban in 1985.)

The only judicial ruling about the legality of this harsh treatment for gambling came in the following antitrust suit filed by an ex-NBA player, who charged that his lifetime expulsion constituted an illegal conspiracy of all teams in the league to boycott his services.

P   Δ

MOLINAS v. NATIONAL BASKETBALL ASS'N.

United States District Court, Southern District of New York, 1961.

190 F.Supp. 241.

KAUFMAN, DISTRICT JUDGE.

Facts

Plaintiff, Jack Molinas, is a well-known basketball player. In 1953, upon his graduation from Columbia University, Molinas was 'drafted' by the Fort Wayne Pistons, then a member of the defendant National Basketball Association (now the Detroit Pistons). Subsequently, in the fall of 1953, he signed a contract to play with the Pistons. In January of 1954, however, he admitted, in writing, that he placed several bets on his team, the Pistons, to win. The procedure he followed was that he contacted a person in New York by telephone, who informed him of the "point spread" on the particular game in question. The plaintiff [Molinas] would then decide whether or not to place a bet on the game. The plaintiff admitted that he received some $400 as a result of these

---

11. These events are dramatized in Eliot Asinof, *Eight Men Out* (New York: Henry Holt, 1963), which was later made into a movie of the same name.

wagers, including reimbursement of his telephone calls to New York. After the plaintiff admitted this wagering, Mr. Podoloff, the president of the league, acting pursuant to a clause (Section 15) in plaintiff's contract and a league rule (Section 79 of the League Constitution) prohibiting gambling, indefinitely suspended the plaintiff from the league. This suspension has continued until the present date. Since the suspension, plaintiff has made several applications, both oral and written, for reinstatement. All of these have been refused, and Mr. Podoloff has testified that he will never allow the plaintiff to re-enter the league. He has characterized the plaintiff as a "cancer on the league" which must be excised.

Facts (con't.)

In the meantime, plaintiff attended and graduated from the Brooklyn Law School, and was then admitted to the New York State Bar. He had also been playing basketball for Williamsport and Hazelton of the Eastern Basketball League.

* * *

With respect to plaintiff's suspension from the league in January of 1954, and the subsequent refusal by the league to reinstate him, plaintiff has patently failed to establish an unreasonable restraint of trade within the meaning of the anti-trust laws. A rule, and a corresponding contract clause, providing for the suspension of those who place wagers on games in which they are participating seems not only reasonable, but necessary for the survival of the league. Every league or association must have some reasonable governing rules, and these rules must necessarily include disciplinary provisions. Surely, every disciplinary rule which a league may invoke, although by its nature it may involve some sort of a restraint, does not run afoul of the anti-trust laws. And, a disciplinary rule invoked against gambling seems about as reasonable a rule as could be imagined. Furthermore, the application of the rule to the plaintiff's conduct is also eminently reasonable. Plaintiff was wagering on games in which he was to play, and some of these bets were made on the basis of a "point spread" system. Plaintiff insists that since he bet only on his own team to win, his conduct, while admittedly improper, was not immoral. But I do not find this distinction to be a meaningful one in the context of the present case. The vice inherent in the plaintiff's conduct is that each time he either placed a bet or refused to place a bet, this operated inevitably to inform bookmakers of an insider's opinion as to the adequacy or inadequacy of the point-spread or his team's ability to win. Thus, for example, when he chose to place a bet, this would indicate to the bookmakers that a member of the Fort Wayne team believed that his team would exceed its expected performance. Similarly, when he chose not to bet, bookmakers thus would be informed of his opinion that the Pistons would not perform according to expectations. It is certainly reasonable for the league and Mr. Podoloff to conclude that this conduct could not be tolerated and must, therefore, be eliminated. The reasonableness of the league's action is apparent in view of the fact

Hold

P's Arg

that, at that time, the confidence of the public in basketball had been shattered, due to a series of gambling incidents. Thus, it was absolutely necessary for the sport to exhume gambling from its midst for all times in order to survive.

The same factors justifying the suspension also serve to justify the subsequent refusal to reinstate. The league could reasonably conclude that in order to effectuate its important and legitimate policies against gambling, and to restore and maintain the confidence of the public vital to its existence, it was necessary to enforce its rules strictly, and to apply the most stringent sanctions. One can certainly understand the reluctance to permit an admitted gambler to return to the league, and again to participate in championship games, especially in light of the aura and stigma of gambling which has clouded the sports world in the past few years. Viewed in this context, it can be seen that the league was justified in determining that it was absolutely necessary to avoid even the slightest connection with gambling, gamblers, and those who had done business with gamblers, in the future. In addition, conduct reasonable in its inception certainly does not become unreasonable through the mere passage of time, especially when the same factors making the conduct reasonable in the first instance, are still present. At any rate, plaintiff must show much more than he has here in order to compel a conclusion that the defendant's conduct was in fact unreasonable. Thus, it is clear that the refusal to reinstate the plaintiff does not rise to the stature of a violation of the antitrust laws.

Case dismissed.

Questions for Discussion

1.   *Molinas* introduces us to the Sherman Antitrust Act's proscription (in Section 1) of "contracts, combinations, or conspiracies in restraint of trade," as applied to commissioner discipline. We will explore in later chapters the application of antitrust doctrine to sports. We simply note here that the antitrust "rule of reason" upon which the court relied in *Molinas* does not turn on a court's intuitive judgment of whether a particular practice seems sensible and equitable, but rather on economic analysis of whether the challenged practice is, on balance, procompetitive or anticompetitive; this in turn requires analysis of whether the practice enhances or diminishes consumer welfare (whatever that term means). If one focuses on that economic question, was the court right in its conclusion that suspending Molinas was reasonable?

2.   Recall the federal district court's ruling in *Rose v. Giamatti* that the Cincinnati team was not a true party to the suit for jurisdictional purposes, because the individual member clubs had no control over the commissioner in his exercise of disciplinary authority. If that is so, how could a commissioner's suspension or expulsion of a player ever constitute a "contract, combination, or conspiracy"? Is it simply unilateral action beyond the scope of Section 1 antitrust review?

The *Molinas* decision had an ironic aftermath. While the litigation was underway, Molinas was actually the ringleader in a nationwide point-shaving scheme in college basketball. When the scandal broke in the spring of 1961 and Molinas was indicted and convicted, Judge Kaufman's ruling seemed even wiser.

Unfortunately, one of the nation's best basketball prospects, Connie Hawkins, was victimized by the fallout from this affair.[12] As the top high school player in New York City, Hawkins met Molinas in the summer of 1960 at playground tournaments. Molinas occasionally bought Hawkins dinner and once loaned him $210 (Hawkins repaid the loan soon thereafter). Then Hawkins went off to the University of Iowa where NCAA rules required him to spend the first year on the freshman team. However, when the point-shaving scandal broke in the spring of 1961, Hawkins was named as a participant. Although he could not have shaved points in a college game—he had not played a game yet—Hawkins was described as both an intermediary between Molinas and other players and a part of Molinas' "farm system" of future point-shavers.

Forced to leave college, Hawkins became the top scorer in the short-lived American Basketball League and then barnstormed with the Harlem Globetrotters. Under NBA rules Hawkins became eligible for its draft in 1964, when his college class graduated. However, the league deemed Hawkins ineligible under the *Molinas* precedent. In 1966, Hawkins launched his own antitrust suit, alleging an illegal boycott of his services.

During the discovery process, which took several years, Hawkins starred in the new American Basketball Association. Eventually, however, the lawyers uncovered persuasive evidence (partly from Molinas) that Hawkins had been an innocent bystander. As a result, the NBA finally settled the suit in 1969 by paying Hawkins $1.3 million in damages and removing him from its ineligible list. The Phoenix Suns won his draft rights, and in his first season Hawkins led the Suns to the NBA playoffs and made the all-NBA team. And in 1992 Hawkins was installed in basketball's Hall of Fame, the same year in which Pete Rose was denied eligibility for baseball's Hall in Cooperstown.

Questions for Discussion

1. What are the implications of the Hawkins story? Had the NBA taken the risk of trebled antitrust damages and gone to court, would it—should it—have won, based on the *Molinas* precedent? What if the facts are murky? Who has the burden of proof? What if the facts are clear but the involvement minor? For example, Doug Moe, a consensus All-American at North Carolina, graduated in 1961, was named as someone who had refused to participate in the gambling scheme, but was banned from the NBA for failing to report the bribe offer. Should Moe have been entitled to

12. See David Wolf, *Foul: The Connie*   1972).
Hawkins Story (New York: Holt Rinehart,

sue? (Which Moe did not do: instead, after starring in the ABA, Moe went on to become one of the NBA's most successful coaches.)

2. Why is gambling considered to be "detrimental to the best interests of the sport"? How far should that anti-gambling sentiment take us? Should an Atlantic City casino, for example, be treated differently from the Meadowlands racetrack? Should either of these be treated differently from private, high-stakes gambling, in which Len Dykstra of the Philadelphia Phillies (in poker) and Michael Jordan of the Chicago Bulls (in golf) each reportedly lost tens of thousands of dollars in 1991? Or should the commissioner's target be only betting on games in one's own sport? If so, should there be a distinction between games involving the player's own team and other teams' games, or between betting on one's team to win and betting that one's team will lose? Is there a difference between a manager and a player betting on his own team to win?

3. Wherever one draws the line against gambling, a further question is how serious is this form of "moral turpitude"—that is, how severe a penalty does it warrant? For example, what actions merited the gravest condemnation from Commissioner Giamatti—Pete Rose's gambling or his income tax fraud? In addition, should betting by a player or manager like Rose be treated the same as betting by an owner such as the Phillies' Cox? Is expulsion of a player or manager such as Rose the same tangible punishment as expulsion of an owner such as Cox or Steinbrenner? Which level of punishment was more appropriate for betting on one's team to win—baseball's lifetime ban of Pete Rose or football's one year suspension of Paul Hornung and Alex Karras?

4. In the summer of 1991 Commissioner Rozelle announced a new policy providing for a four-game suspension for any NFL player convicted of drunk driving. Is exclusion from the league on these grounds for one quarter of the season a good idea? Does a suspended player have a viable antitrust suit?

2. WOMEN IN THE LOCKER ROOM

As the Rose case faded from view in the fall of 1990, public attention turned to the Lisa Olson incident. Olson, a sportswriter who covered the New England Patriots, sought to interview Patriots cornerback Maurice Hurst after a practice session. Told that Hurst would be available only in the locker room rather than in the team's media room, Olson went to speak to Hurst at his locker. While there, Olson was confronted by a naked Zeke Mowatt; Mowatt allegedly made an offensive comment to her, which was echoed by several other players in the background. Following a report by his special counsel, Professor Phil Heymann of Harvard Law School, new NFL Commissioner Paul Tagliabue fined Mowatt $14,000 and the other players lesser amounts.

Although Mowatt has challenged the accuracy of Olson's charge and Heymann's report, this behavior was certainly unacceptable if it did take place. In fact, Lisa Olson filed a tort suit which was settled by the Patriots, reportedly for $250,000. What is your reaction to the juxtaposition of baseball Commissioner Giamatti's lifetime ban of Pete

Rose for betting on his own team to win and Tagliabue's fining Zeke Mowatt the equivalent of one quarter of one game's salary for sexual harassment of a sportswriter, a fine that has not yet been collected?

More interesting legal and policy issues are posed by the activities of Cincinnati Bengals' coach Sam Wyche. Soon after the Olson incident, Wyche, citing his players' need for privacy, refused entry to his locker room after a game to a female USA Today sports writer, Denise Toms. Instead Wyche gave Toms priority in interviewing the player of her choice outside the locker room. For that action, which violated the league's written policy on equal access for female and male reporters, Tagliabue fined Wyche approximately $30,000. Many media accounts of this controversy asserted that female sports writers have an equal legal right to be in the locker room with male reporters, a right that had been won in the following case. In reading the opinion, consider whether and to what extent the media's impression is legally correct, especially under the Supreme Court's current "state action" jurisprudence (which we will encounter in Chapter 8 in the litigation between the NCAA and Jerry Tarkanian of UNLV)? Are there other sources of legal relief that might have been available if Tagliabue had emulated baseball Commissioner Bowie Kuhn and sided with Wyche? As a policy matter, should female sports writers have automatic locker room access?

LUDTKE AND TIME, INC., v. KUHN

United States District Court, Southern District of New York, 1978.

461 F.Supp. 86.

MOTLEY, DISTRICT JUDGE.

[In April 1975, Commissioner Bowie Kuhn instituted a general ban against admission of women sports writers to baseball clubhouses. Earlier the National Hockey League and the National Basketball Association had decided to permit women reporters access to players in their locker rooms. Despite the contrary wishes of the Yankee players, Kuhn insisted that Melissa Ludtke, a Sports Illustrated sportswriter covering the 1977 World Series between the Yankees and the Dodgers, not be allowed into the Yankees' clubhouse.

This lawsuit involved exclusion of Ludtke from the Yankees clubhouse at Yankee Stadium. Yankee Stadium was owned by the City of New York, having been acquired by eminent domain in the early 1970s, and renovated at a cost of $50 million. The Yankees rented the Stadium from the city for baseball games, under a lease whose rent formula depended on attendance at games.]

* * *

Central to the resolution of this case is the undisputed fact that all accredited female sports reporters are excluded from the Yankee clubhouse at Yankee Stadium solely because they are women, whereas all accredited male sports reporters (to the extent that space limitations permit) are permitted access to the clubhouse after games for the purpose of interviewing ballplayers.

Defendants say women reporters are excluded in order 1) to protect the privacy of those players who are undressed or who are in various stages of undressing and getting ready to shower; 2) to protect the image of baseball as a family sport; and 3) preservation of traditional notions of decency and propriety.

Another pivotal fact which is also not disputed is that fresh-off-the-field interviews are important to the work of sports reporters and will give a competitive advantage to those who have access to the ballplayers at that juncture, particularly during the World Series games.

Another critical consideration is the admission that there are several other less sweeping alternatives to the present policy of blanket exclusion of women reporters. Counsel for defendants admitted that those players who are desirous of undressing can retreat to their cubicles in the clubhouse. There the players can be shielded from the "roving eyes" of any female reporters by having each cubicle furnished with a curtain or swinging door. It is also conceded that the player who is undressed and wishes to move about in that state can use a towel to shield himself from view.

Since the Kuhn policy determination is based solely on sex, and since that policy results in denial of equal opportunity to plaintiff Ludtke to pursue her profession as a sports reporter, and since there are several less restrictive alternatives to the total exclusion of women, and since the material facts regarding New York City's involvement in Yankee Stadium and the lease of those premises to the Yankees are not disputed, the only questions remaining for decision are questions of law.

A. State Action

The first question is whether New York City's involvement with Yankee Stadium and the lease arrangement with the Yankees is such as to make the Kuhn policy determination state action within the contemplation of the Fourteenth Amendment.

It must by now be regarded as well settled that state action may be found where the direct perpetrator of allegedly discriminatory acts is, though a private entity, "so entwined" with an agency of the state that that agency must be deemed responsible for the private entity's acts. There is, however, no rigid yardstick against which the relationship may be measured to determine the presence of state action. As the Supreme Court has explained:

> Only by sifting facts and weighing circumstances can the nonobvious involvement of the State in private conduct be attributed its true significance.

Burton v. Wilmington Parking Authority, 365 U.S. 715 (1961).

Burton, like the instant case, involved discrimination against the plaintiff on the ground of a class-based characteristic, in that case race. The discrimination there took place on ostensibly private premises (those of the defendant Eagle Coffee Shoppe), operated under lease from a public authority (the Wilmington Parking Authority). Here the discrimination also takes place on ostensibly private premises (the Yankee Clubhouse) located on premises (Yankee Stadium) operated under lease from a public authority (the City of New York). The Court in *Burton* found that the coffee shop, located in an otherwise public building owned by the Wilmington Parking Authority, enjoyed a "symbiotic relationship" with the publicly operated portions of the premises, consisting of parking facilities. The proximity of the coffee shop was found to be essential in establishing the fiscal viability of the parking garage. The Yankee clubhouse in this case has been opened to the press immediately after games, particularly during the World Series, so that players fresh-off-the-field may be interviewed. Moreover, it is undisputed that television cameras were permitted in the clubhouse after the World Series games for the same purpose. Advertising and massive publicity about the Yankees and individual Yankee ballplayers is essential to the profitability of the Yankee Stadium.

* * *

Here, as in *Burton*, the place where the discriminatory acts occurred is owned by the state (the City of New York) and leased pursuant to special legislative provisions to the Yankees. In this case, as in *Burton*, the facility involved is maintained and improved with the use of public funds. The Court noted in *Burton* that the relationship of the public and private entities in that case placed them in a relationship of interdependence. The same observation can be made on these facts, where the annual rentals to be paid to the City for use of the stadium depend directly on the drawing power of Yankee games, and the City has in turn invested substantial sums of public money to enhance that drawing power by modernizing and improving the stadium itself.

In defendants' memorandum, they set forth the objectives underlying baseball's policy of excluding female reporters from the locker room. Among these conceded objectives were the aim "to protect and preserve the national image of baseball as a family game ... and ... to preserve baseball's audience and to maintain its popularity and standing."

It is an undisputed fact that the City's profit from its lease with the Yankees escalates when attendance at Yankee games increases. Thus the City has a clear interest in the preservation and maintenance of baseball's audience, image, popularity and standing.

* * *

B. Sex Discrimination

This court finds that the state action complained of here infringes both equal protection and due process rights of plaintiff Ludtke.

1. Equal Protection

On the basis of the undisputed facts, plaintiff Ludtke, while in pursuit of her profession as a sports reporter, was treated differently from her male counterparts (other properly accredited sports writers) solely because she is a woman.

* * *

"To withstand constitutional challenge . . . classifications by gender must serve important governmental objectives and must be substantially related to achievement of those objectives." Craig v. Boren, 429 U.S. 190, 197 (1976). Defendants have asserted, as justification for the complete exclusion of female reporters from the clubhouse at Yankee Stadium, their interest in protecting the privacy of the ballplayers while undressing in the locker room.

The right to privacy is of constitutional dimension, see Roe v. Wade, 410 U.S. 113 (1973), and its protection is thus undeniably an important objective. It cannot be said on these facts, however, that there is a sufficiently substantial relationship between that objective on one hand and the total exclusion of women from the Yankee locker room on the other to pass constitutional muster. "Inquiry into the actual purposes of the discrimination . . . proves the contrary." Califano v. Goldfarb, 430 U.S. 199, 212 (1977).

At least during World Series games, male members of the news media with television cameras have been allowed to enter the Yankee locker room immediately after the games and broadcast live from that location. In this connection, only a backdrop behind the player standing in front of the camera is provided to shield other players from the "roving eye" of the camera. These locker room encounters are viewed by mass audiences, which include many women and children. This practice, coupled with defendants' practice of refusing to allow accredited women sports reporters to enter the locker room, shows that the latter is "substantially related" only to maintaining the locker room as an all-male preserve.

* * *

2. Due Process

An analysis of these same facts from the perspective of substantive due process leads us to an identical result. The right to pursue one's profession is a fundamental "liberty" within the meaning of the Fourteenth Amendment's due process guarantee. Further, it is settled law that: Even though the governmental purpose be legitimate and substantial, that purpose cannot be pursued by means that broadly stifle fundamental personal liberties when the end can be more narrowly achieved.

As noted above, the Kuhn policy substantially and directly interferes with the right of plaintiff Ludtke to pursue her profession as a sports reporter. Her male counterparts are able to get to the ballplayers fresh-off-the-field when comments about plays may still be in progress, for example. When a statutory classification significantly interferes with the exercise of a fundamental right, it cannot be upheld unless it is supported by sufficiently important state interests and is closely tailored to effectuate only those interests.

The undisputed facts show that the Yankees' interest in protecting ballplayer privacy may be fully served by [a] much less sweeping means than that implemented here. The court holds that the state action complained of unreasonably interferes with plaintiff Ludtke's fundamental right to pursue her profession in violation of the due process clause of the Fourteenth Amendment.

The other two interests asserted by defendants, maintaining the status of baseball as a family sport and conforming to traditional notions of decency and propriety, are clearly too insubstantial to merit serious consideration. Weighed against plaintiff's right to be free of discrimination based upon her sex, and her fundamental right to pursue her profession, such objectives cannot justify the defendants' policy under the equal protection or due process clauses of the Fourteenth Amendment.

Injunction granted.

Note on Racial Discrimination in Sports

An even starker case of sports discrimination was baseball's total exclusion of black players from the major leagues for more than half a century. True, baseball Commissioner Landis piously intoned in 1942:

> There is no rule, formal or informal, or any understanding—unwritten, subterranean or sub-anything—against the hiring of Negro players by the teams of organized baseball.

However, the historical record is to the contrary. By the 1930s, several players had emerged in the Negro Leagues—such as Satchel Paige and Josh Gibson—whose performance against major league stars in off-season exhibition tours had amply demonstrated their superstar skills. Only the cohesive internal structure of the major leagues under the iron-fisted rule of Judge Landis can explain why not a single last-place club was tempted to strengthen its team (at a comparatively cheap price) by signing black players whose caliber later put them in the Hall of Fame. Not until Landis died in 1944, to be succeeded by Kentucky Senator Albert "Happy" Chandler, did the door swing open to Branch Rickey to sign Jackie Robinson in 1945 and thereby break the color bar in baseball.[13]

13. The entire story is told in Jules Tygiel, *Baseball's Great Experiment: Jack-* *ie Robinson and his Legacy* (New York: Random House, 1983).

Suppose, however, that Landis had lived to foil Rickey's integration effort (just as he had thwarted Bill Veeck's wartime plan to buy the last place Philadelphia Phillies and restock the team with star black players). What kind of legal attack might have been mounted against baseball's segregation by Robinson, perhaps as part of Charles Houston's and Thurgood Marshall's contemporary strategy at the NAACP? Remember that this was two decades before the nation was prepared to enact the Civil Rights Act prohibiting racial discrimination.

In the 1990s, happily, there is no shortage of black players in baseball, nor in football and basketball. Blacks now make up 17% of baseball players (Hispanics another 14%), 62% of football players, and 75% of basketball players.[14] Not only in number but also in quality of performance and size of salary, black players now occupy the upper echelons of professional team sports in America.[15] However, blacks still comprise only a small fraction of players in certain key positions: for example, blacks make up just 1% of baseball catchers and 8% of football quarterbacks. Even more troubling is the severe underrepresentation of blacks in leadership positions with the team or in the front office. Though almost all occupants of head coaching or managerial positions come from the playing ranks, there have been only two black head football coaches in the entire history of this sport. Even in basketball with its stronger record of minority coaches and general managers, at the end of 1992 there were only three blacks among the game's 25 head coaches. For decades baseball also lagged behind, with just five black and two Hispanic managers in its history.[16] Suddenly, though, in 1992 four new minority managers (two black and two Hispanic) were added to the two black incumbents—and one of the latter, Cito Gaston, led his Toronto Blue Jays to a World Series triumph. Even in baseball, though, there remains only a handful of minorities in senior front office positions.

This issue was catapulted into the national consciousness in 1987, as a result of televised remarks made by Los Angeles Dodgers' Vice President Al Campanis on ABC's Nightline—ironically, on a special program devoted to the fortieth anniversary of Jackie Robinson's first game with the Brooklyn Dodgers. When asked by Nightline host Ted Koppel why there were so few black managers and general managers in the game, Campanis replied:

> I don't think it's prejudice. I truly believe that [blacks] may not have some of the necessities to be, let's say, a field manager or perhaps a general manager.

Immediately after this exchange, Campanis was fired by Dodgers' President

14. See Richard E. Lapchick with Jeffrey P. Brown, *1992 Racial Report Card: Do Professional Sports Provide Equal Opportunities for All Races?* 4 CSSS Digest 1 (Summer, 1992) (a publication of the Center for the Study of Sport and Society at Northeastern University).

15. For a valuable review of the empirical research about minority athlete representation, performance and pay, see Lawrence M. Kahn, *Discrimination in Professional Sports: A Survey of the Literature*, 44 Industrial and Labor Rel. Rev. 395 (1991).

16. See Lapchick, *1992 Racial Report*, note 14 above.

Peter O'Malley.[17]   More important, following the lead of the NBA's David Stern, MLB Commissioner Peter Ueberroth and NFL Commissioner Pete Rozelle instituted affirmative action programs to try to encourage their leagues' teams to expand the number of minorities in coaching and front office positions, with the modest results noted above.

Unhappily for the sports world, the issue of racism reared its ugly head again at the end of 1992, in a notorious case involving Marge Schott, the managing partner and largest shareholder in the Cincinnati Reds.   A wrongful dismissal suit brought by an ex-Reds employee brought into the open the fact that Schott regularly used such epithets as "dumb niggers" and "money-grubbing Jews" to refer to her players, associates, and rivals. It was later reported that in a conference call with other owners, Schott had asserted that she would "rather have a trained monkey working for her than a nigger."   The ensuing firestorm of protest across the country caught baseball at a bad time, because it was without a commissioner and engaged in an internal struggle about the future structure and direction of the game.   After extensive discussions between her lawyer and baseball's Executive Committee, Schott agreed to accept the penalty of a $25,000 fine and one-year suspension from the day-to-day decisions of the Reds, though she retained her position as managing partner of the club.

The case does raise an important number of questions of principle regarding the governance of sports.   Once Schott was found to have made these racial slurs, did she deserve the same treatment as was meted out to Campanis—dismissal from baseball—and if so, precisely what does such action entail for an owner as contrasted with an employee?   Is it appropriate, though, to punish someone for personal sentiments that, however deplorable, were expressed in private, and just happen to become public because of a lawsuit (one that was dismissed)?   Is it significant in assessing what Schott may have said to take account of what unquestionably she had done—employed just one black among the forty-five members of her front office staff (by comparison with the 16% minority representation in front offices across Major League Baseball)?

Consider now the variety of legal and policy questions raised by minority hiring practices in sports.   Could minority managerial prospects who are not even interviewed for, let alone appointed to, a vacant position, challenge baseball's hiring practices under Title VII of the Civil Rights Act which forbids discrimination in employment?   Should commissioners go even further and institute in their respective sports—pursuant to their "best interests" authority—the kind of numerical hiring and promotion guidelines that are prevalent in much of business enterprise?   How significant can league-wide guidelines be for appraising the decision of a particular team in selecting who will be its manager or head coach?   (Keep this example in mind for later chapters which take up the broader question whether the team or the league is the key entity in the world of sports.)   Is such explicit reference to group status and affirmative preference actually in the best interest of minority participants in the sport.[18]

17. For a description of the Campanis episode, see Philip M. Hoosie, *Necessities: Racial Bias in American Sports*, xv-xviii, *(New York: Random House, 1989).*

18. The broader society is now confronting the same question about the best way

Finally, consider this further form of discrimination depicted in a best-selling 1992 novel—*The Dreyfus Affair* (by Peter Lefcourt). In the midst of the novel's 1995 pennant race, the star shortstop for the pennant-contending Los Angeles Valley Vikings is discovered to have fallen in love—with his second baseman. Would a real-life commissioner be justified in following his fictional counterpart and banning the players for such conduct that he feels is detrimental to the best interests of the game? Would it make a difference if the gay lovers played for opposing teams in the pennant race?

3. DRUG USE AND DRUG TESTING [19]

For commissioners attempting to define and enforce the best interests of their sports, the most intensely debated issue in the last decade has been drug use by athletes. It is estimated that tens of millions of Americans have used marijuana and cocaine; it is unsurprising, therefore, to find a number of users among the approximately 3,000 professional athletes—most of them young men with high salaries. The same sentiment that has impelled presidents to declare an all-out "War on Drugs" also prompts league commissioners to insist that their players "Just Say No"—or else! But one way that drug use differs from gambling, for example, is that the drug problem emerged after players had been organized into unions that engage in collective bargaining under the umbrella of the National Labor Relations Act (which will be canvassed in detail in Chapter 4).[20] Players and their unions naturally took a somewhat different point of view toward this issue—both about teammates who were found to have abused drugs, and even more so, about league institution of mandatory drug testing of all players. As we will see, the legal and contractual framework for collective bargaining furnished a somewhat more effective base for players challenging the initiatives taken by commissioners to address the drug problem.

In addressing the "drug problem", sports has followed the broader polity in assuming that the major dangers are presented by use of illegal substances such as marijuana and cocaine, rather than more

to address the racial question in America. For provocative statements of contrasting views within the minority community on this topic, see Patricia J. Williams, *The Alchemy of Race and Rights* (Cambridge, Mass.: Harvard University Press, 1991), and Steven Carter, *Reflections of an Affirmative Action Baby* (New York: Basic Books, 1991).

19. Useful overviews of this topic in the sports world are Robert Voy, *Drugs, Sports and Politics* (Champaign, Ill.: Leisure Press, 1991) and Glenn M. Wong and Richard J. Ensor, *Major League Baseball and Drugs: Fight the Problem or the Players?* 11 Nova L. Rev. 779 (1987). Again, Bowie Kuhn's autobiography, *Hardball* note 1 above, at 303–322, gives a close-up picture of how this issue looked to one of the major

protagonists. An important depiction of the broader issues of drug use and drug enforcement in American life is Mark A.R. Kleiman, *Against Excess: Drug Policy for Results* (New York: Basic Books, 1991).

20. An early look at the labor law issues raised by drug testing of professional athletes is Ethan Lock, *The Legality Under the National Labor Relations Act of Attempts by National Football League Owners to Unilaterally Implement Drug Testing Programs*, 39 U. of Florida L. Rev. 1 (1987). Marion Crain, *Expanded Employee Drug Testing Programs and the Public Good: Big Brother at the Bargaining Table*, 64 New York U. L. Rev. 1286 (1989), analyzes subsequent major decisions by the National Labor Relations Board and the courts about this topic in American industry generally.

widespread but legal consumption of alcohol. (Alcohol advertising—especially of beer—is a major revenue source for sports.) Then, in the aftermath of Ben Johnson's world-record 100–meter victory and subsequent disqualification at the 1988 Olympic Games, steroid use became a target of both public criminal law and private commissioner's law. Crucial questions to keep in mind when reading and reflecting on the following materials are whether priority in defending the "best interests of sports" should be placed on "mind-altering" drugs such as cocaine or on "performance-altering" drugs such as the anabolic steroids, on illegal drugs such as marijuana or on legal drugs such as alcohol.

In baseball, two of the earliest cases of drug abuse involved Alan Wiggins, a second baseman for the San Diego Padres and Baltimore Orioles, and Steve Howe, then a relief pitcher for the Los Angeles Dodgers. After each player had gone through a lengthy period of drug abuse, attempted treatment, and suspensions from the game, their lives took drastically different turns in 1991—Wiggins dying of AIDS, Howe returning to stardom as a Yankee reliever. But the addictive effect of cocaine was demonstrated once more when Howe was caught in the off-season buying the drug from an undercover Montana police officer—reportedly for "one last party before spring training." After being put on probation by the criminal courts, Howe was banned from baseball for life by Commissioner Fay Vincent.

The first baseball drug case, however, to seize both the public and the commissioner's attention involved four players on the Kansas City Royals—Vida Blue, Willie Wilson, Jerry Martin, and Willie Aikens—who were arrested and convicted in 1983 for possession of cocaine, and sentenced to three months in jail. For each of these players, Commissioner Bowie Kuhn imposed a one-year suspension for the entire 1984 baseball season, pursuant to the following rule that had been posted in all clubhouses:

> Anyone involved in the illegal possession or use of drugs or illegal trafficking with drugs of any sort will be subject to discipline. In serious cases, the discipline may include suspension or dismissal and termination of contract guarantees.

This rule had been issued pursuant to Major League Rule 21(f) which was binding on baseball players under the uniform player contract:

> (1) OTHER MISCONDUCT. Nothing herein contained shall be construed as exclusively defining or otherwise limiting acts, transactions, practices or conduct found not to be in the best interests of Baseball; and any and all other acts, transactions, practices or conduct not to be in the best interests of Baseball are prohibited and shall be subject to such penalties, including permanent ineligibility, as the facts in the particular case may warrant.

However, Wilson and the other players had a legal foothold for challenging the commissioner exercise of his disciplinary authority. The collective agreement negotiated between baseball owners and the Players' Association (the Basic Agreement) ordained that the Major League Agreement and Major League Rules (the source of the commissioner's powers) bound the players only "to the extent they were not inconsistent with this Basic Agreement." With respect to discipline, Article 11 of the Basic Agreement specified:

A. Just Cause

The Parties recognize that a Player may be subjected to disciplinary action for just cause by his Club, League or the Commissioner. Therefore, in Grievances regarding discipline, the issue to be resolved shall be whether there has been just cause for the penalty imposed.

Under this provision, which is commonplace in almost every unionized firm in any industry, a neutral arbitrator selected by the parties decides whether the exercise of the employer's (here the commissioner's) disciplinary authority is, in fact, for "just cause."

In the path-breaking *Wilson* decision of 1984, the arbitrator accepted Commissioner Kuhn's premise that player use of drugs was a matter of legitimate concern regarding "the best interests of baseball":

At its worst, to the extent that cocaine use becomes habitual or addictive, a player risks both an increased chance of physical deterioration, and a dangerous involvement with the criminals who sell the drug. That involvement may lead to control of the player either because of the addiction or because of the risk of exposure. The consequences of such control over any part of the game are so obviously disastrous as to require no elaboration.

* * *

Nor can there be serious doubt that this type of employee misconduct is of serious impact on the employer. Because baseball players are highly skilled, well compensated and constantly visible, they deserve and receive national attention. Neither the players nor the industry escapes the publicity. And drug involvement, because of its threat to athletes' playing abilities, because it is illegal and because of the related connotation of inroads by organized crime, constitutes a serious and immediate threat to the business that is promoted as our national pastime. Because the perception alone of taint is so potentially damaging, baseball has a substantial interest in the implementation and enforcement of drug prohibitions. This much is clear from the evidence and is not seriously in dispute.

The arbitrator stated that even the Players Association did not seriously challenge the owners' concern about drug use, nor the proposition that discipline might be warranted in appropriate cases. The questions were how legitimate was the concern about cocaine as opposed to other drugs, and what measures the arbitrator should find it "just" for the league to use in response. The following cases pose these issues in more concrete terms.

Questions for Discussion

1. The Willie Wilson case involved regular use of cocaine during the 1983 season, and eventually public arrest, conviction, and a jail term. What additional actions by the commissioner were appropriate?

2. Vida Blue's case, while treated in the same fashion by the criminal law, involved more extensive use of cocaine during the 1982 and 1983 seasons, as well as Blue's role as a conduit between his drug supplier and his Kansas City teammates (and occasionally players from other clubs visiting Kansas City). What penalty from the commissioner?

3. In August 1980, Ferguson Jenkins, then a pitcher for the Texas Rangers, was found to have cocaine in his luggage which was opened at Canadian customs when he flew to Toronto to pitch against the Blue Jays. (Ironically, Jenkins is the only Canadian baseball player ever elected to the Hall of Fame.) Following his arrest, a preliminary trial date was set for December in Toronto. When Kuhn's staff sought to question Jenkins about the incident to determine what action the Commissioner should take, on advice of his Canadian counsel Jenkins refused to answer. What action should Kuhn be entitled to take as of September 1980 (look back at the scope of the commissioner's investigative authority in the material quoted in *Rose v. Giamatti*)?

4. Pascual Perez, then pitching for the Atlanta Braves, was arrested in the Dominican Republic in January 1984, convicted of possession of cocaine, and fined and released on April 9. Upon his return to the United States, Perez denied having committed the offense. Should the commissioner be able to rely on the court's conviction, or should he have to establish the facts before an American arbitrator? (By the early 1990s, Perez, like Steve Howe, had found his way to the Yankees' pitching staff. Unhappily, as also happened to Howe, in 1992 Commissioner Fay Vincent suspended Perez for having failed a spot drug test during spring training.)

5. Vincent's lifetime expulsion of Steve Howe for his seventh reported incident of illegal drug use (in a twelve-year career) was taken by the Players Association to arbitration. If you had been baseball's arbitrator, would you have considered Howe's punishment too severe, or long overdue?

————

The preceding problems all reflect disciplinary responses to illegal drug use. The following problems test both the possible use of other measures against drugs, and the comparative disciplinary treatment of drug use and other off-field misbehavior.

Questions for Discussion

1. The Kansas City Royals in the Vida Blue case described above, and the Pittsburgh Pirates in a later case involving Dave Parker's admitted cocaine use in the early 1980s, sought to reduce their salary payments to these players for the seasons during which they had used drugs. How should an arbitrator (or a judge) interpret the language of the standard player contract as it applies to this issue? Should it matter whether the individual player contract was fully guaranteed? Whether the team

sought merely to avoid paying deferred compensation still owed for prior seasons, or to recoup salary payments already made? How feasible is it to determine whether a player's performance during any one season has deteriorated due to drug use as compared with other factors? If available, is such a contract remedy for the club a sufficient response to the problem of drug use, or was Bowie Kuhn correct in asserting that a commissioner simply cannot trust individual clubs to deal firmly with this problem?

Consider the implications of the Otis Nixon case. Nixon, the star center-fielder of the Atlanta Braves during the 1991 pennant race, failed a drug test (required because of earlier cocaine problems) and was suspended by Commissioner Vincent for the rest of that season and the first month of the 1992 season. Though the Braves narrowly escaped with the National League pennant, they lost the World Series to the Minnesota Twins, in part because of a baserunning blunder in the seventh game by Lonnie Smith, Nixon's replacement in the outfield. Then, in the 1991–1992 off-season, the Braves outbid the California Angels for Nixon's future services, by offering him a multi-million dollar salary increase in a guaranteed three-year contract. What does this case imply about the problem of cocaine use by a baseball player?

2. How does drug use compare with other forms of off-field misbehavior? What about late-night drinking that leads to altercations (as happened to a number of major league players, including Mickey Mantle and Billy Martin)? What about driving a car while impaired and getting into an accident that injures the player and a teammate (as happened to Lenny Dykstra of the Philadelphia Phillies) or even kills another person (as happened to Craig McTavish, then of the Boston Bruins, and Reggie Rogers, then of the Detroit Lions)? A tragic irony of the Rogers case is that just two years earlier his brother Don Rogers, a star safety for the Cleveland Browns, died from smoking crack cocaine. The deaths not only of Don Rogers but also of Len Bias (which occurred the day after the Boston Celtics made Bias the second pick in the 1986 NBA college draft) put the dangers of crack cocaine on the front pages of the nation's newspapers; deaths from drunk driving are an everyday occurrence. Finally, what about athletes who are arrested for carrying a gun without a license or in an inappropriate public setting (as happened to Jose Canseco)?

3. The above questions relate to mind-altering drugs, whether illegal drugs such as cocaine or legal drugs such as alcohol. Even more challenging issues are posed by performance-enhancing drugs such as anabolic steroids, which only recently loomed on the sports horizon. Precisely why should we want to prevent athletes such as Ben Johnson in track or Lyle Alzado in football from using steroids to enhance their speed and strength and thus elevate the levels of performance in their sports? Is there something about the nature of athletic competition that makes league efforts to stamp out steroid use a qualitatively different venture in the "best interests" of the sport? [21]

---

21. An illuminating philosophical discussion of these issues can be found in Robert L. Simon, *Fair Play: Sport, Value, and Society* (Boulder Col.: Westview Press, 1991), in particular, Chapter 4, Enhancing Performance Through Drugs. In Chapter 10 of this book, on *Individual Sports*, we will look at the issues of steroid use and

* * *

The drug cases we have noted were all drawn from baseball, but the problem has been widespread in other sports, as fans of Dexter Manley of the Washington Redskins, Michael Ray Richardson of the New Jersey Nets, and Bob Probert of the Detroit Red Wings remember. But the various league drug policies and collective bargaining regimes differ in many interesting ways. The governance structure in the National Football League was exhibited in the following award involving one of the first major drug controversies in football.

NFL MANAGEMENT COUNCIL AND NFL PLAYERS ASSOCIATION (RANDY CROWDER AND DON REESE)

(Arbitration, 1979).

SCEARCE, ARBITRATOR.

* * *

Donald F. Reese and Randolph C. Crowder were professional football players and under contract to the Miami Dolphins when, on [May 5, 1977], they were charged with unlawfully possessing, selling and delivering a controlled substance (cocaine) to two individuals (who were detectives for the City of Miami) in violation of Section 893.13 of the Florida Statutes. Upon being notified of this turn of events, the Miami Dolphins Club suspended the players, without pay, pending the outcome of the trial. The basis for the Club's action was that the players' arrests were detrimental to the Club's well being. Grievances were filed on behalf of the players, through an attorney, which were processed pursuant to Article VII of the CBA [Collective Bargaining Agreement] to the Player–Club Relations Committee (PCRC). The thrust of the grievance was that the Miami Club had erred when it suspended the players, on the basis that the players were entitled, under the American system of justice, to a presumption of innocence until a finding of guilt by the court. The remedy sought was reinstatement and resumption of pay by the Club, until the Court had an opportunity to act.

On July 25, 1977 the PCRC convened, considered the case and rendered a decision upholding the grievance. The PCRC resolved the grievance [by ordering the Dolphins to reinstate both players at full pay or place them on no-recall waivers. The order of reinstatement expressly stated that it does] not affect or influence any future suspension by an NFL club or by the Commissioner.

* * *

On August 10, 1977 the Circuit Court accepted a plea of Nolo Contendere by the players on all counts, but withheld adjudication;

testing in international track and field and other sports that make up the Olympic   Games.

requiring, instead, that the players serve one year in the County Stockade and placed them on five years concurrent probation on all counts. Sentence commenced on August 15, 1977.

[In early August of 1978 Commissioner Rozelle's office notified both players (and the NFLPA) that it intended to convene a hearing upon their impending release to determine whether disciplinary action against them under Article VII of the bargaining agreement was warranted.]

* * *

Punished twice?

The aforementioned [hearing] was convened on August 17, 1978 at NFL headquarters in New York City with the Commissioner present.... [On] August 18, 1978, a letter was directed to Crowder and Reese:

As you acknowledged yesterday, you are now fully aware of the fact that NFL players occupy a unique position in the public's perception. The names and images of NFL players are regularly carried into many millions of American homes on television, on radio, and through the print media. NFL players are the focus of wide-spread public attention and are, for good or bad, objects of admiration and emulation for countless American young people.

These unquestioned circumstances impose on every NFL player certain minimal standards of personal conduct—on the field and off. As one court has stated it:

It is clear that [the NFL has] sought for years to establish a standard of public conduct for professional football participants, including players. This standard (which might be better termed 'image') included the portrayal of players as high-type, admirable young men who are worthy of the respect and emulation of the young.

The resulting obligations of personal conduct are not just owed to the League—they are owed to the public, to the teams with which the players are associated, and to each and every other professional football player. The game itself can be honored—or dishonored— by its own participants.

One such obligation, beyond any doubt, is to avoid criminal involvement with illegal drugs. The use or disposition of illegal drugs, and the seriousness with which it will be viewed by the League, have been repeatedly emphasized within the League in recent years—in team playbooks, locker room notices, and by general discussion.

* * *

[In your] circumstances, I would normally be inclined to impose very severe sanctions. But I recognize that youth and immaturity contributed to the serious mistake you made. I further recognize that the court which heard your case consciously undertook to impose a moderate sentence followed by a strict probation, apparently in a desire to balance deserved punishment against an opportunity for rehabilitation within the line of work you know best. I am also aware that completion of your sentence took you well into the 1978 pre-season training period, and that further suspension action might jeopardize any further opportunity you may have to obtain football employment. Accordingly, I have determined that no suspension from the NFL is warranted at this time. I am proceeding on the premise that you have, as you said yesterday, learned a hard and painful lesson....

I have, however, determined to attach to your return to the NFL [the] condition that you contribute the sum of $5,000 to a drug rehabilitation facility in the state of Florida, subject to approval by this office....

[This mandatory contribution (in effect, a fine) produced another grievance by Crowder and Reese which the NFLPA took to arbitration. In football, the Commissioner's disciplinary authority was based on Article VIII of the NFL constitution and bylaws:]

DISCIPLINARY POWERS OF COMMISSIONER

8.13 (A) Whenever the Commissioner, after notice and hearing, decides that an owner, shareholder, partner or holder of an interest in a member club, or any player, coach, officer, director or employee thereof, or an officer, employee or official of the League has either violated the Constitution or By–Laws of the League, or has been or is guilty of conduct detrimental to the welfare of the League or professional football, then the Commissioner shall have complete authority to:

(1) Suspend and/or fine such person in an amount not in excess of five thousand dollars ($5,000), and/or

(2) Cancel any contract or agreement of such person with the League or with any member thereof.

(3) In cases involving a violation of the prohibitions against tampering and set forth in Sections 9.1(C), 10 and 11, 9.2 and 12.1(B) hereof, award or transfer selection choices and/or deprive the offending club of a selection choice or choices.

(4) In cases involving a violation affecting the competitive aspects of the game, award or transfer players and/or selection choices, and/or deprive the offending club of a selection choice or choices, and/or cancel any contract or agreement of such person with the League or with any member thereof, and/or fine the offending club in an amount not in excess of twenty-five thousand dollars ($25,000) despite the provisions of subsection (1) herein.

[While the NFL–NFLPA collective agreement, just like the agreement in baseball, provided that the collective agreement superceded any conflicting provisions in the NFL constitution and the standard player contract, the grievance procedures within the collective agreement established a rather different division of authority between the commissioner and an outside arbitrator.]

VII. *Non–Injury Grievance Arbitration*

Section 1. *Definition* : Any dispute ... involving the interpretation or application of, or compliance with, any provisions of this Agreement, the Standard Player Contract, the NFL Player Contract, and any provision of the NFL Constitution and Bylaws pertaining to terms and conditions of employment of NFL players, will be resolved exclusively in accordance with the procedure set forth in this Article; provided, however, that any dispute involving Section 1 of Article III, Section 11 of Article VII, Article VIII and Article IX of this Agreement, paragraph 8 of the Standard Player Contract and paragraph 3 of the NFL Player Contract will not be resolved under the procedure of this Article.

* * *

Section 11. *Integrity and Public Confidence:* In the event a matter filed as a grievance in accordance with the provisions of Section 3 above gives rise to issues involving the integrity of, or public confidence in, the game of professional football, the Commissioner may, at any stage of its processing, after consultation with the PCRC, order that the matter be withdrawn from such processing and thereafter be processed in accordance with the procedure provided in Article III of this Agreement on Commissioner Discipline.

* * *

Commissioner Discipline

Section 1. Commissioner Discipline: Notwithstanding anything stated in Article VII of this Agreement, Non–Injury Grievance, all disputes involving a fine or suspension imposed upon a player by the Commissioner for conduct on the playing field, or involving action taken against a player by the Commissioner for conduct detrimental to the integrity of, or public confidence in, the game of professional football, will be processed exclusively as follows: The Commissioner will promptly send written notice of his action to the player, with a copy to the NFLPA. Within 20 days following written notification of the Commissioner's action, the player affected thereby or the NFLPA, with the approval of the player involved, may appeal in writing to the Commissioner. The Commissioner will designate a time and place for hearing, which will be commenced within 10 days following his receipt of the notice of appeal. As soon as practicable following the conclusion of such hearing, the Commissioner will render a written decision, which decision will constitute full, final, and complete disposition of the dispute, and will be binding upon the player[s] and club[s] involved and the parties to this Agreement with respect to that dispute.

[The question posed to the arbitrator, then, was what jurisdiction, if any, he had under Article VII to review the action taken by the

Commissioner toward Crowder and Reese under the umbrella of Article
VIII.]

* * *

A plethora of questions arise in connection with this case, many of
which are related to and dependent upon the findings on a prefatory
one: Does an arbitrator, empowered (and limited) under Article VII,
have authority to consider challenges to the Commissioner's authority
to exact fines, suspensions or other discipline or to review such actions,
where they are taken under the provisions of Article VIII?

Issue

Before engaging this question, it is obvious that, based upon the
record and testimony presented (and the personal knowledge of this
arbitrator in an earlier role as mediator), the question of the Commissioner's ability to discipline players—both on and off the field and both
during and off-season—was probably the most passionate, if not the
most important, concern of the Association during the protracted negotiations of the CBA. It was the "Gordian knot," that insoluble problem
which impeded, delayed or denied progress in reaching an "Agreement." As adamant as the Association was to eliminate the Commissioner's role in this regard, the Council—on behalf of the Clubs, was
equally determined to maintain the Commissioner's authority intact
and unfettered. The skills of collective negotiations and the art of
compromise resulted in the CBA, executed and implemented as of
March 1, 1977 (retroactive to February 1, 1974). This was only one,
albeit an important one, of a multitude of accommodations reached by
the parties. The bargaining history indicates that, until the virtual
close of negotiations—which immediately preceded the signing of the
CBA, this matter remained a sticking point between the parties. It is
also noted that, until that time, Article VIII was a "Section" of Article
VII, although its substance was virtually the same. The removal of the
substance of Article VIII from Article VII and its establishment as a
separate Article was apparently at the behest of the Commissioner.

The bargaining history of a provision has considerable import,
particularly where the provision in dispute lacks clarity or is given to
ambiguous interpretation.

[After reviewing some of this bargaining history and contract
language, the arbitrator continued.]

* * *

The intent of Article VIII is unmistakable in setting it out from the
provisions of Article VII, which defines an "outside arbitrator's" authority. I am unable to ignore language which lends itself to no other
reasonable meaning. I conclude that I have no authority to interpose
my authority into actions emanating under Article VIII.

Hold

Thus, we look to Article VII and the applicability of that provision
to the instant case, specifically, and its potential implications *vis a vis*
the Commissioner's discipline.

* * *

The execution of Article VII contemplates a setting forth of "the specifics of the alleged action or inaction giving rise to the grievance"— a perceived error in action spelled out, usually in writing, calling for a specific remedy. Here, the asserted error was the suspension of Crowder and Reese by the Miami Club, without pay on the basis of a criminal charge; the remedy requested was reinstatement and resumption of pay. The PCRC took cognizance of the case and rendered a decision and order. The Association contends the PCRC action disposed of all further or future discipline of the players. What the PCRC is authorized to do, under the CBA, is to make ... full, final and complete disposition of the [charges and claims set forth in the] grievance. According to the record, it did precisely that—it determined that Crowder and Reese should be reinstated under pay. What relationship, if any, exists between the PCRC's actions and those of the Commissioner over a year later? Cited as important in this regard was the meaning of Item 7 of the PCRC's order, particularly the statement:

> ... It shall not affect or influence any future suspension by an NFL club or by the Commissioner.

[handwritten margin note: Note (Punished twice Allowed?)]

The Association asserts that a proper interpretation of this provision is its aforementioned position that the PCRC order disposed of any and all matters pertaining to discipline of Crowder and Reese; it contends that the statement "it shall not affect or influence any future suspension by the NFL Club or by the Commissioner" was intended to foreclose future possible discipline of the players involved, but also to isolate the remedy in this case from being cited as precedent for future, perhaps similar ones. The Council, on the other hand, contends such language merely carries out the intent of Article VIII—that it disposed of *that* grievance and did not prejudice the potential for subsequent action in this case, particularly by the Commissioner.

It seems obvious that the provision is hardly the paragon of clear draftsmanship: had it been intended to convey the meaning ascribed to it by the Council, its drafters would seemingly have drafted it—"It shall not affect or influence any future suspension [of Crowder and Reese] by an NFL Club or by the Commissioner." Logic would tend to support the Association's claim as to the intent of this statement, insofar as the non-precedential value of this decision on future cases involving other players. Does the Agreement, and particularly Article VII, contemplate any limitation upon the Commissioner's authority to discipline? I am satisfied that it does. Section 11 of Article VII sets a time frame in which the Commissioner must determine to exercise his authority to remove a "grievance," as defined by Sections 1 and 2 (Article VII) from processing, and place it under the aegis of Article VIII. Assume that the Commissioner determined that the Crowder/Reese grievance gave "rise to issues involving the integrity of, or public confidence in, the game of professional football;" by definition, he could exercise his authority, but would have to do so at some point prior to resolution of the issue under the provisions of Article VII. Thus, had the PCRC disposed of that grievance (as it did), the Commissioner could not "reactivate" the matter afterwards.

It is the Association's position that the Commissioner raised again or reopened the case already disposed of by the PCRC. I am not so persuaded. The PCRC quite clearly resolved the grievances that were initiated; the Commissioner's action over a year later was not directed to the resolution of a grievance which dealt with the suspension of Crowder and Reese *from the Miami Club*, without pay, and which sought their *return to the status quo*. It was *that* matter disposed of by the PCRC. As to the Commissioner's authority to take the actions he did in August of 1978, I must conclude that it is beyond my authority to assert jurisdiction and I do not do so here.

While I conclude that the Commissioner's actions are beyond the scope of Article VII, a logical question arises that, assuming the Commissioner did take an action under Section 11 of Article VII, is there an obligation that issues in order for him to do so? I am satisfied there is. It seems both reasonable and logical that the Commissioner's "consultation" with the PCRC before withdrawing a grievance should be a showing of the "integrity/public confidence" rationale upon which such withdrawal is to be used. It seems not sufficient that consultation would merely be a notice that such withdrawal of the grievance is to be effectuated. Failure to demonstrate such a rationale to the satisfaction of the PCRC could be basis for a claim of arbitrary and capricious action or an unreasonable incursion into the dispute resolution process of Article VII, and subject to challenge under the provisions of that Article by a party defined by Article VII, Section 2.

* * *

Grievance dismissed.

Questions for Discussion

1. While the *Crowder–Reese* decision relates only to the specific terms of the 1982 NFL bargaining agreement which expired in 1987, analogous provisions exist in every bargaining agreement in every league sport. Assuming the arbitrator was correct in his interpretation of the NFL bargaining agreement, when, if ever, may a commissioner's exercise of disciplinary authority be challenged in grievance arbitration? To the extent arbitrators lack jurisdiction to hear such cases, presumably a player's only recourse would be in court: how willing should judges be to overturn commissioners on such matters?

2. Although players associations have consistently opposed giving commissioners this nonarbitrable authority, in the end the associations have always agreed to it. Does this acquiescence reflect a sense on the part of players that some such private authority is appropriate to preserve the image and integrity of the sport?

3. In 1986, Tulane's star center John "Hot Rod" Williams was indicted for allegedly taking money from gamblers to throw two college games.

NBA Commissioner David Stern permitted the Cleveland Cavaliers to draft and pay Williams, but not to play him pending trial, in which Williams was ultimately acquitted. Based on the acquittal, Stern took no action against Williams, who has gone on to a highly successful and lucrative career with the Cavaliers. Why? Should the Commissioner have felt entitled to take action after indictment but prior to the criminal trial? Does it depend on the nature of the charge (for example, rape instead of fixing games)? Should the Commissioner's authority be constrained if the criminal proceedings result in a jury acquittal? In dismissal on procedural grounds? Does this imply that in cases where criminal conduct or proceedings are not involved (for example, Pete Rose's gambling as opposed to his tax evasion), the standard of proof for finding the alleged misconduct should be "beyond a reasonable doubt"? In answering these questions, keep in mind that Baseball Commissioner Landis banned the players involved in the "Black Sox" scandal for life even after a jury had acquitted them of all criminal charges related to the alleged "fixing" of the 1919 World Series.

By contrast with the NFL, the NBA in tandem with its Players Association has created an elaborate drug program.[22] Unlike its baseball counterpart, the NBPA has accepted stiff sanctions against its members for drug use. Article 33 of the basketball agreement states that any player detected using, possessing or distributing a listed "prohibited substance" (at present, heroin or cocaine) shall immediately and permanently be disqualified from the league, and neither the league nor the player's club can dilute this sanction. While the Article does allow the player to petition for reinstatement no earlier than two years from expulsion, approval must be given by both the commissioner and the union.

However, the NBA's draconian disciplinary approach to the discovery of drug use is only one component of a policy that emphasizes rehabilitation and education. Under Article 33, any player with a drug problem who comes forward before detection faces no penalty, but instead receives treatment at the club's expense with his salary continued for at least thirty days.

Equally important, the NBA agreement pioneered a new approach to drug testing.[23] The parties jointly appointed an independent, experi-

---

22. In basketball, as in football, the scope of the neutral arbitration clause in the collective agreement is limited by a provision (Article 28(i)(f)) that gives the commissioner the final authority to determine whether a player's actions threaten "the integrity of, or the maintenance of public confidence in, the game of basketball." Until the 1992 negotiations and strike settlement, hockey remained the one sport in which the president of the league retained broad authority under the collective agreement (Section 4.0) not only with respect to discipline of players for misbehavior on and off the ice, but also with respect to interpretation of the key features of relations between the League and its clubs and the players and their Association.

23. On drug testing in professional sports see the articles by Wong and Ensor, note 17 above, and by Lock, note 18 above. The best scholarly explorations of this topic in law reviews have been written by Mark A. Rothstein. See his *Drug Testing*

enced expert in drug detection and enforcement to review confidentially any evidence that a particular player had a drug abuse problem. If the expert finds "reasonable cause" for believing this to be true, he issues an "authorization for testing" of this player without notice. Except for a recent provision that allows for one test of all rookies at training camp, NBA clubs have agreed to forego any other drug testing of their players.

The basketball agreement represents one drug testing model found in contemporary sports. The NHL and its Players Association have favored a different approach to drugs in hockey: no testing beforehand, but immediate indefinite suspension of any player found to have used drugs at any time (even years earlier, as was disclosed at the divorce trial of Grant Fuhr, then the Edmonton Oilers' all-star goalie).

In contrast, for the last decade the owners in baseball and football have strenuously insisted on randomized testing of all players. In 1984, Marvin Miller for the baseball Players Association and Lee MacPhail for the owners' Player Relations Committee negotiated a "reasonable cause-independent review" procedure similar to basketball's. But only a year later, after a notorious criminal trial of the drug supplier to the Pittsburgh Pirates in the early 1980's, the owners exercised their right to terminate that procedure, arguing that baseball needed to test all its players. Under the guidance of new Commissioner Peter Ueberroth, the owners insisted in the winter of 1986 that all new player contracts require the player to submit to random drug testing.

The same year, Commissioner Rozelle instituted a general drug-testing program in football. Rozelle's program was prompted by the disclosure of drug use by members of the New England Patriots in stories that broke just after the Patriots' Super Bowl shellacking at the hands of the Chicago Bears. In both baseball and football, the union challenged through arbitration the propriety under the collective agreement of the commissioner's unilateral action. The next case presents the arbitrator's response in football, under the same league constitution and collective agreement provisions detailed earlier with the *Crowder–Reese* arbitration.

NFLPA AND NFL MANAGEMENT COUNCIL
(Arbitration, 1986).

KASHER, ARBITRATOR.

* * *

[In January 1986, following Super Bowl XX between the Chicago Bears and New England Patriots, the Boston Globe broke the story

in the Workplace: The Challenge to Employment Relations and Employment Law, 63 Chicago–Kent L. Rev. 683 (1987), and Workplace Drug Testing: A Case Study in the Misapplication of Technology, 5 Harvard J. of L. and Tech. 65 (1991). A useful presentation of the different viewpoints on this topic is the Symposium, Drug Testing in the Workplace, 33 William and Mary L. Rev. 1 (1991).

about drug use by six Patriot players. The ensuing public controversy prompted an effort by NFL Commissioner Pete Rozelle and Jack Donlon, head of the NFL Management Council (NFLMC), to try to persuade Gene Upshaw, head of the NFL Players Association, to agree to drug testing of NFL players. While the NFLPA was prepared to accept a variety of anti-drug measures, the union drew the line at random testing. Thus, on July 7 Rozelle unilaterally announced a new drug program, key ingredients of which were two unscheduled urine tests of all players during the season (conducted exclusively by the league's new drug advisor, Dr. Forrest Tennant).

Rozelle purported to act under both Section 8.13(A) of the NFL constitution and Article VIII of the collective agreement, which had last been renegotiated in 1982. When the NFLPA filed a grievance under the agreement, the arbitrator first capsulized his findings about what had transpired in the 1982 negotiations regarding this issue.]

The 1982 Negotiations

The record reflects that the June 14, 1982 article in Sports Illustrated, co-authored by former NFL player Don Reese, had a catalytic effect on the 1982 bargaining sessions. Bargaining for the 1982 contract began in February of that year and the attention of the parties, and the media, was directed to the NFLPA's proposal that their members be compensated based upon "a percentage of the gross" receipts which the League generated.

After the Reese article appeared, and beginning with the bargaining session held on July 13, 1982 in New York, the NFLPA and the NFLMC began to address the question of chemical dependency among NFL players. In part, their attention was focused on this issue as the result of a form letter which Commissioner Rozelle had written to various individuals in response to questions raised by the Reese article. That letter contained the following paragraph

> Regardless of how much the NFL does, there will always be tragic cases like that of Don Reese, who co-authored the recent article in *Sports Illustrated*. Unfortunately his article contains many untruths and distortions of fact, but he makes one undeniable statement when he points out that the NFL does not employ urine tests for the detection of drug use and that the NFL Players Association has long been on record against such tests. I was told recently by a member of Congress that he is unalterably opposed to the Players Association's stance on this issue and that tests of this type have recently been very successful in curbing the drug problem in the U.S. military.

At or about the same time that the bargaining resumed in New York, on July 13, 1982, Commissioner Rozelle issued a memorandum to all Club Presidents and General Managers, which instructed them, as a reminder, that they were to have in place by July 15, 1982 medical assistance programs which were to include (1) the retaining of a doctor who specialized in drug and alcohol problems, (2) arrangements with a facility that could provide comprehensive treatment for persons with alcohol and drug dependency problems, and, (3) use of resources, available through the League office, including lectures or seminars by Carl Eller.

It is clear from the Commissioner's form letter issued in June of 1982, as well as other evidence in the record regarding opposition to urinalysis testing for drugs by former NFLPA Executive Director, Edward Garvey, that when the parties met at the bargaining table in July 1982 there was an outstanding issue regarding the League's and/or member clubs' rights to institute urinalysis testing as part of the existing medical assistance programs; and where those programs addressed the question of drug use, whether urinalysis testing could be conducted without bargaining about the issue with the NFLPA.

* * *

After discussing the NFLPA's proposal regarding counseling for "personal problems," the NFLMC presented a proposal to the NFLPA on July 23, 1982. This proposal, for the first time, addressed the subject of "tests" in writing. Section 6 of the proposal stated:

> Each club maintains its existing right to test or examine players, including for chemical abuse or dependency problems, during its pre-season physical examination and, upon reasonable cause, during any subsequent physical examination.

In our opinion, it is apparent from the reading of Article XXI of the 1982 collective bargaining agreement, which is, obviously, more detailed than the above-quoted proposal, that the NFLMC, bargaining on behalf of the member clubs, and seeking to achieve the League's desire to institute urinalysis testing, was ultimately and totally successful in convincing the NFLPA that pre-season and reasonable cause testing should be included within any drug treatment/educational program established by contract.

It may very well have been that the clubs did have an "existing right" to conduct such testing; however, in our view, when the parties agreed to codify an allegedly pre-existing management right into agreement provisions, the language of those provisions became the "rules of the work place", which the parties were then obligated to follow.

* * *

The NFL and the NFLMC have argued that the Commissioner of the NFL does not exceed his authority when he establishes policies and procedures involving drug programs which are designed to protect the integrity of, and public confidence in, the game of professional football. The NFL and NFLMC have supported this contention by arguing that the Commissioner's "integrity of the game" authority, insofar as it was exercised on July 7, 1986 by the announcement of an augmented drug program, (1) remained wholly intact, since the NFLPA was unsuccessful in limiting any of that authority during the bargaining which led to the 1982 collective bargaining agreement, (2) is so rooted in a long and consistent past practice of establishing rules for dealing with drug abuse problems that it cannot be limited by language in the collective bargaining agreement that does not conflict with that authority, and (3) is only governed, in view of the Commissioner's wide latitude to control conduct which he determines would be detrimental to the image of the League, by the rule of reason.

There can be no question that the Commissioner of the NFL has broad authority under the Constitution and By–Laws, which are incorporated by reference in the collective bargaining agreement, to establish policy and procedure and to take action which would protect the integrity of, and public confidence in, the game of professional football. The Commissioner has the power, recognized by the collective bargaining agreement, to make rules and enforce them. In certain respects, the Commissioner sits as a third party between the employer (the member clubs) and the union (the NFLPA). However, where the Commissioner establishes policies and procedures (rules) which have application to members of the bargaining unit, his right to establish rules is, in some respects, similar to the right other employers have to establish rules in the context of typical bargaining, relationships. . . . Accordingly, we must conclude that when the Commissioner establishes policies or procedures, which have the effect of rules or regulations, that those policies and procedures, which are impacted by the collective bargaining relationship, are not plenary in nature. Plenary authority is "absolute" or "unqualified" authority; that is not the scope of the Commissioner's authority under the terms of the collective bargaining agreement.

Note (Hold)

This finding is not meant to imply that Commissioner Rozelle does not retain broad and special powers to deal with issues that involve the "integrity of the game." Section 11 of Article VII and Article VIII of the collective bargaining agreement bear strong witness to the fact that the Commissioner of the NFL has specifically retained far-reaching authority to address and resolve integrity of the game matters. . . .

Hold

After consideration of evidence, which supports a finding that the current drug program is subject to improvement in certain areas, this Arbitrator concludes that the Commissioner's augmented drug program is reasonable, per se, where it addresses those subject matters. For example, the Commissioner's intention to centralize and standardize drug education and testing, as well as his intention to impose severe penalties for breaches of medically-related confidentiality, are viewed by the Arbitrator as rules or policies that meet any test of reasonableness.

However, the question of the reasonableness, in whole or in part, of the augmented drug program only has some substantive reason for being answered if we conclude that the Commissioner retained his previously-held, unfettered authority to promulgate and enforce policies and procedures regarding drug misuse and abuse. Our reading of the record convinces us that the parties, including the NFL, full well knew in 1982 that the language of the collective bargaining agreement bound the League, as well as the Management Council and the NFLPA, to follow the chemical dependency program, the testing provisions and procedures and the confidentiality provisions of Sections 6, 7 and 8 of Article XXXI. The Commissioner's augmented drug program, issued in accordance with the Commissioner's authority which is derived from the general language of the Constitution and By–Laws and the collective bargaining agreement, is a "document affecting terms and conditions of employment of NFL players," and where it conflicts with certain specific provisions of the collective bargaining agreement, it is superseded in those areas....

The NFLMC has also argued that the Commissioner's authority for establishing policies and procedures regarding drug misuse and abuse is so rooted in consistent and long-term past practice that the Arbitrator is compelled to conclude that this authority is part of the unwritten fabric of the terms and conditions of employment applicable to NFL players. As inventive as this argument is, the Arbitrator is not persuaded that the parties, by mutual intent, contemplated that previous recognition of the Commissioner's broad authority in all areas addressed by Article XXXI of the 1982 collective bargaining agreement would survive the 1982 negotiations. As discussed above, the Commissioner's disciplinary authority in matters involving drug misuse and abuse was left intact; however, certain other subject areas, such as drug testing and the evaluation of chemical dependency treatment facilities, were addressed by the collective bargaining agreement and represented limitations on the clubs' and/or the Commissioner's rights to change those agreements.

* * *

We find the NFLPA's argument, that the League's augmented drug policy cannot be unilaterally developed and implemented by the League without violating the National Labor Relations Act, to be lacking in merit. The parties bargained about a chemical dependency program, testing and confidentiality. Interestingly, they did not include in their bargain subjects such as "prohibited substances," amphetamines, "anabolic steroids," the specifics of aftercare for players who test positive for drugs, the status of players hospitalized for drug treatment and/or their entitlement to pay or the extent to which, if any, players would be disciplined for improper drug involvement. These are only some of the specific subjects addressed by Commissioner Rozelle's augmented drug program which go beyond, and which are on their face not contradictory to, the somewhat skeletal provisions of Article XXXI. The NFLPA knew of, and participated to some extent in, the Commissioner's previous drug programs. Thus, where the Commissioner retained certain historical "integrity of the game" authority, the NFLPA cannot be heard to complain that the continued exercise of such authority violates the duty to bargain provisions of the National Labor Relations Act.

Sub-
Issue

The question now becomes which new procedures of Commissioner Rozelle's augmented drug program conflict with the specific provisions of Article XXXI and which new procedures do not.

* * *

We will first discuss the question of "unscheduled drug testing"; not necessarily because we believe that it is the most important element in the Commissioner's effort to improve the current chemical dependency program, but because this issue received the greatest coverage and since it presented the most serious stumbling block for the parties in their efforts to amend the current drug program....

"Unscheduled testing" is not addressed, contemplated or permitted by Article XXXI of the collective bargaining agreement. It must be remembered that, as a result of the Commissioner's concern in 1982 regarding abuse and misuse of drugs and his desire to establish urinalysis testing, the League proposed that pre-season and reasonable cause testing be included in the collective bargaining agreement. For a period of time the NFLPA resisted any language being incorporated into the collective bargaining agreement which would permit testing of players for chemical abuse or dependency. When the NFLPA finally conceded to permit certain testing, it qualified the right of the clubs to test by requiring that "there will not be any spot checking for chemical abuse or dependency by the club or club physician." The NFL and the NFLMC have argued that if the NFLPA had wished to prohibit unscheduled testing that their negotiators could have readily drafted language which would have provided that "except as permitted under this agreement, there will be no drug testing of players." The NFL and the NFLMC have further contended that the prohibition on "spot checking" does not prevent the implementation of Commissioner Rozelle's proposed two (2) regular Season unscheduled tests, since those tests cannot be construed as "Spot checks."

The Arbitrator is not persuaded by these arguments. In our opinion the NFL and the NFLMC have improperly attempted to "switch the onus of draftsmanship" to the NFLPA. The "spot checking" prohibition directly follows that sentence in Section 7 of Article XXXI which allows the club physician, upon reasonable cause, to direct a player to Hazelden for chemical abuse or dependency problems. In our opinion, the NFLPA ensured that spot checking was not to be permitted as part of the "reasonable cause" testing right, which the NFLMC obtained for the member clubs as a result of its July 23, 1982 proposal. Accordingly, we find that the "spot checking" prohibition modifies the clubs' rights to conduct reasonable cause testing and is not properly construed as the "only" prohibition on the League's or the clubs' rights to test for chemical use or dependency.

Sub-
Hold

Article XXXI establishes the obligation for players to submit to a pre-season drug test and tests for chemical abuse or dependency problems when a club physician has reasonable cause to direct players to submit to such tests. Article XXXI makes no reference to "two (2) regular season unscheduled tests." The language of Article XXXI is not sufficiently broad to permit unscheduled testing. Further, it is clear that Commissioner Rozelle never contemplated unscheduled testing in 1982, and therefore the negotiators could not have intended that players would be subjected to unscheduled testing.

Accordingly, we conclude that that part of Commissioner Rozelle's augmented drug program, which establishes unscheduled testing, is in conflict with the specific provisions of Article XXXI and is therefore superseded by the agreement's language.

Sub,
Hold
(cont.)

RES
Comm. Lost mostly

* * *

Grievance upheld in part.

Questions for Discussion

1. The arbitral verdict was the same in baseball, where the arbitrator rejected the owners' attempt to use the escape valve in the collective agreement that allowed a special covenant to be inserted in an individual player contract if the covenant was for the "actual or potential benefit of the player." Was this result correct—for either non-guaranteed or guaranteed salary contracts?

2. Are the above decisions based on the premise that the players association has not agreed in the labor contract to permit unscheduled drug testing, or that the league has agreed to refrain from drug testing? How significant is the difference in these two readings? Suppose that the drug problem had arisen when the parties' agreement had expired and was being negotiated: should there be a duty to bargain about this subject? (Current treatment of this issue under national labor law will be presented in Chapter 4.)

———

Of course, sports is only one walk of life where employers and politicians have advocated workplace drug testing as a necessary antidote to the "drug scourge." Absent a collective bargaining agreement (as has been the case since 1987 in football, for reasons we will explore in Chapters 3 and 4), private sector employees generally have no legal recourse against such employer initiatives unless there is sufficient state involvement in the employer's operations to trigger federal constitutional protections, or there are state constitutional or statutory protections that apply even as against private actors. Recalling the *Ludtke* case, if a league commissioner unilaterally imposed a random drug testing regime on all players, could players on a team that plays its home games in a publicly-owned stadium argue that there is sufficient state action to raise federal constitutional claims of due process, equal protection, or privacy? Are there any other ways government is involved with professional sports that might trigger claims of state action so that league policies could be constitutionally challenged? See *Hertel v. City of Pontiac*, 470 F.Supp. 603 (E.D. Mich., 1979)(finding sufficient city involvement in the NFL's decision not to televise Lions' home games within 75 miles of the Pontiac Silverdome to constitute state action, although finding no equal protection violation because there was a rational basis for the classification).

Although professional athletes have not challenged commissioner-initiated drug testing on the basis that a state constitution protects people from invasions of privacy by purely private actors, college athletes have challenged an NCAA drug testing program on these grounds, with mixed results.[24] In *O'Halloran v. University of Washington*, 856 F.2d 1375 (9th Cir.1988), a state constitutional claim against mandatory NCAA drug testing connected with championship events or football bowl games was remanded back to state court where it was eventually dismissed. A California appellate court, however, found that the same NCAA program infringed on the state constitutional right of privacy when implemented by Stanford University (a private school) against its athletes. After extensive analysis of the evidence, the court concluded that drug testing procedures were (a) inaccurate, (b) not justified by a compelling public interest (with respect to athletes as compared to other college students), (c) not the least intrusive means of achieving the claimed interest (as compared with drug education and/or testing only upon reasonable suspicion), and (d) overbroad in dealing with substances (for example, marijuana and cocaine) that did not artificially improve athletic performance. *Hill v. NCAA & Stanford University*, 7 Cal.App.4th 1738, 273 Cal.Rptr. 402 (6th Dist. 1990). As of this writing, the California Supreme Court has taken this case for review (appeal granted, ___ Cal. ___, 276 Cal.Rptr. 319, 801 P.2d 1070).

Questions for Discussion

1. The purpose of noting these cases is not to answer, but rather to raise, important policy questions about drug testing.

(a) Is there a serious problem of drug use by professional athletes? With which drugs? Cocaine, Steroids

(b) Is drug testing truly invasive of players' privacy (as compared, for example, to women sportswriters in the locker room)? N

(c) How accurate are drug testing procedures? Fine Can confidence in test results be enhanced?

(d) Are alternatives such as drug education or "reasonable suspicion" testing preferable to random testing of all players?

(e) Why do people consider it important enough to stamp out drug use by athletes that one should use all available measures, even those as intrusive as drug testing? To preserve the health and safety of the athlete? To protect fair competition? The image of the sport? To which drugs do any or all of these rationales apply?

24. For scholarly explorations of the issues posed by compulsory drug testing of college athletes, see John Allen Scanlan, Jr., *Playing the Drug–Testing Game: College Athletics, Regulatory Institutions and the Rhetoric of Constitutional Argument*, 62 Indiana L.J. 863 (1987), and Le Roy Pernell, *Random Drug–Testing of Student Athletes by State Universities in the Wake of* Von Raab *and* Skinner, 1 Marquette Sports L. J. 41 (1990).

2.   Drugs are not the only condition for which testing of athletes might be considered. The shocking news of Earvin "Magic" Johnson's retirement after contracting the HIV virus, then of his return to the basketball court for the NBA All–Star Game and the 1992 Olympics, then his retirement once more just prior to the 1992–93 season, generated widespread discussion about whether athletes with the HIV virus pose a risk to other players, and whether mandatory HIV testing is justified. What are your views on these issues? Does your answer to the second question depend on your answer to the first?

3.   Alternatively, is the case for testing athletes the same case now being made for testing of employees generally? Is this argument for drug testing related to the needs of the workplace or, instead, to a "demand side" approach to drug enforcement? (This was the direction taken by President Reagan's drug policy in the mid–1980s, under which the police try to stamp out the availability of drugs to those who are especially vulnerable to drug abuse by punishing any users whose demand for the substance helps create the market that makes this criminal enterprise possible.) Who should decide whether it is in the "best interests of sport" (or in the "best interests of society") to test all athletes (or employees) for drug use? Why is it more feasible for a sports league to enforce such a policy for its players than, for example, a television network which tried to impose drug testing on its prime-time stars?

You have now seen a much broader sampling of the real-life problems that arise under the rubric of the "best interests of the sport." Consider again George Will's assertion, quoted early in this chapter, that judges should leave these moral dilemmas to commissioners to wrestle with. Agree or disagree?

Chapter Two

CONSTRUCTING A PLAYERS MARKET: FROM CONTRACT TO ANTITRUST LAW [1]

Chapter 1 focused on a specific set of legal issues implicating a broad spectrum of sports participants—players, managers, owners, even sportswriters. We saw how people who felt aggrieved by commissioner rulings under the time-honored but eminently contestable phrase, "best interests of the sport," sought redress through a number of legal vehicles—contract, antitrust, labor, and constitutional law. Now we undertake an in-depth examination of the situation of one vital segment of the sports world—the players—and consider how the fate of professional athletes has been influenced by the legal structure of their marketplace.

The cases and materials in this and the next chapter focus primarily on one crucial issue, the ability of players to move from one club to another, whether in the same or a different league. In any industry, the worker's ability to play off one employer against another can make a profound difference in treatment received, both in monetary compen-

---

1. An informative law review article on both the law and the sports background to the materials in this chapter (and the next two) is Robert C. Berry and William B. Gould, *A Long Deep Drive to Collective Bargaining: Of Players, Owners, Brawls and Strikes*, 31 Case Western Reserve L. Rev. 685 (1981). The historical background to the development of the "reserve system" in baseball is set out in two books by Harold Seymour— *Baseball: The Early Years* (New York: Oxford University Press, 1960), and *Baseball: The Golden Age* (New York: Oxford University Press, 1971). A Congressional study, Subcommittee on the Study of Monopoly Power of the Committee of the Judiciary, 82d Congress, 2d Session, *Report on Organized Baseball* (Washington, D.C., 1952) (Celler Report), meticulously documents the legal and institutional restraints on player mobility in that sport, which blazed the trail for analogous restraints that emerged in other sports. David Harris, *The League: The Rise and Decline of the NFL* (New York: Bantam, 1986), Terry Pluto, *Loose Balls: The Short, Wild Life of the American Basketball Association* (New York: Simon and Schuster, 1990), and David Cruise and Alison Griffiths, *Net Worth: Exploding the Myths of Pro Hockey* (New York: Viking Penguin, 1991), provide helpful background to the contract disputes in those sports that we will encounter in this (and the next two) chapters.

sation and in satisfactory job conditions.[2] In turn, the legal system has its most powerful impact at precisely this point, as the law chooses whether to enforce, prohibit, or redesign obstacles to employee mobility.

Disputes about player movement from one team to another have been the central preoccupation of sports litigation for over a century, litigation that now takes place within a complex interplay of contract, antitrust, and labor law. From the 1880s into the 1960s, the principal focus was on contract law that defined the relationship between individual player and club. Teams regularly sought to enforce, and players to elude, the network of restrictions epitomized by baseball's "reserve system" (which we will describe later in this chapter). By the end of the 1960s, federal antitrust litigation had been launched against this broad regime of player restraints. A particular target was the reciprocal "anti-tampering" agreement among clubs in the league, a private arrangement that provided the real glue to the reserve system whatever kind of enforcement the player contract received in the civil courts.

As we will see in Chapter 3, the plaintiffs in such antitrust litigation (except for baseball players) enjoyed great success in the 1970s. However, the prime movers in these suits were players associations that at the same time were transforming themselves into labor unions and engaging in collective bargaining under national labor law. By the beginning of the 1980s, the players associations in each of the four major team sports—baseball, football, basketball, and hockey—had negotiated in their collective agreements new rules that specified whether and when a player could become a "free agent"—entitled to move to any other team that made him a better contract offer. Since these arrangements also had the legal effect of immunizing the player market from antitrust scrutiny (for reasons explained in Chapter 3), the 1980s were the heyday of labor law in professional sports—a decade that was marked by numerous strikes and lockouts as well as lawsuits. By the end of the decade, though, the National Football League Players Association (NFLPA), which had enjoyed a conspicuous lack of success under labor law, declared itself a *non*-union in an effort to bring antitrust back into play for the 1990s. In the fall of 1992 the NFLPA won an important jury verdict in that quest, though at the time of this writing a host of decisions were still to be taken in that litigation. Whether the Association *should* succeed is a central theme running throughout this chapter and this book.

2. For a short statement of the case for a freely competitive labor market, see Milton Friedman and Rose Friedman, *Free to Choose: A Personal Statement* 218–236 (New York: Harcourt Brace Jovanovich, 1979), which argues that the best source of protection for employees is not their own employer, or their labor union, or their government (legislative or judicial), but *other* employers. For an appraisal of both the force and the limits of this position, see Paul C. Weiler, *Governing the Workplace: The Future of Labor and Employment Law* (Cambridge, Mass.: Harvard University Press, 1990), especially Chapter 4, The Sources and Instruments of Workplace Governance.

A. TORONTO BLUE JAYS v. BOSTON CELTICS AND DANNY AINGE

In line with the historical evolution of this topic, we turn first to contract law's treatment of different versions of the reserve clause in the player contract. To bring into live focus the issues presented by the legal precedents, we first sketch a dispute that produced a jury verdict but no published judicial opinion—the suit brought a decade ago by the Toronto Blue Jays against the Boston Celtics and Danny Ainge.[3]

Danny Ainge's athletic talent made him an early star and eventual professional performer in two sports. First, he was a baseball prospect of some note who was recruited in 1978 by the Toronto Blue Jays, an expansion franchise. After two years in the minor leagues with the Syracuse Nationals, Ainge signed a three-year contract with the Blue Jays for $525,000, including a $300,000 signing bonus. The Blue Jays envisaged Ainge as their third baseman of the future.

Because of NCAA rules that permit professionals in one sport to retain their college eligibility in another sport, Ainge continued playing basketball for Brigham Young University. Although he had been an effective guard in earlier years, Ainge blossomed into a college super-star in the 1980–1981 season. After averaging 25 points per game, he was voted the Eastman Best Player Award by the National Association of Basketball Coaches (in a year in which Ainge's fellow All-Americans were Ralph Sampson, Mark Aguirre, Kelly Tripucka, and Isiah Thomas). However, because of his apparent commitment to the Blue Jays, no NBA team drafted Ainge in the first round of the June 1981 basketball draft. But canny Arnold "Red" Auerbach of the Boston Celtics chose Ainge with his second-round pick as a hedge against the possibility that the Celtics' two first-round selections, Charles Bradley and Tracy Jackson, would not satisfy the team's backcourt needs.

Throughout the summer of 1981, Ainge struggled with his baseball career, batting only .180 for the Blue Jays. Eventually, Ainge decided it made most sense to give up baseball and cast his lot with basketball. Although the $300,000 baseball signing bonus had carried an explicit commitment on his part not to play professional basketball, Ainge offered to repay the Blue Jays $350,000 for his release, because he expected to get a much richer contract from the Celtics—in the range of $1.5 to $2 million over three years. The Blue Jays rejected Ainge's offer, though, and told him that they would hold him to his contract. To enforce their position, the Jays sued the Celtics and Ainge in federal district court in New York.

The standard player contract upon which the Blue Jays relied included both an affirmative promise by Ainge to play baseball for the Jays and an undertaking that he would refrain from playing for other

---

3. This account is drawn from newspaper stories at the time. For a capsule summary of the litigation, see the 1985 Supplement to John C. Weistart and Cym H. Lowell, *The Law of Sports* 70–72 (Indianapolis, Ind.: Bobbs–Merrill, Supp. 1985.)

professional teams—not only in baseball but also in basketball, football, hockey, and other sports "involving a substantial risk of personal injury." For its part, the Blue Jays had agreed to pay Ainge the signing bonus along with a salary that rose over the three years he was to play (from $50,000 to $75,000 to $100,000 per year). The club retained the right to terminate the contract and its obligations if, among other reasons, Ainge "failed, in the opinion of the Club's management, to exhibit sufficient skill or competitive ability to qualify or continue as a member of the Club's team." [4]

Assume that the following questions (drawn from a decision ten years later) [5] fairly reflected the doctrinal standards governing the injunctive relief sought by the Blue Jays.

(1) Have the Blue Jays shown a likelihood of success on the merits?

(2) Have the Blue Jays shown that failure to issue the injunction would cause them "irreparable harm"?

(3) Does the "balance of harms" favor the Blue Jays, or the Celtics and Ainge?

(4) Will granting or withholding the injunction serve the "public interest"?

In analyzing the appropriate judicial ruling under these standards, as well as the appropriate policy views about these standards, consider the following questions:

1. What legal causes of action, if any, are available on these facts?

2. If there is some cause of action available to the Blue Jays, why is not the standard suit for monetary damages the appropriate remedy?

3. If an injunctive remedy is considered, should the judicial order be positive or negative—that is, should the judge order Ainge to play for the Blue Jays or merely not to play for the Celtics? On what legal basis under the contract and the standards governing equitable relief?

4. For a useful synopsis of the wording and operation of this termination clause in the contracts in the various professional sports, see Richard J. Ensor, *Comparison of Arbitration Decisions Involving Termination in Major League Baseball, the National Basketball Association, and the National Football League*, 32 Saint Louis U. L. J. 135 (1987).

5. The decision in question is *Boston Celtics v. Brian Shaw*, 908 F.2d 1041 (1st Cir.1990), which we will discuss shortly. For a comprehensive review of the evolution of the legal background, see Douglas Laycock, *The Death of the Irreparable Injury Rule* (New York: Oxford University Press, 1991), particularly pp. 168–174 and 184–192 on Personal Service Contracts. A capsule summary of the current doctrines and procedures used in the sports context is Gary Uberstine, The Enforceability of Sports Industry Employment Agreements, Chapter 9 of Gary Uberstine ed., *Law of Professional and Amateur Sport* (Deerfield, Ill.: Clark, Boardman, and Callaghan, 1991).

4. What are the practical interests of each party to this dispute, and how do you weigh the competing interests against each other? Can you think of any reason why the Celtics might have been prepared to offer Ainge an especially generous monetary package to sign him to an immediate contract?

5. From the broader perspective of the public interest, what is the ideal legal resolution of cases such as these?

6. What do you surmise was the result in and from the litigation, on the way to Ainge playing a starring role in two NBA championships won by the Celtics in the mid–1980s?

B. EVOLVING STANDARDS FOR CONTRACT ENFORCEMENT

With the Ainge case and these questions in mind, consider the following decisions rendered in cases where clubs sought injunctions against players "jumping" their contracts. The first three decisions portray the unfolding judicial attitude about this contract remedy: at the turn of the century (*Lajoie*), just before the entry of labor and antitrust law in the 1960s (*Barnett*), and, finally, under the present-day collective bargaining regime (*Shaw*). The next two cases present special issues of allegedly "unclean hands" (*Neely*) and "futures" in player contracts (*Bergey*). The following decision (*Chase*) brings into focus the background league arrangements within which individual players signed contracts with their respective teams. This decision serves as a transition to the world of antitrust which we first encounter in the Supreme Court's *Flood* ruling.

PHILADELPHIA BALL CLUB v. LAJOIE

Court of Common Pleas, Philadelphia County, 1902.

202 Pa. 210, 51 A. 973.

POTTER, JUSTICE.

The defendant in this case contracted to serve the plaintiff as a baseball player for a stipulated time. During that period he was not to play for any other club. He violated his agreement, however, during the term of his engagement, and, in disregard of his contract, arranged to play for another and a rival organization. The plaintiff, by means of this bill, sought to restrain him during the period covered by the contract. The court below refused an injunction.

* * *

The learned judge who filed the opinion in the court below, with great industry and painstaking care, collected and reviewed the English and American decisions bearing upon the question involved, and makes apparent the wide divergence of opinion which has prevailed. We

think, however, that in refusing relief unless the defendant's services were shown to be of such a character as to render it impossible to replace him he has taken extreme ground. It seems to us that a more just and equitable rule is laid down in Pom. Spec. Perf. p. 31, where the principle is thus declared: "Where one person agrees to render personal services to another, which require and presuppose a special knowledge, skill, and ability in the employee, so that in case of a default the same service could not easily be obtained from others, although the affirmative specific performance of the contract is beyond the power of the court, its performance will be negatively enforced by enjoining its breach.... The damages for breach of such contract cannot be estimated with any certainty, and the employer cannot, by means of any damages, purchase the same service in the labor market." ... [W]hen, owing to special features, the contract involves peculiar convenience or advantage, or where the loss would be a matter of uncertainty, then the breach may be deemed to cause irreparable injury.

* * *

The court below finds from the testimony that "the defendant is an expert baseball player in any position; that he has a great reputation as a second baseman; that his place would be hard to fill with as good a player; that his withdrawal from the team would weaken it, as would the withdrawal of any good player, and would probably make a difference in the size of the audiences attending the game." We think that, in thus stating it, he puts it very mildly, and that the evidence would warrant a stronger finding as to the ability of the defendant as an expert ball player. He has been for several years in the service of the plaintiff club, and has been re-engaged from season to season at a constantly increasing salary. He has become thoroughly familiar with the action and methods of the other players in the club, and his own work is peculiarly meritorious as an integral part of the team work which is so essential. In addition to these features which render his services of peculiar and special value to the plaintiff, and not easily replaced, Lajoie is well known, and has great reputation among the patrons of the sport, for his ability in the position which he filled, and was thus a most attractive drawing card for the public. He may not be the sun in the baseball firmament, but he is certainly a bright particular star. We feel, therefore, that the evidence in this case justifies the conclusion that the services of the defendant are of such a unique character, and display such a special knowledge, skill, and ability, as renders them of peculiar value to the plaintiff, and so difficult of substitution that their loss will produce "irreparable injury," in the legal significance of that term, to the plaintiff. The action of the defendant in violating his contract is a breach of good faith, for which there would be no adequate redress at law, and the case, therefore, properly calls for the aid of equity in negatively enforcing the performance of the contract by enjoining against its breach.

But the court below was also of the opinion that the contract was lacking in mutuality of remedy, and considered that as a controlling reason for the refusal of an injunction. The opinion quotes the nineteenth paragraph of the contract, which gives to the plaintiff a right of renewal for the period of six months, beginning April 15, 1901, and for a similar period in two successive years thereafter. The seventeenth paragraph also provides for the termination of the contract upon 10 days' notice by the plaintiff. But the eighteenth paragraph is also of importance, and should not be overlooked. It provides as follows:

> In consideration of the faithful performance of the conditions, covenants, undertakings, and promises herein by the said party of the second part, inclusive of the concession of the options of release and renewal prescribed in the seventeenth and nineteenth paragraphs, the said party of the first part, for itself and its assigns, hereby agrees to pay to him for his services for said term the sum of twenty-four hundred dollars, payable as follows, etc.

And, turning to the fifth paragraph, we find that it provides expressly for proceedings, either in law or equity:

> ... [T]o enforce the specific performance by the said party of the second part, or to enjoin said party of the second part from performing services for any other person or organization during the period of service herein contracted for; and nothing herein contained shall be construed to prevent such remedy in the courts, in case of any breach of this agreement by said party of the second part, as said party of the first part, or its assigns, may elect to invoke.'

We have, then, at the outset, the fact that the paragraphs now criticized and relied upon in defense were deliberately accepted by the defendant, and that such acceptance was made part of the inducement for the plaintiff to enter into the contract. We have the further fact that the contract has been partially executed by services rendered, and payment made therefore, so that the situation is not now the same as when the contract was wholly executory. The relation between the parties has been so far changed as to give to the plaintiff an equity, arising out of the part performance, to insist upon the completion of the agreement according to its terms by the defendant. This equity may be distinguished from the original right under the contract itself, and it might well be questioned whether the court would not be justified in giving effect to it by injunction, without regard to the mutuality or nonmutuality in the original contract. The plaintiff has so far performed its part of the contract in entire good faith, in every detail, and it would therefore be inequitable to permit the defendant to withdraw from the agreement at this late day.

The term "mutuality" or "lack of mutuality" does not always convey a clear and definite meaning. As was said in Grove v. Hodges, 55 Pa. 516:

The legal principle that contracts must be mutual does not mean that in every case each party must have the same remedy for a breach by the other.

In the contract now before us the defendant agreed to furnish his skilled professional services to the plaintiff for a period which might be extended over three years by proper notice given before the close of each current year. Upon the other hand, the plaintiff retained the right to terminate the contract upon 10 days' notice and the payment of salary for that time and the expenses of defendant in getting to his home. But the fact of this concession to the plaintiff is distinctly pointed out as part of the consideration for the large salary paid to the defendant, and is emphasized as such; and owing to the peculiar nature of the services demanded by the business, and the high degree of efficiency which must be maintained, the stipulation is not unreasonable. Particularly is this true when it is remembered that the plaintiff has played for years under substantially the same regulations.

We are not persuaded that the terms of this contract manifest any lack of mutuality in remedy. Each party has the possibility of enforcing all the rights stipulated for in the agreement. It is true that the terms make it possible for the plaintiff to put an end to the contract in a space of time much less than the period during which the defendant has agreed to supply his personal services; but mere difference in the rights stipulated for does not destroy mutuality of remedy. Freedom of contract covers a wide range of obligation and duty as between the parties, and it may not be impaired, so long as the bounds of reasonableness and fairness are not transgressed. If the doctrine laid down in Rust v. Conrad, 11 N.W. 265, quoted in the opinion, is to prevail, it would seem that the power of the plaintiff to terminate the contract upon short notice destroys the mutuality of the remedy. But we are not satisfied with the reasoning intended to support that conclusion. We cannot agree that mutuality of remedy requires that each party should have precisely the same remedy, either in form, effect, or extent. In a fair and reasonable contract, it ought to be sufficient that each party has the possibility of compelling the performance of the promises which were mutually agreed upon.

* * *

The court cannot compel the defendant to play for the plaintiff, but it can restrain him from playing for another club in violation of his agreement. No reason is given why this should not be done, except that presented by the argument, that the right given to the plaintiff to terminate the contract upon 10 days' notice destroys the mutuality of the remedy. But to this it may be answered that, as already stated, the defendant has the possibility of enforcing all the rights for which he stipulated in the agreement, which is all that he can reasonably ask. Furthermore, owing to the peculiar nature and circumstances of the business, the reservation upon the part of the plaintiff to terminate upon short notice does not make the whole contract inequitable.

* * *

Upon a careful consideration of the whole case, we are of the opinion that the provisions of the contract are reasonable, and that the consideration is fully adequate. The evidence shows no indications of any attempt at overreaching or unfairness. Substantial justice between the parties requires that the court should restrain the defendant from playing for any other club during the term of his contract with the plaintiff.

Injunction granted.

————

There are several interesting facts about this case that are not apparent on the face of the decision.[6] First, Napoleon Lajoie was not just an "ordinary" superstar. Over his 21–year career Lajoie had 3,251 hits and a .339 batting average, and was the first second baseman ever voted into the Hall of Fame. Second, the $2,400 annual salary payable under his Philadelphia Nationals' contract was the amount of the ceiling imposed on players' salaries by the National League. The reason Lajoie moved crosstown to play in the fledgling American League was to avoid this ceiling. Finally, despite their judicial victory, the Nationals failed to retrieve their star second baseman. The Philadelphia Americans simply traded Lajoie to their Cleveland counterparts, and the Ohio courts refused to grant an injunction. Shortly thereafter, the National and American Leagues settled their wars with the major league agreement that established the foundation for organized baseball to this day.

Questions for Discussion

1. Do you agree with the conclusion in *Lajoie* that there was mutuality in the terms of this player contract? Should courts have a broad discretion to decide whether there is sufficient mutuality to make it equitable to enforce a contract? For all contracts, or only for personal service contracts?

————

The *Lajoie* case was actually one of the few cases in which a baseball team secured an injunction against its own player—and even then, the order had no tangible value. A provocative recent article[7] observes that this judicial reluctance to issue personal services injunctions was exhibited especially in suits against male workers, including professional athletes; judges showed quite a different sentiment in suits against women, especially entertainers such as the British opera singer

6. See Seymour, *Baseball: The Early Years*, note 1 above, at 306–324.

7. Lea S. Vandervelde, *The Gendered Origins of the* Lumley *Doctrine: Binding Men's Consciences and Women's Fidelity*, 101 Yale L. J. 775 (1992).

Johanna Wagner and the American actress Lillian Russell. By the 1950s, though, courts had largely overcome such reticence with respect to athletes. As the next case indicates, the courts' attention had shifted from the supposed inequity of the contract toward the player (its lack of mutuality) to the team's need to retain especially talented athletes.

CENTRAL NEW YORK BASKETBALL, INC. (SYRACUSE NATIONALS) v. BARNETT

Court of Common Pleas of Ohio, Cuyahoga County, 1961.

181 N.E.2d 506.

DANACEAU, JUDGE.

[The Syracuse Nationals of the National Basketball Association (NBA) sued both the Cleveland Pipers of the new American Basketball League (ABL) and Dick Barnett. Barnett had been the Nationals' first-round draft choice in 1959. He signed the standard player contract for the 1959–1960 season, and then played the 1960–1961 season pursuant to the option clause in his written contract (at a salary of $8,500). In May 1961, Barnett and Nationals' President Dan Biasone reached a telephone agreement for a 1961–1962 contract of $11,500, with an agreed-to advance payment that was later mailed to Barnett (although the check was not cashed). During the next two months, Barnett was wooed by the Cleveland team (headed by his old college coach), and in July he signed a contract with the Pipers for $14,000. The Nationals then sued for an injunction to prevent Barnett from playing for the Pipers.

The Nationals chose not to rely on the option clause in the earlier written contract. According to the Nationals' construction of the contract—which the judge adopted as "reasonable, rational, [and] practical"—the contract expired at the end of the 1961 season and could *not* be unilaterally renewed by the club (as it had been the previous year). (By contrast, Barnett and the Pipers had construed the contract to be repeatedly renewable by the club in order to argue that it was void as a perpetual personal services contract.) The case was therefore decided on the basis of the oral agreement between Barnett and Biasone. The Nationals argued that because Barnett's "talents and abilities as a basketball player [were] of a special, unique, unusual and extraordinary character," they were entitled to an injunction preventing him from playing for the Pipers.]

* * *

There is some disagreement in the testimony as to the ability and standing of Barnett as a basketball player. Daniel Biasone, the General Manager of the Syracuse club for the past 16 years, testified that: "As of now I think Richard Barnett is one of the greatest basketball players playing the game." "He is an exceptionally good shooter."

"He is above average ... with other foul shooters in the National Basketball Association and that he ranked 19th in the whole league (approximately 100 players) scoring, playing as a guard." He further testified:

Q. What is your opinion as to his ability, this is, as a guard, now, at driving?

A. Terrific.

Q. What is your opinion as to his ability as play making as a guard?

A. Good. He has all the abilities a good basketball player should have. He has all the talent of a great basketball player. He is terrific all the way around.

Mr. Biasone also testified on cross-examination that he would place Barnett in the group of some specifically-named nine or ten unusual and extraordinary players in the National Basketball Association.

Mr. Biasone also testified that Barnett was a box office attraction and was asked on cross-examination: "on what basis do you say he was a great box office attraction?" He answered:

A. Because he, in my opinion, he is such a tremendous ball handler and he does things that have crowd appeal, he is noticeable. He appeals to the crowd because he does things extraordinary.

Coach McLendon of the Cleveland Pipers is not so generous in his appraisal. Barnett, in his opinion, is not in the class of the specifically-named outstanding basketball players. McLendon concedes that both Barnett and Neuman, now playing for Syracuse in his first year as a professional, are both "pretty good."

* * *

That the defendant Barnett was 19th among the top 25 scorers in the National Basketball Association in the 1960–61 season is confirmed in the statistics published on page 113 of the official Guide. On page 190 of the Guide is the record of Richard Barnett which indicates that he played in 78 games (out of 79) in the 1960–1961 season for a total of 1,970 minutes; that his F.G.M. percentage was .452; that his F.T.M. percentage was .712 and that he scored 1,320 points for an average of 16.9. The Guide also indicates that Barnett was not among the players in the East–West All Star Game on January 17, 1961, nor was he among the players named in the U.S. Basketball Writers' All–NBA Team for 1961.

The defendant Barnett may not be in the same class with the top ten basketball players. The Syracuse manager is not a disinterested witness, and he may have given an immoderate appraisal of the playing abilities of Barnett. On the other hand, neither are McLendon nor Barnett disinterested witnesses. McLendon's eagerness to secure the services of Barnett at a high salary ($13,000) indicates a higher opinion of Barnett's playing abilities than he was willing to concede at the trial of this case. Barnett was understandably under embarrassment when asked to give opinion of his own abilities and to make comparisons with another named player.

The increase of salary from $8,500 to $11,500 agreed to by plaintiff, the Cleveland Basketball Club's willingness to pay $13,000, and the latter's eagerness to secure his services, all point to a high regard for his playing abilities. Whether Barnett ranks with the top basketball players or not, the evidence shows that he is an outstanding professional basketball player of unusual attainments and exceptional skill and ability, and that he is of peculiar and particular value to plaintiff.

His signed contract with Syracuse provides:

9. The Player represents and agrees that he has exceptional and unique skill and ability as a basketball player; that his services to be rendered hereunder are of a special, unusual and extraordinary character which gives them peculiar value which cannot be reasonably or adequately compensated for in damages at law, and that the Player's breach of this contract will cause the Club great and irreparable injury and damage. The player agrees that, in addition to other remedies, the Club shall be entitled to injunctive and other equitable relief to prevent a breach of this contract by the Player, including, among others, the right to enjoin the Player from playing basketball for any other person or organization during the term of this contract.

* * *

The aforesaid provisions are contained in uniform players' contracts and it would seem that mere engagement as a basketball player in the N.B.A., or A.B.L., carries with it recognition of his excellence and extraordinary abilities.

An important growth in the field of equity has been the use of injunctions against the breach of negative agreements, both express and implied. Pomeroy's Specific Performance of Contract, Third Ed. at page 75 reads:

Another class of contracts stipulating for personal acts are now enforced in England by means of an injunction. Where one person agrees to render personal services to another, which require and presuppose a special knowledge, skill, and ability in the employee, so that, in case of a default, the same services could not easily be obtained from others, although the affirmative specific performance of the contract is beyond the power of the court, its performance will be negatively enforced by enjoining its breach. This doctrine applies especially to contracts made by actors, public singers, artists and others possessing a special skill and ability. It is plain that the principle on which it rests is the same with that which applies to agreements for the purchase of land or of chattels having a unique character and value. The damages for the breach of such contracts cannot be estimated with any certainty, and the employer cannot, by means of any damages, purchase the same services in the labor market.

* * *

Professional players in the major baseball, football, and basketball leagues have unusual talents and skills or they would not be so employed. Such players, the defendant Barnett included, are not easily replaced.

The right of the plaintiff is plain and the wrong done by the defendants is equally plain, and there is no reason why the Court should be sparing in the application of its remedies.

Damages at law would be speculative and uncertain and are practically impossible of ascertainment in terms of money. There is no plain, adequate and complete remedy at law and the injury to the plaintiff is irreparable.

Professional baseball, football, and basketball require regulations for the protection of the business, the public and the players, and so long as they are fair and reasonable there is no violation of the laws on restraint of trade. The evidence before this Court does not show any unfair or unreasonable act on the part of the plaintiff and the Court concludes that the claim of the defendant that the contract is in restraint of trade is without merit.

* * *

Injunction granted.

————

An intriguing footnote to *Barnett* is that the principal owner of the Cleveland Pipers was a young George Steinbrenner, demonstrating for the first time his willingness to outbid other teams for the players he wanted. Look closely at the salary figures in this case—both the absolute dollar levels and the relative changes that summer. What do these figures imply about the impact of competition for professional athletes' services? Is this financial impact likely to be the same when competition takes place between two teams in the same league, rather than between two teams in rival leagues?

The heart of Barnett's mutuality claim was that while the contract allowed the club to terminate his services (i.e., cut him from the team) on very short notice, the "option" clause prevented him from ever moving to another club in the same or different league if the club exercised the option and renewed his contract every year. This option clause in Barnett's contract provided:

22(a). On or before September 1st next following the last playing season covered by this contract, the Club may tender to the Player a contract for the term of that season.... If prior to the November 1 next succeeding said September 1, the Player and the Club have not agreed upon the terms of such contract, then on or before 10 days after said November 1, the Club shall have the right by written notice to the Player to renew this contract for the period of one year on the same terms, except that the amount payable to the Player shall be such as the Club shall fix in said notice: provided, however, that said amount shall be an amount payable at a rate not less than 75% of the rate stipulated for the preceding year.

Barnett argued that when a club renewed the contract under this clause, the new contract thereby included the same option clause, thus permitting the club to renew the contract in each future year—a perpetual right of renewal. The Nationals asserted that the option clause was not included in the renewal option contract; thus the club could exercise this option only once. The court agreed with the Nationals' interpretation, and on that footing held the contract to be valid and enforceable. Had the court agreed with Barnett's interpretation, would that have rendered the contract void (or voidable) for lack of mutuality?

In answering the above question, keep in mind that prior to an arbitration decision and an antitrust decree in the mid–1970s, Major League Baseball and the National Hockey League, respectively, had interpreted their option clauses as being perpetually renewable, making this clause the cornerstone of their so-called "lifetime reserve system." By contrast, the National Football League had always interpreted its option clause as allowing a club to exercise the option only one time after the principal contract expired. The NFL did use a stringent intraleague "compensation" system to discourage free agent movement to another NFL club (see the *Mackey v. NFL* case in Chapter 3), but nothing in their contracts prevented NFL players from signing with another league once their option year ended.

For a variety of reasons, the mutuality defense eventually faded from view in sports cases. However, keep the *Barnett* construction of the standard NBA player contract in mind when you read the arbitrators' decisions in the *Messersmith* (baseball) and *Dutton* (football) grievances at the beginning of Chapter 4.

By the 1960s the main focus of debate was on whether the club was likely to suffer "irreparable harm" from losing the services of a player with "exceptional and unique skill and ability." The quoted language of paragraph 9 in Barnett's NBA contract was very similar to the language found in Danny Ainge's Major League Baseball contract, and indeed in the standard contracts in all professional sports. Should this contract wording be decisive in later litigation? In *Barnett*, the court recited pages of testimony relating to Barnett's skills and abilities, but then stated that "mere engagement as a basketball player in the NBA or ABL carries with it recognition of his excellence and extraordinary abilities," and "[p]rofessional players in the major baseball, football, and basketball leagues have unusual talents and skills or they would not be so employed." Are professional clubs irreparably injured just because any athlete breaches his contract (with or without the "unique skill and ability" clause), or is this an issue that should be determined case by case, depending on the special skill and appeal of the particular athlete? If case by case, under what standards should a court or jury make the determination?

In *Winnipeg Rugby Football Club v. Freeman*, 140 F.Supp. 365 (N.D.Ohio 1955), the court enjoined two players from playing for the NFL's Cleveland Browns in breach of an ongoing contract with the Winnipeg Blue Bombers of the Canadian Football League (CFL). In finding that the players had unique skill and ability, the court noted that the players were much more valuable to the CFL team because of the lower calibre of play in that league. Does this imply that it would be easier for teams playing at a lower level of professional ball (e.g., the minor leagues, European basketball, or Japanese baseball, as well as the CFL) to get injunctions against players, especially if the team to which they are jumping is in the established major league? In this regard, see *Connecticut Professional Sports Corp. v. Heyman*, 276 F.Supp. 618 (S.D.N.Y.1967); *Spencer v. Milton*, 159 Misc. 793, 287 N.Y.S. 944 (1936) (both refusing to enjoin movement by a minor league baseball and basketball player, respectively); *Safro v. Lakofsky*, 184 Minn. 336, 238 N.W. 641 (1931) (refusing to enjoin a minor league boxer from performing in matches not procured by a party to whom he was under exclusive contract). However, see *Dallas Cowboys Football Club, Inc. v. Harris*, 348 S.W.2d. 37 (Tex. Civ. App. 1961) (enjoining a player under a one-year option contract with the NFL's Dallas Cowboys from playing for the Dallas Texans in the fledgling American Football League). By the way, should U.S. courts routinely enforce contracts negotiated in foreign countries, such as that of Dino Rajda who was enjoined from jumping from his Yugoslavian team to the Boston Celtics, or Pavel Bure who on the eve of his injunction hearing had to pay several hundred thousand dollars to secure release from his Russian contract to play for the Vancouver Canucks of the NHL?

In the *Winnipeg Rugby Football Club* case, an injunction was also issued to bar the Cleveland Browns from doing anything to interfere with the Blue Bomber's players' contracts. A prerequisite to this injunction was that the Browns were, or should have been, aware of the obligation of the players to the old team. Why would the plaintiff team also want to subject the defendant team to an injunction?

Note that the *Barnett* litigation was a product of a new league appearing on the scene. As we will see in Chapter 7, the early 1960s saw the emergence of a number of such competitors to the established leagues in every sport except baseball.[8] While Barnett's American Basketball League lasted only one year, it was followed five years later

8. In baseball there was a serious threat of a potential competitor, the Continental League, which was being organized by Branch Rickey in the late 1950s. That effort was foiled when the American and National Leagues expanded or relocated in the early 1960s into prime territory in New York, California, Texas, and Minnesota.

by the American Basketball Association (ABA). Hockey saw the World Hockey Association (WHA) challenge the National Hockey League (NHL). The National Football League (NFL), meanwhile, encountered the American Football League (AFL) in the 1960s, the World Football League (WFL) in the 1970s, and the United States Football League (USFL) in the 1980s. Just as had happened with baseball in the late 19th and early 20th centuries, the presence of two leagues competing for the same players produced a burst of contract litigation (exemplified by *Flowers*, *Neely*, and *Bergey*, *infra*). Should the *Barnett* court have focused more squarely on the significance of interleague rivalry? In contrast with the Ainge litigation in which the struggle was between two teams in different sports, should the presence of two different leagues in the same sport make a court more or less willing to grant the requested injunction?

––––––––

The next case presents a player's contract dispute in the contemporary context of a collective agreement negotiated by a players' association and interpreted by a labor arbitrator.[9]

BOSTON CELTICS v. BRIAN SHAW

United States Court of Appeals, First Circuit, 1990.

908 F.2d 1041.

BREYER, CIRCUIT JUDGE.

On January 23, 1990, Brian Shaw signed a contract with the owners of the Boston Celtics (the "Celtics") in which he promised that he would cancel his commitment to play for an Italian basketball team next year so that he could play for the Celtics instead. When Shaw threatened to break his agreement with the Celtics, they immediately sought arbitration. The arbitrator found that Shaw must keep his promise. The Players Association that represents Shaw agreed with the arbitrator. The Celtics then asked the federal district court to enforce the arbitrator's decision. The court ordered it enforced. Shaw now appeals the district court's order.

I. BACKGROUND FACTS

The basic facts, which are not in dispute, include the following:

(a) In 1988, soon after Shaw graduated from college, he signed a one-year contract to play for the Celtics.

(b) In 1989, Shaw signed a two-year contract to play with the Italian team Il Messaggero Roma ("Il Messaggero"). The team

---

9. For a journalistic account of the battle between Brian Shaw and the Celtics, see Harvey Araton and Flip Bondy, *The Selling of the Green: The Financial Rise and Moral Decline of the Boston Celtics* (New York: Harper Collins, 1992), at 1–19. The title of the book should leave no doubt about the authors' point of view on the *Shaw* case.

agreed to pay him $800,000 for the first year and $900,000 for the second year. The contract contains a clause permitting Shaw to cancel the second year (1990–91). It says that Shaw has the right to rescind the second year of this Agreement ... [if he] returns to the United States to play with the NBA ... by delivering a registered letter to [Il Messaggero] ... between June 20, 1990 and July 20, 1990.

(c) At the end of January 1990 Shaw signed a five-year "Uniform Player Contract" with the Celtics. The contract contains standard clauses negotiated by the National Basketball Association ("NBA") franchise owners and the National Basketball Players Association (the "Players Association"). It adopts by cross-reference arbitration provisions contained in the NBA–Players Association Collective Bargaining Agreement. In the contract, the Celtics promise Shaw a $450,000 signing bonus and more than $1 million per year in compensation. In return, Shaw promises the Celtics, among other things, that he will cancel his second year with Il Messaggero. The contract says that:

> The Player [*i.e.*, Shaw] and Club [*i.e.*, the Celtics] acknowledge that Player is currently under contract with Il Messaggero Roma (the "Messaggero Contract") for the 1989–90 & 1990–91 playing seasons. The Player represents that in accordance with the terms of the Messaggero Contract, the Player has the right to rescind that contract prior to the 1990–91 season *and the player hereby agrees to exercise such right of rescission* in the manner and at the time called for by the Messaggero Contract.

(d) On June 6, 1990, Shaw told the Celtics that he had decided to play for Il Messaggero during the 1990–91 season and that he would not exercise his right of rescission.

* * *

II. The Legal Merits

Shaw makes two basic categories of argument in his effort to show that the district court lacked the legal power to enter its order. First, he says that the arbitration award was itself unlawful. Second, he says that regardless of the lawfulness of the award, the district court followed improper procedures. We shall address these arguments in turn and explain why we find each not persuasive.

A. *The Arbitrator's Decision*

Shaw says that the district court should not have enforced the arbitrator's award because that award was itself unlawful, for any of five separate reasons.

1. The termination promise. Shaw argues that the arbitrator could not reasonably find that he broke a contractual promise to the Celtics because, he says, the Celtics had previously agreed with the

Players Association that contracts with individual players such as Shaw would not contain promises of the sort here at issue, namely, a promise to cancel a contract to play with a different team. Shaw says that this previous agreement between the Celtics and the Players Association renders his promise to terminate Il Messaggero "null and void." To support this argument, he points to Article I, section 2 of the Collective Bargaining Agreement, which Shaw and the Celtics, through cross-reference, made part of their individual agreement. Section 2 says, "Any amendment to a Uniform Player Contract [of the type Shaw and the Celtics used], other than those permitted by this [Collective Bargaining] Agreement, shall be null and void." The Agreement permits amendments (a) "in ... respect to the compensation ... to be paid the player," (b) "in respect to specialized compensation arrangements," (c) in respect to a "compensation payment schedule," and (d) in respect to "protect[ion]" of compensation in the event of contract termination. Shaw says that his promise to cancel the Il Messaggero agreement was an amendment to the Uniform Players Contract that does not concern compensation, specialized compensation, compensation schedules, or compensation protection; therefore, it is "null and void."

Shaw's argument, while logical, fails to show that the arbitrator's contrary finding is unlawful. The reasons it fails are fairly straightforward. First, the argument concerns the proper interpretation of a contract negotiated pursuant to a collective bargaining agreement. Second, federal labor law gives arbitrators, not judges, the power to interpret such contracts. The Supreme Court, noting the strong federal policy favoring the voluntary settlement of labor disputes, has written that a labor arbitration award is valid so long as it "draws its essence" from the labor contract. See United Steelworkers v. Enterprise Wheel & Car Corp., 363 U.S. 593, 597, (1960). An award "draws its essence" from the contract so long as the "arbitrator is even arguably construing or applying the contract and acting within the scope of his authority." United Paperworkers Int'l v. Misco, 484 U.S. 29, 38 (1987).

* * *

Third, one can find "plausible arguments" favoring the arbitrator's construction. Shaw's "rescission" promise defines the beginning of the compensation relationship. It also plausibly determines, at the very least, whether Shaw's compensation will begin at $1.1 million (and continue for three years) or whether it will begin at $1.2 million (and continue for only two years). More importantly, and also quite plausibly, Shaw's overall compensation might have been much different had he declined to promise to play for the Celtics in 1990–91, thereby forcing the Celtics, perhaps, to obtain the services of a replacement for that year. The NBA Commissioner, who reviews all player contracts, found that the term was related to "compensation," as did the arbitrator. We cannot say that their findings lack any "plausible" basis.

* * *

In sum, we find the arbitration award lawful; and, in doing so, it has not been necessary for us to consider the Celtics' additional argument that Shaw bears an especially heavy legal burden in this case because the Players Association does not support him.

B. The District Court Proceedings

The district court, as we have pointed out, issued a preliminary injunction requiring Shaw to rescind "forthwith" his contract with Il Messaggero and forbidding him to play basketball for any team other than the Celtics during the term of his Celtics contract. The court also "enforced" an arbitration award containing essentially the same terms. Shaw argues that both the preliminary injunction and the enforcement order are unlawful. Since the district court correctly upheld the award's validity, Shaw's only remaining arguments are that the district court lacked discretion to award preliminary injunctive relief and that it mismanaged the proceedings below. We discuss both points briefly.

1. The preliminary injunction. The disputed award in this case resulted from arbitration procedures contained in a collective bargaining agreement between a labor organization (the Players Association) and an employers' association (the NBA). Shaw bound himself to that collective bargaining agreement in his contract with the Celtics, the terms of which are themselves a product of collective bargaining between employees and employers. Well-established public policy embodied in statute, see 29 U.S.C. § 172(d), in Supreme Court decisions, and in numerous lower court opinions, strongly favors judicial action to "effectuate[ ] ... the means chosen by the parties for settlement of their differences under a collective bargaining agreement...." United Steelworkers of America v. American Mfg. Co., 363 U.S. 564, 566 (1960).

The only legal question before us, therefore, is whether the district court acted outside its broad equitable powers when it issued the preliminary injunction. That is to say, did the court improperly answer the four questions judges in this Circuit must ask when deciding whether to issue a preliminary injunction. They are: (1) have the Celtics shown a likelihood of success on the merits? (2) have they shown that failure to issue the injunction would cause the Celtics "irreparable harm?" (3) does the "balance of harms" favor Shaw or the Celtics? and (4) will granting the injunction harm the "public interest?" Our examination of the record has convinced us that the court acted well within the scope of its lawful powers.

To begin with, the Celtics have shown a clear likelihood of success on the merits.... The Celtics also have demonstrated irreparable harm. Without speedy relief, they will likely lose the services of a star athlete next year, see Wright & Miller § 2948, at 439 & n. 34 (1972) (collecting cases that have found irreparable harm "in the loss by an athletic team of the services of a star athlete"), and, unless they know fairly soon whether Shaw will, or will not play for them, they will find it difficult to plan intelligently for next season. Indeed, in his contract Shaw expressly:

> represents and agrees that he has extraordinary and unique skill and ability as a basketball player ... and that any breach by the Player of this contract will cause irreparable injury to the Club.

Further, the court could reasonably find that the "balance of harms" favors the Celtics. Of course, a preliminary injunction, if ultimately shown wrong on the merits, could cause Shaw harm. He might lose the chance to play in the country, and for the team, that he prefers. On the other hand, this harm is somewhat offset by the fact that ultimate success on the merits—*i.e.*, a finding that Shaw was not obligated to terminate Il Messaggero after all—would likely result in the following scenario: Shaw might still be able to sign with Il Messaggero and, if not, he would always have the Celtics contract of over $5 million to fall back upon. At the same time, the court's failure to issue the injunction, if the merits ultimately favored the Celtics, could cause them serious harm of the sort just mentioned (*i.e.*, significantly increased difficulty in planning their team for next season). Given the very small likelihood that Shaw would ultimately prevail on the merits, and the "comparative" harms at stake, the district court could properly decide that the overall "balance" favored the Celtics, not Shaw.

Finally, the court could properly find that issuing a preliminary injunction would not harm the public interest. Indeed, as we have pointed out, the public interest favors court action that "effectuate[s]" the parties' intent to resolve their disputes informally through arbitration. Where the dispute involves a professional basketball player's obligation to play for a particular team, one could reasonably consider expeditious, informal and effective dispute-resolution methods to be essential, and, if so, the public interest favoring court action to "effectuate" those methods of dispute-resolution would seem at least as strong as it is in respect to work-related disputes typically arising under collective bargaining agreements. See New England Patriots Football Club, Inc. v. University of Colorado, 592 F.2d 1196, 1200 (1st Cir.1979) (collecting cases in which professional sports players were enjoined from playing for rival teams). Shaw, while conceding that the public also has an interest in seeing that contracts between consenting adults are honored, points to a general policy disfavoring enforcement of personal service contracts. That latter policy, however, typically prevents a court from ordering an individual to perform a personal service; it does not prevent a court from ordering an individual to rescind a contract for services and to refrain from performing a service for others.

Shaw makes an additional argument. He notes that courts will not provide equitable relief such as an injunction to a party with "unclean hands," and he argues that the Celtics' hands are not clean. To support this argument, he has submitted an affidavit saying, in effect, that he signed the contract in a weak moment. His trip to Italy had made him "homesick;" he was "depressed" by what he viewed as undeserved and "negative criticism" in the Italian press; he was not represented by an agent; the Celtics had been urging him to sign up; he read the contract only for about 20 minutes while he was driving around Rome with a Celtics official; and no one ever explained to him that if he did not sign and played with Il Messaggero for another year, he would become a "free agent," able to bargain thereafter with any American team, perhaps for an even greater salary than the Celtics were willing to pay him.

Other evidence in the record, however, which Shaw does not deny, shows that he is a college graduate; that he has played under contract with the Celtics before; that the contract is a standard form contract except for a few, fairly simple, rather clear, additions; that he had bargained with the Celtics for an offer that increased from $3.4 million (in December) to $5.4 million (less than one month later); that he looked over the contract before signing it; that he told the American consul in Rome (as he signed it) that he had read and understood it; and that he did not complain about the contract until he told the Celtics in June that he would not honor it.

Given this state of the record, the district court could easily, and properly, conclude that the Celtics' hands were not "unclean." The one case Shaw cites in support of his position, Minnesota Muskies, Inc. v. Hudson, 294 F.Supp. 979, 981 (M.D.N.C.1969), is not on point. The player in Muskies had a contract with Team A that permitted Team A, not the player, to renew the contract for additional years. Team B lured the player away from Team A even though it knew that Team A intended to exercise its contractual right to keep the player. The court held that this contractual interference amounted to "unclean hands" and refused Team B's request for an injunction preventing the player from returning to Team A. Here, in contrast, Il Messaggero has no contractual right to retain Shaw; whether or not the contract is renewed or rescinded is entirely up to Shaw, not Il Messaggero. Under those circumstances, we cannot find anything improper, "unclean," or unfair about the Celtics' convincing Shaw (indeed, paying Shaw) to exercise his contractual right in their favor. Cf. Restatement (Second) of Torts § 768 (1979).

* * *

Injunction upheld.

Questions for Discussion

1. Unlike *Lajoie* and *Barnett*, in *Shaw* there had been an earlier adjudication of the issues, by a labor arbitrator appointed by the NBA and its Players Association under their collective agreement. Should this fact make a court more willing to order equitable relief against a player seeking to move to another league?

2. In the middle of the 1991-1992 season, the Celtics traded Shaw to the Miami Heat for the latter's equally disenchanted point guard, Sherman

Douglas. Such trades are made possible by the assignment clause that gives the team, the player's employer, the right to assign the personal services contract to another team in the same league. Though unthinkable in most other employment contexts, this provision is standard in athletes' contracts unless the player can negotiate a "no-trade" clause, or the collective bargaining agreement gives a veteran player some control over his being traded. Should this feature of the contract influence a court's decision about whether to force the player to play for the team with which he originally signed? For the team to which he was traded?

More generally, is this assignment clause itself fair and reasonable, or should it be void as against public policy? Would your answer hinge on whether the players union had agreed to the inclusion of such a clause in the standard contract? For what reasons do club owners want such a clause? What would be the long term effect on player-club relations if such clauses were not enforced by the courts? Does this provision, along with that requiring commissioner approval before the contract can become valid, essentially mean that the player is as much under contract to the league as to the club? Should the league, then, also be liable for any breach of contract by the club? See *USFL Players Ass'n. v. USFL*, 650 F.Supp. 12 (D.Or.1986).

3. In *Munchak Corp. v. Cunningham*, 457 F.2d 721 (4th Cir.1972), Billy Cunningham had negotiated a "no-trade" clause in his basketball contract with the ABA's Carolina Cougars. Subsequently, the Cougars were sold and all of the team's player contracts were assigned to the new owner. Cunningham sought to avoid being held to his contract by arguing that this assignment voided it. The Fourth Circuit rejected his argument and held that a standard "no assignment" clause merely meant that the player could not be traded to a different club, not that he could not be traded to a different owner of the same club. Is this a fair interpretation of general "no-trade" language? Would your answer be different if the team was sold to a new owner who immediately relocated the franchise to a different city and changed the name of the team?

––––––––

In assessing the equities of these player contract suits, one factor that influences the reaction of judges, let alone fans, is the salaries paid to players for signing contracts with these apparently onerous clauses. Note how dramatically the basketball salary figures in *Shaw* had changed since the days of *Barnett*. This salary escalation was due in considerable part to the emergence of union representation and collective bargaining in sports: the impact and the desirability of unionism in sports is the subject of Chapter 4.

An important feature of the sports world under labor law is that grievance arbitration rather than civil adjudication is the principal method for resolving disputes affecting players (as we saw with drug-testing in Chapter 1). Note the judicial treatment of the arbitration award in *Shaw*, to be recalled in Chapter 4 when we develop the labor law framework for professional sports.

Finally, look carefully at the arbitrator's treatment of whether the collective agreement permitted Shaw to make the special undertaking in his individually negotiated contract. Keep this case in mind when we address the interplay of collective and individual bargaining in sports at the beginning of Chapter 5.

———

The next cases introduce the world of professional football [10] and explore the doctrine of "unclean hands" that was raised at the end of the *Shaw* decision. In *New York Football Giants, Inc. v. Los Angeles Chargers Football Club, Inc.* (*Flowers*), 291 F.2d 471 (5th Cir.1961), Charles Flowers, a star player for the University of Mississippi football team, was signed by the National Football League's New York Giants to a pro football contract. If the December, 1959 contract signing had been made public at that time, Flowers would have lost his eligibility to play in the New Year's Day Sugar Bowl against Mississippi's traditional rival, Louisiana State. Accordingly, Giants' owner Wellington Mara acceded to Flower's request to keep the contract (and signing bonus) secret until January 2nd, 1960; thus, the team did not submit the contract to NFL Commissioner Pete Rozelle for his approval.

Later in December, Flowers was offered more money by the Los Angeles Chargers of the new American Football League. Flowers thereupon notified the Giants that he was withdrawing from their contract and returning their uncashed bonus checks. Flowers signed with the Chargers on January 1st, right after the Sugar Bowl, and the Giants went to court seeking an injunction to enforce its prior agreement. In court, though, the Giants were met with "the age-old but sometimes overlooked doctrine that 'he who comes into equity must come with clean hands'" (at 473).

"Here the plaintiff's [Giants'] whole difficulty arises because it admittedly took from Flowers what it claims to be a binding contract, but which it agreed with Flowers it would, in effect, represent was not in existence in order to deceive others who had a very material and important interest in the subject matter. If there had been a straightforward execution of the document, followed by its filing with the Commissioner, none of the legal problems now presented to this court to untangle would exist. We think no party had the right thus to create problems by its devious and deceitful conduct and then approach a court of equity with a plea that the pretended status which it has foisted on the public be ignored and its rights be declared as if it had acted in good faith throughout."

"When it became apparent from uncontradicted testimony of Mara that this deceit was practiced in order to bring into being the 'contract'

10. For background on the struggle between the National and American Football Leagues that gave rise to the *Flowers* and *Neely* cases, see Harris, *The League*, note 1 above, 56–66, 102–06, 132–33.

sued upon, the trial court should have dismissed the suit without more on the basis of the 'clean hands' doctrine" (at 474).

While *Flowers* reflects the standard approach to this kind of case, the next decision took a different view.

HOUSTON OILERS, INC. v. NEELY

United States Court of Appeals, Tenth Circuit, 1966.

361 F.2d 36.

PICKETT, CIRCUIT JUDGE.

[Ralph Neely of the University of Oklahoma was one of the top senior college football players in 1964. In those days the National Football League (NFL) and the new American Football League (AFL) conducted their college player drafts at the end of the college regular season, before bowl games were played. Neely was drafted by both the NFL's Baltimore Colts and the AFL's Houston Oilers. Immediately after the November 28 draft, Baltimore offered Neely a four-year contract with salaries from $16,000 to $25,000 per year and a $25,000 signing bonus.

On November 30, Houston president K.S. "Bud" Adams offered Neely a four-year, "no-cut" contract for $16,000 per year and a $25,000 signing bonus. Adams also promised to get a job for Neely with a local real-estate firm and to have his oil company build a Phillips '66 gas station (at a cost of $30,000 to $60,000) for Neely to own and operate. Neely accepted the Houston offer and the contracts were executed on December 1. Neely, who apparently knew that by signing the contracts he had forfeited his remaining college eligibility, wanted the contracts kept secret so that he could play in the Gator Bowl game on January 2. However, the contracts and bonus check were dated December 1, and the contracts expressly provided that they were binding upon execution and (pursuant to AFL rules) had to be filed with the AFL commissioner within 10 days (and they were).

Neely then learned that Baltimore had traded the right to negotiate with him to the Dallas Cowboys. Neely's father-in-law, who had been involved in the negotiations with Houston, then began secretly negotiating with Dallas. On December 29, Neely returned the $25,000 bonus check and sent letters to Adams and Houston stating that he was withdrawing from his contracts with them. On December 31, Dallas deposited $15,000 in Neely's bank account, and Neely told his Oklahoma coach about the Houston contracts. The next day Neely was declared ineligible for the Gator Bowl game, and that evening he signed a four-year contract with Dallas.

Houston brought suit seeking an injunction to prevent Neely from playing for Dallas (or any other professional football team). The trial court, finding that Neely's contracts with Houston were tainted with fraud, refused to grant the injunction. By the time the appellate court handed down its decision, Neely had already played the 1965 season for Dallas.]

* * *

Disagreement over the validity of these contracts does not arise out of the provisions contained therein, but from an extrinsic oral understanding that their existence was to be kept secret until after the post-season game. The essence of Neely's contentions before the trial court and here is that the contracts are unenforceable because Houston falsely represented that the effective date of the agreement would be January 2, 1965, and that Houston's filing of the contract copies with the Commissioner was a violation of its promise to keep the matter secret. The trial court was of the opinion that these alleged misrepresentations constituted fraud in the inducement of the contract which would subject it to rescission. As has been heretofore stated, each contract specifically provides otherwise. Neely does not say he was so naive that he did not know his eligibility for further intercollegiate football competition would be destroyed when he signed a professional football contract and received the bonus money.

The record is too clear for any misunderstanding that the purpose of secrecy surrounding the execution of the contracts was not to preserve Neely's eligibility, but rather to prevent his ineligibility from becoming known; otherwise there was no need for secrecy.

* * *

The scheme to mislead Neely's school, his coaches, his team, and the Gator Bowl opponents, no doubt would have succeeded but for Neely's own double dealing with Dallas, resulting in his attempt to avoid the Houston contracts. While we do not for a moment condone the ruthless methods employed by professional football teams in their contest for the services of college football players, including the lavish expenditure of money,[7] it must be conceded that there is no legal impediment to contracting for the services of athletes at any time, and the above-mentioned conduct, while regrettable, does not furnish athletes with a legal excuse to avoid their contracts for reasons other than the temptations of a more attractive offer. Although there are many dismal indications to the contrary, athletes, amateur or professional, and those connected with athletics, are bound by their contracts to the

7. These methods and their adverse effect upon amateur football players were described by Judge Skelly Wright in Detroit Football Company v. Robinson, 186 F.Supp. 933, 934 (D.D.C., 1960), where he said:

This case is but another round in the sordid fight for football players, a fight which begins before these athletes enter college and follows them through their professional careers. It is a fight characterized by deception, double dealing, campus jumping, secret alumni subsidization, semi-professionalism and professionalism. It is a fight which has produced as part of its harvest this current rash of contract jumping suits. It is a fight which so conditions the minds and hearts of these athletes that one day they can agree to play football for a stated amount for one group, only to repudiate that agreement the following day or whenever a better offer comes along.

same extent as anyone else, and should not be allowed to repudiate them at their pleasure.

* * *

The draft system in professional football limited Neely's negotiations initially to Baltimore and Houston. His collegiate football record was such that he and his father-in-law could anticipate that his services would be in demand and would command a premium contract. The opportunity presented to Neely would come but once in his lifetime, and it is understandable that the situation would be exploited to the maximum. It was with this background that Neely negotiated with Houston and Baltimore. Neely, a bright young man, ably advised by his father-in-law, knew exactly what he wanted.

* * *

There is insufficient evidence to sustain a finding of material misrepresentation on the part of Houston amounting to fraud which would affect the validity of the contracts. It is true that Neely testified that it was his understanding that the contracts were not to become effective until after the game on January 2nd. The contracts, however, provided otherwise, and we are not at liberty to rewrite then. Furthermore, the letter of employment, the filling station arrangement, and the $25,000 bonus check which was delivered upon the execution of the contracts, were all dated December 1, 1964.

The trial court, in denying the relief sought, apparently applied the equitable maxim that "he who comes into equity must come with clean hands." This doctrine, fundamental in equity jurisprudence, means that equity will not in any manner aid a party whose conduct in relation to the litigation matter has been unlawful, unconscionable, or inequitable. But the doctrine does not exclude all wrongdoers from a court of equity nor should it be applied in every case where the conduct of a party may be considered unconscionable or inequitable. While it is not contended here that Houston did not have a legal right to sign Neely to a professional player's contract, it is urged that when Houston participated in a scheme to conceal that for the purpose of permitting an ineligible player to participate in a post-season game, it was such deceit upon others that a court of equity should not intervene to assist in the enforcement of the contract. With this argument we cannot agree. It is neither unlawful nor inequitable for college football players to surrender their amateur status and turn professional at any time. Neely was free to bind himself to such a contract on December 1, 1964 as he would have been after January 2, 1965. Nor was Houston under any legal duty to publicize the contract or to keep it secret. Its agreement to keep secret that which it had a legal right to keep secret cannot be considered inequitable or unconscionable as those terms are ordinarily used in contract negotiations. Neely relies on the case of New York Football Giants v. Los Angeles Chargers, 291 F.2d 471 (5th Cir.1961), where, in a somewhat similar situation, the court applied the clean hands doctrine. It is quite apparent that the player contract in that case was acquired under circumstances much different from those in this case, but if the rule announced in that case was intended to apply to every instance in which a contract is entered into with a college football player before a post-season game with an understanding that it be kept secret to permit that player to compete in the game, then we must respectfully disagree with the conclusion.

Injunction granted.

The facts in these cases provide a glimpse of the relationship between professional and intercollegiate football. Do you find anything familiar in Judge Skelly Wright's lament about the "sordid" state of affairs thirty years ago—before there were player agents to blame? By the way, do not assume, as did the Fifth Circuit, that there was nothing unlawful in the Houston Oilers signing Neely and keeping that fact secret from his school and the NCAA. We will read a good deal more in Chapters 5 and 9 on the topic of college athletes, player agents, and professional teams.

Questions for Discussion

1. The war between the NFL and the AFL in the early 1960s produced numerous cases of players trying to renege on a secret pre-bowl game contract (and bonus payment) with a team in one league in order to sign with a team in the other league. In addition to the *Neely* and *Flowers* cases, see *Detroit Football Co. v. Robinson*, 186 F.Supp. 933 (E.D.La.1960) and *Los Angeles Rams Football Club v. Cannon*, 185 F.Supp. 717 (S.D.Cal. 1960). Only in *Neely* did the court not invoke the "clean hands" doctrine to refuse to enforce the initial contract. As between *Neely* and the other cases, which represents the better legal view? Interestingly, in every one of these cases the court ended up siding with the AFL team and against the NFL team. Is that just a coincidence, or did it reflect a judicial desire to assist the upstart football league against the established league that had far greater market power? Is such a consideration proper in these contract enforcement cases?

2. The *Neely* court made a good deal out of the fact that Neely was intelligent, sophisticated, and knew what he was doing when he helped hide the contract from his college and the NCAA. Is this a factor on which the case should turn? What if the deception were proposed by the club, not by the player? What if the player were relatively naive and uninformed and thus more likely to be led by the professional team?

3. The contract Neely signed was for four years and had a "no-cut" clause in it. This type of provision, which requires the team to continue paying the player his salary for the term of the contract even if he is not retained on the playing roster, has been quite rare in professional football, although not in baseball or basketball (or for football coaches). Can you think of reasons why this might be the case? Such a "semi-guarantee" in a contract differentiates it from those the early courts felt might lack

mutuality because the team could terminate them at any time. By contrast to Neely's contract, Flower's two-year agreement with the Giants would have allowed the Giants to "cut" him at will. Should the fact that the contract a player was trying to back out of did or did not contain such a semi-guarantee affect the equities and perhaps the outcome of the case?

4. Note that in these early 1960's cases (contemporaries of *Barnett*), "unique skill and ability" was not an issue. Courts by this time had apparently adopted the *Barnett* position that the contract clause by which the player represented that he had such skill and ability, plus the very fact of the player being on a professional team roster, satisfied this requirement for an injunction.

––––––

The next case brings the story in football up to the 1970s and the challenge launched against the NFL by the World Football League (WFL). In the course of his opinion, the judge describes comparable litigation involving basketball stars Rick Barry and Billy Cunningham, who were the objects of affection of both the NBA and the American Basketball Association (ABA), a competitor that emerged in the late 1960s.[11] The interesting legal question is whether it is consistent with a player's contractual obligations to his present team to sign a contract to play for another team in the future.

CINCINNATI BENGALS v. BERGEY

United States District Court, Southern District of Ohio, 1974.

453 F.Supp. 129.

PORTER, DISTRICT JUDGE.

[Bill Bergey, a star linebacker for the Cincinnati Bengals of the NFL, earned slightly less than $40,000 per year under a non-guaranteed contract for 1974 that gave the Bengals an option on his services for 1975. In April 1974 Bergey signed a no-cut, three-year contract with the Virginia Ambassadors of the newly formed WFL, who agreed to pay Bergey $125,000 per year plus a $150,000 signing bonus. This WFL contract was designed to begin with the 1976 football season, but would be accelerated forward if the Bengals released Bergey for any reason. Bergey was one of several Bengal stars pursued by the WFL (including starting linemen such as Bob Trumpy, Bob Johnson, and Rufus Mayes), as part of a WFL effort to stockpile a large number of NFL players for the new league. The threat of competition from the WFL moved NFL teams to elevate sharply their salary levels—the Bengals offered Bergey a new five-year contract for a total of $400,000. Unsuccessful in that bidding war, the Bengals sued Bergey, the Ambas-

––––––

11. On the football background, see Harris, *The League*, note 1 above, 149–50, 168–70, 185–86, and 215–16. On the bas-ketball rivalry, see Pluto, *Loose Balls*, note 1 above.

sadors, and the WFL, on the grounds that Bergey's future service agreement with the WFL team undermined and interfered with the Bengals' rights under their existing contract with Bergey.

Extensive testimony was offered about the special character of football as a sport and as an enterprise, particularly from Bengals' founder and head coach, Paul Brown, and its assistant coach, Bill Walsh. The judge concluded that notwithstanding the special emotional demands of football, Bergey's signing of a "futures" contract with another team would not reduce his effectiveness with the Bengals during his existing contract. However, the judge felt there likely would be an adverse impact if several other Bengals' stars were to follow Bergey's lead, because "a football team is a sort of delicate mechanism, the success of whose operation is dependent upon the coordination of various cohesive units."

On the other side of the ledger, though, was the harmful effect on the WFL if its teams were barred from signing NFL contract players for promotion of this new venture.]

* * *

The Court finds that starting a new franchise and a new league is a risky business. In 1960 there were twelve teams in the NFL and eight in the AFL (American Football League). Now there are twenty-six NFL teams in twenty-five cities. This limits the availability of stadiums to a new league. For example, the Virginia Ambassadors were originally known as the Washington Ambassadors and were based in the District of Columbia. The Ambassadors left Washington upon learning that they would have to pay an amount well in excess of $1.5 million to the Washington Redskins of the NFL in order for that team to agree to waive its exclusive rights to play in R.F.K. Stadium. That price was more than the Ambassadors wanted to pay, and there being no other suitable facility in Washington, D.C., the team moved to Virginia.

Increased television coverage of professional football games has produced a sophisticated audience. The costs of fielding a competitive team are much higher today than in 1960. The cost of acquiring players of exceptional ability has contributed significantly to the substantial increase in ticket prices (though these price increases have not been proportionately as great as the increase in costs). The higher ticket prices mean that sports fans expect major league entertainment for their sports dollar. Faced with the stiff competition for the sports dollar by the NFL, as well as other professional sports organizations, the WFL seeks to ensure its future by signing established NFL players to give the new league "credibility" in the eyes of the public. The signing of professional players is also necessary to overcome the doubts of college players as to the future of the league.... Mr. Putnam stated that the signing of name players to future contracts is "essential" to the WFL's success, since the league's financial future is dependent in great part on the earliest possible public acceptance of the WFL as a marketer of "major league" professional football.

[Turning to the legal issues, the court considered two earlier precedents involving Rick Barry and Billy Cunningham, who had been the subject of a similar tug of war between the National Basketball Association and the American Basketball Association in the late 1960s.

Barry's case was extremely entangled. While under contract with the NBA's San Francisco Warriors for 1967–1968, Barry signed a three-year deal with the ABA's Oakland Oaks. Barry was enjoined from jumping to the Oaks for the 1967–1968 season (see *Lemat Corp. v. Barry*, 80 Cal.Rptr. 240 (Cal. App. 1969), but he did play for Oakland in 1968–69. However, when the Oaks were bought by the Washington Capitols, Barry, wanting to remain in the Bay area, signed a five-year contract with the Warriors. When the Capitols sought injunctive relief against the NBA team, Barry's argument was that the Oakland contract had been tainted from the outset because of the conflict with his earlier agreement with the Warriors. Judge Porter quoted the Ninth Circuit's rejection of this argument in *Washington Capitals Basketball Club v. Barry*, 419 F.2d 472 (9th Cir.1969).]

* * *

Barry signed his contract with Oakland while still under contract to the Warriors, who claim that this act was a breach of Barry's contract to them. The Oakland contract, however, was a contract for future services "for a term of three (3) years commencing on October 2, 1968, or such earlier date as (Barry's) services as a basketball player are not enjoined." Performance and consideration therefor were to begin only upon the termination of the Warrior contract. Neither Barry's signing nor Oakland's inducement of him to sign was an illegal act rendering the Oakland contract illegal. Associate Justice Hufstedler of the California Court of Appeal, now Judge Hufstedler of this Court, stated in Diodes, Inc. v. Franzen, 67 Cal.Rptr. 19, 25–26 (1968): "Even though the relationship between an employer and his employee is an advantageous one, no actionable wrong is committed by a competitor who solicits his competitor's employees or who hires away one or more of his competitor's employees who are not under contract, so long as the inducement to leave is not accompanied by unlawful action." In each of these cases, the hired-away employee was not under contract to his employer. Barry was under contract to the Warriors at the time he signed with Oakland but his performance under the Oakland contract was not to begin until after his obligations to the Warriors ceased on October 1, 1968. This fact distinguishes cases in which courts have found an actionable wrong where an employee was encouraged to terminate his contract prior to its termination date.

[A similar ruling was rendered in *Munchak Corp. v. Cunningham*, 457 F.2d 721 (4th Cir.1972), in which the court refused to nullify Cunningham's contract to play for the Carolina Cougars in the 1971–1972 season, even though the three-year agreement had been signed in

August 1969 when Cunningham was under contract to the Philadelphia 76ers. The judge in the *Bergey* case then addressed and rejected the Bengals' argument that judicial precedents from basketball should not govern the assertedly different world of professional football.]

* * *

When *Barry* and *Cunningham* are applied to the case at bar, the Court can only conclude that neither the WFL nor Bergey committed a tortious or otherwise unlawful act in entering into negotiations for and reaching agreement upon a contract for Bergey's personal services to commence after the expiration of his contract with the Bengals. In the language of *Cunningham*, there are no more obligations to be protected by either party to the Bengals contract after May 1, 1976.

Plaintiff argues that the acceleration clause of Bergey's WFL contract induces Bergey to seek his release prior to his NFL contract's expiration. We reject this argument, however, because we accept as true Bergey's testimony that he has no intention of seeking an early release. And, notwithstanding plaintiff's interpretation of *Barry*, we do not read the Ninth Circuit's opinion in that case as granting to Barry the right to breach his contract. Bergey will be liable should he breach his contract while its terms are still in effect.

* * *

In short, we conclude that *Barry* and *Cunningham* support the proposition that it is not illegal for either the player or the sports organization, at the time when the player is under a valid contract to one team, to negotiate and enter into a contract with a different, competing, team and league, under the terms of which the player agrees to render his services at the expiration of his current contract.

* * *

Harm To Public Interest

Next, we flesh out the bare-bones conclusion that plaintiff has failed to show an absence of harm to the public interest if an injunction is granted herein. As we view it, the "public interest" within the meaning of that phrase as it is used here is the policy such as that behind the antitrust laws to encourage to the fullest extent practicable free and open competition in the marketplace. Restraints on competition are not favored.

This Court recognizes such public interest would probably not stand in the way of plaintiff's obtaining injunctive relief if it is able to establish that the contractual rights it has with its players have been tortiously, i.e., maliciously interfered with (plus irreparable harm and no adequate remedy at law). On the facts of this case the Court cannot conclude that such interference as there may be was due to unfair competition. On the contrary, it seems to the Court that the threatened harm is due to competition, and an injunction would therefore not be in the public interest.

The Court would be blind if it did not recognize that there is a public interest of another sort. This is the concern among fans over the actual and prospective loss of key members of a team of which they are devoted followers and the effect this may have on that team's "chances." It is clear that the Court cannot take such "public interest" into consideration. The only public interest that can properly be taken into account is the policy of the law to encourage free competition in the marketplace. Hence, the denial of an injunction is not a case of the Court's turning its back on the fans and the owners of the plaintiff's franchise, as the plaintiff improperly suggested in final argument that it might be.

HARM TO WFL AND PLAINTIFF

Plaintiff has not demonstrated an absence of harm to the WFL defendants or "other persons." We consider the other persons the players, and are of the opinion that if an injunction is issued they will be harmed by the postponement of the time when there is bidding for their future services. Plaintiff concedes that the Bengal players have a First Amendment right to "talk" now to WFL teams about their future services. We are sure that the plaintiff also recognizes that the right of contract is not far behind. What the plaintiff contends, and the Court cannot accept, is that the signing before a player has performed his last game is a tortious interference with its contractual rights.

* * *

The conclusion that plaintiff has not made a clear showing of irreparable injury to itself is a difficult one to make. One reason it is, is that there is nothing to go on because this case is unique. As pointed out by Coach Brown, in all his forty years: "I've never had one like this, where I had a football player playing for me who is also under contract to somebody else." For another, while it may be too late to close the barn door as far as Bergey and Chomyszak are concerned, the threatened damage from the loss of Bob Johnson, et al., may not occur, and will not occur, if the Bengals match any offer they get from a WFL team. The Bengals argue that the fact that in order to match WFL offers they may have to tear up existing contracts and pay more for present services is evidence of irreparable injury.

We recognize that it will cost the Bengals something to bid for the future services of its players to preserve the continuity of the team's performance when present contracts expire. We do not, however, follow the argument that that is evidence of irreparable injury. Prior to the emergence of the World Football League, the teams in the National Football League could rest in relative assurance that the services of their players presently under short-term contracts would remain available beyond the termination dates should the clubs desire to offer players further contracts. The absence of a competitor league justified that self-assurance, for the NFL, until now, has been "the only game in town." With the rise of the WFL, the NFL can no longer rely upon the absence of a competitor for protection of its claims to the future services of players, for which the established teams have neither bargained nor paid consideration.

It is not the players' present services for which the clubs will have to pay more, for those are protected by contracts which can presumably be enforced in the usual manner. It is only when the NFL chooses (and such decision is likely) to join the competition for the later services of its players that it will incur these higher costs. In our best judgment, such higher costs will be attributable to competition and not unfair competition.

* * *

Injunction denied.

Questions for Discussion

1. Several years ago, a dispute arose within the National Hockey League when Pat Quinn, coach of the Los Angeles Kings, signed a contract in mid-season to become president and coach of the Vancouver Canucks at the end of that season. If the Kings had sued for an injunction against this contract, should *Bergey* govern the result? Why do you think the Kings did not need to bring such a suit? (On judicial enforcement of a coach's contracts against recruiting efforts by a team outside the league, see *New England Patriots Football Club v. University of Colorado and Fairbanks*, 592 F.2d 1196 (1st Cir.1979).)

2. Suppose that the league (with or without union approval) decided to incorporate in its standard player contract a provision which specified that during the term of the agreement, the player (or coach) promised not to sign a contract with any team in another league or in another sport. How would you draft this clause to make it enforceable? Would or should a court enforce it by injunction? Would your answers differ if such a provision were incorporated in the employment contract of a business executive? In the partnership agreement of a law firm?

———

As the judge observed in *Bergey*, this legal dispute involved not only the interests of the player and the two teams competing for his services, but also a struggle between the fledgling WFL and the dominant NFL. A similar inter-league conflict surfaced in the legal battles between the National Hockey League (NHL) and the new World Hockey Association (WHA) which began play in 1970–1971.[12] A number of NHL teams went to court seeking injunctions to prevent star players such as Bobby Hull, Derek Sanderson, and Gerry Cheevers from jumping to the upstart WHA. See e.g., *Boston Professional Hockey Ass'n v. Cheevers*, 348 F.Supp. 261 (D.Mass.1972), vacated and remanded, 472 F.2d 127 (1st Cir.1972). This concerted contract litigation effort by the NHL in turn provoked an antitrust suit by the WHA, which accused

---

12. On the struggle between the WHA and the NHL, see David Cruise and Alison Griffiths, *Net Worth*, note 1 above, in particular, Chapters 10 and 11.

the NHL of violating Section 2 of the Sherman Antitrust Act by hoarding hockey-playing talent to preserve the NHL's monopoly over the sport. The decision of the court in this important case, *Philadelphia World Hockey Club v. Philadelphia Hockey Club*, 351 F.Supp. 462 (E.D.Pa.1972), is included in Chapter 7.

After the decisions in *Bergey*, the *Barry* and *Cunningham* cases discussed in *Bergey*, as well as *World Football League v. Dallas Cowboys Football Club*, 513 S.W.2d 102 (Tex. Civ. App. 1974), the judicial consensus seems to be that "futures" contracts will not be held improper unless they interfere with the player's performance of his current contract. This was illustrated in *Minnesota Muskies v. Hudson*, 294 F.Supp. 979 (M.D.N.C.1969), a case with facts similar to *Barry*. Upon graduating from the University of Minnesota in 1966, Hudson signed a one-year contract with the NBA's St. Louis Hawks for the 1966–67 season, with an option clause for the 1967–68 season. However, in May of 1967, with his option year in St. Louis still ahead of him, Hudson signed a three-year contract with the ABA's Minnesota Muskies covering the 1967–68 through 1969–70 seasons. That contract provided that if Hudson were unable to play for the Muskies in 1967–68 because of his option year obligation to the Hawks, he would receive $25,000 for that year from the Muskies for sitting out the year and he would then play the next two seasons under the Muskies contract. One month after signing this contract and being sued by the Hawks, Hudson signed a new five-year contract with the Hawks, beginning with 1967–68. The Muskies—by then the Miami Floridians and under new ownership—did not object to Hudson playing with the Hawks in 1967–68, the option year of the first contract. However, the ABA team sought to enjoin Hudson from playing for the Hawks during the next two seasons. The court declined to rule on whether the contract the Muskies had signed with Hudson was valid, but it refused to grant the injunction.

> The fact remains that the Muskies, knowing that Hudson was under a moral, if not legal, obligation to furnish his services to St. Louis for the 1967–68 and subsequent seasons, if St. Louis chose to exercise its option, sent for Hudson and induced him to repudiate his obligation to St. Louis. Such conduct, even if strictly within the law because of the St. Louis contract being unenforceable, was so tainted with unfairness and injustice as to justify a court of equity in withholding relief." (Id. at 990)

The only material difference between *Hudson* and *Barry* is that in the former case, the Muskies paid Hudson not to play in his option year for the Hawks should he become obligated to the Hawks for that year, whereas in *Barry* the Oakland Oaks contract was merely delayed a year and Rick Barry was given no inducement to sit out his option year with the Warriors. (It should be noted that the NBA's option clause did not have a tolling provision in it such as the NFL's, see *Dallas Cowboys v. Harris*, 348 S.W.2d 37 (Tex. Civ. App. 1961), so an NBA player who elected to sit out his option year thereafter became a free agent.) Is this factual difference—i.e., that the Muskies induced Hudson not to perform his contract obligation to the Hawks—the reason the two cases come out differently? Is this a valid distinction?

In that connection, consider the *Cunningham* case in which the ABA's Carolina Cougars sought to enforce a contract between themselves and Billy Cunningham under which Cunningham was to be given $80,000 if he elected to sit out his 1970–71 option year with the NBA Philadelphia 76ers, and he would then play the next three seasons for the Cougars. The contract thus compensated Cunningham if he did not fulfill the option year obligation, but, unlike Hudson's contract with the Muskies, it did not contractually require him to do so. Then, like Hudson, Cunningham turned around and signed a multi-year contract with the 76ers in violation of his contract with the Cougars. The trial court denied the Cougars an injunction, claiming that the team had unclean hands in interfering with the 76er's first contract. Citing *Barry*, the Fourth Circuit reversed and entered the injunction, arguing that there was no misconduct by the Cougars because if Cunningham did play the option year he would earn up to $20,000 more than if he sat out, and therefore the Cougars contract was really an incentive for him to play his option year for the 76ers, not to sit it out. Do you believe that these cases were correctly decided? Was *Cunningham* more like *Barry* or like *Hudson*, or are they all basically the same?

———

Litigation about player contracts vividly poses the conflict between two visions of contract and its enforcement. One view pictures contracts as personal promises that create moral obligations and entitlements and are worthy of as much legal teeth as the law can sensibly provide. From this perspective, while judges might reasonably be cautious about issuing a specific order forcing a player to play for the team to which he is under contract, they should not hesitate to enjoin him from playing for another team, even if the resulting financial pressures soon yield the first result.

An alternative conception of contract pictures this institution as an economic instrument for whose enforcement the law should be deployed only to the extent such judicial intervention produces an efficient allocation of society's resources. Under this theory, a player should be entitled to break an initial commitment to one team as long as he is willing to pay that team for its financial losses suffered through loss of the player's services. The assumption is that such contract breaches will be committed only when it is socially efficient to do so—in other words, when someone else finds the player's services more valuable and thus worth enough extra money to leave the player better off after compensation damages are paid to the original team.[13]

13. For a helpful appraisal of these two competing viewpoints, see Laycock, *The Death of the Irreparable Injury Rule*, note 5 above, in particular, Chapter 11 on Holmes, Posner, and Efficient Breach.

The cases we have read leave no doubt that in terms of bottom-line results, if not underlying rationale, the courts have embraced the first view about player contracts. But is this judicial verdict socially desirable? Consider these specific questions about sports cases:

i. Is society (at least the sports community) better off with the athlete playing for the original team or the new team?

ii. Is it possible to calculate the actual damages inflicted on a team if a player defects? By analogy, how would you go about calculating the tort damages payable to a team that lost a star player because of physical injuries due to someone else's fault? (As we will see in Chapter 11, precisely that challenge was faced by the court in a suit brought by the NBA Houston Rockets against the Los Angeles Lakers when star Rockets' forward Rudy Tomjanovich was severely injured by a punch thrown by the Lakers' Kermit Washington.)

iii. Suppose that the court issues an injunction that forbids a player to move to another team. Is the player likely to stay and perform effectively for his original team? If not, has litigation been fruitless for that team? Or has the club nonetheless gained something of tangible value from the judicial order? Recall the Coase Theorem which you may have encountered in your first year courses, and for which Coase won the 1992 Nobel Prize in Economics: the law's initial allocation of the right to an asset does not dictate its ultimate destination so long as some voluntary transactions are permitted about disposition of the asset. What does this theorem [14] imply for the way these legal doctrines play themselves out in sports over the longer run?

iv. An alternative way of characterizing the issue is the following: whereas limiting the team's remedy to damages treats the contract as simply a *liability* rule, giving the club injunctive relief means that the contract has, in effect, conferred on the team a *property* right in the player's services.[15] In the sports world, the latter term is not merely a rhetorical label. As we noted earlier, a standard feature of the player contract in every sport has been a right of the team to sell or trade the player's services to another team. Owners have used that right to sell even the greatest players in the game—Babe Ruth was sold by the Boston Red Sox to the New York Yankees in 1919 and Wayne Gretzky was sold by the Edmonton Oilers to the Los Angeles Kings in 1988. As long ago as *Lajoie*, however, courts have observed that players are paid more than generously for giving the teams that prerogative. Is this judicial sentiment apt?

14. Which, interestingly, was anticipated in one of the key early articles on the economics of sports: Simon Rottenberg, *The Baseball Players' Labor Market*, 64 J. of Political Economy 242 (1956).

15. See Guido Calabresi and A. Douglas Melamed, *Property Rules, Liability Rules, and Inalienability: One View of the Cathedral*, 85 Harvard L. Rev. 1089 (1972).

C. RESERVE SYSTEM AND RESTRAINT OF TRADE

The cases and materials up to this point of the chapter have provided a rather truncated picture of the sports industry setting in which player contracts are initially signed. The next case brings that setting to the fore—in particular, the key ingredients in the reserve system first developed by baseball and then copied in varying ways by the other professional sports.[16] To ease reading of the *Chase* opinion, which dwells on the technical language of the reserve system, we provide this capsule summary of that contractual regime:

1. Each team in a league was entitled to list a certain number of players with whom it had a contract relationship and to which the team claimed exclusive rights.

2. All other teams in the league agreed to respect the reserve lists of their fellow league members and not to "tamper" with another team's players by inducing them to move.

3. All teams in the league agreed to sign players only to a single standard form contract. A key provision in that contract was that when its term expired, the team retained an option to renew the contract for another season with the same provisions as before—including this option clause—except for salary. In case of disagreement over salary, the team had the prerogative to set the salary for the upcoming year.

4. A further feature of the reserve system was the draft, whereby major league teams agreed to select (in reverse order of finish in the previous season) from among minor league players talented enough to play in the major league. The modern rookie draft was actually first developed in football in the 1930s, emulated in basketball in the late 1940s, and adopted by baseball and hockey only in the mid–1960s, under which players selected were reserved to the drafting club even before they signed the first standard form contract.

With this background, you will now encounter a rather different judicial perspective on the enforceability of player contracts signed in such an environment.

---

16. On the historical evolution of the reserve clause in baseball, see *Report on Organized Baseball*, note 1 above, and Seymour, *Baseball: The Early Years*, note 1 above. For the emergence of the Federal League that gave rise to the *Chase* decision, see Seymour, *Baseball: The Golden Age*, note 1 above, at 196–213.

AMERICAN LEAGUE BASEBALL CLUB
OF CHICAGO v. CHASE

Supreme Court, Erie County, New York, 1914.

186 Misc. 441, 149 N.Y.S. 6.

BISSELL, JUDGE.

The game of baseball, which began as an athletic sport of youthful players attending the schools and colleges throughout the country, has continued as the favorite athletic sport of America during the past half century, and has been commercialized and organized as professional baseball and developed into a big business conducted for profit under the name of "Organized Baseball."

The National Agreement for the government of professional baseball, together with the Rules of the National Commission, present to the court the scheme of co-operation and management of baseball leagues and baseball clubs and the control of baseball players.

The defendant, Chase, signed with the plaintiff the Player's Contract, as prescribed for the American League of Professional Baseball Clubs by the National Commission; and on the 15th day of June, 1914, gave notice in writing to the plaintiff of his intention to avoid, cancel, and annul the agreement entered into by him with the plaintiff on the 26th day of March, 1914. Thereafter and on the 20th day of June, 1914, he entered into a contract to play baseball for a rival club, to wit, the Buffalo Club of the Federal League. It is a well-established general rule that equity will not specifically enforce a contract of service, either directly by means of a decree directing the defendant to perform it, or by an injunction restraining the defendant from violating it, except in cases where services contracted for are of a special, unique, and extraordinary character, and a substitute for the employee cannot readily be obtained who will substantially answer the purpose of the contract.

*   *   *

[Having concluded that Chase's playing abilities more than satisfied this condition, the court continued.]

The jurisdiction of equity, therefore, is clear in this case, and its power should be exercised by injunction enforcing the negative covenant of the defendant's contract, providing the contract does not lack mutuality and is not a part of an illegal scheme or combination.

The first question, therefore, to be determined is whether the contract between the plaintiff and the defendant is a mutual contract which furnishes a consideration for the negative covenant sought to be enforced in this action. The Player's Contract, which was signed by the parties, provides:

7. The club may, at any time after the beginning and prior to the completion of the period of this contract, give the player ten days' written notice to end and determine all its liabilities and obligations hereunder; in which event the liabilities and obligations undertaken by the club shall cease and determine at the expiration of said ten days. The player, at the expiration of said ten days,

shall be freed and discharged from all obligations to render service to the club.

It thus appears that the defendant could rely upon only 10 days of compensated service with the plaintiff under the contract.

For the purpose of determining to what extent, and for how long a period, the defendant is bound by this contract, as affected by the National Agreement and the Rules of the National Commission, it will be necessary for us to consider analytically what the whole transaction represented by the three instruments, namely, the Player's Contract, the National Agreement, and the Rules and Regulations of the National Commission, undertakes to accomplish, and, in practice, actually does accomplish, as shown by the papers read on this motion.

[The court then quoted a number of provisions from baseball's National Agreement that gave each team "absolute right and title" to players it had "selected" (or drafted), required all players to enter into the standard contract prescribed by the National Commission that oversaw baseball, and incorporated in this contract a term that gave the team the option to renew its player's contract (if the team so chose) on the same terms as in the previous year.]

* * *

It appears that originally the defendant was a "selected" player; but whether he was a selected player at the time he entered the service of the plaintiff is immaterial. Had he come from the vacant lots of the cities, or the fields of the country, or from the college campus, and therefore been "a free agent," at the time he made his entry into "organized baseball," the result would have been the same. If a sale or trade is to be made by one major league club to another, section 3 of article VI governs, and "The right and title of a major league club to its players shall be absolute."

If a sale or trade is to be made by a major league club to a minor league club, section 9 of article VI governs, and the sale or trade is not absolute until waivers have been obtained from the other major league clubs. Thus a player in the highest league, without the exercise of any individual choice, may be required to take service with a club of a lower league where smaller salaries are paid, and where both the aggregate of the salary list and the salary of each individual player is subject to strict limitation under the terms of the National Agreement. No opportunity is afforded the player to solicit employment upon his own account. No right is afforded to enable him to resist an unjust limitation upon his power to earn. No consideration is afforded either himself or his family with respect to choosing a home. In short, he is placed where he must, at all times while playing in "organized baseball," consider that his home is only the place in which his services are for the time being controlled.

The baseball player, even though about to be discharged, is still a thing of value to the club owner. The termination of the obligations by the club owner pursuant to the 10–day provision, is not accomplished by him without securing some return. If the player goes to another major league club, it is either in exchange for some other more desired player or players, or for the waiver price; and the same is true if the discharged player is sent to a league of lower grade.

It seems that the promotion of the ball player is also hedged about with such limitations as to make the property in him absolute whether he will accept terms or not, and to make those terms when arrived at only liberal enough to prevent the player from seeking other means of earning his livelihood.

* * *

"Organized baseball" as conducted under the terms of the National Agreement further seeks to enforce and perpetuate its title to and control of its players as follows:

Section 1, Article VI, of the National Agreement provides:

All parties to this agreement pledge themselves to recognize the right of reservation and respect contracts between players and clubs under its protection. No club operating under this agreement shall at any time negotiate for the purchase or lease of the property of another club without first securing the consent of such club.

Section 2 of Article VI is as follows:

Any club or league which harbors a player who refuses to observe his contract with a club member of any party to this agreement, or to abide by its reservation, shall be considered an outlaw organization, and its claim to contractual and territorial rights ignored.

Thus the baseball player is made a chattel; the title of the club to the player ... is made absolute.

Section 2 of Article VI recognizes the property of the club in the player as existing under two conditions: First, under a contract; and, second, under reserve without a contract.

* * *

If the player has ideas of his own, which fail to accord with those of the club, the National Agreement enables the club to enforce its own terms, leaving the player the option to enter some other trade, calling, or profession, if he is not satisfied.

The scheme of the National Agreement to perpetuate control over a player by means of contracts apparently legal is interesting and pertinent. Each term contract, as appears by Section 1 of Article VIII, must contain a reserve clause or option to renew, and this article of the National Agreement is further enforced by Section A, Rule 17, of the National Commission, which is as follows:

A nonreserve clause in the contract of a major league player without the approval of the commission or of a minor league player without the approval of the National Board shall not be valid.

So that each new contract of the player must contain a reserve clause, and so by a series of contracts, "organized baseball" is able to perpetuate its control over the services of the player. But if, upon the other hand, a contract is at any time unobtainable, or even in fact not in good faith sought to be obtained, as the club owner might offer an immoderately low salary, then the provisions for reservation and the respecting thereof, apply and safeguard the "absolute title" of the club.

But why should a player enter into a contract when his liberty of conduct and of contract is thus curtailed? The answer is that he has no recourse. He must either take the contract under the provisions of the National Agreement, whose organization controls practically all of the good ball players of the country, or resort to some other occupation.

[The court then quoted several provisions of the National Agreement and Rules promulgated by the National Commission which prohibited teams from using players who had not signed formal playing contracts that contained the renewable option clause.]

* * *

This somewhat extended analysis shows to what extent the contract between the plaintiff and the defendant presents reciprocal and mutual, enforceable obligations. The plaintiff can terminate the contract at any time on 10 days' notice. The defendant is bound to many obligations under the remarkable provisions of the National Agreement. The Player's Contract executed in accordance with its terms, binds him, not only for the playing season of six months from April 14th to October 14th, but also for another season, if the plaintiff chooses to exercise its option, and if it insists upon the requirement of an option clause in each succeeding contract, the defendant can be held for a term of years. His only alternative is to abandon his vocation. Can it fairly be claimed that there is mutuality in such a contract? The absolute lack of mutuality, both of obligation and of remedy, in this contract, would prevent a court of equity from making it the basis of equitable relief by injunction or otherwise. The negative covenant, under such circumstances, is without a consideration to support it, and is unenforceable by injunction.

[The court then addressed the question of whether this contractual regime in baseball violated federal antitrust law.]

The novel argument is presented with much earnestness by the learned counsel for the defendant that the combination formed by the operation of the National Agreement and the rules and regulations of the National Commission thereunder, with which the defendant is connected through his contract with the plaintiff, is in direct violation of an act to protect trade and commerce against unlawful restraints and monopolies, in force July 2, 1890, and popularly known as the

Sherman Antitrust Law. It is apparent from the analysis already set forth of the agreement and rules forming the combination of the baseball business, referred to as "organized baseball," that a monopoly of baseball as a business has been ingeniously devised and created in so far as a monopoly can be created among free men; but I cannot agree to the proposition that the business of baseball for profit is interstate trade or commerce, and therefore subject to the provisions of the Sherman Act. An examination of the cases cited by the defendant confirms rather than changes my conclusion.

* * *

Baseball is an amusement, a sport, a game that comes clearly within the civil and criminal law of the state, and it is not a commodity or an article of merchandise subject to the regulation of Congress on the theory that it is interstate commerce.

[The court then turned to the question of what was the appropriate treatment under the common law of player contracts entered into within this baseball structure.]

Another question to be determined upon this motion is whether so-called "organized baseball," operating under the provisions of the National Agreement and the Rules and Contracts subsidiary thereto, is an illegal combination or monopoly in contravention of the common law. The affidavits read on the hearing of this motion show that a combination of 40 leagues, major and minor, has been formed under the terms of the National Agreement, controlling for profit the services of 10,000 players of professional baseball, practically all of the good or skillful players in the country. The analysis of the National Agreement and the Rules of the Commission, controlling the services of these skilled laborers, and providing for their purchase, sale, exchange, draft, reduction, discharge, and blacklisting, would seem to establish a species of quasi peonage unlawfully controlling and interfering with the personal freedom of the men employed. It appears that there is only one league of any importance operating independently of the National Commission, and that is the newly organized Federal League which comprises eight clubs in eight cities. "Organized baseball" is now as complete a monopoly of the baseball business for profit as any monopoly can be made. It is in contravention of the common law, in that it invades the right to labor as a property right, in that it invades the right to contract as a property right, and in that it is a combination to restrain and control the exercise of a profession or calling.

* * *

If a baseball player like the defendant, who has made baseball playing his profession and means of earning a livelihood, desires to be employed at the work for which he is qualified and is entitled to earn his best compensation, he must submit to dominion over his personal freedom and the control of his services by sale, transfer, or exchange, without his consent, or abandon his vocation and seek employment at some other kind of labor. While the services of these baseball players are ostensibly secured by voluntary contracts, a study of the system as hereinabove set forth, and as practiced under the plan of the National Agreement, reveals the involuntary character of the servitude which is imposed upon players by the strength of the combination controlling the labor of practically all of the players in the country. This is so great as to make it necessary for the player either to take the contract prescribed by the commission or abandon baseball as a profession and seek some other mode of earning a livelihood. There is no difference in principle between the system of servitude built up by the operation of this National Agreement, which as has been shown, provides for the purchase, sale, barter, and exchange of the services of baseball players—skilled laborers—without their consent, and the system of peonage brought into the United States from Mexico and thereafter existing for a time within the territory of New Mexico. The quasi peonage of baseball players under the operations of this plan and agreement is contrary to the spirit of American institutions, and is contrary to the spirit of the Constitution of the United States. It is time to heed the warning of that great jurist, the former Chief Judge of the Court of Appeals, Judge Cullen, who thought it advisable to take for the subject of his annual address at the last meeting of the New York State Bar association "The Decline of Personal Liberty in America," as evidenced by recent legislation and judicial decisions. The sanction by the courts of the system here outlined would indeed be further evidence of "The Decline of Personal Liberty."

The system created by "organized baseball" in recent years presents the question of the establishment of a scheme by which the personal freedom, the right to contract for their labor wherever they will, of 10,000 skilled laborers, is placed under the dominion of a benevolent despotism through the operation of the monopoly established by the National Agreement. This case does not present the simple question of a laborer who has entered into a fair contract for his personal services.

While the question of the dissolution of this combination on the ground of its illegality is not before this court for decision, it has nevertheless been thought necessary for the purpose of ascertaining whether or not this plaintiff comes into a court of equity with clean hands to inquire into the organization and operations of the combination to which the plaintiff is a party. A court of equity, insisting that "he who comes into equity must come with clean hands," will not lend its aid to promote an unconscionable transaction of the character which the plaintiff is endeavoring to maintain and strengthen by its application for this injunction. The court will not assist in enforcing an agreement which is a part of a general plan having for its object the maintenance of a monopoly, interference with the personal liberty of a citizen, and the control of his free right to labor wherever and for whom he pleases, and will not extend its aid to further the purposes and practices of an unlawful combination, by restraining the defendant from working for any one but the plaintiff.

Injunction vacated.

———

The court refers to Hal Chase as a "special, unique, and extraordinary baseball player." How extraordinary the judge simply did not realize. In his definitive history of baseball, Harold Seymour characterizes Chase as a "malignant genius."[17] While only Lou Gehrig and George Sisler were comparable first basemen on the field, Chase was the "archetype of all crooked ballplayers ... a full-fledged fixer and gambler." Indeed, at the end of the 1918 baseball season, Chase was charged by his manager, Hall of Famer Christy Mathewson, with having tried to persuade his teammates to lose games on which Chase had bets riding. Though three players on his team testified to this effect in a hearing before the National League President, the President absolved Chase by saying that the players had misunderstood the superstar's joking comments. Chase returned to play for the Giants the next season and to serve as the intermediary between the gamblers and the White Sox players who were involved in the fixing of the 1919 World Series. Chase was indicted by a Chicago grand jury for his role in this affair but the State of California refused to extradite him for trial.[18]

———

Whether or not Chase himself was a deserving candidate for the judicial sentiment expressed in the prior decision—a victim of "quasi peonage"—his case does cast in a rather different light the contracts signed by Lajoie a decade earlier or even by Barnett fifty years later. One question is whether the league arrangements justify the court's refusal to enforce individual contracts through injunctions. While over the years most courts have answered "no," a more important question is whether even a hands-off approach by courts to player contracts would be a sufficient response to the problems players have with these league arrangements. The next case introduces the potential leverage that antitrust law might give players in their struggle against the reserve system. (As noted earlier, Chapter 7 examines the possible use by rival leagues of antitrust law against that system.)

In *Chase*, the player used antitrust policy as a *shield* against a contract injunction sought by the American League Club that had reserved his services. That tactic was sufficient for Chase's purposes because another club in the rival Federal League had been prepared to bid handsomely for his services. However, since the demise of the Federal League just a few years later, Major League Baseball has faced

17. See Seymour, *Baseball: The Golden Age*, note 1 above, 288–93.

18. See Eliot Asinof, *Eight Men Out* (Henry Holt: New York, 1963).

no such competition in its players market, and other professional leagues have encountered rivals only intermittently. Regardless, then, of whether a judge enforces the restrictive terms in a contract between a player and his team, if the other teams in the league have agreed not to "tamper" with the services of their respective players except under strictly defined rules and conditions (an agreement enforced by the commissioner), there will be no effective market for the players' services. That is why players have tried to use antitrust law as a *sword* against such an intraleague arrangement.

Federal antitrust law dates back to 1890, the year the Sherman Antitrust Act was enacted. Section 1 of that Act makes illegal any "contract, combination, or conspiracy in restraint of trade," and Section 2 prohibits the effort by any person to "monopolize or attempt or conspire to monopolize trade." The Justice Department is authorized to proceed either criminally or civilly against antitrust violators, but it has done so only once in the sports setting (in 1953, against the National Football League's broadcasting restrictions: see Chapter 6). In addition, the Federal Trade Commission (FTC) can issue cease and desist orders against antitrust violators, a power that the FTC staff is seeking (so far unsuccessfully) to use for the first time in sports against the American Broadcasting Corporation (ABC) and the College Football Association (CFA) for their television contract (see Chapter 9). In sports, then, enforcement of antitrust law has been left to suits brought by private parties, who can win either treble damages or an injunction (the latter remedy first authorized by the Clayton Antitrust Act of 1914).

Very little use was made of antitrust law in sports until the late 1960s. One reason is that most professional sports did not become thriving business enterprises until that decade. Professional baseball, however, was already becoming a substantial sport and financial presence when the Sherman Act was passed in 1890.[19] The reasons for the lack of antitrust scrutiny of baseball's reserve clause and its other restrictive arrangements must be found within antitrust law itself.

The vast majority of antitrust suits, especially about the players market, have been brought under Section 1 of the Sherman Act. There are three key components of this provision: there must be a *contract*, *combination*, or *conspiracy* ; the combination must have produced a *restraint of trade* ; and the restraint must affect *trade and commerce among the several states*. The last ingredient became the main obstacle to antitrust litigation against baseball, in a ruling handed down by the Supreme Court in *Federal Base Ball Club v. National League*, 259 U.S. 200 (1922), in the aftermath of the failure of the Federal League. The history and the current antitrust status of baseball are depicted in the following case.[20]

---

19. See Seymour, *Baseball, The Early Years*, note 1 above.

20. The memoirs of two of the key protagonists of the *Flood* litigation contain interesting and naturally conflicting per-

Ṗ   Δ

FLOOD v. KUHN

Supreme Court of the United States, 1972.

407 U.S. 258, 92 S.Ct. 2099, 32 L.Ed.2d 728.

JUSTICE BLACKMUN delivered the opinion of the Court.

For the third time in 50 years the Court is asked specifically to rule that professional baseball's reserve system is within the reach of the federal antitrust laws.[1] Collateral issues of state law and of federal labor policy are also advanced.

I ssue

I

THE GAME

It is a century and a quarter since the New York Nine defeated the Knickerbockers 23 to 1 on Hoboken's Elysian Fields June 19, 1846, with Alexander Jay Cartwright as the instigator and the umpire. The teams were amateur, but the contest marked a significant date in baseball's beginnings. That early game led ultimately to the development of professional baseball and its tightly organized structure.

The Cincinnati Red Stockings came into existence in 1869 upon an outpouring of local pride. With only one Cincinnatian on the payroll, this professional team traveled over 11,000 miles that summer, winning 56 games and tying one. Shortly thereafter, on St. Patrick's Day in 1871, the National Association of Professional Baseball Players was founded and the professional league was born.

The ensuing colorful days are well known. The ardent follower and the student of baseball know of General Abner Doubleday; the formation of the National League in 1876; Chicago's supremacy in the first year's competition under the leadership of Al Spalding and with Cap Anson at third base; the formation of the American Association and then of the Union Association in the 1880s; the introduction of

spectives on the case. One book was by Marvin Miller, the head of the Major League Baseball Players' Association which actually brought and financed the antitrust litigation. See *A Whole Different Ball Game: The Sport and Business of Baseball* (New York: Birch Lane Press, 1991), in particular Chapter 10, Flood Gate. The other book was by Bowie Kuhn, then Commissioner of Baseball who defended the suit. See *Hardball: The Education of a Baseball Commissioner* (Times Books: New York, 1987), in particular, Chapter 6—Curt Flood, Meet Marvin Miller. The brief vignette on the *Flood* case in Bob Woodward & Scott Armstrong, *The*

Brethren: Inside the Supreme Court 189–92 (New York: Simon and Schuster, 1979), explains why we have reproduced an apparently irrelevant section of the opinion— "The Game." Apparently, the justices spent as much time debating this list of star players as they did the legal issues. Indeed, it was not until Justice Marshall observed the total absence in the draft opinion of any black baseball players that Justice Blackmun added Jackie Robinson, Roy Campanella, and Satchel Paige. Still Justice Blackmun was chagrined to learn later that he had omitted Mel Ott from his list of greats.

1. The reserve system, publicly introduced into baseball contracts in 1887, centers in the uniformity of player contracts; the confinement of the player to the club that has him under the contract; the assignability of the player's contract; and the ability of the club annually to renew the contract unilaterally, subject to a stated salary minimum. . . .

Sunday baseball; interleague warfare with cut-rate admission prices and player raiding; the development of the reserve "clause"; the emergence in 1885 of the Brotherhood of Professional Ball Players, and in 1890 of the Players League; the appearance of the American League, or "junior circuit," in 1901, rising from the minor Western Association; the first World Series in 1903, disruption in 1904, and the Series' resumption in 1905; the short-lived Federal League on the majors' scene during World War I years; the troublesome and discouraging episode of the 1919 Series; the home run ball; the shifting of franchises; the expansion of the leagues; the installation in 1965 of the major league draft of potential new players; and the formation of the Major League Baseball Players Association in 1966.

Then there are the many names, celebrated for one reason or another, that have sparked the diamond and its environs and that have provided tinder for recaptured thrills, for reminiscence and comparisons, and for conversation and anticipation in-season and off-season: Ty Cobb, Babe Ruth, Tris Speaker, Walter Johnson, Henry Chadwick, Eddie Collins, Lou Gehrig, Grover Cleveland Alexander, Rogers Hornsby, Harry Hooper, Goose Goslin, Jackie Robinson, Honus Wagner, Joe McCarthy, John McGraw, Deacon Phillippe, Rube Marquard, Christy Mathewson, Tommy Leach, Big Ed Delahanty, Davy Jones, Germany Schaefer, King Kelly, Big Dan Brouthers, Wahoo Sam Crawford, Wee Willie Keeler, Big Ed Walsh, Jimmy Austin, Fred Snodgrass, Satchel Paige, Hugh Jennings, Fred Merkle, Iron Man McGinnity, Three–Finger Brown, Harry and Stan Coveleski, Connie Mack, Al Bridwell, Red Ruffing, Amos Rusie, Cy Young, Smokey Joe Wood, Chief Meyers, Chief Bender, Bill Klem, Hans Lobert, Johnny Evers, Joe Tinker, Roy Campanella, Miller Huggins, Rube Bressler, Dazzy Vance, Edd Roush, Bill Wambsganss, Clark Griffith, Branch Rickey, Frank Chance, Cap Anson, Nap Lajoie, Sad Sam Jones, Bob O'Farrell, Lefty O'Doul, Bobby Veach, Willie Kamm, Heinie Groh, Lloyd and Paul Waner, Stuffy McInnis, Charles Comiskey, Roger Bresnahan, Bill Dickey, Zack Wheat, George Sisler, Charlie Gehringer, Eppa Rixey, Harry Heilmann, Fred Clarke, Dizzy Dean, Hank Greenberg, Pie Traynor, Rube Waddell, Bill Terry, Carl Hubbell, Old Hoss Radbourne, Moe Berg, Rabbit Maranville, Jimmie Foxx, Lefty Grove. The list seems endless.

And one recalls the appropriate reference to the "World Serious," attributed to Ring Lardner, Sr.; Ernest L. Thayer's "Casey at the Bat"; [4] the ring of "Tinker to Evers to Chance"; [5] and all the other

4. Millions have known and enjoyed baseball. One writer knowledgeable in the field of sports almost assumed that everyone did until, one day, he discovered otherwise:

I knew a cove who'd never heard of Washington and Lee,

Caesar and Napoleon from the ancient jamboree,

But, bli'me, there are queerer things than anything like that,

For here's a cove who never heard of 'Casey at the Bat'!

Ten million never heard of Keats, or Shelley, Burns or Poe;

But they know "the air was shattered by the force of Casey's blow"

They never heard of Shakespeare, nor of Dickens, like as not,

5. See note 5 on page 111.

happenings, habits, and superstitions about and around baseball that made it the "national pastime" or, depending upon the point of view, "the great American tragedy."

II

THE PETITIONER

The petitioner, Curtis Charles Flood, born in 1938, began his major league career in 1956 when he signed a contract with the Cincinnati Reds for a salary of $4,000 for the season. He had no attorney or agent to advise him on that occasion. He was traded to the St. Louis Cardinals before the 1958 season. Flood rose to fame as a center fielder with the Cardinals during the years 1958–1969. In those 12 seasons he compiled a batting average of .293. His best offensive season was 1967 when he achieved .335. He was .301 or better in six of the 12 St. Louis years. He participated in the 1964, 1967, and 1968 World Series. He played errorless ball in the field in 1966, and once enjoyed 223 consecutive errorless games. Flood has received seven Golden Glove Awards. He was co-captain of his team from 1965—1969. He ranks among the 10 major league outfielders possessing the highest lifetime fielding averages.

Flood's St. Louis compensation for the years shown was:

1961	$13,500 (including a bonus for signing)
1962	$16,000
1963	$17,500
1964	$23,000
1965	$35,000
1966	$45,000
1967	$50,000
1968	$72,500
1969	$90,000

These figures do not include any so-called fringe benefits or World Series shares.

But they know the somber drama from old Mudville's haunted lot.
He never heard of Casey! Am I dreaming? Is it true?
Is fame but windblown ashes when the summer day is through?
Does greatness fade so quickly and is grandeur doomed to die.
That bloomed in early morning, ere the dusk rides down the sky?
  "He Never Heard of Casey," Grantland Rice, The Sportlight, New York Herald Tribune, June 1, 1926, p. 23.

5.   "These are the saddest of possible words,
'Tinker to Evers to Chance.'
Trio of bear cubs, and fleeter than birds,
'Tinker to Evers to Chance.'
Ruthlessly pricking our gonfalon bubble,
Making a Giant hit into a double—
Words that are weighty with nothing but trouble:
'Tinker to Evers to Chance."
  Franklin Pierce Adams, Baseball's Sad Lexicon.

Facts

But at the age of 31, in October 1969, Flood was traded to the Philadelphia Phillies of the National League in a multi-player transaction. He was not consulted about the trade. He was informed by telephone and received formal notice only after the deal had been consummated. In December he complained to the Commissioner of Baseball and asked that he be made a free agent and be placed at liberty to strike his own bargain with any other major league team. His request was denied.

C° A

Flood then instituted this antitrust suit[7] in January 1970 in federal court for the Southern District of New York. The defendants (although not all were named in each cause of action) were the Commissioner of Baseball, the presidents of the two major leagues, and the 24 major league clubs. In general, the complaint charged violations of the federal antitrust laws and civil rights statutes, violation of state statutes and the common law, and the imposition of a form of peonage and involuntary servitude contrary to the Thirteenth Amendment and 42 U.S.C. § 1994, 18 U.S.C. § 1581, and 29 U.S.C. §§ 102 and 103. Petitioner sought declaratory and injunctive relief and treble damages.

Flood declined to play for Philadelphia in 1970, despite a $100,000 salary offer, and he sat out the year. After the season was concluded, Philadelphia sold its rights to Flood to the Washington Senators. Washington and the petitioner were able to come to terms for 1971 at a salary of $110,000. Flood started the season but, apparently because he was dissatisfied with his performance, he left the Washington club on April 27, early in the campaign. He has not played baseball since then.

* * *

IV

THE LEGAL BACKGROUND

A. *Federal Baseball Club v. National League,* 259 U.S. 200 (1922), was a suit for treble damages instituted by a member of the Federal League (Baltimore) against the National and American Leagues and others. The plaintiff obtained a verdict in the trial court, but the Court of Appeals reversed. The main brief filed by the plaintiff with this Court discloses that it was strenuously argued, among other things, that the business in which the defendants were engaged was interstate commerce; that the interstate relationship among the several clubs, located as they were in different States, was predominant; that organized baseball represented an investment of colossal wealth; that it was an engagement in moneymaking; that gate receipts were divided by agreement between the home club and the visiting club; and that the business of baseball was to be distinguished from the mere playing of the game as a sport for physical exercise and diversion.

Mr. Justice Holmes, in speaking succinctly for a unanimous Court, said:

---

7. Concededly supported by the Major League Baseball Players Association, the players' collective-bargaining representative.

The business is giving exhibitions of baseball, which are purely state affairs.... But the fact that in order to give the exhibitions the Leagues must induce free persons to cross state lines and must arrange and pay for their doing so is not enough to change the character of the business.... [T]he transport is a mere incident, not the essential thing. That to which it is incident, the exhibition, although made for money would not be called trade or commerce in the commonly accepted use of those words. As it is put by the defendant, personal effort, not related to production, is not a subject of commerce. That which in its consummation is not commerce does not become commerce among the States because the transportation that we have mentioned takes place. To repeat the illustrations given by the Court below, a firm of lawyers sending out a member to argue a case, or the Chautauqua lecture bureau sending out lecturers, does not engage in such commerce because the lawyer or lecturer goes to another State.

If we are right the plaintiff's business is to be described in the same way and the restrictions by contract that prevented the plaintiff from getting players to break their bargains and the other conduct charged against the defendants were not an interference with commerce among the States.[10]

* * *

B. In the years that followed, baseball continued to be subject to intermittent antitrust attack. The courts, however, rejected these challenges on the authority of *Federal Baseball*. In some cases stress was laid, although unsuccessfully, on new factors such as the development of radio and television with their substantial additional revenues to baseball. For the most part, however, the Holmes opinion was generally and necessarily accepted as controlling authority. And in the 1952 Report of the Subcommittee on Study of Monopoly Power of the House Committee on the Judiciary, H.R. Rep. No. 2002, 82d Cong., 2d Sess., 229, it was said, in conclusion:

On the other hand the overwhelming preponderance of the evidence established baseball's need for some sort of reserve clause. Baseball's history shows that chaotic conditions prevailed when there was no reserve clause. Experience points to no feasible substitute to protect the integrity of the game or to guarantee a comparatively even competitive struggle. The evidence adduced at the hearings would clearly not justify the enactment of legislation flatly condemning the reserve clause.

10. "What really saved baseball, legally at least, for the next half century was the protective canopy spread over it by the United States Supreme Court's decision in the Baltimore Federal League antitrust suit against Organized Baseball in 1922.... It should be noted that, contrary to what many believe, Holmes did call baseball a business; time and again those who have not troubled to read the text of the decision have claimed incorrectly that the court said baseball was a sport and not a business." 2 H. Seymour, *Baseball* 420 (1971).

C. The Court granted certiorari, in the *Toolson, Kowalski,* and *Corbett* cases, and, by a short per curiam (Warren, C.J., and Black, Frankfurter, Douglas, Jackson, Clark, and Minton, JJ.), affirmed the judgments of the respective courts of appeals in those three cases. Toolson v. New York Yankees, Inc., 346 U.S. 356 (1953). *Federal Baseball* was cited as holding "that the business of providing public baseball games for profit between clubs of professional baseball players was not within the scope of the federal antitrust laws," and:

> Congress has had the ruling under consideration but has not seen fit to bring such business under these laws by legislation having prospective effect. The business has thus been left for thirty years to develop, on the understanding that it was not subject to existing antitrust legislation. The present cases ask us to overrule the prior decision and, with retrospective effect, hold the legislation applicable. We think that if there are evils in this field which now warrant application to it of the antitrust laws it should be by legislation. Without re-examination of the underlying issues, the judgments below are affirmed on the authority of Federal Baseball Club of Baltimore v. National League of Professional Baseball Clubs, supra, so far as that decision determines that Congress had no intention of including the business of baseball within the scope of the federal antitrust laws.

This quotation reveals four reasons for the Court's affirmance of *Toolson* and its companion cases: (a) Congressional awareness for three decades of the Court's ruling in *Federal Baseball*, coupled with congressional inaction. (b) The fact that baseball was left alone to develop for that period upon the understanding that the reserve system was not subject to existing federal antitrust laws. (c) A reluctance to overrule *Federal Baseball* with consequent retroactive effect. (d) A professed desire that any needed remedy be provided by legislation rather than by court decree. The emphasis in *Toolson* was on the determination, attributed even to *Federal Baseball*, that Congress had no intention to include baseball within the reach of the federal antitrust laws.

[Justice Blackmun then described and quoted from *United States v. Shubert*, 348 U.S. 222 (1955), in which the Court refused to extend professional baseball's antitrust immunity to a nationwide theatre company. Chief Justice Warren's opinion stresses that the result in *Toolson* was based on *Federal Baseball* and stare decisis and concluded that "[i]f the *Toolson* holding is to be expanded—or contracted—the appropriate remedy lies with Congress."]

* * *

E. United States v. International Boxing Club, 348 U.S. 236 (1955), was a companion to *Shubert* and was decided the same day. This was a civil antitrust action against defendants engaged in the business of promoting professional championship boxing contests. Here again the District Court had dismissed the complaint in reliance upon *Federal Baseball* and *Toolson*. The Chief Justice observed that "if it were not for Federal Baseball and Toolson, we think that it would be too clear for dispute that the Government's allegations bring the defendants within the scope of the Act." He pointed out that the defendants relied on the two baseball cases but also would have been content with a more restrictive interpretation of them than the Shubert defendants, for the boxing defendants argued that the cases immunized only businesses that involve exhibitions of an athletic nature. The Court accepted neither argument. It again noted that "*Toolson* neither overruled *Federal Baseball* nor necessarily reaffirmed all that was said in *Federal Baseball*." It stated:

> The controlling consideration in *Federal Baseball* and *Hart* was, instead, a very practical one—the degree of interstate activity involved in the particular business under review. It follows that stare decisis cannot help the defendants here; for, contrary to their argument, *Federal Baseball* did not hold that all businesses based on professional sports were outside the scope of the antitrust laws. The issue confronting us is, therefore, not whether a previously granted exemption should continue, but whether an exemption should be granted in the first instance. And that issue is for Congress to resolve, not this Court.

The Court noted the presence then in Congress of various bills forbidding the application of the antitrust laws to "organized professional sports enterprises"; the holding of extensive hearings on some of these; subcommittee opposition; a postponement recommendation as to baseball; and the fact that "Congress thus left intact the then-existing coverage of the antitrust laws."

Mr. Justice Frankfurter, joined by Mr. Justice Minton, dissented. "It would baffle the subtlest ingenuity," he said, "to find a single differentiating factor between other sporting exhibitions ... and baseball insofar as the conduct of the sport is relevant to the criteria or considerations by which the Sherman Law becomes applicable to a trade or commerce." He went on:

> The Court decided as it did in the Toolson case as an application of the doctrine of stare decisis. That doctrine is not, to be sure, an imprisonment of reason. But neither is it a whimsy. It can hardly be that this Court gave a preferred position to baseball because it is the great American sport. . . . If stare decisis be one aspect of law, as it is, to disregard it in identical situations is mere caprice.

> Congress, on the other hand, may yield to sentiment and be capricious, subject only to due process. . . .

> Between them, this case and Shubert illustrate that nice but rational distinctions are inevitable in adjudication. I agree with the Court's opinion in Shubert for precisely the reason that constrains me to dissent in this case.

Mr. Justice Minton also separately dissented on the ground that boxing is not trade or commerce. He added the comment that "Congress has not attempted" to control baseball and boxing. The two dissenting Justices, thus, did not call for the overruling of Federal Baseball and Toolson; they merely felt that boxing should be under the same umbrella of freedom as was baseball and, as Mr. Justice Frankfurter said, they could not exempt baseball "to the exclusion of every other sport different not one legal jot or tittle from it."

F. The parade marched on. Radovich v. National Football League, 352 U.S. 445 (1957), was a civil Clayton Act case testing the application of the antitrust laws to professional football. The District Court dismissed. The Ninth Circuit affirmed in part on the basis of *Federal Baseball* and *Toolson*. The court did not hesitate to "confess that the strength of the pull" of the baseball cases and of International Boxing "is about equal," but then observed that "[f]ootball is a team sport" and boxing an individual one.

This Court reversed with an opinion by Mr. Justice Clark. He said that the Court made its ruling in *Toolson* "because it was concluded that more harm would be done in overruling *Federal Baseball* than in upholding a ruling which at best was of dubious validity." He noted that Congress had not acted. He then said:

> All this, combined with the flood of litigation that would follow its repudiation, the harassment that would ensue, and the retroactive effect of such a decision, led the Court to the practical result that it should sustain the unequivocal line of authority reaching over many years.
>
> [S]ince *Toolson* and *Federal Baseball* are still cited as controlling authority in antitrust actions involving other fields of business, we now specifically limit the rule there established to the facts there involved, i.e., the business of organized professional baseball. As long as the Congress continues to acquiesce we should adhere to—but not extend—the interpretation of the Act made in those cases....
>
> If this ruling is unrealistic, inconsistent, or illogical, it is sufficient to answer, aside from the distinctions between the businesses, that were we considering the question of baseball for the first time upon a clean slate we would have no doubts. But *Federal Baseball* held the business of baseball outside the scope of the Act. No other business claiming the coverage of those cases has such an adjudication. We therefore, conclude that the orderly way to eliminate error or discrimination, if any there be, is by legislation and not by court decision. Congressional processes are more accommodative, affording the whole industry hearings and an opportunity to assist in the formulation of new legislation. The resulting product is therefore more likely to protect the industry and the public alike. The whole scope of congressional action would be known long in advance and effective dates for the legislation could be set in the future without the injustices of retroactivity and surprise which might follow court action.

* * *

G. Finally, in Haywood v. National Basketball Assn., 401 U.S. 1204 (1971), Mr. Justice Douglas, in his capacity as Circuit Justice, reinstated a District Court's injunction pendente lite in favor of a professional basketball player and said, "Basketball ... does not enjoy exemption from the antitrust laws."

H. This series of decisions understandably spawned extensive commentary, some of it mildly critical and much of it not; nearly all of it looked to Congress for any remedy that might be deemed essential.

I. Legislative proposals have been numerous and persistent. Since *Toolson* more than 50 bills have been introduced in Congress relative to the applicability or nonapplicability of the antitrust laws to baseball. A few of these passed one house or the other. Those that did would have expanded, not restricted, the reserve system's exemption to other professional league sports. And the Act of Sept. 30, 1961, Pub. L. 87–331, 75 Stat. 732, and the merger addition thereto effected by the Act of Nov. 8, 1966, Pub. L. 89–800, § 6(b), 80 Stat. 1515, 15 U.S.C. § 1291–1295, were also expansive rather than restrictive as to antitrust exemption.

V

In view of all this, it seems appropriate now to say that:

1. Professional baseball is a business and it is engaged in interstate commerce.

2. With its reserve system enjoying exemption from the federal antitrust laws, baseball is, in a very distinct sense, an exception and an anomaly. *Federal Baseball* and *Toolson* have become an aberration confined to baseball.

3. Even though others might regard this as "unrealistic, inconsistent, or illogical," the aberration is an established one, and one that has been recognized not only in *Federal Baseball* and *Toolson*, but in *Shubert, International Boxing,* and *Radovich,* as well, a total of five consecutive cases in this Court. It is an aberration that has been with us now for half a century, one heretofore deemed fully entitled to the benefit of stare decisis, and one that has survived the Court's expanding concept of interstate commerce. It rests on a recognition and an acceptance of baseball's unique characteristics and needs.

4. Other professional sports operating interstate—football, boxing, basketball, and, presumably, hockey and golf—are not so exempt.

5. The advent of radio and television, with their consequent increased coverage and additional revenues, has not occasioned an overruling of *Federal Baseball* and *Toolson.*

6. The Court has emphasized that since 1922 baseball, with full and continuing congressional awareness, has been allowed to develop and to expand unhindered by federal legislative action. Remedial legislation has been introduced repeatedly in Congress but none has

ever been enacted. The Court, accordingly, has concluded that Congress as yet has had no intention to subject baseball's reserve system to the reach of the antitrust statutes. This, obviously, has been deemed to be something other than mere congressional silence and passivity.

Hold
(cont.)

7. The Court has expressed concern about the confusion and the retroactivity problems that inevitably would result with a judicial overturning of *Federal Baseball*. It has voiced a preference that if any change is to be made, it come by legislative action that, by its nature, is only prospective in operation.

8. The Court noted in *Radovich* that the slate with respect to baseball is not clean. Indeed, it has not been clean for half a century.

This emphasis and this concern are still with us. We continue to be loath, 50 years after *Federal Baseball* and almost two decades after *Toolson*, to overturn those cases judicially when Congress, by its positive inaction, has allowed those decisions to stand for so long and, far beyond mere inference and implication, has clearly evinced a desire not to disapprove them legislatively.

Accordingly, we adhere once again to *Federal Baseball* and *Toolson* and to their application to professional baseball. We adhere also to *International Boxing* and *Radovich* and to their respective applications to professional boxing and professional football. If there is any inconsistency or illogic in all this, it is an inconsistency and illogic of long standing that is to be remedied by the Congress and not by this Court. If we were to act otherwise, we would be withdrawing from the conclusion as to congressional intent made in *Toolson* and from the concerns as to retrospectivity therein expressed. Under these circumstances, there is merit in consistency even though some might claim that beneath that consistency is a layer of inconsistency.

The petitioner's argument as to the application of state antitrust laws deserves a word. Judge Cooper rejected the state law claims because state antitrust regulation would conflict with federal policy and because national "uniformity [is required] in any regulation of baseball and its reserved system." The Court of Appeals, in affirming, stated, "[A]s the burden on interstate commerce outweighs the states' interests in regulating baseball's reserve system, the Commerce Clause precludes the application here of state antitrust law." As applied to organized baseball, and in the light of this Court's observations and holding in *Federal Baseball*, in *Toolson*, in *Shubert*, in *International Boxing*, and in *Radovich*, and despite baseball's allegedly inconsistent position taken in the past with respect to the application of state law, these statements adequately dispose of the state law claims.

* * *

[W]hat the Court said in *Federal Baseball* in 1922 and what it said in *Toolson* in 1953, we say again here in 1972: the remedy, if any is indicated, is for congressional, and not judicial, action.

The judgment of the Court of Appeals is affirmed.

R&s

Δ won

Justice Marshall, with whom Justice Brennan concurs, dissenting.

* * *

To non-athletes it might appear that petitioner was virtually enslaved by the owners of major league baseball clubs who bartered among themselves for his services. But, athletes know that it was not servitude that bound petitioner to the club owners; it was the reserve system. The essence of that system is that a player is bound to the club with which he first signs a contract for the rest of his playing days. He cannot escape from the club except by retiring, and he cannot prevent the club from assigning his contract to any other club.

* * *

We have only recently had occasion to comment that:

Antitrust laws in general, and the Sherman Act in particular, are the Magna Charta of free enterprise. They are as important to the preservation of economic freedom and our free-enterprise system as the Bill of Rights is to the protection of our fundamental personal freedoms.... Implicit in such freedom is the notion that it cannot be foreclosed with respect to one sector of the economy because certain private citizens or groups believe that such foreclosure might promote greater competition in a more important sector of the economy.

The importance of the antitrust laws to every citizen must not be minimized. They are as important to baseball players as they are to football players, lawyers, doctors, or members of any other class of workers. Baseball players cannot be denied the benefits of competition merely because club owners view other economic interests as being more important, unless Congress says so.

Has Congress acquiesced in our decisions in *Federal Baseball Club* and *Toolson*? I think not. Had the Court been consistent and treated all sports in the same way baseball was treated, Congress might have become concerned enough to take action. But, the Court was inconsistent, and baseball was isolated and distinguished from all other sports. In *Toolson* the Court refused to act because Congress had been silent. But the Court may have read too much into this legislative inaction.

Americans love baseball as they love all sports. Perhaps we become so enamored of athletics that we assume that they are foremost in the minds of legislators as well as fans. We must not forget, however, that there are only some 600 major league baseball players. Whatever muscle they might have been able to muster by combining forces with other athletes has been greatly impaired by the manner in which this Court has isolated them. It is this Court that has made them impotent, and this Court should correct its error.

We do not lightly overrule our prior constructions of federal statutes, but when our errors deny substantial federal rights, like the right to compete freely and effectively to the best of one's ability as guaranteed by the antitrust laws, we must admit our error and correct it. We have done so before and we should do so again here.

* * *

To the extent that there is concern over any reliance interests that club owners may assert, they can be satisfied by making our decision prospective only. Baseball should be covered by the antitrust laws beginning with this case and henceforth, unless Congress decides otherwise.

Accordingly, I would overrule *Federal Baseball Club* and *Toolson* and reverse the decision of the Court of Appeals.

* * *

[Justice Marshall went on to explain that if the Court were to hold baseball subject to antitrust as a general matter, this did not mean that Flood's claim was necessarily actionable. In particular, baseball would still be entitled to offer as a defense the fact that the terms of Flood's player contract were mandatory subjects of collective bargaining between Major League Baseball and its Players Association, and thus arguably protected by the labor exemption from antitrust liability. The unfolding of that argument in other sports is covered in detail in Chapter 3.]

Appeal dismissed.

———

Justice Oliver Wendell Holmes, Jr., who wrote the Supreme Court's opinion in *Federal Base Ball*, had earlier made the following observations about *stare decisis* in his famous lecture on "The Path of the Law" [21]:

> It is revolting to have no better reason for a rule of law than that it was laid down in the time of Henry IV. It is still more revolting if the grounds upon which it was laid down have vanished long since, and that rule simply persists from blind imitation of the past.

How would (should) Justice Holmes have reacted to Justice Blackmun's adherence in *Flood* to Holmes' decision in *Federal Base Ball*, given that *Flood* rejected every one of the premises upon which *Federal Base Ball* was founded?

Can the Court's ruling be explained by a judicial feeling that baseball needed a system such as the reserve clause to flourish—remember Justice Blackmun's opening paean to The Game—but that such a restrictive system was difficult to square with the Court's standard antitrust analysis? Imagine what Justice Blackmun thought about this comment in the lower court's opinion:

21. Oliver Wendell Holmes, Jr., *The Path of the Law*, 10 Harvard L. Rev. 457, 469 (1887).

[O]rganized baseball existed almost as an enclave or feudal barony throughout the years, managing its own affairs as best calculated to preserve the sport and maintaining its own officialdom for self-regulation purposes—and, except for the brief scandal of the so-called Chicago Black Sox of 1919, apparently has handled its little kingdom and its subjects very well.... As I analyzed the history of organized baseball over the last 50 years, it has shown without Court interference remarkable stability under self-discipline. The Supreme Court in 1922 undoubtedly felt that it should adopt a "hands off" policy as to this one particular sport which had attained such a national standing that only Congress shared the power to tamper with it. And properly so. Baseball's welfare and future should not be for politically insulated interpreters of technical antitrust statutes, but rather should be for the voters through their elected representatives. If baseball is to be damaged by statutory regulation, let the Congressman face his constituents the next November and also face the consequences of his baseball voting record.

Flood v. Kuhn, 443 F.2d 264, 269, 272 (1971)

In contrast, consider whether Justice Marshall in his dissent felt some empathy with the following comment by Judge Frank, who was doubtful even in 1949 that *Federal Base Ball* retained much precedential value:

[W]e have here a monopoly which, in its effect on ball-players like the plaintiff, possesses characteristics shockingly repugnant to moral principles that, at least since the War between the States have been basic in America, as shown by the Thirteenth Amendment to the Constitution, condemning "involuntary servitude," and by subsequent Congressional enactments on that subject. For the "reserve clause," as has been observed, results in something resembling peonage of the baseball player. By accepting the "reserve clause"—and all players in organized baseball must "accept" it—a player binds himself not to sign a contract with, or play for, any club other than the club which originally employs him or its assignee. Although many courts have refused to enforce the "reserve" clause, yet severe and practically efficacious extra-legal penalties are imposed for violation. The most extreme of these penalties is the blacklisting of the players so that no club in organized baseball will hire him. In effect, this clause prevents a player from ever playing with any team other than his original employer, unless that employer consents. Since the right to play with organized baseball is indispensible to the career of a professional baseball player, violations of the clause by such players are infrequent. The violator may perhaps become a judge (a less exciting and often less remunerative occupation) or a bartender or a street-sweeper, but his chances of ever again playing baseball are exceedingly slim.... I may add that, if the players be regarded as quasi-peons, it is of no moment that they are well paid; only the totalitarian-minded will believe that high pay excuses virtual slavery.

Gardella v. Chandler, 172 F.2d 402, 409–10 (2d. Cir.1949)

Questions for Discussion

1. How would the *Toolson* Court in 1953 (or the *Flood* Court in 1972) have reacted if, instead of allowing Jackie Robinson to play, baseball had tried to protect its Jim Crow segregation policies from federal antitrust scrutiny. Keep in mind that the Court had greatly expanded the scope of Congress' "trade and commerce" power in the later stages of the New Deal.

2. What is the precise scope of baseball's present exemption from antitrust? Does it include the league's business dealings with concessionaires (see *Twin City Sportservice, Inc. v. Charles O. Finley (Oakland Athletics)*, 365 F.Supp. 235 (N.D.Cal.1972), reversed on other grounds, 512 F.2d 1264 (9th Cir.1975)), broadcast outlets (see *Henderson Broadcasting Corp. v. Houston Sports Ass'n (Houston Astros)*, 541 F.Supp. 263 (S.D.Tex.1982)), and memorabilia merchandisers (see *Fleer v. Topps Chewing Gum & Major League Baseball Players Ass'n*, 658 F.2d 139 (3d Cir.1981))?

3. If baseball's antitrust immunity is principally applicable to the game's internal relationships, should it exempt Major League Baseball's dealings with the minor leagues, most of whose teams have agreements with a Major League club? See *Portland Baseball Club v. Kuhn*, 491 F.2d 1101 (9th Cir.1974).

4. Currently, Major League Baseball prohibits teams from selling television rights to their games to cable systems located outside the teams' designated home viewing areas. Given that *Federal Base Ball*, *Toolson*, and *Flood* refused to apply antitrust law to baseball's rules governing the structure and production of the game, would this antitrust exemption insulate league restraints on sale of the product via the commercial media of radio and television?

D. APPLICATION OF STATE LAW

Flood did more than merely maintain baseball's immunity from federal antitrust law—it also established, almost offhandedly, a new exemption for baseball from state antitrust law. How does the Court justify this combination of holdings? Suppose the Court had arrived at the opposite conclusion regarding the availability of state antitrust relief against baseball player restraints; what would have been the likely political impact upon federal immunity?

Baseball's immunity from state antitrust law was based on the Court's application of the "dormant Commerce Clause" in the Constitution. The federal antitrust immunity is clearly limited to the sport of baseball. See *International Boxing Club v. United States*, 358 U.S. 242, 79 S.Ct. 245, 3 L.Ed.2d 270 (1959) (holding that professional boxing is not exempt); *Radovich v. NFL*, 352 U.S. 445, 77 S.Ct. 390, 1 L.Ed.2d 456 (1957) (holding that football and other professional sports except baseball are not exempt); *Amateur Softball Ass'n of America v. United States*, 467 F.2d 312 (10th Cir.1972) (holding that amateur softball is not exempt). However, courts have extended the immunity from state antitrust law to all league-wide rules in all league sports. The following case is an illustration.

PARTEE v. SAN DIEGO CHARGERS FOOTBALL CO.

Supreme Court of California, 1983.

34 Cal.3d 378, 194 Cal.Rptr. 367, 668 P.2d 674.

BROUSSARD, JUSTICE.

[Dennis Partee, a kicker for the San Diego Chargers of the National Football League, challenged the NFL's version of the reserve system under California antitrust law. After Partee won a trial verdict, the Chargers and the NFL appealed.]

To promote athletic competition by providing a means of keeping the teams on a par with each other and to foster the business success of the member teams, the NFL has certain operating rules, many of which are embodied in the NFL constitution and bylaws. Partee's antitrust action concerns five of these operating rules as they existed in 1974: the draft, option clause, Rozelle rule, tampering rule and one-man rule. These rules are applied nationwide to all of the teams in the league. The court found all but the option clause to violate California antitrust laws.

* * *

The Chargers contend that professional football is a unique activity of interstate commerce which requires nationally uniform governance, that only federal antitrust laws apply, that interstate commerce would be unreasonably burdened if state antitrust laws were applied to professional football's interstate activities, and that application of the Cartwright Act was a violation of the commerce and supremacy clauses of the Constitution.

The Chargers do not claim federal antitrust laws, the Sherman and Clayton Acts, "occupy" the field of antitrust regulation, or that the federal and state antitrust laws so conflict as to require preemption of the state scheme. The federal and California antitrust laws, having identical objectives, are harmonious with each other.

The commerce clause is a limitation upon the power of the states without implementing legislation by Congress. "Not every exercise of state power with some impact on interstate commerce is invalid. A state statute must be upheld if it 'regulated even-handedly to effectuate a legitimate local public interest, and its effects on interstate commerce are only incidental ... unless the burden imposed on such commerce is clearly excessive in relation to the putative local benefits.'" The burden on interstate commerce will ordinarily be found unreasonable where the state regulation substantially impedes the free flow of commerce from state to state or governs "those phases of the national commerce which, because of the need of national uniformity, demand their regulation, if any, be prescribed by a single authority." The commerce clause permits only incidental regulation of interstate commerce by the states; direct regulation is prohibited.

* * *

Following *Flood v. Kuhn*, state antitrust regulation has been held inapplicable to professional basketball (Robertson v. National Basketball Association (S.D.N.Y.1975); HMC Management v. New Orleans Basketball Club (La.App.1979) and professional football (Matuszak v. Houston Oilers, Inc. (Tex.Civ.App.1974)). No case has been found applying state antitrust laws to the interstate activities of professional sports.

Professional football is a nationwide business structured essentially the same as baseball. Professional football's teams are dependent upon the league playing schedule for competitive play, just as in baseball. The necessity of a nationwide league structure for the benefit of both teams and players for effective competition is evident as is the need for a nationally uniform set of rules governing the league structure. Fragmentation of the league structure on the basis of state lines would adversely affect the success of the competitive business enterprise, and differing state antitrust decisions if applied to the enterprise would likely compel all member teams to comply with the laws of the strictest state.

We are satisfied that national uniformity required in regulation of baseball and its reserve system is likewise required in the player-team-league relationships challenged by Partee and that the burden on interstate commerce outweighs the state interests in applying state antitrust laws to those relationships.

Partee seeks to distinguish Flood v. Kuhn, on the ground that professional baseball enjoys a unique exemption from federal antitrust law and that the United States Supreme Court in upholding baseball's exemption from state law relied on the cases establishing baseball's federal exemption and stated that its holding applied to baseball. However, the high court specifically relied upon the court of appeals' statement: " '[A]s the burden on interstate commerce outweighs the states' interests in regulating baseball's system, the Commerce Clause precludes the application of state antitrust law.' " The high court also relied upon the district court judge's statement that "national 'uniformity [is required] in a regulation of baseball and its reserve system.' " There is no justification to conclude that the United States Supreme Court did not fully consider the brief statements from the lower court opinions it chose to quote, approve, and rely upon. The statements are clear and unequivocal, and we are not free to disregard them.

Because in all relevant respects the burden on interstate commerce and the state interest resulting from the player-team-league relationship in professional football attacked by Partee is substantially the equivalent of that resulting from the reserve clause in professional baseball, the statements are applicable to professional football.

Appeal allowed.

Questions for Discussion

1. Does the holding in this case apply only to attempts by players to challenge league rules on state *antitrust* grounds? Consider Bobby Hebert's challenge in 1991 to the NFL's compensation/right-of-first-refusal system under California's Labor Code, which makes it unlawful for any business to deprive a person of the opportunity to earn his livelihood. Hebert alleged that the Los Angeles Raiders would have signed him to a contract when his contract with the New Orleans Saints expired, but that the Raiders did not do so because they would have had to compensate the Saints with two first-round draft choices. Hebert alleged that this NFL rule violated the state Business and Professions Code. Does the reasoning in *Flood* and *Partee* apply when the state statute sued under is not an antitrust statute? See *Hebert v. Los Angeles Raiders,* 2 Cal.Rptr.2d 489, 820 P.2d 999 (1991).

2. In *Postema v. National League of Professional Baseball Clubs,* 799 F.Supp. 1475, 59 Empl. Prac. Dec. (CCH) ¶ 41,683 (1992), a woman umpire filed suit complaining of gender discrimination in contravention of New York's Human Rights and Restraint of Trade laws (as well as of Title VII of the federal Civil Rights Act). In *Salerno v. American League,* 429 F.2d 1003 (2d. Cir.1970), the Second Court held that baseball's dealings with its umpires were not governed by federal antitrust law. Does that decision (rendered prior to *Flood v. Kuhn*) dictate baseball immunity from state law governing gender (or other) discrimination claims?

3. Does the nonapplicability of state law under *Flood* and *Partee* hinge on a finding of preemption by a federal statute covering the challenged conduct, or merely on the theory that Congress has exclusive jurisdiction, whether or not exercised, over these "inherently nationwide" matters? See *State of Wisconsin v. Milwaukee Braves, Inc.,* 31 Wis.2d 699, 144 N.W.2d 1 (1966), cert. denied, 385 U.S. 990, 87 S.Ct. 598, 17 L.Ed.2d 451 (1966) (considering the application of Wisconsin antitrust law to the relocation of the Milwaukee Braves baseball team to Atlanta).

As we will see in Chapter 4, the free agency for baseball players that was unsuccessfully pursued under antitrust law in *Flood* was won shortly thereafter through labor law (in the *Messersmith* arbitration ruling). But whatever its limitations with respect to outside actors such as television stations or concessionaires, the antitrust immunity confirmed in *Flood* does shelter baseball in its dealings with non-union personnel such as Pete Rose, a manager, or George Steinbrenner, a team owner. It also removes from judicial scrutiny league decisions that restrict individual franchise decisions about a host of matters—in particular, whether to relocate teams such as the Giants from San Francisco to Tampa Bay.

In early 1992, a vigorous debate took place in baseball about whether the Japanese owner of Nintendo should be allowed to purchase a majority interest in the Seattle Mariners: the Japanese industrialist's son-in-law lived in and ran Nintendo America from Seattle and sought to keep the team in that city. To prod baseball owners to agree to at least some version of this purchase of the Mariners, the political leaders of the State of Washington (including the Speaker of the U.S. House of Representatives, Thomas Foley) threatened to strip baseball of its antitrust immunity. Regardless of your views about whether Japanese (or other foreign) investment is in the "best interests" of baseball,[22] do you think that bringing antitrust into the picture would actually enhance the likelihood of a team staying in a market such as Seattle (rather than move to St. Petersburg, for example)? Keep this case in mind when you encounter in Chapter 6 the saga of the Oakland–to–Los Angeles Raiders.

How do you think the *Flood* court, or the current Court, would deal with facts similar to those in *Federal Base Ball*—the established league adopting measures in concert to ensure that a competitor league goes out of business? If the courts were to reaffirm the baseball exemption in a case such as this, how would Congress react? Except for intra-league player restraints, does political deterrence constrain Major League Baseball from excessive use of its antitrust immunity? Are such repeated threats of congressional action an appropriate use of the legislative power?

---

22. In fact, the dispute was eventually resolved on the basis that Nintendo would supply the bulk of the $110 million purchase price of the Mariners, but that John Ellis, president of the local power company, would be the team's chief executive officer.

Chapter Three

FROM ANTITRUST TO
LABOR LAW [1]

A. ANTITRUST BACKGROUND

The *Flood* decision (reproduced at the end of Chapter 2) had two major implications for the world of sports. First, the Supreme Court reiterated that baseball enjoys a broad immunity from antitrust law, which could be removed only by congressional action. As we will see in the next chapter, however, the Major League Baseball Players Association did not need congressional help to dismantle baseball's reserve clause—collective bargaining under labor law proved up to that challenge. Second, the Court confirmed that all other sports are subject to antitrust law. With that assurance, a burst of antitrust litigation was launched in the 1970s against restrictive practices across the spectrum of professional sports.[2] But by the end of the 1970s, players in each of the major professional team sports still faced substantial restraints on their freedom to deal with and move to other teams. This chapter recounts the legal features of that story.

One possible source of insulation of intraleague affairs from section 1 of the Sherman Act is the requirement of a "contract, combination, or conspiracy." In contrast with section 2, which speaks of "every person

1. The best overall account of what happened in both the courts and the various sports in this area is Robert C. Berry, William B. Gould IV, and Paul D. Staudohar, *Labor Relations in Professional Sports* (Dover, Mass: Auburn House, 1986), as updated by Paul Staudohar, *The Sports Industry and Collective Bargaining* (Ithaca, N.Y.: ILR Press, 1989).

Three excellent collections of articles, written principally by economists, give us a picture of the sports labor market before and after the arrival of antitrust and labor law: Roger Noll ed., *Government and the Sports Business* (Washington, D.C.: Brookings, 1974); Paul Staudohar and James A. Mangan, eds., *The Business of Professional Sports* (Urbana, Ill.: University of Illinois Press, 1991); and Paul Sommers, ed., *Diamonds Are Forever: The Business of Baseball* (Washington, D.C.: Brookings, 1992).

2. In addition, as we will see in Chapter 9, the world of intercollegiate sports saw a number of antitrust challenges by students, coaches, and colleges against restrictions imposed by the National Collegiate Athletic Association (NCAA).

who shall monopolize," section 1 requires that there be at least two distinct legal persons who are parties to a collusive arrangement that restrains trade. The obvious question, then, is whether the league—the NFL, the NBA or the NHL—when it adopts intraleague policies is a single entity subject only to section 2 of the Act, or a combination of separate clubs whose internal arrangements are exposed to section 1 scrutiny. While this question is clearly relevant to litigation about league practices regarding the players market, it has been most seriously pressed in litigation about league restraints that was brought by franchise holders (people who themselves are parties to and beneficiaries of this arrangement). Thus we will postpone detailed treatment of the "single entity" issue to Chapter 6 on the franchise market.

Still lurking within section 1 (and also section 2) is another potential barrier to antitrust suits by players—the argument that the "trade and commerce" that is protected against collusive restraint (or monopolization) does not include the labor market. The sports arena, including the cases below on the rookie draft and on veteran free agency, constitutes the main category of antitrust litigation about the employment relationship in any industrial setting. Except for one recent district court decision excerpted below, the courts in the sports cases have assumed with little or no discussion that the Sherman Act bars restraint of trade in the labor as well as in the product market. That conclusion, however, raises significant questions within contemporary scholarly and judicial analysis which presumes that the principal, if not exclusive, aim of antitrust law is to enhance consumer welfare through a more efficient allocation of economic resources.[3]

The immediate target of antitrust law is excessive market power, whether in the hands of a single firm or a group of firms that jointly acquire such market power through anticompetitive agreements. Normally when one thinks of market power and its adverse effects, one does so in the context of a firm operating in the product market—selling its goods or services to consumers. Market power exists when consumers have few if any alternatives to the seller's product, thus enabling the seller to dictate terms based on profit maximization rather than competitive pressure. Economists have identified two general consequences of such market power. First, customers who purchase the product have to pay higher prices (or obtain lower quality products at the same price); this entails a transfer of wealth from customers to producers. In addition, the amount of the good or service produced for and used by consumers will drop. This inflicts a "dead weight loss" upon the economy as a whole, because some factors of production (labor, materials, capital, land, or equipment) that would be most efficient at

---

3. Compare Robert Bork, *The Antitrust Paradox: A Policy at War with Itself* (New York: Basic Books, 1978), with Robert H. Lande, *Wealth Transfers as the Original and Primary Concern of Antitrust*, 34 Has- tings L. J. 65 (1982). See generally Louis Kaplow, *Antitrust, Law and Economics, and the Courts*, 50 Law & Contemp. Probs. 181 (1987).

making the monopolist's product are diverted into producing other goods and services for which they are less well-suited.

There is disagreement about whether the first-mentioned effect of market power—wealth transfer—is the type of harm that antitrust law is concerned with. Conservative "Chicago school" theorists argue that antitrust should not be concerned with who enjoys the fruits of society's output, but only with maximizing the total value of that output. More populist scholars argue that since Congress was concerned about exploitation of consumers when it passed our antitrust laws, wealth transfers from generally less-wealthy consumers to generally more-wealthy producers are properly the concern of antitrust enforcement. There is consensus, however, that the second effect—restriction of output and consequent diversion of resources into less efficient uses—is harmful and should be the target of antitrust law.

Consider, now, the situation in which market power is wielded by the purchaser of a good or service: sellers have few if any other options to deal with. The effect of such "monopsony" power is the converse of monopoly power. Sellers are forced to accept lower purchase prices or to invest more effort and resources in production of a higher quality good for the same price; this effects a wealth transfer from sellers to buyers. Faced with that less favorable market environment, sellers will tend to restrict the amount of the good or service sold; again this means that the total value of society's output will be lower because factors of production are diverted into less efficient uses.

Again, there is scholarly agreement that the latter type of deadweight loss from monopsony power is a legitimate concern of antitrust enforcement, but no such consensus exists about the wealth transfer effect. In addition, the political connotations of monopsonistic wealth transfers are more obscure than those due to monopoly power. Excess market power wielded by monopoly sellers victimizes the broader population of consumers. But excess power wielded by a firm purchasing goods or services for production may actually lower the cost and enhance the quality of output of that factor of production—in particular, labor—for the benefit of consumers who almost invariably outnumber the producers of any one product.

Consider *Kartell v. Blue Shield of Massachusetts, Inc.*, 749 F.2d 922 (1st Cir.1984), where the court held that Blue Shield, the dominant provider of health insurance in Massachusetts, did not violate the Sherman Act by requiring all doctors who performed services for patients insured by the defendant to accept its fee schedule as full payment for the service, and not charge the patient any more. There was some evidence that this restriction caused some young doctors not to practice in Massachusetts (in other words, it reduced the quantity of medical services available), and caused other doctors not to utilize advanced but more costly treatment techniques indicated for patient conditions (in other words, it reduced the quality of medical services). However, the court found no antitrust violation because, among other things, the overall impact of this insurer practice was to hold medical and insurance costs down for consumers.

> [T]he prices at issue here are low prices, not high prices. Of course, a buyer, as well as a seller, can possess significant market power; and courts have held that *agreements* to fix prices—whether maximum or minimum—are unlawful. Nonetheless, the Congress that enacted the Sherman Act saw it as a way of protecting consumers against prices that were too *high*, not too low. And the relevant economic conditions may be very different when low prices, rather than high prices, are at issue. These facts suggest that courts at least should be cautious—reluctant to condemn too speedily—an arrangement that, on its face, appears to bring low price benefits to the consumer (pp. 930–31).

Kartell, then, implies that excess monopsony power—because it may improve the situation of consumers in the marketplace—does not warrant the same kind of close antitrust scrutiny as does monopoly power—which always threatens the interests of consumers.

This analogy is significant for player restraint cases in sports. Players are sellers of a factor of production—their labor—to a league that usually is the only employer in their particular sport. Players associations object to the draft and to restrictions on free agent movement because by thereby limiting players' options to a single team, the league creates monopsony market power; buying teams can force players to accept salaries that are less than the players could get in a market where all teams could bid for any one player. Players are not primarily concerned about the impact of such practices on consumer welfare—the prices that fans pay for tickets, or that networks pay for broadcasting rights, or the quality of the product people watch at the park or on the screen. Players are concerned about enhancing their income and avoiding a transfer of wealth from themselves to team owners. The question, though, is whether antitrust law should be concerned about this type of conflict between players and owners. Relevant to that broad question are these specific issues:

1. Would elimination of the rookie draft and limits on veteran free agency substantially raise player salaries? If both restrictions were dispensed with, how would this influence the pattern of salary distribution? With what effect on the supply of players to the league?

2. Assuming that average player salaries would rise to some extent, would higher payroll costs reduce team profits or raise ticket prices and television fees? If both, which effect would predominate?

3. Does league restraint on player mobility, and thence on team competition for players' services, serve to improve competitive athletic balance within the league—thus enhancing the attractiveness of the league product to fans? Or might such restraints actually inhibit the ability of weaker clubs to upgrade the quality

of their teams? Again, if both are possible, which would predominate?

* * *

The foregoing gives some flavor of the difficult theoretical and empirical questions implicated in the effort to introduce antitrust law into the sports labor market. Following are excerpts from the one sports decision that addresses at even a rudimentary level the question of whether antitrust belongs here at all. (This case involved a suit lodged against the National Football League's maximum salary limit of $1,000 per week for players on a team's development squad, rather than on the regular roster. Further details about the case and its trial outcome will be presented later in this chapter.)   (Facts)

BROWN v. PRO FOOTBALL, INC. (WASHINGTON REDSKINS)

United States District Court, District of Columbia, 1991.

1992–1 Trade Cases (CCH) ¶ 69,747, 1992 WL 88039.

LAMBERTH, DISTRICT JUDGE.

* * *

Contrary to the [NFL teams'] assertion, wage-fixing restraints which affect the labor market are considered price-fixing restraints subject to the antitrust laws. Section 6 of the Clayton Act [which states that "the labor of a human being is not a commodity or article of commerce"] does not exempt such restraints from antitrust liability:

> It is readily apparent that Congress, in enacting § 6, was concerned with the right of labor and similar organizations to continue engaging in [activities that otherwise would be considered antitrust violations], including the right to strike, not with the right of employers to band together for joint action in fixing the wages to be paid by each employer. There is no evidence of the existence of any necessity to protect the latter type of activity at the time when § 6 was enacted. It seems clear that if Congress had wanted to exempt agreements between employers as to the money or compensation that would be paid to their employees, it would not have limited § 6 to exemption of "[t]he labor of a human being" which can be restrained only by the employees or unions controlling the labor itself. Congress would also have provided that compensation offered or paid by employers to employees is not a commodity or article of commerce. This it did not do.

Cordova v. Bache & Co., 321 F.Supp. 600, 606 (S.D.N.Y.1970) (Judge Mansfield). The principle that wage-fixing restraints are price-fixing restraints cognizable under the Sherman Act has been accepted by several courts.

* * *

Moreover, the Supreme Court has noted that price fixing by purchasers of goods "is the sort of combination condemned by the [Sherman] Act." *Mandeville Island Farms, Inc. v. American Crystal Sugar Co.*, 334 U.S. 219, 235 (1948). The court finds no discernible reason, given that the Sherman Act applies to services as well as goods, *United States v. National Association of Real Estate Boards*, 339 U.S. 485, 490 (1950) (Sherman Act "aimed at combinations organized and directed to control of the market by suppression of competition 'in the marketing of goods and services'"), why wage-fixing by purchasers of services should be treated differently than price-fixing by sellers of goods.

Other precedent lends further support to the application of the Sherman Act to wage-fixing restraints. The Supreme Court has noted the "broad remedial and deterrent objectives" of the Clayton Act and has recognized that the statute "does not confine its protection to consumers, or to purchasers, or to sellers.... The Act is comprehensive in its terms and coverage, protecting all who are made victims of the forbidden practices by whomever they may be perpetrated." *Blue Shield of Virginia v. McCready*, 457 U.S. 465, 472 (1982). The Supreme Court has clearly stated that the exchange of a "service for money is 'commerce' in the most common usage of that word" and that the Sherman Act applies to restraints involving the sale of services. *Goldfarb v. Virginia State Bar*, 421 U.S. 773, 787–88 (1988).

Furthermore, the Supreme Court has noted that a consumer is injured in his or her business or property when the price of "goods or services is artificially inflated by reason of the anticompetitive conduct complained of." *Reiter v. Sonotone Corp.*, 442 U.S. 330, 339 (1979). By analogy, and applying the broad remedial and deterrent objectives of the Clayton Act, a service provider is injured in his business or property when buyers of those services artificially deflate the price of services through cooperative anticompetitive conduct. See *Chattanooga Foundry & Pipe Workers v. Atlanta*, 203 U.S. 390, 396 (1960) (recognizing that a city can be injured in its "business of furnishing water" by an antitrust violation). The law in the District of Columbia Circuit recognizes "that athletes have standing to challenge player restrictions in professional sports since the restraints operate directly on, and to the detriment of, the employee." *Smith v. Pro Football, Inc.*, 593 F.2d 1173, 1175 n.2 (D.C.Cir.1978). Based on the authority cited above, this court finds that wage-fixing is an antitrust violation to which the Sherman Act applies.

Argument rejected.

———————

How persuasive is the court's analysis of the monopsony issue, especially its conclusion that "wage-fixing" is always an antitrust violation? Is this conclusion compatible with the First Circuit's position in *Kartell*, referred to earlier, in which Blue Shield used its market power to reduce the price paid for doctors' services?

────────

Later in this chapter we will return to the question of the proper role of antitrust in the labor market, with a selection from the voluminous jurisprudence on the labor law exemption of collective bargaining from normal antitrust scrutiny. However, even if antitrust law can be used to challenge league restrictions on players, not all restraints of trade are illegal, but only those judged to be unreasonable (see *Standard Oil v. United States*, 221 U.S. 1, 31 S.Ct. 502, 55 L.Ed. 619 (1911)). Until well into the 1970s, though, courts tended to find various business arrangements unreasonable *per se*—price fixing (see *United States v. Socony Vacuum*, 310 U.S. 150, 60 S.Ct. 811, 84 L.Ed. 1129 (1940)), market allocation (see *United States v. Topco Assocs.*, 405 U.S. 596, 92 S.Ct. 1126, 31 L.Ed.2d 515 (1972)), group boycotts (see *Klor's, Inc. v. Broadway–Hale Stores*, 359 U.S. 207, 79 S.Ct. 705, 3 L.Ed.2d 741 (1959)), resale price maintenance (see *Dr. Miles Medical Co. v. John D. Parks & Sons Co.*, 220 U.S. 373, 31 S.Ct. 376, 55 L.Ed. 502 (1911)), and vertical territorial restrictions (see *United States v. Arnold, Schwinn & Co.*, 388 U.S. 365, 87 S.Ct. 1856, 18 L.Ed.2d 1249 (1967)). Because these categories were vaguely defined, section 1 jurisprudence allowed courts to condemn forms of conduct that the judges disapproved of for social, political, or economic reasons. In this era the Supreme Court delivered several judgments finding various joint venture rules to be illegal *per se*, even though the resulting enterprises appeared to offer consumers lower prices and greater product quality or output. See *United States v. Sealy*, 388 U.S. 350, 87 S.Ct. 1847, 18 L.Ed.2d 1238 (1967), *United States v. Topco Assocs.*, 405 U.S. 596, 92 S.Ct. 1126, 31 L.Ed.2d 515 (1972), and *Silver v. New York Stock Exchange*, 373 U.S. 341, 83 S.Ct. 1246, 10 L.Ed.2d 389 (1963). These cases are occasionally cited in the sports cases included in this chapter.

Beginning in the mid–1970s, the Supreme Court sharply altered its antitrust stance by either expressly overruling or drastically limiting application of the various *per se* categories. Here we summarize only a few such decisions—the ones most relevant for analyzing sports cases.

In *Broadcast Music Inc. v. Columbia Broadcasting System, Inc.*, 441 U.S. 1, 99 S.Ct. 1551, 60 L.Ed.2d 1 (1979), the Supreme Court narrowed the *per se* approach to price fixing by holding that an organization that held nonexclusive copyright licenses for the musical compositions of hundreds of composers did not automatically violate antitrust law by selling the right to play all of its licensed music to commercial broadcasters at a set price. The Court reasoned that this "blanket license" achieved major cost savings for purchasers, who otherwise would have had to traverse the globe to obtain individual licenses from the composer of every musical piece they wished to broadcast.

This substantial lowering of costs, which is of course potentially beneficial to both sellers and buyers, differentiates the blanket license from individual use licenses. The blanket license is composed of the individual compositions plus the aggregating service. Here, the whole is truly greater than the sum of its parts; it is, to some extent, a different product. The blanket license has certain unique characteristics: it allows the licensee immediate use of covered compositions, without the delay of prior individual negotiations, and great flexibility in the choice of musical material.... Thus, to the extent the blanket license is a different product, ASCAP is not really a joint sales agency offering the individual goods of many sellers, but is a separate seller offering its blanket license, of which the individual compositions are raw material. ASCAP, in short, made a market in which individual composers are inherently unable to compete fully effectively.

Next, the Court limited "group boycott" illegality in *Northwest Wholesale Stationers, Inc. v. Pacific Stationery & Printing Co.*, 472 U.S. 284, 105 S.Ct. 2613, 86 L.Ed.2d 202 (1958), by holding that a wholesale purchasing cooperative formed by a group of small stationery retailers was not guilty of a *per se* antitrust violation when it expelled one of its members for secretly operating a wholesale stationery supply business in competition with the cooperative. The Court reasoned that the cooperative created purchasing efficiencies for its members, which in turn produced lower prices to consumers, and that enforcement of the rule against members competing against the cooperative was arguably important for the cooperative to be able to provide these economic advantages. The Court concluded that "[u]nless the cooperative possesses market power or exclusive access to an element essential to effective competition, the conclusion that expulsion [for violating the rule] is virtually always likely to have an anticompetitive effect is unwarranted."

In *Continental T.V., Inc. v. GTE Sylvania Inc.*, 433 U.S. 36 (1977), the Supreme Court expressly overturned the *per se* rule against a manufacturer placing territorial restrictions on its distributors. The Court reasoned that such restrictions on distributors might improve the firm's overall marketing strategy and make the company more competitive vis-a-vis its rivals, and such competition among producers would ultimately produce lower prices and higher quality for consumers. The Court thus drew a distinction between competition among sellers of one manufacturer's brand (intrabrand competition) and competition among sellers of different manufacturers' brands (interbrand competition):

> The market impact of vertical restrictions is complex because of their potential for simultaneous reduction of intrabrand competition and stimulation of interbrand competition.

* * *

Vertical restrictions reduce intrabrand competition by limiting the number of sellers of a particular product competing for the business of a given group of buyers. Location restrictions have this effect because of practical constraints on the effective marketing area of retail outlets. Although intrabrand competition may be reduced, the ability of retailers to exploit the resulting market may be limited both by the ability of consumers to travel to other franchised locations and, perhaps more importantly, to purchase the competing products of other manufacturers....

Vertical restrictions promote interbrand competition by allowing the manufacturer to achieve certain efficiencies in the distribution of his products.... Economists have identified a number of ways in which manufacturers can use such restrictions to compete more effectively against other manufacturers. For example, [manufacturers] can use the restrictions in order to induce competent and aggressive retailers to make the kind of investment on capital and labor that is often required in the distribution of products unknown to the consumer, [or] to induce retailers to engage in promotional activities or to provide service and repair facilities necessary to the efficient marketing of their products.... The availability and quality of such services affect a manufacturer's goodwill and the competitiveness of his product. Because of market imperfections such as the so-called "free rider" effect, these services might not be provided by retailers in a purely competitive situation, despite the fact that each retailer's benefit would be greater if all provided the services than if none did.

These and similar decisions protected antitrust defendants from *per se* rulings of illegality on motions for summary judgment. In each of the cases described above, on remand from the Supreme Court the lower courts found the challenged conduct to be legal after careful Rule of Reason review, thus corroborating the Court's view that productive efficiencies generated by the challenged agreements might render them socially desirable. No longer, then, does the fact that an agreement decreases "competition" in a general sense automatically result in antitrust illegality.

Another noteworthy case was *National Society of Professional Engineers v. United States*, 435 U.S. 679 (1978), which established the relevant factors for Rule of Reason review. The Justice Department had charged the society governing civil engineers with a *per se* violation of section 1 for adopting a rule that prohibited engineers from quoting a price in their project bid. The society defended its price ban as necessary to protect the public from unsafe structures that engineers might design if they became too cost conscious in order to win bids and jobs. Again rejecting *per se* analysis, the Court established the test for the Rule of Reason: an agreement is unlawful if the anticompetitive injury it causes outweighs the procompetitive benefits it generates. From that premise the Court concluded that the society's ban on competitive bidding violated the Rule of Reason as a matter of law:

The Society's affirmative defense confirms rather than refutes the anticompetitive purpose and effect of its agreement. The Society argues that the restraint is justified because bidding on engineering services is inherently imprecise, would lead to deceptively low bids, and would thereby tempt individual engineers to do inferior work with consequent risk to public safety and health. The logic of this argument rests on the assumption that the agreement will tend to maintain the price level; if it had no such effect, it would not serve its intended purpose. The Society nonetheless invokes the Rule of Reason, arguing that its restraint on price competition ultimately inures to the public benefit by preventing the production of inferior work and by insuring ethical behavior....

The Sherman Act does not require competitive bidding; it prohibits unreasonable restraints on competition. Petitioner's ban on competitive bidding prevents all customers from making price comparisons in the initial selection of an engineer, and imposes the Society's views of the costs and benefits of competition on the entire marketplace. It is this restraint that must be justified under the Rule of Reason, and petitioners' attempt to do so on the basis of the potential threat that competition poses to the public safety and the ethics of the profession is nothing less than a frontal assault on the basic policy of the Sherman Act.

The Sherman Act reflects a legislative judgment that ultimately competition will produce not only lower prices, but also better goods and services.... The assumption that competition is the best method of allocating resources in a free market recognizes that all elements of a bargain—quality, service, safety, and durability—and not just the immediate cost, are favorably affected by the free opportunity to select among alternative offers. Even assuming occasional exceptions to the presumed consequences of competition, the statutory policy precludes inquiry into the question whether competition is good or bad.

The fact that engineers are often involved in large scale projects significantly affecting the public safety does not alter our analysis. Exceptions to the Sherman Act for potentially dangerous goods and services would be tantamount to repeal of the statute. In our complex economy the number of items that may cause serious harm is almost endless—automobiles, drugs, foods, aircraft components, heavy equipment, and countless others, cause serious harm to individuals or to the public at large if defectively made. The judiciary cannot indirectly protect the public against this harm by conferring monopoly privileges on the manufacturers.

It is now clear, then, that the Rule of Reason requires judges and juries to balance only an agreement's effects on economic competition. Courts must weigh the injury to the consumer stemming from any increase in defendants' market power due to the arrangement (allocative inefficiency) against any benefits to the consumer that occur because defendants can make and sell their product(s) at a lower price or make more and higher quality products at the same price (productive efficiency).

The difficulty is that this approach requires fact finders to compare apples and oranges, neither of which can be easily identified or precisely quantified. Because economists invariably differ sharply over both the market power and the efficiency effects of any particular business arrangement, this balancing exercise is problematic for judges, let alone lay juries. In such cases, the crucial—and still largely unresolved—issues are who has the burden of proving each side of the equation and what presumptions apply when the balance of welfare effects appears roughly equal. Keep these questions in mind as you consider the sports cases presented throughout this chapter.

Consider also the specific lessons derived from the four cases excerpted above. Does a group of separate teams generate large benefits by coming together as a single league, such that the league's distinctive product is more valuable than anything individual teams can offer fans by themselves? (See *Broadcast Music*.) Does a challenged rule produce a superior league product that is more competitive in the (interbrand) entertainment market and thus outweighs whatever antitrust concerns are raised by reduced (intrabrand) competition among league members? (See *GTE Sylvania*.) Does a challenged league rule confer monopoly power on the league in its market, and if so, how should that finding affect the antitrust analysis under section 1? (See *Northwest Wholesale Stationers*.) And do the harms allegedly suffered by the plaintiffs from a particular rule, or the league's asserted justifications for the rule, reflect only the economic effects that are relevant to Rule of Reason analysis? (See *Professional Engineers*.) These questions are raised by the numerous sports antitrust cases that follow in this chapter and in the rest of this book.

B. ANTITRUST AND THE PLAYERS MARKET

1. ROOKIE DRAFT

With that doctrinal prelude, we now turn to the key substantive issues raised in antitrust litigation by players against restraints imposed by the leagues' reserve system.[4] The major cases have taken

4. There has been remarkably little analysis in the legal literature of the specific question whether one or other version of the rookie draft or restraints on veteran free agency are compatible with the principles of antitrust law. Valuable treatments of this subject are found in John C. Weistart and Cym H. Lowell, *The Law of Sports* 500–524, 590–627 (Indianapolis: Bobbs–Merrill, 1979), and Stephen S. Ross, *Mo-*

nopoly Sports Leagues, 77 *Minnesota L. Rev.* 647, 667–695 (1989). There is, however, no shortage of economic literature on this topic, perhaps because it seems more an economic than a legal inquiry to judge whether such league restraints on competition in the players market are reasonably necessary for a successful league operation and/or risk undue exploitation of players by clubs in the league. Besides the works

place in football, one involving the rookie draft, the second, development squads, and the third, restraints on veteran free agency.

The draft of college players originated in football in the 1930s and later spread to other professional sports. While there are variations across the sports, the basic structure of the draft is simple. Proceeding in reverse order of finish from the prior season, each team selects a player from the pool of new players available that year. The consequence is that the player can either negotiate a contract to play with the team that selected him or not play in the league at all. When there is no other league in which to play that sport, one would expect an antitrust suit eventually to be lodged by a player unhappy with the contract offer he was able to secure from the team that drafted him. That is what happened in the following case.

SMITH v. PRO FOOTBALL, INC.

United States Court of Appeals, District of Columbia Circuit, 1978.

593 F.2d 1173.

WILKEY, CIRCUIT JUDGE.

[James "Yazoo" Smith, an All–American defensive back at Oregon, was selected by the Redskins as the twelfth pick in the first round of the 1968 draft. He signed a one-year contract for a total of $50,000—$22,000 in salary and $28,000 in bonuses. Smith suffered a career-ending neck injury in the last game of the 1968 regular season, and the Redskins paid him an additional $19,800 (the amount he would have received had he played out the option year of his contract).

Two years later Smith filed this lawsuit attacking the legality of the rookie draft under antitrust law. Smith contended that but for the draft he would have secured a more lucrative contract that would have better protected him from the financial consequences of his injury. The district court ruled that the draft violated federal antitrust law and awarded Smith $92,000, the amount the judge calculated to be the difference between what Smith would have received in a "free market" without a draft and what he actually received.]

I. BACKGROUND

The NFL draft, which has been in effect since 1935, is a procedure under which negotiating rights to graduating college football players are allocated each year among the NFL clubs in inverse order of the clubs' standing.... In 1968 there were 16 succeeding rounds in the yearly draft, the same order of selection being followed in each round. Teams had one choice per round unless they had traded their choice in

referred to in note 1 above, there are two book-length treatments of this issue in connection with baseball. One, Jesse W. Markham and Paul Teplitz, *Baseball Economics and Public Policy* (Lexington Mass.: Lexington Books, 1981), finds such league restraints reasonable. The other, Gerald Scully, *The Business of Major League Baseball* (Chicago,Ill.: University of Chicago Press, 1989), reaches the opposite verdict.

that round to another team (a fairly common practice). When Smith was selected by the Redskins there were 26 teams choosing in the draft.

The NFL draft, like similar procedures in other professional sports, is designed to promote "competitive balance." By dispersing newly arriving player talent equally among all NFL teams, with preferences to the weaker clubs, the draft aims to produce teams that are as evenly-matched on the playing field as possible. Evenly-matched teams make for closer games, tighter pennant races, and better player morale, thus maximizing fan interest, broadcast revenues, and overall health of the sport.

The draft is effectuated through the NFL's "no-tampering" rule. Under this rule as it existed in 1968, no team was permitted to negotiate prior to the draft with any player eligible to be drafted, and no team could negotiate with (or sign) any player selected by another team in the draft. The net result of these restrictions was that the right to negotiate with any given player was exclusively held by one team at any given time. If a college player could not reach a satisfactory agreement with the team holding the rights to his services he could not play in the NFL.

* * *

The NFL player draft differs from the classic group boycott in two significant respects. First, the NFL clubs which have "combined" to implement the draft are not *competitors* in any economic sense. The clubs operate basically as a joint venture in producing an entertainment product—football games and telecasts. No NFL club can produce this product without agreements and joint action with every other team. To this end, the League not only determines franchise locations, playing schedules, and broadcast terms, but also ensures that the clubs receive equal shares of telecast and ticket revenues. These economic joint venturers "compete" on the playing field, to be sure, but here as well cooperation is essential if the entertainment product is to attain a high quality: only if the teams are "competitively balanced" will spectator interest be maintained at a high pitch. No NFL team, in short, is interested in driving another team out of business, whether in the counting-house or on the football field, for if the League fails, no one team can survive.

The draft differs from the classic group boycott, secondly, in that the NFL clubs have not combined *to exclude competitors or potential competitors* from their level of the market. Smith was never seeking to "compete" with the NFL clubs, and their refusal to deal with him has resulted in no decrease in the competition for providing football entertainment to the public. The draft, indeed, is designed not to insulate the NFL from competition, but to improve the entertainment product by enhancing its teams' competitive equality.

In view of these differences, we conclude that the NFL player draft cannot properly be described as a group boycott, at least not the type of group boycott that traditionally has elicited invocation of a *per se* rule. The "group boycott" designation, we believe, is properly restricted to concerted attempts by competitors to exclude horizontal competitors; it should not be applied, and has never been applied by the Supreme Court, to concerted refusals that are not designed to drive out competitors but to achieve some other goal.

* * *

Whether the draft is a group boycott, or not, we think it is clearly not the type of restraint to which a *per se* rule is meant to apply. A *per se* rule is a judicial shortcut: it represents the considered judgment of courts, after considerable experience with a particular type of restraint, that the rule of reason, the normal mode of analysis, can be dispensed with.... A court will not indulge in this conclusive presumption lightly. Invocation of a *per se* rule always risks sweeping reasonable, pro-competitive activity within a general condemnation, and a court will run this risk only when it can say, on the strength of unambiguous experience, that the challenged action is a "naked restraint [ ] of trade with no purpose except stifling of competition." ...

The NFL player draft, we think, quite clearly fails to satisfy the "demanding standards" of *Northern Pacific Railway*. Given that the draft's restrictive effect is temporally limited, we would hesitate to describe its impact on the market for players' services as "pernicious." More importantly, we cannot say that the draft has "no purpose except stifling of competition" or that it is without "any redeeming virtue." Some form of player selection system may serve to regulate and thereby promote competition in what would otherwise be a chaotic bidding market for the services of college players. The Redskins, moreover, presented considerable evidence at trial that the draft was designed to preserve, and that it made some contribution to preserving, playing-field equality among the NFL-teams with various attendant benefits. The draft, finally, like the vertical restraints challenged in *Continental T.V.*, is "widely used" in our economy and has both judicial and scholarly support for its economic usefulness.

This is not to say, of course, that the draft in any one of its incarnations may not violate the antitrust laws. It is only to say that the courts have had too little experience with this type of restraint, and know too little of the "economic and business stuff" from which it issues, confidently to declare it illegal without undertaking the analysis enjoined by the rule of reason....

In antitrust law, as elsewhere, we must heed Justice Cardozo's warning to beware "the tyranny of tags and tickets." When anticompetitive effects are shown to result from a particular player selection system "they can be adequately policed under the rule of reason."

* * *

B.   *Rule of Reason*

Under the rule of reason, a restraint must be evaluated to determine whether it is significantly anticompetitive in purpose or effect.... If, on analysis, the restraint is found to have legitimate business purposes whose realization serves to promote competition, the "anticompetitive evils" of the challenged practice must be carefully balanced against its "procompetitive virtues" to ascertain whether the former outweigh the latter.   A restraint is unreasonable if it has the "net effect" of substantially impeding competition.

* * *

The draft that has been challenged here is undeniably anticompetitive both in its purpose and in its effect.   The defendants have conceded that the draft "restricts competition among the NFL clubs for the services of graduating college players" and, indeed, that the draft "is designed to limit competition" and "to be a 'purposive' restraint" on the player-service market.   The fact that the draft assertedly was designed to promote the teams' playing-field equality rather than to inflate their profit margins may prevent the draft's purpose from being described, in subjective terms, as nefarious.   But this fact does not prevent its purpose from being described, in objective terms, as anticompetitive, for suppressing competition is the Telos, the very essence of the restraint.

The trial judge was likewise correct in finding that the draft was significantly anticompetitive in its *effect*.   The draft inescapably forces each seller of football services to deal with one, and only one buyer, robbing the seller, as in any monopolistic market, of any real bargaining power.   The draft, as the District Court found, "leaves no room whatever for competition among the teams for the services of college players, and utterly strips them of any measure of control over the marketing of their talents."   The predictable effect of the draft, as the evidence established and as the District Court found, was to lower the salary levels of the best college players.   There can be no doubt that the effect of the draft as it existed in 1968 was to "suppress or even destroy competition" in the market for players' services.

The justification asserted for the draft is that it has the legitimate business purpose of promoting "competitive balance" and playing-field equality among the teams, producing better entertainment for the public, higher salaries for the players, and increased financial security for the clubs.   The NFL has endeavored to summarize this justification by saying that the draft ultimately has a "procompetitive" effect, yet this shorthand entails no small risk of confusion.   The draft is "procompetitive," if at all, in a very different sense from that in which it is anticompetitive.   The draft is anticompetitive in its effect on the market for players' services, because it virtually eliminates economic competition among buyers for the services of sellers.   The draft is allegedly "procompetitive" in its effect on the playing field; but the NFL teams are not economic competitors on the playing field, and the draft, while it may heighten athletic competition and thus improve the entertainment product offered to the public, does not increase competition in the economic sense of encouraging others to enter the market and to offer the product at lower cost. Because the draft's "anticompetitive" and "procompetitive" effects are not comparable, it is impossible to "net them out" in the usual rule-of-reason balancing. The draft's "anticompetitive evils," in other words, cannot be balanced against its "procompetitive virtues," and the draft be upheld if the latter outweigh the former. In strict economic terms, the draft's demonstrated procompetitive effects are nil.

The defendants' justification for the draft reduces in fine to an assertion that competition in the market for entering players' services would not serve the best interests of the public, the clubs, or the players themselves. This is precisely the type of argument that the Supreme Court only recently has declared to be unavailing. In *National Society of Professional Engineers v. United States*, the Court held that a professional society's ban on competitive bidding violated § 1 of the Sherman Act. In so holding the Court rejected a defense that unbridled competitive bidding would lead to deceptively low bids and inferior work "with consequent risk to public safety and health," terming this justification "nothing less than a frontal assault on the basic policy of the Sherman Act." Ending decades of uncertainty as to the proper scope of inquiry under the rule of reason, the Court stated categorically that the rule, contrary to its name, "does not open the field of antitrust inquiry to any argument in favor of a challenged restraint that may fall within the realm of reason," and that the inquiry instead must be "confined to a consideration of (the restraint's) impact on competitive conditions." The purpose of antitrust analysis, the Court concluded, "is to form a judgment about the competitive significance of the restraint; it is not to decide whether a policy favoring competition is in the public interest, or in the interest of the members of an industry. Subject to exceptions defined by statute, that policy decision has been made by Congress."

Confining our inquiry, as we must, to the draft's impact on competitive conditions, we conclude that the draft as it existed in 1968 was an unreasonable restraint of trade. The draft was concededly anticompetitive in purpose. It was severely anticompetitive in effect. It was not shown to have any significant offsetting procompetitive impact in the economic sense. Balancing the draft's anticompetitive evils against its procompetitive virtues, the outcome is plain. The NFL's defenses, premised on the assertion that competition for players' services would harm both the football industry and society, are unavailing; there is nothing of procompetitive virtue to balance, because "the Rule of Reason does not support a defense based on the assumption that competition itself is unreasonable."

We recognize, on analogy with the Supreme Court's reasoning in *Goldfarb* and *Professional Engineers*, that professional football "may differ significantly from other business services, and, accordingly [that] the nature of the competition" for player talent may vary from an absolute "free market" norm. Given the joint-venture status of the NFL clubs, we do not foreclose the possibility that some type of player selection system might be defended as serving "to regulate and promote . . . competition" in the market for players' services. But we are faced here, as the Supreme Court was faced in *Professional Engineers*, with what amounts to a "total ban" on competition, and we agree with the District Court that this level of restraint cannot be justified. The trial judge concluded, with pardonable exaggeration, that the draft system at issue was "absolutely the most restrictive one imaginable." Even though the draft was justified primarily by the need to disperse the best players, it applied to all graduating seniors, including average players who were, in a sense, fungible commodities. It permitted college players to negotiate with only one team. If a player could not contract with that team, *he could not play at all.*

Without intimating any view as to the legality of the following procedures, we note that there exist significantly less anticompetitive alternatives to the draft system which has been challenged here. The trial judge found that the evidence supported the viability of a player selection system that would permit "more than one team to draft each player, while restricting the number of players any one team might sign." A less anticompetitive draft might permit a college player to negotiate with the team of his choice if the team that drafted him failed to make him an acceptable offer. The NFL could also conduct a second draft each year for players who were unable to reach agreement with the team that selected them the first time. Most obviously, perhaps, the District Court found that the evidence supported the feasibility of a draft that would run for fewer rounds, applying only to the most talented players and enabling their "average" brethren to negotiate in a "free market." The least restrictive alternative of all, of course, would be for the NFL to eliminate the draft entirely and employ revenue-sharing to equalize the teams' financial resources a method of preserving "competitive balance" nicely in harmony with the league's self-proclaimed "joint-venture" status.

We are not required in this case to design a draft that would pass muster under the antitrust laws. We would suggest, however, that under the Supreme Court's decision in *Professional Engineers*, no draft can be justified merely by showing that it is a relatively less anticompetitive means of attaining sundry benefits for the football industry and society. Rather, a player draft can survive scrutiny under the rule of reason only if it is demonstrated to have positive, economically procompetitive benefits that offset its anticompetitive effects, or, at the least, if it is demonstrated to accomplish legitimate business purposes and to have a net anticompetitive effect that is insubstantial. Because the NFL draft as it existed in 1968 had severe anticompetitive effects and no demonstrated procompetitive virtues, we hold that it unreasonably restrained trade in violation of § 1 of The Sherman Act.

C. Damages

The trial court found that plaintiff would have negotiated a more remunerative contract but for the draft as it existed in 1968, and estimated his damages (before trebling) at $92,200 the difference between plaintiff's actual compensation and what his "services would have brought in a free market." Plaintiff urges that this estimate was too low.... Defendants urge that the estimate was too high. They contend that Pat Fischer, an eight-year veteran and twice all-pro, was not comparable to plaintiff, an untried "rookie"; and that the trial court's hypothesis of a three-year "fully guaranteed" contract was speculative, since no Redskins' first-round draft choice and no defensive back in NFL history rookie or veteran had ever negotiated such advantageous terms.

The computation of damages in antitrust cases invariably has a certain Alice-in-Wonderland quality to it....

* * *

For these reasons, we conclude that the trial judge's hypothesis of a fully guaranteed, three-year contract can be characterized only as a "speculative guess." There is no evidence on which this hypothesis could be founded, no evidence from which it could be inferred. We accordingly remand this case to the District Court for recomputation of damages.

Affirmed in part, reversed in part, and remanded for proceedings consistent with this opinion.

[*Smith* is the key appellate court decision on the rookie draft's legality under antitrust law. The majority ruling elicited a lengthy and vigorous dissent by Judge Mackinnon, which is the most effective judicial statement of the antitrust point of view consistently presented by all professional sports leagues. It remains to be seen whether the Supreme Court will embrace these arguments when it finally accepts a case raising substantive antitrust issues in professional sports.]

* * *

MACKINNON, CIRCUIT JUDGE, dissenting.

* * *

The Nature of the Business.

A critical fact "peculiar to the business" as presently constituted is that the component members of the NFL are not economically competitive with each other. In 1968, the NFL operated through 26 separate corporations in an economic joint venture which fielded teams and thereby furnished entertainment and continue to do so today to paid spectators and a large television audience. Each team has a substantial economic stake in the financial success of all the other teams.

* * *

Professional sports teams are in some respects traditional economic units seeking to sell a product to the public. But economic competition between teams is not and cannot be the sole determinant of their behavior. Professional sports leagues are uniquely organized economic entities; the ultimate success of the league depends on the economic cooperation rather than the economic competition of its members. The product being offered to the public is more than an isolated exhibition, it is a series of connected exhibitions that culminate in the annual grand finale contest between the two teams with the best records in the League, which have demonstrated their prowess in organized, rigidly scheduled League competition. The product being offered the public is the "league sport," and the value of this product at the stadium gate and to the television networks depends on the competitive balance of the teams in the league. Spectators and television viewers are not interested in lopsided games or contests between weak teams.

In many respects, the business of professional football as carried on by the NFL resembles a "natural monopoly." The structure of the League as a single entity outside the antitrust laws was also specifically authorized in 1966 by Act of Congress. As defined by two authorities, a natural monopoly is a monopoly resulting from economies of scale, a relationship between the size of the market and the size of the most efficient firm such that one firm of efficient size can produce all or more than the market can take at a remunerative price, and can continually expand its capacity at less cost than that of a new firm entering the business. In this situation, competition may exist for a time but only until bankruptcy or merger leaves the field to one firm; in a meaningful sense, competition here is self-destructive. At the present time, the NFL, as an organized association of various teams (or firms), has a statutorily recognized monopoly over production of the "league sport" of major professional football. Anyone who wishes to watch a major professional football game must watch an NFL game, played under NFL rules with NFL teams and players. History suggests that it is easier for the NFL to expand the number of teams than it is for another league to form and operate successfully. Competition may exist for a time, as the experiences of the American Football League and the World Football League demonstrate, but in the long run such competition is destructive and many teams fail, even as they did within the NFL in its free market formative years.

The History and Effect of the Draft.

[Here Judge Mackinnon detailed a number of features of life in the NFL in the mid–1930s at the time the draft was adopted. There were just 9 teams with squads of 22 to 26 players. Though a free market existed for players coming out of college, a career in professional football was not that attractive to many players as they graduated from college. Many opted to go on to graduate or professional school, to go into business, or into college or high school football coaching. These alternatives were attractive as compared to the NFL, where salaries were modest, careers were short, and there was always a possibility of a permanently disabling injury.]

* * *

Prior to the first draft, there was a "free market" for players' services. Even so, players' salaries were very modest, and limited club incomes made many franchises precarious. The League would go through 40 franchises before it reached its present stability, with 28 teams. The testimony shows that the Chicago Bears, even though they won the League Championship in 1932, lost $18,000; George Halas, their coach and owner, at the end of the season had to give promissory notes for $1,000 each to Bronko Nagurski and Red Grange for the balance due on their salaries.

The college player draft was adopted in 1935 at the suggestion of Bert Bell, after Cincinnati (which finished the season as the St. Louis Gunners), the bottom team in the Western Division in 1934, had been forced to drop out of the then 10–team league. The 1935 draft as adopted was a pure draft simple, uncomplicated, and complete. The team with the poorest winning record drafted first; the others followed in inverse order to their won-lost record; the team with the best record in the prior season drafted last. In its early years, the draft covered 30 rounds, but was later reduced to 17 rounds.

The draft was first conducted in 1936 and has continued annually for the last 42 years. If we assume that roughly 400 players have been drafted each year, approximately 17,000 players have been drafted by professional football teams. What is significant about this large number is that, although a great many players have been affected by the draft, there have been a relatively insignificant number of lawsuits challenging the validity of the draft as conducted by the NFL. This case is stated to be one of first impression attacking the legality of the draft under the antitrust laws. It is also a material fact, of considerable significance, that no case has been pointed to where the Antitrust Division of the Department of Justice has ever attacked the validity of a player draft in any professional sport.

In my view, there are compelling reasons why the draft has continued so long without serious challenge. In effect a player draft is *natural* for league sports. Competitive equality among the component teams is an inherent requirement for meaningful sports competition and the survival of a conference or league high school, college, or professional and all of its members. Close rivalries are the backbone of any successful sport. When the NFL established the draft, its objective was to give each team the same fair *opportunity* to be competitive; it sought to achieve a competitive balance among all the League's teams, that is, to "try to equalize the teams." The intended result was to create a situation where each League game would become a closer contest, where spectator interest in the game and the players themselves would be increased, where the interesting individual contests would create an interesting League championship race, and where ultimately the teams and their players would benefit from the greater income resulting from the increased fan interest.

* * *

All major sports, in recognition of the need for competitive balance, have drafts. Hockey and basketball have drafts, and baseball instituted a draft when it became clear from the long domination of the New York Yankees that the farm system was not producing competitive balance.

Since the first college football player draft was held in 1936, the results sought to be accomplished have clearly been achieved. Some argue that this has been caused by other factors, but the preponderance of the factual testimony and record evidence supports a conclusion that the college player draft was the key factor which produced the competitive balance of the teams, which in turn brought about the exciting games and interesting championship races and increased public interest in the sport, which ultimately led to the huge gate receipts and large television contracts that are presently producing enormous benefits for the players themselves. There was no showing to the contrary in the 2,000 page record. The majority argue that it is television that produces the interest and the revenues but the balanced teams produced by the draft came first and caused the close contests which attracted the public and eventually television.

Since 1935, the number of teams has increased from 9 to today's League of 28 teams, and the number of players per team has also been increased substantially. Instead of the small squads of around 26 players in the early days of the sport, the modern team's roster once swelled to 47 and was later reduced to 43 players. This has increased the total number of active players in the League as a whole to slightly over 1,200. Gate receipts have increased tremendously due to the increased popular interest in the game. Also important are the television revenues, which constitute a large part of each team's annual income. The NFL television contracts between the League and the television networks have distributed hundreds of millions of dollars to all teams in the League; and current news reports indicate that the payments are to be substantially increased. The lucrative television contract, made possible by an *exemption* from the antitrust laws enacted by Congress, is negotiated for all teams by the League Commissioner. These moneys are distributed *equally* to each team in the League without regard to the size of the team's local television market. In 1968 the revenues from television accounted for approximately 30 percent of the total revenue of the Redskins and this was approximately the same percentage as the average for all NFL teams in that year. Team revenue from gate receipts, television contracts, and other sources has increased tremendously since 1935, and the NFL teams and their players are the direct recipients of the benefits of the increased national interest in NFL games. College players, 22 years old, coming out of college in 1976 and playing in the NFL were making $20,000 to $150,000 their first year.

* * *

Due to the increased benefits afforded professional football players, the competition for graduating college football players that previously existed from lucrative coaching positions and numerous other business and professional opportunities has been successfully met, if not altogether eliminated as a practical matter. The increasing popularity of pro football and its attractiveness to graduating college players assures those interested in the success of the game, such as television and radio broadcasters and networks, stadium owners, team owners, and players already playing in the NFL, that the best college football players year after year will continue to join the professional ranks and assure the quality and attractiveness of their games. In fact, a great many players now go to college for the sole purpose of establishing a playing record which will result in their being drafted by one of the professional teams; a first-round draft choice in the professional league is viewed by many as the substantial equivalent of *summa cum laude* and first-round draft choices are generally paid much higher starting salaries.

* * *

From my analysis, the testimony of record overwhelmingly supports the conclusion that the growth of football between 1935 and 1968 was largely due to the competitive balance that the League achieved during those years and to the creation of a quality product, the "league sport." This competitive balance, and the consequential tremendous growth in public interest, which has inured greatly to the benefit of the players themselves, is in large part a result of the college player draft.... The draft created the competitive balance, that created the public interest, that led other cities to organize teams, that led to national expansion of the league, that enlarged the total gate receipts, that led to the large revenue producing television contracts.

[The dissent then addressed the majority's argument that a less restrictive draft system should have been devised by the NFL.]

* * *

A pure draft takes all of the college players that are coming into the market with the teams with the poorest records having preference in the order of their won and lost records. The draft as it existed in 1968 was a pure draft, and it is submitted that the draft should be that extensive if the opportunity for maximum competitive balance is to be assured. If the draft only lasts two rounds, as the trial court here suggested, the rest of the players are left for the free market and the preponderance of those players, or at least the preponderance of the better players in that group, would go to teams with special attractions and the teams owned by super-wealthy millionaires who desire very greatly to own a winning team. Not even a complete sharing of team revenues could overcome the unfair advantage posed by wealthy owners and collateral attractions of a few cities. Large cities such as New York, Chicago, Los Angeles, and Washington offer special advantages for publicity, endorsements, and lucrative off-field jobs in business. Cities with better weather are more attractive to some players, and teams with better prospects of winning in a particular season furnish a certain attraction for some players. Larger cities with larger stadiums realize more income and hence are somewhat able to offer larger salaries than teams with smaller cities and stadiums. So are teams owned by wealthy sportsmen who place a premium on winning and are willing to support their desires with almost unlimited financial resources. The draft has substantially reduced the ability of these owners to dominate the league.

Given these factors that would permit a few teams to corner the "developing players" that in a great many instances eventually surpass developed players, drafted in the earlier rounds, it is necessary to have a draft that reaches the *maximum number of potential players who are absolutely necessary to preserve competitive balance.* When the draft does not reach that many players, the few stronger teams with the natural advantages will be able to corner the best remaining prospects who become free agents. The testimony indicated that a few "super wealthy" owners with a very deep pocketbook could obtain a very substantial advantage if there were a substantial pool of free market players.

* * *

The Rule of Reason and the College Player Draft.

* * *

[T]he important consideration is the *effect* of the draft. The majority concludes that the draft strips the players of "any real bargaining power," lowers their salaries, and suppresses if not destroys competition for their services. I disagree. The majority opinion and the trial court only looked at the draft from the players' side and only at a portion of that. As for bargaining power, the operation of the draft also restrains the team from dealing with other players (even though there are exceptions, discussed below). This is particularly true when a team drafts for a position, as the Redskins did in drafting Smith as their first-round choice in 1968. The Redskins drafted Smith in the first round to fill a need at the "free safety position." In using their first-round draft choice to select a player for that particular position, they practically put all of their eggs in one basket for that year. In selecting Smith, they passed over or did not reach, all other players of nearly equal ability for that position. After the Redskins had exercised their first draft selection, these other players would be chosen by other teams with later picks, and would thus not be available in later rounds. Even if another player was later available, it would be a waste of a valuable draft choice for the Redskins to use any subsequent choice to draft for that same position, since the position needed only one player and the team had other needs to fill as well. That is the way the 1968 player draft went for the Redskins. After they had drafted Smith first to fill that position, the team practically had to sign him if they wanted to fill what they considered was a vital team vacancy. These circumstances gave Smith very substantial bargaining leverage, as his professional negotiating agent frequently reminded the Redskins. Also, a first-round draft choice commands considerable publicity in the locality, and the team is under very considerable pressure from its fans to sign the player and thereby put the first-round pick in a uniform. Smith was the beneficiary, as a first-round choice, of such public pressure.

While in a free market a player could negotiate with several teams, a team could also negotiate with several players of nearly equal ability and play one off against the others. If Smith had negotiated with the Redskins in a free market, the Redskins could also have simultaneously negotiated with the next-best prospect for free safety as well and the availability of the other player might have served to reduce the salary offers to Smith. Then if Smith and the Redskins could not come to terms, the Redskins could always opt for one of the other prospects they considered to be close to Smith in ability, well realizing, as experience has many times proven, that the ultimate development and performance of the second or third choice might eventually eclipse that of their first favored choice. Drafting college players is not an exact science.

* * *

Simply because the draft is essential to the vitality of the business does not mean that players entering the League, as opposed to veterans already playing in the League, have no interest in the existence of a draft. It would be error to suggest otherwise because without a draft a less stable League with fewer franchises and lower salaries would result. Incoming players receive salaries and bonuses far in excess of what they could command in a free market of teams in a league that did not have the competitive balance which a player draft produces. The vitality of the League, which is admittedly dependent in large measure on the balanced team competition produced by the draft, has attracted so great a public interest that the public in most localities, as referred to above, has subsidized the teams by the erection of huge stadiums without full contribution to their cost by the teams that use them. This fact has enabled salaries paid to draftees to be higher than what they would be in a free market with the attendant destructive competition, unequal competitive balance, and resulting shaky franchises. It cannot be said that rookie players have no interest in the existence of the college player draft.

In short, in my opinion, the evidentiary record here supports the conclusion that the draft also has a favorable effect on the bargaining position of players, which to a considerable extent nets out the adverse effect it has in limiting the players' right to negotiate with other teams.

And this bargaining equivalency vitiates the assertion that players' salaries are depressed on account of the draft.

Questions for Discussion

1. Is the *Smith* majority's analysis in the first part of the opinion, which defends the competitive values of the draft against a charge of *per se* illegality, fully compatible with its analysis in the second part of the opinion, which condemns the anticompetitive effect of the draft under the Rule of Reason?

2. In several very long footnotes, the *Smith* majority and dissent debated a number of the factual underpinnings to their respective arguments:

   a) Was it the player draft, instituted in 1935, or network television, which emerged in the late 1950s, that was the true source of pro football's economic success?

   b) How much competitive balance can really be contributed by the rookie draft (or restraints on veteran free agency), given the team dynasties associated with head coaches such as Paul Brown, Vince Lombardi, Tom Landry, Don Shula, Chuck Noll, and Bill Walsh? Does the NFL need comparable restraints on free agency for coaches (who almost invariably negotiate multi-year no-cut contracts)?

   c) Is the true secret of evenly balanced athletic competition the sharing of revenues, not just from network and cable television but also, in the NFL, from gate receipts? What effect might such league "socialism" have on teams' ability and incentive to pay their players higher salaries?

3. The *Smith* majority seems to state that it is irrelevant for Rule of Reason analysis that a league practice such as the draft enhances competitive balance within the league. Is that position compatible with the Supreme Court's observations quoted earlier in this chapter, to the effect that improvements in the economic efficiency of an enterprise may actually be procompetitive for the broader economy? Indeed, if a league cannot defend the legality of restrictive internal practices on the grounds that they improve the quality of the product offered to its fans, how could a less restrictive draft pass muster, as the *Smith* majority intimates in the latter part of its decision?

4. The principal argument for the draft is that this system is necessary to preserve balanced athletic competition against the threat posed by big market teams. But is there any guarantee that the draft will have that effect, at least as long as teams can sell their top picks to other clubs? Consider, for example, the significance of the Quebec Nordiques dealing Eric Lindros to the Philadelphia Flyers in 1992, for $15 million and five players. (The Nordiques franchise was purchased in 1989 for $15 million.) In addition, is it possible that the draft also obstructs achievement of such competitive balance? Does not the football draft guarantee the Super Bowl winner's rights to valued players that may obstruct the ability of weaker teams to make rapid improvements in their relative strength? Can you

think of ways to restructure the draft to enhance its contribution to equality on the playing field?

5. Opponents of the draft assert that it permits exploitation of new players, who are left with no choice but to accept a "take it or leave it" offer by the drafting team, the only team they are permitted to deal with. Yet in sports like football or basketball, top rookie draft picks have been signing multiyear contracts worth tens of millions of dollars: for example, in 1992, Shaquille O'Neal received a $40 million, 7–year deal from the Orlando Magic. Even in a less wealthy sport such as hockey, Eric Lindros signed that same year a $21 million, 6–year contract with the Philadelphia Flyers. Why do teams feel compelled to make such lucrative offers to their draft picks? Does player leverage have anything to do with league rules that define how long an unsigned draft pick remains on the reserve list of the club that drafted him? In any event, do today's rich offers by teams suggest that players may be worth even more to the franchises than the large sums they are currently receiving? If so, are there ways one might restructure the draft to ensure that teams do offer drafted players their full economic value, while still preserving sufficient competitive balance among teams on the playing field?

6. The previous questions suggest the possibility of "more reasonable" or "less restrictive" alternatives to the current "restraint of trade" flowing from the draft. How does the concept of "less restrictive alternative" fit within antitrust law as envisaged by the Supreme Court in *Professional Engineers*? Is such an alternative simply a factor to be considered, or one that dictates the ultimate antitrust result?

For example, if a court believes that pro football with the existing draft is more procompetitive (more attractive to fans) than football without a draft, does the possibility of a less restrictive draft (one that has less anticompetitive impact on the players market) make the existing system illegal? How does one judge which version of the draft is more or less restrictive as far as players are concerned; compare a three-round draft with players tied to the drafting team for two years to a six-round draft with players tied to the team for just one year? How does one then compare the incremental gains to players from relaxing the draft's prohibition against teams bidding for rookies to the incremental losses to fans from a reduction in competitive athletic balance within the league (on the assumption that the draft does contribute at least some measure of competitive equality)? Does the process of antitrust litigation about these issues give the league sufficient guidance in designing its system for allocating new players to the teams? Does the threat of litigation give the league the incentive to explore more optimal solutions along both dimensions of this issue?

7. The NFL's 1993 litigation settlement, which authorizes a seven-round annual draft, establishes for the first time in professional sports a maximum limit on the amount of money that a team can pay each year to its entire group of first year players. This comes close to establishing, *de facto,* a rookie wage scale. Unless this system is entitled to an antitrust exemption, it would surely be challenged as a violation of section 1. With what result? If you believe the previous draft system without a rookie

salary cap was exploitative, is this system more or less so? Why would the players association be willing to agree to this limitation on the salary amounts rookies can negotiate? Consider these questions as you read the next case involving salary restraints.

Note on Draft Eligibility

Player draft rules specify not only what happens to the players after the draft, but also which players are eligible to be drafted in the first place.[5] Traditionally, the key eligibility rule in football and basketball was that a player was not included in the draft until four years had elapsed after his high school class had graduated (thus dovetailing with the standard four-year eligibility period in college sports). This historic practice was challenged in 1970 by Spencer Haywood. After graduating from high school in 1967, Haywood starred in junior college basketball for one year, in the 1968 Olympic Games, and then at the University of Detroit for one year (where he was an All–American). Granted a "hardship" exemption by the new American Basketball Association (*whose* hardship?), Haywood won ABA rookie of the year and most valuable player honors in the 1969–1970 season. In 1970, Haywood was interested in playing for the Seattle Supersonics in the NBA, but he was barred by Commissioner Walter Kennedy under the NBA's four-year rule. In response, Haywood launched and won an antitrust suit striking down this eligibility rule in one of the first-ever successful player antitrust cases. See *Denver Rockets v. All–Pro Management, Inc.*, 325 F.Supp. 1049 (C.D.Cal.1971). *Haywood* was followed by *Linseman v. World Hockey Ass'n*, 439 F.Supp. 1315 (D.Conn.1977), which struck down the WHA's (and implicitly the National Hockey League's) age–20 eligibility rule (which dovetailed with the "graduation" age from Canadian junior hockey), and *Boris v. United States Football League*, 1984–1 Trade Cases (CCH) ¶ 66,012, 1984 WL 894 (C.D.Cal.1984), which invalidated a USFL rule that (like the pre–1990 NFL rule) required football players to exhaust their college eligibility before being drafted.

In *Haywood*, *Linseman*, and *Boris*, though, the federal district judges applied rather strange versions of the *per se* antitrust ban on group boycotts to these eligibility rules, an approach clearly incompatible with the Rule of Reason analysis now used in all appellate sports cases (including *Smith* above and *Mackey* below). In 1990, to some extent because of the specter of antitrust litigation, the NFL finally relaxed its own four-year eligibility rule for the football draft. We now have a good deal of experience with drafting young players in basketball and hockey, and some experience in football. For example, in the first three years in football, approximately 35 players a year opted for the draft. While a considerable number were not selected by any team in any of the twelve rounds, in 1992 four of the first five picks and 11 of the 28 chosen in the first round were underclassmen.

Questions for Discussion

1. Should a court reach the same result as in *Haywood* if it now undertook a full-blown Rule of Reason analysis, one that takes into account

---

5. See Robert A. McCormick & Matthew C. McKinnon, *Professional Football's Draft Eligibility Rule: The Labor Exemp-* *tion and the Antitrust Laws*, 33 Emory L.J. 375 (1984).

the interests of the young players (both those drafted and those not) and the leagues (both professional and college or junior leagues)? Suppose, for example, the NFL were to follow the suggestion of Bill Walsh, a great coach in both professional and college football, and set a minimum *age* for draft eligibility. How would one go about determining the appropriate age?

2. Consider also the other side of the coin. Both the professional and the college leagues presently require a player who petitions for inclusion in the professional draft to renounce his college eligibility. What are the likely market effects of these parallel arrangements? Are they questionable under antitrust law? We shall take this issue up in more detail in Chapter 9.

3. It is more than historical coincidence that professional leagues' draft rules dovetailed with college eligibility periods. Professional leagues wanted to maintain good relations with colleges who have provided minor league training free of charge to future professional football and basketball players. Now a large group of college football coaches, unhappy with premature loss of an increasing number of their underclassmen, have agreed on a plan to deny NFL scouting combines easy access to *all* their college players (seniors as well as underclassmen). Does this agreement raise some antitrust concerns?

4. Professional leagues have other reasons for excluding certain players from their rosters. One important factor was discussed in Chapter 1— the athlete's involvement in gambling scandals or other indices of poor moral character that threaten the "best interests of the sport." Another reason is the desire to protect players from serious injury (and the league from serious liability)—for example, a young hockey player with sight in only one eye (see *Neeld v. NHL*, 594 F.2d 1297 (9th Cir.1979)). We will address the latter problem in Chapter 11.

2. SALARY RESTRAINTS

In 1987 the NFL devised a "development squad" system under which each team was permitted to sign as many as six rookies or first-year free agents who could practice but not play with the team. The league fixed the salaries payable to each development squad player at $1,000 per week, rather than permit individual teams to negotiate amounts that had ranged up to $7,000 per week for some of these players in their previous rookie year. The NFL's stated objective was to "promote competitive equality under fiscally responsible circumstances." However, the federal district judge granted the plaintiffs summary judgment on their antitrust claim, on the grounds that this salary rule was both anticompetitive and not justifiable under the Rule of Reason.

BROWN v. PRO FOOTBALL, INC.
(WASHINGTON REDSKINS)

United States District Court, District of Columbia, 1992.

1992–1 Trade Cases (CCH) ¶ 69,747, 1992 WL 88039.

LAMBERTH, DISTRICT JUDGE.

* * *

Defendants cannot claim that the uniform salary provision was not significantly anticompetitive in its effect. The uniform salary provision prohibited clubs from paying Developmental Squad players anything but $1,000 per week. This prohibition necessarily eliminated all competition and prevented prospective Developmental Squad players from negotiating salary terms among interested NFL clubs. The salary restraint robbed each seller of football services of any bargaining power, left no room "for competition among the teams for the services of [rookie and first year] players, and utterly strip[ped] them of any measure of control over the marketing of their talents." While the impact of the restraint on any given plaintiff, whether positive or negative, is not presently before the court, the effect of the uniform salary provision was to "suppress or even destroy competition."

* * *

Defendants' primary procompetitive claim is that [its] Resolution "promotes competitive balance in the league by eliminating (1) 'stashing' of quality players and (2) consequent disparities in the number of players available for practice purposes." This procompetitive purpose allegedly "enhances the quality of the [NFL's] entertainment product and benefits 'consumers' of NFL football."[14] Defendants claim that "[b]y stashing quality players and consequently accumulating extra players for practice purposes, [some] teams secured an 'unfair' advantage that threatened to undermine the competitive balance crucial to producing the NFL's popular entertainment product." This Circuit has expressly found defendants' proffered "competitive balance" and "better product" purposes to be irrelevant to the rule of reason analysis. *Smith*, 593 F.2d at 1186.

Because the discussion in *Smith* directly addresses and disposes of the issues presently before this court, the discussion will be reproduced in its entirety below, replacing the draft restraint in *Smith* with the fixed salary restraint involved in the present case:

> The NFL has endeavored to summarize this justification by saying that the [fixed salary] ultimately has a "procompetitive" effect, yet this shorthand entails no small risk of confusion. The [fixed

---

14. While the court acknowledges some correlation between the "stashing" point and the salary restraint, the court does not see the correlation of the number of practice players each team has to the salary restraint itself. Because the basis for both the stashing and equalization objectives (promoting competitive balance among the NFL clubs), is irrelevant to the rule of reason inquiry, however, the court need not address the correlation or lack thereof. The court also notes that the rule of reason analysis "does not open the field of antitrust inquiry to any argument in favor of a challenged restraint that may fall within the realm of reason.... [The] inquiry instead must be confined to a consideration of the restraints' impact on competitive conditions." *Smith*, 593 F.2d at 1186.

salary] is "procompetitive," if at all, in a very different sense from that in which it is anticompetitive. The [fixed salary] is anticompetitive in its effect on the market for players' services because it virtually eliminates economic competition among buyers for the services of sellers. The [fixed salary] is allegedly "procompetitive" in its effect on the playing field.... Because the [fixed salary's] "anticompetitive" and "procompetitive" effects are not comparable, it is impossible to "net them out" in the usual rule-of-reason balancing. The [fixed salary's] "anticompetitive evils," in other words, cannot be balanced against its "procompetitive virtues," and the [fixed salary restraint can] be upheld [only] if the latter outweigh the former. In strict economic terms, the [fixed salary's] demonstrated procompetitive effects are nil.

Smith, 593 F.2d at 1186 (citing *National Soc'y of Professional Eng'rs v. United States*, 435 U.S. 679 (1978)).[15] The court finds that the NFL's alleged procompetitive purposes are either insufficient as a matter of law because they fail to justify the necessity of the salary restraint or they are not relevant to the rule of reason analysis.

Judgment granted.

———————

Irrespective of the final verdict about the antitrust legality of the NFL's development squad system, is this court's dismissal of the league's competitive balance argument for its antitrust Rule of Reason analysis compatible with the Supreme Court's recent pronouncements about the value of economic efficiency in antitrust and the potentially procompetitive impact of certain kinds of internal organizational restraints?

3. VETERAN FREE AGENCY

The following case, *Mackey v. NFL*, posed two different kinds of issues. One issue was the compatibility with substantive antitrust policy of the "Rozelle Rule," the NFL's practice of requiring the team that signed a veteran free agent to provide "fair and equitable" compensation (by way of players, draft choices, or both) to the team that had lost the player off its roster. This practice developed in football in the early 1960s (as well as in basketball after the *Barnett* ruling in Chapter 2), in place of the apparently perpetual option contained in baseball's (and hockey's) lifetime reserve system that figured in the *Chase* and *Flood* cases in Chapter 2. The players' objection to the

---

15. Any claim that the fixed salary provision made the developmental squads themselves more competitive or comparable with each other is likewise rejected. Because the developmental squads did not compete with each other directly, it is obvious that the purpose of any claimed competitive balance among the developmental squads was to promote greater competitive equality among the parent NFL clubs. Such a competitive equality argument, as discussed above, is irrelevant to the antitrust balancing analysis presently before the court.

Rozelle Rule was that while football players formally became free agents at the end of their contracts, as a practical matter they had no more ability to sign with other teams than did baseball players bound by the reserve clause—and, unlike baseball, football is subject to antitrust law.

A second key issue introduced in *Mackey* stemmed from the fact that several years after Commissioner Rozelle instituted the compensation rule, this practice was incorporated in the first collective agreement negotiated between the NFL and its Players Association. The question was whether this free agency restriction had thereby gained a "labor exemption" from antitrust scrutiny.

We first reproduce the portion of *Mackey* that addressed the substantive issue of the compatibility of the Rozelle Rule with antitrust law's bar on "unreasonable restraints of trade."

MACKEY v. NATIONAL FOOTBALL LEAGUE (PART 1)

United States Court of Appeals, Eighth Circuit, 1976.

543 F.2d 606.

LAY, CIRCUIT JUDGE.

* * *

HISTORY.

Throughout most of its history, the NFL's operations have been unilaterally controlled by the club owners. In 1968, however, the NLRB recognized the NFLPA as a labor organization, and as the exclusive bargaining representative of all NFL players. Since that time, the NFLPA and the clubs have engaged in collective bargaining over various terms and conditions of employment. Two formal agreements have resulted. The first, concluded in 1968, was in effect from July 15, 1968 to February 1, 1970. The second, entered into on June 17, 1971, was made retroactive to February 1, 1970, and expired on January 30, 1974. Since 1974, the parties have been negotiating; however, they have not concluded a new agreement.

For a number of years, the NFL has operated under a reserve system whereby every player who signs a contract with an NFL club is bound to play for that club, and no other, for the term of the contract plus one additional year at the option of the club. The cornerstones of this system are § 15.1 of the NFL Constitution and By-laws, which requires that all club-player contracts be as prescribed in the Standard Player Contract adopted by the League, and the option clause embodied in the Standard Player Contract. Once a player signs a Standard Player Contract, he is bound to his team for at least two years. He may, however, become a free agent at the end of the option year by playing that season under a renewed contract rather than signing a new one. A player "playing out his option" is subject to a 10% salary cut during the option year.

Prior to 1963, a team which signed a free agent who had previously been under contract to another club was not obligated to compensate the player's former club. In 1963, after R. C. Owens played out his option with the San Francisco 49ers and signed a contract with the Baltimore Colts, the member clubs of the NFL unilaterally adopted the following provision, now known as the Rozelle Rule, as an amendment to the League's Constitution and By-laws:

Rule

> Any player, whose contract with a League club has expired, shall thereupon become a free agent and shall no longer be considered a member of the team of that club following the expiration date of such contract. Whenever a player, becoming a free agent in such manner, thereafter signed a contract with a different club in the League, then, unless mutually satisfactory arrangements have been concluded between the two League clubs, the Commissioner may name and then award to the former club one or more players, from the Active, Reserve, or Selection List (including future selection choices) of the acquiring club as the Commissioner in his sole discretion deems fair and equitable; any such decision by the Commissioner shall be final and conclusive.

This provision, unchanged in form, is currently embodied in § 12.1(H) of the NFL Constitution. The ostensible purposes of the rule are to maintain competitive balance among the NFL teams and protect the clubs' investment in scouting, selecting and developing players.

During the period from 1963 through 1974, 176 players played out their options. Of that number, 34 signed with other teams. In three of those cases, the former club waived compensation. In 27 cases, the clubs involved mutually agreed upon compensation. Commissioner Rozelle awarded compensation in the four remaining cases.

* * *

Antitrust Issues.

Issue

We turn, then, to the question of whether the Rozelle Rule, as implemented, violates § 1 of the Sherman Act, which declares illegal "every contract, combination ... or conspiracy, in restraint of trade or commerce among the several States." The district court found the Rozelle Rule to be a *per se* violation of the Act. Alternatively, the court held the Rule to be violative of the Rule of Reason standard.

Players' Services as a Product Market.

The clubs and the Commissioner first urge that the only product market arguably affected by the Rozelle Rule is the market for players' services, and that the restriction of competition for players' services is not a type of restraint proscribed by the Sherman Act. In support of this contention, defendants rely on § 6 of the Clayton Act, 15 U.S.C.

§ 17, and on language construing that statute in Apex Hosiery Co. v. Leader. Section 6 of the Clayton Act provides:

> The labor of a human being is not a commodity or article of commerce. Nothing contained in the antitrust laws shall be construed to forbid the existence and operation of labor, agricultural, or horticultural organizations, instituted for the purposes of mutual help, and not having capital stock or conducted for profit, or to forbid or restrain individual members of such organizations from lawfully carrying out the legitimate objects thereof; nor shall such organizations, or the members thereof, be held or construed to be illegal combinations or conspiracies in restraint of trade, under the antitrust laws.

Based on this section, the Supreme Court, in Apex, observed:

> [I]t would seem plain that restraints on the sale of the employee's services to the employer, however much they curtail the competition among employees, are not in themselves combinations or conspiracies in restraint of trade or commerce under the Sherman Act.

On the surface, the language relied on by defendants lends merit to the defense. However, we cannot overlook the context in which the language arose. Section 6 of the Clayton Act was enacted for the benefit of unions to exempt certain of their activities from the antitrust laws after courts had applied the Sherman Act to legitimate labor activities. . . . In Apex, the Court condoned restrictions on competition for employee services imposed by the employees themselves, not by employers.

In other cases concerning professional sports, courts have not hesitated to apply the Sherman Act to club owner imposed restraints on competition for players' services. . . . In other contexts, courts have subjected similar employer imposed restraints to the scrutiny of the antitrust laws. We hold that restraints on competition within the market for players' services fall within the ambit of the Sherman Act.

Per Se Violation.

We review next the district court's holding that the Rozelle Rule is *per se* violative of the Sherman Act.

* * *

The district court found that the Rozelle Rule operates to significantly deter clubs from negotiating with and signing free agents. By virtue of the Rozelle Rule, a club will sign a free agent only where it is able to reach an agreement with the player's former team as to compensation, or where it is willing to risk the awarding of unknown compensation by the Commissioner. The court concluded that the Rozelle Rule, as enforced, thus constituted a group boycott and a concerted refusal to deal, and was a *per se* violation of the Sherman Act.

There is substantial evidence in the record to support the district court's findings as to the effects of the Rozelle Rule. We think, however, that this case presents unusual circumstances rendering it inappropriate to declare the Rozelle Rule illegal *per se* without undertaking an inquiry into the purported justifications for the Rule.

[T]he line of cases which has given rise to *per se* illegality for the type of agreements involved here generally concerned agreements between business competitors in the traditional sense. Here, however, as the owners and Commissioner urge, the NFL assumes some of the characteristics of a joint venture in that each member club has a stake in the success of the other teams. No one club is interested in driving another team out of business, since if the League fails, no one team can survive. Although businessmen cannot wholly evade the antitrust laws by characterizing their operation as a joint venture, we conclude that the unique nature of the business of professional football renders it inappropriate to mechanically apply *per se* illegality rules here, fashioned in a different context. This is particularly true where, as here, the alleged restraint does not completely eliminate competition for players' services.

* * *

Rule of Reason.

The focus of an inquiry under the Rule of Reason is whether the restraint imposed is justified by legitimate business purposes, and is no more restrictive than necessary.

In defining the restraint on competition for players' services, the district court found that the Rozelle Rule significantly deters clubs from negotiating with and signing free agents; that it acts as a substantial deterrent to players playing out their options and becoming free agents; that it significantly decreases players' bargaining power in contract negotiations; that players are thus denied the right to sell their services in a free and open market; that as a result, the salaries paid by each club are lower than if competitive bidding were allowed to prevail; and that absent the Rozelle Rule, there would be increased movement in interstate commerce of players from one club to another.

We find substantial evidence in the record to support these findings. Witnesses for both sides testified that there would be increased player movement absent the Rozelle Rule. Two economists testified that elimination of the Rozelle Rule would lead to a substantial increase in player salaries. Carroll Rosenbloom, owner of the Los Angeles Rams, indicated that the Rams would have signed quite a few of the star players from other teams who had played out their options, absent the Rozelle Rule. Charles De Keado, an agent who represented Dick Gordon after he played out his option with the Chicago Bears, testified that the New Orleans Saints were interested in signing Gordon but did not do so because the Bears were demanding unreasonable compensation and the Saints were unwilling to risk an unknown award of compensation by the Commissioner. Jim McFarland, an end who played out his option with the St. Louis Cardinals, testified that he had endeavored to join the Kansas City Chiefs but was unable to do so because of the compensation asked by the Cardinals. Hank Stram, then coach and general manager of the Chiefs, stated that he probably would have given McFarland an opportunity to make his squad had he not been required to give St. Louis anything in return.

In support of their contention that the restraints effected by the Rozelle Rule are not unreasonable, the defendants asserted a number of justifications. First, they argued that without the Rozelle Rule, star players would flock to cities having natural advantages such as larger economic bases, winning teams, warmer climates, and greater media opportunities; that competitive balance throughout the League would thus be destroyed; and that the destruction of competitive balance would ultimately lead to diminished spectator interest, franchise failures, and perhaps the demise of the NFL, at least as it operates today. Second, the defendants contended that the Rozelle Rule is necessary to protect the clubs' investment in scouting expenses and player developments costs. Third, they asserted that players must work together for a substantial period of time in order to function effectively as a team; that elimination of the Rozelle Rule would lead to increased player movement and a concomitant reduction in player continuity; and that the quality of play in the NFL would thus suffer, leading to reduced spectator interest, and financial detriment both to the clubs and the players. Conflicting evidence was adduced at trial by both sides with respect to the validity of these asserted justifications.

The district court held the defendants' asserted justifications unavailing. As to the clubs' investment in player development costs, Judge Larson found that these expenses are similar to those incurred by other businesses, and that there is no right to compensation for this type of investment. With respect to player continuity, the court found that elimination of the Rozelle Rule would affect all teams equally in that regard; that it would not lead to a reduction in the quality of play; and that even assuming that it would, that fact would not justify the Rozelle Rule's anticompetitive effects. As to competitive balance and the consequences which would flow from abolition of the Rozelle Rule, Judge Larson found that the existence of the Rozelle Rule has had no material effect on competitive balance in the NFL. Even assuming that the Rule did foster competitive balance, the court found that there were other legal means available to achieve that end: e.g., the competition committee, multiple year contracts, and special incentives. The court further concluded that elimination of the Rozelle Rule would have no significant disruptive effects, either immediate or long term, on professional football. In conclusion the court held that the Rozelle Rule was unreasonable in that it was overly broad, unlimited in duration, unaccompanied by procedural safeguards, and employed in conjunction with other anticompetitive practices such as the draft, Standard Player Contract, option clause, and the no-tampering rules.

We agree that the asserted need to recoup player development costs cannot justify the restraints of the Rozelle Rule. That expense is an ordinary cost of doing business and is not peculiar to professional football. Moreover, because of its unlimited duration, the Rozelle Rule is far more restrictive than necessary to fulfill that need.

We agree, in view of the evidence adduced at trial with respect to existing players turnover by way of trades, retirements and new players entering the League, that the club owners' arguments respecting player continuity cannot justify the Rozelle Rule. We concur in the district court's conclusion that the possibility of resulting decline in the quality of play would not justify the Rozelle Rule. We do recognize, as did the district court, that the NFL has a strong and unique interest in maintaining competitive balance among its teams. The key issue is thus whether the Rozelle Rule is essential to the maintenance of competitive balance, and is no more restrictive than necessary. The district court answered both of these questions in the negative.

We need not decide whether a system of inter-team compensation for free agents moving to other teams is essential to the maintenance of competitive balance in the NFL. Even if it is, we agree with the district court's conclusion that the Rozelle Rule is significantly more restrictive than necessary to serve any legitimate purposes it might have in this regard. First, little concern was manifested at trial over the free movement of average or below average players. Only the movement of the better players was urged as being detrimental to football. Yet the Rozelle Rule applies to every NFL player regardless of his status or ability. Second, the Rozelle Rule is unlimited in duration. It operates as a perpetual restriction on a player's ability to sell his services in an open market throughout his career. Third, the enforcement of the Rozelle Rule is unaccompanied by procedural safeguards. A player has no input into the process by which fair compensation is determined. Moreover, the player may be unaware of the precise compensation demanded by his former team, and that other teams might be interested in him but for the degree of compensation sought.

* * *

In sum, we hold that the Rozelle Rule, as enforced, unreasonably restrains trade in violation of § 1 of the Sherman Act.

* * *

Appeal dismissed.

Questions for Discussion

1. Essentially the same questions as were posed earlier about the rookie draft can also be asked about the system that requires clubs who sign veteran free agents to compensate the players' former teams. Does this arrangement really contribute to stronger competition on the field, or does it inhibit the ability of weaker teams to catch up to their stronger

rivals? What lessons can be drawn from the experience within baseball before and after 1976 when (as we will see in the next chapter) free agency rights were given to six-year veterans? Or the lessons drawn from comparing the level of competitiveness in baseball with that in football over the last fifteen years, with football having reintroduced in 1977 an even more restrictive system than the Rozelle Rule (pursuant to the labor exemption we will explore in the next part of *Mackey*)?

2. Do limits on competition really produce unacceptable exploitation of players by the teams? Keep in mind that salaries paid by NFL clubs have soared over the same fifteen-year period. True, the average football player earns only about half the salary of the average baseball player. But what is more important—the *average* or the *median* salary in a sport? The average player *salary* or the average club *payroll*? The proportion of either salary figure to average club *revenues* ?

———

Whereas the rookie draft remained virtually the same in the years from *Smith* to the 1993 settlement in football, the period since *Mackey* (and *Flood*) has witnessed constant innovation and experimentation in the several leagues with different modes of free agency. Almost all of those variations were produced through collective bargaining with the players' association. One new model, however, was introduced unilaterally by NFL owners in 1988—Plan B. Under Plan B, each team was entitled to protect 37 players on its reserve list. Protected players, even if their contract had expired, were permitted to move to other NFL teams only if their current team chose not to match new offers received, and even though subject to the new team paying compensation to the player's current team (in the form of draft picks whose number and round vary with the size of the new salary offer). However, during the months of February and March, all unprotected players could try to negotiate a better deal with another club, which paid no compensation to the team that lost the player. If a player did not receive a better offer from another club, he could return to his existing team under whatever contract he enjoyed or was able to negotiate with the latter. In the four years of Plan B, many veteran players moved to other clubs for sizable signing bonuses and salary increases.

In 1989, eight players, backed by the NFLPA, challenged the NFL's Plan B restrictions on each team's 37 protected players, in a case styled *McNeil v. NFL.* As we will see in the next section, the players were able to avoid application of the labor exemption defense after the district judge held that the NFLPA had successfully renounced its status as a union bargaining agent. The merits of the antitrust issues were tried during the summer of 1992. On September 10, 1992, the jury returned a verdict finding that the NFL's veteran free agent rules violated the Rule of Reason. In responding to a series of special interrogatories, the jury indicated that Plan B harmed players by diminishing competition by NFL clubs for their services, that nonetheless the system contributed significantly to competitive balance among

NFL teams, but that the system was unreasonable because it was more restrictive than necessary for that purpose. The jury found that only four of the eight plaintiffs actually suffered damages—totalling $1.6 million. Once Judge Doty rendered a final judgment with an injunctive order, the NFL indicated it would appeal the verdict on several grounds, including that the jury's Rule of Reason analysis reflected in the special interrogatories and dictated by the court's instructions did not properly apply the *Professional Engineers* balancing test discussed earlier in this chapter. If an appeal were pursued, how should this issue have been resolved on appeal?

The reason these questions are posed as hypotheticals is that just before this book was completed, the NFL and the Players Association worked out a voluntary resolution of their long-standing legal and labor relations conflict. These settlement efforts were spurred by a burst of litigation that ensued after the *McNeil* verdict involving players other than the eight *McNeil* plaintiffs. A crucial issue presented in all of these cases was whether the NFL would be collaterally estopped by *McNeil* from relitigating the issue of whether the Plan B system violates the rule of reason, or alternatively, whether a different set of restrictions (Plan C) was permissible. One such suit filed in Minneapolis by ten unsigned veteran free agents several weeks into the season sought an injunction declaring them to be unrestricted free agents. After finding that the NFL would likely be estopped by *McNeil* from denying liability, Judge Doty entered a temporary restraining order giving the plaintiffs five days during which they would be unrestricted in negotiating with other teams. Three plaintiffs (Keith Jackson, Garin Veris, and Webster Slaughter) then signed contracts with new teams for significantly more money than their original clubs had been offering them. The remaining plaintiffs were either released by or signed new contracts with their clubs, resulting in dismissal of their suits as moot. Still another case was filed in Minneapolis with Philadelphia Eagles' Reggie White as the named plaintiff in a class action seeking to have the Plan B system declared illegal as to all players not otherwise involved in various suits pending around the country. Judge Doty deliberately withheld his judgment about this claim while he prodded both sides to negotiate a voluntary settlement of the overall conflict. The terms of this settlement package will be sketched at the end of this chapter.

C. LABOR EXEMPTION FROM ANTITRUST [6]

We now turn to the second key feature of the *Mackey* decision, the labor exemption from antitrust scrutiny. This version of the labor

---

6. Unlike the substantive antitrust questions posed about the rookie draft and veteran free agency, this topic has produced a voluminous legal literature.

Among the most notable pieces are, in chronological order, Michael S. Jacobs and Ralph Winter, *Antitrust Principles and Collective Bargaining: Of Superstars in Pe-*

exemption poses a different question from the one we raised earlier about *Brown* and *Smith*—whether antitrust's intrinsic focus on "consumer welfare" implies a lack of antitrust concern about employer power in the labor market. Under *Mackey*, the question was whether, even if the Sherman Act was meant to apply to collusive restraints in the labor market, antitrust policy must still be subordinate to a separate federal labor policy that has evolved through a number of statutes designed to foster and protect labor organizations and collective bargaining. This question took on real urgency in the sports world in the 1970s because almost all the important antitrust litigation about free agency restraints was either launched or backed by the player unions that had emerged by the late 1960s in all four major professional sports.

As *Mackey* and succeeding decisions exemplify, for the last two decades the sports arena has been the main battleground in the struggle over the purpose and scope of the labor exemption. Before reading these cases, then, we provide this capsule summary of the broader legal background.

There is a fundamental tension between antitrust law—which bars any "contract, combination, or conspiracy in restraint of trade"—and labor unions—whose *raison d'etre* is to organize and coordinate the efforts of employees in dealing collectively with their employer. Indeed, for the first two decades of its existence, judges used the Sherman Act more often against trade unions than against business corporations, and in *Loewe v. Lawlor*, 208 U.S. 274, 28 S.Ct. 301, 52 L.Ed. 488 (1908), the Supreme Court made it clear that this Act did apply to unions and their activities (there to a national consumer boycott against a nonunion hat manufacturer in Danbury, Connecticut).

Concerned about this threat to their very existence, let alone their effectiveness, unions belonging to the American Federation of Labor persuaded new Democratic President Woodrow Wilson (and his chief advisor on antitrust and labor issues, Louis Brandeis) to include in the 1914 Clayton Act amendments to the Sherman Act a new Section 6 which declared:

onage, 81 Yale L. J. 1 (1971); John C. Weistart, *Judicial Review of Labor Agreements: Lessons From the Sports Industry*, 44 Law and Contemp. Probs. 109 (Autumn, 1981); Philip J. Closius, *Not at the Behest of Non Labor Groups: A Revised Prognosis for a Maturing Sports Industry*, 24 Boston College L. Rev. 341 (1983); Gary R. Roberts, *Reconciling Federal Labor and Antitrust Policy: The Special Case of Sports League Labor Market Restraints*, 75 Georgetown L. J. 19 (1986); Gary R. Roberts, *Sports League Restraints on the Labor Market: The Failure of Stare Decisis*, 41 U. of Pittsburgh L. Rev. 337 (1986); Lee Gold-man, *The Labor Exemption to the Antitrust Laws as Applied to Employers' Labor Market Restraints in Sports and Non–Sports Markets*, (1989) Utah L. Rev. 617; and Ethan Lock, *The Scope of the Labor Exemption in Professional Sports*, (1989) Duke L. J. 339. Valuable recent treatments of this issue that are not specifically focused on sports include Douglas L. Leslie, *Principles of Labor Antitrust*, 66 Virginia L. Rev. 1183 (1980), and Robert H. Jerry and Donald E. Knebel, *Antitrust and Employer Restraints in Labor Markets*, 6 Indus. Rel. L. J. 173 (1984).

That the labor of a human being is not a commodity or article of commerce. Nothing contained in the anti-trust law shall be construed to forbid the existence and operation of labor ... organizations, instituted for the purposes of mutual help ... or to forbid or restrain individual members of such organizations from lawfully carrying out the legitimate objects thereof; nor shall such organizations, or the members thereof, be held or construed to be illegal combinations or conspiracies in restraint of trade, under the antitrust laws.

Samuel Gompers, founder and president of the AFL, celebrated this new section as the "Magna Charta of labor!" To buttress its legal force, Section 20 of the Clayton Act went on to state that in disputes between employers and employees about terms and conditions of employment, collective action undertaken by employees through strikes, picketing, and boycotts, should not "be considered or held to be violations of any law of the United States."

Despite the apparent breadth of this legislative directive, the Supreme Court held in *Duplex Printing Press Co. v. Deering*, 254 U.S. 443, 41 S.Ct. 172, 65 L.Ed.2d 349 (1921), that the Clayton Act protected unions and their members from antitrust liability and federal court injunctions only when the union members were pursuing the "normal and legitimate objects" of a union, not when they "engage in an actual combination or conspiracy in restraint of trade." In *Duplex*, the Court held that a secondary boycott of the only major non-union printing press manufacturer in the country was outside the scope of Clayton Act protection and therefore could be enjoined under Section 1 of the Sherman Act.

During the Great Depression and the New Deal of the 1930s, labor was in a political position to secure the protection it thought it had won two decades earlier. Labor's first victory was the Norris–LaGuardia Act of 1932 (authored by then Harvard Law Professor Felix Frankfurter). This Act made it clear that regardless of whether a labor dispute went beyond the normal bounds of conflict between an employer and its immediate employees, federal courts could not enjoin strikes, pickets, and other forms of employee self help. Although the language of the Norris–LaGuardia Act referred only to issuance of federal *injunctive* remedies, nine years later now Justice Frankfurter authored the Supreme Court's decision in *United States v. Hutcheson*, 312 U.S. 219, 232, 61 S.Ct. 463, 466, 85 L.Ed. 788 (1941), involving a criminal antitrust prosecution, which read the Act as having tacitly overruled *Duplex* and restored the Clayton Act's intended protection of labor disputes from substantive antitrust *liability*:

> So long as a union acts in its self-interest and does not combine with non-labor groups, the licit and the illicit under Section 20 [of the Clayton Act] are not to be distinguished by any [judicial] judgment regarding the wisdom or unwisdom, the rightness or

wrongness, the selfishness or unselfishness of the end of which the particular union activities are the means.

This controversial reading of the Norris–LaGuardia Act was sufficient to give economic pressure by unions a blanket immunity from antitrust liability. Subsequent lower court decisions have held that employer self help through lockouts and strike insurance is similarly protected.[7] A question remained, though, whether the collective agreement that the union signs with the employer was also insulated from antitrust scrutiny. Although *Hutcheson* had extended its antitrust protection to the union only when the latter "does not combine with non-labor groups," it makes little sense to allow a union to strike to get a collective agreement from the employer, but then to subject the agreement itself to antitrust liability. This result seems even more anomalous from the perspective of the second leg of New Deal labor policy, the 1935 Wagner Act, which enacted the National Labor Relations Act (NLRA). The next chapter examines in depth the NLRA as it applies to the world of sports. For now it is sufficient to say that the Wagner Act created an affirmative right of employees to organize themselves into unions, and then imposed on the employer a duty to bargain in good faith with the union to arrive at a collective agreement. In the 1947 Taft–Hartley amendments to the NLRA, the duty to bargain in good faith was also imposed on unions. Both in practice and under the law, such bargaining is often conducted on a wide-ranging multi-employer basis.

The Supreme Court has not, however, been prepared to grant collective agreements the same blanket antitrust exemption that it has extended to strikes and lockouts. Perhaps the most important reason is that unions and employers may find it in their own interest to agree upon restrictive practices whose major impact is felt by outside compet-

---

7. For example, *Kennedy v. Long Island R.R. Co.,* 319 F.2d 366 (2d Cir.1963), dealt with a union antitrust suit against the railroads that collectively agreed to and financed a plan to insure their members against strikes (including a strike by the charging union in this case). To the argument that this multi-employer agreement constituted a "conspiracy in restraint of trade," the court of appeals responded:

> ... These assertions must also fail, for the fundamental reason that the named statutes were designed principally to outlaw restraints upon commercial competition in the marketing and pricing of goods and services and were not intended as instruments for the regulation of labor-management relations.

> Even were we to assume that the strike insurance plan in some way was the "cause" of an interruption in interstate commerce, the Supreme Court has clearly stated that "the Sherman Act ... does not condemn all combinations and conspiracies which interrupt interstate transportation," and that "the end sought was the prevention of restraints to free competition in business and commercial transactions which tended to restrict production, raise prices or otherwise control the market to the detriment of purchasers or consumers of goods and services." Appellants urge, however, that the price of labor is artificially manipulated whenever a railroad is permitted to avail itself of the proceeds of strike insurance. The answer lies in the clear language of section 6 of the Clayton Act, 15 U.S.C. § 17: "The labor of a human being is not a commodity or article of commerce." As an outstanding scholar in the field of labor law has noted: "No one seriously suggests that antitrust policy should be concerned with the labor market per se." Cox, *Labor and the Antitrust Laws—A Preliminary Analysis,* 104 U. of Pa. L. Rev. 252, 254 (1955).

itors to the immediate parties. In three key decisions, *Allen Bradley Co. v. IBEW*, 325 U.S. 797, 65 S.Ct. 1533, 89 L.Ed. 1939 (1945), *UMWA v. Pennington*, 381 U.S. 657, 85 S.Ct. 1585, 14 L.Ed.2d 626 (1965), and *Connell Construction Co. v. Plumbers and Steamfitters*, 421 U.S. 616, 95 S.Ct. 1830, 44 L.Ed.2d 418 (1975), the Supreme Court struggled to formulate a legal test to be applied to collective agreements having such external impact. The same problem has also arisen in the sports context when the operation of a collectively bargained lifetime reserve clause denies a new league access to the available supply of top-flight athletes whom the new league needs to survive as a serious competitor to the established league (see *Philadelphia World Hockey Club v. Philadelphia Hockey Club*, 351 F.Supp. 462 (E.D.Pa.1972)). We will return to this issue and this decision in Chapter 7 when we consider the implications of antitrust for interleague competition.

The problem in *Mackey*, and similar litigation in the sports world, is whether there can be antitrust liability when the principal impact of the terms of a collective agreement is felt by the parties themselves. For this problem, the single Supreme Court precedent is *Local Union No. 189, Amalgamated Meat Cutters v. Jewel Tea Co.*, 381 U.S. 676, 85 S.Ct. 1596, 14 L.Ed.2d 640 (1965). In that case, the union had insisted on inserting in its collective agreement with the Chicago grocery stores a provision that restricted to daytime hours the sale of fresh meat, in order to protect the unionized butchers from employer pressures to work in the evenings. When one of the stores that was subject to this agreement sued to strike down the provision as an antitrust violation, a divided Supreme Court held that this contract term was protected by the labor exemption. Justice White's plurality opinion contains this oft-cited passage (at 689–90) on the scope of the exemption:

> Thus the issue in this case is whether the marketing-hours restriction, like wages, and unlike prices, is so intimately related to wages, hours and working conditions [mandatory subjects of collective bargaining under the NLRA] that the union's successful attempt to obtain that provision through bona fide, arms' length bargaining in pursuit of their own labor union policies, and not at the behest of or in combination with non-labor groups, falls within the protection of the National Labor Policy and is therefore exempt from the Sherman Act.

With this judicial formula and its background in mind, as you read *Mackey* and the following cases consider the ways that courts have treated agreements by players associations to various restrictions on veteran free agency in professional sports.

MACKEY v. NATIONAL FOOTBALL LEAGUE (PART 2)

United States Court of Appeals, Eighth Circuit, 1976.

543 F.2d 606.

LAY, CIRCUIT JUDGE.

THE LABOR EXEMPTION ISSUE.

We review first the claim that the labor exemption immunizes the Commissioner and the clubs from liability under the antitrust laws.... *(Issue)*

HISTORY.

* * *

The players assert that only employee groups are entitled to the labor exemption and that it cannot be asserted by the defendants, an employer group. We must disagree. Since the basis of the nonstatutory exemption is the national policy favoring collective bargaining, and since the exemption extends to agreements, the benefits of the exemption logically extend to both parties to the agreement. Accordingly, under appropriate circumstances, we find that a non-labor group may avail itself of the labor exemption.

The clubs and the Commissioner claim the benefit of the nonstatutory labor exemption here, arguing that the Rozelle Rule was the subject of an agreement with the players union and that the proper accommodation of federal labor and antitrust policies requires that the agreement be deemed immune from antitrust liability. The plaintiffs assert that the Rozelle Rule was the product of unilateral action by the clubs and that the defendants cannot assert a colorable claim of exemption.

To determine the applicability of the nonstatutory exemption we must first decide whether there has been any agreement between the parties concerning the Rozelle Rule.

* * *

THE 1968 AGREEMENT.

At the outset of the negotiations preceding the 1968 agreement, the players did not seek elimination of the Rozelle Rule but felt that it should be modified. During the course of the negotiations, however, the players apparently presented no concrete proposals in that regard and there was little discussion concerning the Rozelle Rule. At trial, Daniel Shulman, a bargaining representative of the players, attributed their failure to pursue any modifications to the fact that the negotiations had bogged down on other issues and the union was not strong enough to persist.

The 1968 agreement incorporated by reference the NFL Constitution and By-laws, of which the Rozelle Rule is a part. Furthermore, it expressly provided that free agent rules shall not be amended during the life of the agreement.

THE 1970 AGREEMENT.   *I mplied*

At the start of the negotiations leading up to the 1970 agreement, it appears that the players again decided not to make an issue of the Rozelle Rule. The only reference to the Rule in the union's formal proposals presented at the outset of the negotiations was the following:

> The NFLPA is disturbed over reports from players who, after playing out their options, are unable to deal with other clubs because of the Rozelle Rule. A method should be found whereby a free agent is assured the opportunity to discuss contract with all NFL teams.

There was little discussion of the Rozelle Rule during the 1970 negotiations.

Although the 1970 agreement failed to make any express reference to the Rozelle Rule, it did contain a "zipper clause":

> [T]his Agreement represents a complete and final understanding on all bargainable subjects of negotiation among the parties during the term of this Agreement. . . .

While the agreement did not expressly incorporate by reference the terms of the NFL Constitution and By-laws, it did require all players to sign the Standard Player Contract, and provided that the Standard Contract shall govern the relationship between the clubs and the players. The Standard Player Contract, in turn, provided that the player agreed at all times to comply with and be bound by the NFL Constitution and By-laws. At trial, Tex Schramm, a bargaining representative of the club owners, and Alan Miller, a bargaining representative of the players, testified that it was their understanding that the Rozelle Rule would remain in effect during the term of the 1970 agreement.

Since the beginning of the 1974 negotiations, the players have consistently sought the elimination of the Rozelle Rule. The NFLPA and the clubs have engaged in substantial bargaining over that issue but have not reached an accord. Nor have they concluded a collective bargaining agreement to replace the 1970 agreement which expired in 1974.

Based on the fact that the 1968 agreement incorporated by reference the Rozelle Rule and provided that free agent rules would not be changed, we conclude that the 1968 agreement required that the Rozelle Rule govern when a player played out his option and signed with another team. Assuming, without deciding, that the 1970 agreement embodied a similar understanding, we proceed to a consideration of whether the agreements fall within the scope of the nonstatutory labor exemption.

GOVERNING PRINCIPLES.

Under the general principles surrounding the labor exemption, the availability of the nonstatutory exemption for a particular agreement turns upon whether the relevant federal labor policy is deserving of pre-eminence over federal antitrust policy under the circumstances of the particular case.

Although the cases giving rise to the nonstatutory exemption are factually dissimilar from the present case, certain principles can be deduced from those decisions governing the proper accommodation of the competing labor and antitrust interests involved here.

We find the proper accommodation to be: First, the labor policy favoring collective bargaining may potentially be given pre-eminence over the antitrust laws where the restraint on trade primarily affects only the parties to the collective bargaining relationship. Second, federal labor policy is implicated sufficiently to prevail only where the agreement sought to be exempted concerns a mandatory subject of collective bargaining. Finally, the policy favoring collective bargaining is furthered to the degree necessary to override the antitrust laws only where the agreement sought to be exempted is the product of bona fide arm's-length bargaining.

APPLICATION.

Applying these principles to the facts presented here, we think it clear that the alleged restraint on trade effected by the Rozelle Rule affects only the parties to the agreements sought to be exempted. Accordingly, we must inquire as to the other two principles: whether the Rozelle Rule is a mandatory subject of collective bargaining, and whether the agreements thereon were the product of bona fide arm's-length negotiation.

MANDATORY SUBJECT OF BARGAINING.

* * *

In this case the district court held that, in view of the illegality of the Rozelle Rule under the Sherman Act, it was "a nonmandatory, illegal subject of bargaining." We disagree. The labor exemption presupposes a violation of the antitrust laws. To hold that a subject relating to wages, hours and working conditions becomes nonmandatory by virtue of its illegality under the antitrust laws obviates the labor exemption. We conclude that whether the agreements here in question relate to a mandatory subject of collective bargaining should be determined solely under federal labor law.

On its face, the Rozelle Rule does not deal with "wages, hours and other terms or conditions of employment" but with inter-team compensation when a player's contractual obligation to one team expires and he is signed by another. Viewed as such, it would not constitute a mandatory subject of collective bargaining. The district court found, however, that the Rule operates to restrict a player's ability to move from one team to another and depresses player salaries. There is substantial evidence in the record to support these findings. Accordingly, we hold that the Rozelle Rule constitutes a mandatory bargaining subject within the meaning of the National Labor Relations Act.

Bona Fide Bargaining.

The district court found that the parties' collective bargaining history reflected nothing which could be legitimately characterized as bargaining over the Rozelle Rule; that, in part due to its recent formation and inadequate finances, the NFLPA, at least prior to 1974, stood in a relatively weak bargaining position vis-a-vis the clubs; and that "the Rozelle Rule was unilaterally imposed by the NFL and member club defendants upon the players in 1963 and has been imposed on the players from 1963 through the present date."

On the basis of our independent review of the record, including the parties' bargaining history as set forth above, we find substantial evidence to support the finding that there was no bona fide arm's-length bargaining over the Rozelle Rule preceding the execution of the 1968 and 1970 agreements. The Rule imposes significant restrictions on players, and its form has remained unchanged since it was unilaterally promulgated by the clubs in 1963. The provisions of the collective bargaining agreements which operated to continue the Rozelle Rule do not in and of themselves inure to the benefit of the players or their union. Defendants contend that the players derive indirect benefit from the Rozelle Rule, claiming that the union's agreement to the Rozelle Rule was a *quid pro quo* for increased pension benefits and the right of players to individually negotiate their salaries. The district court found, however, that there was no such *quid pro quo*, and we cannot say, on the basis of our review of the record, that this finding is clearly erroneous.[17]

In view of the foregoing, we hold that the agreements between the clubs and the players embodying the Rozelle Rule do not qualify for the labor exemption. The union's acceptance of the status quo by the continuance of the Rozelle Rule in the initial collective bargaining agreements under the circumstances of this case cannot serve to immunize the Rozelle Rule from the scrutiny of the Sherman Act.[18]

17. Appellants' *quid pro quo* argument rests primarily on the following testimony of Alan Miller, a bargaining representative of the players, concerning the 1970 negotiations:

There were times when I personally can recall, for example, one point when the NFL owners were taking the position that the NFL players must bargain their individual salaries collectively, for example, all quarterbacks are here to here, all tight ends are here to here, the flankers are making so much, a bonus for anything over three touchdowns, et cetera, et cetera. I remember specifically at that point telling somebody that if that's the way they wanted to bargain that we would, you know, consider making the Rozelle Rule and the abolishment of that rule a direct issue in the negotiations, that's the only recollection I have of that actually coming up; in itself it was not a major topic of discussion.

We cannot agree that this testimony is indicative of a *quid pro quo*. First, the colloquy related by Miller seems to have been a side discussion rather than a focal point of the negotiations. Second, at the time this interchange occurred, the clubs had already agreed to individual salary negotiations in a separate agreement.

18. In view of our holding, we need not decide whether the effect of an agreement extends beyond its formal expiration date for purposes of the labor exemption.

* * *

Conclusion.

In conclusion, although we find that non-labor parties may potentially avail themselves of the nonstatutory labor exemption where they are parties to collective bargaining agreements pertaining to mandatory subjects of bargaining, the exemption cannot be invoked where, as here, the agreement was not the product of bona fide arm's-length negotiations. Thus, the defendants' enforcement of the Rozelle Rule is not exempt from the coverage of the antitrust laws.

* * *

It may be that some reasonable restrictions relating to player transfers are necessary for the successful operation of the NFL. The protection of mutual interests of both the players and the clubs may indeed require this. We encourage the parties to resolve this question through collective bargaining. The parties are far better situated to agreeably resolve what rules governing player transfers are best suited for their mutual interests than are the courts. However, no mutual resolution of this issue appears within the present record. Therefore, the Rozelle Rule, as it is presently implemented, must be set aside as an unreasonable restraint of trade.

Trial verdict upheld.

———

John Mackey was the best tight end in professional football for a decade. He was also the President of the National Football League Players Association (NFLPA) and hence the named plaintiff in the above litigation. Not until 1992 was Mackey finally inducted into professional football's Hall of Fame—ironically, the same year as the Raiders' owner, Al Davis, who was the victor in the other major antitrust battle lost by the NFL (regarding Davis' move of the Raiders from Oakland to Los Angeles), a case we examine in depth in Chapter 6.

The *Mackey* court essentially ignored the statutory labor exemption that protects the conduct of unions and, in some cases, at least, employers who are involved in a "labor dispute." Instead, the court focussed its analysis solely on the nonstatutory exemption recognized by the Supreme Court in *Jewel Tea*—one that protects provisions in collective bargaining agreements from attack. Is that focus appropriate? Doesn't the factual context in *Mackey* look like a fight between parties to a labor dispute? How does your answer influence your view of the three-pronged test that *Mackey* laid down for judging the applicability of the nonstatutory exemption in sports cases? For example, if you are a league negotiator, how could you ensure that the contract concessions you are extracting from the players association really are the product of "bona fide arms-length bargaining," so as to qualify for antitrust immunity? Should the statutory exemption (Clayton § 6 and Norris–LaGuardia) apply, instead, in a case like *Mackey*?

The aftermath of *Mackey* was quite different from what happened with respect to the Raiders—who are now ensconced in Los Angeles. Shortly after it won *Mackey*, the NFLPA agreed to a new collective agreement with the league. In return for restoration of the Association's "union security" clause (see Chapter 4) and generous improvements in the league's pension and disability plans, the Association agreed to new restrictions on veteran free agency—giving the player's present team either a right of first refusal or compensation in the form of specified future draft picks rather than current players.[8] Over the objections of some dissenting players, the Eighth Circuit approved the new system under the *Mackey* standard. See *Reynolds v. NFL*, 584 F.2d 280 (8th Cir.1978). However, since the compensation for a free agent ranged as high as two first-round draft picks from the signing team, this new system proved far more restrictive than the old Rozelle Rule. Of several thousand players who became free agents from 1977 through 1987, only a tiny handful even received offers from another team and only one player actually changed teams for compensation. (This experience is documented in the *Powell* litigation examined later in this chapter.)

Essentially, the same divergence between antitrust verdict and labor relations outcome occurred in the other sports.[9] In the initial wave of player antitrust litigation in the early 1970s, while baseball players lost in *Flood*, the players won in football (in *Smith, Mackey,* and elsewhere), in hockey (in *Philadelphia World Hockey Club v. Philadelphia Hockey Club,* 351 F.Supp. 457 (E.D.Pa.1972)), and in basketball (in *Robertson v. NBA,* 389 F.Supp. 867 (S.D.N.Y.1975)). As described in Chapter 4, soon after *Flood* baseball players secured from a labor arbitrator full freedom from the historic reserve clause. Their Players Association then gave six years of free agency back to the owners (although players had a right to salary arbitration of their salaries from years three through six), and the Association has since preserved the essentials of that lucrative system in bargaining under labor law. In hockey and basketball, as well as in football, the players gave back "equalization" rights to teams that lost free agents: such compensation took the form of players as well as draft picks, but in an amount determined by a neutral arbitrator (*not* the league commissioner). In basketball, such compensation was available for only a five-year period that ended in 1981. Uncompensated free agency in basketball was initially accompanied by a right of first refusal for the player's prior team, and it is now constrained by the salary cap arrangement described in Chapter 5.

8. See David Harris, *The League: The Rise and Decline of the NFL* 255–57 (New York: Bantam Books, 1986).

9. See Berry, Gould, and Staudohar, *Labor Relations in Professional Sports,* note 1 above, for detailed accounts of what took place in both litigation and negotiation in each of the major professional team sports.

The next decision, *McCourt* from the world of hockey, illustrates the judicial response to a second wave of antitrust litigation about the product of collective bargaining over free agency. In reading *McCourt* and rereading *Mackey*, consider the pros and cons of the following alternative formulations of the nonstatutory labor exemption, each of which has been advanced by at least one judge or scholar (all these options have been advanced on the assumption that the direct impact of the restrictive practice is felt only inside, not also outside, the immediate employment relationship):

1. There should be no nonstatutory exemption from antitrust at all—unions and employers should have no right to do through their agreement what would otherwise be illegal by statute.

2. There should be exemption only for provisions that have been inserted in the agreement at the behest of the union for the benefit of the players—the historic purpose of the labor exemption is to help employees, not employers.

3. The exemption should protect all, but only, the terms within an existing collective agreement—the essential condition for relief from antitrust must be actual consent to the practice by the employees through their union.

4. The exemption should protect all employment practices that exist in an employee unit represented by a union—since the employees now have the right under labor law to force the employer to negotiate about the practice, they should not also enjoy the right to litigate about the practice under antitrust law.

5. There should be no antitrust liability at all for restraints in employment—as Section 6 of the Clayton Act stated, "the labor of a human being is not a commodity or article of commerce" for purposes of antitrust law.

As we will see, the formulation of the initial source and purpose of the labor exemption is also crucial for determining the exemption's scope (see *Wood*, below) and its duration (see *Powell*, below).

DALE McCOURT v. CALIFORNIA SPORTS, INC. & THE LOS ANGELES KINGS

United States Court of Appeals, Sixth Circuit, 1979.

600 F.2d 1193.

ENGEL, CIRCUIT JUDGE.

[Rogatien Vachon, after six years as the star goal-tender of the Los Angeles Kings, became a free agent in 1978 and signed a five-year $1.9 million contract with the Detroit Red Wings. Under National Hockey League By–Law Section 9A, the Red Wings were then obligated to make an "equalization payment" to the Kings in the form of players, draft picks, or "as a last resort," cash. Unlike the "Rozelle Rule" in football, the amount of compensation payable under the collective agreement was determined not by the NHL President, but by a neutral arbitrator (named by the League Board of Governors). In this case, the arbitrator awarded the Kings Dale McCourt who in his rookie year had led the Red Wings in scoring. Rather than report to the Kings, McCourt sued, alleging that this NHL version of the "reserve system" violated federal antitrust law. He was met by the defense that the compensation system was both incorporated in the standard player contract and expressly approved by Section 9.03 of the NHL's collective agreement with its Players' Association. Nevertheless, the trial judge granted McCourt injunctive relief, finding that the free agent compensation system was per se illegal under Section 1 and that the nonstatutory labor exemption did not apply. The basis for the labor exemption ruling was that "[t]he preponderance of evidence ... establishes that By-law 9A was not the product of bona fide arm's length bargaining over any of its anticompetitive provisions. The evidence establishes that the by-law was unilaterally imposed upon the NHLPA and was incorporated into the collective bargaining agreement in the identical language it contained when it was first adopted by the League." This appeal followed.]

B. APPLICATION OF LEGAL STANDARDS

We have little difficulty in determining that the first two policy considerations [from *Mackey*] favor the exemption. Clearly here the restraint on trade primarily affects the parties to the bargaining relationship. It is the hockey players themselves who are primarily affected by any restraint, reasonable or not. Second, the agreement concerning the reserve system involves in a very real sense the terms and conditions of employment of the hockey players both in form and in practical effect. . . .

The issue, therefore, in our judgment is narrowed to whether, upon the facts of this case, the agreement sought to be exempted was the product of bona fide arm's-length bargaining.

* * *

On May 4, 1976, the NHL and the NHLPA signed their first collective bargaining agreement retroactive from September 15, 1975. The collective bargaining agreement provides that paragraph 17 of the Standard Player's Contract and By-Law Section 9A are "fair and reasonable terms of employment."

We believe that in holding that the reserve system had not been the subject of good faith, arm's-length bargaining, the trial court failed to recognize the well established principle that nothing in the labor law compels either party negotiating over mandatory subjects of collective bargaining to yield on its initial bargaining position. Good faith bargaining is all that is required. That the position of one party on an issue prevails unchanged does not mandate the conclusion that there was no collective bargaining over the issue. NLRB v. American National Insurance Co., 343 U.S. 395, 404 (1952).

* * *

Contrary to the trial judge's conclusion, the very facts relied upon by him in his opinion illustrate a classic case of collective bargaining in which the reserve system was a central issue. It is apparent from those very findings that the NHLPA used every form of negotiating pressure it could muster. It developed an alternate reserve system and secured tentative agreement from the owner and player representatives, only to have the proposal rejected by the players. It refused to attend a proposed meeting with the owners to discuss the reserve system further. It threatened to strike. It threatened to commence an antitrust suit and to recommend that the players not attend training camp.

For its part, the NHL, while not budging in its insistence upon By–Law Section 9A, at least in the absence of any satisfactory counter proposal by the players, yielded significantly on other issues. It agreed as a price of By–Law Section 9A to the inclusion in the collective bargaining agreement of a provision that the entire agreement could be voided if the NHL and the World Hockey Association should merge. The undisputed reason for this provision was player concern that with a merger of the two leagues, the reserve system would be rendered too onerous because the players would, by the merger, lose the competitive advantage of threatening to move to the WHA. Likewise, the NHL team owners obtained a provision voiding the entire agreement should the reserve system be invalidated by the courts.

The trial court, while acknowledging that the new collective bargaining agreement contained significant new benefits to the players, held that they were not "directly related to collective bargaining on By-law 9A." This observation and the trial court's conclusion that "the NHLPA never bargained for By-law 9A in the first instance" typifies its approach. It is true that the NHLPA did not "bargain for" By–Law Section 9A; it bargained "against" it, vigorously. That the trial judge concluded the benefits in the new contract were wrung from management by threat of an antitrust suit to void the By–Law merely demonstrates that the benefits were bargained for in connection with the reserve system, although he opined that the threat of a suit was a more effective bargaining tool than the threat of a strike. And while we agree with the trial judge that inclusion of language in the collective bargaining agreement that the reserve system provisions were "fair and reasonable" would not immunize it from antitrust attack, it is manifest from the entire facts found by the court that there was no collusion between management and the players association.

* * *

From the express findings of the trial court, fully supported by the record, it is apparent that the inclusion of the reserve system in the collective bargaining agreement was the product of good faith, arm's-length bargaining, and that what the trial court saw as a failure to negotiate was in fact simply the failure to succeed, after the most intensive negotiations, in keeping an unwanted provision out of the contract. This failure was a part of and not apart from the collective bargaining process, a process which achieved its ultimate objective of an agreement accepted by the parties.

Injunction vacated.

EDWARDS, CHIEF JUDGE, dissenting.

I respectfully dissent. My basic disagreement with the majority opinion is planted on the proposition that if sports clubs organized for profit are to be exempted from the antitrust laws, this should be accomplished by statutory amendment, in accordance with the Constitution of the United States. Any such amendment would necessarily follow extensive hearings on the possible implications of the exemption, not only on organized sports, but also on the whole of the American economy a process not available to the Judicial Branch.

* * *

The essence of the restriction on competition involved in this case is an agreement between all National Hockey League clubs not to hire any hockey player who has become a free agent (by refusing reemployment contract terms offered by his previous club) without undertaking to "equalize" the loss to his former club by agreed on or arbitrated transfer of players or cash.

The restriction by its terms is upon the NHL constituent clubs. Its impact, however, is clearly upon star hockey players. Clause 9A.6 obviously diminishes the hockey star's bargaining power, both with his previous employer and any prospective employer. It also may require any player who is transferred under the equalization clause to live in a city and play for a club against his professional (or private) best interests.

The legal question posed by this case is whether an association of employers may in the organized sports industry (here it is hockey) gain exemption from the antitrust laws for an agreement among themselves to restrict otherwise free competition in employment of hockey players by imposing their employer-devised agreement upon a union representing that class of employees through use of economic inducement or compulsion. Before we give judicial sanction to such a practice as consistent with the antitrust and labor-management laws of this country, we should take a long, hard look at the implications for sections of the national economy other than organized sports.

Superstars whose services are at a high premium can be found in many areas of industry and commerce other than the world of sports. Is there any distinction to be drawn between Clause 9A and similar restrictions in, for example, the field of dress manufacturing for the services of highly talented designers, or in the metalworking industries for the services of highly talented engineers, designers, or die shop leaders, or the entertainment field for highly talented personnel, or in the publishing field for highly talented writers?

Such a restriction on freedom of competition (and human freedom in choice of employment) in the interest of promotion or maintenance of business profits, has a distinctly predatory ring.

* * *

Appellants' defense of 9A is cast principally in public policy argument. It runs: Star players like McCourt produce the victories and championships for the club. They also attract the paying customers and generate profits. When star players are monopolized by one club, that club gains profits at the expense of all other clubs in the league. When the star players are distributed somewhat evenly throughout the league, team competition is enhanced and the well-being of the league as a whole is protected. The result is beneficial to the league and to the league's sports-minded public.

The point of this dissent is not to disagree with this public policy argument. Congress, which adopted the antitrust laws in the first instance, may choose to exempt nationally organized sports leagues from the antitrust laws by allowing carefully devised controls over player contracts designed to prevent league imbalance. My problem is that I cannot find any rationale for this court's devising such a policy which is 1) consistent with the antitrust statutes, or 2) which could be limited to the field of sports, or 3) which is supported by decisions on antitrust issues in the United States Supreme Court.

* * *

Until this case, I do not know of any instance where profit making businesses have succeeded in justifying a cartel arrangement which suits their purposes by dint of securing that arrangement's introduction into a collective bargaining agreement and thus acquiring the right to the "labor union exemption." The majority's approval of this arrangement in this case in fact stands the labor union exemption squarely on its head.

Questions for Discussion

1. *Mackey* involved a situation where the union was suing the league over free agency rules that were at issue in ongoing collective bargaining. *McCourt* was a case in which a single player was challenging a free agency rule contained in an existing collective agreement, and about which both the union and league were satisfied. Given this factual distinction, is it correct that the same legal test should be used in both cases to determine whether the labor exemption (statutory or nonstatutory) applies? If not, in which case should a different test be used and what should that test be? If yes, what other distinctions, if any, are there in the collective bargaining scenarios in these two cases that would justify the different results?

The NHL free agency rules returned to prominence in the early 1990s. Collective bargaining in hockey in the 1980s [10] had produced some leeway for players to move to other teams, at least if the signing team was prepared to give up what an arbitrator determined to be equal playing talent (if the signed player was under 25 years of age) or a large number of rookie draft picks (if the player was between 25 and 30 years of age). Then, in the summer of 1990, the St. Louis Blues lured Scott Stevens away from the Washington Capitols with a million dollar per year contract, and in return had to give the Capitals their first round draft picks for the next *five* years. The following summer, the Blues signed Brendan Shanahan, a 22–year–old budding star with the New Jersey Devils. Through the "final offer selection" arbitration model used for Category I equalization, Judge Houston, the arbitrator, awarded Scott Stevens to the Devils. Stevens, very upset, initially refused to report to the Devils and threatened to sue for having been made part of a forced trade for a "free" agent. Perhaps because Stevens' agent then read the *McCourt* case, his client soon relented.

These events, however, placed the issue of free agency squarely on the hockey agenda during the 1991–1992 negotiations for a new agreement. This time the NHL Players Association was headed by Bob Goodenow, a former labor lawyer and player agent. After a brief 10–day strike on the eve of the 1992 Stanley Cup playoffs, the parties reached a settlement that set up a complex system of free agency:

Free Agency in Hockey

Category	Consequence
Players under 24 years or with less than 5 years professional play.	Player chooses either team compensation by draft picks or equalization by playing talent. If former, team has right to match competing offer, if its offer was at least 15% more than player's prior salary.
Players 24 to 29 years or with at least 5 years professional play.	Player chooses either mode of team compensation. Team has right to match offer only if its qualifying bid exceeded both $351,000 and 15% more than player's prior salary.

10. For sharply different accounts of the course of labor relations in hockey, see David Cruise & Alison Griffiths, *Net Worth: Exploding the Myths of Pro Hockey* (New York: Viking Press, 1991); and Alan Eagleson (with Scott Young), *Power Play: The Memoirs of a Hockey Czar* (Toronto, Canada: McClelland and Stewart, 1991) (Eagleson founded the NHLPA and negotiated these free agency rules). For more scholarly treatments, see Jan C. Pulver, *A Face Off Between the National Hockey League and the National Hockey League Players' Association: The Goal a More Competitively Balanced League*, 2 Marquette Sports L.J. 39 (1991), and Joseph M. Weiler, *Legal Analysis of NHL Players' Contracts* 3 Marquette Sports Law Journal 59 (1992) (forthcoming).

Players 30 years and older.	Team must make qualifying offer (as above). Player then chooses whether team has right to match new offer or to receive compensation.
Players with 10 years professional service and earning less than average league salary ($368,000 in 1991–92).	Losing team gets no compensation and has no right to match offer.

The reason why there was only this modest relaxation of free agency restraints was that midway through the labor negotiations, the parties realized that average hockey player salaries had soared over $360,000—up 55% in just two years despite the supposed highly restrictive rules in the old agreement. Why did this salary spiral occur? [11] The answer, in part, is to be found in the system of salary arbitration that hockey shares with baseball, which is described in the next chapter.

———

The next case deals with an antitrust challenge to a collateral feature of one of the important innovations in sports labor relations— the salary cap, which was developed in professional basketball and is being seriously considered in the 1992 negotiations in professional football.[12] We will describe the NBA salary cap in detail in Chapter 5. Suffice it to say here that the NBA and its Players Association has negotiated a maximum (and a minimum) salary budget that can be spent by any team in signing new players—whether veteran free agents from other teams or rookie draft selections.

In addition, as prelude to the decision below, the reader should know that its author, Judge Ralph Winter, was previously a professor of antitrust and labor law at Yale Law School. While at Yale, not only did Professor Winter write one of the major scholarly examinations of the interplay between these two legal regimes, *Collective Bargaining and Competition: The Application of Antitrust Standards to Union Activities*, 73 Yale L.J. 14 (1963), but he also co-authored the first important analysis of this issue in the sports context, at a time when *Flood v. Kuhn* was still wending its way up to the Supreme Court (see Jacobs & Winter, *Antitrust Principles in Collective Bargaining by Ath-*

---

11. The precise extent of the increase in average hockey salaries produced an arbitration dispute before the parties had even drafted the precise language of their new collective agreement. In *NHL Players Association and the National Hockey League Member Clubs* (1992), Arbitrator St. Antoine ruled that "average league salary" for purposes of determining free agency status was to be calculated by counting all compensation (including bonus money) paid to any player who participated in any NHL game, but each player's salary would be weighted to the number of games played.

12. See Staudohar, *The Sports Industry and Collective Bargaining*, note 1 above, at 123–129, for a brief account of the 1983 and 1988 negotiations in basketball, in which the salary cap was first devised and then considerably revised.

letes: Of Superstars in Peonage, 81 Yale L.J. 1 (1971)). Read the following case closely to see whether his professorial background led Judge Winter to a somewhat different judicial perspective than we saw in both *Mackey* and *McCourt*. If so, for better or worse?

LEON WOOD v. NATIONAL BASKETBALL ASSOCIATION

United States Court of Appeals, Second Circuit, 1987.

809 F.2d 954.

WINTER, CIRCUIT JUDGE.

[Leon Wood, a star point guard on the 1984 gold-medal U.S. Olympic basketball team, was the first-round pick by the Philadelphia 76ers in the 1984 college draft. Despite these laurels, the 76ers offered Wood just a $75,000 one-year contract. The reason was that this was the maximum amount permitted to the 76ers, who were over the specified salary ceiling in the newly-negotiated NBA salary cap system. The NBA and its Players Association had negotiated the new salary cap arrangement (based on a guaranteed share for player salaries of 53 percent of total league revenues) to give the clubs some relief from the severe financial difficulties many were experiencing under the previous free agency-first refusal system. The latter system had been created by the consent decree that settled the antitrust litigation in Robertson v. National Basketball Ass'n, 72 F.R.D. 64 (S.D.N.Y.1976), aff'd, 556 F.2d 682 (2d Cir.1977).

In any event, the 76ers qualifying offer to Wood was something of a formality, since the club made it clear to both the player and his agent that adjustments would be made in the team roster to free up salary room for a more generous contract for Wood. Eventually, Wood signed a four-year, $1 million contract with the 76ers, who then traded him. In the meantime, though, Wood had filed an antitrust suit challenging the salary cap; the trial judge dismissed the suit on the basis of the labor exemption. This was Wood's appeal.]

* * *

The draft and salary cap are not the product solely of an agreement among horizontal competitors but are embodied in a collective agreement between an employer or employers and a labor organization reached through procedures mandated by federal labor legislation. Their legality, therefore, cannot be assessed without reference to that legislation. The interaction of the Sherman Act and federal labor legislation is an area of law marked more by controversy than by clarity. We need not enter this debate or probe the exact contours of the so-called statutory or non-statutory "labor exemptions," however, because no one seriously contends that the antitrust laws may be used to subvert fundamental principles of our federal labor policy as set out in the National Labor Relations Act. Wood's claim is just such a wholesale subversion of that policy, and it must be rejected out of hand. As a result, whether the draft and salary cap are *per se* violations of the antitrust laws or subject to rule of reason analysis need not be decided.

Although the combination of the college draft and salary cap may seem unique in collective bargaining (as are the team salary floor and 53 percent revenue sharing agreement), the uniqueness is strictly a matter of appearance. The nature of professional sports as a business and professional sports teams as employers calls for contractual arrangements suited to that unusual commercial context. However, these arrangements result from the same federally mandated processes as do collective agreements in the more familiar industrial context. Moreover, examination of the particular arrangements arrived at by the NBA and NBPA discloses that they have functionally identical, and identically anticompetitive, counterparts that are routinely included in industrial collective agreements.

Among the fundamental principles of federal labor policy is the legal rule that employees may eliminate competition among themselves through a governmentally supervised majority vote selecting an exclusive bargaining representative. Section 9(a) of the National Labor Relations Act explicitly provides that "[r]epresentatives ... selected ... by the majority of the employees in a unit ... shall be the exclusive representatives of all the employees in such unit for the purposes of collective bargaining." Federal labor policy thus allows employees to seek the best deal for the greatest number by the exercise of collective rather than individual bargaining power. Once an exclusive representative has been selected, the individual employee is forbidden by federal law from negotiating directly with the employer absent the representative's consent, NLRB v. Allis–Chalmers Mfg. Co., 388 U.S. 175, 180, (1967), even though that employee may actually receive less compensation under the collective bargain than he or she would through individual negotiations. J.I. Case Co. v. NLRB, 321 U.S. 332, 338–39 (1944).

The gravamen of Wood's complaint, namely that the NBA–NBPA collective agreement is illegal because it prevents him from achieving his full free market value, is therefore at odds with, and destructive of, federal labor policy.[2] It is true that the diversity of talent and specialization among professional athletes and the widespread exposure and discussions of their "work" in the media make the differences in value among them as "workers" more visible than the differences in efficiency and in value among industrial workers. High public visibility, however, is no reason to ignore federal legislation that explicitly prevents employees, whether in or out of a bargaining unit, from seeking a better deal where that deal is inconsistent with the terms of a collective agreement.

---

2. The assumed fact that several competing employers have agreed to the draft and salary cap is of no legal significance because that agreement is embodied in a collective agreement. Multi-employer bargaining is authorized by the National Labor Relations Act and is commonplace. NLRB v. Truck Drivers Local Union, No. 449, International Brotherhood of Teamsters, 353 U.S. 87, 94–96, (1957).

Indeed, examination of the criteria that Wood advances as the basis for striking down the draft and salary cap reveals that there is hardly a collective agreement in the nation that would survive his legal theory. For example, Wood emphasizes his superior abilities as a point-guard and his selection in the first round of the college draft as grounds for enabling him to bargain individually for a higher salary. However, collective agreements routinely set standard wages for employees with differing responsibilities, skills, and levels of efficiency. Wood's theory would allow any employee dissatisfied with his salary relative to those of other workers to insist upon individual bargaining, contrary to explicit federal labor policy. As one commentator has noted, "Congress gave to the majority representative the task of harmonizing and adjusting the conflicting interests of employees within the bargaining unit, no matter how diverse their skills, experience, age, race or economic level." And the Supreme Court has observed, "The complete satisfaction of all who are represented is hardly to be expected." Ford Motor Co. v. Huffman, 345 U.S. 330, 338 (1953).

Wood also attacks the draft and salary cap because they assign him to work for a particular employer at a diminished wage. However, collective agreements in a number of industries provide for the exclusive referral of workers by a hiring hall to particular employers at a specified wage. The choice of employer is governed by the rules of the hiring hall, not the preference of the individual worker. There is nothing that prevents such agreements from providing that the employee either work for the designated employer at the stipulated wage or not be referred at that time. Otherwise, a union might find it difficult to provide the requisite number of workers to employers. Such an arrangement is functionally indistinguishable from the college draft.

Wood further attacks the draft and salary cap as disadvantaging new employees. However, newcomers in the industrial context routinely find themselves disadvantaged vis-a-vis those already hired. A collective agreement may thus provide that salaries, layoffs, and promotions be governed by seniority, Ford Motor Co. v. Huffman, 345 U.S. at 337–39, even though some individuals with less seniority would fare better if allowed to negotiate individually.

Finally, Wood argues that the draft and salary cap are illegal because they affect employees outside the bargaining unit. However, that is also a commonplace consequence of collective agreements. Seniority clauses may thus prevent outsiders from bidding for particular jobs, and other provisions may regulate the allocation or subcontracting of work to other groups of workers. See Fibreboard Paper Products Corp. v. NLRB, 379 U.S. 203, 210–15 (1964). Indeed, the National Labor Relations Act explicitly defines "employee" in a way that includes workers outside the bargaining unit.

If Wood's antitrust claim were to succeed, all of these commonplace arrangements would be subject to similar challenges, and federal labor policy would essentially collapse unless a wholly unprincipled, judge-made exception were created for professional athletes. Employers would have no assurance that they could enter into any collective agreement without exposing themselves to an action for treble damages. Moreover, recognition of a right to individual bargaining without the consent of the exclusive representative would undermine the status and effectiveness of the exclusive representative, and result in individual contracts that reduce the amount of wages or other benefits available for other workers. Wood's assertion that he would be paid more in the absence of the draft and salary cap also implies that others would receive less if he were successful. It can hardly be denied that the NBA teams would be more resistant to benefits guaranteed to all, such as pensions, minimum salaries, and medical and insurance benefits. In fact, the salary cap challenged by Wood is one part of a complex formula including minimum team salaries and guaranteed revenue sharing.

The policy claim that one can do better through individual bargaining is nothing but the flip side of the policy claim that other employees need unions to protect their interests. Congress has accepted the latter position, and we are bound by that legislative choice.

The fact that one cannot alter important provisions of a collective agreement without undermining other provisions demonstrates that Wood's antitrust claim fundamentally conflicts in yet another way with national labor policy. That policy attaches prime importance to freedom of contract between the parties to a collective agreement. Freedom of contract is an important cornerstone of national labor policy for two reasons. First, it allows an employer and a union to agree upon those arrangements that best suit their particular interests. Courts cannot hope to fashion contract terms more efficient than those arrived at by the parties who are to be governed by them. Second, freedom of contract furthers the goal of labor peace. To the extent that courts prohibit particular solutions for particular problems, they reduce the number and quality of compromises available to unions and employers for resolving their differences.

Freedom of contract is particularly important in the context of collective bargaining between professional athletes and their leagues. Such bargaining relationships raise numerous problems with little or no precedent in standard industrial relations. As a result, leagues and player unions may reach seemingly unfamiliar or strange agreements. If courts were to intrude and to outlaw such solutions, leagues and their player unions would have to arrange their affairs in a less efficient way. It would also increase the chances of strikes by reducing the number and quality of possible compromises.

The issues of free agency and entry draft are at the center of collective bargaining in much of the professional sports industry. It is to be expected that the parties will arrive at unique solutions to these problems in the different sports both because sports generally differ from the industrial model and because each sport has its own peculiar economic imperatives. The NBA/NBPA agreement is just such a unique bundle of compromises. The draft and the salary cap reflect the interests of the employers in stabilizing salary costs and spreading talent among the various teams. Minimum individual salaries, fringe benefits, minimum aggregate team salaries, and guaranteed revenue sharing reflect the interests of the union in enhancing standard benefits applicable to all players. The free agency/first refusal provisions in turn allow individual players to exercise a degree of individual bargaining power.[4] Were a court to intervene and strike down the draft and salary cap, the entire agreement would unravel.[5] This would force the NBA and NBPA to search for other avenues of compromise that would be less satisfactory to them than the agreement struck down. It would also measurably increase the chances of a strike. We decline to take that step.

We also agree with the district court that all of the above matters are mandatory subjects of bargaining under 29 U.S.C. § 158(d). Each of them clearly is intimately related to "wages, hours, and other terms and conditions of employment." Indeed, it is precisely because of their direct relationship to wages and conditions of employment that such matters are so controversial and so much the focus of bargaining in professional sports. . . .

It is true that the combination of the draft and salary cap places new players coming out of college ranks at a disadvantage. However, as noted earlier, that is hardly an unusual feature of collective agreements. In the industrial context salaries, promotions, and layoffs are routinely governed by seniority, with the benefits going to the older employees, the burdens to the newer. Wood has offered us no reason whatsoever to fashion a rule based on antitrust grounds prohibiting agreements between employers and players that use seniority as a criterion for certain employment decisions. Even if some such arrangements might be illegal because of discrimination against new employees

4. At oral argument, counsel for Wood argued that because players are allowed a limited right by the collective agreement to bargain individually, the antitrust laws somehow compel that the right be unqualified. We perceive neither logic, policy, nor legal authority supporting this claim. No one denies that a union and employer, including the NBPA and NBA, may set a fixed salary for an employee, an agreement that might well be far worse for Wood than the provisions he now challenges. To hold that the NBPA and NBA must as a matter of law opt either for fixed salaries or unlimited individual bargaining would further no legitimate goal. One might well speculate that only a destructive impasse would result.

5. This discussion is for illustrative purposes only and does not imply that a particular quid pro quo must be proven to avoid antitrust liability. Invalidation of any provision that goes to the bottom line may affect seemingly unrelated provisions. Nor does it imply that a party may not insist upon a deal that is more one-sided than the NBA–NBPA arrangement. See NLRB v. American National Ins. Co., 343 U.S. 395, 402 (1952) (noting that National Labor Relations Act does not "regulate the substantive terms governing wages, hours and working conditions which are incorporated in an agreement"). Any claim of unreasonable bargaining behavior must be pursued in an unfair labor practice proceeding charging a refusal to bargain in good faith, not in an action under the Sherman Act.

(players), the proper action would be one for breach of the duty of fair representation.

Wood relies for legal support primarily upon the Supreme Court's decisions in Connell Construction Co. v. Plumbers and Steamfitters Local Union No. 100, 421 U.S. 616 (1975); Local Union 189, Amalgamated Meat Cutters v. Jewel Tea Co., 381 U.S. 676 (1965); and United Mine Workers v. Pennington, 381 U.S. 657 (1965). He reads those decisions as holding generally that a person outside the bargaining unit, in his case an unsigned first-round draft choice, who is injured in an anticompetitive fashion by a collective agreement may challenge that agreement on antitrust grounds. However, these cases are so clearly distinguishable that they need not detain us. Each of the decisions involved injuries to employers who asserted that they were being excluded from competition in the product market. Wood cites no case in which an employee or potential employee was able to invalidate a collective agreement on antitrust grounds because he or she might have been able to extract more favorable terms through individual bargaining. We need not determine the precise limits of the rules laid down by the cases cited or consider fine distinctions going to whether product- or labor-market activities are in issue. Wood's claim is beyond peradventure one that implicates the labor market and subverts federal labor policy. It must, therefore, be rejected.

Affirmed.

Questions for Discussion

1. How is the *Mackey* test different from Judge Winter's approach in *Wood*; that regardless of factual context or legal characterization (i.e., statutory or nonstatutory), application of the labor exemption turns on whether permitting an antitrust suit would undermine a basic tenet of federal labor policy? How would Judge Winter have analyzed and decided *Mackey*? *McCourt*? Which approach is preferable?

2. *Wood* dismissed an antitrust challenge to apparently stringent restraints on the negotiating leverage of rookie draft picks. Keep this case in mind when you read in Chapter 4 about the labor law framework for professional sports, and in particular about possible protection of players in Woods' position by the union's "duty of fair representation." As we saw earlier in Chapter 2, the limits imposed on rookie salaries by the NBA salary cap were a significant factor in the events leading to the *Brian Shaw* case. Still, most clubs make a serious effort to find room within their salary allotment to sign first-round picks (including Wood) to lucrative contracts. Why do they go to this trouble?

―――――

If *McCourt* and *Wood* illustrate the second wave of antitrust litigation about the player market in sports—individual player challenges to agreements produced in reasonably mature collective bargaining by a union that continued to support the restriction at issue—the next case, *Powell v. NFL*, illustrates the third phase. Here, a players association has become disenchanted after years of experience with the limitations on free agency to which it had voluntarily agreed. However, the Association finds itself unable to secure major changes through direct negotiations with the league under the labor law. Thus, once the existing agreement expires, the union challenges the restrictions in court by arguing that the labor exemption expired along with the contract.

Powell, an offshoot of the ill-fated NFLPA strike of 1987, is the most dramatic, long-playing illustration of that scenario. The same effort was made, however, by the NBA Players Association in *Bridgeman v. NBA*, 675 F.Supp. 960 (D. N.J. 1987).[14] Unlike *Powell*, the basketball litigation proved only a skirmish on the way to a peacefully negotiated relaxation of the NBA's free agency system, which operates within the parameters of the salary cap upon which the NBA owners now place their principal reliance.

In determining whether and when the labor exemption expires, there are several legal options from which to choose:

> 1. The exemption expires with the collective agreement.

> 2. The exemption expires when the parties have reached a deadlock (an "impasse") in their negotiations, either about a particular contract term or about renewal of the agreement generally.

> 3. The exemption continues as long as a bargaining relationship exists between league and union—i.e., until the union itself expires.

> 4. Once a formal player restraint has been negotiated by the players union, it is forever protected from antitrust challenge. Under this model, what happens when there is a partial relaxation of the restraint, such as the NFL's Plan B which in 1988 removed for marginal players the first refusal and equalization provisions in the prior agreement with the NFLPA?

The *Powell* litigation, which has produced several decisions other than those included here, provides ample material to evaluate the above options, from the perspective of both labor and antitrust policy.

POWELL v. NATIONAL FOOTBALL LEAGUE (# 1)

United States District Court, District of Minnesota, 1988.

678 F.Supp. 777.

DOTY, DISTRICT JUDGE.

[In 1987, the NFL Players Association undertook extended negotiations, culminating in a strike, to remove the restrictions on free agency

---

14. For a brief description of what happened in both football and basketball labor relations in 1987–1988, see Staudohar, *Collective Bargaining in Professional Sports*, note 1 above, at 78–83 (football), 127–29 (basketball).

in professional football. The three-week strike was unsuccessful, especially when the NFL used replacement players (as we will see in Chapter 4). When its members returned to work empty-handed, the NFLPA launched yet another antitrust suit. Its target was the right of first refusal/compensation system that had been developed through collective bargaining in 1977 in the aftermath of the *Mackey* decision.

Unfortunately for the players, that system proved even more restrictive than the prior Rozelle Rule. During the 1977–1982 agreement, only a handful of offers were made to free agents (usually when both teams were interested in a trade), and only once did compensation become payable. In the 1982 negotiations, the NFLPA focused its efforts on a guaranteed revenue share and salary scale and secured a $1.2 billion package from the NFL for the next five years. The free agent compensation system proved even more restrictive during the 1982–1987 agreement: of 1415 veterans who became free agents, just one received an offer from another team.

The key issue posed in the decisions reproduced here was whether the NFL could win summary dismissal of the NFLPA suit on the grounds that the labor exemption protected the NFL's free agency restraints, even after the collective agreement had expired and labor negotiations had not produced a renewal.]

Issue

* * *

Basic principles of labor law dictate that provisions relating to mandatory subjects of bargaining "survive" formal expiration of the collective bargaining agreement. Typically, the parties to an expired agreement have an obligation to maintain the status quo as to these provisions until a new agreement is concluded or until the parties reach "impasse." The governing principle is that until impasse is reached, an employer is not free unilaterally to change the essential provisions of an expired collective bargaining agreement but must keep those provisions in effect and bargain with the union as to their possible modification.

* * *

The reason for this emphasis on maintaining the status quo is to provide the parties with a stable environment in which to negotiate a new collective bargaining agreement. "Freezing the status quo ante after a collective agreement has expired promotes industrial peace by fostering a noncoercive atmosphere that is conducive to serious negotiations on a new contract."

In order to properly accommodate the antitrust policy promoting free competition with the labor law obligation requiring the parties to maintain the status quo following expiration of a collective bargaining agreement, the Court holds that the nonstatutory labor exemption must also "survive" expiration of the Agreement. A New Jersey district court recently reached the same conclusion on nearly identical facts. In *Bridgeman v. National Basketball Association*, 675 F.Supp. 960

(D.N.J.1987), a group of professional basketball players sued the National Basketball Association, alleging that various player restraints imposed by the NBA violated the antitrust laws. After balancing the competing interests of the antitrust and labor laws, the Court concluded that there was no merit in the players' contention that restrictions included in a collective bargaining agreement should lose their antitrust immunity the moment the agreement expires....

> [S]uch a rule is unrealistic in light of the requirement that employers must bargain fully and in good faith before altering a term or condition of employment subject to mandatory bargaining even after the collective bargaining agreement expires.... This obligation to maintain the status quo until impasse means that, in a practical sense, terms and conditions of employment that are subjects of mandatory bargaining survive expiration of the collective bargaining agreement.

* * *

Having determined that the labor exemption "survives" expiration of the collective bargaining agreement, the Court must now determine the period of time for which the exemption remains in effect.

* * *

After balancing the various competing interests, the Court concludes that proper accommodation of labor and antitrust interests requires that a labor exemption relating to a mandatory bargaining subject survive expiration of the collective bargaining agreement until the parties reach impasse as to that issue; thereafter, the term or condition is no longer immune from scrutiny under the antitrust laws, and the employer runs the risk that continued imposition of the condition will subject the employer to liability.

The test applied in determining whether the parties have reached impasse as to a particular issue is the same as that applied in determining impasse in the negotiations as a whole.[20] The test is simply whether, following intense, good faith negotiations, the parties have exhausted the prospects of concluding an agreement. Impasse is generally synonymous with deadlock: it occurs when the parties have discussed the matter and, despite their best efforts to achieve agreement, neither is willing to move from its position. No impasse can occur until there appears no realistic possibility that continuing discussions concerning the provision at issue would be fruitful.

Under the Court's formulation, a determination that the parties have reached impasse as to a particular issue results in termination of the labor exemption protecting that particular provision. In the instant case, once the parties reach impasse concerning the player re-

---

20. In *Taft Broadcasting Co.*, the National Labor Relations Board enumerated some of the considerations in making an "impasse" determination:

Whether a bargaining impasse exists is a matter of judgment. The bargaining history, the good faith of the parties in negotiations, the length of the negotiations, the importance of the issue or issues as to which there is disagreement, the contemporaneous understanding of the parties as to the state of negotiations are all relevant factors to be considered in deciding whether an impasse in bargaining existed.

straint provisions, those provisions will lose their immunity and further imposition of those conditions may result in antitrust liability.[21]

Summary dismissal refused.

———

Shortly after this ruling, the National Labor Relations Board found that the NFLPA had not bargained in bad faith during the summer of 1987 (as we will see in Chapter 4). Judge Doty thus concluded that an "impasse" had been reached and that the NFL's nonstatutory labor exemption had expired. The NFLPA then moved for an interim injunction to bar the NFL from applying the compensation system to the 300 free agents still unsigned in June, 1988. The NFLPA contended that the most likely result of a full trial was a ruling based on *Mackey* that the current NFL compensation system also ran afoul of antitrust law. Intriguingly, Judge Doty rejected the injunction request, on the grounds that the parties were still embroiled in a "labor dispute" that qualified for the Norris–LaGuardia Act's ban on federal labor injunctions.

POWELL v. NATIONAL FOOTBALL LEAGUE (# 2)

United States District Court, District of Minnesota, 1988.

690 F.Supp. 812.

DOTY, DISTRICT JUDGE.

* * *

With limited exceptions, the Norris–LaGuardia Act deprives federal courts of jurisdiction to issue injunctions in cases "involving or growing out of labor disputes." The term "labor dispute" is defined broadly in the statute as "any controversy concerning terms or conditions of employment.... The Act's scope is intentionally broad, covering any case ... in which 'the employer-employee relationship [is] the matrix of the controversy.'"

It is clear that the issue of player movement relates to a term or condition of employment and the players do not challenge application of the Act on that basis. Rather, the players argue that any "dispute" which existed over free agency ended once the parties reached a bargaining impasse on that issue. The players contend that restrictions on player movement are now being unilaterally imposed by the owners, and that the controversy therefore has ceased to be a "labor dispute" and is now governed exclusively by the antitrust laws.

---

21. Of course, liability will attach only if the challenged practices do in fact violate the antitrust laws.

While the Court agrees that existing restrictions on free agency are being unilaterally imposed by the owners, and that such restrictions are now subject to the antitrust laws, the Court does not agree that the presence of a bargaining impasse signifies the end of a "labor dispute." Indeed, a bargaining impasse is by definition a "labor dispute." As this Court noted in its earlier opinion, an impasse merely signifies a stalemate in negotiations—it does not mark the end of labor relations generally. For at least a decade, the players and owners have consistently treated the free agency issue as a negotiable term or condition of employment.[7] Under these circumstances, and where the bargaining relationship and the collective bargaining process remains intact, a controversy regarding terms or conditions of employment constitutes a labor dispute. Accordingly, the Court concludes that the current controversy surrounding the free agency issue constitutes a "labor dispute" as contemplated by the Norris–LaGuardia Act.

* * *

The strong federal labor policy embodied in the Norris–LaGuardia Act dictating non-interference in the bargaining process also compels denial of the players' request for injunctive relief.

In 1932, Congress enacted the Norris–LaGuardia Act primarily to curb widespread management attempts to subvert labor strength by obtaining injunctions against various labor activities. In Boys Markets, Inc. v. Retail Clerks Union (1970), the United States Supreme Court described the situation which the Norris–LaGuardia Act was enacted to redress:

In the early part of this century, the federal courts generally were regarded as allies of management in its attempt to prevent the organization and strengthening of labor unions; and in this industrial struggle the injunction became a potent weapon that was wielded against the activities of labor groups. The result was a large number of sweeping decrees, often issued ex parte, drawn on an ad hoc basis without regard to any systematic elaboration of national labor policy.

In 1932 Congress attempted to bring some order out of the industrial chaos that had developed and to correct the abuses that had resulted from the interjection of the federal judiciary into union-management disputes on the behalf of management. Congress, therefore, determined initially to limit severely the power of

7. The instant case is distinguishable from *Mackey*, in which the Court of Appeals stated that "[i]t is not clear that the instant controversy constitutes ... a labor dispute [under the Norris–LaGuardia Act]." 543 F.2d at 623. In *Mackey*, the challenged system of player restraints (the Rozelle Rule) had been imposed by the NFL outside the collective bargaining context before the players had even unionized, and the restraint had "remained unchanged since it was unilaterally promulgated by the clubs...." Moreover, the Rozelle Rule had not been a concrete issue in collective bargaining, with "nothing which could be legitimately characterized as bargaining over the Rozelle Rule...." *Mackey* is "thus properly read as a case in which the disputed restraint had not yet entered the sphere of collective bargaining" because "there had been no exchange, no bargaining, and no consent."

the federal courts to issue injunctions "in any case involving or growing out of any labor dispute...."

The Court also noted that "[a]s labor organizations grew in strength and developed toward maturity, congressional emphasis shifted from protection of the nascent labor movement to the encouragement of collective bargaining and to administrative techniques for the peaceful resolution of industrial disputes." Since the Court's pronouncement in *Boys Markets*, courts have increasingly recognized the broad policy underlying the Norris–LaGuardia Act to encourage collective bargaining and prevent judicial interference in management-labor relations. Given the current status of management-labor relations in the United States, it appears that where judicial intervention would undermine the bargaining process, it is the general intent of Congress to deprive the courts of jurisdiction to issue injunctive relief.

After careful consideration, it is the opinion of the Court that granting the players a preliminary injunction to secure unrestricted free agency would wholly subvert the collective bargaining process and thereby offend a central purpose of the Norris–LaGuardia Act.

Collective bargaining involves agreements on, and trade-offs among, a broad range of different items affecting the terms and conditions of employment. For a court to align itself with one of the parties by, in effect, eliminating from bargaining one of the major items in the bargaining mix, would work a wholesale subversion of the collective bargaining process....

In any event, it would be highly destructive to collective bargaining if major issues could be removed from the bargaining table and preliminarily resolved in isolation in antitrust litigation. If one of the parties to the bargaining relationship were able to secure the substance of its bargaining objectives by obtaining a preliminary injunction, there would be very little motivation for that party to bargain in good faith toward reaching an agreement. Judicial intervention at this stage of the bargaining process would give one side a preliminary victory while effectively disabling the other.

Injunction denied.

———

In his decision Judge Doty noted that a permanent injunction (and presumably liability for damages) might be available to NFLPA members if and when a final ruling was made that the NFL's restrictions on free agency violated antitrust law. Is this view consistent with what courts have held the Norris LaGuardia Act implies for the labor exemption from antitrust? Look back at the text and cases earlier in this chapter—in particular, *Hutcheson*—depicting the evolution of the labor exemption.

With the NFLPA having been denied preliminary injunctive relief, and the usual delays before a jury trial on the merits of the antitrust claim, the Eighth Circuit allowed the NFL an interlocutory appeal on Judge Doty's first labor exemption ruling adopting the "impasse" test.

POWELL v. NATIONAL FOOTBALL LEAGUE (# 3)

United States Courts of Appeals, Eighth Circuit, 1989.

930 F.2d 1293.

GIBSON, CIRCUIT JUDGE.

* * *

The League concedes that agreements among competing employers to impose salary or other restraints in labor markets may be subject to the Sherman Act when they are imposed outside of the collective bargaining process and without regard to the labor laws. It argues, however, that the restraints involved in cases supporting this rule were not developed in the collective bargaining process and the employment relationships in those cases were not controlled by the labor laws. The League further recognizes that the antitrust laws may apply to collectively bargained restraints when such agreements directly restrict business competition in product markets. It further contends that product market effects are an essential predicate for applying the antitrust laws, and that the employment terms challenged in this case do not impose any such product market restraints. In short, the League argues that in this lawsuit the Players challenge management practices wholly governed by the federal labor laws, and that the Players' sole remedy against such practices lies in the economic pressure that the Players may exert against the League under the labor laws.

Our evaluation of the district court's impasse standard cannot proceed without a firm appreciation of the remedies available under the federal labor laws to the parties involved in labor negotiations or disputes. After the expiration of a collective bargaining agreement, a comprehensive array of labor law principles govern union and employer conduct. For both sides, there is a continuing obligation to bargain. Before the parties reach impasse in negotiations, employers are obligated to "maintain the status quo as to wages and working conditions." Such conduct is often conducive to further collective bargaining and to stable, peaceful labor relations. After impasse, an employer's continued adherence to the status quo is authorized. At the same time, once an impasse in bargaining is established, employers become entitled to implement new or different employment terms that are reasonably contemplated within the scope of their pre-impasse proposals. If employers exceed their labor law rights in implementing employment terms at impasse, the full range of labor law rights and remedies is available to unions.

The Supreme Court has recognized that disputes over employment terms and conditions are not the central focus of the Sherman Act. For example, in holding that a union did not have standing to assert antitrust claims against a multi-employer bargaining association with which it had a collective bargaining relationship, the Court stated that Congress has developed "a separate body of labor law specifically designed to protect and encourage the organizational and representational activities of labor unions." Associated Gen. Contractors of Cal. v. California State Council of Carpenters, 459 U.S. 519 (1983). Under these laws, a union "will frequently not be part of the class the Sherman Act was designed to protect, especially in disputes with employers with whom it bargains." In this context, we must decide the extent to which a labor union may employ the antitrust laws to attack restraints imposed by management which are derived from an expired collective bargaining agreement.

A collective bargaining agreement is not always essential to a finding that challenged employment terms fall within the labor exemption. In Amalgamated Meat Cutters v. Wetterau Foods, 597 F.2d 133 (8th Cir.1979), employer agreements adopted in response to a strike caused plaintiffs to be denied employment. After first determining that the challenged employer conduct was lawful under the labor laws, this court affirmed the dismissal of plaintiffs' treble damage claims:

> Since any injury to [plaintiffs] would flow naturally from the replacement of striking workers, which conduct federal labor policy sanctions, see [NLRB v. Mackay Radio & Tel. Co., 304 U.S. 333 (1938)], the agreement ... cannot constitute a violation of the antitrust law. Federal labor policy sanctions both the goal of resisting union demands and the method of replacing striking workers and the magnitude and nature of any restraint of trade or commerce in this case directly follows from the sanctioned conduct. The agreement had no anticompetitive effect unrelated to the collective bargaining negotiations.

Other courts have concluded that in certain circumstances labor market restraints imposed in a collective bargaining context do not raise Sherman Act issues. In Prepmore Apparel v. Amalgamated Clothing Workers, 431 F.2d 1004, 1007 (5th Cir.1970), the Fifth Circuit held that an employer's refusal to deal with a union with respect to terms of employment was ordinarily governed by the National Labor Relations Act and did not state a claim for violation of the Sherman Act. Similarly, in Mid–America Regional Bargaining Association v. Will County Carpenters, 675 F.2d 881, 893 (7th Cir.1982), the Seventh Circuit held that an escrow agreement which was implemented after a collective bargaining agreement expired was protected by both the statutory and nonstatutory labor exemptions.

While the League invites us to read these cases as establishing a rule to the effect that the Sherman Act is concerned only with product markets and not those for player services, we need not read them so broadly. We do, however, interpret them as precedent supporting the proposition that, in certain circumstances, such as in this case, the

Note (Hdd)

nonstatutory labor exemption may be invoked even after a collective bargaining agreement has expired.

Hold

Our reading of the authorities leads us to conclude that the League and the Players have not yet reached the point in negotiations where it would be appropriate to permit an action under the Sherman Act. The district court's impasse standard treats a lawful stage of the collective bargaining process as misconduct by defendants, and in this way conflicts with federal labor laws that establish the collective bargaining process, under the supervision of the National Labor Relations Board, as the method for resolution of labor disputes.

In particular, the federal labor laws provide the opposing parties to a labor dispute with offsetting tools, both economic and legal, through which they may seek resolution of their dispute. A union may choose to strike the employer. Further, either side may petition the National Labor Relations Board and seek, for example, a cease-and-desist order prohibiting conduct constituting an unfair labor practice. To now allow the players to pursue an action for treble damages under the Sherman Act would, we conclude, improperly upset the careful balance established by Congress through the labor law.

Both relevant case law and the more persuasive commentators establish that labor law provides a comprehensive array of remedies to management and union, even after impasse. After a collective bargaining agreement has expired, an employer is under an obligation to bargain with the union before it may permissibly make any unilateral change in terms and conditions of employment which constitute mandatory subjects of collective bargaining. After impasse, an employer may make unilateral changes that are reasonably comprehended within its pre-impasse proposals.

* * *

The labor arena is one with well established rules which are intended to foster negotiated settlements rather than intervention by the courts. The League and the Players have accepted this "level playing field" as the basis for their often tempestuous relationship, and we believe that there is substantial justification for requiring the parties to continue to fight on it, so that bargaining and the exertion of economic force may be used to bring about legitimate compromise.

The First Refusal/Compensation system, a mandatory subject of collective bargaining, was twice set forth in collective bargaining agreements negotiated in good faith and at arm's length. Following the expiration of the 1982 Agreement, the challenged restraints were imposed by the League only after they had been forwarded in negotiations and subsequently rejected by the Players.[10] The Players do not

10. On November 17, 1988, the League delivered two proposals to the Players. The first of these modified player benefits but maintained the First Refusal/Compensation system for all players, and strongly resembled a management proposal of September 7, 1987, that the players had rejected before striking. The second proposal, which offered

contend that these proposals were put forward by the League in bad faith. We therefore hold that the present lawsuit cannot be maintained under the Sherman Act. Importantly, this does not entail that once a union and management enter into collective bargaining, management is forever exempt from the antitrust laws, and we do not hold that restraints on player services can never offend the Sherman Act. We believe, however, that the nonstatutory labor exemption protects agreements conceived in an ongoing collective bargaining relationship from challenges under the antitrust laws.[11] "[N]ational labor policy should sometimes override antitrust policy," and we believe that this case presents just such an occasion.

Upon the facts currently presented by this case, we are not compelled to look into the future and pick a termination point for the labor exemption. The parties are now faced with several choices. They may bargain further, which we would strongly urge that they do. They may resort to economic force. And finally, if appropriate issues arise, they may present claims to the National Labor Relations Board. We are satisfied that as long as there is a possibility that proceedings may be commenced before the Board, or until final resolution of Board proceedings and appeals therefrom, the labor relationship continues and the labor exemption applies. . . .

HEANEY, SENIOR CIRCUIT JUDGE, dissenting.

Today, the majority permits the owners to violate the antitrust laws indefinitely. Because such a result is not justified by the labor laws, I dissent.

* * *

The majority purports to reject the owners' argument that the labor exemption in this case continues indefinitely. The practical effect of the majority's opinion, however, is just that—because the labor exemption will continue until the bargaining relationship is terminated either by a NLRB decertification proceeding or by abandonment of bargaining rights by the union.

* * *

The only basis for NLRB action ... would appear to be a petition for decertification. Certainly, the owners will not file such a petition knowing full well that, if they do, they will subject themselves to antitrust scrutiny. Certainly, the Union will not file such a petition when the price will be the loss of collective bargaining rights. The only likely source for a petition to decertify is a group of high-salaried,

---

free agency to some players but retained the First Refusal/Compensation system for many others, was similar to a management proposal offered to the Players in September and October of 1987. After the Players had rejected both proposals, the League implemented a new "free agency" system effective February 1, 1989, which was substantially identical to the terms of the second proposal.

11. The dissent argues that the court's action today deprives the union of the threat of antitrust laws, "the antitrust lever" and removes this issue from the bargaining table. This is precisely the thrust of the nonstatutory labor exemption to the antitrust laws.

highly skilled players who believe that they could do better without a union. It follows that the end result of the majority opinion is that once a union agrees to a package of player restraints, it will be bound to that package forever unless the union forfeits its bargaining rights. Certainly, *Mackey* does not suggest such a result.

The majority also suggests that the union can strike to eliminate or modify the player restraints. This is, of course, an alternative, but should players be forced to strike to alter owner conduct which violates the antitrust laws? I think not.[8]

Neither scenario, decertification nor economic strife, harmonizes the antitrust laws with the labor laws. The majority opinion will, moreover, discourage collective bargaining. Players will be considerably less likely to enter into any agreement with respect to player restraints because of the certainty that the terms of the agreement will become the terms of employment ad infinitum, unless they strike and win. In practical terms the majority has eliminated the owners' fear of the antitrust lever; therefore, little incentive exists for the owners to ameliorate anticompetitive behavior damaging to the players.

* * *

It may be argued that both successful and unsuccessful strikes and lockouts are normal parts of the collective bargaining process and that this Court should not give the players through court action what they are unable to win at the bargaining table or through economic action. I subscribe to that view, but this view cannot be controlling where the employers are engaging in practices which may well be illegal. There must be a point at which the validity of the package of player restraints can be tested without the union resorting to a strike or terminating its collective bargaining rights. In my view, impasse is the appropriate point at which to do this.

Appeal upheld.

———

8. See Lock, *The Scope of the Labor Exemption in Professional Sports*, 1989 Duke L.J. 339. Lock notes that there are several features that distinguish the professional athletes' unions from the great majority of industrial unions. First, professional athletes do not possess homogeneous skills; a wide range of ability and expertise exists among players. Thus, different players have dramatically different needs from a union. Second, the nature of professional sports presumes that the owners retain nearly complete discretion to make necessary personnel changes to produce a winning team. Typically, a professional athlete has virtually no job security. For example, the NFL standard player contract contains no injury protection beyond the season in which the injury occurs and grants the team sole discretion to terminate a player's contract at any time for lack of skill. Only five percent of all NFL players have been able individually to limit this discretion. In addition, the professional life of an athlete is short, resulting in high turnover of union members. The NFL Players Association experiences an average yearly turnover of twenty-five percent. Thus, a strike jeopardizes a significant portion of the career and earning potential of many athletes. Moreover, most professional athletes possess highly specialized skills that are rarely marketable in any other industry. As a result, players are extremely vulnerable to explicit and implicit management pressure.

After losing its bid for a rehearing by the Eighth Circuit *en banc* and its petition for certiorari before the Supreme Court,[15] the NFLPA declared itself no longer a union representing players in collective bargaining and instigated yet another antitrust suit against the NFL's player restraints—this suit filed in New Jersey on behalf of Freeman McNeil and five other players. Venue in the case was transferred to Minnesota where, along with the remnants of the *Powell* case, the NFL had also filed a suit asking for a declaratory judgment that its free agency rules were still exempt from antitrust enforcement, and in any event did not violate antitrust laws.[16] All three cases were assigned to Judge Doty. Meanwhile, the legal consequences of the NFLPA declaring itself no longer a "union" were the subject of still another important ruling in this ongoing struggle.

POWELL v. NFL (# 4); McNEIL v. NFL

United States District Court, District of Minnesota, 1991.

764 F.Supp. 1351.

DOTY, DISTRICT JUDGE.

[In November, 1989, immediately after receiving the Eighth Circuit's decision (and notwithstanding its further petition for review by the Supreme Court), the NFLPA's Executive Committee told the NFL it would no longer engage in collective bargaining with the league, more than 60% of the players signed a petition revoking any authority of the NFLPA to act as their bargaining agents and the NLFPA revised its bylaws to remove any authority of its officers to negotiate with the NFL or its member clubs. Then, in early 1990, Freeman McNeil and seven other free agent players whose contracts had expired on February 1, 1990 launched yet another antitrust suit (backed by the NFLPA) against restrictions on free agency in football. The players here sought partial summary judgment that the labor exemption had finally expired. The NFL disagreed, contending that the NFLPA must first obtain a determination from the NLRB "that its certification is no longer operative."]

15. The issue of the termination of the labor exemption had been the subject of sustained scholarly analysis after the district court and prior to the appeals court rulings in *Powell*. See Lee Goldman, *The Labor Exemption to the Antitrust Laws*, note 6 above, and Ethan Lock, *The Scope of the Labor Exemption in Professional Sports*, note 6 above. For commentary on the appeals court ruling, see the exchange between Neil K. Roman, *Illegal Procedure: The National Football Players Union's Improper Use of Antitrust Litigation for Purposes of Collective Bargaining*, 67 Denver U. L. Rev. 111 (1990) and Ethan Lock, *Powell v. National Football League: The Eighth Circuit Sacks the National Football League Players Association*, id. 135. See also Note (by David Nahmias), *Releasing Superstars from Peonage: Union Consent and the Nonstatutory Labor Exemption*, 104 Harvard L. Rev. 874 (1991).

16. That case, *The Five Smiths v. NFLPA*, 788 F.Supp. 1042 (D.Minn.1992), was later amended to add a claim that if the union was decertified and the league's policies rendered unlawful conspiracies, then efforts by the NFLPA and player agents to share information and coordinate salary negotiations were equally illegal conspiracies. This claim by the NFL, which was dismissed in March 1992, is considered in Chapter 5.

* * *

The NFL defendants' position regarding decertification, however, finds no support in labor law. The National Labor Relations Act "guarantees the employees the right to bargain collectively with representatives of their own choosing." The existence of a bargaining relationship does not depend on NLRB certification, but rather depends on whether a majority of the employees in a bargaining unit supports a particular union as their bargaining representative. This majority status may be achieved through an NLRB election and certification procedure, but a union may also demonstrate majority status "by showing convincing support, for instance, by a union-called strike or strike vote, or ... by possession of cards signed by a majority of the employees authorizing the union to represent them for collective bargaining purposes." NLRB v. Gissel Packing Co., 395 U.S. 575, 596–97 (1969). An employer's obligation to bargain thus is not restricted "solely to those unions whose representative status is certified after a Board election."

* * *

Just as certification is not required to create a collective bargaining relationship, a decertification proceeding is not required to end it.... A decertification election proceeding may be conducted when either an employer or a competing union seeks to contest a union's majority status and the union disagrees. In the present case, a majority of players have voted to end collective bargaining. The NFLPA also concedes that it has lost its majority status and may no longer bargain on the players' behalf. Thus, there is no need for the NLRB to decertify the NFLPA.

The NFL defendants further argue that even if the NLRB decertified the NFLPA, this procedure would be insufficient to end the labor exemption. They do not, however, state what acts they believe would suffice to end the exemption, reflecting perhaps a belief that the labor exemption never ends. The *Powell* court, however, expressly rejected the idea that the NFL defendants enjoy endless antitrust immunity. Moreover, such protection is contrary to the fundamental labor law principle that, just as employees have a right to bargain collectively through a labor organization, they also have a corresponding right not to do so. Thus, the NFL defendants may not argue that they have been denied their opportunity to bargain with plaintiffs because plaintiffs have exercised their right to refrain from union representation.

Based on the foregoing, the court holds that the plaintiffs are no longer part of an "ongoing collective bargaining relationship" with the defendants. The NFLPA no longer engages in collective bargaining and has also refused every overture by the NFL defendants to bargain since November of 1989. The NFLPA further has abandoned its role in all grievance arbitrations and has ceased to regulate agents, leaving them free to represent individual players without NFLPA approval. The plaintiffs have also paid a price for the loss of their collective bargaining representative because the NFL defendants have unilaterally changed insurance benefits and lengthened the season without notifying the NFLPA.

Because no "ongoing collective bargaining relationship" exists, the court determines that the nonstatutory labor exemption has ended. In the absence of continued union representation, the Eighth Circuit's rationale for the exemption no longer applies because the parties may not invoke any remedy under the labor laws, whether it be collective bargaining, instituting an NLRB proceeding for failure to bargain in good faith or resorting to a strike.

Motion granted.

Questions for Discussion

1. You have now witnessed the real-life impact of the doctrinal ruling in *Powell*. Recall that the aim of the labor exemption is to accommodate antitrust policy—a competitive marketplace—to labor law policy—collective action. What policy of federal labor law is served by telling the parties that the labor exemption expires if, and only if, the players association goes out of the business of collective bargaining as a union? At the same time, do not forget the question posed earlier in this chapter; precisely what antitrust policy is served by allowing players associations to sue the owners about employment policies agreed-to within the league?

2. At the same time that Judge Doty was determining the legal effect of the NFLPA's deunionization effort in *Powell* (# 4), a federal district judge in the District of Columbia was deciding *Brown v. Pro Football, Inc. (Washington Redskins)*—holding that the Association's self-inflicted demise as a labor union was not necessary to assert the players' antitrust rights. As we saw from another decision in this litigation excerpted earlier in this chapter, *Brown* dealt with establishment by the NFL in 1989 of six-player development squads for each team at league-mandated salary levels. This league initiative had not been the subject of collective bargaining (let alone agreement) in the past. The NFLPA (which in early 1989 was still acting as the players' bargaining agent) applauded the creation of these squads, but insisted that developmental players' salaries be individually negotiated. When the NFL went ahead with its fixed salary scale of $1,000 per week, the Association filed an antitrust suit. In rejecting the NFL's labor exemption defense to this suit, the district judge concluded, contrary to the various alternatives embraced in *Bridgeman* and *Powell* above, that the appropriate point for terminating the exemption was expiration of the agreement. (And as we saw earlier in the chapter, the judge later found that this salary arrangement violated antitrust law.)

BROWN v. PRO FOOTBALL, INC.

United States District Court, District of Columbia, 1991.

782 F.Supp. 125.

LAMBERTH, DISTRICT JUDGE.

* * *

While this court recognizes the precedent which establishes that the nonstatutory labor exemption survives expiration of a collective bargaining agreement, this court questions the wisdom of continued application of that court-made doctrine beyond expiration due to the fact that such an exemption hinders rather than facilitates the execution of new collective bargaining agreements. The present case provides a good example. The NFL and NFLPA signed a collective bargaining agreement in 1982. That agreement expired in 1987. It is now 1991 and the parties have not negotiated a new collective bargaining agreement. The court has no indication as to when the parties will execute a new agreement. For the past four years, by continuing to hold parties to the terms of the expired collective bargaining agreement, courts have been treating the parties as if they had a current agreement. Such treatment results not from any legislation or express assent of the parties, but from a judicial fiction ostensibly fashioned to promote the negotiation of a new collective bargaining agreement with terms mutually acceptable to both parties.

Unfortunately, the nonstatutory labor exemption actually provides a disincentive for the NFL to sign a new collective bargaining agreement. If the NFL is satisfied with the terms in the expired agreement, all it need do is maintain the status quo and continue to receive exemption from antitrust liability for restraints to which the union no longer agrees. As mentioned earlier, the stated purpose of extending the terms of an expired collective bargaining agreement was to foster a "non-coercive environment that is conducive to serious negotiations on a new contract." Rather than creating an atmosphere conducive to serious negotiations, extension of the terms of an expired collective bargaining agreement actually discourages serious negotiations on a new collective bargaining agreement. As long as the employer is satisfied with the status quo, that employer has no incentive to negotiate a new agreement. Moreover, such an extension apparently removes the firm deadline necessary for fruitful negotiation. The certainty that treble damages under the antitrust laws would attach after a date would create the atmosphere of economic certainty and urgency necessary for the parties to negotiate seriously and sign a new collective bargaining agreement.

* * *

The unions have every right to seek treble damages for unlawful NFL antitrust restraints. It is this court's view that the NFL's antitrust liability should attach at expiration of the collective bargaining agreement, not at some indeterminate point beyond expiration which is labelled "impasse." Antitrust exemption should end at expiration because the reason for the exemption no longer exists: the union no longer agrees to the restraint and therefore continuation of the restraint violates the Sherman Act. Moreover, extension beyond expiration of the collective bargaining agreement breeds uncertainty for the parties and the courts and also inhibits negotiation on a new collective bargaining agreement. If the terms and the nonstatutory exemption don't end at expiration, parties don't have deadlines after which they can be certain that antitrust liability properly applies. Without such certainty, no new agreement will be executed.

Without an endpoint at expiration, the terms of a collective bargaining agreement and the applicability of the nonstatutory labor exemption remain in perpetual limbo. Even if a court were to set expiration at impasse, this would not foster execution of a new collective bargaining agreement or remove any uncertainty because courts would still have to determine the existence of "impasse" and whether court intervention at that point would be appropriate—determinations as to which different courts will likely differ.

* * *

Extending the nonstatutory labor exemption beyond expiration also deprives labor of an important bargaining right and impinges on labor's freedom of contract. The threat of treble damages under the antitrust laws is one of the union's economic weapons in its collective bargaining arsenal. Exempting employers from application of the antitrust laws in the absence of a collective bargaining agreement deprives unions of a statutorily created bargaining chip in the negotiating process. This chip may well be labor's strongest weapon insofar as labor has the power to subject employers to great economic risk under the antitrust and labor laws for activities which Congress has determined are unlawful restraints. This economic force is a lawful chip the union has to induce employers to reach agreement on collective bargaining terms so that the exemption would apply.

At the same time, extension of the nonstatutory labor exemption beyond expiration of the collective bargaining agreement is inconsistent with the primary policy behind the labor laws and the nonstatutory labor exemption. As discussed earlier, that goal is to promote the execution of new collective bargaining agreements. Under the nonstatutory labor exemption, employers are exempt from certain applications of the antitrust law. Such exemption is consistent with the policies behind labor laws and the exemption which together seek to encourage employers and unions to agree on terms relating to conditions of employment. Terms included within a collective bargaining agreement are protected. Extension of the exemption beyond expiration of that agreement frustrates the relevant policies because it treats the parties as if there is a collective bargaining agreement when in fact there is none. If the parties have not expressly agreed to terms relating to conditions of employment, this court can find no discernible justification for granting the employer any exemption from the antitrust laws. To do so would reward employers simply for being part of a collective bargaining relationship where employers and labor had at one time agreed on terms relating to conditions of employment.

Summary dismissal denied.

————

Is this formulation of the termination of the labor exemption more or less persuasive than those seen earlier in *Powell* and *Bridgeman*? In any event, is *Brown* distinguishable on the grounds that development squad salaries had never been negotiated with the NFLPA, unlike the restraints on veteran free agency in football which the NFL had actually relaxed in the Plan B attacked in *McNeil* or the salary cap in basketball which had been maintained as it was in the NBA's expired agreement with the Players Association before being attacked in *Bridgeman*?

After the district court judge had rejected the NFL's labor exemption defense in *Brown*, and then granted the plaintiffs summary judgment on the antitrust violation issue, a week-long trial was held in the fall of 1992 on the issue of damages. The jury determined that $10 million in damages had been caused to the 235 development squad players, an assessment that was trebled to $30 million (plus legal costs). The NFL announced, of course, that it would appeal. Ironically, Tony Brown, the lead plaintiff who was now out of football, won $460,000 in his suit which had been backed by the NFLPA, even though Brown had been one of the replacement players who enabled the NFL to break the Players Association strike in 1987.

Throughout the entire *McNeil* (and *Brown*) litigation, the NFL had been intensely pursuing settlement of these issues and resumption of a collective bargaining relationship with the NFLPA. In January 1993, the parties reached agreement on a long-term pact involving substantial compromises by both sides in their legal and labor relations positions. Just to synopsize the terms of this settlement (which is depicted in detail in the Supplement), veteran players will become free agents after five years of service, though NFL clubs can protect designated "franchise" player who is guaranteed a spot in the upper echelons of player salaries. In return, the Association agreed to continue the rookie draft, though with the number of rounds reduced from twelve to seven. Most important, the Association agreed to a salary cap if the league's overall salary payments reached a certain percentage of designated league revenues. (The nature and evolution of the salary cap arrangement is detailed in Chapter 5.) In the event a salary cap comes into effect, veteran free agency will ensue after four years of service. Teams losing free agents would be compensated by extra draft picks, but not at the expense of the teams signing the free agents. Finally, the NFL agreed to pay a total of $195 million (including $20 million in legal fees) to resolve the claims of players whose free agency had been restricted by Plan B.

Why did the parties' negotiating postures evolve in this direction? To what extent did they reflect an accurate perception of the parties' respective legal positions? If you had been counsel advising the

NFLPA, would you have felt there were good *legal* reasons to settle for something considerably short of total free agency? Would you have thought that there were good *practical* reasons for constructing a different system? Do your reasons reflect the interests of all Association members, or just some? If the latter, which types of member? Now put yourself in the shoes of the NFL and its counsel, and go through the same legal and pragmatic analysis. Why was there a negotiating zone for creative resolution of this problem, which had bedeviled football for the last quarter century?

One final note about this new settlement. The agreement states that (a) the parties do not waive their right to make antitrust claims about provisions in the settlement after it expires, (b) that the parties recognize that the labor exemption applies throughout the term of the new collective agreement and that neither party will sue the other for any antitrust violations until impasse is reached in bargaining or six months after the contract's expiry, whichever comes later, and (c) that if the NFLPA decides to decertify after impasse, the NFL will not invoke the labor exemption on the ground that the union had not really decertified. Consider the difficulties posed for the NFL by the NFLPA's decision to decertify after *Powell.* The absence of a union certainly made it harder for the two sides to settle all the player litigation and enter into a new collective agreement. Would not both parties have found it in their mutual interest to agree that the NFL would waive any right to invoke the labor exemption in an antitrust suit brought by the NFLPA at some point after the new agreement expired? Why might the NFL have opposed such a provision?

Chapter Four

LABOR LAW AND COLLECTIVE BARGAINING IN PROFESSIONAL SPORTS [1]

Two comparisons between baseball and football underscore the significance of the subject matter of this chapter. In 1967, the average salary of Major League Baseball players was $19,000, of National Football League players, $25,000. In the early 1970s, baseball players failed in their effort in *Flood* to secure the assistance of antitrust law in improving their economic condition. By contrast, football players won lower court decisions in both the *Smith* case involving the rookie draft and the *Mackey* case involving restraints on veteran free agency. But by the early 1990s average baseball players' salaries had soared slightly over $1 million, while football players lagged far behind, averaging $495,000 in 1992. A major part of the explanation for this conjunction of financial and legal developments lies in the course taken by union representation and collective bargaining in the two sports conducted under the auspices of the National Labor Relations Act (NLRA). Indeed, as the *Powell* and *McNeil* litigation showed, football players are engaged in a concerted effort to dispense with labor law and return to what they believe are the friendlier confines of antitrust.

1. The principal reference source for both the labor relations history and doctrinal issues in this area is Robert C. Berry, William B. Gould and Paul D. Staudohar, *Labor Relations in Professional Sports* (Dover, Ma.: Auburn House, 1986), as supplemented by Paul D. Staudohar, *The Sports Industry and Collective Bargaining* (Ithaca, N.Y.: I.L.R. Press, 2d ed.1989). See also Lee Lowenfish, *The Imperfect Diamond: A History of Baseball's Labor Wars* (New York: Da Capo Press, rev. ed. 1991) and David Harris, *The League: The Rise and Decline of the NFL* (New York: Bantam, 1986) for interesting depictions of what happened in collective bargaining in those two sports. The recently published memoirs of the two principal protagonists in baseball in the critical period, Marvin Miller, the players association's leader, and Bowie Kuhn, baseball's commissioner, offer a provocative counterpoint on the key decisions made in that sport. See Marvin Miller, *A Whole Different Ballgame: The Sport and Business of Baseball* (New York: Birch Lane Press, 1991), and Bowie Kuhn, *Hardball: The Education of a Baseball Commissioner* (New York: Times Books, 1987). Andrew Zimbalist, *Baseball and Billions* (New York: Basic Books, 1992), particularly in Chapters 1 and 4, presents a sophisticated but readable analysis of the evolution and current state of baseball's labor relations and economics.

The first organizations of professional athletes developed more than a century ago with the formation of the National Brotherhood of Baseball Players, a body that shortly thereafter tried to establish a Players' League to free its members from the shackles of the established National League's reserve clause and $2,000 per year salary cap. However, the seeds of modern collective action by professional athletes were sowed in the 1950s, with the formation of player organizations in all four team sports. In each sport these bodies were deliberately named *associations* rather than *unions*, because the latter term was considered appropriate only for the teams' concession vendors or maintenance crews, not for elite athletes. Not until the mid–1960s did players realize that for all their status in the outside world, to force owners to change the structure of the players' market they would have to engage in full-fledged collective bargaining under professional leadership—the leadership of Marvin Miller in baseball, Ed Garvey in football, Larry Fleisher in basketball, and Alan Eagleson in hockey.

A major preoccupation of the player unions in the 1970s was antitrust litigation, as reflected in the cases in the previous chapter. Both before and after this litigation, though, all the unions established allegiance among the players and engaged in direct negotiations with the leagues. This effort took place under the umbrella of the NLRA.

The NLRA, first enacted in 1935 as the Wagner Act and sweepingly revised by the Taft–Hartley Act of 1947, confers on employees (by Section 7) the rights to organize themselves into a union, to engage in collective bargaining with their employer, and to go on strike or take other concerted action for their mutual aid and protection. The employees' right to engage in (or refrain from) this bargaining process is secured in Section 8 by several unfair labor practice provisions that prohibit particular forms of employer (or union) interference and intimidation. The primary responsibility for interpreting and administering the Act, both to protect these employee rights and to preserve a legitimate sphere of action for employers and unions, is conferred on the National Labor Relations Board (NLRB), whose decisions are subject to a measure of judicial review by the federal appellate courts.

Over the last half century, the NLRB and the courts have developed an elaborate labor law jurisprudence. In the less than 25 years of active union representation in professional sports, this industry has produced decisions that illustrate virtually all the major doctrinal spheres in contemporary labor law. Reading the sports labor law cases also gives us a bird's-eye view of the tumultuous course taken by labor relations in sports. Finally, the cases provide a revealing perspective of labor law itself, as the NLRB tries both to resolve conflicts between leagues and unions and to reconcile tensions on each side of the bargaining table—on the league side, among the various clubs and their commissioner, and on the union side, between veterans and rookies, superstars and journeymen.

Perhaps the most important question posed by these materials stems from juxtaposition of these two facts. The National Football League Players Association (NFLPA), together with its affiliate that represented players in the short-lived North American Soccer League, has produced the lion's share of sports labor litigation and jurisprudence. As we saw in the previous chapter, in the late 1980s the NFLPA decided that collective bargaining under the NLRA was so fruitless an exercise that the players' lot would be improved if the association abandoned its statutory labor role in an effort to restore the halcyon days of antitrust. What does this tell us about the effectiveness of the national labor laws and about the resources of the rival parties in football (as compared with baseball, a sport in which antitrust has always been unavailable)?

A. FREE AGENCY VIA LABOR ARBITRATION

Before detailing the distinctive jurisprudence that has evolved for sports labor relations, we present two decisions that exhibit the starkly contrasting fate of baseball and football unions operating under the self-same labor statute. These two judgments were actually rendered by labor arbitrators, rather than by the NLRB. Under the statutory framework, once a union has been able to win a collective agreement from an employer, the standard mechanism for administering this agreement is through private arbitration. Traditionally in the sports world, this role of arbitrator—of private judge—had been performed by the commissioner under both the uniform player contract and the league rules. However, in the early collective agreements negotiated by the player associations, the commissioner was replaced by an independent arbitrator as the person who would finally resolve grievances arising under the agreement or standard player contract.[2]

This little-noticed institutional change, under which Peter Seitz replaced Commissioner Bowie Kuhn as interpreter of both the baseball labor agreement and player contract, had a profound effect on the sport. Just three years after the Supreme Court in the *Curt Flood* case had once again refused to subject baseball's "reserve system" to antitrust scrutiny, Seitz was presented with the following case, which required that he construe the meaning and scope of the key components of that system.

---

2. As we saw in Chapter 1, though, this displacement was not absolute. Commissioners have retained in varying degrees their responsibility as final arbiter of the "best interests of the sport."

NATIONAL & AMERICAN LEAGUE PROFESSIONAL BASEBALL CLUBS v. MAJOR LEAGUE BASEBALL PLAYERS ASSOCIATION

(Messersmith and McNally Grievances).

66 Labor Arbitration 101 (1976).

SEITZ, ARBITRATOR.

[Andy Messersmith of the Los Angeles Dodgers and Dave McNally of the Montreal Expos had both refused to sign new player contracts at the end of the 1974 season; instead they played the 1975 season under the terms of Section 10(c) of the Uniform Player Contract, which gave their clubs the right to renew the old contract "on the same terms" (except for salary, the amount of which had recently been subjected to arbitration in cases of dispute). The question posed to the arbitrator was whether the contract as renewed by the club contained this option clause as well. If it did, the player could be included indefinitely on the club's reserve lists through use of this perpetually renewable option. If on the other hand, the reserve option clause was spent after its first use, the two players had now become free agents.

In addition to that issue of interpretation, the arbitrator faced a preliminary question of whether he even had jurisdiction to entertain this issue, because of the presence of the following provision in the collective agreement:

> Except as adjusted or modified hereby, *this agreement does not deal with the reserve system.* The Parties have different views as to the legality and as to the merits of such system as presently constituted. This agreement shall in no way prejudice the position or legal rights of the parties or of any player regarding the reserve system.
>
> During the term of this agreement neither of the parties will resort to any form of concerted action with respect to the issue of the reserve system, and there shall be no obligation to negotiate with respect to the reserve system.

(Emphasis supplied.)

In the first half of his decision, Seitz wrestled with the meaning of this apparent exclusion of the reserve clause from the agreement upon which his authority rested. Eventually, he concluded that he did have jurisdiction to resolve grievances about the meaning of different provisions in the collective agreement and the standard player contract, even though some of these provisions served as more or less important features of the reserve system. The merits of that judgment will be examined later in this chapter, with the decision in *Kansas City Royals v. Major League Baseball Players Ass'n.*, 532 F.2d 615 (8th Cir.1976), in which a federal appeals court reviewed the correctness of the arbitrator's jurisdictional ruling. Here we present the arbitrator's analysis of the crucial question of the scope of the reserve clause in baseball.

The arbitrator first reviewed the origins and development of the reserve clause.]

* * *

The Reserve System of the leagues is nowhere defined in a sentence or a paragraph. Reference is commonly and frequently made in the press and by the news media to a "Reserve Clause"; but there is no such single clause encompassing the subject matter. It seems fair to say, on the basis of what has been presented, that the "Reserve System" refers to a complex and a congeries of rules of the leagues (and provisions in the collective Basic Agreement and the Uniform Players Contract) related to the objective of retaining exclusive control over the service of their players in the interest of preserving discipline, preventing the enticement of players, maintaining financial stability and promoting a balance or a relative parity of competitive skills as among clubs. Such "exclusive control," it is said, is exercised by a Club placing the name of a player on its "reserve list" which is distributed to the other clubs in both leagues. A player on such a list, assert the leagues, cannot "play for or negotiate with any other club until his contract has been assigned or he has been released" (Rule 4–A(a)) and may not be the subject of "tampering" as described in Rule 3(g).

This system of reservation of exclusive control is historic in baseball and is traceable to the early days of the organized sport in the 19th century. Over the years, the scheme and structure of provisions designed to establish and maintain that control has been changed in expression. The leagues assert that the system was designed, initially, to combat the institutional chaos that resulted when players under contract with one club defected to another. In an effort to deal with the problem, it is represented, various versions of reserve clauses had been adopted.

The problems facing the National League in the closing years of the 19th century, however, in respect of defecting players, were not limited to the circumstances of a player defecting to another club in the league. Other leagues came into being from time to time and disappeared. The League, in 1899, in an effort to prevent defection of players to other leagues, placed in the individual player's contract a "renewal clause," so-called. This clause, according to the leagues, was the legal basis for clubs applying to the courts of equity to enjoin players from "jumping" to a rival league. As Club Exhibit 16 evidences, contract renewal clauses, over time, differed in their provisions; but all gave an option to a Club to renew its contracts with players for stated periods.

* * *

In 1947 the renewal clause in the Uniform Players Contract (which had been in effect since 1930) was amended for that reason to provide as follows:

> 10(a) On or before February 1st (or if a Sunday, then the next preceding business day) in the year of the last playing season covered by this contract, the Club may tender to the Player a contract for the term of that year by mailing the same to the Player.... If prior to the March 1 next succeeding said February, the Player and the Club have not agreed upon the terms of the contract, then on or before 10 days after said March 1, *the Club*

shall have the right by written notice to the Player ... to renew this contract for the period of one year on the same terms, except that the amount payable to the Player shall be such as the Club shall fix in such notice; provided, however, that said amount, if fixed by a Major League Club shall be an amount payable at a rate of not less than 75% of the rate stipulated for the preceding year. (Emphasis supplied.)

This provision, except as amended as indicated in the accompanying footnotes, was carried forward in all forms of the Uniform Player Contract subsequently used, including those signed by these grievants.

* * *

[The arbitrator then summarized the positions of the parties to the present dispute.]

Messersmith signed a one-year contract with the Los Angeles Dodgers in 1974. This contract was duly renewed by the Club for what is commonly called the "renewal year" of 1975. The renewal was effected under Section 10(a) of the Uniform Players Contract.

The Players Association claims that Messersmith, having served out and completed his renewal year on September 29, 1975, was no longer under contract with the Los Angeles Club and, accordingly, was a free agent to negotiate for the rendition of his services with any of the other clubs in the leagues; but that the clubs "have conspired to deny Mr. Messersmith that right and have maintained the position that the Los Angeles Club is still exclusively entitled to his services."

As an affirmative defense, it is the position of the leagues that, by virtue of having sent its reserve list on November 17, 1975 to the appropriate officials and the subsequent promulgation of that list by them, the Los Angeles Club has reserved Messersmith's services for its own use, exclusively, for the ensuing season. This position is based on Major League Rule 4–A(a) which provides:

(a) FILING. On or before November 20 in each year, each Major League Club shall transmit to the Commissioner and to its League President *a list not exceeding forty (40) active and eligible players, whom the club desires to reserve for the ensuing season....* On or before November 30 the League President shall transmit all of such lists to the Secretary–Treasurer of the Executive Council, who shall thereupon promulgate same, *and thereafter no player on any list shall be eligible to play for or negotiate with any other club until his contract has been assigned or he has been released* .... (Emphasis supplied.)

This Major League Rule is supported and supplemented by Major League Rule 3(g), which reads as follows:

(g) TAMPERING. To reserve discipline and competition and to prevent the enticement of players ... *there shall be no negotiations or dealings respecting employment, either present or prospective between any player ... and any club other than the club with which he is under contract or acceptance of terms, or by which is reserved ...   unless the club or league with which he is connected shall have in writing, expressly authorized such negotiations or dealings prior to their commencement.   (Emphasis supplied.)*

* * *

[After a brief statement of the narrowness of his ruling, arbitrator Seitz presented his conclusions on the two issues. He first ruled that the option clause was *not* included in the renewed contract—and hence that Messersmith and McNally were not under contract to the Dodgers and Expos, respectively, after the 1975 season.]

It deserves emphasis that this decision strikes no blow emancipating players from claimed serfdom or involuntary servitude such as was alleged in the *Flood Case*. It does not condemn the Reserve System presently in force on constitutional or moral grounds. It does not counsel or require that the System be changed to suit the predilections or preferences of an arbitrator acting as a Philosopher–King intent upon imposing his own personal brand of industrial justice on the parties. To go beyond this would be an act of quasi-judicial arrogance!

* * *

However, the scope and effect of a reserve system is for the *Parties* to determine, not the Panel. As stated, the Panel's role is restricted to an interpretation and application of the agreement of the parties.

* * *

No one challenges the right of a Club to renew a Player's contract with or without his consent, under Section 10(a), "for the period of one [renewal] year." I read the record, however, as containing a contention by the leagues that when a Club renews a Player's contract for the renewal year, the contract in force during that year contains the "right of renewal" clause as one of its terms, entitling the Club to renew the contract in successive years, to perpetuity, perhaps, so long as the Player is alive and the Club has duly discharged all conditions required of it. This is challenged by the Players Association whose position it is that the contractual relationship between the Club and the Player terminates at the end of the first renewal year. Thus, it claims that there was no longer any contractual bond between Messersmith and the Los Angeles Club on September 29, 1975.

The league's argument is based on the language in Section 10(a) of the Player's Contract that the Club "may renew this contract for the period of one year *on the same terms* "; and that among those "terms" is the right to further contract renewal.

In the law of contract construction, as I know it, there is nothing to prevent parties from agreeing to successive renewals of the terms of their bargain (even to what had been described as "perpetuity"), provided the contract expresses that intention with explicit clarity and the right of subsequent renewals does not have to be implied....

There is nothing in Section 10(a) which, explicitly, expresses agreement that the Players Contract can be renewed for any period beyond the first renewal year. The point the leagues present must be based upon the implication or assumption, that if the renewed contract is "on the same terms" as the contract for the preceding year (with the exception of the amount of compensation) the right to additional renewals must have been an integral part of the renewed contract. I find great difficulties, in so implying or assuming, in respect of a contract providing for the rendition of personal services in which one would expect a more explicit expression of intention. There are numerous provisions and terms in the Uniform Players Contract that are renewed in the renewal year when a Club exercises its renewal rights under Section 10(a). Provision of the right to make subsequent and successive renewals is in an entirely different category, however, than the numerous terms in the Players Contract which deal with working conditions and duties which the Club and the Player owe to each other. That right, critically, concerns and involves the continued existence of *the contract itself* as expressing the mutual undertakings of the parties and the bargain which they struck. All of the other "terms" of the Player–Club relationship stand or fall according to whether the contract, as such, is renewed.

[The arbitrator then discussed two basketball cases—*Lemat Corp. v. Barry*, 80 Cal.Rptr. 240 (Cal. Ct.App.1969) and *Central New York Basketball v. Barnett*, 181 N.E.2d 506 (Ohio C.P. Ct. 1961) (both of which we saw in Chapter 2)—involving similar renewal clauses. In *Barnett*, the *club* had argued and the court agreed, that the option clause in basketball's standard player contract was for one renewal year only, not perpetual, and *Barry* followed *Barnett*.]

* * *

In this connection it is also pertinent to observe that the "no tampering rule" (which, in baseball, is contained in Major League Rule 3(g)), has its equivalent, in NBA basketball, in Section 35 of the NBA constitution. The prohibition there, however, applies to any player "who is *under contract* to any other member of the Association." (Emphasis supplied.) Thus, in the "reserve system" of the NBA basketball league, the player must have been under contract to be reserved; but in this case, the leagues argue that even if the contract be construed to have expired, the player may be reserved.

In these circumstances I find that Section 10(a) falls short of reserving to a Club the right to renew a contract at the end of the renewal year. Accordingly, I find that Messersmith was not under contract when his renewal year came to an end.

[On the second issue, the arbitrator concluded that the major league rules did *not* prevent other teams from attempting to sign

Messersmith and McNally—in short they were free agents within the league.]

We now turn to the Major League Rules, as to which it has already been stated that, by virtue of Section 9(a) of the Uniform Players Contract and Article XIII of the Basic Agreement, they are a part of the agreements of the parties if not inconsistent with the provisions of the Basic Agreement and the Players Contract.

The parties are in sharp conflict on this. The leagues claim that there is exclusive reservation of a player's services under Rule 4–A(a) regardless of the continued existence of any contractual relationship between the Club and the Player. Thus, Counsel for the National League asserted that:

> The club may continue the pattern of career-long control over the player and that this pattern of career-long control is not essentially dependent upon the renewal clause (Section 10–A) at all.

The Players Association, on the other hand, asserts that in the absence of a nexus or linkage of contract between the Player and the Club, there can be no exclusive reservation of the right to his future services.

* * *

These provisions and others in the very Rules which, allegedly, establish the kind of reservation of services for which the leagues contend, all subsume the existence of a *contractual relation*. The leagues would have it that it is only when there is a release or assignment that a contract must have been in existence; but even if there were no contract in existence (the players' contract having expired) a Club, by placing the name of a player on a list, can reserve exclusive rights to his services from year to year for an unstated and indefinite period in the future. I find this unpersuasive. It is like the claims of some nations that persons once its citizens, wherever they live and regardless of the passage of time, the swearing of other allegiances and other circumstances, are still its own nationals and subject to the obligations that citizenship in the nation imposes. This "status" theory is incompatible with the doctrine or policy of freedom of contract in the economic and political society in which we live and of which the professional sport of baseball ("the national game") is a part.

* * *

Finally, on this point, it is evident that traditionally, the leagues have regarded the existence of a contract as a basis for the reservation of players. In Club's Exhibit No. 15 there is set forth the Cincinnati Peace Compact of the National and American Leagues, signed January 10, 1903—probably the most important step in the evolution and development of the present Reserve System. In that document it provided:

> Second—A *reserve rule* shall be recognized, by which each and every club may reserve *players under contract*, and that a uniform

contract for the use of each league shall be adopted. (Emphasis supplied.)

This emphasis on the existence of a contract for reservation of a player to be effective was perpetuated in the Major League Rules to some of which I have referred. It is even found in Rule 3(g) in which, however, it is referred to disjunctively along with acceptance of terms "or by which he was reserved." However, *even in Rule 3(g)*, reading it analytically and construing it syntactically, one may reasonably reach the conclusion:—*no contract, no reservation*. The provision says there shall be no dealings between a player and a club other than the one "with which he is under *contract*, or acceptance of terms, *or by which he is reserved*." (Emphasis supplied.) ...

Thus, I reach the conclusion that, absent a contractual connection between Messersmith and the Los Angeles Club after September 28, 1975, the Club's action in reserving his services for the ensuing year by placing him on its reserve list was unavailing and ineffectual in prohibiting him from dealing with other clubs in the league and to prohibit such clubs from dealing with him.

In the case of McNally whom the Montreal Club had placed on its disqualified list, a similar conclusion has been reached.

* * *

[Finally, arbitrator Seitz addressed the League's concern that the absence of a lifetime reserve system would devastate baseball.]

I am not unmindful of the testimony of the Commissioner of Baseball and the Presidents of the National and American League given at the hearings as to the importance of maintaining the integrity of the Reserve System. It was represented to me that any decision of the Arbitration Panel sustaining the Messersmith and McNally grievances would have dire results, wreak great harm to the Reserve System and do serious damage to the sport of baseball.

Thus, for example, it was stated that a decision favoring these grievants would encourage many other players to elect to become free agents at the end of the renewal years; that this would encourage clubs with the largest monetary resources to engage free agents, thus unsettling the competitive balance between clubs, so essential to the sport; that it would increase enormously the already high costs of training and seasoning young players to achieve the level of skills required in professional baseball and such investments would be sacrificed if they became free agents at the end of a renewal year; that driven by the compulsion to win, owners of franchises would over-extend themselves financially and improvident bidding for players in an economic climate in which, today, some clubs are strained, financially; that investors will be discouraged from putting money in franchises in which several of the star players on the club team will become free agents at the end of a renewal year and no continuing control over the players' services can be exercised; and that even the integrity of the sport may be placed in hazard under certain circumstances.

I do not purport to appraise these apprehensions. They are all based on speculations as to what may ensue. Some of the fears may be imaginary or exaggerated; but some may be reasonable, realistic and sound. After all, they were voiced by distinguished baseball officials with long experience in the sport and a background for judgment in such matters much superior to my own. However, as stated above, at length, it is not for the Panel (and especially the writer) to determine what, if anything, is good or bad about the reserve system. The Panel's sole duty is to interpret and apply the agreements and undertakings of the parties. If any of the expressed apprehensions and fears are soundly based, I am confident that the dislocations and damage to the reserve system can be avoided or minimized through good faith collective bargaining between the parties. There are numerous expedients available and arrangements that can be made that will soften the blow—if this decision, indeed, should be regarded as a blow. This decision is not the end of the line by any means. The parties, jointly, are free to agree to disregard it and compose their differences as to the reserve system in any way they see fit.

* * *

Grievance upheld.

————

Early in his opinion, arbitrator Seitz emphatically stated that his role was not to evaluate the merits of baseball's reserve system, but merely to interpret the meaning of its constituent provisions. Look closely at the passages in which the arbitrator considers and selects from the alternative interpretations advanced by the Association and the League about the proper interpretation of the option clause in the player's contract and the reserve clause in the major league rules. Is there such a sharp distinction between evaluation and interpretation of these legal documents?

The legal implication of the *Messersmith* ruling was that any baseball player could become a free agent simply by playing out his option year without signing a new contract. As the *Messersmith* decision was being rendered and judicially reviewed in the winter of 1975–1976, the baseball collective agreement was itself expiring and being renegotiated. Naturally enough, free agency became the central issue in these negotiations. After a seventeen-day owner lockout of the players during spring training—a work stoppage that was unilaterally ended by Commissioner Kuhn in the "best interests of the sport"—the Players Association and the owners' Player Relations Committee reached a new collective agreement in the summer of 1976. The new contract modified free agency considerably. During his first two years in the league, a player had to accept his club's unilateral contract offers, and for years three through six the player was still contractually bound to his initial club, but he had the right to final-offer arbitration about the appropriate amount of salary (see later in the chapter). Only after six years' service did full free agency begin. We saw in Chapter 1 how owners such as Charles Finley and Ted Turner reacted to this new regime and how Commissioner Kuhn responded. Later in this chapter, we will see how the baseball commissioner and owners collaborated in the mid–1980s to stifle competition for free agents, and how the Players Association and Seitz's successor arbitrators responded. Despite these struggles, however, the basic structure of the baseball player market remains the same as fashioned fifteen years ago.

Messersmith and its progeny stand in stark contrast to what happened in football. As we saw in Chapter 3, shortly after the arbitral ruling in the *Messersmith* grievance, federal appeals courts held in *Mackey* and *Smith* that football's restraints on competition for players violated federal antitrust laws. Like their counterparts in basketball and hockey, though, the NFL Players Association subsequently agreed in collective bargaining to alternative restraints on free agency.

This regime in football gave the incumbent owner a right of first refusal regarding any offer made by another club to one of the team's free agent players. If the incumbent team chose not to match the offer, it was awarded specified draft picks intended to compensate for the value of the player being lost. Unlike baseball, then, football did not establish any time at which a veteran player would enjoy untrammelled free agency. Experience soon made it clear that there would be little or no competitive bidding for players under this new system, and as a result the NFLPA sought to emulate their baseball counterpart's success in labor arbitration.

NFL PLAYERS ASSOCIATION v. NFL MANAGEMENT COUNCIL

(John Dutton grievance).

Arbitration, 1980.

LUSKIN, ARBITRATOR.

* * *

[John Dutton, a defensive lineman with the Baltimore Colts, played out his contract in 1978, received no offers as a free agent, and then played the next season pursuant to a one-year contract at 110 percent of his previous year's salary as provided for in Section 17 of the collective agreement. At the expiration of that season Dutton again sought offers from other NFL clubs as a free agent. He again received no offers, because the NFL interpreted the agreement as providing the old club of *any* free agent with a right of first refusal or a right to receive draft choice compensation from the new club. Dutton and the

NFLPA then filed a grievance alleging that these rights in the old club were intended under the bargaining agreement to apply only in the first year after a player's negotiated contract had expired, not year after year (that is, in years in which the expiring contract was itself a contract that had been renewed pursuant to Section 17). The question the football arbitrator had to decide was whether after that second season, Dutton—like Messersmith in baseball—was an unrestricted free agent. The Players Association argued that if the parties to the collective bargaining agreement—who undoubtedly were aware of the ruling in *Messersmith*—intended to create a perpetually renewable option, the agreement would have said so explicitly. Since it did not, Section 17 must be construed as leaving a veteran who played out his option year a free agent, not subject to either a right of first refusal or compensation to his former team. The League retorted that Section 17 was just part of the broader Article XV Right of First Refusal/Compensation provision, and that Section 1 of that Article subjected all "Veteran Free Agents" to these rights in their former team. The one exception to that principle was found in Section 18, cases of Extreme Personal Hardship, and this section excluded just first refusal, not compensation for players who fitted within the Section's terms. Both sides also produced evidence of the circumstances of negotiations to support their claims about what the other side actually understood this Article to mean.]

* * *

During the entire period of the series of negotiating meetings that began with the New Orleans meetings in January 1977, and continued thereafter in Washington and New York, the Management Council negotiators did not state that they would construe the ultimately agreed-upon language in Article XV, Section 17, in a manner which would permit a team to exercise continuing options in accordance with the procedures set forth therein. The NFLPA did not, at any time, state to the Management Council negotiators that it would interpret the agreed-upon language in a manner which would provide a veteran free agent with complete and total freedom to contract with another team without being restricted by a right of first refusal or compensation in instances where a player had gone through the Section 17(b) procedures for a second time.

* * *

The evidence would conclusively indicate that there was a meeting of the minds in almost every major respect. The parties did agree upon a system. They reached agreements based upon the views expressed by the 8th Circuit Court of Appeals in *Mackey*, when the Court referred to the fact that a reserve system was a mandatory subject for negotiations and that there was the need for reasonable restrictions relating to player transfers as "necessary for the successful operations of the NFL." The Court then proceeded to "encourage" the parties to resolve that question through collective bargaining since the parties were far better situated to agreeably resolve "what rules governing players' transfers are best suited for their mutual interests than are the courts."

* * *

The parties to this Agreement had been negotiating under different circumstances and in different bargaining climates for approximately three years. They were at all times well aware of the agreements reached between the parties in baseball and basketball, and they were at all times aware of the arbitration awards in baseball. They were aware of the decisions of the Courts in the lawsuits that were filed that challenged the legality of the football draft, the standard players contract, the Rozelle Rule, and other forms of restrictions alleged to constitute violations of the anti-trust laws. Both parties were mindful of the need for meaningful movement away from previously fixed and rigid positions. The NFLPA demanded, negotiated and received substantial benefits upon the conclusion of the negotiations and the settlement of the pending litigation. There is evidence in this record that the settlement of the class action in *Alexander* involved the payment of approximately $16,000,000 by the NFL to the members of the class. The obligations assumed by the NFL for retroactive pension benefits and other forms of compensation involved costs to the NFL of in excess of $100,000,000. The member clubs obtained a "system" which they believed that they had to have and could live with. In return, the NFLPA obtained a contractual procedure whereby, under the established system, any player completing his contract would have the right to "test the market" and determine what his services might be worth to other clubs that would be willing to negotiate with that player. The fact that the system may not have worked as effectively as the NFLPA may have expected, would not necessarily indicate the existence of a conspiracy by the teams to engage in concerted action to refuse to make "offers" and to thereby nullify the system.

The primary issue in this proceeding must, therefore, turn on the interpretation to be placed upon the contractual language appearing in the applicable provisions of Article XV.

Article XV establishes certain precise procedures that must be followed by a team in order to retain its right of first refusal/compensation. A failure to follow those procedures could result in permitting a player to sign a contract with a new team without providing his former team with right of first refusal or compensation. In each instance, however, where that occurs, controlling contractual language is clear, precise and unambiguous. Under Article XV, Section 18 (Extreme Personal Hardship), the "outside arbitrator," under an established set of facts and circumstances, could find that there had been a substantive violation of Article V, Section 1, or the existence of extreme personal hardship, in which event the arbitrator could deny to the player's old club its "right of first refusal." The parties have explicitly agreed that in the event first refusal rights are denied (under Section 18) because of extreme personal hardship, the club's last written contract offered to the player constitutes a "qualifying offer" for compensation pursuant to Article XV, Section 11. It should be noted that the last sentence of Article XV, Section 17 (Re-signing), permits a player to be free to negotiate and sign a contract or contracts with any NFL club without first refusal rights or compensation between clubs under circumstances where a player's old club does not advise him in writing by June 1st that it desires to re-sign him. That procedure appears in the Agreement immediately after that portion of Section 17(b) upon which the Union relies when it contends that a player becomes a free agent with a right to contract with any other team in the NFL without any provision for his old team to receive compensation or to have a right of first refusal. The language of Section 17(b) does not serve to support the Union's contention in this case. The fact that provision is made for a salary of 110 percent of the salary provided in the last preceding year, or 120 percent if the player has played out the option year, does not necessarily mean that a team's contractual right to first refusal/compensation has ended at that point in time.

Article XV, Section 1 (Applicability), clearly and unambiguously concerns itself with players "who play out the options in their contracts or whose contracts otherwise expire ... and with respect to veteran free agents through at least 1982...." All of the sections of Article XV apply to those persons. The various sections establish precise procedures that are to be followed with respect to a teams' right to exercise rights of first refusal or to receive compensation for the loss of the services of a veteran free agent based upon the timetables, the procedures and the salaries. Section 17 serves to define the rights and obligations of a veteran free agent who receives no offer to sign a contract with a different NFL club (pursuant to Article XV) and he is advised by his old club that the old club desires to resign him. The player has an option which he may exercise within fifteen days thereafter to sign a contract or contracts with his old club at its last best written offer or to sign a one-year contract (with no option year) with his old club at 110 percent of the salary provided in his contract for the last preceding year. There then follows a parenthetical provision which increases the salary to 120 percent if the player has just played out the option year. Nowhere within the language of Section 17(b) are there words or phrases which could be interpreted in a manner which places a limitation upon the option rights of a player's old club to one option or two options following the expiration of his contract or contracts.

It could very well be argued that the absence of language in Section 17 that specifically establishes a limitation upon the team's option rights or the absence of language that would provide annual options that a team may exercise by paying a player an additional ten percent each year that the option is exercised would create the existence of an ambiguity. Section 17(b) may not be a model of clarity, but the fact remains that Article XV, Section 1, becomes completely controlling since the general applicability of that provision has neither been modified nor amended by the language of Section 17(b).

In instances where the parties made provision for total free agent status, the contractual language explicitly provides for a team's loss of first refusal or compensation rights. The last sentence of Article XV, Section 17, illustrates the procedures adopted by the parties throughout Article XV. In an instance where a team may lose its right of first refusal and retain its compensation rights, the language of Article XV, Section 18, is illustrative of that understanding. The arbitrator cannot infer from the absence of affirmative or negative language that the parties reached an agreement or understanding that would serve to confer total free agent status to a veteran player who had completed a year of service pursuant to a Section 17(b) contract....

Grievance denied.

————

These critical arbitration rulings in baseball and in football were starkly different in outcome. Are the textual differences in the collective agreement language sufficient to explain the contrasting results? Or is it more likely that other factors—perhaps the rather different bargaining scenarios leading up to adoption of the contract language or the differing philosophical inclinations of the arbitrators—account for the ultimate verdicts?

The NFLPA was not able to retrieve through arbitration what it had given up through negotiation. And whereas the MLBPA preserved the core of its *Messersmith* victory in bargaining struggles and work stoppages in 1976, 1981, 1985, and 1990, the NFLPA made no appreciable headway in modifying, let alone eliminating, the "equalization" principle through a bruising seven-week strike in 1982 and a disastrous three-week strike in 1987. For that reason, the NFLPA formally disclaimed any interest in serving as a union under labor law in the 1990's, in the hope this step would restore to football players a chance to take advantage of the antitrust principles secured through litigation in the mid–1970s. As we saw in Chapter 3, the affirmative verdict in the *McNeil* case in the fall of 1992 finally gave football players the legal leverage they needed to secure meaningful (though not unrestricted) free agency in that sport.

B. APPLICATION OF THE NLRA TO SPORTS

We now return to the content of labor law for the sports industry. Congress enacted the National Labor Relations Act (NLRA) pursuant to its power to regulate interstate commerce. When *Federal Base Ball Club of Baltimore v. National League of Professional Baseball Clubs*, 259 U.S. 200, 42 S.Ct. 465, 66 L.Ed. 898 (1922), was decided, "interstate commerce" usually was construed quite narrowly; for that reason baseball was considered too localized a form of business enterprise to be subject to federal antitrust law. Only a razor-thin 5–4 majority of the Supreme Court in *NLRB v. Jones & Laughlin Steel Corp.*, 301 U.S. 1, 57 S.Ct. 615, 81 L.Ed. 893 (1937), which upheld the validity of the NLRA itself, released Congress from this "dual federalism" constraint on its authority over the national economy.

A side effect of the New Deal constitutional revolution was that the open-ended NLRA gained considerably broader reach over private business and employment than Congress had initially contemplated. As a result, the NLRB has consistently exercised some measure of discretion to decide whether and when certain industries will be subjected to the national labor law. Not until the early 1970s were higher education and health care, for example, brought within the Board's purview. Notwithstanding the changing orientation of player associations in the mid–1960s, then, it was by no means inevitable that sports would come under the umbrella of the NLRA. (In fact, the NLRB refused to apply the Act to horse racing tracks in *Walter A. Kelley*, 139 N.L.R.B. 744 (1962)). Ironically, the decision that cast this legal die in favor of professional athletes was an application for union certification by *umpires*.

THE AMERICAN LEAGUE OF PROFESSIONAL BASEBALL CLUBS & ASS'N OF NATIONAL BASEBALL LEAGUE UMPIRES

National Labor Relations Board, 1969.

180 N.L.R.B. 190.

* * *

[The Board first ruled that baseball sufficiently involved interstate commerce that the NLRA could apply.]

* * *

The Board's jurisdiction under the Act is based upon the commerce clause of the Constitution, and is coextensive with the reach of that clause.

* * *

[Notwithstanding *Federal Base Ball* and *Toolson*] since professional football and boxing have been held to be in interstate commerce and thus subject to the antitrust laws, it can no longer be seriously contended that the Court still considers baseball alone to be outside of interstate commerce. Congressional deliberations regarding the relationship of baseball and other professional team sports to the antitrust laws likewise reflect a Congressional assumption that such sports are subject to regulation under the commerce clause. It is, incidentally, noteworthy that these deliberations reveal Congressional concern for the rights of employees such as players to bargain collectively and engage in concerted activities.   Additionally, legal scholars have agreed, and neither the parties nor those participating as *amici* dispute, that professional sports are in or affect interstate commerce, and as such are subject to the Board's jurisdiction.   Therefore, on the basis of the above, we find that professional baseball is an industry in or affecting commerce, and as such is subject to Board jurisdiction under the Act.

* * *

Section 14(c)(1) of the National Labor Relations Act, as amended, permits the Board to decline jurisdiction over labor disputes involving any "class or category of employers, where, in the opinion of the Board, the effect of such labor dispute on commerce is not sufficiently substantial to warrant the exercise of its jurisdiction...."   The Employer and other employers contend that because of baseball's internal self-regulation, a labor dispute involving the American League of Professional Baseball Clubs is not likely to have any substantial effect on interstate commerce; and that application of the National Labor Relations Act to this Employer is contrary to national labor policy because Congress has sanctioned baseball's internal self-regulation.   The Employer also contends that effective and uniform regulation of baseball's labor relations problems is not possible through Board processes because of the sport's international aspects.

LAW
(ISSUE)

* * *

We have carefully considered the positions of the parties, and the *amicus* briefs, and we find that it will best effectuate the mandates of the Act, as well as national labor policy, to assert jurisdiction over this Employer.   We reach this decision for the following reasons:

Hold

Baseball's system for internal self-regulation of disputes involving umpires is made up of the Uniform Umpires Contract, the Major League Agreement, and the Major League Rules, which provide, among other things, for final resolution of disputes through arbitration by the Commissioner.   The system appears to have been designed almost entirely by employers and owners, and the final arbiter of internal disputes does not appear to be a neutral third party freely chosen by both sides, but rather an individual appointed solely by the member club owners themselves.   We do not believe that such a system is likely either to prevent labor disputes from arising in the future, or, having once arisen, to resolve them in a manner susceptible or conductive to voluntary compliance by all parties involved.   Moreover, it is patently contrary to the letter and spirit of the Act for the Board to defer its undoubted jurisdiction to decide unfair labor practices to a disputes settlement system established unilaterally by an employer or group of employers. Finally, although the instant case involves only umpires employed by the League, professional baseball clubs employ, in addition to players, clubhouse attendants, bat boys, watchmen, scouts, ticket sellers, ushers, gatemen, trainers, janitors, office clericals, batting practice pitchers, stilemen, publicity, and advertising men, grounds keepers and maintenance men. As to these other categories, there is no "self-regulation" at all. This consideration is of all the more consequence for of those employees in professional baseball whose interests are likely to call the Board's processes into play, the great majority are in the latter-named classifications.

We can find, neither in the statute nor in its legislative history, any expression of a Congressional intent that disputes between employers and employees in this industry should be removed from the scheme of the National Labor Relations Act.

* * *

[W]e are not here confronted with the sort of small, primarily intrastate employer over which the Board declines jurisdiction because of failure to meet its prevailing monetary standards. Moreover, it is apparent that the Employer, whose operations are so clearly national in scope, ought not have its labor relations problems subject to diverse state laws.

The Employer's final contention, that Board processes are unsuited to regulate effectively baseball's international aspects, clearly lacks merit, as many if not most of the industries subject to the Act have similar international features.

* * *

We further find that the following employees of the Employer constitute a unit appropriate for the purposes of collective bargaining within the meaning of Section 9(b) of the Act:

> All persons employed as umpires in the American League of Professional Baseball Clubs, but excluding all other employees, office clerical employees, guards, professional employees and supervisors as defined in the Act.

Petition granted.

———————

MEMBER JENKINS, dissenting:

My colleagues advance as a reason for asserting jurisdiction herein the absence of a Congressional intent to resolve labor disputes in baseball in a different manner from that established in the NLRA. In my opinion, the question is not whether Congress intended that disputes between employers and employees in the professional baseball industry should be resolved in the same or in a different manner from that established for other industries covered by the Act, but whether Congress, in enacting the NLRA, intended to include such disputes within the reach of the Board's jurisdiction at all. If any inference is to be drawn from Congressional silence on the matter, a very compelling reason exists for nonassertion of jurisdiction.

* * *

Whether fortuitous or otherwise, professional baseball's unique and favored status [in both the Nation's social and business community] had already gained judicial approval long before enactment of the NLRA. It is irrefutable, therefore, that Congress in 1935 harbored no intent to include the labor relations of professional baseball within the reach of the Board's jurisdiction. And while the Supreme Court has since rejected the narrow conception of commerce on which *Federal Baseball* was premised, in large measure prior to any amendments to the Act, my colleagues point to no legislative history in the subsequent amendments to the Act which would support a legislative intent thereafter to include baseball's labor relations within the reach of the Act. Indeed, it would appear that in the present posture, an amendment expressly including the baseball industry within the Act would be required to warrant the Board's assertion of jurisdiction.

* * *

Even assuming in agreement with my colleagues that professional baseball is subject to the Board's jurisdiction, and further, that the Board has the discretion under Section 14(c)(1) of the Act to assert or decline jurisdiction, I am of the opinion that no compelling reasons exist for exercising that discretion to assert jurisdiction in the instant case. There is no showing that this industry is wracked with the kinds of labor disputes which are likely to constitute a burden on commerce. Nor am I satisfied that the majority's conclusion, that baseball's "commissioner" system for internal self-regulation of disputes is not likely to prevent such burden or disruption of commerce, constitutes a ground for our taking jurisdiction over the industry. Indeed, I question the propriety of prejudging baseball's arbitral system in this representation proceeding, particularly in view of the fact that the matter has not been litigated and in the absence of an issue which calls for a close scrutiny of the efficacy of that system based on facts spread on the record. In any event, the pendency of a single [unfair labor practice] charge, even assuming it arose as a direct result of the failure of baseball's arbitral system, is hardly ground for discrediting that system any more than it is for rejecting arbitration procedures in any industry. Moreover, my colleagues appear to shoot wide of the mark when they note that other employees, such as clubhouse attendants, bat boys, watchmen, scouts, ticket sellers, ushers, gatemen, trainers, janitors, grounds keepers and maintenance men, are not covered by baseball's arbitral system. Unlike umpires, these employees appear to be directly employed by the individual baseball clubs and it appears that their labor relations would be so handled. While baseball players are likewise hired directly by the individual clubs, the entire league has an interest in the relations between the players and their employers because of the very nature of the game and the need to maintain competition. Thus, there is an urgent need for ultimately settling problems dealing with the players on a league level while no such need is apparent in the case of stadium-oriented employees. Furthermore, it appears from the record that some of the latter employees are already represented by labor organizations in single-employer units and presumably have their own dispute settlement procedures. Finally, there is no showing that any labor disputes of national importance exist among these employees.

For the foregoing reasons I would dismiss the petition herein.

Questions for Discussion

1. What is your reaction to the contrasting observations by the NLRB members to baseball's system of internal self-regulation via the commissioner, in light of what you read in Chapter 1?

2. In the following portion of its decision in the above case, the NLRB dealt with the league's argument that umpires are "supervisors" as defined in Section 2(ii) of the NLRA, and thus not "employees" entitled to union representation:

> It is not contended that umpires have authority to hire, fire, transfer, discharge, recall, promote, assign, or reward. We think it equally apparent that umpires do not "discipline" or "direct" the work force according to the common meaning of those terms as used in the Act.
>
> The record indicates that an umpire's basic responsibility is to insure that each baseball game is played in conformance with the predetermined rules of the game. Thus, the umpire does not discipline except to the extent he may remove a participant from the game for violation of these rules. Testimony shows that after such a removal the umpire merely reports the incident to his superiors and does not himself fine, suspend, or even recommend such action. As the final arbiter on the field, the umpire necessarily makes decisions which may favor one team over another, and which may determine to some extent the movements of various players, managers, and other personnel on the ball field. The umpire does not, however, direct the work force in the same manner and for the same reasons as a foreman in an industrial setting. As every fan is aware, the umpire does not—through the use of independent judgment—tell a player how to bat, how to field, to work harder or exert more effort, nor can he tell a manager which players to play or where to play them. Thus, the umpire merely sees to it that the game is played in compliance with the rules. It is the manager and not the umpire who directs the employees in their pursuit of victory.
>
> Accordingly, we find that the umpires are not supervisors, and thus the Employer's motion to dismiss on this ground is hereby denied.

Even if one assumes that a baseball manager (like Tom Lasorda of the Dodgers) or a football head coach (like Joe Gibbs of the Redskins) are excluded from the Act, would a coach in baseball, or an assistant coach in football, basketball, or hockey, be eligible for union representation under the NLRA (by the players' associations or some other body)? N

C. UNION SUPPORT AND EMPLOYER RETALIATION [3]

One tangible result of NLRA coverage is that employees gain federal legislative protection against employer retaliation for supporting their union and its actions. For most workers, this legal protection is most important in the early days of union organization, in the face of employers determined to stay union-free. In professional sports, however, players had already organized their associations and secured rudimentary collective agreements before they could be sure of NLRA coverage. In addition, sports clubs and leagues are unusual employers because they need and want a union for their players in order to secure and retain the benefit of the labor exemption. (This explains the peculiar posture of the parties in the *Powell* litigation, in which the NFL, the employer, was vigorously resisting the efforts of the NFLPA to deunionize football.)

However, the Section 7 rights of employees extend beyond initial organization to encompass support of the union in its bargaining efforts—for example, by trying to rally fellow employees in favor of the union and against the employer during a strike. Section 8 of the Act makes it an unfair labor practice for the employer to "interfere with, restrain, or coerce" employees engaged in such "concerted activities", and Section 8(a)(3) forbids "discrimination in tenure of employment" (that is, dismissal) on account of such union support.

While these half-century old employee rights and employer obligations are firmly embedded in labor jurisprudence, they are inevitably murky in application. Even the most determined antiunion employer, recognizing the presence of the NLRA in the background, is careful to direct such retaliation only against employees whose work history provides some colorable basis for discharge or other punitive action. As a result, unfair labor practice charges based on Section 8 involve difficult and time-consuming examinations of the employer's true motivation for its actions and the employee's record of performance.

This difficulty is greatly exacerbated in professional sports. Unlike workers in almost every other walk of life, athletes have no expectation of keeping their positions just because they are doing a reasonably competent job. Every pre-season—indeed, throughout the season—veteran players face the threat of release and replacement by rookie challengers. Under the standard NFL player contract, for example:

---

3. Unlike the relationship between antitrust law and sports, there has been little systematic scholarly work done about the various aspects of labor law as applied to professional sports. Thus, in this chapter we will provide references to some of the recent scholarly work on debates within labor law generally. With respect to the topic in this immediate section, one of us has written extensively: see, Paul C. Weiler, *Promises to Keep: Securing Workers' Rights to Self–Organization Under the NLRA*, 96 Harvard L. Rev. 1769 (1983), and Paul C. Weiler, *Governing the Workplace: The Future of Labor and Employment Law* (Cambridge, Ma.: Harvard University Press, 1990), Chapters 3 and 6.

Skill, Performance and Conduct. Player understands that he is competing with other players for a position on Club's roster within the applicable player limits. If at any time, in the sole judgment of Club, Player's skill or performance has been unsatisfactory as compared with that of other players competing for positions on Club's roster, or if Player has engaged in personal conduct reasonably judged by Club to adversely affect or reflect on Club, then Club may terminate this contract.

A severe test is posed to the NLRB, then, when the Board must decide whether a club's exercise of this judgment about a player's relative skill was contaminated by animus against his union activities. This problem is magnified by the fact that union representatives tend to be respected veterans who may have passed their peak performance years. The following case illustrates the difficulty of this issue.

SEATTLE SEAHAWKS v. NFLPA & SAM McCULLUM

National Labor Relations Board, 1989.

292 N.L.R.B. No. 110.

[From 1976 through 1981, Sam McCullum was a starting wide receiver for the Seattle Seahawks. In 1981, McCullum was selected by his teammates to be their union player representative. McCullum's prominent role in union activities in the following bargaining year (leading up to the lengthy players' strike during the 1982 season) produced severe tensions with Seahawks' coach Jack Patera. In particular, Patera was upset by McCullum's orchestration of the "solidarity handshake" by his teammates with members of the opposing team at the beginning of their first preseason game. Nevertheless, McCullum started all of the August 1982 preseason games for the Seahawks. In a trade made at the end of training camp, however, the Seahawks obtained from the Baltimore Colts another wide receiver, Roger Carr, and McCullum was cut from the team's final roster. An unfair labor practice charge was then filed by McCullum and the NFLPA.

The evidence at trial showed that the Seahawks' Director of Football Operations, Mike McCormick, and its General Manager, John Thompson, had been trying for months to trade for Carr on favorable terms. Also, Jerry Rhome, the offensive coordinator, had been closely involved in deciding which of the team's four wide receivers should be let go to make room for Carr. However, the Administrative Law Judge found that both of these team decisions were influenced by the Seahawks'—and especially Patera's—antiunion sentiments directed at McCullum. In this decision, a divided NLRB grapples with the Seahawks' appeal from the ALJ's ruling.

In *Wright Line*, 251 N.L.R.B. 1083 (1980), enf'd, 662 F.2d 899 (1st Cir.1981), cert. denied, 455 U.S. 989 (1982), the NLRB clarified its test for determining when an employer has committed an unfair labor practice by firing an employee. Rather than stopping with the judgment whether antiunion motivation was a cause "in part" of the firing, the Board required the employee first to show that his union activities were a "motivating factor" in the employer's decision to fire him, and then the employer could defend by showing that the employee would have been fired even if he had not engaged in union activities. The Supreme Court accepted this "but for" test in *NLRB v. Transportation Management Corp.*, 462 U.S. 393, 400–03 (1983). The Seahawks first challenged the ALJ's ruling on the ground that it misapplied the *Wright Line* test by finding no more than that McCullum's union activities were "in part" a factor in his release.]

* * *

It is incontestable that the judge, notwithstanding his occasional use of the term "in part" to describe the extent of the Respondent's unlawful motivation, found that antiunion considerations were a motivating factor in the decision that produced McCullum's release, and that he fully considered the Respondent's *Wright Line* defense. We therefore find that his analysis fully comports with the *Wright Line* standard.

The Respondent has also excepted to the judge's implicit finding that certain remarks that Sam McCullum made in his role as the team's player representative at a February 19, 1982 press conference and that produced negative reactions from both the team's general manager, John Thompson, and its head coach, Jack Patera, are in fact protected under Section 7 of the Act. In particular, the Respondent argues that McCullum's expression of his view that team doctors, whom he saw as identified with management, released injured players for games too soon, when the players were not fully recovered, constituted "disloyal" disparagement of the employer, which, pursuant to the theory of NLRB v. Electrical Workers Local 1229 IBEW (Jefferson Standard), 346 U.S. 464 (1953), is not protected activity under Section 7. The Respondent also argues, as to the "solidarity handshake" episode, that any hostility would naturally be against the Union—as the author of this activity throughout the league—rather than against McCullum. We disagree with both contentions.

In *Jefferson Standard*, the Supreme Court held that a union's public attacks on the quality of the employer's product were not protected under Section 7 when they had no connection with the employee's working conditions or any current labor controversy. It seems indisputable, however, that the relative haste with which injured players are returned to the football field is a matter that directly affects the players' working conditions. Although McCullum's views may have been exaggerated or not soundly based, that does not withdraw the protection of the Act from them. Indeed, employees and employers frequently differ greatly in their views whether the employees are properly treated.

We do not mean to suggest, of course, that it was unlawful for either Thompson or Patera to take issue with McCullum's statements. The fact remains, however, that McCullum established himself at this press conference as a fairly aggressive union spokesman. McCullum's role as player representative was highlighted again when he and two other players approached Patera in August to apprise him of the players' intention to support the Union's "solidarity handshake" plan by engaging in such a handshake with the opposing team in the upcoming August 13 game with St. Louis. Although it was another player who mentioned the "union solidarity" symbolism of the handshake, it was McCullum who—after Patera had expressed his opposition—said that the players might go ahead and do it anyway. We agree with the judge that Patera's prediction of the subsequent fines ('I'll fine you as much as I can') and the heavy fines that the Respondent sought to impose reveal animus toward union activity for which, at this point, McCullum was the obvious focus on the team.

* * *

The Respondent attacks the judge's discrediting of Patera—which is essential to his findings of unlawful motive—by insisting that it rests fundamentally not on observations of witness demeanor but rather on a flawed logical analysis of the plausibility of Patera's account of an urgent search, beginning as early as January 1982, for a "deep threat" wide receiver.

* * *

We, of course, recognize that the judge's evaluation of all the testimony was influenced by his view of how it fit together logically or failed to do so, but we are necessarily reluctant to disregard the demeanor component of credibility resolutions by a trier of fact. We therefore decline the Respondent's invitation to reverse the judge's assessment of the credibility of Patera's testimony.

Finally, we address two of the Respondent's arguments concerning alleged inconsistencies between the judge's factual findings and the record evidence. These are both matters raised also by our dissenting colleague.

First, the Respondent argues that a finding that it was seeking to obtain Carr in order to rid itself of McCullum is inconsistent with the evidence that the Respondent had declined to accept Baltimore's offer of Carr in late spring for a first round draft choice, that it had declined another Baltimore offer in August for a "high" draft choice, and that the Respondent had even toughened its position by insisting on September 2 that it would give up only a fourth round draft choice for Carr. We do not see that conduct as inconsistent with the judge's motivation finding for the reasons essentially given by the judge.

An employer may harbor an unlawful intent to rid itself of a troublesome employee but still wish to do so on the most advantageous terms possible. Furthermore, the testimony of the Respondent's own witnesses shows that they reasonably believed that Baltimore wanted to be rid at all costs of the injury-prone Carr.

* * *

It is undeniable that Rhome was responsible for rating the wide receivers throughout training camp and the preseason games and that Patera would reasonably take seriously his judgment, after the Carr trade, that McCullum should be released rather than Steve Largent, Byron Walker, or Paul Johns. But it is clear from Rhome's testimony that he was not consulted about the desirability of having Carr, as opposed to McCullum, at the point in the season that Carr was finally acquired. Thus, Rhome testified that he could not rate Carr because he had not seen him play very recently. Rhome obviously approached the evaluation process with the realization that Carr was not for cutting. As he testified, "You can't just eliminate Roger Carr because you just got through trading for him." Hence, having Carr as one of the wide receivers going into the new season was essentially imposed on Rhome by the trade. He made no considered judgment that an injury-prone player who had not participated in any training camp that summer and did not know Seattle's system of offensive plays would be more valuable than McCullum.

Although Carr's name was first mentioned by McCormick when he joined the Respondent's organization in March and the initial decision to make inquiries about Carr occurred after a conversation among McCormick, Patera, and Thompson about the matter, Patera made the initial call, while subsequent negotiations with Baltimore were carried out first by McCormick and later by Thompson. But Patera's role was crucial. As Thompson testified, Patera was the one to decide who would make the team. Given the time at which Carr was finally acquired—just before the opening of the season—it was clear that, as Rhome recognized, acquiring him meant bringing him onto the team. Nothing in the record suggests that efforts to acquire players would have been made without continuing consultation with the head coach. Thus, it had to be up to Patera whether negotiations to acquire Carr would continue just before the start of the season, when cuts were to be made....

Given the reports that Rhome says he made to Patera about the progress of players Walker and Johns in the training camp and preseason games, the continued pursuit of Carr is suspect. McCullum was rated a very good wide receiver in many respects—allegedly all except for the ability to go deep and catch "the bomb." But this was an area in which Johns and Walker were now rated highly, so the need to obtain Carr for that particular skill was diminishing rapidly according to the Respondent's own witnesses.

The Respondent simply has not shown that the acquisition of Roger Carr on September 3 would have occurred even in the absence of the animus of the Respondent's management—more notably, but not solely, the animus of Patera—against McCullum as an outspoken representative of union sentiment on the team. The animus against the Union's solidarity had been powerfully expressed, but thwarted in August, when the Respondent imposed fines for the 'solidarity handshake' that greatly exceeded those imposed by any other NFL team and then was forced to rescind the fines. The opportunity for the Respondent to rid itself of the most visible team symbol of that solidarity was finally seized upon in September through the acquisition of Carr.

Charges upheld.

————

MEMBER JOHANSEN, dissenting

Despite the undisputed facts regarding the timing and progress of the Carr-trade talks—notably the early initial efforts of McCormick, the hard bargaining techniques of Thompson, and the absence of any role in the process by Patera—the judge and my colleagues nevertheless conclude that the Carr acquisition was central to a carefully designed pretext to justify McCullum's elimination. I cannot agree. The judge's analysis is flawed by his failure to account for Patera's lack of participation in effecting the trade. The judge imputed Patera's apparent hostility toward McCullum to the Respondent generally. By so doing, however, the judge ignored the fact that the Respondent did not stand accused of having committed any unfair labor practices independent of the McCullum discharge, and that there is no union animus on the part of those within the Respondent's organization, i.e., McCormick and Thompson, who actually played a direct personal role in the Carr acquisition.

The judge's analysis also too readily discounts the fact that the attempts to deal for Carr were initiated right after McCormick joined the Seattle organization after leaving the Colts, and well in advance of McCullum's most "anti-Patera" confrontation, i.e., the "solidarity handshake" incident; and it leaves unexplained the unwillingness of the Respondent's trade negotiators to conclude the Carr-deal quickly so as to assure an excuse for dismissing McCullum. Indeed, it was the Colts who, in the end, were the party most eager to make a trade for Carr.... Yet the Seahawks twice passed by Colt deadlines for trading for Carr.

The judge's analysis also does not refute the Respondent's evidence that it cut McCullum for sound business reasons. In this regard, as with the Carr acquisition itself, the judge again overemphasized Patera's responsibility in the selection process ... failed to account fully for the role of the Respondent's offensive coordinator, Jerry Rhome, in the decision to let McCullum go.

* * *

Rhome proceeded to rate Largent as the [Seahawks'] star. He stated that he could not rate Carr because he had not seen him play in preseason. He declared that Johns, Walker, and McCullum were very close, but that he would take Walker over McCullum. Rhome testified that he had earlier told Patera that Johns should probably be given the starting position over McCullum. Rhome also testified that retaining five players at the wide receiver position would not have been tenable because the extra receiver would cost the team a player at another slot; the team could not afford cutting back on the strength of their offensive line; the possibility of an injury to a quarterback precluded having only two at that position; the tight end position was thought to require three active players; and the Respondent had traditionally carried just four wide receivers. Rhome averred that his fellow assistant coaches agreed with his assessment on the number of receivers that should be carried. Rhome further commented that in any event McCullum was not likely to be happy in a backup role, spending the bulk of the game time on the bench. Rhome stated that the decision boiled down to a choice between McCullum and Walker and that developing the potential of a youthful Walker was an appealing prospect for the team.

After giving his perspective to Patera the decision to terminate McCullum seemed logically to emerge: (1) Largent, as the Respondent's premier wide receiver, would obviously be kept; (2) Carr would be retained in view of the fact that the trade for him had just been effected; (3) Johns was projected as a probable starter over McCullum; (4) Johns was needed as the punt returner—a matter independent of his role as wide receiver; (5) Walker displayed promise as a young talent with his best playing years ahead; and (6) McCullum's starting role was challenged and he was facing the declining years of his playing abilities.

* * *

For all the foregoing reasons, the Respondent's choice of McCullum as the expendable player emerges as one based on a business judgment of the team's personnel needs that would have been made even in the absence of antiunion motivation. Accordingly, I find that the Respondent has met its *Wright Line* burden and I would reverse the judge's conclusion that the Respondent's termination of McCullum violated the Act.

Questions for Discussion

1. Note that the NLRB rendered this decision in 1989, seven years after McCullum's release. Not until March 1991 did the Board's Administrative Law Judge issue his decision calculating the amount of back pay owed McCullum by the Seahawks—$250,000. Even the latter decision was still under appeal to the Board as of the end of 1992. What is the probable effect of these administrative delays on implementation of the policies of the Act? Is the effect of delay more or less significant in the sports context? [4]

4. See Ethan Lock, *Employer Unfair Labor Practices During the 1982 National* *Football League Strike: Help on the Way*, 6 U. of Bridgeport L. Rev. 189 (1985).

2.   What does this issue suggest to the average player who is deciding whom to vote for as the club's union representative? Should he vote for a younger star player who is unlikely to be released, but also less likely to be sympathetic to the union's goals on behalf of journeymen players, or for an older journeymen player who is more susceptible to being cut by the team, but more committed to union activities?

D.   CERTIFICATION OF THE PLAYERS' BARGAINING AGENT

The aim of a union organizing drive is to win the right to represent employees in collective bargaining with their employer. Absent voluntary recognition by the employer (as was extended by the various sports leagues in the late 1960s to what were then comparatively weak player associations), a union enjoying substantial allegiance among the employees must petition the NLRB to conduct a secret ballot election among the employees. If the union wins a majority of the votes cast, the Board then certifies the union as the exclusive bargaining agent for all the employees (Section 9(a)). But before any such election can be conducted, the Board must define the scope of the relevant employee constituency—that is, the "unit appropriate for purposes of collective bargaining" (Section 9(b)).

Again, the NLRB and the courts have developed an elaborate jurisprudence for determining which of the many possible employee groupings exhibit the ideal "community of interest" for bargaining together.[5] Although these conclusions were not preordained by precedents from other industrial settings, no one has challenged the assumption that the appropriate unit in professional sports comprises *only* the players (thus excluding all other employees of the clubs), and *all* the players (thus not distinguishing higher-priced positions such as quarterback from lower-priced positions such as defensive back). Just like antitrust law, however, labor law must decide whether the center of gravity in the union's bargaining relationship will be with the individual club or with the entire league. The answer was rendered in a certification petition for players in the North American Soccer League.

NORTH AMERICAN SOCCER LEAGUE v. NLRB

United States Court of Appeals, Fifth Circuit, 1980.

613 F.2d 1379.

RONEY, CIRCUIT JUDGE.

The correct collective bargaining unit for the players in the North American Soccer League is at issue in this case. Contrary to our first

5. See Douglas L. Leslie, *Labor Bargaining Units,* 70 Virginia L. Rev. 353 (1984).

impression, which was fostered by the knowledge that teams in the League compete against each other on the playing fields and for the hire of the best players, our review of the record reveals sufficient evidence to support the National Labor Relations Board's determination that the League and its member clubs are joint employers, and that a collective bargaining unit comprised of all NASL players on clubs based in the United States is appropriate. Finding petitioners' due process challenge to be without merit, we deny the petition for review and enforce the collective bargaining order on the cross-application of the Board.

The North American Soccer League is a non-profit association comprised of twenty-four member clubs. The North American Soccer League Players Association, a labor organization, petitioned the NRLB for a representation election among all NASL players. The Board found the League and its clubs to be joint employers and directed an election within a unit comprised of all the soccer players of United States clubs in the League. Excluded from the unit were players for the clubs based in Canada, because the Board concluded its jurisdiction did not extend to those clubs as employers.

* * *

The settled law is not challenged on this petition for review. Where an employer has assumed sufficient control over the working conditions of the employees of its franchisees or member-employers, the Board may require the employers to bargain jointly. The Board is also empowered to decide in each case whether the employee unit requested is an appropriate unit for bargaining. The Board's decision will not be set aside unless the unit is clearly inappropriate. Thus the issues in this case are whether there is a joint employer relationship among the League and its member clubs, and if so, whether the designated bargaining unit of players is appropriate.

JOINT EMPLOYERS.

Whether there is a joint employer relationship is "essentially a factual issue," and the Board's finding must be affirmed if supported by substantial evidence on the record as a whole.

The existence of a joint employer relationship depends on the control which one employer exercises, or potentially exercises, over the labor relations policy of the other. In this case, the record supports the Board's finding that the League exercises a significant degree of control over essential aspects of the clubs' labor relations, including but not limited to the selection, retention, and termination of the players, the terms of individual player contracts, dispute resolution and player discipline. Furthermore, each club granted the NASL authority over not only its own labor relations but also, on its behalf, authority over the labor relations of the other member clubs. The evidence is set forth in detail in the Board's decision and need be only briefly recounted here.

The League's purpose is to promote the game of soccer through its supervision of competition among member clubs. Club activities are governed by the League constitution, and the regulations promulgated thereunder by a majority vote of the clubs. The commissioner, selected and compensated by the clubs, is the League's chief executive officer. A board of directors composed of one representative of each club assists him in managing the League.

The League's control over the clubs' labor relations begins with restrictions on the means by which players are acquired. An annual college draft is conducted by the commissioner pursuant to the regulations, and each club obtains exclusive negotiating rights to the players it selects. On the other hand, as the Board recognized, the League exercises less control over the acquisition of "free agent" players and players "on loan" from soccer clubs abroad.

The regulations govern interclub player trades and empower the commissioner to void trades not deemed to be in the best interest of the League. Termination of player contracts is conducted through a waiver system in accordance with procedures specified in the regulations.

The League also exercises considerable control over the contractual relationships between the clubs and their players. Before being permitted to participate in a North American Soccer League game, each player must sign a standard player contract adopted by the League. The contract governs the player's relationship with his club, requiring his compliance with club rules and the League constitution and regulations. Compensation is negotiated between the player and his club, and special provisions may be added to the contract. Significantly, however, the club must seek the permission of the commissioner before signing a contract which alters any terms of the standard contract.

Every player contract must be submitted to the commissioner, who is empowered to disapprove a contract deemed not in the best interest of the League. The commissioner's disapproval invalidates the contract. Disputes between a club and a player must be submitted to the commissioner for final and binding arbitration.

Control over player discipline is divided between the League and the clubs. The clubs enforce compliance with club rules relating to practices and also determine when a player will participate in a game. The League, through the commissioner, has broad power to discipline players for misconduct either on or off the playing field. Sanctions range from fines to suspension to termination of the player's contract.

Although we recognize that minor differences in the underlying facts might justify different findings on the joint employer issue, the record in this case supports the Board's factual finding of a joint employer relationship among the League and its constituent clubs.

Having argued against inclusion of the Canadian clubs in the NLRB proceeding, petitioners contend on appeal that their exclusion renders the Board's joint employer finding, encompassing 21 clubs, inconsistent with the existence of a 24–club League. The jurisdictional determination is not before us on appeal, however, and the Board's decision not to exercise jurisdiction over the Canadian clubs does not undermine the evidentiary base of its joint employer finding.

Even assuming the League and the clubs are joint employers, they contend that *Greenhoot, Inc.*, 205 N.L.R.B. 250 (1973), requires a finding of a separate joint employer relationship between the League and each of its clubs, and does not permit all the clubs to be lumped together with the League as joint employers. In *Greenhoot*, a building management company was found to be a joint employer separately with each building owner as to maintenance employees in the buildings covered by its contracts. The present case is clearly distinguishable, because here each soccer club exercises through its proportionate role in League management some control over the labor relations of other clubs. In Greenhoot, building owners did not exercise any control through the management company over the activities of other owners.

Appropriate Unit.

The joint employer relationship among the League and its member clubs having been established, the next issue is whether the leaguewide unit of players designated by the Board is appropriate. Here the Board's responsibility and the standard of review in this Court are important.

The Board is not required to choose the most appropriate bargaining unit, only to select a unit appropriate under the circumstances. The determination will not be set aside "unless the Board's discretion has been exercised 'in an arbitrary or capricious manner.'"

Notwithstanding the substantial financial autonomy of the clubs, the Board found they form, through the League, an integrated group with common labor problems and a high degree of centralized control over labor relations. In these circumstances the Board's designation of a leaguewide bargaining unit as appropriate is reasonable, not arbitrary or capricious.

In making its decision, the Board expressly incorporated the reasons underlying its finding of a joint employer relationship. The Board emphasized in particular both the individual clubs' decision to form a League for the purpose of jointly controlling many of their activities, and the commissioner's power to disapprove contracts and exercise control over disciplinary matters. Under our "exceedingly narrow" standard of review, no arguments presented by petitioners require denial of enforcement of the bargaining order.

Thus the facts successfully refute any notion that because the teams compete on the field and in hiring, only team units are appropriate for collective bargaining purposes. Once a player is hired, his working conditions are significantly controlled by the League. Collective bargaining at that source of control would be the only way to

effectively change by agreement many critical conditions of employment.

Order enforced.

———————

The result of the *NASL* decision was to require all the soccer teams
to bargain as a single unit with the players association. In that
respect, the labor law treatment of sports leagues is distinctive. The
general principle of labor law is that multiemployer bargaining is a
purely consensual undertaking, one that must initially be agreed to by
the union and each of the employers participating.[6] The principal
constraint imposed by the law is that once all affected parties have
voluntarily moved towards such an arrangement, no one party can
unilaterally withdraw during a particular round of bargaining just
because negotiations have not gone as that party hoped. (In *Charles D.
Bonanno Linen Service v. NLRB*, 454 U.S. 404, 102 S.Ct. 720, 70 L.Ed.2d
656 (1982), the Supreme Court held that even an impasse reached in
negotiations did not warrant an employer leaving the larger multiemployer unit.) Note the way in which the court in *NASL* characterized
the relevant employer entity in the sports context in order to distinguish the broader doctrinal principles just mentioned. Recall this labor
law treatment of this issue when we take up in Chapter 6 the analogous
question of whether the club or the league is the relevant entity under
antitrust law.

Though voluntary in origin, multiemployer bargaining is now a
common feature of the industrial relations landscape, particularly in
industries such as trucking or construction where there are hosts of
small firms dealing with a few large unions such as the Teamsters or
the Carpenters. Both employers and unions in these industries find
they have a complementary long-term interest in putting their relationship on that broader footing. What might these interests be in the
sports context? How is league-wide bargaining helpful or harmful to
the clubs or to the players? Does sports differ from other industries in
that certain types of issues can only be addressed effectively through
league-wide, rather than individual club, bargaining?

A further legal complication affects the bargaining structure of
hockey and baseball. Two of the teams in baseball (the Toronto Blue
Jays and the Montreal Expos) and eight of the teams in hockey are
located in Canadian cities. Though the basic labor law model in
Canada resembles that in the United States,[7] there are a number of
significant variations in the operation of labor law in the two countries.

---

6. See Douglas L. Leslie, *Multiemployer
Bargaining Rules*, 75 Virginia L. Rev. 241
(1989) and Jan Vetter, *Commentary on
'Multiemployer Bargaining Rules': Search-
ing for the Right Questions*, 75 Virginia L.
Rev. 285 (1989).

7. See Paul C. Weiler, *Reconcilable Differences: New Directions in Canadian Labor Law* (Toronto: Carswell, 1980).

(Indeed, a fundamental constitutional difference is that Canadian labor law is principally a matter of provincial rather than national jurisdiction, so that the labor law in Quebec governing the Expos is itself somewhat different from that of Ontario which covers the Blue Jays.) Canadian laws, for example, tend to require mandatory government mediation and secret ballot strike votes before a strike or lockout is legal, and then the law bars permanent—in the case of Quebec, even temporary—replacement of the struck or locked-out employees. Though negotiating impasses and work stoppages have been a regular occurrence in baseball for two decades, and though the same fate overtook hockey in the spring of 1992, neither the leagues nor the unions in these sports have sought to take advantage of these special features of Canadian labor law. Why might that be so?

E. UNION'S EXCLUSIVE BARGAINING AUTHORITY [8]

Once the NLRB has certified the union as the majority choice of the employees, the union becomes the "exclusive representative of *all* the employees in the unit for purposes of collective bargaining" (Section 9(a)). Though not inevitable from the Act's bare language, in its crucial decision in *J.I. Case Co. v. NLRB*, 321 U.S. 332, 338, 64 S.Ct. 576, 580, 88 L.Ed. 762 (1944), the Supreme Court read the congressional intent under this provision to make the collective agreement paramount to any individually-negotiated employment conditions:

> It is equally clear since the collective trade agreement is to serve the purpose contemplated by the Act, the individual contract cannot be effective as a waiver of any benefit to which the employee otherwise would be entitled under the trade agreement. The very purpose of providing by statute for the collective agreement is to supersede the terms of separate agreements of employees with terms which reflect the strength and bargaining power and serve the welfare of the group. Its benefits and advantages are open to every employee of the represented unit, whatever the type or terms of his pre-existing contract of employment.

The following decision from the sports context illustrates the doctrine of exclusive union authority in operation.

---

8. See George Schatzki, *Majority Rule, Exclusive Representation, and the Interests of Individual Workers: Should Exclusivity be Abolished?* 123 U. of Pennsylvania L. Rev. 897 (1975), and Eileen Silberstein, *Union Decisions on Collective Bargaining Goals: A Proposal for Interest Group Participation*, 77 Michigan L. Rev. 1485 (1979).

MORIO v. NORTH AMERICAN SOCCER LEAGUE

United States District Court, Southern District of New York, 1980.

501 F.Supp. 633.

MOTLEY, DISTRICT JUDGE.

* * *

[In the period following NLRB certification of the NASLPA as bargaining agent for professional soccer players, and while the NASL was challenging the Board's league-wide unit determination in court (see the previous case), the League refused to bargain collectively with the union and instead continued to negotiate new contracts with individual players. The union filed unfair labor practice provisions with the Board which then petitioned a federal district court for a Section 10(j) injunction to stop these individual negotiations.]

* * *

Commencing on or about October 19, 1978, until on or about March, 1979, and continuing thereafter, Respondents by-passed the Union and dealt directly with employees in the unit. Respondents solicited employees to enter into individual employment contracts, negotiated individual employment contracts, and actually entered into individual employment contracts with the employee members of the unit.

The evidence introduced at the hearing conducted by the court established that Petitioner has reasonable cause to believe that Respondents have entered into individual contracts with employees since September 1, 1978, and continue to do so and that these individual contracts constitute 96.8% of the existing individual contracts. The other 3.2% of the current individual player contracts were entered into prior to the Union's certification on September 1, 1978.

Respondents conceded that they have unilaterally changed the conditions of employment by requiring employees to obtain permission from their respective clubs before wearing a particular brand of footwear other than that selected by each Respondent Club; that they have changed the conditions of employment by initiating plans for a new winter indoor soccer season which began in November, 1979, and ended in March, 1980; that they unilaterally changed conditions of employment by requiring employees to play or otherwise participate in the winter indoor soccer season; they they unilaterally changed conditions of employment by initiating plans to increase the 1980 summer outdoor soccer season by two games and two weeks over the 1979 format, which is presently in operation; and that they unilaterally changed employment conditions by initiating plans to reduce the maximum roster of all the Respondent Clubs during the regular summer outdoor season from 30 players to 26 players beginning on or about October 16, 1979, and continuing to the present.

* * *

The unilateral changes which Respondents admit have occurred since September 1, 1978, in the terms and conditions of employment, may violate the employer's obligations to bargain with the exclusive bargaining representative of the players. The duty to bargain carries with it the obligation on the part of the employer not to undercut the Union by entering into individual contracts with the employees. In NLRB v. Katz, 369 U.S. 736 (1962), the Supreme Court noted:

> A refusal to negotiate in fact as to any subject which is within § 8(d) and about which the Union seeks to negotiate violates § 8(a)(5).

It is undisputed that Respondents have since September 1, 1978, refused to bargain with the Union. Respondents claim that they had a right to refuse to bargain with the Union since they were pursuing their right to appeal the Board's determination that all of the players referred to above constitute a unit for collective bargaining purposes. Respondents' duty to bargain with the Union arose from the time the Union was certified as the exclusive bargaining representative of the players—September 1, 1978. The fact that Respondents were pursuing their right to appeal did not, absent a stay of the Board's order, obviate their duty to bargain with the Union and does not constitute a defense to an application for relief under Section 10(j) of the Act where, as here, Respondents have apparently repeatedly refused to bargain with the Union and have continued to bypass the Union and deal directly with employees. As Petitioner says, Respondents could have bargained subject to later court decision adverse to Petitioner and the Union and can do so now. Negotiations between Respondents and the Union were scheduled to commence August 12, 1980, notwithstanding Respondents' petition for a writ of certiorari.

Respondents' most vigorous opposition comes in response to Petitioner's application for an order requiring Respondents to render voidable, at the option of the Union, all individual player contracts, whether entered into before or after the Union's certification on September 1, 1978. Respondents' claim that such power in the hands of the Union, a non-party to this action, would result in chaos in the industry and subject Respondents to severe economic loss and hardship since these individual contracts are the only real property of Respondents.

It should be noted, at the outset, that the relief requested by Petitioner is not a request to have all individual contracts declared null and void. It should be emphasized that Petitioner is not requesting that the "exclusive rights" provision of the individual contracts, which bind the players to their respective teams for a certain time, be rendered voidable. Moreover, the Board seeks an order requiring Respondents to maintain the present terms and conditions in effect until Respondents negotiate with the Union—except, of course, for the unilateral changes—unless and until an agreement or a good faith impasse is reached through bargaining with the Union. Petitioner does not, however, seek to rescind that unilateral provision which provided for the present summer schedule. The Board has consciously limited its request for relief to prevent any unnecessary disruption of Respondents' business. The Board is seeking to render voidable only those unilateral acts taken by the Respondents, enumerated above, which Respondents admit have in fact occurred.

These unilateral changes appear to modify all existing individual contracts entered into before September 1, 1978, in derogation of the Union's right to act as the exclusive bargaining agent of all employees in the unit.

The court finds that Petitioner is entitled to the temporary injunctive relief which it seeks with respect to all of the individual contracts. The individual contracts entered into since September 1, 1978, are apparently in violation of the duty of the Respondents to bargain with the exclusive bargaining representative of the players. The Act requires Respondents to bargain collectively with the Union. The obligation is exclusive. This duty to bargain with the exclusive representative carries with it the negative duty not to bargain with individual employees. Medo Photo Supply Corp. v. NLRB, 321 U.S. 678.

* * *

In National Licorice Co. v. NLRB, 309 U.S. 350 (1940), the Supreme Court held that the Board has the authority, even in the absence of the employees as parties to the proceeding, to order an employer not to enforce individual contracts with its employees which were found to have been in violation of the NLRA. Petitioner is seeking temporary relief to this effect as to those individual contracts entered into before September 1, 1978, as well as relief with respect to those contracts entered into prior to September 1, 1978. The evidence discloses that Petitioner has reasonable cause to believe that Respondents have used, and will continue to use, the individual contracts entered into prior to September 1, 1978, to forestall collective bargaining.

* * *

The Board is, therefore, entitled to the relief which it seeks requiring Respondents to render voidable certain provisions in the existing individual contracts which the Union requests, as set forth above. The Union has been permitted by the court to intervene in this action as a party petitioner. The court finds that it is not the intent of the Petitioner, as Respondents claim, to visit punitive actions on Respondents and that the requested relief with respect to the individual contracts has been carefully tailored to avoid chaos in Respondents' industry and to avoid any economic hardship to Respondents.

Injunction granted.

———

By virtue of Section 9(a), then, the union is entitled to eliminate all individual bargaining, even bargaining to secure better terms than the collectively-negotiated minimum. But collective bargaining in sports, as in the entertainment industry generally, has followed a different path, under which the union agreement sets out guaranteed benefits and a minimum salary scale and permits a Patrick Ewing (like a Bill Cosby) to negotiate whatever extra remuneration the market will bear. Such individual freedom of contract operates at the sufferance of, and within parameters set by, the collective agreement—with the performer's agent serving, in a sense, as delegate for the union.

That free market orientation is most pronounced in the case of baseball, with its free agency system developed post-*Messersmith*. The consequence is that not only are baseball salaries in the early 1990s dramatically higher than they were two decades earlier, but so also is the salary range—at the moment, running from the $109,000 minimum to Ryne Sandberg's $7 million-a-year contract. Nor are these figures just isolated extremes.[9] In 1967, when Marvin Miller was appointed Executive Director of the MLBPA and set out to turn the organization into a true union, the average baseball salary was $19,000 a year and the median salary, $17,000; in 1976, just before free agency became operative, the average salary was $52,000, the median $40,000; but by the opening of the 1992 season, while the average salary was $1.09 million the median was less than half that—$525,000. Of 719 players on the opening team rosters, 177 were earning $2 million or more, while 208 players earned $200,000 or less.

In that respect the outcome of baseball collective bargaining is sharply different than what one finds in most unionized sectors, where the salary scale tends to tilt towards the average career veteran rather than the exceptional star.[10] How would the salary structure in baseball be different if there were no association and no basic agreement? Does this suggest that the *raison d'etre* for a players union is different from that for a traditional trade union?

The one occasion when a players association sought to act like a mainstream labor union was the 1982 negotiations in football. That year the NFLPA tried to establish a salary scale weighted towards seniority and specific accomplishments, and thereby restructure the existing salary pattern that turns more on playing position (for example, quarterback as opposed to defensive back) or original draft position (for example, early in the first round rather than in a later round). The policy rationale for allowing a union to have legal authority to negotiate such constraints on individual salary negotiations was expressed by the Supreme Court in *J.I. Case, supra*.

> But it is urged that some employees may lose by the collective
> agreement, that an individual workman may sometimes have, or be
> capable of getting, better terms than those obtainable by the group

---

9. For close empirical analysis of this phenomenon, see Rodney Fort, Pay and Performance: Is the Field of Dreams Barren?, in Chapter 8 of Paul M. Sommers, ed., *Diamonds Are Forever: The Business of Baseball*, (Washington, D.C.: Brookings, 1992).

10. See Richard B. Freeman and James L. Medoff, *What Do Unions Do?* (New York: Basic Books, 1984), in particular, Chapter 5, Labor's Elite: The Effect of Unionism on Wage Inequality.

and that his freedom of contract must be respected on that account. We are not called upon to say that under no circumstances can an individual enforce an agreement more advantageous than a collective agreement, but we find the mere possibility that such agreements might be made no ground for holding generally that individual contracts may survive or surmount collective ones. The practice and philosophy of collective bargaining looks with suspicion on such individual advantages. Of course, where there is great variation in circumstances of employment or capacity of employees, it is possible for the collective bargain to prescribe only minimum rates or maximum hours or expressly to leave certain areas open to individual bargaining. But except as so provided, advantages to individuals may prove as disruptive of industrial peace as disadvantages. They are a fruitful way of interfering with organization and choice of representatives; increased compensation, if individually deserved, is often earned at the cost of breaking down some other standard thought to be for the welfare of the group, and always creates the suspicion of being paid at the long-range expense of the group as a whole. Such discriminations not infrequently amount to unfair labor practices. The workman is free, if he values his own bargaining position more than that of the group, to vote against representation; but the majority rules, and if it collectivizes the employment bargain, individual advantages or favors will generally in practice go in as a contribution to the collective result. We cannot except individual contracts generally from the operation of collective ones because some may be more individually advantageous.

Ironically, having beaten back that players association effort in the 1982 negotiations and strike, the NFL in 1992 proposed a salary scale for rookies (in return for somewhat relaxed veteran free agency). Though the NFLPA did agree to limit the total amount of money that could be spent by a team on rookies, the leaders of players associations in all sports find the idea of direct constraints on individual player negotiations to be anathema. Why do you think the players associations take this position? Do you agree with their point of view? As we will see in the next chapter, the NBA has negotiated a cap on the size of a club's total payroll (an amount that is adjusted every year in light of changing revenues for the sport). Would it be equitable for the union also to agree to a cap on the highest salary payable—a multiple of the minimum salary adjusted every year to league revenue—in return for a sizable hike in lower salary levels? Would that step be undesirable from the point of view of economic efficiency within the sports labor market? Alternatively, do you think that lower echelon players actually secure a "trickle down" benefit from new salary peaks scaled each year by players such as Jose Canseco, Roger Clemens, Bobby Bonilla, Ryne Sandberg, and Bobby Bonds?

F. DUTY TO BARGAIN IN GOOD FAITH

Once an employee bargaining agent has been selected, both employer and union come under a statutory duty to bargain collectively with each other. Section 8(d) of the NLRA defines that obligation as follows:

> (T)o bargain collectively is ... to meet at reasonable times and confer in good faith with respect to wages, hours, and other terms of employment, ... but such obligation does not compel either party to agree to a proposal or require the making of a concession.

Many volumes of labor law cases and commentary have been written to spell out the meaning and application of the duty to bargain.[11] For our purposes it is sufficient to state that the principal focus of the duty is procedural rather than substantive. As long as a party does not engage in *surface* bargaining—that is, go through the motions with no real intent to arrive at a settlement—the party is perfectly free to engage in *hard* bargaining—to remain unyielding in its negotiating position, whatever the arguments made by the other side. The statutory policy of free collective bargaining presumes that the ultimate way to break a deadlock at the bargaining table should be through the economic pressure of a strike or a lockout, not through an unfair labor practice charge in which one party tries to persuade the Board that its position is more reasonable than the other side's. As the Supreme Court observed in *NLRB v. Insurance Agents' Int'l Union*, 361 U.S. 477, 488–89, 80 S.Ct. 419, 426–27, 4 L.Ed.2d 454 (1960):

> It must be realized that collective bargaining under a system where the Government does not attempt to control the results of negotiations, cannot be equated with an academic collective search for truth—or even with what might be thought to be the ideal of one. The parties ... still proceed from contrary and to an extent antagonistic viewpoints and concepts of self interest. The system has not reached the ideal of the philosophic notion that perfect understanding among people would lead to perfect agreement among them on values. The presence of economic weapons in reserve, and their actual exercise on occasion by the parties, is part and parcel of the system that the Wagner and Taft–Hartley Acts have recognized.

There is no better illustration of the Court's pessimistic appraisal of collective bargaining than the history of such bargaining over free agency in baseball and football over the last two decades.

But while the law has adopted a hands-off attitude to the content of collective bargaining, it has been more interventionist in prescribing standards of behavior in the bargaining process. Perhaps the two most

---

11. See Archibald Cox, *The Duty to Bargain in Good Faith*, 71 Harvard L. Rev. 1401 (1958), and Paul C. Weiler, *Striking a New Balance: Freedom of Contract and the Prospects for Union Representation*, 98 Harvard L. Rev. 351 (1984).

important such doctrines are (i) an obligation of the employer (and, on occasion, the union) to supply all relevant information that is "needed by the bargaining representative for the proper performance of its duties" (see *NLRB v. Acme Industrial Co.*, 385 U.S. 432, 435–36, 87 S.Ct. 565, 567–68, 17 L.Ed.2d 495 (1967)),[12] and (ii) the obligation to refrain from unilateral changes in matters under discussion, at least until "impasse" has been reached in bargaining (see *NLRB v. Katz*, 369 U.S. 736, 743, 745, 82 S.Ct. 1107, 1111, 1112, 8 L.Ed.2d 230 (1962)).[13]

An essential component of each doctrine is whether the issue in dispute comes within the phrase "terms and conditions of employment" under Section 8(d), such that the employer must provide information and refrain from unilateral action about it. The inevitable substantive judgments that must be made about the appropriate scope of "mandatory" bargaining *subjects*, if not the legitimate content of bargaining *proposals*, preoccupied the Board and the courts for several decades. The important recent Supreme Court decision in *First National Maintenance Corp. v. NLRB*, 452 U.S. 666, 673, 101 S.Ct. 2573, 2578, 69 L.Ed.2d 318 (1981), held that key management decisions "about the scope and direction of the enterprise" were not mandatory subjects of bargaining, regardless of their direct impact on employee lives.[14] In this respect, the Court majority echoed the sentiment in Justice Stewart's earlier concurring opinion in *Fibreboard Paper Products v. NLRB*, 379 U.S. 203, 223, 226, 85 S.Ct. 398, 409, 411, 13 L.Ed.2d 233 (1964), that Section 8(d) does not detract from the prerogative of private business management under "the traditional principles of free enterprise" to make decisions that "lie at the core of entrepreneurial control." On the other hand, management's prerogative not to bargain about its original *decision*, for example, to close down a facility, does not relieve the employer of its duty to bargain with the union about the *effects* of that action on its employees.

The fact that bargaining about a particular topic is not *mandatory* does not imply that such bargaining is *illegal*. Indeed, purely voluntary negotiation about such *permissive* topics takes place regularly in different bargaining relationships. But the line drawn between mandatory and permissive subjects is significant not only because the employer has no duty to discuss the latter topics (nor to supply information and remain inactive about them), but also because the union is not entitled to insist—in particular, to the point of a strike—in bargaining about them (see *NLRB v. Wooster Division of Borg–Warner Corp.* 356 U.S. 342, 78 S.Ct. 718, 2 L.Ed.2d 823 (1958)).

12. See Leslie K. Shedlin, *Regulation of Disclosure of Economic and Financial Data and the Impact on the American System of Labor–Management Relations*, 41 Ohio State L. J. 441 (1980), and Lee Modjeska, *Guess Who's Coming to the Bargaining Table*, 39 Ohio State L. J. (1978).

13. Peter G. Earle, *The Impasse Doctrine*, 66 Chicago–Kent L. Rev. 407 (1988).

14. See Michael C. Harper, *Leveling the Road From* Borg–Warner *to* First National Maintenance: *The Scope of Mandatory Bargaining*, 68 Virginia L. Rev. 1447 (1982), and Thomas C. Kohler, *Distinctions without Differences: Effects Bargaining in Light of* First National Maintenance, 5 Ind. Rel. L. J. 402 (1983).

With this capsule summary of the basic concepts of the duty to bargain in mind, consider the following case which gives us a glimpse of baseball collective bargaining in 1980 as the parties wrestled with the free agency system they had constructed in 1976 after the *Messersmith* ruling.

SILVERMAN v. MAJOR LEAGUE PLAYER RELATIONS COMM.

United States District Court, Southern District of New York, 1981.

516 F.Supp. 588.

WERKER, DISTRICT JUDGE.

[Following the arbitrator's ruling in the *Messersmith* grievance, in 1976 Major League Baseball (MLB) and its Players Association agreed to a four-year contract that gave free agency status to players with six years of big-league service. (Players with between two and six years service had a right to salary arbitration instead.) If a team lost a free agent, it was entitled to receive from the signing club only an amateur draft pick as "compensation." Under this new system, average player salaries rose sharply, from approximately $52,000 in 1976 to $197,000 in 1981.

With the agreement expiring at the end of 1979, the Player Relations Committee (PRC), the clubs' official bargaining arm headed by Ray Grebey, sought to change the compensation system for free agents who met certain specified standards of high performance. A team losing such a "premium" or "ranking" free agent would be entitled to select from the roster of the signing team a player who had not been put on the latter team's "protected" list of its top fifteen players.

The Players Association, led by Marvin Miller, objected strongly to the PRC's proposal on the ground that it would deter free agent signings and thus depress overall player salaries. On the eve of the strike in May 1980, the two sides agreed, in effect, to postpone the issue for one year. A joint committee was established to study the issue and report back during the next winter. Absent agreement at that time between the two sides, the owners were left free to implement the new compensation system, and if they did, the players could strike over it during the 1981 season.

There were a number of highly publicized comments made in the winter of 1980–1981 by Commissioner Bowie Kuhn and by club owners such as Ted Turner of the Atlanta Braves and Ray Kroc of the San Diego Padres, to the effect that escalating player salaries were causing serious financial problems to the game and even threatening certain clubs with bankruptcy. When Miller formally requested financial data to substantiate this claim, Grebey refused, saying that the owners were seeking expanded compensation for free agents in order to maintain better player balance between the clubs. Rather than have to rely on the vagaries of the amateur draft and minor league prospects, a club losing a free agent would receive a major league player in return. The Players Association then filed a bargaining in bad faith charge with the NLRB. The Board found the charge meritorious and sought immediate injunctive relief from a federal district court in New York.]

CpA

* * *

The Board alleges in its petition that the public statements by club owners regarding claims of financial difficulties created a reasonable belief on the part of the Players Association that respondents' bargaining position during this second round of negotiations was based, "at least in part, on the present or prospective financial difficulties of certain of Respondents' member clubs." Although Marvin Miller has expressed some doubt as to club owners' inability to pay rising player salaries, he nevertheless takes the position that the Players Association must have the financial information it requests if it is to fulfill its duty of fair representation. If deprived of that information, the Association claims that it must blindly decide whether to press its demands and risk the loss of jobs for its members if the clubs cannot survive under the "compensation" terms proposed by the Association, or to recede from its position and accept the PRC's proposal without verifying owners' claims of financial distress caused by "free agency." Thus, the Association brought an unfair labor practice charge against the PRC for its failure to disclose the requested financial data after the clubs allegedly put into issue their inability to pay.

C5A
(cont.)

In NLRB v. Truitt Manufacturing Co., 351 U.S. 149 (1956), the Supreme Court laid to rest the question of whether an employer, bound by the National Labor Relations Act to bargain in good faith, could claim that it was financially unable to pay higher wages and then refuse a union's request to produce financial data to substantiate the claim. Holding that such conduct supported a finding of failure to bargain in good faith, the Court explained:

Issue

> Good-faith bargaining necessarily requires that claims made by either bargainer should be honest claims. This is true about an asserted inability to pay an increase in wages. If such an argument is important enough to present in the give and take of bargaining, it is important enough to require some sort of proof of its accuracy.

However, *Truitt's* progeny have held that an employer is required to disclose its financial condition only when the employer claims an inability to pay, however phrased, during the course of bargaining.

Petitioner admits that at no time during bargaining sessions have respondents made a claim of inability to pay. Nevertheless, petitioner urges the Court to find that public statements made by several club owners as well as the Commissioner of Baseball about the financial condition of the industry are sufficient to support a finding of reasonable cause to believe that respondents have injected the inability to pay into the negotiations.

* * *

Petitioner concedes, as it must, that the Board and courts have never found that an employer has injected financial condition into negotiations, absent statements or conduct by the employer at the bargaining table. Nevertheless, it urges this Court to find, on the basis of statements by Commissioner Kuhn and various owners, that the financial issue has become relevant to the negotiations regarding "compensation" because of the unique nature of collective bargaining in baseball. Mindful that this Court must be "hospitable" to the views of the Regional Director, however novel, I am nevertheless convinced that the Board's position is wrong, and thus will not "defer to the statutory construction urged by (it)."

It is the PRC Board of Directors which is charged with the exclusive authority to formulate the collective bargaining position of the clubs and to negotiate agreements with the Players Association. Indeed, Grebey, the official spokesman for the PRC in collective bargaining matters, has consistently denied that the clubs' financial status is at issue in the current negotiations.

Commissioner Kuhn's remarks in December 1980 at the convention cannot be imputed to the PRC as a statement of its bargaining position. First, petitioner's attempt to establish an agency relationship between the Commissioner and the PRC is unavailing. As Commissioner of Baseball, Kuhn presides at the regular joint meetings of the Major Leagues, but does not request nor preside at special meetings called by the PRC. Moreover, while Kuhn is responsible for disciplining players who may then file grievances against him in his capacity as Commissioner, he has likewise ordered the clubs to cease certain action when the interests of baseball warranted his intercession, as when he directed the clubs to open their training camps in the spring of 1976.

* * *

In a multi-employer bargaining unit as large and publicly visible as the Major League Baseball Clubs, it is inevitable that extraneous statements will be made by individuals affiliated in some way with the group which are inconsistent with the official position of the unit. This only underscores the necessity, recognized by the PRC, for centralized bargaining responsibility and authority. Clearly, individual expressions of opinion cannot serve to bind the entire bargaining unit in the absence of authority to speak for the group.

Petitioner and the Association strain to emphasize the uniqueness of collective bargaining in the baseball industry to avoid the consequences of the established labor law regarding the inability to pay. However, this Court cannot accept "collective bargaining through the press" as a basis for a 10(j) injunction.

The Act has provided for collective bargaining between the parties through their authorized representatives. If this Court were to find that the several public statements by club officials and the Commissioner were sufficient to support a finding that the PRC and its negotiating team view the respondents' "compensation" proposal as related to the financial condition of the clubs, it would do violence to the intent and purpose of the Act which limits the jurisdiction of this Court.

To accept petitioner's argument would permit disgruntled employers in a multi-employer unit who disagreed with the negotiation policies of their representatives to force negotiation issues into the courts, thereby "conducting labor management relations by way of an injunction," a result clearly contrary to the purpose of the Act. The Players Association and the PRC entered into a valid contract on May 23, 1980. As part of that contract they agreed that if the parties were unable to reach an agreement on the "compensation" issue, the PRC could implement its proposal, thereby triggering one of the Players Association's options, that is, to reopen the agreement on that issue and set a strike deadline of no later than June 1, 1981. This Court will not alter the terms of this contract for which the parties freely bargained by delaying implementation of the proposal and a possible strike on the basis of a tortured reading the law regarding inability to pay.

Thus, I cannot find that the comments by several club officials and the Commissioner, relied upon by petitioner, are statements of policy on behalf of the PRC which would support a claim of inability to pay.

Moreover, the issue of salary, above a minimum rate, is not a subject of collective bargaining between the Players Association and the PRC. Rather, individual players negotiate independently with the clubs as to their salary. Indeed, it is the high player salaries which have resulted from the negotiation of individual contracts by players and clubs which Commissioner Kuhn addressed in his 1980 speech. Noting that player salaries are increasing at a more rapid rate than revenues, he opined that bargaining of individual contracts has led to this problem. He called upon players and owners to cooperate in this regard to arrest the trend and avoid loss to all, including the fans who will be required to pay higher ticket prices.

The evidence adduced at the hearing is insufficient to support a finding that the replacement player "compensation" proposal implemented by the PRC presents economic issues. Rather, the proposal is addressed to the inequities which flowed from the "compensation" for "free agents" as provided for in the 1976 agreement. Specifically, the proposal implemented by the PRC in February 1981, recognized the difference in skill and ability among "free agents" by the type of compensation provided to a club losing the player. In addition, the proposal is designed to more adequately assist the clubs in replacing players lost in the "free agent" draft. Under the 1976 agreement, clubs were unable to replace lost players through the Minor League and amateur systems within a meaningful time period, if at all.

* * *

The court is mindful that a strike may result from its denial of petitioner's request for a 10(j) injunction. Indeed, the industry has suffered a strike in the past. Nevertheless, in struggling with a temptation and even compulsion to prevent a strike in the public interest, I am bound by the law. The possibility of a strike, although a fact of life in labor relations, offers no occasion for this Court to distort the principles of law and equity. The resolution of the "compensation" issue is left to the parties through the negotiation process.

PLAY BALL!!!

SO ORDERED.

————

Contrary to the hopes of the district judge, his decision was quickly followed by a strike that shut baseball down for much of the summer of 1981. The contract dispute was finally settled on the basis that teams losing free agents would receive replacement players drawn from a pool of players left unprotected for this purpose by all teams that had retained the right to sign free agents in that off-season. This compromise arrangement provided some compensation to the team losing a player via free agency, but without directly deterring any team bidding for that player.

The most notable instance of this compensation system in operation took place in 1984. When the Toronto Blue Jays signed Dennis Lamp, a free agent from the Chicago White Sox, the White Sox selected as compensation Tom Seaver who had been left unprotected by the New York Mets. The result was that when Seaver, the most illustrious player in Mets' history, won his 300th game in the summer of 1985, he did so while pitching in New York's Yankee Stadium, rather than in Shea Stadium. Even more ironic, Seaver won that game for the White Sox on the eve of yet another baseball strike, in whose settlement the owners scrapped their 1981 innovation and returned to the older model of amateur draft picks payable by the team that won, to the team that lost, a premium free agent. By this time, baseball owners had become more concerned about the salary arbitration process, for which the association agreed to postpone player eligibility until completion of three, rather than just two, years of service.

Silverman was decided favorably for the baseball owners only because the PRC itself had carefully avoided making any claims of financial difficulty during negotiations. It is not uncommon, though, in sports bargaining for the league to claim financial troubles that may trigger the obligation to provide supporting data. Furthermore, other types of documents that leagues would like to keep confidential may have to be produced for the union. For example, in 1982 the NFLPA won an unfair labor practice claim against the NFL Management Council because the Council refused to produce its television and radio contracts—thereby depriving the union of information it needed to represent the players whose working conditions might be affected by league or club obligations contained in the contracts. Thus, if information is relevant to a bargaining issue, either during collective bargaining or during the administration of an existing agreement, the employer must produce that information if requested by the union.

Questions for Discussion

1. Suppose a players association asks the league for detailed information about team revenues and costs for purposes of bargaining for a fixed percentage share of the gross for the players. Does the league have to supply this data, and if so, in what form? Is it a good idea for sports leagues to disclose their financial situation voluntarily to their players' representatives? (In the summer of 1985, Commissioner Peter Ueberroth overrode the objection of a number of owners and ordered baseball's books opened to the Players Associations' auditors and economists.)

———

Recall from cases in Chapter 3 such as *Mackey, McCourt, Wood,* and *Powell* that the rookie draft and restraints on veteran free agency have been held "mandatory" subjects of bargaining. Thus, not only are both parties entitled to bargain about these issues, but the results of such negotiations are protected by the labor exemption from antitrust attack by players unhappy with the system.

Players do, of course, retain the power to attack league decisions through labor law procedures. For example, in the summer of 1992, the MLB Players Association won an arbitration award striking down a change in baseball's amateur draft. Previously, a team drafting a high school graduate had to sign the player before he enrolled in college. That deadline gave highly-rated draft picks some negotiating leverage—for example, Brian Taylor, the number one pick in the 1991 draft, was able to extract a $1.5 million bonus from the New York Yankees on the eve of his enrollment in junior college. In the 1991–92 offseason, baseball's owners amended the draft rules to allow teams to retain their rights until players had completed college—allegedly to encourage high school graduates to pursue higher education.

Though neither the amateur draft nor minor league players (like Taylor) are covered by the major league collective agreement, such a rule would likely be insulated from antitrust challenge by baseball's post-*Flood* exemption. However, the Players Association persuaded baseball's labor arbitrator, George Nicolau, that any such improvement in the value of a draft pick violated the free agency provisions in the labor agreement by intensifying the penalty inflicted on teams who signed a free agent. In the 1992–93 off-season, baseball owners were reportedly considering removal of any draft pick payment by teams signing veteran free agents in order to retain the owners' freedom to tighten constraints on amateur draftees.

Questions for Discussion

1. Consider whether the following items should be considered mandatory subjects for bargaining:

(i) Enlarging the regular schedule or playoffs.

(ii) Institution (or elimination) of the designated hitter in baseball.

(iii) Institution (or elimination) of overtime to break ties in hockey or football.

(iv) Installation of artificial turf in football or baseball parks.

(v) Hockey's repeal (in 1992) of its rule that players must wear helmets during a game.

(vi) Use of instant replay (vis-a-vis either the players or the umpires association).

(vii) The league's no-gambling policies.

(viii) Relocation of a team to a new city (for example, the NFL Raiders to Los Angeles) or expansion into new cities (e.g., the National [Baseball] League into Miami and Denver).

(ix) Who the commissioner will be, and whether a sitting commissioner can be fired.

G.   ECONOMIC CONFLICT IN SPORTS LABOR RELATIONS [15]

We observed earlier that under our national labor law the principal means for breaking deadlocks at the bargaining table are supposed to be the economic pressures of a work stoppage, not the legal pressures of an unfair labor practice charge. Section 7 of the original NLRA protected the employees' right "to engage in concerted activities for the purpose of collective bargaining"—that is, to strike. After thirty years of doctrinal evolution, the Supreme Court read the Act as affording employers a reciprocal economic weapon—a lockout of their employees to force the union to compromise at the bargaining table (see *American Ship Building Co. v. NLRB*, 380 U.S. 300, 85 S.Ct. 955, 13 L.Ed.2d 855 (1965)). From the fans' perspective, both leagues and players associations have been only too ready to exercise these prerogatives in their periodic negotiations.

While each side enjoys the legal right to stop work and thereby try to alter the balance of power in negotiations, the other side does not have to sit back and absorb the economic punishment. In particular, ever since the crucial Supreme Court decision in *NLRB v. Mackay Radio and Telegraph*, 304 U.S. 333, 58 S.Ct. 904, 82 L.Ed.2d 1381 (1938), employers have been told that they are free to continue operating during a strike (if they can), to hire replacements for this purpose, and

---

15. See generally, Weiler, *Striking a New Balance*, note 11 above, and Weiler, *Governing the Workplace*, note 3 above, in particular, Chapter 6.

even to give these replacements priority over the strikers in the jobs available when the strike ends. Interestingly, the issue of "permanent" status for replacements has tended to dominate in popular and political debates about the strike issue over the last decade (in labor disputes ranging from the air traffic controllers in 1981 to the Daily News in 1991). However, the NFL battle in 1987 shows that the employer's principal weapon is simply the power to recruit and use replacements without any guarantees of job security. And an employer can hire *temporary* replacements even when it is the *employer* that initiates the work stoppage through a lockout. See *Local 825 International Union of Operating Engineers v. NLRB (Harter Equipment)*, 829 F.2d 458 (3d Cir.1987).

Under current federal law, then, both employers and unions have wide leeway to do whatever they can economically to secure a contract settlement on their preferred terms. At some outer point, though, the law draws a boundary line between legitimate weapons of self-defense and impermissible forms of retaliation against the exercise of the statutory right. An interesting exploration of where that line should be located is this recent decision by the NLRB in yet another legal exhibit from the troubled bargaining relationship in football.

NFL MANAGEMENT COUNCIL AND NFLPA

National Labor Relations Board, 1992.

309 N.L.R.B. No. 10.

[After its experience with the lengthy players' strike in 1982, the NFL Management Council (NFLMC) decided that if the NFLPA went on strike during the 1987 contract negotiations, the league would continue its regular schedule using replacement players. The Council Executive Committee (CEC) and its Executive Director, Jack Donlan, asked CEC official (and former NFL quarterback), Eddie Lebaron, to coordinate this effort, under which the clubs would rely mainly on players who were at their training camps in August that year but who had failed to make the regular roster. The NFL players did go on strike after the third game of the 1987 season. After cancelling the next week's games, the NFL clubs were able to present replacement games in each of the next two weeks. The pressures thereby exerted on the union membership forced the Association to call off the strike, and send the players back to work on Thursday, October 15th. (At that time the Association announced that it would use the legal rather than the strike route, via litigation that produced the *Powell* rulings set out in Chapter 2.) However, pursuant to a CEC policy, all the clubs refused to use any of their striking veterans for that weekend's games, because these players had not reported by 1:00 p.m. on Wednesday. However, the clubs did use replacement players who signed as late as 4:00 p.m. on Saturday, October 17th for that Sunday's games (or by 4:00 p.m. Monday for the Monday night game). The NFLPA then filed unfair labor charges with the NLRB on the ground that this NFL policy discriminated against those players who had exercised their statutory right to strike, and thus deprived strikers of one-sixteenth of their annual salaries for the sixteen game season.]

* * *

The Supreme Court has recognized that "there are some practices which are inherently so prejudicial to union interests and so devoid of significant economic justification ... that the employer's conduct carries with it an inference of unlawful intent so compelling that it is justifiable to disbelieve the employer's protestations of innocent purpose." *American Ship Building Co. v. NLRB*, 380 U.S. 300 (1965). If an employer's conduct falls within this category, "the Board can find an unfair labor practice even if the employer introduces evidence that the conduct was motivated by business considerations." *NLRB v. Great Dane Trailers*, 388 U.S. 26, 34 (1967).

On the other hand, if the impact on employee rights of the discriminatory conduct is:

> comparatively slight, an antiunion motivation must be proved to sustain the charge if the employer has come forward with evidence of legitimate and substantial business justifications for the conduct. Thus, in either situation, once it has been proved that the employer engaged in discriminatory conduct which could have adversely affected employee rights to some extent, the burden is upon the employer to establish that it was motivated by legitimate objectives since proof of motivation is most accessible to him.

Applying these principles to this case, we find as an initial matter that the Wednesday deadline rule clearly constitutes discriminatory conduct which adversely affects employee rights. On its face, the rule discriminates against strikers by applying different, and more stringent, standards for eligibility to participate in NFL games (and to be paid for such participation). Moreover, the rule also adversely affects one of the most significant rights protected by the Act—the right to strike. The Board and the courts, applying the priciples of *Great Dane*, have long recognized that the right to strike includes the right to full and complete reinstatement upon unconditional application to return. *NLRB v. Fleetwood Trailer Co.*, 389 U.S. 375, 380–381 (1967); see also *Laidlaw Corp.*, 171 NLRB 1366, 1368–1369 (1968), enf. 414 F.2d 99 (7th Cir.1969), cert. denied 397 U.S. 920 (1970).

As in *Laidlaw*, the Respondents—in reliance on their Wednesday reporting deadline—offered the striking employees who reported for work on October 15 "less than the rights accorded by full reinstatement" (i.e., the right to participate in the games scheduled for October 18–19 and to be paid for those games). Thus, the Wednesday deadline adversely affected the striking employees in the exercise of their right to strike or to cease participating in the strike, by prohibiting the full and complete reinstatement, for the October 18–19 games, of those employees who chose to return to work after the Respondents' deadline had passed.

* * *

The Respondents assert that the Wednesday deadline was justified by the Clubs' need for sufficient time to prepare returning players for game conditions. In this regard, the Respondents presented evidence that the strikers' physical condition would be expected to deteriorate as the strike progressed. In addition, NFL Management Council official Eddie LeBaron testified that players could not maintain their "football condition" without participating in practices involving physical contact. The Respondents also assert that they particularly did not wish to risk injuries to so-called franchise players.

The Respondents also assert that the rule is justified by their goal of ensuring that each Club operates from the same competitive position. Thus, the Wednesday deadline would give each Club the same amount of preparation time with returning players, prevent situations in which a replacement squad was "mismatched" against a squad composed of veterans who had reported late in the week, and ensure that Clubs could prepare for specific players during the Wednesday and Thursday practices when game plans were typically practiced.

Finally, the Respondents assert that the Wednesday deadline was justified in light of substantial administrative difficulties allegedly posed if strikers returned at a late date in the week....

In evaluating the Respondents' justifications, we initially note the unprecedented nature of the Wednesday deadline and the absence of any evidence that the Respondents have imposed a deadline of this type on employees outside of a strike setting. In particular, the record shows that players who withheld their services in pursuit of individual goals (i.e., players holding out for a more lucrative contract) are not subject to comparable restraints on their status on their return. Rather, such players are eligible to play immediately so long as they are included in the Club's active roster. If the Club determines that the player is not in shape to play, he may be placed on an Exempt list, as noted above. However, there is no automatic disqualification from participation in NFL games, or from being paid for a game while on the Exempt list, as was the case with the striking employees in 1987. This is so whether or not the individual is considered a "franchise player." Likewise, after the 1982 strike, players were immediately restored to their prestrike status—including players who did not report or practice until the Thursday prior to the next weekend's games....

It is undisputed that the Wednesday deadline was only applicable to striking players. The Respondents could and did sign nonstrikers to contracts subsequent to the date the strikers were declared ineligible; the nonstrikers were eligible to play in and were paid for the October 18–19 games....

Under these circumstances, we find that the Respondents have not established legitimate and substantial justifications for the deadline rule. While it may be true that some striking employees' physical conditioning declined during the strike, the same considerations were present in the case of holdouts and of replacement players. Likewise, safety concerns did not preclude the immediate reinstatement of the striking players in 1982, even though they had been out for 57 days, while the 1987 strike lasted only 25 days....

We also find that the Respondents' asserted competitiveness concerns are unpersuasive. Although the Respondents were entitled to ensure that all clubs operated under the same rules, adopting a deadline which discriminated against strikers was unnecessary to the achievement of this goal. The Respondents' argument that Clubs needed the practice time provided by the Wednesday deadline to prepare the strikers to play (and, for the purpose of those practices, needed to know who would be playing for its opponent) is contradicted by their willingness to allow nonstrikers with substantially less preparation time to play in those games. Moreover, the Respondents' claim that late-returning strikers would have a disproportionate impact on the game unless Clubs had an opportunity to prepare their players to face them would seem to contradict their prior claim that these same players were so out of shape that it would be unsafe to play them. Again, in the case of returning holdouts, replacement players, and the players returning from the 1982 strike, competitiveness concerns did not dictate the imposition of an eligibility deadline like the Wednesday deadline at issue here. We find that such concerns did not justify that deadline in 1987 either.

In addition, we find that the logistical and administrative burden of reinstating the strikers does not justify the rule either. In this regard, the Respondents' arguments are premised entirely on the burden of reinstating the entire 1100 player complement, even though the rule on its face would apply to a single striker who elected to return to work. The Respondents provide no justification for the application of the rule in these circumstances.[24] We also note that the Respondents maintained a substantial complement of replacement players well after the strikers had been fully reinstated. Accordingly, we find that any administrative burden associated with maintaining two separate squads

24. Indeed, we note that the deadline rule was anomalous in other respects as well. Thus, as the judge noted, it was applied to preclude even specialty players such as kickers from participation in the games, notwithstanding the lack of any evidence that the Respondents' asserted justifications applied in their case. Likewise, the rule was applied to players on injured reserve throughout the strike even though those players would not have been eligible in any event and the only effect of the Wednesday deadline was to prevent them from receiving compensation to which they would otherwise have been entitled as injured players. The Wednesday deadline was also applied to players whose next scheduled game was on Monday, October 19 even though they had as much time to prepare for a Sunday game. The Respondents admit that safety or logistical reasons could not justify the application of the rule to these individuals.

for the games on October 18–19 is not a legitimate and substantial justification for the Wednesday deadline.

* * *

Complaint upheld.

————

The NLRB directed NFL teams to compensate each striking player for the salary lost (plus interest) as a result of this unfair labor practice—estimated to total $30 million for 1100 players. In that same first week in October 1992, a jury found the NFL liable for $30 million in damages to 235 development squad players whose salaries had been limited to $1,000 a week by the league (in the *Brown* litigation described in Chapter 3). The NFL immediately announced it would appeal both the Board order and the jury verdict. Just a few months earlier, though, the NFL had lost its final appeal of another $30 million judgment for disputed contributions (and interest) payable to the players' pension fund. See *Bidwill v. Garvey*, 943 F.2d 498 (4th Cir.1991).

Questions for Discussion

1. In the portion of the *NFL Management Council* decision excerpted above, the Board ruled that players who were on the active roster when the strike began were entitled to be paid for the "deadline games" played after the strike ended, despite the League's contention that they would not be ready to play that weekend. Therefore, players who were on "injured reserve" when the strike began and ended—and who were paid their normal salaries before the strike—were even more clearly entitled to payment for the "deadline games," since there was no issue about their readiness to play. But should these players also have been entitled to be paid for games cancelled or played during the strike? Does the answer to this question depend on whether injured reserve players were also on strike? If so, how would you determine whether an injured player was on strike? If you were an association official, would you encourage injured players to "report" for work during a strike or to maintain "solidarity" with the striking players?

2. Consider the broader industrial relations factors that influence the protagonists in deciding how to exercise their statutory rights in a sports strike. Why did the NFL choose to use temporary rather than permanent replacements in the 1987 strike? Why did Major League Baseball choose not to use (or even threaten to use) any replacements in its 1990 lockout (even if the spring training lockout had reached the regular season stage)? To what extent does the effectiveness of these tactical collective bargaining weapons turn on such background features of the sport as the number of games in the season, the existence of minor leagues, and the sources and distribution of league revenues?

3. There was some criticism of the NFLPA in 1987 to the effect that it did not utilize the most potent economic weapons at the Association's disposal. Can you think of any strategies a players' union could follow in

orchestrating a work stoppage that might be more effective in pressuring owners to make concessions?

H. ADMINISTRATION OF THE LABOR AGREEMENT [16]

However acrimonious the bargaining struggle and work stoppage, eventually labor disputes are settled and contracts signed. The collective agreement almost invariably contains promises by the union not to strike, and by the employer not to lock out, during the contract's term. Because the interest in labor peace is so intense in the sports world, labor agreements there tend to run for four or five years, rather than the two-year or three-year norm in other industries.

During the life of any agreement, though, especially one that lasts five years, a host of problems inevitably arises—for example, disputes about player discipline or the proper interpretation of contract language (including language in the standard player contract that is incorporated by reference in the collective agreement). While the parties are able to resolve most of these disputes through direct discussions, some differences are not easily reconciled. Having waived their statutory right to strike as a means of breaking the deadlock, employees instead must rely on a system of final and binding arbitration by a neutral person selected by both sides.

This development presented a further challenge to labor law: what should be the judicial approach to this institution of grievance arbitration? In its celebrated *Steelworkers Trilogy*, 363 U.S. 564, 80 S.Ct. 1343, 4 L.Ed.2d 1403 (1960), the Supreme Court told lower courts in no uncertain terms that they must defer to the parties' choice of this alternative dispute resolution procedure. Therefore, when one side seeks to compel the other to arbitrate a claim (a grievance) under the agreement, the court should—irrespective of its views of the contractual merits of the claim—strongly presume the matter to be arbitrable unless the contract language creating the grievance procedure makes it unmistakable that no such claim of this type was meant to be arbitrated. Likewise, to protect the integrity of the arbitration process, a court may issue injunctions to preserve the status quo pending the outcome of an arbitration. Finally, once the arbitrator has rendered a decision, the court must enforce the decision right or wrong, as long as the award appears "to draw its essence from the collective bargaining agreement." The Supreme Court's rationale was that:

> It is the arbitrator's construction which was bargained for and so far as the arbitrator's decision concerns construction of the con-

---

16. See David B. Feller, *A General Theory of the Collective Bargaining Agreement*, 61 California L. Rev. 663 (1973); Theodore St. Antoine, *Judicial Review of Labor Arbitration Awards*, 75 Michigan L. Rev. 1137 (1977); and William B. Gould, *Judicial Review of Labor Arbitration Awards: The Aftermath of* AT & T *and* Misco, 64 Notre Dame L. Rev. 464 (1989).

tract, the courts have no business overruling him because their interpretation of the contract is different from his.

In the sports context, these principles have been applied on several occasions. See, e.g., *Davis v. Pro Basketball, Inc.*, 381 F.Supp. 1 (S.D.N.Y.1974), and *Erving v. Virginia Squires Basketball Club*, 349 F.Supp. 716 (E.D.N.Y.1972). However, the most vivid illustration of this judicial hands-off attitude toward arbitration awards—an attitude the Supreme Court emphatically restated in *United Paperworkers Int'l. Union v. Misco Inc.*, 484 U.S. 29, 108 S.Ct. 364, 98 L.Ed.2d 286 (1987)— occurred when Major League Baseball sought judicial reversal of the *Messersmith* reading of the baseball agreement to contract sharply the traditional scope of the reserve system. The Kansas City Royals, representing Major League Baseball, are here appealing a federal district court decision upholding arbitrator Seitz's ruling which we read at the beginning of this chapter.

C∂A

KANSAS CITY ROYALS v. MAJOR LEAGUE BASEBALL PLAYERS ASS'N

United States Court of Appeals, Eighth Circuit, 1976.

532 F.2d 615.

HEANEY, CIRCUIT JUDGE.

Facts ↓

[The Players Association and the Owners had entered into two collective bargaining agreements (prior to the 1973 agreement at issue in the *Messersmith* arbitration) that dealt with the arbitrability of the reserve system. The 1968 Basic Agreement established the arbitration procedure for grievances, designated the Commissioner as arbitrator, and specifically excluded two types of disputes (neither relating to the reserve system) from arbitration. With respect to the reserve system, the agreement provided that:

> The parties shall review jointly ... possible alternatives to the reserve clause as now constituted....

> The joint review of the reserve clause shall be completed prior to the termination date of this Agreement....

> [I]t is mutually agreed that the Clubs shall not be obligated to bargain or seek agreement with the Players Association on [the reserve clause] during the term of this Agreement.

The 1970 Basic Agreement replaced the Commissioner as arbitrator with an independent three-judge panel (such as the one used in *Messersmith*) and added two more specific exclusions from arbitration (again neither involved the reserve system). During the negotiations of this agreement, Curt Flood filed suit (ultimately decided in the Supreme Court opinion discussed in Chapter 2) challenging the reserve system under federal antitrust laws. In the face of this pending litigation, and unable to reach agreement on modifications to the reserve system, the parties inserted the following provision in Article XIV of the Basic Agreement:

> Regardless of any provision herein to the contrary, this Agreement does not deal with the reserve system. The parties have differing views as to the legality and as to the merits of such system as presently constituted. This Agreement shall in no way prejudice the position or legal rights of the Parties or of any Player regarding the reserve system.
>
> It is agreed that until the final and unappealable adjudication (or voluntary discontinuance) of *Flood v. Kuhn* now pending in the federal district court of the Southern District of New York, neither of the Parties will resort to any form of concerted action with respect to the issue of the reserve system, and there shall be no obligation to negotiate with respect to the reserve system. Upon the final and unappealable adjudication (or voluntary discontinuance) of *Flood v. Kuhn* either Party shall have the right to reopen the negotiations on the issue of the reserve system....

A lawyer for the National League claimed that Players Association leader Marvin Miller said during the negotiations that the reserve system "is going to be outside the Agreement. It will not be subject to the Agreement, but we will acquiesce in the continuance of the enforcement of the rules as house rules and we will not grieve over those house rules." Miller denied making the statement.

During the term of the 1970 agreement, players filed grievances involving one or more of the provisions that comprise the reserve system. The owners did not challenge the arbitrator's jurisdiction to rule on these grievances because they felt that the grievances did not concern the "core" or "heart" of the reserve system.

During the negotiations of the 1973 Basic Agreement, the parties agreed to two modifications of the reserve system: the "five-and-ten" rule (a player with ten years of big-league experience, the last five years with the same team, could veto a trade to any other team) and much more significantly, the arbitration of salary disputes. However, the parties failed to reach agreement on other modifications to the reserve system proposed by the Players Association. Therefore, Article XIV of the 1970 agreement became Article XV of the 1973 agreement, except that the reference to the Flood litigation was removed and the phrase "except as adjusted or modified hereby"—which both parties recognized to be ambiguous—was inserted before "this Agreement does not deal with the reserve system" (The owners wanted some recognition of the agreed-upon changes in the reserve system as a safeguard against Miller's efforts to get Congress to repeal baseball's antitrust exemption, which had been upheld by the Supreme Court in the *Flood* case.) In addition, the owners agreed in a letter to Miller that "[n]otwithstanding [Article XV], it is hereby understood and agreed that the Clubs will not during the term of the Agreement make any unilateral changes in the Reserve System which would affect player obligations or benefits."]

* * *

IV

We cannot say, on the basis of the evidence discussed above, that the record evinces the most forceful evidence of a purpose to exclude the grievances hereinvolved from arbitration.

(a) The 1968 agreement clearly permitted the arbitration of grievances relating to the reserve system. It, therefore, cannot be said that the Club Owners never consented to the arbitration of such grievances. The Club Owners might have argued that they agreed to arbitrate such grievances because the Commissioner of Baseball was designated as the arbitrator, and that he, recognizing the importance of the reserve system to baseball, would interpret the disputed provisions to allow perpetual control by a Club Owner over its players. That argument, however, was not advanced before either the arbitration panel, the District Court or this Court. Moreover, the argument would not be particularly flattering to any Commissioner of Baseball.[19]

(b) Article XIV, the predecessor to Article XV, was suggested by the Players Association for rather specific purposes and the Club Owners clearly did what they could to preserve their right to argue that the reserve system remained a part of the collective bargaining agreement. Indeed, if the Club Owners' counterproposals with respect to Article XIV had been accepted, the reserve system would clearly have remained subject to arbitration.

Article XV was clearly designed to accomplish the same purposes as Article XIV. If in accomplishing these purposes the players had clearly agreed to exclude disputes arising out of the operation of the reserve system from arbitration, the Messersmith–McNally grievances would not be arbitrable. For the reasons discussed in this opinion, however, no such agreement can be found.

(c) From 1970 to 1973, a number of grievances concerning the reserve system were submitted to arbitration. The Club Owners raised no jurisdictional objections. While this fact alone is not of controlling significance, because the grievances submitted did not go to what the Club Owners regard as the "core" or "heart" of the reserve system, the submission of grievances relating to the reserve system is certainly a fact that detracts from the Club Owners' contention that the parties

19. Mr. Bowie Kuhn, the present Commissioner of Baseball, testified, in substance, that he felt that Article X of the 1973 agreement gave him the power to withdraw a grievance from arbitration if he felt that the grievance involved the "preservation of the integrity of, or the maintenance of public confidence in, the game of baseball." He testified further that he did not withdraw these grievances from arbitration because he didn't want to do anything to adversely affect the collective bargaining process: he respected the reputation of Mr. Seitz, the impartial arbitrator, and he respected the arbitration process.

clearly understood Article XIV to mean that grievances relating to the reserve system would not be subject to arbitration.

(d) The fact that Marvin Miller may have given assurances, during the 1970 negotiations, that the players would not grieve over house rules cannot be viewed as the most forceful evidence of a purpose to exclude the Messersmith–McNally grievances from arbitration. First, there is some dispute in the record as to whether Miller made such a statement. Second, assuming he did, the term "house rules" is ambiguous. Third, and we think most important, the weight of the evidence, when viewed as a whole, does not support the conclusion that Article XV was intended to preclude arbitration of any grievances otherwise arbitrable.

(e) The essence of the Club Owners' arguments on the question of arbitrability was perhaps best articulated in the testimony of Larry McPhail, President of the American League, in which he stated: "Isn't it fair to say that our strong feelings on the importance of the core of the reserve system would indicate that we wouldn't permit the reserve system to be within the jurisdiction of the arbitration procedure?" The weaknesses in this argument have been previously discussed in paragraphs (a), (b) and (c) above. We add only that what a reasonable party might be expected to do cannot take precedence over what the parties actually provided for in their collective bargaining agreement.

V

The Club Owners contend that even if the arbitration panel had jurisdiction, the award must be vacated. They argue that the award exceeded the scope of the panel's authority by "fundamentally altering and destroying the Reserve System as it historically existed and had been acquiesced in by the Association."

As we have previously noted, our review of the merits of an arbitration panel's award is limited. The award must be sustained so long as it "draws its essence from the collective bargaining agreement."

The nub of the Club Owners' argument is that both they and the Players Association understood the reserve system to enable a club to perpetually control a player, that this understanding was reflected in the 1973 agreement, and that the arbitration panel was without authority to alter the agreed upon operation of the reserve system.

We cannot agree that the 1973 collective bargaining agreement embodied an understanding by the parties that the reserve system enabled a club to perpetually control a player. First, the agreement contained no express provision to that effect. Second, while there is evidence that the reserve system operated in such a manner in recent years,[21] the record discloses that various Players Association represen-

---

21. In Flood v. Kuhn, both the majority opinion and Mr. Justice Marshall's dissent viewed the reserve system as involving perpetual player control, although that issue was not squarely before the Court.

tatives viewed the system as allowing a player to become a free agent by playing under a renewed contract for one year.

Moreover, it can be argued that the arbitration panel's award did not "alter" the reserve system. To the extent that the reserve system did enable a club to perpetually control a player, it was not necessarily by virtue of successive invocations of the renewal clause, or application of the reserve list and no-tampering rules in the absence of a contractual obligation. Other provisions operate to deter a player from "playing out his option," as is evidenced by the fact that few players have done so. On this basis, it may be said that the arbitration panel's decision did not change the reserve system, but merely interpreted various elements thereof under circumstances which had not previously arisen.

The 1973 agreement empowered the arbitration panel to "interpret, apply or determine compliance with the provisions of agreements" between the players and the clubs. We find that the arbitration panel did nothing more than to interpret certain provisions of the Uniform Player's Contract and the Major League Rules. We cannot say that those provisions are not susceptible of the construction given them by the panel. Accordingly, the award must be sustained.

Conclusion

We hold that the arbitration panel had jurisdiction to hear and decide the Messersmith–McNally grievances, that the panel's award drew its essence from the collective bargaining agreement, and that the relief fashioned by the District Court was appropriate. Accordingly, the award of the arbitration panel must be sustained, and the District Court's judgment affirmed. In so holding, we intimate no views on the merits of the reserve system. We note, however, that Club Owners and the Players Association's representatives agree that some form of a reserve system is needed if the integrity of the game is to be preserved and if public confidence in baseball is to be maintained. The disagreement lies over the degree of control necessary if these goals are to be achieved. Certainly, the parties are in a better position to negotiate their differences than to have them decided in a series of arbitrations and court decisions. We commend them to that process and suggest that the time for obfuscation has passed and that the time for plain talk and clear language has arrived. Baseball fans everywhere expect nothing less.

* * *

Appeal dismissed.

Questions for Discussion

1. Having read the contractual and historical materials in both the arbitral and judicial opinions, what do you think was the proper construction of baseball's reserve clause? To what extent are your views influenced by your sentiments about the equities of the issue? If you feel that Arbitrator Seitz's reading may have been somewhat dubious, does this

affect your evaluation of the *Steelworker Trilogy's* hands-off approach to arbitral construction of labor agreements, an approach that is quite different from judicial sentiment towards an administrative agency's (such as the NLRB's) construction of a statute?

2. Recall that the parties mutually select their arbitrator and either party can terminate the appointment if displeased with any one ruling. In Chapter 1, we saw such dismissal befall Tom Roberts, the baseball arbitrator in 1986, following his decision striking down the drug testing covenants in individual player contracts. The same fate overtook Peter Seitz following his *Messersmith* decision. Of even greater interest, though, the baseball owners almost dismissed Seitz *before* the *Messersmith* hearing because of Seitz' decision in the Jim "Catfish" Hunter case. Indeed, Commissioner Bowie Kuhn, in his autobiography, *Hardball*, relates that the owners rejected Kuhn's recommendation that Seitz be replaced. The Player Relations Committee felt that Seitz, having ruled for the Players Association in *Hunter*, would likely lean towards the owners in *Messersmith*, with that case's quite different contract footing and more momentous implications.

3. Even though a party may guess wrongly how its current arbitrator will rule, a second key difference between contract arbitration and statutory administration is that the parties can renegotiate the contractual language that an outside arbitrator may have misconstrued, a step the parties certainly cannot take with respect to an administrative interpretation of a statute. In fact, the baseball agreement expired just a few months after the *Messersmith* decision was rendered, and the agreement was being renegotiated long before any more players reached free agent status. According to the Coase theorem so favored within the Law and Economics movement, Seitz's interpretation of the reserve clause, right or wrong, was largely irrelevant to the real-world outcome of those negotiations. Do you agree?

4. In order to re-establish its reserve system after *Messersmith*, did Major League Baseball need to have the consent of the Players Association? Recall that there were two contractual features of the traditional system, the renewable option in the player contract and the anti-tampering clause in the league rules. Could baseball have simply amended its own rules to address this problem? With what risks under antitrust law? Under labor law? In industrial relations?

5. Coming back to the issue of judicial review, compare the legal standard used by the court in *Kansas City Royals*, supra, with the standard formulated by the court in *Charles O. Finley v. Bowie Kuhn*, 569 F.2d 527 (7th Cir.1978), to govern judicial review of baseball commissioner's decisions under the owners' major league agreement. (The *Finley* case, as you will recall from Chapter 1, dealt with Bowie Kuhn's rejection of Oakland A's owner, Charles Finley's, attempt to sell several of his team's star players before they became free agents post-*Messersmith*.) Should there be more, less, or similar judicial deference to these two types of private rulings?

I. UNION AND INDIVIDUAL PLAYER [17]

The deference given to private arbitration in administration of the labor agreement accentuates the dominance of the association over individual player in the day-to-day life of the bargaining relationship. Thus, a player in a contract dispute with his own club cannot go off to court where he and his attorney might feel more comfortable: he must rely on the private arbitration mechanism endorsed in the *Steelworkers Trilogy* (see *Davis v. Pro Basketball, Inc. (Portland Trailblazers)*, 381 F.Supp. 1 (S.D.N.Y., 1974), and *Cincinnati Bengals v. Jack Thompson*, 553 F.Supp. 1011 (S.D.Ohio 1983)).[18] When the player seeks to use arbitration, he will find in some sports, such as football, that the Association alone controls access to this procedure (see *Chuy v. NFLPA*, 495 F.Supp. 137 (E.D.Pa.1980)). Even in sports such as baseball, where the player has the legal right to take his case to the arbitrator irrespective of the Player Association's views about its merit, as a practical matter the player must rely on the experienced Association staff to have any real prospect in front of the arbitrator. Does all of this mean that the player associations are free to wield their legal authority and real-life clout in disregard of the individual player's interests?

The answer is that unions are anything but free in this regard. In a companion decision to *J.I. Case*, supra, described and quoted from earlier, *Steele v. Louisville and Nashville R.R. Co.*, 323 U.S. 192, 65 S.Ct. 266, 89 L.Ed.2d 173 (1944), the Supreme Court held that the exclusive authority conferred on unions by statute could be upheld as constitutional only if the Act were read as implicitly creating a duty of fair representation (DFR) owed by the union to individual employees. The authoritative judicial statement about the content of this duty is found in *Vaca v. Sipes*, 386 U.S. 171, 87 S.Ct. 903, 17 L.Ed.2d 842 (1967):

> [A] breach of the statutory duty of fair representation occurs only when a union's conduct toward a member of the collective bargaining unit is *arbitrary, discriminatory, or in bad faith* (emphasis added).

The precedent-setting unfair representation decision, *Steele*, involved a union's negotiation of a collective agreement that put black railroad workers on the bottom rung of the seniority ladder. Absent

---

17. See Matthew W. Finkin, *The Limits of Majority Rule in Collective Bargaining*, 64 Minnesota L. Rev. 183 (1980); Michael C. Harper and Ira C. Lupu, *Fair Representation as Equal Protection*, 98 Harvard L. Rev. 1211 (1985); and Clyde W. Summers, *The Individual Employee's Rights Under the Collective Bargaining Agreement: What Constitutes Fair Representation?* 127 U. Pennsylvania L. Rev. 251 (1977).

18. The statement in the text holds true when the agreed-upon adjudicator is an outside neutral, rather than the League Commissioner, or the NHL President who still decides most player contract disputes in hockey. If the adjudicator of a particular dispute is the commissioner or president appointed by the owners, the player is more likely to be able to take the dispute to court. See *Dryer v. Los Angeles Rams*, 40 Cal.3d 406, 220 Cal.Rptr. 807, 709 P.2d 826 (1985); compare *Erving v. Virginia Squires*, 349 F.Supp. 716 (E.D.N.Y.1972); *Morris v. New York Football Giants, Inc.*, 150 Misc.2d 271, 575 N.Y.S.2d 1013 (1991).

such clearly illegitimate discrimination, the courts have been loath to overturn the results of collective bargaining between the union and an employer (who, as we saw earlier, owes no corresponding substantive obligations to the employees under its duty to "bargain in good faith.") Thus, in its recent decision in *Air Line Pilots Ass'n v. O'Neill*, ___ U.S. ___, 111 S.Ct. 1127, 113 L.Ed.2d 51 (1991), the Supreme Court stated that in applying the *Vaca v. Sipes* "arbitrary, discriminatory, or bad faith" standard to the intense bargaining struggle over the content of the labor contract, courts must offer unions latitude "within a wide range of reasonableness."

Even assuming such a deferential attitude on the part of the courts, though, one can imagine sports cases in which an arguable DFR charge might be filed.

Questions for Discussion

1. Recall from Chapter 3 the situation in *Wood v. National Basketball Association*, 809 F.2d 954 (2d Cir.1987), in which a rookie draft pick objected to the feature of the NBA–NBPA salary cap that required teams above the cap to offer just the league's minimum salary even to the team's first round draft pick. Suppose that instead of suing the NBA under antitrust and losing because of the labor exemption, Wood had sued the NBPA for unfair representation of rookies in negotiating such a severe constraint on their salaries. What result?

2. Alternatively, suppose the players association and owners in a particular sport took up an idea floated earlier in this chapter: they negotiated a salary peak for individual player contracts that reduced amounts potentially payable to a Michael Jordan or Wayne Gretzky, for example, in return for significantly higher minimum salaries for less illustrious performers in that sport. Would the superstars have a valid DFR suit against the players association? A stronger or weaker claim than the rookies' case above?

3. Suppose a players association agreed to permit the league to revise the players' pension plan so as to remove an inflation-generated earnings "surplus" that would otherwise have been used to raise the amounts paid to retired players in order to keep these benefits level with inflation. In return, the owners agree to spend a sizable share of this surplus to pay for a new fringe benefit for active players—severance pay. An Ontario Supreme Court judge found that such a scenario did take place in hockey in the 1980s, and constituted a violation by the league of the terms of its pension plan: the judge awarded approximately $50 million (including interest) in a suit brought by such former NHL greats as Gordie Howe and Bobby Hull: see *Bathgate et al. v. NHL Pensions' Society et al.*, 98 D.L.R. (4th) 327 (1992). As of the time of writing, a similar lawsuit under U.S. pension law is pending in a Pennsylvania district court. Suppose, though, that the wording of the pension agreement would permit such league action if the players association gave its explicit consent, and the retired players then filed a duty of fair representation charge against the association under federal labor law. Does a players association have an obligation to represent fairly the interests of retired players in negotiations with the league?

Does the answer turn on whether the association is entitled to negotiate with clubs on behalf of former players? See *Allied Chemical & Alkali Workers v. Pittsburgh Plate Glass Co.*, 404 U.S. 157, 92 S.Ct. 383, 30 L.Ed.2d 341 (1971).

In sports, as in labor relations generally, the vast majority of DFR claims involve complaints about the union's handling of an individual contract grievance. One important reason is that the terms of the collective agreement negotiated between union and employer give the court (or the NLRB) some guidance for appraising the union's treatment of the employee in the unit. The following case illustrates the judicial struggle with the content of the duty of fair representation in a concrete sports situation.

PETERSON v. KENNEDY, BERTHELSEN AND NFLPA

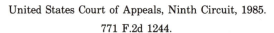

United States Court of Appeals, Ninth Circuit, 1985.

771 F.2d 1244.

REINHARDT, CIRCUIT JUDGE.

[James Peterson of the Tampa Bay Buccaneers signed one-year contracts for each of the 1976, 1977, and 1978 football seasons. Besides the standard injury protection clause that provided for payment of that year's salary in case of an injury occurring during any one season, Peterson's contract contained a special clause that entitled him to his salary for the 1977 and 1978 seasons if he were unable to play because of a football-related injury in a previous year. Peterson did injure his knee early in the 1976 season and missed the entire year because of surgery. When Peterson reported to training camp in the summer of 1977, he was cut from the team after one week drills. This was done pursuant to the standard player contract provision that allows the club to terminate the contract if a player's performance appears "unsatisfactory" compared to other players competing for positions on the squad.

After contacting the NFLPA and allegedly talking to its employee, Harold Kennedy (a recent law graduate), in August 1977, Peterson's agent filed a grievance under the "injury grievance procedure" in the NFL–NFLPA collective agreement in order to recover the salary due for the 1977 and 1978 seasons. The parties disputed whether the NFLPA had been informed at the outset of a special "injury protection" clause in Peterson's contract. However, when Richard Berthelson, the NFLPA General Counsel, learned of that clause in 1978, he sought to channel the grievance into the "non-injury" grievance procedure. Unfortunately, because the switch took place after the sixty days permitted for filing non-injury grievances, the contract arbitrator found the non-injury grievance to be time-barred. Meanwhile, the arbitrator under the injury grievance procedure found against Peterson's claim on the ground that this particular procedure was only to claim salary payments owed for the year during which the injury occurred.

Having lost both sides of his contract claim against the Buccaneers, Peterson sued the NFLPA for breach of the labor law duty of fair representation. Although the jury found in favor of Peterson's legal claim, the trial judge granted the NFLPA's motion for judgment notwithstanding the verdict (JNOV). The principal ground was that the union's conduct amounted to no more than negligence, and negligence could not constitute unfair representation under the NLRA. Peterson appealed that ruling.]

* * *

Peterson's breach of duty claim is based principally on allegations that the union, through its representatives, erroneously advised him to file an injury grievance and that the union failed to rectify its error while there still was time to do so. We assume arguendo that the advice was in fact erroneous, although it is not entirely clear that such was the case.

* * *

The district court concluded that the evidence presented was legally insufficient to sustain the jury's verdict that the union breached its duty of fair representation. We agree. After reviewing all of the evidence in the light most favorable to Peterson, we conclude that the union did not breach its duty of fair representation; the record is devoid of evidence that the union acted in an arbitrary, discriminatory, or bad faith manner.

The duty of fair representation is a judicially established rule imposed on labor organizations because of their status as the exclusive bargaining representative for all of the employees in a given bargaining unit. The Supreme Court [in DelCostello v. International Bthd. of Teamsters, 462 U.S. 151, 164 n. 14, 103 S.Ct. 2281, 2290 n.14, 76 L.Ed.2d 476 (1963)] recently explained the basis and scope of the duty:

> The duty of fair representation exists because it is the policy of the National Labor Relations Act to allow a single labor organization to represent collectively the interests of all employees within a unit, thereby depriving individuals in the unit of the ability to bargain individually or to select a minority union as their representative. In such a system, if individual employees are not to be deprived of all effective means of protecting their own interests, it must be the duty of the representative organization to "serve the interests of all members without hostility or discrimination toward any, to exercise its discretion with complete good faith and honesty, and to avoid arbitrary conduct.

A union breaches its duty of fair representation only when its conduct toward a member of the collective bargaining unit is "arbitrary, discriminatory, or in bad faith." The duty is designed to ensure that unions represent fairly the interests of all of their members without exercising hostility or bad faith toward any. It stands "as a bulwark to prevent arbitrary union conduct against individuals stripped of traditional forms of redress by the provisions of federal labor law."

The Supreme Court has long recognized that unions must retain wide discretion to act in what they perceive to be their members' best interests. To that end, we have "stressed the importance of preserving union discretion by narrowly construing the unfair representation doctrine." We have emphasized that, because a union balances many collective and individual interests in deciding whether and to what extent it will pursue a particular grievance, courts should "accord substantial deference" to a union's decisions regarding such matters.

Note
(Hold)
Rule

A union's representation of its members "need not be error free." We have concluded repeatedly that mere negligent conduct on the part of a union does not constitute a breach of the union's duty of fair representation.

* * *

(Issue)

Whether in a particular case a union's conduct is "negligent", and therefore non-actionable, or so egregious as to be "arbitrary", and hence sufficient to give rise to a breach of duty claim, is a question that is not always easily answered. A union acts "arbitrarily" when it simply ignores a meritorious grievance or handles it in a perfunctory manner, for example, by failing to conduct a "minimal investigation" of a grievance that is brought to its attention. We have said that a union's conduct is "arbitrary" if it is "without rational basis," or is "egregious, unfair and unrelated to legitimate union interests." In Robesky v. Qantas Empire Airways Ltd., 573 F.2d 1082, 1089–90 (9th Cir.1978), we held that a union's unintentional mistake is "arbitrary" if it reflects a "reckless disregard" for the rights of the individual employee, but not if it represents only "simply negligence violating the tort standard of due care."

There are some significant general principles that emerge from our previous decisions. In all cases in which we found a breach of the duty of fair representation based on a union's arbitrary conduct, it is clear that the union failed to perform a procedural or ministerial act, that the act in question did not require the exercise of judgment and that there was no rational and proper basis for the union's conduct.

* * *

We have never held that a union has acted in an arbitrary manner where the challenged conduct involved the union's judgment as to how best to handle a grievance. To the contrary, we have held consistently that unions are not liable for good faith, non-discriminatory errors of judgment made in the processing of grievances. We have said that a union's conduct may not be deemed arbitrary simply because of an error in evaluating the merits of a grievance, in interpreting particular provisions of a collective bargaining agreement, or in presenting the grievance at an arbitration hearing. In short, we do not attempt to second-guess a union's judgment when a good faith, non-discriminatory judgment has in fact been made. It is for the union, not the courts, to decide whether and in what manner a particular grievance should be pursued. We reaffirm that principle here.

Sound policy reasons militate against imposing liability on unions for errors of judgment made while representing their members in the collective bargaining process. In Dutrisac, we recognized that holding unions liable for such errors would serve ultimately to "defeat the employees' collective bargaining interest in having a strong and effective union." If unions were subject to liability for "judgment calls," it would necessarily undermine their discretion to act on behalf of their members and ultimately weaken their effectiveness. In the long run, the cost of recognizing such liability would be borne not by the unions but by their memberships. Not only would the direct costs of adverse judgments be passed on to the members in the form of increased dues, but, more importantly, unions would become increasingly reluctant to provide guidance to their members in collective bargaining disputes. Such a result would be inconsistent with our oft-repeated commitment to construe narrowly the scope of the duty of fair representation in order to preserve the unions' discretion to decide how best to balance the collective and individual interests that they represent.

* * *

Whether liability for a loss occasioned by ordinary negligence of the union might be spread more equitably among the membership as a whole, rather than be borne by the individual member who is harmed, is no longer an open question.

In applying the foregoing principles to the case at hand, we conclude, as a matter of law, that Peterson failed to establish that the NFLPA breached its duty of fair representation.... The alleged error was one of judgment. Viewing the evidence in the light most favorable to Peterson, the most that can be said is that the union provided him with incorrect advice and did not alter its judgment until it was too late to rectify the error. In this case, deciding whether to file an injury or a non-injury grievance was not a purely mechanical function; the union attorneys were required to construe the scope and meaning of the injury and non-injury grievance provisions of the collective bargaining agreement and to determine which of the two grievance procedures was more appropriate. As we have indicated earlier, the answer was not as simple as a literal reading of the two contract sections might indicate.

* * *

Although the union's representatives may have erred in initially advising Peterson to file an injury grievance and in failing to recognize its mistake in time to file a non-injury grievance in its stead, we are unwilling to subject unions to liability for such errors in judgment. Accordingly, we affirm the district court's conclusion that the evidence presented was insufficient, as a matter of law, to support the jury's verdict against the union.

Appeal Denied.

———

Suppose that a player files a grievance alleging that his release violated a "no-cut" guarantee in his contract. (This was the contract claim advanced in *Dryer v. Los Angeles Rams*, 40 Cal.3d 406, 220 Cal.Rptr. 807, 709 P.2d 826 (1985).) The Players Association agrees with the Club and the League that the contract language will not bear that interpretation and drops the grievance rather than take it to arbitration. Does the player have any legal right to take his claim before an outside adjudicator?

In response to the above question, the Supreme Court devised a carefully qualified remedial structure in *Vaca v. Sipes*, 386 U.S. 171, 87 S.Ct. 903, 17 L.Ed.2d 842 (1967). The player would have to sue in court both the association and the club, establish first that the union's judgment in dropping the grievance was "arbitrary, discriminatory, or in bad faith" (that is, breached the duty of fair representation owed by the union to the player), and *then* try to sustain the merits of his contract claim against the team (in court, not in arbitration). If the player succeeded on both counts, the club would be responsible for the damage done by the contract violation and the union for the additional costs attributable to use of this more complex procedure, such as legal fees incurred in the lawsuit and additional salary losses incurred because it took longer to get a ruling in litigation than in arbitration (see *Bowen v. United States Postal Service*, 459 U.S. 212, 103 S.Ct. 588, 74 L.Ed.2d 402 (1983)). For a sports case illustrating this process, see *Chuy v. NFLPA*, 495 F.Supp. 137 (E.D.Pa.1980).

J. SALARY ARBITRATION [19]

When most sports fans think of arbitration, what comes to mind is not *grievance*, but *salary*, arbitration. These two collectively bargained procedures resemble each other in presentation of the claims and arguments of player and club through a private, informal proceeding in front of a neutral arbitrator. One difference is that the player's case in salary arbitration is presented by his personal agent, although the players association has a representative present to assist the player's agent. A more fundamental jurisprudential difference, though, is that

---

19. See James B. Dworkin, *Owners versus Players: Baseball and Collective Bargaining*, 136–172 (Dover, Mass.: Auburn House, 1981) and David M. Frederick, William H. Kaempfer, and Richard L. Wobbekind, Salary Arbitration as a Market Substitute, Chapter 2 of *Diamonds Are Forever*, note 9 above.

whereas grievance arbitration interprets and enforces contract rights already created by the collective agreement, salary arbitration itself establishes this key term in the individual player's contract.

Salary arbitration first emerged in the early 1970's in hockey, rather than baseball. Unlike football or basketball, hockey resembled baseball (at least prior to *Messersmith*) in the assumption that the player contract was perpetually renewable. That posed the question of how to fix the salary figure in each year's contract. Traditionally, that prerogative had been reserved to the owners. With the emergence of independent players associations in the late 1960s, the perceived unfairness in the traditional practice led to substitution of a neutral as salary arbitrator—in hockey in 1970 and in baseball in 1973.

The procedures operate quite differently in the two sports. Hockey utilizes the more conventional arbitration model in which hearings are conducted by named arbitrators at various times throughout the year, and after listening to both sides' arguments the arbitrator issues a detailed written decision several weeks (even months) later. In baseball, by contrast, each salary arbitration is conducted before one of a large number of arbitrators during a three-week period in February, and each arbitrator simply gives his final verdict on the day after the hearing. Again underlying that procedural difference, hockey arbitrators must decide what they think is the appropriate salary amount, typically somewhere between the numbers proposed by each side. The baseball arbitrator, by contrast, can only select one or other of the two figures proposed, rather than compromise between them.

Baseball salary arbitration is perhaps the most visible and most studied example of this model of "final offer selection" which emerged in 1960s theorizing about dispute resolution. The assumption of that theory is that such a constraint on the arbitrator's decision-making authority expands the incentives felt by the parties to agree to a voluntary settlement without outside adjudication. What do you think is the logic of that theory? In actual practice, whereas in its first two years of use in baseball half the salary cases were settled, in the early 1990s, of approximately 160 players entering the process only 20 or so needed an arbitral ruling.

It is argued that the availability of this procedure is a major contributor to spiralling baseball salaries. Though owners typically win more verdicts than they lose, the entire class of players eligible for arbitration secures an average salary increase of slightly over 100 percent. In 1992, even the players "losing" their cases secured average annual salary increases of 75 percent, amounting to a $450,000 raise.[20]

---

20. The cash value of salary arbitration is demonstrated even more clearly by recent econometric research which finds that after taking account of actual performance on the field, the mere fact of becoming eligible for arbitration raises the salaries of players by anywhere from 55% to 90%, depending on the player's position: see Paul C. Burgess and Daniel L. Marburger, Bargaining Power and Major League Baseball, Chapter 3 of *Diamonds Are Forever*, note 9 above.

For that reason, salary arbitration has recently eclipsed even free agency as the principal object of the owner's ire. In 1985, the owners took a strike to get eligibility for arbitration lifted from two to three years of service; then, in 1990 the owners locked out the players to hold any reduction in eligibility time to just the highest one-sixth of players with between two and three years service. And in hockey, that sport's little-noticed (but regularly used) arbitration procedure is credited with driving salaries upward in 1990 and 1991, thus contributing to the first-ever hockey strike on the eve of the 1992 Stanley Cup playoffs. Growing numbers of owners in both sports are now saying they would like to scrap entirely the salary arbitration system devised two decades earlier.

It is easy to understand such owner sentiment in the unlikely event that the alternative would be the previous system of *owner* determination of the player's salary in the case of a negotiating deadlock. The more interesting question, though, concerns the comparative effects of salary arbitration and free agency. Do you think that salary arbitration would be inflationary if there were no free agency? Alternatively, might players fare better if they gave up neutral salary arbitration entirely, in return for unrestricted free agency and competition by all teams for all players' services? Does the current system in baseball, which every year combines a right of free agency for a few players and salary arbitration for many more, provide a reasonable balance between the two sides, or does it tilt in one direction or the other?

Another significant feature of salary arbitration are the factors an arbitrator may take into account in making the award. The Basic Agreement in baseball provides that the relevant criteria are:

> the quality of the Player's contribution to his Club during the past season, the length and consistency of his career contribution, the record of the Player's past compensation, comparative baseball salaries, the existence of any physical or mental defects on the part of the Player, and the recent performance record of the Club including but not limited to its League standing and attendance as an indication of public acceptance.

Of these criteria, the salaries of players of comparable position, skill, and seniority seem to get the most attention during hearings.[21] However, the Basic Agreement expressly prohibits arbitrators from hearing evidence relating to a club's financial position or ability to pay. This means that clubs with very different revenue levels are plugged into a standardized pay scale generated by salary arbitration. Is this appropriate? What impact does this have on baseball's overall salary structure? What implications might it have for competitive team balance? For whether and to what extent the teams should agree to share

---

21. For econometric analysis of those factors that actually have the most influence on arbitration verdicts, see David J. Faurot and Stephen McAllister, *Salary Ar-* *bitration and Pre–Arbitration Negotiation in Major League Baseball*, 45 Ind. and Lab. Rel. Rev. 697 (1992).

revenues? Keep this general issue in mind as you consider in Chapter 6 whether for antitrust purposes leagues are single entities or a collection of competing businesses.

K. UNION SECURITY IN SPORTS [22]

A final component of labor law addresses the other side of the tension between the individual interests of particular players and the group interests of players as a whole. The duty of fair representation we described earlier requires the players association to pursue the interests of each member of the bargaining unit, regardless of whether the player has joined and supports the association selected by the majority. Whatever the fate of individual grievances, such as in *Peterson*, supra, all players inevitably enjoy the benefits of the collectively bargaining regime governing their sport—under which average baseball player salaries, for example, have soared from $19,000 in 1967 to just over $1 million in 1992.

On the other side of the coin, what can the players association do to protect the majority of players from the temptation felt by individuals to "free ride"—to take full advantage of the labor contract but not to bear any share of the costs of negotiating and administering the agreement? In response to this problem, players associations, like unions in all other industries, have sought to negotiate "union security" arrangements.

Under Sections 8(a)(3) and 8(b)(2) of the National Labor Relations Act, unions and employers are forbidden from requiring actual membership in the union. The practical significance of that statutory ban is that the union can do nothing to employees who choose to go back to work during a strike called by the majority. See *Pattern Makers' League of North America v. NLRB*, 473 U.S. 95, 105 S.Ct. 3064, 87 L.Ed.2d 68 (1985). However, unions can secure from each employee a contribution to the financial cost of the representation effort by requiring even non-members to pay to the union the financial equivalent of the union dues paid by members (see *NLRB v. General Motors Corp.*, 373 U.S. 734, 83 S.Ct. 1453, 10 L.Ed.2d 670 (1963)). A recent Supreme Court decision held, however, that to the extent any union funds are expended on activities not directly related to the fate of the unit (such as political campaigns or organizing drives among non-union workers), a dissenting employee can insist on a *pro rata* rebate of part of this "agency fee" (see *Communication Workers of Am. v. Beck*, 487 U.S. 735, 108 S.Ct. 2641, 101 L.Ed.2d 634 (1988)). Finally, in the twenty or so states (largely in the south or southwest) that have "right-to-work" laws, unions cannot insist on even this limited financial contribution

22. See Kenneth G. Dau–Schmidt, *Union Security Agreements Under the NLRA: The Statute, the Constitution, and the* *Court's Opinion in* Beck, 27 Harvard J. on Legis. 51 (1990).

(see *Retail Clerks Int'l Ass'n, Local 1625 v. Schermerhorn*, 373 U.S. 746, 83 S.Ct. 1461, 10 L.Ed.2d 678 (1963)).

Union security in the form of the agency shop has on occasion been a significant feature of labor relations in sports. In particular, the desperate fiscal straits of the NFL Players Association in 1977 was a significant factor in its agreeing in the wake of *Mackey* to give the owners the restraints on free agency that became the target of the *McNeil* litigation. In return, the union was able to secure a collective agreement and agency-shop-dues checkoff clause that would restore its financial life blood. As we saw in Chapter 3, though, in the aftermath of the 1987 strike which failed to liberalize veteran free agency, the NFLPA was ready to forego not simply a collective agreement, but even its union status, in order to prevail in the *McNeil* litigation. The explanation for that change of heart is that the NFLPA, as other players associations, now relies on another lucrative source of monetary support—trading cards.

This avenue was first discovered in the late 1960s by Marvin Miller, head of the baseball players association.[23] Up to that time, baseball players had sold rights to their likenesses on these cards on an individual basis—and for a pittance. Miller persuaded the players to sign over licensing rights to their associations which marketed the rights collectively. The $60 million or so the MLBPA now annually realizes from this source provides ample support for the association's expenses (including its strike fund), and also returns a handsome dividend to the players every year. Now that such promotional activities have come to other sports, so also has this association source of revenue. In the early 1990s the NFLPA has realized over $20 million a year from group licensing of its members names and likenesses, up from $1 million in 1985, and more than enough to finance free agency antitrust litigation against the NFL (whose costs ran at about $9 million in 1991).

The other side of this coin is that when the owners realize that group licensing is the financial base of a strong union adversary, the league will take steps to reduce this cash flow. Precisely that owner effort was a key factor in the National Hockey League strike in April 1992, before the parties agreed on a new agreement that made explicit the NHLPA's right to sell its members' likenesses to trading card companies. Meanwhile, the NFL is challenging the NFLPA in a different fashion. NFL Properties, a licensing/publishing corporation wholly owned by NFL clubs, is actively bidding against the NFLPA to obtain the players' licensing rights, both from new rookies and from veteran players already under contract with the NFLPA. NFL Properties began with a Quarterback Club that included such name players as John Elway, Dan Marino, Randall Cunningham, and Warren Moon who were signed to lucrative, exclusive contracts. These efforts vis-a-vis veteran players have elicited Association suits for breach of contract

---

23. See Miller, *A Whole Different Ball Game*, note 1 above, 91–94, 142–152.

against certain of the players and for tort and antitrust violations against the League. Whatever the outcome of such litigation in football, this sequence of events displays the same tension between the immediate interests of players as individuals and their long-term interests as a group that underlies the broader topic of union security.

L. COLLUSION IN BASEBALL [24]

The material in this chapter and in the preceding one has shown how union representation under the labor laws can create a favorable marketplace for athletes: most notably so in the case of baseball where the players association has never been able to draw upon the legal resources of antitrust law. In the mid–1980s, though, under newly elected Commissioner Peter Ueberroth, the baseball owners sought to undermine the "free agency" regime that the owners had been unable to modify through collective bargaining with the union. The owners' venture in "collusion" spawned multiple arbitration proceedings in the next five years and produced more than 1,000 days of hearings and 17,000 pages of transcript. The final punctuation point was payment by the owners of $280 million in damages to the players. It is impossible to depict these events here through even selected portions of the several lengthy arbitration decisions. However, the story is sufficiently interesting, and the lessons sufficiently important, that we provide the following synopsis of what transpired.

Under the auspices of free agency inspired by the *Messersmith* ruling, baseball salaries had soared from an average of approximately $50,000 in 1976 to $370,000 in 1985. Baseball owners were so troubled by this perceived threat to their fiscal viability that at the outset of collective bargaining in 1985, they voluntarily opened their books to the Players Association. The owners asked the Association to have its own accountants and economists appraise the validity of the their financial plight. That posture was in marked contrast to the same owners' refusal in 1980–1981 to let the players examine their balance sheets, a refusal that in *Silverman* supra was held legal under the NLRA only (because in the earlier negotiations it was the commissioner, not the PRC, that had claimed hardship.)

After a brief work stoppage in the summer of 1985, the owners succeeded in securing a modest concession that postponed players' eligibility for salary arbitration from two to three years of service. In return, the owners agreed to establish a modified regime for bidding for

---

24. For an overview of these events, see Stephen L. Willis, *Comment: A Critical Perspective on Baseball's Collusion Decisions*, 1 Seton Hall J. of Sports Law 109 (1991). For contrasting economic analyses see Dan Durland Jr. and Paul M. Sommers, *Collusion in Major League Baseball: An Empirical Test*, 14 J. of Sport Behavior 19 (1991); Robert A. Baade and Carolyn Tuttle, *Owner Collusion or Sound Fiscal Management: An Analysis of Recent Events in Baseball's Labor Market*, 1 Seton Hall J. of Sports Law 41 (1991); and Andrew Zimbalist, Salaries and Performance: Beyond the Scully Model, Chapter 7 of *Diamonds are Forever*, note 9 above.

free agents. When a player declared for free agency before the end of October, his incumbent (or "home") team was given until December 7th to offer the player salary arbitration. If arbitration was not offered, or if the player did not accept the offer within a few weeks, the home team had to re-sign the player by January 8th or lose all rights to negotiate with him until May 1st. The Association's objective was to remove what it felt was a sentiment among the owners to defer to the interests of the home team in deciding whether to bid for a free agent's services.

Subsequently, Commissioner Ueberroth convened the owners for a series of meetings at the end of the 1985 season. His aim was to document why it was bad business for teams to engage in bidding for free agents by offering players not only very high salaries, but also guaranteed long-term contracts. Such behavior by one club forced all the other clubs to adopt similar measures, to the ultimate detriment of the owners collectively.

The owners' response to the Commissioner's message was dramatic. In the previous off-season—in the winter of 1984–1985—26 of 46 veteran free agents switched teams, and 16 of the 26 clubs signed at least one free agent. The average salary increase of free agents and of other veteran players who signed that year was roughly 14 percent. In the 1985–1986 off-season, by contrast, only 4 of 32 free agents signed with other clubs, and all 4 players had been told by their home team that it was not interested in signing them. The home team had expressed an ongoing interest in each of the other 28 free agents; none received a single offer from another team. Feeling that strong pressure, all of these players accepted their home club's final offer by the January 8th deadline. One player, Kirk Gibson, did so by phone from New Zealand, five minutes before midnight. The average salary negotiated by veteran players that year was 6 percent *lower* than it had been in the previous year.

Similar events occurred in the next off-season, 1986–1987, but with some interesting variations. There were more free agents, 79 in total, who as a group tended to be of somewhat higher quality (including all-stars such as Jack Morris, Tim Raines, Andre Dawson, and Lance Parrish). A few more players changed teams that year, but none of the 79 free agents received a higher outside offer. For example, Jack Morris, was arguably the best pitcher ever to enter the free agent market, before or since. However, Morris received no offer from any club other than his home team, the Detroit Tigers. Not one outside club (including Morris' preferred choice, his hometown Minnesota Twins) would even accept Morris' offer to sign at a salary to be determined by a neutral arbitrator. Only the Tigers took that offer, and so Morris reluctantly signed with them before the January 8th deadline.

Eight players, though, did not sign before the January 8th deadline. Most experienced the fate of Tim Raines. Even with his home team, the Montreal Expos, apparently shut out of the market for his services, Raines, the 1986 National League batting champion, received no outside offers, before or after January 8th. Eventually he returned to the Expos on May 1st, after missing the first month of the season.[25] In total, the salaries of that year's cohort of free agents declined 15 percent, and the vast majority signed only one-year contracts.

The consequence for the owners was that overall players' salaries increased at a far lower rate for the next several years than total league revenues and club profits. Under *Flood*, baseball players could not challenge this pattern of concerted owner behavior under antitrust law. The Players Association was, however, able to lodge a series of grievances under the following provision in the "free agency" article of baseball's collective agreement:

H. INDIVIDUAL NATURE OF RIGHTS

The utilization or non-utilization of rights under this Article XVIII is an individual matter to be determined solely by each player and each club for his or its own benefit. Players shall not act in concert with other Players and Clubs shall not act in concert with other Clubs.

Ironically, this clause had been inserted into the agreement at the owners' insistence in 1976, when the parties were designing their new free agent system after the *Messersmith* ruling. The owners had been troubled by earlier episodes of the Dodgers' Sandy Koufax and Don Drysdale, and then of the Phillies' Mike Schmidt and Larry Bowa, who had negotiated with their clubs as a tandem: one player would not sign without his friend and teammate also being signed. The owners' concern was that with both free agency and the proliferation of player agents representing multiple players (see Chapter 5), the use of this tactic would spread. The aim of Paragraph H was to ensure that each player negotiated as an individual, not as part of a package. Marvin Miller, Executive Director of the Players Association, eventually agreed to the proposal, but only with the anti-concerted action undertaking being made reciprocal on the part of the teams.

The first Association grievance under this section, filed in January 1986, was temporarily derailed in August 1986 when the owners tried to remove the arbitrator, Tom Roberts, because of his recent ruling that the clubs had violated the labor contract in following Commissioner Ueberroth's directive to insert a random drug-testing clause in new individual contracts (see Chapter 1). Another arbitrator eventually

---

25. Bob Horner, instead of returning to the Atlanta Braves, finally signed with the Yakuit Swallows in the Japanese Baseball League. Andre Dawson, who desperately wanted to move from the Expos to a team with a natural grass playing surface that would preserve his knees, eventually got an offer from the Chicago Cubs, but only in the following bizarre fashion. His agent offered the Cubs a contract signed by Dawson, but with the salary left blank. The agent then called a press conference to tell the Chicago fans that the Cubs could have Dawson at whatever price the *team* thought was fair. After a written apology to the league's Player Relations Committee, the Cubs signed the contract with Dawson at *their* figure of $500,000, less than half Dawson's salary with the Expos in the previous year. For that price, the Cubs got a player who won the 1987 Most Valuable Player Award.

ruled that while the owners (and the Association) were free to fire their designated arbitrator for the future, they could not terminate the incumbent's jurisdiction in cases which had already been put before him. As a result, not until December 1987 did Roberts finally complete and issue his ruling that in the winter of 1985–1986, the owners had violated the "in concert" clause.

One consequence of this delay was that the owners followed essentially the same pattern of behavior in the winter of 1986–1987. In turn, the Association filed a second collusion grievance, and in the ensuing arbitration the new arbitrator, George Nicolau, issued the same ruling as had his predecessor. Both arbitrators rejected the League's argument that while the teams may have been acting in a "consciously parallel" fashion, each was doing so as a response to its own financial and competitive needs, not as part of a broader reciprocal arrangement with its colleagues:

MLB PLAYERS ASSOCIATION AND THE 26 MAJOR LEAGUE CLUBS

(Collusion Grievance No. 2).

Arbitration, 1987.

NICOLAU, ARBITRATOR.

* * *

The differentiating factor [in a team making an offer to a free agent] was not the player's agent, the player's prominence, the loss or retention of a draft choice, or the possibility of a long-term contract, but whether the former club wanted that player. When it did, there was no competitive bidding such as there had been in the past. Unlike the pre–1985 years, no club sought to challenge a former club's "right" to a player though any such right had expired with the expiration of his contact.

Article VIII(H) does not guarantee any particular level of market activity and it may well be, as the Clubs assert, that a growing awareness of the economics of the game and the "learning curve" of free-agent performance would lead to fewer offers, perhaps at lower prices. But the period at issue was not one of "declining activity"; the Record demonstrates that there was literally no market; no bid, save one: that of the former club. Those players who only received that one bid "surely had a value [to other clubs] at some price," in Chairman Robert's words, yet there were no other bidders "at any price." Only when the former club no longer wanted "its" player, did other clubs "feel free" to bid.

The impact of this uniform behavior cannot be overstated. Unlike the pre–1985 years, when several clubs participated in the free-agent market bidding against former clubs that retained negotiating rights, in 1986, like 1985, no club entered that market. This "no bid, no bargain-

ing" forcing of players back to their former clubs cannot be attributed
to individualized notions of hard bargaining or independent implemen-
tations of sophisticated economic analysis. What transpired in 1986
occurred because everyone "understood" what was to be done. By
common consent, exclusive negotiating rights were, in effect, ceded to
former clubs. There was no vestige of a free market, as that term is
commonly understood. The object was to force players back to their
former clubs and the expectation was that all would go back in a
replication of 1985, requiring nothing more to be done. California
could go down to the wire with Downing, DeCinces, and Boone; Toronto
could put a "little heat" on Clancy; and Montreal could publicly "one
offer" Raines and Dawson because they knew with a certainty there
would be no other bidders to interfere.

* * *

In any one year, there may be a great deal of bidding between
former clubs and other clubs; in another year, substantially less. But
the abrupt cessation of activity in 1985 and the repetition of that
pattern, with only minor post-January 8 deviations in 1986, cannot be
attributed to the free play of market forces. Clubs have different
personalities, different fiscal realities, different budgets, and different
needs. Rather than reactions on the basis of those realities and those
needs, there was a patent pattern of uniform behavior, a uniformity
simply unexplainable by the rubric of financial responsibility or by any
other factors on which the Clubs have relied in this proceeding. In my
opinion, their conduct with respect to the 1986 free agents was in
deliberate contravention of Club obligations as embodied in Article
XVIII (H), for which an appropriate remedy is fully justified.

Grievance upheld.

———

The remedial phase of these collusion proceedings was as lengthy,
complex, and illuminating as was the liability phase. The simple
remedy the arbitrators initially adopted was to offer each of the
directly affected veteran players a "second look" at free agency. The
consequence, though, was that when arbitrator Roberts made this order
in January 1988 for the original free agent class of 1985–1986, ongoing
collusion by the owners caused these players to fare little better the
second time than they had the first. Only Kirk Gibson signed with
another team, the Dodgers, and he did so for essentially the same
salary that he received under his old contract with the Tigers. (The
following 1988 season Gibson was the National League's Most Valuable
Player.)

By the winter of 1987–1988 the Roberts ruling had come down, the
second arbitration hearing was well under way, and the owners had
modified their program to establish an "Information Bank" under the
auspices of the Player Relations Committee. Under this arrangement,

every team in the league provided detailed information about each and every offer it made (or perhaps even contemplated making) to any player. This permitted every team to get an immediate picture of the demand for the services of every player in the free agent market. Any team could know, then, precisely how much it had to bid to gain an edge on its competitors, if not for one player, then for another.

In response to the Association's third grievance, Arbitrator Nicolau found that this arrangement, too, violated Article XVIII's bar against concerted owner action. The 76 free agents in 1987–1988 did receive twelve offers from other teams in competition with their home teams, and three of these players switched clubs. However, the Information Bank was found to have limited considerably the salary offers made by competing teams that year.

When the arbitrators turned to the task of awarding monetary damages to affected players, their calculations required several analytical judgments. Some judgments involved the interlocking features of salary determination. For example, contracts signed by free agents early in the off-season had a demonstrable spillover effect on salary arbitration that winter. Thus, the sizable cohort of players with 3 to 5 years of service were also affected even though these players were not yet entitled to free agency. Similarly, artificial restraints imposed on salary levels for any one year's class of free agents had a depressing effect on the subsequent year's salaries; this effect would endure even after collusion had ended because free agents (or arbitration candidates) in those later years would begin their negotiations with considerably lower salary benchmarks than a fully competitive marketplace would have produced. Finally, the removal of effective competition for free agents not only depressed actual salary amounts, but also cut back on valuable contract perquisites such as long-term guaranteed contracts, performance bonuses, and no-trade clauses.

With respect to each group of affected players, there remained an even more difficult problem of how to calculate the actual financial losses. Without going into the details of the econometric models used to do the analysis, suffice it to say that damages awarded by the arbitrators amounted to $10 million for lost 1986 salaries, $38 million for lost 1987 salaries (the product of collusion in both 1986 and 1987), and $65 million for lost 1988 salaries. Further damage awards for salary losses in 1989 and 1990 were forthcoming, as well as damages for the lost value of the contract features such as performance bonuses and no-trade clauses. By 1990, baseball had a new commissioner, Fay Vincent, and a somewhat more cooperative cast to its labor-management relationship (the latter sentiment emerging in the aftermath of still another lockout of players from spring training camps in early 1990.) Having received and read several hundred pages of arbitration decisions, the owners and the Players Association finally agreed in the fall of 1990 to a settlement of all claims during the entire collusion period, for a total of $280 million. In addition, several players were given yet another chance at free agency, this time in a much more competitive marketplace. (After collusion ended, average salaries leaped from $430,000 in 1988 to over $1 million in 1992.) Of the "second look" free agents who switched teams in return for considerably more lucrative contracts, the most significant was Jack Morris who signed with the Minnesota Twins and became the Most Valuable Player in the Twins' thrilling 1991 World Series triumph.

The settlement agreement and payments completed the owners' involvement in the collusion case. The Players Association still has the daunting task of devising a formula for distributing this $280 million among its members. The dimensions of the challenge became clearer in the summer of 1991, when it was announced that 800 players had filed claims totalling over $1 billion to a share in the settlement. Reportedly, the two largest bids were by Jack Morris (for $4.5 million) and Andre Dawson (for $3.5 million). Association leaders may soon experience what the Supreme Court observed in *Ford Motor Co. v. Huffman*, 345 U.S. 330, 338, 73 S.Ct. 681, 686, 97 L.Ed. 1048 (1953) (as a reason for subjecting unions to a rather relaxed standard of fair representation): "The complete satisfaction of all who are represented is hardly to be expected."

As a postscript, in their 1990 collective bargaining round the parties amended the "in concert" provision to provide that if the owners (though not the players) violated this clause in the future, affected players would be entitled to receive three times their "lost baseball income," plus full legal fees and interest.

The five-year period of baseball owner collusion and union response vividly demonstrates how a system of private negotiation and adjudication undertaken within the umbrella of labor law can replicate the role of public antitrust law in defining and enforcing the conditions for a competitive marketplace. The episode suggests several intriguing questions.

For example, why do we need trebled damages, rather than simply full compensation for actual damages, to enforce a ban on collusion? Is payment of $280 million—$11 million per club—not a sufficient deterrent to future incidents of this kind of contract violation?

A second question concerns the owners' use of the "Information Bank" to collect and disseminate salary offers to free agent players. This practice constituted the owners' violation in the third collusion year after Arbitrator Nicolau gave a rather literal reading to the "in concert" clause in the collective agreement. In the absence of such a clause, though—and in a sport other than baseball—such information sharing could be challenged under antitrust law. Why should this be so? Isn't the assumption of "perfect knowledge" a fundamental ingredient of the free market model? What is wrong with each bidder and seller knowing exactly what everyone else thinks a particular player is worth as long as they do not have an agreement to act collusively with that information (as in traditional bid-rigging conspiracies)?

Information sharing, however, is not a tactic limited to one side of the bargaining table—player agents, as well as owners, can agree to communicate salary offers to one another in order to drive up the "going rate" of certain types of players, such as first-round draft choices. Indeed, in a recent lawsuit the NFL alleged that the NFLPA and agents representing NFL and college players did just this.

THE FIVE SMITHS v. NFL PLAYERS ASSOCIATION

United States District Court, District of Minnesota, 1992.

788 F.Supp. 1042.

DOTY, DISTRICT JUDGE.

[The NFL's complaint asserted that the agents' practice of exchanging information about current salaries and offers was a "combination and conspiracy ... the purpose and effect of which [was] to fix [and] raise ... compensation paid to NFL players." The NFL argued that this conspiracy was both a "per se" violation of antitrust law as price (i.e., wage) fixing and an unreasonable restraint of trade. In ruling on the NFLPA's motion to dismiss, the court first rejected the NFL's "per se" theory. The court concluded that the "per se" rule should not apply because most players do not compete "for the same jobs on the same teams" due to the college draft and restrictions on veteran free agents—thus there was no conspiracy among "competitors." Even if the players were "competitors," though, the court found that the exchange of salary information is not so manifestly anticompetitive as to warrant per se condemnation. The court's reasoning implies that the NFL's "per se" theory would have prevailed only if the court had found that the players were "competitors" *and* the NFL had made specific allegations of a salary-fixing conspiracy.

The court then turned to the NFL's argument that the agents' information sharing was an unreasonable restraint of trade. The NFL's complaint alleged that each club "has been damaged financially by the combination and conspiracy between the NFLPA and player-agents." The court used this allegation to reject the "unreasonable restraint of trade" claim: "Plaintiffs thus allege only injury to themselves; they fail to allege any injury to competition or to define a relevant market in which such injury occurred." As if to run up the score, so to speak, the court then rejected this claim on its merits.]

* * *

Even if the plaintiffs were to plead a relevant market, the court determines that their claim would nonetheless fail under the rule of reason because they are unable to allege the only type of price information exchange that the Supreme Court has determined constitutes a violation under the rule of reason. As previously discussed, plaintiffs allege only one specific example of concerted action, that the NFLPA and player-agents have acted in concert to share information on player compensation. The Supreme Court has determined that, absent some agreement between competitors to restrain price, the exchange of price and other market information is generally benign conduct that facilitates efficient economic activity.

Plaintiffs argue, however, that the alleged agreement between the NFLPA and player-agents to share information on player compensation constitutes an antitrust violation like that found in United States v. Container Corp., 393 U.S. 333 (1969). *Container Corp.* ruled that an exchange of price information among competitors, without an agreement to fix prices, was sufficient to raise antitrust concerns, but only in markets where certain structural conditions exist. Those characteristics are: (1) a highly concentrated market dominated by relatively few sellers; (2) a fungible product; (3) competition that is primarily based on price; and (4) inelasticity of demand because buyers tend to order for their immediate short term needs. Examining those characteristics, the court concludes that such market conditions do not exist in the present case. Plaintiffs neither allege nor can allege that there is a highly concentrated relevant market of competing sellers of players' services because there are over 1,500 professional football players, many of whom are represented in salary negotiations by agents, of whom there are hundreds. In addition, most football players do not compete by selling a fungible product as to which purchasing decisions are primarily made on the basis of price, additional structural factors which are necessary for an information exchange to violate the rule of reason. See *Container Corp.*, 393 U.S. at 337. Rather, each player has his own unique attributes and skills, which are of varying desirability to the different teams. Moreover, each player's salary is arrived at during negotiations with his employer club.[1] Finally, the court concludes that there is no inelasticity of demand due to a market of buyers who purchase only for their immediate short term needs. To the contrary, the teams generally sign players to multi-year contracts and the system of player restraints essentially ties each player to his employer club for the duration of his career. Based on the foregoing, the court concludes that the market structure of the National Football League does not have the characteristics required by *Container Corp.* and thus the plaintiffs cannot allege the requisite factors to establish a rule of reason violation based solely on the exchange of salary information.

The court further concludes that the alleged salary exchange fails to state a rule of reason violation because any such exchange can have no anticompetitive effect given the present system of player restraints. Plaintiffs' theory of rule of reason liability is essentially that information concerning the salaries of comparable players is a relevant factor in contract negotiations between an agent and the player's employer

---

1. As a result of the plaintiffs' players restraints, specifically the college draft and the first refusal/compensation system, most players are also unable to compete with each other for the same position on the same team because they are bound to their assigned clubs for the duration of their careers.

club and that having access to such information enables agents to negotiate higher salaries for their players than they would otherwise be able to obtain if forced to negotiate in the dark. Plaintiffs therefore contend that agents' access to such information is somehow anticompetitive. The court, however, rejects that contention. First, plaintiffs fail to allege any anticompetitive effect to either themselves as competitors or the market as a whole. Moreover, as previously discussed, the existing restraints have virtually eliminated competition among plaintiffs for player services and also between players for positions. As a result, players have little leverage in their salary negotiations. Moreover, it is undisputed that the alleged salary information exchange merely provides agents and players with information that plaintiffs already possess. Although plaintiffs contend that it somehow violates the antitrust laws for agents to have independent access to that same negotiating information, the court determines that the availability of such information can only make the negotiation process fairer because the negotiations can take place without any misunderstanding or misrepresentation about what other players are earning. The court thus concludes that the dissemination of salary information has no anticompetitive effect and may actually benefit competition because it provides players with the same type of information concerning other players' salaries that the plaintiffs already possess.

Summary dismissal granted.

Questions for Discussion

1. Near the end of the above opinion, the court argues that rather than restrain competition, the agents' information sharing actually enhances it by creating a level playing field between the clubs and the agents. Is this argument sound? If so, does this suggest that the flexible "rule of reason" approach under antitrust law is preferable to the rigid, literal interpretation of a contractual provision such as the "in concert" clause in the baseball collective agreement?

2. Recall that the court's first ground for rejecting the NFL's "unreasonable restraint of trade" argument was that the NFL failed to allege "any injury to competition." Why do you suppose the NFL would be reluctant to argue that its clubs are competitors (except, of course, on the playing field)? Look back at the antitrust cases against the NFL in Chapter 3 and keep this question in mind when you read *Los Angeles Memorial Coliseum Comm'n v. National Football League* in Chapter 6.

3. In rejecting the NFL's restraint of trade argument, Judge Doty kept emphasizing that the players were not competitors because of the restrictions on free agency in the league. Since the players were able to obtain a substantially greater degree of free agency in the 1993 settlement with the NFL and the subsequent collective agreement, would a league antitrust challenge to players sharing detailed contract information have more validity under the court's analysis? If not, would the clubs be able to share salary information lawfully?

Consider the broader significance of the club revenue-player salary equation and its relationship to the governing legal rules. From 1985 through 1988, while player salaries rose from an average of $370,000 to $430,000, total baseball revenues soared from $650 million to $1 billion. When owner collusion ended, average salaries spiraled from $430,000 in 1988 to more than $1 million in 1991, but league revenues were also shooting up throughout this period, to over $1.6 billion by 1992.

In this respect, baseball owners today do not appear to claim that spiraling salaries are out of line with total league revenues (indeed, they are around 45 percent of league revenues while player costs in the NBA and the NFL are well over 50 percent). What they do claim, however, is that because all the teams compete in the same free agent market and are subject to the same criteria in salary arbitration, teams in small markets like Milwaukee, Seattle, and Pittsburgh, earning less than a third of the total revenues of teams in the major markets, are being squeezed out of the star player market altogether. A committee co-chaired by Brewers' owner Allan "Bud" Selig and MLBPA Executive Director Don Fehr is currently studying this issue, and will present conclusions and recommendations in the near future.

Do you agree that this poses a problem for baseball's competitive balance or the financial viability of small market teams? If so, what do you think is the optimal solution—holding down player salaries through restraints on free agency or salary arbitration, greater revenue sharing among the clubs (which today share no local television, concessions or marketing revenues and give visiting teams an average of just 15% of gate receipts), or some combination of the two?

Alternatively, baseball could require small market teams to relocate to more populous areas where they can generate sufficient revenue; probably more than two teams in the New York, Chicago, and Los Angeles markets, and more than one team in areas like Philadelphia, Boston, and Toronto. Assuming the owners would ever permit it, would gravitation of teams to fewer but more populous communities be desirable? As yet another alternative, perhaps the small markets would keep their teams, but the mega-markets would be given several new expansion teams to dilute the revenues of the teams currently there. Would that be desirable? What impact would such expansion have on average player salaries? On the quality of team play? Keep all these questions in mind when we explore monopolization in professional sports in Chapter 7.

Finally, in his 1991 memoirs, *A Whole Different Ballgame: The Sport and Business of Baseball*, Marvin Miller, founder of the baseball players' union, asserted that the collusive behavior of Commissioner Ueberroth and the owners was a more serious violation of the "best interests of the game" than was Pete Rose's gambling. Miller's point was not so much that the owners violated their contractual undertakings to the players (as would also have been true if the owners had paid less than their proper contribution to the players' pension plan). Miller said that what was special about owner collusion, and worse than Rose trying to make money by betting on his team to win, was that owners such as George Steinbrenner tried to make money by, in effect, choosing to let their teams lose. Is that a valid comparison? What arguments could one make against Miller's assertion?

Chapter Five

AGENT REPRESENTATION OF THE ATHLETE [1]

This chapter introduces another important participant in the sports world—the player agent. Agents have long been a key factor in the entertainment industry, by helping to secure work and earnings for actors, musicians, and writers. However, because of the tradition in sports that the player was the "property" of the club that originally brought him to the major leagues, there was far less room for effective representation of the player's interests *vis-a-vis* the team. Indeed, one of the first reported instances of athlete representation, by Bob Woolf of Earl Wilson, a pitcher for the Boston Red Sox in the mid–1960s, came about because Wilson happened to consult Woolf about a minor automobile accident. In those early days, general managers often refused to deal directly with Woolf and his colleagues in salary negotiations, which forced agents to advise their clients from behind the scenes.[2] As a measure of how dramatically this field has been transformed in the last quarter century, in televising the 1991 NFL draft ESPN had a remote camera and announcer in the quarters of Leigh Steinberg, the high-profile agent for several first-round selections that day.

The reason for the current prominence of agents is the variety of roles they now play for their clients. The principal role is negotiating the player's contract with the team. This task is far more important now because of the huge amounts of money involved in such negotiations—thanks to the interplay of labor and antitrust law described in the previous chapters. We mentioned at the start of Chapter 4 that baseball players now average over $1 million a year and football

1. This part of the law of sports has produced a considerable body of legal scholarship. Valuable overviews are provided by Kenneth Shropshire, *Agents of Opportunity: Sports Agents and Corruption in Collegiate Sports* (Philadelphia: University of Pennsylvania Press, 1990) and Lionel S. Sobel, The Regulation of Player Agents and Lawyers, Chapter 1 of Gary Uberstine ed., *Law of Professional and Amateur Sports* (Deerfield, Ill: Clark, Boardman, and Callaghan, 1991) (an earlier version of Sobel's piece appeared at 39 Baylor L. Rev. 701 (1987).

2. Bob Woolf, *Behind Closed Doors* 42–46 (New York: Atheneum, 1976).

players nearly $500,000. In basketball as well, average salaries have now surpassed a million dollars (versus $20,000 a quarter century ago), and even in hockey, a sport without a lucrative national television contract, average salaries leaped from $225,000 in 1989–90 to $370,000 in 1991–92.

The sports marketplace is different not only because of much higher average salary levels, but also because of the huge spread between the minimum and maximum amounts earned by different players (ranging in 1992 from $109,000 to nearly $7 million in baseball). Because far more money rides on the outcome of individual salary negotiations, it is worthwhile for players to pay someone with talent and experience in this work to deal with the seasoned general managers who bargain on behalf of their "clients," the team owners. Added to this financial value is an emotional factor—minimizing the impact on the player's personal feelings and team morale of frank discussion (about the player's shortcomings as well as strengths) that takes place in such negotiations to determine where the player fits within the game's overall salary scale.

While negotiating contracts with teams is at the core of the sports agent's role, many agents now do much more on behalf of their clients.[3] Just as is true in the entertainment industry, good agents can secure lucrative endorsements and promotional activities for their clients. In non-team sports such as golf and tennis, athletes' direct earnings from the sport depend on how they fare in the tournaments; thus the principal focus of people like Mark McCormack of International Management Group (who began with Arnold Palmer) and Donald Dell of Pro–Serv (who began with Arthur Ashe) has been to generate revenue opportunities for their clients outside the sport.[4] Even in team sports, the outside earnings of a star athlete such as Michael Jordan ($38 million in 1992) dwarf what he receives directly from his team for accomplishments on the court.

Full-service agents are concerned not only with revenue generation, but also with revenue management for their clients. This task may involve simply planning the athlete's budget for daily living and seeing that his bills are paid. More importantly, it usually involves development and execution of an investment program (including tax planning) that maximizes the long-term value of monies that are saved by the player. This financial management role is crucial now that high draft picks in all sports regularly receive more money from their signing bonuses alone than their families could ever have dreamed of saving from a lifetime of work. Invested wisely, this money can

3. See Lloyd Z. Remick and David S. Eisen, *The Personal Manager in the Entertainment and Sports Industries*, 3 Ent. and Sports L. J. 57 (1986), and W. Michael Robertson, Financial Planning and Professional Money Management for the Athlete, Chapter 3 of Uberstine, ed., *Law of Professional and Amateur Sports*, note 1 above.

4. See Mark McCormack, *What They Don't Teach You at Harvard Business School* (New York: Bantam, 1984), and Donald Dell, *Minding Other People's Business* (New York: Villard, 1989).

provide long-term financial security for the player, regardless of what fate has in store for him in the usually short and always unpredictable career of a professional athlete.

A. UNION AND AGENT REPRESENTATION OF ATHLETES

Because of the glamour and financial prospects from representing star athletes, the number of agents has spiraled in recent years. No one knows the exact number of practitioners, but it is safe to say that there are nearly as many, if not more, agents as professional athletes. One reason that there is no precise count of agents is that no formal training—in particular, no legal training—is required to become one. Indeed, it is sometimes observed that the only qualification for practicing in this profession is that one have a client.

Yet, most prominent agents are lawyers, however little they may have learned about negotiating, promoting, and investment planning while they were at law school. There is, however, an important element of legal expertise in athlete representation: knowledge not only of the general law of contract and taxes, but also of the distinctive law of the collective agreement for a sport. The agreement negotiated by the players association and the league in each sport exercises considerably greater influence on the outcome of individual player contracts than does statutory labor and antitrust law upon the terms of the collective agreements themselves.

As a brief reminder of what we saw in Chapter 4, a union selected by a majority of the employees has the exclusive authority to negotiate all terms and conditions of employment for all members in the bargaining unit. Like their counterparts in the entertainment industry, though, players associations have exercised this statutory authority only to the extent of negotiating minimum salaries, benefits, and job protection—a level of basic compensation that is guaranteed to every player, whether rookie or superstar. The collective agreement thus allows every player to try to negotiate more advantageous terms—in particular, high guaranteed salaries. A critical step was taken in the 1970 baseball agreement, which opened the door to agents by giving the player a positive right to have a representative negotiate his individual contract.

The collective agreement exerts a powerful influence on the outcome of such individual negotiations.[5] The share of league revenues channeled into team payrolls through collective bargaining—in minimum salaries and fringe benefits—determines how much is left for individual bargaining. Moreover, the manner in which the collective agreement structures the individual player market shapes the leverage

---

5. The best theoretical statement of how this happens—albeit written for a different setting—is Robert M. Mnookin and Lewis A. Kornhauser, *Bargaining in the Shadow of the Law: The Case of Divorce*, 88 Yale L. J. 950 (1979).

that can be deployed by individual players and teams in their direct dealings. There is no better example of this impact of collective action than the salary results of the free agency enjoyed by baseball players after the *Messersmith* arbitration, as compared with what football players received after the *Dutton* ruling (see Chapter 4 supra). An equally prominent shadow is cast over player negotiations in baseball by the availability of salary arbitration, and in basketball by the terms of the salary cap and revenue-sharing arrangement that emerged from NBA collective bargaining in the 1980's. Finally, the collective agreement and its arbitration jurisprudence define the meaning of crucial terms in the player contract—such as incentive clauses and long-term guarantees. Representatives of both the players and the teams must be fully aware of these legal nuances to know precisely what rides on their negotiation of particular contract language.

We will not attempt to present a detailed picture of the background law of the player contract in every sport—to do so would require another book of nearly the same size as this one.[6] However, the following excerpts from arbitration awards and notes about key contract provisions should give some sense of the importance of this branch of the law of sports in the day-to-day work of a player agent. The first case depicts the manner and degree to which the collective agreement leaves room for individual bargaining.[7]

ALVIN MOORE & ATLANTA BRAVES
(Arbitration, 1977).

PORTER, ARBITRATOR.

Facts

On April 1, 1977, a contract was entered into by the Atlanta Braves and Alvin E. Moore, which contained the following special covenant:

The Atlanta Club and player Alvin Earl Moore agree that should player Moore not be satisfied with his playing time by June 15, 1977, that the Atlanta Club will initiate a trade that would not be consummated without the prior written consent of Alvin Moore. Notification of player Alvin Moore's dissatisfaction should be submitted in writing to the Atlanta Club prior to June 15, 1977.

Should a trade not be consummated by the end of the 1977 championship baseball season Alvin Moore will become a free agent if he so desires.

6. That task has actually been undertaken in four separate chapters in Uberstine, ed., *Law of Professional and Amateur Sports*, note 1 above: Chapter 5, by Jeffrey S. Moorad, on Major League Baseball, Chapter 6, by Leigh Steinberg, on the National Football League, Chapter 7, by Ted Steinberg, on the National Basketball Association, and Chapter 8, by John Chapman, on the National Hockey League.

7. At issue in this case was the first set of rules drafted for free agency in baseball,

following the *Messersmith* decision. That 1976 contract settlement not only specified when a player could become a free agent and what compensation (in the form of draft picks) was owed to the losing team, but also created a draft procedure whereby a specified number of teams could secure the right to bid for the free agents the teams wanted to pursue. That last feature of the free agency system was dispensed with in the 1981 baseball agreement.

Should player Alvin Moore be satisfied with his playing time by June 15, 1977, this covenant of this contract will be declared null and void with all other aspects of this contract being in full force according to major league rules and the basic agreement.

On April 28, 1977, National League President Charles S. Feeney approved the contract but disapproved the special covenant in a letter to General Manager Bill Lucas of the Braves. The text of President Feeney's letter is as follows:

The Special Covenant contained in Alvin Moore's contract is disapproved because it contains provisions inconsistent with the Reserve System Article of the new Basic Agreement.

Please be sure that Player Moore receives a copy of this letter.

The present grievance was filed on June 7, 1977, challenging the propriety of President Feeney's action in disapproving the covenant and requesting that the covenant "immediately be reinstated."

The [Players] Association's position is grounded in the recognition article, Article II of the Basic Agreement, which provides:

ARTICLE II—RECOGNITION

The Clubs recognize the Association as the sole and exclusive collective bargaining agent for all Major League Players, and individuals who may become Major League Players during the term of this Agreement, with regard to all terms and conditions of employment except (1) individual salaries over and above the minimum requirements established by this Agreement and (2) Special Covenants to be included in individual Uniform Player's Contracts, *which actually or potentially provide additional benefits to the Player.* (Emphasis added).

The Association argues that the special covenant in question clearly provides "actual or potential benefits" to player Moore and, hence, is a permissible subject for negotiation and agreement between Moore and his Club....

According to the Association, there are only three valid reasons for a League President to disapprove a special covenant. He may do so: (1) if the covenant does not meet the test of Article II in that it does not "actually or potentially provide additional benefits to the Player"; (2) if the covenant violates an applicable law or is specifically prohibited by a Major League rule which is not inconsistent with the Basic Agreement, e.g., if the covenant provides for the giving of a bonus for playing, pitching or batting skill or a bonus contingent on the Club's standing, types of bonuses specifically prohibited by Major League Rule 3[a]; or (3) if the covenant purports to bind some third party whom the Club and the Player have no authority to bind (e.g., a covenant stating that, regardless of what a Player does on the field, an Umpire cannot eject him from a game or the League President or the Commissioner cannot discipline him)....

The Clubs reply that the Moore covenant strikes at the very heart of the reserve system which the parties negotiated following the Arbitration Panel's Decision No. 29, the so-called "Messersmith–McNally" case. In the wake of the Messersmith–McNally case, all players were theoretically free to play out their contracts and become free agents after an additional renewal year. Confronted by the impending collapse of the reserve system, the Clubs observe, the parties, for the first time, jointly negotiated a new reserve system and incorporated the new system in Article XVII of the 1976–1979 Basic Agreement. In the Clubs' view, Article II of the Basic Agreement does not provide authority for an individual Club and Player to negotiate what, in their opinion, is an entirely new reserve system, merely because such a system would provide a benefit to the Player. . . .

Club's
(N.L. Pres.)
Arg

The Clubs concede that, in practice, the League Presidents have approved particular covenants which differ from and hence are arguably "inconsistent" with the provisions of the Basic Agreement. In their view, however, the inconsistencies in these approved covenants involved interests of the individual Clubs and Player alone—e.g., covenants guaranteeing a player's salary for one or more years, covenants waiving a Club's rights regarding commercial endorsements, medical examinations, etc. They did not involve covenants, such as the Moore covenant, wherein the Club and the Player sought to waive the interests of others—in this case the 25 other Clubs' interest in maintaining the kind of competitive balance among the various Clubs which the Reserve System of Article XVII was and is designed to provide.

Club's
Support
for
Arg

The Moore covenant is said by the Clubs to contravene the scheme of Article XVII in three main respects. First, it grants to Moore, who presently has less than one year of Major League service, a conditional right to demand a trade, should he "not be satisfied with his playing time by June 15, 1977." . . .

1

Second, if a trade is not consummated by the end of the 1977 season, the Moore covenant renders Moore eligible to become a free agent, if he so desires, despite the fact that he will then have only a little more than a year's Major League service. . . .

2

Third, the Moore covenant does not expressly make him subject to the re-entry procedure, with its quota and compensation provisions. . . .

3

The objective of this re-entry procedure, the Clubs contend, is to provide for an even and equitable distribution of players among all the Clubs and prevent a few of the richer Clubs from buying up a disproportionate share of the available free agent talent. To permit the Atlanta Club and Player Moore to by-pass the re-entry procedure would defeat this objective and allow the Atlanta Club to waive the rights which the other 25 Clubs have in maintaining the competitive balance which the re-entry procedure is designed to foster, the Clubs conclude. They ask, accordingly, that league President Feeney's disapproval of the Moore covenant be sustained by the Panel.

* * *

In the Chairman's judgment, both parties have advanced sound positions in support of their respective claims, but each has pushed his position to an unsound extreme. For reasons to be given more fully below, the Chairman is convinced the Moore covenant can be interpreted in a way which does not impinge upon the legitimate interests of the other Clubs and could and should have been approved on that basis. No reason appears why the Atlanta Club may not accord to Moore conditional rights to demand a trade and to become a free agent under Article XVII, B(2), despite the fact that he does not have the requisite years of Major League service to claim these rights unilaterally. The 5- and 6-year service requirements for Players seeking to exercise such rights unilaterally under Article XVII, D and B(2), respectively, are for the individual Club's benefit; and no persuasive evidence or argument has been presented to show why the benefit of long-term title and reservation rights to Moore's contract may not be waived by his club. But if Atlanta may waive the length of service requirements designed for its benefit, it may not waive the reentry procedure designed for the benefit of all 26 Clubs. . . .

Negotiations between individual Clubs and Players are not, however, conducted in a vacuum. To the contrary, and at the risk of belaboring the obvious, individual Player–Club negotiations are conducted not only within the framework of applicable law but within the framework of organized professional baseball and the attendant rules, agreements and regulations by which the sport or industry is governed and by which the Association on behalf of the Players and the Clubs comprising the two Major Leagues have agreed to be bound. Within the latter framework are innumerable matters affecting the interests and rights of all the Clubs and Players, such as the number of Player contracts to which each Club may have title and reservation rights, the number of Players each Club may retain on its active roster, the length of the intra or interleague trading periods, etc. Variations in any one of these provisions might give a Player "additional benefits" but are beyond the Club's power to make. . . .

To the extent the Association seeks to push its "additional benefit" argument to the point where the Moore covenant is to be interpreted as exempting Moore from the free agent quota system and other aspects of the reentry procedure designed to protect the interests of all 26 Clubs, the Chairman believes it presses its argument too far.

* * *

Grievance upheld in part.

Questions for Discussion

1. Suppose the individual contract specifies that at its termination the player becomes a free agent without compensation—that is, the team waives its right to whatever draft pick it would receive from a new team

signing the player. Is this provision valid (see *Mike Marshall and Minnesota Twins* (Arbitration, 1978))?

2. The basketball collective agreement adopts a different approach to the permissible language in individual contracts. Article I of the NBA agreement states "that the player and team can supplement the provisions of the Uniform Player Contract, but may not agree upon terms that contradict, change, or are inconsistent with a [Uniform Player Contract] UPC provision, nor provide for a waiver by a player of any benefit or sacrifice of any right to which the player is entitled under the collective agreement." The agreement then goes on to list numerous provisions in the individual contract that can be amended, and presents the carefully-drafted contract terms that can be inserted in their place. Recall the arbitrator's decision in the *Brian Shaw* case (in Chapter 2) about the compatibility with the NBA labor agreement of a specific clause that had been inserted in Shaw's contract with the Boston Celtics.

3. A unique feature of baseball's Major League Rules, incorporated by reference in the collective agreement, prohibits (through Rule 3(A)) "the giving of a bonus for playing, pitching or batting skills; or which provides for the payment of a bonus contingent on the standing of the club at the end of the championship season." That is why incentive clauses in baseball contracts are always defined in terms of number of games played, at-bats, pitching starts, or other kinds of appearances. What is the rationale for this contract restriction, which does not exist in other sports? Is it a sensible policy? What was the proper outcome of the grievance filed by Dennis "Oil Can" Boyd, whom the Montreal Expos promised an extra $300,000 if he started 32 games in the 1990 season, when rather than start Boyd for the 32nd time at his regular turn in the rotation on the final day of the season, the Expos used a rookie pitching prospect?

As we saw in the *Danny Ainge* case and decisions following in Chapter 2, the standard sports contract gives the team the right to terminate the contract if the "player fails, in the opinion of the Club's management, to exhibit sufficient skill or competitive ability to qualify or continue as a member of the Club's team" (this is the language in baseball's player contract). Under such a provision, can a team release a veteran player with a high salary in favor of a less-accomplished younger player with a much lower salary, when the team judges the gap in performance insufficient to warrant the salary differential?

To avoid such problems players negotiate "guaranteed" contracts if they have the market leverage to do so. The following case illustrates an important problem in the interpretation of such guarantees.

DANTE PASTORINI & OAKLAND RAIDERS

(Arbitration, 1984).

KAGEL, ARBITRATOR.

[In 1981 the Raiders released quarterback Dan Pastorini with two years left on his guaranteed contract. After the Philadelphia Eagles picked Pastorini up for those two years, the question arose whether salary payments by the Eagles should offset amounts otherwise owed by the Raiders.]

* * *

[T]here is no language in Pastorini's contract supporting the Raiders' right to an offset; and, as will be noted herein, the Raiders, when they wanted the right of an offset, provided for such contract language, as they did in [quarterback Jim] Plunkett's contract....

LEAGUE POLICY

Joel Bussert, a witness for the Management Council, who is the Director of Personnel for the National Football League, testified as to what he contends is the past practice of the League on the question of offsets. He testified on direct examination as follows:

A. The League's policy, as I attempted to say earlier, was that when a player was released from a guaranteed contract and signed with a second club, any amounts earned from that second club would be offset against the guaranteed amounts he was entitled to receive from the first club.

On cross-examination, Bussert testified as follows:

Q. Have you ever communicated to the NFL Players Association in written form or any other form this policy that you testified to about what the custom and practice of the League is?

A. No.

He further testified on cross-examination:

Q. Could you indicate for us what written information there may be as to this policy of offsets that you testified about? Is it in the Constitution and By–Laws?

A. It's not in the Constitution and By–Laws.

Q. Is it in the Rules and Regulations of the League?

A. No.

Q. Where is it?

A. As I attempted to explain earlier, it's been the policy of the League.

* * *

MITIGATION

The Raiders argue that Pastorini had a duty to mitigate damages as an offset to a terminated guaranteed contract under common law and California case law. In this regard, they cite Parker v. Twentieth Century–Fox Film Corp., 474 P.2d 689 (Cal.1970).

The Court in that case stated a rule which is cited in the Raiders' brief, as follows:

> The general rule is that the measure of recovery by a wrongfully discharged employee is the amount of salary agreed upon for the period of service, less the amount which the employer affirmatively proves the employee has earned or with reasonable effort might have earned from other employment.

That rule is not applicable in the Pastorini case. There is no claim that Pastorini was "wrongfully discharged." In fact, Pastorini was not discharged—he was waived, an action *authorized* by the contract. The Raiders had a right to waive Pastorini but they also had an obligation to pay the salaries provided for in the contracts which they assumed from Houston.

This case does not concern itself with an alleged breach of the contracts between the Raiders and Pastorini at the time of the waiver; it is not a case seeking damages; but it is an action on the contracts themselves for the agreed-upon compensation which is set forth in the contracts between the Raiders and Pastorini. What Pastorini is seeking is the payment of a debt owed to him by the Raiders as a result of the contracts and the concept of offset by way of mitigation is not applicable in this instance.

SUMMARY

The record shows with reference to so-called "custom and practice," that whatever that custom and practice is claimed to have been, as among the Clubs themselves regarding offsets in guarantee cases, no such custom or practice was considered by the Management Council and the Players Association in the *Davis* and *Smith* decisions [and] it is not part of the Collective Bargaining Agreement since it was not accepted by both Parties to the Collective Bargaining Agreement.

The record establishes that when an offset is intended, the League and Management Council have provided for such language in Paragraph 10 of the NFL Player Contract form. Paragraph 10 of that form thus sets forth a specific offset against the Player's salary for any Workers' Compensation benefits received by the Player.

The Collective Bargaining Agreement also provides specific language dealing with offsets, such as the provision which limits a Club's liability for certain benefits once a released Player has re-signed with another NFL Club, as Pastorini did. In Article X, the Parties have provided that injury protection payments to a released Player will stop when he signs with another NFL Club. In Article XXXV, the Agreement provides that a Player will not get his termination pay, a collectively bargained "skill" guarantee, if he resigns with another Club for the same season . . . .

It must be concluded that in Pastorini's case his contracts do not provide for an offset, nor does League "policy," nor do PCRC decisions insert offset provisions into his contracts; and the concept of "mitigation" does not apply to Pastorini's case.

Grievance upheld.

Questions for Discussion

1. Do you agree with the result in this case? After a similar arbitral ruling in *Rudy Hackett and Denver Nuggets* (Arbitration, 1977), the NBA and its Players Association amended their collective agreement to provide for an offset against guaranteed compensation of "any amounts earned by the Player (for services as a player) from any NBA member during the period covered by the terminated contract."

2. Except for periods of interleague competition, football players have rarely enjoyed the benefit of contracts that are guaranteed against loss of skill and lowered performance, or even for disability that lasts beyond the season in which the injury occurred. The practice in football is to negotiate a series of one-year agreements, rather than a single multi-year agreement. That means that if a player's skill level drops off (or he is overtaken by a younger, cheaper competitor), his football team is free to release the player at the end of each training camp free of any salary obligation for this and future years. The absence of guaranteed contracts in football and their presence in baseball was an important feature of the *McNeil* litigation described in Chapter 3 regarding the impact of free agency. Indeed, at the trial, plaintiffs' attorneys pointed out to defenders of the NFL's Plan B, such as George Young, general manager of the New York Giants, and Don Shula, coach of the Miami Dolphins, that these witnesses enjoyed salary guarantees in their contracts that were negotiated within a free agency environment enjoyed by coaches and managers. Young and Shula responded that the main explanation for the lack of guarantees in football player contracts was not Plan B, but the special nature of football and the more intense motivation this sport demanded of it athletes. Do you agree?

3. As noted above, the presence or absence of guaranteed multi-year agreements is relevant not simply to a decline in player performance but also to an inability to perform because of injury. While the NFL's uniform player contract provides for payment of salary for the entire contract period during which a player is disabled, the practice of multiple one-year contracts means that the team can simply release the player before future contracts begin and thereby terminate that injury salary protection. See *Sample v. Gotham Football Club (Jets)*, 59 F.R.D. 160 (S.D.N.Y.1973); but compare *Chuy v. Philadelphia Eagles Football Club*, 595 F.2d 1265 (3d Cir.1979)). Knowing of this league practice and its consequences, what should football player agents do in negotiating contracts for their clients?[8]

4. When a team agrees to a no-cut contract with a salary guarantee, must it continue to pay the players' salary during a strike called by the Players Association? During a lockout initiated by the league's Player

---

8. See Kenneth Lehn, *Property Rights, Risk Sharing, and Player Disability in Ma-* *jor League Baseball*, 25 J. of Law and Econ. 343 (1982).

Relations Committee? See *California Angels and Frank Tanana; Milwaukee Braves and Larry Hisle* (Arbitration, 1983).

B. THE SALARY CAP [9]

Another product of collective bargaining is sufficiently interesting and sufficiently important to warrant a more extended note—the NBA salary cap. This formula was developed in negotiations in 1983 between NBPA leader Larry Fleisher and Commissioner Larry O'Brien. That was a time when basketball was in a rather sorry financial state, with two-thirds of its teams losing money and a few teams (for example, the Cleveland Cavaliers) losing a great deal of money. Now, with the NBA enjoying unprecedented popular appeal and financial prosperity, the salary cap is given a large share of the credit, and other sports are adopting similar arrangements.

The salary cap provision takes up forty or so densely-written pages in the NBA collective agreement and appendices. It is sufficient for our purposes here just to capsulize the rather simple core of this idea. Every year the league and players association add up the total revenues of all the clubs (exclusive of a few sources such as concessions, parking, and, much more significant now, NBA Properties), calculate 53 percent of that revenue total, deduct a portion (approximately 3 percent) for the league's payment to the player benefits funds, and then divide the net figure by the number of clubs in the league. That final number constitutes a presumptive ceiling upon the amount of money any one individual club can spend on player salaries.

The figure is not, however, a totally binding ceiling, because clubs are not limited in the amount they are permitted to spend to re-sign their own veteran players to new contracts. Right from the outset, a considerable number of teams have had payrolls that were above the supposed cap amount, with consequences we shall mention shortly. In addition, this article in the labor agreement imposes not just a ceiling upon the amount teams *may* pay their players, but also a floor amount that a team *must* pay in salaries. The manner in which this floor is calculated is by adding up the total dollar expenditures by teams above the ceiling, deducting this excess figure from the 53 percent of total league revenues calculated earlier, and then dividing that smaller aggregate figure by the number of teams in the league. The product of this calculation is the minimum amount that must be spent on player salaries by every team in the league.

The combination of these two numerical exercises means that this contract provision actually functions more to give players a guaranteed *share* in aggregate league revenues than to set a fixed *cap* on the dollar amount that must be spent on player salaries. And to make that

9. On the development of the salary cap in professional basketball, see Robert C. Berry, William B. Gould, and Paul D. Stau-dohar, *Labor Relations in Professional Sports* 181–188 (Dover, Mass: Auburn House, 1986).

salary floor-revenue sharing arrangement effective, if any one team does not pay its players the specified minimum (perhaps because the team does not have sufficient revenues of its own to do so), the league as a whole has undertaken to step in and make up the difference (presumably out of league-wide revenues from national television, marketing, and so on).

The salary cap provision has become the major defining feature for individual player negotiations in basketball, and has created a marketplace with a markedly different flavor than one sees in other sports. For example, once these formulas had been developed and used for several years, the NBA agreed in 1988 collective bargaining to reduce the length of its draft from seven to two rounds, and to make every player a free agent after his first contract expired. The home team does retain a right of first refusal with respect to players at the end of their rookie contracts, though not thereafter. In addition, in meeting such an outside offer (which the Cleveland Cavaliers did in 1990 with respect to the Miami Heat's $26.5 million bid to make the Cavaliers' John Williams the highest-paid player in the game), the home team is not limited by the salary cap. The broader reality, then, is that even though veteran NBA players formally enjoy full free agency (with no compensation made to the losing team), players still feel strong financial ties to the incumbent teams. The reason is that the current team is limited only by its own budget, not by the league's labor contract, in determining how much it can afford to pay for this player's services.

There are a host of special wrinkles to operation of the salary cap, with which player agents and team general managers must be totally familiar in order to operate effectively in this environment. One such feature we saw earlier in the *Leon Wood* case excerpted in Chapter 3. For purposes of the cap, rookies are treated like free agents from other teams, not like the team's own players. That means that if a club is over the cap amount, the most it can offer is the league's minimum salary to sign a rookie, even to sign the top pick in that year's college draft. On the other hand, if the player is forced to accept that specified minimum, he is bound by no more than a one-year agreement, at the end of which the player becomes an unrestricted free agent. The problem, of course, is that such free agency rights must still be exercised in an environment where other clubs are constrained in bidding for his services by the salary cap. Fortunately for star college players, the emergence of European basketball as a reasonably lucrative option (exercised, for example, by Duke's Danny Ferry in 1990) is the more likely reason why clubs feel pressure to pare down their rosters and payroll in order to be able to sign their draft picks at more attractive prices (as the Orlando Magic did for Shaquille O'Neal in 1992).

While it was the NBA that first adopted the technique of allocating a guaranteed share of league revenues to player salaries, the idea first originated in the 1982 negotiations in football, as the brain-child of then NFLPA leader Ed Garvey. At that time (and during that strike)

NFL owners totally rejected this idea as a form of socialism in disguise, as an unacceptable inroad upon their property rights in a capitalist economy (though football owners have always practiced a high degree of revenue sharing among fellow team-owners). Ironically, ten years later the NFL, under its new Commissioner Paul Tagliabue, had become a firm devotee of the salary sharing idea as the mechanism for finally resolving the league's long-standing legal and labor relations dispute with the NFLPA (in the aftermath of the *Powell* and *McNeil* litigation depicted in Chapter 3). And just before this book was finished, Tagliabue and Gene Upshaw, Garvey's successor as NFLPA leader, were able to resolve the *McNeil* litigation depicted in Chapter 3 with a broad-ranging settlement that gave veteran players ample free agency rights, but with a salary cap that provided financial protection to the owners. The special features of the NFL salary cap formula are depicted in the Supplement.

In the NBA, Commissioner David Stern and the owners have always been the strongest advocates of this idea. For a number of years, the NBPA was prepared to accept the salary cap, though it was certainly not a fervent supporter. The simple explanation for the Association's acquiescence is this fact: whereas the cap began at a level of $3.6 million a club in 1984–85, permitting salaries to average $340,000 that season, by the 1992–93 season the cap was set at $14.5 million, permitting salaries to average well over $1 million (depending on how many teams are above the cap, and how many players are rotated through the 12–man active roster limits). However, significant issues have now begun to emerge about the design and operation of the salary cap, of which we mention three here.

Questions for Discussion

1. One issue is how to define and calculate league revenues. For example, how should one deal with accounting decisions made by a team that also owns one of its key revenue sources, e.g., the television or radio station upon which the team's games are broadcast. An even bigger issue is whether a particular revenue source, e.g., the marketing ventures of NBA Properties, should be shared with the players. Indeed, if the players are to be limited to a specified share of the league's revenues, should they also be entitled to participate in the *marketing* of the league's licensing, television, and other revenue sources?

2. Even assuming that one can arrive at a consensus about what and how much revenues are to be counted, an even more difficult question is selecting the relevant percentage figure for the salary share. The natural tendency, as occurred in basketball in 1983, is to agree on a number that is reasonably close to the status quo at the time. Certainly that number will be very different from sport to sport. For example, football and basketball do not have the substantial expenditures of baseball or hockey in running a farm system to develop new players, rather than just pay the salaries of their current major league players. (As we shall see later in Chapter 9, America's colleges now run and pay for the farm teams that develop professional football and basketball players.) But there is no reason to

suppose that the same percentage figure—e.g., the 53 percent used in basketball—continues to be appropriate in 1993, when aggregate league revenues are running over $800 million, as it was in 1983 when revenues totalled roughly $150 million. But that leaves the question of how exactly one should go about deciding what are to be the respective shares of owners and players in this financial bonanza.

3. The following real-life case graphically displays the complexities of the NBA's salary cap (which has become almost as convoluted as the Internal Revenue Code). In 1990–91, the top rookie point guard in the league was Sherman Douglas, the second round draft pick of the Miami Heat who played under a one-year contract at a comparatively modest salary (for reasons indicated by the *Leon Wood* case in Chapter 3). As a free agent Douglas was able to extract from the Los Angeles Lakers a contract offer of $16.5 million over seven years, even though the Lakers were far above the salary cap. The Lakers could make that offer to Douglas because an exception to the salary cap system allowed it to use half the salary of one of its own players who had just retired—in this case, Magic Johnson. Then the Heat was able to match the Lakers' offer without regard to its own salary cap status, because the cap does not limit the amount a team is able to pay its own players whose contracts have expired. Having retained their rights to Douglas, the Heat then traded him to the Boston Celtics for Brian Shaw who was paid a comparable salary, but had not played up to the Celtic's expectations after being forced to return to them via the *Shaw* litigation depicted in Chapter 2.

The Douglas case explains why the NBA system is called a *soft cap*—a system that places some restraints on spiralling salaries but permits most NBA teams to have player payrolls in excess of the supposed $14.5 million ceiling for 1992–93. The NFL, in its negotiations with the Players Association to settle the *McNeil* case, was able to secure a *hard cap* that will place an absolute ceiling on each team's total salary budget. What are the arguments that could be advanced by either the league or the association in favor of one or other of these options?

A final question concerns not what is in the salary cap, but something that is left out. As we made clear earlier, the term "cap" is actually something of a misnomer for this arrangement. What the NBA really has is an agreement between clubs and players associations about what "share" of league revenues is to be spent on player salaries and other kinds of compensation. The question is why there are no further criteria for salary sharing amongst the players themselves.

With the exception of the minimum salary levels (in baseball, for example, set at $109,000 for 1992, or 1.5% of the $7.3 million salary peak reached by Barry Bonds in late 1992), the players and their union exercise no direct collective voice in how club payrolls are distributed among the players on the team rosters. That allocation is the cumulative product of individual players seeking to maximize their individual bargaining power with the help and representation of their agents. It is true that the collectively bargained rules of this salary negotiation game—for example, who is entitled to salary arbitration or free agency and on what terms—obviously have a powerful indirect role on individual salary outcomes. So far, though, players associations have made little or no effort to specify what the market should bear for individual players.

Still, we have just seen that a collectively-negotiated ceiling and floor can be placed on the amounts that a club will spend on its entire payroll (in amounts that are adjusted each year to take account of changing revenues for the game). It obviously would be technically feasible for the collective agreement to go on to specify a ceiling on the amount that can be spent on the salary of any one player, at the same time raising the floor amount paid to players on the bottom rung of the salary ladder. (Indeed, the recent NFL agreement that denies free agency to designated "franchise" players may operate as an implicit salary ceiling for other top-flight players.) Perhaps the ceiling would be a designated multiple of the minimum salary (25 times?), with both figures adjusted annually in accordance with total league revenues. Is this approach more or less consistent with the traditional role and purpose of trade unions? What are the pros and cons of this idea? Is there a tension here between equity and efficiency? Can you think of refinements that might improve the concept? What do you imagine would be the reaction of agents?

C. BREAKDOWNS IN THE AGENT– PLAYER RELATIONSHIP

The preceding sections convey some of the flavor of the sports agent's role and expertise. The principal focus of this chapter, though, is not the law used by agents in their dealings with clubs, but rather the law governing the relationship between agents and players. The cases selected for this section provide a further glimpse of the working life of an agent and illustrate the types of conflict that can arise between an agent and his client.

A heavily publicized legal proceeding against an agent in the mid–1970s rated only a brief notation in the law reports: *People v. Sorkin*, 64 A.D.2d 680, 407 N.Y.S.2d 772 (1978). There a New York appeals court upheld a substantial jail term meted out to Richard Sorkin, a prominent New York representative of hockey players. Sorkin misappropriated over $1 million of his clients' funds, which he then lost in gambling at the race track and on the stock market.

While the Sorkin affair cast a blemish on the reputation of sports agents generally, the more important question posed by that case and the ones that follow is whether such misconduct is merely the occasional abuse that occurs in any type of commercial undertaking, or instead is symptomatic of a deeper imbalance in the player-agent relationship. Can we trust the marketplace to drive out most of the bad agents in favor of the good, relying on general criminal or civil law to deal with the few "bad apples" that remain? Or should we devise a systematic regulatory program targeted at sports agents generally? If we should, who should devise and enforce the program, and with what objectives?

1. STANDARDS FOR AGENT COMPETENCE [10]

ZINN v. PARRISH

United States Court of Appeals, Seventh Circuit, 1981.

644 F.2d 360.

BARTELS, SENIOR DISTRICT JUDGE.

FACTS

For over two decades the appellant Zinn had been engaged in the business of managing professional athletes. He stated that he was a pioneer in bringing to the attention of various pro football teams the availability of talented players at small black colleges in the South. In the Spring of 1970, Parrish's coach at Lincoln University approached Zinn and informed him that Parrish had been picked by the Cincinnati Bengals in the annual National Football League draft of college seniors, and asked him if he would help Parrish in negotiating the contract. After Zinn contacted Parrish, the latter signed a one-year "Professional Management Contract" with Zinn in the Spring of 1970, pursuant to which Zinn helped Parrish negotiate the terms of his rookie contract with the Bengals, receiving as his commission 10% of Parrish's $16,500 salary. On April 10, 1971 Parrish signed the contract at issue in this case, which differed from the 1970 contract only insofar as it was automatically renewed from year to year unless one of the parties terminated it by 30 days' written notice to the other party. There were no other restrictions placed on the power of either party to terminate the contract.

Under the 1971 contract, Zinn obligated himself to use "reasonable efforts" to procure pro football employment for Parrish, and, at Parrish's request, to "act" in furtherance of Parrish's interests by: a) negotiating job contracts; b) furnishing advice on business investments; c) securing professional tax advice at no added cost; and d) obtaining endorsement contracts. It was further provided that Zinn's services would include, "at my request efforts to secure for me gainful off-season employment," for which Zinn would receive no additional compensation, "unless such employment (was) in the line of endorsements, marketing and the like," in which case Zinn would receive a 10% commission on the gross amount. If Parrish failed to pay Zinn amounts due under the contract, Parrish authorized "the club or clubs that are obligated to pay me to pay to you instead all monies and other

10. For an outline of the legal framework to the player-agent relationship, see Gregory W. McAleenan, Agent–Player Representation Agreements, Chapter 2 of Uberstine, ed., *Law of Professional and Amateur Sports*, note 1 above.

considerations due me from which you can deduct your 10% and any other monies due you...."

Over the course of Parrish's tenure with the Bengals, Zinn negotiated base salaries for him of $18,500 in 1971; $27,000 in 1972; $35,000 in 1973 (plus a $6,500 signing bonus); and a $250,000 series of contracts covering the four seasons commencing in 1974 (plus a $30,000 signing bonus). The 1974–77 contracts with the Bengals were signed at a time when efforts were being made by the newly-formed World Football League to persuade players in the NFL to "jump" to the WFL to play on one of its teams. By the end of 1973 season Parrish had become recognized as one of the more valuable players in the NFL. He was twice selected for the Pro Bowl game, and named by Sporting News as one of the best cornerbacks in the league. Towards the end of the 1973 season, the Bengals approached Parrish with an offer of better contract terms than he had earlier been receiving. By way of exploring alternatives in the WFL, Zinn entered into preliminary discussions with the Jacksonville Sharks in early 1974, but decided not to pursue the matter once he ascertained that the Sharks were in a shaky financial position. In retrospect, Zinn's and Parrish's decision to continue negotiating and finally sign with the Bengals was a sound one, for the Sharks and the rest of the WFL with them folded in 1975 due to a lack of funds.

Shortly after signing the 1974 series of contracts, Parrish informed Zinn by telephone that he "no longer needed his services." By letter dated October 16, 1975 Parrish reiterated this position, and added that he had no intention of paying Zinn a 10% commission on those contracts. In view of its disposition of the case, the district court made no specific fact finding as to the amounts Parrish earned during the 1974–77 seasons. Zinn claims that the total was at least $304,500 including bonus and performance clauses. The 1971 contract by its terms entitled Zinn to 10% of the total amount as each installment was paid, and Zinn claims that he has only received $4,300 of the amounts due him. Accordingly, this suit was filed to recover the balance, plus interest at the rate of 5% per annum for vexatious delay in payment.

In addition to negotiating the Bengals contracts, Zinn performed a number of other services at Parrish's request. In 1972 he assisted him in purchasing a residence as well as a four-unit apartment building to be used for rental income; he also helped to manage the apartment building. That same year Zinn negotiated an endorsement contract for Parrish with All–Pro Graphics, Inc., under which Parrish received a percentage from the sales of "Lemar Parrish" T-shirts, sweat-shirts, beach towels, key chains, etc. The record shows that Zinn made a number of unsuccessful efforts at obtaining similar endorsement income from stores with which Parrish did business in Ohio. He also tried, unsuccessfully, to obtain an appearance for Parrish on the Mike Douglas Show. Zinn arranged for Parrish's taxes to be prepared each year by H & R Block.

The evidence showed that, despite his efforts, Zinn was unable to obtain off-season employment for Parrish. In this connection, however, it was Zinn's advice to Parrish that he return to school during the off-season months in order to finish his college degree, against the time when he would no longer be able to play football. With respect to Zinn's obligation to provide Parrish with advice on "business investments," he complied first, by assisting in the purchase of the apartment building; and second, by forwarding to Parrish the stock purchase recommendations of certain other individuals, after screening the suggestions himself. There was no evidence that Zinn ever forwarded such recommendations to any of his other clients; he testified that he only did so for Parrish. In summing up Zinn's performance under the contract, Parrish testified as follows: Q: Did you ever ask Zinn to do anything for you, to your knowledge, that he didn't try to do? A: I shall say not, no.

[The appeals court first rejected the district court's conclusion that the contract between Zinn and Parish was void under federal securities law on the grounds that this was a contract for investment advice and Zinn was not a registered adviser. The court said that isolated transactions with a client as an incident to the main purpose of his management contract to negotiate football contracts did not constitute engaging in the business of advising others on investment securities.]

* * *

We consider next the district court's judgment that Zinn failed to perform the terms and conditions of his contract. . . .

EMPLOYMENT PROCUREMENT

Zinn's obligation under the 1971 Management Contract to procure employment for Parrish as a pro football player was limited to the use of "reasonable efforts." At the time the contract was signed, Parrish was already under contract with the Cincinnati Bengals for the 1970–1971 season, with a one-year option clause for the 1971–1972 season exercisable by the Bengals. Parrish could not, without being in breach of his Bengals contract, enter into negotiations with other teams for the 1971–72 season. The NFL's own rules prevented one team from negotiating with another team's player who had not yet attained the status of a "free agent." At no time relevant to this litigation did Parrish become a free agent. Thus, unless he decided to contract for future services for the year following the term of the option clause with the Canadian or World Football League, Parrish's only sensible course of action throughout the time Zinn managed him was to negotiate with the Bengals.

Parrish had no objection to Zinn's performance under the professional management contract for the first three years up to 1973, during which time Zinn negotiated football contracts for Parrish. A drastic change, however, took place in 1974 when a four-season contract was negotiated with the Bengals for a total of $250,000 plus a substantial signing bonus. At that time, the new World Football League came into existence and its teams, as well as the teams of the Canadian Football League, were offering good terms to professional football players as an inducement to jump over to their leagues from the NFL. In order to persuade Parrish to remain with the team, the Bengals club itself first initiated the renegotiation of Parrish's contract with an offer of substantially increased compensation. This was not surprising.

Parrish claims, however, that Zinn should have obtained offers from the World Football League that would have placed him in a stronger negotiating position with the Bengals. This is a rather late claim. It was not mentioned in Parrish's letter of termination, and is entirely speculative. Given what Zinn accurately perceived as the unreliability of any offers he might have obtained from the WFL, his representation of Parrish during this period was more than reasonable.

* * *

OTHER OBLIGATIONS

We focus next on the other obligations, all incidental to the main purpose of the contract. The first of these refers to "[n]egotiating employment contracts with professional athletic organizations and others." ... [T]he evidence clearly shows that Zinn performed substantial services in negotiating with the Bengals by letter, telephone, and in person when he and Parrish were flown at the Bengals' expense to Cincinnati for the final stage of negotiations on the 1974–1977 series of contracts.

Zinn was further obligated to act in Parrish's professional interest by providing advice on tax and business matters, by "seek[ing] ... endorsement contracts," and by making "efforts" to obtain for Parrish gainful off-season employment. Each of these obligations was subject to an implied promise to make "good faith" efforts to obtain what he sought. Under Illinois law, such efforts constitute full performance of the obligations. Until Parrish terminated the contract, the evidence was clear that Zinn made consistent, good faith efforts to obtain off-season employment and endorsement contracts. Indeed the district court found that Zinn at all times acted in good faith, with a willingness "to provide assistance within his ability." The district court confused success with good faith efforts in concluding that Zinn's failure to obtain in many cases jobs or contracts for Parrish was a failure to perform. Moreover, Zinn did give business advice to Parrish on his real estate purchases, and he did secure tax advice for him.

Parrish fully accepted Zinn's performance for the years 1970, 1971, 1972, and 1973 by remitting the 10% due Zinn under the contract. Parrish was at all times free to discharge Zinn as his agent before a new season began. Instead, he waited until Zinn had negotiated a series of contracts worth a quarter of a million dollars for him before letting Zinn know over the phone that his services were no longer required. That call, coupled with Parrish's failure to make the 10%

commission payments as they came due, was a breach of the 1971 contract.... Therefore Zinn has a right to recover a 10% commission on all amounts earned by Parrish under the 1974, 1975, 1976, and 1977 Bengals contracts.

Appeal allowed.

————

How does the court formulate the standard of performance expected of a sports agent? How does this standard compare with the duty of "fair representation" imposed by labor law on the players association (see Chapter 4 supra)? With the standard of care required of a lawyer who represents a player in any transaction? Is the standard used in *Zinn* appropriate for the sports agent business?

A recent suit alleging negligent performance by an agent was *Bias v. Advantage International, Inc.*, 905 F.2d 1558 (D.C.Cir.1990). This case was an outgrowth of the tragic death of Len Bias from cocaine use, only two days after the Boston Celtics had made the Maryland star the second pick in the 1986 NBA draft. The Bias estate sued his agent, Lee Fentriss, for allegedly not moving quickly enough to finalize a million-dollar insurance policy and an endorsement contract with Reebok. The suit was summarily dismissed on the grounds that, even though agent and client had discussed these contracts before the rookie draft, the agent could not reasonably have been expected to finalize arrangements before Bias' death made that impossible.

2. AGENT FEE FORMULAS

BROWN v. WOOLF

United States District Court, Southern District of Indiana, 1983.

554 F.Supp. 1206.

STECKLER, DISTRICT JUDGE.

* * *

Plaintiff alleges that prior to the 1973–1974 season he had engaged the services of defendant, a well-known sports attorney and agent, who represents many professional athletes, has authored a book, and has appeared in the media in connection with such representation, to negotiate a contract for him with the Pittsburgh Penguins of the National Hockey League. Plaintiff had a professionally successful season that year under the contract defendant negotiated for him and accordingly again engaged defendant's services prior to the 1974–1975 season. During the negotiations in July 1974, the Penguins offered plaintiff a two-year contract at $80,000 per year but plaintiff rejected the offer allegedly because defendant asserted that he could obtain a better, long-term, no-cut contract with a deferred compensation feature with the Indianapolis Racers, which at the time was a new team in a new league. On July 31, 1974, plaintiff signed a five-year contract with the Racers. Thereafter, it is alleged the Racers began having financial difficulties. Plaintiff avers that Woolf continued to represent plaintiff and negotiated two reductions in plaintiff's compensation including the loss of a retirement fund at the same time defendant was attempting to get his own fee payment from the Racers. Ultimately the Racers' assets were seized and the organizers defaulted on their obligations to plaintiff. He avers that he received only $185,000 of the total $800,000 compensation under the Racer contract but that defendant received his full $40,000 fee (5% of the contract) from the Racers.

Plaintiff alleges that defendant made numerous material misrepresentations upon which he relied both during the negotiation of the Racer contract and at the time of the subsequent modifications. Plaintiff further avers that defendant breached his fiduciary duty to plaintiff by failing to conduct any investigation into the financial stability of the Racers, failing to investigate possible consequences of the deferred compensation package in the Racers' contract, failing to obtain guarantees or collateral, and by negotiating reductions in plaintiff's compensation from the Racers while insisting on receiving all of his own. Plaintiff theorizes that such conduct amounts to a prima facie case of constructive fraud for which he should receive compensatory and punitive damages and have a trust impressed on the $40,000 fee defendant received from the Racers.

* * *

Indiana cases contain several formulizations of the tort of constructive fraud. Generally it is characterized as acts or a course of conduct from which an unconscionable advantage is or may be derived, or a breach of confidence coupled with an unjust enrichment which shocks the conscience, or a breach of duty, including mistake, duress or undue influence, which the law declares fraudulent because of a tendency to deceive, injure the public interest or violate the public or private confidence. Another formulization found in the cases involves the making of a false statement, by the dominant party in a confidential or fiduciary relationship or by one who holds himself out as an expert, upon which the plaintiff reasonably relies to his detriment. The defendant need not know the statement is false nor make the false statement with fraudulent intent.

The Court believes that both formulizations are rife with questions of fact, inter alia, the existence or nonexistence of a confidential or fiduciary relationship, and the question of reliance on false representations, as well as questions of credibility.

Defendant argues that despite the customary existence of such fact questions in a constructive fraud case, judgment is appropriate in this instance because plaintiff has produced nothing to demonstrate the existence of fact questions. He makes a similar argument in the motion for partial summary judgment on the punitive damages issue.

In this case, defendant has offered affidavits, excerpts of depositions, and photocopies of various documents to support his motions. He contends that such materials demonstrate that reasonable minds could not conclude that defendant did the acts with which the complaint charges him. In response, plaintiff rather belatedly offered portions of plaintiff's depositions as well as arguing that issues such as those raised by a complaint based on constructive fraud are inherently unsuited to resolution on a motion for summary judgment.

Having carefully considered the motions and briefs and having examined the evidentiary materials submitted, the Court concludes that summary judgment would not be appropriate in this action. The Court is not persuaded that there are no fact questions remaining unresolved in this controversy such that defendant is entitled to judgment as a matter of law.

Summary dismissal refused.

———

Was the true source of this dispute the player's fee arrangement with his agent? What precisely was the problem with the fee formula? How would you recast the formula? [11]

3. AGENT CONFLICTS OF INTEREST [12]

DETROIT LIONS AND BILLY SIMS v. JERRY ARGOVITZ

United States District Court, Eastern District of Michigan, 1984.

580 F.Supp. 542.

DEMASCIO, DISTRICT JUDGE.

[This lawsuit arose when Billy Sims, a star running back for the Detroit Lions, signed a contract with the Houston Gamblers of the USFL and then, less than six months later, signed a contract with the Lions. Sims and the Lions sued to have his contract with the Gamblers declared unenforceable.

Sim's agent was Jerry Argovitz. As Argovitz was negotiating a new contract for Sims and the Lions in the spring of 1983, he became part owner and president of the Gamblers. Sims knew that Argovitz had applied for the Gamblers franchise, but he did not know the extent

---

11. See Saul Levmore, *Commissions and Conflicts in Agency Arrangements*, J. of Law and Econ. ___ (1993), for an illuminating analysis of the incentives and conflicts generated by fee structures in a variety of principal-agent relationships—for example, personal injury litigation, real estate, and securities underwriting.

12. See Robert E. Fraley and Fred Russell Harwell, *The Sports Lawyer's Duty to Avoid Differing Interests: A Practical Guide to Responsible Representation*, 11 Hastings Comm. and Ent. L. J. 165 (1989).

of Argovitz's interest in the Gamblers and, according to the court, he would not have understood the conflicts of interest inherent in Argovitz's dual roles as owner and agent.

When negotiating with the Lions, on April 5 Argovitz asked for $6 million over four years, a $1 million interest-free loan, and guarantees that Sims would be paid in case of injury or decline in skills. By May 30 Argovitz had reduced his demands to $3.5 million over five years, an interest-free loan, an injury (but not a skills) guarantee, and $400,000 to purchase an annuity. The court found that on June 1, "Argovitz and the Lions were only $500,000 apart" and on June 22, "the Lions and Argovitz were very close to reaching an agreement on the value of Sims' services."]

* * *

Apparently, in the midst of his negotiations with the Lions and with his Gamblers franchise in hand, Argovitz decided that he would seek an offer from the Gamblers. Mr. Bernard Lerner, one of Argovitz's partners in the Gamblers, agreed to negotiate a contract with Sims. Since Lerner admitted that he had no knowledge whatsoever about football, we must infer that Argovitz at the very least told Lerner the amount of money required to sign Sims and further pressed upon Lerner the Gamblers' absolute need to obtain Sims' services. In the Gamblers' organization, only Argovitz knew the value of Sims' services and how critical it was for the Gamblers to obtain Sims. In Argovitz's words, Sims would make the Gamblers' franchise.

On June 29, 1983, at Lerner's behest, Sims and his wife went to Houston to negotiate with a team that was partially owned by his own agent. When Sims arrived in Houston, he believed that the Lions organization was not negotiating in good faith; that it was not really interested in his services. His ego was bruised and his emotional outlook toward the Lions was visible to Burrough and Argovitz. Clearly, virtually all the information that Sims had up to that date came from Argovitz. Sims and the Gamblers did not discuss a future contract on the night of June 29th. The negotiations began on the morning of June 30, 1983, and ended that afternoon. At the morning meeting, Lerner offered Sims a $3.5 million five-year contract, which included three years of skill and injury guarantees. The offer included a $500,000 loan at an interest rate of 1 percent over prime. It was from this loan that Argovitz planned to receive the $100,000 balance of his fee for acting as an agent in negotiating a contract with his own team. Burrough testified that Sims would have accepted that offer on the spot because he was finally receiving the guarantee that he had been requesting from the Lions, guarantees that Argovitz dropped without too much quarrel. Argovitz and Burrough took Sims and his wife into another room to discuss the offer. Argovitz did tell Sims that he thought the Lions would match the Gamblers financial package and asked Sims whether he (Argovitz) should telephone the Lions. But, it is clear from the evidence that neither Sims nor Burrough believed that the Lions would match the offer. We find that Sims told Argovitz not to call the Lions for purely emotional reasons. As we have noted, Sims believed that the Lions' organization was not that interested in him and his pride was wounded. Burrough clearly admitted that he was aware of the emotional basis for Sims' decision not to have Argovitz phone the Lions, and we must conclude from the extremely close relationship between Argovitz and Sims that Argovitz knew it as well. When Sims went back to Lerner's office, he agreed to become a Gambler on the terms offered. At that moment, Argovitz irreparably breached his fiduciary duty. As agent for Sims he had the duty to telephone the Lions, receive its final offer, and present the terms of both offers to Sims. Then and only then could it be said that Sims made an intelligent and knowing decision to accept the Gamblers' offer.

During these negotiations at the Gamblers' office, Mr. Nash of the Lions telephoned Argovitz, but even though Argovitz was at his office, he declined to accept the telephone call. Argovitz tried to return Nash's call after Sims had accepted the Gamblers' offer, but it was after 5 p.m. and Nash had left for the July 4th weekend. When he declined to accept Mr. Nash's call, Argovitz's breach of his fiduciary duty became even more pronounced. Following Nash's example, Argovitz left for his weekend trip, leaving his principal to sign the contracts with the Gamblers the next day, July 1, 1983. The defendants, in their supplemental trial brief, assert that neither Argovitz nor Burrough can be held responsible for following Sims' instruction not to contact the Lions on June 30, 1983. Although it is generally true that an agent is not liable for losses occurring as a result of following his principal's instructions, the rule of law is not applicable when the agent has placed himself in a position adverse to that of his principal.

During the evening of June 30, 1983, Burrough struggled with the fact that they had not presented the Gamblers' offer to the Lions. He knew, as does the court, that Argovitz now had the wedge that he needed to bring finality to the Lions' negotiations.

* * *

The evidence here convinces us that Argovitz's negotiations with the Lions were ongoing and it had not made its final offer. Argovitz did not follow the common practice described by both expert witnesses. He did not do this because he knew that the Lions would not leave Sims without a contract and he further knew that if he made that type of call Sims would be lost to the Gamblers, a team he owned.

On November 12, 1983, when Sims was in Houston for the Lions game with the Houston Oilers, Argovitz asked Sims to come to his home and sign certain papers. He represented to Sims that certain papers of his contract had been mistakenly overlooked and now needed to be signed. Included among those papers he asked Sims to sign was a waiver of any claim that Sims might have against Argovitz for his blatant breach of his fiduciary duty brought on by his glaring conflict of interest. Sims did not receive independent advice with regard to the wisdom of signing such a waiver.

* * *

Argovitz's negotiations with Lustig, Jim Kelly's agent, illustrates the difficulties that develop when an agent negotiates a contract where his personal interests conflict with those of his principal. Lustig, an independent agent, ignored Argovitz's admonishment not to "shop" the Gamblers' offer to Kelly. Lustig called the NFL team that he had been negotiating with because it was the "prudent" thing to do. The Gamblers agreed to pay Kelly, an untested rookie quarterback, $3.2 million for five years. His compensation was $60,000 less than Sims', a former Heisman Trophy winner and a proven star in the NFL. Lustig also obtained a number of favorable clauses from Argovitz; the most impressive one being that Kelly was assured of being one of the three top paid quarterbacks in the USFL if he performed as well as expected. If Argovitz had been free from conflicting interests he would have demanded similar benefits for Sims. Argovitz claimed that the nondisclosure clause in Kelly's contract prevented him from mentioning the Kelly contract to Sims. We view this contention as frivolous. Requesting these benefits for Sims did not require disclosure of Kelly's contract. Moreover, Argovitz's failure to obtain personal guarantees for Sims without adequately warning Sims about the risks and uncertainties of a new league constituted a clear breach of his fiduciary duty.

* * *

We are mindful that Sims was less than forthright when testifying before the court. However, we agree with plaintiff's counsel that the facts as presented through the testimony of other witnesses are so unappealing that we can disregard Sims' testimony entirely. We remain persuaded that on balance, Argovitz's breach of his fiduciary duty was so egregious that a court of equity cannot permit him to benefit by his own wrongful breach. We conclude that Argovitz's conduct in negotiating Sims' contract with the Gamblers rendered it invalid.

* * *

Rescission granted.

———

Argovitz was one of the protagonists in another highly-publicized tug of war between the NFL and the USFL, this one for Arkansas star Gary Anderson.[13] The 1983 first round draft pick of both the NFL's San Diego Chargers and the USFL's Tampa Bay Bandits, Anderson

13. See David Harris, *The League: The Rise and Decline of the NFL* 574–76 (New   York: Bantam, 1986).

became an Argovitz client without being told of Argovitz's USFL interests in Houston. Argovitz succeeded in channeling Anderson to the Bandits without giving the Chargers a real chance to outbid its USFL rival.

Shortly thereafter, though, Anderson became friendly with Lloyd Wells, an ex-Kansas City Chiefs' scout and an aspiring agent. When Anderson switched allegiance to Wells, the Chargers' owner, Gene Klein, loaned Wells $30,000 to finance his representation of Anderson. Wells soon negotiated a new four-year, $1.5 million contract with the Chargers, which topped the Bandits' $1.375 million deal. The Bandits, however, secured an injunction against Anderson playing for the Chargers from a Texas judge who did not find the Bandits' contract to be flawed by Argovitz' wearing these two hats as agent and owner. (Also of interest was the evidence at trial that despite four years at the University of Arkansas, Anderson had not learned to read; that is one reason he could not understand the various documents he kept signing.)

Questions for Discussion

1. Is the *Anderson* case different from *Sims* as far as Argowitz was concerned? Of what relevance to the Bandits case is the reported fact that Wells, Anderson's second agent, took loan money from the Chargers' owner. Would an agent ever be able to represent an athlete properly with a team if the team owner is the agent's creditor? With any team in that league?

2. Contrast the *Argovitz* cases with the following situations:

(a) Jerry Kapstein, one of the most prominent baseball agents for two decades, married the daughter of Joan Kroc, then owner of the San Diego Padres, and regularly advised his mother-in-law about her ownership interests. Should that relationship have barred Kapstein from representing players on the Padres? On the Dodgers? On the Yankees? On the Chicago Bears?

(b) Larry Fleisher and Alan Eagleson were the founders and long-time leaders of the NBA and NHL Players Associations, respectively. They also had full rosters of individual clients among their association members. Was this appropriate? See *Major Indoor Soccer League & Professional Soccer Players Ass'n (PROSPA)*, NLRB Ruling, Nov. 15, 1983?

(c) Suppose that Leigh Steinberg is asked to represent George Seifert, coach of the 49ers, whose star quarterback, Joe Montana, is also a Steinberg client: a conflict of interest? If Steinberg represents Bears coach Mike Ditka? Or the Hendricks' brothers seek to represent Ricky Henderson and Dave Henderson of baseball's Oakland A's? Or David Falk, Patrick Ewing's agent, wants to add another Knicks player to his client roster despite the NBA salary cap?

(d) Multifaceted firms such as International Management Group (IMG) and ProServ not only represent many tennis players but they also promote, manage, and even sponsor tournaments on the tennis tour. Is this dual representation legitimate? Should the body responsible for the tour be able to impose limitations on such inter-relationships? See *Volvo North American Corp. v. Men's International Professional Tennis Council (MIPTC)*, 857 F.2d. 55 (2d Cir.1988) (also Chapter 10).

3. With respect to each of the potential conflicts suggested above (including Argovitz'), if the player is explicitly told of the situation and still enters into or maintains a relationship with his agent, should the player then be bound to contracts negotiated by the agent? Should the agent be immune from malpractice suits brought by the player alleging poor performance by the agent due to the conflict? Should the agent's conduct be deemed "proper" according to the rules of professional ethics enforced by bar associations? What might lead a player to make such a choice?

4. AGENT RECRUITING OF COLLEGE ATHLETES [14]

The next decision is just one of several legal proceedings brought against the same pair of agents for the same behavior—recruiting college athletes to become their clients while they were still eligible to play at college. Norby Walters had been a successful representative of many musicians and entertainers, including Marvin Gaye, Dionne Warwick, Lou Rawls, Luther Vandross, and Patti Labelle. At the suggestion of a young acquaintance, Lloyd Bloom, Walters decided to begin representing athletes as well, especially young football players. The technique Walters and Bloom adopted was to approach the player while he was still in college and offer him a cash sum and subsequent monthly payments, in return for which the player signed an agency contract post-dated to January 2nd of the player's senior year. The whole arrangement was to be kept confidential so that the player would not lose his collegiate eligibility, which would diminish his professional marketability.

Walters and Bloom quickly enjoyed remarkable success. They signed ten players in 1985, two of whom (Ron Harmon of Iowa and Tim McGee of Tennessee) were 1986 first-round NFL draft picks. In 1986, the two signed up 35 players, of whom eight were 1987 first round draft picks (including Brent Fullwood by the Packers, Reggie Rogers by the Lions, and Rod Woodson by the Steelers) and several others (such as, Jerry Ball and Ron Morris) were prominent early round picks. All in all, Walters and Bloom invested roughly $800,000 in recruiting some 60 college players (a few of whom, such as Brad Sellers and Derrick McKey, were star basketball players).

However, this economic venture unraveled and spawned numerous legal proceedings for reasons exhibited in the next case.

14. The best treatment of this broad topic is Shropshire, *Agents of Opportunity*, note 1 above. A very interesting account of the *cause celebre* described in this section and later on in this chapter is Chris Mortensen, *Playing for Keeps: How One Man Kept the Mob From Sinking its Hooks Into Pro Football* (New York: Simon and Schuster, 1991).

NORBY WALTERS AND LLOYD BLOOM
v. BRENT FULLWOOD

United States District Court, Southern District of New York, 1987.

675 F.Supp. 155.

BRIEANT, CHIEF JUDGE.

[In the summer of 1986, Norby Walters and Lloyd Bloom induced Brent Fullwood, star running back for Auburn University, to sign a post-dated representation agreement in return for an immediate payment of $4,000 (secured by a promissory note) and another $4,000 during the fall football season. This modest investment by the new agency partnership seemed highly worthwhile when the Packers selected Fullwood as the fourth pick in the 1987 NFL draft. By that time, however, Fullwood had defected to another agent, George Kickliter of Alabama, and had repudiated his deal with Walters and Bloom. Thus Walters and Bloom sued Fullwood, seeking not only to recover the $8,000 they had already paid him but also to collect the promised five percent commission on Fullwood's multi-million dollar contract. The key issue posed to the federal judge was whether the secret arrangement between the agents and Fullwood, which had put the player in violation of NCAA regulations, was an enforceable contract under New York law.]

* * *

"We are living in a time when college athletics are honeycombed with falsehood, and when the professions of amateurism are usually hypocrisy. No college team ever meets another today with actual faith in the other's eligibility."—President William Faunce of Brown University, in a speech before the National Education Association, 1904.

The N.C.A.A. was organized in 1906 largely to combat such evils. Its constitution provides in relevant part that:

Any individual who contracts or who has ever contracted orally or in writing to be represented by an agent in the marketing of the individual's athletic ability or reputation in a sport no longer shall be eligible for intercollegiate athletics in that sport.

N.C.A.A. Constitution, sec. 3–1–(c).

Section 3–1–(a) prohibits any player from accepting pay in any form for participation in his college sport, with an exception for a player seeking, directly without the assistance of a third party, a loan from an accredited commercial lending institution against future earnings potential solely in order to purchase insurance against disabling injury.

This Court concludes that the August 1986 loan security agreement and the W.S. & E. agency agreement between Fullwood and the plaintiffs violated sections 3–1–(a) and 3–1–(c) of the N.C.A.A. Constitution, the observance of which is in the public interest of the citizens of New York State, and that the parties to those agreements knowingly betrayed an important, if perhaps naive, public trust. Viewing the parties as *in pari delicto*, we decline to serve as "paymaster of the wages of crime, or referee between thieves". We consider both defendant Fullwood's arbitration rights under the N.F.L.P.A. Agents' Regulations, and plaintiffs' rights on their contract and promissory note with Fullwood, unenforceable as contrary to the public policy of New York. "The law 'will not extend its aid to either of the parties' or 'listen to their complaints against each other, but will leave them where their own acts have placed them.' "

Absent these overriding policy concerns, the parties would be subject to the arbitration provisions set forth in section seven of the N.F.L.P.A. Agents' Regulations, and plaintiffs' rights under the contract and promissory note with Fullwood also would be arbitrable. However, under the "public policy" exception to the duty to enforce otherwise- valid agreements, we should and do leave the parties where we find them.

It is well settled that a court should not enforce rights that arise under an illegal contract.

* * *

An agreement may be unenforceable in New York as contrary to public policy even in the absence of a direct violation of a criminal statute, if the sovereign has expressed a concern for the values underlying the policy implicated. In re Estate of Walker, 476 N.E.2d 298, 301 (1985), the Court of Appeals refused to enforce a bequest of adoption decrees to the testator's adopted daughters, concluding that such a bequest, though not criminal, was contrary to public policy. The court concluded, " '[W]hen we speak of the public policy of the state, we mean the law of the state, whether found in the Constitution, the statutes or judicial records'. Those sources express the public will and give definition to the term. A legacy is contrary to public policy, not only if it directly violates a statutory prohibition ... but also if it is contrary to the social judgment on the subject implemented by the statute."

* * *

The New York State legislature has spoken on the public policies involved in this case, by expressing a concern for the integrity of sporting events in general, and a particular concern for the status of amateur athletics. See, e.g., New York Tax Law sec. 1116(a)(4) (McKinney's supp. 1987) (granting tax exemption to any organization "organized and operating exclusively ... to foster national or international amateur sports competition"); New York Penal Law Secs. 180.35, 180.40 (McKinney's supp. 1987) (establishing criminal sanctions for sports bribery).

Even were we not convinced of the legislative concern for the values underlying sec. 3–1–(c) of the N.C.A.A. Constitution, New York case law prevents judicial enforcement of contracts the performance of which would provoke conduct established as wrongful by independent commitments undertaken by either party. Not all contracts inducing breaches of other agreements fall within this rule, but those requiring fraudulent conduct are unenforceable as contrary to the public policy of New York.

In the case before us, no party retains enforceable rights. To the extent plaintiffs seek to recover on the contract or promissory note signed by Fullwood, their wrongful conduct prevents recovery[2]; to the extent Fullwood seeks to compel arbitration, as provided for in the N.F.L.P.A. Agents' Regulations, his own wrongs preclude resort to this Court.

All parties to this action should recognize that they are the beneficiaries of a system built on the trust of millions of people who, with stubborn innocence, adhere to the Olympic ideal, viewing amateur sports as a commitment to competition for its own sake. Historically, amateur athletes have been perceived as pursuing excellence and perfection of their sport as a form of self-realization, indeed, originally, as a form of religious worship, with the ancient games presented as offerings to the gods. By demanding the most from themselves, athletes were believed to approach the divine essence. Through athletic success, the Greeks believed man could experience a kind of immortality.[3]

There also is a modern, secular purpose served by Secs. 3–1–(a) and 3–1–(c) of the N.C.A.A. Constitution. Since the advent of intercollegiate sports in the late 19th century, American colleges have struggled, with varying degrees of vigor, to protect the integrity of higher education from sports-related evils such as gambling, recruitment violations, and the employment of mercenaries whose presence in college athletic programs will tend to preclude the participation of legitimate scholar-athletes.

Sections 3–1–(a) and 3–1–(c) of the N.C.A.A. Constitution were instituted to prevent college athletes from signing professional contracts while they are still playing for their schools. The provisions are rationally related to the commendable objective of protecting the academic integrity of N.C.A.A. member institutions. A college student already receiving payments from his agent, or with a large professional contract signed and ready to take effect upon his graduation, might well be less inclined to observe his academic obligations than a student, athlete or not, with uncertainties about his future career. Indeed, he might not play at his college sport with the same vigor and devotion.

2. We note in passing that, as a provisionally certified N.F.L.P.A. agent, Bloom was bound by sec. 5(C)(1) of the N.F.L.P.A. Agents' Regulations, which forbids a contract advisor from "[p]roviding or offering to provide anything of significant value to a player in order to become the contract advisor for such player".

3. As expressed by the classical poet Pindar of Thebes (518–438 B.C.): "Creatures of a day/ What is someone?/ What is no one?/ Man is merely a shadow's dream/ But when god-given glory comes upon him in victory/ A bright light shines on us and life is sweet/ When the end comes the loss of flame brings darkness/ But his glory is bright forever." C. Boara, Classical Greece, at 23.

The agreement reached by the parties here, whether or not unusual, represented not only a betrayal of the high ideals that sustain amateur athletic competition as a part of our national educational commitment; it also constituted a calculated fraud on the entire spectator public. Every honest amateur player who took the field with or against Fullwood during the 1986 college football season was cheated by being thrown in with a player who had lost his amateur standing.

In August 1986, Brent Fullwood was one of that select group of college athletes virtually assured of a lucrative professional sports contract immediately upon graduation, absent serious injury during his senior year. The fruits of the system by which amateur players become highly paid professionals, whatever its flaws, were soon to be his. That is precisely why plaintiffs sought him out. Both sides of the transaction knew exactly what they were doing, and they knew it was fraudulent and wrong. This Court and the public need not suffer such willful conduct to taint a college amateur sports program.

Suit dismissed.

————

Far more unsavory features of the Walters–Bloom style of sports practice were not adverted to in the above proceeding. In the background as partners and investors in this venture were Sonny and Michael Franzese, key members of the Colombo organized crime family in New York. Apparently Walters and Bloom drew upon these backers for help in enforcing their contracts with threats of physical violence against players who reneged on their deal and against agents such as Kickliter who had wooed the players away. Indeed, the whole scheme came to light in March 1987 when a masked man beat Kathy Clements, wife of the former Notre Dame quarterback, Tom Clements, and herself an associate of Steve Zucker, a Chicago-based sports agent. Zucker had been among the first agents to attract a client away from Walters and Bloom (Tim McGee, the Bengals first round pick in 1986) and he had just done the same with two others (Reggie Rogers of Washington and Doug Dubose of Nebraska). When rumors of an organized crime connection with college and professional athletes emerged, the Chicago offices of U.S. Attorney and FBI took charge of the investigation, with legal ramifications we will see later in this chapter.

While Walters and Bloom might have been unique in their "gangland" approach, they certainly were not unique in paying college players money to sign post-dated agency contracts. The key to the success of such an arrangement was keeping it secret. Neither the agent nor the client would disclose the contract or the payments which, under NCAA rules, made the player ineligible for future collegiate competition; as a result the player's college risked costly NCAA sanctions for using an ineligible player, even unknowingly. This not uncommon practice invited not only judicial nullification of the agency contract, as in *Fullwood*, but also criminal prosecution of both the players and the agents engaged in such a practice.

Even aside from its deceptive nature, this practice raised significant ethical and legal questions. Why would Walters and Bloom believe it was financially worthwhile to pay clients to sign with them? If a player takes a "signing bonus" from an agent, should the player not be held to that contract later on—is there any difference from a contract entered into by the player with a team? Suppose that the agent offers no money. Is it proper for an agent to pursue college athletes as potential clients? Should it matter whether the athlete's college eligibility has expired? Consider the following Model Rule of Professional Conduct:

> 7.3. A lawyer may not solicit professional employment from a prospective client with whom the lawyer has no family or prior professional relationship, by mail, in person or otherwise, when a significant motive for the lawyer's doing so is the lawyer's pecuniary gain.

To what extent should a sports agent who happens to be a lawyer feel constrained by this rule?

D. EMERGENCE OF AGENT REGULATION [15]

The foregoing materials raise the question whether we can rely on market competition within the general law (especially contract law) to secure a sufficiently high quality of player representation by sports agents. If you are dubious on that score, what are your specific concerns about the agent marketplace? Still, whatever answer emerges from that discussion of economic principle, there is a widespread popular impression that things are seriously wrong with this profession. For example, Leigh Steinberg has been quoted as characterizing his business as "the ultimate sleazoid profession of the eighties." For the last decade, perceived problems with agents have attracted the attention of both state legislatures and players associations, whose regulatory responses we will see shortly.

Interestingly, an analogous brand of athletic representation, by boxing managers, has long been the target of administrative licensing and regulation.[16] The following case offers a revealing vignette of this precedent for modern restraints on sports agents.

---

15. An illuminating perspective on the broader issues posed by these materials is David B. Wilkins, *Who Should Regulate Lawyers?* 105 Harvard L. Rev. 799 (1992). This article's in-depth analysis of the promise and the limits of different institutional candidates for the regulation of lawyers is of interest not simply by way of analogy. Most agents may not be lawyers, but because the most successful and visible are, most players tend to have a lawyer as their agent.

16. See John C. Weistart and Cym H. Lowell, *The Law of Sports* (Indianapolis: Bobbs–Merril, 1979), in particular § 2.14, Manager's or Agent's Contracts.

GEORGE FOREMAN ASSOCS., LTD.
v. GEORGE FOREMAN

United States District Court, Northern District of California, 1974.

389 F.Supp. 1308.

PECKHAM, DISTRICT JUDGE.

[In 1971, an aspiring heavyweight boxer, George Foreman, signed a contract with Martin Erlichman, who acted through an entity titled George Foreman Associates ["Associates"]. In return for guaranteeing Foreman $10,000 a year in training expenses and $25,000 a year in living expenses (paid as an advance out of Foreman's future boxing earnings), Erlichman was promised 25% of Foreman's total future earnings from boxing matches and other promotions. In January, 1973, that agreement suddenly became far more valuable when Foreman, in an upset, knocked out Joe Frazier in the second round and became heavyweight champion. Foreman then sued to have the agreement declared null and void under the governing California law because Erlichman had not secured from the State Athletic Commission a license as "manager." Erlichman defended on the ground that Associates was not Foreman's manager within the meaning of the statute.]

* * *

Section 18674(b) characterizes as a manager any person who "directs or controls the professional boxing activities of any professional boxer." As we have seen, paragraph 1(b) of the 1972 Agreement requires that all financial arrangements for Foreman's fights be approved by Associates, subject to the qualification that this approval not be unreasonably withheld. Even with this qualification of reasonableness, the approval power is a significant one; a partner in Associates has characterized this power as the right "to utilize its judicious and reasonable withholding of approval to obtain better and more favorable financial terms for such fight contracts," and in their legal arguments Associates recognize their approval power as a "substantive right to evaluate the offer on the merits, grant approval if warranted, or deny approval if such denial is reasonably called for under the particular circumstances." This approval is evidently not envisioned as a technical formality or a perfunctory matter; and the very real element of control which Associates derives from its approval right is in no way lessened by the prospect that the interests of Associates and Foreman will normally coincide, since there are situations in which, as counsel for Foreman has suggested, these interests may diverge, or in which the parties may differ in their perceptions of their short-term and long-term interests. The fact that disputes will be submitted to arbitration is likewise immaterial here, since the position of Associates may well be upheld by the arbitrator, and a control approved as "reasonable" is not thereby rendered any less of a restraint.

Another potential source of control over Foreman's boxing activities is found in paragraph 5 of the 1972 Agreement, which gives

Associates a like power of approval or disapproval over Foreman's choice of a successor to Sadler [his manager], in the event that selection of a successor becomes necessary. Certainly the selection of a manager and trainer is one of a boxer's most important decisions.

Associates has volunteered, in its points and authorities, to waive the approval provisions of Paragraph 1(b); such a waiver is provided for in Paragraph 10 of the 1972 Agreement, which permits either party to waive the right to performance owed to it in the event that such performance is found to violate the laws of any jurisdiction. Such a waiver will not help Associates here, however, since we find below that the payment provisions of the Agreement are also sufficient to confer "manager" status upon Associates.

Section 18674(c) characterizes as a manager any person who is entitled to receive more than 10 percent of the gross purse of any professional boxer for services relating to such boxer's participation in a professional boxing contest. Associates quite rightly points out that one purpose of the 1972 Agreement was to eliminate Associates from the role of providing services in the negotiation and promotion of fights and various related rights; however, the Agreement does obligate Associates to advance money for training expenses and for travel expenses incident to training and boxing, and to guarantee Foreman $25,000 per year as compensation for his services as an employee of Associates. This court finds no reason why such payments should not, in keeping with the intent and purpose of the statute, be considered services relating to Foreman's boxing activities.

This interpretation derives considerable support and force from the history of state regulation of professional boxing in California and elsewhere. For many years, boxing was plagued by revelations of sordid abuses. Managers were accused of living off the earnings of impoverished fighters who received virtually nothing in return, having bartered away the right to their future earnings in exchange for the most meager present returns; close underworld connections often resulted in defrauding the public through the "fixing" of fights. These abuses ultimately prompted the extensive statutory and regulatory framework administered by the State Athletic Commission, a framework which has been described by the California Supreme Court as evincing "an unusually strong policy" of public regulation, one of whose primary goals is "to provide safeguards for the protection of persons engaging in the activity." The statutes and regulations indicate a clear purpose to safeguard boxers against the temptation to mortgage their futures in exchange for relatively meager present consideration;[1] in light of that purpose, it is appropriate and even necessary to interpret advance payments (such as those made to Foreman under the 1972

1. Cf. P. Simon, "The Boxer," (Columbia 1969, BMI): "I have squandered my resistance/For a pocketful of mumbles,/Such are promises/All lies and jest/Still, a man hears what he wants to hear/And disregards the rest."

agreement) as falling within the scope of the "services" which trigger the licensing requirement and other statutory protections.

In at least two respects therefore, this court finds that Associates falls within the statutory definition of "manager," and is hence subject to the jurisdiction of the State Athletic Commission. Once this determination is made, it is evident that the 1972 Agreement fails in numerous respects to comply with the applicable regulations governing boxer-manager contracts. The most significant violation was the failure of the parties to appear together before the Commission and secure its approval of the Agreement as required by 4 Cal.Admin.Code 258; in addition, the Agreement was not filed with the Commission (257), was not on a proper printed form or other approved form (256), and substantially exceeded the maximum term of three years (258).

These violations necessarily render the Agreement invalid and unenforceable, both by the express terms of the Commission's own regulations (258: "A contract is not valid between manager and boxer unless....") and by the recognized principle that a contract which violates the law cannot be enforced in an action founded upon the contract. No matter what their intentions or understandings may have been, the parties are not at liberty to waive or ignore the requirements of the law, particularly where the law in question is founded upon an "unusually strong" public regulatory policy designed in part to protect both the general public and some of the parties themselves.

* * *

Motion granted.

———

In recent years, a bigger agency problem in boxing has been presented by the long-term contractual commitments extracted from boxers by promoters in return for giving the fighter a chance at a big-time match. The fiduciary issues are accentuated here by the fact that a few promoters thereby secure control over a number of boxers pursuing the same championship belt. For a glimpse of the practical and legal issues that were raised about Don King's role in the Mike Tyson–Buster Douglas heavyweight title fight, see *Don King Productions, Inc. v. James "Buster" Douglas, et al.*, 742 F.Supp. 741 (S.D.N.Y. 1990).

———

It was not until the early 1980s that systematic regulation of the sports agent business was undertaken. This effort was pursued along two parallel tracks: one in the state legislatures, the other in the players associations. The pioneers for each were the California legislature, which in 1982 enacted the Athletic Agents Act (set forth in the Supplement), and the NFL Players Association, which in 1983 adopted a set of regulations for what it labeled "contract advisors." With some interesting variations, the NFLPA example was followed by the NBPA in 1985 and the MLBPA in 1987. While a few state legislatures (such as Alabama and North Carolina) have emulated the broad-based California model, the majority of the more than 20 states that have now passed some form of agent regulation have focused on just the single problem area exemplified by the *Walters & Bloom* case—agent recruiting of college athletes whose eligibility has not yet expired. (See the Minnesota and Florida statutes excerpted in the Supplement.) Such regulation, which addresses the rights and expectations of a third party to the player-agent relationship—the college—will be treated separately in the next section. Here we canvass the issues posed by the efforts of legislatures and unions to protect athletes from possible harm inflicted by their own agents.

Regardless of whether the regulations are adopted within the legislative or the player association forum, they are remarkably similar in the manner in which they tackle the issues posed in the cases and problems depicted earlier in this chapter.[17] There are, however, important differences in the authority and the competence of these respective regulatory sources. The authority of the state legislature is reasonably clear. The representation of athletes is an occupation that can be subjected to the kinds of legal controls that now govern activities ranging from medicine to hairdressing. Thus, California requires any aspiring agent to apply for registration (on payment of a fee) by the state Department of Labor. After investigation, the agency grants a license (which must be periodically renewed) to practice in this field, subject to a variety of legal constraints regarding fees, bonds and agency contracts.

While state constitutional authority to adopt some occupational regulations now seems clear (see *Williamson v. Lee Optical*, 348 U.S. 483, 75 S.Ct. 461, 99 L.Ed.2d 563 (1955)), the scope of that authority is murkier. A particular question posed in professional sports is whether, given the national cast to this market, any one state's regulatory reach should depend on the agent's home base, or the player's, or that of the college from which the player is coming, or of the professional team to which the player is going, or any and all of the above. State legislatures are naturally prone to spread their regulatory net as far as possible, but such action poses a serious difficulty to agents. If too many states follow the California model—each requiring its own registration fees, surety bonds, and administrative paperwork—the cumulative cost of such regulation might reduce considerably the number of agents competing to work for athletes. Nor is it clear that state government bureaucrats have the expertise needed to develop general standards for agent practice or to review the qualifications and prior work of applicants for an agent's license (or renewal). If they lack such

17. For a comprehensive overview, see   *Lawyers*, note 1 above.
Sobel, *The Regulation of Player Agents and*

expertise, we are unlikely to secure the benefits from regulation that justify its costs. Indeed, there is substantial evidence that in most states requiring agent registration, virtually no agents are now complying—apparently without legal consequence.

While some agents have argued that these regulatory schemes violate the federal Constitution's "dormant" commerce clause by imposing an unreasonable burden on interstate commerce, this argument seems unlikely to prevail under current constitutional standards. See *CTS Corp. v. Dynamics Corporation of America*, 481 U.S. 69, 107 S.Ct. 1637, 95 L.Ed.2d 67 (1987). Perhaps a more serious claim is that the state schemes are preempted by federal labor law which makes NLRB certified unions the exclusive bargaining representatives of the employees; since the players associations delegate some of their exclusive bargaining authority to certified agents, state regulation may infringe upon congressionally-granted union authority. Whatever the merits of this argument, no serious constitutional challenge has been launched against any of these state statutes, perhaps because states have made almost no effort to enforce them. For the same reason, little has resulted from the calls by some agents for Congress to regulate agents federally so that state regulations would be expressly preempted.

Players associations seem better equipped to regulate agents than do state governments. Once an agent has learned and complied with the single set of requirements adopted by the association, he can represent any players and deal with any team in that sport (and the players associations in the major team sports have cooperated in developing similar requirements). In addition, players associations have both the incentive and the resources to develop regulatory competence needed to improve the quality of agent representation.

Regulation by players associations, however, faces a legal problem—the source of an association's authority to impose binding regulations on agents. The solution comes from labor law. Recall from Chapter 3 that under the NLRA, a union such as a players association has the exclusive authority to represent all employees in its unit (members or not) for purposes of collective bargaining about the terms and conditions of employment (see *J.I. Case Co. v. NLRB*, 321 U.S. 332, 64 S.Ct. 576, 88 L.Ed. 762 (1944)). Under labor law, unions are free to limit the scope of the labor agreement to a set of guaranteed employment terms, and to permit individual bargaining about salaries and benefits above these minimum standards. In sports, as in other entertainment industries, individual negotiation has become the established practice. But while unions can and do delegate their exclusive authority to the individual employee and his agent, a union may choose to waive its statutory prerogatives conditionally and only in favor of agents of whom the union approves. When players associations adopt the latter posture, both the collective agreement and the labor laws preclude a club from negotiating individual contracts with agents who are not certified for that purpose by the association. In effect, then, the clubs become the enforcer of the association's regulatory program, because they must refuse to deal with any agent who has not secured and retained the association's stamp of approval. (The NFLPA even made football "contract advisors" agents of the Association itself, not just of the players, a tactic that the NBPA and the MLBPA chose *not* to adopt. What are the pros and cons of this particular arrangement?)

But while its bargaining relationship with the league may give the players association the leverage to impose its certification program on agents, this power secured under labor law does not necessarily insulate the regime from challenge under other laws—in particular, antitrust law.[18] Indeed, player regulation of agents bears an ironic resemblance to the traditional "reserve clause" system under which owners sharply constrained player prerogatives. In effect, the association members agree to a standard set of terms upon which they will purchase the service of player agents—one term being the maximum agency fee—and the players collectively require agents to subscribe to these terms as a condition of doing business in this sport. Should such restraints on the agent market be considered an illegal restraint of trade under the Sherman Act? As one might suspect, players associations answer this question in the negative. The associations assert the same labor exemption from antitrust that leagues have relied on to protect existing limitations on player mobility. In the following case, the NBPA attempted to ward off the first, and as yet only, legal challenge to association regulation of agents.

COLLINS v. NBPA & GRANTHAM

United States District Court, District of Colorado, 1991.

[Unpublished decision, affirmed *per curiam*, 976 F.2d 740 (10th Cir.1992).]

MATSCH, DISTRICT JUDGE.

[Starting in the mid–1970s, Thomas Collins had become a successful agent for several NBA stars, including Ralph Sampson, Terry Cummings, Alex English, Lucius Allen, and, most prominently, Kareem Abdul–Jabbar. Collins received certification by the NBPA in 1986, soon after the latter's regulations came into force. Shortly thereafter, though, Collins allowed his certification to lapse because he had become the target of a highly publicized lawsuit by Jabbar. The suit alleged a variety of breaches of fiduciary duty on the part of Collins:

—Failure to prepare and file Jabbar's tax returns for several years, which eventually cost Jabbar $300,000 in interest and penalties.

—Commingling of various clients' funds, including transfer of approximately $200,000 of Jabbar's money to the accounts of other players from which it could not later be recouped.

—Converting a corporate indebtedness of $290,000 into a personal debt of Jabbar's, without the latter's authorization.

18. See Lori J. Lefferts, *The NFL Players Association's Agent Certification Plan: Is it Exempt from Antitrust Review?* 26 Arizona L. Rev. 599 (1984).

—Most costly to Jabbar, investing much of his assets in speculative and ill-fated real estate ventures (such as in hotels and restaurants), rather than in the conservative and more secure investments that Jabbar said he had requested.

Eventually in late 1989, Collins and Jabbar settled their litigation before trial. The terms of that settlement were kept confidential, with the exception of a specific acknowledgement by Jabbar that "there has been no finding that [Collins] engaged in misrepresentation, misappropriation, conversion, breach of fiduciary duty or negligence." Although a separate suit by Lucius Allen was still pending, Collins then applied for recertification. At the personal request of Terry Cummings, the NBPA Committee on Agent Representation (which included NBPA Executive Director Charles Grantham) granted Collins interim certification to represent Cummings in his contract negotiations with the San Antonio Spurs.

The Committee, however, undertook an extensive informal investigation of the Jabbar–Collins affair. This involved not only examining the documents and speaking to the lawyers and accountants, but also a lengthy personal meeting with Collins and Jabbar together, without their lawyers. On that basis, the Committee eventually decided, in October 1990, *not* to recertify Collins. The latter was informed of his right to challenge this decision in an evidentiary hearing before a named arbitrator. Instead, Collins brought suit under antitrust law, alleging that the NBPA was guilty of a concerted boycott of his services as an agent, pursuant to an Association effort to monopolize representation of professional basketball players. The following decision considered the NBPA's motion for summary dismissal of Collins' suit.]

* * *

Like other sports and entertainment unions, the NBPA believes that the collective good of the entire represented group is maximized when individualized salary negotiations occur within a framework that permits players to exert leverage based on their unique skills and personal contributions. The NBPA therefore has authorized the players or their individually selected agents to negotiate individual compensation packages. This delegation of representational authority to individual players and their agents has always been limited solely to the authority to negotiate individual compensation packages, and to enforce them through the grievance-arbitration procedure established by the NBPA–NBA Agreement.

Player agents were unregulated by the NBPA before 1986. By the mid–1980s, a substantial number of players had complained to the officers of the NBPA about agent abuses. Specifically, players complained that the agents imposed high and non-uniform fees for negotiation services, insisted on the execution of open-ended powers of attorney giving the agents broad powers over players' professional and financial decisions, failed to keep players apprised of the status of negotiations with NBA teams, failed to submit itemized bills for fees and services, and, in some cases, had conflicts of interest arising out of representing coaches and/or general managers of NBA teams as well as players. Many players believed they were bound by contract not to dismiss their agents regardless of dissatisfaction with their services and fees, because the agents had insisted on the execution of long-term agreements. Some agents offered money and other inducements to players, their families and coaches to obtain player clients.

In response to these abuses, the NBPA established the Regulations, a comprehensive system of agent certification and regulation, to insure that players would receive agent services that meet minimum standards of quality at uniform rates. First, the Regulations provide that a player agent may not conduct individual contract negotiations unless he signs the "Standard Player Agent Contract" promulgated by the Committee. The "Standard Player Agent Contract" limits player agent fees by prohibiting any fee or commission on any contract which entitles the player to the minimum salary and by limiting agent fees on all contracts. Second, the Regulations contain a "code of conduct" which specifically prohibits an agent from providing or offering money or anything of value to a player, a member of a player's family or a player's high school or college coach for the purpose of inducing the player to use that agent's services. The code also prohibits agents from engaging in conduct that constitutes an actual or apparent conflict of interest (such as serving as an agent for a player while also representing an NBA team, general manager or head coach), engaging in any unlawful conduct involving dishonesty, fraud, deceit, misrepresentation, or engaging in any other conduct that reflects adversely on his fitness to serve in a fiduciary capacity as a player agent or jeopardizes the effective representation of NBA players.

Third, the Regulations restrict the representation of players to individuals who are certified player agents, and set up a program for the certification of agents who are then bound by the Regulations' fee restrictions and code of conduct. Prospective player agents must file the "Applications for Certification as an NBPA Player Agent" with the Committee. The Committee is authorized to conduct any informal investigation that it deems appropriate to determine whether to issue certification and may deny certification to any applicant:

(1) Upon ... determining that the applicant has made false or misleading statements of a material nature in the Application;

(2) Upon ... determining that the applicant has ever misappropriated funds, or engaged in other specific fraud, which would render him unfit to serve in a fiduciary capacity on behalf of players;

(3) Upon ... determining that the applicant has engaged in any other conduct that significantly impacts adversely on his credibility, integrity or competence to serve in a fiduciary capacity on behalf of players; or

(4) Upon ... determining that the applicant is unwilling to swear or affirm that he will comply with these Regulations and any

amendments thereto and that he will abide by the fee structure contained in the standard form player-agent contract incorporated into these Regulations.

Any prospective agent whose application for certification is denied may appeal that denial by filing a timely demand for arbitration.... The arbitrator is empowered to order certification if he determines, based on the evidence, that the Committee did not meet its burden of establishing a basis for denying certification. The arbitrator's decision is final and binding on all parties and is not subject to judicial review....

After unilaterally promulgating the Regulations, the NBPA obtained, in arms length collective bargaining, the NBA's agreement to prohibit all member teams from negotiating individual player salary contracts with any agent who was not certified by the NBPA.

* * *

Both the Regulations and Article XXXI are within the statutory exemption from antitrust regulation. When promulgating the Regulations and when negotiating Article XXXI, the NBPA acted in its own interest, independently of any employers and without denying access to rival employers. The number and identity of the employers remains unchanged regardless of the Regulations or Article XXXI. A union's actions are in its "self-interest" if they bear a reasonable relationship to a legitimate union interest. *Adams, Ray & Rosenberg v. William Morris Agency, Inc.*, 411 F.Supp. 403 (C.D.Cal.1976). The NBPA regulatory program fulfills legitimate union purposes and was the result of legitimate concerns: it protects the player wage scale by eliminating percentage fees where the agent does not achieve a result better than the collectively bargained minimum; it keeps agent fees generally to a reasonable and uniform level, prevents unlawful kickbacks, bribes, and fiduciary violations and protects the NBPA's interest in assuring that its role in representing professional basketball players is properly carried out. Although Collins claims any benefit is in the *player's* self-interest, not the union's, it is impossible to separate the two—the union is composed of its members and exists solely to serve the players. When the players benefit, the union benefits as well.

The second prong of the [labor exemption] test is also met. Collins incorrectly claims that when enacting the Regulations, the NBPA combined with a non-labor group and thus fails to earn a statutory exemption. The most analogous case is *H.A. Artists and Associates v. Actors' Equity Assn.*, 451 U.S. 704 (1981), in which the Supreme Court upheld similar regulations against an antitrust challenge. In *H.A. Artists*, theatrical agents who represented members of Actors Equity Association for purposes of procuring employment and negotiating individual salaries above the collectively bargained minimum, challenged that union's licensing system, which regulated the agents and required union members to employ only union-licensed agents. The Equity regulations, like the NBPA regulations at issue here, permitted only those agents who were licensed by the union to represent union members in individual salary negotiations with employers. The Equity regulations protected and sought to maximize wages by requiring agents to renounce any commission on any portion of a contract under which an actor or actress received no more than the collectively bargained minimum wages, and by limiting commissions in other respects. The Equity regulations also allowed actors to terminate their representation contracts with agents, and required agents to honor their fiduciary obligations. The Equity regulations were a response to historical abuses by agents, and were designed to secure better services from agents at lower rates.

The Court held that the Actors' Equity regulations met the *Hutcheson–Allen Bradley Co.* test for the statutory labor exemption. First, the Regulations were designed to promote the union's legitimate self-interest. Second, there was no combination with either a non-labor group or a non-party to a labor dispute. The Court held there was no combination between the union and the employers—the theatrical producers—to create or maintain the regulation system. Rather, the union unilaterally developed the regulatory system in response to agent abuses and to benefit union members. The Court concluded that although some agents agreed to the regulations, there was no combination with a non-labor group or persons who were not party to a labor dispute. The agents themselves were a labor group because they had an "economic interrelationship" with the union and its members "affecting legitimate union interest." That is, "the[y] represented ... union members in the sale of their labor ... [a function] that in most nonentertainment industries is performed exclusively by unions." Thus, any dispute between the agents and the union regarding the representation of union workers was a "labor dispute"—which was outside of the purview of the antitrust laws.

The NBPA Regulations similarly meet the second part of the *Hutcheson–Allen Bradley Co.* test. The NBPA did not combine with a non-labor group or a non-party to a labor dispute when promulgating the Regulations or negotiating Article XXXI. The NBPA unilaterally developed its Regulations in response to agent abuses and to benefit its members. It did not develop them in collusion with the employer group or to assist the employer group effort to restrain competition or control the employer group's product market.

Like the Equity agents, the player agents are a labor group. Although basketball players, unlike actors, can and do obtain employment without an agent, most players employ agents to negotiate their salaries and can fall victim to unscrupulous agent behavior. The player agents have a clear economic interrelationship with the players they represent; their remuneration is directly dependent on the relationship set up with the player and the salary obtained for him. Because they represent persons in the negotiation of terms of employment, the agents are clearly parties to a labor dispute within the meaning of the NLRA. As such, they would meet the second prong of the test regardless of whether there is a combination with a non-labor group.

Article XXI of the NBPA–NBA Agreement also meets the second prong and is entitled to the statutory exemption. Article XXI was obtained in arms-length collective bargaining at the urging of the NBPA after it unilaterally promulgated the Regulations. It was not agreed to at the behest of or in combination with the NBA, the employer group. Regardless of Article XXXI, pursuant to § 9 of the NLRA, the NBA member teams may not negotiate salaries with anyone other than the NBPA without NBPA approval. It therefore follows that Article XXXI of the NBPA–NBA Agreement does little more than memorialize in explicit terms what the NBA member teams' legal duty would be under the NLRA: to deal only with the NBPA or agents specified by the NBPA. The provision adds no new requirements to the NBA and thus creates no problem for the statutory exemption of the Regulations.

Article XXXI of the NBPA–NBA Agreement presents none of the concerns contained in the cases in which employer-union activities have been found to fall outside of the statutory exemption. Unlike *Allen Bradley*, the union activity is not designed to help employers control competition and prices. In fact, Article XXXI which requires teams to negotiate only with NBPA certified agents has no effect on the market for teams' services or on the market relating to any team. There is no combination with employer interests. With respect to the teams, the situation after the agreement is identical to the situation before it. The union serves its legitimate goals of protecting its representational function and the employer group's market is unchanged.

* * *

Even if Article XXXI of the Agreement were not entitled to the statutory exemption, it would be immune from antitrust review under the nonstatutory exemption to the antitrust laws. The Supreme Court has determined that when a union-employer agreement falls within the protection of the national labor policy, a proper accommodation between the policy favoring collective bargaining under the NLRA and the congressional policy favoring free competition in business markets requires that some agreements be accorded a limited nonstatutory labor exemption from antitrust sanctions. Connell Construction Inc. v. Plumbers and Steam Fitters Local 100, 421 U.S. 616, at 622; Meat Cutters v. Jewel Tea Co., 381 U.S. 676 (1975). Unlike the statutory exemption which immunizes activities that are expressly described in the Clayton and Norris LaGuardia Acts, the nonstatutory exemption immunizes labor arrangements that are the ordinary implication of activities contemplated by the federal labor laws. When the agreement is reached through bona fide, arms-length bargaining between the union and the employers, and the terms of the agreement are not the product of an initiative by the employer group but were sought by the union in an effort to serve the legitimate interests of its members, it is free from antitrust scrutiny.

In *Jewel Tea*, the butchers' union sought from the Jewel grocery store chain a provision—which it had already obtained from a multiemployer grocery association encompassing most other grocers in the area—restricting meat sales to limited weekday and Saturday hours. Jewel ultimately capitulated, agreeing to include the meat sale hours restriction in its contract with the union. The effect of the collective bargaining agreements was to limit competition among grocers. They were contractually committed not to sell meat after 6 P.M. or on Sunday. Because the union sought the marketing restriction to serve its members' concern of limiting working hours, an issue well within the terms and conditions of employment over which they were entitled to negotiate, the Court held that the union's efforts to obtain the restriction "through bona-fide, arms' length bargaining in pursuit of their own labor union policies, falls within the protection of the national labor policy and is therefore exempt from the Sherman Act." The Court recognized that the agreements affected competition among employers but held that the NLRA allowed the union to negotiate those issues.

The nonstatutory exemption similarly immunizes the Regulations from Sherman Act scrutiny. The Regulations were unilaterally developed in response to player complaints and to further NBPA labor policies. The NBPA–NBA Agreement, including Article XXXI, was agreed to in arms-length collective bargaining. The provision was not sought "at the behest of or in combination with" any employer or other non-labor group as forbidden by *Jewel Tea*. There is no economic benefit to the NBPA or the NBA member teams as a result of this provision and there is no effect on the employer's product or service market as a result of the provision.

Summary dismissal granted.

Questions for Discussion

1. Questions have been raised, however, about the applicability of *H.A. Artists and Associates v. Actors' Equity Ass'n.*, 451 U.S. 704, 101 S.Ct. 2102, 68 L.Ed.2d 558 (1981) (and the earlier precedents upon which this decision relied) to the sports context. In *H.A. Artists*, the Supreme Court emphasized the peculiar features of the theatrical world: actors are employed on an intermittent basis for specific productions; agents serve as a vital link in securing scarce work for performers (in place of the union hiring hall that performs this function in other industries in which workers move from job to job and employer to employer); and the primary aim of the Actors' Equity regulations was to ensure that in return for a chance at getting a job through an agent, actors were not required to pay the agent a fee that left net earnings from the job below the union-negotiated minimum scale. In addition, the Court emphasized that not only did Actors' Equity act unilaterally in devising its program of agent regulation, but it relied on

self-compliance by its own members for enforcement, rather than on a collective agreement negotiated with producer-employers.

In each of these respects, the sports industry is quite different from the theatrical industry (and also from the music industry, where an analogous union program passed Supreme Court muster in *American Fed'n of Musicians v. Carroll*, 391 U.S. 99, 88 S.Ct. 1562, 20 L.Ed.2d 460 (1968)). Should these variations make a legal difference? What arguments could sports agents advance that the policy behind the labor exemption for collectively negotiated restraints on players (or owners) does not apply to restraints imposed on agents? If the labor exemption were held not to protect player association regulation of sports agents, would antitrust law apply to the program in baseball (notwithstanding *Flood v. Kuhn*)?

2. One further aspect of the Collins case was adverted to by the Tenth Circuit in its brief *per curiam* decision: nobody ever alleged that Collins was incompetent at or acted improperly in negotiating player contracts with his clients' professional teams, though this is the function over which unions have exclusive authority and the role that gives players associations the legal hook to regulate agents. The NBPA's refusal to certify Collins only prevented him from negotiating with NBA teams; it did not prevent Collins from handling a player's endorsements, taxes, or investments. Thus, the grounds for not certifying Collins were unrelated to the function that he was being prevented from performing for a player who wanted him to perform it. Is this appropriate? Should unions be allowed to regulate agents for misconduct or incompetence other than as a contract negotiator? If not, should certification be denied to an agent because, for example, he is convicted of drug use? Publicly disagrees with the union's bargaining strategy? On the other hand, what is an appropriate standard of incompetence in contract negotiations; could certification be denied because an agent negotiated a contract the union believed was far below market value?

3. Recall from Chapter 3 that in 1989, as part of its litigation strategy, the NFLPA decertified as a union and thereby surrendered its legal foothold for regulating agents. The NFLPA called itself a trade association; it invited agents voluntarily to pay dues as nonvoting members and to comply with all the previously obligatory regulations, thereby entitling the agents to all of the organization's support services.

4. In the fall of 1992, a suit was filed in the Pennsylvania state court by several football players (mostly from the Pittsburgh Steelers), alleging that the NFLPA should not have certified as a "contract advisor" the players' agent and investment counsellor who subsequently misappropriated their funds. (The agent is now facing criminal charges and presumably is judgment-proof.) What is the basis for and standard of liability for such a suit—the common law tort of negligence or a labor law duty of fair representation (which we saw applied in the *Berthelsen* case in Chapter 4)? Is there any way that a players association can insulate itself from such litigation while still endeavoring to screen and certify agents for its members (or for players in the league who are not association members)?

———

Whatever the ultimate answer to these legal policy questions, players association regulation has evoked remarkably little complaint from established practitioners in this field, many of whom have served as advisers in the development and administration of these programs. One reason for this acceptance among the target group might be the reasonably relaxed character of the programs, which we will see in operation later in this chapter. At this point it is useful to highlight the key issues in the design of any regulatory program by either states or unions.[19]

1. *Coverage.* Who is an "agent" for purposes of such regulation? Should "agents" include only the people who negotiate player contracts with teams, or also people who pursue promotional opportunities for the player or manage his money? Should such regulation (particularly by state legislatures) apply to agents who are also lawyers licensed to practice in the relevant jurisdiction? Should the regulations govern dealings between agents and college players or graduates who are not yet on a professional roster?

2. *Eligibility.* What qualifications should be demanded of someone seeking certification as an approved agent? A law degree? Participation in a training program? A passing score on a test of knowledge of the relevant material in this area of practice? A probationary term until successful negotiation of a certain number of player contracts?

3. *Financial Responsibility.* Should the agent have to demonstrate financial responsibility to practice in this field? Through posting a surety bond? How high an amount? Just for money managers or also for contract negotiators?

4. *Solicitation of Business.* Should any active solicitation of players by agents be permitted? Should the agent be permitted to provide something of value to a player as an inducement to sign the agency contract? Should the agent be able to pay third parties for referrals of players? Most important of all, should agents be restricted from contacting college players whose eligibility has not yet expired?

5. *Fees.* Within the players associations, the driving force behind regulatory efforts tends to be player concerns about the size of agent fees. An important issue is whether any ceiling at all should be imposed on agent fees, especially a ceiling devised by the players' own association. If there is to be such a fee scale, should it be based on an hourly rate or a percentage figure? If a percentage, a flat rate or one that rises or falls depending on the size of the underlying contract? What is the appropriate percentage figure? Should the base exclude the minimum salary amounts mandated by the collective agreement or amounts paid as incentive bonuses? What about non-guaranteed con-

19. Besides the pieces noted earlier, helpful analyses of these problems can be found in Bart I. Ring, *An Analysis of Athlete Agent Certification and Regulation: New Incentives With Old Problems*, 7 Loyo- la Ent. L. J. 321 (1987), and Miriam Benitez, *Of Sports, Agents, and Regulations— The Need for a Different Approach*, 3 Ent. and Sports L. J. 199 (1986).

tract amounts, especially those contained in long-term deals? Is the same fee percentage appropriate for the negotiation of a player's contract with the team as for the negotiation of an endorsement contract with a product manufacturer or a promotional contract with an outside business? How will the players association's answer to these issues likely influence the agent's incentives in negotiations (e.g., to pursue incentive bonuses and long-term deals)?

There are many other problems addressed by one or other of these regulatory schemes (including the issue of potential conflicts of interest, about which we posed a number of questions immediately after the *Argovitz* case). A broader question of principle, however, runs through all these topics. A players association (and to a lesser extent a state authority) can gather together all the relevant material about agent qualifications, experience, financial responsibility, fee levels, and potential conflicts of interest, and then make this data available and reasonably comprehensible to players in the sport, ideally on a comparative basis. Is the facilitation of such "comparison shopping" by players— veterans or rookies—a sufficient response to the problems seen in the earlier cases? Is there any danger in having an association or state authority go farther and mandate a set of rules that govern all player-agent relationships? The following decision that shows agent regulation in operation offers further material for reflection on this fundamental question of legal policy. (And by the way, this decision was rendered by a private arbitrator, selected and paid for by the players associations, pursuant to the dispute resolution procedure mandated in the standard player-agent representation agreement.)

COORDINATED SPORTS MANAGEMENT
v. GUTIERREZ

(Arbitration, 1988).

St. Antoine, Arbitrator.

Facts

On January 6, 1987 Jackie Gutierrez signed a "Player's Agent Authorization Form," empowering Bill Moore of Coordinated Sports Management Group, Inc. to act as exclusive representative in negotiating "for inclusion in a Uniform Player's Contract the salary and Special Covenants, if any, which actually or potentially provide additional benefits to me as defined by the Basic Agreement...." This authorization was to remain in effect "until the aforementioned Uniform Player's Contract is executed, or until the authorization is revoked by me [player] in writing, whichever is the earlier." Gutierrez was the only person who signed this document.

Also on January 6, 1987 Gutierrez as "Player" signed an "Agreement" with Coordinated Sports Management Group, Inc. Fernando Cuza signed on behalf of Coordinated. The term of this Agreement was stated as "two (2) years."   Paragraph 3 described the "DUTIES" of Coordinated. . . .

Paragraph 4 of the Agreement read as follows:

> CONSIDERATION : In consideration of the services outlined in paragraph 3, above, CSMG shall be entitled to a sum of five percent (5%) of any and all compensation received by Player pursuant to an Employment Contract negotiated by CSMG.

Both the Authorization and the Agreement were in English only, although Coordinated provides a Spanish translation of the printed, illustrated brochure promoting its services for professional athletes. Gutierrez's native language is Spanish and his English is somewhat limited. He insisted that he talked (in Spanish) only with Fernando Cuza, not Moore, about signing an agency contract. Gutierrez further testified he told Cuza he would sign "just for one year," the same as he had signed with another agent in the past. He did not read the documents before signing them and denied that Cuza explained that the Agreement was for two years.

Earlier, on December 16, 1986 while Gutierrez was unrepresented by a player agent, the Baltimore Orioles had tendered him a contract for the 1987 season. It provided for a base salary of $134,000 and certain incentive bonuses. That amounted to the maximum allowable cut from the $167,500 he received from the Orioles in 1986.

Bill Moore of Coordinated informed the Orioles shortly after January 6 of his status as Gutierrez's player agent. In part because of some concern about the player's prior history of mental problems, Moore did not file for salary arbitration before the deadline of January 15, thus concededly leaving Gutierrez "without any bargaining power at all." Eventually, on March 5, 1987, Moore secured a contract for Gutierrez with the Orioles at the same base salary of $134,000 they had offered in December 1986, but with a somewhat improved set of performance bonuses, and with a provision that he would be paid at the rate of $150,000 for any time spent on a major league active playing roster during 1987. Gutierrez testified that he signed his 1987 contract as it was presented to him by Orioles' general manager Henry Peters, with no one else present, but Peters vouched for Moore's involvement in the negotiations. During 1987 Gutierrez played about 33 days in the major leagues and then was sent to Rochester for the rest of the season. His total earnings from the Orioles during 1987 were $136,812.76.

On February 10, 1987 Coordinated sent a letter and folder to Gutierrez in care of his sister-in-law in Miami, which was apparently the player's standard mailing address in the United States. The folder contained 1986 tax preparation workpapers, and the letter instructed Gutierrez on its use. On July 13, 1987 Coordinated wrote Gutierrez in care of the Rochester Red Wings, noting that it had not received his 1986 tax return information, indicating that it had extended his filing deadline to August 15, 1987, and asking him to contact Coordinated immediately if he wished it to prepare his 1986 returns. There is no evidence Coordinated had anything further to do with Gutierrez's tax returns for any year, nor that it "regularly"—or ever—provided him with "investment counselling and tax planning" as spelled out in paragraph 3 of the January 6, 1987 Agreement.

Gutierrez was released by the Baltimore Orioles during spring training in March 1988. He signed a minor league contract on May 28, 1988 with the Philadelphia Phillies organization, paying $5,000 a month, and played with a Maine club until he was recalled to the majors on July 15, at which time he again signed a major league contract at a seasonal rate of $70,000. Meanwhile, Fernando Cuza had left Coordinated in May 1987 and moved to Speakers of Sport. On July 7, 1987, Gutierrez signed a player agent authorization form with Cuza and five other individuals, most or all of whom are associated with Speakers of Sport. Gutierrez did not sign an authorization form with Coordinated for 1988, and there is no positive evidence Coordinated asked him for one.

ISSUE

Is player Gutierrez in breach of the Agreement with player agent Coordinated Sports Management Group, Inc., dated January 6, 1987? If so, what should be the remedy? If not, what should be the disposition of this grievance?

DISCUSSION

The position of the grievant player agent is simple and straightforward. On January 6, 1987 it signed an express written two-year contract with player Gutierrez whereby grievant agreed to negotiate any employment contracts and handle certain financial affairs for the player, and the player in turn agreed to pay grievant five percent of all compensation received by the player under any employment contract negotiated by grievant. Grievant has either performed or been ready, able, and willing at all times to perform. But the player has failed to pay in accordance with its contractual commitment, and is thus indebted to the grievant in an amount initially calculated as $13,575.28. The player must have been satisfied with the services of Fernando Cuza, his main contact at grievant, because he followed Cuza to Speakers of Sport.

The player responds that under the "realities" of the situation, a Spanish-speaking person like himself did not truly understand what he was signing. He meant to contract with Fernando Cuza, not grievant, and he meant to contract for only one year. In 1987 grievant negotiated a contract with Baltimore little better than what Baltimore offered on its own. Grievant didn't even obtain an authorization form from the player in 1988. It provided scant tax assistance in 1987 and none in 1988, and no investment counseling of any kind in either year.

The arbitrator finds several aspects of this case especially troubling. First, the relationship is inherently confusing between the Player's Agent Authorization Form, which expires upon execution of the player's contract, and the Agreement, which has a stated term of two years. The arbitrator can easily understand why anyone, and particularly someone whose native language is not English, would not realize that the Agreement might continue even after the authorization ended. Second, by the literal terms of the Agreement, an agent could collect five percent of a player's total employment compensation while adding absolutely nothing to the benefits guaranteed under the Basic Agreement, and while providing only the most modest amount of tax and investment assistance. Third, Moore, apparently the principal negotiator with Baltimore, concededly left Gutierrez "without any bargaining power at all" when he decided not to file for salary arbitration. Although it is true Moore testified he thought he was thus acting in the player's own best interests, the fact is he did not discuss this "very personal matter" with Gutierrez before deciding not to file for arbitration. Finally, I assign little importance to the player's apparent attachment to Fernando Cuza. Cuza, as a fellow Latin, was the natural contact person for Gutierrez. But Moore and others were the key negotiators and decision-makers for grievant.

A central doctrine of modern contract law is that even an agreement meeting all formalistic requirements for legal validity should not be enforced to the extent that it is "unconscionable." The hallmarks of unconscionability include great disparity in the knowledge, skill, and education possessed by the parties; gross inequality of bargaining power; and, perhaps preeminently, contract terms that are unreasonably favorable to one of the parties. See, e.g., Henningsen v. Bloomfield Motors, Inc., 32 N.J.358, 161 A.2d 69 (1960); Williams v. Walker–Thomas Furniture Co., 350 F.2d 445 (D.C.Cir.1965); 1 A. Corbin, Contracts § 128 (1963). For the reasons set forth in the preceding paragraph, I find the Agreement in the present case so grossly one-sided both as written and as performed as to be unconscionable. It should therefore not be enforced according to its terms.

Nonetheless, grievant has provided the player with some benefits. It is thus entitled to a certain amount of compensation, either as partial enforcement of the Agreement or under a theory of restitution. I shall first provide grievant with five percent of any amount on the 1987 uniform contract that it obtained for the player *above* the mandated minimum. The player's counsel calculated this, on the basis of 33 days in the major leagues at the special $150,000 annual rate instead of $134,000, as $3,011. Figures provided by the Baltimore Orioles indicate that Gutierrez received $2,812.76 in excess of $134,000 during 1987. I leave that to the parties, in the first instance, to work out. Furthermore, in light of my sharp reduction of the base on which the five percent agent's fee is to operate, I believe the grievant should also receive any actual, provable, out-of-pocket expenses (travel, telephones, etc.) it incurred in negotiating the 1987 player's contract with the Baltimore Orioles (*not* the expenses incurred in obtaining the original Agreement with the player himself). Finally, although grievant did little in the way of tax assistance and nothing in the way of investment advice, at least it stood ready to provide the former service. I shall add $500 as a reasonable value of that benefit, chargeable to the player.

In reaching this decision and setting forth this remedy, I shall emphasize what I trust should be recognized anyway: the facts of this particular case are controlling, and the same result would not necessarily follow in other situations. Specifically, I am definitely not suggesting that a five percent agent's fee based on a principal's total compensation would be unconscionable in all circumstances. Even with a mandated minimum, for example, there might be cases where a serious question exists about the willingness of the employer to enter into a contract at all. But here that issue does not arise. The Orioles had tendered the player a contract at $134,000 a year even before grievant and the player agreed on an agency arrangement.

Grievance upheld only in part.

————

Another interesting case involved yet another episode in the Walters and Bloom drama, this time involving Ron Harmon from the University of Iowa and the Buffalo Bills. Harmon was one of the first athletes Walters and Bloom recruited. At a March 1985 meeting (which was secretly taped by Harmon's father), Harmon signed a post-dated representation contract, in return for which he received an immediate $2,500 evidenced by a promissory note and an additional $250 per month until he left Iowa. In addition, Walters and Bloom paid travel expenses for Harmon and his family and friends, a "finder's fee" for putting Walters and Bloom in touch with one of his Iowa teammates, and a $32,000 down payment on a new Mercedes as he left school in June 1986. Despite the receipt of more than $50,000 from Walters and Bloom, Harmon switched agents midway through his negotiations with the Bills in the summer of 1986. As in *Fullwood*, Walters and Bloom filed suit against their former client to recover their promised five percent of Harmon's 4–year $1.425 million contract (a $70,000 commission), plus their payments to and expenditures on behalf of Harmon. This time, however, the New York state judge sent the case to arbitration under the NFLPA's agent certification regime (see *Walters v. Harmon*, 135 Misc.2d 905, 516 N.Y.S.2d 874 (1987).

The arbitrator, John Culver, a former U.S. Senator from Iowa, first indicated that even though the contract between Harmon and World Sports & Entertainment, Inc. ("WSE"—Bloom and Walters' firm) violated NCAA rules, it was not illegal or in violation of the NFLPA regulations. Thus, the arbitrator did not take the NCAA rules into consideration in his decision. Likewise, he did not regard Harmon as an innocent victim of fraud or unequal bargaining power. Harmon understood exactly what he was doing and the terms of the agreement, which he signed over the objections of his father. Nonetheless, the arbitrator voided the agreement between Harmon and WSE because Walters and Bloom had induced Harmon to sign it by payments of substantial amounts of cash and travel expenses, all in violation of the NFLPA regulations.

> The fact that Mr. Harmon may have freely accepted or even requested the money does not make their conduct acceptable under the Regulations.... [T]he correct remedy is to render the Agreement null and void. Otherwise, if the Agreement were enforced, the Contract Advisor who provided something of significant value to an NFL player in order for the player to execute a representation agreement would benefit from his or her wrongful conduct.... If such unfettered "bribery" were permitted, the result could be bidding wars between contract advisors for the rights to represent athletes.

Following the same tack as *Gutierrez*, the arbitrator did find that Bloom and Walters had provided services of value to Harmon and should be paid quantum meruit of $125 per hour for 25.23 hours of work, or $3,153.75. He also required Harmon to reimburse WSE for its out-of-pocket representation expenses, and to repay the $2,500 loan evidenced by a promissory note (although not the other $54,000 unmemorialized payments by WSE on Harmon's behalf).

Interesting questions emerge from these and other arbitration decisions involving soured relationships between players and agents. Should agents who have behaved in reproachable fashion and/or in violation of the union's regulations be awarded fees on a quantum meruit basis and reimbursement of expenses and loans? Or should they get no redress as a punitive deterrent against such behavior? To what extent should your answer depend on the degree of "innocence" of the player involved?

In addition, we noted earlier that Walters and Bloom spent roughly $800,000 to induce nearly 60 players to sign agency contracts, and 10 of their clients (including Harmon and Fullwood) were selected in the first round of the 1986 and 1987 NFL drafts. Look closely at the hours and dollar figures in the *Harmon* case to understand why such a large amount seemed a sensible investment in starting up this new enterprise.

E. AGENTS, COLLEGE ATHLETES AND NCAA RULES [20]

Both the *Harmon* arbitration ruling and the earlier *Fullwood* decision testify to a weakness in the legal sanctions available against agent impairment of college eligibility. The agent who signs a college

---

20. Besides the books by Shropshire, *Agents of Opportunity*, note 1 above, and Mortensen, *Playing for Keeps*, note 14 above, see also Robert J. Ruxin, *Unsportsmanlike Conduct: The Student–Athlete, the NCAA, and Agents*, 8 J. of Coll. and Univ. Law 347 (1981–82), and Charles W. Ehrhardt and J. Mark Rodgers, *Tightening the Defense Against Offensive Sports Agents*, 16 Florida State U. L. Rev. 633 (1988).

player—especially the agent who pays money to get the player's signature—does risk that the contract will not be legally enforced and the money paid will be lost. However, this risk will materialize only if the player becomes sufficiently dissatisfied with his agent's performance to go elsewhere. Thus, both judge-made contract law and player association regulatory law directly protect the interests only of the athlete, not of the college that is not a party to this agency relationship. (Would the college, however, have the right to bring a tort action against the agent for interfering with its "contractual" relationship with its student-athletes?) [21]

Agents do not appear to have been greatly deterred by the lack of legal enforceability of their players' commitments. It is estimated that a large majority of top draft picks in football and basketball have signed with agents before their eligibility has expired, many of these players in return for money. The elaborate nature of these arrangements is exemplified by the 1987 deal between Kevin Porter, a star cornerback for Auburn University, and an agent named Jim Abernethy. Just before his senior year at Auburn, Porter signed an agreement with Abernethy that promised the latter five percent of Porter's professional salary and ten percent of his endorsement earnings, in return for an immediate $2,000 "signing bonus" paid to Porter, $900 monthly payments, Thanksgiving and Christmas bonuses, and $100 for each interception that season.

These kinds of deals not only constitute symbolic violations of the NCAA principles of "amateur" intercollegiate sports—they also subject the college to a considerable risk of tangible loss. For example, although Walters and Bloom had secretly signed Alabama's star basketball forward, Derrick McKey, to an agency contract, the school used McKey in the next NCAA tournament. When the NCAA discovered this fact it required Alabama to forfeit two games it had won and repay the $250,000 the university had received from the tournament. And even if the university does learn of an agency contract in time to declare the player ineligible (as happened with Porter prior to Auburn's appearance in the Sugar Bowl), the university loses one of its best players and thus the chance at a successful season, both artistically and financially.

Understandably, then, there is widespread popular sentiment in favor of putting some legal teeth behind the NCAA eligibility rules. However, the NCAA is a private body and its rules are not directly enforceable in court. The attitude of many agents was candidly ex-

21. See Richard P. Woods and Michael R. Mills, *Tortious Interference With an Athletic Scholarship: A University's Remedy for the Unscrupulous Sports Agent*, 40 Alabama L. Rev. 141 (1988), and Marianne M. Jennings and Lynn Zioiko, *Student-Athletes, Athlete Agents and Five Year Eligibility: An Environment of Contractual Interference, Trade Restraint and High-*

pressed by Mike Trope, one of the early exponents of this behavior: [22]

> The NCAA rules are not the laws of the United States. They are simply a bunch of hypocritical and unworkable rules set up by the NCAA. I would no sooner abide by the rules and regulations of the NCAA than I would with the Ku Klux Klan.

Norby Walters echoed Trope, saying that he considered ignoring the NCAA code to be "no different than bending the Knights of Columbus rules." (Indeed, both Trope and Walters could have cited statements in the 10th Circuit's decision in the *Neely* case (in Chapter 2) to the effect that there was nothing illegal in the Houston Oilers signing a college player to a professional contract and trying to keep it secret so that he could play in a bowl game.) The next set of legal proceedings demonstrated to Walters and his partner—and to sports agents and college athletes generally—that there *is* a difference between the two.

As mentioned above, it was organized crime's intrusion with physical threats and violence that brought the federal authorities into this picture. However, to establish its jurisdiction in the case, the Chicago U.S. Attorney's office developed the theory that it was a legal fraud for the player and his agent to hide their relationship to maintain the player's scholarship and his NCAA eligibility. This became a breach of the federal Mail Fraud Act when the school mailed the player's annual signed eligibility form to the NCAA head office.[23] And as far as agents were concerned, their repeated use of this practice constituted a violation of the Racketeer Influenced and Corrupt Organizations Act (RICO) (to which, of course, were added the allegations of extortion).

When the case came to trial, the jury found both Walters and Bloom guilty of mail fraud with respect to Michigan (their client being Robert Perryman) and Indiana (Rod Woodson), though not with respect to Michigan State (Adrian White) or Iowa (Ron Harmon) (for reasons we will mention later). On appeal, the Seventh Circuit overturned these convictions (see 913 F.2d 388 (7th Cir.1990)). In the case of Walters, the reason was an inadequate instruction regarding his "advice of counsel" defense. Apparently Walters—whose cousin, Len Trost, was head of the sports department of a New York law firm, Shea, Gould—had received advice from the firm that while secretly signing players might flout the NCAA's private rules, it did not violate any public laws. Ironically, Bloom's conviction was reversed on the ground that he should have been granted a separate trial, since only Walters had relied on this "advice of counsel" defense and thereby waived his attorney-client privilege.

Late in 1991, though, Walters pleaded guilty to the charge of mail fraud. Walters may have feared that the next jury would reject the

---

Stake Payments, 66 U. of Detroit L. Rev. 179 (1989).

22. Mike Trope, *Necessary Roughness* (Chicago: Contemporary Books, 1987), at 68.

23. See Landis Cox, *Targeting Sports Agents With the Mail Fraud Statute:* United States v. Norby Walters & Lloyd Bloom, 41 Duke L.J. 1157 (1992).

"advice of counsel" defense since he apparently had concealed from his lawyer many of the unsavory tactics that he and Bloom routinely employed in recruiting players. In return for Walters' guilty plea to the mail fraud charges, the government dropped the more serious RICO charges (in particular, for threats and extortion). As a result Walters received an 18–month jail sentence, rather than the earlier five-year term. A separate prosecution of Bloom resulted in lengthy probation and community service for him.

Equally crucial to Walters' plea bargain, and of much broader significance, was the following district court ruling rejecting Walters' legal defense against the validity of the mail fraud indictment. The court's reasoning makes such agent practice a federal offense irrespective of the especially seamy features of the Walters and Bloom venture. Indeed, this legal theory also makes it criminal for college players to sign and conceal their agency contracts. In fact, all of Walters and Bloom's clients eventually did plead guilty to this charge, in return for which they were put on probation on the conditions that they repay their schools for the scholarship funds they received while they were ineligible, and that they perform a number of hours of community service.

UNITED STATES v. NORBY WALTERS

United States District Court, Northern District of Illinois, 1991.

775 F.Supp. 1173.

LEINENWEBER, DISTRICT JUDGE.

* * *

SCOPE OF THE FEDERAL MAIL FRAUD STATUTE

Defendant challenges the indictment on the ground that it does not charge him with an offense under the mail fraud statute. The federal mail fraud statute provides in relevant part that "whoever, having devised or intending to devise any scheme or artifice to defraud, or for obtaining money or property by means of false or fraudulent pretenses ... for the purpose of executing such scheme or artifice ... places in any post office ... any matter or thing whatever ... shall be fined not more than $1000 or imprisoned not more than five years, or both." 18 U.S.C. § 1341. Defendant maintains that the indictment does not properly allege that the scheme was "devised ... for obtaining money or property."

Defendant advances two analytically distinct arguments. First, defendant contends that the mail fraud statute, as interpreted by the United States Supreme Court in McNally v. U.S., 483 U.S. 350, 356 (1987), only applies where the "affirmative goal" of a scheme is to obtain money or property through fraud. According to defendant, the scheme alleged was not affirmatively designed to deprive the colleges of scholarship funds. Defendant maintains that, at most, his conduct only incidentally effected such a deprivation.

Second, defendant argues that the colleges did not suffer a deprivation of property or money as a result of his activity, because the scholarship money would have been paid to the players even in the absence of the alleged scheme.

* * *

McNally

McNally involved a mail fraud prosecution of two Commonwealth of Kentucky officials. The relevant portion of the indictment charged the defendants with a scheme "to defraud the citizens and government of Kentucky of their right to have the Commonwealth's affairs conducted honestly...." *McNally*, 483 U.S. at 353. At trial, the jury was not told that in order to convict they had to find that the Commonwealth of Kentucky had actually been defrauded of money or property. Both defendants were convicted on the mail fraud counts. On appeal, the petitioners argued that the mail fraud convictions were invalid because the jury did not find that the scheme was devised to obtain money or property.

The United States Supreme Court agreed. Although the statute was drafted in the disjunctive, the court held that its legislative history and traditional application required that it be read in the conjunctive. In order for an indictment to stand under 18 U.S.C. § 1341, the offense charged must involve a scheme that was devised to defraud and to obtain money or property by false or fraudulent pretenses. As the court stated, "rather than construe the statute in a manner that leaves its outer boundaries ambiguous ... we read § 1341 as limited in scope to the protection of property rights."

A) Meaning of "for Obtaining Money or Property"

Following the Supreme Court's decision in *McNally*, a number of courts had the opportunity to address the applicability of the mail fraud statute in cases where the offense charged involved a non-economic deprivation. Many of these cases were post-*McNally* challenges to indictments or convictions which had been handed-up or entered before the *McNally* decision was issued. Invariably, the underlying scheme involved the bribery of a governmental official or the use of political clout to influence a certain governmental decision. The courts rejected the use of the mail fraud statute in these so-called "intangible rights" prosecutions, explaining that the statute only reached schemes "that had as their goal the transfer of something of economic value to the defendant." U.S. v. Baldinger, 838 F.2d 176 (6th Cir.1988).

The operative language in *Baldinger* is "economic value." To come within the scope of Section 1341, the scheme must have been devised to obtain "money or property." However, by quoting language out of context, defendant manipulates the plain meaning of a number of post-

McNally decisions. Defendant argues that Section 1341 only punishes a scheme that has "as its goal" the deprivation of money or property. Defendant maintains that since his "goal" was not to deprive the colleges of scholarship money, his activity does not come within the punitive ambit of the mail fraud statute.

* * *

The case of U.S. v. Holzer, 840 F.2d 1343 (7th Cir.1988) involved the bribery prosecution of an Illinois state trial judge. The judge had allegedly solicited bribes in the form of "loans" from attorneys with cases before him and from persons seeking appointments by the court as receivers. The government argued that by taking bribes Holzer became the constructive trustee of the bribe money. By failing then to turn the money over to the state, he deprived the state of its right to the property in violation of Section 1341.

In rejecting the government's argument, the court explained that "taking one's employer's property by fraud ... and failing to convey the receipts of bribery to one's employer are not the same acts. The bribe became the employer's property through the fiction of a constructive trust not because he bargained for them but to make sure that the dishonest employee does not profit from them." *Holzer*, 840 F.2d at 1347.

The crux of the holding in *Holzer* distinguished "deprivation" in the bribery context from traditional mail fraud, where the defendant deprives a party of that party's own money or property. Here, the indictment charges defendant with the latter offense. Defendant's reliance upon constructive-trust principles to buttress his argument is therefore misplaced. If anything is to be garnered from *Holzer*, it is that an individual who defrauds an employee's (here athlete's) employer (here college) of the employer's own money, may be prosecuted under the mail fraud statute.

* * *

In the present case, the misrepresentations were made to the colleges after the players were ineligible to participate in intercollegiate athletics. The colleges were thus induced to continue financial support through fraud. These affirmative misrepresentations are analogous to an initial fraudulent inducement to contract, since the continuation of scholarship payments was dependent upon continued eligibility. Walters' offense was that he executed agreements which, by their very existence, made the players ineligible to receive scholarship money. At the same time, he allegedly knew 1) that misrepresentations would subsequently be made to insure that the players continued to receive the aid, and 2) that those misrepresentations were necessary to the success of his scheme.

Defendant has failed to support his position that a scheme must have as its "affirmative objective" the deprivation of money or property in order to make out an offense under the mail fraud statute. A more sensible interpretation of the statute would indicate that a scheme is devised "for obtaining" money or property when the defendant knows that its success requires a specific fraudulent deprivation of money or property. That deprivation need not be the "affirmative goal" or the "ultimate objective" of the schemers. Indeed, the deprivation of money or property need not directly benefit the schemers, so long as it advances the scheme.

B) Relevance of Pre-Scheme Eligibility

Defendant also maintains that this prosecution is precluded by the fact that the scholarship money would have been paid to the players in the absence of defendant's scheme. Neither existing case law nor the language of the mail fraud statute support defendant's interpretation. The statute punishes a scheme devised to obtain money or property by fraud. It does not follow that in order to constitute mail fraud the money or property would not have been obtained without the scheme. Here, once the representation agreements were executed, the players could only obtain scholarship money by fraudulently representing that they were eligible to play football.

Furthermore, a brand new deprivation occurred as a result of defendant's scheme: the colleges were deprived of their right to allocate athletic scholarships on the basis of truthful representations as to each player's eligibility. The right to control the allocation of athletic scholarships is a right protected by the mail fraud statute.

* * *

THE "IN FURTHERANCE OF" REQUIREMENT

Finally, defendant argues that the indictment should be dismissed because the mailings were not made "in furtherance of" the scheme. In order for defendant to prevail on his motion, the court must believe that "there is no conceivable evidence that the government could produce at trial" to substantiate its allegation that the eligibility forms were mailed in furtherance of the scheme.

* * *

The court is not without guidance on this question. Bloom argued this very point in a pre-trial motion to dismiss the indictment in Walters I. At that time Judge Marovich explained how the mailings could have been used to execute the alleged scheme

> [A] jury could reasonably conclude that the mailings in this case are an essential part of the scheme because they facilitated concealment of the scheme. If the universities or the Big Ten Conference had been given truthful information on the forms, the universities could have terminated the student-athletes' football scholarships and prevented the athletes from playing with the team. Such an occurrence could seriously affect a particular athlete's value to defendants.

Walters, 711 F.Supp. at 1440.

Defendant does not provide the court with any reason to believe that Judge Marovich's analysis is unsound. NCAA regulations did not prevent defendant's stable of players from signing contracts and foregoing their college eligibility for immediate entrance into the pro draft. Very few players, however, avail themselves of that opportunity. A player in his junior year of college is unlikely to have demonstrated the proven ability necessary to justify a lucrative professional contract. The fact that the players signed by defendant chose not to forego their senior year adds weight to this observation. If a player's prospect of signing such a contract was diminished because he was rendered ineligible to play intercollegiate football, defendant's commission under the representation agreement would be adversely affected. The players' misrepresentations concerning their eligibility were therefore "essential to the perpetration and concealment of the alleged fraud."

Furthermore, the government is not required to show that defendant actually intended to use the mails, only that their use was reasonably foreseeable. See Pereira v. U.S., 347 U.S. 1, 8–9 (1954). The eligibility statements which the players were asked to sign were forms provided by the Big Ten. The regulations required the colleges to submit these forms to the Big Ten headquarters in Schaumburg, Illinois. From these facts a jury could certainly conclude that the use of the mails to effect the submission of the forms was reasonably foreseeable.

Dismissal rejected.

———

State prosecutors have also attempted to use provisions of their criminal laws to punish such agent misbehavior. The State of Alabama was unsuccessful in its prosecution of Jim Abernethy for supposedly "tampering with a sporting contest" by paying Auburn's Kevin Porter (see *Abernethy v. State*, 545 So.2d 185 (Ala.Crim.App.1988)). However, the threat of such a prosecution against Walters proved an effective lever in getting the latter to reimburse the University of Alabama for the $250,000 the school had to repay the NCAA for playing Walters' client, Derrick McKey, in the 1987 NCAA basketball championship.

In addition to technical questions about the scope of particular criminal statutes, these proceedings pose broader questions about whether it is appropriate to use the criminal law in this sphere. Answering the latter question requires study and analysis of the current state of big-time college sports, a subject treated in Chapters 8 and 9. As some indication of the moral complexity of the underlying situation, the apparent reason why the jury acquitted Walters and Bloom of the charges involving Ron Harmon and University of Iowa was the dubious quality of Harmon's academic record at that school, a record that probably left him ineligible under Big Ten, if not also NCAA, regulations. Is it appropriate to prosecute (for example, for mail fraud) college athletic or academic officials who play fast and loose with such academic regulations, or who are guilty of recruiting violations? Is such prosecution likely? Should agents be treated differently than coaches? Should players who knowingly participate in any scheme that violates NCAA rules, but take scholarships and conceal the violation, be subject to criminal prosecution?

———

In recent years state legislatures have actually pursued a quite different track—more than twenty states have enacted legislation specifically targeted at the problem of college eligibility.[24] (Unsurprisingly, almost every one of these states has one or more colleges that are traditional powers in either football or basketball.) A number of these statutes adopt licensing programs that, in theory at least, seek to ensure high-quality representation for their departing student-athletes. But with or without such a certification scheme, each of these statutes adopts one or more of the following restraints on agent dealings with college athletes.

1. Some states require an explicit warning, in bold print on the face of the agency contract, that by entering into this agreement the player is forfeiting any further NCAA eligibility. Most of these laws give the athlete a "cooling off" period within which to change his mind and cancel the agreement (for example, fifteen days in Maryland).

2. A few states (such as Florida) require the agent and/or the athlete to notify the institution immediately after having signed the contract. Most, however, provide that such notification must be given to the institution (to its athletic director) a minimum number of days (for example, thirty days in Georgia) *before* the agency contract is to be signed.

3. Many states (such as Illinois) make it illegal, both civil and criminal, for an agent to give anything of value to the athlete or his family as an inducement to signing the representation contract.

4. Ten states (Iowa, Kentucky, Louisiana, Maryland, Michigan, Mississippi, Oklahoma, Pennsylvania, Texas, and Virginia) flatly prohibit the agent from signing any contract with an athlete who has not yet completed his college eligibility. Indeed, some states (such as Texas) prohibit any contact or communication between an agent and a college player that might lead to loss of the player's eligibility:

> A registered athlete agent shall not directly contact an athlete who is participating in a team sport at an institution of higher education located in the state to discuss the athlete agent's representation of the athlete in the marketing of the athlete's athletic ability or reputation or the provision of financial services by the athlete agent, or enter into any agreement, written or oral, by which the

24. See Jan Stiglitz, *NCAA–Based Agent Regulation: Who are We Protecting?* 67 North Dakota L. Rev. 215 (1991).

athlete agent will represent the athlete, until after the completion of the athlete's last intercollegiate contest, including postseason games, and may not enter into an agreement before the athlete's last intercollegiate contest that purports to take effect at a time after that contest is completed.

(Texas Code, Ann. art. 8871, para. 6(b)(5))

The most visible use of this Texas law took place in 1990 when former Heisman Trophy winner Johnny Rodgers, who worked for a Nebraska firm called Total Economic Athletic Management (TEAM), took out for dinner and shopping in New York the mother of Andrew Ware, the Houston quarterback who had just won the 1989 Heisman Trophy as a junior, and told Mrs. Ware that TEAM could make $20 million for her son if he were to leave college that year. Both Rodgers and TEAM were fined $10,000 by the Texas Secretary of State (a Houston alumnus) for violating the above-quoted law, fines that they are now appealing. Could one fashion a persuasive constitutional basis for the Rodgers appeal (see *Shapero v. Kentucky Bar Ass'n*, 486 U.S. 466, 108 S.Ct. 1916, 100 L.Ed.2d 475 (1988))?

These various restrictions on agent dealings with college athletes are enforced by a variety of sanctions, in some states against the athlete as well as the agent: not only criminal prosecution and fines, but also a right conferred on the college to sue for any damages it suffers as the result of the agent's signing of one of its athletes. In Tennessee, for example, such damages include all lost television revenues, lost ticket sales from regular season athletic events, lost revenues from not qualifying for postseason athletic events such as football bowl games and NCAA tournaments, and an amount equal to three times the value of the athlete's scholarship.

The foregoing conveys the intensity of state legislative interest in the subject. It also poses important questions of legal principle. Should there be *any* legislative enforcement of the NCAA's rules regarding player-agent relationships? If so, which of the above models is best? Or does the problem lie in the NCAA eligibility rules themselves, rather than in the efforts by athletes and agents to avoid them? Keep your views on that last question tentative for the moment, until we examine the entire sphere of intercollegiate athletics in Chapters 8 and 9.

––––––

In conclusion, reflect for a moment about all the materials presented in the first five chapters of this book about the legal and institutional framework for the player market in professional team sports. How would you compare the value of contract, antitrust, and labor law in securing the key interests of athletes? The contributions made by players associations or agents in elevating player salaries and benefits?

Chapter Six

FRANCHISE, LEAGUE, AND COMMUNITY

A. THE NATURE OF THE LEAGUE

The previous four chapters presented the legal framework governing the players' market in professional sports. The next two chapters undertake a detailed examination of the manner in which the law treats the relationship of clubs and leagues.[1]

The significance of this franchise side of the ledger can be capsulized in these financial figures. As most sports fans know, average player salaries have soared over the last quarter century—in baseball, for example, from $19,000 in 1967 to over $1 million in 1992, and in football from $25,000 in 1967 to $450,000 in 1992. Despite such spiralling player costs, baseball and football franchises that sold for approximately $7 million in 1967 were being sold for $100 million or more in 1992—and these were the prices paid for less profitable teams such as baseball's Seattle Mariners and football's New England Patriots. Even steeper escalation took place in franchise values in the NBA and the NHL.

Recognition of these financial trends is important for two reasons. First, although a more favorable legal environment has enabled players to secure a larger share of the game's revenues—player salaries have gone up somewhat more than franchise prices—the lion's share of salary increases is attributable to increases in the game's revenues that were also enlarging ownership profits. Sports over the past few dec-

---

1. There has been a good deal of scholarly commentary in the law reviews about the legal issues raised in these chapters, and we shall provide citations at the appropriate points in the text. Here we refer the reader to three valuable book-length treatments of the personalities and the economics in the background to the legal disputes in football and baseball respectively: David Harris, *The League: The Rise and Decline of the NFL* (New York: Bantam Books, 1986), James Edward Miller, *The Baseball Business: Pursuing Pennants and Profits in Baltimore* (Chapel Hill, N.C: University of North Carolina Press, 1990), and Andrew Zimbalist, *Baseball and Billions* (New York: Basic Books, 1992).

ades serve as an apt illustration of what the eminent British economist Alfred Marshall called the first "law" of labor economics: the employer's demand for labor is derived from the consumer's demand for the goods and services produced by that labor.

The second reason why we must be conscious of this explosion in team values—of the fact, for example, that the NHL charged $2 million for an expansion franchise in 1967 and $50 million in 1992—is because the law has left its imprint on that economic trend as well. The next two chapters explore the legal structure of sports ownership, both within a league and between leagues, and how it influences franchise values and the amount of revenue generated by fans who attend the games, broadcasters and advertisers that televise the games, and communities that subsidize the facilities for playing the games.

Chapter 1 provided a glimpse of the distinctive structure of the sports league.[2] In every sport the league rests on an elaborate contractual agreement among all the member teams—its "constitution." Each owner is given both a franchise which the team runs in its (usually) exclusive territory and a vote in the governance of the league. Through its governing bodies, the league in turn develops by-laws and rules that define the rights and obligations of all participants in the enterprise—in particular, the division of revenues from gate receipts, television contracts, and marketing of the league and team names. At the apex of this structure is a commissioner who wields broad authority to determine and enforce "the best interests of the sport," including adjudication of disputes between league participants. Illustrative of the latter role was baseball Commissioner Fay Vincent's ruling in the summer of 1991, in connection with the National League's expansion into Miami and Denver, about what proportion of the players would be contributed and expansion fees received by American League and National League clubs, respectively.

As we saw in Chapter 1, when objections are launched against the commissioner's formulation of the league's "best interests," courts have generally displayed a very deferential attitude towards decisions reached through these internal league councils. Courts have exhibited a much different legal posture, however, when attacks are launched against the underlying validity of the league contract—particularly challenges under antitrust law. As we saw in Chapter 3's depiction of antitrust litigation in the players' market, there are two potential bases for legal attacks under the Sherman Antitrust Act: section 1, which

---

2. For analyses of the special economic features of sports leagues, see Walter C. Neale, *The Peculiar Economics of Professional Sports: A Contribution to the Theory of the Firm in Sporting Competition and in Market Competition*, 78 Quarterly J. of Econ. 1 (1964); James Quirk & Mohammed El Hodiri, The Economic Theory of a Professional Sports League, Chapter 1 of Roger Noll ed., *Government and the Sports* *Business* (Washington, D.C.: Brookings, 1974); Henry G. Demmert, *The Economics of Professional Team Sports* (Lexington, Mass.: D.C. Heath, 1973); and George G. Daly, The Baseball Player's Labor Market Revisited, Chapter 1 of Paul M. Sommers ed., *Diamonds Are Forever: The Business of Baseball* (Washington, D.C.: Brookings, 1992).

bars any "contract, combination, or conspiracy ... in restraint of trade," and section 2, which bars any effort to "monopolize or attempt to monopolize" a market. In turn, three different types of challengers may be found against league practices. One group consists of third parties attempting to deal with the existing league, such as players, fans, stadiums, aspiring club owners, and television networks. The second group includes team owners who may oppose a rule or policy of their league. The third type of challenger is a new league trying to develop and maintain itself as a viable competitor to the established league. This chapter considers how the law has treated the first two groups; the next chapter examines the third.

Chapter 3 gave a detailed picture of the manner in which section 1 of the Sherman Act enabled courts to strike down league restraints on the players' market. This chapter takes another look at the antitrust "rule of reason"—here as applied to league decisions about team owners, franchise locations, and television policies. In this setting we will also focus on a crucial legal issue that underlies all section 1 sports litigation within both the product and the labor markets. Does a sports league consist of a collection of distinct and economically competitive clubs who have come together to cooperate in some aspects of otherwise autonomous businesses—akin to NUMMI Motors, formed by General Motors and Toyota? Or is the sports league more aptly treated as a single integrated entity, analogous to a national law firm with partners based in several cities, which is thus incapable of *conspiracy* in restraint of trade when it establishes its internal operating rules and structure?[3] Logically, the "single entity" defense was potentially available against the antitrust suits by players and their associations in the 1970s. However, the argument was not seriously advanced by league defendants until the early 1980s in response to section 1 antitrust suits brought by individual owners who objected to particular decisions made

---

3. Except for the labor exemption issue studied in Chapter 3, the "single entity" issue has produced more scholarly debate than any other question in sports law. The issue was first explored in a series of articles in the early 1980s. Compare Myron C. Grauer, *Recognition of the National Football League as a Single Entity Under Section 1 of the Sherman Act: Implications of the Consumer Welfare Model*, 82 Michigan L. Rev. 1 (1983), *and* Gary R. Roberts, *Sports Leagues and the Sherman Act: The Use and Abuse of Section 1 to Regulate Restraints on Intraleague Rivalry*, 32 UCLA L. Rev. 219 (1984) (both arguing for single entity treatment), *with* Daniel E. Lazaroff, *The Antitrust Implications of Franchise Relocation Restrictions in Professional Sports*, 53 Fordham L. Rev. 1157 (1984) (arguing against the single entity theory); see also Gary R. Roberts, *The Single Entity Status of Sports Leagues Under*

Section 1 of the Sherman Act: An Alternative View, 60 Tulane L. Rev. 562 (1986) (rebutting Lazaroff). A second round took place at the end of the 1980s. See Daniel E. Lazaroff, *Antitrust and Sports Leagues: Re-Examining the Threshold Questions*, 20 Arizona State L. J. 953 (1988) (against); Lee Goldman, *Sports, Antitrust, and the Single Entity Theory*, 63 Tulane L. Rev. 751 (1989) (against); Myron C. Grauer, *The Use and Misuse of the Term "Consumer Welfare": Once More to the Mat on the Issue of Single Entity Status for Sports Leagues Under Section 1 of the Sherman Act*, 64 Tulane L. Rev. 71 (1989) (in favor); Gary R. Roberts, *The Antitrust Status of Sports Leagues Revisited*, 64 Tulane L. Rev. 17 (1989) (in favor); and Michael S. Jacobs, *Professional Sports Leagues, Antitrust, and the Single-Entity Theory: A Defense of the Status Quo*, 67 Indiana L. J. 25 (1991) (against).

by their own leagues, under constitutions to which the plaintiffs themselves were parties.

The main battleground in this antitrust war concerned efforts by one NFL club to move the team—in particular, the site of its home games—from one metropolitan area to another. An interesting rehearsal, though, for the basic arguments about league authority versus club autonomy came from a decade-long effort by the National Football League to erect strict barriers against any of its club owners, CEOs, or their families owning an interest in clubs in other sports leagues.[4] In terms of antitrust policy, this league effort would have its major impact (if any) on competition between the NFL and the leagues in other sports, such as baseball, basketball, hockey, and soccer. However, the North American Soccer League framed its legal challenge to the NFL's proposed rule under section 1 of the Sherman Act. The NFL argued, and the trial judge agreed, that no section 1 recourse was available against policies agreed-upon by participants in a single league entity. See *NASL v. NFL*, 505 F.Supp. 659 (S.D.N.Y.1980). The following opinion was the first appellate court ruling to address this issue.

NASL v. NFL

United States Court of Appeals, Second Circuit, 1982.

670 F.2d 1249.

MANSFIELD, CIRCUIT JUDGE.

[Beginning in the 1950s, the NFL had an informal policy against any of its club owners controlling teams in other leagues. That policy became controversial in the late 1960s when the NASL was formed with Lamar Hunt, owner of the NFL's Kansas City Chiefs, serving as major promoter of the NASL and owner of its Dallas Tornados. Some time later, Miami Dolphins' owner Joe Robbie gained a controlling interest (through his wife) in the NASL's Fort Lauderdale franchise. Two of Hunt's and Robbie's most vocal critics were Leonard Tose of the Philadelphia Eagles and Max Winter of the Minnesota Vikings, who each faced considerable competition from NASL teams in his city. Finally, the NFL amended its by-laws in October 1978 to impose substantial fines and ultimate divestiture upon any football owner who by himself or through his family owned or operated a team in another league. The NASL, backed by Hunt and Robbie, then filed this antitrust suit raising the single entity issue.]

* * *

The NFL is an unincorporated joint venture consisting of 28 individually owned separate professional football teams, each operated through a distinct corporation or partnership, which is engaged in the business of providing public entertainment in the form of competitive

---

4. On the background, see Harris, *The*   108–11, 317–24.
League, note 1 above, at 91–92, 94–100,

football games between its member teams. It is the only major league professional football association in the United States. Upon becoming a member of the NFL a team owner receives a non-assignable franchise giving him the exclusive right to operate an NFL professional football team in a designated home city and "home territory," and to play football games in that territory against other NFL members according to a schedule and terms arranged by the NFL.

The success of professional football as a business depends on several factors. The ultimate goal is to attract as many people as possible to pay money to attend games between members and to induce advertisers to sponsor TV broadcasts of such games, which results in box-office receipts from sale of tickets and revenues derived from network advertising, all based on public interest in viewing games. If adequate revenues are received, a team will operate at a profit after payment of expenses, including players' salaries, stadium costs, referees, travel, maintenance and the like. Toward this goal there must be a number of separate football teams, each dispersed in a location having local public fans willing to buy tickets to games or view them on TV; a group of highly skilled players on each team who are reasonably well-matched in playing ability with those of other teams; adequate capital to support the teams' operations; uniform rules of competition governing game play; home territory stadia available for the conduct of the games; referees; and an apparatus for the negotiation and sale of network TV and radio broadcast rights and distribution of broadcast revenues among members.

To perform these functions some sort of an economic joint venture is essential. No single owner could engage in professional football for profit without at least one other competing team. Separate owners for each team are desirable in order to convince the public of the honesty of the competition. Moreover, to succeed in the marketplace by attracting fans the teams must be close in the caliber of their playing ability. As one commentator puts it: "there is a great deal of economic interdependence among the clubs comprising a league. They jointly produce a product which no one of them is capable of producing alone. In addition, the success of the overall venture depends upon the financial stability of each club." J. Weistart & C. Lowell, The Law of Sports 757–58 (1979).

Earlier in this century various professional football leagues existed, outstanding of which were the NFL and AFL (American Football League). In 1970 the AFL merged into the NFL, after receiving Congressional approval to avoid violation of antitrust laws that would otherwise occur.[2] Since then the NFL has assumed full responsibility

2. Although Congress has exempted from antitrust scrutiny the mergers of professional team sports leagues, 15 U.S.C. § 1291, it specifically provided, in adopting this exemption, that "[n]othing contained in this [exemption] shall be deemed to change, determine, or otherwise affect the applicability or nonapplicability of the antitrust laws" to such leagues.

for national promotion of professional football, granting of team franchises, negotiation of network TV contracts for broadcast rights with respect to its members' games, employment of referees, adoption of game rules, scheduling of season games between members leading up to the league championship game known as the Super Bowl, and many other matters pertaining to the national sport. Although specific team profit figures were not introduced at trial, the record is clear that the NFL and most of its members now generally enjoy financial success. The NFL divides pooled TV receipts equally among members. Preseason gate receipts from each game are shared on a 50/50 basis between opposing teams, and regular season gate receipts are divided on the basis of 60% for the home team and 40% for the visiting team.

Although NFL members thus participate jointly in many of the operations conducted by it on their behalf, each member is a separately owned, discrete legal entity which does not share its expenses, capital expenditures or profits with other members. Each also derives separate revenues from certain lesser sources, which are not shared with other members, including revenues from local TV and radio, parking and concessions. A member's gate receipts from its home games varies from those of other members, depending on the size of the home city, the popularity of professional football in the area and competition for spectators offered by other entertainment, including professional soccer. As a result, profits vary from team to team. Indeed as recently as 1978, the last year for which we have records, 2 of the 28 NFL teams suffered losses. In 1977, 12 teams experienced losses. Thus, in spite of sharing of some revenues, the financial performance of each team, while related to that of the others, does not, because of the variables in revenues and costs as between member teams, necessarily rise or fall with that of the others. The NFL teams are separate economic entities engaged in a joint venture.

[With that picture of the NFL's organizational structure, the appeals court summarily rejected the single-entity theory.]

* * *

The characterization of the NFL as a single economic entity does not exempt from the Sherman Act an agreement between its members to restrain competition. To tolerate such a loophole would permit league members to escape antitrust responsibility for any restraint entered into by them that would benefit their league or enhance their ability to compete even though the benefit would be outweighed by its anticompetitive effects. Moreover, the restraint might be one adopted more for the protection of individual league members from competition than to help the league. For instance, the cross-ownership ban in the present case is not aimed merely at protecting the NFL as a league or "single economic entity" from competition from the NASL as a league. Its objective also is to shield certain individual NFL member teams as discrete economic entities from competition in their respective home territories on the part of individual NASL teams that are gaining economic strength in those localities, threatening the revenues of such individual teams. . . . The NFL members have combined to protect and restrain not only leagues but individual teams. The sound and more just procedure is to judge the legality of such restraints according to well-recognized standards of our antitrust laws rather than permit their exemption on the ground that since they in some measure strengthen the league competitively as a "single economic entity," the combination's anticompetitive effects must be disregarded.[5]

[Having acknowledged that the interdependence of team owners in a league required a "rule of reason" analysis of the league's restrictive policies, the court then decided that the anticompetitive effect of the NFL ban on common ownership outweighed its procompetitive values.]

Hld

Because of the economic interdependence of major league team owners and the requirement that any sale be approved by a majority of the league members, an owner may in practice sell his franchise only to a relatively narrow group of eligible purchasers, not to any financier. The potential investor must measure up to a profile having certain characteristics. Moreover, on the supply side of the sports capital market the number of investors willing to purchase an interest in a franchise is sharply limited by the high risk, the need for active involvement in management, the significant exposure to publicity that may turn out to be negative, and the dependence on the drawing power and financial success of the other members of the league. The record thus reveals a market which, while not limited to existing or potential major sports team owners, is relatively limited in scope and is only a small fraction of the total capital funds market. The evidence further reveals that in this sports capital and skill market, owners of major professional sports teams constitute a significant portion. Indeed the existence of such a submarket and the importance of the function of existing team owners as sources of capital in that market are implicitly recognized by the defendants' proven intent in adopting the cross-ownership ban. If they believed, as NFL now argues, that all sources of capital were fungible substitutes for investment in NASL sports teams and that the ban would not significantly foreclose the supply of sports capital, they would hardly have gone to the trouble of adopting it.

Unless the ban has procompetitive effects outweighing its clear restraint on competition, therefore, it is prohibited by § 1 of the Sherman Act. That law does not require proof of the precise boundaries of the sports capital market or the exact percentage foreclosed; it is sufficient to establish, as was done here, the general outlines of a separate submarket of the capital market and that the foreclosed portion of it was likely to be significant.

Rule

5. Even if the NFL were a single firm, that fact would not immunize from § 1 scrutiny the restraint involved here. Vertical agreements between a corporation and its distributors are subject to the rule of reason, Continental TV, Inc. v. GTE Sylvania Inc., 433 U.S. 36, (1977), and we see no reason why an agreement between a corporation and its owners (as the NFL teams owners would be under this assumption) should be treated differently.

NFL argues that the anticompetitive effects of the ban would be outweighed by various procompetitive effects. First it contends that the ban assures it of the undivided loyalty of its team owners in competing effectively against the NASL in the sale of tickets and broadcasting rights, and that cross-ownership might lead NFL cross-owners to soften their demands in favor of their NASL team interests. We do not question the importance of obtaining the loyalty of partners in promoting a common business venture, even if this may have some anticompetitive effect. But in the undisputed circumstances here the enormous financial success of the NFL league despite long-existing cross-ownership by some members of NASL teams demonstrates that there is no market necessity or threat of disloyalty by cross-owners which would justify the ban. Moreover, the NFL was required to come forward with proof that any legitimate purposes could not be achieved through less restrictive means. This it has failed to do. The NFL, for instance, has shown no reason why it could not remedy any conflict of interest arising out of NFL–NASL competition for broadcast rights by removing cross-owners from its broadcast rights negotiating committee.

For the same reasons we reject NFL's argument that the ban is necessary to prevent disclosure by NFL cross-owners of confidential information to NASL competitors. No evidence of the type of information characterized as "confidential" is supplied. Nor is there any showing that the NFL could not be protected against unauthorized disclosure by less restrictive means. Indeed, despite the existence of NFL cross-owners for some years there is no evidence that they have abused confidentiality or that the NFL has found it necessary to adopt confidentiality rules or sanctions. Similarly, there is no evidence that cross-ownership has subjected the personnel and resources of NFL cross-owners to conflicting or excessive demands. On the contrary, successful NFL team owners have been involved in ownership and operation of other outside businesses despite their equal potential for demands on the owners' time and resources. Moreover, a ban on cross-ownership would not insure that NFL team owners would devote any greater level of their resources to team operations than they otherwise would.

Reversed.

———————

Interestingly, in his dissent from the Supreme Court's refusal to review this ruling, then Justice Rehnquist took issue with precisely that last feature of the Second Circuit's decision.

The NFL owners are joint venturers who produce a product, professional football, which competes with other sports and other forms of entertainment in the entertainment market. Although individual NFL teams compete with one another on the playing field, they rarely compete in the marketplace. The NFL negotiates its television contracts, for example, in a single block. The revenues from broadcast rights are pooled. Indeed, the only interteam competition occurs when two teams are located in one major city, such as New York or Los Angeles. These teams compete with one another for home game attendance and local broadcast revenues. In all other respects, the league competes as a unit against other forms of entertainment.

This arrangement, like the arrangement in Broadcast Music, Inc. v. Columbia Broadcasting System, Inc., 441 U.S. 1 (1979), is largely a matter of necessity. If the teams were entirely independent, there could be no consistency of staffing, rules, equipment, or training. All of these are at least arguably necessary to permit the league to create an appealing product in the entertainment market. Thus, NFL football is a different product from what the NFL teams could offer independently, and the NFL, like ASCAP, is "not really a joint sales agency offering the individual goods of many sellers, but is a separate seller offering its [product], of which the individual [teams] are raw material. [The NFL], in short, made a market in which individual [teams] are inherently unable to compete fully effectively."

The cross-ownership rule, then, is a covenant by joint venturers who produce a single product not to compete with one another. The rule governing such agreements was set out over 80 years ago by Judge (later Chief Justice) Taft: A covenant not to compete is valid if "it is merely ancillary to the main purpose of a lawful contract, and necessary to protect the covenantee in the enjoyment of the legitimate fruits of the contract, or to protect him from the dangers of an unjust use of those fruits by the other party." United States v. Addyston Pipe and Steel Co., 85 F. 271, 281 (6th Cir.1898), *aff'd as modified*, 175 U.S. 211 (1899).

The cross-ownership rule seems to me to meet this test. Its purposes are to minimize disputes among the owners and to prevent some owners from using the benefits of their association with the joint venture to compete against it. Participation in the league gives the owner the benefit of detailed knowledge about market conditions for professional sports, the strength and weaknesses of the other teams in the league, and the methods his co-venturers use to compete in the marketplace. It is only reasonable that the owners would seek to prevent their fellows from giving these significant assets, which are in some respects analogous to trade secrets, to their competitors.

The courts have not, to my knowledge, prohibited businesses from requiring employees to agree not to compete with their employer while they remain employed. I cannot believe the Court of Appeals would expect a law firm to countenance its partners working part time at a competing firm while remaining partners. Indeed, this Court has noted that the Rule of Reason does not prohibit a seller of a business from contracting not to compete with the buyer in a reasonable geographic area for a reasonable time *after* he has terminated his relationship with the business. It is difficult for me to understand why the cross-ownership rule is not valid under this standard.

The anticompetitive element of the restraint, as found by the Court of Appeals, is that competitors are denied access to "sports capital and skill." In defining this market, the Court of Appeals noted that although capital is fungible, the skills of successful sports entrepreneurs are not. This entrepreneurial skill, however, is precisely what each NFL owner, as co-venturer, contributes to every other owner.

* * *

In any event, it seems to me that the cross-ownership rule was narrowly drawn to vindicate the legitimate interests described above. The owners are limited only in areas where the special knowledge and skills provided by their co-owners can be expected to be of significant value. They are not prohibited from competing with the NFL in areas of the entertainment market other than professional sports. An owner may invest in television movies, rock concerts, plays, or anything else that suits his fancy.

See 459 U.S. 1073, 1077–80 (1982).

Does Justice Rehnquist's reasoning change your mind about the appeals court's judgment on this score? How is consumer welfare, now a primary policy goal of antitrust law, enhanced or diminished by the Second Circuit's decision?

Questions for Discussion

1. Shortly after this judicial ruling, Ed DeBartolo Sr., whose son Ed Jr. owned the San Francisco 49ers, decided to buy and operate an expansion franchise, the Pittsburgh Maulers, in the new United States Football League (USFL). Similarly, Edward Bennett Williams, minority owner and president of the Washington Redskins, purchased a majority interest in baseball's Baltimore Orioles. If the NFL passed and enforced a rule against these specific forms of cross-ownership, would these bars survive antitrust scrutiny? What variables does *NASL* allow a court to consider in determining whether application of a cross-ownership restriction is lawful under the rule of reason? Are these distinctions sensible?

2. Abstracting from the external legal questions, what are the pros and cons of a ban on cross-ownership from the point of view of the league itself? Unlike the NFL, major league baseball (which does not have to worry about antitrust litigation after *Flood*) has welcomed owners from other leagues and sports. For example, in the summer of 1992 when the Detroit Tigers were sold by one pizza baron, Tom Monaghan (Domino's) to another, Mike Ilitch (Little Caesars), the other baseball owners quickly and unanimously approved Ilitch's entry into baseball even though he was also the owner of the NHL's Detroit Red Wings. If you were the commissioner of a sports league, what policy would you advocate on this score, and why?

3. The *NASL* ruling is arguably relevant to more than just restrictions on cross-ownership. The NFL (again unlike other leagues) has long had a ban on corporate ownership of any of its franchises. A lawsuit has been filed by Billy Sullivan, former owner of the New England Patriots, charging that the NFL violated antitrust law by enforcing this policy against Sullivan when he put the Patriots up for sale in 1988 (and eventually sold the team to Victor Kiam). What do you think will be—what should be—the result of that litigation? What are the values served by such a policy (which again exists only in the NFL)? What are its costs (and how might these figure in calculation of potential antitrust damages)?

4. The single-entity issue is conceptually confounding. What criteria should courts use to determine whether the cooperation of more than one person or corporation is the permissible joint behavior of a single economic entity? For each possible criterion, consider how it would apply to corporations with multiple divisions or to law partnerships. Also consider whether and how each criterion promotes antitrust policy.

The true nature of a sports league—as either a joint venture of independent clubs or a single entity comprised of separately managed divisions—has arisen in other contexts. For example, recall from Chapter 4 that the National Labor Relations Board held (and the Fifth Circuit agreed) that the North American Soccer League was a "joint employer" subject to a single bargaining unit of players represented by its Players' Association. A few years later the USFL Players' Association brought suit against the League to collect the unpaid salaries of players for the defunct Portland Breakers' franchise. In ruling against the Players Association the judge emphasized the difference between *joint* and *single* employer status and held that a sports league did not exhibit the integrated operation under common ownership and management that warranted "single employer" treatment. See *USFLPA v. USFL*, 650 F.Supp. 12 (D.Or.1986). Having seen in earlier chapters the league policies that establish uniform player contracts, entry-level drafts, waiver and trade rules, and restrictions on veteran free agency, do you agree that players left unpaid by one franchise should have no recourse against the league as a whole? Is this relevant to whether a league is a single entity for antitrust purposes?

In another case, *Professional Hockey Corp. v. World Hockey Ass'n*, 143 Cal.App.3d 410, 191 Cal.Rptr. 773 (1983), a California court held that the representatives of each franchise on the Board of Trustees of the WHA (a corporate entity) had a fiduciary duty to act for the benefit of the league as a whole when making decisions about common league goals—in this case whether to approve a new league owner whose financial strength or weakness could affect the league-wide venture. The court explicitly rejected the argument that merely because the San Diego Chargers, for example, were involved in fierce athletic competition with the Los Angeles Raiders, this meant Gene Klein, then owner of the Chargers, owed no duty of "obedience, diligence, and loyalty" to his bitter rival, Raiders' owner Al Davis.

In the WHA case, the court did not have to decide how far the fiduciary duty of corporate directors extends because the judge found no factual basis for any breach of such a duty. However, under general partnership law, which treats joint ventures as a type of partnership, each partner has a fiduciary duty to place the interests of the venture above his own interests unless the partnership agreement or the other partners allow otherwise. The case next-described from the summer of 1992—a case we considered in Chapter 1 with reference to the authority of the commissioner—raises the question of how far that fiduciary duty of the team might go.

The National League baseball owners as a whole favored having the Chicago Cubs and the Atlanta Braves switch places in the League's eastern and western divisions, both to enhance geographic rivalries and to reduce travelling time and costs. However, the Cubs' owner, the Chicago Tribune, exercised its power under the National League constitution to veto the proposed realignment, reportedly because it feared that adding late-starting west coast games to the Cubs' schedule would detract from the television ratings of the Cubs' games broadcast on the team's corporate sibling, the Chicago superstation WGN. Then Commissioner Vincent overrode the Cubs' veto because he believed the new alignment was in the best interests of baseball. As we saw in Chapter 1, the Cubs persuaded a federal judge in Chicago to block the Commissioner's action, and in the aftermath of Vincent's forced resignation the matter was dropped pending a study of broader realignment in baseball. But whether or not a commissioner has authority to override individual team prerogatives, should each owner have a judicially enforceable duty to vote in favor of the interests of the league at the expense of its own team's financial rewards? If so, should the Chicago Tribune (with its Cubs and WGN), owner Ted Turner (who owns both the Atlants Braves and the first cable superstation, WTBS), and George Steinbrenner (who owns the New York Yankees' and enjoys a lucrative television contract with Madison Square Garden network), be under a fiduciary duty to vote in favor of sharing of their teams' television revenues with poorer teams such as the Seattle Mariners, the Kansas City Royals, and the Pittsburgh Pirates? How does revenue-sharing relate to the single entity issue?

B. ADMISSION AND RELOCATION OF SPORTS FRANCHISES

Perhaps the most hotly contested sports law question in the 1980s concerned league control over admission of new franchises to the league, and relocation of those franchises once admitted.[5] The constitu-

---

5. Besides the articles cited in note 3 above, see John C. Weistart, *Control of* *Market Opportunities: A Perspective on Competition and Cooperation in the Sports*

tional documents and practices in all sports leagues have always required at least super-majority (if not unanimous) consent to the creation of any new franchise and the acceptance of a new owner into the league. Once part of the league, the franchisee enjoys an exclusive right to operate a team in the immediate geographic location. However, any attempt by an owner to move its team to another area would also require consent of the league as a whole. The most recent illustration of this constitutional condition is the decision of Major League Baseball in late 1992 to deny approval of the proposed sale and move of the San Francisco Giants to Tampa Bay—a decision that immediately precipitated litigation in both the Florida and California courts.

An early legal challenge to this traditional league prerogative came in *San Francisco Seals v. NHL*, 379 F.Supp. 966 (C.D.Cal.1974). One of the six NHL expansion franchises created in 1967, the Seals had enjoyed little success in the San Francisco Bay area and so in 1969 sought to move to what was then still vacant territory in Vancouver, British Columbia. The League's board of governors (comprised of one representative from each team) refused to approve the move, and the Seals sued under section 1 of the Sherman Act. The trial court summarily rejected this claim in a brief decision; the key passage was the following:

> What then is the relevant market? I find that the relevant product market with which we are here concerned is the production of professional hockey games before live audiences, and that the relevant geographical market is the United States and Canada.

> Now let us examine plaintiff's relationship with the defendants within the relevant market. Plaintiff, of course, wishes to participate in this market, but not in competition with the defendants. It expects to maintain its league membership and to accept and enjoy all of the exclusive territorial benefits which the National Hockey League affords. As a member team, it will continue cooperating with the defendants in pursuit of its main purpose, i.e., producing sporting events of uniformly high quality appropriately scheduled as to both time and location so as to assure all members of the league the best financial return. In this respect, the plaintiff and defendants are acting together as one single business enterprise, competing against other similarly organized professional leagues.

> The main thrust of the Sherman Act is to prohibit some competitors from combining with other competitors to gain a competitive advantage over other competitors by creating impermissible restraints upon trade or commerce. It is fundamental in a

Industry, 1984 Duke L. J. 1013, and Gary R. Roberts, *The Evolving Confusion of Professional Sports Antitrust, The Rule of Reason, and the Doctrine of Ancillary Restraints*, 61 Southern Calif. L. Rev. 943 (1988). See also James Quirk, *An Economic Analysis of Team Movements in Professional Sports*, 38 L. & Contemp. Prob. 42 (Winter 1973).

section 1 violation that there must be at least two independent business entities accused of combining or conspiring to restrain trade.

Within the relevant market in which we are here concerned, plaintiff and defendants are not competitors in the economic sense. It is of course true that the member teams compete among themselves athletically for championship honors, and they may even compete economically, to a greater or lesser degree, in some other market not relevant to our present inquiry. But, they are not competitors in the economic sense in this relevant market. They are, in fact, all members of a single unit competing as such with other similar professional leagues. Consequently, the organizational scheme of the National Hockey League, by which all its members are bound, imposes no restraint upon trade or commerce in this relevant market, but rather makes possible a segment of commercial activity which could hardly exist without it.

See 379 F.Supp. at 969–70

A decade later came what has aptly been called the "Super Bowl of Sports Litigation." This was the struggle between Commissioner Pete Rozelle and the National Football League and Al Davis, owner of the Raiders, over whether the Raiders were free to leave Oakland, where the team had enjoyed marked athletic and financial success, and move its home base south to Los Angeles, where Davis felt his prospects were even rosier.[6] Of the ten or so judicial rulings reported from this single sports law saga, the following decision is perhaps the most important. In reading this opinion, keep two questions in mind. One is whether the Supreme Court's pending *Copperweld* judgment (excerpted later in this chapter) would have made a difference in the Ninth Circuit's treatment of the "single entity" question. The other is whether this appellate panel's appraisal of the franchise movement issue under "rule of reason" antitrust analysis indicates that relocation is best left to internal league governance or should be subject to outside judicial scrutiny.

LOS ANGELES MEMORIAL COLISEUM COMM'N. v. NFL (RAIDERS I)

United States Court of Appeals, Ninth Circuit, 1984.

726 F.2d 1381.

ANDERSON, CIRCUIT JUDGE.

[This case was precipitated by the 1978 decision of Carroll Rosenbloom, owner of the Los Angeles Rams, to move his team from the Los Angeles Coliseum to Anaheim, attracted by a lucrative lease arrange-

---

6. The Raiders case is treated in depth throughout Harris, *The League*, note 1   above.

ment offered by that city. At the same time, Al Davis had reached a stalemate in efforts to negotiate the terms for renewal of the Raiders' lease with the Oakland Coliseum. Conversations thus began between Davis and L.A. Coliseum officials about a possible Raiders' move to the Coliseum.

Alerted to possible legal difficulties with its relocation procedures, the NFL moved in late 1978 to amend its rules. Rule 4.1 had defined "home territory" as extending for a 75–mile radius from the boundaries of the team's home city as designated in the NFL Constitution. (Thus, Los Angeles was still the home city of the Rams playing in Anaheim.) Rule 4.3 provided that any team proposing to move into another's home territory needed unanimous approval from all other teams. Other relocations required only a three-quarters vote. The amended Rule 4.3 applied the three-quarters formula to all relocations regardless of the new site, which removed the possibility of a veto by the incumbent club.

On March 1, 1980, Davis signed a "memorandum of agreement" to move the Raiders to the L.A. Coliseum. On March 10, 1980, the NFL took a vote on the proposed move (over Davis's objections). The verdict was 22–0 against, with five teams (including the Rams) abstaining.

Shortly thereafter, the Raiders joined a suit filed in 1978 by the Coliseum against the NFL. Over the objections of the NFL (and the Oakland Coliseum, which intervened as a party), Los Angeles was retained as the venue for the jury trial. After a three-month jury trial on liability alone, a trial that focused largely on the single entity defense, Judge Harry Pregerson, who had just become a Ninth Circuit judge, granted a directed verdict for plaintiffs on this issue, and thus removed it from jury consideration. Nonetheless, the jury could not reach a rule of reason verdict and a mistrial was declared. A second lengthy liability trial resulted in a verdict finding that the NFL's action was an unreasonable restraint of trade. An injunction was entered barring the league from blocking the Raiders' relocation, and the NFL immediately appealed. The first issue addressed by the Ninth Circuit panel was the single-entity defense.]

* * *

It is true, as the NFL contends, that the nature of an entity and its ability to combine or conspire in violation of § 1 is a fact question. It would be reversible error, then, to take the issue from the jury if reasonable minds could differ as to its resolution. Here, however, the material facts are undisputed. How the NFL is organized and the nature and extent of cooperation among the member clubs is a matter of record; the NFL Constitution and Bylaws contain the agreement. Based on the undisputed facts and the law on this subject, the district court correctly decided this issue.

The district court cited three reasons for rejecting the NFL's theory. Initially, the court recognized the logical extension of this argument was to make the League incapable of violating Sherman Act

§ 1 in every other subject restriction—yet courts have held the League violated § 1 in other areas. Secondly, other organizations have been found to violate § 1 though their product was "just as unitary . . . and requires the same kind of cooperation from the organization's members." Finally, the district court considered the argument to be based upon the false premise that the individual NFL "clubs are not separate business entities whose products have an independent value." We agree with this reasoning.

NFL rules have been found to violate § 1 in other contexts. Most recently, the Second Circuit analyzed the NFL's rule preventing its member-owners from having ownership interests in other professional sports clubs. North American Soccer League v. National Football League, 670 F.2d 1249, 1257–1259 (2d Cir.1982).

* * *

Cases applying the single entity or joint venture theory in other business areas also contradict the NFL's argument. As stated by the Supreme Court.

> Nor do we find any support in reason or authority for the proposition that agreements between legally separate persons and companies to suppress competition among themselves and others can be justified by labelling the project a "joint venture." Perhaps every agreement and combination in restraint of trade could be so labeled.

Timken Roller Bearing Co. v. United States, 341 U.S. 593, 598, (1951). *Timken* involved an allegation of territorial division among three companies that shared partial common ownership. In Perma Life Mufflers, Inc. v. International Parts Corp., 392 U.S. 134, 141–42 (1968), the Court reiterated that common ownership will not suffice to preclude the application of § 1. While these cases and others have been the subject of some criticism, they remain the law. In recognition that a broad application of *Timken* and *Perma Life* could subvert legitimate procompetitive business associations, this circuit has found the threshold requirement of concerted activity missing among "multiple corporations operated as a single entity" when "corporate policies are set by one individual or by a parent corporation." The facts make it clear the NFL does not fit within this exception. While the NFL clubs have certain common purposes, they do not operate as a single entity. NFL policies are not set by one individual or parent corporation, but by the separate teams acting jointly.

It is true the NFL clubs must cooperate to a large extent in their endeavor in producing a "product"—the NFL season culminating in the Super Bowl. The necessity that otherwise independent businesses cooperate has not, however, sufficed to preclude scrutiny under § 1 of the Sherman Act.

* * *

The case of United States v. Sealy, Inc., 388 U.S. 350 (1967), is closely on point. Sealy licensed manufacturers to sell bedding products under the Sealy name and allocated territories to the licensees. The facts showed, however, that this arrangement was not vertical but horizontal; the 30 licensees, owning all of the stock of Sealy, controlled all its operations. Describing the Sealy organization as a joint venture, the Court nonetheless found it a per se violation of the Sherman Act.

The NFL structure is very similar to that in *Sealy*. The League itself is only in very limited respects an identity separate from the individual teams. It is an unincorporated, not-for-profit "association." It has a New York office run by the Commissioner, Pete Rozelle, who makes day-to-day decisions regarding League operations. Its primary functions are in the areas of scheduling, resolving disputes among players and franchises, supervising officials, discipline and public relations. The decision involved here on territorial divisions is made by the NFL Executive Committee, which is comprised of a representative of each club. Even though the individual clubs often act for the common good of the NFL, we must not lose sight of the purpose of the NFL as stated in Article I of its constitution, which is to "promote and foster the primary business of League members." Although the business interests of League members will often coincide with those of the NFL as an entity in itself, that commonality of interest exists in every cartel. As in *Sealy*, we must look behind the label proffered by the defendants to determine the substance of the entity in question.

Our inquiry discloses an association of teams sufficiently independent and competitive with one another to warrant rule of reason scrutiny under § 1 of the Sherman Act. The NFL clubs are, in the words of the district court, "separate business entities whose products have an independent value." The member clubs are all independently owned. Most are corporations, some are partnerships, and apparently a few are sole proprietorships. Although a large portion of League revenue, approximately 90%, is divided equally among the teams, profits and losses are not shared, a feature common to partnerships or other "single entities." In fact, profits vary widely despite the sharing of revenue. The disparity in profits can be attributed to independent management policies regarding coaches, players, management personnel, ticket prices, concessions, luxury box seats, as well as franchise location, all of which contribute to fan support and other income sources.

In addition to being independent business entities, the NFL clubs do compete with one another off the field as well as on to acquire players, coaches, and management personnel. In certain areas of the country where two teams operate in close proximity, there is also competition for fan support, local television and local radio revenues, and media space.

(H.W.)

These attributes operate to make each team an entity in large part distinct from the NFL. It is true that cooperation is necessary to produce a football game. However, as the district court concluded, this does not mean "that each club can produce football games only as an NFL member." This is especially evident in light of the emergence of the United States Football League.

[Just like the Second Circuit in the *NASL* case, the Ninth Circuit majority recognized that the operation of the NFL as a joint venture required a rule of reason analysis of Rule 4.3 and its application.]

In a quite general sense, the case presents the competing considerations of whether a group of businessmen can enforce an agreement with one of their co-contractors to the detriment of that co-contractor's right to do business where he pleases. More specifically, this lawsuit requires us to engage in the difficult task of analyzing the negative and positive effects of a business practice in an industry which does not readily fit into the antitrust context. Section 1 of the Sherman Act was designed to prevent agreements among competitors which eliminate or reduce competition and thereby harm consumers. Yet, as we discussed in the context of the single entity issue, the NFL teams are not true competitors, nor can they be.

The NFL's structure has both horizontal and vertical attributes. On the one hand, it can be viewed simply as an organization of 28 competitors, an example of a simple horizontal arrangement. On the other, and to the extent the NFL can be considered an entity separate from the team owners, a vertical relationship is disclosed. In this sense the owners are distributors of the NFL product, each with its own territorial division. In this context it is clear that the owners have a legitimate interest in protecting the integrity of the League itself. Collective action in areas such as League divisions, scheduling and rules must be allowed, as should other activity that aids in producing the most marketable product attainable. Nevertheless, legitimate collective action should not be construed to allow the owners to extract excess profits. In such a situation the owners would be acting as a classic cartel. Agreements among competitors, i.e., cartels, to fix prices or divide market territories are presumed illegal under § 1 because they give competitors the ability to charge unreasonable and arbitrary prices instead of setting prices by virtue of free market forces.

On its face, Rule 4.3 divides markets among the 28 teams, a practice presumed illegal, but, as we have noted, the unique structure of the NFL precludes application of the per se rule. Instead, we must examine Rule 4.3 to determine whether it reasonably serves the legitimate collective concerns of the owners or instead permits them to reap excess profits at the expense of the consuming public.

1. RELEVANT MARKET

The NFL contends it is entitled to judgment because plaintiffs failed to prove an adverse impact on competition in a relevant market.

* * *

The relevant market provides the basis on which to balance competitive harms and benefits of the restraint at issue. Such evidence is essential in a Section 1 case.

* * *

In the antitrust context, the relevant market has two components: the product market and the geographic market. Product market definition involves the:

> process of describing those groups of producers which, because of the similarity of their products, have the ability—actual or potential—to take significant amounts of business away from each other. A market definition must look at all relevant sources of supply, either actual rivals or eager potential entrants to the market.

Two related tests are used in arriving at the product market: first, reasonable interchangeability for the same or similar uses; and second, cross-elasticity of demand, an economic term describing the responsiveness of sales of one product to price changes in another. Similar considerations determine the relevant geographic market, which describes the "economically significant" area of effective competition in which the relevant products are traded.

The claims of the Raiders and the L.A. Coliseum, respectively, present somewhat different market considerations. The Raiders attempted to prove the relevant market consists of NFL football (the product market) in the Southern California area (the geographic market). The NFL argues it competes with all forms of entertainment within the United States, not just Southern California. The L.A. Coliseum claims the relevant market is stadia offering their facilities to NFL teams (the product market) in the United States (the geographic market). The NFL agrees with this geographic market, but argues the product market involves cities competing for all forms of stadium entertainment, including NFL football teams.

That NFL football has limited substitutes from a consumer standpoint is seen from evidence that the Oakland Coliseum sold out for 10 consecutive years despite having some of the highest ticket prices in the League. A similar conclusion can be drawn from the extraordinary number of television viewers—over 100 million people—that watched the 1982 Super Bowl, the ultimate NFL product. NFL football's importance to the television networks is evidenced by the approximately $2 billion they agreed to pay the League for the right to televise the games from 1982–1986. This contract reflects the networks' anticipation that the high number of television viewers who had watched NFL football in the past would continue to do so in the future.

To some extent, the NFL itself narrowly defined the relevant market by emphasizing that NFL football is a unique product which can be produced only through the joint efforts of the 28 teams. Don

Shula, coach of the Miami Dolphins, underscored this point when he stated that NFL football has a different set of fans than college football.

The evidence from which the jury could have found a narrow pro football product market was balanced, however, with other evidence which tended to show the NFL competes in the first instance with other professional sports, especially those with seasons that overlap with the NFL's. On a broader level, witnesses such as Pete Rozelle and Georgia Frontierre (owner of the L.A. Rams) testified that NFL football competes with other television offerings for network business, as well as other local entertainment for attendance at the games.

In terms of the relevant geographic market, witnesses testified, in particular Al Davis, that NFL teams compete with one another off the field for fan support in those areas where teams operate in close proximity such as New York City–New Jersey, Washington, D.C.- Baltimore, and formerly San Francisco–Oakland. Davis, of course, had firsthand knowledge of this when his team was located in Oakland. Also, the San Francisco Forty–Niners and the New York Giants were paid $18 million because of the potential for harm from competing with the Oakland Raiders and the New York Jets, respectively, once those teams joined the NFL as a result of the merger with the American Football League. Al Davis also testified at length regarding the potential for competition for fan support between the Raiders and the Los Angeles Rams once his team relocated in Los Angeles.

Testimony also adequately described the parameters of the stadia market. On one level, stadia do compete with one another for the tenancy of NFL teams. Such competition is shown by the Rams' move to Anaheim. Carroll Rosenbloom was offered what he considered to be a more lucrative situation at the Big A Stadium, so he left the L.A. Coliseum. In turn, the L.A. Coliseum sought to lure existing NFL teams to Los Angeles. Competition between the L.A. Coliseum and the Oakland Coliseum for the tenancy of the Raiders resulted.

It is true, as the NFL argues, that competition among stadia for the tenancy of professional football teams is presently limited. It is limited, however, because of the operation of Rule 4.3. Prior to this lawsuit, most teams were allowed to relocate only within their home territory. That is why Carroll Rosenbloom could move his team to Anaheim. This is not to say the potential for competition did not previously exist. There was evidence to the effect that the NFL in the past remained expressly noncommitted on the question of team movement. This was done to give owners a bargaining edge when they were renegotiating leases with their respective stadia. The owner could threaten a move if the lease terms were not made more favorable.

The NFL claims that it is places, not particular stadia, that compete for NFL teams. This is true to a point because the NFL grants franchises to locales (generally a city and a 75 mile radius extending from its boundary). It is the individual stadia, however, which are most directly impacted by the restrictions on team movement. A stadium is a distinct economic entity and a territory is not.

It is also undoubtedly true, as the NFL contends, that stadia attempt to contract with a variety of forms of entertainment for exhibition in their facilities. In the case of the L.A. Coliseum, this includes college football, concerts, motorcycle races and the like. An NFL football team, however, is an especially desirable tenant. The L.A. Coliseum, for example, had received the highest rent from the Rams when they played there. We find that this evidence taken as a whole provided the jury with an adequate basis on which to judge the reasonableness of Rule 4.3 both as it affected competition among NFL teams and among stadia.

We conclude with one additional observation. In the context of this case in particular, we believe that market evidence, while important, should not become an end in itself. Here the exceptional nature of the industry makes precise market definition especially difficult. To a large extent the market is determined by how one defines the entity: Is the NFL a single entity or partnership which creates a product that competes with other entertainment products for the consumer (e.g., television and fans) dollar? Or is it 28 individual entities which compete with one another both on and off the field for the support of the consumers of the more narrow football product? Of course, the NFL has attributes of both examples and a variety of evidence was presented on both views. In fact, because of the exceptional structure of the League, it was not necessary for the jury to accept absolutely either the NFL's or the plaintiff's market definitions. Instead, the critical question is whether the jury could have determined that Rule 4.3 reasonably served the NFL's interest in producing and promoting its product, i.e., competing in the entertainment market, or whether Rule 4.3 harmed competition among the 28 teams to such an extent that any benefits to the League as a whole were outweighed. As we find below, there was ample evidence for the jury to reach the latter conclusion.

2. The History and Purpose of Rule 4.3

The NFL has awarded franchises exclusive territories since the 1930s. In the early days of professional football, numerous franchises failed and many changed location in the hope of achieving economic success. League members saw exclusive territories as a means to aid stability, ensuring the owner who was attempting to establish an NFL team in a particular city that another would not move into the same area, potentially ruining them both.

Rule 4.3 is the result of that concern. Prior to its amendment in 1978, it required unanimous League approval for a move into another team's home territory. That, of course, gave each owner an exclusive territory and he could vote against a move into his territory solely because he was afraid the competition might reduce his revenue. Notably, however, the League constitution required only three-quarters approval for all other moves. The 1978 amendment removed the double-standard, and currently three-quarters approval is required for all moves.

That the purpose of Rule 4.3 was to restrain competition among the 28 teams may seem obvious and it is not surprising the NFL admitted as much at trial. It instead argues that Rule 4.3 serves a variety of legitimate League needs, including ensuring franchise stability. We must keep in mind, however, that the Supreme Court has long rejected the notion that "ruinous competition" can be a defense to a restraint of trade. Conversely, anticompetitive purpose alone is not enough to condemn Rule 4.3. The rule must actually harm competition, and that harm must be evaluated in light of the procompetitive benefits the rule might foster.

3. ANCILLARY RESTRAINTS AND THE REASONABLENESS OF RULE 4.3

The NFL's primary argument is that it is entitled to judgment notwithstanding the verdict because under the facts and the law, Rule 4.3 is reasonable under the doctrine of ancillary restraints. The NFL's argument is inventive and perhaps it will breathe new life into this little used area of antitrust law, but we reject it for the following reasons.

The common-law ancillary restraint doctrine was, in effect, incorporated into Sherman Act section 1 analysis by Justice Taft in *United States v. Addyston Pipe & Steel Co.*, 85 F. 271 (6th Cir.1898), aff'd as modified, 175 U.S. 211 (1899). Most often discussed in the area of covenants not to compete, the doctrine teaches that some agreements which restrain competition may be valid if they are "subordinate and collateral to another legitimate transaction and necessary to make that transaction effective."

Generally, the effect of a finding of ancillarity is to "remove the per se label from restraints otherwise falling within that category." R. Bork, Ancillary Restraints and the Sherman Act, 15 Antitrust L.J. 211, 212 (1959). We assume, with no reason to doubt, that the agreement creating the NFL is valid and the territorial divisions therein are ancillary to its main purpose of producing NFL football. The ancillary restraint must then be tested under the rule of reason, the relevance of ancillarity being it "increases the probability that the restraint will be found reasonable." As we have already noted, the rule of reason inquiry requires us to consider the harms and benefits to competition caused by the restraint and whether the putative benefits can be achieved by less restrictive means.

The competitive harms of Rule 4.3 are plain. Exclusive territories insulate each team from competition within the NFL market, in essence allowing them to set monopoly prices to the detriment of the consuming public. The rule also effectively foreclosed free competition among stadia such as the Los Angeles Coliseum that- wish to secure NFL tenants. The harm from Rule 4.3 is especially acute in this case because it prevents a move by a team into another existing team's market. If the transfer is upheld, direct competition between the Rams and Raiders would presumably ensue to the benefit of all who consume the NFL product in the Los Angeles area.

The NFL argues, however, that territorial allocations are inherent in an agreement among joint venturers to produce a product. This inherent nature, the NFL asserts, flows from the need to protect each joint venturer in the "legitimate fruits of the contract, or to protect him from the dangers of an unjust use of those fruits by the other party." We agree that the nature of NFL football requires some territorial restrictions in order both to encourage participation in the venture and to secure each venturer the legitimate fruits of that participation.

Rule 4.3 aids the League, the NFL claims, in determining its overall geographical scope, regional balance and coverage of major and minor markets. Exclusive territories aid new franchises in achieving financial stability, which protects the large initial investment an owner must make to start up a football team. Stability arguably helps ensure no one team has an undue advantage on the field. Territories foster fan loyalty which in turn promotes traditional rivalries between teams, each contributing to attendance at games and television viewing.

Joint marketing decisions are surely legitimate because of the importance of television. Title 15, U.S.C. § 1291 grants the NFL an exemption from antitrust liability, if any, that might arise out of its collective negotiation of television rights with the networks. To effectuate this right, the League must be allowed to have some control over the placement of teams to ensure NFL football is popular in a diverse group of markets.

Last, there is some legitimacy to the NFL's argument that it has an interest in preventing transfers from areas before local governments, which have made a substantial investment in stadia and other facilities, can recover their expenditures. In such a situation, local confidence in the NFL is eroded, possibly resulting in a decline in interest. All these factors considered, we nevertheless are not persuaded the jury should have concluded that Rule 4.3 is a reasonable restraint of trade. The same goals can be achieved in a variety of ways which are less harmful to competition.

As noted by Justice Rehnquist, a factor in determining the reasonableness of an ancillary restraint is the "possibility of less restrictive alternatives" which could serve the same purpose. See Justice Rehnquist's dissent from the denial of certiorari in *North American Soccer League*, 459 U.S. 1074 (1982). This is a pertinent factor in all rule of reason cases. Here, the district court correctly instructed the jury to take into account the existence of less restrictive alternatives when determining the reasonableness of Rule 4.3's territorial restraint. Because there was substantial evidence going to the existence of such alternatives, we find that the jury could have reasonably concluded that the NFL should have designed its "ancillary restraint" in a manner that served its needs but did not so foreclose competition.

The NFL argues that the requirement of Rule 4.3 that three-quarters of the owners approve a franchise move is reasonable because it deters unwise team transfers. While the rule does indeed protect an owner's investment in a football franchise, no standards or durational limits are incorporated into the voting requirement to make sure that concern is satisfied. Nor are factors such as fan loyalty and team rivalries necessarily considered.

The NFL claims that its marketing and other objectives are indirectly accounted for in the voting process because the team owners vote to maximize their profits. Since the owners are guided by the desire to increase profits, they will necessarily make reasonable decisions, the NFL asserts, on such issues of whether the new location can support two teams, whether marketing needs will be adversely affected, etc. Under the present Rule 4.3, however, an owner need muster only seven friendly votes to prevent three-quarters approval for the sole reason of preventing another team from entering its market, regardless of whether the market could sustain two franchises. A basic premise of the Sherman Act is that regulation of private profit is best left to the marketplace rather than private agreement. The present case is in fact a good example of how the market itself will deter unwise moves, since a team will not lightly give up an established base of support to confront another team in its home market.

The NFL's professed interest in ensuring that cities and other local governments secure a return on their investment in stadia is undercut in two ways. First, the local governments ought to be able to protect their investment through the leases they negotiate with the teams for the use of their stadia. Second, the NFL's interest on this point may not be as important as it would have us believe because the League has in the past allowed teams to threaten a transfer to another location in order to give the team leverage in lease negotiations.

Finally, the NFL made no showing that the transfer of the Raiders to Los Angeles would have any harmful effect on the League. Los Angeles is a market large enough for the successful operation of two teams, there would be no scheduling difficulties, facilities at the L.A. Coliseum are more than adequate, and no loss of future television revenue was foreseen. Also, the NFL offered no evidence that its interest in maintaining regional balance would be adversely affected by a move of a northern California team to southern California.

It is true, as the NFL claims, that the antitrust laws are primarily concerned with the promotion of interbrand competition. To the extent the NFL is a product which competes with other forms of entertainment, including other sports, its rules governing territorial division can be said to promote interbrand competition. Under this analysis, the territorial allocations most directly suppress intrabrand, that is, NFL team versus NFL team, competition. A more direct impact on intrabrand competition does not mean, however, the restraint is reasonable. The finder of fact must still balance the gain to interbrand competition against the loss of intrabrand competition. Here, the jury could have found that the rules restricting team movement do not sufficiently promote interbrand competition to justify the negative impact on intrabrand competition.

To withstand antitrust scrutiny, restrictions on team movement should be more closely tailored to serve the needs inherent in producing the NFL "product" and competing with other forms of entertainment. An express recognition and consideration of those objective factors espoused by the NFL as important, such as population, economic projections, facilities, regional balance, etc., would be well advised. Fan loyalty and location continuity could also be considered. Al Davis in fact testified that in 1978 he proposed that the League adopt a set of objective guidelines to govern team relocation rather than continuing to utilize a subjective voting procedure.

Some sort of procedural mechanism to ensure consideration of all the above factors may also be necessary, including an opportunity for the team proposing the move to present its case. See Silver v. New York Stock Exchange, 373 U.S. 341 (1963) (without procedural safeguards, the collective act of the Exchange in disconnecting the wire service to a broker constituted a boycott, per se illegal under § 1); cf. Deesen v. Professional Golfers Ass'n, 358 F.2d 165 (9th Cir.1966) (where PGA had reasonable rules governing eligibility of players for tournaments, there was not a § 1 violation). In the present case, for example, testimony indicated that some owners, as well as Commissioner Rozelle, dislike Al Davis and consider him a maverick. Their vote against the Raiders' move could have been motivated by animosity rather than business judgment.

Substantial evidence existed for the jury to find the restraint imposed by Rule 4.3 was not reasonably necessary to the production and sale of the NFL product. Therefore, the NFL is not entitled to judgment notwithstanding the verdict.

Affirmed.

[The appeals court majority concluded, then, that the jury's verdict about the unreasonableness of this restraint—the opinion labelled this a "paradigm fact question"—was based on adequate evidence in the record. The majority judgment elicited the following vigorous dissent, which focused on the single-entity question.]

JUDGE WILLIAMS, dissenting.

* * *

The only realistic manner in which to define what constitutes a single entity for antitrust review is to focus upon the purpose the definition is to serve. "Single entity" taken in a functional sense begins and ends with an analysis of formal organizational and operational aspects of an enterprise, reconciled with the realities of the economic competition in the marketplace. If the aim of the Sherman Act § 1 is consumer-dictated supply, unfettered by conspiracy between competing producers—and, I submit that it is—extreme caution is warranted in defining precisely what competitive units exist in the marketplace. It is equally as important to permit collaboration and concerted action among branches of a single economic entity in the marketplace with impunity from the Sherman Act § 1, as it is to police conspiracies between economic competitive entities. Nonetheless, all economic units remain susceptible to challenge under the antitrust laws from those external entities injured by acts violative of § 1, or competitive entities injured as result of monopoly, or attempted monopoly, in an industry under Sherman Act § 2 tenets.

Resolving whether the NFL is a single entity requires consideration of many factors, including formalistic aspects of operations such as ownership, overlapping directorates, joint marketing or manufacturing, legal identity, corporate law autonomy, and substantive aspects such as de facto autonomy of member clubs, chains of command over policy decisions, public perception and economic interdependency rendering otherwise independent member clubs subordinate to the integrated whole. When the entities in question are to be evaluated under the antitrust laws, the crucial criterion is whether the formally distinct member clubs compete in any economically meaningful sense in the marketplace.

* * *

The district court placed an unwarranted emphasis upon the formalistic aspects of the relationship of the NFL and the member clubs, ignoring the subtle, but yet more significant interdependency of the member clubs and the indivisibility of the clubs with the NFL. For example, the district court makes much of two such formal organizational characteristics: separate incorporation and management. But, when viewed from the mundane perspective of daily operations, emphasis upon these legal formalisms obscures the reality of life in the NFL. Only the athletic strategems are autonomous—albeit tightly constrained by league guidelines on eligibility, medical and physical condition and exploitation of player talent. The NFL cannot truly be separated from its member clubs, which are simultaneously franchisees and franchisors. The Raiders did not, and do not now, seek to compete with the other clubs in any sense other than in their win/loss standings; they do not challenge the plethora of other ancillary regulations attendant to the league structure, including the draft, regulation and scheduling of meetings between teams, and the system of pooled and shared revenues among the clubs because they wish to remain within its beneficial ambit.

* * *

[F]unctionally distinct units that cannot produce separate, individual goods or services absent coordination are inextricably bound in an economic sense, and must adopt certain intra-league instrumentalities to regulate the whole's "downstream output." In the case of the member clubs, this "downstream output" is professional football, and the organ of regulation is the unincorporated, not-for-profit, association commonly known as the NFL. There is virtually no practical distinction between the League, administered by the appointed Commissioner, per se and the member clubs; the NFL represents to all clubs, including the Raiders, the least costly and most efficient manner of reaching day-to-day decisions regarding the production of their main, and collectively produced, product.

Although the NFL determines matters of scheduling, resolving player disciplinary matters and inter-club disputes as well as other routine matters, critical league decisions, such as the matter of franchise location, are submitted to an Executive Committee comprised of a representative of each club. There can be no instance of the Executive Committee acting in other than the collective interests of the member clubs, since by definition, that body's decisions are the consensus of NFL members. There is no distinct interest of the NFL, since it exists solely to coordinate the members' participation in the joint production of professional football.

By riveting its attention upon the "single entity" issue, as a sort of talismanic affirmative defense to the appellees' charges here, the district court overlooked the dispositive inquiry of whether Rule 4.3, as an instrument of the NFL member clubs, violated the Sherman Act § 1, by restricting any economically independent entities from supplying goods or services related to professional football to the individual clubs. I use "upstream flow" as shorthand for products and services like players and coaches, television services, potential investors and the myriad of other integrated industries; member clubs do have independent and economically significant identities apart from the collective NFL for the limited purposes of their extra-league dealings with those upstream suppliers. Thus, § 1 can and should protect the competitive aspects of player drafts, disallow cross-ownership bans and exclusive television and equipment contracts, by insuring that any one club's interaction outside the confines of intra-league regulation of production of the sport is unfettered by the working of any intraleague rule.

This is the critical distinction between cases which invalidate various intraleague rules, and those which uphold them. That member clubs compete for investors and the services of talented players is underscored by the fact that, although aggregate revenues are shared among all member clubs, there is no intra-league regulation upon the form of investment by a member club's financial backers, the dividend policy, or operating expenses and expenditures of any member for player services. League regulations comport with economic reality in this sense; courts have merely applied a similar philosophy to other aspects of the professional leagues' operations, including, inter alia, club-player relationships.

The paradox to which I return, as the root of why the NFL, as well as other sports leagues, must be regarded as a "single entity" is that the keener the on-field competition becomes, the more successful their off-the-field, and ultimately legally relevant, collaboration. The formal entities, including the member clubs—including the Raiders—which the district court ruled to be competitors cannot compete, because the only product or service which is in their separate interests to produce can only result as a fruit of their joint efforts. This systemic cooperation trickles down to all members of the league, regardless of their on-the-field record, at least to the extent of the shared revenues....

A ruling that the NFL cannot enforce Rule 4.3 is effectively ruling that it may not enforce any collective decision of its member clubs over the dissent of a club member, although this is precisely what each owner has contractually bargained for in joining the enterprise. Without power to reach collective decisions, the NFL structure becomes superfluous, and professional sports, without a cost-effective policing mechanism such as the league, will dissolve in the face of uncontrollable free-riding and loss of economies of scale.

Not only did the district court underrate the business scenario in which the member teams cooperate far more than they compete in the legally irrelevant on-field sense, but its directed verdict on the single entity issue ignored two significant aspects of the NFL's organization. First, the NFL member clubs pool their revenues to a degree unique even among sporting leagues. By focusing upon the separate calculation of profits and loss by members, the district court elevated form over substance. Profit, as currently understood in the accounting profession, is a term of art, and as such is inherently subjective, often manipulated by equity interests to serve legally irrelevant business motives. The relevant consideration, as the NFL has recognized by implementation of its shared revenue concept, is total infusion of consumer dollars into the sport, and some predictable and centrally administered allocation of those jointly earned revenues among member clubs. After that purpose, the members adopt the only workable model for earning and distributing the revenues from sale of a non-severable and indistinct product—professional football.

The product distributed by the member clubs is not analogous to ball bearings (*Timken Roller Bearing Co. v. U.S.*), mattresses (*U.S. v. Sealy, Inc.*), or groceries (*U.S. v. Topco Associates*), because stripped of the NFL rules, participation in a regulated draft, orderly schedules and league standings, professional football is indistinguishable from sand lot follies. This inescapable fact of interdependence distinguishes the NFL franchisees and professional football from other industries comprised of "separate business entities whose products have independent value."

There was no evidence before the district court establishing that a member club of the NFL could, or would seek to, defect to the USFL, thereby transferring its assets in quest of greater exploitation. Only such a showing, or an alternative theory, supported by evidence in the record could illustrate that any particular member club had an intrinsic value shorn of its affiliation with the NFL, and thus could support the district court's result. We find no such evidence in the record. There is no evidence that any of the member clubs' investors would have committed time or capital investment without the existing league structure. Without the league, professional football becomes a pursuit no more substantial than a group of finely-tuned athletes traveling haphazardly about, in search of playing competition.

* * *

Holding that the NFL is not a single entity, but rather an aggregation of economic competitors, is tantamount to ruling that the NFL structure is itself per se invalid under the Sherman Act § 1; this will spell the end of sporting leagues as are currently used in football, hockey, golf, soccer, basketball and countless other associations in industries with similar endemic characteristics.

To elevate formal corporate characteristics of ongoing economic entities above the substance of what purpose and function the structure serves, and what product(s) emerge from the process, would not only destroy the NFL, professional sports leagues, and the goodwill that results from continuity in national allocation of the sport throughout the country, but would create a rule of law casting all franchise/wholesale distribution relationships into inescapable doubt.

Rather than avoid creating an "exemption" from the Sherman Act for professional sporting leagues, failing to account for the substantial and unique characteristics extant in professional sports by refusing the NFL review as a single entity creates turmoil and dissolves the analytic framework within which courts scrutinize agreements under Sherman Act § 1. It is unrealistic and inaccurate to lump intra-NFL rules in with agreements binding separate economic entities which produce independent products and accrue independent revenues. Rule 4.3 is no more a restraint on trade in professional football for Sherman Act § 1 purposes, than is an intra-corporate directive regulating the location or operation of its headquarters, franchise, or branch of a multi-outlet business.

No "antitrust exemption" for the NFL would be created by holding that it is a single economic entity for purposes of regulating franchise location. Section 2 of the Sherman Act, prohibiting monopolies and attempts to monopolize, remains fully applicable to all NFL intra-league rules and activities.

Many present NFL practices, including Rule 4.3, are highly suspect under the Sherman Act § 2 prohibitions, because notwithstanding the form or substance of the NFL's style of organization and operation, some practices appear calculated to create barriers to entry for would-be rival leagues in profitable geographical markets. In short, Sherman Act § 2 is the proper curb upon the NFL's successful exploitation of its intra-firm economies of scale and competitive advantages. Radovich v. NFL, 352 U.S. 445 (1957) and particularly American Football League v.

NFL, 323 F.2d 124, 131 (4th Cir.1963) suggest the possibility of true economic competitors challenging the effect of intra-league rules upon nascent competition under § 2 of the Sherman Act.

* * *

As always, § 1 remains a viable theory under which those "upstream" aspects of member clubs' operations—those activities [for] which the NFL and previous courts acknowledge the individual members as economically distinct entities—could be challenged. An oft-tried, and frequently successful example of this theory has been the player draft litigation; the distinction between instances in which the NFL acts as a collective monitor of intra-league affairs, and those in which it intercedes at the behest of a member club for anti-competitive advantage over "upstream" bargaining entities outside the NFL.

The purposes for which the NFL should be viewed as a single entity, impervious to § 1 attack, must be functionally defined as those instances in which member clubs must coordinate intraleague policy and practices if the joint product is to result. Prohibiting the NFL from attempting to exploit a monopolistic position in the industry, or from cloaking concerted anti-competitive pressure upon extrinsic "upstream" suppliers in the guise of "league" restrictions, does not require that we strike ancillary terms of the franchise agreements between member clubs as anti-competitive. A principled approach requires that we distinguish one situation from the other, and protect both competitive markets for football players and television coverage, as well as the integrity of terms Al Davis agreed to as salient aspects of his arms' length negotiations with the other member clubs. Davis has received no more or less than he has bargained for, as a franchisee of the NFL.

To hold the NFL a single entity for purposes of intraleague regulation of relocation of existing franchises, thereby cutting off Sherman Act § 1 liability in this instance, is fully consistent with the prior cases that address the validity of league regulation of member clubs. In such cases, the leagues' power has consistently been upheld.

––––––

With respect to the single-entity issue, is this a question of fact, of law, or of mixed fact and law? Recall that in *NASL*, the appellate court reversed the trial judge's finding that the NFL was a single entity, while in *Raiders I*, despite labelling the issue one of fact, the appellate court upheld the trial judge's directed verdict against the league on this issue. Should this question still be open to litigation, before juries or judges, in any section 1 antitrust suit brought against the NFL (or any other sports league)?

Because the next decision reproduced in this chapter also focuses on the single-entity question, we postpone further discussion of that issue. However, regardless of whether courts rule that the NFL (or any other league) is a single entity and thereby insulated from any section 1 antitrust scrutiny, the teams are in a reasonably close and cooperative relationship in producing and selling their games. As Justice Rehnquist stated in *NASL* about the NFL's ban on interleague cross-ownership, the success of a joint venture may require significant restrictions on each member's individual freedom of action. The Supreme Court explained in *Continental T.V., Inc. v. GTE Sylvania Inc.*, 433 U.S. 36, 97 S.Ct. 2549, 53 L.Ed.2d 568 (1977), why such restraints can be compatible with antitrust's objective of market competition. In that case the Court rejected *per se* illegality of "vertical restraints" imposed by a manufacturer on the territories in which its distributors could market the manufacturer's products. The Court reasoned that such limitations on "intrabrand competition"—one distributor competing against another to sell a particular manufacturer's brand of television set—may be necessary to sustain the manufacturer's presence in the broader competitive market for all brands of television sets. (For a more detailed discussion of and excerpts from *GTE Sylvania*, see Chapter 3).

How would you apply this line of analysis to the analogous problem of a restriction imposed by a sports league on the freedom of individual clubs to change the territory in which they play their home games (in other words, distribute the league's product)? What might a team owner hope to gain, artistically or financially, from moving his club to a new location? What tangible reasons might lead other clubs to resist such a relocation? In comparing the interests of an individual owner and the group of owners, whose are more compatible with the consumer welfare that antitrust law is supposed to promote? Does your answer vary depending on the circumstances of the proposed move, and if so, what are the relevant circumstances?

Questions for Discussion

1. Why was the jury asked to define a relevant market? *Professional Engineers* and other Supreme Court decisions since the mid–1970s (discussed in Chapter 3) make it clear that rule of reason analysis turns on the totality of competitive effects, not merely on the effects in some isolated submarket. *Raiders I* thus notes that the jury was required to consider all interbrand and intrabrand competitive effects. What was the purpose, then, of identifying a relevant product and geographic market? The answer may lie in the trial judge's instruction that the jury should determine the competitive effects of the NFL blocking the Raiders move only in what the jury identified as the relevant market. Was this instruction reversible error?

2. How is the jury supposed to balance effects to both interbrand and intrabrand competition? As for intrabrand competition, would the Raiders' presence in Los Angeles affect the competitive behavior of either the Rams or the Raiders? If so, would the Raiders absence from the San Francisco area affect the 49ers' competitive behavior in the opposite manner? As for interbrand competition, what does this mean? Does a "monopolist" that increases its efficiency enhance interbrand competition by making a higher quality or less expensive product, or does it diminish interbrand competi-

tion by raising barriers to entry? In the Raiders case, how would you have balanced the intrabrand competitive effects in Los Angeles and San Francisco and the interbrand effects in the larger entertainment market?

3. What would be the balance of intrabrand and interbrand competitive effects if the NFL had blocked an attempt by Al Davis to move the Raiders to Memphis instead of to Los Angeles? To Green Bay, Wisconsin? To Tokyo? What if the Pittsburgh Steelers had proposed to move to Los Angeles? To Memphis? To Green Bay? To Tokyo? In making these determinations, should juries undertake *de novo* evaluation of the competitive effects, or should they give some deference to the judgment of the league's owners?

4. The *Raiders I* majority noted that one factor in determining reasonableness was whether there were less restrictive alternatives that could serve the same purpose. What does this mean? How would a jury use such an instruction in its deliberations? After the case was concluded, the NFL amended Rule 4.3 to include a list of "objective factors" that club owners should consider in deciding whether to approve a franchise relocation—for example, market size, stadium adequacy, and attendance. Had this language been in the rule prior to the teams' 22–0 vote against the Raiders move, would the rule or its application in the Raiders case have been less restrictive? Would it have changed any votes?

5. The *Raiders I* majority rejected the NFL's claim that Rule 4.3 was inherently reasonable as a restraint ancillary to a larger lawful contract. The court stated that classification of a restraint as ancillary means only that the restraint is not *per se* illegal. How should a restraint's ancillary nature be considered in subsequent rule of reason analysis? What instructions should a trial court give to a jury? What inherent rights should partners in a joint venture (all of whom have a fiduciary duty to the venture) have to control the business activity of their partners in the conduct of the venture's business? Keep this question in mind as you consider *Raiders II* later in this chapter.

6. Lawyers for the Oakland–Alameda County Coliseum had prepared an antitrust complaint that they would have filed if the NFL had approved the Raiders' move to Los Angeles; the draft complaint alleged that such a move would restrain competition in the San Francisco Bay area. The suit would have been tried before a jury in Oakland. Under the legal theory that the Los Angeles jury used to find the NFL guilty of an antitrust violation for not approving the move, how would the NFL have fared in the Oakland suit had it approved the move? Knowing what you know now, had you been an NFL owner at the meeting to vote on the proposed Raiders' move, how would you have cast your vote?

7. Note that the dissenting judge in *Raiders I* argued that the NFL was a single entity immune from section 1 attack against franchise location decisions, but he agreed with the implicit finding in cases such as *Smith* and *Mackey* (included in Chapter 3 above) that the league is a section 1 combination with respect to its decisions about player personnel matters. Does that distinction appeal to you as a matter of legal logic? As a matter of practical common sense?

———

So far, the Supreme Court has rejected all attempts (for example, in both *Raiders I* and *NASL*) to have it consider the substantive antitrust issues presented by professional sports leagues. Ironically, shortly after the appellate courts' decisions in those cases, the Court delivered a major ruling on antitrust law, *Copperweld v. Independence Tube*. In this case the Court considered whether a parent corporation and its wholly owned, but separately incorporated, subsidiary were distinct entities legally capable of conspiring with each other under section 1 of the Sherman Act. The Court held that they were not. Because of the central importance of this issue to the legal status of sports leagues, we reproduce here extended excerpts from *Copperweld*.

COPPERWELD CORP. v. INDEPENDENCE TUBE CORP.

Supreme Court of the United States, 1984.

467 U.S. 752, 104 S.Ct. 2731, 81 L.Ed.2d 628.

CHIEF JUSTICE BURGER for the Court.

* * *

Petitioners, joined by the United States as amicus curiae, urge us to repudiate the intra-enterprise conspiracy doctrine. The central criticism is that the doctrine gives undue significance to the fact that a subsidiary is separately incorporated and thereby treats as the concerted activity of two entities what is really unilateral behavior flowing from decisions of a single enterprise. We limit our inquiry to the narrow issue squarely presented: whether a parent and its wholly owned subsidiary are capable of conspiring in violation of § 1 of the Sherman Act. We do not consider under what circumstances, if any, a parent may be liable for conspiring with an affiliated corporation it does not completely own.

A.

The Sherman Act contains a "basic distinction between concerted and independent action." The conduct of a single firm is governed by § 2 alone and is unlawful only when it threatens actual monopolization. It is not enough that a single firm appears to "restrain trade" unreasonably, for even a vigorous competitor may leave that impression. For instance, an efficient firm may capture unsatisfied customers from an inefficient rival, whose own ability to compete may suffer as a result. This is the rule of the marketplace and is precisely the sort of competition that promotes the consumer interests that the Sherman Act aims to foster. In part because it is sometimes difficult to distinguish robust competition from conduct with long-run anti-competitive effects, Congress authorized Sherman Act scrutiny of single firms only when they pose a danger of monopolization. Judging unilateral conduct in this manner reduces the risk that the antitrust laws will dampen the competitive zeal of a single aggressive entrepreneur.

Section 1 of the Sherman Act, in contrast, reaches unreasonable restraints of trade effected by a "contract, combination ... or conspiracy" between separate entities. It does not reach conduct that is "wholly unilateral." Concerted activity subject to § 1 is judged more sternly than unilateral activity under § 2. Certain agreements, such as horizontal price fixing and market allocation, are thought so inherently anticompetitive that each is illegal per se without inquiry into the harm it has actually caused. Other combinations, such as mergers, joint ventures, and various vertical agreements, hold the promise of increasing a firm's efficiency and enabling it to compete more effectively. Accordingly, such combinations are judged under a rule of reason, an inquiry into market power and market structure designed to assess the combination's actual effect. Whatever form the inquiry takes, however, it is not necessary to prove that concerted activity threatens monopolization.

The reason Congress treated concerted behavior more strictly than unilateral behavior is readily appreciated. Concerted activity inherently is fraught with anticompetitive risk. It deprives the marketplace of the independent centers of decisionmaking that competition assumes and demands. In any conspiracy, two or more entities that previously pursued their own interests separately are combining to act as one for common benefit. This not only reduces the diverse directions in which economic power is aimed but suddenly increases the economic power moving in one particular direction. Of course, such mergings of resources may well lead to efficiencies that benefit consumers, but their anticompetitive potential is sufficient to warrant scrutiny even in the absence of incipient monopoly.

B.

The distinction between unilateral and concerted conduct is necessary for a proper understanding of the terms "contract, combination ... or conspiracy" in § 1. Nothing in the literal meaning of those terms excludes coordinated conduct among officers or employees of the same company. But it is perfectly plain that an internal "agreement" to implement a single, unitary firm's policies does not raise the antitrust dangers that § 1 was designed to police. The officers of a single firm are not separate economic actors pursuing separate economic interests, so agreements among them do not suddenly bring together economic power that was previously pursuing divergent goals. Coordination within a firm is as likely to result from an effort to compete as from an effort to stifle competition. In the marketplace, such coordination may be necessary if a business enterprise is to compete effectively. For these reasons, officers or employees of the same firm do not provide the plurality of actors imperative for a § 1 conspiracy....

C.

For similar reasons, the coordinated activity of a parent and its wholly owned subsidiary must be viewed as that of a single enterprise for purposes of § 1 of the Sherman Act. A parent and its wholly owned subsidiary have a complete unity of interest. Their objectives are common, not disparate; their general corporate actions are guided or determined not by two separate corporate consciousnesses, but one. They are not unlike a multiple team of horses drawing a vehicle under the control of a single driver. With or without a formal "agreement," the subsidiary acts for the benefit of the parent, its sole shareholder. If a parent and a wholly owned subsidiary do "agree" to a course of action, there is not sudden joining of economic resources that had previously served different interests, and there is no justification for § 1 scrutiny....

The intra-enterprise conspiracy doctrine looks to the form of an enterprises's structure and ignores the reality. Antitrust liability should not depend on whether a corporate subunit is organized as an unincorporated division or a wholly owned subsidiary. A corporation has complete power to maintain a wholly owned subsidiary in either form. The economic, legal, or other considerations that lead corporate management to choose one structure over the other are not relevant to whether the enterprise's conduct seriously threatens competition. Rather, a corporation may adopt the subsidiary form of organization for valid management and related purposes. Separate incorporation may improve management, avoid special tax problems arising from multi-state operations, or serve other legitimate interests. Especially in view of the increasing complexity of corporate operations, a business enterprise should be free to structure itself in ways that serve efficiency of control, economy of operations, and other factors dictated by business judgment without increasing its exposure to antitrust liability. Because there is nothing inherently anticompetitive about a corporation's decision to create a subsidiary, the intra-enterprise conspiracy doctrine "impose[s] grave legal consequences upon organizational distinctions that are of de minimis meaning and effect."

Questions for Discussion

1. The Supreme Court emphasized at the outset of *Copperweld* that it was focusing only on the possibility of section 1 antitrust conspiracy between a corporation and a wholly, not a partially, owned subsidiary. But what do the Court's policy arguments for rejecting intra-enterprise conspiracy in that pure form imply for the special case of sports leagues?[7] To what extent are the actual interests of clubs within a league unified or disparate? Hierarchically ordained or voluntarily negotiated? Does the degree of unity depend on the league's tradition, culture, and leadership. Compare, for example, baseball under Judge Landis in the 1920s and the 1930s with baseball under Fay Vincent in the 1990s. Does it depend on the degree of revenue-sharing among clubs in the leagues? Compare the NFL,

---

7. The implications of *Copperweld* for the antitrust status of sports leagues are a major preoccupation of the second round of scholarly debate on the single entity issue. See the later articles by Lazaroff, Goldman, Grauer, Roberts, and Jacobs cited in note 3 above.

which divides more than ninety percent of its revenues according to league-determined formulas, with the NHL, where less than ten percent of revenues are shared among the clubs.[8]

2.   To the extent that individual club interests are disparate instead of uniform, does this disparity result from inherent independence ("separate sources of economic power," in the words of the *Copperweld* opinion), or from the voluntary choice of a single economic unit to use a decentralized mode of operation? What products does a sports league produce? Who owns the trademarks under which a league or its teams market their products? Do member clubs of a sports league compete with each other like independent oil companies or auto manufacturers, or like divisions of a single corporation in which each division's economic rewards are based on its varying performance?

3.   Do players have an interest in the relocation of teams? Should player interests (if any) be advanced under antitrust law or labor law? If labor law, should relocation be a mandatory subject of bargaining under the National Labor Relations Act. See *Dubuque Packing Co.*, 303 N.L.R.B. No. 66 (1991)?

The *Raiders I* decision concerned only the NFL's antitrust liability for rejecting the Raiders' proposed move to Los Angeles. Following a second trial on the damages question, the jury awarded the Raiders $11.55 million for profits lost due to the two-year delay in their move south. The NFL appealed this sizable damage award (which was trebled under the Sherman Act) on the ground that the benefits the Raiders realized by taking from the NFL the opportunity to create an expansion franchise in Los Angeles should be deducted from the team's lost profits. The appellate court ruled as follows.

LOS ANGELES MEMORIAL COLISEUM COMM'N v. NFL (RAIDERS II)

United States Court of Appeals, Ninth Circuit, 1986.

791 F.2d 1356.

WILLIAMS, DISTRICT JUDGE.

* * *

Prior to 1980, the NFL as a whole owned the right to expand into the Los Angeles area. As evidence at both phases of the trial in this case demonstrated, the Los Angeles opportunity represented an extremely valuable expansion possibility for the league. The value of the Los Angeles opportunity arose not only from the economic potential of

8. See Scott E. Atkinson, Linda R. Stanley, & John Tschirhart, *Revenue Sharing as an Incentive in an Agency Problem: An*   *Example From the National Football League*, 19 RAND J. of Econ. 27 (1988).

one of the nation's largest media markets, but also from the NFL's well-established and widely followed nation-wide entertainment product....

As indicated above, the value of the league's expansion opportunities belonged to the league as a whole, or in other words, was owned in part by each franchise owner. Unquestionably, when the Raiders moved to Los Angeles, they appropriated for themselves the expansion value that had accumulated in Los Angeles. Although by moving out of Oakland the Raiders "gave back" an expansion opportunity to the NFL, the uncontradicted testimony at trial showed the Los Angeles market to be a significantly more lucrative franchise opportunity. Indeed, the Raiders' managing general partner, Al Davis, testified that the Raiders increased their value by some $25 million by moving to Los Angeles.

If, as the Raiders contend and we have found, the jury decided that Rule 4.3 was illegal only as applied in 1980, then the NFL's development of the Los Angeles expansion opportunity until 1980 cannot be said to be illegal in the eyes of the antitrust laws.... [T]he accumulated value of that business opportunity is not something to which the Raiders became entitled as a result of the liability verdict. As a result, the injunction permitting the Raiders to play NFL football in Los Angeles provided them with a windfall benefit beyond the scope of the antitrust verdict.

* * *

Because the Raiders' gross damages from their two year delay in moving to Los Angeles have been, as we have found, properly determined, the remaining task for the district court on remand will be to calculate the value of the Raiders' injunctive relief that exceeded the scope of the liability verdict, and offset that value against the Raiders' monetary award. As indicated above, the excess portion of the injunctive relief can be measured as the value of the NFL's Los Angeles expansion opportunity in 1980, prior to the NFL's legal conduct, less the value of the Oakland opportunity returned to the league.

* * *

Application of this offset rule is consistent with, and indeed, virtually compelled by, this court's *Raiders 1* opinion. In analyzing the "unique" nature of professional athletic leagues vis-a-vis the antitrust laws, this panel expressly acknowledged that "the nature of NFL football requires some territorial restrictions in order both to encourage participation in the venture *and to secure each venturer the legitimate fruits of that participation*." Here, the league owners collectively possessed the value that had accumulated in the Los Angeles expansion opportunity. This value, as indicated above, was created at least in part through the NFL's development, over the years, of a popular spectator sport with a national following. Although this panel upheld the liability jury's conclusion that Rule 4.3 as it was applied to the Raiders' move was an unreasonable restraint of trade, the opinion noted several less onerous forms of territorial restrictions that could pass muster under the rule of reason. Among these were standards restricting team movement that expressly recognized certain objective factors such as population, economic projections and the like, that the league could legitimately consider in deciding whether to permit a team to move. If such restrictions, applied in a non-arbitrary manner, would be reasonable under the Sherman Act, then *a fortiori*, a rule requiring merely an objectively-determined payment to league members as compensation for the right to take a valuable, jointly-owned franchise opportunity out of the league's hands, would also be a reasonable restriction.

Thus, by taking possession of the Los Angeles expansion opportunity from the NFL, the Raiders reaped a windfall benefit beyond the scope of the antitrust verdict. For this reason, and also because the NFL, in the absence of its antitrust violation, would have been justified in requiring the Raiders to compensate the NFL for the excess value represented by the Los Angeles expansion opportunity, that excess value should have been offset against the Raiders' lost profits from the two years they were precluded from moving to Los Angeles. The district court therefore erred in refusing to admit evidence of the full benefits of the Los Angeles expansion opportunity received by the Raiders, and in refusing to instruct the jury on the NFL's offset defense. The court incorrectly limited the NFL's offset evidence in this regard to the "negotiating advantage" the Raiders received during the 1980–82 period by virtue of the fact that Rule 4.3 discouraged other teams from moving to Los Angeles during that period. On remand, the scope of the offset should be broadened to include the full value of the Los Angeles opportunity that had accrued prior to 1989, less the value of the "Oakland opportunity" that was returned to the NFL.

See 791 F.2d at 1371–73

Questions for Discussion

1. *Raiders I* and *Raiders II* were both decided by the same three judge panel. The second opinion reasoned that the NFL owned the expansion market in Los Angeles, and the Raiders, move to Los Angeles gave them a windfall benefit. Is this reasoning consistent with the first opinion's conclusions on the single-entity and the rule of reason issues? Both the NFL and the Raiders filed certiorari petitions after *Raiders II*, and argued that the two decisions were irreconcilable, but the Supreme Court again declined to hear the case. See 484 U.S. 826 (1987).

2. In another part of the *Raiders II* opinion, the court reversed the jury's verdict finding that the NFL had breached a state law duty of good faith and fair dealing with the Raiders:

> The evidence presented in this case, taken as a whole, permits only one of two conclusions: either (1) neither the Raiders nor the NFL

breached the duty of good faith with respect to the contemplated franchise move from Oakland to Los Angeles, or (2) both parties so breached.... The Raiders and their managing general partner Al Davis expressed, on various occasions ... their refusal to forego these relocation plans regardless of the wishes of the NFL. They in essence denied any contractual obligation to submit their relocation plans to the League for approval, and deliberately sought to avoid or circumvent the prescribed procedure for obtaining a vote of the other teams. In fact, the Raiders even notified the League, prior to the owners' vote, that they had officially and unilaterally "moved" to Los Angeles.... It cannot reasonably be maintained that the NFL's subsequent withholding of authorization, but not these actions of the Raiders, constituted a breach of the implied promise of good faith and fair dealing.

See 791 F.2d at 1361–62

Again, are *Raiders I* and *Raiders II* compatible? How does the finding that all NFL teams have reciprocal duties of good faith toward one another affect the single-entity issue? If the NFL's disapproval of the Raiders' move violated federal antitrust law, how could the Raiders' refusal to submit their proposed move to such a vote be a breach of that duty?

3. *Raiders II* held that the jury found Rule 4.3 illegal only as applied in the specific case, not on its face. Of what relevance, then, was the court's discussion in *Raiders I* about less restrictive alternatives, objective standards for reviewing proposed franchise moves, and ancillary restraints? Is it significant that the NFL owners disapproved the Raiders proposed vote by a vote of 22–0? Suppose that the vote had been 12–10 in favor, but short of the special 3/4ths majority needed for franchise relocation?

Raiders II was significant not just in sharply reducing the size of the NFL's damage liability to the Raiders, but also in offering somewhat greater support for league constraints upon unilateral team movements. The latter effect became apparent soon afterwards in litigation involving the National Basketball Association and the San Diego Clippers. The Clippers decided to move their operations from San Diego to the Los Angeles Sports Arena (which, ironically, was also owned by the Los Angeles Memorial Coliseum Commission) where the Clippers would compete with the Los Angeles Lakers playing in their Forum. After *Raiders I*, but before *Raiders II*, the NBA decided not to risk trebled damages by refusing to schedule Clippers' games in Los Angeles. Instead, the league sued the Clippers, and sought a judicial declaration that the league could lawfully prohibit this relocation. The following is the Ninth Circuit's interpretation of its holdings in *Raiders I* and *Raiders II*.

NBA v. SAN DIEGO CLIPPERS BASKETBALL CLUB

United States Court of Appeals, Ninth Circuit, 1987.

815 F.2d 562.

FERGUSON, CIRCUIT JUDGE.

* * *

The antitrust issues are directly controlled by the two *Raiders* opinions, although the district judge had the benefit only of *Raiders I* when he rendered judgment. Collectively, the *Raiders* opinions held that rule of reason analysis governed a professional sports league's efforts to restrict franchise movement. More narrowly, however, *Raiders I* merely held that a reasonable jury could have found that the NFL's application of its franchise movement rule was an unreasonable restraint of trade. *Raiders II* confirmed that the jury's liability verdict affirmed in *Raiders I* "held Rule 4.3 [the franchise movement rule] invalid only as it was applied to the Raiders' proposed move to Los Angeles." The Clippers' and the Coliseum's efforts to characterize *Raiders I* as presenting guidelines for franchise movement rules are thus unavailing. Neither the jury's verdict in *Raiders*, nor the court's affirmance of that verdict, held that a franchise movement rule, in and of itself, was invalid under the antitrust laws.

Raiders I did establish the law of this circuit in applying the rule of reason to a sports league's franchise relocation rule, "a business practice in an industry which does not readily fit into the antitrust context." Any antitrust plaintiff "must prove these elements: '(1) An agreement among two or more persons or distinct business entities; (2) which is intended to harm or unreasonably restrain competition.' " The *Raiders I* panel carefully examined the structure of professional football in applying [this] standard, a structure in which the "teams are not true competitors, nor can they be." The *Raiders I* panel concluded that the relevant market for professional football, the history and purpose of the franchise-movement rule, and the lack of justification of the rule under ancillary-restraint doctrine all supported the jury's verdict. In so doing, of course, the panel set down no absolute rule for sports leagues. Instead, it examined the facts before it and concluded that the jury's conclusion that the NFL violated the antitrust laws was supported by the record.

Yet the Clippers argue, as they must to support summary judgment, that the "NBA three-quarters rule ... is illegal under *Raiders I*"—i.e., either that the NBA rule is void as a matter of law under *Raiders I*, or that the NBA has not adduced genuine issues of fact to allow the rule to stand. The Clippers assert that the rule "is illegal as applied ... [but that under *Raiders I*], a professional sports league's club relocation rule must at least be 'closely tailored' and incorporate objective standards and criteria such as population, economic projections, playing facilities, regional balance, and television revenues." Putting to the side, for the moment, the NBA's adamant and repeated assertions that such standards have been incorporated in the evaluation of franchise movements, the Clippers misperceive the effect of the *Raiders* cases. The Clippers' confusion, and that of a number of commentators, may derive from the *Raiders I* panel's painstaking efforts to guide sports leagues toward procedures that might, in all cases, withstand antitrust analysis. The objective factors and procedures recounted by the Clippers are "well advised," and might be sufficient to demonstrate procompetitive purposes that would save the restriction from the rule of reason. They are not, however, necessary conditions to the legality of franchise relocation rules.

Since a careful analysis of *Raiders I* makes it clear that franchise movement restrictions are not invalid as a matter of law, for the district judge to grant summary judgment against the NBA, he must have found that the NBA had adduced no facts upon which a reasonable jury could have found that NBA consideration of the Clippers' move was a reasonable restraint of trade. As we have demonstrated, antitrust analysis under *Raiders I* indicates that the question of what restraints are reasonable is one of fact. We believe that numerous issues of fact remain.

The NBA asserts a number of genuine issues of fact: (1) the purpose of the restraint as demonstrated by the NBA's use of a variety of criteria in evaluating franchise movement, (2) the market created by professional basketball, which the NBA alleges is substantially different from that of professional football, and (3) the actual effect the NBA's limitations on movements might have on trade. The NBA's assertions, if further documented at trial, create an entirely different factual setting than that of the Raiders and the NFL. Further, as the NBA correctly notes, the antitrust issue here is vastly different than that in the *Raiders* cases: the issue here is "whether the mere requirement that a team seek [NBA] Board of Governor approval before it seizes a new franchise location violates the Sherman Act." The NBA here did not attempt to forbid the move. It scheduled the Clippers in the Sports Arena, and when faced with continued assertions of potential antitrust liability, brought this suit for declaratory relief. Given the *Raiders I* rejection of per se analysis for franchise movement rules of sports leagues, and the existence of genuine issues of fact regarding the reasonableness of the restraint, the judgment against the NBA must be reversed.

Summary judgment reversed.

After this decision had been rendered, the NBA and the Clippers settled their litigation on the terms that the Clippers make a substantial payment to the league for the right to remain in Los Angeles.[9] What are the broader guidelines that emerge from *Raiders* and from *Clippers* for the benefit of leagues and teams that naturally want to

9. For analysis of both the *Raiders* damages decision and the *Clippers* liability decision, see Kenneth L. Shropshire, *Opportunistic Sports Franchise Relocations: Can Punitive Damages in Actions Based Upon Contract Strike a Balance?*, 22 Loyola of L.A. L. Rev. 569 (1989).

know *before* antitrust litigation whether a team's proposed move from one city to another can either be made or be blocked? What kind of legal liability does the league—or the club—face if it guesses incorrectly about the state and application of the law?

———————

Along with the question of relocation is the equally vital antitrust problem regarding league expansion. Suppose that a city builds an expensive new sports facility (as St. Petersburg, Florida, built its Suncoast Dome) in the hope of attracting a sports franchise, but no existing team is prepared to move there. However, a local entrepreneur with the appropriate background and resources has indicated firm interest in filling this vacant facility and territory, which has the requisite population and fan interest. Should the entrepreneur and/or the city have a right under antitrust law to insist that the league offer an expansion franchise?

A preliminary rehearsal of an analogous question took place in the early 1970s, in the case of *Levin v. NBA*, 385 F.Supp. 149 (S.D.N.Y. 1974). The plaintiff had entered into an agreement to purchase the Boston Celtics. The NBA, like other sports leagues, required approval of such transactions by three-fourths of the other teams acting as the league's Board of Governors. The Board rejected Levin's bid to purchase the Celtics, and Levin sued. The federal district judge did not venture into the merits of the contrary views asserted by the parties about the nature and legitimacy of the grounds for rejection, which apparently were related in some way to Levin's long-standing business relationship with Sam Schulman, the maverick owner of the Seattle Supersonics. Instead, the judge summarily dismissed the claim on the ground that this case presented no antitrust concerns:

> While it is true that the antitrust laws apply to a professional athletic league, and that joint action by members of a league can have antitrust implications, this is not such a case. Here the plaintiffs wanted to join with those unwilling to accept them, not to compete with them, but to be partners in the operation of a sports league for plaintiffs' profit. Further, no matter which reason one credits for the rejection, it was not an anti-competitive reason. Finally, regardless of the financial impact of this rejection upon the plaintiffs, if any, the exclusion of the plaintiffs from membership in the league did not have an anticompetitive effect nor an effect upon the public interest. The Celtics continue as an operating club, and indeed are this year's champion.

> The law is well established that it is competition, and not individual competitors, that is protected by the antitrust laws....

It is also clear that where the action the plaintiffs attack, the rejection from co-partnership, has neither anticompetitive intent nor effect, that conduct is not violative of the antitrust laws....

See 385 F.Supp. at 152.

Remember, though, that a decade after the equally abrupt dismissal of the *San Francisco Seals* relocation case, Al Davis was able to persuade an appellate court that he did have an antitrust right to move his Oakland Raiders team to Los Angeles. In tandem with Davis, three owners from the World Football League sought to persuade a different federal appellate court that they were entitled to admission to the National Football League—not as purchaser of an existing team, but as creator of a new team. And as the main survivor of the ill-fated World Football League venture in the 1970s (recall the *Bergey* case from Chapter 2), these owners brought with their application not just a city, a stadium, and a fan base, but also a team of players looking for a league in which to play.

MID–SOUTH GRIZZLIES v. NFL

United States Court of Appeals, Third Circuit, 1983.

720 F.2d 772.

GIBBONS, CIRCUIT JUDGE.

[The Memphis Southmen were one of the few successful franchises in the World Football League, which opened in 1974 and closed midway through the 1975 season. The team then reorganized with players from two other WFL teams (in the Philadelphia Bell and the Southern California Sun), named itself the Grizzlies, and applied for a franchise in the National Football League. The Grizzlies claimed that they were an established football enterprise operating in a city, Memphis, that had demonstrated strong popular demand for professional football, and was not included in the 75–mile "home territory" of any existing NFL franchise. The NFL rejected the Grizzlies' application; the reasons given were recent expansion to Seattle and Tampa, the scheduling need for an even number of teams, and an uncertain labor relationship with the NFLPA. The Grizzlies then filed an antitrust suit in Philadelphia. The suit relied not only on the Sherman Act, but also upon 15 U.S.C. § 1291 (Public Law 87–331), which gave professional sports leagues a limited antitrust exemption to pool and sell their television rights, and upon Public Law 89–800, which in 1966 amended § 1291 to permit the merger of the National and American Football Leagues "if such agreement increases rather than decreases the number of professional football clubs." The trial judge granted the NFL's motion for summary dismissal, and the Grizzlies appealed.]

* * *

Public Law 89–800 establishes as a matter of law that the merger which produced the NFL from two formerly competing leagues did not violate the antitrust laws. Public Law 87–331 establishes as a matter of law that the members may lawfully pool revenues from the sale of television rights. The parties agree that in other respects a rule of reason analysis is appropriate....

Under a rule of reason analysis a section 1 violation ... can be established by proof: (1) that the defendants contracted, combined, or conspired among each other; (2) that the combination or conspiracy produced adverse, anticompetitive effects within relevant product and geographic markets; (3) that the objects of and conduct pursuant to that contract or conspiracy were illegal; and (4) that the plaintiff was injured as a proximate result of that conspiracy. In this case there is no dispute about the requisite concert of action among the defendants. The defendants do deny injury to competition in any relevant market from their rejection of the Grizzlies' application. They urge that any limitations on actual or potential competition in any relevant market were insulated from antitrust scrutiny by the 1961 and 1966 statutes referred to, or, are reasonable as a matter of law. They also urge that as a matter of law there was no competition among league members or between league members and non-members in other markets to which the Grizzlies point.

The Grizzlies identify as the relevant product market major-league professional football, and as the relevant geographic market the United States. The trial court found these markets to be relevant. The court observed as well that "[t]here is no doubt that the NFL currently has a monopoly in the United States in major league football." The Grizzlies pose as the question on this appeal "whether it can be said as a matter of law that defendants neither acquired nor maintained monopoly power over any relevant market in an unlawful manner."

As to the acquisition of dominant position and monopoly power, the facts are undisputed. Long before the Grizzlies and the World Football League came into existence, Congress authorized the merger of the two major football leagues extant in 1966, and granted to the merged league the power to pool television revenues. That congressional decision conferred on the NFL the market power which it holds in the market for professional football. Congress could not have been unaware that necessary effect of the television revenue sharing scheme which it approved for the NFL would be that all members of that league would be strengthened in their ability to bid for the best available playing and coaching personnel, to the potential disadvantage of new entrants.

* * *

But, the Grizzlies urge, the 1966 statute did not confer the authority to abuse the market power, even though it may have authorized its acquisition. Rather, the merger was approved only "if such agreement increases rather than decreases the number of professional clubs so operating." Paraphrasing their argument, it is the Grizzlies' contention that the statute which authorized NFL acquisition of monopoly power in the professional football market required not only that the league members refrain from abusing that power against potential competitors, but that it take affirmative steps to share its market power with others.

This reading of the 1966 legislation is at least plausible. It poses two separate issues. One is the issue of abuse of monopoly power against potential rivals of the NFL in the business of promoting professional football as a spectator spectacle. The other is the issue of admitting others to a share in the NFL's dominant market position. Although the Grizzlies' briefs, both here and in the district court, tend to blur the distinction between those issues, the complaint makes clear that only the second is presented in this case. The only basis on which the Grizzlies seek recovery under Section 4 of the Clayton Act is that they were denied admission to the monopoly, and thus were deprived of a share of the NFL's monopoly power. No claim is made that abuse of NFL market power led to the demise of the World Football League, and no issue is before us concerning activities of the NFL, since that demise, which may have inhibited the development of competition by another football league. The NFL structure as a barrier to entry to the market by another football league is relevant in this case only to the extent that it bears on the obligation to permit entry to the NFL.[7]

There are two possible sources of any NFL obligation to permit entry to its shared market power; the 1966 statute, and the Sherman Act. Each will be considered separately.

The provision in the 1966 statute that "such agreement increases rather than decreases the number of professional football clubs so operating" cannot reasonably be construed as addressing competition, the preservation of which is the object of the Sherman Act. The basic thrust of the 1966 statute is to authorize an arrangement which eliminated competition among the only two viable competitors then in the professional football market. The reference to an increase in the number of professional football teams "so operating" is a reference to professional teams operating under the antitrust exemption for television revenue sharing provided in the 1961 statute. Thus what the 1966 statute suggests is that more home team territories would be added, not to increase competition in professional football, but to permit geographic enlargement of the NFL's market power.

The Grizzlies urge that home team regions derive important economic benefits from the presence of a professional football team, in the form of hotel, restaurant and travel business, stadium employment, and the like. Undoubtedly that is so, and probably such derivative economic benefits were in the minds of those Senators and Congressmen interested in NFL expansion. Those benefits, however, do not result

---

7. There is no doubt that the NFL structure authorized by the 1961 and 1966 legislation in itself presents a formidable barrier to entry by a competitive football league. That legally countenanced barrier might well, if abused against extra-league competitors, result in antitrust liability. But the issue of competition by another league is not presented here, except to the limited extent noted.

from competition with the NFL or even from competition, other than athletic, among its members. Rather they result from the presence of a franchisee which shares the NFL market power over professional football. Moreover, even if one assumes that Congress intended in the 1966 statute to extend incidental economic benefits on businesses in new home territory areas, it is difficult to see what standing the Grizzlies have to rely on that intent with respect to their claim for league membership. Finally, even if there was a congressional intent to confer economic benefits in some new home territories, nothing in the 1966 statute or its sparse legislative history suggests a basis for concluding that businesses in Memphis, Tennessee, rather than in other metropolitan areas were to receive them.

Since the 1966 statute is not directed at preservation of competition in the market for professional football, and cannot be construed as conferring any economic benefit on the class to which the Grizzlies belong, we conclude that it does not oblige the NFL to permit entry by any particular applicant to the NFL shared market power.

We turn, therefore, to the Sherman Act. As noted above, Sherman Act liability requires an injury to competition. In this case the competition inquiry is a narrow one, because the Grizzlies are not seeking recovery as potential competitors outside the NFL. They identify as the antitrust violation the league's negative vote on their application for membership.

* * *

Assuming, without deciding, that the summary judgment record presents disputed fact issues with respect to the actual motivation of the NFL members, those disputed facts are not material, under Section 1 of the Sherman Act, if the action complained of produced no injury to competition.

As to competition with NFL members in the professional football market, including the market for sale of television rights, the exclusion was patently pro-competitive, since it left the Memphis area, with a large stadium and a significant metropolitan area population, available as a site for another league's franchise, and it left the Grizzlies' organization as a potential competitor in such a league. If there was any injury to competition, actual or potential, therefore, it must have been to intra-league competition.

The NFL defendants' position is that the summary judgment record establishes conclusively the absence of competition, actual or potential, among league members. Rather, they urge, the league is a single entity, a joint venture in the presentation of the professional football spectacle.

For the most part the congressionally authorized arrangements under which the NFL functions eliminate competition among the league members. Indeed it is undisputed that on average more than 70% of each member club's revenue is shared revenue derived from sources other than operations at its home location. The Grizzlies do not challenge the legality of the NFL's revenue sharing arrangements, and seek to participate in them. The Grizzlies emphasize that there nevertheless remains a not insignificant amount of intra-league non-athletic competition. We need not, in order to affirm the summary judgment, accept entirely the NFL's position that there is no intra-league competition. Conceivably within certain geographic submarkets two league members compete with one another for ticket buyers, for local broadcast revenue, and for sale of the concession items like food and beverages and team paraphernalia. Thus rejection of a franchise application in the New York metropolitan area, for example, might require a different antitrust analysis than is suggested by this record. But the Grizzlies were obliged, when faced with the NFL denial of the existence of competition among NFL members and a potential franchisee at Memphis, to show some more than minimal level of potential competition, in the product markets in which league members might compete. They made no such showing. The record establishes that the NFL franchise nearest to Memphis is at St. Louis, Mo., over 280 miles away. There is no record evidence that professional football teams located in Memphis and in St. Louis would compete for the same ticket purchasers, for the same local broadcast outlets, in the sale of team paraphernalia, or in any other manner.

The Grizzlies contend on appeal, although they did not so contend in the trial court, that league members compete in what they call the "raw material market" for players and coaching personnel. Entirely apart from the propriety of considering a legal theory not presented in the trial court, there are major defects in this Grizzlies' argument. First, the Grizzlies exclusion from the league in no way restrained them from competing for players by forming a competitive league. Second, they fail to explain how, if their exclusion from the league reduced competition for team personnel, that reduction caused an injury to the Grizzlies' business or property.

One final Grizzlies' argument in support of their section 1 Sherman Act claim bears mentioning. Relying on the essential facilities doctrine ..., they urge that because the NFL is a practical monopoly it had an obligation to admit members on fair, reasonable, and equal terms, absent some procompetitive justification for their exclusion. This Grizzlies argument suffers from the same defect as the others. The essential facilities doctrine is predicated on the assumption that admission of the excluded applicant would result in additional competition, in an economic rather than athletic sense. The Grizzlies have simply failed to show how competition in any arguably relevant market would be improved if they were given a share of the NFL's monopoly power.

Since on the record before us the Grizzlies have shown no actual or potential injury to competition resulting from the rejection of their application for an NFL franchise, they cannot succeed on their section 1 Sherman Act claim.

Affirmed.

A similar antitrust suit to force expansion in hockey was summarily dismissed in *Seattle Totems v. National Hockey League*, No. C 75–804 (W.D.Wash.1985).

Questions for Discussion

1. Can one square the antitrust logic of *Grizzlies* with that of *Raiders I* or *II*, or both? What specific features of the NFL's refusal to expand in *Grizzlies* influenced the court's assessment of the effect upon market competition? How do these features compare with the attempted refusal to allow relocation in *Raiders*? What did the reasoning of *Raiders* and *Grizzlies* imply about the legal right of the Baltimore Colts to move to Indianapolis or of the St. Louis Cardinals to move to Phoenix? Alternatively, suppose that after the demise of the United States Football League (which we will examine in the next chapter), Donald Trump had sought admission to the NFL for his New Jersey Generals, bringing with him Herschel Walker and Doug Flutie to play in Yankee Stadium. If the NFL had refused to admit the Generals, did the antitrust analysis in *Raiders* and *Grizzlies* give Trump any hope of winning admission in court?

2. The court concluded in *Grizzlies* that the NFL's refusal to add the Grizzlies did not affect market competition because no other NFL teams were located near Memphis. This reasoning assumes that the only place NFL teams compete economically with one another is in the local market. The Grizzlies argued there was also nationwide competition among NFL clubs for players and coaches. Are there other ways that NFL teams arguably compete on a national level? If the NFL is not considered a single entity, is the Grizzlies claim persuasive? How does the court deal with this argument? Is the court's response persuasive?

3. Many people react to the rather abstract antitrust demand for market competition with the feeling that it is a far bigger step for a court to order addition of a new franchise to the league than simply to require that an existing franchise be permitted to move to a more profitable site. Does that imply that a golfer (for example, a foreign golfer such as Nick Faldo or Seve Ballesteros) should have no legal right to be admitted to play in tournaments on the Professional Golfers Association Tour? (We will consider the organization of individual sports such as golf and tennis in Chapter 10.)

4. There are, of course, practical differences in the way in which new golfers and tennis players gain access to their respective tours, and the manner in which new expansion franchises are added. Generally, new golfers and tennis players are accepted for tournaments when they prove more competitive at the game than the people they replace. In contrast, new league franchises are added when the existing owners agree that expansion to a particular area is in the league's best economic or political interests, and then only upon payment of huge expansion fees (as of 1991, $95 million in baseball and $50 million in hockey). Even if a court were

inclined to support the hypothetical expansion claim by Donald Trump's New Jersey Generals, how would the judge decide that New York City was the best place for NFL expansion, and how would the judge calculate the appropriate franchise fee? Could the court be guided by how clubs now decide these issues?

———

Step back from these technical legal issues and consider the broader economic significance of *Raiders* and *Grizzlies* taken as a pair. Cities have been told by the courts that no new sports franchises will be created unless the league agrees to that step, something that leagues do sparingly. Yet, the NFL's Raiders, Colts, and Cardinals have proved that an existing franchise has considerable leeway to move to an attractive vacant site. Is this not a significant factor in the fierce financial bidding seen over the last decade between cities competing for a scarce number of sports franchises? The result of these bidding wars is that many teams, whether or not they move, are regularly favored with large public subsidies through luxurious new stadiums built at public expense and leased at low rentals, generous concession and parking rights, tax holidays, and even substantial direct payments. Indeed the Raiders scenario illustrated precisely that phenomenon: the City of Anaheim lured the Rams out of the L.A. Memorial Coliseum by offering Rams' owner Carroll Rosenbloom 95 acres of valuable real estate for commercial development right next to a refurbished Anaheim Stadium. Nor could Los Angeles legitimately complain about that action since the city had pioneered in this tactic by offering 300 acres in Chavez Ravine to the Brooklyn Dodgers to come west and build their own park to replace an outmoded Ebbetts Field.[10] This leverage by clubs over communities anxious to keep or acquire a professional franchise is a textbook example of the exercise of monopoly power— driving the "price" of franchises up by artificially restricting supply in the face of growing demand.

Local governments do have some legal power with which to try to block departures of their "home" teams. One method is to enforce an existing stadium lease between the team and the city. The question is what remedy the city may receive if the team would be breaking its lease contract with the proposed move. Should the city (or its stadium authority) be entitled to injunctive relief or limited to damages for lost rental and concession revenue, an amount that presumably is more than matched by the money being offered by another community.

---

10. See Harris, *The League*, note 1 above, *passim* (describing in detail how NFL owners—including Ram's owner Carroll Rosenbloom—extracted more and more favorable stadium deals from communities anxious to attract or retain a professional football team); Miller, *The Baseball Business*, note 1 above, at 293–303 (describing similar negotiations undertaken by Ed-

ward Bennett Williams, owner of baseball's Baltimore Orioles, to secure a highly attractive stadium—the new Camden Yards—and lease arrangement for his team); and Neil J. Sullivan, *The Dodgers Move West* (New York: Oxford University Press, 1987) (recounting the relocation of the baseball Dodgers from Brooklyn to Los Angeles).

(Recall the same issue with respect to enforcement of player contracts discussed in Chapter 2.) Interestingly, some courts have found the city-lessor's damages from a team's breach of contract are not irreparable and that monetary damages are sufficient. Others have granted equitable relief based on the unique and irreplaceable value of the franchise. Compare *City of New York v. New York Jets*, 90 Misc.2d 311, 394 N.Y.S.2d 799 (1977), with *HMC Management v. New Orleans Basketball Club*, 375 So.2d 712 (La.App.1979).

An injunction, however, even if granted, has only short-term value. Indeed, the prospect of injunctive enforcement may make clubowners less willing to sign long-term leases. Therefore cities have turned to a more potent legal weapon—eminent domain—to hold on to their present teams at no more than a "fair" market value.[11] Unsurprisingly, exploration of that possibility took place in yet another legal episode in the long-running Saga of the Lost Raiders. The City of Oakland attempted to use California's extremely broad eminent domain law to keep the Raiders in Oakland by condemning the Raiders' NFL franchise and immediately reselling it to a local owner approved by the NFL. The state trial court dismissed the City's petition, and the case eventually reached to the California Supreme Court.

CITY OF OAKLAND v. OAKLAND RAIDERS (I)

Supreme Court of California, 1982.

32 Cal.3d 60, 183 Cal.Rptr. 673, 646 P.2d 835.

RICHARDSON, JUSTICE.

... [T]wo issues are herein presented, the first dealing with the intangible nature of the property proposed to be taken, and the second focusing on the scope of the condemning power as limited by the doctrine of public use.

* * *

Because the power to condemn is an inherent attribute of general government, we have observed that "constitutional provisions merely place limitations upon its exercise." The two constitutional restraints are that the taking be for a "public use" and that "just compensation" be paid therefor. No constitutional restriction, federal or state, purports to limit the nature of the property that may be taken by eminent domain. In contrast to the broad powers of general government, "a municipal corporation has no inherent power of eminent domain and can exercise it only when expressly authorized by law." We examine briefly the source of that statutory power.

* * *

The new law appears to impose no greater restrictions on the exercise of the condemnation power than those which are inherent in

11. See Charles Gray, *Keeping the Home Team at Home*, 74 California L. Rev. 1329 (1986); Ellen Z. Mufson, *Jurisdiction-* *al Limitations on Intangible Property in Eminent Domain*, 60 Indiana L. J. 389 (1985).

the federal and state constitutions. Further, the power which is
statutorily extended to cities is not limited to certain types of property,
nor was it intended to be. In discussing the broad scope of property
rights which are subject to a public taking under the new law, the Law
Revision Commission comment significantly notes that "Section 1235.-
170 is intended to provide the broadest possible definition of property
and to include any type of right, title or interest in property that may
be required for public use."

* * *

Over 125 years ago, the United States Supreme Court rejected a
similar claim that intangible property could not be condemned. In The
West River Bridge Company v. Dix et al. (1848) 47 U.S. 507, 533, the
high court carefully explained:

> A distinction has been attempted ... between the power of a
> government to appropriate for public uses property which is corpo-
> real ... and the like power in the government to resume or
> extinguish a franchise. The distinction thus attempted we regard
> as a refinement which has no foundation in reason, and one that,
> in truth, avoids the true legal or constitutional question in these
> causes; namely, that of the right in private persons, in the use or
> enjoyment of their private property, to control and actually to
> prohibit the power and duty of the government to advance and
> protect the general good. We are aware of nothing peculiar to a
> franchise which can class it higher, or render it more sacred, than
> other property. A franchise is property, and nothing more; it is
> incorporeal property....

A century later, the high court reaffirmed the principle. Reasoning that "the intangible acquires a value ... no different from the
value of the business' physical property," it concluded that such intan-
gibles as trade routes of a laundry were condemnable, upon payment of
just compensation therefor, when properly taken for a public use.
(Kimball Laundry Co. v. United States (1949) 338 U.S. 1, 10–11, 16).

* * *

For eminent domain purposes, neither the federal nor the state
constitution distinguishes between property which is real or personal,
tangible or intangible. Nor did the 1975 statutory revision. Bearing in
mind that the Law Revision Commission, after an extensive national
study, made its legislative recommendations, including a definition of
condemnable property which it characterized as "the broadest possible," we conclude that our eminent domain law authorizes the taking of
intangible property. To the extent that the trial court based its
summary judgment on a contrary conclusion it erred.

In fairness it must be said that the trial court fully acknowledged
"the intent of the Legislature to allow the taking of any type of
property, real or personal, if it was in fact necessary for a public use."
But the court concluded as a matter of law that (1) no statutory or

charter provision specifically authorized the taking of a professional football franchise, and (2) the operation of such a franchise is not a recognized public use which would permit its taking under general condemnation law. Assuming, for purposes of discussion, the propriety of the first premise, this fact alone is insufficient to support summary judgment, and we cannot agree with the second premise which we now explore.

* * *

Is City's attempt to take and operate the Raiders' football franchise a valid public use? We have defined "public use" as "a use which concerns the whole community or promotes the general interest in its relation to any legitimate object of government." On the other hand, "It is not essential that the entire community, or even any considerable portion thereof, shall directly enjoy or participate in an improvement in order to constitute a public use." Further, while the Legislature may statutorily declare a given "use, purpose, object or function" to be a "public use" (§ 1240.010), such statutory declarations do not purport to be exclusive.

* * *

The United States Supreme Court established years ago that "what is a public use frequently and largely depends upon the facts and circumstances surrounding the particular subject-matter in regard to which the character of the use is questioned." Further, "public uses are not limited, in the modern view, to matters of mere business necessity and ordinary convenience, but may extend to matters of public health, recreation and enjoyment."

No case anywhere of which we are aware has held that a municipality can acquire and operate a professional football team. May it do so? In our view, several decisions concerning recreation appear germane. In City of Los Angeles v. Superior Court, 333 P.2d 745 (1959), we noted that a city's acquisition of a baseball field, with recreational facilities to be constructed thereon to be used by the city, was "obviously for proper public purposes." Similarly, in County of Alameda v. Meadowlark Dairy Corp., 38 Cal.Rptr. 474 (1964), the court upheld a county's acquisition by eminent domain of lands to be used for a county fair, reasoning that "Activities which promote recreation of the public constitute a public purpose." Considerably earlier, in Egan v. San Francisco, 133 P. 294 (1913), in sustaining a city's power to build an opera house, we declared:

> Generally speaking, anything calculated to promote the education, the recreation or the pleasure of the public is to be included within the legitimate domain of public purposes.

The examples of Candlestick Park in San Francisco and Anaheim Stadium in Anaheim, both owned and operated by municipalities, further suggest the acceptance of the general principle that providing access to recreation to its residents in the form of spectator sports is an appropriate function of city government. In connection with the latter stadium, the appellate court upheld the power of the City of Anaheim to condemn land for parking facilities at the stadium on the ground that "the acquisition, construction, and operation of a stadium by a county or city represents a legitimate public purpose."

Several of our sister jurisdictions are in accord.

* * *

The obvious difference between managing and owning the facility in which the game is played, and managing and owning the team which plays in the facility, seems legally insubstantial. If acquiring, erecting, owning and/or operating a sports stadium is a permissible municipal function, we discern no valid legal reason why owning and operating a sports franchise which fields a team to play in the stadium is not equally permissible.

* * *

While it is readily apparent that the power of eminent domain formerly may have been exercised only to serve certain traditional and limited public purposes, such as the construction and maintenance of streets, highways and parks, these limitations seem merely to have corresponded to an accepted, but narrower, view of appropriate governmental functions then prevailing. The established limitations were not imposed by either constitutional or statutory fiat. Times change. Apparently acknowledging the evolving nature of public use, as we have noted, the Law Revision Commission specifically recommended against the retention of the list of possible public uses in the new law, explaining, "The scheme of the Eminent Domain Law renders a listing of public uses in the general condemnation statute, as under former Section 1238, unnecessary...."

From the foregoing we conclude that the acquisition and, indeed, the operation of a sports franchise may well be an appropriate municipal function. That being so, the statutes discussed herein afford City the power to acquire by eminent domain any property necessary to carry out that function.

We caution that we are not concerned with the economic or governmental wisdom of City's acquisition or management of the Raiders' franchise, but only with the legal propriety of the condemnation action. In this period of fiscal constraints, if the city fathers of Oakland in their collective wisdom elect to seek the ownership of a professional football franchise, are we to say to them nay? And, if so, on what legal ground? Constitutional? Both federal and state Constitutions permit condemnation requiring only compensation and a public use. Statutory? The applicable statutes authorize a city to take any property, real or personal. Decisional? Courts have consistently expanded the eminent domain remedy permitting property to be taken for recreational purposes with the public either as playing participants or observing spectators.

* * *

Respondents urge, further, that because the NFL constitution bars a city from holding a franchise and being a member, the expenditure of any public monies for acquisition of the Raiders' franchise cannot be deemed in the public interest. On the other hand, an affidavit filed by the NFL commissioner avers that "a brief interim ownership" by City "would not be inconsistent with the NFL Constitution. . . ." We, of course, are not bound by such an interpretation. Assuming its validity, however, respondents answer that if City contemplates the prompt transfer to private parties of the property interests which it seeks to condemn, after such brief ownership, that transfer would vitiate any legitimate "public use" which is a prerequisite to condemnation in the first place. In turn, City points to the statute which, as previously noted, expressly authorizes that to which respondents object: "[A] person may acquire property under subdivision (a) with the intent to sell, lease, exchange or otherwise dispose of the property or an interest therein," provided such retransfer is made "subject to such reservations or restrictions as are necessary to protect or preserve the attractiveness, safety, and usefulness of the project." So long as adequate controls are imposed upon any retransfer of the condemned property, there is no reason why the "public purpose" which justifies a taking may not be so served and protected. We envision that the adequacy of any such controls can only be determined within the factual context of a specific retransfer agreement.

* * *

Reversed and remanded.

* * *

BIRD, C.J., concurring and dissenting.

The power of eminent domain claimed by the City in this case is not only novel but virtually without limit. This is troubling because the potential for abuse of such a great power is boundless. Although I am forced by the current state of the law to agree with the result reached by the majority, I have not signed their opinion because it endorses this unprecedented application of eminent domain law without even pausing to consider the ultimate consequences of their expansive decision. It should be noted that research both by the parties and by this court has failed to disclose a single case in which the legal propositions relied on here have been combined to reach a result such as that adopted by the majority.

There are two particularly disturbing questions in this case. First, does a city have the power to condemn a viable, ongoing business and sell it to another private party merely because the original owner has announced his intention to move his business to another city? For example, if a rock concert impresario, after some years of producing concerts in a municipal stadium, decides to move his productions to another city, may the city condemn his business, including his contracts with the rock stars, in order to keep the concerts at the stadium? If a small business that rents a storefront on land originally taken by the city for a redevelopment project decides to move to another city in order to expand, may the city take the business and force it to stay at its original location? May a city condemn any business that decides to seek greener pastures elsewhere under the unlimited interpretation of eminent domain law that the majority appear to approve?

Second, even if a city were legally able to do so, is it proper for a municipality to drastically invade personal property rights to further the policy interests asserted here?

The rights both of the owners of the Raiders and of its employees are threatened by the City's action. Thus, one unexplored aspect of the majority's decision is the ruling that contract rights can be taken by eminent domain. The cases relied on by the majority in support of this holding chiefly concerned inverse condemnation suits. Those cases essentially held that when a state condemns a business, the government is obligated to compensate the business owner for the value of the contract rights destroyed by the taking. In this case, the City seeks to condemn employment contracts between the Raiders and dozens of its employees. Can the City acquire personal employment contracts as simply as it can acquire a tract of land? Are an employee's rights violated by this non-consensual taking of an employment contract or personal services agreement?

At what point in the varied and complex business relationships involved herein would this power to condemn end? In my view, this court should proceed most cautiously before placing a constitutional imprimatur upon this aspect of creeping statism. These difficult questions are deserving of more thorough attention than they have yet received in this litigation.

It strikes me as dangerous and heavy-handed for the government to take over a business, including all of its intangible assets, for the sole purpose of preventing its relocation.

* * *

. . . [T]he wisdom of the City's decision here may not be successfully challenged in the courts unless it can be shown that the municipality acted in an arbitrary or capricious fashion, or its act represents a "gross abuse of discretion." Given this present state of the law, on this limited record, respondents have not demonstrated that there has been a violation of these standards. Unless it can be shown that the City's decision to use its power of eminent domain in this fashion was completely irrational, there is no relief available for respondents in the courts. Any relief must come from legislatively imposed restrictions.

The court is further constrained because this case is before us on appeal from a dismissal entered after the granting of a motion for summary judgment. On such an appeal, this court must give the benefit of any doubt to the City. Given the far-reaching potential of this decision, a final conclusion as to the legal validity of the City's action should await a full record and complete factual presentation.

At this stage of the proceedings, there is no constitutional or statutory ground for barring the City's action. Despite my serious misgivings about the wisdom of the City's action and the possible future ramifications of a holding that the state has the power to take an ongoing business to prevent it from leaving a particular area, I am constrained by the law to join, albeit reluctantly, the judgment entered here.

Questions for Discussion

1. Is the majority correct that if it is legitimate to use eminent domain to take someone's land to build a stadium to attract a sports franchise, it is equally legitimate to use eminent domain to take a franchise (at fair compensation) in order to keep the team in the community? On the very broad scope of a government's "public use" prerogative under the federal constitution, see the Supreme Court's subsequent decision in *Hawaii Housing Auth. v. Midkiff*, 467 U.S. 229 (1984).

2. How would one measure the value of a team for purposes of providing fair compensation in the eminent domain proceedings? Is it the value of the Raiders in Oakland or in Los Angeles? With or without favorable lease offers from the two cities competing for the franchise?

3. What precisely is the *public* use for which the municipality exercises its governmental authority either to attract or to keep a professional sports franchise? Recently, some economists have expressed skepticism at the oft-heard claim that it is a good investment of the taxpayers' scarce dollars to lure or to keep a major league team in the area.[12] What are the tangible financial benefits from having a sports franchise in town? Consider how much of a team's revenues come from local sources (gate and concessions) as opposed to national sources (network television)? Where and upon whom does the team spend its revenues? Who tends to go to the games, local residents or tourists, and with what effect on the local economy? Even within a single metropolitan area, are there conflicting interests between the central city—Detroit, for example—and surrounding suburban communities—such as Auburn Hills—seeking to lure one of the city's long-time teams? What are the implications of that analysis for your judgment about who should pay for sports facilities—the taxpayer or the fan? If the fans should pay, how could they do so? Through premium payments for rental of skyboxes and club seats? But what "fans" actually rent many of these kinds of seats, and does this imply that a different taxpayer bears at least part of the cost?

---

12. See, e.g., Arthur T. Johnson, The Sports Franchise Relocation Issue and Public Policy Response, Chapter 12 of Arthur T. Johnson & James Frey eds., *Government and Sports* (Totawa, N.J.: Rownen & Allenheld, 1985); Robert A. Baade & Richard F. Dye, *Sports Stadiums and Area Development: A Critical Review*, 2 Econ. Dev. Q. 265 (1988); Mark S. Rosentraub & David Swindell, *"Just Say No": The Economic and Political Realities of a Small City's Investment in Minor League Baseball*, 5 Econ. Dev. Q. 152 (1991).

4. Are there intangible public values derived from the presence of a sports team in a locality? What are they? Do they affect your judgment about the public finance issues noted above?

———

The force of the *City of Oakland I* ruling was felt soon thereafter on the other side of the country. Robert Irsay, owner of the Baltimore Colts, had been negotiating with Baltimore, Phoenix, and Indianapolis to secure the best new stadium offer upon the expiry of his Baltimore Memorial Stadium lease. After the State of Maryland enacted an amendment to its eminent domain legislation that would explicitly authorize such proceedings against the Colts by the City of Baltimore, Irsay promptly decamped late one night in moving vans that took all the Colt's personnel and tangible property to a hearty welcome in Indianapolis the next day. A federal district court in Maryland eventually ruled that Irsay had thereby eluded the reach of the Baltimore City Council's eminent domain ordinance. See *Mayor & City Council of Baltimore v. Baltimore (Colts) Football Club*, 624 F.Supp. 278 (D.Md. 1985). If the intangible property to be condemned is the NFL franchise assigned in the NFL constitution to Baltimore, was this ruling correct?

Of course, only a few teams can make the sudden getaway accomplished by the Colts. States could enact explicit legislation to authorize eminent domain proceedings if a team threatened to move in the midst of negotiations for a lease renewal and improved facilities. Why then was the Oakland action not emulated by Chicago, for example, when threatened with loss of its White Sox to St. Petersburg (unless a new Comiskey Park were built at public expense)? Part of the answer, at least, can be found in the next decision (which was summarily affirmed by the California Supreme Court) addressing a federal constitutional argument raised against Oakland on remand from *City of Oakland I*.[13]

CITY OF OAKLAND v. OAKLAND RAIDERS (II)

California Court of Appeals, First District, 1985.

174 Cal.App.3d 414, 220 Cal.Rptr. 153.

SABRAW, ASSOCIATE JUSTICE.

We turn first to the trial court's commerce clause determination. United States Constitution, article 1, section 8, clause 3, grants Congress the power "[t]o regulate commerce ... among the several States...." This provision was intended to foster development and maintenance of a national common market among the states and to eradicate trade barriers. Indeed, "[r]ecognition of [this] predominant

---

13. See Gray, note 11 above; Lisa J. Tobin–Rubio, *Eminent Domain and the Commerce Clause Defense*, 41 U. of Miami L. Rev. 1185 (1987); Edward P. Lazarus, *The Commerce Clause Limitation on the Power to Condemn a Relocating Business*, 96 Yale L.J. 1543 (1987).

goal ... has permeated judicial interpretations of state power to regulate commerce."

It is today established that state or local regulation of interstate commerce will be upheld if it " 'regulates even-handedly to effectuate a legitimate local public interest, and its effects on interstate commerce are only incidental ... unless the burden imposed on such commerce is clearly excessive in relation to putative local benefits.' " Still, "experience teaches that no single conceptual approach identifies all of the factors that may bear on a particular [commerce clause] case." One additional, albeit less recently relied-on approach to review of state or local action under the commerce clause provides that burdens will be voided if the regulation governs "those phases of the national economy which, because of the need of national uniformity, demand their regulation, if any, be prescribed by a single authority." The absence of Congressional action respecting such economic matters is not controlling because, as has been long established, the commerce clause limits state power by its own force.

* * *

Plaintiff contends exercise of eminent domain power can never violate the commerce clause and notes that no previous case has precluded an eminent domain taking under that constitutional provision. The lack of such case law, however, is unremarkable; it serves merely to point out that eminent domain cases have traditionally concerned real property, rarely implicating commerce clause considerations which deal primarily with products in the flow of interstate commerce. Whether the commerce clause precludes taking by eminent domain of intangible property, however, is a novel question posed, it seems, for the first time in this case.

It is well established that a state may exercise eminent domain power even though by so doing it indirectly or incidentally burdens interstate commerce. Defendants, however, contend that professional football is such a nationwide business and so completely involved in interstate commerce that acquisition of a franchise by an individual state through eminent domain would impermissibly burden interstate commerce. A recent Supreme Court decision, *Partee v. San Diego Chargers Football Co.*, 194 Cal.Rptr. 367 (1983), supports this view.

Partee held that the NFL required nationally uniform regulation and that interstate commerce would be unreasonably burdened if state antitrust laws applied to a League franchise located in this state. Uniform nationwide regulation was called for because:

> Professional football's teams are dependent upon the league playing schedule for competitive play.... The necessity of a nationwide league structure for the benefit of both teams and players for effective competition is evident as is the need for a nationally uniform set of rules governing the league structure. Fragmentation of the league structure on the basis of state lines would

adversely affect the success of the competitive business enterprise, and differing state antitrust decisions if applied to the enterprise would likely compel all member teams to comply with the laws of the strictest state.

The same situation is presented here. Indeed, the trial court's findings track and amplify on *Partee*. Regarding the interdependent character of the NFL, the court noted that each member team is substantially dependent for its income on every other team: League television contract proceeds are divided equally and gate receipts nearly equally; a team's drawing power is therefore a financial benefit to the other teams as well as to itself; hence the capacity and quality of the facility in which games are played is a component of the League's financial success. The court also found evidence of the necessity of a nationwide League structure: based on the above factors, each League franchise owner has an important interest in the identity, personality, financial stability, commitment, and good faith of each other owner. Thus, under League bylaws, new members must first be approved by the current members. In short, although the clubs compete to an important degree, the League is also a joint venture of its members organized for the purpose of providing entertainment nationwide. Finally, the court found that a bar to relocation on the basis of state eminent domain law would adversely affect the League enterprise. An involuntarily acquired franchise could, at the local government's pleasure, be permanently indentured to the local entity. The League's interests would be subordinated to, or at least compromised by, the new owner's allegiance to the local public interest in matters such as lease agreements, ticket prices, concessions, stadium amenities, scheduling conflicts, etc. As the trial court found, it must also be anticipated that a single precedent of eminent domain acquisition would pervade the entire League, and even the threat of its exercise elsewhere would seriously disrupt the balance of economic bargaining on stadium leases throughout the nation.

Plaintiff's proposed action would more than indirectly or incidentally regulate interstate commerce: plaintiff claims authority—pursuant to authorization found in state eminent domain statutes—to bar indefinitely defendant's business from relocating out of Oakland. This is the precise brand of parochial meddling with the national economy that the commerce clause was designed to prohibit.

As shown above, relocation of the Raiders would implicate the welfare not only of the individual team franchise, but of the entire League. The spectre of such local action throughout the state or across the country demonstrates the need for uniform, national regulation. In these circumstances, ... if relocation threatens disproportionate harm to a local entity, regulation—if necessary—should come from Congress; only then can the consequences to interstate commerce be assessed and a proper balance struck to consider and serve the various interests involved in a uniform manner.

Case dismissed.

————

In a major constitutional ruling handed down two years after the above decision, a divided Supreme Court held in *CTS Corp. v. Dynamics Corp. of Am.*, 481 U.S. 69, 107 S.Ct. 1637, 95 L.Ed.2d 67 (1987), that neither the federal securities laws nor the interstate commerce clause preempted Indiana legislation to control hostile takeover bids launched from outside the state against corporations legally domiciled within the state. Yet the appellate court in *City of Oakland II* held that a local government, exercising state legislative authority, was precluded by the "dormant" commerce clause from trying to block the Raiders' move from one city to another city within the same state. Can one square this holding with *CTS Corp.* by finding an intrinsic difference in the relationship between an individual club and the overall league, as compared to the operation of our national securities market? But is any such argument on behalf of the Raiders against Oakland's eminent domain claim compatible with the Raiders earlier position in support of its intraleague conspiracy claim against the NFL?

————

The NFL's generally unhappy experience with the various kinds of litigation depicted in this chapter sent Commissioner Rozelle to Congress in the early 1980s to seek legislative relief. In particular, the NFL sought enactment of a law that would explicitly exempt from section 1 challenge the League's internal policies and decisions regarding revenue sharing, approval of new owners, expansion, and most importantly, franchise relocation. In an (unsuccessful) effort to avoid opposition from the players association, the NFL did not ask for legislative relief from section 1 suits about the players market.

In the Senate Commerce Committee, at least, the NFL succeeded in winning majority approval of a bill called the *Professional Sports Community Protection Act* of 1985. Though for a variety of reasons, this Act did not get any farther down the legislative path, it is worthwhile sketching the range of positions taken about the bill, to focus discussion about the underlying issues.[14]

• Senator DeConcini of Arizona favored total deregulation—in the sense of granting the league immunity from any section 1 antitrust liability for its franchise decisions.

14. See Glenn M. Wong, *Of Franchise Relocation, Expansion, and Competition in Professional Sports: The Ultimate Political Football*, 9 Seton Hall L.J. 1 (1985); Daniel S. York, *The Professional Sports Community Protection Act: Congress' Best Response to Raiders*, 38 Hastings L.J. 345 (1987); John A. Gray, *Section 1 of the Sherman Act and Control Over NFL Franchise Locations: The Problem of Opportunistic Behavior*, 25 Amer. Bus. L.J. 123 (1987); John Beisner, *Sports Franchise Relocation: Competitive Markets and Taxpayer Protection*, 6 Yale L. & Pol. Rev. 429 (1988).

• Senator Danforth of Missouri (for the committee majority) proposed granting a league substantial immunity from section 1 antitrust liability if its constitution were worded so as to allow relocation only if the proposed move was "reasonable and appropriate" in light of some or all of the following factors: a history of low public financial support for the team; low fan support; significant operating losses at the present site; the responsibility of team management for the team's declining financial and popular success; and the presence or absence of other league teams in the current and proposed locations. A judge could overturn the league's relocation decision only if it was not based on "substantial evidence."

• Senator Gorton of Washington, while accepting the above substantive factors, wanted a crucial procedural change. Any party objecting to the league's decision about a proposed relocation would have a right to full review before a tripartite arbitration board to decide whether the proposed team move was *necessary* (not just *reasonable*) and appropriate.

• Senator Spector of Pennsylvania wanted to grant antitrust immunity only if the league's constitution restricted franchise moves to cases in which the stadium was demonstrably inadequate for profitable operations, or the stadium authority had consistently violated major terms in the lease agreement, or the team had a history of operating losses that endangered its long-term profitability.

Questions for Discussion

With respect to the above approaches and any others that may occur to you, ask yourself:

1. Do the cases we have read present a serious legal problem requiring a legislative solution?

2. If there is a problem, is the best solution to return control to the league? What criteria should the league use to make these decisions? Can one trust the deliberations of autonomous league councils to produce decisions that are truly in "the best interests of the sport." Or, do we need some measure of—perhaps searching—judicial scrutiny of the league's verdict? Can one trust a court, sitting in a community greatly affected by the result, to make a fully dispassionate judgment? (Might the Raiders' case have come out differently had it been tried before an Oakland judge and jury?) If neither leagues nor local courts are the best decision makers, what process would you recommend?

3. Suppose that a league incorporated in its constitution relocation criteria such as those proposed in the Danforth bill. Without congressional action, do those criteria pass antitrust muster in the courts?

4. With respect to the substantive merits, why is so much emphasis placed on the claims of fans in the team's current community? If our objective is the broader public welfare, is it not as good a test as any to see whether fans in other communities are willing to pay more to get a

particular team? Do people have a special moral entitlement to keep an existing team, as opposed to securing a new team?

———

All the above questions are premised on the assumption that this issue should be viewed through the lens of section 1 of the Sherman Act. Suspend final judgment about the questions of franchise relocation and expansion until we consider in Chapter 7 a sharply different conception of these issues, under section 2 of the Sherman Act, which deals with monopolization.

Note on Tax Treatment of Franchise Values

While professional sports leagues have been unsuccessful so far in securing statutory protection for their decisions about franchise relocation, they have won special congressional treatment in several areas. The most important of these areas is the sale of television rights, which is the topic of the next section. Here we briefly describe the favorable treatment federal tax law provides for the purchase and sale of sports franchises.[15]

These rather esoteric tax rules are a key part of the explanation for an otherwise puzzling phenomenon—the continued escalation in franchise prices over the last quarter century while owners regularly lament the "losses" they experience in running their teams (losses that owners invariably attribute to rising player salaries). For example, in 1988 Victor Kiam purchased the New England Patriots for $85 million. The Patriots then dropped to the bottom of the National Football League both on the playing field and in fan attendance. Eventually Kiam was forced to sell the team in 1992 because of its reported deficits. Surprisingly, though, the new purchaser, Jim Orthwein, paid approximately $105 million for the Patriots.

The explanation for this apparent financial discrepancy stems from the way in which purchasers of a team are entitled to allocate and depreciate the assets that make up a sports franchise. Assuming that the club does not own the stadium in which it plays, the team's only tangible assets are its playing and office equipment (which is of modest value). One could plausibly argue that the bulk of the purchase price—particularly for a brand-new expansion team should be attributed to the "franchise" itself. It is this contractual regime that gives the team the exclusive rights to play in its territory (usually in a publicly owned and subsidized facility) and to share in the league's national television and marketing contracts. However, because the useful life and economic value of a franchise lasts indefi-

15. In-depth analyses of this topic can be found in Benjamin Okner, Taxation and Sports Enterprises, Chapter 5 of Roger G. Noll, ed., *Government and the Sports Business* (Washington, D.C.: Brookings, 1974), and Stafford Matthews, Taxation of Sports; Chapter 22 of Gary Uberstine, ed., *Law of Professional and Amateur Sports* (Deerfield, Ill: Clark, Boardman & Callaghan, 1991) (particularly § 22.04 on "Sale or Transfer of a Sports Franchise"). For an up-to-date synopsis of the financial significance of this issue see Zimbalist, *Baseball and Billions*, note 1 above, at 34–36. And for a brief description of how this tax device was originally used, by the person who claims to have "invented" it, see William Veeck, *Hustler's Handbook*, 328–332 (New York: Putnam, 1965).

nitely, it is a nondepreciable asset for tax purposes, just like the land on which stands Wrigley Field, owned by the Chicago Cubs.

Thus, beginning in the 1960s club owners took the position that much of the purchase price should be allocated to the player contracts that came with the franchise. By the late 1970s both the courts and Congress had accepted that theory, overriding the contrary views of the Internal Revenue Service (IRS). In *Selig v. United States*, 740 F.2d 572 (7th Cir.1984), the Seventh Circuit ruled that of the $10.8 million that Allan "Bud" Selig paid in 1969 to buy the insolvent Seattle Pilots and move them to Milwaukee (as the Brewers), $10.2 million (approximately 95%) was properly attributable to the 150 major and minor league players that came with the team. In *Laird v. United States*, 556 F.2d 1224 (5th Cir.1977), the Fifth Circuit held that of the $8.45 million paid by the Smith family in 1966 for an NFL expansion franchise in Atlanta, $3.05 million (approximately 40%) was attributable to the player contracts. (The disparity in the two rulings was due to the district court's appraisal in *Laird* of the value of the Smiths' share of the NFL's national television contract.) These appellate court rulings were not rendered until fifteen years after the original team purchase. In the meantime, as part of its Tax Reform Act of 1976, Congress had enacted § 1056 of the Internal Revenue Code, which created a presumption that no more than 50% of the sale price of a franchise should be attributed to its players. Currently, at least when the club's purchase price does not include a playing facility, this 50% figure operates more as a floor than as a ceiling.

The reason why this tax treatment is financially significant is that player contracts are a depreciable asset that can be amortized over the five-year period that is the typical professional career. Thus, when Victor Kiam bought the Patriots for $85 million in 1988, he could readily impute $40 million of this price to his player contracts and write off $8 million each year against any operating profits earned by the team over the next five year span. If the club's operating profits totalled less than $8 million in any one year, the extra book losses could be set off against Kiam's earnings from any other business he owned, such as Remington Rand.

The Fifth Circuit in *Laird* (echoed by the Seventh Circuit in *Selig*) had rejected the IRS position that only a modest portion of the club's purchase price should be allocated to the players who came with the team:

> [I]t is clear that the players are the primary assets of a professional football club. Without them, there could not be a game. As Texas E. Schramm, the widely-respected President and General Manager of the Dallas Cowboys, testified:
>
>> The players are the principal product and it is players who are responsible for your winning. They are responsible for the fans coming to your stadium. They are responsible for the income that you receive on television.
>>
>> Without the players, in professional football, you don't have anything.
>
> 556 F.2d, at 1277.

While players are obviously the crucial factor in a team's success on the field, how relevant is that fact to the tax question of whether player contracts should be deemed a depreciable asset of the team? Is not the crucial athletic asset that comes with the purchase of a franchise the right to participate in the rookie draft, the veteran reserve system, and other features of the players market that allow teams to restock their rosters as current players leave? Keep in mind that clubs include in their operating expenses the money they spend on player salaries owed under the contracts, as well as expenditures made for scouting, drafting, and training new playing prospects (including the minor league operations in baseball and hockey). Should the buyer of a Hollywood studio be entitled to write off 50% of the purchase price as payment for the movie stars the studio has under contract for ongoing film productions (as well as deduct from taxable income all salary payments made under these contracts)?

When the concept of player depreciation first emerged on the tax accounting scene in the 1960s, the owners' practice was to write off the value of players *presently* on their rosters. When the team was later sold after these players had retired, none of the sale price would be attributed to these assets that had been fully depreciated and literally disappeared from the game. Section 1245 of the Internal Revenue Code (as amended by the 1976 Tax Reform Act) blocked that loophole. Now, if a team is sold for more than its base value after the write-off of player contracts, the gains are recaptured and taxed as of the date of sale. In effect clubs can postpone, rather than eliminate, tax liability for any operating profits the team had written off. This tax break still constitutes a valuable, long-term, interest-free "loan" from the government in the amount of the taxes that would otherwise have been payable on operating profits, analogous to the tax savings gained from contributions made to pensions and other retirement plans. And if the owner holds on to the franchise until he dies, this loan is forgiven by the government, because tax law deems the heirs to assume title to this (and other) assets at their current market value.

The tax reforms of the 1980s further reduced the legal value of this tax benefit by reducing the top marginal income tax rates for individuals and corporations from their 1970s levels of 70% and 52%, respectively, to the 31% and 34% rates that prevail in the early 1990s. On the other hand, the financial value of such a depreciable asset has increased much faster because of sharply higher franchise sale prices. There is no better illustration than the Nintendo group's purchase of the Seattle Mariners in 1992 for more than $100 million—ten times the amount paid by Bud Selig in 1969 for the Seattle Pilots.

C. LEAGUE–WIDE TELEVISION CONTRACTS [16]

The earliest antitrust problems encountered by sports leagues in their internal dealings concerned league policy toward a new medium,

16. On the broader financial and social implications of sports on television, see David A. Klatell & Norman Marcus, *Sports* *for Sale: Television, Money, and the Fans* (New York: Oxford University Press, 1988). For an excellent, but now factually-

television. In the early 1950s, the right to broadcast a game on radio or television belonged to and was sold by either of the teams playing in the game (see *Liberty Broadcast Sys. v. National League Baseball Club of Boston, Inc.*, 1952 Trade Case (CCH) ¶ 67,278 (N.D.Ill.)). However, television posed a special threat to the fundamental principle of territorial exclusivity embodied in league constitutions, a principle that insulated franchise owners from intrusion by other clubs into their home markets. Broadcasts of games involving the more successful teams (such as the New York Yankees in baseball and the Cleveland Browns in football) could be beamed into any part of the country. Thus, the earliest league television policy sought to limit the breadth of broadcasts of games played by any one team, a policy that attracted the unfavorable attention of the Justice Department in the first case in this section.

Not long afterwards, it became evident that league-wide pooling and sale of broadcast rights would help the league enlarge the total revenues it derived from television and would permit a more equitable distribution of these funds among all clubs in the league. To facilitate such arrangements for the National Football League, in particular, the Congress enacted the Sports Broadcasting Act (SBA) of 1961, the first ever antitrust exemption fashioned for sports by the legislative—as opposed to the judicial—branch of our national government. The second decision in this section depicts the immense role played by sports television in the 1980s and the complex legal and policy problems television poses for both the leagues and their fans.

UNITED STATES v. NFL

United States District Court, Eastern District of Pennsylvania, 1983.

116 F.Supp. 319.

GRIM, DISTRICT JUDGE.

[The NFL's initial stance was to permit each individual team to contract for the telecasting of games in which that team was participating. However, the League's by-laws contained a blanket prohibition against teams broadcasting their games into the home territories of other teams. The Justice Department charged that this league policy constituted an agreement in restraint of trade in violation of Section 1 of the Sherman Antitrust Act.]

dated, economic analysis of televised sports, see Ira Horowitz, Sports Broadcasting, Chapter 8 of Roger G. Noll, ed., *Government and the Sports Business*, (Washington, D.C.: Brookings, 1974). See also Joan M. Chandler, Sport as T.V. Product: A Case Study of "Monday Night Football," Chapter 2 of Paul D. Staudohar & James A. Mangan eds., *The Business of Professional Sport* (Urbana, Ill.: University of Illinois Press, 1991). The legal framework for these issues is detailed in Robert Alan Garrett & Philip R. Hochberg, Sports Broadcasting, Chapter 11 of Gary Uberstine ed., *Law of Professional and Amateur Sports*, note is above. The best treatment of the contemporary antitrust issues to be found is Stephen F. Ross, *An Antitrust Analysis of Sports League Contracts with Cable Networks*, 39 Emory L.J. 463 (1990).

I.

Is the provision which prevents the telecasting of outside games into the home territories of other teams on days when the other teams are playing at home illegal?

There can be little doubt that this provision constitutes a contract in restraint of trade. The market for the public exhibition of football no longer is limited to the spectators who attend the games. Since the advent of television and radio, the visual and aural projections of football games can be marketed anywhere in the world where there are television or radio facilities to transmit and receive them. When a football team agrees to restrict the projection of its games in the home areas of other teams, it thereby cuts itself off from this part of its potential market. Since the clubs of the National Football League have agreed at certain times not to project their games into the home territories of other clubs, they have given that part of their market at those certain times exclusively to other teams. In return, each of them has been given the right to market its own games without competition in its own home area under the same circumstances. The purpose and effect of this is to restrict outside competition on the part of other teams in the home area of each club. This, therefore, is a clear case of allocating marketing territories among competitors, which is a practice generally held illegal under the anti-trust laws.

An allocation of marketing territories for the purpose of restricting competition, however, is not always illegal.... The principal question in the present case is whether the particular restraints imposed by Article X are reasonable or unreasonable.

Professional football is a unique type of business. Like other professional sports which are organized on a league basis, it has problems which no other business has. The ordinary business makes every effort to sell as much of its product or services as it can. In the course of doing this it may and often does put many of its competitors out of business. The ordinary businessman is not troubled by the knowledge that he is doing so well that his competitors are being driven out of business.

Professional teams in a league, however, must not compete too well with each other, in a business way. On the playing field, of course, they must compete as hard as they can all the time. But it is not necessary and indeed it is unwise for all the teams to compete as hard as they can against each other in a business way. If all the teams should compete as hard as they can in a business way, the stronger teams would be likely to drive the weaker ones into financial failure. If this should happen not only would the weaker teams fail, but eventually the whole league, both the weaker and the stronger teams, would fail, because without a league no team can operate profitably.

It is particularly true in the National Football League that the teams should not compete too strongly with each other in a business way. The evidence shows that in the National Football League less than half the clubs over a period of years are likely to be financially successful. There are always teams in the League which are close to financial failure. Under these circumstances it is both wise and essential that rules be passed to help the weaker clubs in their competition with the stronger ones and to keep the League in fairly even balance.

The winning teams usually are the wealthier ones and unless restricted by artificial rules the rich get richer and the poor get poorer (as Commissioner Bell put it). Winning teams draw larger numbers of spectators to their games than do losing teams and from the larger gate receipts they make greater profits than do losing teams. With this greater wealth they can spend more money to obtain new players, they can pay higher salaries, and they can have better spirit among their players than can the weaker teams. With these better and happier players they will continue to win most of their games while the weaker teams will continue to lose most of their games. The weaker teams share in the prosperity of the stronger teams to a certain extent, since as visiting teams they share in the gate receipts of the stronger teams. But in time even the most enthusiastic fans of strong home teams will cease to be attracted to home games with increasingly weaker visiting teams. Thus, the net effects of allowing unrestricted business competition among the clubs are likely to be, first, the creation of greater and greater inequalities in the strength of the teams; second, the weaker teams being driven out of business; and, third, the destruction of the entire League.

In order to try to keep its teams at approximately equal strength and to protect weaker teams from stronger teams, a league theoretically might use a number of devices. It might (1) limit the bonus price which could be paid to new players, (2) give the weaker teams a prior right over stronger teams to draft new players, (3) prohibit the sale of players after a certain day in the playing season, (4) limit the number of players on each team, (5) limit the total amount of salaries which a team can pay, (6) give the lowest team in the league the right to draft a player from the highest team, when and if the highest team has won a certain number (three for instance) of consecutive championships, and (7) reasonably restrict the projection of games by radio or television into the home territories of other teams.

It is easy to see that the first six devices would make it easier for weaker teams to compete with stronger ones. The usefulness of the seventh device, however, in the protection of the weaker teams may not be so obvious, particularly since it prevents the weaker teams from televising into the home territories of the stronger teams as much as it prevents the stronger teams from telecasting into the home territories of the weaker ones. The evidence indicates that television audiences and sponsors have so little interest in games between weak teams that it is very difficult to obtain sponsors for outside telecasts of such games. Consequently, the weaker teams lose practically nothing by this television restriction. But they benefit greatly from it in that the restriction adds to their home game attendance by preventing potential spectators from staying at home to watch on television exciting outside head-on games between strong teams. The competitive position of the weaker teams is improved by this increase in home attendance, while the competitive position of the stronger teams is weakened somewhat by their inability to sell to sponsors the right to televise their desirable head-on games into the home territories of the weaker teams when the weaker teams are playing at home.

A large part of defendants' evidence was directed to the question of whether the televising of a team's own home games in that team's home territory has an adverse effect on attendance at these home games. The evidence on this point, particularly the evidence relating to the great decrease in home attendance of the Los Angeles Rams during the 1950 season when all its home games were televised at home, shows quite clearly that the telecasting of a home game into a home territory while the home game is being played has an adverse effect on the attendance at the game. This clearly indicates by implication that the telecast of an outside game, particularly a head-on game, also adversely affects attendance at a home game.

* * *

The greatest part of the defendant clubs' income is derived from the sale of tickets to games. Reasonable protection of home game attendance is essential to the very existence of the individual clubs, without which there can be no League and no professional football as we know it today.

This is not a case of one industry fighting the competition of another, as for instance coal fighting the competition of oil, or railroads fighting the competition of trucks, or moving pictures fighting the competition of television. Football provides a magnificent spectacle for television programs and television provides an excellent outlet and market for football. They both can use and indeed need each other. By working together intelligently each will be an important adjunct to the other. The objective of the clubs in agreeing to a television blackout of the home territory (except for the remote possibility of a home game telecast) during the day a home game is played is not to restrain competition among the individual clubs in the sale of television rights or competition among television stations and networks and advertisers and advertising agencies in the purchase of such rights. This particular restriction promotes competition more than it restrains it in that its immediate effect is to protect the weak teams and its ultimate effect is to preserve the League itself. By thus preserving professional football this restriction makes possible competition in the sale and purchase of television rights in situations in which the restriction does not apply.

The purposes of the Sherman Act certainly will not be served by prohibiting the defendant clubs, particularly the weaker clubs, from protecting their home gate receipts from the disastrous financial effects of invading telecasts of outside games. The member clubs of the

National Football League, like those of any professional athletic league, can exist only as long as the league exists. The League is truly a unique business enterprise, which is entitled to protect its very existency by agreeing to reasonable restrictions on its member clubs. The first type of restriction imposed by Article X is a reasonable one and a legal restraint of trade.

II.

Is the restriction on telecasting outside games in home territories when the home teams are playing away games and telecasting them in their home territories illegal?

The reasonableness of this particular restriction must also be tested by its effect on the attendance and gate receipts of a team's home games. It is obvious that on a day when the home team is playing an away game there is no gate attendance to be harmed back in its home area and the prohibition of outside telecasts within its home area cannot serve to protect gate attendance at the away game, which is played in the opponent's home territory.

Several of defendants' witnesses attempted to justify the restriction with the opinion that it is necessary in this situation to protect the home team's "good will" by which they meant that the restriction is necessary to protect the home team from loss in gate receipts at subsequent home games. However, there is not one shred of evidence, not one specific example based on actual experience, to support this opinion which, more accurately stated, is nothing more than conjecture.

It is probably true, though not proved by the evidence, that the simultaneous telecasting of an outside game and an away game in the home area of the team playing away would result in a division of the television audience between the two games. Obviously the existence or the prospect of such competition would make the television rights to the home club's away games less attractive to sponsors and consequently less profitable to the club. But this does not concern attendance at football games. Indeed, the testimony of defendants' witnesses consistently indicates that the primary reason for the restrictions in this situation actually is to enable the clubs in the home territories to sell monopoly rights to purchasers of television rights to away games.

The record in this case contains no factual justification for Article X's suppression of competing telecasts of League games when, for example, the Philadelphia Eagle's away game is being televised in its home territory. Defendants' speculation or conjecture that without such restriction gate attendance would decline a week or two later at the Eagles' home game has little probative value. Article X's restriction on this type of competition is an unreasonable and illegal restraint of trade.

Charge upheld in part.

The district court issued a decree that prohibited the National Football League and its clubs from adopting any rules or entering into any television contract that restricted the area in which any team's games would be broadcast, except into a team's home territory on a day it was playing a home game. In 1960, the American Football League (AFL) started operations and immediately negotiated a leaguewide television contract with ABC. At this time, each NFL club was still selling its television rights separately. The new NFL Commissioner, Pete Rozelle, believed that if the AFL was going to operate with the advantage of a league-wide television package, the NFL had to do the same. Such a contract under which revenues were shared equally by all clubs was becoming more important to the NFL because teams in the large markets (New York, Chicago, and Los Angeles) were getting much greater revenues for their television rights than were teams in smaller cities (Green Bay, Pittsburgh, and Baltimore). The resulting disparity in income, coupled with competition for players from the AFL, threatened the ability of small-market clubs to field good teams. (An even greater disparity in income from local television revenues is having a similar effect in major league baseball today.) Thus, Rozelle promptly negotiated a league-wide television contract with CBS. The NFL then petitioned Judge Grim to approve the new CBS contract.

However, because a provision of the NFL–CBS contract barred individual teams from selling television rights for their games to competing broadcasters, Judge Grim held (at 196 F.Supp. 445 (E.D.Pa. 1961)) that the contract violated the terms of his 1953 antitrust decree. The NFL went to the Congress and persuaded it to pass the Sports Broadcasting Act (SBA). The key provisions of the SBA were as follows:

> § 1291. The antitrust laws ... shall not apply to any joint agreement by or among persons engaging in or conducting the organized professional team sports of football, baseball, basketball, or hockey, by which any league of clubs ... sells or otherwise transfers all or any part of the rights of such league's member clubs in the sponsored telecasting of the games of football, baseball, basketball, or hockey as the case may be, engaged in or conducted by such clubs....
>
> § 1292. Section 1291 of this title shall not apply to any joint agreement described in the first sentence in such section which prohibits any person to whom such rights are sold or transferred from televising any games within any area, except within the home territory of a member club of the league on a day when said club is playing at home.

Questions for Discussion

1. As we saw in the *NFL* decision, the Justice Department alleged and the court agreed that the league's television policies constituted a "conspiracy in restraint of trade" by the clubs, in violation of section 1 of the Sherman Act. Does the SBA, which grants professional sports leagues

special antitrust immunity for television contracts, constitute tacit congressional recognition of the "economically divisible" as opposed to "single entity" character of a sports league in all its other policy decisions—in particular, when the league limits the free agency enjoyed by either its players or its owners? But what are the implications of the following section of the SBA?

> § 1294. Nothing contained in this chapter shall be deemed to change, determine, or otherwise affect the applicability or nonapplicability of the antitrust laws to any act, contract, agreement, rule, course of conduct, or other activity by, between, or among persons engaging in, conducting, or participating in the organized professional team sports of football, baseball, basketball, or hockey, except the agreements to which section 1291 of this title shall apply.

2. Section 1292 of the SBA limits the antitrust immunity granted by section 1291 to television contracts that restrict blacked-out games to those being played by member clubs at home on the day of the telecast. Given that the NFL definition of "home territory" is the area within a 75–mile radius of the franchise city, does this exemption cover a league requirement that a network to black out broadcasts of Miami Dolphins games from a television station located 100 miles from Miami whose signal reaches as close as 40 miles to Miami? See *WTWV v. NFL*, 678 F.2d 142 (11th Cir.1982). What if the signal reached Miami only after bouncing off a satellite and could be received only with a satellite dish?

3. All NFL regular season games are televised pursuant to national network contracts. If the Dolphins unilaterally decided to have one of their non-sellout games blacked out in New York (assuming the network contract permitted such a black-out), so that section 1292 was triggered and the section 1291 exemption was vitiated, what would be the legal implications? Is section 1 of the Sherman Act thereby violated? Is Judge Grim's decree (which has never been lifted) violated? What if the Dolphins sold the rights to one of its preseason home games to CBS but required that it be blacked out in both Miami and New York—would that eliminate the exemption? Would the black-out be illegal? What would happen if the visiting team sold the rights to the same game to NBC and allowed the telecast to be shown in Miami and New York?

4. Are league contracts with cable networks covered by the SBA? By its terms, section 1291 extends antitrust immunity to a league's sale of pooled rights for "sponsored telecasting of games." The major sports cable networks such as ESPN, TNT, and SportsChannel America are funded partially by subscriber's fees and partially by advertising revenues. In addition, the transmission by cable programming from event to television screen fits within the term "telecasting." The legislative history of the SBA, however, casts doubt on whether Congress intended to grant antitrust immunity to any league contracts other than those with the "free" television networks. When the SBA was enacted in 1961, its chief proponent, NFL Commissioner Pete Rozelle, told Congress that "[T]his bill covers only the free telecasting of professional sports contests, and does not cover pay TV." In 1982, then-NFL counsel (and now Commissioner) Paul Tagliabue reiterated to a Senate Committee that "the words 'sponsored telecasting'

were intended to exclude pay and cable. This is clear from the legislative history and from the committee reports. So, that statute does not authorize us to pool and sell to pay and cable." In light of these comments before and after enactment of the SBA, how should a court interpret the Act with respect to the NFL's current television contracts with ESPN and TNT? With reference to the NHL's contract with SportsChannel America? With respect to any attempts to put the Super Bowl, or the NBA playoffs, or regular season games, on pay-per-view television?

5. If the SBA does not provide antitrust immunity for the NFL's contracts with ESPN and TNT, or the NHL's contract (from 1988 to 1992) with SportsChannel America, do these contracts, under a rule of reason analysis, violate section 1 of the Sherman Act?

6. Does an NFL restriction on the telecasting of a playoff game or the Super Bowl violate section 1 under the reasoning of *United States v. NFL*? If such restrictions are a violation, does the SBA exempt them? See *Blaich v. National Football League*, 212 F.Supp. 319 (S.D.N.Y.1962).

7. Does the SBA have any implications for league revenue sharing. Article 10.3 of the NFL constitution provides that all member clubs share equally in the league's television revenues. (It was a major political accomplishment of new Commissioner Pete Rozelle to persuade the Mara family (New York Giants), George Halas (Chicago Bears), and Dan Reeves (Los Angeles Rams) to agree to this policy, which transferred significant dollar revenues from their clubs to those in smaller media markets. Similar suggestions over the years in other major sports leagues have been quickly killed by large market owners.) Even though the legislative history makes it clear that one important rationale for the SBA was to allow NFL teams to share television revenues, does the SBA's language exempt the sharing of network television revenues? If not exempt, is such revenue sharing, or the sharing of any other type of revenue (such as local radio and television revenues, gate receipts, luxury box rental fees, parking and concessions revenues, and trademark licensing fees), a section 1 antitrust violation?

8. Even if the SBA does not offer special antitrust shelter to a particular league television package, that gap is not necessarily filled by affirmative antitrust liability. For example, does major league baseball's judicially-fashioned antitrust immunity apply to its contract with ESPN? See *Henderson Broadcast Corp. v. Houston Sports Association*, 541 F.Supp. 263 (S.D.Tex.1982)?

The more fundamental question is how judges should treat current league television policies, which have progressed far beyond the primitive state displayed to Judge Grim in 1953, under modern principles of antitrust analysis that have also become more sophisticated. Sports television revenues from contracts negotiated under the protective umbrella of the SBA have experienced phenomenal growth. The first exclusive NFL contract with CBS, signed in 1962, paid the 14 teams a total of $4.65 million ($320,000 per team). Thirty years later, the

NFL's five network contracts earned its 28 teams a total of $950 million ($34 million per team). Similarly, major league baseball's network contracts in the early 1960s netted a little more than $3 million per year, while the early 1992 combination of CBS and ESPN contracts paid $350 million per year (in addition to the $350 million that baseball teams cumulatively received from sales of their local broadcasting rights). In the 1980s, the National Basketball Association (NBA) teams began to share in those television riches (as did their players through the salary cap arrangement). It was the NBA's television policy that finally provided another, more up-to-date look at the legal issues.

CHICAGO PROFESSIONAL SPORTS LIMITED PARTNERSHIP & WGN v. NBA

United States Court of Appeals, Seventh Circuit, 1992.

961 F.2d 667.

[The factual background is drawn from the district court opinion (at 754 F.Supp. 1336 (E.D. Ill.1991).]

The National Basketball Association ("NBA"), acting through its Board of Governors, limits the number of games NBA teams may broadcast over "superstations." Superstations are independent, over-the-air television stations that broadcast in their local market areas and are also carried by cable systems to other parts of the country. WTBS in Atlanta, WGN TV in Chicago and WWOR in New York are all examples of superstations. The NBA's rules, including those limiting games on superstations, of which there have been several over the years, are enacted by vote of the NBA's Board of Governors, a body consisting of one representative from each of the 27 NBA teams.

During each of the last five seasons, the NBA's superstation rules allowed every NBA team to broadcast up to 25 games on a superstation. But effective this season, the Board of Governors has adopted a new rule reducing that number from 25 to 20. Chicago Professional Sports Limited Partnership, owners of Chicago's NBA franchise, the Chicago Bulls, and WGN Continental Broadcasting Co. ("WGN"), to whom the partnership ("the Bulls") had licensed 25 Bulls games for this season, seek to enjoin the league from enforcing the new 20–game rule so that the Bulls may sell and WGN may buy rights to televise 25 rather than only 20 Bulls games for broadcast nationwide.

This is an antitrust case. The Bulls and WGN allege that the league's decision to reduce the number of superstation games permitted to any team constitutes a horizontal agreement among the NBA teams to restrict output and to boycott superstations, in violation of Section 1 of the Sherman Act.

* * *

I

The NBA is a joint venture of its 27 professional basketball teams, based in cities and television markets as large as New York, Los

Angeles and Chicago and as comparatively small as Charlotte, North Carolina and Salt Lake City, Utah. As joint venturers the teams have understandably entered into agreements about how many players are allowed on the basketball court, how high the basket should be, how many seconds should run on the shot clock and the like. Obviously, agreements on game rules are essential to producing basketball games at all. But the teams have also entered into league-wide agreements on a great many other subjects, including collective bargaining with the players, the college draft, group insurance, the licensing of products, and television contracts with the national networks. Those agreements are not strictly necessary to produce basketball games. The NBA is not simply a rule-making organization. It has an economic significance of its own and controls some competition between the teams off the court as well as on it.

In several areas, the league has virtually preempted economic activity by the individual teams. In marketing, for instance, the merger of the teams into the league is almost complete. It is undisputed that the league controls the trademarks and logos of all the teams and that, outside their own arenas, the teams have few if any rights to license the sale of merchandise—jackets or pennants or posters—with team or NBA logos. Through licensing agreements with the league's marketing arm, NBA Properties, Inc., each team has granted the league the sole and exclusive worldwide right, subject only to narrow exceptions, to license and use its "symbols"....

In substantial measure, the league acts as an integrated firm. Revenues generated from contracts for licensed products entered into by the league are split evenly among the teams, and the even split is redistributive. Not all teams contribute equally to sales. Last year, Bulls paraphernalia outsold every other team's products. Notwithstanding, the Bulls receive the same 1/27th draw of the net as all the other teams.

The teams also pool and market some of their television rights jointly, through the league, under an exemption from the antitrust laws granted by Congress. See 15 U.S.C. §§ 1291–1295 (the "Sports Broadcasting Act"). For this season and the next three seasons, the NBA has sold broadcast rights, on behalf of all the teams, both to the National Broadcasting Company ("NBC") and Turner Network Television ("TNT"), a cable network. Revenues from those contracts will be shared jointly and the share to each team from the combined rights fees received from NBC and TNT this season will come to $6.8 million.

These fees from NBC and TNT represent the single largest source of shared revenues among the teams, and their agreement to pool certain TV rights, sell them jointly, and split the proceeds evenly reflects a kind of nonaggression pact among all the teams, an agreement not to compete in an area where they otherwise might. In a free open market, with each team doing its own bargaining, strong teams like the Bulls, the Detroit Pistons, the Los Angeles Lakers and the

Boston Celtics would command more money this season than weaker teams like the Sacramento Kings or the Miami Heat. Under their agreement to pool TV broadcast rights, however, each team will receive the same amount. Whether the strongest teams could negotiate on their own for as much money as their pro rata share of what the league has obtained for them by pooling their rights is an open question.

The income of all the teams is significantly enhanced by the revenues from their joint projects. Combining the revenues from all their joint projects, broadcast and other, each team will receive nearly $8.5 million from the league this season as shared profits of their joint venture. For many teams the revenues from the shared ventures may mean the difference between operating in the black and net operating losses. The NBA Commissioner, David Stern, estimated that but for the $8.5 million they will receive from the league, 20 of the 27 teams would run net operating losses this season. Stern also testified that, even with the shared revenues, one or two teams might still finish the season in the red.

It is not disputed, and it is plain from the financial figures, that the prosperity of the league currently depends on the volume of the shared revenues generated by the league's economic activity on behalf of the teams and particularly on the revenues generated by the broadcast contracts with the national networks....

Nevertheless, and despite the substantial economic collaboration among the teams, the NBA is only a partially integrated venture. The level of contractual integration among the teams lies somewhere in between what would be tolerated under the antitrust laws among wholly separate firms, on the one hand, and what one would expect from a fully merged or integrated firm on the other. Joint enterprises like NBA Properties, Inc. and the network contracts with NBC and TNT show the teams acting together as a single economic unit, pooling resources, agreeing not to compete with each other or the league and sharing the risks and benefits of their joint endeavors. But the teams also remain very much separate entities, each one with economic significance in its own right.

Head-to-head direct competition in the marketplace is clearest in New York and Los Angeles. The New Jersey Nets compete against the New York Knicks and the Los Angeles Lakers compete against the Los Angeles Clippers in the same geographic market. All the teams compete for media attention, for coaching staffs and front office personnel and, with some restraints, for players.

The most significant sign of their economic independence is the fact that all the teams calculate their own profits and that what they earn on their own and keep for themselves is more substantial than what they produce together and share. In four of the last five years, from the 1985–86 season through 1989–90, the average NBA team collected slightly better than 50% of its total revenues from a single source, gate receipts for regular season home games. In the fifth season, 1987–88, the proportion was 49.1%. Only minuscule amounts of those revenues are shared. This season, each team will keep 94% of its regular season home gate, giving up only 6% to the league. The teams earn more independently than they receive in shared revenues.

Although Commissioner Stern estimated that the $8.5 million that the league will distribute to each team this season may effectively double the gross revenues of the poorest teams, he also said that same amount would represent only 15–20% of the gross revenues of the richest teams. Last year, when the distribution from the league was much smaller, because television revenues from the league's national television contracts were less than half of what they will be this year, the proportion of its gross revenues which any team received from the league was also smaller. Shared revenues are not the primary source of income for many teams.

It is instructive, too, that fifteen to fifty percent income from revenue sharing is not the rule among professional sports leagues. Some leagues show greater economic integration than the NBA does. Thus, revenue sharing among the teams in the National Football League ("NFL") runs much deeper than in the NBA. Of the total revenue of the 28 NFL clubs, roughly 70% flows from the league's network contracts and is shared equally. The NFL teams, unlike NBA teams, share their gate receipts 60–40 between the home team and the away team. The Commissioner of football, Paul Tagliabue, estimated that only 5–10% of an NFL team's revenues "is not shared in any way."

All NBA teams depend on their own entrepreneurship and some teams do much better in the marketplace than others. The disparities among the teams' year-end financial statements are substantial. Last season, for instance, the Lakers recorded total revenues of $42.8 million dollars, which is more than three times as much as the Washington Bullets, who grossed a league low, $11.9 million. For the 26 teams other than the Lakers, average revenues for the '89–90 season were $21 million—almost twice as much as the Bullets grossed but not even half of what the Lakers made.

As a general trend, these disparities in revenues have an impact on competition on the court. Teams with impressive records tend to show bigger revenues than teams in the cellar. On the very most basic level, going to the playoffs means more games, and therefore more gate receipts, and more fan following and therefore higher rights fees from local broadcasting (which belong 100% to the teams)—in other words, more money. In 1989–90, the league champions, the Pistons, collected playoff revenues of $2.9 million dollars, net of the playoff revenues they shared with the league. In addition, and to complete the circle, more money means a better chance at making the playoffs again. The richest teams enjoy competitive advantages on the court over the poorest teams—in the ability to bid for free agents or to pay to keep their own players who opt for free agency, and so field a strong team; in the ability to charter flights for away games, and so field an alert team; in the ability to hire top notch staffs, and so field a well-coached team, and more.

The teams in the NBA cooperate in some ventures, but they engage in many others, on the court and off, as independent firms.

II

This season the NBA will gross more than $180 million from its network television contracts with NBC and TNT. NBC will carry 22 regular season games, TNT will carry 50 and each network will carry up to 30 playoff games. Time was, however, that the league's appeal to the networks was nowhere near what it is now. In 1981, CBS aired the NBA's premier event, its championship series, on tape delay rather than carrying it live and in prime time. League revenues from television, over-the-air and cable, were less than $23 million in 1981–82, increasing to $27.5 million in 82–83, but in both cases amounting to less than 16% of the projected revenues for this season.

Today, the league is in full blooming financial health. Total league revenues this season are projected at $700 million. In 1982, they were $128 million. The economic resurgence of the NBA is nothing short of phenomenal, and as the league explains it, "[w]hile a number of factors have contributed to the resurgence of the League, one of the principal reasons for its current success has been a sound and consistent television policy." NBA Commissioner David Stern has obviously done a superb job.

A significant strategic part of the league's television policy since 1982 has been to restrict the number of games in the market which compete with the league's national contracts. In particular, the league has taken several steps to limit local broadcasts and the independent rights of the teams to sell games, in order to maximize the value of the rights it sells to the national networks for national broadcast.

[In 1979 the NBA Board of Governors resolved that all future local television contracts entered into by NBA teams would be subject to the league's constitution and by-laws; the resolution gave the league the exclusive right to negotiate national cable contracts. In 1980 the Board further resolved that no team could broadcast more than 41 of its 82 regular season games on "free" local television (including superstations), and gave the commissioner broad power to enforce this rule with sanctions ranging from forfeiture of games to fines of $100,000 for each violation. The Bulls voted for both the 41–game limit and the commissioner's enforcement powers.]

* * *

In June 1985, the Board of Governors put further restraints on superstations, this time voting to limit the teams to 25 superstation games a year, beginning with the 1985–86 season, down from the 41 that had been allowed in each of the previous four seasons. The Bulls voted for the resolution. In October 1989, the governors approved a permanent resolution "blacking out" superstation games on nights when an NBA game is shown nationally on cable as part of the league's national cable package, which, by this time, had moved from USA and ESPN to TNT. Most recently, in April 1990, the Board of Governors voted, over the objections of the Bulls and the New Jersey Nets, to reduce superstation broadcasts by any team from 25 to 20, giving rise to this lawsuit.

The NBA's television strategy has not been mimicked by other professional sports leagues. The NBA, the NFL and Major League Baseball have each approached selling and regulating TV rights in different ways. All three leagues are currently in the first year of four-year contracts with the networks, running through their 1993 seasons, and each league read and played the market differently. Still, the networks agreed to substantial increases in rights fees for all of them.

The NFL negotiates all television rights deals for its teams and prohibits them from negotiating television contracts on their own, with the exception of contracts for certain pre-season games. The NFL's teams retain no rights and no games.... All regular season NFL games are produced for network television; every NFL game is televised every week under one of the NFL's five network contracts. There are no superstation broadcasts of NFL games.

The NFL's new contracts are its most lucrative ever and the NFL was able to negotiate the increases despite the fact that ratings for NFL games, as a percentage of total households, have declined.

The NBA's broadcast strategy also differs from Major League Baseball's. Baseball recently signed a contract with ESPN for 175 games a season for four seasons, in its first move ever into national cable rights and exposure. At the same time, baseball has moved to limit its over-the-air exposure. Baseball's new 1990–93 deal with CBS gives the over-the-air network only 16 regular games this season, down from 40 games last year, leaving 24 new Saturday afternoon slots open to the teams. By contrast, since 1982 the NBA has steadily reduced the size of its national cable package from 80 games to 50 and upped its over-the-air package from 7 games to a possible 26, aiming for more exposure on the major over-the-air networks and less on national cable.

Major league baseball regulates superstation broadcasts by imposing a surcharge rather than limiting the number of games directly.

[The district court then detailed the recent history of television contracts in basketball, both between the league and networks and between the Bulls and local television stations. The key findings were as follows:

    1. Under the network contract that expired in 1989–1990, the NBA received $47.5 million per season from CBS. Under the new contract with NBC, the league received $150 million per season for a somewhat higher number of games. The NBA contract with TNT rose from $27 million per season to $69 million per season for the same number of games. After a deduction for league expenses,

these network revenues are divided evenly among all teams. These contracts were negotiated before any changes were made by the NBA in its superstation policy.

2.   Each team was permitted to sell television rights for up to 41 games on local "free" television and the rest on cable (but not games shown on, or conflicting with, NBC's game telecasts).   In 1988–1989, the Bulls' contract with WFLD Channel 32 in Chicago yielded $1.6 million for 37 games ($43,000 per game).   In 1989–1990, the Bulls moved to WGN Channel 9 for the maximum 25 games permitted on a superstation.   Bulls ratings doubled on WGN—Chicago's identifiably "sports" station—and the Bulls earned $3.2 million for the year (or $128,000 per game).   All the other Bulls games not shown on NBC or WGN were telecast locally on cable, via SportsChannel Chicago.

3.   Because of WGN's availability to approximately thirty percent of American homes, total Bulls viewership nearly doubled from its Chicago audience to a national average of 650,000 a game, slightly less than TNT's usual cable audience of 750,000, and far less than NBC's regular season viewership of 4.7 million on Sunday afternoons.

4.   While each team keeps all revenues derived from contracts with local stations, including superstations, the NBA received approximately $4 million in royalty payments from cable operators who retransmitted superstation games—not only from Chicago's WGN, but also from Atlanta's WTBS (the Atlanta Hawks) and New York's WWOR (the New Jersey Nets).   These royalty revenues were divided evenly among all teams.

On these facts, the legal issues were whether the NBA's new policy, reducing the maximum number of superstation games from 25 to 20, was covered by the antitrust exemption under the Sports Broadcasting Act (SBA), and if not, whether this policy constituted an unreasonable restraint of trade under antitrust law.

After the trial judge granted the Bulls and WGN an injunction, the NBA appealed.   Its first argument to the Seventh Circuit Court of Appeals was that as a basketball league, the NBA was entitled to the protection of the SBA.]

EASTERBROOK, CIRCUIT JUDGE.

* * *

[T]he Sports Broadcasting Act applies only when the league has "transferred" a right to sponsored telecasting".   Neither the NBA's contract with NBC nor its contract with Turner Network Television transfers to the network a right to limit the broadcasting of other contests.   Both contracts and, so far as we can tell, the league's articles and bylaws, reserve to the individual clubs the full copyright interest in all games that the league has not sold to the networks.   As the "league of clubs" has not transferred to the networks either the right to show, or the right to black out, any additional games, the Sports Broadcasting Act does not protect its 20–game rule.

The NBA protests that such an approach is arbitrary. What if the league had assumed control of all broadcast rights and licensed only 20 of the Bulls' games to WGN? That would have been a "transfer" by a "league of clubs." What could be the point of forbidding a different mechanism (the rule limiting to 20 the number of games teams may sell to superstations) that leads to the same result? Other mechanisms to achieve similar outcomes abound. The league might have put a cap of 20 superstation games in its contracts with NBC and Turner, or it might have followed the path of professional baseball and allowed unlimited broadcasting over superstations while claiming a portion of the revenues for distribution among the clubs. (Sharing of revenues occurs in all team sports, although less so in the NBA than other leagues.)

Whether there are ways to achieve the NBA's objective is not the question. Laws often treat similar things differently. One has only to think of tax law, where small differences in the form of a business reorganization have large consequences for taxation. Substance then follows form. Antitrust law is no exception: agreements among business rivals to fix prices are unlawful per se, although a merger of the same firms, even more effective in eliminating competition among them, might be approved with little ado. Such distinctions are not invariably formal. The combined business entity might achieve efficiencies unavailable to the cartelists. But then the line in the Sports Broadcasting Act is not entirely formal either. Perhaps the reason the NBA has not commandeered all of the telecasting rights and sold limited numbers of games to superstations is that it cannot obtain the approval of the clubs to do this—for a change in the allocation of rights is apt to affect the allocation of revenues, making the bargaining problem difficult with 27 clubs. A league's difficulty in rearranging its affairs to obtain the protection of the Sports Broadcasting Act is one source of protection for competition.

What the NBA might have done, it did not do. The Sports Broadcasting Act is special interest legislation, a single-industry exception to a law designed for the protection of the public. When special interests claim that they have obtained favors from Congress, a court should ask to see the bill of sale. Special interest laws do not have "spirits," and it is inappropriate to extend them to achieve more of the objective the lobbyists wanted. What the industry obtained, the courts enforce; what it did not obtain from the legislature—even if similar to something within the exception—a court should not bestow. Compromises draw unprincipled lines between situations that strike an outside observer as all but identical. The limitation is part of the price of the victory achieved, a concession to opponents who might have been able to delay or block a bill even slightly more favorable to the proponents. Recognition that special interest legislation enshrines results rather than principles is why courts read exceptions to the antitrust laws narrowly, with beady eyes and green eyeshades.

III

The merits of the case turn on the characterization of the NBA. Is a sports league a single entity? In that event its decisions about telecasting are effectively unreviewable. Copperweld Corp. v. Independence Tube Corp., 467 U.S. 752 (1984). True, its operating divisions (the teams) have separate owners, but on this view the league's method of hiring capital is no more relevant than would be the decision of a single firm to obtain loans from different banks in different cities, or the decision by a large retailer to compensate managers of its stores with a percentage of the local profits. Is the NBA instead a joint venture adopting strategies that foster its competition with other entertainments? In that event pro basketball on TV is not fundamentally different from "Star Trek: The Next Generation," a series created by cooperation among many persons who are competitors at other times. Producers of a television series commit the episodes exclusively to one network (or one station in a local market) in order to compete against the offerings of other ventures. No program, indeed no producer's entire menu of programs, commands a substantial share of the market in televised entertainment. Marketing strategies such as exclusivity and limits on the number of episodes produced per year then must be understood as ways to compete rather than ways to exploit consumers. Perhaps, however, the NBA is a joint venture only in the production of games; in the hiring of inputs (from basketballs to players) and in the sale of their product, the owners are competitors. In that event the television rules look more like a reduction in output, the work of a cartel, and only an exemption from the antitrust laws permits the owners to act cooperatively.

Characterization is a creative rather than exact endeavor. Appellate review is accordingly deferential. The district court held a trial, heard the evidence, and concluded that the best characterization of the NBA is the third we have mentioned: a joint venture in the production of games but more like a cartel in the sale of its output. Whether this is the best characterization of professional sports is a subject that has divided courts and scholars for some years, making it hard to characterize the district judge's choice as clear error.

Parts of the NBA's brief verge on the argument that a sports league is a single entity as a matter of law. Justice Rehnquist's opinion dissenting from the denial of certiorari in [NASL] 459 U.S. 1074 (1982), supports such a position, to which Copperweld added weight two years later. There is a lively debate in the academic press on the subject. All agree that cooperation off the field is essential to produce intense rivalry on it—rivalry that is essential to the sport's attractiveness in a struggle with other sports, and other entertainments in general, for audience. The persons denominated owners of teams may not own them in an economic sense. Many of their actions are subject to review by the league's board, so that the "owners" may be no more than financier-managers of the league's branch offices. How much cooperation at the league level is beneficial is an interesting question in economics as well as law. See Jesse W. Markham & Paul v. Teplitz, Baseball Economics and Public Policy (1981). But the NBA did not contend in the district court that the NBA is a single entity, let alone that it is a single entity as a matter of law. It does no more than allude to the possibility here. Whether a sports league is a single entity for antitrust purposes has significance far beyond this case, and it would be imprudent to decide the question after such cursory dialog. Perhaps the parties will join issue more fully in the proceedings still to come in the district court. For now we treat the NBA as a joint venture, just as the parties do in the bulk of their arguments.

[The appellate panel, assuming for the sake of this case that the NBA was a joint venture governed by the rule of reason, next assessed the league's market power.]

* * *

As the NBA points out, sports is a small fraction of all entertainment on TV, and basketball a small fraction of sports televising. Viewers of basketball games do not have qualities uniquely attractive to advertisers—and if they do, the advertisers can reach them via other sports programs and many other programs too. NBC advertises basketball games during sitcoms and other programs, implying that the market in viewers extends well beyond weekend sports programming. Higher prices, the hallmark of a reduction in output, are missing: advertisers pay no more per thousand viewers of NBA basketball than they do for other sports audiences, and substantially less than they pay per thousand viewers of other entertainment. During 1990 the cost per thousand viewers (CPM) of a regular-season NBA network game was $8.17. NCAA football fetched $11.50, and viewers of prime-time programs were substantially more expensive. The CPM for "L.A. Law" was $19.34, the CPM for "Coach" $13.40. The NBA hardly has cornered the market on the viewers advertisers want to reach.

According to the NBA, this means that its rules do not injure viewers or advertisers, and it makes more sense to understand them as ways to compete against other suppliers of entertainment programming, all of which—right down to the smallest producers of syndicated programs—find it in their interest to sell exclusive rights to a small number of episodes. The NBA contends that until it tried to adopt a rational structure for television it had a much smaller audience than it does now. During 1980 and 1981 CBS carried the final game of the championship series by delayed broadcast! In 1982 only five NBA games appeared on network TV. A "restraint" that in the end expands output serves the interests of consumers and should be applauded rather than condemned. Rules keeping some popular games off superstations may help weaker teams attract the support of their local audiences, something that (like the sharing of revenues) in the longer run promotes exciting, competitive games. Teams in smaller markets depend more on live gate to finance operations that will compete with the Bulls, Lakers, and Knicks on the court. Rivalry makes for a more attractive product, which then attracts a larger audience—the very expansion of output that the antitrust laws foster.

A market defined by TV viewers is not the only way to look at things. The district court in *NCAA* defined a market of games shown. If "basketball games" are the product, then the NBA's plan cuts output by definition even if more persons watch the fewer (and more attractive) games shown on TV. The NCAA tried to persuade the Supreme Court that the plaintiffs should be required to establish power in a viewership market. The Court replied:

> We must reject this argument for two reasons, one legal, one factual. As a matter of law, the absence of proof of market power does not justify a naked restriction on price or output.... This naked restraint on price and output requires some competitive justification even in the absence of a detailed market analysis."

468 U.S. at 109–10

Although this passage is not entirely clear, we understand it as holding that any agreement to reduce output measured by the number of televised games requires some justification—some explanation connecting the practice to consumers' benefits—before the court attempts an analysis of market power. Unless there are sound justifications, the court condemns the practice without ado, using the "quick look" version of the Rule of Reason advocated by Professor Areeda and by the Solicitor General's brief in *NCAA*.

The district court proceeded in this fashion, examining the league's justifications; finding each wanting, the judge enjoined the 20–game rule without defining a market. In this court, the league's lead-off justification is that the telecasting rule prevents the clubs from "misappropriating" a "property" right that belongs to the NBA: the right to exploit its symbols and success. The district court properly rejected this argument on two grounds. First, it mischaracterizes the NBA's articles and bylaws, which leave with the teams the intellectual property in their games. The NBA could acquire a property interest in all broadcasting rights but has not done so. The 20–game rule does not transfer any broadcasting rights to the league; instead it shortens the list of stations to which clubs may sell rights the teams concededly possess. Second, it has nothing to do with antitrust law. We want to know the effects of the TV policy on consumers' welfare, not whether the league possesses sufficient contractual rights that it has become the "owner" of the copyright. See Continental T.V., Inc. v. GTE Sylvania Inc., 433 U.S. 36, 52–53 & n. 21 (1977) (rejecting an argument that legality of restraints under the antitrust laws depends on the characterization of a transaction in the law of property). A cartel could not insulate its agreement from the Sherman Act by giving certain producers contractual rights to sell to specified customers. Agreements limiting to whom, and how much, a firm may sell are the defining characteristics of cartels and may not be invoked as justifications of a cutback in output. That the NBA's cutback is only five games per year is irrelevant; long ago the Court rejected the invitation to inquire into the "reasonableness" of price and output decisions. Competition in markets, not judges, sets price and output. A court applying the Rule of Reason asks whether a practice produces net benefits for consumers; it is no answer to say that a loss is "reasonably small." (What is more, if five superstation games is tiny in relation to the volume of telecasting, the benefits from the limitation are correspondingly small.)

[The court then addressed the NBA's argument that the reduction to twenty games that might be broadcast on superstations was justified as a restraint on "free riders."]

* * *

It costs money to make a product attractive against other contenders for consumers' favor. Firms that take advantage of costly efforts without paying for them, that reap where they have not sown, reduce the payoff that the firms making the investment receive. This makes investments in design and distribution of products less attractive, to the ultimate detriment of consumers. Control of free-riding is accordingly an accepted justification for cooperation.

Three forms of free-riding characterize the Bulls' telecasting, according to the NBA. First, the contracts with NBC and TNT require these networks to advertise NBA basketball on other shows; the Bulls and WGN receive the benefit of this promotion without paying the cost. Second, the NBA has revenue-sharing devices and a draft to prop up the weaker teams. The Bulls took advantage of these while they were weak (and through the draft obtained their current stars) but, according to the league, are siphoning viewers (and thus revenues) to their own telecasts, thus diminishing the pot available for distribution to today's weaker teams. Third, the Bulls and WGN are taking a free ride on the benefits of the cooperative efforts during the 1980s to build up professional basketball as a rival to baseball and football—efforts that bore fruit just as the Bulls produced a championship team, and which the Bulls would undermine.

Free-riding is the diversion of value from a business rival's efforts without payment. Consider the classic example of free-riding in retail distribution. Manufacturer produces a product or improvement that requires explanation or demonstration—perhaps a television set with an improved degaussing coil. Retailer # 1 demonstrates the effects to consumers in a showroom filled with TV sets, some with and some without the feature. Such a demonstration is costly in merchandise, in staff time, in floor space. Neither Manufacturer nor Retailer # 1 can charge the consumer for this information. Its value is too uncertain to expect the consumer to pay for access to the sales floor, and a retailer is not apt to gain customers by threatening to charge them if they leave without buying. So a consumer may leave the store with valuable information; Retailer # 1 recovers the cost of supplying this information in the purchase price of the product, not with a separate charge. Yet a consumer armed with the information may order the product from Retailer # 2, which offers no information. Retailer # 2 can make a profit at a lower price than does Retailer # 1, for Retailer # 2 has lower costs. To compete, Retailer # 1 must lower its own price, and that means lowering its costs too—cutting cost by cutting services that consumers value. Restrictions on the price, territory, or customers of Retailer # 2 may restore the profitability of point-of-sale services, to consumers' benefit.

What gives this the name free-riding is the lack of charge. Retailer # 1 does not charge the customer for a valuable service; Retailer # 2 does not pay Retailer # 1 for delivering this service. Put the retailers in a contractual relation, however, and they could adjust their accounts so that the person providing a valuable service gets paid. When payment is possible, free-riding is not a problem because the "ride" is not free. Here lies the flaw in the NBA's story. It may (and does) charge members for value delivered. As the NBA itself emphasizes, there are substantial revenue transfers, propping up the weaker clubs in order to promote vigorous competition on the court. Without skipping a beat the NBA may change these payments to charge for the Bulls' ride. If the $40 million of advertising time that NBC will provide during the four years of its current contract also promotes WGN's games, then the league may levy a charge for each game shown on a superstation, or require the club to surrender a portion of its revenues. Major league baseball does exactly this and otherwise allows its teams access to superstations. Avoidance of free-riding therefore does not justify the NBA's 20–game limit.

Doubtless there is irony in saying that the limit violates the antitrust laws because the defendants could adopt a system of charges for making sales. Revenue-pooling and pass-over payments are the usual tools of cartels.... Charges for the privilege of putting games on superstations will lead to fewer such broadcasts; by selecting the tax carefully, the NBA could induce the Bulls to broadcast 20 games, neither more nor less, on WGN. Plaintiffs have hinted that they will ask the district court to ban all revenue-sharing procedures for telecasting. Yet we do not suppose that the Bulls are going to ask the court to hold that the draft of college players, the cap on their payroll, the distribution of revenues from the NBC and TNT contracts, and other sharing devices all violate the Sherman Act. Sharing is endemic in league sports. The prevalence of what is otherwise a hallmark of a cartel may suggest the shakiness of treating the clubs, which must cooperate to have any product to sell, as rival "producers" in the first place.

Because of the way in which issues have become separated in this litigation, we do not decide whether revenue-sharing from superstation broadcasts is consistent with the antitrust laws. Needless to say, we also do not decide whether any of the cooperative arrangements by which the league hires the services of the players comports with the Sherman Act. (The National Basketball Players Association, concerned that we might do some such thing by accident, has filed a brief urging us to guard our tongues.) It is enough to say that if the league may levy a tax on superstation broadcasts, then there is no free-riding. And if the league may not levy a tax, then a direct limit with the same effect as a tax is unjustifiable. Either way the NBA comes up short, and under *NCAA* the failure of its justifications eliminates the need for the district judge to define a market.

The NCAA argued that restrictions on the number of games telecast spread revenues and exposure among universities, helping to produce balanced competition on the field and hence making the games actually telecast more exciting, to the benefit of fans. Distributing telecasts among schools served, in the NCAA's view, as a substitute for the draft and other controls professional leagues deployed to the same end. The Supreme Court found the argument unpersuasive. It is hard to see how similar balance arguments by professional leagues, which make the most of drafts, trades, and revenue-pooling to foster exciting games, could be more compelling. Unless the Supreme Court is prepared to modify NCAA, the district court did not commit clear error in applying the "quick look" version of the Rule of Reason and rejecting the NBA's arguments.

Affirmed.

———

Ironically, as a notable law and economics scholar at Chicago, then Professor Easterbrook was counsel for the National Collegiate Athletic Association (NCAA) in its unsuccessful appeal to the Supreme Court in *NCAA v. Board of Regents of the University of Oklahoma*, 468 U.S. 85, 104 S.Ct. 2948, 82 L.Ed.2d 70 (1984), a decision that is referred to at numerous points in the *WGN* opinion.[17] In that case—the only Supreme Court decision on the substantive antitrust treatment of any aspect of sports—the Court ruled that the NCAA's sale of an exclusive package of college football telecasts violated Section 1 of the Sherman Act. Though neither *WGN* judgment adverted to this fact, the *NCAA* case provided the most graphic evidence we have of the economic impact of sports teams collectively restricting the sale of their television rights. In 1983, just before the Supreme Court ruling, the NCAA received and distributed to its members approximately $85 million for the ninety football games that were shown pursuant to several network contracts (on both free and cable television). In 1984, immediately after the *NCAA* decision, all the schools together received less than $50 million for the broadcasts of nearly 200 games on different forms of

17. For an illuminating exchange about the virtues and vices of antitrust law generally, see Frank A. Easterbrook, *The Limits of Antitrust*, 63 Texas L.Rev. 1 (1984), and Richard S. Markovits, *The Limits to Simplifying Antitrust: A Reply to Professor Easterbrook*, 63 Texas L.Rev. 41 (1984).

television. The price paid by ABC and CBS to show a national game dropped from $1.3 million in 1983 to $600,000 or less in 1984.

Questions for Discussion

1. Given Judge Easterbrook's opinion, are there steps that the NBA can take to bring its superstation policy under the protective umbrella of the Sports Broadcasting Act? Can the NBA require a "transfer" to the league of the television rights of all its teams? What does Judge Easterbrook's theory of statutory interpretation imply for SBA coverage of cable television contracts? Is there a rationale for distinguishing between free and cable television?

2. Three decades after its enactment, is the SBA good public policy toward sports broadcasting? What are the benefits secured by affording sports leagues this prerogative in the sale of their television rights? What has been the SBA's affect on franchise values? What are the costs of this policy? What effects has the SBA had on the number and price of games that fans can watch? Are there other ways to secure the legitimate interests of the clubs while reducing any harmful impact on fans? Keep these questions and this material from professional sports in mind when we consider in Chapter 9 the analogous problem in intercollegiate sports, and when we read the *NCAA* decision.

3. Judge Easterbrook's opinion in the *WGN* case illustrates the trend toward antitrust analysis founded on classic microeconomic theory and a focus on consumer welfare, rather than the more populist approach of the pre–1970s era. *WGN* also provides an insight into how a conservative antitrust judge might view the single-entity issue, which Judge Easterbrook ultimately declined to resolve on the ground that the NBA had not raised it clearly at the trial level. In light of his comments and his "Chicago School" law-and-economics approach, how would Judge Easterbrook decide the single-entity question if it were squarely presented? Are his comments in *WGN* an invitation to sports leagues to raise this issue more forcefully?

4. Note that the trial judge determined that the NBA was like a single firm in production of the league product but like a cartel in marketing and selling that product; Judge Easterbrook deferred to this finding given the sketchy state of the record. Under this theory, what league rules or policies are immune from section 1 attack as unilateral conduct? Player restraints such as the NFL's Plan B that was at issue in *McNeil*? Franchise relocation restrictions like the NFL's Rule 4.3 at issue in *Raiders*?

Suppose that the several television networks formed a broadcast association to make single bids for league television rights (with games to be distributed across the broadcast spectrum, free and cable). The practical effect of such collaboration is vividly displayed in recent bidding for Olympic television rights. All the networks in the European Community agreed on a single bid for the 1992 Summer Games from Barcelona: the result was that the International Olympic Committee received $75 million for television rights for the entire European market. By contrast, the IOC received $401 from NBC as the outcome of competitive bidding by U.S. networks for the American market. Should sports leagues be entitled to attack such a network arrangement under antitrust law? Should the presence of the SBA permitting cooperation by teams in the league-wide sale of broadcast rights legitimate network cooperation in buying rights offered by the league under the SBA umbrella?

More fundamentally, recall the line of analysis sketched earlier in Chapter 3—about the consumer welfare orientation of modern antitrust law and the latitude this may imply for the exercise of monopsony power that reduces production costs ultimately passed on to consumers. Is it fair to equate the position of teams in a league collectively deciding on the allocation of or price paid for the services of players, with the position of networks purchasing from the teams in this same league the right to show these players and games to fans across the country? Or are there critical differences between the two settings that make this parallel inappropriate?

Note on Revenue Sharing

The *WGN* case illustrates not only the impact of league policy on the sports television market, but also the relationship between league economic cooperation and the quality of the league's athletic competition. Suppose that the NBA used a different policy to deal with superstation broadcasts: rather than cut back on the number of games telecast on superstations to fans across the country, the league "taxed" the extra revenues derived by a team from this source (the amount exceeding what a purely local television station was prepared to offer for broadcast rights).

If the NBA imposed such a "tax" only on revenues from superstation broadcasts, the policy would probably attract antitrust litigation as an attempt to do indirectly what WGN said the league could not do directly. Suppose, though, that the league went further and required that *all* revenues derived from local broadcast rights be shared among all NBA teams—an extension of the principle of revenue sharing developed earlier by the NBA and its players association under their collectively bargained "salary cap."

In all sports except football (which sells all television rights through league-wide contracts), the current distribution of local broadcasting revenue is a major source of inequality in club earnings. (Another source, present also in football, is the quality of the stadium lease with the local community.) The problem is especially acute in baseball, where the disparity in local broadcast revenues has risen even faster than their absolute amounts. In 1971, for example, when the 24 baseball teams earned less than $30 million from local broadcasting, the maximum ratio was roughly 4:1 (from the Dodgers' $1.8 million to the Pirates' $450,000). In 1991, when total local broadcast revenues had soared over $300 million, the maximum ratio was 16:1 (from the Yankees' $56 million to the Mariners' $3.5 million). Because the clubs can no longer rely on the reserve system to insulate equality of team playing talent from inequality in team earnings, there is considerable interest in league-wide revenue sharing in major league baseball—particularly sharing of local broadcast revenues.

Peter Bavasi, former president of the Toronto Blue Jays and the Cleveland Indians, recalled that when the subject of revenue sharing was brought up in league meetings, one of the owners of a large-market team would stand up, begin his comments with "Comrades!," and after embarrassed laughter the topic would quickly be dropped. If and when the idea receives more serious consideration in baseball (or basketball or hockey), the owners will have to address the following tangible concerns.

1. Is extensive revenue sharing fair to the teams in larger markets? Do the Yankees have a "right" to all revenues from broadcasts of their games in New York? Is there a special problem of fair treatment of the owners who recently purchased teams in big city markets (for example, the Mets who were bought in 1986)? Is there a way of dealing with that latter concern? [18]

2. Is extensive revenue sharing an efficient way to run a league, particularly from the point of view of consumer welfare? Should the league's main concern be how to divide up the current revenue pie or how to enlarge the pie? Does revenue sharing contribute to or detract from the latter objective? How could a revenue-sharing scheme be designed to maximize its contribution to revenue expansion?

3. Would revenue sharing among owners generate economic exploitation of players by creating an indirect form of the reserve system? What would be your reaction if you were Donald Fehr, executive director of the MLB Players Association? Would some of your constituents be helped and some hurt by such a league policy; if so, how? Again, could a revenue-sharing plan be designed to minimize any harmful impact on the players' interests?

4. Suppose that after considerable thought and effort a new revenue-sharing scheme was devised, it proved attractive to a majority of the owners, but it could not get the necessary three-quarters approval because of opposition from the large-market clubs. Could the commissioner step in under his "best interests of baseball" authority we studied in Chapter 1 to impose the scheme on all owners? Is there a difference between Commissioner Vincent barring George Steinbrenner from pocketing the money he received by selling Yankees' games to the Madison Square Garden cable network, and Commissioner Bowie Kuhn prohibiting Oakland A's owner Charles Finley from pocketing the money from sale of his star players to Steinbrenner's Yankees (and to Tom Yawkey's Red Sox)? Regardless of the similarities or differences between the two cases as a matter of principle, is it likely that a commissioner would impose his revenue-sharing views in such a fash-

18. See Louis Kaplow, *An Economic Analysis of Legal Transitions*, 99 Harvard L. Rev. 509 (1986), for a valuable analysis of this general type of problem.

ion? What does reflection on this problem suggest about the "single-entity" issue we have been tracing through this chapter? [19]

———

The experience under the Sports Broadcasting Act may provide revealing lessons about other congressional efforts to benefit professional sports leagues. Consider these comments by Vice President Al Gore, made while he was a Senator from Tennessee, when he dissented from the Senate Commerce Committee's proposed Professional Sports Community Protection Act of 1985 (which was described earlier in this chapter):

> The fundamental cause of franchise instability in professional football is scarcity of franchises. The NFL has refused to expand to meet legitimate demand and this has occasioned intense bidding by cities to lure and maintain existing franchises. Professional team owners are positioned to extract enormous benefits and subsidies from municipalities and they are taking advantage of these opportunities. So long as the NFL refuses to expand, the current situation with its frenzied bidding and disappointed sports fans will persist even if the committee bill becomes law.

> It is not surprising that concerned parties have looked to the Congress for help because it is an earlier Congressional waiver of the antitrust laws for the NFL that has contributed to the current problems. What is surprising is that the Committee has ignored the real cause of the problem and instead asked to further protect the NFL from the antitrust laws. To my mind, the Committee has missed the point.

* * *

> By entering into contracts with all three networks, the NFL has been able to effectively eliminate the opportunity for a competing league to establish itself in the fall season. With no competition, they have been free to limit the available franchises and to ignore justifiable claims from municipalities for teams. Since the merger 15 years ago, the NFL has enjoyed an increase in annual television revenues per team from close to $1,500,000 in 1970 to $15 million in 1985. With the supply of franchises limited, the value of NFL franchises has increased dramatically. It is no wonder that the owners have been reluctant to establish new franchises. This would only decrease their share of available television revenues and diminish competition for, and accordingly the resale value of, their franchises.

19. For a post-*Copperweld* argument that the degree of league revenue sharing should be crucial to the characterization of a sports league as a single entity or a joint venture, see Note, *A Substantive Test for Sherman Act Plurality: Applications for Professional Sports Leagues*, 52 U. of Chicago L. Rev. 99 (1985). Does this argument square with the Court's statement in *Copperweld* that single-entity status should not turn on the structural and operational choices of a business pursuing optimal efficiency?

* * *

   While I share the Chairman's and the Committee's interest in allowing the NFL and other professional sports leagues to better control the movement of franchises, I am of the view that legislative action in that area alone does nothing to solve the real cause of the problem. If you take the simple step of limiting the NFL antitrust exemption to operate consistent with the Congress' original intention, you would establish a competitive environment which in due course would bring more professional football, including NFL franchises, to more cities. This would put a quick halt to the frenzied bidding between competing cities for the existing number of limited franchises, which is only making owners richer, taxpayers poorer, and sports fans feel betrayed.

It is likely that the Senator was moved to make these comments by his constituents' sense of grievance about the NFL's denial of a franchise to Memphis (recall the *Grizzlies* case earlier). The merits of our Vice President's views are explored in the following chapter.

Chapter Seven

MONOPOLY IN PROFESSIONAL SPORTS

In appraising the legal policies fashioned for professional sports by both legislatures and courts, it is of paramount importance that there is only one major professional league in each sport. This "monopoly" state, in turn, is the principal source of many of the conflicts that arise between the league and its constituents and of the difficult problems that these disputes pose for traditional legal doctrines.[1]

Previous chapters have described how player salaries and franchise values have soared during the last quarter century. Underlying both trends has been an equally startling rise in the total revenues flowing into professional sports. In 1950, for example, major league baseball's revenues from all sources barely totalled $30 million. By the early 1990s, baseball's revenues surpassed $1.5 billion annually—a fifty-fold increase. To some extent, this revenue growth was produced by increased fan attendance at games: from 21 million in the early 1950s (an average of 18,000 per game) to 57 million in 1991 (an average of 27,000 for a considerably larger number of games). As we saw at the end of Chapter 6, an even greater source of financial growth in baseball has been the explosion in its broadcasting revenues: from $4 million in 1950 to nearly $700 million in 1991.

The same kind of financial bonanza has been tapped in football, starting in the late 1950s, and in basketball and hockey, especially since the early 1980s. The legal doctrines we have traced up to this point exert their influence upon the division of this expanding pie between team owners and players, or owners and stadium authorities. This chapter considers whether the total size of the pie is due at least in

---

1. The most important legal treatment of this topic is Stephen F. Ross, *Monopoly Sports Leagues*, 73 Minnesota L. Rev. 643 (1989) (a shorter version of which appears as Chapter 8 of Paul D. Staudohar and James A. Mangan eds., *The Business of Professional Sports* (Urbana, Ill: Universi-ty of Illinois Press, 1991)). For a contrast-ing point of view to Ross' on many of the issues, see Thane N. Rosenbaum, *The Anti-trust Implications of Professional Sports Leagues Revisited: Emerging Trends in the Modern Era*, 41 U. of Miami L. Rev. 729 (1987).

part to the fact that there is only one major league in each sport selling this product to a more enthusiastic fandom—and if so, what is the law's responsibility for that state of affairs.

This broad theme is an undertone to many of the cases we have already read, in which courts applying "rule of reason" analysis under section 1 of the Sherman Act have struggled to strike an appropriate balance between the league's interest in fashioning internal rules that promote vigorous athletic competition on the field or floor, and the claims of players, fans, and communities to fair economic treatment at the hands of member clubs. Consider how some of the cases analyzed earlier would look if there had been two, three, or even four leagues presenting viable alternatives for the plaintiffs.

Players—Suppose that "Yazoo" Smith, after being drafted by the Redskins, or John Mackey, after playing out his option with the Colts, had had the option of signing with teams in other football leagues. Similarly, suppose Curt Flood had had available to him other baseball leagues in which to play when he had to decide whether to sign a contract that permitted the Cardinals to trade him to the Phillies without his consent.

Television—Suppose that there were several professional basketball leagues seeking exposure and revenue from television networks and superstations. Would the NBA still have tried to reduce the number of Bulls games on WGN? If it had done so, would the availability of other leagues and games have ameliorated the competitive impact of the NBA's policy on television viewers who wanted to watch professional basketball?

Franchises—Suppose that the American Football League had continued as a rival to the National Football League, perhaps accompanied by one or more of the other leagues that have sought to challenge the NFL's dominance. Would there have been only one professional football team in the Los Angeles area in the late 1970s, so that the city of Anaheim had to offer Rams' owner Carroll Rosenbloom 95 acres of prime real estate to induce him to move his team from the Coliseum? When the Rams decided to move out of the Coliseum, would not the AFL have actively encouraged one of its teams—though perhaps not Oakland's highly successful Raiders—to fill the football vacuum left in the nation's second largest city? Similarly, following the demise of the WFL in the mid–1970s, would not the Memphis Grizzlies have been eagerly sought after by at least one football league wanting to establish a presence in the football-mad South?

Products—Although league resistance to innovations that may improve the quality of the sport only rarely generates antitrust litigation on the part of product suppliers,[2] such innovation is an important value

---

2. An example is the prohibition by the Professional Golfers Association Tour against players using the new, square-grooved PING irons in tournaments, a decision that produced ongoing litigation in *Bob Gilder v. PGA Tour, Inc.*, 727 F.Supp. 1333 (D.Ariz.1989), affirmed 936 F.2d 417 (9th Cir.1991). Chapter 10 contains a de-from the point of view of consumer welfare. The competitive pressures generated by a challenger league create an incentive for innovations that enhance enjoyment of the sport. Perhaps the best example is the American Basketball Association, whose heritage for professional basketball included not only the *Oscar Robertson* case and thence veteran free agency, but also the three-point shot and the slam dunk.

Earlier chapters have described an emerging sentiment among antitrust scholars and judges such as Robert Bork, Ralph Winter, and Frank Easterbrook that courts should be loath to scrutinize closely the reasonableness of restrictive practices developed within a business enterprise. The assumption of the law and economics movement is that the best guarantee that social welfare will be enhanced rather than harmed by such arrangements is the force of market competition faced by such businesses. Courts have, however, been unwilling to embrace that position fully in sports cases because the undeniable lesson from history is that interleague competition is very much the exception, not the rule, in sports.[3]

For example, while organized baseball regularly faced rival leagues during its first fifty years of existence, no new league has surfaced since the demise of the Federal League in 1915 (that league's principal legacy being the Supreme Court decision that produced baseball's antitrust immunity). Similarly, once the National Hockey League (formed in 1917) established its dominance in that sport in the 1920s, only one competitor has come on the scene. The World Hockey Association (WHA) operated for only six seasons before a 1979 agreement under which the NHL absorbed four WHA teams—the Edmonton Oilers, Winnipeg Jets, Hartford Whalers, and Quebec Nordiques—while the other WHA teams folded. In basketball, the National Basketball Association (formed in 1949) faced the short-lived American Basketball League for only the 1961–1962 season (recall from Chapter 2 the ABL's legal legacy, the *Barnett* decision), and then struggled against the American Basketball Association for nine seasons (1967–1976) before a peace treaty brought four teams—the New Jersey Nets, Denver Nuggets, Indiana Pacers, and San Antonio Spurs—into the NBA, with the other ABA teams folding.

The National Football League (formed in 1920) has faced by far the most vigorous interleague competition. The most serious challenges came from the All American Football Conference, which lasted from 1946 to 1949, when the NFL absorbed three AAFC teams—the Cleve-

---

tailed treatment of this issue, which has surfaced mainly on organized tours for individual sports.

3. Books describing that history in the several sports include Harold Seymour, *Baseball: The Early Years* (New York: Oxford, 1960) and *Baseball: The Golden Years* (New York: Oxford, 1971) (on baseball); David Cruise and Alison Griffiths, *Net Worth: Exploding the Myths of Pro Hockey* (New York: Viking Press, 1991) (on

hockey); Terry Pluto, *Loose Balls: The Short Wild Life of the American Basketball Association* (New York: Simon and Schuster, 1990) (basketball); and David Harris, *The League: The Rise and Decline of the NFL* (New York: Bantam Books, 1986); and Jim Byrne, *The $1 League: The Rise and Fall of the USFL* (New York: Simon and Schuster, 1986) (football).

land Browns, San Francisco 49ers, and Baltimore Colts—and then from the American Football League, whose growing success from 1960 through 1966 led the NFL to merge with the AFL and take in all eight AFL teams (with the blessing of an express antitrust exemption granted by Congress). This larger, more powerful NFL, with its annual Super Bowl championship, had little trouble in fending off subsequent challenges from the World Football League in the mid–1970s and the United States Football League in the mid–1980s. At the present time in football, as in all the other major professional team sports, the established league faces no visible prospect of serious competition.

While the factual record is clear, the explanation for it is not. Does the historic tendency toward monopoly indicate that this is the "natural" state for professional sports, or does it reveal a failure to implement the legal policy against monopolization? This is the underlying question posed in the cases and materials in this chapter.

A. MONOPOLY POWER AND THE RELEVANT MARKET

The principal source of law in this area is section 2 of the Sherman Act which prohibits firms from endeavoring to "monopolize trade and commerce," supplemented by Section 7 of the Clayton Act which forbids mergers that "lessen competition or tend to create a monopoly." A monopolization charge consists of two elements: the possession of monopoly market power, and the use of unacceptable means to acquire, entrench or maintain that market power.[4] Here we address the first issue—the meaning of monopoly power in the sports marketplace.

From an economic point of view, monopoly is not to be equated with "bigness" as such. Companies as huge as General Motors have learned to their chagrin that mere size is no guarantee against the forces of market competition. A firm has a measure of monopoly power only if it has the ability to raise prices significantly above marginal production costs without experiencing a decrease in profits, if not sales. The immediate source of such market power is "inelasticity of demand": few consumers will substantially reduce their purchases of the firm's products when prices are raised or product quality (ergo, costs of production) is lowered. A long-run source is "inelasticity of supply": despite the presence of monopoly profits in this market, barriers to entry obstruct the emergence of new competitors that would give consumers an alternative source of supply.

In practice, however, it is difficult to detect and measure monopoly power in the precise economic sense of the term, and even more difficult to demonstrate such market reality in the artificial setting of a

---

4. For a more detailed treatment of monopolization see Herbert Hovenkamp, *Economics and Federal Antitrust Law*, 135 ff.(St. Paul, Minn.: West Publishing, 1985).

courtroom.[5] Consequently, courts have adopted a surrogate test for monopoly power. Does the firm have a large majority of the total production and sales in the relevant market, which is defined by both a product type and a geographical area within which the products in question are viable alternatives for most buyers (or sellers)—e.g., television rights to football games in the northeastern United States, tickets to sporting events in southern California, or professional football players in the United States? Once the plaintiff demonstrates such a large market share, the burden shifts to the defendant to show that it does not actually have the power to raise prices above their competitive levels without a sharp decline in sales. Few defendants can meet the burden of proving this negative—the absence of market power.

The key issue in the legal determination of monopoly power, therefore, is determining the precise scope of the market within which the defendant is alleged to have too large a share. Defining the relevant product market is not as easy a task as it might appear. What initially looks like an insulated enclave for a particular firm if the market is viewed narrowly, often can be a strongly competitive environment when one takes account of the entire array of choices available to participants in the broader marketplace. The following case illustrates an appeals court wrestling with the geographic contours of the sports market, as the court considered a complaint by the fledgling American Football League that the National Football League had adopted tactics designed to stifle its potential rival from the outset.

AFL v. NFL

United States Court of Appeals, Fourth Circuit, 1963.

323 F.2d 124.

HAYNSWORTH, CIRCUIT JUDGE.

[Shortly after the American Football League began operations in 1960, the AFL launched this antitrust suit against its established rival, the National Football League. The AFL charged that the NFL had offered expansion franchises to the cities of Dallas and Minneapolis in order to frustrate the AFL's plan to move into these two prime football sites. A trial judge dismissed the antitrust suit, and the AFL appealed.]

* * *

The National Football League was organized in 1920. For a number of years its existence was precarious. Until the last ten years, its membership was far from static, and until 1946 every major league professional football team operating in the United States was associated with it. In 1945, the All American Football Conference was organized, and it operated through the four seasons of 1946–1949 with eight teams, except that two of the teams were merged in 1949, and in the last

---

5. See Hovenkamp, *Economics and Federal Antitrust Law*, note 4 above, at 55 ff.

season, there were but seven teams. Thereafter the All American Football Conference disbanded, but three of its teams were received into the National Football League, and teams franchised in those three cities, Baltimore, Cleveland and San Francisco, were operated under National League franchises when this action was commenced.

In 1959, the National Football League operated with twelve teams located in eleven cities. There were two teams in Chicago and one each in Cleveland, New York, Philadelphia, Pittsburgh, Washington, Baltimore, Detroit, Los Angeles, San Francisco, and Green Bay, Wisconsin. In 1960, two additional franchises were placed, one in Dallas and one in Minneapolis–St. Paul, the Dallas team beginning play in 1960 and the Minneapolis–St. Paul team in 1961. In 1961, one of the Chicago teams, the Cardinals, was transferred to St. Louis.

The American Football League was organized in 1959, and began with a full schedule of games in 1960. Affiliated with it were eight teams located in eight cities, Boston, Buffalo, Houston, New York, Dallas, Denver, Los Angeles and Oakland. After the 1960 season, the Los Angeles team was moved to San Diego.

* * *

[Discussion of expansion in the NFL (National) began as early as 1956; the early favorites were Dallas and Houston because of their good weather and potential rivalry. In 1959, however, one of the applicants for a Dallas franchise, Lamar Hunt, decided to form a new league instead. By the end of 1959, the AFL (American) had been organized with eight teams, including teams in Dallas (the Texans), Houston (the Oilers), and Minneapolis. Meanwhile, in late 1959 the NFL announced that it would grant expansion teams to Dallas (the Cowboys) and Houston in 1960, but the Houston franchise was conditioned on the availability of an adequate stadium. It soon became known that the Houston team would not be able to play in Rice University's stadium (the only adequate stadium in Houston at the time), so the NFL eliminated Houston from consideration. Instead, the prospective owners of the AFL Minneapolis franchise (who had already paid a $25,000 franchise fee to AFL founder, Lamar Hunt) withdrew from the AFL and were granted an NFL team (the Vikings).]

It thus came to pass that in the 1960 season, teams of the two leagues were in direct competition in New York, Dallas, Los Angeles, and in the San Francisco–Oakland area. Each league had teams in other cities in which there was no direct competition between the leagues. The two leagues were competing on a national basis for television coverage, outstanding players and coaches, and the games of each league competed for spectators with the televised broadcast of a game of the other.

The first and most important question on appeal, therefore, is a review of the District Court's determination of the relevant market. The District Court recognized that the two leagues and their member teams competed with each other in several ways, and that the relevant market with respect to one aspect of their competition would not necessarily be the relevant market with respect to another. Since each league recruited players and coaches throughout the nation, he concluded that the relevant market with respect to their competition in recruiting was nationwide. He necessarily found that their competition for nationwide television coverage, with a blackout only of the area in which the televised game was played, was nationwide. As for the competition for spectators, he found the relevant market to be those thirty-one metropolitan areas in the United States having a population of more than 700,000 people according to the 1960 census. This determination was based upon testimony that a metropolitan area of that size might be expected to support a major league professional football team. Indeed, [Lamar] Hunt, of the American League, had testified that a metropolitan area of 500,000 might support such a team. The District Court's determination was influenced by American's contention that the bare existence of the National League and its member teams foreclosed certain markets to it and limited its capacity to operate successfully. It is reinforced by the evidence of many applications from other cities which were actively pressed upon American, some of which, at least, were thought worthy of real consideration.

In addition to those cities in which American actually placed franchises, Hunt testified that there was substantial interest in a franchise in Vancouver, Seattle, Kansas City, Louisville, Cincinnati, Philadelphia, Jacksonville, Miami, Atlanta, St. Louis and Milwaukee. The eighth franchise was placed in Oakland only after consideration of the "strong case" made by Atlanta. In short, it abundantly appears that cities throughout the United States and one Canadian city were actively competing for league franchises, there being many more applicants than available franchises.

In this Court, the plaintiffs contend that the relevant market is composed of those seventeen cities in which National now either has operating franchises, or which it seriously considered in connection with its expansion plans in 1959. They would thus include in the relevant market New York, Chicago, Philadelphia, Cleveland, Pittsburgh, Washington, Los Angeles, San Francisco, Baltimore, Detroit and Green Bay, in which National teams were operating in 1959, plus Dallas and Minneapolis–St. Paul, in which franchises were authorized in 1960, plus Houston, Buffalo and Miami, which were considered by National for expansion, and St. Louis, to which the Chicago Cardinals were transferred in 1961 after American's first operating season. They include in the relevant market all of the closed cities in which there is a National League team, but no American League team, but exclude from the relevant market all of those closed cities in which there is an American League team but no National League team, and all of those other cities in which there is now no major league professional football team, but which would be hospitable to a franchise and which have a potential for adequate support of a professional football team. They advance the unquestioned principle that the relevant market should be geographically limited to the area in which the defendants operate, or the area in which there is effective competition between the parties.

In very different contexts, the relevant market has been found to be a single city, a group of cities, a state, or several states. In considering an attempt to monopolize, it, of course, is appropriate to limit the relevant geographic market to the area which the defendant sought to appropriate to itself, and, if monopoly power has been acquired in a separably identifiable and normally competitive market, it is irrelevant that the defendant did not possess the same monopoly power in an unrelated market elsewhere.

Plaintiff's contention here, however, is a simple fractionalization of a truly national market. Each league has teams franchised to cities on the Atlantic, on the Pacific and in the midlands. Each team in each league travels back and forth across the country to play before many different audiences in many different cities. Most of the official season games are played in a city in which there is a franchised team, but that is not invariable, and most of the preseason exhibition games are played in cities in which there is no franchised team. In locating franchises, neither league has restricted itself to any geographic section of the country or limited itself to any particular group of cities. In American's brief history, it has moved one team from Los Angeles to San Diego, and the many changes which have occurred in National's franchises belie any notion of geographic limitation.

Though we may concentrate our attention upon competition between the leagues for franchise locations and lay aside for the moment clearly national aspects of their competition for players, coaches and television coverage, location of the franchise is only a selection of a desirable site in a much broader, geographically unlimited market. It is not unlike the choice a chain store company makes when it selects a particular corner lot as the location of a new store. It preempts that lot when it acquires it for that purpose, but, as long as there are other desirable locations for similar stores in a much broader area, it cannot be said to have monopolized the area, or, in a legal sense, the lot or its immediate vicinity.

The National League was first upon the scene. In 1959, it had franchises in eleven cities, the two Chicago teams being in direct competition with each other. It now has franchises in fourteen cities, some of which the District Court found capable of supporting more than one professional football team. Obviously, the American League was of that opinion, for it placed teams in New York, Los Angeles, and the San Francisco–Oakland area, where National, at the time, had well-established teams. Most of the other cities in which each league operates, however, are incapable of supporting more than one professional football team. In such a city, a professional football team, once located there, enjoys a natural monopoly, whether it be affiliated with the National or American League, but the fact that National had teams located in such cities before American's advent does not mean that National had the power to prevent or impede the formation of a new league, or that National's closed cities should be included in the relevant market if American's closed cities are to be excluded. The fact is that the two leagues are in direct competition for regular season spectators only in New York, Dallas, and the San Francisco–Oakland area, and, during the 1960 season, in Los Angeles. If the relevant market is not to be limited to those cities, it must be, geographically, at least as broad as the United States, including Hawaii and portions of Canada.

Though there may be in the nation no more than some thirty desirable sites for the location of professional football teams, those sites, scattered throughout the United States, do not constitute the relevant market. The relevant market is nationwide, though the fact that there are a limited number of desirable sites for team locations bears upon the question of National's power to monopolize the national market.

The District Court's finding that National did not have the power to monopolize the relevant market appears plainly correct. In 1959, it occupied eleven of the thirty-one apparently desirable sites for team locations, but its occupancy of some of them as New York and San Francisco–Oakland was not exclusive, for those metropolitan areas were capable of supporting more than one team. Twenty of the thirty-one potentially desirable sites were entirely open to American. Indeed, the fact that the American League was successfully launched, could stage a full schedule of games in 1960, has competed very successfully for outstanding players, and has obtained advantageous contracts for national television coverage strongly supports the District Court's finding that National did not have the power to prevent, or impede, the formation of the new league. Indeed, at the close of the 1960 season, representatives of the American League declared that the League's success was unprecedented.

American advances a theory, however, that, since the National League won Minneapolis–St. Paul in competition with American, National could have taken several other cities away from American had it undertaken to do so. This is only a theory, however, unsupported by evidence. It ignores the fact that American won Houston over National's competition, and that each league has won one and lost one in their direct competition for franchise locations. It ignores the fact that National was committed to expansion from twelve to sixteen teams in two separate steps, two teams at a time, so that it had but two franchises to place at the time American was being organized. American questions the finding that sixteen teams is a maximum that one league can efficiently accommodate, but the finding is based upon evidence and was not clearly erroneous. In short, there is no basis for a contention that the evidence required a finding that National, had it wished, could have placed a team in every location sought by American, or in a sufficient number of them to have destroyed the league.

American complains that National, the first upon the scene, had occupied the more desirable of the thirty-one potential sites for team locations. Its occupancy of New York and San Francisco–Oakland was not exclusive, however, and the fact that its teams in other locations, such as Baltimore and Washington, enjoyed a natural monopoly does not occasion a violation of the antitrust laws unless the natural monopoly power of those teams was misused to gain a competitive advantage for teams located in other cities, or for the league as a whole. It frequently happens that a first competitor in the field will acquire sites which a latecomer may think more desirable than the remaining available sites, but the firstcomer is not required to surrender any, or all, of its desirable sites to the latecomer simply to enable the latecomer to compete more effectively with it. There is no basis in antitrust laws for a contention that American, whose Boston, Buffalo, Houston, Denver and San Diego teams enjoy natural monopolies, has a right to complain that National does not surrender to it other natural monopoly locations so that they too may be enjoyed by American rather than by National. When one has acquired a natural monopoly by means which are neither exclusionary, unfair, nor predatory, he is not disempowered to defend his position fairly.

* * *

We conclude, therefore, that the District Court properly held that the plaintiffs have shown no monopolization by the National League, or its owners, of the relevant market, and no attempt or conspiracy by them, or any of them, to monopolize it or any part of it. No violation of the Sherman Act having been established, the judgment of the District Court is affirmed.

Affirmed.

———

Despite its lack of success in this litigation, the upstart AFL proved a worthy competitive force against the established NFL. Buoyed by the first big network television contract with ABC for regular season sports—the contract that forced the NFL to petition Congress for enactment of the Sports Broadcasting Act—the AFL undertook a dramatic bidding war for NFL players, especially star quarterbacks such as John Brodie. By 1966 the NFL was ready to make peace, and the two leagues agreed to a merger. However, in light of the Fourth Circuit's reasoning in the above decision, the leagues had grave doubts about the legality of their plans. But by dangling the promise of expansion into New Orleans to powerful committee chairs from Louisiana, Senator Russell Long and Representative Hale Boggs, the leagues were able to secure congressional blessing for this new league venture through an amendment to the Sports Broadcasting Act, 15 U.S.C. § 1291. We have seen this amendment discussed in Chapter 6 in the *Memphis Grizzlies* case (post-World Football League), and we will encounter it later in this chapter in litigation arising out of the demise of the United States Football League (below).

It is important in thinking about section 2's ban on monopolization to remember that the two elements of a violation—monopoly market power and improper conduct—are wholly separate. The conduct constituting the monopolizing act does not have to involve directly the market being monopolized. Given this doctrinal reality, why was the entire focus of *AFL v. NFL* the geographic market in which franchises were being awarded? The fact that the alleged unlawful conduct was strategic placement of new NFL franchises and the threat to add two more in other potential AFL cities does not mean that the market being monopolized has to be the one in which franchises are granted. If you were an upstart league alleging that an established league was trying to prevent you from becoming a viable competitor, in what market would you allege that the established league clearly held monopoly (or monopsony?) market power that it most wanted to maintain? In what market are the competitive effects of a second league most immediately apparent and dramatic? What do established leagues fear most from new leagues?

In assessing the presence of monopoly power, there is a *functional* as well as a *geographic* cast to the relevant market. The National Football League, for example, has regularly argued (though without much success) that professional football faces market competition from college football, that football faces competition from baseball, basketball, and other sports, and that all sports face competition from movies, concerts, theater, and other forms of entertainment.[6] The major judicial precedent in this regard is *United States v. E.I. du Pont de Nemours & Co.*, 351 U.S. 377, 76 S.Ct. 994, 100 L.Ed. 1264 (1956). This case involved a section 2 complaint against du Pont which produced 75% of the country's cellophane; cellophane, though, constituted just 20% of all "flexible packaging materials." The following passages indicate how the Supreme Court analyzes such market definition issues:

> Market delimitation is necessary under du Pont's theory to determine whether an alleged monopolist violates § 2. The ultimate consideration in such a determination is whether the defendants control the price and competition in the market for such part of trade or commerce as they are charged with monopolizing. Every manufacturer is the sole producer of the particular commodity it makes but its control in the above sense of the relevant

---

6. Indeed, an antitrust complainant against the NFL also failed in his effort to characterize football tickets as merely one product available in the "general entertainment market," where such a judgment was essential to his charge that the Buffalo Bills illegally "tied" availability of season ticket packages for regular season games to the purchase of tickets for exhibition games. See *Coniglio v. Highwood Services,* *Inc.*, 495 F.2d 1286, 1292 (2d Cir.1974). Also, to the same effect, *Driskill v. Dallas Cowboys Football Club*, 498 F.2d 321 (5th Cir.1974); *Laing v. Minnesota Vikings Football Club*, 372 F.Supp. 59 (D.Minn. 1973), affirmed, 492 F.2d 1381 (8th Cir. 1974); *Pfeiffer v. New England Patriots*, 1973–1 Trade Cases ¶ 74,267, 1972 WL 647 (D.Mass.1972).

market depends upon the availability of alternative commodities for buyers: i.e., whether there is a cross-elasticity of demand between cellophane and the other wrappings. This interchangeability is largely gauged by the purchase of competing products for similar uses, considering the price, characteristics and adaptability of the competing commodities.

* * *

If a large number of buyers and sellers deal freely in a standardized product, such as salt or wheat, we have complete or pure competition. Patents, on the other hand, furnish the most familiar type of classic monopoly. As the producers of a standardized product bring about significant differentiations of quality, design, or packaging in the product that permit differences of use, competition becomes to a greater or less degree incomplete and the producer's power over price and competition greater over his article and its use, according to the differentiation he is able to create and maintain. A retail seller may have in one sense a monopoly on certain trade because of location, as an isolated country store or filling station, or because no one else makes a product of just the quality or attractiveness of his product, as for example in cigarettes. Thus one can theorize that we have monopolistic competition in every nonstandardized commodity with each manufacturer having power over the price and production of his own product. However, this power that, let us say, automobile or soft-drink manufacturers have over their trademarked products is not the power that makes an illegal monopoly. Illegal power must be appraised in terms of the competitive market for the product.

Determination of the competitive market for commodities depends on how different from one another are the offered commodities in character or use, how far buyers will go to substitute one commodity for another. For example, one can think of building materials as in commodity competition, but one could hardly say that brick competed with steel or wood or cement or stone in the meaning of the Sherman Act litigation; the products are too different. This is the interindustry competition emphasized by some economists. On the other hand, there are certain differences in the formulae for soft drinks, but one can hardly say that each one is an illegal monopoly.

* * *

What is called for is an appraisal of the "cross-elasticity" of demand in the trade. The varying circumstances of each case determine the result. In considering what is the relevant market for determining the control of price and competition, no more definite rule can be declared than that commodities reasonably interchangeable by consumers for the same purposes make up that "part of the trade or commerce," monopolization of which may be illegal.

351 U.S., at 380–81, 392–96, 76 S.Ct. at 999, 1005–07.

Shortly after *du Pont*, the Supreme Court rendered its second decision in *International Boxing Club v. United States*, 358 U.S. 242, 79 S.Ct. 245, 3 L.Ed.2d 270 (1959). In its first decision in these proceedings, at 348 U.S. 236 (1955), the Supreme Court had ruled for the first time that any sport was subject to antitrust law (thereby beginning the scenario whereby the immunity won earlier by baseball would be confined to that sport by *Flood v. Kuhn)*. This second decision dealt with the merits of the antitrust complaint concerning boxing. Apparently James Norris, owner of Detroit's Olympia Arena and hockey Red Wings, and Willard Wirtz, owner of Chicago's Stadium and Black Hawks, had formed International Boxing Club (IBC) to try to dominate professional boxing. IBC used Joe Louis and Sugar Ray Robinson as the levers to win exclusive control of the champions and contenders in boxing's heavyweight, middleweight and welterweight divisions, and bought Madison Square Garden to secure control of all the major sites for big time fights. The Justice Department charged IBC with monopolizing and restraining trade in *championship* boxing, and the District Court found violations of both sections 1 and 2 of the Sherman Act. The following is the key passage from the Supreme Court's analysis of the merits of IBC's appeal:

> Appellants launch a vigorous attack on the finding that the relevant market was the promotion of *championship* boxing contests in contrast to *all* professional boxing events. They rely primarily on *United States v. du Pont & Co.*, 351 U.S. 377 (1956).... In testing for the relevant market in Sherman Act cases, the Court said:
>
> > ... no more definite rule can be declared than that commodities reasonably interchangeable by consumers for the same purposes make up that 'part of the trade or commerce,' monopolization of which may be illegal.

The appellants argue that the "physical identity of the products here would seem necessarily to put them in one and the same market." They say that any boxing contest, whether championship or not, always includes one ring, two boxers and one referee, fighting under the same rules before a greater or lesser number of spectators either present at ringside or through the facilities of television, radio, or moving pictures.

> We do not feel that this conclusion follows. As was also said in *du Pont*, supra, at 404:
>
> > The 'market' ... will vary with the part of commerce under consideration. The tests are constant. That market is composed of products that have reasonable interchangeability for the purposes for which they are produced—price, use and qualities considered.

With this in mind, the lower court in the instant case found that there exists a "separate, identifiable market" for championship boxing contests. This general finding is supported by detailed findings to the effect that the average revenue from all sources for appellants' championship bouts was $154,000 compared to $40,000 for their nonchampionship programs; that television rights to one championship fight brought $100,000, in contrast to $45,000 for a nontitle fight seven months later between the same two fighters; that the average "Nielsen" ratings over a two-and-one-half-year period were 74.9% for appellants' championship contests, and 57.7% for their nonchampionship programs (reflecting a difference of several million viewers between the two types of fights); that although the revenues from movie rights for six of appellants' championship bouts totaled over $600,000, no full-length motion picture rights were sold for a non-championship contest; and that spectators pay "substantially more" for tickets to championship fights than for nontitle fights. In addition, numerous representatives of the broadcasting, motion picture and advertising industries testified to the general effect that a "particular and special demand exists among radio broadcasting and telecasting [and motion picture] companies for the rights to broadcast and telecast [and make and distribute films of] championship contests in contradistinction to similar rights to non-championship contests."

In view of these findings, we cannot say that the lower court was "clearly erroneous" in concluding that nonchampionship fights are not "reasonably interchangeable for the same purpose" as championship contests.... The case which most squarely governs this case is *United States v. Paramount Pictures*, 334 U.S. 131 (1948). There, the charge involved, *inter alia*, extensive motion picture theatre holdings. The District Court had refused to order a divestiture of such holdings on the grounds that no "national monopoly" had been intended or obtained. This Court felt that such a finding was not dispositive of the issue, saying:

First, there is no finding as to the presence or absence of monopoly on the part of the five majors [defendants] in the *first-run* field for the entire country, in the *first-run* field in the 92 largest cities of the country, or in the *first-run* field in separate localities. Yet the *first-run* field, which constitutes the cream of the exhibition business, is the core of the present cases....

Similarly, championship boxing is the "cream" of the boxing business, and, as has been shown above, is a sufficiently separate part of the trade or commerce to constitute the relevant market for Sherman Act purposes.

76 S.Ct. at 249–52, 358 U.S. at 249–52.

Questions for Discussion

1. In light of the *du Pont* and *IBC* line of analysis, how much weight should be given to the NFL's product market argument sketched earlier in

antitrust litigation against the league? Recall Judge Easterbrook's observations in the *WGN* decision in Chapter 6; should the sports *television* market be treated differently from the sports *ticket* market?

2. A sports league operates in markets other than those in which it sells its product to customers—the markets for live event tickets and television and radio broadcast rights. It also sells franchises in the league and trademark licenses, and purchases equipment and the services of coaches and players. In which of the major markets in which an established league operates does it probably hold substantial market power? In which does it likely hold little market power? Does your answer hinge on unstated variables—which sport is involved, whether an upstart league is operating at the time, or whether the market is national or local (in which case market power can vary from city to city)?

3. In considering the labor or equipment markets, review the discussion of "monopsony" in Chapter 3—a buyer has so much market power over sellers of some factor of production that they have virtually no alternative buyer. In such a case, the monopsonist can force prices down to artificially low levels, which ultimately hurts the consumer by causing some suppliers to cut back the amount of the input they are willing to supply and thereby shifts resource allocation toward goods and services less desired by consumers. That may, however, also benefit consumers who do buy the product by reducing the monopsonist's production costs that in some part (depending on the elasticity of demand for the product) will be passed through to consumers. If a league monopsonizes an input market, should that be as automatic a section 2 violation as if it had monopolized a product market? Or should a court have to go one step further and determine whether the monopsony benefits or injures consumers on balance?

B. MONOPOLY RESOURCES AND MONOPOLIZING CONDUCT

The mere existence of monopoly power in the relevant market, however defined, is not sufficient to establish a violation of section 2 of the Sherman Act. As the Supreme Court put it in *United States v. Grinnell Corp.*, 384 U.S. 563, 570–71, 86 S.Ct. 1698, 1704, 16 L.Ed.2d 778 (1966), a section 2 violation also requires "the willful acquisition or maintenance of that power as distinguished from growth or development as a consequence of a superior product, business acumen, or historic accident." Over the last century, courts have developed a sizable jurisprudence regarding how to distinguish legitimate from illegitimate sources of monopoly power.

From the point of view of antitrust policy, the question is not whether a monopolistic firm has exploited its power by raising prices or lowering output to maximize its profits. While this practice harms consumers in the short run (and may be subject to government regulation on that account), the presence of monopoly profits in a particular market often serves as an inducement to other firms to enter the market if they can, which in the long run creates a competitive environment for the benefit of consumers. Indeed, the prospect of new entry may discourage the established firm from fully exploiting its monopoly power in the first place. The true evil aimed at by antitrust law, then, is action by the monopolist that excludes others from entering the market and providing competitive balance.

However, not all exclusionary practices warrant legal prohibition. If the size or competence of an established firm allows it to develop high quality products sold at low prices that cannot be matched by its rivals, it hardly enhances consumer welfare for a judge to penalize the firm for making such an effort to satisfy its customers. The challenge in this area of antitrust law is to distinguish between those exclusionary practices by the dominant firm that benefit consumers, and hence are legally tolerable, from exclusionary practices that are anticompetitive, and thus warrant legal prohibition.

A good deal of this antitrust jurisprudence is displayed in the following cases. In sports, such litigation has been targeted at the established league's use of its control over assets vital to the emergence of a competitive sports venture. We saw this in the *AFL* case above, which involved desirable franchise cities, and in the *NASL* case in Chapter 6 (in which the charge was brought under section 1 of the Sherman Act), which involved the allegedly scarce supply of sports capital and entrepreneurial talent. The next three decisions deal with other resources indispensable in present-day professional sports—players, facilities, and television contracts.

1. PLAYERS

Chapter 3 presented an in-depth look at the role of antitrust law in the player market. The focus of that chapter's analysis was very different from our concern here. In cases such as *Flood*, *Mackey*, and *McCourt*, the players and their associations used section 1 of the Sherman Act to attack the variety of legal practices—capsulized as the "reserve system"—that limited player mobility and bargaining leverage within the established league. This chapter examines the established leagues' use of their control over players—including control obtained through collective bargaining—to foil potential competitors by denying new leagues access to the most vital of all sports assets—player talent, especially well-known, high-quality talent.

Such control tends to be less effective in football and basketball because every year the intercollegiate "farm clubs" in these sports "graduate" a new class of athletes of demonstrated quality and considerable renown. Perhaps this is one of the reasons why the NFL and NBA never included provisions in their player contracts that perpetually bound players to the team and prevented them from signing with teams *in a different league* (if one existed) when the contract expired. By contrast, in baseball and hockey, the intercollegiate game is much less prominent; thus the major leagues have created their own farm systems to develop player talent for parent clubs. Since a network of contract restrictions bound every young player from the time he entered the minor leagues to the time he retired from the big leagues,[7] it was crucial to the success of new leagues aspiring to big-time status to break that stranglehold. The appropriate legal vehicle was Section 2 of the Sherman Act; the following decision is the principal example of its use.

PHILADELPHIA WORLD HOCKEY CLUB v. PHILADELPHIA HOCKEY CLUB

United States District Court, Eastern District of Pennsylvania, 1972.

351 F.Supp. 462.

HIGGINBOTHAM, DISTRICT JUDGE.

[This decision concerned an antitrust suit filed by the fledgling World Hockey Association against its established rival, the National Hockey League. The WHA's primary objective was to secure a federal court injunction against the NHL and its clubs from seeking state court injunctions to prevent over 60 NHL players who had signed WHA contracts from moving to the WHA in apparent violation of their NHL standard player contracts.[1] The trial judge provided an elaborate description of the structure of professional hockey, relations between the NHL and amateur and minor professional hockey leagues, the reserve system and the standard player contract, expansion of the NHL in the late 1960s, and the emergence of the WHA in the early 1970s. Here we distill this lengthy decision into the key items relevant to the legal analysis reproduced here. We begin, however, by quoting the prelude to the trial judge's decision.]

* * *

In 1917, the National Hockey League was born with Montreal and Toronto as its only members. In 1924, Boston was added, followed in 1926 with Chicago, Detroit and New York. In 1967, Los Angeles, Philadelphia, Pittsburgh, California, Minnesota, and St. Louis entered the League and in 1970 Buffalo and Vancouver. In 1972, Nassau (New York) and Atlanta joined this now famous League. Since 1966, the National Hockey League has received in excess of $36,000,000 for the sale of the rights to play major league professional hockey in their league. When in 1970 the National Hockey League admitted Vancouver and Buffalo, each of these two new clubs paid in excess of $8,000,-

---

7. Bobby Orr, for example, became the property of the Boston Bruins when he was just 14 years old, because the Bruins, recognizing his talent, took over sponsorship of the midget league in which Orr was then playing in his hometown of Parry Sound, Ontario.

1. [See *Boston Professional Hockey Ass'n v. Cheevers*, 348 F.Supp. 261 (D. Mass.1972), reversed on other grounds, 472 F.2d 127 (1st Cir.1972), and *Nassua Sports v. Hampson*, 355 F.Supp. 733 (D.Minn.1972) (both denying the negative injunction); contra, *Nassua Sports v. Peters*, 352 F.Supp. 870 (E.D.N.Y.1972) (granting the injunction).]

000 for the acquisition of the minor professional league clubs in their locality and for distribution to National Hockey League clubs.

Thus, from what in 1917 was a relatively minor sports attraction, the National Hockey League has skated into the 1970s to a position of substantial wealth, power, broad spectator interest, international recognition and many superstars, all crescendoing into huge profits for both its owners and players.

One writer observes:

"What has happened is this: the intrinsic speed and excitement of hockey has made it the game of the second half of this century."

Maybe in 1922 when the Supreme Court decided the baseball case, hockey was also, as Mr. Justice Holmes then described baseball, primarily an effort to give exhibitions with profits and interstate commerce contacts as mere incidentals. But today, as I review the instant record, hockey is primarily a multi-state, bi-national business, where the fundamental motive is the making of money. From its multiple interstate contacts it is a business in commerce subject to the federal antitrust laws.

Despite the thousands of words uttered on this record by all parties about the glory of the sport of hockey and the grandeur of its superstars, the basic factors here are not the sheer exhilaration from observing the speeding puck, but rather the desire to maximize the available buck.

* * *

[The judge then described how almost all major league hockey players came from amateur teams governed by the Canadian Amateur Hockey Association, although some came from U.S. clubs operating under the auspices of the Amateur Hockey Association of the United States. While traditionally NHL clubs had directly sponsored individual amateur teams in Canada, especially at the Junior A level, since 1967 there had been an umbrella NHL–CAHA agreement under which NHL clubs contributed over $1 million per year for amateur player development. At the same time, the NHL began to conduct an annual draft of all the approximately 7,000 amateur players turning twenty years of age, 150 of whom were drafted, with specified payments to CAHA club members for each player drafted, and each of the 45 or so players who signed an NHL contract.

Almost all newly drafted players began professional hockey in one of three minor hockey leagues—the American, the Western, and the Central Hockey Leagues—all of whose teams were either directly sponsored by an NHL club or had an affiliation or player loan arrangement. There were sharp differences in both profitability and caliber of play between the NHL and the three minor leagues. Whereas NHL teams averaged near sellout crowds of 14,000 per game at more than $5 per ticket, minor league teams averaged 4,000 fans per game at $2.50

per ticket. These differences in gate revenues, together with the emergence of local and network television contracts, permitted NHL teams to pay their players an average annual salary of $24,000 in 1971–1972, compared to $11,000–12,000 for minor league players. Thus, while the WHA planned to recruit a significant number of players from the minor professional leagues, the judge concluded that in order to succeed the WHA also needed access to players who had developed the ability to excel in the NHL.

The major obstacle to the WHA's recruiting of NHL players was the NHL standard player contract. Under clause 17 of that contract, the club was entitled to renew the contract on the same terms as before, with the exception of the salary amount, which was set anew each year. Since one of the terms in the existing contract was clause 17 itself, the player contract was perpetually renewable. Similar terms were included in the standard contracts in the AHL, the WHL, and the CHL constitutions, which led the trial judge to find as follows:]

The similarities of phraseology and basic incorporation of Clause 17 in the Standard Player's Contract of the AHL, CHL, WHL, and NHL is the result of a common agreement, mutual understanding, and conspiracy by the NHL and its affiliated minor leagues to maintain a monopolistic position so strong that the NHL precludes effective competition by the entry of another major professional hockey league. Through the totality of many interlocking arrangements, including the Joint Affiliation Agreement, the Pro–Amateur Agreement, and Clause 17 in the Standard Player's Contract, the NHL perpetuates a conspiracy and combination with the intent to monopolize and which monopolizes major league professional hockey. These concerted efforts were done not solely to maintain a high level of professional competition among the NHL teams, but rather the major reason was the desire to preclude others from ever having immediate access to the reservoir of players who could become part of another major professional hockey league which could be a material and viable competitor to the NHL. In the words of Mr. Clarence Campbell, President of the NHL, part of the NHL's purpose was to make certain that the NHL would always be " … the only major professional hockey league operating from coast-to-coast in the United States or Canada."

* * *

[In the late 1960s there were some negotiations about the terms of this standard player contract between the NHL and its long-time president, Clarence Campbell, and the new NHL Player Association under its founding leader, Alan Eagleson. These labor negotiations, though, focussed only on the mechanism for settling differences about salary amounts in the renewed option contract. Previously, salary disputes between teams and veteran players were adjudicated by NHL President Campbell; as of 1972, however, the NHL agreed to neutral salary arbitration. With that exception, hockey's basic reserve system remained untouched, enforced by a vigorous anti-tampering section in the NHL by-laws. Any team that publicly indicated interest in acquiring a player on another team's reserve list, let alone negotiated with that player, was subject to fines and loss of draft choices.]

THE NECESSITY FOR SOME FORM OF RESERVE CLAUSE.

Every major professional team sport utilizes some form of "reserve" clause in its standard player's contract. Some of the purported justifications for a "reserve" clause (e.g., the need for competitive balance within the league) apply to all sports. A less anti-competitive "reserve" clause than the present one may be needed in hockey.

In order to be successful, a professional hockey league normally must have some of the qualities of parity among its member teams which make other sports successful. That is, the public must believe that there is relative parity among the member teams and that each team has the opportunity of becoming a contender over a reasonable cycle of years and a reasonable chance of beating any other team on any given night.

The history of the NHL's Stanley Cup Series, the "World Series" of hockey, indicates that relative parity does not exist within the NHL. In the last twenty years, Montreal has won the Stanley Cup on twelve occasions, Toronto has won four times, Detroit has won three times, and Chicago has won once.

The founders of the WHA believe that even if the quality of the hockey played by its member teams is not as high as in the NHL, the WHA will still be successful if it can maintain sufficient parity of quality among its own teams.

* * *

[The judge then described the expansion of major-league professional hockey. The NHL, which was formed in 1917, achieved a permanent base in six cities by 1942. Not until 1967 did expansion occur, this time into six new cities. For the $2 million franchise fee, each new club obtained the right to select 20 players each from the established teams' reserve lists, except for 20 protected players for each of the latter teams. Three years later, in 1970, the NHL expanded again into Buffalo and Vancouver, this time at a price of $8 million per franchise, and the clubs selected players from those left off 15–player protected lists.

In August 1971, the NHL learned of the imminent formation of the WHA. In reaction, the NHL took two major steps. One was to authorize further expansion into Atlanta and Long Island, at $6 million per franchise. Long Island was crucial because the WHA had been actively negotiating for a franchise lease in the newly-constructed Nassau Coliseum, the only site available for a hockey team in the New York metropolitan area (other than Madison Square Garden, which had an exclusive hockey lease with the NHL Rangers). When the NHL awarded a franchise to Roy Boe (who also paid $4 million in territorial indemnity to the Rangers), the Nassau Coliseum signed a lease with the NHL's New York Islanders.

The NHL's other step was to form a Legal Committee that, through the Washington law firm of Covington and Burling, coordinated vigorous enforcement of the reserve clause through injunction proceedings against NHL players seeking to move to the WHA for much higher salaries.

The WHA's response was to launch this antitrust suit against the NHL. One claim rested on section 1 of the Sherman Act. Judge Higginbotham was loath to grant an injunction to the WHA on that ground.]

On the basis of the present record as to the § 1 issues, I have some doubts on the WHA's probability of ultimate success. The sports field is in some ways a hybrid, in that it is both similarly and dissimilarly affected by the normal economic variables governing business success. For a corporation producing aluminum, any entrant in the field is a competitor. From a traditional oligopolist's or monopolist's view, one might consider any new entrant as an adversary and thus undesirable. But by the nature of a sports contest, there must always be an adversary. By analogy, who would enjoy Vida Blue blazing strikes across home plate when the batter's box was empty, or Mark Spitz' triumphs, if he were the only one in the pool. Sports teams need competition, and if there are more than two teams, some type of league is probably desirable.

For maximum customer receptivity and profit it is in the best interest of any club that its opponents not generally be viewed by the public as totally incompetent and utterly unable to compete effectively. For if the latter occurs, thousands of customers will not spend their dollars for tickets to view hundreds of games when the contest seems to present no more of a challenge than an ant confronting an elephant. Thus, if it is not possible to keep the competitive challenge of all teams within some reasonable parameters, some type of intraleague reserve clause or system may be desirable and in fact necessary.

* * *

[At the heart of the WHA's case, though, was section 2 of Sherman, which prohibited monopolization, or attempted monopolization, and which the trial judge believed gave the WHA much firmer legal ground.]

To determine whether the WHA has shown that the NHL falls within the test articulated in *United States v. Grinnell*, one must first understand the history and impact of the reserve clause and the various arbitration agreements.

A.   The Reserve Clause—Its History and Application.

*   *   *

An examination of the record discloses that prior to 1969, the only mechanism existing for the resolution of salary disputes when the player and the respective NHL member team were unable to mutually agree, would be for the President of the NHL, Clarence Campbell, to serve as the final arbiter.   Prior to 1969, there were no contractual impediments whatsoever to the NHL club having and exercising a perpetual option over any player once he had been drafted by a NHL team and had signed a Standard Player's Contract.   It is unequivocally clear that, in view of the monopolistic power of the NHL, this arrangement would have violated Section 2 of the Sherman Act, since a player, for his entire professional career, would be contractually bound to play for the team which then held his contract.

Prior to 1969, the operation of Clause 17 would have permitted the club to tender to the player a new contract every year, and that player would be required to sign, with any dispute over salary to be ultimately decided by the President of the NHL.   Any dispute apart from salary would also be finally determined by the President of the NHL, as authorized by Clause 18 of that same Standard Player's Contract.   It is therefore necessary to examine the events since 1969 to determine whether any subsequent, alleged modifications of Clause 17 have diluted its previously, fatally defective, anti-competitive effects.

[A]lthough between 1969 and 1972 negotiations occurred on the issue of the arbitrability of salaries, it was not until June, 1972, that any of the Standard Player's Contracts formally reflected and incorporated the requirement that an independent arbitrator would conclusively decide salary disputes.   In 1969, as previously noted, the President of the NHL ultimately decided salary.   In 1970, the Standard Player's Contract stated salary was to be determined by mutual agreement.

Looking only to the language of the 1970 Standard Player's Contract, one can alternatively conclude that, rather than being mandatorily compelled to submit to arbitration, the President of the NHL, pursuant to clause 18, could decide salary, as in 1969.   Thus, with that construction, when one examines only those provisions which have been actually embodied in the 1970 Contract, and read clause 18 together with clause 17, then the 1970 Contract, in terms of its scope and indefinite duration, is precisely identical to the 1969 Contract in all material respects.   If the existence of a mechanism to determine compensation is deemed to be legally dispositive as to whether there is a valid, enforceable contract, then such a scheme did, in fact, exist. The "right to renew" aspect of Clause 17, therefore, continued to operate in 1970 uncurbed and unrestrained and, consequently, was equally violative of Section 2 of the Sherman Act due to the same vitiating, anti-competitive results discussed above.   While this fact will be reiterated below, the 1970 version of the Standard Player's Contract was the form utilized during the 1971–1972 playing season.

To continue this chronology of events since 1969, one has to specifically focus on the two Arbitration Agreements executed between the NHL and the NHL Players' Association, and ascertain in what ways, if any, was the Standard Player's Contract altered or modified, thus arguably curing any antitrust defect. More important, however, attention must be directed to the allocation of authority vested in the NHL Players' Association by the players.

* * *

Initially, it should be stressed that the labor relations history between the NHL and the NHL Players' Association has often proceeded in a most informal fashion in terms of the failure to execute "formalized" agreements. As an example, Charles Mulcahy, the NHL owner-representative to the NHL Owner–Player Council, while discussing the method of operation of that Council, stated: "The history of hockey has been on a handshake basis, and if I tell you something, I am not going to go back on my word...." It was his understanding that such oral agreements could be regarded as provisions of a player's contract even though unrecorded and not specifically ratified by any particular player.

Mr. Alan Eagleson, Executive Director of the Players' Association, testified before the Senate Commerce Committee on June 28, 1972, that: "There is no formal collective bargaining agreement as such between the members of the Players' Association and the League. For purposes of direct discussion between players and owners, the format of our negotiations with the owners includes a Player–Owner Council." Mr. Eagleson has further testified:

> The aim of the [A]ssociation is to eventually extend that arbitration [of salary disputes] to include an independent arbitration of all problems between players and owners. But it is a first step. And in this fashion we feel that it gives the club perhaps a little better advantage, but gives the players significant advantage over what— over the position he has previously been in. Because a player can still say, all right, that is the position of my association, and my association has agreed that the arbitration will be binding, but I may decide after having heard the decision on arbitration to say to hell with my association and the owners, I am not going to play for that kind of money. This happened, I think, only on one occasion, and it only lasted for a matter of a day and a half before we were able to express to the player that, look, fair ball is fair ball. As a result, things have gone rather smoothly in the past two years in this year.

With such nebulousness, it is impossible to reconstruct the full context of the relationship of the parties and the binding effect, if any, of their agreements. Because of the informality of these discussions, some agreements have been finalized by a handshake, many of them have never been reduced to writing. Therefore, in view of this past cloudy collective bargaining history, the various parties may honestly reconstruct their "understanding" of these transactions differently.

In considering the impact the Arbitration Agreements have wrought upon the Standard Player's Contract, as well as examining the legal significance of any collective bargaining negotiations, I recognize that, at a minimum, one is always dealing with a quadripartite relationship:

(1) The National Hockey League (which presumably can speak for the owners);

(2) The NHL Players' Association (which purportedly speaks for the players en masse);

(3) A specific individual hockey player, who has his own specific contract with a single identifiable club; and

(4) A particular NHL team which has drafted certain players and negotiated individual contracts with each player.

Thus, the critical issue before me is whether any agreement reached by the National Hockey League Players' Association and the NHL teams is legally binding on an individual hockey player so that it modifies his currently existing contract to incorporate those new terms. I find that unless the individual player has specifically agreed to the amendment of his current contract, the March 29, 1972 Arbitration Agreement executed between the NHL and the NHL Players' Association is not legally binding on an individual player and, hence, does not modify his current contract. Of course, a player may ratify the agreement of the Players' Association and the Club owners, but absent precise ratification, I find that any agreement between the Players' Association and the owners does not result in an automatic modification of a pre-existing, specific player's contract. If one were to permit the Players' Association and the NHL to possess such power to amend an individual's current contract without the individual's express authorization or express ratification, one can imagine a player's one-year contract being extended for an indefinite period of time beyond the player's expressed original intent.

* * *

Even if, arguendo, the 1972 Arbitration Agreement is automatically incorporated into an existing individual player's contract and is not solely a device for determining salary, and even if the 1972 Arbitration Agreement expires in 1975 without having been extended by the NHL and the NHLPA (thus arguably making the reserve clause unenforceable after 1975 because no mechanism will then exist for determining the amount of compensation), I hold that in the circumstances of this case, the three year restraint following the expiration of a current contract (considering this factor along with the other numerous interlocking agreements the NHL has fashioned and shaped over the years to monopolize a hockey player's professional career) is unreasonable, and in violation of Section 2 of the Sherman Act.

Finally, apart from the collective bargaining negotiations relative to the arbitration of salary, there have been no modifications of Clause 17 of the Standard Player's Contract which have altered or eliminated the basic perpetual option which the NHL has over any hockey player once he has first signed a Standard Player's Contract.

B. Monopoly Power.

In view of the impact of the reserve clause, an additional issue for determination is whether the NHL possesses monopoly power in the relevant market. In United States v. E. I. du Pont De Nemours & Co., supra, 351 U.S. at 391, the Court defined monopoly power as " . . . the power to control prices or exclude competition."

Further, in American Tobacco Co. v. United States, 328 U.S. 781, 811 (1946), the Court stated:

> The authorities support the view that the material consideration in determining whether a monopoly exists is not that prices are raised and that competition actually is excluded but that power exists to raise prices or to exclude competition when it is desired to do so.

Here, through the use, inter alia, of (1) Standard Players' Contracts, including the "reserve clause" in paragraph 17 of that contract, (2) the agreements between the NHL and three of the major semi-professional leagues, and (3) the agreements between the professional and semi-professional leagues and the amateur leagues, it is clear that the NHL overwhelmingly controls the supply of players who are capable and available for play in a new league where the level of internal competitions fairly approaches the levels currently existing in the NHL. In an attempt to minimize the NHL's extraordinary degree of control over the players, the NHL asserts that there are many other available players who will shortly be able to play major league professional hockey. However, the relevant market place is the market place of today, not the market place of 1980 or even the market place of 1975. A monopolist may not today excuse his present predatory practices because someday in the future his total domination of the market place may be lessened.

The NHL's monopoly power is their power to control overwhelmingly the supply of hockey players who are today available for play in any major professional league. It is that total control by the NHL which I hold is proscribed by § 2 of the Sherman Act. One who builds the most modern steel mill cannot operate without an adequate supply of iron ore. The 50,000 amateur hockey players allegedly available to the WHA are the "iron ore" from which viable competition can be built. If the WHA is to compete effectively for attendance and television rights with commensurate payments, the WHA must have a "show" which is equal or nearly equal to that of the NHL today. Since the WHA is a newcomer, the quality of play need not instantly equal that of the NHL, but there must be a prospect that the product will be nearly equal in a relatively short period of time.

Of course, I recognize that the NHL has neither prevented the birth of the infant WHA nor has the NHL caused the WHA to sustain a premature demise, but monopoly power may be restrained before its full wrath is felt.

C. *Willfulness & Intent.*

The mere possession of monopoly power in the relevant market does not alone constitute a violation of Section 2 of the Sherman Act, 15 U.S.C. Section 2. There must also be "(2) the willful acquisition or maintenance of that power as distinguished from growth or development as a consequence of a superior product, business acumen, or historic accident." United States v. Grinnell, 384 U.S. 563, 570–71 (1966).

The activities of the NHL go beyond mere possession of monopoly power in the relevant market to breach these aforementioned prohibitions articulated in *United States v. Grinnell.*

The NHL has willfully acquired and maintained its monopoly power through the use of the many agreements detailed in Findings of Fact 35–89. Its continuing and overriding goal is to maintain a monopoly over the supply of major league professional hockey players.

The NHL employs devices such as reserve clauses, Standard Player Contracts, an NHL semi-professional league Joint–Affiliation Agreement, and control over the amateurs through the Pro–Am Agreement in which the amateurs agreed to recognize the NHL as the "sole and exclusive governing body of professional hockey." If the NHL reserve clause were valid for those players whose contracts terminated in September, 1972, then the NHL would have the power, directly or indirectly, to prevent any player under "contract" to the NHL or one of its affiliated minor professional leagues from playing with any other team or league outside the NHL System.

Upon reading the self-serving tributes for its expenditure of millions of dollars to develop amateur and minor league hockey, one might infer that the millions were spent solely for the honor and glory of amateur and minor league hockey. The NHL's motives were not quite so noble; these expenditures to develop the amateur and minor professional leagues were essential to maintain the NHL's monopolistic position.

In *American Football League v. National Football League* the Court noted:

In 1959 the NFL had most of the ablest players under contract. However, colleges graduate annually large numbers of talented players, and, because after the season starts professional football rosters are usually limited to around 35 players, many good players are released each year after the training season and are available to be signed by clubs in any league. Moreover, NFL players become free agents after a period of years.

In contrast to the above picture of relative openness and availability of players in professional football, the NHL has a system which controls access to all professional and semi-professional players for at least three years. As my discussion, *supra*, concerning the reserve clause conclusively demonstrates, if the operation of the NHL's current reserve clause is not restrained, the NHL's control over the players is absolute for at least three years after the expiration of any current contract. Further, the value of the minor league professional hockey players as a source of supply to the major leagues is not the equivalent of college-level players in football. Moreover, the minor league professional hockey players are likewise bound by standard player contracts which contain reserve clauses materially identical to the NHL standard player contract. Finally, the general practice is that if a minor professional league player does not make the NHL team, nevertheless he is still bound by his former minor professional league contract and is thus not free to sign with another club or any other league. These differences between the football and hockey reserve systems are crucial.

Secondary evidence of the NHL's intent to maintain its control over professional hockey is its continuing policy of expansion tied to the increasing demand for hockey in the United States and also in Canada. Of course, if even this burgeoning interest in hockey in North America could nonetheless support only one supplier, then this court would be bound to conclude that the NHL enjoys a "natural monopoly." In Ovitron Corp. v. General Motors Corp., 295 F.Supp. 373, 378 (S.D.N.Y. 1969), the Court noted "the natural monopolist is entitled to compete vigorously and fairly in a struggle for a market which cannot support more than one supplier."

* * *

Keeping in mind both the many agreements employed by the National Hockey League and its continuing expansion, it is apparent that the National Hockey League's intent is and was the willful acquisition and maintenance of a position as the only major professional hockey league in the United States and Canada.

* * *

Here the NHL intended to keep, and did keep, a complete and exclusive hold upon the market of major league professional hockey players which the NHL acquired soon after its creation. The fact that the WHA is attempting to enter that market does not mitigate the instant WHA claims that the NHL currently enjoys monopoly power in the relevant market; for there is no evidence before me that under the present circumstances, the WHA will be an effective competitor.

* * *

The expansion of the NHL during the WHA's formative period and the creation of the WHA itself are both responses to an increased market for the sport and thus increased economic attractiveness for those entering as well as those already in the field.

Here, I do not rely solely on the expansion of the NHL to show that it had the intent to monopolize; for the President of the NHL, Clarence Campbell, has explained his league's intent as a determined drive to assure that the NHL is 'the only major professional hockey league operating from coast to coast in the United States or Canada.'

Expansion of the NHL was one factor indicative of the wrongful intent of the older league to totally monopolize hockey and remain the only major professional hockey league operating with the United States, but expansion was only one of the several threads spun in the monopolistic fabric of the NHL to blanket players from entry to another league.

Injunction granted.

———

In other portions of his lengthy decision, Judge Higginbotham described negotiations about hockey's reserve clause that had taken place between the NHL and its newly formed Players Association in the previous three to four years. The NHLPA had succeeded in adding to the standard player contract a procedure for neutral arbitration of the salary amount when a team exercised its option to renew one of its player's contracts. It was clear, though (as NHLPA Executive Director Alan Eagleson testified in *Flood v. Kuhn*), that hockey clubs continued to enjoy the same perpetually renewable rights to their players' services as was then understood to exist in baseball (prior to the *Messersmith* arbitration ruling). Because the perpetually renewable option clause was accepted by the NHLPA and included in the collective bargaining agreement, it is necessary briefly to revisit the nonstatutory labor exemption that shields collectively bargained provisions from antitrust attack (see Chapter 3), an exemption that Judge Higginbotham held did not protect the NHL in this case. The following is an excerpt from the opinion on this issue.

From my examination of the foregoing cases (*Hutcheson, Allen Bradley, Pennington,* and *Jewel Tea*), several conclusions can be drawn. First, those cases all involved situations where the union had been sued for its active, conspiratorial role in restraining competition in a product market, and the union, not the employer, sought to invoke the labor exemptions. Here there is no evidence that the Players' Association was a joint-conspirator with the National Hockey League in creating and retaining the reserve clause. The evidence establishes the Players' Associations' persistent opposition to the present form of reserve system. The reserve clause, in fact, was more than a sturdy teenager when the Players' Association was born. The reserve clause was fathered by the

NHL, and the Players' Association has repeatedly sought to exclude it in its present form.

Second, the cases cited above pertained to issues which furthered the interests of the union members and on which there had been extensive collective bargaining. Again, that is not true in this litigation. The National Hockey League has not come forward with any substantial evidence which could warrant this Court finding that the reserve clause—as it presently operates in conjunction with the other interlocking agreements—was ever a subject of serious, intensive, arm's-length collective bargaining. When the Players' Association was recognized in 1967, some variation of the reserve system had existed for probably sixteen years prior thereto. Subsequent efforts by the Association to markedly revamp the reserve system have been continually rebuffed by the NHL. The discussions revolving around the Arbitration Agreements related only to resolving salary disputes, and did not in any way alter or affect the basic perpetual option of the reserve system.

Finally, even if, arguendo, there had been substantial arm's-length collective bargaining by the National Hockey League and the Players' Association to revise the perpetual option provision of the reserve clause ..., those negotiations would not shield the National Hockey League from liability in a suit by outside competitors who sought access to players under the control of the National Hockey League.

* * *

Even if the benefits of the labor exemptions can be extended to encompass the employer's activities, that outcome is not changed merely because the employer is a member of a multi-employer association. A multi-employer group will not be accorded any greater protections than a single employer. Though a multi-employer organization will be insulated from unfair labor practice prosecutions only if it acts in good faith and takes only the limited steps necessary to protect itself, however restraining, anti-competitive acts will not be immunized from the Sherman Act. Cf. Kennedy v. Long Island R.R. (2nd Cir.1963); Prepmore Apparel, Inc. v. Amalgamated Clothing Workers of America (5th Cir.1970). While the employer activities in the two latter cases were not subject to the Sherman Act, the Courts clearly intimated that employer efforts to monopolize a particular product market would not be similarly treated.

* * *

The labor exemption which could be defensively utilized by the union and employer as a shield against Sherman Act proceedings when there was bona fide collective bargaining, could not be seized upon by either party and destructively wielded as a sword by engaging in monopolistic or other anti-competitive conduct. The shield cannot be transmuted into a sword and still permit the beneficiary to invoke the narrowly carved out labor exemption from the antitrust laws. To allow and condone such conduct would frustrate Congress' carefully orchestrated efforts to harmoniously blend together two opposing public policies.

In sum, the National Hockey League, as it stands before me in the instant action, is not the most ideal candidate to be a beneficiary of the labor exemptions. The National Hockey League itself was primarily responsible for devising and perpetuating a monopoly over the system. Not only did it enforce and implement its restraints against players and member clubs of the National Hockey League, but, moreover, it sought to enforce it against outside competitors who wanted to enter the competition at the professional level.

I reject the argument that an employer (National Hockey League) can conspire with or take advantage of a union to restrain competition and seriously impair the business dealings and transactions of competitors.

351 F.Supp. at 498–500.

Questions for Discussion

1. Which of the reasons that the judge gave for not applying the labor exemption in this case seems most valid in light of the subsequent circuit court decisions in *Mackey*, *McCourt*, *Wood*, and *Powell*? In answering, review the three prongs of the *Mackey* test. Would this same result follow if a players association negotiated a full free agency system within the boundaries of its own league, but with the proviso that teams in this league enjoyed a "right of first refusal" if one of its players signed a contract with a team in a rival league?

2. Facilitated by the above decision, the WHA's entry on the hockey scene resulted in a fierce bidding war for players that sent average salaries soaring and team balance sheets into the red. The same scenario took place in football and basketball, whose established leagues faced the challenge of new competitors without a perpetually renewable option in their standard player contracts (recall the *Barnett*, *Bergey*, and *Neely* decisions in Chapter 2). Why were teams willing to spend huge sums of money on players, irrespective of the effect on their balance sheets? Does this practice make good business sense for teams in the new league? For teams in the established league? Is there—or should there be—a legal barrier to such spending, especially by the established league? Consider the analogy of illegal "predatory pricing" by a dominant firm faced by a new rival—i.e., deliberately pricing a product below cost to force weaker firms out of the market. Should there be a similar bar to "predatory salary-paying"? If so, how would a court determine when a salary had escalated above the player's legitimate competitive market value (i.e., his marginal revenue product) and become an illegitimate predatory wage level? And by the way, why does an established league such as the NFL, the NBA, and the NHL always choose to compete by paying higher salaries to its players,

rather than by charging lower prices to its fans? The explanation is crucial to understanding the peculiar features of monopoly in sports.

3. The culmination of the legal and financial struggle between the NHL and the WHA was a 1979 agreement under which four WHA clubs moved into the NHL and the other WHA owners received monetary compensation. The NHL Players Association agreed not to challenge the legality of this arrangement under the Sherman Act in return for a collective agreement containing the "free agency" rules we described in the *Dale McCourt* case in Chapter 3. An almost identical scenario occurred in basketball—absorption of a number of ABA teams into the NBA with the consent of the NBA Players Association—producing the collective agreement at issue in the *Leon Wood* case (also in Chapter 3). Is consent by the players through their union a sufficient response to public policy concerns about interleague mergers? If not, who should challenge such arrangements? In what circumstances, if any, should sports mergers be allowed to occur?

2. STADIUMS

Expansion into desirable cities targeted by a new league is a favorite tactic of established leagues, not only in hockey (see *Philadelphia World Hockey Club*) and in football (see *AFL v. NFL*), but also in baseball. Indeed major league baseball, threatened in the late 1950s by Branch Rickey's proposed Continental Baseball League, hastily undertook its first expansion in this century, into New York and Houston in the National League and Washington and Kansas City in the American League.[8]

However effective these preemptive steps may be against the new sporting venture, judges understandably feel qualms about erecting absolute bars against such league action. Such a rule would forever deny fans in "virgin" cities the opportunity to secure a team in the established major league; even assuming an upstart league came along, at best these fans would acquire a team in the less attractive league that would still be the city's only team in that sport. Ideally there should be two or more major league teams in each sport playing in the same city, at least if the population is not so small that it effectively constitutes a natural monopoly market. Fans would then have a choice of which team to patronize and clubs would face pressure to be more productive managers and to charge lower ticket prices. There is, however, a major obstacle to accomplishing that end—the limited number of stadiums and arenas available for play. We have already seen that typically such sports facilities are provided by the municipality at a heavily subsidized price; sometimes the city even gives the team valuable land upon which to build a privately owned facility, such as the Dodgers secured in Chavez Ravine when the team was induced to move from Brooklyn to Los Angeles. The next case considers whether once the established team has secured a stadium through either full

---

8. See Lance E. Davis, Self–Regulation in Baseball: 1909–71, Chapter 10 of Roger Noll, ed., *Government and the Sports Business*, (Washington D.C.: Brookings, 1974).

ownership or an exclusive long-term lease, a newcomer team can demand access to this "essential facility".[9]

HECHT v. PRO–FOOTBALL, INC.

United States Court of Appeals, District of Columbia, 1977.

570 F.2d 982.

WILKEY, CIRCUIT JUDGE.

[With the successful launching of their eight-team football venture in 1960, the American Football League owners began planning in 1965 for expansion into two new cities, one of which was to be in a current National Football League city. Hecht and his partners believed that Washington, D.C. was a prime candidate for an AFL team they wanted to start, but they needed a stadium in which to play. The one existing facility in the area, RFK Stadium, was owned by the U.S. Government, but was subject to a 30–year lease under which Pro–Football Inc.'s Redskins were the exclusive tenant for professional football. Although the federal Interior Department wanted to offer a lease to an AFL franchise, the Redskins were unwilling to grant explicit permission for that step. Having lost out on expansion (the AFL went into Miami instead), Hecht sued the Redskins and the NFL, alleging a violation of Section 2 of the Sherman Act. This decision considered Hecht's appeal from the trial jury's verdict in favor of the defendant.

The target of the appeal was a number of jury instructions made by the trial judge. The first concerned whether even if professional football was the appropriate product market, the entire country or only the D.C. area was the relevant geographic market.]

* * *

The relevant geographic market is "the area of effective competition," the area "in which the seller operates, and to which the purchaser can practically turn for supplies." It is well settled that the relevant market "need not be nationwide," and that "where the relevant competitive market covers only a small area the Sherman Act may be invoked to prevent unreasonable restraints within that area." Indeed, courts have regularly identified relevant geographic markets as single cities or towns, and even portions thereof.

In this case Hecht sought to enter the market for professional football in Washington, D.C. He argues that the Redskins frustrated his entry by denying him use of RFK stadium, access to which was a condition precedent to his submitting a successful franchise application. Given this posture of the case, it seems evident that the relevant geographical market is the D.C. metropolitan area: it is here that "the seller operates"; it is here alone that the Redskins' customers (primarily, their ticket purchasers) can "practically turn" for the supply of

9. See generally James R. Ratner, *Should There Be an Essential Facility Doc-* *trine?,* 21 U.C. Davis L. Rev. 327 (1988).

professional football. Hecht sought to compete for these customers by obtaining a franchise of his own, and it can scarcely be doubted that "the area of effective competition" between him and the Redskins would be the nation's capital.

The trial court, however, defined the relevant geographical market as "the area of effective competition for the acquisition, location and operation of a professional football franchise in the years 1965 and 1966." It is true, of course, that Hecht had to "compete" with other cities before he could assure himself of a franchise for Washington; yet this is hardly the competition that is at issue here. Hecht is not complaining that the Redskins' restrictive covenant prevented him from entering "the national market for football franchises"; obviously, Hecht could have entered that market, notwithstanding the Redskins' lease, from any other city. Hecht is complaining, rather, that the restrictive covenant on RFK Stadium in Washington, D.C. prevented him from entering the market for professional football in Washington; this is "the area which the alleged restraints affect." The "national competition" was but a preliminary, if necessary, step to a distinctly local end. We hold, therefore, that the trial judge erred in failing to instruct the jury that the relevant geographic market is the area of metropolitan Washington, D.C., in which Hecht and the Redskins would have effectively competed for customers.[21]

Monopolistic Intent and "Natural Monopoly."

The offense of "monopolization" under Sherman Act § 2 implicates both the possession of monopoly power, "monopoly in the concrete," and an element of willfulness or intent. To demonstrate intent to monopolize, however, a plaintiff need not always prove that the defendant acquired or maintained his monopoly power by means of exclusionary, unfair, or predatory acts. At least since *Alcoa*, it has been clear that the requisite intent can be inferred if a defendant maintains his power by conscious and willful business policies, however legal, that inevitably result in the exclusion or limitation of actual or potential competition. In accordance with *Alcoa*, Hecht requested an instruction that the jury could find monopolistic intent if it found that the Redskins had consciously engaged in acts or contracts, whether lawful or unlawful, that "maintained and protected" their monopoly over professional football in Washington. The trial judge refused to give this instruction. Instead, he ruled that the *Alcoa* theory of intent (viz., an inference of monopolistic intent without a showing of specific unfair

21. These customers would include potential season ticket holders and occasional ticket buyers, and, to a lesser extent, purchasers of local radio and pre-season television broadcasting rights. Most of a professional football team's broadcasting revenue, of course, derives from the national television contract, which is negotiated by the league. As testimony at trial indicated, however, individual teams have very little control over the revenue they derive from this contract, and thus the most important factor in considering location of a franchise is the potential "gate" in the home city. For this reason, national television audiences and national television contract revenues should be ignored in ascertaining the relevant market here....

practices) was not available to Hecht unless he proved that the Washington metropolitan area could support two professional football teams. We hold that this instruction was error.

In order to explain the trial judge's chain of reasoning, it is necessary to elaborate somewhat the teaching of *Alcoa*. In that opinion, Judge Hand recognized, as noted above, that monopolistic intent may be inferred from conscious business practices that inevitably produce or maintain monopoly power. Judge Hand also recognized, of course, that there are situations in which an inference of monopolistic intent absent a showing of specific unfair practices would be improper. One such situation is where defendant has a "natural monopoly" where, in Judge Hand's words, "[a] market [is] so limited that it is impossible to produce at all and meet the cost of production except by a plant large enough to supply the whole demand." [26] In the wake of *Alcoa*, accordingly, a substantial body of case law has developed, holding that the "characteristics of a natural monopoly make it inappropriate to apply the usual rule that success in driving competitors from the market is evidence of illegal monopolization." These cases hold, in short, that a natural monopolist does not violate § 2 unless he "acquired or maintained [his] power through the use of means which are 'exclusionary, unfair or predatory.'" In this case, therefore, the trial judge properly told the jury that if it found the Redskins to have a natural monopoly, "such a monopoly does not violate the antitrust laws unless it was acquired or maintained by exclusionary, unfair, or predatory means."

The trial judge further instructed the jury, however, that Hecht bore the burden of proving that the Redskins did not have a natural monopoly.

* * *

This part of the instruction, we think, was incorrect. It is the clear thrust of *Alcoa* that, once a plaintiff has proven the defendant's maintenance of its monopoly power through conscious business practices, a rebuttable presumption is established that defendant has the requisite intent to monopolize. The defendant can defeat this presumption by showing that it had monopoly, as some have greatness, "thrust upon it,"—that its power derives from "superior skill, foresight and industry" or (as is particularly relevant here) from the advantages of natural monopoly conditions. Both the Supreme Court and the lower courts have echoed this position. We are not called upon in this case to elaborate the various circumstances under which the burden of proof in § 2 cases might shift to defendant; we hold merely that when, as here,

26. United States v. Aluminum Co. of America, 148 F.2d at 430. See C. Kaysen & D. Turner, *Antitrust Policy* 191 (1959):

Natural monopoly. In the economic sense, natural monopoly is monopoly resulting from economies of scale, a relationship between the size of the market and the size of the most efficient firm such that one firm of efficient size can produce all or more than the market can take at a remunerative price, and can continually expand its capacity at less cost than that of a new firm entering the business.

a defendant seeks to avoid a charge of monopolization by asserting that it has a natural monopoly owing to the market's inability to support two competitors, the defendant, and not the plaintiff, bears the burden of proof on that score.

This holding finds firm grounding in antitrust policy. To hold otherwise could effectively mean that a defendant is entitled to remain free of competition unless the plaintiff can prove, not only that he would be a viable competitor, but also that he and defendant both would survive. This result would be ironic indeed: we cannot say that it is in the public interest to have the incumbent as its sole theatre, or its sole newspaper, or its sole football team, merely because the incumbent got there first. Assuming that there is no identity of performance, the public has an obvious interest in competition, "even though that competition be an elimination bout." "It has been the law for centuries," Justice Holmes once wrote, "that a man may set up a business in a small country town, too small to support more than one, although thereby he expects and intends to ruin some one already there, and succeeds in his intent." The newcomer and the incumbent may both succeed, or either or both may fail; this is what competition is all about.

ESSENTIAL FACILITY.

Hecht contends that the District Court erred in failing to give his requested instruction concerning the "essential facility" doctrine. We agree. The essential facility doctrine, also called the "bottleneck principle," states that "where facilities cannot practicably be duplicated by would-be competitors, those in possession of them must allow them to be shared on fair terms. It is illegal restraint of trade to foreclose the scarce facility." [36] This principle of antitrust law derives from the Supreme Court's 1912 decision in United States v. Terminal R. R. Ass'n,[37] and was recently reaffirmed in Otter Tail Power Co. v. United States; [38] the principle has regularly been invoked by the lower courts.

---

36. A. D. Neale, *The Antitrust Laws of the United States* 67 (2d ed. 1970); id. at 66–69, 127–31. See L. A. Sullivan, *Antitrust* 131 (1977):

> [I]f a group of competitors, acting in concert, operate a common facility and if due to natural advantage, custom, or restrictions of scale, it is not feasible for excluded competitors to duplicate the facility, the competitors who operate the facility must give access to the excluded competitors on reasonable, non-discriminatory terms.

37. 224 U.S. 383 (1912). In *Terminal R.R.*, a group of railroads had won control of all railroad switching facilities in St. Louis; topographical factors prevented potential competitors from gaining access to the city via other routes. The Court held:

> [W]hen, as here, the inherent conditions are such as to prohibit any other reasonable means of entering the city, the combination of every such facility under the exclusive ownership and control of less than all of the companies under compulsion to use them violates both the first and second sections of the [Sherman Act].

The Court ordered the railroads to amend their agreement to provide "for the admission of any existing or future railroad to joint ownership and control of the combined terminal properties" on equal terms.

38. 410 U.S. 366, 377–78 (1973). In *Otter Tail*, municipalities sought to compete with defendant power company by building their own electric facilities. The municipalities could not afford to construct their own subtransmission lines, however, and defendant

To be "essential" a facility need not be indispensable; it is sufficient if duplication of the facility would be economically infeasible and if denial of its use inflicts a severe handicap on potential market entrants. Necessarily, this principle must be carefully delimited: the antitrust laws do not require that an essential facility be shared if such sharing would be impractical or would inhibit the defendant's ability to serve its customers adequately.

In this case Hecht presented evidence that RFK stadium is the only stadium in the D.C. metropolitan area that is suitable for the exhibition of professional football games. He also presented evidence that proper agreements regarding locker facilities, practice sessions, choice of playing dates, and so forth would have made sharing of the stadium practical and convenient. Accordingly, Hecht requested an instruction that if the jury found (1) that use of RFK stadium was essential to the operation of a professional football team in Washington; (2) that such stadium facilities could not practicably be duplicated by potential competitors; (3) that another team could use RFK stadium in the Redskins' absence without interfering with the Redskins' use; and (4) that the restrictive covenant in the lease prevented equitable sharing of the stadium by potential competitors, then the jury must find the restrictive covenant to constitute a contract in unreasonable restraint of trade, in violation of Sherman Act §§ 1 and 3. This instruction was substantially correct and failure to give it was prejudicial error.

Remanded for new trial.

———

In *Fishman v. Estate of Wirtz*, 807 F.2d 520 (7th Cir.1986) (with Judge Easterbrook dissenting at length), the court considered a claim that Chicago Stadium was an "essential facility" for the NBA Chicago Bulls, which could not lawfully be withheld from Fishman, a prospective buyer of the Bulls, by the Wirtz family, owners of the Stadium and the NHL Chicago Black Hawks, in their competition to purchase the Bulls (in 1972, for $3.3 million). What is the appropriate antitrust verdict?

In *USFL v. NFL*, 634 F.Supp. 1155, 1176–80 (S.D.N.Y.1986), the district judge granted summary judgment to the defendant NFL against a feature of the USFL's wide-ranging antitrust claim—the allegation that NFL teams had hampered efforts by potential USFL franchises to play in stadiums where NFL teams had leases. Most of the alleged offenders were NFL teams that leased municipally-owned stadiums (for example, the Minneapolis Metrodome, the Pontiac Silverdome, and Denver's Mile High Stadium). The judge held that any NFL team's effort to persuade the public stadium authority not to grant a lease to a

refused to "wheel" power for them over its own lines. The court found that Otter Tail's subtransmission lines were a scarce facility and that its refusal to share them violated § 2.

USFL rival, or at least not a lease on favorable terms, was insulated from antitrust scrutiny by the *Noerr–Pennington* doctrine. That doctrine, based on a pair of Supreme Court decisions of these names, holds that a private actor's effort to persuade a public body to exercise its prerogative favorably to the petitioner's position cannot violate the Sherman Act even if done for an anticompetitive purpose. The USFL did not appeal this feature of the trial judge's ruling, which held that such First Amendment immunity to antitrust regulation applied to municipal decisions made in a commercial or a proprietary (as opposed to a regulatory) capacity. (The Second Circuit's opinion on the USFL's appeal of other aspects of this litigation is reproduced next in this chapter.)

3. TELEVISION CONTRACTS

The last essential ingredient for a viable sports league is a reasonably lucrative television contract. This source of guaranteed revenue is needed not so much to pay the new league's stadium rentals and administrative expenses as to pay the players for whose services the new league is bidding against its entrenched rival. The 1961 Sports Broadcasting Act permitted the NFL (and other leagues) to sell in a single exclusive package the right to televise their games. The amounts received by leagues from networks for these television rights have risen at a remarkable pace: from approximately $325,000 a club in the NFL's first exclusive network contract in 1962 to $34 million a year in 1992, under contracts with three "free" and two cable networks. A practical question is whether *not* having such a television deal presents an insurmountable barrier to any new league. A second question is whether there is anything the law can or will do about this barrier. The next case offers some extended judicial reflections on the latter question.

USFL v. NFL [10]

United States Court of Appeals, Second Circuit, 1988.

842 F.2d 1335.

WINTER, CIRCUIT JUDGE.

[We saw in earlier chapters that challenges launched against the National Football League's dominance of professional football by the American Football League in the 1960s and the World Football League in the 1970s produced important antitrust (and player contract) decisions. This pattern continued with the United States Football League's abortive challenge in the 1980s. The USFL began as a spring football league in March 1983, bolstered by television contracts with ABC and

10. On the rise and demise of both the USFL and its lawsuit, see Byrne, *The $1 League*, note 3 above. The legal issues are presented in Lori J. Brown, *The Battle:* *From the Playing Field to the Courtroom —* United States Football League v. National Football League, 18 Toledo U. L. Rev. 871 (1987).

ESPN. However, after losing $200 million in three years, the League played its last game in July 1985. At the urging of Donald Trump, owner of the New Jersey Generals, the USFL made an effort to move to a fall schedule in 1986, supposedly the more natural time for fans to watch football. However, the League was unable to secure a network television contract and it folded. Blaming the NFL for its failure, the USFL sued.

Though the case did go to trial and the jury found that the NFL violated section 2 of the Sherman Act in a number of its actions, the USFL won only a Pyrrhic victory because the jury's damage verdict was for just $1.00—which was trebled by statute to $3.00. The reason was that the jury rejected the USFL's principal allegation—that the NFL had denied the USFL access to the essential resource of network television. The following decision deals with the USFL's appeal on that issue.]

THE HISTORY OF MAJOR-LEAGUE PROFESSIONAL FOOTBALL.

* * *

The USFL was founded in May 1982 by David Dixon as a league that would play spring football. The league began play in March 1983 with teams in Birmingham, Boston, Chicago, Denver, Los Angeles, Michigan, New Jersey, Oakland, Philadelphia, Phoenix, Tampa and Washington. In part because of the location of its teams in major television markets, the USFL was able to obtain multimillion dollar network and cable television contracts with ABC and ESPN. Nevertheless, for reasons explored in detail infra, the USFL demonstrated little stability. Over its three seasons of spring football (one of which was a "lame-duck" season commenced after an announced decision to shift to fall play), the USFL clubs played in twenty-two cities, and had thirty-nine principal owners. None of the majority owners of an original USFL team was a majority owner by 1986 when a planned fall schedule was aborted by the $1.00 verdict.

* * *

THE NFL'S TELEVISION CONTRACTS.

The growth of the NFL was closely related to the growth of television. Beginning in 1951, the Dumont network televised five regular season games (twelve by 1954), as well as the championship game each year. In the mid–1950's, the Columbia Broadcasting System ("CBS") began broadcasting certain NFL regular season games for $1.8 million per year, and the National Broadcasting Company ("NBC") acquired the right to televise the NFL championship game. The broadcast rights to games were controlled by individual teams during the 1950's, however.

In 1961, the NFL teams agreed to sell their collective television rights as a single package and to share broadcast revenues equally among all franchises. This decision was in response to arguments by

Commissioner Rozelle that the league's competitive balance on the field would eventually be destroyed if teams in major television markets continued to sell their broadcast rights individually. In the long run, he believed, great differentials in television revenues among teams would lead to a competitive imbalance that would diminish the overall attractiveness of the NFL's product. Rozelle's arguments were bolstered by the policy of the recently organized AFL to pool television rights and revenues in its first broadcast contract with ABC.

Before the NFL could enter a pooled-rights television contract, however, it had to overcome several legal obstacles.

[Here the court described the 1953 antitrust decision against the NFL's earlier television policy, reproduced in Chapter 6.]

* * *

Specifically intending to alter Judge Grim's order, Congress enacted the Sports Broadcasting Act of 1961, which exempted from the antitrust laws pooled-rights agreements entered into by professional sports leagues....

The first NFL pooled-rights contract was with CBS. For the 1962 and 1963 seasons, CBS was the only network permitted to bid for this contract because it had individual rights contracts running through 1963 with nine teams. The NFL received $4,650,000 per season from CBS during these two seasons. For the 1964–65 NFL contract, CBS outbid NBC and ABC with an offer of $14,100,000 per season. In 1964, the AFL, which had had a contract with ABC, entered into a five-year, $36 million contract with NBC.

In 1966, Congress amended the Sports Broadcasting Act specifically to confer antitrust immunity on the NFL–AFL merger.... In passing this legislation, Congress was plainly informed that, upon consolidation of the two leagues, the NFL would have broadcast contracts with at least two networks.

In 1970, the NFL entered into a contract with ABC to televise a game nationally on Monday nights. Since then, all three major television networks have broadcast NFL games, and the NFL's annual revenues from television have increased by more than 800 percent. The NFL teams received approximately $186 million for the 1970–73 seasons; $268 million for the 1974–77 seasons; $646 million for the 1978–81 seasons; and $2.1 billion over the five-year period 1982–86.

The ABC, CBS and NBC contracts from 1970 onward have given each network rights of first negotiation and first refusal to decide whether to continue its NFL contract for subsequent years. The NFL's 1982–86 contracts were nonexclusive and did not forbid a network from televising another football league's games at any time when it was not broadcasting NFL games.... Because the NFL was forbidden by its network contracts to televise games on cable, cable television contracts were open to a competing league, although such contracts are less lucrative than network contracts. When the NFL's network contracts expired in 1981 and 1986, the networks were free to contract with a competing league's games for all time slots.

* * *

MANAGEMENT OF THE USFL.

The USFL was conceived and organized in 1981 to play in the spring rather than the fall. Its founders believed that public demand for football was not satisfied by the NFL's and the colleges' fall seasons; that cable television, which could not televise NFL games under the existing NFL-network contracts, would offer unique opportunities for television revenues and exposure; that a spring football league would face limited competition; that there was a sufficient supply of football players for two leagues; and that a spring league could draft college players and put them on the field even before the NFL draft.

The USFL's founders placed a high priority on the fans' perception of the quality of play. They intended to use major stadiums and to hire well-known coaches. At the same time, they wanted the league to control costs. For its first season, therefore, the USFL established budget guidelines for player salaries of between $1.3 and $1.5 million per team.

The USFL's founders did not seek to obtain a television contract for fall play. Before fielding a team, however, the USFL received bids for a spring television contract from ABC and NBC and from two cable networks, ESPN and the Turner Broadcasting System. The league entered a four-year contract with ABC, and a two-year contract with ESPN. The ABC agreement provided for ABC to pay the USFL $18 million for the 1983 and 1984 seasons, with options exercisable by ABC at $14 million for 1985 and at $18 million for 1986. ESPN contracted to televise USFL games for two years at rights fees of $4 million for 1983 and $7 million for 1984. The USFL began with eight of its twelve teams in the nation's top ten television markets. The ABC contract required the USFL to field teams in the three largest television markets (New York, Los Angeles and Chicago) and in at least four of the five other top-ten television markets in which teams were originally located (Philadelphia, Boston, Detroit, San Francisco/Oakland and Washington).

The USFL's first year of play, 1983, was a mixed success. The league received extensive media exposure when it signed Heisman Trophy winner Herschel Walker to a three-year, $3,250,000 contract. The Nielsen television rating for the first week of games was 14.2, a figure comparable to NFL ratings. As the season went on, however, the USFL's television ratings declined; average television ratings for the year were 6.23 on ABC and 3.28 on ESPN. Average attendance for the year was approximately 25,000. Nevertheless, these figures were consistent with the league's and networks' preseason projections.

On the financial side, the picture was not as bright. The USFL lost a total of almost $40 million, or an average of $3.3 million per team.

The league had projected losses of only about $2 million per year for each team over the first three years. The unanticipated financial losses were chiefly the result of the failure to stay within the original salary guidelines. Indeed, in a November 1983 letter to other owners, Tad Taube of the Oakland team warned that: "If we are not successful in establishing player [salary] caps I can guarantee you that there will not be a USFL within three years, irrespective of improved revenue [from] television.... We have sighted the enemy and they are us!"

The USFL's second year was marked by change. Four teams shifted locations. For example, the owner of the Chicago franchise exchanged that franchise for the Phoenix franchise, taking his winning Chicago coach and players while the original Phoenix team moved to Chicago under a new owner. The league, over the objection of some owners, expanded from twelve teams to eighteen. Five of the original owners left the league. Some of the new owners, notably Donald Trump of the New Jersey Generals, believed that the USFL ought to play in the fall. Thereafter, the issue of when to play became divisive, and several owners came to believe that Trump was trying to bring about a merger with the NFL that would include only some USFL teams.

The NFL introduced extensive evidence designed to prove that the USFL followed Trump's merger strategy, and that this strategy ultimately caused the USFL's downfall. The merger strategy, the NFL argued, involved escalating financial competition for players as a means of putting pressure on NFL expenses, playing in the fall to impair NFL television revenues, shifting USFL franchises out of cities where NFL teams played into cities thought to be logical expansion (through merger) cities for the NFL, and, finally, bringing the antitrust litigation now before us.

Throughout the second half of 1983 and early 1984, several USFL owners escalated spending on player salaries. USFL teams, for example, signed established NFL players such as running back Joe Cribbs and defensive back Gary Barbaro. Trump, in particular, signed a number of players who were still under contract with the NFL to future contracts, including superstar Lawrence Taylor of the New York Giants. USFL owners also signed many top players coming out of college, for example, wide receiver Anthony Carter and quarterback Jim Kelly. The USFL's spending on players greatly outpaced its revenues. The owner of the Los Angeles team, for example, committed the team to $13.1 million in salaries and bonuses for just one season. He even entered into a multiyear, $40 million contract with just one player, Steve Young of Brigham Young University.

By the end of the 1984 season, USFL franchises in two of the top three television markets, Chicago and Los Angeles, had failed, and only four of the original owners remained in the league. The league was not a failure as entertainment, however. Despite a decline in the USFL's television ratings to 5.7 on ABC and 2.8 on ESPN, ABC exercised its option to carry the USFL in the spring of 1985 at $14 million and offered a new contract worth $175 million for four years in the spring beginning in 1986. ESPN offered a contract worth $70 million over three years.

Nevertheless, during an August 1984 owners' meeting, the USFL decided to move to the fall in 1986. This decision was made despite: (i) ABC's warning that such a move would breach its contract for the spring of 1985 and 1986; (ii) the contrary recommendations of a management consulting firm, McKinsey & Company, which the USFL had retained for $600,000 to consider the advisability of a fall season; and (iii) the contrary recommendations of the USFL's directors of operations and marketing.

Moreover, Eddie Einhorn, a USFL owner who was to represent the USFL in negotiations to secure a network contract for the fall, warned that moving from large television markets to "merger" cities too quickly might preclude the securing of a network contract. Nevertheless, in the ensuing months, the USFL withdrew from Chicago, Detroit, Philadelphia, Pittsburgh and Washington, D.C.—each a large television market with an NFL team—and moved into Baltimore (which had lost its NFL team in 1984) and Orlando (which had no NFL team). Through mergers, the USFL bolstered franchises in Oakland (which had lost the NFL Raiders to Los Angeles) and Phoenix (which had been discussed as a possible NFL expansion city). The decision to move to the fall damaged the USFL's relations with ABC and ESPN. The former withheld a significant portion of the USFL's rights fees for the 1985 season, while the latter demanded a renegotiation of its proposed 1985–87 USFL contract.

In October 1984, the instant litigation was begun. The USFL's 1985 "lame-duck" spring season appears to have been affected adversely by the now publicly announced move to the fall. The league's television ratings declined to 4.1 on ABC and 2.0 on ESPN. By the end of the season, several owners had withdrawn financial support for their teams, and a number of clubs were no longer meeting their payrolls and other bills. The USFL scheduled eight teams for its fall 1986 season, which was ultimately cancelled after the verdict in this case. Only one team (New Jersey), was in a top-ten television market. One other team (Tampa Bay) was in a top-twenty market. Three teams were located in Florida (Jacksonville, Orlando and Tampa Bay) but only one was west of the Mississippi River (Phoenix). In three years, USFL teams had left fourteen of the twenty-two cities in which they had played.

* * *

[At trial, the jury found that the NFL had violated section 2 of the Sherman Act in a number of ways. One violation was an effort to co-opt potential USFL owners such as Donald Trump or franchise locations such as Oakland (a strategy sketched in a presentation to NFL executives by Harvard Business School Professor Michael Porter, called

"Conquering the USFL"). Another was expanding NFL rosters from 45 to 49 players and conducting a draft of USFL players, in line with a memorandum prepared by NFL labor negotiator, Jack Donlan, called "Spending the USFL Dollar" by bidding up player salaries. But the jury rejected the USFL argument that the NFL had monopolized access to television in the fall, a key predicate to the USFL's damages claim. The following is the appellate court's analysis of that crucial issue.]

1. *Liability*

A. *The Sports Broadcasting Act.*

The USFL contends that the Sports Broadcasting Act of 1961 limits the antitrust exemption for pooled-rights contracts to a single contract with one network. Therefore, it argues, the NFL's multiple contractual arrangements with three networks violates the injunction in *United States v. National Football League*, a decision claimed by the USFL collaterally to estop the NFL from denying that its arrangements with the networks violate Section 1 of the Sherman Act.

The Sports Broadcasting Act states that:

> The antitrust laws ... shall *not* apply to any joint agreement by or among persons engaging in or conducting the organized professional team sport ... of football, ... by which any league of clubs participating in professional football ... contests sells or otherwise transfers all or any part of the rights of such league's member clubs in the sponsored telecasting of the game ... of football.

This statutory language thus neither states nor implies that the exemption limits the NFL to a contract with only one network. Moreover, the legislation does contain express limitations on the exemption designed to protect college football from televised competition with the NFL, which suggests by implication that no other limitations exist.

Faced with statutory language unambiguously hostile to its claims, the USFL resorts to alleged ambiguities in the legislative history. Upon examination, however, the legislative history offers no reason to depart from the statutory language.

* * *

In any event, the passage of the 1966 NFL–AFL merger statute provides conclusive evidence that Congress did not intend the 1961 Act to prohibit NFL contracts with more than one network. When considering this legislation, Congress was explicitly informed that the merged league would continue to broadcast its games on "at least 2 networks," [18] and no concern whatsoever was expressed in Congress that

---

18. During the hearings on the merger bill, Commissioner Rozelle testified "that because of the logistics of handling perhaps 13 or 14 games on a Sunday afternoon, [the NFL] would require at least 2 networks." In response to the question of whether New York City residents would be able to see professional football on television when the other New York club was playing a home game, Rozelle said that the league would try to do so, "which is why I feel we will probably have to go to two networks, to assure that each of the 26 or 28 teams has all of its road games brought back to its home city." Moreover,

such conduct was either undesirable or would go beyond the scope of the 1961 Act's exemption. Moreover, while permitting the merger, Congress added a further limitation to the exemption to protect high school games from televised competition with the NFL. The lack of a "one network" limitation in the 1966 merger bill thus dooms the USFL's claims. Accordingly, we hold that the mere existence of the NFL contracts with the three networks does not violate the antitrust laws. Having made this determination, we need not consider whether the decree in United States v. National Football League has any collateral-estoppel effect.

B. *The "Dilution Effect."*

* * *

Because the [USFL's next two] claims are based on the so-called "dilution effect" of the NFL's contracts with the three networks, a separate discussion of the concept of a "dilution effect" and its role in the professional football industry is necessary.

The term "dilution effect" comes from a CBS business study ordered by Neil Pilson, CBS Sports' President, and completed in June 1984. CBS conducted the study because it was apprehensive over ABC's signing a USFL fall contract and desired the leverage a second league would afford it in its negotiations with the NFL. The study estimated the economic impact on CBS of the televising of USFL games in the fall under various scenarios....

As explained by Pilson, the value of a USFL fall contract to CBS was determined (in simplified fashion) as follows. From the estimated gross advertising revenues would be subtracted estimates of: (i) expenses related to production; (ii) losses in revenues that would otherwise have been earned by programs preempted by USFL games, or "preemptive impact"; (iii) decreases in advertising revenues from NFL games resulting from the addition of USFL games, or "dilution effect"; and (iv) rights fees to the USFL. Pilson testified that when these estimates were made in June 1984, the resultant calculation, CBS's profit, was negative. The USFL argues that, but for the "dilution effect" of $50 million, the sum would have been sufficiently positive to make a USFL contract attractive. The USFL assumes that the "dilution effect" was experienced equally by all three networks and thus concludes that the effect of NFL's network contracts was to exclude all competition.

the NFL and AFL submitted a memorandum to the subcommittee concerning whether the merger would result in reduced broadcasts of football games:

> Because a single network cannot practically establish as many as twenty-eight regional networks and because the expanded league desires to maintain its present level of club television income, the plan contemplates the continued use of two networks by the expanded league, e.g., on a conference or other divisional basis. Thus, both during the period prior to the expiration of the existing television contracts and afterwards, it is contemplated that there will be continued home viewer access to duplicate broadcasts, including telecasts of other league games into home cities on days when the home team is playing at home.

The district court instructed the jury to analyze the NFL's television contracts in light of the CBS study. Specifically, the jury was told to consider "[t]he high NFL rights fees charged to the networks, which plaintiffs allege triggered a dilution effect that makes it economically infeasible for any network to offer a satisfactory television contract to any professional football league other than the NFL." The jury rejected the USFL's claims as to the "dilution effect" in finding that the NFL had not monopolized a television submarket, that the NFL television contracts were not an unreasonable restraint, and that the NFL did not have the power to exclude a competing league from obtaining a network contract. There was ample evidence to support these conclusions.

First, the USFL concedes, as it must, that the "dilution effect" is nonexistent when the NFL network contracts expire and negotiations over new contracts are under way.... The district court's instructions directed the jury to consider the length of these contracts, then five years, in determining whether they were reasonable. Its verdict, therefore, is dispositive because the duration of the contracts was hardly unreasonable as a matter of law.

Second, there was no evidence that the result of the calculations described above would be the same for ABC as for CBS. ABC's contract was largely confined to televising a single NFL game in prime time on a weekday night. Its Sundays were free of football, and it would not encounter the scheduling problems faced by CBS in televising both NFL and USFL games on Sunday afternoons. ABC was thus free to schedule games so as to maximize revenue.... The USFL, which bore the burden of proof on this issue, called two witnesses from ABC in a position to testify about the "dilution effect" on ABC. Neither witness was questioned about the "dilution effect." Both did testify, however, that the USFL's exodus from major television markets and its other difficulties greatly diminished the value of USFL telecasts by 1985 and 1986.

Third, the conduct of the NFL and the networks indicates that neither believed their contracts to be exclusionary. Notwithstanding the early opinion of the NFL's Moyer about a network without a contract being an "open invitation to a new league," the NFL's actual conduct displayed no marked desire to lock up all three networks. Prime-time weekday telecasts were offered to NBC and CBS, both of whom already had NFL contracts, before ABC was approached. It was the testimony of both the ABC executives and CBS's Pilson, elicited by counsel for the USFL, that Rozelle routinely used the threat of leaving them without an NFL contract in order to extract from them the largest possible rights fees. If the "dilution effect" theory of exclusion were correct, the NFL could not credibly threaten to leave one network without a contract. If the theory were correct, moreover, the last network to sign with the NFL would have a bargaining advantage because its agreement would be essential to the NFL's monopoly, much as the owner of the last lot in a tract of land needed for a construction project can demand the highest price. In the NFL-network negotiations, the opposite was the case, and the last network to sign was at a bargaining disadvantage. Thus, in 1982, the NFL first signed agreements with ABC and NBC and then approached CBS. According to Pilson, CBS regarded itself as being in a very disadvantageous bargaining position. As a result, CBS paid $736 million for the new contract, an increase of more than 100% over its previous contract. On the basis of this evidence, therefore, the jury would have been hard-pressed to conclude that the NFL needed a contract with CBS to freeze out a competing league, a circumstance that would have precluded a credible threat to leave CBS without a contract and the resultant hefty increase in rights fees.

Fourth, even if the "dilution effect" theory were alive and well in 1986, the jury could have found that that "effect" was not a cause of the USFL's failure to get a network contract in that year. The CBS study was made in 1984 and was based on estimates of revenues that were plainly excessive given the circumstances of 1986. Immediately after the study was completed, the Supreme Court decided National Collegiate Athletic Association v. Board of Regents, 468 U.S. 85 (1984), invalidating the NCAA's exclusive control over the televising of college football games. This decision had the effect of multiplying greatly the number of college games telecast and of reducing advertising revenue generally for football games. An ABC witness also testified there was a proliferation of sporting events on network and cable television after the fall of 1984 that also reduced the advertising fees that could be charged for professional football. In addition, there were the problems of the USFL itself. The league had failed to establish fan loyalty in most places because of repeated franchise moves. Most importantly, the USFL had abandoned most major television markets, thereby rendering telecasts of its games much less valuable than had been estimated by the earlier CBS study. Finally, the disagreements among the USFL owners, the financial condition of some of the franchises, and the "lame-duck" spring season of 1985 further lessened the value of USFL telecasts in 1986. In fact, Pilson himself testified that by 1986 the events described above had rendered the "dilution effect" irrelevant to CBS's decision not to televise the USFL. In light of this evidence, the jury was free to conclude that the revenues to be expected from USFL telecasts were so low that no network would purchase them even if there were no "dilution effect."

C. "Intent and Effect" Charge.

We now consider the district court's instruction regarding liability on the USFL's television-related claims. The USFL contends that it should not have been required to show that the intent and effect of the NFL's television contracts with the major networks were exclusionary (rather than simply intent or effect) in order to prove a Section 2 claim. . . .

The district court gave the following charge with respect to the USFL's Section 2 television-related claims:

A company may not be found to have wilfully acquired or main- tained monopoly power if it has acquired that power solely through the exercise of superior foresight and skill or because of natural advantages ... or because of economic or technological efficiency; ... or by laws passed by Congress.... In this regard, you should be aware that in 1966 Congress passed a law permitting the merger of the two major football leagues then existing.... Accordingly, I instruct you that the 1966 merger of the AFL and the NFL cannot be the basis for inferring that the NFL acquired monopoly power unlawfully. In addition, in 1961 Congress passed a statute that provides that a contract between a professional sports league and a television network for the sale of pooled telecast rights is not a restraint of trade in violation of the antitrust laws. Accordingly, I instruct you that the making of these contracts by the NFL with the television networks constitutes the lawful acquisition of power, [e]ven if you were to find that these contracts gave the NFL monopoly power, unless you found that the intent and effect of these agreements is to exclude a competing league or its members from selling any of their television rights.

This instruction was consistent with the Sports Broadcasting Act, discussed infra, as exempting from antitrust scrutiny a league's pooled- rights contracts with networks unless they constitute illegal monopoli- zation or an unreasonable restraint of trade so far as competing leagues are concerned. More importantly, the intent-and-effect charge was consistent with the legal standards for illegal monopolization under Section 2.

The Supreme Court has repeatedly defined monopolization as the "willful acquisition or maintenance" of monopoly power. The willful- ness element certainly requires proof of intent. Proof of effect is required by definition alone to satisfy the "acquisition or maintenance" requirement.

A requirement that both intent and effect be proven is necessary to enable a trier of fact to make the critical distinction between conduct that defeats a competitor because of efficiency and consumer satisfac- tion, and conduct that "not only (1) tends to impair the opportunities of rivals, but also (2) either does not further competition on the merits or does so in an unnecessarily restrictive way." Hopes and dreams alone cannot support a Section 2 claim of monopolization. If they did, the nationwide advertisement "Ford wants to be your car company" would constitute an open-and-shut Section 2 case. Success alone is not enough or the antitrust laws would have their greatest impact on the most efficient entrepreneurs and would injure rather than protect consumers.

Proof of intent and effect is also of evidentiary value. Distinguish- ing between efficient and predatory conduct is extremely difficult because it is frequently the case that "[c]ompetitive and exclusionary conduct look alike." Evidence of intent and effect helps the trier of fact to evaluate the actual effect of challenged business practices in light of the intent of those who resort to such practices. As Justice Stevens stated in *Aspen Skiing*,

> [E]vidence of intent is merely relevant to the question whether the challenged conduct is fairly characterized as "exclusionary" or "anticompetitive"—to use the words in the trial court's instructions—or "predatory," to use a word that scholars seem to favor. Whichever label is used, there is agreement on the proposition that "no monopolist monopolizes unconscious of what he is doing." As Judge Bork stated more recently: "Improper exclusion (exclusion not the result of superior efficiency) is always deliberately intended."

The present case is in fact a useful example of the intent-and-effect approach to determining whether certain practices are predatory. As the preceding discussion of the "dilution effect" indicates, the jury's conclusion that the NFL's three network contracts were not exclusionary was supported by evidence that a quality league could either have overcome the "dilution effect" or have acquired a contract when the NFL's contracts expired. The conduct of the NFL itself and the networks showed their disbelief in any exclusionary effect by the NFL's threatening to leave a network without NFL games and the networks' taking the threat seriously. The evidence also supported the conclusion that when the NFL locked up the third network, CBS, in the 1982 negotiations, it did so to obtain $736 million in rights fees, not to exclude competitors.

* * *

D. Legitimate Business Opportunities and Profit-Maximization Charge.

The USFL further argues that the district court erroneously charged the jury that the NFL's three network contracts were lawful if motivated by any "legitimate" purpose, including profit maximization. The pertinent charge reads as follows:

> Plaintiffs allege that the NFL coerced the networks not to give the plaintiffs a contract.... So long as they have a legitimate business purpose in doing so, defendants have no duty to limit themselves in entering into the television contracts so that other football leagues would have an easier time entering the market, or to foresee that other leagues might do so, or for any reasons to decline a profitable business opportunity.

This charge was consistent with settled precedent. "[A] firm with lawful monopoly power has no general duty to help its competitors, whether by holding a price umbrella over their heads or by otherwise pulling its competitive punches." A monopolist may not, of course, use its market power, whether obtained lawfully or not, to prevent or impede competition in the relevant market. The jury was thus properly instructed that:

A monopoly achieved or maintained as a result of ... legitimate good business practices is not unlawful. A monopolist has the same right to compete as any other company. Under the antitrust laws, a monopolist is encouraged to compete vigorously with its competitors and to remain responsive to the needs and demands of its customers. At the same time, a monopolist cannot use its lawfully acquired power to maintain its monopoly. In addition, there is nothing in the antitrust laws that requires a monopolist to act against its own self interest so long as the monopolist does not at the same time exercise its power to maintain that power. Thus, a monopolist is under no duty affirmatively to help or aid its competitors and is free to set as its legitimate goal the maximization of its own profits so long as it does not exercise its power to maintain that power.

The USFL challenges this charge on the ground that setting prices at a profit-maximizing level is an anticompetitive act. We disagree. Prices not based on superior efficiency do not injure competitors, but rather invite competitive entry. As we stated in *Berkey Photo*:

Setting a high price may be a use of monopoly power, but it is not in itself anticompetitive. Indeed, although a monopolist may be expected to charge a somewhat higher price than would prevail in a competitive market, there is probably no better way for it to guarantee that its dominance will be challenged than by greedily extracting the highest price it can.

* * *

H. Essential–Facilities Charge.

Finally, the USFL contends that it was held to an improperly high standard of proof on its "essential-facilities" claim. We set out the pertinent charge:

Plaintiffs allege that defendants violated Sections [1] and [2] of the Sherman Act by conspiring to and in fact denying plaintiffs access to a satisfactory national broadcast television contract for future seasons, with any one of the three networks. The legal basis for this particular claim by plaintiffs is that a network contract is an essential facility which the USFL or any other professional football league needs in order to compete in major league professional football. You should only consider this claim if you have already found, pursuant to my earlier instructions, that defendants possess monopoly power in a relevant market or submarket. If you have not found that defendants possess monopoly power, you must return a verdict in defendants' favor on this claim. In order to prove their essential "facilities" claim, plaintiffs must prove all of the following elements by a preponderance of the evidence: First: That a national broadcast television contract with at least one of the three networks, CBS, NBC or ABC, is essential to the ability of a professional football league to compete successfully in the United

States; Second[:] that potential competitors of the NFL cannot as a practical matter duplicate the benefits of a network contract; Third: That the defendants control access to each of the three networks, that is, the defendants themselves have the ability by their actions to deny actual or potential competitors, such as the USFL, access to national broadcast television—access to a national broadcast television contract; Fourth: That the defendants through their actions have exercised their ability to deny actual or potential competitors access to a national broadcast television contract by denying the USFL such access; Fifth: That a national broadcast television contract between one or more of the networks and a professional football league other than the NFL would not interfere with any of the defendants' lawful dealings with those networks.

The USFL argues first that this charge erred in failing to distinguish between a network television contract in the spring and one in the fall. The charge did, however, address the USFL's denial of "access to a satisfactory national broadcast contract for future seasons." The jury was well aware of the USFL's claim that a spring contract was unsatisfactory as an "inferior facility" or "minor league." It thus either rejected that characterization of spring football or rejected the USFL's claim that the NFL could deny the USFL access to a network in the fall. The spring-fall issue was thus before the jury.

The USFL next claims that it was error for the district court to require a showing of monopoly power in a relevant submarket or market before considering the essential-facilities claim. We fail to see why the USFL challenges this instruction because the jury did find monopoly power in a relevant market and therefore did consider the essential-facilities claim. Had the challenged instruction been omitted, the verdict would have been exactly the same.

[On the basis of this analysis of the television liability issue, the appeals court found no reason to overturn the jury's purely nominal damage award for other antitrust violations found against the NFL. The court also rejected the USFL's request to use these antitrust findings as a basis for sweeping injunctive relief—restructuring the NFL into two leagues, each limited to a single network contract.]

* * *

What the USFL seeks is essentially a judicial restructuring of major-league professional football to allow it to enter. Because of the explicit congressional authorization in 1966 for the NFL–AFL merger and single-league operation, the USFL does not attack the league structure directly. Instead, the USFL asks us to prevent networks from broadcasting, and fans from watching, NFL games in the hope that they will turn to the USFL. Absent a showing of an unlawful barrier to entry, however, new sports leagues must be prepared to make the investment of time, effort and money that develops interest and fan loyalty and results in an attractive product for the media. The jury in the present case obviously found that patient development of a loyal following among fans and an adherence to an original plan that offered long-run gains were lacking in the USFL. Instead, the USFL quickly changed to a strategy of competition with the NFL in the fall, hoping thereby to force a merger of a few USFL teams into the NFL. That led to a movement of USFL teams out of large television markets and a resultant reduction in value of USFL games to television. As USFL owner and negotiator Einhorn predicted, abandoning major television markets precluded the possibility of obtaining a network contract. The USFL hoped, however, that if a merger did not occur, a jury verdict in the instant litigation followed by a decree effectively forcing a network to televise its product would save the day. Instead, the jury found that the failure of the USFL was not the result of the NFL's television contracts but of its own decision to seek entry into the NFL on the cheap.

Verdict affirmed.

————

Following this appellate decision, the NFL argued that the USFL was not a "prevailing plaintiff" in this litigation and hence was not entitled to have the NFL pay its attorney fees as mandated by the Clayton Act. The trial judge held (at 704 F.Supp. 474 (S.D.N.Y.1989) that notwithstanding the USFL's inability to persuade the jury of financial damages from the NFL's actions—as opposed to the USFL's managerial mistakes—the jury had found significant enough violations of the Sherman Act by the NFL to warrant a fee award to the USFL's attorneys of $5.5 million.

C. BREAK UP THE BIG LEAGUES?

Having added this final piece to the existing legal mosaic of professional sports, step back and speculate about a possible future course for the game. In particular, consider a position that has been seriously advanced by some scholars,[11] that the major leagues within each sport should be broken up into three or four separate leagues that would compete against each other (on the model of the judicial break-up of A.T. & T.'s historic monopoly over telephone services).[12] The following questions will help focus your analysis of this proposal and its implications for our understanding of the status quo in sports.

1. To what extent are the legal, economic, and personal conflicts seen in prior chapters attributable to the current monopoly position enjoyed by the established league in each sport?

11. In particular, by Stephen Ross in the articles cited in note 1 above.

12. *United States v. American Telephone and Telegraph Company*, 552 F.Supp. 131 (D.D.C.1982). See Glen O. Robinson, *The Titanic Remembered: AT & T and the Changing World of Telecommunications*, 5 Yale J. on Reg. 517 (1988), for a review of the AT & T litigation and break-up.

2. Is there any prospect of competitive leagues emerging on their own to challenge seriously the dominant power within any sport? Why has no upstart league in any sport ever been able to survive for more than a few years as a viable counterweight to the market power of the established league?

3. Is the current sports monopoly attributable in significant measure to barriers created by the "exclusionary" conduct of the established leagues or barriers deriving from the variety of special legal prerogatives and immunities that we have seen extended to the various leagues? By the way, why have government officials—in the federal and state legislative, executive, and judicial branches of government—been forthcoming with so many privileges and subsidies for the dominant sports leagues?

4. Alternatively, is the more likely explanation for the uniform pattern displayed in all sports over the last century, that sports is a natural monopoly? We mean "natural" not only in the strict economist's definition of that term,[13] but also in the practical sense that the essence of sports is competition, the high point of athletic competition is the crowning of a champion, and the league whose champion is generally recognized by fans as supreme inevitably receives the lion's share of gate attendance and television revenues—funds the league can use to attract the best players to its teams and thereby reinforce its dominant image with fans. In other words, is a single "major" league what sports consumers really want?

5. Whatever your diagnosis of the causes of the current sports monopoly, would it be desirable, would it be feasible, for Congress or an antitrust court to break up the established leagues, all of whose current divisions enjoy "big league" status in the popular mind? Each such division would be made an independent entity headed by its own commissioner: no agreements would be permitted with the other new leagues for allocation of players or franchises, or sale of television rights and marketing licenses. If that policy course were to be followed, should the several new leagues be entitled to (or required to) cooperate in staging a single championship playoff? In effect, should the Super Bowl or the World Series be deemed an "essential facility" that must be made accessible to each league in order to preserve a competitive sports marketplace (by analogy to the appeals court ruling in *Aspen Highlands Skiing Corp. v. Aspen Skiing Co.*, 738 F.2d 1509 (10th Cir.1984), affirmed on somewhat different grounds, 472 U.S. 585, 105 S.Ct. 2847, 86 L.Ed.2d 467 (1985))?

6. Among the different constituencies observed in earlier chapters—owners, players, players associations, agents, municipalities, television networks, and fans—who would win and who would

---

13. See John Cirace, *An Economic Analysis of Antitrust Law's Natural Mo-* *nopoly Cases*, 88 West Virginia L. Rev. 677 (1986).

lose from such a dramatically different structure to the sports world? Why?

* * *

The foregoing is a purely speculative exercise, at least for the foreseeable future. Nevertheless, reflecting upon this possible "brave new world" of competitive sports leagues is important to cast into sharper relief the economic and human conflicts, and the resulting legal puzzles, depicted in the previous chapters. Recall the case of *Rose v. Giamatti*, with which this book began. What is the ultimate source of the commissioner's authority to define the "best interests of the sport"? Is that authority purely private or public, or some blend of the two? How does George Will's observation—that the courts should stay out of sports—look to you now?

Chapter Eight

INTERCOLLEGIATE SPORTS: DUE PROCESS AND ACADEMIC INTEGRITY

We now begin exploring the law's impact on intercollegiate sports. As in professional sports, the last two decades have witnessed an explosion of litigation by the people and institutions involved in intercollegiate athletics. There are interesting similarities and contrasts between college sports and their professional counterparts. Whatever points of comparison are emphasized, the materials from the world of college athletics presented in the next two chapters cast light on the broader role of law in shaping the governance of sports.[1]

For this purpose the telling comparison is not how the game is played on field or floor, even though, for example, the rules of football are essentially the same in the NFL and the Big Ten. Rather, the key similarity between professional and college sports that has helped fuel the bulk of litigation is the vast sum of money generated from fans intensely interested in watching the games, whether live or on television.

---

1. The subject of college sports has produced a growing number of popular book-length treatments. These books, typically written by journalists, exhibit a rather jaundiced attitude towards various features of intercollegiate athletics, an attitude that is visible in titles such as *A Hundred Yard Lie*, *Win At Any Cost*, and *Undue Process*. While these and other books provide interesting glimpses of the real life practices that lead to litigation and judicial opinions, a more balanced picture of the fundamental issues can be found in scholarly works such as Wilford S. Bayley and Taylor D. Littleton, *Athletics and Academe: An Anatomy of Abuses and a Prescription for Reform* (New York: American Council on Education, MacMillan Publishing, 1991); *Symposium, The Reform of Big–Time Intercollegiate Athetics*, 20 Capital L. Rev. 541 (1991); Rodney K. Smith, *An Academic Game Plan for Reforming Big–Time Intercollegiate Athletics*, Denver U. L.Rev. 213 (1990); and John C. Weistart, *Legal Accountability and the NCAA*, 10 J. of Col. and Univ. L., 167 (1983). Perhaps the most informative of the more popular books are Murray Sperber, *College Sports Inc., The Athletic Department versus the University* (New York: Henry Holt, 1990), and Gary Funk, *Major Violation: The Unbalanced Priorities in Athletics and Academics* (Champaign, Ill: Leisure Press, 1991).

An especially vivid number in that regard is the billion-dollar contract signed by the Columbia Broadcasting System (CBS) with the National Collegiate Athletic Association (NCAA) to televise the NCAA's men's basketball tournament—sports fans' annual March Madness—for the next seven years. Postseason college football bowl games generate almost $75 million a year in revenues for participating schools and their conferences. The University of Washington's football program has earned nearly $10 million in annual profits for the school in recent years, and in 1991 Notre Dame signed a $37.5 million contract with the National Broadcasting Corporation (NBC) for the rights to televise the school's home football games for five years. The University of Southern California has raised from alumni and booster groups $250,000 endowments for each of fifty positions on the school's football team. In aggregate, major college sports (Division 1, and Division 1–A in football) generate roughly one billion dollars in annual revenues, more than half from football programs.[2]

These soaring financial figures have jeopardized the principles that supposedly make intercollegiate sports unique. Article I of the NCAA's constitution proclaims:

> The competitive athletics programs of member institutions are designed to be a vital part of the education system. A basic purpose of this Association is to maintain intercollegiate athletics as an integral part of the education program and the athlete as an integral part of the student body and, by so doing, retain a clear line of demarcation between intercollegiate athletics and professional sports.

However, the financial temptation of this commercial athletic venture often causes serious tension with the NCAA's stated purpose of conducting intercollegiate sports "in a manner designed to protect and enhance the physical and educational welfare of student-athletes" (Article 2.2). In particular, the prospect of lucrative championship teams makes it difficult to treat student-athletes as "amateurs" whose participation is "motivated primarily by education and by the physical, mental, and social benefits" of athletics, and who are to "be protected from exploitation by professional and commercial enterprises" (Article 2.6).

Beneath the surface of these stated objectives, intercollegiate sports has much the same structural features as we earlier saw exhibited by professional sports. The NCAA has approximately 800 member colleges and universities. The Association was formed early in the twentieth century in response to the dangerous state of college football.[3] With nearly 20 fatal and 150 seriously disabling injuries befalling

2. The principal source of financial data for intercollegiate sports is Mitchell H. Raiborn, *Revenues and Expenses of Intercollegiate Athletic Programs: Analysis of Financial Trends and Relationships, 1985–1989* (Overland Park, Kansas: NCAA, 1990).

3. A first-rate historical treatment of the early years of intercollegiate sports is Ronald Smith, *Sports and Freedom: The Rise of Big–Time College Athletics* (New York: Oxford University Press, 1988).

participants in college football games every year, in 1906 President Theodore Roosevelt called together the heads of major universities to get them to agree on a set of playing rules that would outlaw dangerous tactics such as the "flying wedge." After considerable bickering, the schools agreed to create the NCAA as a forum for reshaping the rules for football (e.g., bringing in the forward pass), and, later, for standardizing the rules for basketball and other sports.

With respect to the rules of the game off the field, Association members agreed upon broad principles of student amateurism in college sports. However, the operating constitutional regime was "home rule" by each institution in determining what these principles meant for admission, academic progress, and financial assistance of its student-athletes. Only after World War II and an initially unsuccessful effort to implement a "Sanity Code" intended to eliminate perennial abuses in college programs, did the NCAA members agree to empower the Association (and its newly-hired Executive Director) with authority over the *enterprise* (and not merely the *game*) of college sports. Four decades later, the NCAA Manual consists of 400 pages of intricate regulations authored, interpreted, and enforced by a complex interplay of the legislative, executive, and judicial branches of the Association.

Just as was historically true in professional sports, establishing a detailed body of private law for the governance of intercollegiate sports has been the preserve of the colleges and universities who, along with the conferences to which they belong, constitute the membership of the Association. Unsurprisingly, the member schools have displayed a strong interest in maintaining other NCAA objectives such as the principles of "equity in competition" (Article 2.7) and "economy of athletics program operation" (Article 2.13). This institutional interest has become much more intense recently because athletic program expenditures have been rising even faster than revenues. In 1989, for example, the University of Michigan had a football team that won the Rose Bowl and a basketball team that won the NCAA championship, and also had a $2 million deficit in its overall athletic budget. The two revenue-producing sports, football and men's basketball, can produce profits ranging as high as $10 million, but a considerable number of schools show a loss even in these two supposedly lucrative sports programs.

These dollar amounts on their balance sheets generate intense concern on the part of school officials who collectively decide in the NCAA's annual conventions what constitutes the "best interests" of intercollegiate sports. That institutional perspective inevitably clashes with the interests not only of dissident NCAA members, but also of athletes and coaches whose sporting careers are governed by the NCAA regime, but who have no vote in the formulation or enforcement of NCAA policy. The last two decades have witnessed growing recourse to the courts by people dissatisfied with the decisions made within the NCAA hierarchy. The cases and materials in this chapter depict both the judicial response to specific conflicts, and the uneasy equilibrium in the autonomy the law has left to the NCAA in governing the college sports enterprise.

A. THE TARKANIAN SAGA [4]

The most celebrated legal challenge to NCAA autonomy was launched by Jerry Tarkanian of the University of Nevada at Las Vegas (UNLV). After a successful but contentious career at Long Beach State, in the fall of 1973 Tarkanian was recruited to be head coach for the struggling UNLV basketball program. On his arrival, Tarkanian found that the NCAA had embarked on a full-scale examination of rule violations by UNLV. The investigation lasted four years, during which time Tarkanian took his Running Rebels to a 29–3 regular season record and the Final Four championship playoffs in 1977. At the end of that season, however, UNLV announced that pursuant to an NCAA directive, the school was suspending Tarkanian for two years because he had been found personally guilty of major violations of NCAA rules.

The two main charges against Tarkanian were that he had arranged for payment of a flight home for one of his players and that he had arranged for an instructor to give another player a passing grade in a course the player did not attend. The NCAA investigators asserted that these infractions had been disclosed by the player and the instructor. Upon learning of the charges, Tarkanian, the University, and the Nevada Attorney General's office undertook their own investigations and obtained contrary affidavits from both the alleged participants and several corroborating witnesses. But production of this new material simply elicited a new and more serious charge against Tarkanian, that he had pressured witnesses to give false evidence in NCAA proceedings.

At Tarkanian's hearing before the NCAA's Committee on Infractions, the evidence against him consisted merely of assertions made by NCAA staff investigators of what they recalled people saying to them in the previous three years, matched against the affidavits and supporting documents offered by Tarkanian and UNLV. No oral testimony or cross-examination of witnesses was permitted. At the end of the proceeding, after a private consultation with the enforcement staff, the five-member Committee (of which the chair and two other members were law professors) found that the violations had occurred. The Committee put UNLV's basketball program on probation for two years, and required the university to suspend Tarkanian as coach for those two years or face further penalties. UNLV's appeal to the NCAA Council was dismissed a few months later. (Tarkanian himself had no right of appeal since he was not a member of the NCAA.)

---

4. A revealing look at the entire Tarkanian case, written from a very pro-Tarkanian vantage point, is Don Yaeger, *Shark Attack: Jerry Tarkanian and His Battle With the NCAA and UNLV* (New York: Harper Collins, 1992). A scholarly treatment of the legal issues is John P. Sahl, *College Athletes and Due Process Protection: What's Left After* NCAA v. Tarkanian, 21 Arizona St. L. J. 621 (1989).

As a state university, UNLV was required by both federal constitutional and state statutory law to give Tarkanian, its tenured coach, a hearing before suspending him. Although the hearing officer did not believe that any violations had occurred, he concluded that UNLV had no choice but to suspend Tarkanian if the school wanted to remain part of the NCAA. On the eve of his suspension Tarkanian went to court, eventually suing both UNLV and the NCAA. The Nevada courts found that the NCAA proceedings had denied Tarkanian "due process." Operating on the assumption that the NCAA was a "state actor" governed by the federal constitution, the trial court issued injunctions barring UNLV's suspension of Tarkanian and NCAA retaliation against UNLV. The Nevada Supreme Court affirmed. The case finally reached the United States Supreme Court in 1988; by then Tarkanian had accumulated more wins than any other active coach in college basketball (and had become Nevada's highest paid public employee), and the Supreme Court had considerably narrowed its view of what constitutes "state action."

NATIONAL COLLEGIATE ATHLETIC ASS'N. v. TARKANIAN

Supreme Court of the United States, 1988.

488 U.S. 179, 109 S.Ct. 454, 102 L.Ed.2d 469.

JUSTICE STEVENS for the Court.

* * *

II

Embedded in our Fourteenth Amendment jurisprudence is a dichotomy between state action, which is subject to scrutiny under the Amendment's Due Process Clause, and private conduct, against which the Amendment affords no shield, no matter how unfair that conduct may be. As a general matter the protections of the Fourteenth Amendment do not extend to "private conduct abridging individual rights." Burton v. Wilmington Parking Authority, 365 U.S. 715, 722 (1961).

"Careful adherence to the 'state action' requirement preserves an area of individual freedom by limiting the reach of federal law" and avoids the imposition of responsibility on a State for conduct it could not control. When Congress enacted § 1983 as the statutory remedy for violations of the Constitution, it specified that the conduct at issue must have occurred "under color of" state law; thus, liability attaches only to those wrongdoers "who carry a badge of authority of a State and represent it in some capacity, whether they act in accordance with their authority or misuse it."

In this case Tarkanian argues that the NCAA was a state actor because it misused power that it possessed by virtue of state law. He claims specifically that UNLV delegated its own functions to the NCAA, clothing the Association with authority both to adopt rules governing UNLV's athletic programs and to enforce those rules on behalf of UNLV. Similarly, the Nevada Supreme Court held that UNLV had delegated its authority over personnel decisions to the NCAA. Therefore, the court reasoned, the two entities acted jointly to deprive Tarkanian of liberty and property interests, making the NCAA as well as UNLV a state actor.

These contentions fundamentally misconstrue the facts of this case. In the typical case raising a state action issue, a private party has taken the decisive step that caused the harm to the plaintiff, and the question is whether the State was sufficiently involved to treat that decisive conduct as state action. This may occur if the State creates the legal framework governing the conduct; if it delegates its authority to the private actor; or sometimes if it knowingly accepts the benefits derived from unconstitutional behavior. Thus, in the usual case we ask whether the State provided a mantle of authority that enhanced the power of the harm-causing individual actor.

This case uniquely mirrors the traditional state action case. Here the final act challenged by Tarkanian—his suspension—was committed by UNLV. A state university without question is a state actor. When it decides to impose a serious disciplinary sanction upon one of its tenured employees, it must comply with the terms of the Due Process Clause of the Fourteenth Amendment to the Federal Constitution. Thus when UNLV notified Tarkanian that he was being separated from all relations with the University's basketball program, it acted under color of state law within the meaning of 42 U.S.C. § 1983.

The mirror image presented in this case requires us to step through an analytical looking glass to resolve it. Clearly UNLV's conduct was influenced by the rules and recommendations of the NCAA, the private party. But it was UNLV, the state entity, that actually suspended Tarkanian. Thus the question is not whether UNLV participated to a critical extent in the NCAA's activities, but whether UNLV's actions in compliance with the NCAA rules and recommendations turned the NCAA's conduct into state action.

We examine first the relationship between UNLV and the NCAA regarding the NCAA's rulemaking. UNLV is among the NCAA's members and participated in promulgating the Association's rules; it must be assumed, therefore, that Nevada had some impact on the NCAA's policy determinations. Yet the NCAA's several hundred other public and private member institutions each similarly affected those policies. Those institutions, the vast majority of which were located in States other than Nevada, did not act under color of Nevada law. It necessarily follows that the source of the legislation adopted by the NCAA is not Nevada but the collective membership, speaking through an organization that is independent of any particular State.

State action nonetheless might lie if UNLV, by embracing the NCAA's rules, transformed them into state rules and the NCAA into a state actor. UNLV engaged in state action when it adopted the

NCAA's rules to govern its own behavior, but that would be true even if UNLV had taken no part in the promulgation of those rules. In Bates v. State Bar of Arizona, 433 U.S. 350 (1977), we established that the State Supreme Court's enforcement of disciplinary rules transgressed by members of its own bar was state action. Those rules had been adopted in toto from the American Bar Association Code of Professional Responsibility. It does not follow, however, that the ABA's formulation of those disciplinary rules was state action. The State Supreme Court retained plenary power to reexamine those standards and, if necessary, to reject them and promulgate its own. So here, UNLV retained the authority to withdraw from the NCAA and establish its own standards. The University alternatively could have stayed in the Association and worked through the Association's legislative process to amend rules or standards it deemed harsh, unfair, or unwieldy.[15] Neither UNLV's decision to adopt the NCAA's standards nor its minor role in their formulation is a sufficient reason for concluding that the NCAA was acting under color of Nevada law when it promulgated standards governing athlete recruitment, eligibility, and academic performance.

Tarkanian further asserts that the NCAA's investigation, enforcement proceedings, and consequent recommendations constituted state action because they resulted from a delegation of power by UNLV. UNLV, as an NCAA member, subscribed to the statement in the Association's bylaws that NCAA "enforcement procedures are an essential part of the intercollegiate athletic program of each member institution." It is, of course, true that a state may delegate authority to a private party and thereby make that party a state actor. Thus, we recently held that a private physician who had contracted with a state prison to attend to the inmates' medical needs was a state actor. But UNLV delegated no power to the NCAA to take specific action against any University employee. The commitment by UNLV to adhere to NCAA enforcement procedures was enforceable only by sanctions that the NCAA might impose on UNLV itself.

Indeed, the notion that UNLV's promise to cooperate in the NCAA enforcement proceedings was tantamount to a partnership agreement or the transfer of certain University powers to the NCAA is belied by the history of this case. It is quite obvious that UNLV used its best efforts to retain its winning coach—a goal diametrically opposed to the NCAA's interest in ascertaining the truth of its investigators' reports. During the several years that the NCAA investigated the alleged violations, the NCAA and UNLV acted much more like adversaries than like partners engaged in a dispassionate search for the truth. The

---

15. Furthermore, the NCAA's bylaws permit review of penalties, even after they are imposed, "upon a showing of newly discovered evidence which is directly related to the findings in the case, or that there was a prejudicial error in the procedure which was followed in the processing of the case by the Committee." UNLV could have sought such a review, perhaps on the theory that the NCAA's investigator was biased against Tarkanian, as the Nevada trial court found in 1984. The NCAA Committee on Infractions was authorized to "reduce or eliminate any penalty" if the University had prevailed.

NCAA cannot be regarded as an agent of UNLV for purposes of that proceeding. It is more correctly characterized as an agent of its remaining members which, as competitors of UNLV, had an interest in the effective and evenhanded enforcement of NCAA's recruitment standards. Just as a state-compensated public defender acts in a private capacity when she represents a private client in a conflict against the State, the NCAA is properly viewed as a private actor at odds with the State when it represents the interests of its entire membership in an investigation of one public university.

The NCAA enjoyed no governmental powers to facilitate its investigation.[17] It had no power to subpoena witnesses, to impose contempt sanctions, or to assert sovereign authority over any individual. Its greatest authority was to threaten sanctions against UNLV, with the ultimate sanction being expulsion of the University from membership. Contrary to the premise of the Nevada Supreme Court's opinion, the NCAA did not—indeed, could not—directly discipline Tarkanian or any other state university employee.[18] The express terms of the Confidential Report did not demand the suspension unconditionally; rather, it requested "the University ... to show cause" why the NCAA should

---

17. In Dennis v. Sparks, 449 U.S. 24 (1980), on which the dissent relies, the parties had entered into a corrupt agreement to perform a judicial act. As we explained:

[H]ere the allegations were that an official act of the defendant judge was the product of a corrupt conspiracy involving bribery of the judge. Under these allegations, the private parties conspiring with the judge were acting under color of state law; and it is of no consequence in this respect that the judge himself is immune from damages liability. Immunity does not change the character of the judge's action or that of his co-conspirators. Indeed, his immunity is dependent on the challenged conduct being an official judicial act within his statutory jurisdiction, broadly construed. Private parties who corruptly conspire with a judge in connection with such conduct are thus acting under color of law....

In this case there is no suggestion of any impropriety respecting the agreement between the NCAA and UNLV. Indeed the dissent seems to assume that NCAA's liability as a state actor depended not on its initial agreement with UNLV, but on whether UNLV ultimately accepted the NCAA's recommended discipline of Tarkanian. In contrast, the conspirators in *Dennis* became state actors when they formed the corrupt bargain with the judge, and remained so through completion of the conspiracy's objectives.

18. Tarkanian urges us to hold, as did the Nevada Supreme Court, that the NCAA by its rules and enforcement procedures has usurped a traditional, essential state function. Quite properly, he does not point to the NCAA's overriding function of fostering amateur athletics at the college level. For while we have described that function as "critical," NCAA v. Board of Regents of the University of Oklahoma, 468 U.S. 85, 120 (1984), by no means is it a traditional, let alone an exclusive, state function. Cf. San Francisco Arts & Athletics, Inc. v. United States Olympic Committee, 483 U.S. 522, 545, (1987) ("Neither the conduct nor the coordination of amateur sports has been a traditional government function."). Tarkanian argues instead that the NCAA has assumed the state's traditional and exclusive power to discipline its employees. "[A]s to state employees connected with intercollegiate athletics, the NCAA requires that its standards, procedures and determinations become the State's standards, procedures and determinations for disciplining state employees," he contends. "The State is obligated to impose NCAA standards, procedures and determinations making the NCAA a joint participant in the State's suspension of Tarkanian." This argument overlooks the fact that the NCAA's own legislation prohibits it from taking any direct action against Tarkanian. Moreover, suspension of Tarkanian is one of many recommendations in the Confidential Report. Those recommendations as a whole were intended to bring UNLV's basketball program into compliance with NCAA rules. Suspension of Tarkanian was but one means toward achieving that goal.

not impose additional penalties if UNLV declines to suspend Tarkanian. Even the University's vice president acknowledged that the Report gave the University options other than suspension: UNLV could have retained Tarkanian and risked additional sanctions, perhaps even expulsion from the NCAA, or it could have withdrawn voluntarily from the Association.

Finally, Tarkanian argues that the power of the NCAA is so great that the UNLV had no practical alternative to compliance with its demands. We are not at all sure this is true,[19] but even if we assume that a private monopolist can impose its will on a state agency by a threatened refusal to deal with it, it does not follow that such a private party is therefore acting under color of state law.

In final analysis the question is whether "the conduct allegedly causing the deprivation of a federal right [can] be fairly attributable to the State." It would be ironic indeed to conclude that the NCAA's imposition of sanctions against UNLV—sanctions that UNLV and its counsel, including the Attorney General of Nevada, steadfastly opposed during protracted adversary proceedings—is fairly attributable to the State of Nevada. It would be more appropriate to conclude that UNLV has conducted its athletic program under color of the policies adopted by the NCAA, rather than that those policies were developed and enforced under color of Nevada law.

Reversed.

JUSTICE WHITE dissented and filed an opinion in which JUSTICES BRENNAN, MARSHALL and O'CONNOR joined.

All agree that UNLV, a public university, is a state actor, and that the suspension of Jerry Tarkanian, a public employee, was state action. The question here is whether the NCAA acted jointly with UNLV in suspending Tarkanian and thereby also became a state actor. I would hold that it did.

I agree with the majority that this case is different on its facts from many of our prior state action cases. As the majority notes, in our "typical case raising a state action issue, a private party has taken the decisive step that caused the harm to the plaintiff." In this case, however, which in the majority's view "uniquely mirrors the traditional state action case," the final act that caused the harm to Tarkanian was committed, not by a private party, but by a party conceded to be a state actor. Because of this difference, the majority finds it necessary to "step through an analytical looking glass" to evaluate whether the NCAA was a state actor.

But the situation presented by this case is not unknown to us and certainly is not unique. In both *Adickes v. S.H. Kress & Co.*, 398 U.S.

---

19. The University's desire to remain a powerhouse among the nation's college basketball teams is understandable, and nonmembership in the NCAA obviously would thwart that goal. But that UNLV's options were unpalatable does not mean that they were nonexistent.

144 (1970), and *Dennis v. Sparks*, 449 U.S. 24 (1980), we faced the question of whether private parties could be held to be state actors in cases in which the final or decisive act was carried out by a state official. In both cases we held that the private parties could be found to be state actors, if they were "jointly engaged with state officials in the challenged action."

The facts of *Dennis* are illustrative. In *Dennis*, a state trial judge enjoined the production of minerals from oil leases owned by the plaintiff. The injunction was later dissolved on appeal as having been issued illegally. The plaintiff then filed suit under 42 U.S.C. § 1983, alleging that the judge had conspired with the party seeking the original injunction—a private corporation—the sole owner of the corporation, and the two sureties on the injunction bond to deprive the plaintiff of due process by corruptly issuing the injunction. We held unanimously that under the facts as alleged the private parties were state actors because they were "willful participant[s] in joint action with the State or its agents." ...

On the facts of the present case, the NCAA acted jointly with UNLV in suspending Tarkanian. First, Tarkanian was suspended for violations of NCAA rules, which UNLV embraced in its agreement with the NCAA. As the Nevada Supreme Court found in its first opinion in this case, "[a]s a member of the NCAA, UNLV contractually agrees to administer its athletic program in accordance with NCAA legislation." Indeed, NCAA rules provide that NCAA "enforcement procedures are an essential part of the intercollegiate athletic program of each member institution."

Second, the NCAA and UNLV also agreed that the NCAA would conduct the hearings concerning violations of its rules. Although UNLV conducted its own investigation into the recruiting violations alleged by the NCAA, the NCAA procedures provide that it is the NCAA Committee on Infractions that "determine[s] facts related to alleged violations," subject to an appeal to the NCAA Council. As a result of this agreement, the NCAA conducted the very hearings the Nevada Supreme Court held to have violated Tarkanian's right to procedural due process.

Third, the NCAA and UNLV agreed that the findings of fact made by the NCAA at the hearings it conducted would be binding on UNLV. By becoming a member of the NCAA, UNLV did more than merely "promise to cooperate in the NCAA enforcement proceedings." It agreed, as the University Hearing Officer appointed to rule on Tarkanian's suspension expressly found, to accept the NCAA's "findings of fact as in some way superior to [its] own." By the terms of UNLV's membership in the NCAA, the NCAA's findings were final and not subject to further review by any other body, and it was for that reason that UNLV suspended Tarkanian, despite concluding that many of those findings were wrong.

In short, it was the NCAA's findings that Tarkanian had violated NCAA rules, made at NCAA-conducted hearings, all of which were agreed to by UNLV in its membership agreement with the NCAA, that resulted in Tarkanian's suspension by UNLV. On these facts, the NCAA was "jointly engaged with [UNLV] officials in the challenged action," and therefore was a state actor.

* * *

The majority states in conclusion that "[i]t would be ironic indeed to conclude that the NCAA's imposition of sanctions against UNLV—sanctions that UNLV and its counsel, including the Attorney General of Nevada, steadfastly opposed during protracted adversary proceedings—is fairly attributable to the State of Nevada." I agree. Had UNLV refused to suspend Tarkanian, and the NCAA responded by imposing sanctions against UNLV, it would be hard indeed to find any state action that harmed Tarkanian. But that is not this case. Here, UNLV did suspend Tarkanian, and it did so because it embraced the NCAA rules governing conduct of its athletic program and adopted the results of the hearings conducted by the NCAA concerning Tarkanian, as it had agreed that it would. Under these facts, I would find that the NCAA acted jointly with UNLV and therefore is a state actor.

———

While the NCAA won this major legal victory over Tarkanian, it was not thereby able to remove him from the college basketball court. Further litigation in the lower courts kept Tarkanian in place through the 1989–1990 season, which UNLV capped with its first national championship. (Tarkanian's coaching contract entitled him to ten percent of the $1.4 million UNLV won from the NCAA's tournament.) In the summer of 1990, UNLV and the NCAA reached a settlement whereby UNLV accepted additional probation for its basketball team in lieu of suspending Tarkanian, the coach. However, this ban on television and postseason appearances was postponed until the 1991–1992 season. It was the Duke Blue Devils, not NCAA investigators, who ended Tarkanian's bid in March 1991 for an unbeaten season and a second consecutive national championship. In the summer of 1991, faced with further troubles, including public criticism from UNLV's president and another major NCAA investigation (this one involving the recruiting of Lloyd Daniels in the mid–1980s), Tarkanian finally announced his intention to resign from UNLV in 1992, eighteen years after he began. Although his basketball team had lost its major stars to the NBA, Tarkanian's final season was highly successful—UNLV finished the regular season ranked seventh in the national polls. But because of offenses allegedly committed in the mid–1970s, this unheralded group of players was denied the chance to play for the NCAA's 1992 basketball championship.

The U.S. Supreme Court has settled the NCAA's status as a matter of legal doctrine, but important questions of constitutional principle remain.[5] In the 1970s the lower courts had treated the NCAA as a "state actor" in connection with both private and public universities. See, e.g., *Howard University v. NCAA*, 510 F.2d 213 (D.C.Cir.1975). After the Supreme Court's "state action" trilogy of 1982,[6] the Fourth Circuit reversed the judicial course in *Arlosoroff v. NCAA*, 746 F.2d 1019 (4th Cir.1984); the appeals court held the NCAA to be a private actor and thereby dismissed a constitutional challenge against an NCAA rule restricting the eligibility of foreigners brought by a student at Duke University, a private institution. The *Tarkanian* case was the first major case in the 1980s involving a state university.

Suppose that the Supreme Court had found the NCAA a "state actor" owing constitutional due process to Tarkanian (as UNLV, a public university, clearly did owe its employee). What legal obligations were riding on this label? Courts have interpreted the Fourteenth Amendment due process requirement to require that governmental action meet minimum standards of fairness such as adequate notice or an opportunity to be heard before the state makes a decision. To succeed on a due process claim under the Fourteenth Amendment, a litigant must prove that state action has deprived him or her of a liberty or property interest and that the procedures employed by the state were less than what was "due." There is a developed (and confusing) jurisprudence defining liberty or property interests and the procedures mandated by the Constitution in specific circumstances. Generally, state law determines whether a litigant has a protected property interest, and federal constitutional law determines the amount of required process.[7]

In *Tarkanian* the Nevada Supreme Court held that Tarkanian's contractual relationship with UNLV, a state institution, created a protected property interest in his tenured coaching job. See *Tarkanian v. NCAA*, 103 Nev. 331, 741 P.2d 1345 (1987). That ruling was based on Supreme Court jurisprudence that if state law provides "a legitimate claim of entitlement" to a job, a protected property interest exists. See *Board of Regents of State Colleges v. Roth*, 408 U.S. 564, 92 S.Ct. 2701, 33 L.Ed.2d 548 (1972) (ruling that a non-tenured instructor at a state university had no property interest in his position because state law created no legitimate basis for him to claim that he was entitled to renewal of his contract). The Nevada Supreme Court also found that Tarkanian's liberty interests were implicated because termination of his employment would stigmatize him and alter or extinguish a "right

---

5. For a critique, see *The Supreme Court, 1988 Term—Leading Cases*, 103 Harv.L.Rev. 137, 193 (1989).

6. The three decisions were *Rendell–Baker v. Kohn*, 457 U.S. 830, 102 S.Ct. 2764, 73 L.Ed.2d 418 (1982); *Lugar v. Edmonson Oil Company, Inc.*, 457 U.S. 922, 102 S.Ct. 2744, 73 L.Ed.2d 482 (1982); and

Blum v. Yaretsky, 457 U.S. 991, 102 S.Ct. 2777, 73 L.Ed.2d 534 (1982).

7. See generally, Laurence H. Tribe, *American Constitutional Law* §§ 10–9 to 10–14, at 685–718 (Foundation Press: Mineola, N.Y., 2d ed. 1988).

or status previously recognized by state law" (quoting *Paul v. Davis*, 424 U.S. 693, 96 S.Ct. 1155, 47 L.Ed.2d 405 (1976)).

As we will see later in this chapter, courts before *Tarkanian* struggled with the question whether student-athletes have a property interest in their intercollegiate athletic eligibility, as a means of obtaining either a career in professional sports or at least a college education. Some courts answered in the affirmative. See, e.g., *Hall v. University of Minnesota*, 530 F.Supp. 104 (D.Minn.1982), finding that college eligibility was a protected property interest because it was an essential step on the way to a professional sports career. Most courts, however, refused to find a property interest in athletic eligibility, believing that a college athlete's prospects for securing professional employment were too "speculative and not of constitutional dimensions." *Colorado Seminary v. NCAA*, 417 F.Supp. 885 (D.Colo.1976), affirmed, 570 F.2d 320 (10th Cir.1978).[8]

The Nevada Supreme Court also ruled that, as a matter of federal law, the NCAA did not provide the requisite amount of process in its investigation of Tarkanian. The court found that at a minimum, evidence against Tarkanian collected during interviews conducted by the NCAA enforcement staff should be in the form of written affidavits, relying on an oft-cited passage from the Supreme Court about what factors courts should balance in determining the procedures required in a given situation:

> First, the private interest that will be affected by the official action; second, the risk of erroneous deprivation of such interest through the procedures used, and the probable value, if any, of additional or substitute safeguards; and finally, the Government's interest, including the function involved and the fiscal and administrative burdens that the additional or substitute procedural requirement would entail.

Mathews v. Eldridge, 424 U.S. 319, 335, 96 S.Ct. 893, 47 L.Ed.2d 18 (1976).

When considering legal challenges to NCAA revocation of the eligibility of student-athletes, those courts that have treated the NCAA as a state actor have generally found NCAA procedures to be adequate under the Due Process Clause. See, e.g., *Regents of University of Minnesota v. NCAA*, 560 F.2d 352 (8th Cir.1977); *Howard University v. NCAA*, 510 F.2d 213 (D.C.Cir.1975); *Justice v. NCAA*, 577 F.Supp. 356 (D.Ariz.1983). Although *Tarkanian* bars federal due process claims against the NCAA, these cases may be relevant in determining the procedures required by state statutes (which we will examine later in this chapter) imposing due process requirements on the NCAA. In addition, the constitutional analysis in the cases cited presumably still applies to suits brought by students or coaches against public universities, which are state actors.

---

8. See Brian L. Porto, *Balancing Due Process and Academic Integrity In Intercollegiate Athletics: The Scholarship Ath-* *lete's Property Interest in Eligibility*, 62 Indiana L.J. 1151 (1987).

Questions for Discussion

1. In appraising the merits of the *Tarkanian* ruling, consider the following issues:

(i) Should NCAA action toward a student-athlete at a private school such as Duke or Notre Dame be treated any differently under the Constitution than a baseball commissioner's action toward a Pete Rose or a George Steinbrenner? Is there anything special about the function of regulating sports in educational institutions? Are there any material differences in the structures of the NCAA and of a professional sports league and in the manner in which the respective members conduct their athletic businesses? And by the way, after *Tarkanian*, would a successor to Melissa Ludtke likely win a suit to gain access of women reporters to the New York Yankees clubhouse? Note that the public-private relationship in *Ludtke* (in Chapter 1) was the reverse of the relationship in *Tarkanian*.

(ii) When the NCAA takes action against a state university such as UNLV, is there a stronger case for judicial scrutiny? How much choice did UNLV have to defy the NCAA and respect Tarkanian's due process rights? Are there legal instruments more appropriate than the Constitution for challenging NCAA restraints on institutional or personal choices?

2. Suppose that UNLV had not been able to reach a settlement with the NCAA and had eventually suspended Tarkanian (after the Supreme Court's ruling). Would Tarkanian have had any legal remedies against UNLV? Since UNLV clearly is a state actor, could Tarkanian have sued the university for violating his due process rights by acceding to the demands of a private association to deprive him of a protected property right without a hearing, especially when the university doubted the factual basis for the NCAA's demand? If such a suit succeeded, what remedies would be available? Would the threat of such remedies place public colleges that belong to the NCAA in a Catch–22 situation when the NCAA orders one of their employees disciplined—either do it and violate the constitution or refuse and face NCAA sanctions? Could private schools follow the NCAA's directives without legal consequence? What are the possible implications for the NCAA of such a dual legal standard?

3. Whether or not Tarkanian could have sustained such a suit against UNLV, could he successfully have sued the NCAA, not for itself denying him due process, but for inducing UNLV to breach his constitutional rights under his employment contract? (Recall the tort action brought by the Toronto Blue Jays against the Boston Celtics in the Danny Ainge case in Chapter 2.) There is limited support for such a legal claim against the NCAA in the preliminary injunction ruling in *Regents of the University of Minnesota v. NCAA*, 422 F.Supp. 1158 (D.Minn.1976), involving a basketball player who had sold his complimentary tickets at more than their face value. The court of appeals reversed this ruling on the specific facts of the case, and expressed no view about the legal principle. See *Regents*, 560 F.2d 352 (8th Cir.1977). Is such a claim consistent with the state action policies underlying *Tarkanian*?

The following case, drawn from a quite different side of the intercollegiate sports enterprise, illustrates both the strengths and weaknesses of such a tort claim against the NCAA as an "outside" third party allegedly interfering with the plaintiff's rights *vis-a-vis* a public university.

NCAA v. HORNUNG

Supreme Court of Kentucky, 1988.

754 S.W.2d 855.

LAMBERT, JUSTICE.

[This case was an appeal of a $1.1 million tort award won by Paul Hornung against the NCAA. Hornung, a former Notre Dame Heisman trophy winner and Green Bay Packer star, had become a television sports broadcaster. When the Atlanta superstation WTBS was awarded the rights to telecast a package of college football games in 1982 and 1983, it seriously considered Hornung as its color analyst. However, when the NCAA exercised its rights under the television contract with WTBS to veto Hornung as a candidate, Hornung sued the NCAA for the tort of improper interference with his potential contractual relationship with WTBS.]

* * *

At trial, Committee Chairman Hallock testified that the reasons for Hornung's disapproval were:

> My own experience with the Committee, and you find this in the Constitution and By–Laws of the NCAA, was first of all to protect the objective of keeping a strong demarcation between amateur—college football and professional football. There are strong resolutions and actions within the NCAA By–Laws, statements against gambling. I felt very definitely that the combination of the identification, the primary identification since—pretty much since Paul Hornung graduated in 1956 was with professional football. I felt personally that the unfortunate suspension of Mr. Hornung for gambling activity was not something that the NCAA wanted to simply overlook in the selection of people to represent college football on television. I had a personal feeling that the national image as continually being represented by Miller Beer of Paul Hornung's life-style was not in keeping with any positive— certainly any positive quality that the NCAA was interested in condoning in any way. Those were my personal feelings.

The NCAA makes a number of attacks upon the orders and rulings of the trial court and the opinion of the Court of Appeals. Principally, however, it contends that Hornung failed to prove that it "improperly" interfered with his prospective contractual relation with WTBS. Admitting that its actions were intentional, the NCAA argues that before recovery may be allowed, proof of malice is required. According to the

NCAA, there was no proof of malice; its disapproval of Hornung being a legitimate exercise of its contract right with WTBS. Hornung argues to the contrary that a showing of malice is not required for recovery. He argues that it is sufficient to prove that the NCAA's interference with his prospective contract was intentional and without reasonable justification. The trial court and the Court of Appeals held that the NCAA had a right to approve or disapprove Hornung, but was required to exercise "good faith," and that in light of the factors set forth in Section 767 of the Restatement (Second) of Torts, sufficient evidence was presented to permit a determination by the trier of fact that the NCAA breached its duty.

* * *

Our law is clear that a party may not recover under the theory presented in the absence of proof that the opposing party "improperly" interfered with his prospective contractual relation. To determine whether the interference is improper, Section 767 sets forth seven factors to be considered by the court in ruling on the motion for directed verdict and, if the case is submitted, considered by the jury. Unless there is evidence of improper interference, after due consideration of the factors provided for determining such, the case should not be submitted to the jury. Even if evidence is presented which would otherwise make a submissible case, the party whose interference is alleged to have been improper may escape liability by showing that he acted in good faith to assert a legally protected interest of his own.

* * *

From [the] authorities, it is clear that to prevail a party seeking recovery must show malice or some significantly wrongful conduct. In Prosser and Keeton on Torts § 130 (W.P. Keeton ed. 5th ed. 1984), this is stated as follows:

> [T]he [interference] cases have turned almost entirely upon the defendant's motive or purpose, and the means by which he has sought to accomplish it.... [S]ome element of ill will is seldom absent from intentional interference; and if the defendant has a legitimate interest to protect, the addition of a spite motive usually is not regarded as sufficient to result in liability.

* * *

Returning to the evidence, the most significant fact presented by Hornung was that after the vote, Crowder was mentioned as a possible announcer by two members of the Committee in a hallway discussion with Wussler and Hanson. Hornung argues that from this it may be inferred that he was rejected so that Crowder could have the job. Even if this incident stood alone, which it does not, and there was no other evidence to explain the action of the Committee, such an inference would not be reasonable. After all, the Committee had seventeen other members and, despite the presence of Wussler and Hanson at the meeting, there was no evidence of improper influence upon the deliberations. No evidence was presented that the other members of the Committee had any knowledge of the hallway conversation or that the two spoke on behalf of the Committee.

Moreover, Hallock explained the reasons for the Committee's rejection of Hornung as "the unfortunate episode in his professional playing career when he was suspended by the NFL for gambling activity," the inconsistency between the image the NCAA sought to promote and the image of Hornung portrayed in the Miller Lite Beer commercial, and the opinion that Hornung was too closely associated with professional football. Hornung argues that these reasons are subterfuge, but nothing more than speculation was presented to contradict the reasons given.

It is undisputed that during his professional football career Hornung was suspended for gambling activity and that in the Miller Lite Beer commercial, Hornung was portrayed as a playboy. These were certainly legitimate matters for consideration by the NCAA. In view of Hornung's long and outstanding career in the National Football League, it is not unreasonable to hold the opinion that he is more closely associated with professional football than college football. Contrary to Hornung's argument, its acceptance of advertising revenue from the Miller Brewing Company does not render the NCAA's objection to the commercial incredible. The objection was not Hornung's promotional activity on behalf of the brewing company; it was the image portrayed in the commercial. Likewise, Hornung's previous broadcast of college football games is irrelevant as the NCAA did not have "announcer approval rights" as it had here. Finally, Hallock's vote in 1985, three years after the Committee vote, in favor of Hornung's election to membership in the College Football Hall of Fame and the fact that the Committee took only ten minutes to disapprove Hornung do not conflict with the testimony given by Hallock. From the foregoing, we conclude that Hornung failed to prove that the NCAA "improperly" interfered with his prospective contractual relation with WTBS.

Even if our conclusion about improper interference were otherwise, the NCAA would nevertheless prevail upon its defense under Restatement Section 773. The NCAA was entitled to assert "in good faith" its right of announcer approval. This right had been bargained for and was an essential element in the contract with WTBS. The NCAA was entitled to assert its right even to the detriment of Hornung's prospective contractual relation. If the NCAA believed that employment of Hornung was contrary to its interest, even if such belief was mistaken, it was justified in disapproving Hornung pursuant to the terms of the agreement with WTBS.

* * *

Trial verdict reversed.

In light of *Hornung*, how far could the commissioner of baseball go in barring Pete Rose from working for firms doing business with Major League Baseball? Recall the cases noted in Chapter 1 in which Commissioner Bowie Kuhn banned Willie Mays and Mickey Mantle from associating with baseball teams because they worked for Atlantic City casinos. Similarly, could the NCAA bar Jerry Tarkanian from ever working in any capacity for an NCAA member school (inside or outside the athletic department)? Is there a difference between "interfering" with a prospective employment opportunity and ordering suspension or dismissal of someone already employed (as the NCAA did to Tarkanian)?

At a more fundamental level, both the Pete Rose and the Paul Hornung cases reveal the difficulties with characterizing these litigants as third parties. On the one hand, players and coaches neither make the rules nor appoint the commissioners who govern professional and intercollegiate sports. On the other hand, they sign contracts with their teams that incorporate by reference the league's or association's governing rules and authorities. The question, then, is how much the courts should defer to judgments made by the league or association about the "best interests" of its sport, when these judgments will defeat the contractual expectations of individuals who have no role in this private governing structure? Suppose, for example, that a professional league or college conference exercised its contractual right to reject a television analyst on the ground that he was openly gay. Under the *Hornung* standard, is such a veto legal?

As just a preliminary glimpse of the substantive issues that lead to litigation about NCAA procedures, recall that the rule allegedly broken in the *University of Minnesota* case (mentioned above before the *Hornung* decision) dealt with the players' complimentary game tickets. The evolution of NCAA policy towards such tickets displays the constant tug of war between rule-making at the NCAA and temptations felt on campus. The initial rule was simply that each player could receive four tickets for every game in which his team participated. While players were prohibited from selling their tickets, many players broke that rule in return for substantial payments, especially for more attractive games. The NCAA then instituted a "pass" system under which the players could list four people who had to identify themselves at the gate to obtain their seats for the game. This system made it more difficult, but by no means impossible, for players to sell (to school boosters, for example) a favored position on the pass list. Eventually, the NCAA turned to the current rule, which specifies that three of the four passes must be designated for the player's family members or fellow students. Is this a sensible solution? What exactly is the problem?

B. PROCEDURAL DUE PROCESS [9]

As the preceding section indicates, the Supreme Court's insulation of the NCAA from direct constitutional constraints did not end the debate about the obligations this organization owes to its constituents. After the original *Tarkanian* decision in 1977, Congress conducted a lengthy inquiry into NCAA enforcement procedures. The Report [10] threatened legislation unless the NCAA voluntarily improved its procedures (and in certain respects the Association did so). Following the Supreme Court's second *Tarkanian* ruling in 1988, a number of states (including Nebraska, Florida, Illinois, and, unsurprisingly, Nevada) passed legislation requiring the NCAA to comply with federal and state due process principles as a matter of statutory law.

The Nebraska and Nevada laws provide an interesting contrast in legislative approaches to this issue. Instead of specifying the procedures necessary to afford due process, the Nebraska legislation, passed in 1990, provides only that "all proceedings of a collegiate athletic association, college, or university that may result in the imposition of a penalty for violation of such association's rule or legislation shall comply with due process of law as guaranteed by the Constitution of Nebraska and laws of Nebraska." The procedures the NCAA must follow are to be derived from general Nebraska case law defining due process, which presumably is influenced by federal constitutional precedents such as *Mathews v. Eldridge*. That leaves open the key question, though, of whether the procedures appropriate for NCAA investigations are those used for administrative determination of welfare entitlements or those used by courts in resolving criminal charges. The Nebraska statute allows the parties to sue the NCAA for injunctive relief or damages, and makes NCAA decisions and penalties reviewable in state court like the decisions of state agencies.

In contrast, the Nevada legislation, passed in 1991, noted that "substantial monetary loss, serious disruption of athletic programs and significant damage to reputations and careers result from the imposition of sanctions on member institutions, its employees, [and] student-athletes ... for violations of [NCAA] rules." In an NCAA proceeding which results in the imposition of a sanction for violation of an NCAA rule, "all parties against whom a sanction may be imposed must be afforded an opportunity for a hearing after reasonable notice." The law also provides that 1) the NCAA must give detailed notice of the

---

9. For an extended journalistic critique of NCAA procedures, see Don Yaeger, *Undue Process: The NCAA's Injustice For All* (Champaign, Illinois: Sagamore Publishing, 1991). Contrasting scholarly views are presented by Frank Remington, NCAA Rule Enforcement Procedures, Chapter 12 of Gary Uberstine, ed., *Law of Professional and Amateur Sports*, (Deerfield, Illinois: Clark, Boardman, and Callaghan, 1991) (the author was a long-time member of the NCAA Committee on Infractions as well as

an eminent criminal law professor at Wisconsin Law School), and Burton F. Brody, *NCAA Rules and Their Enforcement: Not Spare the Rod and Spoil the Child; Rather Switch the Values and Spare the Sport*, 1982 Arizona St. L.J. 109.

10. *NCAA   Enforcement   Program*: Hearings Before the Subcomm. on Oversight and Investigation of the Comm. on Interstate and Foreign Commerce, House of Representatives, 95th Cong. (1978).

charge against the party; 2) the party charged with violating an NCAA rule may be represented by counsel and "is entitled to respond to all witnesses and evidence related to the allegations against him and may call witnesses on his own behalf"; 3) "all written statements introduced as evidence at a proceeding must be notarized and signed under oath by the person making the statement"; 4) a record must be kept of all the proceedings; 5) parties may make objections to evidence; 6) the adjudicator must be impartial and avoid ex parte communications with the parties; 7) "the decision and findings of fact must be based on substantial evidence in record, and must be supported by a preponderance of such evidence"; and 8) NCAA sanctions must be "reasonable in light of the nature and gravity of the violation" and "consistent with penalties and sanctions previously imposed" by the NCAA. Like the Nebraska statute, the Nevada legislation affords injunctive and damage remedies to those harmed by violations of these procedures, as well as affording judicial review of the merits of the NCAA decision.

Faced with these varying state limitations on its investigative procedures, the NCAA sought a federal court injunction barring Nevada's enforcement of its law in connection with the NCAA's ongoing investigation of UNLV's and Tarkanian's recruitment of Lloyd Daniels. The NCAA's constitutional challenge to the state law focused on the need for national uniformity in NCAA enforcement proceedings. In the summer of 1992, the Nevada district court entered an injunction against the state.

NCAA v. MILLER

United States District Court, District of Nevada, 1992.

795 F.Supp. 1476.

McKIBBEN, JUDGE.

The NCAA seeks an order of the court enjoining the application of Nev. Rev. Stat. §§ 398.155–398.255 [the Nevada statute] to an infractions case involving the NCAA, UNLV, Ronald Ganulin, Tim Grgurich, Jerry Tarkanian, and Shelley Fischer.

* * *

[NCAA] enforcement programs are administered by the NCAA Committee on Infractions. This committee supervises an investigative staff, makes factual determinations relating to any possible rules violations, and imposes appropriate penalties on member institutions found to be in violation of NCAA rules.

* * *

When allegations of a rule violation come to the attention of the NCAA enforcement staff, a notice of preliminary inquiry is delivered to the member institution involved. If, after investigation, the NCAA staff determines that a possible rule violation has occurred, the institution is advised and an official inquiry is commenced. The institution is requested to investigate the allegations, and the institution then reports its findings to the Committee on Infractions and suggests appropriate corrective action.

A pre-hearing conference is held with the institution, the affected individuals, and NCAA staff. At the pre-hearing conference, the NCAA staff is required to advise the parties of information it intends to use to support the allegations in the official inquiry before the committee, and the parties are permitted to review memoranda and documents relating to the alleged infractions prior to the official inquiry. The institution and the affected parties are permitted to appear at the official hearing before the Committee on Infractions. There, those involved may contest the allegations and present arguments and information to the committee. However, the NCAA has no power to issue subpoenas or to compel a witness to appear or give sworn testimony.

After the official hearing and private deliberation, the committee issues written findings of violations and recommends corrective action. The NCAA does not take corrective action against individual representatives or student athletes of the institution. Instead, the NCAA takes corrective action against the member institution itself.

Appeals may be taken from the committee's findings to the NCAA council. Finally, the NCAA rules provide for a further appeal to the full membership of the NCAA.

In this case, the NCAA received information of possible rule violations at UNLV and, on December 17, 1990, sent a notice of official inquiry to UNLV describing the possible violations. Between December 17, 1990, and April, 1991, the NCAA staff and UNLV conducted separate investigations of the UNLV intercollegiate basketball program. Witnesses were interviewed, information was exchanged, and documents were secured in preparation for the official hearing before the Committee on Infractions (which was set for September 27–29, 1991).

Meanwhile, on July 11, 1991, Defendants Tim Grgurich and Ron Ganulin, through written correspondence, demanded ... that the NCAA conduct the investigation and hearing in complete accord with [the Nevada statute]. On August 5, 1991, and August 15, 1991, respectively, Defendants Jerry Tarkanian and Shelley Fischer made similar written demands on the NCAA for compliance with the new Nevada law. . . . [Defendants'] demands included: (1) that at least thirty (30) days prior to the prehearing conference the NCAA give each defendant copies of all documents the NCAA intends to rely upon or use in any manner; (2) that each defendant be given the opportunity to confront all witnesses; (3) that the NCAA provide the defendants all exculpatory statements obtained by the NCAA; (4) that ... an independent and impartial entity be selected to adjudicate the facts and take corrective actions; (5) that all proceedings of the NCAA hearing be open to the public, recorded and transcribed; and (6) that all other provisions of [the Nevada statute] be complied with.

* * *

THE COMMERCE CLAUSE

The NCAA contends in count one of its complaint that [the Nevada statute] violates the Commerce Clause of the United States Constitution. Under Article I of the United States Constitution, Congress is granted the power "to regulate commerce ... among the several States...." Although the Commerce Clause is phrased as an affirmative grant of power to Congress, the Supreme Court has long recognized that "the Commerce Clause even without implementing legislation by Congress is a limitation upon the power of the States." This aspect of the Commerce Clause limits state interference with interstate commerce.

In this case, the threshold inquiry is whether the regulatory activities of the NCAA involve interstate commerce for purposes of Commerce Clause protection in light of the educational objectives of the NCAA. A principal purpose of the NCAA is to promote amateurism in intercollegiate athletics and to ensure that athletics are an integral part of the academic process through the cooperative and collective efforts of the member institutions. Yet, as the Fifth Circuit observed, "[w]hile the participating athletes may be amateurs, intercollegiate athletics in its management is clearly business, and big business at that." Hennessey v. NCAA, 564 F.2d 1136, 1150 (5th Cir.1977). The NCAA and its member institutions are "significantly involved in interstate commerce in the conduct of the athletic programs." The record before this court amply supports these conclusions.

* * *

The court must next consider whether the statute violates the Commerce Clause. In *Brown–Forman Distillers Corp. v. New York Liquor Auth.*, 476 U.S. 573 (1986), the Supreme Court, drawing from its earlier Commerce Clause decisions, articulated a two-tiered approach to be used when determining the validity of a state statute under the Commerce Clause. The Court instructed that "when the statute directly regulates or discriminates against interstate commerce, or when its effect is to favor in-state economic interests over out-of-state interests ... [the statute is] generally struck down ... without further inquiry." However, when "a statute has only indirect effects on interstate commerce and regulates evenhandedly, ... [the court examines] whether the State's interest is legitimate and whether the burden on interstate commerce clearly exceeds the local benefits."

Initially, therefore, the court must consider whether the Nevada law directly discriminates against interstate commerce or amounts to "economic protectionism." If so, the statute must be considered per se invalid under the Commerce Clause....

In this case [the Nevada statute] does not fit the Supreme Court's model of a state statute which is per se invalid under the Commerce Clause. The challenged statute seeks to impose certain minimum "due process" procedural standards on the NCAA when the NCAA is investigating a Nevada NCAA member institution. The statute does not facially or directly discriminate against interstate commerce, nor does it sound of economic protectionism. Further, the statute's effect on interstate commerce is only indirect; that is, it does not overtly thwart or block the NCAA's relationship with the Nevada member institutions or its relationship with member institutions in other states. Accordingly, the court concludes that [the Nevada statute] is not per se invalid under the Commerce Clause.

Next, the court turns to an analysis of the statute under the "balancing" approach. Under this approach the court must first identify the state's interests in its legislation, ensure that those interests are legitimate, and then determine whether the state law imposes an excessive burden on interstate commerce in relation to those legitimate interests.

... According to the defendants, the public purpose to be served by the enactment of the statute is to afford basic due process safeguards to the careers, livelihoods, and reputations of all Nevadans, including students and employees of Nevada NCAA member institutions, the alumni of these institutions, and the fans and boosters of Nevada intercollegiate sports. While these are narrowly tailored interests, they are, nevertheless, matters of legitimate local public interest. This conclusion, however, does not end the inquiry.

Even though a state statute addresses an area of legitimate state concern, it may still violate the Commerce Clause if it imposes an improper burden on interstate commerce. The state statute must not be "excessive in relation to the local interests served by the statute." Edgar v. MITE Corp., 457 U.S. 624, 643 (1982).

The NCAA persuasively argues that its ability to accomplish its goals of scholarship, sportsmanship, and amateurism depends to a substantial degree on the creation of nationally uniform rules under which teams can compete on an equal basis. In order to satisfactorily achieve these goals, the NCAA's enforcement procedures must be applied evenhandedly and uniformly on a national basis.

The Nevada statute, however, mandates procedures which are both substantially different from those contained in the NCAA bylaws and significantly burdensome on the NCAA's objective of maintaining a "level playing field" within intercollegiate athletics. For example, Section 398.155(2) of the statute provides that "[a] party to a proceeding ... is entitled to confront and respond to all witnesses and evidence related to the allegation against him...." Yet, the NCAA bylaws contain no comparable provision because the NCAA lacks subpoena power. Thus, since the NCAA does not have the ability to subpoena witnesses or otherwise require their cooperation, an infractions proceeding could not practicably be processed in compliance with the provisions of the Nevada statute.

In addition, [the Nevada statute] requires that the hearings be conducted by an "impartial" hearing officer. However, under existing NCAA rules, only the membership convened at conventions may authorize someone other than the Committee on Infractions to conduct an infractions hearing. Therefore, the NCAA would be unable to comply with this provision of the Nevada law absent membership approval at a convention.

Finally, [the Nevada statute] precludes the NCAA from expelling its Nevada institutions if those institutions refuse to comply with the provisions of the bylaws and constitution of the NCAA which are in conflict with the statute. This provision and similar provisions in other states would strip the NCAA of the authority to freely adopt its own procedural regulations. Because the NCAA enforcement proceedings would clearly be paralyzed by these procedural requirements, the NCAA would likely be reluctant to use its resources to enforce rules evenhandedly in the several venues in this country.

A statute's effect beyond the enacting state's borders is also relevant in balancing the affected interests. The court must closely scrutinize a statute which controls commerce outside its borders. An extraterritorial regulation exceeds the inherent limits of the enacting state's authority and is invalid regardless of whether the statute's extraterritorial reach was intended by the legislature....

Here, the extraterritorial effect of the Nevada statute is substantial. It severely restricts the NCAA from establishing uniform rules to govern and enforce interstate collegiate practices associated with intercollegiate athletics. The likely practical effect of the statute would be to compel the NCAA to adopt the procedural rules enacted by the Nevada Legislature, thereby allowing the Nevada Legislature to effectively dictate enforcement proceedings in states other than Nevada. Further, ... as the record reflects, a strong possibility exists that other states will adopt legislation inconsistent with the Nevada statute, thus precluding the NCAA from having a uniform rule and procedural basis for conducting its investigation and review of member institutions.[4]

While the concerns the Nevada law is designed to address are legitimate, and while similar concerns have been expressed by the

4. In South–Central Timber Dev., Inc. v. Wunnicke, 467 U.S. 82 (1984), the Supreme Court expressed its concern regarding a state statute which has extraterritorial reach:

Unrepresented interests will often bear the brunt of regulations imposed by one State having a significant effect on persons or operations in other States. Thus, "when the regulation is of such a character that its burden falls principally upon those without the state, legislative action is not likely to be subjected to those political restraints which are normally exerted on legislation where it affects adversely some interests within the state." On the other hand, when Congress acts, all segments of the country are represented, and there is significantly less danger that one State will be in a position to exploit others.

legislatures of other states,[5] any narrow interests the State of Nevada may have in imposing the requirements of [its statute] for the protection of institutions and individuals residing in Nevada is outweighed by the general harm to the uniform enforcement of regulations by the NCAA and its member institutions throughout the country. [The Nevada statute] effectively invalidates the NCAA's system of internal governance and enforcement and imposes procedural requirements with which the NCAA cannot comply.

* * *

Therefore, the court concludes that applying the provisions of [the Nevada statute] to the pending infractions case involving UNLV and the individual defendants violates Article I, Section 8, Clause 3 of the United States Constitution.

THE CONTRACT CLAUSE

The NCAA asserts [that the Nevada statute] substantially impairs existing contractual relations between itself and the Nevada member institutions in violation of the Contract Clause of Article I, Section 10 of the United States Constitution. The Contract Clause provides that "[n]o State shall ... pass any ... Law impairing the Obligation of Contracts...."

* * *

Analysis of a Contract Clause claim proceeds in two steps. First, the court must determine whether the state law "substantially impairs the contractual relationship." This inquiry involves three components: whether there is a contractual relationship; whether a change in law impairs that contractual relationship; and whether the impairment is substantial. If the impairment is minimal, the inquiry ends and the state law is allowed to stand.

Second, if the impairment is substantial, then the court must decide whether the degree of that impairment is both "reasonable and necessary to achieve a valid state interest."

* * *

[T]he record establishes that the NCAA and the Nevada NCAA member institutions have a contractual relationship sufficient to trigger review under the Contract Clause.

The court next turns to the question of whether [the Nevada statute] impairs the obligations under this contractual relationship and, if so, whether that impairment is substantial. Total destruction of

---

5. To date four states have enacted legislation directed to the NCAA enforcement proceedings. These states are Nebraska, Illinois, Florida, and Nevada. The states of Kansas, Ohio, Missouri, South Carolina, and Kentucky are considering similar legislation. In addition, the NCAA itself is taking steps to modify its procedural system of internal governance.

contractual expectations is not necessary for a finding of substantial impairment.

The primary purpose of the NCAA, as set forth in detail in the discussion of the Commerce Clause, is to promote amateur intercollegiate athletics and to ensure that intercollegiate competition takes place on a level and fair playing field. To achieve these goals, the NCAA has promulgated certain substantive rules and regulations relating to, among other things, recruiting, academic eligibility and rules of play. Every NCAA member has voluntarily and contractually agreed to abide by these rules and regulations. If all the members were not bound by these agreed upon rules and regulations, the effectiveness of the NCAA in attaining national uniformity in compliance with these rules and regulations would be severely restricted.

The defendants contend that the Nevada law does not modify or alter the substantive requirements that bind NCAA member institutions. The statute, instead, modifies the process by which the NCAA conducts investigations of alleged substantive violations by its membership by providing for certain "minimum" procedural standards.

However, the substantive effect of these statutory provisions is significant. Investigative and enforcement proceedings, followed by sanctions if warranted, are an important component in the NCAA's ongoing effort to foster fair play in intercollegiate athletics. Yet, as the record reflects, and as the court has discussed in depth under the Commerce Clause analysis, the NCAA cannot comply with certain procedures mandated by the statute in carrying out its investigations of alleged NCAA violations.... Thus, enforcement proceedings against Nevada member institutions are effectively precluded, or severely restricted, thereby allowing Nevada institutions to gain an unfair competitive advantage over other members. This result is both inconsistent with the core purpose of the NCAA and indirectly allows Nevada institutions to circumvent the central substantive requirements it contractually agreed to honor. In this court's view, the provisions of [the Nevada statute], when considered as a whole, substantially impair the contractual relationship between Nevada member institutions and the NCAA.

* * *

The burden ... is on the defendants to show that the contractual impairment was "necessary to achieve an important public purpose." The apparent purpose of the statute, as discussed above, is to afford basic due process safeguards to the careers, livelihoods, and reputations of all Nevadans which include students, alumni, and employees of UNR and UNLV, and the fans and boosters of Nevada intercollegiate sports. While the statute does represent a legitimate exercise of police power, its singular narrow purpose does not elevate it to the level of state laws necessary to protect the health and safety of the people.

* * *

[Moreover] in this case, the Nevada law does not attempt to alleviate a broad societal problem; it specifically targets the NCAA and directs the NCAA to treat Nevada member institutions differently than it treats the other member institutions in contravention of preexisting contractual agreements. The Nevada law's purpose is to adjust the rights and responsibilities of contracting parties. Further, the State of Nevada is attempting to enter a field it had never before sought to regulate; it attempts to bring about a permanent and significant alteration of the contract relationship of those entities within its coverage.

* * *

Accordingly, the court concludes that the Nevada legislation unconstitutionally impairs the contractual relationship which exists between the NCAA and its Nevada member institutions in violation of Article I, Section 10 of the United States Constitution.

* * *

CONCLUSION

Therefore, the court finds and concludes that the provisions of [the Nevada statute] violate Article I, Section 8, Clause 3 and Article I, Section 10 of the United States Constitution and are invalid and unenforceable against the NCAA.

* * *

Injunction granted.

———

Nevada has appealed the district court's decision to the Ninth Circuit and the Supreme Court may yet have another role in the saga of the NCAA and Jerry Tarkanian. If affirmed, this case will be the third time we have seen efforts to apply state law to a sports conflict frustrated by the "dormant" Commerce Clause, on the ground that applying state law would impermissibly impose one state's standards on an inherently nationally business. The other two cases were *Partee v. San Diego Chargers* (in Chapter 2), in which California antitrust law was held inapplicable to the NFL's player restraints, and *City of Oakland v. Oakland Raiders (II)* (in Chapter 6), in which the city was told it could not use California's eminent domain statute to take the Raiders NFL franchise.

A major Commerce Clause decision is *CTS Corp. v. Dynamics Corp. of Am.*, 481 U.S. 69, 107 S.Ct. 1637, 95 L.Ed.2d 67 (1987), which involved an Indiana law that regulated tender offers made for Indiana-chartered corporations, whether or not the offer came from in-state or out-of-state bidders. The Supreme Court upheld the Indiana law against the constitutional argument that the state had unduly interfered with the national securities market. Are there differences between the sports industry and the securities industry that might explain why the federal district court in *Miller* did not even cite *CTS Corp.*?

Questions for Discussion

1. Suppose that Nevada (following the lead of Montana) enacted a statute that forbade wrongful dismissal or suspension of employees working in the state, and specified in the law what kind of due process must be extended to employees before such disciplinary action was taken. Can such a law be applied to national corporations that have employees working in the state? Would the answer differ if the employer—perhaps a securities firm—belonged to a national association that required different procedures for employees suspected of specific offenses, such as fraud? Again, is there a difference between employment in sports and employment in other industries that is relevant to the issues of constitutional federalism?

2. In *Hill v. NCAA & Stanford University*, 7 Cal.App.4th 1738, 273 Cal.Rptr. 402 (6th Dist.1990), review granted, 276 Cal.Rptr. 319, 801 P.2d 1070, a California appellate court held that the NCAA's drug-testing program for student-athletes violated the right of privacy of students in California schools protected by that state's law. That ruling has now been appealed to the California Supreme Court. Irrespective of what is the proper interpretation of California's privacy law, does *Miller* imply that application of such a state law to an NCAA regulation is precluded by the dormant commerce clause? Might the answer differ if the targets of the testing program are performance-enhancing drugs such as anabolic steroids, or mind-altering drugs such as marijuana?

————

Although state efforts to regulate NCAA enforcement procedures may not be effective, former Rep. Tom McMillen introduced legislation in Congress that would require the NCAA to provide "due process" in all enforcement proceedings. Such national legislation would not be subject to dormant Commerce Clause (or probably Contract Clause) attack. Whether or not Congress ever passes such legislation, which at the moment seems unlikely, the McMillen bill raised both practical and policy questions about what role the law and courts should play in securing fair and effective "law" enforcement by a private body. In response to political and popular pressures, the NCAA appointed a blue-ribbon committee to review its procedures. The Special Committee, which was headed by Rex Lee (former U.S. Solicitor–General and the NCAA's counsel in the *Tarkanian* appeal before the Supreme Court) and included former Chief Justice Warren Burger, announced its recommendations in late 1991. As we will see, some of the proposals are being implemented.

————

These developments cast a somewhat different light on the question posed earlier about whether it is necessary to constitutionalize the NCAA to secure proper safeguards for its members. After all, why would the member-schools of the NCAA tolerate procedures that truly deny them "due process"? The answer, at least in part, lies in the regular scandals that afflict the world of college sports.

Two of the most widely publicized scandals from the 1980s produced litigation. One involved the football program at Southern Methodist University (SMU),[11] which was revived under the leadership of Ron Meyer (who, ironically, had previously been a coaching colleague of Jerry Tarkanian at UNLV). In order to recruit star high school prospects (such as Eric Dickerson who gave SMU the best five-year record in college football in the early 1980s), the SMU athletic staff and a cadre of Dallas boosters instituted a program of bonus payments to high school seniors to induce them to sign letters of intent to enroll at SMU. They also made regular monthly payments to SMU players and arranged for a Dallas dealership to provide expensive cars to star players. It was later learned that these expenditures had been authorized by William Clements during his tenure as Chairman of the SMU Board of Governors, between Clements' two terms as governor of Texas. As we will see in the next chapter, the NCAA's imposition of the "death penalty"[12] on SMU football produced an important antitrust challenge to the NCAA's authority.

Shortly after SMU's practices and penalties became public, the even more successful and prestigious Kentucky basketball program was literally enveloped in scandal.[13] Inside an Emery Delivery envelope addressed by Kentucky assistant coach Dwayne Casey to the father of Chris Mills, one of the nation's most heavily recruited basketball players in the spring of 1988, was found a basketball video tape—and $1,000 in cash. National publicity of this discovery by Emery's Los Angeles warehouse staff precipitated an NCAA investigation that also uncovered apparent cheating on the ACT college entrance examination by Eric Manuel, another star Kentucky recruit that year. Manuel, who scored only 3 (out of a possible 35) when he first took the ACT in his native Georgia, received an 18 the next time he took the test, in Kentucky. Investigation of the second answer sheet revealed that almost every one of Manuel's answers (right or wrong) were identical to those of another Kentucky student sitting behind him. Still another Kentucky recruit, Sean Kemp, was caught with jewelry that had been reported stolen from a teammate, Sean Sutton, son of Kentucky coach Eddie Sutton. Despite these and other unpleasantries, Kentucky bas-

11. See David Whitford, *A Payroll to Meet: A Story of Greed, Corruption and Football at SMU* (New York: MacMillan, 1989).

12. The "death penalty" rule allows the NCAA to terminate for two years a school's program in a sport in which a major rules violation is committed within five years of another major rules violation in any sport.

13. See Alexander Wolff & Armen Keteyian, *Raw Recruits: The High Stakes Game Colleges Play to Get Their Basketball Stars—And What It Costs to Win* (New York: Simon and Schuster, 1990).

ketball escaped the "death penalty" visited on SMU after the school fired its athletic director and coaching staff.[14] The new coach was Rick Pitino, who was wooed away from the NBA's New York Knicks of the NBA for a reported $6 million, seven-year contract.

The SMU and Kentucky cases are just the tip of the iceberg of what is taking place in big-time college sports. During the 1980s alone, more than half of the 105 Division 1–A schools received sanctions, many being put on probation and banned from postseason play.[15] The problem is not merely that schools violate the numerous technical requirements of a voluminous NCAA rulebook. In a 1989 survey of NFL players, one-third admitted that they had received cash payments while in college, and half said that they knew teammates who had received money under the table.[16] Coaches such as Bobby Knight of Indiana and Jerry Tarkanian publicly lament that top high school basketball prospects are offered financial packages of $100,000 or more to choose one school over its competitors. Even legitimate recruiting expenditures (such as departmental salaries and travel expenses) cost as much as $40,000 for each athlete who enrolls in the school. And Rick Pitino's compensation package at Kentucky puts him just slightly ahead of the earnings of college coaching luminaries such as Lou Holtz of Notre Dame and John Thompson of Georgetown. (These packages include not only salary, but also revenues from shoe contracts, radio and television shows, summer clinics, and speaking engagements across the country.)

Why are institutions prepared to expend this much money on sports—$10 million per year for the average Division 1 athletic program and $25 million for the largest? The explanation is complex. While many Division 1 programs apparently suffer a financial loss from athletic operations, the institutions retain the programs because of the tremendous marketing, public relations, and political benefits that athletics generate. However, there are limits on the amount that schools can afford to lose in subsidizing their "auxiliary" athletic programs, and the only way to limit those losses (or for some schools, to maximize their profits) is to have winning football and men's basketball teams that frequently appear on television and regularly fill their stadiums and arenas with paying fans.[17] In addition, the intangible public relations values of these programs are greatly increased when the school's teams are winning.

14. The assistant coach, Casey, sued Emery for its handling of the envelope and the money. The settlement of the suit, according to Casey, will keep him "comfortable for a long, long time." USA Today, Oct. 29, 1990, at 13C.

15. See Bayley & Littleton, *Athletics and Academe*, note 1 above, at 25.

16. See Sperber, *College Sports Inc.*, note 1 above, at 257.

17. To give just some sense of the potential rewards or losses from Division 1–A football alone, in 1989 the most successful programs earned net profits of around $10 million while the least successful lost nearly $2 million. In Division 1 basketball, the most profitable team earned $4.5 million, while the biggest loser was out approximately $600,000. See Raiborn, *Revenues and Expenses*, note 2 above, at 56–60.

Given the multi-million dollar differences between the winning and losing "revenue-sport" programs, as well as the intangible benefits from victory, institutions put great pressure on their coaches and athletic department personnel to win games. And because their careers, reputations, and chances for celebrity status are at stake, many coaches and others involved in athletics succumb to the temptation to bend or break the rules to attract the best athletes to their schools and keep them eligible once they are there.[18] This is why the NCAA decided after World War II that it would no longer rely on voluntary "home rule" adherence to the Association's principles. An enforcement staff of one employee in the early 1950s became three by the late 1960s and now consists of 15 full-time employees; the NCAA has even used ex-FBI agents as part-time investigators. The enforcement problem faced by the NCAA (and thence by courts and legislatures scrutinizing the NCAA) is that the targets of the NCAA rulebook are "crimes without victims"—consensual behavior that takes place in private and is very hard to detect and deter even for governments that can use compulsory investigative techniques unavailable to a private body such as the NCAA.

Almost all the cases in the next two sections were considered under the constitutional state action rubric since overruled by the Supreme Court in *Tarkanian*. The decisions still provide illuminating glimpses of some problematic issues presented to the NCAA and its reformers about how the Association does and should conduct its supervision of intercollegiate sports. This section examines NCAA procedures for enforcing its rules, and the next section explores the content of these rules. Having thus exposed the problems, we will then review the legal resources still available for addressing these problems.

BERST v. CHIPMAN

Supreme Court of Kansas, 1982.

232 Kan. 180, 653 P.2d 107.

SCHROEDER, CHIEF JUSTICE.

[This case involved an NCAA investigation of the recruiting of high school basketball star Bobby Lee Hurt by the University of Alabama. The Birmingham Post wrote a series of stories about the case (both before and after the NCAA investigation), stories that eventually produced libel suits against the Post by Hurt and his high school principal. The Post then sought to compel discovery of the NCAA's investigative files, which contained several off-the-record statements made to NCAA staff. The question posed to the court was whether there was a sufficient public interest in protecting the confidentiality of the

---

18. Nor should one think this is a recent phenomenon. The first intercollegiate sporting event was a Harvard–Yale rowing regatta in 1852. In the second such competition between these schools in 1855, Harvard included an ex-student in its crew. See Smith, *Sports and Freedom*, note 3 above, at 176.

NCAA's investigative reports to outweigh a private party's (ironically, a newpaper's) right to discovery in litigation.]

* * *

Whether the petitioners have a protectable interest in maintaining the confidentiality of their private investigation into possible infractions of NCAA rules undoubtedly presents a legal question of significant public interest. Substantially affected are the privacy interests of those persons to whom information in the file relates or who have passed on information to the NCAA under a pledge of confidentiality, as well as the NCAA's ability to perform one of its primary functions, that of policing its own ranks to prevent corruption in collegiate athletics.

* * *

Investigations by the NCAA of possible rules infractions are conducted in the strictest of confidence pursuant to internal rules of the NCAA. It is undisputed that investigators must rely on confidential sources for much of their information. Generally, any information an investigator comes across during his inquiries is placed in the NCAA's confidential file on that investigation. In any one of the NCAA's investigation files there may be allegations and speculation about an individual's sexual preferences, mental capacity, drug and alcohol use, and financial condition; academic records of students, anonymous letters and memoranda of telephone calls, and internal memoranda of interviews which contain the investigator's mental impressions, speculations, and conclusions.

* * *

The NCAA maintains that its policy of confidentiality has been central to the success of this self-policing system in effect for the past 30 years. The NCAA strongly argues loss of this confidentiality will destroy the system, causing intercollegiate athletics to suffer. Because of the extent of national interest and involvement in intercollegiate athletics, the NCAA asserts there is a strong public interest in preserving the means by which the NCAA can investigate and supervise the area of college level sports, which outweighs the petitioners' interest in obtaining the information sought for their defense in the libel action. Furthermore, the NCAA is concerned about potential harm to innocent persons not parties to the Alabama lawsuit, who either disclosed information contained in the file or about whom the information relates.

The subpoena duces tecum served on the NCAA, Smith and Berst required them to make available at their depositions: "[A]ll documents and correspondence relating to the initiation, prosecution and results of any investigation by the National Collegiate Athletic Association concerning Bobby Lee Hurt, Edward Seal, Butler High School, Huntsville,

Alabama or the recruiting of Bobby Lee Hurt by the University of Alabama."

* * *

[A] determination must be made whether, as petitioners argue, the interest in maintaining the confidentiality of the NCAA's file outweighs the interest and need of the Birmingham Post Company to discover these documents.

* * *

Where the parties have conflicting interests in material sought to be discovered, the protective power of the court may be sought by a party under this provision, and the court must balance the litigant's interest in obtaining the requested information with the resisting party's interest, as well as the public interest in maintaining the confidentiality of the material.

In balancing the interests involved herein it must be recognized the parties involved in the lawsuit have a great interest in the revelation of all pertinent facts. It is an oft-quoted doctrine that the public has a right to every man's evidence; there is a general duty to give what information one is capable of and any exemptions are exceptional, being in derogation of a positive general rule.

* * *

We recognize this case presents a conflict between highly valued interests. On the one hand there is an interest in confidentiality, both to prevent embarrassment to persons who have relied on pledges of secrecy in disclosing information to the NCAA or about whom information in the file may relate, and to promote the public interest in the supervision of intercollegiate athletics to prevent corruption in that area and retain a clear line of demarcation between college athletics and professional sports. On the other hand is the interest in disclosure of all facts relevant to the petitioners' defense in the libel action which will contribute to a full and fair determination of the issues in that case. This case presents a situation where a compromise solution must be reached which will sufficiently serve the interests of both parties.

* * *

Of the information contained in the NCAA's file which pertained to the litigants and the subject matter of the libel action, we required the disclosure of oral statements and comments of the litigants, their employers and fellow employees from Butler High School, made in person or by telephone to Dale Smith and reduced to written memoranda bearing the typed signature of Smith. These memoranda contain information directly relating to a central issue in the Alabama lawsuit, that of the truth or falsity of the information reported in the subject publications. . . . [E]ven a strong interest in confidentiality is outweighed when the information sought goes to the very essence, or "heart," of the issues in the case. This is the situation presented here. Therefore, while we recognize the interest in preserving the confidential nature of these memoranda is substantial, it must give way to assure all the facts will be available for a fair determination of the issues in the libel action.

* * *

Discovery ordered.

HERD, JUSTICE, dissenting.

When I weigh the conflicting interests in the material sought to be discovered, I come down on the side of protecting the public interest. The public has an overwhelming interest in fostering and supporting the self-regulation engaged in by the Colleges and Universities under the auspices of the NCAA. Television has injected such a large amount of money into college athletic programs the temptation to cheat in recruitment of athletes is overwhelming. In the absence of NCAA regulations and sanctions, the so-called "athlete factories" consisting of twenty to thirty major universities would outbid all others for talent, then pay for it with television exposure. Such would ring the death knell of college athletics as presently constituted. I consider the present system worth maintaining. This can be accomplished only through regulation, investigation and sanctions, either by the NCAA or the government.

Since the NCAA does not have subpoena power, its investigation of complaints is dependent upon a pledge of confidentiality. The majority opinion successfully removes that technique and will ultimately eliminate NCAA regulation or force it to obtain subpoena power. I prefer self-regulation to other options, therefore I dissent.

———

Although directly material NCAA records can usually be discovered in litigation, often subject to protective orders requiring litigants to keep their contents confidential, a more troubling prospect for the NCAA is that its investigative records (or those compiled by its conferences and member schools) might be published pursuant to state "freedom of information" laws that allow private parties (usually newspapers) access to most "public records." Such laws present two questions. First, are the NCAA's files "public records"? (A state institution's files almost surely are public.) See *Kneeland v. NCAA*, 850 F.2d 224 (5th Cir.1988) (holding NCAA and Southwest Conference documents compiled during investigations of the SMU "death penalty" case were not "public records" under the Texas Open Records Act). Second, if they are public records, does the state law provide any exceptions that allow these files to be kept confidential? See *Combined Communications Corp. of Oklahoma v. Boger*, 689 F.Supp. 1065 (W.D.Okla.1988) (holding that there is no public right of access to a state university's letter of intent under the First Amendment or the

Oklahoma Open Records Act). However these questions are resolved, the underlying policy issues are often the same for both freedom of information laws and discovery demands in the litigation. What impact would public disclosure of such records have on the ability of the NCAA or its members to investigate infractions?

Does the value placed by NCAA investigators on off-the-record tips help explain the procedures we saw used in *Tarkanian*? Is it justifiable for the NCAA to use such unattributed material in a hearing about alleged rules violation? The following provision from the NCAA Manual states the Association's present policy.

> 32.6.5.5.1 Information from Confidential Sources. In presenting information and evidence for consideration by the committee during an institutional hearing, the enforcement staff shall present only information that can be attributed to individuals who are willing to be identified. Information obtained from individuals not wishing to be identified shall not be relied upon by the committee in making findings of violations. Such confidential sources shall not be identified to either the Committee on Infractions or the institution.

Another issue relating to NCAA power has been the extent to which courts should protect the rights of student-athletes (and of coaches such as Tarkanian) against an organization whose only constituent members are colleges and universities.[19] It seems especially unfair, for example, when the NCAA sanctions an athletic program for violations that occurred several years earlier. As a result, student-athletes who had nothing to do with the infractions may lose their chance to compete in postseason games or on national television. This happened to the 1991–92 UNLV basketball team which was not allowed to play in the NCAA tournament because of rules violations committed fifteen years earlier, and to the SMU football team which received the "death penalty" for earlier rules violations.

In 1987 Hersey Hawkins and his Bradley University teammates sued the NCAA after it barred the team from the NCAA basketball tournament because of earlier school violations. The players asserted that imposing such a penalty on them was so fundamentally unfair that it violated the Equal Protection and Due Process Clauses of the Constitution. The district court dismissed the suit on the grounds that no fundamental rights were implicated and that the NCAA had a rational basis for imposing penalties on innocent players in order to maintain the integrity of intercollegiate athletics. See *Hawkins v. NCAA*, 652 F.Supp. 602 (C.D.Ill.1987). Today, presumably the suit would also be

---

19. For a critique of the historical exclusion of student-athletes from NCAA decision-making, see Rodney K. Smith, *The National Collegiate Athletic Association's* *Death Penalty: How Educators Punish Themselves and Others*, 62 Indiana L.J. 985, 1050–57 (1985).

dismissed pursuant to the *Tarkanian* decision because NCAA sanctions are not state action. However, the case raises the basic policy questions whether it is fair for student-athletes to be penalized for "crimes" committed by others, and if not, whether the NCAA could alter its enforcement procedures to avoid such unfairness while effectively enforcing its substantive rules.

Another question is what procedures the NCAA should provide to players or coaches accused of violations. The NCAA recently adopted procedural protections for individual students (and coaches) who may lose their eligibility to play (or coach) intercollegiate sports. For example, players and coaches have the right to be represented by legal counsel during an interview with NCAA investigators (Article 32.3.5) and to participate with counsel at Committee on Infractions hearings in which their eligibility (or employment) is at stake (Article 32.6.4). However, only staff members faced with disciplinary sanctions have the right of appeal to the NCAA Council; the university must exercise the right to appeal a denial of its student-athlete's eligibility (Article 32.8.3). Are these procedures sufficient? If not, what alternatives exist that would also provide effective enforcement of NCAA rules?

In 1991, a Special Committee appointed by the NCAA to review its investigative and adjudicative process recommended major changes in the Association's procedures.[20] The Committee suggested that the NCAA use retired judges to serve as hearing officers and to determine whether violations have occurred, based on taped transcripts of investigative interviews and legal arguments. The Committee on Infractions would no longer determine whether wrongdoing has in fact occurred, but would decide only whether to accept or alter the penalties recommended by the hearing officer. Jerry Tarkanian's reaction to the Committee Report was that his case "has been a catalyst for bringing this reform about. This is a magnificent day for those who want and expect fairness within the most powerful athletic body in the world."

Was Tarkanian right? Should the accused also have a right to confront and cross-examine witnesses who provide evidence to be used in this hearing process? If so, does the NCAA need a subpoena power to force recalcitrant witnesses to testify? Should the NCAA have that power, and if so, would that turn the Association back into a "state actor?" The crucial theme that runs through all these cases and questions is the extent to which expanded procedural rights for the targets of NCAA investigations are compatible with effective enforcement of NCAA rules regulating the billion-dollar world of intercollegiate sports.

---

20. See *Report and Recommendations of the Special Committee to Review the* *NCAA Enforcement and Infractions Process* (Overland Park, Kansas: NCAA, 1991).

C. ELIGIBILITY REQUIREMENTS

Reflection on that last question, the enforcement costs of due process, brings into focus the content and value of the rules which the NCAA is trying to enforce in the first place. The bulk of the NCAA's investigations and penalties involve promises made to players in recruiting and payments made or benefits received while they are at college. The NCAA deems these practices improper and "illegal" because they violate the basic principles stated earlier—that intercollegiate sports, unlike professional sports, are an integral part of the academic mission of the college, played by students for the love of the game (i.e., as "amateurs") rather than for pay. To define the meaning of a "student amateur athlete" takes several hundred pages in the NCAA Manual. The scandals at Southern Methodist University and the University of Kentucky epitomized the continual threat to the *amateur* quality of intercollegiate sports. A contemporaneous scandal at the University of Georgia revealed the sometimes dubious *academic* quality of this enterprise.[21] The case of *Kemp v. Ervin*, 651 F.Supp. 495 (N.D.Ga.1986), was a lawsuit by an instructor at Georgia who was fired for speaking out about practices used by the university to maintain its football players' academic eligibility.

Jan Kemp was the coordinating instructor of English in Georgia's Division of Developmental Studies, which provided remedial education to academically underqualified students to whom the school had granted special admission. Athletic director and football coach Vince Dooley regularly used this program for many of his recruits (sometimes twenty or more players in a single year); for example, Dooley's intervention resulted in Herschel Walker's admission via this program in 1980, a week *after* Walker had starred for Georgia in his first game as a supposed freshman playing against Tennessee. In December 1981, the school promoted nine football players out of the developmental program into regular academic studies in order to keep them eligible for the New Year's Day Sugar Bowl, even though all the players had received D's in remedial English and school policy required a grade of C to exit the remedial program.

Kemp, leading a protest by the Division's faculty, complained about the implications of this practice for the academic treatment of the school's black football players (more than 60% of the players in the program were black). Kemp attacked decisions made by her supervisor, Dr. Leroy Ervin, head of Developmental Studies, who was black, and Ervin's supervisor, Dr. Virginia Trotter, the University's Vice President of Academic Affairs (and former Undersecretary of Education for President Gerald Ford). After receiving Kemp's letter of protest, Ervin (with Trotter's support) removed Kemp from her position as English coordinator and then refused to renew her oral contract as an

---

21. See Francis X. Dealy, Jr., *Win At Any Cost: The Sellout of College Athletics*   78–95 (New York: Birch Lane Press, 1990).

instructor in the Division. Ervin apparently called Kemp "a liar and bigot" and asked her whether she thought she was more important to the school than a football player. Kemp, after attempting suicide, eventually sued and won a $2.6 million verdict against Ervin, Trotter, and the University of Georgia. Following the defendants' appeal, a settlement reduced the award to a $1 million cash payment and Kemp's reinstatement.

Kemp v. Ervin dramatically portrays the problem of maintaining the academic quality of intercollegiate sports. Widespread publicity about the scandal and litigation coincided with the NCAA's effort to enhance academic standards for both admission and progress at school. The NCAA's proposal in turn, produced heated controversy about the disparate impact of these new standards on black athletes. The following cases and notes provide a snapshot of the key NCAA judgments about who should be eligible to play in intercollegiate sports, and the practical problems and conflicts generated by these official judgments.

1. ADMISSION STANDARDS

NCAA rules specify the academic credentials required from athletes who graduate from high school and want to play in intercollegiate athletics. In the athletic setting, as in university admissions generally, a continuing struggle has been waged over the use of standardized admissions tests.[22] In 1964, the NCAA shifted from its traditional posture of university "home rule" in admission policies, and adopted a minimum standard for athletes of a *predicted* 1.6 grade point average (GPA) in college, based on their high school record and test scores. The debate about that rule surfaced in the following case involving Robert Parish, who two decades later was still the starting center for the Boston Celtics.

PARISH v. NCAA

United States District Court, Western District of Louisiana, 1973.

361 F.Supp. 1220.

DAWKINS, CHIEF JUDGE.

* * *

These student athletes had been recruited by Centenary College to play basketball on athletic scholarships. The primary plaintiff, Robert L. Parish, as later will be shown, probably was the most sought-after college basketball prospect in the nation at the end of his last high school year.

Plaintiffs request declaratory and injunctive relief against defendant to prevent NCAA from applying the "1.600 Rule" against them

22. For an account of the earlier debates, see Ron Waicukauski, *The Regula-* *tion of Academic Standards in Intercollegiate Athletics*, 1982 Arizona L. J. 79.

and declaring them ineligible to play on the Centenary basketball team. They seek injunctive relief against NCAA from applying its January 9, 1973 resolution, as it applies to Centenary and them insofar as it required Centenary to find them ineligible to play.

* * *

One of the specifically promulgated goals of NCAA is to insure that college athletes are an integral part of the student body of the college or university they attend. The by-law enacted to attain this objective was 4–6–(b)–(1), which is known as the 1.600 Rule. This by-law was amended at the NCAA annual convention January 13, 1973, by changing its requirement that a student predict a 1.600 grade-point average before being declared by his college or university to be eligible to participate in intercollegiate athletics. This requirement was that a student need only graduate from high school with a minimum 2.00 grade-point average (on a 4.00 level) in order to be declared eligible to participate in athletics.

* * *

Under the prediction tables, a student athlete's grade-point is predicted on the basis of a formula utilizing either high school grades or rank in high school class and a score on the Scholastic Aptitude Test (SAT) or the American College Test (ACT). It is quite apparent that one must score sufficiently high enough on either test to meet the minimum requirement of the 1.600 Rule.

* * *

Parish, 7′ 1″ in height, denominated a "super-athlete," was recognized during his last high school year by national magazines, newspapers, and sports columnists as probably the number one or number two leading basketball prospect in the United States, in the manner of Wilt Chamberlain and Lew Alcindor. He was named to several All–American high school teams and chosen by the Basketball News as the number one high school graduate basketball player in the country. Of course, he was recruited, even courted, by almost every major college in the nation.

In order to fulfill the requirements of NCAA's 1.600 Rule, Parish took the ACT twice, his score being an 8. Regrettably, before achieving such prominence, he had been somewhat deprived, both educationally and economically; and probably began to aspire ambitiously toward a full higher education only after "the baskets began to swish." With this score, most colleges "backed off" because they felt Parish could not meet the 1.600 requirement.

* * *

With these facts before us, we now turn to the recruitment of Robert Parish by Centenary. NCAA, knowing that he was going to be a highly recruited prospect, had familiarized itself with Parish's high school record before the summer of 1972, well prior to his being signed to an athletic scholarship contract by Centenary. During June of 1972, NCAA received information that Centenary was going to sign Parish, and one of its representatives, Berst, called then Coach Wallace and asked him how Parish was going to predict a 1.600 score. Wallace replied that the school was going to convert the ACT test score to an SAT score, whereupon Berst informed him this was prohibited by the rules. Subsequently, NCAA advised Centenary through its coaching staff and its Director of Athletics (who has "resigned" since the controversy arose), orally and by written correspondence, that the College could not convert ACT scores to SAT scores. As "water runs from a duck's back," so did these warnings fall on deaf ears and failed to prevent Centenary's Athletic Department successfully from proceeding with its efforts to sign Parish upon a scholarship contract.

The College signed Parish August 17, 1972, to a four-year athletic scholarship. It is interesting to note that Centenary's athletic agents-in-charge informed Parish that this scholarship award was made " . . . in accordance with the provisions of the Constitution of the National Collegiate Athletic Association, pertaining to the principles of amateurism, sound economic standards, and financial aid to student athletes."

Subsequently, Centenary informed NCAA that in taking such action it had converted test scores of other athletes at the school, i.e., the remaining plaintiffs in this action. It is worthy of note that, as stated, even by using the most favorable conversion table, as did Centenary, Parish still failed to predict 1.600. Ironically, he and all other plaintiffs have maintained a higher scholastic grade-point average throughout their respective college careers than required by the Rule.

* * *

Now, unfortunately, we have before us the single, not so simple, question of whether we should issue a preliminary injunction against defendants—a "Hobson's choice," which we do not relish at all, considering the empathy we hold for all of these competing interests: 1) the careers of these young athletes; 2) their present and future prospects; 3) the outstanding degree of culture contributed by the institution known as Centenary College, locally, regionally, and nationally, since well before the War Between the States; and finally, 4) the nationwide elevation of scholastic and athletic standards developed by NCAA for so many years.

* * *

Addressing the merits, even if this is a right or privilege protected by the Constitution, we hold that the 1.600 Rule withstands the denial of equal protection attack because it has a rational relationship to legitimate State (or national) purposes. Obviously, the challenged action by NCAA is not subject to strict judicial scrutiny. Therefore, we turn to the traditional standard of review which requires only that the NCAA's system be shown to bear some rational relationship to legitimate purposes. NCAA adopted the 1.600 Rule as a means of insuring that the athlete be an integral part of the student body and to maintain intercollegiate athletics as an integral part of the education program. Mr. Byars, of NCAA, summarized the need for these rules, as establishing a minimum standard which would prevent exploitation of athletes by the college or university, that is, setting up and agreeing to the prediction process by NCAA's members in order to prevent recruitment for athletic purposes alone of young men who had relatively poor chances of obtaining academic degrees; to encourage institutions with lower standards to elevate those standards to be more compatible with other institutions; and to discourage the unsound academic and economic practices of the past which had allowed indiscriminate granting of scholarships, resulting in too many athletes dropping out after their freshman or sophomore years. This rule was adopted to prevent abuses and at the time it was thought that this rule would solve the problem.

Notwithstanding, NCAA now has determined (since its action involving Centenary, Parish, and his teammates) that the rule was inadequate. This is based upon the fact that the 1.600 Rule was repealed and the 2.00 Rule was enacted in its stead. In Associated Students v. NCAA (May 25, 1973, Civil No. S–2754, E.D. Cal.), Judge McBride stated:

"Without deciding the question, it appears that this classification is reasonably related to the purposes of the 1.600 Rule."

However, he concluded that the 1.600 Rule, as interpreted by Official Interpretation 418 (O.I. 418) did not meet muster as to equal protection constitutional requirements. We agree that the 1.600 Rule's classification is reasonable, not arbitrary, and rests upon a ground having a fair and substantial relation to NCAA's object in enacting the legislation, so that all persons similarly circumstanced shall be treated alike, i.e., the Rule bears a rational relationship to the legitimate purposes for which it was enacted. Although application of the Rule may produce seemingly unreasonable results in certain situations, this is not unusual for use of generalized rules frequently produces irrational results in isolated circumstances. Such results do not condemn those rules under traditional equal protection scrutiny. Here, NCAA has advanced one step at a time, addressing itself to the phase of the problem which then seems most acute to it.

Plaintiffs also presented evidence to show that the SAT and ACT tests discriminated against all of them in some form. One (Parish) came from a minority group, one from a rural school, etc. This type of evidence was rejected as having no weight in Murray v. West Baton Rouge Parish School Board, 472 F.2d 438 (5th Cir.1973):

"Plaintiffs have made a broad-based attack on the use of psychological testing at Port Allen Elementary School. The focus of the attack appears to be that the tests are being used to discriminate against the black students. There is absolutely no evidence that the testing is being used to foster segregation in the class rooms, ... and despite conclusionary allegations to the contrary, there is no evidence whatsoever that the tests are being administered in a discriminatory manner. If, as plaintiffs claim, there are a few black students whose educational progress has been wrongly retarded because of this testing, it is most unfortunate. But as a federal court we cannot intervene absent some well defined constitutional deprivation. There is no factual showing that the tests are culturally biased, discriminatorily conceived, or even that they had a discriminatory effect. That the tests might not be an educationally valid one for a few individual children does not, in and of itself, give rise to constitutional deprivation. On the record before us, we can find no constitutional fault with the testing in the Port Allen Elementary School.

We take judicial notice of the fact that, at the time in question, the particular tests involved here under NCAA's Rule 1.600 were administered throughout the nation; almost every college in the United States required a score from one test or the other for admission purposes. We, therefore, must reject plaintiffs' claim as to this issue. We also note that members of the black race have been perhaps the greatest beneficiaries of numerically disproportionate participation in intercollegiate athletics; and they have done so under the aegis of the 1.600 Rule.

In *Associated Students*, supra, the Court stated:

* * *

Bearing in mind that the central purpose of the 1.600 Rule is to insure that the individual who participates in intercollegiate athletics is capable of succeeding academically at the college level, this new classification is overinclusive and not rationally related to the objective of the rule insofar as it declares ineligible not only those student athletes who fail to predict a minimum 1.600 grade point average and who have not yet completed their first year in college, and not only those student athletes who fail to achieve a minimum 1.600 grade point average for the first year in college, but additionally those student athletes who demonstrated by the conclusion of the first year that they have the ability to achieve academic success by actually earning at least a 1.600 grade point average. Once a student has an earned grade point average achieved over a reasonable period of time, then it is unreasonable, in light of the purposes of the rule, to impose sanctions against the student based on the fact that he failed to predict a certain grade point average. Instead, any sanctions imposed should be predicated on the actual grade point average attained by the student.

* * *

With this conclusion, we respectfully but regretfully disagree. It is our considered view that the Court in the just quoted decision overlooked the fact that one of the purposes of the official interpretation of the 1.600 Rule is to prevent schools from granting scholarships to those students who, after taking part in testing procedures, do not show a possibility of attaining a degree before entering college.

Under that decision, all member schools could recruit all those athletes whose entrance examinations did not predict successful graduation and then, if they did obtain a higher grade-point average than 1.600 after the first year in school, they would be entitled to participate in NCAA sponsored athletic events thenceforth. The Court's decision there effectively would prevent enforcement of the 1.600 Rule, which the Court already had determined to be rational in order to achieve NCAA's stated objective.

We cannot fathom how the official interpretation creates a classification which is in nonconformance with equal protection standards. In order to meet that objective, determination of eligibility must be made at the time of application and certification; to make it at a later date simply destroys the classification which the Court already had conceded to be reasonable. This decision in effect would allow colleges to recruit ineligible athletes and hope they will meet graduation prediction standards after their first year grades are in, thus becoming eligible for their entire collegiate athletic life. As stated, it is our considered opinion that NCAA's official interpretation of its 1.600 Rule does not create a classification which violates the equal protection requirements of the Constitution.

Case dismissed.

Note on Proposition 48

While the court's decision in favor of the NCAA was upheld on appeal (see *Parish v. NCAA*, 506 F.2d 1028 (5th Cir.1975)), the NCAA repealed the 1.600 Rule in the early 1970s and instead required scholarship athletes to have only a minimum 2.0 GPA from high school. After a decade of experience with that standard, the Association adopted Proposition 48 over vigorous opposition, especially from its black colleges.[23] Stated simply, Proposition 48 required at least a 2.00 high school GPA in an 11–course core curriculum and a minimum SAT score of 700 or ACT score of 15. (The NCAA statement of the rule in Article 14.3 is not at all simple, taking up ten pages in the Manual.) Among the cases epitomizing concerns at the time were Chris Washburn and John Williams who each had 470 SAT scores (400 is the score for writing one's name on the test), but were hotly recruited by more than 100 schools for their basketball prowess. Washburn enrolled at North Carolina State and Williams at Tulane, where the average SAT scores of the freshman classes were 1020 and 1120.[24]

23. See Funk, *Major Violation*, note 1 above, at 106–24, for a description and evaluation of Proposition 48. Interestingly, one major source of support for this new NCAA regulation was the University of Georgia and its fellow-members of the Southeastern Conference. Popular outrage about the Jan Kemp case had forced the SEC to adopt somewhat stiffer admissions requirements within the conference, and these schools naturally preferred to have their competitors around the country bound by the same standards in recruiting student-athletes for their teams.

24. See Sperber, *College Sports Inc.*, note 1 above, at 218.

Under the original version of Proposition 48 (incorporated in Article 14.3), the student-athlete who met either the minimum GPA or test score requirement but not both (the "partial qualifier") could still enroll in college on an athletic scholarship, but was not eligible to play for one year during which he had to demonstrate satisfactory academic progress in the college. Two early examples of partial qualifiers were Rumeal Robinson and Terry Mills, who both starred on Michigan's 1989 championship basketball team and went on to play in the NBA. In the late 1980s, the NCAA adopted an even more controversial version of the rule, Proposition 42. Proposition 42 barred colleges from giving financial aid to partial qualifiers during their freshman year. Proposition 42 drew even more vigorous criticism than Proposition 48 for its allegedly discriminatory impact on blacks. That protest movement, led by John Thompson at Georgetown University (but strongly opposed by Arthur Ashe), produced further amendment by Proposition 26, which makes Proposition 48 partial qualifiers eligible for non-athletic, need-based financial aid. All efforts to repeal Proposition 48 have, however, been overwhelmingly defeated.

Endorsing the proposals of the President's Commission, a key part of the NCAA's policy-making structure created in the mid–1980s, the Association in early 1992 further tightened up admissions standards for athletes by increasing the minimum high school GPA to 2.5 in a core curriculum of 13 specified courses. Athletes who had high test scores could have a lower GPA (for example, the minimum GPA for an athlete who scored 900 on the SAT is 2.00). However, the President's Commission successfully opposed the recommendation of the NCAA's Academic Requirements Committee to lower the test score requirement for athletes with high GPA's (to 650 on the SAT, for example, for a GPA of 3.00).

With that background, consider the arguments pro and con any flat NCAA rule telling colleges whom they can admit and whom they cannot admit to play on the college's team on a scholarship.[25] A rule based only on GPA in a core curriculum, or a rule involving only test scores, or a rule combining the two. A rule that fixes the minimum eligibility requirements at a specified percentage (such as 75%) of the average performance of a school's entire freshman class (this version would erect a much higher admission floor for athletes recruited by Duke than by UNLV). Should failure to meet the standard preclude athletic participation, athletic financial aid, or both? Would it be preferable to have a rule that denies eligibility to all freshman athletes, regardless of their high school GPA and SAT scores, and regardless of whether the student was at college on an athletic scholarship? In

25. For contrasting views of two prominent black scholars, see Linda S. Greene, *The New NCAA Rules of the Game: Academic Integrity or Racism?*, 28 St. Louis Univ. L.J. 101 (1984), and Harry Edwards, The Collegiate Athletic Arms Race: Origins and Implications of the "Rule 48" Controversy, in Richard Lapchick, ed., *Fractured Focus: Sport as a Reflection of Society* 21–43 (Lexington, Mass: D.C. Heath, 1986).

grappling with these questions, consider the relevance of the following data: [26]

1.   White students now average approximately 920 on the SAT, versus 740 for blacks (and 800 for Mexican–Americans and 940 for Asian–Americans).

2.   These differentials in SAT scores are slightly smaller among athletes—white athletes average 890 and black athletes average 740 (and 45 percent of black athletes fall below 700).

3.   Of freshman athletes who did not qualify under Proposition 48 in its first five years of operation, approximately 85% were black. Of these, approximately 85% were ineligible because they failed to meet the minimum SAT requirement (not the GPA requirement).

4.   Among student-athletes admitted to college in 1984 and 1985 (the years just before Proposition 48 went into effect), 52% of white and 27% of black athletes had graduated five years later. Of athletes admitted with SAT scores below 700, 2.5% of the whites and 10.8% of blacks graduated within that time frame.

5.   The percentage of blacks among scholarship athletes in NCAA schools dropped considerably in 1986 (from 24% to 17%), but has risen steadily since then to a point nearly as high as in 1985. There remains, however, a change in the distribution of black athletes under Proposition 48: more blacks in football and men's basketball and fewer in the non-revenue sports.

The racial disparities in SAT scores are not merely a policy problem for the NCAA. They also may pose a legal problem under civil rights law which itself has undergone a major transformation since the *Parish* litigation. A challenge to Proposition 48 might be lodged on both constitutional and civil rights statutory grounds. After *Tarkanian* the NCAA is not a state actor and thus is not subject to the Fourteenth Amendment. Suppose, however, that a constitutional challenge were aimed at state universities that adhere to Proposition 48. This scenario potentially raises the same legal questions as *Tarkanian*. Can the NCAA sanction a state institution for failing to follow NCAA admissions standards that might violate student-athletes' constitutional rights? If not, can the NCAA afford to enforce these minimum admission standards against only its private college members?

These questions are relevant, however, only if Proposition 48 constitutes discrimination in the constitutional sense. The major obstacle to such a finding is *Washington v. Davis*, 426 U.S. 229, 96 S.Ct. 2040, 48 L.Ed.2d 597 (1976), which requires *intentional* discrimination for a violation of constitutional equal protection violation. Could one argue that because NCAA members *knew* of the racial disparities in SAT

---

26. These data are drawn from the 1991 Report of the College Board (which administers the SAT), the series of reports by the American Institute for Research from its 1987–1988 *National Study of In-* *tercollegiate Athletics* (conducted for the NCAA's President's Commission and released in 1989), and another series of reports by the NCAA's own *Academic Performance Study* (released in 1991).

scores, and nonetheless adopted (and have since tightened up on) Proposition 48 over vehement objections from black colleges, that their action amounted to *intentional* discrimination? [27]

A second possible basis for a legal challenge to Proposition 48 is Title VI of the federal Civil Rights Act, which provides that "no person shall, on the grounds of race, color, or national origin, be excluded from participation in, be denied the benefit of, or be subjected to discrimination under any program receiving any federal financial assistance." [28] Under this federal *statutory* law, it is sufficient for a finding of illegal discrimination that use of SAT scores has had a disparate *impact* on blacks, regardless of whether these eligibility criteria were adopted for purposes of disparate *treatment* of blacks. See *Griggs v. Duke Power Co.*, 401 U.S. 424, 91 S.Ct. 849, 28 L.Ed.2d 158 (1971) (so interpreting Title VII, the employment part of the Civil Rights Act), and *Groves v. Alabama State Board of Education*, 776 F.Supp. 1518 (M.D.Ala.1991) (applying Title VII jurisprudence to a Title VI attack on minimum SAT scores for admission to a state teachers' college).

Once a plaintiff shows a disparate impact, the burden shifts to the defendant to justify continued use of the practice in question. For the last several years, there has been a heated legal and political debate about the nature and extent of the required justification, a debate that has been focused on *employment* practices of businesses that are challenged under Title VII of the Civil Rights Act. In its path-breaking *Griggs* decision in the 1970's, the Supreme Court said that the touchstone is "business necessity," and that the employer must "show that any given requirement [has] a manifest relationship to the employment in question," (401 U.S. at 432, 91 S.Ct. at 854). Nearly two decades later in, *Wards Cove Packing Co. v. Atonio*, 490 U.S. 642, 659, 109 S.Ct. 2115, 2125, 104 L.Ed.2d 733 (1989), the Rehnquist Supreme Court articulated a more relaxed "business justification" test, under which it was sufficient that "a challenged practice serves, in a significant way, the legitimate employment goals of the employer," rather than have to be demonstrably "essential to effective job performance," (as the Court had stated earlier in *Dothard v. Rawlinson*, 433 U.S. 321, 331, 97 S.Ct. 2720, 2728, 53 L.Ed.2d 786 (1977)). The *Wards Cove* decision sparked a two-year struggle between former President Bush and the Democratic

---

27. By the time of the 1992 NCAA convention when eligibility standards were raised, the informational base about the racial impact of these eligibility rules had been greatly expanded as a result of studies commissioned or done by the NCAA (see note 26 above). In particular, evidence from the pre-Proposition 48 cohort indicated that the higher requirements then being proposed would have excluded another 4% of white athletes and 6% of blacks.

28. In the mid–1980s there was a major legal and political controversy about whether Title VI covered only the immedi-

ate program or activity that received federal funding, or the entire institution that obtained such aid. In *Grove City College v. Bell*, 465 U.S. 555, 104 S.Ct. 1211, 79 L.Ed.2d 516 (1984), the U.S. Supreme Court opted for the former interpretation, but in 1988 the Congress overrode President Reagan's veto and enacted the Civil Rights Restoration Act which explicitly expanded the law's scope to include the institution as a whole. Thus, all colleges receiving federal financial assistance for any program (virtually every school receives some federal aid) are subject to Title VI.

Congress, which ended in 1991 when the President finally signed a new Civil Rights Act. In disparate impact cases the law now requires the defendant "to demonstrate that the challenged practice is job-related to the position in question and consistent with business necessity." Pub. L. No. 102–66 (codified at 42 U.S.C. § 1981) (1991).

In light of the historical evolution of disparate impact standards in Title VII employment cases, how should a court appraise the legality of the NCAA's Proposition 48 against a Title VI challenge? In particular, what is the appropriate reference point for determining whether there is a disparate impact in the first place? The proportion of black and white high school athletes who fail the minimum eligibility requirements, or the proportion of black and white athletes who secure college scholarships in any event? This question is crucial because the percentage of blacks among student-athletes in NCAA schools had returned by 1990 to close to where it was in 1985 before Proposition 48 came into effect. (As noted earlier, there is actually a slightly higher percentage of blacks in football and men's basketball, and a lower percentage in other sports. What does this tell us about the "market" for college athletes?) It appears, then, that the black athletes who fail to satisfy the minimum eligibility requirements of Proposition 48 are being replaced by other blacks who do pass these tests.

However, in a narrow 5–4 decision in *Connecticut v. Teal*, 457 U.S. 440, 102 S.Ct. 2525, 73 L.Ed.2d 130 (1982), the Supreme Court rejected such a "bottom line" defense to a Title VII lawsuit. The plaintiffs were black state employees who had failed in disproportionate numbers a preliminary test for promotion; the Court rejected the State of Connecticut's defense that its affirmative action program ensured that a proportionate number of black employees (though not the plaintiffs) were in fact promoted.[29] Does this ruling make sense, either as a general matter, or when you consider its possible application under Title VI to decisions made by educational institutions in the admission of student-athletes (or of all students for that matter)?

Assume for the sake of argument that Proposition 48 has had a "disparate impact" under the relevant legal criteria. The question then is whether the NCAA could establish that SAT scores are "related to the practice in question and consistent with [educational] necessity" (according to the new Civil Rights Act wording). Answering this question first requires value judgments about the nature and purpose of the athletic scholarship position for which SAT scores are used as a screening criterion. For example, is it relevant that noted black educators such as Harry Edwards of Berkeley and Henry Gates of Harvard have defended Proposition 48 as a motivator for high school athletes who do *not* secure college scholarships. It would also require careful empirical assessment of any available statistical data to deter-

29. See Martha Chamallas, *Evolving Conceptions of Equality Under Title XII: Disparate Impact and the Demise of the* *Bottom Line Principle*, 31 UCLA L. Rev. 305 (1983).

mine the correlation (if any) between the NCAA's minimum SAT scores and academic performance in college.[30]   Finally, one must consider whether, if it violates the Civil Rights Act for the NCAA and its members to establish minimum SAT scores for athletic scholarship eligibility, it would also be illegal for any college to use minimum test scores in its normal admissions process.

2. ACADEMIC PROGRESS

Even more important than initial admissions standards are rules designed to ensure that student-athletes successfully advance through the school's academic program and ultimately graduate.   Article 14.4 of the NCAA Manual spells out minimum course and GPA requirements that student-athletes must satisfy in making academic progress at college in order to maintain their eligibility to play.   The following case provides an unusual twist on this source of contention within major college sports.

HALL v. UNIVERSITY OF MINNESOTA

United States District Court, District of Minnesota, 1982.

530 F.Supp. 104.

LORD, CHIEF JUDGE.

[The plaintiff, a black senior on the Minnesota basketball team, was denied admission by college officials to the school's University Without Walls (UWW) program, the only "degree program" in which he had a reasonable chance to enroll.   The plaintiff needed to be enrolled in such a program to maintain his athletic eligibility and enhance his prospects in that year's NBA draft.]

* * *

This Court has no hesitation in stating that the underlying reason for the plaintiff's desire to be enrolled in a degree program at the defendant University is the enhancement of his chances of becoming a professional basketball player.   The plaintiff will probably never attain a degree should he be admitted to a degree program since the National Basketball Association draft occurs in April of 1982, well before the plaintiff could accumulate sufficient credits for a degree.   The plaintiff was a highly recruited basketball player out of high school who was recruited to come to the University of Minnesota to be a basketball player and not a scholar.   His academic record reflects that he has lived up to those expectations, as do the academic records of many of the athletes presented to this Court.

The plaintiff applied for admission to the UWW twice, once in August of 1981 and once in October of 1981.   In each case, the UWW

---

30. For preliminary evidence on this score, see American Institute for Research, *Academic Performance and College Sports:* *A Report Based on the 1987–88 National Study of Intercollegiate Athletes* (Palo Alto, Cal.: AIR, 1992).

admissions committee determined, based on the plaintiff's application, that he should be admitted to the UWW introductory program. In each case, the directors of the program (further up in the hierarchy of the UWW) intervened in the admissions process and effectively directed the admissions committee to reject plaintiff's application. This interference by the directors never occurred in any other case as to any other student.

Prior to the intervention of the directors, one of the UWW directors contacted Dean Lupton of the General College concerning the plaintiff. The director summarized the information conveyed by Dean Lupton in a confidential memorandum regarding the plaintiff. The memorandum noted that the following factors bore on the plaintiff's application:

1. The "political aspects" of admitting plaintiff;

2. Plaintiff's "substantial" travel record (one weekend trip to Chicago in fall quarter 1981);

3. The plaintiff had earned "A's" in courses he was not eligible to be in;

4. The General College had found it necessary to monitor plaintiff's work through a Professor Harris;

5. The plaintiff improperly turned in work on Regent's letterhead stationary;

6. The plaintiff turned in work done by others as his;

7. That every "W" (withdrawal) on plaintiff's transcript was originally an "N" (equivalent to an "F");

8. That within four weeks of the commencement of classes, plaintiff typically had earned a grade of "N"; and

9. That plaintiff had put through fake approval forms on more than one occasion.

* * *

This memorandum was passed on to a successor director who, after the plaintiff reapplied and was again accepted by the admissions committee, effectively vetoed the decision of the admissions committee.

* * *

It seems apparent that the plaintiff was not judged solely on the basis of his applications and the information therein. Each time the admissions committee reviewed the plaintiff's application, they recommended that he be admitted. After the intervention of the directors and the communication of the information outlined in the above-mentioned memorandum, the plaintiff was denied admission. However, in both of the rejection letters sent to the plaintiff, none of the allegations noted in the memorandum were listed as reasons for the plaintiff's failure to gain admission to the UWW.

* * *

A student's interest in attending a university is a property right protected by due process. The defendant asserts that while in cases of expulsion, public education may be a property right, in cases of nonadmission, public education is but a mere privilege. However, the right versus privilege distinction has long been abandoned in the area of due process. And in any event, even though the plaintiff was denied admission, the circumstances of this case make it more like an expulsion case than a non-admission case. The plaintiff lost existing scholarship rights; he cannot enroll in another college without sitting out one year of competition under athletic rules; and although he has attended the defendant University for several years, he may no longer register for day classes at the defendant University.

But to say that due process applies in the area of a student's interest in attending a university does not finish the analysis. One must answer the question of what process is due. "Due process is flexible and calls for such procedural protection as the particular situation demands." *Morrissey v. Brewer*, 408 U.S. 471, 481 (1972). Factors balanced to determine what process is due are: 1) the private interest affected by the action; 2) the risk of an erroneous deprivation of such interest through the procedures used and the value of additional procedural safeguards; and (3) the government's interest involved, including fiscal and administrative burdens.

The private interest at stake here, although ostensibly academic, is the plaintiff's ability to obtain a "no cut" contract with the National Basketball Association. The bachelor of arts, while a mark of achievement and distinction, does not in and of itself assure the applicant a means of earning a living. This applicant seems to recognize this and has opted to use his college career as a means of entry into professional sports as do many college athletes. His basketball career will be little affected by the absence or presence of a bachelor of arts degree. This plaintiff has put all of his "eggs" into the "basket" of professional basketball. The plaintiff would suffer a substantial loss if his career objectives were impaired.

The government's interest, i.e., the defendant University's interest, is the administrative burden of requiring a hearing or other due process safeguards for every rejection of every student who applies to the University. This burden would be tremendous and this Court would not require the defendant University to shoulder it.

The key factor in this case which weighs heavily in the plaintiff's favor is the risk of an erroneous deprivation given the nature of the proceedings used in processing the plaintiff's application. This Court is aware that in the area of academic decisions, judicial interference must be minimal. However, an academic decision is based upon established academic criteria. In this case, the plaintiff's applications to the UWW were treated very differently than all other applications. The directors intervened in the process and provided the admissions committee with allegations concerning the plaintiff's conduct, a facet of the proceedings that taints this "academic" process and turns it into something much like a disciplinary proceeding. Given this aspect of the proceedings, it would appear that the plaintiff should have at least been notified that allegations had been made regarding his conduct so that he could have presented evidence in his own behalf. Without this safeguard, there exists a chance that the plaintiff may have been wrongfully accused of actions which then form the basis for his rejection.

This is not to say that all applicants who are rejected by the defendant University must be given an opportunity to rebut evidence used in evaluating a college application; however, if the defendant University intends to interject evidence concerning allegations of improper conduct of the applicant into the admissions process, it must provide the applicant an opportunity to give his or her side of the story.

Finally, one must consider all that has occurred in light of the standards utilized by the Courts in this Circuit in evaluating the propriety of issuing a preliminary injunction. Four factors determine whether a preliminary injunction should issue. They are: (1) the threat of irreparable harm to the moving party, (2) the state of balance between that harm and the injury that granting the injunction will inflict on other parties, (3) the public interest, and (4) the probability that the movant will succeed on the merits of the claim.

With respect to the first factor, if the plaintiff is not eligible to play basketball by January 4, 1982, he will not play his senior year. This poses a substantial threat to his chances for a "no cut" contract in the National Basketball Association, according to his coach, and his overall aspirations regarding a career as a professional basketball player. It would be difficult indeed to measure the loss to the plaintiff in terms of dollars and cents. The injury is substantial and not really capable of an accurate monetary prediction. Thus, it would be irreparable.

The harm to the other parties, i.e., the defendant University, is difficult to assess. On the one hand, this Court doubts that the University men's intercollegiate varsity basketball team and coaching staff would characterize the reinstatement of the plaintiff to the team in terms of "harm." But the defendant University academic wing argues that if this Court orders the plaintiff into a degree program, its academic standards and integrity would be undermined. The plaintiff and his fellow athletes were never recruited on the basis of scholarship and it was never envisioned they would be on the Dean's List. Consequently we must view with some skepticism the defendant University's claim, regarding academic integrity. This Court is not saying that athletes are incapable of scholarship; however they are given little incentive to be scholars and few persons care how the student athlete performs academically, including many of the athletes themselves. The exceptionally talented student athlete is led to perceive the basketball, football, and other athletic programs as farm teams and proving grounds for professional sports leagues. It well may be true that a good academic program for the athlete is made virtually impossible by the demands of their sport at the college level. If this situation causes harm to the University, it is because they have fostered it and the institution rather than the individual should suffer the consequence.

It appears from the record that there is a "tug of war" going on over this plaintiff. The academicians are pulling toward higher standards of achievement for all students while the athletic department must tug in the direction of fielding teams who contribute to paying a substantial share of the university's budget. In this tug of war the academic department will suffer substantially no ill effects if it loses. On the other hand, the athletic department, directors, coaches and personnel under this system are charged with the responsibility of at least maintaining and fielding teams which are capable of competing with the best in their conference or in the nation. This Court is not called upon to determine any long term solution to the dilemma posed. It is called upon to determine if the rights of an individual caught up in the struggle have been violated.

* * *

Injunction granted.

Is the above the kind of message judges should send college administrators about student-athletes? Recalling the Jan Kemp case, how often do you think college officials are too rigorous in enforcing internal academic standards and thereby threatening a star athlete's eligibility?

Or is the case of Ronnie Harmon at the University of Iowa more representative? [31] Apparently Harmon maintained a 1.62 GPA at Iowa with help from courses such as billiards, soccer, bowling, and football coaching. To try to meet the minimum 1.85 GPA required by the Big Ten, Harmon took a summer school course in watercolor painting, but he received only a D. Yet Iowa ignored both Big Ten requirements and the NCAA rule that students must obtain course credits that demonstrate real progress toward a degree. What eventually cost Harmon his eligibility was his acceptance of cash advances from agents Norby Walters and Lloyd Bloom in return for signing a contract with them.

Consider also the case of Brent Fullwood, a star running back at Auburn University and another Walters and Bloom client whose litigation was depicted in Chapter 5. The NFL had Fullwood and other potential draft picks take the standard Wunderlic Personality Test of general verbal, mathematical, and spatial reasoning skills. On a scale

31. We saw Harmon earlier in Chapter 5, in a legal battle with his ill-starred agents, Norby Walters and Lloyd Bloom. A recent account of the entire Walters–Bloom affair, including the sorry academic performance of Harmon and many other clients of these agents, is Chris Mortenson, *Playing for Keeps: How One Man Kept the Mob from Sinking Its Hooks into Pro Football* (New York: Simon and Schuster, 1991).

that deems a person scoring 25 or higher as having "management potential," someone scoring 14 as qualified for a janitorial job, and someone scoring 10 as "functionally illiterate," Fullwood, who was enrolled for four years at Auburn, scored only a 9.

Faced with mounting criticism about such cases, the NCAA continues to refine and enforce its requirement that athletes make meaningful progress toward a legitimate degree in the institution. An offshoot of this NCAA effort has been a proliferation of "sports management" courses taught by members of the athletic department. That development, in turn, raises the question whether playing the sport should itself be considered a key component of a college degree program, presumably accompanied by a few academic courses. Before dismissing this option, compare the requirements for college degree programs in music, dance, the visual arts, and architecture. Why not allow students to major in football, or basketball, or in athletics generally? [32] What place should sports—in particular, *intercollegiate* sports—have in American college life? [33]

3. AGE AND EXPERIENCE

Having been admitted to and performed acceptably in the college's academic program, the student-athlete is permitted to participate in intercollegiate competition for no more than four seasons in any one sport (see Article 14.2). This eligibility period expires after five calendar years from first registration, with a variety of exceptions for the Peace Corps, church missions, pregnancy, and international sports competition (the Olympics and the Pan–American games). A special rule states that "any participation . . . in organized sports competition . . . after the student's 20th birthday and prior to full-time enrollment in a collegiate institution shall count as one year of varsity competition in that sport" (Article 14.2.5). The following case illustrates both the general rationale for the rule and the problems it can cause when put side by side with the NCAA's academic admission requirements.

32. In thinking about that issue, consider the implication of these two pieces of data. First, the odds of a high school athlete making a college team are approximately 1 in 16 in football and 1 in 40 in basketball, and the odds of college players going on to play for a professional team are just 1 in 75 in football and 1 in 70 in basketball. (These odds were calculated from 1989 figures presented in Bayley & Littleton, *Athletics and Academe*, note 1 above, at 84.) On the other hand, a study done by Clifford Adelman of the Office of Research of the U.S. Department of Education, *Light and Shadows on College Athletes: College Transcripts and Labor Market History* (1990), traced the experience of college athletes who did not go on to professional sports as part of a larger national cohort of the high school class of 1972. By 1986, when the class had reached the average age of 32, students who had played intercollegiate sports (including blacks) had fared significantly better in subsequent employment than had their non-athlete counterparts. In contrast, the students who had fared worst economically were performing arts majors.

33. See Robert Simon, *Fair Play: Sports, Values, and Society* (Westview Press: Boulder, Col. 1991), in particular, Chapter 4, Do Intercollegiate Sports Belong on Campus?; and Gregory M. Travalio, *Values and Schizophrenia in University Athletics*, 20 Capital Univ. L. Rev. 587 (1991), for thoughtful discussions of the last issue.

BUTTS v. NCAA & LASALLE UNIVERSITY

United States Court of Appeals, Third Circuit, 1984.

751 F.2d 609.

HIGGINBOTHAM, CIRCUIT JUDGE.

I

[Albert Butts, an outstanding high school basketball player in Philadelphia who had deficiencies in his academic record, spent both his senior year and an extra year enrolled in a private Virginia preparatory school (on scholarship). Butts' twentieth birthday took place during that second year. Having enrolled in and played for three years at LaSalle University, Butts sued to avoid the "competition after 20 rule;" he argued that the rule discriminated on account of both age and race. A district court judge refused to issue an injunction and Butts appealed.]

* * *

The district court concluded that appellant had shown a strong likelihood that the bylaw has a racially disparate impact, and thus that they could make out a prima facie case under § 2000d, but that the NCAA had advanced a legitimate, nondiscriminatory reason for the bylaw:

> [T]he bylaw is designed and intended to promote equality of competition among its members at each level so as to prevent college athletics and access to athletic scholarships from being dominated by more mature, older, more experienced players, and to discourage high school students from delaying their entrance into college in order to develop and mature their athletic skills.

The district court held that, in response to this justification, appellants had the burden of showing that it was pretextual or that "some other, less intrusive, rule would accomplish the stated objects of the present rule." The district court found that they had not shown a reasonable likelihood of being able to meet this burden. [In addition] the district court concluded that under relevant regulations, age combined with experience could be legitimately used as measures of the "maturity and level of athletic skill of the athlete."

II

Though there have been many changes since, in December of 1891, James Naismith first nailed two peach baskets to the balcony ten feet above the floor at the International Young Men's Christian Association Training School, now Springfield College, Springfield, Massachusetts, basketball is still the only major sport of strictly United States origin.[2]

---

2. An incident in a rugby contest convinced Naismith, as he later wrote, that "there might be more effective ways of doing good besides preaching." Thus, he decided to "drop the ministry and go into this other work."

The game was an almost instant success at the scholastic level. However, not surprisingly, it was the "acceptance by Yale in 1894 that induced other institutions to follow suit." In these early years the rules of the game varied greatly from institution to institution, with Cornell, for example, playing with 50 men per side. The first collegiate basketball game with five men on a side was played on March 20, 1897 between Yale University and the University of Pennsylvania. Approximately eight years after the first intercollegiate basketball game the NCAA was born and since then it has played an important role in the regulation of amateur collegiate sports. It had adopted and promulgated playing rules, standards of amateurism, standards for academic eligibility, regulations concerning recruitment of athletes, and rules governing the size of athletic squads and coaching staffs. During the eighty years since the NCAA's birth, collegiate basketball and the NCAA have grown as dominant institutions in America at a level which Naismith could never have contemplated when he invented this sport to appease the students at Springfield who were bored with "the Swedish, German and French forms of calisthenics of that period," and because he wanted to "fill the void that existed between football and baseball."

In this case we are confronted with a clash of many intensely felt interests. No one has captured the student-athlete's interests better than Professor Linda Greene in her seminal article, *The New NCAA Rules of the Game: Academic Integrity or Racism?*, 28 St. Louis U. L.J. 101, 137 (1984), where she wrote that "athletic activities are an important and integral facet of the educational process. In addition, participation in sports activities does bestow upon the athlete important psychological, social and physical benefits." Yet, as Professor Greene goes on to note:

> The substantiality of the interest increases at the college level. This is due in part to the economic stake of the student in certain important college sports. In addition, not only is the athlete often exchanging his prowess for an education, "the chance to display ... athletic prowess in college stadiums and arenas throughout the country [may be] worth more in economic terms than the chance to get a college education." Even if the college athlete does not reach the professional ranks, our sports-dominated culture often rewards outstanding college athletes in both tangible and intangible ways. Viewed from several different perspectives, the interests of athletes cannot be lightly disregarded.

When stripped of legal verbiage, the competing interests in this case are those of: (1) a talented young man who fervently desires to show his athletic prowess—not primarily for success in academia but for what could be the success on the highly remunerative courts of the National Basketball Association; (2) a distinguished college that would like to demonstrate its highest excellence on the basketball floor and thereby rise as close as it can to a local, regional or maybe even a national championship; and (3) a powerful collegiate association which, according to its brief, wants to thwart "professionalism" in college sports, "maintain intercollegiate athletics as an integral part of the educational process," and "ensure that athletes are representative of, and thus an integral part of, the student body as a whole."

Despite the exalted nomenclature which today's basketball aficionado might use in describing the college game, with its adroit "full-court press" defensive maneuver, or the exhilarating offensive "slam dunks," "high percentage shooters" from the outside, "good moves" to the basket, and players who can go "either way," we recognize that there is far more involved in this case than merely the joy of the sport. At stake are the size of Mr. Butts' future bank account,[3] the additional luster that could be added to LaSalle's legend of success in basketball, and the limits of the NCAA's power to curb "a persistent and perhaps inevitable desire to 'win at all costs,' " and prevent "a wide range of competitive excesses that prove harmful to students and institutions alike."

III

* * *

Mindful of our narrow scope of review, we have carefully considered the record, Judge Fullam's thoughtful memorandum opinion, and the briefs and arguments presented by counsel in this expedited appeal. We appreciate that all parties have advanced substantial factual and legal bases for their respective positions. Each party has indicated that it may wish to introduce additional evidence at trial on the merits. Thus, we do not now intimate any view of what the final disposition of Mr. Butts' and LaSalle's complaints should be. On the record as it stands, however, we cannot say that the district court abused its discretion, committed an obvious error in applying the law, or made a serious mistake in considering the proof.

Affirmed.

———————

Is the NCAA policy sound? Is a hands-off judicial posture appropriate? In thinking about this rule, recall the case of Andrew Gaze, a 23–year–old Australian who arrived at Seton Hall University in October 1988, enrolled in courses such as First Aid, Creative Motion, and Youth Activities, and then led Seton Hall to the 1989 NCAA champion-

3. At oral argument Mr. Butts' attorney claimed that:

This case is moot if we do not get our preliminary injunction. Mr. Butts and the testimony from the 76ers general manager was that he is definitely a pro prospect. He cannot play today, he cannot even be considered to play in the pros today and will not be considered unless he is screened by the pros this year. We put into evidence that he is considered by the pros in one of the top 75 . . . and will likely go, since he is there, in the first three rounds. Where he will go or whether he will go at all completely depends, based on that testimony, on the professional people seeing him this year. Twenty-seven games are to be played. Six have been played. He dies a little bit with each game he misses.

ship final game which they lost to Michigan (on a shot in the final seconds of overtime by Rumeal Robinson, Proposition 48's most notable partial qualifier). Immediately after that game, Gaze left for Australia to play for his father's professional basketball team in Melbourne.[34]

4. COLLEGE TRANSFER

The denouement of the massive recruiting campaigns conducted by colleges for star high school athletes is that on or after the national Letter–of–Intent day, the athlete commits himself in writing to one school, in return for which the school undertakes to provide financial aid. Once the student-athlete enrolls in the school, NCAA rules erect a significant hurdle to athletes choosing to transfer to other schools.[35] No athletic representative of another college may contact the student-athlete without permission from his current college (Article 13.1.1.3). Without such permission, no financial aid can be provided to a transferee until at least one year has passed. And even with permission from the first institution, the basic rule (in Article 14.6.1) is that a transferring student is ineligible to compete until after a full academic year in residence at the new school. (Recall that there is a maximum eligibility period of five calendar years.) The NCAA's transfer regulations take up another ten pages in its Manual. The following case concerns a student-athlete who thought he had found a loophole in these regulations.

ENGLISH v. NCAA

Court of Appeals of Louisiana, Fourth Circuit, 1983.

439 So.2d 1218.

Schott, Judge.

* * *

[Jon English, a highly rated high school quarterback, was recruited by and enrolled at Michigan State for the 1979–1980 school year. Realizing that his playing prospects at Michigan State were poor, English dropped out for a year to enroll at a junior college in Pittsburgh, the city where his father was an assistant college football coach. English then went to Iowa University, where he played in the fall seasons of 1981 and 1982. After having little success at Iowa, English spent the winter and spring of 1983 at a junior college in New Orleans, and then sought to enroll and play for Tulane in the fall of 1983, a school where his father was now head coach. English considered himself eligible because the NCAA rule at the time, as well as the summary of the rule in the NCAA Guide for the College–Bound Student–Athlete, referred to a year elapsing "since the transfer from

34. See Sperber, *College Sports Inc.,* note 1 above, at 235.

35. See Michael J. Cozzillio, *The Athletic Scholarship and the College National* *Letter of Intent: A Contract by Any Other Name,* 35 Wayne L. Rev. 1275 (1989).

the *first* four-year college." Having failed to persuade the NCAA of his position, English brought suit.]

* * *

Plaintiff's due process argument is based on the theory that the NCAA did not adequately inform him of the rules regarding his eligibility. He argues that the rule as quoted in the NCAA Guide literally entitled him to play ball with Tulane in 1983 because a year had elapsed since his transfer from the first four-year college, Michigan State, in 1980. Thus, he attacks the interpretation placed on the rule by William Hunt, head of the NCAA's Legislation and Enforcement Section, as being unreasonable in defining "first" to be the last four-year college. He argues further that the Guide's references to residence and semester hours completed at junior colleges further confuse the transfer rule and create further ambiguity. Finally, he rejects the notion that he would have sought further interpretation of the rule even if he had read the introduction because it was so clear to him that he was eligible.

The record does not support this argument. First, it is clear from the testimony of plaintiff's father, Coach English, that there was from the very beginning a question in plaintiff's mind about his eligibility notwithstanding the way he wanted to read the rule. He was plainly aware of the underlying and laudable policy of the NCAA to prevent a student from playing for two different colleges in successive years. Second, while he pretends to a sincere belief that the rule plainly declared him eligible, his first move after seeing the rule was to raise a question about it with his father who in turn raised questions about it with Petersen and Wall. He was squarely in the teeth of the Guide's introduction, i.e., he had questions about NCAA legislation, and was obliged to contact the NCAA national office for answers. But he failed to avail himself of this opportunity. Instead, he embarked on a course which he knew was perilous and preferred to take a chance that somehow his interpretation might be accepted by the NCAA.

It is well to note here that plaintiff was determined to play for his father at Tulane if at all possible. His prospects at Iowa State, as at Michigan State previously, were poor and not at all conducive to his being considered for a professional football contract upon his graduation from college. He explained that his skills as a quarterback could be best developed under the tutelage of his father who was a pass oriented coach. Since this would be his last year of college ball it was important for him to make the most of it. Only his interpretation of the transfer rule would make all of this possible.

We find Hunt's interpretation of the rule to be absolutely correct. The rule is dealing with a present college attempting to certify a player as eligible when he has played for a previous college. It contemplates two colleges, the first and the second. If one plays for a college one year he can't play for another college the next year. He must sit out for a year after playing for the first college. The rule does not and need not concern itself with the bizarre kind of a situation where one had played for yet a third college in the distant past. Reduced to its simplest terms a player may not jump from one college to another in successive years. We repeat that plaintiff on his own and again after speaking to his father was generally aware of the rule's meaning and while hoping to have found a loophole had questions about his theory.

* * *

There is no support in the record for plaintiff's contention that the NCAA was arbitrary, capricious, unfair, or discriminatory in dealing with his case. Had he inquired of the NCAA as to his plans before he left Iowa State he would have been told that he could not play at another college in 1983. Some 900 colleges belong to the NCAA and thousands of players abide by its rules. They do so voluntarily apparently convinced that constraints on their freedom to move about from college to college are a fair price to pay for protection against the evils which would emerge from untrammeled recruiting practices and uncontrolled pirating of players among the colleges. The word "arbitrary" connotes acting without reason or judgment, or determined by whim or caprice. "Capricious" is virtually synonomous. The record reflects that the NCAA, in adopting and implementing the transfer rule at issue here, acted quite reasonably in its efforts to prevent players from jumping from one school to another in successive years. Plaintiff was not dealt with unfairly. He was the victim only of his own plans and his own hope for special treatment. As to discrimination, Hunt testified that in all his years with the NCAA he never saw a case like plaintiff's and plaintiff failed to produce proof of any case like his which would provide a basis for his charge. He did show that some years ago the NCAA adopted the present rule to add the "first four-year college" language to close a loophole which previously existed and which enabled players to move from one four year college to another in successive years, but this is not plaintiff's situation and his charge of discrimination gets no support from these facts.

* * *

Appeal dismissed.

BARRY, JUSTICE, dissenting.

This case involves a very unique and isolated situation involving a very narrow question of interpretation of one word in an NCAA bylaw which may determine the eligibility for a student-athlete's last year of intercollegiate football competition.

* * *

[After reviewing the relevant materials and agreeing with English's reading of the rule, the dissent continued.]

The NCAA virtually controls football in over 900 colleges. Its purpose is to regulate sports programs and maintain the integrity of amateur athletics. Member schools must adhere to rigid rules or suffer severe sanctions. Considering the NCAA's enormous control (and its laudable purposes), it must also bear some burden to account for its heavy hand options.

Along with the NCAA's privileges goes the duty to provide clear and accurate information when disseminating its many rules and regulations. Jon English's interpretation of [the NCAA rule] was reasonable because the language is clear. His conclusion was supported by Mr. Wall. "First" still means "first," not "last," contrary to what Mr. Hunt would have us believe. What the NCAA intended, and what it published, were two different things. "Intent" is immaterial when the expression is unambiguous.

The majority's opinion is a Monday morning quarterback's opinion of what should be, but wasn't; what was intended, but not expressed. The NCAA goofed on the English language (no pun intended). Jon English relied on the NCAA bylaw and changed his position to his detriment. He was supported and encouraged in his belief by his more sophisticated superiors. Surely he has a right to protect his interests based on these extraordinary facts. That right should permit his eligibility [the NCAA rule].

––––––––

Consider how odd this NCAA rule would be if applied to restrict student participation in other extracurricular college activities. Would anyone have been concerned if Jon English wanted to be a reporter covering sports for the Tulane school newspaper or to participate in a college drama group? The historic reason why the NCAA adopted such strict controls on mobility for student-athletes was concern about the practice of "tramp athletes." One of the most highly publicized of these incidents occurred in the 1890s, when Fielding Yost, then a third-year law student at West Virginia, enrolled as a freshman at Lafayette on a Wednesday in order to help Lafayette's football team beat its arch-rival Pennsylvania that Saturday.[36] Yost then withdrew from Lafayette in time to return to West Virginia for classes on Monday. (He later became one of the most successful head coaches in college football history, at Michigan.) Today, the stated reason for retaining the rule is the fear that top athletes enrolled at one college will constantly be recruited by other schools. Once a student-athlete chooses a school and signs a letter of intent, the NCAA wants the student left alone to pursue his or her studies and sports without being wooed by other schools, with the possibility that the "tampering" schools will be tempted to offer improper inducements. Are these legitimate concerns that justify a transfer rule?

Consider also the breadth of the transfer rule. Is a two-year ban on eligibility without the consent of the "home team" university excessive? Or even a full one-year ban if the student-athlete transfers with

36. See Smith, *Sports and Freedom,* note 3 above, at 139.

his prior school's consent? How does such a restriction affect the treatment received by athletes from their current schools? Why is this two (or one) year hiatus on eligibility applied only to athletes in college football, basketball, and hockey? What should be the operation of the rule in cases where the program is put on NCAA probation? When a player's personal circumstances or relationship with the coach changes? When the head coach leaves a particular school, especially in the case of a student who has signed a letter of intent but not yet even enrolled at the school?

An argument occasionally made (although not officially by the NCAA) in favor of transfer restrictions is that they are necessary to preserve competitive balance among intercollegiate athletic programs. Others argue that, especially in football, allowing a talented substitute player to transfer to a school where he could be a starter would actually improve competitiveness in the college game. This is the same issue that has been at the heart of the debate about free agency in professional sports. Keep these transfer rules in mind for the next chapter, which focuses explicitly on college sports as an economic enterprise whose "labor market" some would like to subject to antitrust law and market competition.

Some have argued that the NCAA should make coaches live by the same transfer rules as students—namely, that unless the coach has completed five years at a school, he or she may not leave one institution for another without sitting out a year. What policy would be advanced by such a rule? What reasons exist for opposing such a rule?

D. JUDICIAL SCRUTINY OF INSTITUTIONAL DECISIONS

The next three cases evidence some awareness by courts of a judicial responsibility to take an independent look at decisions rendered inside the college athletic establishment. Recall, in this connection, the views expressed by the courts who were asked to review commissioner decisions about the best interests of baseball in the *Milwaukee, Finley, Turner,* and *Cubs* cases in Chapter 1.

GULF SOUTH CONFERENCE v. BOYD

Supreme Court of Alabama, 1979.

369 So.2d 553.

BEATTY, JUSTICE.

[The plaintiff, Boyd, entered Livingston University in the fall of 1975 under a one-year scholarship. At the end of the year, Boyd, then suffering from an asthmatic condition, refused Livingston's offer to renew his scholarship, dropped out of this school, and attended a junior college in his home town. Two years later, he wanted to attend and play football for Troy State, but the commissioner of the Gulf South Conference declared him ineligible. Boyd won a trial court ruling that the Commissioner had misinterpreted the Gulf South Conference rule that prohibited transfers except when "a GSC member does not renew the grant-in-aid of an eligible athlete" or when "a prospective student-athlete does not accept the grant-in-aid at that school" and sits out for two years. This appeal followed.]

* * *

The GSC contends that the lower court's order was erroneous for two reasons; the first being that the lower court was without jurisdiction to intervene in the internal affairs of the GSC.

[I]n Scott v. Kilpatrick, 237 So.2d 652 (1970), . . . [t]his Court held that participation in high school athletics was a privilege and not a property right. This Court further found that "[i]f officials of a school desire to associate with other schools and prescribe conditions of eligibility for students who are to become members of the school's athletic teams, and the member schools vest final enforcement of the association's rules in boards of control, then a court should not interfere in such internal operation of the affairs of the association." *Scott*, however, is distinguishable from the instant case.

Scott involved a high school athletic association while the present case involves a college athletic association. There is a vast difference between high school football and college football. A high school athlete receives no present economic benefit from playing high school football, his only economic benefit being the possibility of his receiving an offer of a college scholarship. The *Scott* case held that such a possibility was too speculative to recognize as a property right. In contrast, the college athlete receives a scholarship of substantial pecuniary value to engage in college sports. Such scholarships often cover the complete cost of attending a college or university; therefore, the right to be eligible to participate in college athletics cannot be viewed as a mere speculative interest, but is a property right of present economic value.

The contention by the GSC that the lower court did not have jurisdiction basically stems from a body of common law involving private associations. See Chaffee, *The Internal Affairs of Associations Not For Profit*, 43 Harv. L. Rev. 993 (1930). The general rule is that courts should not interfere with the internal management of such associations. The theory behind this non-interference doctrine is that the individual members of such associations have the freedom to choose their associates and the conditions of their association; further, it is argued, judicial review of the affairs of such associations would violate this basic principle of the freedom to associate. Still another justification asserted for the existence of the non-interference doctrine is that the rules and regulations upon which these associations operate are often unclear, and the courts would have no available standard upon which to determine the reasonableness of their rules. Even though we recognize the existence of this non-interference principle, nevertheless this Court has sanctioned judicial review when the actions of an association are the result of fraud, lack of jurisdiction, collusion, arbitrariness, or are in violation of or contravene any principle of public policy.

We hold that the general non-interference doctrine concerning voluntary associations does not apply to cases involving disputes between college athletes themselves and college athletic associations. There is a cogent reason for this position. In such cases the athlete himself is not even a member of the athletic association; therefore, the basic "freedom of association" principle behind the non-interference rule is not present. The athlete himself has no voice or bargaining power concerning the rules and regulations adopted by the athletic associations because he is not a member, yet he stands to be substantially affected, and even damaged, by an association ruling declaring him to be ineligible to participate in intercollegiate athletics. Thus he may be deprived of the property right eligibility to participate in intercollegiate athletics. While there is a split of authority on the question, we agree with the following statement of the Oklahoma Supreme Court:

> It is asserted by the NCAA that judicial scrutiny of the bylaw is inappropriate. Courts are normally reluctant to interfere with the internal affairs of voluntary membership associations, however, in particular situations, where the considerations of policy and justice are sufficiently compelling judicial scrutiny and relief are available.... The necessity of court action is apparent where the position of a voluntary association is so dominant in its field that the membership in a practical sense is not voluntary but economically necessary. It was proper for the trial court to examine the validity of the bylaw.

* * *

The defendant GSC also contends that the lower court's order was erroneous because it was contrary to the terms of the GSC transfer rule under the undisputed facts of this case. That contention is untenable. The evidence introduced in the lower court tends to show that Boyd was, in fact, eligible under two of the bylaws. GSC Bylaws, Article V, Section 3(C) states in effect that an athlete becomes a free agent and may be signed by any other GSC school if a GSC member school does not renew the grant-in-aid of that athlete. Here Boyd's one-year scholarship was not renewed because, although Livingston offered to renew it, Boyd did not accept that offer of renewal. Since there was no renewal of the scholarship, Boyd became a free agent and was free to sign with whatever school he chose. Livingston University was not obligated to renew or offer to renew Boyd's scholarship, and Boyd was not obligated to accept Livingston's offer. Both parties had performed their obligations to each other and neither party owed any further obligation to the other at the close of the 1975–1976 football season.

Boyd was also eligible under GSC Bylaw, Article VIII, Section 3, which states in pertinent part that "A prospective student-athlete who does not accept the grant-in-aid at that school nor participate becomes a free agent at the end of two (2) years and can be signed by any GSC school." Since Boyd's original scholarship with Livingston was effective only for the 1975–1976 football season, Boyd became a prospective student-athlete for Livingston at the end of his one-year scholarship. Because he did not accept Livingston's offer, did not attend school at Livingston, and did not play football for two years, he became a free agent. The lower court was therefore correct in ruling that Boyd was eligible to play football at Troy State University for the 1978–1979 football season since the 1978 football season occurred at the end of two years after Boyd's refusal to accept the second grant-in-aid offered by Livingston University.

It should be noted that the relationship between a college athlete who accepts an athletic scholarship and the college which awards such an athletic scholarship is contractual in nature. The college athlete agrees to participate in a sport at the college, and the college in return agrees to give assistance to the athlete. The athlete also agrees to be bound by the rules and regulations adopted by the college concerning the financial assistance. Most of these rules and regulations are promulgated by athletic associations whose membership is composed of the individual colleges. The individual athlete has no voice or participation in the formulation or interpretation of these rules and regulations governing his scholarship, even though these materially control his conduct on and off the field. Thus in some circumstances the college athlete may be placed in an unequal bargaining position. The GSC's interpretation of the bylaws in question was that a student football athlete who transfers from one GSC school to another will not be eligible to participate in football at the second school unless the first school drops football or unless the first school does not merely offer to renew the grant-in-aid scholarship of the student-athlete. The lower court rejected this interpretation and, as we have shown, that decision was correct. Accordingly, let the judgment be affirmed.

Judgment affirmed.

————

California courts expressed a similar sentiment in the following case, which dealt with the NCAA's suspension of a school from postseason play because the school had adopted a different interpretation of the minimum test score requirement at issue in the *Parish* case.

CALIFORNIA STATE UNIVERSITY, HAYWARD v. NCAA

Court of Appeals of California, First District, 1975.

47 Cal.App.3d 533, 121 Cal.Rptr. 85.

BRAY, ASSOCIATE JUSTICE.

Defendant NCAA contends that the trial court erred in failing to follow the doctrine of judicial abstention from interference in the affairs of a private voluntary association. However, courts will intervene in the internal affairs of associations where the action by the association is in violation of its own bylaws or constitution.

* * *

In the instant case plaintiffs' complaint alleges that the NCAA decision, that the entire intercollegiate program at CSUH is indefinitely ineligible for post-season competition, is contrary to the NCAA constitution and bylaws, and that the decision is void as against public policy because it would force CSUH to violate constitutional rights of its students guaranteed by the Fourteenth Amendment. The trial court has not yet finally adjudicated these claims but plaintiffs are entitled to have the matter determined.

Defendant NCAA asserts that as a matter of law no interest of any member of the NCAA is sufficiently substantial to justify judicial intervention because the interest affected by the sanction in question is the school's potential participation in NCAA championship events, an interest which is a mere expectancy as it is contingent upon performance during the season. The NCAA claims that California courts have only intervened when a vital interest was affected, such as where a member was expelled from a union, where a professional or trade organization's actions threatened disastrous economic consequences to a member, where substantial property interests were threatened by expulsion from an association, or where someone was totally excluded from becoming a member of a group.

As to the latter point, the court took a position contrary to appellant's in Bernstein v. Alameda Med. Assn., 139 Cal.App.2d 241, 253, when it found that the California Supreme Court had implied:

> that in relation to this subject there is no fundamental distinction between a medical association, a labor union and a fraternal or beneficial association. In each type of organization the relationship between the members and the group is determined by contract, the terms of which find expression in the constitution and bylaws.

Likewise there can be no fundamental distinction between an athletic association and the above associations where, as here, the claim is that the association failed to abide by its own rules or the laws of the land.

As to the claim that CSUH's interest is not sufficiently substantial to justify judicial intervention due to a mere expectancy of participation in championship events, it has already been discussed that a violation by an association of its own bylaws and constitution or of the laws of the land justifies judicial intervention. Further, that CSUH had, and has, more than a mere expectancy that some of its athletes would earn the opportunity to participate in NCAA championship events but for the suspension is evidenced by the fact that at the time of both the hearing on the temporary restraining order and the hearing on the preliminary injunction, there were upcoming NCAA championship events in which CSUH students, without the imposed suspension, were eligible to compete. Additionally, the decision of the NCAA necessarily affects more than just the possibility of being precluded from championship events. The sanction of indefinite probation affects the reputation of CSUH and its entire athletic program, and thereby also affects CSUH's ability to recruit athletes. Judicial notice may be taken that state schools such as CSUH are deeply involved in fielding and promoting athletic teams with concurrent expenditures of time, energy and resources. The school provides and pays for the coaches, supplies and equipment. It finances, equips, trains and fields the teams. And, its funds pay the NCAA membership dues. The contention that CSUH has no substantial interest to justify judicial intervention lacks merit.

* * *

The NCAA also claims that plaintiffs do not contend that the procedural process followed by the NCAA in imposing sanctions on CSUH was not full and fair, and asserts:

> While insisting that voluntary non-profit associations follow their own procedures in disciplining their members, courts have refused to disturb the association's decision when there was no procedural unfairness and the proceedings conformed to the requirements established by the group.

As already discussed the courts will intervene where the action by the association is in violation of its own bylaws and constitution. That this rule applies to substantive as well as procedural questions is supported by cases which appellant itself cites.... NCAA also asserts that judicial intervention in this type of case is undesirable and raises a number of policy arguments to that effect. Because it is clear that courts will intervene if an association violates its own rules or the laws of the land, these arguments have no weight.

Plaintiffs have raised sufficient questions as to whether the NCAA has violated its own rules or the laws of the land by its action to justify intervention by the trial court to determine these questions.

Affirmed.

Despite the sentiments expressed in *Boyd* and *Hayward*, there are limits to the protections athletes (or coaches) can secure through judicial interpretation of NCAA rules. The reason is that even if the

NCAA loses a particular case (or even if the Association feels insecure with victories in cases such as *English*), the NCAA can simply rewrite the rules to make them crystal-clear in support of the same policy. For example, Article 11.2 of the NCAA Manual requires that all contractual agreements or appointments for coaching staffs stipulate that coaches found in violation of NCAA regulations are subject to discipline pursuant to NCAA enforcement procedures, including suspension without pay and even dismissal for "deliberate and serious violations."

Therefore, enduring protections for individuals can be secured only through legal tools that establish binding rights and obligations that cannot be altered during the next NCAA convention. Even after *Tarkanian*, in which the Supreme Court removed federal constitutional scrutiny of the NCAA, there remain several such tools. The next case exemplifies the use of tort litigation in a situation that vividly evokes the academic concerns about the world of big-time college sports.

ROSS v. CREIGHTON UNIV.

United States District Court, Northern District of Illinois, 1990.

740 F.Supp. 1319.

NORDBERG, DISTRICT JUDGE.

One day in July 1987, Kevin Ross, a former college basketball player, barricaded himself in a high-rise hotel room in downtown Chicago and threw assorted pieces of furniture out the window. As Ross currently recalls it, the defenestrated furniture "symbolized" the employees of Creighton University, whose alleged misdeeds he blames for the onset of this "major depressive episode." Ross now sues the university in contract and tort. The gist of Ross's Amended Complaint is that Creighton caused this episode and otherwise injured him by recruiting him to attend the school on a basketball scholarship while knowing that Ross, who scored 9 points out of a possible 36 on the American College Test, was pitifully unprepared to attend Creighton, which is a private school whose average student in the year Ross matriculated, 1978, scored 23.2 points on the ACT.

COMPLAINT

Ross, who is 6 feet and 9 inches tall, was a high school basketball star in Kansas City, Kansas, when Creighton recruited him. Creighton knew that Ross could not handle college-level studies, but kept him eligible for the basketball team by recommending that he enroll in "bonehead" (Ross's description) courses, such as ceramics, marksmanship, and the respective theories of basketball, track and field, and football. Under its rules, the university would not have accepted the pursuit of this esoteric curriculum by a non-athlete. After four years, when his basketball eligibility expired, Ross had earned only 96 of the 128 credits required to graduate, maintaining a "D" average. His reading skills were those of a seventh-grader; his overall language skills, those of a fourth-grader.

In order to get Ross remedial education, representatives of Creighton made arrangements for Ross to attend Chicago's Westside Preparatory School, an elementary and high school whose founder, Marva Collins, has drawn national attention for her abilities as an educator. As its name suggests, Westside Prep is a school for children, not for adults. Ross says that Creighton representatives made four trips to Chicago to discuss Ross's enrollment. The agreement to enroll Ross is spelled out in a letter dated July 29, 1982, from Collins to Creighton's athletic director. The letter, countersigned by a Creighton official and returned to Collins, obligated Creighton to pay for Ross's tuition, special tutoring, books and living expenses. Ross attended Westside in 1982 and 1983. He later attended Roosevelt University, also located in Chicago, but dropped out after 1985 for want of money. Ross's furniture-throwing outburst took place on July 23, 1987. He was arrested and ordered to make restitution in the amount of $7,500.

* * *

Ross's Tort Claim

... Ross says [his tort] claim is a hybrid of "negligent infliction of emotional distress" and "educational malpractice." These strands of tort law "intertwine" to form the novel tort of "negligence in recruiting and repeatedly re-enrolling an athlete utterly incapable—without substantial tutoring and other support—of performing the academic work required to make educational progress," exacerbated by the enrollment of plaintiff in a school with children half his age and size. Before considering the merits of this tort, the Court must unravel its separate threads.

Educational malpractice is a tort theory beloved of commentators, but not of courts. While often proposed as a remedy for those who think themselves wronged by educators (see, e.g., J. Elson, *A Common Law Remedy for the Educational Harms Caused by Incompetent or Careless Teaching*, 73 Nw.U.L.Rev. 641 (1978)), educational malpractice has been repeatedly rejected by the American courts.

* * *

Whether to create a cause of action for educational malpractice is, of course, a question for the Court, which determines as a matter of law whether a duty runs from defendant to plaintiff. It is a matter of considering sound social policy, guided by looking to " '[t]he likelihood of injury, the magnitude of the burden of guarding against it and the consequences of placing that burden upon defendant.' "

* * *

This Court believes the same general concerns would lead the Illinois courts to reject the tort of educational malpractice. Admittedly, the term "educational malpractice" has a seductive ring to it; after all, if doctors, lawyers, accountants and other professionals can be held liable for failing to exercise due care, why can't teachers? The answer is that the nature of education radically differs from other professions. Education is an intensely collaborative process, requiring the interaction of student with teacher. A good student can learn from a poor teacher; a poor student can close his mind to a good teacher. Without effort by a student, he cannot be educated. Good teaching methods may vary with the needs of the individual student. In other professions, by contrast, client cooperation is far less important; given a modicum of cooperation, a competent professional in other fields can control the results obtained. But in education, the ultimate responsibility for success remains always with the student. Both the process and the result are subjective, and proof or disproof extremely difficult.

* * *

It also must be remembered that education is a service rendered on an immensely greater scale than other professional services. If every failed student could seek tort damages against any teacher, administrator and school he feels may have shortchanged him at some point in his education, the courts could be deluged and schools shut down. The Court believes that Illinois courts would avert the flood and the educational loss. This is not to say that the mere worry that litigation will increase justifies a court's refusal to remedy a wrong; it is to say that the real danger of an unrestrained multiplication of lawsuits shows the disutility of the proposed remedy. If poor education (or student laziness) is to be corrected, a common law action for negligence is not a practical means of going about it.

* * *

[Having rejected both the general tort of educational malpractice and Ross' claim for negligent infliction of emotional distress, the court then asked does Ross] nonetheless have a cause of action that is sui generis? Ross argues that he does, contending that "the present case is so unique and egregious that, despite the lack of precedent, a cause of action should be found to exist." Ross basically argues that a special tort be created for the benefit of student athletes, or more precisely, for the benefit of student athletes whose academic performance would not have qualified them to be students had they not been athletes. In Ross's view, "The present case does not question classroom methodology or the competence of instruction. Rather the issue is whether Plaintiff should ever have been admitted to Creighton and whether, once admitted, Creighton had a duty to truly educate Plaintiff and not simply to maintain his eligibility for basketball...."

Ross's inability to plead a cause of action under existing law strongly counsels against creating a new cause of action in his favor. Rules serve little purpose if they are not reasonably predictable and if they do not apply across the board, for one cannot conform behavior to the unknowable. See A. Scalia, *The Rule of Law as a Law of Rules*, 56 U.Chi.L.Rev. 1175, 1178–79 (1989). Even a new rule declared through the evolutionary process of the common law ought fairly be deduced from existing doctrine—something that cannot be said for Ross's claim. The policy reasons considered by the Illinois courts further counsel against recognition of this new duty. Schools would be forced to undertake the delphic science of diagnosing the mental condition of potential recruits. And why should the cause of action be limited to student athletes? Shouldn't all students who actually pay tuition also have an equal right to recover if they are negligently admitted, and once negligently admitted, have a right to recover if the school negligently counsels and educates them? To allow Ross to recover might redress a wrong (assuming, for sake of argument, that he was in fact exploited), but it would also endanger the admissions prospects of thousands of marginal students, as schools scrambled to factor into their admissions calculations whether a potentially "negligent admission" now could cost unforeseeable tort damages later. The Court should not and will not craft a new tort for Ross.

[On appeal, the Seventh Circuit Court of Appeals upheld the summary dismissal of Ross' tort theory of educational malpractice, but took a somewhat different view of Ross' contract claim.]

ROSS v. CREIGHTON UNIV.

United States Court of Appeals, Seventh Circuit, 1992.

957 F.2d 410.

RIPPLE, CIRCUIT JUDGE.

* * *

It is held generally in the United States that the "basic legal relation between a student and a private university or college is contractual in nature. The catalogues, bulletins, circulars, and regulations of the institution made available to the matriculant become a part of the contract." Indeed, there seems to be "no dissent" from this proposition. As the district court correctly noted, Illinois recognizes that the relationship between a student and an educational institution is, in some of its aspects, contractual. It is quite clear, however, that Illinois would not recognize all aspects of a university-student relationship as subject to remedy through a contract action. "A contract between a private institution and a student confers duties upon both parties which cannot be arbitrarily disregarded and may be judicially enforced." However, "a decision of the school authorities relating to the academic qualification of the students will not be reviewed.... Courts are not qualified to pass an opinion as to the attainments of a student ... and ... courts will not review a decision of the school authorities relating to academic qualifications of the students."

There is no question, we believe, that Illinois would adhere to the great weight of authority and bar any attempt to repackage an educational malpractice claim as a contract claim. As several courts have noted, the policy concerns that preclude a cause of action for educational malpractice apply with equal force to bar a breach of contract claim attacking the general quality of an education. "Where the essence of the complaint is that the school breached its agreement by failing to provide an effective education, the court is again asked to evaluate the course of instruction ... [and] is similarly called upon to review the soundness of the method of teaching that has been adopted by an educational institution."

To state a claim for breach of contract, the plaintiff must do more than simply allege that the education was not good enough. Instead, he must point to an identifiable contractual promise that the defendant failed to honor. Thus, ... if the defendant took tuition money and then provided no education, or alternately, promised a set number of hours of instruction and then failed to deliver, a breach of contract action may be available. See *Zumbrun*, 101 Cal.Rptr. 499 (1972) (breach of contract action allowed against university when professor declined to give lectures and final exam, and all students received a grade of "B"). Similarly, a breach of contract action might exist if a student enrolled in a course explicitly promising instruction that would qualify him as a journeyman, but in which the fundamentals necessary to attain that skill were not even presented. In these cases, the essence of the plaintiff's complaint would not be that the institution failed to perform adequately a promised educational service, but rather that it failed to perform that service at all. Ruling on this issue would not require an inquiry into the nuances of educational processes and theories, but rather an objective assessment of whether the institution made a good faith effort to perform on its promise.

We read Mr. Ross' complaint to allege more than a failure of the University to provide him with an education of a certain quality. Rather, he alleges that the University knew that he was not qualified academically to participate in its curriculum. Nevertheless, it made a specific promise that he would be able to participate in a meaningful way in that program because it would provide certain specific services to him. Finally, he alleges that the University breached its promise by reneging on its commitment to provide those services and, consequently, effectively cutting him off from any participation in and benefit from the University's academic program. To adjudicate such a claim, the court would not be required to determine whether Creighton had breached its contract with Mr. Ross by providing deficient academic services. Rather, its inquiry would be limited to whether the University had provided any real access to its academic curriculum at all.

Accordingly, we must disagree respectfully with our colleague in the district court as to whether the contract counts of the complaint can be dismissed at the pleadings stage. In our view, the allegations of the complaint are sufficient to warrant further proceedings. We emphasize, however, the narrow ground of our disagreement. We agree—indeed we emphasize—that courts should not "take on the job of supervising the relationship between colleges and student-athletes or creating in effect a new relationship between them." We also recognize a formal university-student contract is rarely employed and, consequently, "the general nature and terms of the agreement are usually implied, with specific terms to be found in the university bulletin and other publications; custom and usages can also become specific terms by implication." Nevertheless, we believe that the district court can adjudicate Mr. Ross' specific and narrow claim that he was barred from any participation in and benefit from the University's academic program without second-guessing the professional judgment of the University faculty on academic matters.

Affirmed in part, remanded in part.

Questions for Discussion

1. If courts are unwilling to allow tort claims by student-athletes, and prepared to accept contract claims only for explicit and specific promises, how will future scholarship agreements be worded? Should courts allow suits for breach of alleged verbal promises (for example, by recruiters) that are not contained in the written agreement?

2. Can one distinguish between a university's legal and educational obligations to the general student body [37] and its obligations to student-athletes, especially those on athletic scholarships in revenue-producing football and basketball? In what legal direction should the factual differences incline courts? [38]

3. From reading this case, earlier cases, and the general media, are you comfortable with the judicial conclusion in *Ross* that supervision of educational quality is best left to the NCAA "which presumably possesses the staff and expertise to carry out the job"?

———

Congress has not been prepared to place full reliance on the NCAA. Over the NCAA's opposition, a Student–Athlete Right–to–Know Act was enacted in 1990 (Pub. Law 101–542, Title I, §§ 102, 104 (Nov. 8, 1990) (codified at 20 U.S.C. § 1092(e) (1991)). This Act, which was propelled through the Congress by Senator Bill Bradley and Representative Tom McMillan, two former basketball All–Americans and Rhodes Scholars, requires the Department of Education to assemble and publish comparative athlete graduation rates at different colleges. With this bill pending, the NCAA adopted a similar regulation of its own (Articles 13.3 and 30.1), under which this data will be collected and distilled into a form that will be given to athletes and their families.

In the fall of 1992, the NCAA published its Report on *1991–92 NCAA Division 1 Graduation Rates*, which offers a statistical perspective on the educational problem to which these measures are addressed.

---

37. See John G. Culhane, *Reinvigorating Educational Malpractice Claims: A Representational Focus*, 67 Washington L. Rev. 349 (1992).

38. As to athletes, see Timothy Davis, *Examining Educational Malpractice Jurisprudence: Should a Cause of Action Be Created for Student Athletes?* 69 Denver U. L. Rev. 57 (1992).

Of all freshman athletes enrolled in Division 1 colleges in the fall of 1984, 52% had graduated from that college by the spring of 1991—a rate just slightly less than the 53% of all freshmen who enrolled in those colleges in the fall of 1984, but considerably less than the 75% graduation rate for students who attended college full-time for five consecutive years (as do almost all scholarship athletes). The graduation rate of male athletes, 47%, was much lower than that of female athletes, 62%. An even greater disparity was found between the graduating rates of white and black athletes, which were 59% and 35% respectively. Unsurprisingly, the trouble spots were the revenue-producing sports of football (46% overall, 56% for whites and 34% for blacks), and men's basketball (38% overall, 53% for whites and 29% for blacks).[39]

The foregoing figures capsulize the record of Division 1 schools taken as a whole. The several hundred pages of the NCAA Report are principally devoted to recording the situation at each school. Unsurprisingly, graduation records of individual colleges vary dramatically above and below the Division 1 average. For example, the University of Houston graduated a dismal 14% of its football players and zero percent of its men's basketball players.

Is publication and distribution of comparative graduation data across sports and colleges likely to improve the educational situation disclosed above? Should schools also be required to provide data regarding the odds of a college athlete going on to a professional sports career (see note 32 above) with a view to motivating student-athletes to work at least as hard in the classroom as on the field? Is development by both Congress and the NCAA of such a database for "informed consent" by college applicants (and their parents) a sufficient answer to those who advocate educational malpractice suits by athletes such as Kevin Ross? (Would informed consent preclude patients suing hospitals for medical malpractice? See *Tunkl v. Regents of the Univ. of California*, 60 Cal.2d 92, 32 Cal.Rptr. 33, 383 P.2d 441 (1963).)

Consider yet another possible solution, designed to provide even stronger institutional incentives than publication of graduation rates. Suppose that the NCAA abolished all its mandatory rules regarding

---

39. The NCAA Report also sets out "refined" figures that exclude student-athletes "who did not graduate within six years but were either in good academic standing when they left the institution, or were still in school at the beginning of the seventh year" (p.4). These refinements served to raise the overall athlete graduation rate to 68%, without materially altering its internal distribution by gender, race, and sport. Because the NCAA Report did not make the same adjustments in all-student graduation rates, these higher "refined" numbers are not useful in comparing the academic performance of athletes and non-athletes.

Indeed, even if we did have the comparative data, using such "refined" rates is troublesome because of questions about why a student-athlete leaves the institution in good academic standing. If students who leave are not counted in calculating graduation rates, coaches do not face at least this disincentive not to renew scholarships or otherwise force athletes to leave school when they are doing well academically, but not playing as well as someone else the coach wants to recruit with his limited number of scholarships.

which athletes can be admitted to college and how they must progress academically while at school. Instead, athletes would take a standardized test (such as the GRE test) when they finish their third (or fourth) year. If the athlete received at least a certain minimum score on this test of knowledge and skill acquired while at college, the school would be entitled to offer a scholarship to his replacement. If, however, the athlete failed (or refused to take) the test, the college would lose one of its scholarships in that sport for the next four years. How might this regime influence relations between the athletic and the academic departments in the university?

———

In March 1991, the Report of the Knight Foundation's blue-ribbon Commission on Intercollegiate Athletics was issued—*Keeping Faith with the Student–Athlete: A New Model for Intercollegiate Athletics.* The following passage captures the Commission's model for reforming college sports:

> The reform we seek takes shape around what the Commission calls the "one-plus-three" model. It consists of the "one"—presidential control—directed toward the "three"—academic integrity, financial integrity and accountability through certification. This model is fully consistent with the university as a context for vigorous and exciting intercollegiate competition. It also serves to bond athletics to the purposes of the university in a way that provides a new framework for their conduct.

You have now been exposed to a variety of materials about the problems of academic integrity and due process in college sports. Has this chapter left you confident that we can entrust responsibility for these issues to college presidents? Are there parallels with the questions posed earlier about the role of commissioners in determining the "best interests" of professional sports? These questions may be even more urgent when we confront in the next chapter the problem of financial integrity in the increasingly commercialized world of intercollegiate athletics.

Chapter Nine

INTERCOLLEGIATE SPORTS: COMMERCIALISM AND AMATEURISM

The previous chapter traced the tension between the NCAA's efforts to foster academic values in intercollegiate sports and the interests of students and coaches who are affected by the definition and enforcement of NCAA rules. This chapter considers the even starker conflict between the amateur ideal and the commercial reality of big-time college sports, and explores the availability of antitrust, antidiscrimination, and other legal regimes to parties who dislike the balances struck by the NCAA.[1]

In Chapter 8 we mentioned the large sums of money being generated by and spent on college sports in the 1990s; perhaps the most remarkable figure is the *billion*-dollar, seven-year television contract for the NCAA's men's basketball tournament. Just twenty-five years ago the television rights for this tournament earned a mere $190,000, and as late as 1981 the television rights were sold for $9 million per year. During the 1980s total sports revenues reached $22 million for one school (in 1989) and an average of nearly $10 million apiece for the 106 Division 1–A schools.[2] Division 1 (1–A in football) consists of schools with large programs in football and men's basketball, which earn almost all the direct athletic revenues for their schools—an average of approximately $6 million between the two sports apiece for

1. Besides the works cited in the opening footnote of the previous chapter, see Nand Hart–Nibbing & Clement Cottingham, *The Political Economy of College Sports*, (Lexington, Mass.: D.C. Heath, 1986); Paul R. Lawrence, *Unsportsmanlike Conduct: The National Collegiate Athletic Association and the Business of College Football* (New York: Praeger, 1987); Arthur A. Fleisher III, Brian L. Goff & Robert D. Tollison, *The National Collegiate Athletic Association: A Study in Cartel Behavior* (Chicago: Univ. of Chicago Press, 1992); Richard B. McKenzie & E. Thomas Sullivan, *Does the NCAA Exploit College Athletes? An Economics and Legal Interpretation*, Antitrust Bulletin 373 (Summer 1987).

2. The figures in this and the next paragraph are drawn from Mitchell H. Raiborn, *Revenues and Expenses of Intercollegiate Athletics Programs: Analysis of Financial Trends and Relationships, 1985–1989* (Kansas: NCAA, 1990).

the Division 1–A schools in 1989, compared to a total of $350,000 per school from all the other men's and women's sports combined. The University of Washington generated as much as $15 million in revenue and $10 million in profits from football alone, and other schools earned nearly $10 million in revenues and $5 million in profits from men's basketball.

Unfortunately for NCAA members, though, accompanying these expanding revenues has been a corresponding escalation in expenditures on intercollegiate sports. Though the big-time programs earn the lion's share of sports revenues, the average Division 1–A school ended with only a tiny surplus of $39,000 from athletics. The average balance sheet for schools in all other NCAA Divisions showed a deficit; for example, the typical school in Division 1–AA lost $800,000 on sports. Indeed, while football and men's basketball usually produce profits for their schools, even in these two sports many of the larger universities have experienced substantial deficits in recent years. When one includes expenditures on sports that produce little or no revenue on their own, more than one-third of Division 1–A schools reported an athletic deficit in 1989, ranging as high as $4 million at Auburn University.[3]

The foregoing financial figures produce an obvious interest on the part of schools in the NCAA's stated principle regarding "Economy of Athletics Program Operation":

> Intercollegiate athletics programs shall be administered in keeping with prudent management and fiscal practices to assure the financial stability necessary for providing student-athletes with adequate opportunities for athletic competition as an integral part of a quality educational experience.

(Article 2.13)

A host of NCAA rules are designed to implement this policy, as well as the principle of "Competitive Equity" which "assures that individual student-athletes in institutions would not be prevented unfairly from

3. These are the financial figures reflected in university accounts and reported to the NCAA. Tracking and calculating surpluses or deficits from college sports is a difficult exercise because there is no firm consensus about what revenues or expenditures are properly attributable to a school's athletic program. How much of the university's general overhead—ranging from the president's office to the library to campus security—should be allocated to athletics? What is the true cost to a college of admitting a scholarship athlete into its classes and its housing and eating facilities, and will this cost tend to be more or less than the tuition and room and board fees charged to ordinary students (the latter being the figure depicted as the sports expenditure in university accounts)? How much of the revenues from game concessions, souvenirs, and alumni donations should be credited to the athletic department? There is considerable disparity in the accounting methods and judgments used by different schools with respect to these and a host of other questions posed in this area. The limited amount of in-depth scholarly investigation of the institutions' books finds that schools tend to understate significantly the revenues and correspondingly overstate the expenses from sports: see Fleisher, et al., *The NCAA: A Study in Cartel Behavior*, note 1 above, at 73–94. This empirical finding accords with the expectations of economists that people in charge of any non-profit enterprise will minimize book profits from their programs. What is the likely source of that non-profit managerial incentive? If valid, what are its implications for the world of college sports?

achieving the benefits inherent in participation in intercollegiate athletics" (Article 2.7). The most important such NCAA rules set out to define who is an "amateur" eligible to compete in college sports, and to ban receipt by student-athletes of any extra benefits beyond those permitted by the rules. The first part of this chapter completes our presentation of the main components of the NCAA Manual, with selected cases illustrating the rules in operation. We then turn to the various legal approaches that have been used to challenge these NCAA policies, not only by players and coaches, but also by the fans whose patronage (either at the gate or on television) finances our large college sports establishment.

A. NCAA ELIGIBILITY RULES

1. PAY BEFORE COLLEGE

A key "general principle" (stated at the outset of Article 12) that underlies much NCAA regulation is that "only an amateur student-athlete is eligible for intercollegiate participation in a particular sport," so as to "maintain a clear line of demarcation between college athletics and professional sports." Article 12 goes on to provide that an athlete "loses amateur status and thus shall not be eligible for intercollegiate competition" in a number of specified ways—for example, by payment "in any form for the sport" or "a promise of pay even if such pay is to be received following completion of intercollegiate athletic competition."

A perennial problem faced by the NCAA concerns hockey players from Canada, many of whom play major Junior A hockey under Canadian Amateur Hockey Association (CAHA) auspices which permit teams to pay room and board and educational expenses for their players (many living away from home). Until the early 1970s, NCAA bylaws simply made any Canadian Junior A hockey player ineligible for U.S. college hockey. That Official Interpretation by the NCAA of its rules was struck down by a district judge in *Buckton v. NCAA*, 366 F.Supp. 1152 (D.Mass.1973), as unconstitutional discrimination against aliens. (Would this case have a different result after the *Tarkanian* decision discussed in Chapter 8?) In 1974, the NCAA substituted a new interpretation of the term "pay" to include "educational expenses not permitted by governing legislation of this Association ... [and any] expenses received from an outside amateur sports team ... in excess of actual and necessary travel and meal expenses and apparel or equipment ... for practice and game competition ..." (Article 12.1.2(e)). This new formula produced a struggle between the NCAA and Denver University, which culminated in the following case.

COLORADO SEMINARY (UNIV. OF DENVER) v. NCAA

United States District Court, District of Colorado, 1976.

417 F.Supp. 885, aff'd, 570 F.2d 320 (10th Cir.1978).

ARRAJ, CHIEF JUDGE.

* * *

In response to the September, 1974 NCAA Memorandum the University of Denver like other hockey-playing institutions had provided the NCAA with the questionnaires executed by its various student-athletes. The information furnished revealed among other things that several of the D.U. hockey players had received room and board expenses from outside amateur teams and thus indicated to NCAA officials that these student-athletes were ineligible. However, unlike the other hockey-playing institutions D.U. refused to declare these students ineligible, instead unequivocally stating that each student-athlete was eligible.

The refusal was based upon the University's own interpretation of applicable NCAA legislation. This interpretation was derived in part from the opinion of the hockey coach, Murray Armstrong, who had previously served on several NCAA committees. Coach Armstrong believed that a hockey player was not a professional if he received an allowance from his team in lieu of, and not in excess of, an amount equal to his "actual and necessary" expenses for travel plus one meal in connection with each practice and game.

The University's Chancellor Maurice Mitchell, who considered Coach Armstrong "extremely familiar" with the situation, likewise determined that D.U. had done nothing wrong. Furthermore, it was his opinion that it would be "cynical" to declare these student-athletes ineligible because this seemed to say that the students were somehow lacking in character. He concluded that to sign the questionnaires declaring the students ineligible merely "to put them on the ice" would violate duties owed by the University to its students. Ultimately, it was his decision to declare the student-athletes eligible.

* * *

EQUAL PROTECTION

Plaintiffs present essentially two claims of violations of their rights to equal protection. The first, on behalf of the student-athletes, is addressed to the official interpretations, the second, on behalf of the University itself, challenges the penalties imposed.

It is first asserted that the prohibition on receipt of compensation for expenses other than travel and one meal from an outside source discriminates between various classes of student-athletes Canadian and American, poor and rich, rural and city. The gist of the claims of discrimination against these shifting and sometime vague classes is that poor rural students, most commonly Canadian, must move to cities where amateur hockey is being played to be able to participate and, to be able to live, must accept compensation from the teams for such expenses as room and board.

It is now well established that the right to an education, though important, is not so fundamental as to require strict scrutiny of classifications allegedly affecting that right....

The same court which struck down the previous official interpretations in *Buckton* while utilizing strict scrutiny has subsequently found, and we believe correctly, that the present classifications in the interpretations apply to all hockey players of all nationalities and are not based on alienage or any other basis requiring strict scrutiny. Indeed, [one of the student-plaintiffs here, Falcone] is an American whose eligibility was lost for having accepted compensation for room and board expenses from an American amateur team. Accordingly, the plaintiff[s][are] entitled to have the NCAA's eligibility regulations invalidated only if they bear no rational relationship to that organization's legitimate objectives.

The objectives of the NCAA have been previously stated. They include maintaining intercollegiate athletics as an integral part of the educational program and the athlete as an integral part of the student body. In furtherance of these objectives Article 3, Section 1 of the NCAA constitution requires in substance that any aid received with minor exceptions be administered by the student-athlete's educational institution....

There is some merit to the argument that those student-athletes who received aid from an outside team while in school were in a substantially similar position to those receiving aid from their school for the same expenses. But this is not to say that the restrictions have no "fair and substantial relation to the object of the legislation." Although explanations for the restrictions have not been presented, an obvious reason would be to avoid the practical difficulties of monitoring and controlling aid received from a nonmember, over which the Association could exercise no authority. It might also be pointed out that it was these student-athletes the NCAA determined to immediately reinstate.

The situation of those student-athletes receiving aid from outside sources while not in school is entirely different. The court in Jones v. National Collegiate Athletic Association [392 F.Supp. 295 (D.Mass. 1975)] observed that play during the periods while not in school cannot be considered as coincidental to or in conjunction with obtaining an education.

* * *

We concur in the holding of the court in *Jones* that the present regulations do not unconstitutionally discriminate against those in any of the classes suggested by plaintiffs, particularly not against those plaintiffs receiving compensation for room and board while not in school.

The Court is not oblivious to the less advantageous position in which a student-athlete without means may be placed by the effect of the NCAA regulations. But neither the Equal Protection Clause of the Fourteenth Amendment, nor the counterpart equal protection requirement embodied in the Fifth Amendment, guarantees "absolute equality or precisely equal advantages." This Court cannot use the Constitution as a vehicle to alleviate the consequences of differences in economic circumstances that exist wholly apart from any NCAA action.

* * *

This Court is one of expressly limited jurisdiction whose statutory duties do not include sitting as a final arbiter of disputes between an association and its membership. A disturbing aspect of this litigation is the attempt to rely upon the federal judiciary to resolve essentially private disputes because of the refusal of the Association and member institution to deal with each other on a reasoning and where necessary compromising basis.

* * *

Most importantly, because of the refusal of Association and member institution to cooperate, student-athletes in all sports must suffer the consequences. We cannot constitutionalize amateur sports to protect their interests. The result may well be to develop new levels of cynicism in young students who are so often the pawns in the games of power between associations, and associations and member institutions. But if nothing else, this case may well demonstrate that defiance in the name of principle can prove to be inflexibility disguised as a virtue.

Case dismissed.

———

Given the stringency of the NCAA's definition of an "amateur" student-athlete as applied to Canadian hockey players wanting to play U.S. college hockey, should NCAA rules have permitted Danny Ainge to play basketball for Brigham Young University while he was also playing third base for the Toronto Blue Jays (as we saw in Chapter 2)?

2. PAY AT COLLEGE

Although the NCAA has drawn a line, then, against the typical kind of compensation provided Canadian Junior A hockey players, the Association's rules make it clear that "[p]ay is the receipt of funds, awards or benefits not permitted by the governing legislation of the Association for participation in athletics" (Article 12.02.3), and that a "grant-in-aid administered by an educational institution is not considered to be pay ..., provided it does not exceed the [Association's] financial aid limitations" (Article 12.01.4). Article 15 of the NCAA Manual then uses twenty pages to spell out the precise kind of tuition, fees, room and board, and books that a college may provide as financial aid to its athletes. Article 16 is equally detailed regarding permissible "awards, benefits and expenses." A crucial rule, Article 16.02.03, bans "extra benefits" for student-athletes—that is, benefits not "generally available to the institution's students." (This is the rule that Jerry Tarkanian allegedly violated by reimbursing the air fare home for one of his UNLV players.) A recurring issue is how to treat athletes who, while receiving an athletic scholarship, are also able to draw on external sources of financial support while at college.

WILEY v. NCAA

United States Court of Appeals, Tenth Circuit, 1979.

612 F.2d 473.

McKay, Circuit Judge.

Wiley was a student-athlete at the University of Kansas. Coming from a desperately poor background, he sought to meet his education costs through a federal Basic Education Opportunity Grant (BEOG) pursuant to 20 U.S.C. § 1070a. He was awarded $1,400 for the 1975–1976 school year. In addition, he received an athletic scholarship from the University of Kansas in the amount of $2,621. In the spring of 1976, plaintiff was declared ineligible to compete in intercollegiate athletic events because his athletic award plus his BEOG exceeded National Collegiate Athletic Association (NCAA) limitations. The University of Kansas unsuccessfully appealed to the NCAA to restore plaintiff's eligibility but did not pursue its right to appeal further.

Wiley then brought suit in the United States District Court for the District of Kansas to enjoin, inter alia, the inclusion of his BEOG in the calculation of the maximum financial assistance permissible under the NCAA Constitution. He alleged violation of the Equal Protection Clause and the Supremacy Clause.

* * *

We observe that the case does not implicate the right to a college education, or even to participate in intercollegiate athletics. Wiley's interest is instead the right to attend college and play sports under a certain favorable financing arrangement, i. e., a full athletic scholarship plus a full BEOG grant.[6]

This court has consistently found that, unless clearly defined constitutional principles are at issue, the suits of student-athletes dis-

6. Wiley admits to several available options that would have permitted attending college. Wiley insists that "[a]s a student with complete need at the university, [he would be] entitled to $3,800 aid" from various programs. Indeed, Wiley could have remained on the university's track team and under NCAA rules met his residual needs through federal educational loans or other student loans. Wiley was also free under NCAA rules to obtain employment during periods either before or between his years in college. Finally, while it may have required an "austere" life style, Wiley could have survived in college on his athletic scholarship alone. The athletic scholarship available to Wiley in 1975–1976 included tuition, books, housing, food and, had Wiley chosen to do various jobs for the athletic department, $15.00 per month extra.

pleased with high school athletic association or NCAA rules do not present substantial federal questions. [L]anguage contained in these cases may be too sweeping if applied where access to an education or other similarly substantial interest is at stake. Nonetheless, we find neither Wiley's personal interest nor the character of the alleged misclassification, even under Hagans, to require alteration of our cases.

Appeal upheld.

HOLLOWAY, CIRCUIT JUDGE dissenting.

* * *

Everyone concerned admits that neither a suspect classification nor deprivation of a fundamental constitutional right is involved in this case. But even so, Wiley is a person entitled to "equal protection" against state action under a rule not rationally related to a legitimate purpose of the acting agency.

* * *

Under the NCAA rule a student-athlete may receive a full grant even though his or her parents are millionaires and are providing any level of support. Student-athletes also can receive without penalty government payments under the GI Bill of Rights, military reserve training programs, the War Orphans Educational Program, Social Security Insurance Program and Non–Service–Connected Veteran's Death Pension Program. Thus, the rule distinguishes between student-athletes receiving money from BEOG's and those receiving money from their parents or these government sources.

The NCAA regulations concerning limitations on aid to athletes, as applicable here, clearly have as their principal purpose the promotion of amateurism in athletics by prohibiting pay for play. The NCAA concludes, and I think permissibly, that any aid which can be manipulated by the university or its supporters to supplement the basic athletic grant-in-aid to student-athletes falls into the play-for-pay category. The regulations also seem to prevent one member institution from using its access to economic resources (through endowment funds, alumni or otherwise) to obtain an advantage over other member institutions in the fielding of athletic teams. These are legitimate purposes, I believe. The question then is whether the regulation applied here is rationally related to these purposes.

Appellants argue that the exclusion of the assistance received from parents, from the GI Bill of Rights, or from social security, veterans or other death benefits is justified as "earned" by the athlete or the athlete's family prior to matriculation. That does not explain, of course, the exclusion of payments for student-athletes' participation in military reserve training programs. What is foreclosed or taken into account in determining the amount of assistance permitted is payment for employment of the student during the semester or term time, and all grants and scholarships (government or otherwise) that possibly can be controlled by the university or its athletic supporters. Thus, the line drawn is to permit support that is totally beyond the control of the university and its supporters, that has no possible relationship to the student's athletic ability or participation, that does not provide an advantage to one university over another, and that can have no bearing upon the principal aim of the regulations prohibiting pay for play.

The key question then becomes whether the university or its supporters can manipulate the BEOG's, and, perhaps, whether these grants are more available to students in some member universities than in others. The BEOG legislation provides a minimum base of financial support for economically deprived college students. BEOG's are based solely on need, considering only the resources the student's family can be expected to provide. Athletic ability or participation is totally irrelevant to the grants; neither is scholastic nor other ability a factor. The program operates under an entitlement concept that all eligible students receive awards without regard to any other student financial aid. The student apparently may attend any college or university. It has been described as a "G.I. Bill for all Americans." All this appears to be admitted by the NCAA and the other appellants, who have appended to their reply brief a letter setting out much of that policy, written by the Chief of the Program Policy and Analysis Branch of the Department of Health, Education & Welfare.

A university can enter into an agreement with the United States Commissioner of Education to administer the BEOG's, and to calculate and disburse funds to qualifying students enrolled in that institution. But disbursement must be in accordance with very strict requirements of federal regulations; these requirements eliminate the exercise of any significant discretion. Under statutory and regulatory BEOG guidelines the university cannot administer the grants in a manner calculated to benefit student-athletes without violating federal law.

There was absolutely no indication that the University of Kansas could manipulate the BEOG program to provide any semblance of pay for play. Applications need not be made through any university; Wiley applied for his grant through a public library in Maryland. Neither is there any indication that the University of Kansas, nor any other university member of the NCAA, could derive a special benefit from the BEOG's that would help the institution secure an advantage over any similar institution in the recruitment of or assistance to student-athletes. The NCAA appears to have recognized these conclusions because it has now changed its regulations to permit student-athletes to receive BEOG grants along with athletic scholarships.[2]

2. Under the 1977 amendment to the NCAA rules, the amount available under a BEOG, when added to the athletic scholarship, may not exceed an allowable maximum. Apparently the amount of the athletic scholarship must be reduced in such event. I express no opinion upon whether the new rule bears a rational relationship to the legitimate purposes of the NCAA regulation.

Wiley is not entitled to a university education as a fundamental right, and certainly not to participation in college athletics, but as a member of an identifiable class he is protected under the Equal Protection Clause from arbitrary state action. Although the test to be applied in this instance is the "rational relationship" test, requiring great deference to the formulators, this appears to be one of those perhaps rare cases in which there is no rational basis for the NCAA's rule. I would affirm the district court decision.

———

After the Supreme Court holding in *Tarkanian* (see Chapter 8) that the NCAA is not a state actor, the Association's rules now appear to be immune from direct constitutional challenges to such NCAA rules. Does this mean that the NCAA is now free to adopt "irrational" rules without fear of judicial review? Might a court be tempted to read *Tarkanian* as applying only to challenges of NCAA disciplinary procedures, but not in cases involving substantive NCAA rules affecting important constitutional rights? If not, is there any other legal theory that an "ineligible" player (especially one at a private school) might use to challenge an "irrational" NCAA rule?

Ironically, the NCAA was in the process of reversing its position about this issue at the same time as the case was being litigated. The most recent amendment, which was passed in 1992, permits a Division 1 student-athlete to "receive a Pell Grant in combination with other institutional financial aid, provided the overall grant does not exceed the value of a full grant-in-aid plus $1700...." (Article 15.2.4.1). Is this a sensible resolution of the problem? Consider that according to an NCAA-commissioned survey more than 60% of black football and basketball players, and 40% of white athletes in these revenue-producing sports, reported that they had less than $25 per month for personal expenses while at college.[4]

Before the 1992 amendment, poor student-athletes could and did apply for Pell Grants from the government, but because NCAA rules did not let them keep the grants for themselves, the money was paid to their school's athletic departments. Member schools had opposed efforts to amend the rule to allow students to keep up to $1,700 of their Pell Grants, not because the schools felt that poor athletes did not need the money, but because the institutions could not afford to lose this source of revenue.

Recall from the *Wiley* dissent that the stated purpose of the NCAA's ban on various types of financial assistance to student-athletes is to prevent institutions and their boosters from manipulating the amount of money awarded to star players. This policy has recently

4. See American Institutes for Research, *Studies of Intercollegiate Athletics, Report No. 3: The Experiences of Black Intercollegiate Athletes at NCAA Division 1 Institutions* (Palo Alto, Cal: AIR, 1989).

been given a new twist in connection with the debate about Proposition 42 and NCAA admission standards (see Chapter 8). Recall that Proposition 48 originally allowed "partial qualifiers" (students who had either a 2.00 high school GPA or a 700 SAT score, but not both) to attend college on an athletic scholarship, although they lost their freshman year of eligibility. The first version of Proposition 42 would have eliminated the financial grant-in-aid for partial qualifiers, as well as their right to play during their freshman year. Vehement protests by black leaders forced the NCAA to modify Proposition 42 to bar only *athletic* scholarships during the freshman year, and to permit partial qualifiers to receive financial support from a variety of institutional sources not based on athletic ability. But this has caused concern about what steps institutions will now take in recruiting star athletes who are marginally qualified for college. Where do you think that financial assistance for such athletes will probably come from, and at whose expense?

Another source of financial support is a job. NCAA rules (Article 15.2.6) require, though, that "earnings from the student-athlete's employment during semester or term time [be counted] in determining whether his or her full grant-in-aid has been reached," (Article 15.2.6). Only student-athletes who receive no athletic scholarship "may earn legitimate income in excess of a full grant-in-aid" (and then only if no one from the athletic department helped arrange the job). What is the problem for which these rules are an attempted solution? Is it a fair solution or not?

Besides cash payments to athletes, the NCAA strictly forbids any benefits "in kind" over and above the carefully-delineated grant-in-aid for tuition, fees, books, and room and board. Article 16 spends fifteen pages of the NCAA Manual elaborating on the general principle that "extra benefits" may not be provided to athletes and their families or friends if the same benefit is not "generally available to the institution's students or their relatives or friends." This rule prohibits, for example, a school from providing athletes with notebook paper or pocket calculators, and a coach from giving an injured player a ride (even to class or practice) in a severe storm when the coach is going in the same direction; also student-athletes cannot receive complimentary tickets to an awards dinner for their parents or spouses, transportation home during holidays or for family emergencies, free long-distance telephone calls, pay TV movies charged to an athlete's hotel bill for a road game, or legal assistance for any personal problem with the law. After much adverse publicity, the NCAA recently amended this rule to allow athletes to receive transportation to and from a teammate's funeral (Art. 16.10.1.5) and—from only one of three designated faculty or staff members—advice about their prospective professional careers (Art. 16.3.2(e)). A very sizable proportion of the infractions found by the NCAA enforcement branch rests on violations of this rule. Is there a need for such close scrutiny of benefits for student-athletes, or do these cases trivialize NCAA policy?

3.　PROFESSIONAL CONTRACTS

Under NCAA rules, an athlete loses amateur status not only for receiving pay or a promise of pay for current athletic competition, but also for "sign[ing] a contract or commitment of any kind to play professional athletics" in the future (Article 12.1.1(c)).　Recall the *Neely* case in Chapter 2, in which the Houston Oilers tried to keep confidential their signing of Ralph Neely so that he could play for the Oklahoma Sooners in a New Year's bowl game.　The next case also illustrates this rule in operation.

SHELTON v. NCAA

United States Court of Appeals, Ninth Circuit, 1976.

539 F.2d 1197.

Wright, Circuit Judge.

The principal issue in this appeal is whether the NCAA rule declaring ineligible for intercollegiate athletics in a particular sport any student who has ever signed a contract to play that professional sport violates the Equal Protection Clause of the constitution.

The basic facts are not in dispute.　The NCAA constitution declares as one of its goals the promotion and preservation of amateurism in college athletics.　In order to advance this goal, the NCAA constitution contains a rule which distinguishes between amateur and professional athletes on the basis of whether an individual has signed a contract to play professional sports.　The rule provides that a student who has signed such a contract, regardless of its enforceability, is ineligible to participate in intercollegiate athletics in that sport.

Appellee Shelton does not deny that he signed a professional contract with an American Basketball Association team which resulted in his being declared ineligible by Oregon State University.　Indeed, he contends that the contract is unenforceable because he was induced to sign it by fraud and undue influence.　The legal enforceability of the contract is the subject of a separate action brought by Shelton against the professional team which is now pending before the district court. Shelton urges that the NCAA rule making him ineligible despite the alleged defects in the contract creates an impermissible classification in violation of the Equal Protection Clause.　He wants the rule suspended while his litigation and the college basketball season continue.

Our review on such questions is limited.　None of the parties contends that the NCAA rule infringes upon a fundamental right which would necessitate strict judicial scrutiny.　Instead, we must examine the rule to determine whether it rationally furthers some legitimate purpose.　If it does, then our review is complete.

The rule purports to promote and protect amateurism in intercollegiate athletics.　None of the parties seriously contends that this goal is illegitimate. Instead they dispute the means chosen by the NCAA to achieve it.

Shelton believes that it is unreasonable to treat as a professional one who alleges that the contract which he signed is unenforceable. In effect, he contends that the NCAA rule is overinclusive because if he is successful in his other action and the contract is declared unenforceable he is not nor would he ever have been a professional.

In a similar case two years ago, Associated Students, Inc. v. NCAA, 493 F.2d 1251 (9th Cir.1974), this court reviewed another NCAA eligibility rule which was challenged on equal protection grounds. We recognized that the application of such rules may produce unreasonable results in certain situations. Nonetheless, we found that the rule did not violate the equal protection clause. Moreover, we did so although we recognized that the rule and its enforcement provisions might not be the best means for achieving the desired goal. It is not judicial business to tell a voluntary athletic association how best to formulate or enforce its rules.

We believe that the present appeal is controlled by *Associated Students*. The general rule under which Shelton was declared ineligible may from time to time produce unfortunate results. If an individual were subsequently successful in gaining a legal declaration that a professional contract was in fact void from its inception, a ruling that he was ineligible in the interim between his signing and the court's judgment might cause hardship. But the potential hardship does not make the rule irrational or unrelated to its goal. Moreover, hardship could be avoided by not signing a pro-contract. Reliance on a signed contract as an indication that a student's amateur status has been compromised is rationally related to the goal of preserving amateurism in intercollegiate athletics.

While our function is to determine only if the NCAA has selected a method of protecting amateurism which is reasonably related to that goal, an examination of the alternatives suggested by Shelton supports the conclusion that the rule in question withstands an equal protection challenge. Shelton argues that the rule should allow for cases such as his own where alleged defects in formation of the contract render it a nullity. The NCAA and its member institutions cannot simply take an athlete's word that his signed contract is void. An eligibility rule limited to contracts that would withstand a court test would be no rule at all. One could sign a contract, then allege that it was unenforceable and participate at will in college athletics while maintaining an option to enter the professional ranks at any time. Clearly, this would obliterate any remaining distinctions between amateur and professional athletes.

The alternative would be extremely burdensome. In the context of this appeal, for instance, the NCAA and its member institutions would be placed in the position of having to predict the outcome of Shelton's action against the professional basketball team. In order to do so they would likely have to undertake extensive investigations of the facts and time consuming hearings involving the parties. Even then, they would have no assurance that their decision would be compatible with the ultimate determination of the courts.

We hold that an effort to avoid this tangled set of affairs through the use of an easily applied and generally reliable criterion is rationally related to a legitimate purpose and does not, therefore, violate the equal protection clause.

Case dismissed.

————

After *Shelton*, the NCAA amended the rule to make clear that merely *signing* a professional contract will cost the student-athlete his amateur status, "regardless of [the contract's] legal enforceability or any consideration received" (Article 12.1.3). If *Tarkanian* had not foreclosed a constitutional challenge, would this rule be rationally related to a legitimate objective? What is the objective? Are there circumstances under which the application of this rule would not further the objective? Should the NCAA be required to create exceptions for every conceivable irrational application of a rule that is generally reasonable?

Two other controversial rules cause players to lose eligibility as a professional. The first renders a player ineligible if he "asks to be placed on the draft list ... of a professional league in that sport" (Art. 12.2.4.2). This rule creates a dilemma for basketball and football players since the NBA and NFL do not draft players with eligibility remaining unless they expressly petition to be put on the draft list. (In contrast, underclassmen in baseball and hockey are drafted without the players' consent and thus never have to lose their eligibility to determine whether they will be drafted (and if so, by which team and in which round).) The rule works a special hardship on players who declare themselves eligible for the NBA or NFL draft and then are not drafted by any team. This problem led to two antitrust suits against the NCAA, *Banks v. NCAA*, 977 F.2d 1081 (7th Cir.1992), and *Gaines v. NCAA*, 746 F.Supp. 738 (M.D.Tenn.1990), which will be explored later in this chapter. NCAA committees are considering legislation to relax the rule (despite objection from the NBA and NFL) by giving players thirty days after the draft to renounce their professional status and return to their college as an amateur; no action is expected, however, before the 1994 convention.

The other such "professionalism" rule renders a player ineligible if he or she has "ever agreed (orally or in writing) to be represented by an agent for the purpose of marketing his or her athletics ability or reputation in that sport," (Art. 12.3.1). Why does the NCAA consider a player a professional if he or she merely agrees to be represented in the future by an agent?   Does this rule rationally further a legitimate NCAA objective?[5]

Has the NCAA's strict definition of amateur status succeeded in "maintain[ing] a clear line of demarcation between college athletics and professional sports"?   In what ways are Division 1–A and NFL football similar?   In what ways dissimilar?   Why is it vital to maintain such a "clear line of demarcation," even to the extent of frowning on a *future* professional contract?   Recall the case of Danny Ainge, who played professional baseball for the Toronto Blue Jays at the same time he was playing college basketball for Brigham Young University.   Also consider that college coaches of these "amateur" sports receive generous compensation with the NCAA's blessing (recall Rick Pitino's $5 million, 7–year contract at Kentucky), and that movement between college and professional coaching ranks occurs regularly: Larry Brown and Pitino in basketball, for example, and Bill Walsh and Jack Pardee in football.

The broader question that runs through all the cases in this chapter is whether, given the financial stakes riding on big-time college sports, courts should defer to NCAA efforts to maintain the amateur status of the players (as contrasted, for example, to the players' academic status which we considered in the previous chapter).

B. JUDICIAL READING OF THE SCHOLARSHIP CONTRACT [6]

Having seen a variety of NCAA rules in operation, we now consider the legal resources still available to aggrieved parties who wish to challenge NCAA policies after the Supreme Court's *Tarkanian* decision which sharply inhibits constitutional attacks.   Just as in professional sports, one possible route is to ask for an independent judicial interpretation of the contractual relationship between the parties, consisting of both the contract between student (or coach) and institution and, in the background, the implicit contract among the institutions making up the Association (the latter agreement incorporated by reference in the former).

---

5. See Marianne M. Jennings & Lynn Zioko, *Student–Athletes, Athlete Agents and Five Year Eligibility: An Environment of Contractual Interference, Trade Restraint and High–Stake Payments*, 66 Univ. of Detroit L. Rev. 179 (1989).

6. For careful analyses of the legal issues presented by these cases, see Michael J. Cozzillio, *The Athletic Scholarship and the College National Letter of Intent: A Contract By Any Other Name*, 35 Wayne L. Rev. 1275 (1989), and Alfred Dennis Mathewson, *Intercollegiate Athletics and the Assignment of Legal Rights*, 35 St. Louis Univ. L.J. 39 (1990).

TAYLOR v. WAKE FOREST

Court of Appeals of North Carolina, 1972.

16 N.C.App. 117, 191 S.E.2d 379.

CAMPBELL, JUDGE.

[Greg Taylor was recruited by and signed a letter of intent to play football for Wake Forest University. The Grant–in–Aid, or athletic scholarship, provided as follows:

This Grant, if awarded, will be for 4 years provided I conduct myself in accordance with the rules of the Conference, the NCAA, and the Institution. I agree to maintain eligibility for intercollegiate athletics under both Conference and Institutional rules. Training rules for intercollegiate athletics are considered rules of the Institution, and I agree to abide by them. If injured while participating in athletics supervised by a member of the coaching staff, the Grant or Scholarship will be honored; and the medical expenses will be paid by the Athletic Department. This grant, when approved, is awarded for academic and athletic achievement and is not to be interpreted as employment in any manner whatsoever.

Taylor played for Wake Forest's football team in his freshman year. During the fall semester he compiled a grade point average of 1.0 (out of 4.0), far below the 1.35 the school required all students to have at the end of the freshman year. Taylor did not attend the spring football practices, and his GPA for the spring semester rose to 1.9. He then decided not to play football in the fall of his sophomore year; his GPA rose again, to 2.4.

Because of his refusal to play football, Wake Forest's Scholarship Committee, on the recommendation of the Faculty Athletic Committee, revoked his scholarship as of the end of his sophomore year. Taylor nevertheless remained at Wake Forest and graduated on time. He sued to recover $5,500 in expenses incurred during his last two years because he lost his scholarship.]

* * *

Plaintiffs contend that there was a genuine issue as to a material fact and that a jury should determine whether Gregg Taylor acted reasonably and in good faith in refusing to participate in the football program at Wake Forest when such participation interfered with reasonable academic progress.

The plaintiffs' position depends upon a construction of the contractual agreement between plaintiffs and Wake Forest. As stated in the affidavit of George J. Taylor, the position of the plaintiffs is that it was orally agreed between plaintiffs and the representative of Wake Forest that:

[I]n the event of any conflict between educational achievement and athletic involvement, participation in athletic activities could be limited or eliminated to the extent necessary to assure reasonable academic progress.

And plaintiffs were to be the judge as to what "reasonable academic progress" constituted.

We do not agree with the position taken by plaintiffs. The scholarship application filed by Gregg Taylor provided:

> I agree to maintain eligibility for intercollegiate athletics under both Conference and Institutional rules. Training rules for intercollegiate athletics are considered rules of the Institution, and I agree to abide by them.

Both Gregg Taylor and his father knew that the application was for "Football Grant–In–Aid Or A Scholarship," and that the scholarship was "awarded for academic and athletic achievement." It would be a strained construction of the contract that would enable the plaintiffs to determine the "reasonable academic progress" of Gregg Taylor. Gregg Taylor, in consideration of the scholarship award, agreed to maintain his athletic eligibility and this meant both physically and scholastically. As long as his grade average equaled or exceeded the requirements of Wake Forest, he was maintaining his scholastic eligibility for athletics. Participation in and attendance at practice were required to maintain his physical eligibility. When he refused to do so in the absence of any injury or excuse other than to devote more time to studies, he was not complying with his contractual obligations.

Summary judgment granted.

Questions for Discussion

1. Some time after *Taylor* (and a similar verdict in *Begley v. Mercer University*, 367 F.Supp. 908 (E.D.Tenn.1973)), the NCAA amended its rules to provide that "where a student's athletic ability is taken into consideration in any degree in awarding financial aid, such aid shall not be awarded in excess of one academic year" (Article 15.3.3.1). While high school athletes may be informed that the practice of the athletic department is to recommend renewal of financial aid, this rule explicitly forbids any assurance that renewal is automatic (even for an athlete who suffers a career-ending injury). Why does the NCAA impose these constraints on its own members' freedom of action? Can these constraints be justified? Recall from Chapter 8 the NCAA rules that impose substantial eligibility costs on athletes who want to transfer to another school from the one to which they first committed themselves with a Letter of Intent.

2. Under what circumstances is it ethically and legally appropriate for a school not to renew a scholarship for a student who has neither exhausted eligibility nor graduated? Because he or she was a poor player? Injured? Academically ineligible? Missed practice once a week in order to attend chemistry lab? If the school refuses to renew the scholarship for an inappropriate reason, does the student-athlete have any legal remedy against the school? Would your answer differ if the NCAA had not prohibited its member schools from assuring their student-athletes automatic renewal of their scholarships?

3. Given the NCAA practices and judicial precedents just described, along with the contractual features of the athletic scholarship described

earlier, what is the nature of the legal relationship between college and athlete? In particular, should an athlete playing football or basketball on scholarship be treated as an *employee* of the institution? This question arises in a variety of contexts. For example, as we will see in Chapter 11, a severely injured athlete might file a claim for workers' compensation on the ground that the injury arose out of and in the course of employment. See *Rensing v. Indiana State Univ.*, 437 N.E.2d 78 (Ind. App.1982), affirmed, 444 N.E.2d 1170 (Ind.1983). Similarly, under current income tax law (section 117(b)(2) of the Internal Revenue Code), the part of an athletic scholarship that covers room and board rather than tuition, fees and books, is deemed to be *taxable* income.[7] Finally, under labor law, a group of athletes might seek to engage in "concerted activities ... for purposes of mutual aid or protection" under section 7 of the National Labor Relations Act—that is, they might unionize and strike. How does the student-athlete compare with the medical resident, for example, and how should the two be treated under the NLRA? See *Cedars–Sinai Medical Center and Cedars–Sinai Housestaff Ass'n.*, 224 N.L.R.B. No. 90 (1976). Should the governing criterion be the "student" label applied by the university to this relationship, or the practical economic reality? How does the real-life situation of the college football player compare to that of the professional football player or to that of the college cafeteria worker in terms of time spent, mandatory conditions for being "paid," degree of supervision, and control and value of the services to the institution?

* * *

C. ANTITRUST SCRUTINY OF NCAA RULES [8]

The cases examined so far have all involved efforts by individual players or institutions to retain the athletes' eligibility to participate in intercollegiate sports within the framework of NCAA rules. These cases reflect a recurring tension between the expectations and obligations created in the relationship between the athlete (or coach) and the school and the school's commitment to the NCAA. The reason why that tension is so strong, and why the school ultimately feels compelled to live by the edicts of the NCAA, is because otherwise the school could not participate in major college sports—in the NCAA basketball tournament, football bowl games, and other lucrative post-season championships. All colleges with major athletic programs are members of the NCAA, and they have all agreed to abide by the NCAA's rules and not to play against any school the Association declares ineligible. Thus, in

7. See David Williams, *Is the Federal Government Suiting Up to Play in the Reform Game?* 20 Capital Univ. L. Rev. 621, 623–24 (1991).

8. The most important scholarly article in this area is Lee Goldman, *Sports and Antitrust: Should College Athletes Be Paid to Play?*, 65 Notre Dame L. Rev. 206 (1990). See also the more recent analysis in Note (by George Kokkines), *Sherman Act Invalidation of the NCAA Amateurism Rules*, 105 Harvard L. Rev. 1299 (1992). Early treatments of this topic include John C. Weistart, *Antitrust Issues in the Regulation of College Sports*, 5 J. of College & Univ. L. 77 (1978–79), and Note, *Tackling Intercollegiate Athletics: An Antitrust Analysis*, 87 Yale L.J. 655 (1978).

antitrust parlance, NCAA membership is an "essential facility" for a school to participate in major college athletics, and the NCAA cannot lawfully withhold access to this "facility" unless granting it would be impractical or inhibit the other members' ability to operate their business adequately (recall the *Hecht* case in Chapter 7).

1. PRODUCT MARKET

In earlier chapters we saw a comparable structure agreed to by the owners of teams in each sport's only professional league challenged under antitrust law, sometimes successfully. A similar antitrust challenge to one aspect of the intercollegiate structure was launched in the early 1980s. Intriguingly, this suit was filed by two universities that were part of the group of football powers comprising the College Football Association (CFA), and were chafing under the restrictive television policies adopted by the NCAA's broader membership. (The CFA consists of virtually all Division 1–A football institutions except for the members of the Big Ten and Pac–Ten conferences, which have separate television contracts.) The Supreme Court's opinion in this case is the only Supreme Court decision to consider how to apply substantive antitrust law to the sports industry.

NCAA v. BOARD OF REGENTS OF THE UNIV. OF OKLAHOMA & UNIV. OF GEORGIA ATHLETIC ASS'N.

Supreme Court of the United States, 1984.

468 U.S. 85, 104 S.Ct. 2948, 82 L.Ed.2d 70.

JUSTICE STEVENS for the Court.

* * *

History of the NCAA Television Plan

In 1938, the University of Pennsylvania televised one of its home games.[3] From 1940 through the 1950 season all of Pennsylvania's home games were televised. That was the beginning of the relationship between television and college football.

On January 11, 1951, a three-person "Television Committee," appointed during the preceding year, delivered a report to the NCAA's annual convention in Dallas. Based on preliminary surveys, the committee had concluded that "television does have an adverse effect on college football attendance and unless brought under some control threatens to seriously harm the nation's overall athletic and physical system." The report emphasized that "the television problem is truly a national one and requires collective action by the colleges."

---

3. According to the NCAA football television committee's 1981 briefing book: "As far as is known, there were [then] six television sets in Philadelphia: and all were tuned to the game."

[In 1951 the NCAA adopted a television plan that permitted only one game per week to be broadcast in each area and limited each school to two television appearances per season. The University of Pennsylvania at first insisted on televising all its home games, but after the NCAA declared it a member in bad standing and the four schools scheduled to play at Pennsylvania that year threatened to cancel the games, the school agreed to follow the NCAA plan.

Studies in each of the next five years also indicated that television had an adverse effect on attendance. The NCAA continued to formulate a television policy for all its members. From 1965 to 1977, ABC held the exclusive rights to network broadcasts of NCAA football games.]

* * *

The Current Plan

The plan adopted in 1981 for the 1982–1985 seasons is at issue in this case. This plan, like each of its predecessors, recites that it is intended to reduce, insofar as possible, the adverse effects of live television upon football game attendance....

In separate agreements with each of the carrying networks, ABC and the Columbia Broadcasting System (CBS), the NCAA granted each the right to telecast the 14 live "exposures" described in the plan, in accordance with the "ground rules" set forth therein.[9] Each of the networks agreed to pay a specified "minimum aggregate compensation to the participating NCAA member institutions" during the 4–year period in an amount that totaled $131,750,000.

* * *

The plan also contains "appearance requirements" and "appearance limitations" which pertain to each of the 2–year periods that the plan is in effect. The basic requirement imposed on each of the two networks is that it must schedule appearances for at least 82 different member institutions during each 2–year period. Under the appearance limitations no member institution is eligible to appear on television more than a total of six times and more than four times nationally, with the appearances to be divided equally between the two carrying networks. The number of exposures specified in the contracts also sets an absolute maximum on the number of games that can be broadcast.

Thus, although the current plan is more elaborate than any of its predecessors, it retains the essential features of each of them. It limits the total amount of televised intercollegiate football and the number of games that any one team may televise. No member is permitted to

9. In addition to its contracts with the carrying networks, the NCAA has contracted with Turner Broadcasting System, Inc. (TBS), for the exclusive right to cablecast NCAA football games. The minimum aggregate fee for the initial two-year period of the TBS contract is $17,696,000.

make any sale of television rights except in accordance with the basic plan.

Background of This Controversy

Beginning in 1979 CFA members began to advocate that colleges with major football programs should have a greater voice in the formulation of football television policy than they had in the NCAA. CFA therefore investigated the possibility of negotiating a television agreement of its own, developed an independent plan, and obtained a contract offer from the National Broadcasting Co. (NBC). This contract, which it signed in August 1981, would have allowed a more liberal number of appearances for each institution, and would have increased the overall revenues realized by CFA members.

In response the NCAA publicly announced that it would take disciplinary action against any CFA member that complied with the CFA–NBC contract. The NCAA made it clear that sanctions would not be limited to the football programs of CFA members, but would apply to other sports as well. On September 8, 1981, respondents commenced this action in the United States District Court for the Western District of Oklahoma and obtained a preliminary injunction preventing the NCAA from initiating disciplinary proceedings or otherwise interfering with CFA's efforts to perform its agreement with NBC. Notwithstanding the entry of the injunction, most CFA members were unwilling to commit themselves to the new contractual arrangement with NBC in the face of the threatened sanctions and therefore the agreement was never consummated.

* * *

II

There can be no doubt that the challenged practices of the NCAA constitute a "restraint of trade" in the sense that they limit members' freedom to negotiate and enter into their own television contracts. In that sense, however, every contract is a restraint of trade, and as we have repeatedly recognized, the Sherman Act was intended to prohibit only unreasonable restraints of trade.

It is also undeniable that these practices share characteristics of restraints we have previously held unreasonable. The NCAA is an association of schools which compete against each other to attract television revenues, not to mention fans and athletes. As the District Court found, the policies of the NCAA with respect to television rights are ultimately controlled by the vote of member institutions. By participating in an association which prevents member institutions from competing against each other on the basis of price or kind of television rights that can be offered to broadcasters, the NCAA member institutions have created a horizontal restraint—an agreement among competitors on the way in which they will compete with one another. A restraint of this type has often been held to be unreasonable as a matter of law. Because it places a ceiling on the number of games member institutions may televise, the horizontal agreement places an artificial limit on the quantity of televised football that is available to broadcasters and consumers. By restraining the quantity of television rights available for sale, the challenged practices create a limitation on output; our cases have held that such limitations are unreasonable restraints of trade. Moreover, the District Court found that the minimum aggregate price in fact operates to preclude any price negotiation between broadcasters and institutions, thereby constituting horizontal price fixing, perhaps the paradigm of an unreasonable restraint of trade.

Horizontal price fixing and output limitation are ordinarily condemned as a matter of law under an "illegal per se" approach because the probability that these practices are anticompetitive is so high; a per se rule is applied when "the practice facially appears to be one that would always or almost always tend to restrict competition and decrease output." In such circumstances a restraint is presumed unreasonable without inquiry into the particular market context in which it is found. Nevertheless, we have decided that it would be inappropriate to apply a per se rule to this case. This decision is not based on a lack of judicial experience with this type of arrangement, on the fact that the NCAA is organized as a nonprofit entity, or on our respect for the NCAA's historic role in the preservation and encouragement of intercollegiate amateur athletics. Rather, what is critical is that this case involves an industry in which horizontal restraints on competition are essential if the product is to be available at all.

As Judge Bork has noted: "[S]ome activities can only be carried out jointly. Perhaps the leading example is league sports. When a league of professional lacrosse teams is formed, it would be pointless to declare their cooperation illegal on the ground that there are no other professional lacrosse teams." R. Bork, The Antitrust Paradox 278 (1978). What the NCAA and its member institutions market in this case is competition itself—contests between competing institutions. Of course, this would be completely ineffective if there were no rules on which the competitors agreed to create and define the competition to be marketed. A myriad of rules affecting such matters as the size of the field, the number of players on a team, and the extent to which physical violence is to be encouraged or proscribed, all must be agreed upon, and all restrain the manner in which institutions compete. Moreover, the NCAA seeks to market a particular brand of football—college football. The identification of this "product" with an academic tradition differentiates college football from and makes it more popular than professional sports to which it might otherwise be comparable, such as, for example, minor league baseball. In order to preserve the character and quality of the "product," athletes must not be paid, must be required to attend class, and the like. And the integrity of the "product" cannot be preserved except by mutual agreement; if an institution adopted such restrictions unilaterally, its effectiveness as a competitor on the playing field might soon be destroyed. Thus, the NCAA plays a vital role in enabling college football to preserve its character, and as a result enables a product to be marketed which might otherwise be unavailable. In performing this role, its actions widen consumer choice—not only the choices available to sports fans but also those available to athletes—and hence can be viewed as procompetitive....

Respondents concede that the great majority of the NCAA's regulations enhance competition among member institutions. Thus, despite the fact that this case involves restraints on the ability of member institutions to compete in terms of price and output, a fair evaluation of their competitive character requires consideration of the NCAA's justifications for the restraints.

Our analysis of this case under the Rule of Reason, of course, does not change the ultimate focus of our inquiry.... Under the Sherman Act the criterion to be used in judging the validity of a restraint on trade is its impact on competition.

III

Because it restrains price and output, the NCAA's television plan has a significant potential for anticompetitive effects.[28] The findings of the District Court indicate that this potential has been realized. The District Court found that if member institutions were free to sell television rights, many more games would be shown on television, and that the NCAA's output restriction has the effect of raising the price the networks pay for television rights. Moreover, the court found that by fixing a price for television rights to all games, the NCAA creates a price structure that is unresponsive to viewer demand and unrelated to the prices that would prevail in a competitive market. And, of course, since as a practical matter all member institutions need NCAA approval, members have no real choice but to adhere to the NCAA's television controls.

The anticompetitive consequences of this arrangement are apparent. Individual competitors lose their freedom to compete. Price is higher and output lower than they would otherwise be, and both are unresponsive to consumer preference.[33] This latter point is perhaps the

---

28. In this connection, it is not without significance that Congress felt the need to grant professional sports an exemption from the antitrust laws for joint marketing of television rights. See 15 U.S.C. §§ 1291–1295. The legislative history of this exemption demonstrates Congress' recognition that agreements among league members to sell television rights in a cooperative fashion could run afoul of the Sherman Act, and in particular reflects its awareness of the decision in United States v. National Football League, 116 F.Supp. 319 (E.D.Pa.1953), which held that an agreement between the teams of the National Football League that each team would not permit stations within 75 miles of the home city of another team to telecast its games on a day when that team was playing at home violated § 1 of the Sherman Act.

33. The District Court provided a vivid example of this system in practice:

A clear example of the failure of the rights fees paid to respond to market forces occurred in the fall of 1981. On one weekend of that year, Oklahoma was scheduled to play a football game with the University of Southern California. Both Oklahoma and USC have long had outstanding football programs, and indeed, both teams were ranked

most significant, since "Congress designed the Sherman Act as a 'consumer welfare prescription.'" A restraint that has the effect of reducing the importance of consumer preference in setting price and output is not consistent with this fundamental goal of antitrust law.[34] Restrictions on price and output are the paradigmatic examples of restraints of trade that the Sherman Act was intended to prohibit. At the same time, the television plan eliminates competitors from the market, since only those broadcasters able to bid on television rights covering the entire NCAA can compete. Thus, as the District Court found, many telecasts that would occur in a competitive market are foreclosed by the NCAA's plan.

Petitioner argues, however, that its television plan can have no significant anticompetitive effect since the record indicates that it has no market power—no ability to alter the interaction of supply and demand in the market. We must reject this argument for two reasons, one legal, one factual.

As a matter of law, the absence of proof of market power does not justify a naked restriction on price or output. To the contrary, when there is an agreement not to compete in terms of price or output, "no elaborate industry analysis is required to demonstrate the anticompetitive character of such an agreement." Petitioner does not quarrel with the District Court's finding that price and output are not responsive to demand. Thus the plan is inconsistent with the Sherman Act's command that price and supply be responsive to consumer preference. We have never required proof of market power in such a case. This naked restraint on price and output requires some competitive justification even in the absence of a detailed market analysis. As a factual matter, it is evident that petitioner does possess market power. The District Court employed the correct test for determining whether college football broadcasts constitute a separate market—whether there are other products that are reasonably substitutable for televised NCAA football games. Petitioner's argument that it cannot obtain supracompetitive prices from broadcasters since advertisers, and hence broadcasters, can switch from college football to other types of programming simply ignores the findings of the District Court. It found that intercollegiate football telecasts generate an audience uniquely attractive to advertisers and that competitors are unable to offer programming that can

among the top five teams in the country by the wire service polls. ABC chose to televise the game along with several others on a regional basis. A game between two schools which are not well-known for their football programs, Citadel and Appalachian State, was carried on four of ABC's local affiliated stations. The USC–Oklahoma contest was carried on over 200 stations. Yet, incredibly, all four of these teams received exactly the same amount of money for the right to televise their games.

34. As the District Court observed:

Perhaps the most pernicious aspect is that under the controls, the market is not responsive to viewer preference. Every witness who testified on the matter confirmed that the consumers, the viewers of college football television, receive absolutely no benefit from the controls. Many games for which there is a large viewer demand are kept from the viewers, and many games for which there is little if any demand are nonetheless televised.

attract a similar audience. These findings amply support its conclusion that the NCAA possesses market power. Indeed, the District Court's subsidiary finding that advertisers will pay a premium price per viewer to reach audiences watching college football because of their demographic characteristics is vivid evidence of the uniqueness of this product. Moreover, the District Court's market analysis is firmly supported by our decision in International Boxing Club v. United States, 358 U.S. 242 (1958), that championship boxing events are uniquely attractive to fans and hence constitute a market separate from that for non-championship events. Thus, respondents have demonstrated that there is a separate market for telecasts of college football which "rest[s] on generic qualities differentiating" viewers. It inexorably follows that if college football broadcasts be defined as a separate market—and we are convinced they are—then the NCAA's complete control over those broadcasts provides a solid basis for the District Court's conclusion that the NCAA possesses market power with respect to those broadcasts. "When a product is controlled by one interest, without substitutes available in the market, there is monopoly power."

Thus, the NCAA television plan on its face constitutes a restraint upon the operation of a free market, and the findings of the District Court establish that it has operated to raise price and reduce output. Under the Rule of Reason, these hallmarks of anticompetitive behavior place upon petitioner a heavy burden of establishing an affirmative defense which competitively justifies this apparent deviation from the operations of a free market.

IV

[P]etitioner argues that its television plan constitutes a cooperative "joint venture" which assists in the marketing of broadcast rights and hence is procompetitive....

The District Court did not find that the NCAA's television plan produced any procompetitive efficiencies which enhanced the competitiveness of college football television rights; to the contrary it concluded that NCAA football could be marketed just as effectively without the television plan. There is therefore no predicate in the findings for petitioner's efficiency justification. Indeed, petitioner's argument is refuted by the District Court's finding concerning price and output. If the NCAA's television plan produced procompetitive efficiencies, the plan would increase output and reduce the price of televised games. The District Court's contrary findings accordingly undermine petitioner's position. In light of these findings, it cannot be said that "the agreement on price is necessary to market the product at all." ... Here production has been limited, not enhanced. No individual school is free to televise its own games without restraint. The NCAA's efficiency justification is not supported by the record.

Neither is the NCAA's television plan necessary to enable the NCAA to penetrate the market through an attractive package sale.

Since broadcasting rights to college football constitute a unique product for which there is no ready substitute, there is no need for collective action in order to enable the product to compete against its nonexistent competitors. This is borne out by the District Court's finding that the NCAA's television reduces the volume of television rights sold.

V

Throughout the history of its regulation of intercollegiate football telecasts, the NCAA has indicated its concern with protecting live attendance. This concern, it should be noted, is not with protecting live attendance at games which are shown on television; that type of interest is not at issue in this case. Rather, the concern is that fan interest in a televised game may adversely affect ticket sales for games that will not appear on television.[56]

Although studies in the 1950s provided some support for the thesis that live attendance would suffer if unlimited television were permitted, the District Court found that there was no evidence to support that theory in today's market....

There is, however, a more fundamental reason for rejecting this defense. The NCAA's argument that its television plan is necessary to protect live attendance is not based on a desire to maintain the integrity of college football as a distinct and attractive product, but rather on a fear that the product will not prove sufficiently attractive to draw live attendance when faced with competition from televised games. At bottom the NCAA's position is that ticket sales for most college games are unable to compete in a free market. The television plan protects ticket sales by limiting output—just as any monopolist increases revenues by reducing output. By seeking to insulate live ticket sales from the full spectrum of competition because of its assumption that the product itself is insufficiently attractive to consumers, petitioner forwards a justification that is inconsistent with the basic policy of the Sherman Act. "[T]he Rule of Reason does not support a defense based on the assumption that competition itself is unreasonable."

VI

Petitioner argues that the interest in maintaining a competitive balance among amateur athletic teams is legitimate and important and that it justifies the regulations challenged in this case. We agree with the first part of the argument but not the second.

Our decision not to apply a per se rule to this case rests in large part on our recognition that a certain degree of cooperation is necessary if the type of competition that petitioner and its member institutions

---

56. The NCAA's plan is not even arguably related to a desire to protect live attendance by ensuring that a game is not televised in the area where it is to be played. No cooperative action is necessary for that kind of "blackout." The home team can always refuse to sell the right to telecast its game to stations in the immediate area. The NCAA does not now and never has justified its television plan by an interest in assisting schools in "blacking out" their home games in the areas in which they are played.

seek to market is to be preserved. It is reasonable to assume that most of the regulatory controls of the NCAA are justifiable means of fostering competition among amateur athletic teams and therefore procompetitive because they enhance public interest in intercollegiate athletics. The specific restraints on football telecasts that are challenged in this case do not, however, fit into the same mold as do rules defining the conditions of the contest, the eligibility of participants, or the manner in which members of a joint enterprise shall share the responsibilities and the benefits of the total venture.

The NCAA does not claim that its television plan has equalized or is intended to equalize competition within any one league.[62] The plan is nationwide in scope and there is no single league or tournament in which all college football teams complete. There is no evidence of any intent to equalize the strength of teams in Division I–A with those in Division II or Division III, and not even a colorable basis for giving colleges that have no football program at all a voice in the management of the revenues generated by the football programs at other schools.[63] The interest in maintaining a competitive balance that is asserted by the NCAA as a justification for regulating all television of intercollegiate football is not related to any neutral standard or to any readily identifiable group of competitors.

The television plan is not even arguably tailored to serve such an interest. It does not regulate the amount of money that any college may spend on its football program, nor the way in which the colleges may use the revenues that are generated by their football programs, whether derived from the sale of television rights, the sale of tickets, or the sale of concessions or program advertising. The plan simply imposes a restriction on one source of revenue that is more important to some colleges than to others. There is no evidence that this

62. It seems unlikely, for example, that there would have been a greater disparity between the football prowess of Ohio State University and that of Northwestern University in recent years without the NCAA's television plan. The District Court found that in fact the NCAA has been strikingly unsuccessful if it has indeed attempted to prevent the emergence of a "power elite" in intercollegiate football. Moreover, the District Court's finding that there would be more local and regional telecasts without the NCAA controls means that Northwestern could well have generated more television income in a free market than was obtained under the NCAA regime.

63. Indeed, the District Court found that the basic reason the television plan has endured is that the NCAA is in effect controlled by schools that are not restrained by the plan:

The plaintiffs and other CFA members attempted to persuade the majority of NCAA members that NCAA had gone far beyond its legitimate role in football television. Not surprisingly, none of the CFA proposals were adopted. Instead the membership uniformly adopted the proposals of the NCAA administration which "legitimized" NCAA's exercises of power. The result was not surprising in light of the makeup of the voting membership. Of approximately 800 voting members of the NCAA, 500 or so are in Divisions II and III and are not subjected to NCAA television controls. Of the 275 Division I members, only 187 play football, and only 135 were members of Division I–A at the time of the January Convention. Division I–A was made up of the most prominent football-playing schools, and those schools account for most of the football games shown on network television. Therefore, of some 850 voting members, less than 150 suffer any direct restriction on their right to sell football games to television.

restriction produces any greater measure of equality throughout the NCAA than would a restriction on alumni donations, tuition rates, or any other revenue producing activity. At the same time, as the District Court found, the NCAA imposes a variety of other restrictions designed to preserve amateurism which are much better tailored to the goal of competitive balance than is the television plan, and which are "clearly sufficient" to preserve competitive balance to the extent it is within the NCAA's power to do so. And much more than speculation supported the District Court's findings on this score. No other NCAA sport employs a similar plan, and in particular the court found that in the most closely analogous sport, college basketball, competitive balance has been maintained without resort to a restrictive television plan.

Perhaps the most important reason for rejecting the argument that the interest in competitive balance is served by the television plan is the District Court's unambiguous and well supported finding that many more games would be televised in a free market than under the NCAA plan. The hypothesis that legitimates the maintenance of competitive balance as a procompetitive justification under the Rule of Reason is that equal competition will maximize consumer demand for the product. The finding that consumption will materially increase if the controls are removed is a compelling demonstration that they do not in fact serve any such legitimate purpose.[68]

VII

The NCAA plays a critical role in the maintenance of a revered tradition of amateurism in college sports. There can be no question but that it needs ample latitude to play that role, or that the preservation of the student-athlete in higher education adds richness and diversity to intercollegiate athletics and is entirely consistent with the goals of the Sherman Act. But consistent with the Sherman Act, the role of the NCAA must be to preserve a tradition that might otherwise die; rules that restrict output are hardly consistent with this role. Today we hold only that the record supports the District Court's conclusion that by curtailing output and blunting the ability of member institutions to respond to consumer preference, the NCAA has restricted rather than enhanced the place of intercollegiate athletics in the Nation's life. Accordingly, the judgment of the Court of Appeals is

Affirmed.

JUSTICE WHITE with whom JUSTICE REHNQUIST joins, dissenting.

* * *

I

"While it would be fanciful to suggest that colleges are not concerned about the profitability of their ventures, it is clear that other,

---

68. This is true not only for television viewers, but also for athletes. The District Court's finding that the television exposure of all schools would increase in the absence of the NCAA's television plan means that smaller institutions appealing to essentially local or regional markets would get more exposure if the plan is enjoined, enhancing their ability to compete for student athletes.

non-commercial goals play a central role in their sports programs." J. Weistart & C. Lowell, The Law of Sports § 5.12 (1979). The NCAA's member institutions have designed their competitive athletic programs "to be a vital part of the educational system." Deviations from this goal, produced by a persistent and perhaps inevitable desire to "win at all costs," have in the past led, and continue to lead, to a wide range of competitive excesses that prove harmful to students and institutions alike....

The NCAA, in short, "exist[s] primarily to enhance the contribution made by amateur athletic competition to the process of higher education as distinguished from realizing maximum return on it as an entertainment commodity." In pursuing this goal, the organization and its members seek to provide a public good—a viable system of amateur athletics—that most likely could not be provided in a perfectly competitive market. "Without regulation, the desire of member institutions to remain athletically competitive would lead them to engage in activities that deny amateurism to the public. No single institution could confidently enforce its own standards since it could not trust its competitors to do the same." Note, Antitrust and Nonprofit Entities, 94 Harv. L. Rev. 802, 817–18 (1981). The history of intercollegiate athletics prior to the advent of the NCAA provides ample support for this conclusion. By mitigating what appears to be a clear failure of the free market to serve the ends and goals of higher education, the NCAA ensures the continued availability of a unique and valuable product, the very existence of which might well be threatened by unbridled competition in the economic sphere.

In pursuit of its fundamental goal and others related to it, the NCAA imposes numerous controls on intercollegiate athletic competition among its members, many of which "are similar to those which are summarily condemned when undertaken in a more traditional business setting." J. Weistart & C. Lowell, supra, at § 5.12.b. Thus, the NCAA has promulgated and enforced rules limiting both the compensation of student-athletes, and the number of coaches a school may hire for its football and basketball programs; it also has prohibited athletes who formerly have been compensated for playing from participating in intercollegiate competition, restricted the number of athletic scholarships its members may award, and established minimum academic standards for recipients of those scholarships; and it has pervasively regulated the recruitment process, student eligibility, practice schedules, squad size, the number of game played, and many other aspects of intercollegiate athletics. One clear effect of most, if not all, of these regulations is to prevent institutions with competitively and economically successful programs from taking advantage of their success by expanding their programs, improving the quality of the product they offer, and increasing their sports revenues. Yet each of these regulations represents a desirable and legitimate attempt "to keep university athletics from becoming professionalized to the extent that profit making objectives would overshadow educational objectives." Significantly, neither the Court of Appeals nor this Court questions the validity of these regulations under the Rule of Reason.

Notwithstanding the contrary conclusion of the District Court, and the majority, I do not believe that the restraint under consideration in this case—the NCAA's television plan—differs fundamentally for anti-trust purposes from the other seemingly anticompetitive aspects of the organization's broader program of self-regulation. The television plan, like many of the NCAA's actions, furthers several complementary ends. Specifically, the plan is designed "to reduce, insofar as possible, the adverse effects of live television ... upon football game attendance and, in turn, upon the athletic and related educational programs dependent upon the proceeds therefrom; to spread football television participation among as many colleges as practicable; to reflect properly the image of universities as educational institutions; to promote college football through the use of television, to advance the overall interests of intercollegiate athletics, and to provide college football television to the public to the extent compatible with these other objectives." More generally, in my view, the television plan reflects the NCAA's funda-mental policy of preserving amateurism and integrating athletics and education. Nor does the District Court's finding that the plan is intended to maximize television revenues, warrant any implication that the NCAA and its member institutions pursue this goal without regard to the organization's stated policies.

* * *

[I]t is essential at this point to emphasize that neither the Court of Appeals nor this Court purports to hold that the NCAA may not (1) require its members who televise their games to pool and share the compensation received among themselves, with other schools, and with the NCAA; (2) limit the number of times any member may arrange to have its games shown on television; or (3) enforce reasonable blackout rules to avoid head-to-head competition for television audiences. As I shall demonstrate, the Court wisely and correctly does not condemn such regulations. What the Court does affirm is the Court of Appeals' judgment that the NCAA may not limit the number of games that are broadcast on television and that it may not contract for an overall price that has the effect of setting the price for individual game broadcast rights.[2] I disagree with the Court in these respects.

* * *

2. This litigation was triggered by the NCAA's response to an attempt by the College Football Association (CFA), an organization of the more dominant football-playing schools and conferences, to develop an independent television plan. To the extent that its plan contains features similar to those condemned as anticompetitive by the Court, the CFA may well have antitrust problems of its own. To the extent that they desire continued membership in the NCAA, moreover, participation in a television plan developed by the CFA will not exempt football powers like respondents from the many kinds of NCAA controls over television appearances that the Court does not purport to invalidate.

III

Even if I were convinced that the District Court did not err in failing to look to total viewership, as opposed to the number of televised games, when measuring output and anticompetitive effect and in failing fully to consider whether the NCAA possesses power to fix the package price, as opposed to the distribution of that package price among participating teams, I would nevertheless hold that the television plan passes muster under the Rule of Reason. The NCAA argues strenuously that the plan and the network contracts "are part of a joint venture among many of the nation's universities to create a product— high-quality college football—and offer that product in a way attractive to both fans in the stadiums and viewers on [television]. The cooperation in producing the product makes it more competitive against other [television] (and live) attractions." The Court recognizes that, "[i]f the NCAA faced 'interbrand' competition from available substitutes, then certain forms of collective action might be appropriate in order to enhance its ability to compete." It rejects the NCAA's proffered procompetitive justification, however, on the ground that college football is a unique product for which there are no available substitutes and "there is no need for collective action in order to enable the product to compete against its nonexistent competitors." This proposition is singularly unpersuasive.

It is one thing to say that "NCAA football is a unique product," that "intercollegiate football telecasts generate an audience uniquely attractive to advertisers and that competitors are unable to offer programming that can attract a similar audience." It is quite another, in my view, to say that maintenance or enhancement of the quality of NCAA football telecasts is unnecessary to enable those telecasts to compete effectively against other forms of entertainment. The NCAA has no monopoly power when competing against other types of entertainment. Should the quality of the NCAA's product "deteriorate to any perceptible degree or should the cost of 'using' its product rise, some fans undoubtedly would turn to another form of entertainment.... Because of the broad possibilities for alternative forms of entertainment," the NCAA "properly belongs in the broader 'entertainment' market rather than in ... [a] narrower marke[t]" like sports or football.

The NCAA has suggested a number of plausible ways in which its television plan might enhance the ability of college football telecasts to compete against other forms of entertainment. Although the District Court did conclude that the plan is "not necessary for effective marketing of the product," its finding was directed only at the question whether college football telecasts would continue in the absence of the plan. It made no explicit findings concerning the effect of the plan on viewership and thus did not reject the factual premise of the NCAA's argument that the plan might enhance competition by increasing the market penetration of NCAA football. The District Court's finding that network coverage of NCAA football would likely decrease if the plan were struck down, in fact, strongly suggests the validity of the NCAA's position. On the record now before the Court, therefore, I am not prepared to conclude that the restraints imposed by the NCAA's television plan are "such as may suppress or even destroy competition" rather than "such as merely regulat[e] and perhaps thereby promot[e] competition."

IV

Finally, I return to the point with which I began—the essentially noneconomic nature of the NCAA's program of self-regulation. Like Judge Barrett, who dissented in the Court of Appeals, I believe that the lower courts "erred by subjugating the NCAA's educational goals (and, coincidentally, those which Oklahoma and Georgia insist must be maintained in any event) to the purely competitive commercialism of [an] 'every school for itself' approach to television contract bargaining." Although the NCAA does not enjoy blanket immunity from the antitrust laws, it is important to remember that the Sherman Act "is aimed primarily at combinations having commercial objectives and is applied only to a very limited extent to organizations ... which normally have other objectives."

The fact that a restraint operates on nonprofit educational institutions as distinguished from business entities is as "relevant in determining whether that particular restraint violates the Sherman Act" as is the fact that a restraint affects a profession rather than a business. The legitimate noneconomic goals of colleges and universities should not be ignored in analyzing restraints imposed by associations of such institutions on their members, and these noneconomic goals "may require that a particular practice, which could properly be viewed as a violation of the Sherman Act in another context, be treated differently." The Court of Appeals, like the District Court, flatly refused to consider what it termed "noneconomic" justifications advanced by the NCAA in support of the television plan. It was of the view that our decision in National Society of Professional Engineers v. United States, 435 U.S. 679 (1978), precludes reliance on noneconomic factors in assessing the reasonableness of the television plan. This view was mistaken, and I note that the Court does not in so many words repeat this error.

Professional Engineers did make clear that antitrust analysis usually turns on "competitive conditions" and "economic conceptions." Ordinarily, "the inquiry mandated by the Rule of Reason is whether the challenged agreement is one that promotes competition or one that suppresses competition." The purpose of antitrust analysis, the Court emphasized, "is to form a judgment about the competitive significance of the restraint; it is not to decide whether a policy favoring competition is in the public interest, or in the interest of the members of an industry." Broadly read, these statements suggest that noneconomic values like the promotion of amateurism and fundamental educational objectives could not save the television plan from condemnation under the Sherman Act. But these statements were made in response to "public interest" justifications proffered in defense of a ban on competitive bidding imposed by practitioners engaged in standard, profit-motivated commercial activities. The primarily noneconomic values pursued by educational institutions differ fundamentally from the "overriding commercial purpose of [the] day-to-day activities" of engineers, lawyers, doctors, and businessmen, and neither *Professional Engineers* nor any other decision of this Court suggests that associations of nonprofit educational institutions must defend their self-regulatory restraints solely in terms of their competitive impact, without regard for the legitimate noneconomic values they promote.

When these values are factored into the balance, the NCAA's television plan seems eminently reasonable. Most fundamentally, the plan fosters the goal of amateurism by spreading revenues among various schools and reducing the financial incentives toward professionalism. As the Court observes, the NCAA imposes a variety of restrictions perhaps better suited than the television plan for the preservation of amateurism. Although the NCAA does attempt vigorously to enforce these restrictions, the vast potential for abuse suggests that measures, like the television plan, designed to limit the rewards of professionalism are fully consistent with, and essential to the attainment of, the NCAA's objectives.... The collateral consequences of the spreading of regional and national appearances among a number of schools are many: the television plan, like the ban on compensating student-athletes, may well encourage students to choose their schools, at least in part, on the basis of educational quality by reducing the perceived economic element of the choice; it helps ensure the economic viability of athletic programs at a wide variety of schools with weaker football teams; and it "promot[es] competitive football among many and varied amateur teams nationwide." These important contributions, I believe, are sufficient to offset any minimal anticompetitive effects of the television plan.

———

The majority and dissenting opinions in the preceding case are among the most important in this book, both because they constitute a primer on the application of antitrust law and its rule of reason to the peculiar business of marketing athletically competitive sports entertainment, and because they highlight the fundamental conflict of values that permeates all the legal policy issues surrounding college athletics. The questions raised and/or left unresolved by the decision in the *Board of Regents* case are among the most complex and confounding in all of the law of sports.

Perhaps the most fundamental question about intercollegiate sports is how to reconcile the conflict between academic and amateur values and commercial market values. Both the majority and dissent recognize that the NCAA's promotion of amateur and educational goals is legitimate. From that premise the dissent argued that this "higher" goal justifies virtually any agreement among NCAA members about producing and marketing their various sports. The majority opinion, however, appears to draw a sharp line of demarcation between rules defining the nature of the product (the hundreds of pages of rules described earlier about academic eligibility and recruiting and compensating players)—which are lawful because they allow the NCAA schools to offer a unique type of product—and rules regarding how the schools market and sell their games, which must conform to antitrust restrictions against collaboration to reduce output and raise prices. Is it sensible for the majority to distinguish between the labor market for student-athletes and the product market for fans? Or is the dissent correct that the NCAA should be free to govern both the labor and product markets in college sports. If neither view is appealing, how should courts determine when rules that promote competing values should escape the antitrust requirement of market competition?

This question is complicated by the fact that while most college officials involved in athletics truly believe that amateurism and academics are important values, maximizing revenue is undeniably a crucial factor in athletic decision-making at every Division 1 school. If colleges must compete for revenues, the financial (and public relations) benefits of winning (and the consequences of losing) are magnified. Thus, by commercializing the product market, the Court has created a huge incentive for schools and coaches to win, which jeopardizes the standards designed to promote amateurism and academics. Does the Supreme Court draw the proper balance between these competing values in the application of antitrust law? How should courts balance these values in determining when different athletic programs should be required to compete and when they should be allowed to cooperate?

Questions for Discussion

1. Recall the holding in *Professional Engineers* (see Chapter 3) that only Congress, not private producers, should be allowed to structure an industry on the premise that other values are more important than market competition. Is Justice White's dissent correct that nonprofit entities such as colleges should be exempt from this rule? Or is the majority correct that the NCAA cannot lawfully decide to stifle competition in order to promote what its members (with their own economic interests) perceive to be in the best interests of their educational mission? In thinking about this question, ask yourself how antitrust law should apply to an agreement by the only three hospitals in a city, all of which are nonprofit, to fix common prices for their medical services or not to perform certain types of controversial medical procedures. Should hospitals be allowed to agree to hire employees at defined salaries and benefits? Should the Justice Department have succeeded in its 1992 prosecution of the Massachusetts Institute of Technology for participating in a group of elite private colleges that agreed to specify the amount of financial aid that would be offered to any student accepted by more than one of the colleges. See *United States v. Brown Univ. et al.*, 805 F.Supp. 288 (E.D. Pa., 1992). (All the defendant

schools except MIT agreed to abandon the Ivy Overlap Group while they sought explicit congressional exemption for it.)

2. Given the requirement that colleges compete in selling their product (at least through television), are there any steps the NCAA can take to alleviate the adverse effects that such competition has on the academic and amateur values it seeks to foster in student athletics? The dissent suggests some possibilities, such as forced sharing of all revenues and limiting each school's number of television appearances. Would such steps be lawful under the majority opinion? Why has the NCAA not adopted these or similar measures?

3. Putting aside the question of whether and when it is appropriate to allow alternative social values to trump market competition, the majority suggests—in line with *Broadcast Music* (see Chapter 3)—that many NCAA rules are actually procompetitive because they are important to the creation of a unique product that would not otherwise be available—amateur athletics. Is college football intrinsically different from NFL football? Is college tennis intrinsically different from professional tennis? Are you persuaded by the Court's arguments that the NCAA's television rules did not significantly contribute to the preservation of amateur athletics?

4. Since this decision, the CFA (as well as the Pac–Ten and Big Ten conferences) has entered into network contracts that give exclusive network rights to broadcast members' football games and thus prevent individual schools from negotiating their own television deals. (Almost every college basketball conference has negotiated similar television packages.) If, as the Court holds, any agreement among different colleges that has the effect (indeed, the express purpose) of reducing output and raising prices violates the rule of reason, are the CFA's contracts any more legal than the NCAA's? See *Regents of the Univ. of Calif. v. American Broadcasting Co.*, 747 F.2d 511 (9th Cir.1984); and *Association of Independent Television Stations, Inc. v. College Football Ass'n.*, 637 F.Supp. 1289 (W.D.Okl.1986).

Justice White noted in his dissent that the antitrust victory won by these CFA members might come back to haunt the CFA in its own dealings with the television networks.[9] In the immediate aftermath of the *Board of Regents* ruling, the price of network television packages, which had risen from $5 million per year in the early 1960s to $75 million per year in the early 1980s, dropped sharply in value. Although there were many more college football games on television in 1984 than in 1983 (under a CFA contract with ABC, a Big Ten–Pac 10 contract with CBS, and a host of deals between individual schools and cable networks or television sports distributors), the price of a national game was cut nearly in half. Not until 1990 was the CFA able to negotiate a $70 million per year deal with ABC and ESPN, to go along with the Big Ten–Pac 10 package (which by now had been awarded to

9. See David Greenspan, *College Football's Biggest Fumble: The Economic Impact of the Supreme Court's Decision in* National Collegiate Athletic Association v. Board of Regents of the University of Oklahoma, 33 Antitrust Bulletin 1 (1988).

ABC). Toward the end of those negotiations, Notre Dame broke away and signed a separate 5–year, $35 million deal with NBC for the rights to telecast its home games, to the great displeasure of its fellow CFA members.

The Federal Trade Commission is now considering a complaint that the CFA's exclusive contract with ABC and ESPN violates the Sherman Act. The FTC, though, can enforce antitrust laws only against an entity that is "organized to carry on business for its own profit or that of its members" (see 15 U.S.C. § 44 (1988)). Does this wording encompass the CFA? Regardless of the scope of the FTC's administrative jurisdiction, should the CFA–ABC television package be considered a "restraint of trade" under section 1 of the Sherman Act (in a complaint filed in court by the Justice Department, for example)? Note that the NCAA, the CFA, and intercollegiate sports generally do not enjoy the protective exemption from antitrust enjoyed by professional sports' television packages under the Sports Broadcasting Act (SBA) at issue in the *WGN* decision in Chapter 6. Ironically, the NFL invited the NCAA to co-sponsor the SBA and be included in the list of protected organizations, but NCAA officials, believing that their policies were beyond antitrust question, declined. The NCAA's only statutory protection is § 1293 of the SBA, which rescinds the exemption for a professional league if its games are telecast into any area where a college game is being played on a Saturday.

Questions for Discussion

1. Unlike what has happened in college football, the NCAA continues to sell a single television package for its men's basketball tournament. The annual value of "March Madness" on television has risen from $9 million in 1981 to $145 million in 1991. Suppose the NCAA, building on that experience, replaced football bowl games with (or incorporated them into) an NCAA football championship. Would that event bring more money from network bidders than the $75 million now derived from both television and gate receipts for all the current bowl games? Would such an Association initiative be legal under *Board of Regents*?

2. The majority opinion asserts that the complaining universities, Oklahoma and Georgia, had no real choice but to adhere to the NCAA's television rules. Recall, however, that in *Tarkanian* the Court found that the NCAA was not a "state actor" in ordering UNLV to suspend Coach Tarkanian because, the Court reasoned, UNLV had a choice, "however unpalatable," whether to comply with the NCAA's directives. Are these judicial observations, just four years apart, incompatible? Or is there a difference in the circumstances (legal or factual) that explains these contrasting sentiments?

3. What implications, if any, does the *Board of Regents* decision have for the question of whether professional sports leagues should be treated as single entities for section 1 "conspiracy" purposes? Are there material differences between the structure and product of the NFL or NBA and that of the NCAA?

4. The *Board of Regents* ruling involved the use of antitrust law to eliminate restrictive agreements that affected the supply and price of a product offered to consumers, the principal constituency of antitrust policy. A key step in rule of reason analysis is the determination of the market in which the defendant's product competes. Study the majority opinion closely. Does the Court indicate whether any one league's games should be considered as just one of the many sports and entertainment products that compete for consumer patronage, either at the live gate or on the television screen?

Let us turn away from antitrust law for a moment. The Internal Revenue Service has treated revenues derived from intercollegiate sports telecasts—as well as from gate receipts—as non-taxable income earned by colleges and universities that are non-profit enterprises. The IRS has accepted the schools' argument that, for purposes of sections 511–513 of the Internal Revenue Code, college sports are "related" to the institutions' tax-exempt educational purposes.[10] In the winter of 1992, however, the IRS ruled that funds received from the corporate sponsors of a bowl game (for example, from Mobil Oil for the Cotton Bowl) were unrelated and therefore taxable. Competing bills have been introduced in the Congress that would either overturn this ruling or extend it to all television revenues from college sports. Which of these options makes the most sense as a matter of tax policy? Educational policy? Sports policy?

---

2. ATHLETE MARKET

The sports industry provides the major judicial evidence that the product market is not the exclusive concern of antitrust law and that section 1 prohibits unreasonable restraints on the labor market (at least absent a labor exemption drawn from federal labor law policy). The labor market in intercollegiate sports includes both players and coaches. College coaching staffs occasionally encounter NCAA restraints imposed on the employment market for their services (in addition to the requirement that coaches comply with the NCAA recruiting and eligibility rules described earlier). For example, the NCAA has imposed limits on the size of coaching staffs, a ceiling that has required especially sizable programs to dismiss some assistant coaches. See *Hennessey v. NCAA*, 564 F.2d 1136 (5th Cir.1977).

The overall operation of the college coaching market, though, demonstrates what free agency can do for those who make a difference between winning and losing programs. Total compensation for college football and basketball coaches includes not only base salary, but also shoe contracts, radio and television shows, summer clinics (often at the

10. See Williams, *Suiting up for the Game*, note 7 above, 625–26.

school's facilities), endorsements, and speaking engagements. Earnings from all these sources for well known college coaches such as Bobby Bowden, Lou Holtz, John Thompson and Rick Pitino range from $500,-000 to $1 million dollars per year (comparable to the amounts earned by professional coaches).[11] At its 1992 convention, the NCAA adopted a modest procedural change that requires coaches to get written approval from school officials for their outside sources of income. In a future year, though, one might imagine the President's Commission pressing for a uniform rule that limits coaching earnings to the basic salary paid by the college, and channels much of the extra revenue to the schools to help defray athletic program expenses. How much would such a rule actually reduce coaches' compensation? If the coaches attacked this hypothetical rule on antitrust grounds, they would find a few judicial rulings favorable to the NCAA in the 1970s, but these decisions were short and sparsely reasoned. In any event, these cases all preceded the Supreme Court's holding in *Board of Regents* that at least some NCAA policies are subject to antitrust control. Consider, then, what arguments might be advanced by the NCAA for mandating such common coaching staff policies for its members, and how any such arrangements should fare under present-day antitrust scrutiny. Suppose the NCAA went further to establish a ceiling on the income coaches could receive from all sources, and on the amount of time they could spend on activities not directly related to the school. Would this pass antitrust muster?

The much larger antitrust question, though, concerns the student-athlete, whose terms of service in the sport are closely regulated by the NCAA Manual and enforcement procedures. An appellate court case that considered an antitrust challenge to these NCAA policies was *McCormack v. NCAA*. The case involved a class action brought by a lawyer-alumnus of Southern Methodist University (SMU), who complained on behalf of the school's alumni, cheerleaders, and athletes about the "death penalty" the NCAA imposed on the SMU football program in 1981 for repeated major infractions of NCAA rules prohibit-

---

11. An example is the financial package secured by Bill Frieder when he was lured away from Michigan by Arizona State on the eve of the 1989 NCAA basketball tournament (which the Wolverines proceeded to win under the direction of Frieder's former assistant):

Coach Frieder received a contract that included an incentive of $10,000 for graduation rates, but that incentive was dwarfed by incentives tied to winning and commercial success. The academic incentive in Coach Frieder's contract was miniscule in comparison to incentives related to winning basketball games. Coach Freider received a salary of $154,000; a guarantee of $350,000 in annual income from summer camps, a sneaker company contract and television and radio deals; $20,000 if the Sun Devils win at least ten conference games; an extra week's salary if they win one game in the conference tournament or get an NIT bid; two week's additional salary if they get an NCAA berth; three week's salary if they reach the NCAA regionals; four week's salary if they reach the "Final Four"; five week's salary if they win the National Championship; $20,000 if the average attendance at home games is at least 7,5000; $30,000 if the average attendance is at least 11,000.

Rodney K. Smith, *An Academic Game Plan for Reforming Big–Time Intercollegiate Athletics*, 67 Denver Univ. L. Rev. 213, n.213 (1990)

ing payments and extra benefits to athletes.[12] The Fifth Circuit spent most of its decision doubting whether McCormack or the class he claimed to represent had standing to complain of an antitrust violation. Assuming, for the sake of argument, that at least the players might have standing to challenge NCAA restraints on compensation of student-athletes, the Fifth Circuit panel briefly discussed the merits of such a claim.

McCORMACK v. NCAA

United States Court of Appeals, Fifth Circuit, 1988.

845 F.2d 1338.

RUBIN, CIRCUIT JUDGE.

* * *

The Supreme Court has recently considered the antitrust laws in relation to college football. In NCAA v. Board of Regents of the University of Oklahoma, the Court held that the antitrust laws apply to some aspects of college football competition and that the NCAA had violated those laws by placing restrictions on the ability of member schools to sell the rights to televise the schools' football games.

The NCAA argues that, despite the holding in *Board of Regents*, its eligibility rules are not subject to the antitrust laws because, unlike the television restrictions in *Board of Regents*, the eligibility rules have purely or primarily noncommercial objectives. The NCAA's argument finds some support in the caselaw, but we need not address it here. Assuming, without deciding, that the antitrust laws apply to the eligibility rules, it does not follow that the rules violate those laws. The Sherman Act does not forbid every combination or conspiracy in restraint of trade, only those that are unreasonable. We hold that the NCAA's eligibility rules are reasonable and that the plaintiffs have failed to allege any facts to the contrary.

The plaintiffs argue that the eligibility rules constitute price fixing by a cartel of buyers of labor and so should be conclusively presumed to be unreasonable and therefore illegal. In *Board of Regents*, however, the Supreme Court held that the NCAA's rules prescribing the way in which its members compete with one another should be analyzed under the rubric of reasonableness, rather than condemned as per se illegal. The Court recognized that in college football, horizontal restraints on competition are essential if the product is to be available at all.... What the NCAA and its member institutions market in this case is competition itself—contests between competing institutions. Of course, this would be completely ineffective if there were no rules on which the competitors agreed to create and define the competition to be marketed.

---

12. On the SMU case generally, see Chapter 8, and also David Whitford, *A Payroll to Meet: A Story of Greed, Corrup-* *tion and Football at SMU* (New York: MacMillan, 1989).

Similarly, this court has recognized that "in some sporting enterprises a few rules are essential to survival." We have held that if indicia of anticompetitive intent are lacking, the rule-of-reason analysis applies.

The essential inquiry under the rule-of-reason analysis is whether the challenged restraint enhances competition. Applying this test, we have little difficulty in concluding that the challenged restrictions are reasonable. The Supreme Court indicated strongly in *Board of Regents* that such was the case. In a paragraph mentioning the eligibility rules expressly, the majority stated:

> It is reasonable to assume that most of the regulatory controls of the NCAA are justifiable means of fostering competition among amateur athletic teams and therefore procompetitive because they enhance public interest in intercollegiate athletics.

The Court further explained:

> [T]he NCAA seeks to market a particular brand of football—college football. The identification of this "product" with an academic tradition differentiates college football from and makes it more popular than professional sports to which it might otherwise be comparable, such as, for example, minor league baseball. In order to preserve the character and quality of the "product," athletes must not be paid, must be required to attend class, and the like. And the integrity of the "product" cannot be preserved except by mutual agreement; if an institution adopted such restrictions unilaterally, its effectiveness as a competitor on the playing field might soon be destroyed. Thus, the NCAA plays a vital role in enabling college football to preserve its character, and as a result enables a product to be marketed which might otherwise be unavailable. In performing this role, its actions widen consumer choice—not only the choices available to sports fans but also those available to athletes—and hence can be viewed as procompetitive.

* * *

The NCAA markets college football as a product distinct from professional football. The eligibility rules create the product and allow its survival in the face of commercializing pressures. The goal of the NCAA is to integrate athletics with academics. Its requirements reasonably further this goal.

After amending their complaint once and withdrawing another amendment, the plaintiffs still produce only two allegations to support their claim that the NCAA's rules are designed to stifle competition: that the NCAA permits some compensation through scholarships and allows a student to be a professional in one sport and an amateur in another. Accepting these facts as true, however, they do not undermine the rationality of the eligibility requirements. That the NCAA has not distilled amateurism to its purest form does not mean its attempts to maintain a mixture containing some amateur elements are unreasonable. We therefore conclude that the plaintiffs cannot prove any set of facts that would carry their antitrust claim and that the motion to dismiss was properly granted.

Because the eligibility rules do not violate the antitrust laws, enforcement of them through suspension and other restrictions does not constitute an illegal group boycott.

Summary judgment granted.

————

A much more substantial antitrust challenge to NCAA policy was mounted by the Public Citizens Litigation Group on behalf of Braxston Banks, a former Notre Dame football player. This suit targeted the NCAA eligibility rules that deny "amateur status" to any player who "enters into a professional draft or an agreement with an agent ... to negotiate a professional contract" (Article 12.1.1(f)). This is the rule that courts and legislatures attempted to enforce against agents to protect colleges from premature loss of their players (see Chapter 4).[13] The question posed in the *Banks* litigation is whether the underlying NCAA policy unreasonably deprives college players of the opportunity to participate in the draft and receive the advice and representation of an agent.

P   Δ

BANKS v. NCAA

United States Court of Appeals, Seventh Circuit, 1992.

977 F.2d 1081.

COFFEY, CIRCUIT JUDGE.

[Braxston Banks entered Notre Dame in 1986 as a highly rated football prospect. By the end of his freshman year he was the starting fullback on the varsity team. But Banks injured his knee early in his sophomore year and started only a handful of games during that season and the next one. Banks decided to sit out his entire senior year (1989) to give his knee a chance to recover fully. By that time, Banks' classmate, Anthony Johnson, had become Notre Dame's starting fullback and the top-rated NFL prospect at that position.

In the winter of 1990, Banks debated whether to turn professional with Johnson or to return to Notre Dame for a fifth year, for which he was eligible under NCAA rules and for which Notre Dame was ready to give him another year's full scholarship. After extensive discussions

Facts

---

13. Recall in particular, the case of Norby Walters and Lloyd Bloom, which is recounted in Chris Mortenson, *Playing for Keeps: How One Man Kept the Mob From Sinking Its Hooks Into Pro Football* (New York: Simon and Schuster, 1991). In fact, Walters and Bloom sought to have their criminal indictment quashed on the ground that the NCAA rules whose violations the agents and their clients had concealed were themselves illegal under antitrust law. The district court tersely rejected this argument in a decision that focused primarily on mail fraud issues. See *United States v. Walters & Bloom*, 711 F.Supp. 1435 (N.D. Ill.1989).

with NFL scouts and a player-agent known to his family, Banks decided in March 1990 to enter the NFL draft and to sign a representation agreement with the agent. To make himself eligible for the draft, the NFL required Banks to sign a form whereby he "irrevocably renounced any and all remaining college eligibility." As far as the NCAA was concerned, its own Bylaws 12.2.4 and 12.3 dictated that either of Banks' actions—entering the draft or signing an agent representation contract—would cost Banks his future college eligibility.

Unfortunately, the condition of Banks' knee hampered his performance at the NFL tryout camp in Indianapolis in early April. Thus no team selected Banks in any of the twelve rounds of the late April draft, and no team was willing to sign him to a free-agent contract. Though Banks returned to Notre Dame in the summer of 1990 to finish his degree, the NCAA would not give him a waiver from its rules to permit Banks to play for Notre Dame that fall. As a result, Banks launched this antitrust suit against the NCAA. The judge granted the NCAA's motion under Rule 12(b)(6) for summary dismissal because of Banks' failure to state a valid antitrust claim.]

* * *

IV. Rule 12(b)(6) Dismissal of a Rule-of-Reason Case

Banks' primary contention on appeal is that because the record is not thoroughly developed, it was inappropriate for the district court to decide that the NCAA no-draft and no-agent rules were pro-competitive in ruling on a Rule 12(b)(6) motion to dismiss. . . . The district court decided the case not on the basis of the relative anti-competitive effect of the rules versus the pro-competitive impact, but on the ground of Banks' absolute failure to allege an anti-competitive effect. . . . Since the district judge's decision was based on Banks' failure to allege an anti-competitive effect on an identifiable market, the argument that the court improperly determined that the rules were reasonable on a motion to dismiss is without merit.

V. The Validity of the Antitrust Claim

* * *

[Plaintiff's] allegations identify two markets: (1) NCAA football players who enter the draft and/or employ an agent and (2) college institutions that are members of the NCAA. Another reading of the complaint might even have deduced a third market, the NFL player recruitment market. But regardless of how charitably the complaint is read, it has failed to define an anti-competitive effect of the alleged restraints on the markets.

The dissent reasons that Banks has alleged that the NCAA no-draft rule has an anti-competitive effect in the market for college football players. The dissent claims this anti-competitive effect is the no-draft rule "foreclosing players 'from choosing a major college football team based on the willingness of the institution to waive or change [the no-draft] rule.' " This allegation can at best be described as inaccurate and further fails to allege an anti-competitive impact. First, as Banks states in his amended complaint, the NCAA has adopted the no-draft, no-agent, and other substantive rules to which all NCAA member institutions "have agreed, and do in fact, adhere." Contrary to Banks' erroneous allegation, an NCAA member institution may not waive or change the no-draft rule at its discretion, for it is rather obvious that only the National Collegiate Athletic Association can waive or change one of its substantive rules. Any school that sought to waive or change the rules would forfeit its ability to participate in NCAA sanctioned events.

Second, as the district court held, the complaint has failed to allege an anti-competitive impact. The failure results from Banks' inability to explain how the no-draft rule restrains trade in the college football labor market. The NCAA Rules seek to promote fair competition, encourage the educational pursuits of student-athletes and prevent commercialism. . . .

As the Supreme Court in *Board of Regents* stated: "most of the regulatory controls of the NCAA [are] a justifiable means of fostering competition among the amateur athletic teams and therefore are pro-competitive because they enhance public interest in intercollegiate athletics." The Court further explained:

> The NCAA seeks to market a particular brand of football—college football. The identification of this "product" with an academic tradition differentiates college football from and makes it more popular than professional sports to which it might otherwise be comparable, such as, for example, minor league baseball. In order to preserve the character and quality of the "product," athletes must not be paid, must be required to attend class, and the like. And the integrity of the "product" cannot be preserved except by mutual agreement; if an institution adopted such restrictions unilaterally (restrictions on eligibility rules), its effectiveness as a competitor on the playing field might soon be destroyed. Thus, the NCAA plays a vital role in enabling college football to preserve its character, and as a result enables a product to be marketed which might otherwise be unavailable. In performing this role, its actions widen consumer choice—not only the choices available to sports fans but also those available to athletes—and hence can be viewed as procompetitive.

The no-draft rule has no more impact on the market for college football players than other NCAA eligibility requirements such as grades, semester hours carried, or requiring a high school diploma. They all constitute eligibility requirements essential to participation in NCAA sponsored amateur athletic competition. Banks might just as well have alleged that only permitting a student five calendar years in which to participate in four seasons of intercollegiate athletics restrains trade. Banks' allegation that the no-draft rule restrains trade is absurd. None of the NCAA rules affecting college football eligibility restrain trade in the market for college players because the NCAA does not exist as a minor league training ground for future NFL players but rather to provide an opportunity for competition among amateur students pursuing a collegiate education.[12] Because the no-draft rule represents a desirable and legitimate attempt "to keep university athletics from becoming professionalized to the extent that profit making objectives would overshadow educational objectives," the no-draft rule and other like NCAA regulations preserve the bright line of demarcation between college and "play for pay" football. We consider college football players as student-athletes simultaneously pursuing academic degrees that will prepare them to enter the employment market in non-athletic occupations, and hold that the regulations of the NCAA are designed to preserve the honesty and integrity of intercollegiate athletics and foster fair competition among the participating amateur college students.

Hold
(con 4.)

In order for the NCAA Rules to be considered a restraint of trade in violation of § 1 of the Sherman Act, Banks must allege that the no-draft and no-agent rules are terms of employment that diminish competition in the employment market (i.e., college football).

The dissent refers to NCAA member colleges as "purchasers of labor" in the college football player market and the players as "suppliers" in this market.[13] After likening colleges to "purchasers of labor," the dissent extends the analogy to conclude that colleges offer material terms of employment to their college players and that the no-draft rule is a "material term of employment" that harms competition in the college football labor market.

In contrast to professional football, NCAA student-athletes are required to attend class, maintain a minimum grade point average, and enroll and complete a required number of courses to obtain a degree. The no-draft rule is evidence of the academic priority of the NCAA because it forecloses a student-athlete from hiring an agent or entering the NFL draft and after failing to meet the professional standards, returning to play college football to improve his football skills in hopes

---

12. This conclusion is buttressed by the fact that a very small number of college athletes go on to participate in professional athletics. Of the over 12,000 Division 1–A college football players, less than 300 go on to the NFL each year. In fact, it has been calculated that of the elite 336 players drafted each year, only 49 percent make NFL teams and after 5 years only 35 percent are still with an NFL team.

13. We disagree with Banks' allegation in paragraph 22(c) of his Amended Complaint that the NCAA no-draft and no-agent Rules give the college player only one realistic chance of being drafted in the NFL, because the college player (1) can enter the draft any time during his college career (Tommy Maddox of UCLA was just drafted by Denver although he had two more years of eligibility); (2) enter the draft, then play for another league like the CFL, WFL, or ARENA or even sit out for a year and then reenter the draft (Bo Jackson was a first round draft choice of Tampa Bay, but he chose to play baseball instead, the next year he was drafted by the Los Angeles Raiders with whom he signed); or (3) complete his eligibility before entering the draft.

Recently 97 of the 107 NCAA Division 1–A football programs imposed strict guidelines on NFL scouts to prevent plucking student-athletes from colleges.

of entering an upcoming draft. In denying a college football player the right to play professional football (entering the NFL draft) and then return to college football, the no-draft rule merely serves as an NCAA eligibility requirement and precludes the existence of a college football labor market for athletes who are ineligible by NCAA standards.

Secondly, we disagree with the dissent's allegation that NCAA member schools are "purchasers of labor," as the operation of the NCAA eligibility and recruiting requirements prohibits member colleges from engaging in price competition for players. We fail to understand how the dissent can allege that NCAA colleges purchase labor through the grant-in-aid athletic scholarships offered to college players when the value of the scholarship is based upon the school's tuition and room and board, not by the supply and demand for players. Elimination of the no-draft and no-agent rules would fly in the face of the NCAA's amateurism requirements. Member schools might very well be exposed to agents offering the services of their football playing clients to the highest bidder. In representing their "pro athlete" clients, the agents would in all probability attempt to bargain with the NCAA school and might very well expect the school to offer their client an attractive contract, possibly involving automobiles, condominiums, and cash as compensation in contravention of the NCAA amateurism rules. Such arrangements might involve cash compensation payable only in the future after the player has completed his college eligibility and continues with an NFL club. The involvement of professional sports agents in NCAA football would turn amateur intercollegiate athletics into a sham because the focus of college football would shift from educating the student-athlete to creating a "minor-league" farm system out of college football that would operate solely to improve players' skills for professional football in the NFL. We should not permit the entry of professional athletes and their agents into NCAA sports because the cold commercial nature of professional sports would not only destroy the amateur status of college athletics but more importantly would interfere with the athletes' proper focus on their educational pursuits and direct their attention to the quick buck in pro sports.

The no-agent and no-draft rules are vital and must work in conjunction with other eligibility requirements to preserve the amateur status of college athletics, and prevent the sports agents from further intruding into the collegiate educational system.

Note
(Hold)

* * *

The dissent takes a surprisingly cynical view of college athletics and contends that "colleges squeeze out of their players one or two more years of service" because the no-draft rule forces the player to choose between continued collegiate eligibility and entering the draft. This description of players "selling their services" to NCAA colleges stands in stark contrast to the academic and amateurism requirements of the vast majority of college athletic programs that, in compliance with the NCAA rules and regulations, are foreclosed from offering cash compensation or "non-permissible awards, extra benefits, or excessive or improper expenses not authorized by NCAA legislation...." The fact that a minority of schools (such as the University of Houston) [17] "use" athletes rather than encourage and foster their students' academic pursuits, does not negate the fact that all NCAA member colleges encourage and require their student-athletes to carry a minimum number of semester credits and maintain a minimum grade point average equivalent to the academic program the university's non-athletic students follow.

* * *

We agree with the district court's finding that the plaintiff has failed to allege an anti-competitive effect on a relevant market; at best Banks has merely attempted to frame his complaint in antitrust language. While Banks alleges a restraint on the market of college football players, college institutions who are members of the NCAA, and perhaps an NFL player recruitment market, the complaint fails to explain how these alleged restraints diminish competition in or among the markets. In our review of Banks' arguments in his appellate briefs as well as our review of the oral argument, we have been unable to discern a cogent argument articulated even on appeal that the alleged restraints impose an anti-competitive effect on the alleged markets. The appellant merely claims that there is an anti-competitive effect, but he fails to explain what it is. While Banks might possibly have been able to allege an anti-competitive impact on a relevant market through a more carefully drafted complaint or an amendment to his complaint, he failed to do so. It is not for us, as appellate judges, to restructure his complaint for him.

Affirmed.

FLAUM, CIRCUIT JUDGE, concurring in part and dissenting in part.

* * *

As the NCAA concedes, Banks defined two markets in his complaint, only one of which it is necessary to address here: the nationwide labor market for college football players. NCAA member colleges are the purchasers of labor in this market, and the players are the suppliers. The players agree to compete in football games sponsored by the colleges, games that typically garner the colleges a profit, in exchange for tuition, room, board and other benefits.

---

17. Recently, the NCAA released the graduation rates of Division I NCAA member schools. These statistics reveal that only 14 percent of scholarship athletes in football graduated from the University of Houston within six years of their matriculation in 1983–84 or 1984–85. In addition, the NCAA reported that zero percent of black football athletes at the University of Houston graduated within six years of their enrollment in 1983–84 or 1984–85, whereas 33 percent of white football players at Houston graduated within six years of their enrollment in 1983–84 or 1984–85.

It is hardly a revelation that colleges fiercely compete for the most promising high school football players—the players who, incidentally, are most likely to feel constrained by the challenged rules two or three years down the line. If the no-draft rule were scuttled, colleges that promised their athletes the opportunity to test the waters in the NFL draft before their eligibility expired, and return if things didn't work out, would be more attractive to athletes than colleges that declined to offer the same opportunity. The no-draft rule eliminates this potential element of competition among colleges, the purchasers of labor in the college football labor market. It categorically rules out a term of employment that players, the suppliers of labor in that market, would find advantageous.

* * *

It should come as no surprise that the no-draft rule operates to the detriment of the players, and that colleges benefit from the fact that their athletes feel tied to the institution for four years. Consider, for example, athletes who are known in the vernacular as "bubble" players. These athletes are excellent competitors at the collegiate level, but for various reasons are considered less than certain NFL prospects. Bubble players who wish to market their wares in the professional market after their sophomore or junior year will forego entry into the NFL draft because, if they are not selected (or fail to join a team after being selected), the rule will prevent them from returning to college to hone their skills and try again in subsequent years. See Note, Sherman Act Invalidation of the NCAA Amateurism Rules, 105 Harv. L. Rev. 1299, 1311 (1992). The rule permits colleges to squeeze out of their players one or two more years of service, years the colleges might have lost had the ability to enter the draft without consequence to eligibility been the subject of bargaining between athletes and colleges. The rule thereby distorts the "price" of labor in the college football labor market to the detriment of players.

The NCAA disputes this characterization, maintaining that the no-draft rule is not "anticompetitive" as the term is employed under the Sherman Act. At the heart of its argument is the contention that "there is no price competition as such among colleges for players because the 'price,' the value of grant-in-aid, is determined by the school's tuition, room, and board, not by the supply of and demand for players." This analysis of the college football labor market is partially correct; in that market, players exchange their labor for in-kind benefits, not cash. At least ideally. But see Johnson, Defense Against the NCAA, U.S. News & World Rep., Jan. 13, 1992, at 25 (improper cash payments made to football players at Auburn University); Johnson, Playing for Pay in Texas, Newsweek, Mar. 16, 1987, at 32 (same at Southern Methodist University).

It is unrealistic, however, to suggest that the value of those in-kind benefits is limited solely to tuition, room and board. If this were true, the best football players would attend the most expensive private universities that would admit them, for these universities would offer, under the NCAA's analysis, the most "valuable" compensation for their services. Assuming some regional loyalties, private colleges such as Syracuse University, the University of Southern California, and Notre Dame would consistently outrecruit public colleges such as Penn State, UCLA and the University of Michigan. As anyone familiar with college football well knows, this is not the case. The reason is simple. Athletes look to more than tuition, room and board when determining which college has offered them the most attractive package of in-kind benefits. Some athletes look primarily to the reputation of a particular program or coach as a "feeder" into the NFL; others believe that the quality of a university's academic program and the commitment of the coaching staff to scholarly pursuits is more important. Some athletes look to whether a college will offer them a cushy, high-paying job during the summer or school year; others might be attracted by state-of-the-art training facilities. And some athletes, if given the chance, would look to whether a college would allow them to enter the NFL draft and return if they did not join a professional team.

All of these things—with the exception of the last item—are "terms of employment" that currently sweeten the pot for athletes choosing among college football programs. They provide, apart from tuition, room and board, the means by which colleges, as purchasers of labor, attract and compensate their players, the suppliers of labor. That the medium of exchange is non-monetary does not alter the fact that these benefits constitute the "price" of labor in the college football market, or that the categorical elimination of one of those benefits harms competition in that market. The NCAA's protestations notwithstanding, there can be no doubt that Banks has alleged an anticompetitive effect in a relevant market.

* * *

Banks easily clears the threshold ["of connecting the injury claimed to the purposes of the antitrust laws"]. The no-draft rule, as noted, is anticompetitive because it constitutes an agreement among colleges to eliminate an element of competition in the college football labor market. The purposes of the antitrust laws are served when employers are prevented from tampering with the employment market in this precise way. "Just as antitrust law seeks to preserve the free market opportunities of buyers and sellers of goods, so also it seeks to do the same for buyers and sellers of employment services...." Banks' injury—namely, the revocation of his eligibility and consequent loss of his athletic scholarship during his final year at Notre Dame—"flows from" the precise anticompetitive aspects of the NCAA rules that he set out in his complaint.

The NCAA also raises the issue of harm to consumers; it contends that Banks' complaint is deficient because it does not "reasonably support the inference that consumers are harmed by the operation of the no-draft and no-agent rules." Whether harm to consumers is the sine qua non of antitrust injury is an issue over which there is currently a split in this circuit. Some of our cases hold that a plaintiff, to satisfy the antitrust injury requirement, must demonstrate that the challenged practice causing him harm also harms consumers by reducing output or raising prices. *Stamatakis Indus., Inc. v. King*, 965 F.2d 469, 471 (7th Cir.1992); *Chicago Professional Sports Ltd. Partnership v. National Basketball Ass'n.*, 961 F.2d 667, 670 (7th Cir.1992). Others hold that application of the antitrust laws "does not depend in each particular case upon the ultimate demonstrable consumer effect." *Fishman v. Estate of Wirtz*, 807 F.2d 520, 536 (7th Cir.1986); see also *Chicago Professional Sports*, 961 F.2d at 677 (Cudahy, J., concurring).

One can dispense with the NCAA's contention without choosing sides in this dispute. To see why, it is important first to identify the consumers and the market at issue in this case. By "consumers," the NCAA apparently means people who watch college football. These individuals certainly are consumers in the college football product market, but the market at issue here is the college football labor market, and the NCAA member colleges are consumers in that market. It would be counterintuitive to require Banks to demonstrate that the no-draft and no-agent rules harm the colleges, the very entities that established those rules. I doubt very strongly that the rule laid out in *Chicago Professional Sports*, to the extent it is valid elsewhere, was intended to apply in this context. Concerted action among consumers that lowers prices harms competition as much as concerted action among producers that raises prices. The distinction should be irrelevant to any discussion of antitrust injury. Professors Areeda and Turner, when discussing the right of laborers to challenge antitrust violations in the labor market, put things nicely:

> It would be perverse ... to hold that the very object of the law's solicitude and the persons most directly concerned—perhaps the only persons concerned—could not challenge the restraint....
> The standing of such plaintiffs is undoubted and seldom challenged.

Banks has alleged that the NCAA rules harm competition to the detriment of producers in the college football labor market, and that his injuries are directly related to that harm. This is sufficient to establish "antitrust injury" in this context.

I add here a caveat to avert any potential misunderstandings. My point is only that Banks has properly alleged an anticompetitive effect in a relevant market and has demonstrated antitrust injury, and hence that his damages action should survive the NCAA's motion to dismiss. But this is, of course, only the first step. To ultimately prevail, Banks also must demonstrate, under the rule of reason, that the no-agent and no-draft rules, despite their anticompetitive effects, are not "justifiable means of fostering competition among amateur athletic teams and therefore procompetitive" on the whole. It may very well be that the no-draft and no-agent rules are essential to the survival of college football as a distinct and viable product, in which case Banks would lose. A lively debate has arisen among those who have already considered this matter. I opt not to join the fray here, for I think it unwise to weigh pro- and anticompetitive effects under the rule of reason on a motion to dismiss.

Today's decision, by holding that Banks has not alleged that the rules are anticompetitive in the first instance, deprives him of the opportunity to join this issue on remand. As I have discussed, it is difficult to reconcile this holding with a sound reading of Banks' complaint. On a broader level, I am also concerned that today's decision—unintentionally, to be sure, for it suggests that a "more artfully drafted complaint" could have alleged an anticompetitive effect in this market—will provide comfort to the NCAA's incredulous assertion that its eligibility rules are "noncommercial." The NCAA would have us believe that intercollegiate athletic contests are about spirit, competition, camaraderie, sportsmanship, hard work (which they certainly are) . . . and nothing else. Players play for the fun of it, colleges get a kick out of entertaining the student body and alumni, but the relationship between players and colleges is positively noncommercial. It is consoling to buy into these myths, for they remind us of a more innocent era—an era where recruiting scandals were virtually unknown, where amateurism was more a reality than an ideal, and where post-season bowl games were named for commodities, not corporations. On the flip side, it is disquieting to think of college football as a business, of colleges as the purchasers of labor, and of athletes as the suppliers.

The NCAA continues to purvey, even in this case, an outmoded image of intercollegiate sports that no longer jibes with reality. The times have changed. College football is a terrific American institution that generates abundant nonpecuniary benefits for players and fans, but it is also a vast commercial venture that yields substantial profits for colleges. The games provide fans with entertaining contests to watch, and athletes with an opportunity to display and develop their strength, skills and character, but they are saleable products nonetheless. An athlete's participation offers all of the rewards that attend vigorous competition in organized sport, but it is also labor, labor for which the athlete is recompensed. The no-draft and no-agent rules may, ultimately, pass muster under the rule of reason. But, putting the adequacy of Banks' complaint to the side, contending that they have no commercial effect on competition in the college football labor market, or that there is no market of that type at all, is chimerical:

> The true stake is this decades-long gentleman's agreement between the NFL and the college powers-that-be that has kept all but a handful of football playing collegians from turning pro before their four-year use to their schools is exhausted. The pros get a free farm system that supplies them with well-trained, much publicized employees. The colleges get to keep their players the equivalent of barefoot and pregnant.

Klein, College Football: Keeping 'em Barefoot, Wall St. J., Sept. 4, 1987, at 15.

When confronted with the clash between soothing nostalgia and distressing reality, it is oftentimes difficult to resist the call of tennis champion Andre Agassi, who when hawking cameras off the court tells us that "image is everything." But we must remember that Agassi's domain, at least in this instance, is television. What may be true there is decidedly not under the lens of the antitrust laws. Having found that Banks has cleared the threshold of alleging an anticompetitive effect in a relevant market, I would reverse the district court's dismissal of his damages action and remand for further proceedings.

————

Was the holding in *Banks*[14] based upon a deficiency in pleadings, or upon the court's view that the nature of college sports made it impossible for a student-athlete to formulate an antitrust claim against the NCAA's amateurism and academic eligibility rules? If the former, how should Banks have crafted his complaint to satisfy the court? If the latter, do you agree with that substantive position? Consider, in particular, the majority's assertion that college athletes are not employees and there is no labor market in which NCAA members might compete for them. Is the fact that NCAA rules prohibit schools from competing for athletes with cash evidence that there is no athletic labor market, or evidence that NCAA members have combined to establish their favored uniform terms for competition in that market?

Having observed the impact that these NCAA rules have on athletes who make no secret of their actions, we can now revisit the real policy questions that were disguised somewhat in the Chapter 5 cases involving underhanded behavior by players and agents. Is it fair for the NCAA to take away an athlete's eligibility because he requests inclusion in the NFL or NBA draft? In neither baseball nor hockey does the professional league require a positive election by the athlete before he can be drafted. At its 1992 convention the NCAA made it clear that an athlete would not lose his eligibility for negotiating with a professional club that had drafted him if he had not taken an affirmative step to be part of the draft. (Eligibility would be lost if the player employed an agent in the negotiations or if the player actually signed a professional contract.) While an NCAA Committee has proposed that football and basketball players be allowed to participate in the professional drafts in these sports without compromising their college eligibility, consideration of that proposal has been postponed until at least the 1994 convention. In football and basketball, who actually gains and

---

14. An almost identical suit was resolved in the same manner as *Banks* by a district court in Tennessee. See *Gaines v. NCAA*, 746 F.Supp. 738 (M.D.Tenn.1990). For a trenchant critique of the district court decision in *Banks*, see Ethan Lock, *Unreasonable NCAA Eligibility Rules Send Braxston Banks Truckin*, 20 Capital Univ. L. Rev. 643 (1991).

who loses from the complementary efforts of the NCAA and the professional leagues to force college players to make an irrevocable election between the college and professional ranks, in order to maintain the NCAA's "clear line of demarcation"?

Consider the experience of young Brian Taylor, a high school graduate selected by the Yankees as the first pick in the 1991 baseball draft. After a summer of negotiating, on the eve of his enrollment date in junior college, Taylor signed a contract with the Yankees for an unprecedented $1.5 million bonus. The reaction of Major League Baseball in the winter of 1992 was to modify its draft rules to preserve the drafting team's rights to a high school graduate during the player's college career. Why did the owners do this? Since then, the baseball labor arbitrator, George Nicolau, has ruled that the owners' unilateral adoption of the new draft rules violated the collective bargaining agreement with the Players Association because they infringed upon the rights of current major league players. How can rules for drafting high school players affect current major league players?

As the *Banks* court acknowledges, the case illustrates a phenomenon of broader significance for the role of sports in higher education. Only a tiny number of college athletes can make a career of professional sports. The odds of a college player making the cut as a rookie on a professional team are 1 in 75 in football and 1 in 70 in basketball.[15] Fortunately, Banks had the ability and motivation to return to college and get a degree to equip him for a different career path. Too often, though, that is not the result of the student-athlete's stay in college.

Questions for Discussion

1. The *Banks* majority argued that if the NCAA's "no draft" and "no agent" rules were held illegal under section 1, the same fate must befall all other NCAA eligibility requirements. If a court found unreasonable the NCAA's bar against Banks' returning for his senior year, must the same antitrust verdict follow for the NCAA rules that limit Notre Dame's (and other colleges') financial expenditures for athletes to reimbursement of standard educational expenses? Or can these two features of NCAA "amateurism" be distinguished under the antitrust Rule of Reason?

2. Should the long-standing NCAA bar on payments to college athletes be maintained,[16] or should each school determine whether this is how it wants to conduct its athletic program? Consider these two analogies to the situation of college athletes. Suppose that the NFL (without agreement from the Players Association) adopted a league policy limiting salaries and bonuses that teams could pay to draft picks. Would this policy be acceptable under the antitrust rule of reason (assuming that the NFL is not a single entity)? Alternatively, suppose that the nation's universities

---

15. These odds were calculated from 1989 figures presented in Wilford S. Bailey & Taylor D. Littleton, *Athletics and Academe: An Anatomy of Abuses and a Prescription for Reform* 84 (New York: MacMillan, 1991).

16. For contrasting views on this issue, compare Goldman, *Sports and Antitrust*, note 8 above (no), with Smith, *An Academic Game Plan*, note 11 above, at 274–77 (yes).

agreed on the amount and terms of financial aid they would give to students. On the amount of money they would pay to teaching and research assistants? On the amount of money that teaching hospitals would offer to prospective interns and residents? Would any such intercollegiate agreement be acceptable under antitrust law? See *United States v. Brown Univ. et al.*, 805 F. Supp. 288 (E.D.Pa.1992). Is there anything distinctive about the student-athlete, by comparison to these examples?

In *Banks*, the Seventh Circuit majority relied heavily on the Supreme Court's *Board of Regents* decision applying antitrust law to the NCAA's dealings with television networks, in which the Court intimated that NCAA regulation of student-athletes was distinctive (dicta that were later relied on by the Fifth Circuit in *McCormack*). The judicial assumption is that athlete regulation is designed to develop and market college sports as an activity played by student amateurs—a product that is clearly demarcated from professional sports in consumer appeal. From the very beginning [17] the NCAA philosophy has been that

> [a]n amateur in athletics is one that enters and takes part in athletic contests purely in obedience to the play impulse or for the satisfaction of purely play motives and for the exercise, training, and social pleasures derived. The natural or primary attitude of mind and motives in play determines amateurism.

This philosophy initially led the NCAA to prohibit "the offering of inducements to players to enter colleges or universities because of their athletic abilities and of supporting or maintaining players while students on account of their athletic abilities." As late as 1935, the NCAA Code on Recruiting and Subsidizing of Athletes banned participation in intercollegiate athletics by anyone who had ever "received a loan, scholarship aid, remission of fees, or employment, primarily because he is an athlete, through channels not open to non-athletes equally with athletes." Only after extensive struggles in the late 1940s and early 1950s did the current NCAA regime emerge, under which member schools are permitted to offer scholarships that pay student-athletes their tuition, fees, books, and room and board, supplemented by general need-based financial assistance (up to $1,700), and often by extensive and costly academic tutoring. In light of this evolution of its policy, can the NCAA claim that college athletes are truly "amateurs" for purposes of antitrust law, and that the product it offers to fans is distinctive in that respect from professional sports? Or are college athletes in the revenue sports (Division 1 men's basketball and Division 1–A football) really professionals who, instead of being paid cash in amounts based on free market negotiations, are paid in kind, through

17. For an account of the historical evolution of the NCAA's philosophy of amateurism, see Lawrence, *Unsportsmanlike Conduct*, note 1 above.

fixed amounts of educational services determined by a producer-employer trade association?

Suppose that a court were to find illegal under the Sherman Antitrust Act the battery of rules in the NCAA Manual specifying the "amateur" flavor of college sports. Does it follow that the "academic" features of NCAA eligibility rules—for example Proposition 48—would also be legally improper?

D. GENDER DISCRIMINATION LAW [18]

Whatever one's views about the foregoing questions as a matter of pure antitrust principle, many people would be troubled if a court took it upon itself to transform college sports in this fashion. There has, however, been a good deal of discussion recently about the desirability of adding to the current grant-in-aid for college athletes a sufficient stipend that would enable athletes to enjoy the same amenities of college life as do their fellow students, who are not required to devote 30 to 40 hours per week to football or basketball practices and games. Implementation of such a policy, though, would require adoption of a new NCAA rule, one that spelled out the amounts and conditions of payments permitted from all institutions. Indeed, a significant legal obstacle to the NCAA taking any such action is that once schools make direct cash payments to athletes for playing college sports, it would become far more difficult to invoke the rubric of "amateur" college sports as a defense against antitrust challenges such as *McCormack* and *Banks*. Could the NCAA plausibly argue that college sports are a distinctive product because they are just a little professional?

The consequence of a successful legal attack under antitrust would not be simply to force the NCAA to authorize modest stipends for all college athletes. The result, instead, would be the same kind of competitive bidding by colleges for "free agent" high school players as we have become accustomed to in professional baseball every winter. And unless student athletes were then deemed to be "employees" under the National Labor Relations Act, there could be no labor union

---

18. A popular account of the emergence of women in sports is Mariah Burton Nelson, *Are We Winning Yet? How Women Are Changing Sports and How Sports Are Changing Women* (New York: Random House, 1991). Systematic treatments of the legal issues are to be found in Glenn M. Wong & Richard J. Ensor, *Sex Discrimination in Athletics: A Review of Accomplishments and Defeats*, 2, Gonzaga L. Rev. 343 (1986); Karen L. Tokarz, Sex Discrimination in Amateur and Professional Sports, Chapter 13 of Gary Uberstine ed., *Law of Professional and Amateur Sports* (Deerfield, Ill: Clark, Boardman and Calla-

ghan, 1991); and Diane Heckman, *Women & Athletics: A Twenty Year Retrospective on Title IX*, 9 Univ. of Miami Enter. & Sports L. Rev. 2 (1992). A thoughtful analysis of the philosophical complexities of gender equality in sports is Robert Simon, *Fair Play in Sports, Values and Society* (Boulder, Col.: Westview Press, 1991), in particular Chapter 6, Sex Equality in Sports. Deborah Rhode, *Gender and Justice*, 300–04 (Cambridge, Mass.: Harvard University Press, 1989), situates the issues posed by women, sports and law within the broader legal and feminist debates about gender discrimination.

empowered to waive these antitrust rights and agree to a rookie draft or salary cap in their place.

There is, however, a fundamental difference between college football and major league baseball. Whereas baseball's historic reserve clause put more money in the pockets of wealthy owners such as Walter O'Malley and Gussie Busch, NCAA rules permit "exploitation" of college athletes by not-for-profit institutions such as Notre Dame or Miami University. While big-time college sports has become a highly commercialized enterprise, the net revenues it generates go into the university's coffers, to be spent on the institution's programs.

In practice, athletic revenues are almost all spent on *athletic*, rather than *academic*, programs. (The exception that exemplifies the rule is Notre Dame, which has dedicated all the revenues from its recent NBC television contract to the school's academic life.) Even schools such as the University of Michigan, which customarily fills its 106,000 seat football stadium and makes millions of dollars from both football and men's basketball, regularly experience million-dollar deficits in their overall athletic department budgets. Part of the deficit is due to sizable expenditures on departmental and coaching salaries and amenities. Most of the money, though, goes to support the schools' other athletic programs. Because a star athlete such as Rocket Ismail of Notre Dame or Patrick Ewing of Georgetown received in a scholarship only a fraction of his economic value to his school, the college was able to award full scholarships to marginal players on those teams, and to many players on non-revenue producing teams. In addition, at many schools the general student body gains access to elaborate facilities for use in intramural sports.

These facts raise some interesting social policy questions. At Division 1 schools, blacks make up 37% of the football players, 56% of the men basketball players, and 33% of the women basketball players (and probably an even higher percentage of the stars in these sports). These are the student-athletes whose efforts generate the large revenues used to subsidize both nonrevenue sports (that are only 8% black and typically involve middle or upper-middle class activities like tennis, golf, or swimming) and the general student body (which is only 4% black). Thus, the NCAA system causes a wealth transfer from poor, black student-athletes to middle and upper-class white students. Although football and men's basketball account for 93% of all the revenues directly generated by intercollegiate sports for Division 1–A schools, 60% of black football and basketball players (and 40% of their white teammates) report that they have less than $25 per month for personal expenses while at college.[19] Are these facts relevant to the constitutional, antitrust, and other legal issues discussed earlier?

19. The data on the distribution of black versus white athletes are drawn from American Institutes for Research, *The Experiences of Black Intercollegiate* *Athletes*, note 4 above. The data on revenue generated by different sports are drawn from Raiborn, *Revenues and Expenses*, note 4 above, at 18 (Table 2.11).

For purposes of this chapter, the distributional questions at legal issue involve women student-athletes. Until the early 1970s, women's sports were excluded from the purview of the NCAA and run instead by the Association of Intercollegiate Athletic Women (AIAW): as a result they were seriously underfunded. In 1972, the Congress enacted Title IX of the Education Amendments (20 U.S.C. § 1681 et seq. (1988)):

> No person ... shall, on the basis of sex, be excluded from participation in, be denied the benefit of, or be subjected to discrimination under any education program or activity receiving federal financial assistance.

In 1974, Congress rejected an amendment proposed by Senator John Tower and supported by the NCAA that would have excluded intercollegiate sports from Title IX coverage. In the early 1980s, though, the same result was achieved by judicial interpretation. The Supreme Court ruled, in *Grove City College v. Bell*, 465 U.S. 555, 104 S.Ct. 1211, 79 L.Ed.2d 516 (1984), that Title IX governed only the specific college programs that received federal assistance. Not until the Civil Rights Restoration Act of 1987 (20 U.S.C. § 1681 et seq. (1988)) explicitly extended Title IX coverage to *all* the programs of an institution that received *any* federal aid did Title IX come fully into play for women's college sports. And in 1992, the Supreme Court sharply raised the legal stakes in these cases by permitting private damage suits by anyone asserting that she has been personally harmed by a violation of Title IX. See *Franklin v. Gwinnett County Public Schools*, ___ U.S. ___, 112 S.Ct. 1028, 117 L.Ed.2d 208 (1992) (involving a high school student's claim of sexual harassment by a teacher).

1. RESOURCES

Department of Health, Education, and Welfare regulations and policy interpretations released in the late 1970s fleshed out the content of Title IX somewhat. The position of the Office of Civil Rights, now responsible for Title IX, is that the statutory requirement of "equality" is not necessarily violated by "unequal aggregate expenditures for members of each sex or unequal expenditures for male and female teams." 51 Fed. Reg. 20,524 (1986). Instead, the test for compliance is a comparison of the:

> availability, quality and kinds of benefits, opportunities and treatment afforded members of both sexes. Institutions will be in compliance if the compared program components are equivalent, that is, equal or equal in effect. Under this standard, identical benefits, opportunities or treatment are not required, provided the overall effect of any differences is negligible.

44 Fed. Reg. 71,415 (1979)

For a popular treatment of this issue, see Francis X. Dealy Jr., Black Gladiators, Chapter 5 of his *Win at Any Cost: The* *Sell-Out of College Athletics* (New York: Birch Lane Press, 1990).

For purposes of the judgments that must be made about whether there actually is "equal athletic opportunity," the federal regulations direct that the amounts spent on athletic scholarships be on a "substantially proportional basis to the number of male and female participants in the institution's athletic programs," 44 Fed. Reg. 71,414 (1979). In addition, the following program factors must be taken into account:

1. Whether the selection of sports and levels of competition effectively accommodate the interests and abilities of members of both sexes;
2. Provision of equipment and supplies;
3. Scheduling of games and practice time;
4. Travel and per diem allowance;
5. Opportunity to receive coaching and academic tutoring;
6. Assignment and compensation of coaches and tutors;
7. Provision of locker rooms, practice and competitive facilities;
8. Provision of medical training services;
9. Provision of housing and dining facilities and services;
10. Publicity.

34 C.F.R. § 106.41(c) (1990)

Important issues of principle arise both in applying the above criteria to particular athletic programs and in assessing the compatibility of these sports guidelines with broader visions of gender equality in American law and American life. Until the fall of 1992, there had been no court decisions spelling out the implications of Title IX guidelines for specific disputes. Two significant judicial rulings had been rendered, however, in response to legal challenges launched under analogous state laws in the 1980s, the hiatus period for Title IX. We include here some key aspects of these opinions insofar as they address the broader themes in intercollegiate sports.

In reading these judicial opinions about what the law requires, it is useful to have this snapshot of the facts and figures regarding Division 1–A schools as of 1991.[20]

Category	Male/Female Ratio
Student Enrollment	1.05—1
Student-Athletes	2.49—1
Scholarship Expenditures	2.56—1
Athletic Contests	1.23—1
Participants: Coaches	1.04—1
Participants: Coaching Expenditures	1.26—1

20. These figures are drawn from the *NCAA Gender Equity Study: Summary of* *Results* (Overland Park, Kansas: NCAA, 1992).

BLAIR v. WASHINGTON STATE UNIV.

Supreme Court of Washington (en banc), 1987.

108 Wash.2d 558, 740 P.2d 1379.

DOLLIVER, JUSTICE.

This is a sex discrimination action brought under the state Equal Rights Amendment, Const. Art. 31, § 1 (Amend. 61), and the Law Against Discrimination. Appellants are female athletes and coaches of female athletes at Washington State University.

* * *

The comprehensive findings of fact of the trial court demonstrate that, despite marked improvements since the early 1970's, the women's athletic programs have continued to receive inferior treatment in funding, fundraising efforts, publicity and promotions, scholarships, facilities, equipment, coaching, uniforms, practice clothing, awards, and administrative staff and support. During the 1980–1981 school year, the year before the trial, the total funding available to the men's athletic programs was $3,017,692, and for the women's programs was $689,757, roughly 23 percent of the men's. The funds for the men's programs were derived largely from revenues, both gate admissions ($958,503) and media rights, conference revenues, and guaranties ($943,629). Most of these revenues were derived from football ($1,430,-554). Of the funding available to the women's programs, most was derived from legislative appropriations ($451,082). Very little came from gate admissions ($10,535). Although the number of participation opportunities for men increased by 115 positions from 1973–1974 to 1980–1981, the opportunities made available for women decreased 9 positions during the same period. The budget for men's scholarships increased from $380,056 to $478,052 during that period; the budget for women's scholarships in 1980–81 was $150,000. The trial court observed in its memorandum opinion:

> The non-emphasis on the women's athletic program was demonstrated in many ways, some subtle, some not so subtle.... The message came through loud and clear, women's teams were low priority.... [T]he net result was an entirely different sort of participation opportunity for the athletes.

On the basis of numerous findings of fact detailing the inferior treatment of the women's athletic program, the trial court concluded the university had "acted, or failed to act, in the operation of the University's intercollegiate athletics program in a manner that resulted in discriminatory treatment of females...." The athletes had "suffered unlawful sex discrimination violative of [West] RCW 49.60 and the State Equal Rights Amendment."

The court entered a detailed injunction to remedy the violations. With respect to funding, the court ordered the women's program must receive 37.5 percent of the University's financial support given to intercollegiate athletics during the year 1982–1983. The required minimum percentage for women increased each year by 2 percent until it corresponded to the percentage of women undergraduates at the University, 44 percent at the time of the injunction. The trial court provided, however, the level of support for women's athletics was not required to exceed by more than 3 percent the actual participation rate of women in intercollegiate athletics at the University, excluding football participation from the comparison. The injunction prohibited the total budget for women's athletics ever to be less than the base budget of $841,145 for 1981–1982, unless the expenditures for men's athletics were correspondingly reduced.

The injunction also specified:

In determining the level of University financial support of intercollegiate athletics for purposes of the above calculation, the term "University financial support" shall not include revenue generated by or attributable to any specific sport or program. Such excluded sources of revenue shall specifically include gate receipts, conference revenues, guarantees, sale of media rights, concession and novelty sales at games, coach and athlete work projects, and donations attributable to a sport or program.

The injunction apportioned the funding for athletic scholarships in a similar manner. . . .

The court also ordered the University to allow for increased participation opportunities until female participation, again excluding football participation from the comparison, reached a level commensurate with the proportion of female undergraduate students. The court noted female participation had increased in recent years and stated in its memorandum opinion, "[t]he change in the last ten years is dramatic, and it seems possible that parity will soon arrive."

The court further required the University to take affirmative steps to make opportunities to generate revenue equally available to men's and women's programs, stating:

Because past sex discrimination has afforded women's teams and coaches less opportunity to generate revenue, the University should take affirmative action in providing additional personnel with such knowledge and experience.

The trial court required the University to appoint a [sex equity committee, comprised of students, coaches, and administrators,] to monitor the application of the funding formulas and other elements of the injunction.

* * *

A. Football Exclusion

The first issue raised by the plaintiffs is whether the trial court abused its discretion in creating an injunctive remedy which excluded football from its calculations for participation opportunities, scholarships, and distribution of nonrevenue funds. We conclude the trial court did abuse its discretion and reverse on this issue. The Equal

Rights Amendment and the Law Against Discrimination prohibit such an exclusion.

* * *

The recognized purpose of the Equal Rights Amendment is to end special treatment for or discrimination against either sex. This absolute mandate of equality does not, however, bar affirmative governmental efforts to create equality in fact; governmental actions favoring one sex which are intended solely to ameliorate the effects of past discrimination do not implicate the Equal Rights Amendment.

Neither party disputes that the intercollegiate athletics program at Washington State University is subject to the Equal Rights Amendment and the Law Against Discrimination. The trial court found that the operation of the program resulted in discriminatory treatment of women and the women's athletic program in violation of these laws. Football is a large and essential part of intercollegiate athletics at the University. To exclude football, an all male program, from the scope of the Equal Rights Amendment would only serve to perpetuate the discriminatory policies and diminished opportunities for women.

The trial court attempted to explain the exclusion of football by stating football was a sport "unique in many respects, the combination of which distinguished it from all other collegiate sports...." The court identified such distinguishing characteristics as the number of participants, scholarships, and coaches, amount of equipment and facilities, income generated, media interest, spectator attendance, and publicity generated for the University as a whole. The court concluded:

> Because of the unique function performed by football, it should not be compared to any other sport at the University. Because football is operated for profit under business principles, ... football should not be included in determining whether sex equity exists ...

We do not believe, however, these or any other characteristics of football justify its exclusion from the scope of the injunction remedying violations of the Equal Rights Amendment. It is stating the obvious to observe the Equal Rights Amendment contains no exception for football. The exclusion of football would prevent sex equity from ever being achieved since men would always be guaranteed many more participation opportunities than women, despite any efforts by the teams, the sex equity committee, or the program to promote women's athletics under the injunction.

B. Revenue Retention

The plaintiffs also challenge the portion of the injunction excluding from the division of university financial support the revenue generated by any specific sport or program. The injunction allows each sport to reap the benefit of the revenues it generates. We hold the trial court did not abuse its discretion. Exclusion of sports-generated revenue from the calculations of university financial support is not prohibited under applicable state law and can be supported by several policy considerations. We affirm this portion of the trial court's injunction.

* * *

The trial court's funding plan provides incentive for all sports to develop revenue-generating capability of their own. As the trial court stated in its findings of fact and conclusions of law:

> There is an incentive to coaches and to a lesser extent their athletes to produce as much income as possible from all sources because they are the persons who first benefit from such income. The funding plan encourages the sports to fund their expenses through their own efforts, rather than depend upon direct legislative appropriations.

The injunction specifically requires the sex equity committee to recommend ways to encourage and promote women's sports to increase their own revenues; the funding plan would further promote such a goal. The plan thus requires the University to create equal opportunity to raise revenue for men's and women's sports.

The funding plan allows disproportionate expenses of any particular sports program to be derived from the program itself. The plan is also gender neutral. It provides a solution which does not violate the Equal Rights Amendment and encourages revenue development for all sports while accommodating the needs of the sports program incurring the greatest expenses at this time.

Our decision upholding the trial court's conclusion regarding sports-generated revenues does not in any way modify the University's obligation to achieve sex equity under the Equal Rights Amendment. The trial court's minimum requirements for participation opportunities and scholarships, already discussed, must be achieved; the court's guidelines for distribution of nonrevenue funds must be followed, and the remaining portions of the injunction, including promotion and development of women's sports, must be observed.

In addition, our conclusion allowing each sport to use the revenues it generates does not, of course, require the sport to do so. The record reflects the football program was transferring $150,000 or more per year from its revenues to the women's program before the injunction was entered. We encourage such practices to continue, along with other efforts to foster cooperation within the department.

We therefore reverse the trial court's exclusion of football from its calculations for participation opportunities and scholarships and affirm the trial court's decision to exclude sports-generated revenues from its distribution of financial support. We emphasize the portion of the injunction requiring additional promotion of women's sports and development of their revenue-generating capability and encourage continued cooperation and efforts to bring the University's intercollegiate athletic program into compliance with the Equal Rights Amendment.

* * *

Reversed in part.

Questions for Discussion

1. If revenues earned by each sport could lawfully be excluded from the determination of whether women's sports were being treated unequally, and if the football program was actually earning a profit which the university was using to subsidize other sports, what was the basis for the finding of a violation? How will the overall athletic program differ after the court's requirements are met? Will there merely be many more women participants in sports that have very little money to spend? Who will bear the burden of a judicial decision that requires a school to bring in more women participants in intercollegiate sports?

2. What difference is there between the trial court's exclusion of football as such from the gender equation, and the appellate court's exclusion of revenues generated by football? Compare the treatment of that issue in *Blair* with the judicial analysis in the next case, which dealt with a motion by Temple University for summary dismissal of a suit brought on behalf of female student-athletes under both federal and state constitutions and Title IX.

HAFFER v. TEMPLE UNIV.

United States District Court, Eastern District of Pennsylvania, 1987.

678 F.Supp. 517.

LORD, SENIOR DISTRICT JUDGE.

INTRODUCTION

This is a class action alleging unlawful gender discrimination in Temple University's intercollegiate athletic program. The plaintiff class consists of "[a]ll current women students at Temple University who participate, or who are or have been deterred from participating because of sex discrimination in Temple's intercollegiate athletic program." ... Plaintiffs claim that the treatment of women student athletes in each of [three] areas violates the fourteenth amendment's equal protection clause and the Pennsylvania Equal Rights Amendment. Plaintiffs also claim that the distribution of financial aid violates Title IX of the Education Amendments of 1972, 20 U.S.C. § 1681 et seq. ("Title IX").

* * *

Federal Constitutional Claims

* * *

This court's task is to define the "equality" that is required, and then to determine whether defendants offer equivalent athletic programs to men and women student athletes. The complaint alleges that Temple's separate programs are unequal in almost every conceivable area, including the allocation of opportunities to compete, expenditures, recruiting, coaching, travel and per diem allowances, uniforms, equipment, supplies, training facilities and services, housing and dining facilities, academic tutoring, and publicity. With a few exceptions, the reams of evidence submitted by plaintiffs and defendants raise genuine issues of material fact with respect to whether class members have been discriminated against in the provision of these resources. I will outline many of these factual disputes below.

A) Opportunities to Compete

The gravamen of plaintiffs' complaint is that, despite the fact that Temple's student body is approximately fifty percent female, approximately one-third of the participants in Temple's intercollegiate athletic program are women. Figures produced by defendants in discovery reveal that approximately 450 men and 200 women participate in Temple's intercollegiate athletic program.

* * *

[D]efendants claim that plaintiffs have failed to establish that this participation rate is evidence of gender discrimination. Temple argues that the general student population does not constitute a relevant pool. Rather, Temple contends, the relevant pool consists of "those potential students who possess the special abilities and interests to compete in sports at the Division I intercollegiate level." Temple's argument rests upon the proposition that there is no reason to believe that equal numbers of male and female college students possess the exceptional skills and interests required for Division I intercollegiate athletics.

Although it is true that "[w]hen special qualifications are required to fill particular jobs, comparisons to the general population (rather than to the smaller group of individuals who possess the necessary qualifications) may have little probative value," there exists a genuine issue whether the figures produced by plaintiff evidence a discriminatory impact against women. This is so for at least two reasons. There is evidence that the number of male and female student athletes at Temple who possess the skills and interest required for intercollegiate athletics is not independent of the money Temple devotes to athletic scholarships and recruiting, and the resources devoted to advertising, promotion and sports information activities. . . . Plaintiffs have introduced evidence from which a fact finder could find that defendants discriminate by gender in the provision of these funds and resources. Second, although the relevant pool must possess special qualifications, the record before me does not establish that the population pool is not a proxy for the distribution of athletic talents and interests. Defendants have submitted the National Federation of High School Association's 1986 Sports Participation Survey, a compilation of data received from all fifty state high school athletic associations regarding the number of high school students who participate in interscholastic sports. This survey reveals that approximately 34% of those who participate in interscholastic sports are girls. As the present record does not reveal the percentage of intercollegiate athletes that participated in interscholastic athletics, I am unable to assess fully the significance of the Sports Participation Survey. Plaintiffs have introduced evidence that some intercollegiate athletes did not compete in interscholastic sports, and that "certain sports found at the college level are often organized for high school aged athletes ... through privately sponsored classes and/or privately sponsored competitions, country clubs, Y's, etc." On the record before me, I am unable to appraise fully the significance of this evidence. The present record compels me to conclude that there exists a genuine issue of material fact with respect to the relevant pool. Finally, plaintiffs have produced evidence that talented and interested women student athletes to fill expanded women's teams at Temple "abound," and that Temple could, if it provided the opportunities and devoted the resources, "field an outstanding women's program twice the size of the program it has historically fielded." On this record, viewing all inferences to be drawn from the evidence in the light most favorable to plaintiffs, and resolving all doubts as to the existence of genuine issues of material fact against the defendants, I am unable to conclude that defendants are entitled to judgment as a matter of law on this claim.

Defendants argue, at some length, that plaintiffs cannot prove an intent to discriminate against women on this claim because "Temple's program constitutes discrimination in favor of, and not against, women." Temple argues as follows. If the University sponsored a unisex sports program, virtually no women would participate in intercollegiate athletics. Therefore the existence of a separate women's program is a form of preferential treatment. Temple analogizes to a hypothetical case in the racial area:

> Suppose, for example, that Temple had an overall enrollment which was sixteen percent black but, finding that virtually no black students were able to meet the regular admissions standards for the physics program, instituted a special admissions track to increase the number of black students in that program from zero to ten percent. Could black applicants then successfully challenge this effort as a violation of the Equal Protection Clause[?].... The plaintiffs are challenging Temple's affirmative efforts in *extending* benefits to women on the theory that Temple has not gone far enough.

This argument misses the mark. In the above example, black students were not precluded from applying to the regular admissions program. The separate track represents an additional opportunity to join the physics program. However, the physics program and the men's athletic program are not analogous: both black and white students may apply to the general physics program; only men may try out for the men's sports teams. Thus, the women's teams do not represent an additional opportunity for women to play intercollegiate sports, but rather the only opportunity for women to play intercollegiate sports. . . .

B) Expenditures

Plaintiffs claim that the differences in expenditures for the men's and women's intercollegiate athletic programs violate the equal protection clause. Temple presently spends approximately $2,100 more per male student athlete than per female student athlete. . . .

Defendants' first argument is that because the women's teams, collectively, have a higher winning percentage than the men's teams, collectively, and because the women student athletes have a higher mean cumulative grade point average than do the men student athletes, Temple's spending policies do not adversely affect women. . . . I do not accept the proposition that teams or programs with comparable win-loss records have necessarily been treated equally in terms of expenditures.[10] Similarly, the fact that women student athletes have a higher mean cumulative grade point average has no relevance to the issue of whether unequal expenditures violate the equal protection clause.

Temple argues, in the alternative, that the difference in per student expenditures is caused solely by the enhanced levels of support given the football, men's basketball and women's basketball teams. Temple argues that these three "revenue" teams have the potential to provide "unique benefits" to the University, and that it is thus rational to give "enhanced" support to these teams. Temple argues that the remaining twenty-three intercollegiate athletic teams are "nonrevenue" teams. Defendants have introduced evidence that the total expenditures on men's nonrevenue teams are practically identical to the total expenditures on women's nonrevenue teams. Moreover, as there are substantially more men than women on the nonrevenue teams, the per student expenditures for the nonrevenue teams favor women. Thus, Temple claims, net expenditures on the men's and women's teams do not constitute gender discrimination.

At first blush, Temple's argument is appealing. However, the present record raises material questions regarding defendants' attempt to classify the football and basketball teams as revenue teams, and all other teams as nonrevenue teams. First, the revenue teams produce no net revenue. For example, in 1984–1985, the football team had revenues of $514,015, and expenditures of $1,136,152, for a *net* expenditure of $622,137. In 1985–1986, the football team generated $732,738 against expenditures of $1,360,469, for a net expenditure of $627,731. In each of these years the net expenditures on this revenue team

10. Over the last three years, the football team has won 42% of its games, while the women's badminton team won 96% of its matches. . . . Last year, Temple spent $1,360,-469, or $9514 per student, on the football team, and $9987, or $1248 per student, on the badminton team. I am not, of course, suggesting that the football and badminton teams should receive equal funding. I am suggesting that the relationship between expenditures, win-loss records and equal treatment is not apparent.

exceeded the expenditures on the entire women's intercollegiate athletic program. In each of the last two seasons the purportedly revenue producing men's basketball team had a net expenditure of approximately $200,000....

Even assuming that there were no questions of fact regarding Temple's claim that it sponsors three revenue teams, there exist genuine issues of material fact regarding the "unique benefits" these teams provide. Defendants have introduced evidence that football and men's basketball provide enhanced visibility, revenues and publicity beneficial to Temple's enrollment efforts. Temple believes that some day the football and men's basketball teams may be able to generate enough funds to subsidize the entire intercollegiate athletic program. The portions of the record cited by defendants do not support the proposition that Temple treats the women's basketball team as if it has the potential to provide special benefits to the University. In addition, plaintiffs have produced evidence that revenues are not independent of expenditures on marketing, advertising and promotion, and that various women's teams are capable of generating interest and revenues if the proper investments in them are made.

To be sure, Temple has a legitimate interest in obtaining favorable publicity, and in generating revenues through intercollegiate sports. However, these interests, whether individually or in tandem, cannot override the constitutional right to equal protection of the law. In short, there is a genuine factual issue whether the disparate expenditures are substantially related to Temple's interests. Moreover, it is clear that financial concerns alone cannot justify gender discrimination. However, it is not inappropriate to consider net expenditures when evaluating whether the women's teams are discriminated against in the allocation of funds.

* * *

Summary dismissal denied.

———

After eight years in litigation, the *Haffer* case was finally settled in the midst of trial in June 1988. Under a consent decree, Temple agreed to a host of changes in its athletic program, such as increasing the female proportion of all its student-athletes to 40–45%, awarding athletic scholarships to women in proportion to their athletic participation, and keeping budget expenditures on female programs within ten percentage points of female athletic participation.

As an ironic denouement to this case, in 1991 the Temple faculty voted to drop its football program on the ground that this sport was responsible for half of the large deficit in the school's athletic budget. The administration resisted that pressure, arguing that the football team was beginning to win and that revenues are projected to grow sharply in the new Big East football conference. A university spokesman was quoted in the Chronicle of Higher Education as saying, "Now is not the time to eliminate football. It's time to cash in on the investment we have made." Then, in the aftermath of yet another dismal team record in 1992, with some prodding from Bill Cosby, Temple's most famous alumnus, the university installed as its new coach Ron Dickerson, the only black head coach in any Division 1–A football program at that time.

The Temple story exhibits a problem more and more universities across the country are experiencing—deficits in their athletic programs, sometimes contributed to by their football and men's basketball teams. The following data provide a systematic picture of the situation of Division 1–A schools in 1989: [21]

1. Average athletic revenues were $9.685 million and average expenses were $9.646 million, leaving an average net surplus of $39,000.

2. Of the 87 (of 106) schools reporting, 48 had an athletic surplus (averaging $1.046 million), 35 had a deficit (averaging $1.337 million), and 4 reported a balanced budget.

3. Within men's athletics programs, 69 had a surplus (averaging $1.814 million) while 16 had a deficit ($1.376 million). Women's programs had 5 schools with a surplus (averaging $85,000) and 78 with a deficit (at $1.354 million).

4. Within individual sports, football produced a surplus for 49 schools, averaging $2.77 million (with the ten largest ranging from $4.5 to $9.6 million), and 39 produced a deficit, averaging $638,000 (the largest was $1,713 million). Men's basketball produced a surplus for 55 schools at an average of $1.167 million (the nine largest ranging from $2 to $4.6 million), and a deficit at 28 schools, averaging $238,000 (the largest was $606,000).

At schools experiencing athletic deficits, administrations are reluctant to charge these amounts to their general budgets and thereby use up part of student tuition and alumni donations. Instead, universities are attempting to cut athletic costs, especially by weeding out less popular sports. The question is whether, under the shadow of Title IX, schools can drop existing women's teams.

Certainly the tactics displayed in Oklahoma in 1989 are not to be recommended. The Oklahoma University administration decided to drop the women's basketball program, which cost $280,000 per year and attracted approximately 200 spectators a game, and spend the money it saved on other women's athletics programs (such as soccer). However, when objections were raised to the proposed fate of women's basketball, Oklahoma Governor Henry Bellmon was quoted as saying:

---

21. These data are drawn from various tables in Raiborn, *Revenues and Expenses*, note 2 above.

It doesn't bother me. They'll still have intramural basketball, won't they? We never had total equality in women's athletics, and I don't know that we ever will have. They don't have the same opportunity now. There is no women's baseball or women's wrestling. I guess there is women's mud wrestling![22]

The resulting storm of political protest forced the University to back down and restore the women's basketball team.

More difficult issues are posed by the case of William and Mary College in early 1991. The College had twenty-five intercollegiate teams, twelve for men, twelve for women, and one (fencing) for both. The total athletic budget was $5 million, most of which came from the mandatory student fee of $550 (the school's sports teams did not generate large gate or television revenues). When the state of Virginia's fiscal crisis produced substantial cuts in the College's overall budget, the school decided to drop men's and women's swimming, men's wrestling, and women's basketball. Faced with a threatened lawsuit challenging the legality of dropping the women's basketball team while retaining the men's team in that sport, the College retreated.

As of the end of 1992, the principal judicial finding that a college athletic program violated Title IX focused on a similar question. In 1988 members of the Colgate University women's ice hockey team petitioned to have women's ice hockey upgraded from a student-run "club" sport (one that received only $4,600 per year in university support) to a varsity sport. Men's ice hockey, which was one of the major varsity sports at Colgate, received almost $240,000 per year in support (as compared with $275,000 for football, a total of $140,000 for the other ten men's varsity sports, and a total of $220,000 for the eleven women's varsity sports). When the school's Committee on Athletics denied the petition, the players sued.

In *Cook v. Colgate University*, 802 F.Supp. 737 (N.D.N.Y.1992), the district magistrate judge rejected Colgate's argument that a violation of Title IX must turn on appraisal of relative female and male opportunities and support in the school's overall athletic program, rather than in a single sport such as ice hockey:

> The Statute and Regulations invite a comparison between separate teams in a particular sport because they are designed to protect not only a particular class of persons, but individuals as well.... Otherwise it would be of little consequence for a women's basketball player to know that the overall athletic program is nondiscriminatory if her team is discriminated against through funding or otherwise in comparison to men's basketball. In a similar manner, it would be of little solace for a male member of an under-funded and otherwise discriminated against men's volleyball team, as opposed to a women's volleyball team, to know that the overall athletic program was technically in compliance with Title IX.

---

22. Donna Lopiano, *Fair Play for All (Even Women)*, N.Y. Times (Apr. 15, 1990).

The court then outlined the framework for evaluating charges of discrimination in violation of Title IX:

> [T]he plaintiffs, in order to establish a prima facie case, must demonstrate the following: (1) that the athletic department at Colgate is subject to Title IX; (2) that they are entitled to the protection of Title IX; and (3) that they have not been provided "equal athletic opportunities." If plaintiffs prove a prima facie case, they will have established a rebuttable presumption that Colgate has violated Title IX. This presumption, however, will disappear from the case if Colgate comes forward with legitimate nondiscriminatory reasons for its decision not to upgrade the women's ice hockey team to varsity status. Once Colgate has introduced such evidence, in order to prevail, the plaintiffs must prove that Colgate's proffered reasons are merely a pretext.

Relying on ten factors cited in 34 C.F.R. § 106.41(c)(1–10), the court found an enormous disparity in the treatment of men's and women's ice hockey at Colgate—in particular, in financial expenditures, equipment, locker room facilities, travel, availability of ice time for practice, and coaching. "The men's ice hockey players were treated like princes. The women ice hockey players were treated like chimney sweeps."

The court then considered and rejected as pretextual the various reasons proferred by Colgate for refusing to make women's ice hockey a varsity sport. The court found that the true reason was the substantial expenditures involved, and that this reason was legally invalid:

> [I]f schools could use financial concerns as a sole reason for disparity of treatment, Title IX would become meaningless. Under such circumstances, a school could always use a lack of funds as an excuse to deny equality because it costs money to implement equivalent women's programs with long standing men's programs. This cannot be either the spirit or meaning of Title IX.
>
> History shows that it is not easy to achieve equality. No one said that making things equal would not require some pain and sacrifice. The budget proposed by the plaintiffs in 1988 is probably unrealistic at this time. There is, however, no requirement that the funding be equal for both teams, but Colgate must provide equivalent benefits and opportunities. In this era of more limited resources, it may come down to taking from the men and giving to the women. The men have been given so much, a little "spreading of the wealth" is appropriate.

* * *

> Equal athletic treatment is not a luxury. It is not a luxury to grant equivalent benefits and opportunities to women. It is not a luxury to comply with the law. Equality and justice are not luxuries. They are essential elements which are woven into the very fiber of this country. They are essential elements now codified under Title IX. Many institutions of higher education appar-

ently hold the opinion that providing equality to women in athletics is both a luxury and a burden. The feeling seems to be that to afford such equality to women is a gift and not a right. The women's ice hockey players do not want a gift. They obviously do not consider equivalent treatment to be a luxury. The women only want equal athletic opportunities. That is what the law demands.

Is the court's argument in *Colgate* persuasive? What are its implications? Does it mean that every football-playing NCAA member now faces the prospect of having to establish a women's football team receiving roughly equal funding, or might that be true only if the school already has a women's football team as a club sport? If a school must provide equal opportunity in the same sport for both genders, what did the *Colgate* court mean in saying that funding did not have to be equal but there had to be "equivalent benefits and opportunities"? After *Colgate*, how can a school determine precisely what is its lawful obligation to women in each sport? Because Colgate has appealed the above ruling to the Second Circuit, some of these questions may soon be answered.

A final decision worth noting granted an injunction to members of the women's gymnastics and field hockey teams at Indiana University of Pennsylvania preventing the school in its budget-cutting effort from eliminating these women's sports, along with the men's soccer and tennis teams. See *Favia v. Indiana University of Pennsylvania*, 812 F.Supp. 578 (W.D.Pa.1993). The court's decision was based on a finding that the percentage of women varsity athletes at the university was well below the percentage of women in the student body (38% versus 56%). The court held that such a disparity constitutes a violation of Title IX unless the school can show it is taking strong ongoing corrective action to remedy the imbalance or that "the interests and abilities of [women] have been fully and effectively accommodated by the present program." Even though these budget cuts affected equal numbers of participants of each gender in the school's programs, the effect was to reduce the total percentage of women students involved in athletics, and for that reason the university's actions were illegal under Title IX. Similar rulings were also handed down in late 1992 and early 1993 against Brown University (for eliminating women's gymnastics and volleyball along with two men's sports) and Colorado State University (for eliminating women's softball (18 players) along with men's baseball (55 players)—which actually increased the total percentage of women athletes at the university). Is it appropriate to use the percentage of women in the student body as the benchmark for determining whether women students enjoy equal athletic opportunities?

2. ACCESS

A more fundamental issue lurks beneath the surface of the questions posed above. What if Colgate had responded to the Title IX complaint by adopting a new policy that its one varsity ice hockey team would henceforth be open to female as well as male student-athletes:

would that step successfully finesse the charge of gender discrimination? The tacit assumption of *Blair*, *Haffer*, and *Cook* is that colleges will establish *separate* teams for women and men, and thus the institution must be required to provide *equal* support to the women's and men's teams in order to maintain overall "equality of athletic opportunity for members of both sexes." The federal regulations adopted under Title IX are quite frank on this point:

> (b) *Separate teams.* Notwithstanding the requirements of paragraph (a) of this section, a recipient may operate or sponsor separate teams for members of each sex where selection for such teams is based upon competitive skill or the activity involved is a contact sport. However, where a recipient operates or sponsors a team in a particular sport for members of one sex but operates or sponsors no such team for members of the other sex, and athletic opportunities for members of that sex have previously been limited, members of the excluded sex must be allowed to try-out for the team offered unless the sport involved is a contact sport. For the purposes of this part, contact sports include boxing, wrestling, rugby, ice hockey, football, basketball and other sports the purpose or major activity of which involves bodily contact.

But is "separate but equal" compatible with the constitutional mandate of "equal protection" after *Brown v. Board of Education*, 347 U.S. 483, 74 S.Ct. 686, 98 L.Ed. 873 (1954)? Certainly, it would be unthinkable for colleges to establish separate but equal teams for black athletes, even if the goal was to address the apparent disparate impact of Proposition 48. Why has there been so little debate about the gender-segregation of college sports? [23] As the following cases indicate, though, there has been some litigation about this issue at the high school level.

HOOVER v. MEIKLEJOHN

United States District Court, District of Colorado, 1977.

430 F.Supp. 164.

MATSCH, DISTRICT JUDGE.

[The plaintiff, a 16–year–old eleventh grade student, was barred from playing for her public high school's junior varsity soccer team. She challenged a rule adopted by the Colorado High School Activities Association that limited soccer (but not baseball or cross country running) to males. The Association had relied on advice from its medical committee that girls playing soccer on coed teams risked their health and safety.]

* * *

Primarily, the committee was concerned with risks attendant upon collisions in the course of play. While the rules of soccer prohibit body

---

23. But for an extended critique by a feminist scholar, see Karen L. Tokarz, *Separate but Unequal Educational Sports Programs: The Need for a New Theory of Equality*, 1 Berkeley Women's L.J. 201 (1985).

contact (except for a brush-type shoulder block when moving toward the ball), there are frequent instances when players collide in their endeavors to "head" the ball. In those instances, contact is generally in the upper body area.

There is agreement that after puberty the female body has a higher ratio of adipose tissue to lean body weight as compared with the male, and females have less bone density than males. It is also true that, when matured, the male skeletal construct provides a natural advantage over females in the mechanics of running. Accordingly, applying the formula of force equals mass times acceleration, a collision between a male and a female of equal weights, running at full speed, would tend to be to the disadvantage of the female. It is also true that while males as a class tend to have an advantage in strength and speed over females as a class, the range of differences among individuals in both sexes is greater than the average differences between the sexes. The association has not established any eligibility criteria for participation in interscholastic soccer, excepting for sex. Accordingly, any male of any size and weight has the opportunity to be on an interscholastic team and no female is allowed to play, regardless of her size, weight, condition or skill.

* * *

The defendants on the board of education and the professional educators in control of the activities association have concluded that the game of soccer is among those which serve an educational purpose and governmental funds have been provided for it. It is a matter of common knowledge that athletics are a recognized aspect of the educational program offered at American colleges and universities and that many of them offer scholarships to males and females for their agreement to participate in intercollegiate sports competition. Such offers result from organized recruiting programs directed toward those who have demonstrated their abilities on high school teams. Accordingly, the chance to play in athletic games may have an importance to the individual far greater than the obvious momentary pleasure of the game.

Accordingly, the claim of the plaintiff class in this case is properly characterized as a denial of an equal educational opportunity.

* * *

Brown [v. Board of Education, 347 U.S. 483 (1954)] held that blacks were denied a constitutionally protected equality when they were forced to attend schools established only for those of the same race. As suggested by Justice Brennan in Frontiero v. Richardson, 411 U.S. 677, 686 (1973), a classification according to sex is comparable to race in that it is "an immutable characteristic determined solely by the accident of birth."

* * *

The Supreme Court has exhibited an obvious reluctance to label sex as a "suspect" classification because the consequences of the application of the many "invidious" discrimination precedents to all separations by sex could lead to some absurd results. For example, would the Constitution preclude separate public toilets?

* * *

In a very recent Supreme Court opinion, Craig v. Boren, 429 U.S. 190 (1976), Mr. Justice Brennan, writing for the Court, attempted to define a new standard of review, saying:

> To withstand constitutional challenge, previous cases establish that classifications by gender must serve important governmental objectives and must be substantially related to achievement of those objectives.

That language may be considered a "middle-tier approach," requiring something between "legitimate" and "compelling," viz., "important," and something more than a "rational" relationship but less perhaps than "strict scrutiny," viz., "substantially" related.

* * *

Because of its flexibility and sensitivity to the notion of equality itself, [the following three-pronged] method of analysis is particularly appropriate to the present case.

1. THE IMPORTANCE OF THE OPPORTUNITY BEING UNEQUALLY BURDENED OR DENIED

The opportunity not merely burdened but completely denied to the plaintiff and the class she represents is the chance to compete in soccer as a part of a high school educational experience. Whether such games should be made available at public expense is not an issue. The content of an educational program is completely within the majoritarian control through the representatives on the school board. But, whether it is algebra or athletics, that which is provided must be open to all. The Court in *Brown* expressed a constitutional concern for equality in educational opportunity and this controversy is squarely within that area of concern. Accordingly, without reference to any label that would place this opportunity on one of two or more "tiers," it must be given a great importance to Donna Hoover and every other individual within her class. Surely it is of greater significance than the buying of beer, considered in *Craig,* supra.

2. THE STRENGTH OF THE STATE INTEREST SERVED IN DENYING IT

The defendants in this case have sought to support the exclusionary rule by asserting the state interest in the protection of females from injury in this sport. While the evidence in this case has shown that males as a class tend to have an advantage in strength and speed over females as a class and that a collision between a male and a female would tend to be to the disadvantage of the female, the evidence also shows that the range of differences among individuals in both sexes is greater than the average differences between the sexes. The failure to establish any physical criteria to protect small or weak males from the injurious effects of competition with larger or stronger males destroys the credibility of the reasoning urged in support of the sex classification. Accordingly, to the extent that governmental concern for the health and safety of anyone who knowingly and voluntarily exposes himself or herself to possible injury can ever be an acceptable area of intrusion on individual liberty, there is no rationality in limiting this patronizing protection to females who want to play soccer.

3. The Character of the Group Whose Opportunities Are Denied

Women and girls constitute a majority of the people in this country. To be effective citizens, they must be permitted full participation in the educational programs designed for that purpose. To deny females equal access to athletics supported by public funds is to permit manipulation of governmental power for a masculine advantage.

Egalitarianism is the philosophical foundation of our political process and the principle which energizes the equal protection clause of the Fourteenth Amendment. The emergence of female interest in an active involvement in all aspects of our society requires abandonment of many historical stereotypes. Any notion that young women are so inherently weak, delicate or physically inadequate that the state must protect them from the folly of participation in vigorous athletics is a cultural anachronism unrelated to reality. The Constitution does not permit the use of governmental power to control or limit cultural changes or to prescribe masculine and feminine roles.

It is an inescapable conclusion that the complete denial of any opportunity to play interscholastic soccer is a violation of the plaintiff's right to equal protection of the law under the Fourteenth Amendment. This same conclusion would be required under even the minimal "rational relationship" standard of review applied to classifications which are not suspect and do not involve fundamental rights. The governmental purpose in fielding a soccer team is to enhance the secondary school educational experience. The exclusion of girls to protect them from injury cannot be considered to be in furtherance of that educational objective. If the purpose of the exclusionary rule is the protection of health, safety and welfare of the students, it is arbitrary to consider only the general physiological differences between males and females as classes without any regard for the wide range of individual variants within each class.

While Rule XXI is invalid under either method of analysis, there is a difference between them which is revealed in considering both the remedy required here and the possible ramifications of this case for future controversies.

There is no contention in this case that the Constitution compels soccer competition with teams composed of the best players, regardless of sex. Donna Hoover sought a chance to play on the boys' team only because there is no girls' team. The parties here agree that the effective equalization of athletic opportunities for members of both sexes would be better served by comparable teams for members of each sex and that under current circumstances mixed-sex teams would probably be dominated by males. Accordingly, it is conceded that "separate but equal" teams would satisfy the equality of opportunity required by the Constitution. The "separate but equal" doctrine was articulated in *Plessy v. Ferguson*, 163 U.S. 537 (1896), approving racial separation in transportation facilities. The doctrine was rejected for education in *Brown*, supra, upon the conclusion that racial separation was inherently unequal because it involved a stigmatizing inferiority for the minority race. No such effect is conceivable for a separation of athletic teams by sex.

* * *

Given the lack of athletic opportunity for females in past years, the encouragement of female involvement in sports is a legitimate objective and separation of teams may promote that purpose. It may also justify the sanction of some sports only for females, of which volleyball may be an example.

Separate soccer teams for males and females would meet the constitutional requirement of equal opportunity if the teams were given substantially equal support and if they had substantially comparable programs. There may be differences depending upon the effects of such neutral factors as the level of student interest and geographic locations. Accordingly, the standard should be one of comparability, not absolute equality.

In arriving at the conclusion that the defendants are in violation of the Fourteenth Amendment by providing interscholastic soccer only for male high school students, I am aware that there will be many concerned about the ramifications of this ruling. Football, ice hockey and wrestling are also made available only for males in Colorado, and volleyball is provided only for females. While there is now no reason to rule beyond the specific controversy presented by the evidence, it would seem appropriate to make some general observations about constitutional concerns in athletic programs supported by public funds.

The applicability of so fundamental a constitutional principle as equal educational opportunity should not depend upon anything so mutable as customs, usages, protective equipment and rules of play. The courts do not have competence to determine what games are appropriate for the schools or which, if any, teams should be separated by sex. What the courts can and must do is to insure that those who do make those decisions act with an awareness of what the Constitution does and does not require of them. Accordingly, it must be made clear that there is no constitutional requirement for the schools to provide any athletic program, as it is clear that there is no constitutional requirement to provide any public education. What is required is that whatever opportunity is made available be open to all on equal terms. It must also be made clear that the mandate of equality of opportunity does not dictate a disregard of differences in talents and abilities among individuals. There is no right to a position on an athletic team. There is a right to compete for it on equal terms.

* * *

Order granted.

Questions for Discussion

1. What actions does this ruling allow Colorado high schools to take? Consider each of the following scenarios: (1) a school allows girls to try out for the school's only soccer team, but over a period of several years few girls try out and none make the team; (2) a school requires half the players on the school's only soccer team to be girls; (3) a school has both boys' and girls' soccer teams, but disbands the girls' team when only three girls come out for the team, and then refuses to let the three girls try out for the boys' team; (4) a school has a boys-only soccer team and a girls-only field hockey team (each team has the same number of players).

2. In the 1990s, unlike the 1970s, few would argue that soccer poses a serious risk of injury to young girls. But what about football or ice hockey? Should these sports be mixed-sex or single sex? How should the court rule in a case involving a sixteen-year-old girl who wants to try out for the men's wrestling team when the school has no girl's wrestling program? See *Saint v. Nebraska School Activities Ass'n*, 684 F.Supp. 626 (D.Neb. 1988). How about a case in which a young woman sues to be permitted to compete in the regional Golden Gloves boxing competition? See *Lafler v. Athletic Board of Control*, 536 F.Supp. 104 (W.D.Mich.1982). What should be the result in litigation initiated in 1992 by a Baltimore high school student against her school board, claiming that the school failed to give adequate warning of the danger a crippling injury the girl suffered when she tried out for the school's football team? [24]

3. The opposite question arises if a boy wishes to participate in a sport for which his school offers only a girls' team—for example, in field hockey or volleyball. Should courts allow boys to try out for spots on a "girls'" team if there is no boys' team in that sport? What would likely happen if that were the rule? Should it matter whether the sport is a "contact sport"? Compare *Kleczek v. Rhode Island Interscholastic League*, 612 A.2d 734 (R.I.1992) (holding that boys do not have the right to play on the girls' field hockey team); with *Williams v. School District of Bethlehem*, 799 F.Supp. 513 (E.D.Pa.1992) (holding that denying boys the right to play on a girls' field hockey team violates both Title IX and the Equal Protection clauses of the U.S. and Pennsylvania constitutions).

---

24. *See* Felicity Barringer, *Fullback Sues School Over Her Injury*, New York Times at § D 20 (Aug. 19, 1992).

In *Clark v. Arizona Interscholastic Ass'n.*, 695 F.2d 1126 (9th Cir.1982), a group of boys sued when they were barred by Arizona rules from playing on their school's volleyball team, which was limited to girls. In dismissing the suit, the court asserted:

> As discussed above, the governmental interest claimed is redressing past discrimination against women in athletics and promoting equality of athletic opportunity between the sexes. There is no question that this is a legitimate and important governmental interest.
>
> The only question that remains, then, is whether the exclusion of boys is substantially related to this interest. The question really asks whether any real differences exist between boys and girls which justify the exclusion; i.e., are there differences which would prevent realization of the goal if the exclusion were not allowed.
>
> The record makes clear that due to average physiological differences, males would displace females to a substantial extent if they were allowed to compete for positions on the volleyball team. Thus, athletic opportunities for women would be diminished. As discussed above, there is no question that the Supreme Court allows for these average real differences between the sexes to be recognized or that they allow gender to be used as a proxy in this sense if it is an accurate proxy. This is not a situation where the classification rests on " 'archaic and overbroad' generalizations" or "the baggage of sexual stereotypes." Nor is this a situation involving invidious discrimination against women, or stigmatization of women. The [Arizona Interscholastic Association] is simply recognizing the physiological fact that males would have an undue advantage competing against women for positions on the volleyball team. The situation here is one where there is clearly a substantial relationship between the exclusion of males from the team and the goal of redressing past discrimination and providing equal opportunities for women.
>
> We recognize that specific athletic opportunities could be equalized more fully in a number of ways. For example, participation could be limited on the basis of specific physical characteristics other than sex, a separate boys' team could be provided, a junior varsity squad might be added, or boys' participation could be allowed but only in limited numbers. The existence of these alternatives shows only that the exclusion of boys is not necessary to achieve the desired goal. It does not mean that the required substantial relationship does not exist. . . .
>
> In this case, the alternative chosen may not maximize equality, and may represent trade-offs between equality and practicality. But since absolute necessity is not the standard, and absolute equality of opportunity in every sport is not the mandate, even the existence of wiser alternatives than the one chosen does not serve to invalidate the policy here since it is substantially related to the

goal. That is all the standard demands. While equality in specific sports is a worthwhile ideal, it should not be purchased at the expense of ultimate equality of opportunity to participate in sports. As common sense would advise against this, neither does the Constitution demand it.

695 F.2d, at 1131.

Do you agree with the court's reasoning? Or should sports teams be integrated by gender (as they must be by race)? Does your answer differ depending on whether the level of play is elementary school, high school, college, or professional (recall that private sports activities are covered by the Civil Rights Act)? Is there a stigma of female athletic inferiority created by "separate but equal" teams? If teams were integrated by gender and selected on the basis of ability alone, would this enhance or reduce equality of athletic opportunity? How much of the current differential between female and male athletic performance is due to physiology, and how much is due to resources and socialization?[25] Is integration the ideal way for aspiring female athletes to overcome the latter obstacles?

3. ADMINISTRATION

In intercollegiate sports, at least, the "separate but equal" policy of Title IX helped produce a major expansion in women's sports programs and a significant closing of the gap with their male counterparts. In the early 1970s there were approximately 30,000 intercollegiate women athletes, but now there are now nearly 200,000 who play in roughly the same number of sports as are now offered to men (although the number of participants per sport is smaller for women than for men). While in 1973, NCAA Division 1 schools spent an average of just over $27,000 per year on their women's athletic programs, only 2% of what they spent on men's programs, by 1991 the women's share had increased to 25% of the average for men. The fact that women make up 31% of the number of student-athletes and 50% of the college student body indicates there is considerable work yet to do: however, the level of progress is undeniable.

Ironically, though, while Title IX helped usher in a pronounced expansion in women's participation in college sports, the same era saw a marked decline in women's role in administering college sports. Again, the bare figures tell the story. In the early 1970s women comprised more than 90% of both coaches and administrators of women's teams and programs. Women now coach less than 50% of the women's teams and direct only about 15% of their programs (and make up only 30% of all administrative staff in college athletic programs).[26]

---

25. See Brian J. Whipp & Susan A. Ward, *Will Women Soon Outrun Men?* 355 Nature 25 (Jan. 2, 1992).

26. See Vivian Acosta & Linda Jean Carpenter, *Women in Intercollegiate Sport:*

A Longitudinal Study, Thirteen Year Update 1977–1990 (unpublished manuscript, 1990).

The source of this trend is easy to trace. In the early 1970s, the then separate but unequal women's athletics programs formed their own body, the Association of Intercollegiate Athletics for Women (AIAW), to play a role analogous to the NCAA in the governance of women's sports. In the late 1970s, however, the NCAA, having failed to roll back Title IX, decided to take control of the now burgeoning women's sports programs. Thanks to its greater financial resources and television exposure, the NCAA was successful in its quest. In 1982, having failed in an antitrust suit, see *AIAW v. NCAA*, 558 F.Supp. 487 (D.D.C.1983), affirmed, 735 F.2d 577 (D.C.Cir.1984), the AIAW folded.

At the same time, most schools integrated their men's and women's programs under a single administrative director. Almost invariably, the men's athletic director, a man, became the overall athletic director, and the women's athletic director, a woman, either became his assistant or saw her position eliminated altogether. In the coaching sphere, the men's teams almost always had a male coach (the fewer than one percent of men's teams with a female coach tended to be in sports such as tennis and swimming). However, the women's teams, which had begun to generate greater resources and exposure, had become attractive to male coaches, who gradually filled more than 50% of these positions.

The foregoing developments pose both legal and philosophical questions. On the legal side, what are the possibilities for Civil Rights Act lawsuits alleging denial of equal employment opportunity in the athletic sphere? [27] For example, what are (or should be) the prospects for a suit by a woman denied a position for a football coaching job, when the woman, though never having played football, had a successful coaching record in a variety of sports? See *Oates v. District of Columbia*, 647 F.Supp. 1079 (D.D.C.1986), affirmed, 824 F.2d 87 (D.C.Cir.1987). Or a woman who seeks a job as athletic director of a program whose main attractions are men's football and basketball? See *Wynn v. Columbus Municipal Separate School Dist.*, 692 F.Supp. 672 (N.D.Miss.1988). Or a woman coaching the women's basketball team who complains of a much lower salary than that paid to the male coach of the men's basketball team? See *Burkey v. Marshall County Board of Education*, 513 F.Supp. 1084 (N.D. W.Va. 1981)). Or, shifting the legal focus, a group of women student-athletes who allege a violation of their Title IX right to "equal athletic opportunity" because their school employs predominantly male coaches and administrators in the women's sports programs?

A broader philosophical question is posed by these historical developments. Many feminists look back fondly on the era of the AIAW as exhibiting the possibility of a distinctive women's voice in the gover-

---

27. For an intriguing analysis of the broader questions posed by the athletic case, see Vicki Schultz, *Telling Stories About Women and Work: Judicial Inter-* *pretations of Sex Segregation in the Workplace in Title VII Cases Raising the Lack of Interest Argument*, 103 Harvard L. Rev. 1750 (1990).

nance of sports.[28] Among the features they point to are the AIAW's promotion of a wide range of sports for student participants, without special regard to those that are the most exciting for spectators (to pay) to watch; the equal division of television revenues among all schools, not just among the winning programs; and the denial of special scholarships for athletics as such. (Ironically, that last feature of the AIAW philosophy had to be dropped in the face of threatened Title IX litigation by women athletes who wanted the same kind of scholarship aid as was available to male college athletes.) Do these tenets of the AIAW's philosophy exhibit a distinctively "female" tone? Something of enduring value for the policies of the now-integrated NCAA?

E. AFTERTHOUGHT

Reflecting about these materials and questions on gender discrimination brings back into view the tension traced throughout this chapter. From one point of view, college sports—certainly men's football and basketball—are major commercial ventures. That reality was recognized and reinforced by the Supreme Court in its *Board of Regents* decision. But however attractive and lucrative these sports may be in the consumer market, the students who produce them are supposed to be amateurs who perform for the love of the game and as part of their education, not for monetary reward. Thus colleges defend gender discrimination cases such as *Blair* and *Haffer* by emphasizing the revenue generated by certain favored sports, while the NCAA defends antitrust suits such as *McCormack* and *Banks* by emphasizing the clear demarcation between professional and amateur college sports.

Title IX could prove to be the catalyst for sweeping changes in college athletics. As long as schools have men-only football programs with roughly 85 scholarships and a dozen coaches and trainers, it will be almost impossible for them to provide equal financial support for women's sports. If Title IX is aggressively enforced, either schools will have to cut back dramatically on the size and ambition of their football programs (possibly cutting back on this sport's revenue-generating ability), or they will have to acknowledge that football teams are outright commercial ventures whose players are more like employees than merely students. How likely is either of these scenarios? Would either be desirable?

Recently the NCAA has taken some modest steps to ameliorate the increasingly apparent tension between commercialism and the NCAA's stated mission—in particular, through redistribution of some sports revenues. (An earlier effort along these lines in the late 1970s to

28. See Ann Uhlir, *Athletics and the University: The Post–Woman's Era*, Academe 25 (July–August, 1987); R. Vivian Carpenter & Linda Jean Acosta, *Back to the Future: Reform with a Woman's Voice*, Academe 23 (January–February, 1991); Wendy Olson, *Beyond Title IX: Toward an Agenda for Women and Sports in the 1990s*, 3 Yale J. of L. & Fem. 105 (1991).

redistribute college football television revenues sparked formation of the College Football Association, and thence the antitrust challenge in *Board of Regents.*) In 1991, the NCAA devised a new revenue sharing formula for its men's basketball tournament.[29] A large part of the money is divided among the athletic conferences in light of the conference's overall basketball performances over the previous six years. Another large part is distributed among schools according to how many sports and scholarships they offer to their respective student bodies. The NCAA uses smaller portions of the money to pay the cost of catastrophic injury insurance for all its members' athletes and to create a special fund for emergency assistance to disadvantaged athletes. Finally, a flat sum of $25,000 is distributed to each Division 1 institution for academic programs for student-athletes. As a result of these substantial changes, UNLV's share of the Final Four revenues dropped from $1.4 million in 1990 to $200,000 in 1991, though the 1991 pool was much larger.

The evident aim of this new formula was to reduce sharply the financial premium placed by schools on winning NCAA tournaments. But once the NCAA has started down this path, a more radical step looms as a possibility. Instead of simply sharing the revenues paid to the NCAA for television rights to its basketball tournament, the NCAA could require most or all revenues from games involving NCAA members to be put into a huge pot and distributed to all the member schools on a basis that placed little or no premium on winning. Would such a scheme be desirable? Would it be an antitrust violation? (See Justice White's dissent in *Board of Regents.*)

Another twist involves the way in which shared sports revenues could be spent. Suppose, for example, that rather than share revenues more equally among *athletic* programs, the money was distributed for the benefit of all the colleges' *academic* programs.[30] In other words, all monies included in the revenue sharing scheme would be distributed on a per school (or student) basis among all NCAA members on the conditions that none of it could be spent on intercollegiate athletics and that all of it must be used in the explicitly educational mission of the college. Even further, at least in non-revenue sports such as men's golf or women's tennis, there might be no *athletic* scholarships at all, no longer giving this favored category of student a free ride through college. The antidiscrimination objectives of Title IX could be pursued by redistribution of the net profits from men's football and basketball

29. See Robert N. Davis, *Athletic Reform: Missing the Bases in University Athletics*, 20 Capital Univ. L. Rev. 597, 601–02 (1991).

30. In 1991, legislation was introduced in Congress (the *Collegiate Athletic Reform Act*) to prod the NCAA down that path. This bill, authored by then-Representative Tom McMillen (who was an All–American basketball player, a Rhodes scholar, and an NBA performer of note), would grant the NCAA a carefully tailored exemption from the antitrust restraints imposed by the Supreme Court in *Board of Regents*. In return, the NCAA would have to adopt a revenue distribution plan that rewarded schools for the academic performances of their student-athletes, rather than their teams' win-loss records. For a defense of this proposal by its author, see Tom McMillen, *Out of Bounds* (New York: Simon and Schuster, 1992).

into women's *studies*, rather than women's *sports*. Is this "brave new world" more compatible with the philosophy of the NCAA quoted and relied on in so many of the cases in this and the previous chapter? Or would it ruin college sports to the detriment not only of the athletic establishment, but also of the athletes and fans who derive so much enjoyment from the games? What are your thoughts at the end of this extended examination of the impact of both money and law on the world of intercollegiate athletics?

Chapter Ten

INDIVIDUAL SPORTS

This chapter introduces a different part of the sports world—sports played by individual competitors rather than by teams, sports played in tournaments rather than in leagues. More and more, sports such as golf, tennis, auto racing, boxing, track and field, and bowling have been able to tap spectator interest and generate large revenues from live attendance, television broadcasts, and licensing arrangements. A by-product of this expanding financial success has been increasing litigation.

Individual sports pose the same challenge to courts as do professional and college team sports. How can one accommodate private regulation designed to foster vigorous and appealing athletic competition with public laws designed to protect both participants and outsiders from the misguided or arbitrary exercise of power by those in charge of the sport? This chapter presents a number of judicial variations on this perennial theme, all drawn from the world of individual sports.

As a prelude to these case selections, it is useful to underline some of the distinctive characteristics exhibited by individual sports off—rather than on—the field.

    1. Most important, the athletes compete as individuals rather than as members of a team. In the eyes of the law, this makes tennis players, for example, independent contractors rather than employees.

    2. In several sports, the players have organized themselves into associations that govern their respective sports in the best interests of its performers, as contrasted with team sports where the dominant forces are the owners who contribute capital. The pioneer in this respect has been the Tournament Players Division of the Professional Golfers Association (PGA).

    3. Fan interest focuses much more on individual tournaments than on season-long championship races. The tours in several sports have developed systems for accumulation of points from each

event that entitle the top players to participate in a lucrative final event such as the Association of Tennis Professionals (ATP's) Masters' Championship. However, much greater fan and media interest is aroused by the "Grand Slam" events. Hence authorities in charge of a tournament such as the Masters in golf, Wimbledon in tennis, and the Indianapolis 500 in auto racing, have a great deal of clout in their sports, while sponsors of lesser-known tournaments have substantial economic concerns about how tour officials and players treat the events.

4. For decades many of the major individual sports (but not boxing, golf, or auto racing) were fully committed to the ideal of "amateurism"—athletes playing simply for the love of the game. These sports excluded from major events any players who openly earned their living from playing the sport. However, unlike college football and men's basketball, the tennis world in the early 1970s, and track and field in the early 1980s, responded to the growth of "under the table" payments to top stars in a profitable sports enterprise by accepting professionalism among their performers.

5. The combination of the large sums of money generated by a sport and the professional status of its athletes produces a demand for sports agents. Individual sports have been the setting for some of the most prominent and successful sports agents—Mark McCormack, for example, who represented Arnold Palmer and Jack Nicklaus, and Donald Dell, who represented Arthur Ashe and Jimmy Connors. This agency work served as the stepping stone for McCormack's International Management Group (IMG) and Dell's ProServ becoming major forces in the business of individual sports, managing and promoting the same tournaments their clients played in—which evoked some delicate questions about how these many-sided relationships can be meshed.

6. Equipment used in individual sports can play a much larger role in determining who wins the contest—most conspicuously, the engines in racing cars, but also the rackets, clubs, and balls used in tennis and golf. Such equipment is produced by manufacturers who have a major financial stake in having their products used on professional tours, because of the influence star athletes exert on purchases by the general sporting public. Thus manufacturers are another group with a distinct economic interest in decisions about the rules of the game.

7. The professional and college sports examined in previous chapters are played by teams located almost entirely in the United States. (The exceptions are two baseball teams and eight hockey teams based in Canada, a country whose laws are similar to those in the United States.) In contrast, several of the major individual sports have a large share of their events (as in tennis) or players (as in golf) drawn from numerous countries around the world. More-

over, track and field and swimming, for example, are governed by international federations that control access to the Olympic Games that every four years capture the attention of athletes and fans around the world. This international dimension to individual sports poses a major challenge to American judges asked to apply and enforce domestic laws.

The foregoing provides a capsule summary of the distinctive real world flavor of individual sports. The cases in this chapter exhibit some of the legal differences that these factual distinctions can make.

A.   UMPIRING THE GAME

A revealing illustration of the extent of sports litigation is that in the 1980s auto racing produced *two* appellate court decisions over whether aggrieved contestants could go to court to try to snatch victory from the jaws of defeat. In both cases, suit was brought against the National Association of Stock Car Auto Racing (NASCAR), a privately held, for-profit organization that sanctions and promotes stock car racing throughout the country. To participate in any major stock car race, one must be a member of and pay an annual licensing fee to NASCAR. Membership does not, however, entitle one to elect NAS-CAR officials or participate in its decisions.

CROUCH v. NASCAR

United States Court of Appeals, Second Circuit, 1988.

845 F.2d 397.

MESKILL, CIRCUIT JUDGE.

[The plaintiff, Crouch, was declared the victor in a 1985 stock car race held in Vermont under the auspices of NASCAR. Another driver, LaJoie, actually crossed the finish line ahead of Crouch, but was disqualified by the NASCAR official at the track. LaJoie appealed the official scorer's verdict to NASCAR headquarters on the ground that the scorer had improperly penalized him a lap during a restart of the race; this missing lap had led to LaJoie's disqualification for allegedly passing Crouch's car in the face of the yellow accident caution flag displayed later in the race. NASCAR headquarters first characterized the track rulings as an appealable "scoring," rather than an unappeala-ble "race procedure" decision, and then, after reviewing the race tapes, declared LaJoie the victor.

Crouch took the matter to court even though under the NASCAR constitution, competitors in all races were required to sign entry forms that stipulated that everyone agreed to abide by the decisions of officials relating to the event and "that such decisions are non-appeal-able and non-litigable." The trial judge nonetheless upheld Crouch's claim on the theory that NASCAR's interpretation and application of its rules—in particular its characterization of this dispute as a "scoring" rather than a "race procedure" matter—was "unreasonable and arbitrary." NASCAR and LaJoie appealed to the Second Circuit.]

* * *

The threshold issue that we must resolve is the proper standard for judicial review of NASCAR's interpretation of its own rules. Our decision in Koszela v. National Association of Stock Car Auto Racing, Inc., 646 F.2d 749 (2d Cir.1981), provides some guidance. In that case, we considered claims that NASCAR misapplied its rules in determining the rightful winner of two races and that its decisions regarding the two races were arbitrary and clearly erroneous. We first reasoned that the principle of judicial noninterference set forth in the law of voluntary associations was not strictly applicable, noting that NASCAR was a for-profit company that completely dominated the field of stock car racing and that its members have no rights whatsoever with respect to the internal governance of the organization. We added, however, that a reviewing court is not free to reexamine the correctness of the official track decisions in question because NASCAR's rules "do not provide for any administrative appeal, much less judicial review, of official decisions." We also noted that the only provision granting a competitor the right to challenge occurrences at the track is the protest mechanism, and that "this provision is not intended to be a device by which disappointed competitors may challenge an official's interpretation of the rules or the application of the rules to the facts." We accordingly refused to reexamine the correctness of the official track decisions in question.

In the instant case, the district court cited *Koszela*, and concluded that because of the considerations discussed in that case it was "precluded from reviewing the official decisions of NASCAR officials with respect to the Catamount race." It added that "[t]o allow competitors to challenge the assessment of lap and time penalties or the timing and scoring of laps would result in the same type of protracted disputes that the finality rule is meant to prevent.... By according final weight to the official NASCAR track decisions, this court avoids placing itself in the position of 'super-referee.'"

The court also concluded, however, that the considerations that preclude review of the correctness of the official track decisions do not necessarily prevent the review of the procedures used to implement these decisions. The court added that "[w]hile courts may be hesitant to unnecessarily interject themselves into the private affairs of an association, where the association enforces its rules in a manner that is unreasonable or arbitrary courts may intervene." In applying this standard, the court did not defer to NASCAR's judgment that under its rules, the disputed actions of the local track officials did not constitute the imposition of a lap or time penalty, or to NASCAR's decision that disqualification is not a race procedure decision. Rather, the court apparently believed that under its adopted standard, it was appropriate to undertake a *de novo* review of the NASCAR rules in order to determine whether the national NASCAR officials had acted unreasonably or arbitrarily by reviewing the local track officials' decisions.

* * *

The court's decision in Charles O. Finley & Co. v. Kuhn, 569 F.2d 527 (7th Cir.1978), is relevant. In that case, the court concluded that a waiver of recourse to the courts that was signed by the major league baseball clubs was valid, noting that such a waiver coincides with the common law standard disallowing court interference. The court added that there are exceptions to this general rule of nonreviewability of the actions of private associations, however, "1) where the rules, regulations or judgments of the association are in contravention to the laws of the land or in disregard of the charter or bylaws of the association and 2) where the association had failed to follow the basic rudiments of due process of law."

* * *

In the instant case, Crouch and Wright are not claiming that they were deprived of any procedural safeguards or that their due process rights were violated, however. Rather, the crux of their complaint is that NASCAR improperly provided LaJoie with a procedural safeguard, i.e., review of the local track officials' decisions by the NASCAR headquarters. In fact, LaJoie maintains that if the district court correctly held that the local track officials' actions constituted a disqualification, then he was entitled to be informed of the disqualification and to have the disqualification decision reviewed by NASCAR headquarters pursuant to Section 13 of the rulebook. Section 13 provides that all violations of NASCAR rules are to be reported in writing to the NASCAR Vice President for Competition, and that this Vice President can review these reported violations. We therefore do not believe that the cases discussing the occasional need for a court to intervene in the internal affairs of an association because of the lack of adequate safeguards support the district court's decision.

Although here there was no allegation of inadequate procedural protections, the district court still thought that it was appropriate to conduct its own analysis of NASCAR's interpretation of its procedural rules. Moreover, despite the court's recognition that NASCAR possesses considerable stock car racing expertise upon which it may rely in interpreting its own rules, the court apparently did not give much weight to that expertise in reaching its decision that NASCAR acted unreasonably by overturning a race procedure decision made by a local track official. Rather, the court evidently felt that in order to determine whether NASCAR acted unreasonably or arbitrarily, it should itself delve into NASCAR's rulebook and decide *de novo* whether the lap 68–71 incident involved a disqualification, and whether a disqualification constitutes a lap and time penalty and is therefore a nonreviewable race procedure decision.

We believe the district court erred in making this inquiry. As the Seventh Circuit noted [in *Finley*] when rejecting the argument that the Commissioner of Baseball's actions were "procedurally unfair," certain standards, such as "the best interests of baseball, [and] the interests of the morale of the players and the honor of the game ... are not necessarily familiar to courts and obviously require some expertise in their application." The court accordingly proclaimed that the judiciary should not be professional baseball's "umpire and governor." We believe that federal courts are equally unfamiliar with standards such as "race procedure decision" and "lap and time penalty," and thus should decline the plaintiffs' invitation to become the "super-scorer" for stock car racing disputes. Furthermore, there is no contention that NASCAR acted "in disregard of [its] charter or bylaws." Rather, plaintiffs-appellees contend essentially that NASCAR misinterpreted its own internal regulations. Accordingly, we conclude that the district court should have deferred to NASCAR's interpretation of its own rules in the absence of an allegation that NASCAR acted in bad faith or in violation of any local, state or federal laws.... We believe that adopting any lower standard for reviewing an organization's interpretation of its own procedural rules would create too great a danger that courts will become mired down in what has been called the "dismal swamp"—the area of a group's activity concerning which only the group can speak competently. Indeed, the district court's admitted confusion about the proper interpretation of NASCAR Rule 13–5 is one illustration of how perilously close the court came to the edge of the swamp under its adopted standard of review. As we acknowledged in *Koszela*, "[u]ltimately, the solution for unauthorized or improper officiating lies not in individual challenges seeking to undo what has been done, but rather in pressure brought upon the officials in charge by drivers, owners, fans, and even NASCAR to improve the caliber of [NASCAR's supervision of races]."

* * *

Indeed, the district court implicitly acknowledged that the national officials acted in good faith. Specifically, the court noted that the national officials believed that the local officials' decision to penalize LaJoie in connection with the lap 68–71 incident resulted in part from the scoring error the local officials made in connection with the lap 1–2 incident. The national officials therefore thought it was appropriate to correct both decisions. Moreover, as we noted in *Koszela*, it is common practice to refer race procedure questions to the national NASCAR office. We thus believe that the district court should have deferred to NASCAR's interpretation of its own rules, under which NASCAR had the authority to review and decide the disputed issues.

Reversed.

Notes and Questions

1. What is the formal legal source of a court's authority to review decisions made by a sport's ruling body—especially about who has won an

event? Should the court have dismissed Crouch's suit, regardless of the asserted grounds, because Crouch apparently had agreed (through both his membership in NASCAR and his entry form for the Vermont race) that he would not appeal adverse decisions to the courts? In an earlier decision, *Koszela v. NASCAR*, 646 F.2d 749 (2d Cir.1981), the Second Circuit stated that:

> The policies supporting [judicial] noninterference are considerably weaker where the organization is "primarily a business run for profit" in which the " 'members' have no rights whatsoever with respect to the internal governance of the organization." Moreover, NASCAR's complete dominance in the field of stock car racing leaves competitors little choice but to join. Where an organization has achieved such a "stranglehold," rigid adherence to a "hands off" policy is inappropriate. See Chafee, *The Internal Affairs of Associations Not for Profit*, Harv. L. Rev. 993, 1021–23 (1930).

Id. at 754.

In that light, compare the judicial treatment of NASCAR in *Crouch* to the treatment of decisions rendered by baseball commissioners in the *Finley*, *Turner* and *Chicago Cubs* cases discussed in Chapter 1.

2. If courts are prepared to intervene at least upon occasion, what are the appropriate occasions? Is it relevant, for example, that Crouch was at first named the winner at the end of the race, and that he was challenging a later decision made at NASCAR headquarters that reversed the scorer's decision made at the track? Is it significant that in *Koszela*, a similar scenario took place, but the decision made at headquarter's reversing Koszela's announced victory at the race site was rendered by the Competition Director without hearing from either of the contestants (a hearing would take place only upon further appeal to the NASCAR Commission)?

B. ELIGIBILITY TO PLAY

Before players can win races or tournaments, they must be eligible to compete in the first place. One of the major functions of the organization in charge of any sport is to determine who can play in each event. In team sports the key decisions are made by the management of each team which decides whether to keep an existing player or to bring in a replacement. In individual sports such as golf and tennis, these decisions are now made by a body composed of, or accountable to, the players themselves. In a similar setting, medicine, the Supreme Court has questioned the delegation of authority to committees of doctors to judge whether one of the members of their specialty should gain or retain staff privileges in a hospital where they might compete for the same patients.[1] Judicial concern is likely to be even greater in the world of sports where there is no compelling need to protect patients from risky medical treatment.

1. See *Patrick v. Burget*, 486 U.S. 94, 108 S.Ct. 1658, 100 L.Ed.2d 83 (1988). See also James F. Blumstein and Frank A. Sloan, *Antitrust and Hospital Peer Review*, 51 L. and Contemp. Prob. 7 (1988).

The legal response to this problem is best glimpsed through the world of professional golf, which has undergone a lengthy evolution toward its present regime of player control.[2] Golf came to the United States in the late nineteenth century with creation of several clubs in the northeast. In 1894, two clubs, St. Andrews and Newport Country Club, both attempted to stage a national amateur championship within weeks of each other, each championship producing different winners. To eliminate the confusion and produce one national amateur championship, the Country Club in Brookline, the Chicago Golf Club and the Shinnecock Hills Club, joined with the two tournament clubs to charter the U.S. Golfers Association. The USGA staged its first Open Championship at St. Andrews in 1895 to accompany the first U.S. Amateur Championship.

Almost all of the rising number of clubs employed professionals to keep the course in playing condition, to sell and store equipment, and to teach members how to play the game. In 1916, club professionals formed the Professional Golfers' Association (PGA), which staged its own professional championship, and during the 1920s and 1930s coordinated golf tournaments in several cities. Most of these tournaments were held in the south in the winter, and most of the players were club professionals whose northern clubs were closed for the winter. While there were a few golfing greats who successfully concentrated on tournament golf alone—Walter Hagen, Gene Sarazan, Sam Snead, Byron Nelson, and Ben Hogan—there rarely was a shortage of tournament slots for professionals who wanted to enter.

The situation began to change in the 1950s when the combination of spectator interest and television broadcasting brought much more money into the game—by 1958, total PGA tour prize money surpassed $1 million. For the first time PGA tour officials found that the qualifying event held early in the week of each tournament was not sufficient to reduce the number of entrants to a manageable field. New eligibility rules, which still favored club professionals, resulted in many tournament players being dropped from the tour roster. One such player brought an antitrust suit, *Deesen v. PGA*, 358 F.2d 165 (9th Cir.1966), one of the earliest substantive antitrust decisions rendered about any sport.

By the time Deesen had ended his unsuccessful legal challenge to PGA eligibility rules, the character of the golf enterprise had undergone another major change. Although tour revenues were still soar-

---

2. For a comprehensive picture of the development of the professional golf tours, see Al Barkow, *The History of the PGA Tour* (New York: Doubleday, 1989). The definitive history of the game of golf is Robert Browning, *A History of Golf: The Royal and Ancient Game* (London: J.M. Dent & Sons, Ltd., 1955).

For detailed analysis of the current tours, IMG Chairman Mark McCormack's annual survey of the PGA provides a constantly revised and updated version of such information. See, Mark H. McCormack and Laurence Levy, *The World of Professional Golf* (Cleveland: International Merchandising Corporation, 1993). See also, William Wartman, *Playing Through: Behind the Scenes on the PGA Tour* (New York: William Morrow and Company, Inc., 1990).

ing—to $5 million in prize money by the late 1960s—new stars of the game such as Arnold Palmer, Jack Nicklaus, and Gary Player had become impatient with the continuing role of club professionals. The result was formation of the Tournament Players Division (TPD) of the PGA, which took full charge of the tour under a commissioner (presently Deane Beman, a former tour player) ultimately accountable to players on the tour.

Coincident with this constitutional change was a new set of eligibility rules that sharply reduced access to tournaments by club professionals and based admission to the tour on successful completion of qualifying school and competition. Spots for newcomers (many of whom now come from the lower-ranking Ben Hogan tour) were created by dropping from the eligibility list players who had placed near the bottom of tour winnings in the prior year. This new system produced yet another antitrust challenge, and the closest judicial look yet at tour limits on player eligibility.

WESER v. PGA

United States District Court, Northern District of Illinois, 1979.

1979–2 Trade Cases (CCH) ¶ 78,180.

MARSHALL, DISTRICT JUDGE.

[Between 1949 and 1958, Emil Weser participated in tournament golf as a PGA-approved player—an individual eligible to compete on the pro tour. The PGA terminated his status as an approved player in 1958. Although he did participate in some non-Tournament Player Division (TPD)/PGA tournaments, Weser maintained his involvement with golf primarily through the operation of his driving range and golf shop where he gave golf instructions. In 1976, Weser decided to become active in tournament golf again and to enter the Western Open tournament. The Western Open tournament was co-sponsored by the Western Gold Association (WGA) and the TPD. The WGA and the TPD entered into a written agreement on September 29, 1975 that provided that "[p]layers eligible to apply to enter the Tournament shall be those prescribed in the TPD Tournament Regulations." The TPD Tournament Regulations established ten categories of persons eligible to participate in TPD co-sponsored events. Eligibility for entry into the Western Open was limited to members of the TPD, members of professional golfers' associations that were recognized by the TPD, the Illinois section PGA champion, the head professional at Butler National (the course where the 1976 Western Open was played), 19 members of the Illinois section of the PGA, and the PGA National club professional champion.

Weser had never been a member of the PGA or the TPD. Since he did not fit into any of the eligibility categories, he did not submit the entry form for the Western Open. Instead, he sued the PGA, the TPD, and the WGA for alleged violations of the antitrust laws. This was the district court's ruling on a motion for summary dismissal.]

ELIGIBILITY REQUIREMENTS

* * *

Defendants have asserted that the purpose for the eligibility requirements is not to exclude able competitors from the field of professional golf but rather is to foster competition by guaranteeing to sponsors, participants, and spectators that the golfers participating in tournaments are of the highest caliber. There is no evidence that this purpose is illusory and the regulations support it. The golfing proficiency of each member is constantly reviewed. When a member is consistently defeated in tournament play he must prove his competence as if he were a new player. The regulations, at least on their face, are designed to allow only those golfers of proven ability to participate in TPD events. This purpose is not exclusionary; rather the restrictions are intended to foster the highest degree of competition. Therefore, the proper standard to apply in this case is the rule of reason.

"The focus of an inquiry under the rule of reason is whether the restraint imposed is justified by legitimate business purposes, and is no more restrictive than necessary." The restraint that plaintiff has complained of is the "membership" requirement of the TPD regulations. First it should be noted that membership in the PGA and the TPD are not the only methods for gaining admission into a TPD cosponsored event. Foreign professional golfers are permitted to compete provided the golf association they belong to is recognized by the TPD. Also, the sponsor organization is allowed to invite up to eight non-members to compete in the tournament which they sponsor. However, these other methods for admission into the golf event are *de minimis* compared to the number of positions on the field which are available to members of the TPD and PGA. The proper inquiry is whether there is a legitimate business purpose for limiting the players to members of the PGA and the TPD.

LIMIT ON NUMBER OF PLAYERS

Defendants have provided sufficient evidence which shows that the number of participants in a one-day tournament of professional golf is limited to between 144 and 156 players by the physical and extrinsic factors of the course. Each tournament golf course consists of 18 holes which are played in two waves, one wave starting from the first tee and the second from the tenth. These waves then interchange starting positions after they complete their first nine holes. It takes approximately 4.5 hours for a player to finish the entire 18 holes. Normally, the first two waves start out at 7:30 a.m. and the second two waves of the day start out at noon. It takes approximately two hours to get the last group in a wave off its first tee. The last group in the wave that starts at noon therefore actually tees off around 2:00 p.m. and would be expected to finish at about 6:30 p.m. Each of the four waves consists of

12 to 13 groups of 3 players. Thus if 12 groups comprise a wave, 144 players can be accommodated in 1 day; if 13 groups make up the wave, 156 players can participate. This evidence has not been controverted by plaintiff.

In addition the number of days the tournament may last at each golf course is controlled by the limited resources available to the sponsor. Defendants assert that the tournaments are generally played at private clubs across the country. Any time allotted by the club for a tournament results in the members of that club being deprived of the use of their golf course. At the present time, an 18–hole qualifying competition is held on the Monday preceding the major event if more than 144 applications from "qualified" golfers are received. Therefore many tournaments require a minimum of five days to complete. Many of the TPD tournaments are sponsored by civic and charitable organizations. Functions such as marshalling and scorekeeping are performed by volunteers of these sponsor organizations and the number of available volunteers is naturally limited. Plaintiff has not disputed these facts. We therefore conclude that there are legitimate business reasons for limiting the number of participants in a golf tournament.

METHOD TO SELECT PLAYERS

The next inquiry is whether the method selected by defendants to limit the number of participants is reasonable or whether less restraining alternatives are available. All persons falling into one of the categories set forth in the TPD eligibility regulations are permitted to compete in the Monday pretournament qualifying rounds. Therefore the natural starting place for determining if the field is limited in a manner consistent with the anti-trust laws is with the TPD's eligibility regulations. These regulations will be considered reasonable if they are consistent with the stated purpose of the TPD—to foster competition at the highest level. But if the regulations permit entry to some golfers who have not proven their competitive ability, while denying it to others, or if the regulations are so restrictive that those persons who have proven their competitive ability are refused entry into the tournaments in order to favor less qualified members, the regulation may not be reasonable.

The 1977 TPD regulations set forth ten categories of persons who are eligible to compete in TPD co-sponsored tournaments. The first category consists of "members in good standing of TPD." The methods for becoming a member in the TPD are set forth in the TPD bylaws. The 1977 bylaws specify six divisions of persons who are eligible to apply for membership in the TPD.... These classifications ultimately break down into three categories: approved tournament players, certain PGA members, and major tournament winners. The only method for becoming an "approved tournament player" is to successfully complete a TPD qualifying school. Those PGA members who may join the TPD on the strength of their PGA membership are full-time head professionals. The third category consists of some of the major tournament winners; however, there is clearly a built-in bias for those who participate in the PGA Club Professional Championship, a tournament sponsored by the PGA.

Plaintiff alleges that completing the TPD school is not a reasonable method for determining if one has the requisite skills for competing in the individual tournaments. He has asserted that the schools are held in a limited area of the country each year, and that golfers will fluctuate in ability depending upon the location of the school. However the papers show that the 1977 fall qualifying school, unlike those in years past, was divided into three parts; sectional qualifying, regional qualifying, and then final qualifying rounds. The sectional rounds were scheduled in 24 different locations, the regionals in 4 areas, and then the final competition in 1 location. This evidence has not been expanded upon by either the plaintiff or the defendants.

In addition the papers reveal that the number of persons who may "successfully" complete the school is determined to some extent by the number of openings on the tour. This type of subjective qualifying seems inconsistent with the entire scheme of the TPD and verges on a vertical group boycott as we have before defined that phrase. The effect of this practice would be to restrict entrance of new players in favor of the old pros, and has no relationship to competence.

As we noted in our denial of plaintiff's motion for preliminary injunction, there also seems to be some question of the reasonableness of allowing Class–A PGA members into the TPD without requiring them to complete the TPD school. The defendants have asserted that the 1977 amendments to the regulations restrict automatic eligibility to Class–A PGA members who are also full-time head professionals, and that this amendment alleviates our prior concern. Whether these individuals are given a higher priority than their skills would prove, were they required to complete the TPD school, is still an issue which must be resolved in order to determine whether the regulations co-incide with the purpose of the TPD.

Two of the four remaining categories of persons who may apply for membership in the TPD are geared to the PGA Club Professional Championship. While these persons have undoubtedly proven their ability in tournament golf, we are concerned with the separation of this tournament from other major golf events. Although the sixth category permits automatic eligibility for "winners" of the World Series of Golf, the U.S. Open, the Masters and British Open, there is a definite bias for players in the PGA Championship—in addition to the "winner" of the PGA Championship tournament, the 25 lowest scoring golfers are also automatically eligible. The fifth category of persons who may apply for membership without completing the TPD school are "all current PGA Section Champions." Again the relationship between the PGA and competitive ability has not been sufficiently explained.

The same problems arise in the nine remaining categories of the TPD tournament eligibility regulations. Many of the categories are tied to the PGA and/or the PGA Championship Tournament. Although the skill of these members is not questioned, the differentiation between these members and others similarly situated but unaffiliated with the PGA is questionable and is still a material fact in issue. . . .

Partial dismissal granted.

Questions for Discussion

1. Notice that *Weser* was decided in 1979, during the same period that the Supreme Court was redefining the antitrust Rule of Reason in cases like *Professional Engineers, Broadcast Music, GTE Sylvania,* and *Northwest Wholesale Stationers* (see Chapter 3), none of which were cited in the above opinion. The *Weser* court said that the issue under the Rule of Reason was whether the PGA restraint "was justified by legitimate business purposes and was no more restrictive than necessary." Is this test compatible with the current "procompetitive vs. anticompetitive effects" formula that seeks to balance efficiency benefits from a particular restraint against consumer welfare injury from increased market power? How should *Weser* have been analyzed and resolved under the modern approach?

2. Is it appropriate for a court to decide whether each of the various categories for tournament eligibility furthers the stated TPD purpose of "foster[ing] competition at the highest levels?" To what extent should courts defer to the judgment of the private governing association on this issue? Is the *Weser* court's approach in this respect consistent with that adopted in *Crouch v. NASCAR*?

————

Of some relevance to that last question is an ugly feature of the history of the PGA eligibility rules. From the time of its creation in 1916, the PGA Charter limited membership to "members of the Caucasian" race. From the late 1940s through the late 1950s, there was regular controversy and litigation when PGA tour events refused to accept star golfers from the Negro tour such as Bill Spiller, Ted Rhodes, and Charles Sifford.[3] While none of these cases ever came to trial, and the PGA repealed this membership bar in 1961, this history still poses the question of what would be the legal basis for a challenge against a discriminatory formal rule or actual practice that appears to exclude minority golfers (or players in other sports).

Questions for Discussion

1. Could such a challenge be lodged under Title VII of the Civil Rights Act which bars discrimination in "employment"? Or under Title II of the Civil Rights Act which guarantees "fair and equal treatment [in] the goods, services, facilities, privileges, advantages and accommodation at any place of public accommodation,"—defined to include "sports arenas, stadiums, or

3. See Charlie Sifford with James Gullo, *"Just Let Me Play": The Story of Charlie Sifford, the First Black PGA Golfer* (Latham, N.Y.: British American Publishing, 1992).

other places of entertainment"? Or under section 1 of the Sherman Act (as interpreted in *Weser*)?

2. Suppose that a top-flight woman player wanted to take her chances on the much more lucrative men's PGA tour (where the total prize money now surpasses $50 million), rather than play only on the Ladies PGA tour (where the total prize money is less than $20 million). If Raymond Floyd can now participate in both regular and senior men's golf tour events, why cannot Nancy Lopez play in events on both the women's and the men's tours? Alternatively, could a young male golfer claim a legal right to play on either the women's or the senior men's tour? Are there any relevant legal or philosophical differences between these two claims?

3. One noteworthy case crystallizes many of the issues inherent in gender-based tours. Dr. Renee Richards, formerly a ranking men's tennis player, underwent a transsexual operation to become female. Richards then attempted to enter the women's field in the 1977 U.S. Open. The USTA adopted the Barr sex-chromatin test, which would detect male chromosomes, shortly after Dr. Richards filed for tournament entry. Richards then sought and was granted an injunction against application of the test on the grounds of violation of New York human rights laws. While the court felt that use of this test was justifiable to prevent fraud against women competitors (men masquerading as women), it held that the Barr test should not be used as the sole criterion. *Richards v. USTA*, 93 Misc.2d 713, 400 N.Y.S.2d 267 (1977). Specifically, the court found that Dr. Richards was female externally, internally, endocrinologically, somatically, psychologically, and socially. Thus the USTA's use of the Barr test to exclude a participant who was a woman by so many other standards constituted illegal discrimination. Other than the phobias of tour officials or prospective audiences, does a sports tour have any legitimate grounds for excluding a transsexual? If size and muscle power are significant factors affecting truly equal competition, could the USTA not have adopted a direct standard of size and weight? Should the golf and tennis tours follow the example of boxing and classify competitors according to physical size rather than according to gender?

4. In the late 1980s, the PGA adopted a controversial revision in its rules that denied general eligibility for tour events (above a specified number of sponsor invitations) to foreign players who did not commit themselves to play at least fifteen times on the American tour. Australian players such as Greg Norman were prepared to make that commitment, but star Europeans such as Nick Faldo and Seve Ballesteros were not, because of the conflicting demands of their expanding European tour. Should Faldo and Ballesteros have an antitrust claim if they satisfy all other eligibility requirements with respect to playing ability? How would one characterize the purpose and effects of the PGA rule in connection with the Rule of Reason test?

5. Could the PGA deny admission to the tour to any player who refused to grant the PGA's marketing division the right to offer the player's name and likeness as part of a group licensing package sold by the PGA to manufacturers of golf clubs, clothes, or other paraphernalia? Suppose that a player objected because he had sold (or wanted to sell) an

exclusive endorsement to a manufacturer of a different product line. Suppose that the firm insisted on its endorsement rights because it was a sponsor of the tournament that the player wanted to enter. See *Greenleaf v. Brunswick–Balke–Collender Co.*, 79 F.Supp. 362 (E.D.Pa.1947), and *Washington State Bowling Proprietors Ass'n. v. Pacific Lanes Inc.*, 356 F.2d 371 (9th Cir.1966).

C. DISCIPLINARY AUTHORITY OF THE TOUR

Once courts intervene to protect the right of individual players to compete in golf (or tennis or bowling) tournaments, inevitably courts will be drawn into tour actions that terminate the eligibility of existing players, whether through suspension or permanent expulsion.[4] The pioneering case in this area came from the Ladies PGA Tour. After the men's PGA rebuffed their request in the 1940s for a separate women's division within that organization, in 1950 women golfers created their own tour composed of eleven tournaments and eleven participants. The LPGA struggled through the 1950s and the 1960s, but in 1972 it appeared to have made a major gain in financial backing and popular status when the Colgate Company, sponsor of the highly-rated Dinah Shore television show, decided to create the Dinah Shore Golf Classic, which became one of the Grand Slam events on the women's tour. In the same year, though, one of the top LPGA players, Jane Blalock, was suspended by her peers for her alleged practice of moving her ball during play.

BLALOCK v. LPGA

United States District Court, Northern District of Georgia, 1973.

359 F.Supp. 1260.

Moye, District Judge.

[Following several complaints from competitors, the LPGA tournament director appointed four observers to watch Jane Blalock play during a May 1972 tournament in Louisville. The observers agreed that Blalock was, indeed, moving her ball, including advancing her ball on the green after she had cleaned it. A meeting was convened of the Tour Executive Board comprised of five players—Cynthia Sullivan, Judy Rankin, Linda Craft, Penny Zavichas, and Sharon Miller. The Board initially found Blalock guilty of cheating during play, fined her $500, and placed her on probation for the rest of the season. Two weeks later the Executive Board reconvened, with two other players from the tour's tournament committee, and changed the penalty to a suspension for one full year. Blalock sued, alleging an illegal group boycott under federal antitrust law.]

---

4. On the legal and policy questions, see John C. Weistart, *Player Discipline in Professional Sports: The Antitrust Issues*, 18 William and Mary L. Rev. 703 (1977), and Robert H. Heidt, *"Don't Talk of Fairness": The Chicago School's Approach Toward Disciplining Professional Athletes*, 61 Indiana L.J. 53 (1985).

* * *

Measured by the standard set forth in [previous cases], the Court finds that the purpose and effect of the arrangement in this case (the agreement by defendants Sullivan, Rankin, Craft, Zavichas and Miller to suspend plaintiff from defendant LPGA for one year) was to exclude plaintiff from the market, and is therefore a "naked restraint of trade." Plaintiff is a member in good standing of defendant LPGA. Suspension therefrom is tantamount to total exclusion from the market of professional golf. Not only would plaintiff be excluded from LPGA sponsored tournaments, but, as defendant LPGA's Constitution and By–Laws provide in Article VIII:

> A member of the Ladies Professional Golf Association may not compete for prize money in a tournament, professional-amateur, or qualifying event that is not co-sponsored by the LPGA Tournament Players Corporation, or approved in writing by the LPGA Executive Director. . . .

The suspension was imposed upon plaintiff by defendants Sullivan, Rankin, Craft, Zavichas and Miller in the exercise of their completely unfettered, subjective discretion, as is evident from the fact that they had initially imposed upon plaintiff only probation and a fine, but then, without hearing from plaintiff, determined to impose the suspension at issue here. Furthermore, the suspension was imposed by competitors of plaintiff who stand to gain financially from plaintiff's exclusion from the market.

The Court therefore determines that the arrangement in this case is illegal per se. Consequently, it is not necessary that it inquire as to the reasonableness of the suspension.

* * *

Defendants have cited the cases of *Molinas v. National Basketball Association*, 190 F.Supp. 241 (S.D.N.Y.1961), and *Deesen v. Professional Golfers' Association of America* 358 F.2d 165 (9th Cir.1966). The Court finds these cases to be inapposite. The facts in *Molinas* demonstrate that Molinas, a professional basketball player, was suspended by the president of the National Basketball Association who was acting pursuant to a clause in Molinas's contract and a league rule prohibiting gambling. The suspension was not imposed by Molinas's competitors.

In the *Deesen* case, Deesen, a professional golfer and a member of the Professional Golfers' Association, had his approved tournament player status terminated by the PGA's national tournament committee. The national tournament committee was largely composed of noncompetitors of Deesen (the only exception being Bob Rosburg). Furthermore, the Court of Appeals relied heavily on the fact that notwithstanding that Deesen's tournament status had been terminated, Deesen was not completely excluded from the market (tournaments) as he could still participate therein, if he chose to become a golf teacher employed by a golf club. The termination in *Deesen* was based upon virtually a mathematical application of pre-determined standards. It did not involve a completely unfettered, subjective and discretionary determination of an exclusionary sanction by a tribunal wholly composed of competitors, as here....

Partial summary judgment granted.

Questions for Discussion

1. Look closely at the doctrinal analysis employed in *Blalock*, a case arising early in the evolution of sports antitrust law. Would a present-day court treat this as a question of *per se* illegality, in light of the last twenty years of sports antitrust jurisprudence? Would Rule of Reason analysis make any difference in the final result?

After *Blalock*, most tours, including the LPGA's, altered their disciplinary procedures to ensure that the ultimate decisionmakers are not solely fellow tour competitors of the player being charged. The typical present-day disciplinary model was at issue in the next antitrust suit, *O'Grady v. PGA*, 1986 WL 15389, 1986–2 Trade Cases (CCH) ¶ 67,361 (S.D. Cal.1986). O'Grady had been fined $500 by PGA Commissioner Deane Beman for insulting a worker at a New Orleans tournament. O'Grady was so infuriated by his discipline that he publicly described Beman as a dictator worse than Hitler, Mussolini, or Richard Nixon. O'Grady also made a disparaging comment about the Riviera Golf and Country Club, the site of the Los Angeles Open: O'Grady said that while Riviera had once been "really great," it was now like a "cheap public course that today would make a great runway for L.A.X." Beman then fined O'Grady an additional $5,000 and suspended him from the tour for the next six weeks (and six golf tournaments) for "conduct unbecoming" a PGA tour member. Having lost his appeal to the tour's Appeals Committee (comprised of one tournament player and two non-players, the Chairman of the Tournament Policy Board and the President of the PGA), O'Grady filed an antitrust suit, relying on *Blalock*. The trial judge quoted the following testimony from Jack Nicklaus about the meaning of "conduct unbecoming a professional golfer":

> [B]asically, what it really amounts to is the PGA of America has always had a Code of Ethics and the PGA Tour has always had a Code of Ethics. We felt for the best interests of the game the players should conduct themselves in a manner that is in the best interests of the game. It is in the best interest of the tour. It is a collective image. The best interests of PGA of America, of all the club pros in the country, to be able to [omitted] our position with the sponsor, our position with television, our position dealing with the public in general. I think it is important that the image of the player and the tour be for the good of the Association.

* * *

> If the rules were not there and the players headed in any direction they wanted to head, first of all we would not have had an Association, we would not have had a tour, as we know it, nor do I think the public

would have accepted us in the direction they have, which I think is good. Television contracts we have. The sponsors we have. Everything I think has grown largely because we, as an Association, have worked together for one common goal, which is for the benefit of the tour.

The judge then dismissed O'Grady's antitrust suit:

Mr. O'Grady would better serve himself by polishing his clubs and his golfing skills which are apparently very considerable, and leave off his temptation for verbal engagements.

Do you agree? In a team sport such as the NFL, for example, suppose that Zeke Mowatt had publicly attacked Commissioner Paul Tagliabue as a "dictator" for fining him in the aftermath of the Lisa Olsen incident. Should Tagliabue be able to penalize Mowatt for this added offense? Or suppose that Charles Barkley had publicly criticized the parquet basketball floor in the Boston Garden as "old, in poor shape, and giving the Celtics an unfair advantage because they know where the ruts and cracks are." Is this a disciplinary offense?

2. Recall the cases and problems in Chapter 1. Should baseball and football have a procedure for appealing disciplinary rulings by their commissioners as the *O'Grady* case exemplifies in golf (and as also exists in tennis)? Of course, when there is a players association with a collective bargaining agreement, the suspended player (for example, Steve Howe) can take the case to arbitration. But outside the union context, should Pete Rose have had an avenue to appeal from a decision by Bart Giamatti, or George Steinbrenner from one by Fay Vincent?

———

In thinking about tour disciplinary authority, consider the following case, one of the most important in modern American sports. On April 27, 1967, Muhammad Ali, the world's heavyweight boxing champion and most celebrated athlete, refused to be inducted into the U.S. armed forces on the ground of a conscientious religious objection. On April 28, 1967, the New York State Athletic Commission revoked Ali's license to box, and all the other state commissions soon followed suit. Ali's suit against the New York commission was then dismissed on administrative law grounds. See *Muhammad Ali v. State Athletic Commission of New York*, 308 F.Supp. 11 (S.D.N.Y.1969):

* * *

The visibly barbaric aspects of prize fighting, together with only slightly concealed vices of other kinds, led New York and other States to ban the activity altogether during long periods of modern history. For some time, however, relaxing its scarcely questionable power of total prohibition, New York, again like other States, has permitted the so-called sport, but subjected it to sweeping and rigorous controls administered by a State Athletic Commission. It is much too late in our constitutional history to dwell long upon the obviously sweeping powers of the State to regulate an activity of this kind. The scope of occupational licensing and supervision must vary, of course, with the nature of the business and its impacts. Whether the variations be deemed differences of kind or merely "of degree," it is plain that some fields, including the one before us, are subject to broad powers for the determination and application of state policy judgments.

The peculiar mix of mystique and big business characterizing the world of professional sports is nowhere more complex and bemusing than in the "boxing game." Even judges have some awareness of the brutal, corrupt and dirty chapters in the history of this subject. On the other hand, the blood, sweat and smoke of the fight arena have been the ingredients for producing folk heroes, enshrined as models for the young as well as shrewd investments for others. All such diverse things are reflected in the broad mandate of the Athletic Commission—which is required to watch out for "fixes," for sharp managerial practices and for other corrupt devices while it strives to follow the loftier and still cherished ideals of a simpler age reflected in the notion of a "clean sport." To implement its various objectives, the Commission is entitled to wide freedom both for expert technical controls and for more romantic, even "mid-Victorian" judgments of moral, quasi-aesthetic value.

308 F.Supp. at 16 (citations omitted).

Not until the Supreme Court sustained Ali's constitutional freedom of religion claim and voided his subsequent conviction for draft evasion was he permitted by state authorities to return to the ring.[5]

Questions for Discussion

1. Suppose that a golfer or tennis player had claimed the same exemption from the draft as did Ali. Or suppose that the player had merely attacked the president's war policy in as vigorous a tone as Mac O'Grady employed against Deane Beman. Are either or both of these actions valid grounds under antitrust law for suspension of the player from a privately governed tour whose officials believe the player's conduct to be harmful to the best interests of their sport?

2. A different kind of disciplinary problem arose in 1983 in tennis. The Argentinian star Guillermo Vilas was discovered to have been paid $60,000 to appear at a tournament in Rotterdam. The Men's International Professional Tennis Council (MIPTC), then the governing authority for the men's tour, fined Vilas $20,000 and suspended him for a year for violating its rule against appearance money or guarantees. Vilas exercised his right under the MIPTC constitution to appeal this decision to a three-member

---

5. See Thomas Hauser, *Muhammad Ali: His Life and Times* 142–202 (New York: Simon and Schuster, 1991). On the broader issues posed by the sport of boxing and its regulation (both internally and by state boxing commissions), see Jeffrey T. Sammons, *Beyond the Ring: The Role of Boxing in American Society* (Urbana, Ill.: Univ. of Illinois Press, 1990).

panel composed of one person selected by Vilas, another by MIPTC officials, and the third by these two nominees (all panel members were selected from a larger MIPTC roster). The panel confirmed the Council's finding of a rules violation by Vilas and upheld the fine, but revoked the suspension because this was the first time that which the Council had enforced its rule against the growing practice of paying appearance fees to star attractions. Vilas paid the modest fine and the matter was closed.

Suppose, though, that the suspension had been upheld and Vilas had proceeded with his threatened antitrust suit against the MIPTC. How does a rule that bars individual tournaments from paying individual players more than the official prize money stand up under antitrust scrutiny? Such a rule has always been the norm in men's and women's golf and women's tennis, but as we will see the rule has recently been relaxed somewhat in men's tennis. To what extent does such a rule serve the interests of players (those who are regularly paid appearance fees and those who are not), of tournaments, and of fans?

D. ORGANIZING A SPORTS TOUR

The phenomenon of appearance money is best understood within the broader evolution of tennis (and other non-team) tournament tours. Lawn tennis, as the game was first called, was invented in the 1870s. The All England Lawn Tennis Club staged the first Wimbledon Championship in 1877 and the United States Lawn Tennis Association (now the USTA) staged its first championship in 1881. In 1900, twelve countries agreed to play for the Davis Cup, and in 1913 the national associations from these and other countries formed the International Lawn Tennis Federation (now the ITF) as the game's world-wide governing authority.

Amateurism was the Federation's central principle. Unlike golf tournaments, "open" tennis championships were not open to players who earned their living from the game. Once top players established their reputations, they had to drop out of "Grand Slam" competition and barnstorm around the world playing exhibition matches. Beginning with Suzanne Lenglen in the 1920s, this was the path followed by superstars such as Bill Tilden, Don Budge, Jack Kramer, Pancho Gonzales, and Rod Laver. Meanwhile, ITF tennis had developed into a regime of "shamateurism," as it was labeled. Tournament organizers and national associations had always been permitted to pay players their travel expenses for an event, but it became common practice to pay sums substantially above actual expenses to the top players—in effect, appearance guarantees.

Some tournament tennis players were thus able to make a reasonably decent living from the sport—considerably better than college football players on scholarship, but not as good as avowedly professional golfers on the PGA Tour. By the 1960s, some tennis authorities—particularly the British—wanted to end this hypocrisy and make their events truly "open," but they were always outvoted within the ITF by authorities in smaller countries that were worried about losing money and control. The political logjam was broken not by litigation, but by market competition. In the mid–1960s Lamar Hunt, fresh from his success with the American Football League, organized a new venture, World Championship Tennis (WCT), that successfully recruited most of the top players to a professional tour promising both serious competition and sizable prize money. Faced with that threat, in 1968 the All England Lawn Tennis Club declared Wimbledon open to professionals, and the USTA immediately followed suit with its U.S. Open.

These actions ushered in an era of top-flight tennis, fast-growing spectator and television revenues, constant controversy about the structure of the sport, and periodic litigation among parties fighting for a larger share of the pie. Following are some of the highlights of that history.[6]

In 1968 the ITF voted to allow professionals to enter Grand Slam events and Davis Cup competition. The Federation also developed its own set of Grand Prix tournaments to compete against the WCT Tour. Scheduling conflicts and competition for players between the two tours promoted a fierce rivalry; the ITF, after failing to negotiate cooperation in scheduling with the WCT, banned all WCT pros from ITF events. The absence of the WCT pros from the 1972 Grand Slams promoted a truce between the tours; WCT and ITF officials resolved their conflict by literally dividing the calendar between them.

In 1972, the men players created an Association of Tennis Professionals (ATP) whose first presidents were Cliff Drysdale and Arthur Ashe and first executive director was Jack Kramer. Conflict between the ATP and the ITF produced another boycott of Wimbledon in 1973 by men players supporting one of their members, who had been suspended by the ITF for not playing for his country in the Davis Cup competition.

Soon thereafter, with the help of Donald Dell—Arthur Ashe's agent and the founder of ProServ—the ATP and the ITF agreed to create the MITPC to run the men's game: each party had three members on the Council's governing board. The MIPTC later became a tripartite body with three board members added to represent the various tournaments and their directors.

6. The best treatment of the emergence of the present-day tennis tour is Richard Evans, *Open Tennis: 1968–1989* (New York: Viking, 1990). Other historical portrayals of the professional tennis circuits are Bud Collins, *My Life With the Pros*, (New York: E.P. Dutton, 1989); Jack Kramer with Frank Deford, *The Game: My 40 Years in Tennis* (New York: G.P. Putnam & Sons, 1979); and Pam Shriver, Frank Deford & Susan Adams, *Passing Shots* (New York: McGraw-Hill, 1987). Narrower time frames are described in John Feinstein, *Hard Courts: Real Life on the Professional Tennis Tours* (New York: Villard Books, 1992) and Rich Koster, *The Tennis Bubble: Big-Money Tennis, How It Grew and Where It's Going* (New York: Quadrangle/The New York Times Book Company, 1976). The legal picture prior to the decision excerpted in this section is described in George Matanias, Thomas Cryar, & David Johnson, *A Critical Look at Professional Tennis Under Antitrust Law*, 4 Enter. & Sports L. J. 57 (1987).

Meanwhile, women players had not been faring nearly as well as men financially—women's prizes often amounted to only about 10% of those offered to men in the same Grand Prix tournament events. In response, a new Women's Tennis Association (WTA) was formed, led by Billie Jean King as President and Gladys Heldman as Executive Director. The new WTA successfully launched the Virginia Slims women's tour under the sponsorship of the Phillip Morris Tobacco Company. This challenge to the tennis establishment produced threats of expulsion of women members from Grand Slam tournaments and litigation in response (see *Heldman v. USLTA*, 354 F.Supp. 1241 (S.D.N.Y.1973), until the ITF finally agreed with the WTA to create a Women's International Professional Tennis Council (WIPTC) to govern the women's game.

In 1974 yet another entrant appeared on the scene, World Team Tennis (WTT), which offered fans a schedule of matches between teams of players representing different cities. After the WTT recruited star players such as Jimmy Connors and Evonne Goolagong, the MIPTC threatened suspension of any players deserting its tour. That threat produced yet another lawsuit, Jimmy Connors vs. Arthur Ashe (ATP President) and his colleagues, a suit that was dropped when the MIPTC backed down.

In fact, the new WTT model of teams playing in a league did not prove to be a serious threat to the traditional practice of individual players competing by and for themselves in tournaments. By the mid–1980s, the basic structure of present-day tennis had emerged. Tennis players drawn from around the world competed in tournaments staged around the world. Most tournaments consisted of separate events held on the men's and women's tours respectively; however, the four Grand Slam Tournaments (the Australian, French, All England, and U.S. Opens) and a few other tournaments had both men's and women's competitions; each tournament was staged by a local body with financial support from a local sponsor, but the tour as a whole had a general corporate sponsor; the men's tour, in particular, devised an elaborate system of ranking players by their overall performance throughout the year, paying bonus money for players who did best on tour events, and staging a lucrative year-end Masters Tournament for the best players on the tour that year.

Along with these wider and more lucrative tournament opportunities came an extensive array of regulations by tour authorities, regulations that were embodied in contractual commitments signed by any player who wanted to appear in a tournament and by any organization that wanted to stage a tour event. Recall one example of such regulation—the ban on fees paid by an individual tournament to players to guarantee their appearance at that event. Instead, the tours sought to ensure widespread participation in tournaments by requiring each player to enter a minimum number of events (at least fourteen on the men's tour), and by offering a bonus pool created by contributions from each tournament.

These devices were felt necessary because star players such as John McEnroe and Chris Evert were constantly offered the chance to play in brief exhibition events that paid large sums of money with no risk to their computer rankings. Thus, the tours also imposed stringent limits on when players could perform in special events that conflicted with tournaments and on the ability of any party involved in conducting an official tournament to stage a special event off the tour.

A special target of such regulations were organizations such as Donald Dell's Proserv and Mark McCormack's International Management Group (IMG). Proserv and IMG initially emerged as agencies representing star tennis and golf players, but soon developed the ability to assist, manage, and even stage tour events themselves. Believing that this mix of functions involved a potential conflict of interest (Donald Dell even served as color commentator on telecasts of tournaments involving his clients), the MIPTC barred a player agency from conducting tournaments which, it was feared, would have an unfair advantage in getting the agency's clients to appear at their tour events. (In fact, it was this apparent conflict of interest that led noted agent Lee Fentress to leave ProServ and create his own organization, Advantage International.)

We have provided the foregoing detail about the evolution and structure of the tennis tour as backdrop for the one appellate court decision that addresses the compatibility with American antitrust law of tour organization of individual sports (which in the case of tennis, but not golf, is an international structure). This litigation was actually initiated by the Volvo Corporation which had been the general sponsor of the men's tour as the latter evolved in the late 1970s and early 1980s, before being outbid for sponsorship by Nabisco Brands. Some time after the suit began, the MIPTC satisfied Volvo's concerns by giving favorable schedule treatment to the latter's New England tournament. By then, however, Proserv and IMG had become parties to the litigation and continued the legal attack on MIPTC regulation. After a federal district judge in New York granted summary dismissal of the suit, the plaintiffs appealed to the Second Circuit.

VOLVO NORTH AM. CORP. v. MEN'S INT'L PROFESSIONAL TENNIS COUNCIL (MIPTC)

United States Court of Appeals, Second Circuit, 1988.

857 F.2d 55.

PIERCE, CIRCUIT JUDGE.

[The first question was whether Volvo, IMG, and Proserv had standing under antitrust law to challenge components of the MIPTC system to which they themselves were parties.]

* * *

Appellants claim on appeal that "MIPTC coordinates horizontal competitors banding together to eliminate competition among themselves and to use their collective power to limit the competitive opportunities of outsiders." In other words, appellants view MIPTC as a vehicle through which certain entities, primarily other tournament owners and producers, have established a cartel in the market for men's professional tennis; allegedly, this cartel has not only limited output and raised prices in the market for men's professional tennis events, but has also used its market power to inhibit competition from the owners and producers of Special Events. Proserv and IMG claim that the cartel has injured them, in their capacities as owners and producers of Special Events, (1) by restricting their ability to obtain a sufficient supply of players' services for Special Events; (2) by causing them to own and produce fewer Special Events than they otherwise would have owned and produced; and (3) by causing the Special Events that they have owned and produced to be less profitable than these events otherwise would have been. Volvo claims similar injuries as a potential owner and producer of Special Events. In addition, all three appellants claim that they have been injured ... because compliance with MIPTC's rules has prevented them from competing "freely and vigorously with the events owned and produced by the defendants and their co-conspirators."

In response ... MIPTC raises the following argument in one form or another: if appellants' theory is correct, and MIPTC is the vehicle through which tournament owners and producers have organized a cartel in the market for men's professional tennis, then appellants lack standing to challenge the cartel because, as owners and producers of sanctioned tournaments, appellants themselves are members of the cartel who stand to benefit from the cartel's unlawful activity. Taken to its logical conclusion, appellees' argument suggests that we adopt a per se rule prohibiting putative cartel members from asserting antitrust claims against other members of the cartel.

We decline to adopt a rule precluding cartel members from raising antitrust challenges against the cartel. As one commentator has noted, "even absent legal restraint the cartel is inherently more fragile than the single-firm monopolist. The interests of the cartel as a whole often diverge substantially from the interests of individual members." H. Hovenkamp, *Economics and Federal Antitrust Law* § 4.1, at 83 (1985) ("Hovenkamp"). Individual members of the cartel may face different costs; some may be more efficient than others, and "some may produce slightly different products, which cost either a little less or a little more than the product sold by other cartel members." Thus, even though a particular trade restraint adopted by a cartel presumably operates to the cartel's aggregate benefit, the restraint may operate to the detriment of an individual member.... To the extent a cartel member credibly asserts that it would be better off if it were free to compete—such that the member's interest coincides with the public interest in vigorous competition—we believe that the individual cartel member satisfies the antitrust injury requirement....

2. APPLYING ANTITRUST INJURY ANALYSIS

a. MIPTC's Administration of the Grand Prix Circuit

As noted above, appellants claim that, in administering the Grand Prix, MIPTC has denied appellants "the opportunity to produce tennis events in the manner they seek with respect to matters such as site location, player compensation and scheduling." In response, appellees argue that, to the extent appellants themselves are owners and producers of events sanctioned by MIPTC, they "are only helped by rules minimizing scheduling conflicts," and that "the MIPTC rule limiting the amount of prize money which can be awarded by an event ... cannot possibly hurt appellants in their association with MIPTC sanctioned events" because appellants stand to "benefit from a ceiling on one of the key costs of running an event."

For the following reasons, we conclude that appellants have standing to challenge the administration of the Grand Prix circuit. Because the individual cartel member's interests may diverge from the interests of the cartel as a whole, MIPTC's decisions relating to site location and scheduling might not work to appellants' advantage, even though appellants are owners and producers of sanctioned events. Appellants claim that MIPTC uses its power "to shield tournaments favored by MIPTC from the rigors of competition," and, in our view, this allegation satisfies the antitrust injury requirement. Moreover, as Volvo argues on appeal, the rule limiting the amount of prize money that may be awarded by sanctioned events may injure appellants, as owners and producers of such events, by preventing them from "compet[ing] against other Grand Prix events for the services of highly ranked players by offering more prize money." Once again, although a particular rule may work to the aggregate benefit of the owners and producers of sanctioned events, it may not benefit an individual owner or producer such as Volvo, Proserv, or IMG. Thus, because appellants' individual interests may coincide with the public interest in promoting competition, we believe that appellants have satisfied the first element of the standing analysis.

* * *

c. Commitment Agreements

The amended complaint alleges that the Commitment Agreements inhibit men's professional tennis players from competing in Special Events. Appellees counter the attack on the Commitment Agreements by arguing, first, that "appellants stand only to gain from each of the alleged restrictions on the market for men's tennis playing services," because "any incentives for players to sell their services to the Grand Prix ... can only benefit appellants" in their capacity as owners and producers of MIPTC-sanctioned events. . . .

Notwithstanding the foregoing arguments, we conclude that appellants have standing to challenge the Commitment Agreements. As alleged, the Commitment Agreements discourage players from participating in non-sanctioned events and, therefore, increase the cost of producing these events. Accordingly, IMG and Proserv, in their capacities as owners and producers of non-sanctioned Special Events, may have suffered "injury of the type the antitrust laws were intended to prevent." Moreover, by restricting the supply of players available for non-sanctioned events, the Commitment Agreements also discourage owners and producers from disassociating themselves from MIPTC. To the extent that owners and producers of sanctioned events, such as Volvo, would otherwise find it in their economic interests to compete against the alleged tennis cartel, these owners and producers also have suffered the type of injuries the antitrust laws were intended to forestall. Thus, in our view, all three appellants have satisfied the element of antitrust injury.

* * *

[For similar reasons the court upheld the plaintiffs' standing to challenge the MITPC rules requiring tournament contributions to the bonus pool and restricting special events. The court then turned to the merits of the plaintiffs' antitrust claims. The court first held that the MIPTC, made up of representatives of players, tournaments, and national tennis associations, was the type of joint venture that was capable of an antitrust conspiracy, explicitly following judicial precedents that had characterized the NCAA and professional leagues as single rather than multiple entities for purposes of section 1 of the Sherman Antitrust Act. After noting that the plaintiffs had attacked as horizontal price-fixing the MIPTC rule that specified prize money ranges for different kinds of tournaments, the court made the following comment about the reasonableness of such a practice.]

Assuming that appellants succeed in proving the foregoing allegations, however, we express no opinion at this time as to whether appellees' conduct should be condemned as per se unlawful or, instead, should be analyzed under the Rule of Reason. Normally, "agreements among competitors to fix prices on their individual goods and services are among those concerted activities" that are considered per se illegal under § 1 of the Sherman Act. The relevant inquiry, however, involves more than "a question simply of determining whether two or more potential competitors have literally 'fixed' a 'price.'" Instead, "'price fixing' is a shorthand way of describing certain categories of business behavior to which the per se rule has been held applicable." Moreover, we recognize that professional sporting events cannot exist unless the producers of such events agree to cooperate with one another to a certain extent, and that the antitrust laws do not condemn such agreements when coordination is essential if the activity is to be carried out at all. Thus, on remand, the district court should carefully consider whatever arguments appellees may offer in support of their practices relating to player compensation before deciding whether the per se rule or the Rule of Reason should apply.

[The appeals court made essentially the same judgment about the plaintiff's attack on MIPTC's allocation of different dates to different tours sites and sponsors: this practice could constitute an illegal horizontal division of the tournament market, but no decision was made about whether the MIPTC practice was per se illegal or possibly justifiable under the rule of reason. With respect to the charge that eligibility conditions imposed by the MIPTC on players constituted a potential group boycott, the Appeals Court stated]:

According to appellant Proserv, "the Grand Prix tournaments have collectively agreed not to permit the participation by any player who fails to accept the conditions the group imposes upon the player's activities for an entire year." Thus, men's professional tennis players "confront through the Commitment Agreements a horizontal agreement among competing producers of tennis tournaments setting forth the terms under which they will collectively decline to deal with the players."

Judge Duffy considered the Commitment Agreements to be "essentially employment contracts that require employee players to play only for MIPTC for thirty-six weeks a year." The court then stated that "[e]mployers may impose reasonable employment conditions for a reasonable period of time," and that "[e]ven accepting plaintiffs' assertion that creating an independent tennis event series is not feasible during the remaining weeks of the year, I cannot find that an exclusive employment contract for thirty-six weeks a year is imposed for an unreasonable length of time."

In our view, the amended complaint adequately alleges that appellees have threatened to engage in a group boycott or concerted refusal to deal. Generally, a group boycott is "an agreement by two or more persons not to do business with other individuals, or to do business with them only on specified terms." To prevail on a group boycott or refusal to deal claim, a plaintiff must demonstrate that the defendant intends to restrain competition, or to enhance or expand his monopoly, and has acted coercively.

Whether the threatened boycott alleged in the amended complaint [should be legally appraised by a per se rule] is a matter for the district court to consider in due course.

[Finally, the Court reinstated the appellant's claim that the MIPTC's organization and operation of men's tennis potentially constituted an illegal monopoly under section 2 of the Sherman Act.]

The offense of monopolization under § 2 of the Sherman Act consists of two elements: (1) the possession of monopoly power in the relevant market; and (2) the willful acquisition or maintenance of that power, as distinguished from growth or development as a consequence of a superior product, business acumen, or historic accident. Aspen Skiing Co. v. Aspen Highlands Skiing Corp., 472 U.S. 585, 596 n. 19, (1985). Appellants clearly have alleged that MIPTC possesses monopoly power over the production of first-rate men's professional tennis events. Paragraph 50 of the amended complaint, for example, alleges that in 1985 the top one hundred men's professional tennis players all signed Commitment Agreements. Moreover, the amended complaint alleges that appellees have willfully maintained their monopoly power (1) by merging with WCT in 1983; (2) by requiring players to sign Commitment Agreements; and (3) by requiring owners of sanctioned events to contribute to the bonus pool. Although the facts may eventually bear out the district court's conclusion that MIPTC has not willfully maintained its monopoly power, and that MIPTC instead has benefited from "the recent historical development of men's professional tennis," we do not believe that the district court was correct to draw this conclusion on a motion to dismiss.

Appeal granted.

————

The appellate court thus upheld the plaintiffs' appeal, reinstated the plaintiff's antitrust suit, and returned the case to the district court for trial on the merits. As has happened with almost every law suit launched in the world of tennis, the litigants in *Volvo* soon settled the case without its merits ever being reached in court. Volvo turned its sponsorship attention to the European golf tour (where, by the way, it insisted upon adoption of the ban on appearance fees that previously had rewarded players such as Nick Faldo, Seve Ballesteros, and Ian Woosnam). Player agencies such as Proserv and IMG agreed, after a three year phase-out period, not to be involved in ownership of tournaments, while the MITPC relaxed its rule to allow agencies to sell television and sponsorship rights on a men's tour that itself was changing sharply in character.

In 1990, the ATP broke away from the MIPTC and decided to stage its own tour run by and for the players. Many prominent players felt that the MITPC executive had been unresponsive to their concerns about a tour that had become too long and dispersed to permit regular genuine competition among the top stars. The new regime left the ITF with its four Grand Slam tournaments and the Davis Cup competition, and a new $6 million Grand Slam Championship (for semi-finalists from the four major events) to be staged just after the ATP's season-ending Masters Championship in November of each year. The ATP tour is divided into 24 Championship Series events (with prize money ranging from $600,000 to $2 million) and 54 World Series events (with minimum prize money of $250,000). All top-ten ranked players are required to play in at least nine championship events, and the ATP has guaranteed to each such tournament that at least six top-ten players will participate. In addition, none of its players are permitted to perform in another tournament or special event in competition with the Championship Series. With respect to World Series events for which there is no such commitment or protection, the ATP now allows such tournaments to pay appearance fees. The first such fees paid above-the-board were by the San Francisco tournament in February of 1990: Andre Agassi received $175,000 to appear and $32,000 to win.

Hamilton Jordan, the first Executive Director of the ATP Tour (and formerly Chief of Staff to President Jimmy Carter), lauded this new venture as "one stop shopping" for men's tennis, through which "the pie would get bigger and everybody would benefit." Not only has the tour managed to secure a rich sponsorship deal with IBM, but the ATP has sold (through IMG) its worldwide television rights on a package basis for $110 million a year. For the ATP membership, at least, the outcome has been a happy one: smaller commitments from individual players and a tour whose prize money topped $42 million in 1992 (exclusive of the bonus pool, appearance money, and Grand Slam events). Women tennis players have observed these developments with envy, as they play a comparable schedule for $16 million in total prize money. A combination of division within the WTA ranks and contractual commitments to outside sponsors (such as Kraft) have blocked for the time being any similar venture for the women tennis players.

We have sketched the foregoing developments within tennis in order to pose anew the legal questions that were not finally addressed in *Volvo*.

1. Does the appearance money issue look any different when viewed with this broader historical perspective?

2. Why should individual players—especially the best players—be required to appear at a specified number of tour events around the world (in addition to participation by many in four two-week Grand Slam tournaments, the year-long Davis Cup competition, and the season-ending tour championships)? Should this rule pass the Rule of Reason test?

3. Why should players be barred from participating in special non-tour events held at the same time as Championship Series events, or within a specified distance of contemporaneous World Series events? Now players who violate these rules are simply fined by the governing body (the ATP or the WITPC), and the fines are paid by the special event sponsors as part of the appearance money guarantee. This is what happened to Monica Seles in 1991, when she played at a New Jersey exhibition shortly after her mysterious absence from Wimbledon. What if the ATP or the WITPC put more teeth in this rule by suspending a player for several months for such an infraction. Could the player or the event promoter sue?

4. Is the collective sale of television rights on behalf of the entire tour—with proceeds divided among individual tournaments—consistent with the antitrust doctrines we saw applied to professional leagues in Chapter 6 (in the *WGN* case) and to college sports in Chapter 9 (in the *Oklahoma–Georgia* case)?

5. Would it be legal for the ATP membership to boycott ITF events—on the ground, for example, that most of the money now earned by the USTA from the U.S. Open is paid not as prize money

to professional players, but used to fund the USTA's broader activities promoting tennis in this country?

6. Recall the *Sims v. Argovitz* case from Chapter 5, and related questions about conflicts of interest affecting sports lawyer-agents and their player-clients. Does that material justify tour concern about the fact that, for example, Donald Dell and Proserv were at one and the same time the manager of Volvo's annual New England tennis tournament and the agent of Jimmy Connors and others whom Volvo wanted to play in the tournament?

7. In assessing each of these questions, should the tour organizations in each sport—i.e., the ATP or the PGA—be treated as a single entity offering a single product that must compete in the broader sports and entertainment market, and thus insulated from section 1 scrutiny of its internal decisions and restrictions?

The foregoing questions are as relevant to the golf as to the tennis tours. While private litigation may not soon be forthcoming from among the players, sponsors, broadcasters, and others who participate in and profit from the current tours, the Justice Department and the Federal Trade Commission (FTC) are empowered to launch such proceedings on behalf of the general public. Indeed, the FTC has reportedly undertaken an investigation of the PGA golf tour. Such an investigation raises broader questions about whether restrictive organization of any one (non-team) sport unduly burdens the sports market, and whether American antitrust law enforcement should target a sport such as tennis that operates on a world-wide basis.

A final issue concerns not market restraints but gender disparities. Among the Grand Slam tournaments comprising both men and women events, Wimbledon and the French Open (but not the United States or Australian Opens) pay smaller prize money for the women's than the men's championship. Is that practice discriminatory? Is it relevant that the separate men's tennis tour now offers two and a half times the prize money as the women's tour (this is also true of the PGA versus the LPGA golf tours)? What accounts for these large differentials in the financial rewards for the typical male and female athletes (Monica Seles and Nancy Lopez being exceptions that prove the rule)?[7] Does this have any bearing on the questions posed in Chapter 9 about college sports under Title IX—for example, whether the men's and women's basketball programs should receive equal financial support?

E. REGULATING PLAYING EQUIPMENT

An additional source of protagonists and controversies is the manufacturing of equipment used in a sport. The design of tennis rackets and golf clubs is an obvious target of tour regulation because of the

7. See Lawrence M. Kahn, *Discrimination in Professional Sports: A Survey of the* *Literature*, 44 Indus. and Lab. Rel. Rev. 395, 412–14 (1991).

impact playing equipment can have on athletic competition. But private regulation of the tools that put individual athletes at an advantage displays the historical tensions felt by organizations whose manifest purpose is to serve the welfare of the game, but that also serve the entrepreneurial interests of participants.

An early illustration of a court grappling with these issues was *STP Corporation v. United States Auto Club (USAC)*, 286 F.Supp. 146 (S.D.Ind.1968). In the sport of auto racing, the USAC functioned not as the promoter of races such as the Indianapolis 500, but as a non-profit body that merely sanctioned events, licensed participants, and regulated the safety and appeal of the races—including specifications for racing car engines. In the 1967 Indy 500, Studebaker's new turbine-powered car proved to be much faster than traditional piston-driven engines (although the Studebaker Turbocar had to drop out near the end of that race because of gear box troubles). Shortly thereafter, the USAC introduced a rule that limited the size of turbine-powered engines in order to make them equivalent in speed to piston-powered cars. In dismissing an antitrust suit brought by STP, Studebaker's subsidiary in charge of its racing program, a district judge held that such USAC rulemaking was perfectly acceptable under the rule of reason:

> One of the purposes of the USAC is to encourage the sport of automobile racing, which is a highly competitive sport of a very technical nature. The quickest way to bring about the demise of racing would be to permit a situation that developed for one car with superior qualities or such superior capabilities as to eliminate competition. It would be somewhat like allowing one basketball team to have a large hoop at one end of the court and a small regulation size basketball hoop at the other end for the other team. In order to have a continuation of racing, the Court concludes that USAC acted reasonably in trying to bring about an equivalency between the piston-powered automobiles with turbine-powered cars according to a formula that was prepared and cemented after consultation with those who are considered most expert in the field.... The making of competitive rules is something that any governing body of an organization such as USAC has a right to do. Such action goes to the very purpose of its existence, i.e., to encourage competitive racing.

286 F.Supp. at 151

Ten years later, a similar dispute arose in tennis with two added features. Unlike the USAC, the U.S. Tennis Association itself ran several major tournaments, including the lucrative U.S. Open. In this case the USTA simply adopted a new equipment rule issued by the International Tennis Federation (ITF), which had traditionally exercised responsibility to establish a single set of rules governing tennis matches wherever played.

GUNTER HARZ SPORTS v. USTA

United States District Court, District of Nebraska, 1981.

511 F.Supp. 1103.

SCHATZ, DISTRICT JUDGE.

[The ITF had banned a German manufacturer's new model of tennis racket—called the "spaghetti racket" because it had two layers of vertical strings, one on each side of the horizontal strings. The effect of this "double-stringing" was to impart a very powerful topspin to a tennis ball such that when the ball hit the ground in front of a player it would bounce sharply over his head. When the racket first appeared in European tournaments, it helped produce several astonishing upsets of star players by low-ranked opponents. In the face of a threatened player boycott of the 1977 French Open, the ITF issued a temporary emergency ban of this racket pending in-depth study of its effects; when the study was completed, the ITF permanently banned the double-strung racket. The ITF stated that "the spirit of this rule is to prevent undue spin on the ball that would result in a change in the character of the game." After the USTA had endorsed and adopted both ITF regulations, the racket manufacturer sued the USTA in Nebraska.]

* * *

While the Sherman Act is primarily aimed at conduct which has commercial objectives, ample authority exists for finding the activities of the USTA subject to Section 1. Non-profit voluntary associations which sanction and regulate professional sporting tournaments, races and other contests have been held subject to the antitrust laws in the exercise of their rule-making authority. Similarly, non-profit amateur athletic associations formed for the primary purpose of promoting amateur athletics have been found subject to the prohibitions of Section 1 of the Sherman Act. Courts have proceeded on the theory that while each such sanctioning organization has the primary noncommercial purpose of promoting organized sports in an orderly fashion, "its subsequent actions in carrying out its laudable objectives could trigger the applicability of the Sherman Act if such conduct restrained interstate trade or commerce in an unreasonable manner."

* * *

The actions of the USTA in this case clearly cannot be characterized as the traditional type of group boycott to which the per se doctrine has been applied. The Court accepts plaintiff's contention that the USTA entered into a Sherman Act "agreement" when it joined other member nations of the ITF in the adoption of Rule 4 of the Rules of Tennis, and when it agreed to follow the temporary ban of double-strung rackets. However, the Court rejects any suggestion of "agreement," as that term is used in the Sherman Act, between the USTA or the ITF and any distributors or manufacturers of tennis equipment to prevent the plaintiff from competing in the sale or distribution of rackets or stringing systems. Totally lacking in this case is an agreement between "business competitors in the traditional sense." Nor can the actions of the USTA in adopting a rule defining tennis rackets be labeled as lacking in "any redeeming virtue."

Where the purpose of a "group boycott" has been to protect fair competition in sports and games, courts have eschewed a per se analysis in favor of an inquiry into the reasonableness of the restraint under the circumstances.

* * *

Defendants contend that the actions of the USTA are exempt from this type of analysis under the circumstances of this case because the ITF actually initiated and promulgated the temporary ban and Rule 4, while the USTA was forced to adopt the rule as a condition of its membership. The Court finds that contention without merit.... "[C]ourts have uniformly rejected any defense that an antitrust violation was 'forced' onto the defendant," and the "Supreme Court has held that 'acquiescence in an illegal scheme is as much a violation of the Sherman Act as the creation and promotion of one.'"

The Constitution of the USTA provides that it is "an independent tennis organization and as such cannot take any action at the request of any international tennis body which is inconsistent with the provisions of its Certificate of Incorporation or any By–Laws or Standing Orders issued hereunder." As an independent tennis organization the USTA's membership in the ITF is voluntary, and it cannot take any action at the request of the ITF, or as a condition of its membership in the ITF, which is a violation of the antitrust laws of the United States and escape liability.

* * *

Turning to an analysis of the actions of the USTA under the rule of reason, the Court specifically finds that the collective action of the USTA, ITF, and other member national associations of the ITF was intended to accomplish the legitimate goals of preserving the essential character and integrity of the game of tennis as it had always been played, and preserving competition by attempting to conduct the game in an orderly fashion. The record is totally devoid of any evidence from which an intent to injure the plaintiff or any other manufacturer or distributor of tennis equipment can be inferred. As noted previously, the Court finds no agreement between the USTA or ITF and any manufacturer or distributor of tennis equipment to exclude plaintiff from competing in the market for rackets or stringing systems.

The evidence shows that the ITF solicited, received, and acted upon comments and suggestions from equipment manufacturers, including Fischer and Harz. The original draft of the proposed rule was revised partly in response to comments of manufacturers suggesting that many conventional rackets on the market would be banned by the original draft of the proposed rule, although such rackets did nothing to alter the character of the game. However, the Court finds nothing impermissible in such communication or response. Both the USTA and the ITF had the right to solicit such information and act upon it in attempting to make reasonable informed decisions concerning racket specifications and in attempting to draft the rule so that it would be the least restrictive of technological improvements and developments, but still address the legitimate concern that such development not adversely alter the character of the game of tennis as it had been played historically or artificially enhance the skill and ability of players, thereby harming the integrity of competitive tennis.

Secondly, the Court concludes that the actions of the USTA and the ITF were reasonably related to the goals discussed above. In reaching that conclusion, the Court is not to substitute its own judgment for that of the ITF or the USTA. It is irrelevant whether the Court might or might not independently reach the same decision based on the same evidence. In this regard, the Court agrees with the characterization of the latitude to be given a sanctioning organization contained in *STP Corp. v. United States Auto Club*:

> ... A membership organization ... must be left to legislate its own rules and its own guidelines for participation of its members for the purposes for which it was created so long as that legislation is not done in an unreasonable manner and without malice or intention to harm a single member or segment of membership. Such membership organizations have the right to adopt such rules to protect their very existence.

Plaintiff contends that the actions of the ITF in enacting the temporary ban on double-strung rackets were arbitrary because the basis for the ban was a false and misleading assessment by the German Federation of a study made by the Braunschweig Technical University on the effect of double-strung rackets, and a playing demonstration using poor copies of the Fischer double-strung racket, not strung according to Fischer's specifications on stringing tension.

The Court finds that despite the actual conclusion of the Braunschweig study that double stringing did not revolutionize the character of the game and should not be banned, the study's findings did lend support to the concerns which prompted the temporary ban. The study found that strokes at high speed, as well as stroke types which primarily utilized cross strings, could be played under certain conditions only; that double stringing resulted in strokes with a very strong spin being played almost exclusively since those strokes were most effective; and that on red gravel and coarse fiber courts, when high topspin strokes were played in the baseline area, balls could bounce over the back fence and such balls could only be returned when hit right after they bounced.

* * *

Contrary to plaintiff's assertions, the Court finds that the ITF's temporary ban bore a rational relationship to its goal of attempting to conduct organized tennis competitions in an orderly fashion. The COM at Barcelona acted not only on the basis of the demonstration, and the German Federation's assessment of the Braunschweig study, but also on the basis of actual and threatened players' strikes against use of the double-strung racket, publicity concerning upsets of high-ranking players by virtual unknowns using double-strung rackets, and adverse reports of several national federations based on their experience with the racket in match play and in training situations. This evidence provided an objective basis from which the COM could have concluded that a temporary freeze on the use of the rackets was necessary pending further investigation and subsequent action by the ITF Council.

* * *

The Court finds that a rule on racket specifications designed to prohibit rackets which impart exaggerated topspin to the ball on impact is rationally related to the goal of preserving the character of the game of tennis. In this regard, the Court especially credits the testimony of Cliff Drysdale and Vic Braden, who are both highly qualified to testify as experts on the subject....

Both Drysdale and Braden testified that the ability to impart topspin to a ball is one of the most important skills in the game of tennis. As Braden put it, being able to hit topspin is the "name of the game." Drysdale testified that it was his opinion that a player who has never been able to hit topspin with a conventional racket could, with a double-strung racket, be able to hit great topspin lobs by making a very small adjustment in the way he hit the ball. Drysdale also testified that an average player using a double-strung racket would be able to serve much more effectively than with a conventional racket, making it more difficult for an opponent to return a serve and correspondingly more difficult to get the ball into play.

Similarly, Braden testified that because a player using a double-strung racket could increase spin on a serve, there would not be many service returns, which would change the character of the game tremendously. As a result, the game would lend itself to people who develop a very efficient serve with a double-strung racket. Clearly, the ITF and the USTA could rationally consider a racket's artificial enhancement of fundamental skills of the game a threat to the integrity and character of tennis as it has been historically played.

Drysdale and Braden testified that widespread use of the double-strung rackets could change the character of the game in a number of other ways as well. Since other shots with double-strung rackets are substantially less effective than topspin shots, Drysdale testified that the end result would be a situation where everyone would be playing almost exclusively topspin shots. This tendency to adopt a similar style would reduce the variety of the game as it has been traditionally played, resulting in decreased spectator interest. Additionally, the result of the topspin that a double-strung racket can impart to the ball is a ball that bounces considerably higher, causing an opponent to move back to or past the baseline to get into a position where he can contact the ball. This also prevents an opponent from aggressively "attacking" by coming to the net. In Drysdale's opinion, players being forced to back away from the net would result in administrators of the game either having to expand the dimensions of the court or changing the composition of the ball in some way to accommodate the differences caused by the racket.

Braden also testified to his assumption that as people using double-strung rackets became proficient in hitting topspin lobs, court dimensions and structures would have to be changed. Braden's research indicated that on a typical 120–foot court with a twelve foot fence, a topspin lob hit hard enough with a spaghetti racket could force an opponent to climb to a nine-foot height against the back fence.

While plaintiff presented witnesses who testified that use of double-strung rackets would not change the character of the game, as previously noted, the Court infers from the expert testimony of Drysdale and Braden that the ITF and USTA could have reasonably concluded that rackets or stringing that impart excessive topspin to the ball alter the character of the game. This is all that is necessary since the Court is not to substitute its independent judgment for the ITF or the USTA in weighing the relative opinions of expert witnesses.

The Court also concludes that the actions of the USTA in honoring the temporary ban and adopting Rule 4 were not more extensive than necessary to serve the legitimate goals of the USTA and ITF. Based on the players' strikes and walkouts occasioned by use of the double-strung racket, the Court concludes that the temporary freeze on the use of double-strung rackets in sanctioned play was no more extensive than necessary to further the legitimate goal of conducting the game in an orderly fashion, especially in view of the provision that member nations could apply for permission to experiment with the racket at club level. The Court finds it reasonable for the ITF and USTA to have concluded that the alternative of taking no action and letting the racket have a twenty-four month trial period would not have furthered that goal.

Rule 4 itself was narrowly drawn to proscribe only rackets and stringing systems that imparted exaggerated topspin to the ball, since the ITF concluded that it was that feature which changed the character of the game. The breadth of the rule was additionally narrowed by provision of appeal procedures whereby a racket that failed to conform to the face of the rule could be approved under the standard that it did not impart exaggerated topspin to the ball or change the character of the game.

* * *

Suit dismissed.

[In a brief *per curiam* decision, the Eighth Circuit upheld the district court decision on the merits, while making clear that the USTA, notwithstanding its non-profit status, was governed by antitrust law in making decisions such as this adoption of an ITF rule of the game.]

———

Despite the favorable precedents in the *STP* and *Gunter Harz* cases, in the late 1980s both the USGA and the PGA became embroiled in serious antitrust litigation involving the new square-grooved (or U-shaped) golfing irons. Traditionally, grooves in golfing irons have been shaped like a "V" that angles to a point embedded in the face of the club. In the early 1980s, the USGA and the Royal and Ancient Golf Club of St. Andrew's, Scotland (the rule-making authority for golf outside the United States) had relaxed their traditional ban on square grooves (which are shaped like a "U" inside the iron's face). This provided a major market opportunity for a new club manufacturer, Karsten Manufacturing. Karsten Sollheim, head of the firm, designed a new Ping Eye2 golf iron whose U-shaped grooves helped make it the country's best selling golf club, generating revenues of $100 million per year.

According to golf's ruling authorities, the problem was that the new square-grooved club imparted much more backspin to the ball, especially with shorter irons used to hit balls out of the rough. PGA Tour players such as Jack Nicklaus, Tom Watson, and Greg Norman protested that Ping iron users such as Mark Calcavecchia gained an unfair playing advantage: long but less accurate drivers off the tee did not have to pay the usual price of less control over approach shots hit from the rough toward the pin on the green. The response of the USGA was to adopt a new formula for club design that required a slightly broader gap between the grooves on the surface of the iron. While Karsten initiated an antitrust suit against this USGA rule, he eventually settled on the terms that the firm would manufacture all its new clubs in accordance with USGA specifications, but all existing Ping clubs would be grandfathered as acceptable to the USGA.

Neither the Tournament Players Division (TPD) of the PGA nor its commissioner, Deane Beman, was prepared to accept that compromise. Instead, they instituted a ban on the use of any square-grooved irons in PGA Tour events. Because this was the first time that the PGA itself had imposed special restrictions on equipment used in its tournaments, the step generated some procedural complications. Broader tour decisions such as this were normally made by the TPD's Policy Board, which was composed of ten directors—four players elected by the tour membership, three officials from the PGA, and three independent directors. Since the first seven directors all had endorsement agreements with other golf equipment manufacturers, they abstained from voting on the new rule to avoid the possible conflicts of interest. The three independent directors voted unanimously for the proposed new rule. However, such a small number of votes did not square with the PGA Board's existing quorum rule. Thus, a new meeting was scheduled, at which all members voted to change the procedural requirements for such cases, and the same independent directors again voted for the ban on U-shaped irons.

Unsurprisingly, this course of events produced another lawsuit. The lead plaintiffs were Tour golfers who had used (and been paid to endorse) Ping Eye2 irons, but an additional plaintiff, and the party financing the entire litigation, was Karsten Manufacturing. The plaintiffs won a temporary injunction that has banned PGA enforcement of the tour rule pending trial on the merits in early 1993. See *Gilder v. PGA Tour Inc.*, 727 F.Supp. 1333 (D.Ariz.1989), affirmed, 936 F.2d 417 (9th Cir.1991). On the eve of trial in April 1993, this $100 million lawsuit was settled on the basis that Ping irons could be used on the PGA Tour, but that the Tour Policy Board would establish an independent committee to evaluate the acceptability of golf equipment—including square-grooved irons—for tour competition.

Questions for Discussion [8]

1. Remember that present-day Rule of Reason analysis requires courts to balance procompetitive benefits against anticompetitive harms. How would a sports governing body's decision to ban double-stringed tennis rackets or square grooved golf irons be analyzed under that test? Do the statements in *Gunter Harz* and *STP Corporation* that courts should defer to the good faith judgment of governing bodies make sense for purposes of such balancing of competitive effects? Is a different test appropriate in reviewing the decisions of private sports regulatory bodies? Is the procedural history of the PGA Tour's ban on square grooved irons relevant to such an analysis? What facts should the plaintiffs in *Gilder* have had to establish at trial to warrant a finding that the ban on square grooved irons violated the antitrust Rule of Reason?

2. How could Karsten establish that significant damages would be inflicted on its business if Tour players are not allowed to use the firm's irons in PGA tournaments? Do Bob Gilder, Mark Calcavecchia, and others actually pay for their Ping Eye2 irons?

3. Does the prior question imply that the USGA and the USTA, with their broader regulatory reach, are more exposed to antitrust litigation about their equipment rules than are the PGA and the ATP? Or do the latter bodies display a characteristic antitrust exposure of their own?

---

8. Besides the cases mentioned in the text, other relevant precedents include *Weight–Rite Golf Corp. v. United States Golf Ass'n*, 1990 WL 145594, 1990–2 Trade Cases (CCH) ¶ 69,181 (M.D.Fla.1990) (injunction request), and 766 F.Supp. 1104 (M.D.Fla.1991) (final decision), and *Eureka Urethane, Inc. v. Professional Bowlers Ass'n. of Am.*, 746 F.Supp. 915 (E.D.Mo. 1990).

4. Suppose that the ATP adopted a rule banning use of racket frame designs that imparted high levels of speed and power to the ball, especially on the serve. Why might the ATP be tempted to pass such a rule? Should adoption of such a rule be subject to antitrust challenge by either racket manufacturers or players? More so than if the ATP responded to the growing number of 130 miles-per-hour serves by shortening the service court, or by allowing only one serve per point?

5. Should the PGA Tour consider adopting a standardized golf ball for all its tournaments—a ball designed not to fly as far as existing balls? What practical arguments would be advanced within the Tour for and against such action? Would this be a risky legal step? Should it matter whether the Tour periodically sold to the highest bidder the exclusive right to manufacture and market the ball used in its events (with the PGA distributing the proceeds among Tour members either *per capita* or *pro rata*, depending on the players' performance during the year)?

6. How should a court deal with litigation by a manufacturer complaining that a professional sports league (or the NCAA) had banned its type of equipment from being used in the league's games? In the early 1980s a manufacturer that had developed a laser-beam device to measure for first downs in football brought a section 1 antitrust claim against the NFL for refusing to allow home teams to use the device in its games. In an unpublished opinion, the district court in San Antonio summarily dismissed the case on the ground that the NFL decision had no anticompetitive effects. *Carlock v. NFL*, Case # SA–79–CA–133 (W.D.Tex.1982).

> The NFL's refusal to purchase the plaintiffs' invention was merely a business decision made by an entity charged with the orderly and uniform implementation of the rules of professional football. The decision was based on the League's own business judgment, in consideration of numerous factors, including public acceptance of the chain-and-stakes technique for measuring the progress of the football, the undesirability of over-elaboration of officiating techniques, risks of technical failure, additional cluttering of sidelines, additional training problems, line-of-sight problems, and the costs required for the purchase of such equipment. Disappointed by their rejection, the plaintiffs simply seek to have this court substitute its business judgment for that of the NFL, which the plaintiffs believe failed to appreciate the merits of their invention.
>
> Any purchasing decision by any organization, regardless of its form, has some effect on market conditions. The antitrust laws afford product sellers the right to compete for the sale of their products, but the antitrust laws are not designed to guarantee sales of their products. There is simply no antitrust principle that requires any buyer to purchase and make use of an unwanted product simply because the buyer's failure to do so might negatively affect an individual seller or have some effect on the market for the sale of that product.

Is this reasoning persuasive? Are there any facts Carlock might have proven to change the result? Is the court's analysis applicable to cases involving governing bodies for individual sports?

F. OLYMPIC SPORTS

A recurring theme in this chapter is the tension between external legal regulation and internal governance of a sport, especially where the sport is international and the regulation is carried out by an American court. That tension is sharply heightened for the various sports that make up the quadrennial Olympic games, which are followed with great interest by billions of fans around the world. To understand these issues, one must first understand the extraordinarily complex structure that governs Olympic sports.[9]

At the apex of the Olympic structure is the International Olympic Committee (IOC), which controls the Olympic games. The IOC in turn entrusts the various national Olympic committees with determination of which athletes will compete in the Olympics. In the United States, this governing body is the United States Olympic Committee (USOC). Under the Amateur Sports Act of 1978, 36 U.S.C. § 371 et seq., the USOC is charged with overseeing all matters relating to U.S. participation in both the Olympic and Pan American games, as well as with performing several other specific functions related to the promotion of "amateur athletic activity" in the United States.

Each sport is separately governed by its own international sports federation, now 40 in number, each of which conducts its own world championships and sanctions other independently operated contests. Eligibility standards for participation in any contest sponsored or sanctioned by an international federation are established and enforced by the federation. Eligibility for participation in the Olympic games was originally defined by the IOC in the Olympic Charter, but that responsibility has now been delegated (through Rule 45 of the Olympic Charter) to the international federation that governs each sport, as long as the federation complies with the IOC's requirements. Thus, responsibility for establishing and enforcing criteria for participation in all but unsanctioned events rests exclusively with the various international federations.

As with the IOC, operating under the umbrella of the international federation in each sport is a national federation that exercises many of the eligibility and promotional functions of the international body. The national federation in each sport holds the qualifying events that determine which athletes are to represent the country in the Olympic games (and in many sports, the world championships sponsored by the international federation). The Amateur Sports Act of 1978 instructs the USOC to recognize an appropriate national governing body in each sport. The Act empowers these governing bodies to perform various functions related to their sports: conducting "amateur athletic competi-

---

9. A valuable scholarly history of the Olympic games is Alan Guttman, *The Olympics: A History of the Modern Games* (Urbana, Ill.: University of Illinois Press, 1992). A highly critical journalistic treatment of the way the Olympics are now run is Vyv Simson & Andrew Jennings, *The Lords of the Rings* (London: Simon & Schuster, 1992).

tion" in the United States; sanctioning other such competitions inside and outside the United States; determining eligibility standards for participation in such competitions; selecting the athletes to represent the United States in the Olympic and Pan American games; representing the United States in the international federation; and generally governing all "amateur athletic activities" in their respective sports in the United States.

A crucial legal issue is when, under what legal theories, and under what standard of review an American court should overturn a decision by one of these governing bodies. The following highly publicized case depicts some of the key legal arguments that have been made about this issue.

DEFRANTZ v. UNITED STATES OLYMPIC COMMITTEE (USOC)

United States District Court, District of Columbia, 1980.

492 F.Supp. 1181.

JOHN H. PRATT, DISTRICT JUDGE.

Plaintiffs, 25 athletes and one member of the Executive Board of defendant United States Olympic Committee (USOC), have moved for an injunction barring defendant USOC from carrying out a resolution, adopted by the USOC House of Delegates on April 12, 1980, not to send an American team to participate in the Games of the XXIInd Olympiad to be held in Moscow in the summer of 1980. Plaintiffs allege that in preventing American athletes from competing in the Summer Olympics, defendant has exceeded its statutory powers and has abridged plaintiffs' constitutional rights.

* * *

According to its Rules and By-laws, the International Olympic Committee (IOC) governs the Olympic movement and owns the rights of the Olympic games. IOC Rules provide that National Olympic Committees (NOC) may be established "as the sole authorities responsible for the representation of the respective countries at the Olympic Games," so long as the NOC's rules and regulations are approved by the IOC. The USOC is one such National Olympic Committee.

The USOC is a corporation created and granted a federal charter by Congress in 1950. This charter was revised by the Amateur Sports Act of 1978. Under this statute, defendant USOC has "exclusive jurisdiction" and authority over participation and representation of the United States in the Olympic Games.

* * *

On December 27, 1979, the Soviet Union launched an invasion of its neighbor, Afghanistan. That country's ruler was deposed and killed and a new government was installed....

President Carter termed the invasion a threat to the security of the Persian Gulf area as well as a threat to world peace and stability, and he moved to take direct sanctions against the Soviet Union. These sanctions included a curtailment of agricultural and high technology exports to the Soviet Union, and restrictions on commerce with the Soviets. The Administration also turned its attention to a boycott of the summer Olympic Games [in Moscow] as a further sanction against the Soviet Union.

* * *

[The President put great pressure on the USOC not to send a team to the 1980 Games, even to the point of threatening to withhold federal funding from the USOC, to revoke its tax exemptions, and to invoke the International Emergency Economic Powers Act to forbid any athletes from traveling to the Soviet Union during the games. In addition, the House of Representatives passed a resolution, by a vote of 386 to 12, opposing U.S. participation in the Games.]

* * *

[On April 12, 1980], [a]fter what USOC President Kane describes in his affidavit as "full, open, complete and orderly debate by advocates of each motion," the House of Delegates, on a secret ballot passed, by a vote of 1,604 to 798, a resolution [declaring that the USOC would not send a team to Moscow unless international conditions changed dramatically.]

* * *

1. THE AMATEUR SPORTS ACT OF 1978

Plaintiffs allege in their complaint that by its decision not to send an American team to compete in the summer Olympic Games in Moscow, defendant USOC has violated the Amateur Sports Act of 1978.... Reduced to their essentials, these allegations are that the Act does not give, and that Congress intended to deny, the USOC the authority to decide not to enter an American team in the Olympics, except perhaps for sports-related reasons, and that the Act guarantees to certain athletes [a right to compete in the Olympic Games.] ...

* * *

The principal substantive powers of the USOC are found in § 375(a) of the Act.[12] In determining whether the USOC's authority

---

12. They are to: "(1) serve as the coordinating body for amateur athletic activity in the United States directly relating to international amateur athletic competition; (2) represent the United States as its national Olympic committee in relations with the International Olympic Committee ...; (3) organize, finance, and control the representation of the United States in the competitions and events of the Olympic Games ... and obtain, either directly or by delegation to the appropriate national governing body, amateur representation for summer games." 36 U.S.C. § 375(a)(1), (2), (3). The "objects and purposes" section of the Act includes the provision, also found in the 1950 Act, that the USOC shall "exercise exclusive jurisdiction ... over all matters pertaining to the

under the Act encompasses the right to decide not to participate in an Olympic contest, we must read these provisions in the context in which they were written. In writing this legislation, Congress did not create a new relationship between the USOC and the IOC. Rather, it recognized an already long-existing relationship between the two and statutorily legitimized that relationship with a federal charter and federal incorporation.[13] The legislative history demonstrates Congressional awareness that the USOC and its predecessors, as the National Olympic Committee for the United States, have had a continuing relationship with the IOC since 1896. Congress was necessarily aware that a National Olympic Committee is a creation and a creature of the International Olympic Committee, to whose rules and regulations it must conform. The NOC gets its power and its authority from the IOC, the sole proprietor and owner of the Olympic Games.

In view of Congress' obvious awareness of these facts, we would expect that if Congress intended to limit or deny to the USOC powers it already enjoyed as a National Olympic Committee, such limitation or denial would be clear and explicit. No such language appears in the statute. Indeed, far from precluding this authority, the language of the statute appears to embrace it. For example, the "objects and purposes" section of the Act speaks in broad terms, stating that the USOC shall exercise "exclusive jurisdiction" over " . . . all matters pertaining to the participation of the United States in the Olympic Games. . . ." We read this broadly stated purpose in conjunction with the specific power conferred on the USOC by the Act to "represent the United States as its national Olympic committee in relations with the International Olympic Committee," and in conjunction with the IOC Rules and By-laws, which provide that "representation" includes the decision to participate. In doing so, we find a compatibility and not a conflict between the Act and the IOC Rules on the issue of the authority of the USOC to decide whether or not to accept an invitation to field an American team at the Olympics. The language of the statute is broad enough to confer this authority, and we find that Congress must have intended that the USOC exercise that authority in this area, which it already enjoyed because of its long-standing relationship with the IOC. We accordingly conclude that the USOC has the authority to decide not to send an American team to the Olympics.

Plaintiffs next argue that if the USOC does have the authority to decide not to accept an invitation to send an American team to the Moscow Olympics, that decision must be based on "sports-related considerations." In support of their argument, plaintiffs point to

participation of the United States in the Olympic Games . . . including the representation of the United States in such games." Id., § 374(3).

13. To the extent the USOC was granted extended power by the 1978 Act, the legislative history makes clear, and the plaintiffs do not dispute the fact, that these powers were primarily designed to give the USOC supervisory authority over United States amateur athletic groups in order to eliminate the numerous and frequent jurisdictional squabbles among schools, athletic groups and various national sports governing bodies.

§§ 392(a)(5) and (b) of the Act, which plaintiffs acknowledge "are not in terms applicable to the USOC," but rather concern situations in which national governing bodies of various sports, which are subordinate to the USOC, are asked to sanction the holding of international competitions below the level of the Olympic or Pan American Games in the United States or the participation of the United States athletes in such competition abroad. These sections provide that a national governing body may withhold its sanctions only upon clear and convincing evidence that holding or participating in the competition "would be detrimental to the best interests of the sport." Plaintiffs argue by analogy that a similar "sports-related" limitation must attach to any authority the USOC might have to decide not to participate in an Olympic competition. We cannot agree.

The provision on which plaintiffs place reliance by analogy is specifically concerned with eliminating the feuding between various amateur athletic organizations and national governing bodies which for so long characterized amateur athletics. As all parties recognize, this friction, such as the well-publicized power struggles between the NCAA and the AAU, was a major reason for passage of the Act, and the provisions plaintiffs cite, among others, are aimed at eliminating this senseless strife, which the Senate and House Committee reports indicate had dramatically harmed the ability of the United States to compete effectively in international competition. In order to eliminate this internecine squabbling, the Act elevated the USOC to a supervisory role over the various amateur athletic organizations, and provided that the USOC establish procedures for the swift and equitable settlement of these disputes. As indicated above, it also directed that the national governing bodies of the various sports could only withhold their approvals of international competition for sports-related reasons. Previously, many of these bodies had withheld their sanction of certain athletic competitions in order to further their own interests at the expense of other groups and to the detriment of athletes wishing to participate.

In brief, this sports-related limitation is intimately tied to the specific purpose of curbing the arbitrary and unrestrained power of various athletic organizations subordinate to the USOC not to allow athletes to compete in international competition below the level of the Olympic Games and the Pan American Games. This purpose has nothing to do with a decision by the USOC to exercise authority granted by the IOC to decide not to participate in an Olympic competition.

* * *

We therefore conclude that the USOC not only had the authority to decide not to send an American team to the summer Olympics, but also that it could do so for reasons not directly related to sports considerations.

(b) Athletes' Statutory Right to Compete in the Olympics

* * *

Plaintiffs argue that the Report of the President's Commission on Olympic Sports, which was the starting point for the legislation proposed, and the legislative history support their argument that the statute confers an enforceable right on plaintiffs to compete in Olympic competition. Again, we are compelled to disagree with plaintiffs.

The legislative history and the statute are clear that the "right to compete," which plaintiffs refer to, is in the context of the numerous jurisdictional disputes between various athletic bodies, such as the NCAA and the AAU, which we have just discussed, and which was a major impetus for the Amateur Sports Act of 1978. Plaintiffs recognize that a major purpose of the Act was to eliminate such disputes. However, they go on to argue that the Report which highlighted the need for strengthening the USOC in order to eliminate this feuding, made a finding that there is little difference between an athlete denied the right to compete because of a boycott and an athlete denied the right to compete because of jurisdictional bickering.

The short answer is that although the Congress may have borrowed heavily from the Report of the President's Commission, it did not enact the Report. Instead, it enacted a statute and that statute relates a "right to compete" to the elimination of jurisdictional disputes between amateur athletic groups, which for petty and groundless reasons have often deprived athletes of the opportunity to enter a particular competition. . . .

The Senate Report makes clear that the language relied on by plaintiffs is not designed to provide any substantive guarantees, let alone a Bill of Rights. Further, to the extent that any guarantees of a right to compete are included in the USOC Constitution as a result of this provision, they do not include a right that amateur athletes may compete in the Olympic Games despite a decision by the USOC House of Delegates not to accept an invitation to enter an American team in the competition. This provision simply was not designed to extend so far. Rather, it was designed to remedy the jurisdictional disputes among amateur athletic bodies, not disputes between athletes and the USOC itself over the exercise of the USOC's discretion not to participate in the Olympics.

* * *

Because we conclude that the rights plaintiffs seek to enforce do not exist in the Act, and because the legislative history of the Act nowhere allows the implication of a private right of action, we find that plaintiffs have no implied private right of action under the Amateur Sports Act of 1978 to maintain this suit.[23]

23. Plaintiffs have also alleged as a cause of action that in addition to violating its governing statute, defendant USOC has also violated its Constitution and By-laws,

2. Constitutional Claims

Plaintiffs have alleged that the decision of the USOC not to enter an American team in the summer Olympics has violated certain rights guaranteed to plaintiffs under the First, Fifth and Ninth Amendments to the United States Constitution....

(a) State Action

Although federally chartered, defendant is a private organization. Because the Due Process Clause of the Fifth Amendment, on which plaintiffs place great reliance, applies only to actions by the federal government, plaintiffs must show that the USOC vote is a "governmental act," i.e., state action. In defining state action, the courts have fashioned two guidelines. The first involves an inquiry into whether the state

> ... has so far insinuated itself into a position of interdependence with (the private entity) that it must be recognized as a joint participant in the challenged activity.

Here, there is no such intermingling, and there is no factual justification for finding that the federal government and the USOC enjoyed the "symbiotic relationship" which courts have required to find state action. The USOC has received no federal funding[25] and it exists and operates independently of the federal government. Its chartering statute gives it "exclusive jurisdiction" over "all matters pertaining to the participation of the United States in the Olympic Games...." 36 U.S.C. § 374(3). To be sure, the Act does link the USOC and the federal government to the extent it requires the USOC to submit an annual report to the President and the Congress. But this hardly converts such an independent relationship to a "joint participation."

The second guideline fashioned by the courts involves an inquiry of whether:

injuring plaintiff Shaw, a member of USOC's Executive Board. In particular, plaintiffs argue in their memorandum, at 33, that the USOC has violated its corporate purpose of coordinating amateur sports so as to obtain the "most competent amateur representation" in the Olympic Games. This corporate purpose appearing in the USOC Constitution is identical to that appearing in the Act, s 374(4), and we have already found that defendant has not violated that statute. Just what other specific violations of the USOC Constitution and By-laws plaintiffs are alleging does not appear in the complaint or in the plaintiffs' memoranda. To the extent they allege violations of provisions also contained in the Act, we have already determined that question. To the extent they involve a yielding to "political pressures," we note that on April 23, 1980 the IOC Executive Board reviewed the actions of the USOC and concluded that they were not in violation of IOC Rule 24(C), which requires that NOC's "must be autonomous and must resist all pressures of any kind whatsoever, whether of a political, religious or economic nature." To the extent that plaintiffs are alleging that defendant has violated any provision of its Constitution and By-laws requiring it to be autonomous, we adopt the conclusion of the IOC and find that this resolves any such allegations in favor of defendant.

25. Federal funds were authorized under the Amateur Sports Act of 1978 but have never been appropriated. But the mere receipt of federal funds by a private entity, without more, is not enough to convert that entity's activity into state action. *Spark v. Catholic University of America*, 510 F.2d 1277 (D.C.Cir.1975).

... there is a sufficiently close nexus between the state and the challenged action of the regulated entity so that the action of the latter may be fairly treated as that of the state itself.

... In the instant case, there was no requirement that any federal government body approve actions by the USOC before they become effective.

Plaintiffs argue that by the actions of certain federal officials, the federal government initiated, encouraged, and approved of the result reached (i.e., the vote of the USOC not to send an American team to the summer Olympics). Plaintiffs advance a novel theory. Essentially, their argument is that the campaign of governmental persuasion, personally led by President Carter, crossed the line from "governmental recommendation," which plaintiffs find acceptable and presumably necessary to the operation of our form of government, into the area of "affirmative pressure that effectively places the government's prestige behind the challenged action," and thus, results in state action. We cannot agree.

* * *

Here there is no [requisite governmental] control. The USOC is an independent body, and nothing in its chartering statute gives the federal government the right to control that body or its officers. Furthermore, the facts here do not indicate that the federal government was able to exercise any type of "de facto " control over the USOC. The USOC decided by a secret ballot of its House of Delegates. The federal government may have had the power to prevent the athletes from participating in the Olympics even if the USOC had voted to allow them to participate, but it did not have the power to make them vote in a certain way. All it had was the power of persuasion. We cannot equate this with control. To do so in cases of this type would be to open the door and usher the courts into what we believe is a largely nonjusticiable realm, where they would find themselves in the untenable position of determining whether a certain level, intensity, or type of "Presidential" or "Administration" or "political" pressure amounts to sufficient control over a private entity so as to invoke federal jurisdiction.

We accordingly find that the decision of the USOC not to send an American team to the summer Olympics was not state action, and therefore, does not give rise to an actionable claim for the infringements of the constitutional rights alleged.

(b) Constitutionally Protected Rights

... Were we to find state action in this case, we would conclude that defendant USOC has violated no constitutionally protected right of plaintiffs.

We note that other courts have considered the right to compete in amateur athletics and have found no deprivation of constitutionally protected rights. As the Government has pointed out in Parish v. National Collegiate Athletic Association, 506 F.2d 1028 (5th Cir.1975), basketball players sought an injunction to prevent the NCAA from enforcing its ruling declaring certain athletes ineligible to compete in tournaments and televised games. The court stated that:

> the privilege of participation in interscholastic activities must be deemed to fall ... outside the protection of due process.

Plaintiffs have been unable to draw our attention to any court decision which finds that the rights allegedly violated here enjoy constitutional protection, and we can find none. Plaintiffs would expand the constitutionally-protected scope of liberty and self-expression to include the denial of an amateur athlete's right to compete in an Olympic contest when that denial was the result of a decision by a supervisory athletic organization acting well within the limits of its authority. Defendant has not denied plaintiffs the right to engage in every amateur athletic competition. Defendant has not denied plaintiffs the right to engage in their chosen occupation. Defendant has not even denied plaintiffs the right to travel, only the right to travel for one specific purpose. We can find no justification and no authority for the expansive reading of the Constitution which plaintiffs urge. To find as plaintiffs recommend would be to open the floodgates to a torrent of lawsuits. The courts have correctly recognized that many of life's disappointments, even major ones, do not enjoy constitutional protection. This is one such instance.

Case dismissed.

Questions for Discussion

1. Should the federal government be able to enact a law delegating what in many countries is a governmental function to a private group, then exert enormous political pressure on that group to make a certain decision, and still argue that there is insufficient government involvement to trigger constitutional protections for those adversely affected by that decision? The courts have uniformly refused to recognize as state action the decisions of any of the national or international athletic governing bodies. See, e.g., *Behagen v. Amateur Basketball Ass'n of the United States*, 884 F.2d 524 (10th Cir.1989); *International Olympic Comm. v. San Francisco Arts & Athletics*, 781 F.2d 733 (9th Cir.1986), affirmed, 483 U.S. 522, 107 S.Ct. 2971, 97 L.Ed.2d 427 (1987). Thus, like the NCAA after the *Tarkanian* decision in Chapter 8, these organizations are not required to provide constitutional due process or equal protection to those affected by their decisions. Does this mean that these bodies can do whatever they want? Could the USOC decide not to send a team to the Olympics in retaliation to an IOC decision not to award the Games to an American city, or because the IOC refused to enter a licensing agreement with an American company? If constitutional arguments are unavailable, are there any other legal claims disappointed athletes could make?

2. One question stemming from the Amateur Sports Act is the extent to which the USOC, a national sports governing body, or their international

counterparts, are subject to American antitrust law. The cases presented earlier in this chapter involved antitrust review of a variety of decisions made by the bodies governing professional tours in tennis, golf, and auto racing. The only case so far to challenge a sports federation decision on antitrust grounds was brought in 1989 by Carol Cady and John Powell against The Athletics Congress (TAC) of the USA (as of December, 1992, USA Track and Field). TAC had suspended the athletes for participating in an unsanctioned track meet in South Africa, which was then under an International Amateur Athletic Federation (IAAF) boycott due to its apartheid policies. In an unpublished decision, the district court held that TAC's action was within the scope of the power vested in it by Congress through the Amateur Sports Act and thus was exempt from antitrust challenge. Was this the proper result? What if TAC suspended an athlete for participating in a track meet that TAC has declined to sanction because the meet was held on the same day as a meet sponsored by TAC itself (see Rule 53(iii) of the IAAF Handbook)?

The most controversial decisions by sports federations involve athlete eligibility—either establishing eligibility standards, which is done by the international federation, or applying the standards in individual cases, which can be done by the international or national bodies. The most hotly debated eligibility issue in recent years has involved the use of performance-enhancing drugs and the procedures for testing for these drugs (particularly steroids).[10] The following is one of the most well-known cases posing the difficult legal issues relating to enforcement of anti-drug rules.

REYNOLDS v. INTERNATIONAL AMATEUR ATHLETIC FEDERATION

United States District Court, Southern District of Ohio, 1992.

—— F.Supp. ——.

[The court had granted a temporary restraining order against the IAAF and was now considering whether to issue a preliminary injunction. The IAAF did not participate in the evidentiary hearing on the ground that the court lacked personal jurisdiction over it. The court allowed TAC and three other track and field athletes to intervene as defendants and the USOC to file an amicus brief.]

The Plaintiff, Harry L. Reynolds, Jr. is a world-class amateur track athlete. He is the current world record holder at the 400 meter distance, and won the silver medal at that distance in the 1988 Olympic games in Seoul, Korea.

----

10. See Dr. Robert L. Voy with Kirk D. Deeter, *Drugs, Sports, and Politics*, (Champaign, Ill.: Leisure Press, 1991); Hon. Charles L. Dubin, *Commission of Inquiry Into the Use of Drugs and Banned Practices Intended to Increase Athletic Performance* (Ottawa: Government of Canada, 1990) (Ben Johnson Inquiry).

This action arises out of Reynolds' appearance in the Herculis '90 International track and field competition ("the Herculis meet") in Monte Carlo, Monaco on August 12, 1990. Following the meeting, Reynolds was randomly chosen to submit a urine sample, and on October 18, 1990 he was notified that the sample had tested positive for the anabolic steroid nandrolone. The IAAF immediately suspended Reynolds [for two years—August 12, 1990 to August 11, 1992] pending a hearing by Reynolds' national track and field governing body, TAC.

Rather than seek a hearing from TAC, Reynolds sought the intervention of this Court in a case styled *Reynolds v. The Athletics Congress of the U.S.A.* ("Reynolds I").... On March 19, 1991, this Court held that Reynolds failed to exhaust his administrative remedies and [the case was dismissed on that ground].[3]

Plaintiff then attempted to exhaust the administrative process available to him. Pursuant to the Amateur Sports Act of 1978, 38 U.S.C. §§ 371–396, and the United States Olympic Committee (USOC) Constitution, Reynolds first participated in an expedited American Arbitration Association proceeding on June 7, 1991. On June 10, 1991, the arbitrator issued a decision essentially exonerating Reynolds on the charge of steroid use:

> The arbitrator finds that the Respondent's suspension of Mr. Reynolds was improper; that there is clear and convincing evidence that the "A" sample and the "B" sample did not emanate from the same person and the "B" sample did not confirm the "A" sample; that there is substantial evidence that neither the "A" sample or the "B" sample emanated from the Claimant; and that Claimant should be declared eligible to compete in the qualifying rounds for the World Game Championships on June 12, 1991.

Both TAC and the IAAF refused to accept the arbitrator's decision for the alleged reason that such proceedings are inconsistent with the IAAF's post-suspension administrative adjudication process as provided in IAAF Rule 59. Reynolds' request to the USOC to enforce the decision was denied.

TAC, as the organization required by the IAAF to provide post-suspension administrative adjudication of any dispute, eventually scheduled a hearing for September 13, 1991. After a 12–hour hearing and two weeks of deliberation, the TAC hearing panel announced its decision exonerating Reynolds:

> The panel, after hearing the matters before it, the testimony of witnesses and expert witnesses from both sides, documents and exhibits, hereby finds that Mr. Harry "Butch" Reynolds has cast substantial doubt on the validity of the drug test attributed to him. The panel finds that the "B" sample positive result reported by the

---

3. The Defendant in the current action, IAAF, specially appeared in *Reynolds I* and moved to have the claims against it dismissed for lack of personal jurisdiction. This Court never had occasion to consider the issue.

Lafarge Laboratory has been impeached by clear and convincing evidence.

The IAAF, however, refused to accept TAC's finding. Pursuant to its own Rule 20—which provides for the arbitration of disputes between itself and its member associations—the IAAF ordered, on November 17, 1991, an arbitration of the TAC hearing decision. On May 10 and 11, 1992 the IAAF and TAC presented their positions to a three-member arbitration panel. After only two hours of deliberation, the panel issued a seven page decision finding there to be "no doubt" as to Reynolds' guilt.

On May 27, 1992, Reynolds returned to this Court and filed a Verified Complaint along with an application for emergency injunctive relief. The Complaint, which differs from that filed in *Reynolds I* in that it only names the IAAF as a Defendant, states claims for breach of contract, defamation, tortious interference with a business relationship, and denial of contractual due process.

The next morning this Court held an informal preliminary conference to discuss the possible issuance of a temporary restraining order against the IAAF. Although an official representative of the IAAF was not present, counsel for the IAAF in *Reynolds I* was notified of the conference and did appear to make arguments on the IAAF's behalf, although she expressly informed the Court that she had been unable to contact the IAAF and had not yet been retained to represent the IAAF in the current action. As this Court has already noted, the IAAF thereafter decided not to retain counsel to represent it in this action, and has not made an appearance.

Finding the Plaintiff's application for a temporary restraining order to be meritorious, the Court on May 28, 1992 "restrained and enjoined [the IAAF] from impeding or otherwise interfering with Plaintiff Harry L. Reynolds, Jr.'s participation in all international and national amateur track and field events...."

I. PERSONAL JURISDICTION OF THIS COURT OVER THE IAAF

* * *

For personal jurisdiction to exist over a nonresident defendant ... two basic prerequisites must be satisfied: the defendant must be amenable to suit under the forum state's long-arm statute and the exercise of jurisdiction over the defendant must not violate the Due Process Clause of the United States Constitution.

* * *

[The court concluded that the IAAF is subject to the jurisdiction of Ohio courts under two provisions of the state's long-arm statute—the provisions attaching jurisdiction to nonresident defendants who "transact any business in this state" or who "cause tortious injury" by an act either in the state or outside the state if the defendant regularly engages in business within the state.]

Aside from determining whether the IAAF is amenable to suit in Ohio pursuant to the Ohio long-arm statute, this Court must also determine whether the exercise of jurisdiction over the IAAF comports with the dictates of Due Process:

> Due Process requires only that in order to subject a defendant to a judgment in personam, if he be not present within the territory of the forum, he have certain minimum contacts with it such that the maintenance of the suit does not offend "traditional notions of fair play and substantial justice."

International Shoe Co. v. Washington, 326 U.S. 310, 316 (1945)....

The Court believes that it may constitutionally exercise personal jurisdiction over the IAAF. Initially, the Court must sharply reject the IAAF and TAC's position that the IAAF is not subject to the jurisdiction of *any* court *anywhere* in the world. At the hearing, TAC's counsel expressed the view that the IAAF is "infallible" and its decisions must not be reviewable by this Court—or any other. Indeed, IAAF vice president Arne Ljungqvist has been quoted as stating:

> Civil courts create a lot of problems for our anti-doping work, but we have said we don't care in the least what they say. We have our rules, and they are supreme....

... It is simply an unacceptable position that the courts of this country cannot protect the individual rights of United States citizens where those rights are threatened by an association which has significant contacts with this country, which exercises significant control over both athletes and athletic events in this country, which acts through an agent organization in this country,[6] and which gains significant revenue from its contracts with United States companies.

Regarding the inquiry which this Court must make ..., it is manifest that the IAAF has purposefully availed itself of the privilege of acting in Ohio, and has caused direct consequences to the Plaintiff in Ohio. This Court has previously listed in detail the facts supporting this conclusion and they will not be recounted here. Suffice it to say, as a general matter, Ohio athletes are subject to the Rules of the IAAF, the IAAF gains substantial revenue from the activities of these athletes, and the IAAF has recognized a track and field event to be held in Ohio. With respect to Mr. Reynolds specifically, the IAAF has contributed expense money so that Mr. Reynolds could compete in two events recognized by the IAAF, has published arguably defamatory statements which were circulated in Ohio publications, and has committed acts

---

6. The Court finds untenable what is apparently the tactic of the IAAF to insulate itself from the jurisdiction of any court: despite the incredible power and influence which it directly wields over track and field athletics in the United States and throughout the world, the IAAF continually maintains that it has no direct contact with any country or athlete, and that it only acts or has any outside contact through its member organizations, such as TAC. While that may be true, it must then be conceded that TAC is an agent of the IAAF and personal jurisdiction may be found to exist through TAC's contacts with this forum.

which may be found to have tortiously interfered with Mr. Reynolds' business relationships with both United States and Ohio companies.

Furthermore, this Court believes that as the IAAF acts through its member organizations, it is reasonable to subject the IAAF to jurisdiction anywhere its member organizations may be subject to suit. The evidence before the Court establishes that the IAAF distributes money to athletes through its member organizations, notifies athletes of positive drug test results through its member organizations, and provides adjudication of disputed drug test results in the first instance through its member organizations. Essentially, the IAAF refuses to have any contact with individual athletes, instead forcing such athletes to approach the IAAF through the national organizations. Thus, this Court holds, as the Tenth Circuit held in Behagen v. Amateur Basketball Ass'n, [744 F.2d 731 (10th Cir.1984)], that an international organization which acts through its members may be subject to the jurisdiction of a particular court based upon a member's contacts with, and activity in, the forum. Where, as here, the member organization has intervened as a Defendant in the action, the exercise of personal jurisdiction is beyond question.

Aside from all of the above, the Court holds that the exercise of personal jurisdiction over the IAAF is reasonable, fair, and constitutional because the IAAF has waived its right to contest the exercise of jurisdiction by this Court. In *Reynolds I*, the IAAF appeared in the action and moved, as provided in Federal Rule of Civil Procedure 12(b)(2), to dismiss on the grounds that this Court lacked personal jurisdiction over it. In the current action, however, it has apparently decided *sua sponte* that this Court has no jurisdiction over it and that it need not even appear to argue the matter. Thus, the plaintiff has been denied the ability to obtain discovery from the IAAF in order to support its claim that sufficient contacts exist between the IAAF and Ohio to support this Court's exercise of personal jurisdiction.

* * *

In accordance with all of the foregoing ..., this Court holds that the IAAF's failure to enter a timely objection to personal jurisdiction, which failure resulted in the inability of the Plaintiff to obtain the necessary discovery to establish the facts upon which he asserts the jurisdiction of this Court rests, results in the waiver of the IAAF's right to contest the personal jurisdiction of this Court....

II. THE PRELIMINARY INJUNCTION

* * *

The issue of greatest import to this Court, to the parties, and to *amicus*, is the threat of the IAAF to "contaminate," or in other words, suspend any athlete who competes against Mr. Reynolds knowing that he is currently deemed ineligible to participate in IAAF track and field events. The Court not only finds the threat unconvincing, it finds it to be an inappropriate consideration to weigh against the harm which will befall Mr. Reynolds if he is wrongfully prevented from participating in track and field competitions due to his IAAF Ineligibility status.

The IAAF's threat is unconvincing for several reasons. First, it is not at all clear that IAAF's contamination rule is mandatory in nature. Indeed, documents and testimony adduced at the preliminary injunction hearing cast considerable doubt upon this proposition, and lead this Court to conclude that it is not always strictly enforced. Furthermore, it is equally unclear that the IAAF would attempt to prevent United States track and field athletes uninvolved in this litigation from participating in the Olympics on the basis of Rule 53(ii) alone. The loss of some of the event's top competitors, the resulting public outcry, and the possible loss of substantial revenue to the IAAF, all lead this Court to conclude that widespread "contamination" of American athletes by the IAAF is unlikely.

Even if, however, this Court considered such contamination to be the likely result if an injunction were to issue, the Court finds such a threat *by the Defendant IAAF* to be an entirely inappropriate consideration. It is, of course, axiomatic that in considering the merits of a preliminary injunction, the Court must consider whether the injunction will harm others. However, it is the impassioned conviction of the Court that such harm to others does not, and indeed, should not, include harm to others *caused by the voluntary and intentional acts of the Defendant*. To hold otherwise would be to allow the IAAF to hold the entire American Olympic team against an unfavorable decision from this Court....

This Court also believes that Reynolds has established a likelihood of success on the merits of his claims. With respect to the validity of the drug test performed at the Lafarge Laboratory on the urine sample provided by Reynolds in Monte Carlo, this Court believes—as did the American Arbitration Association arbitrator and the TAC hearing panel—that Reynolds has created a substantial doubt as to the accuracy of the reported results. Not only did Reynolds' expert testify as to numerous deficiencies in the Lafarge Laboratories' testing procedure,[9] he also testified as to several inconsistencies with the actual test results which make it highly unlikely that both samples actually originated with Mr. Reynolds.[10] Finally, and perhaps most egregious of all, Plaintiff's expert testified that nandrolone is known to remain in an individual's body for a considerable period of time, and the fact that

9. For instance, Plaintiff's expert testified that the laboratory failed to attach proper chain of custody documentation to the urine samples provided by Reynolds, failed to use an "internal standard" to assist it in interpreting the results, and failed to use a positive quality control.

10. Plaintiff's expert testified that the "picture" of naturally occurring steroids should be relatively the same for both samples of urine if, as alleged, they were both supplied by Reynolds. He concluded, however, that because the naturally occurring steroids in the two samples created extremely different "pictures," the two could not have originated with the same individual.

Reynolds' urine allegedly tested positive for two metabolites of nandrolone on August 12, 1990, and tested negative for nandrolone one week later on August 19, 1990, casts considerable doubt on the validity of the August 12 test.

With respect to the claims in Reynolds Complaint, the Court finds it likely that they are meritorious. First, it appears likely that a contractual relationship exists between the Plaintiff and both the IAAF and TAC, and it further appears that the IAAF breached this contract when it departed from its own guidelines and regulations regarding appropriate drug testing procedures. Second, it appears likely that the IAAF—with disregard for its own policy of confidentiality—maliciously released to the world media information that Reynolds had tested positive for the steroid nandrolone *before* Reynolds was accorded a hearing before TAC as prescribed by IAAF rules. It is reasonable to infer that the IAAF knew that such information would cause third parties to void existing endorsement contracts and prevent others from entering into such contracts. As such, Reynolds is likely to succeed on his claim of defamation and tortious interference with a business relationship.

* * *

Injunction granted.

———

The court in *Reynolds* enjoined the IAAF and TAC "from interfering, impeding, threatening to impede or interfere in any way [with] the Plaintiff's ability to compete in all international and national amateur track and field competitions, including but not limited to the 1992 United States Olympic Trials and 1992 Summer Olympic Games, as a result of or in any manner connected with tests on any sample of urine attributed to him from the August 12, 1990 Herculis '90 International Track and Field Meet in Monte Carlo, Monaco." After two frantic days of appeals in which a Sixth Circuit judge stayed the injunction, Justice Stevens reinstated the injunction, and the full Supreme Court declined to reconsider Justice Stevens' order, (see 112 S.Ct. 2512 (1992)), TAC allowed Reynolds to run in the 400–meter race at the Olympic trials in New Orleans, at which Reynolds qualified only as an alternate on the 4X400 meter relay team. However, the USOC refused to grant Reynolds credentials to travel with the U.S. Olympic team to Barcelona, based on the IAAF's refusal to allow him to compete there despite the injunction. After the Olympics, the IAAF announced that because of Reynolds' legal challenge, it was extending his suspension from August 1992 through the end of that year.

In December 1992, the district judge, finding that the IAAF had "purposefully avoided the truth," entered a default damages award of $27.3 million (approximately $7 million in compensatory damages and $20 million in punitive damages), and made his earlier injunction permanent. The practical issue now facing Reynolds is how to collect his award. Can he attach money owed to the IAAF by various American sponsors, such as Coca Cola? Can he attach any assets the IAAF might have or accrue in the United States for future track meets, such as the 1996 Olympics in Atlanta? Can he attach assets of TAC, the U.S. governing track federation, which is a member of the IAAF? Can IAAF officials be arrested for contempt when they enter the United States for failing to abide by the court's injunctions? As a footnote, because of this damage award the IAAF threatened for a time to extend Reynolds' suspension again beyond December 31, 1992.

Questions for Discussion

1. Should American—or any country's—courts review and overturn the decisions of an international sports governing body? If so, under what standard of review and on what grounds? The IAAF contends that if the courts of every nation could overturn its decisions, the Federation could not govern effectively because national political interests would influence many courts to overturn any IAAF decision contrary to the interests of their country's athletes. Compare this argument to those invoked in *Partee* in chapter 2 and *NCAA v. Miller* in Chapter 8, in which the courts blocked state laws from governing national sports organizations in the United States.[11]

2. How should the courts of individual countries (or states) deal with international (or national) sports governing bodies? Would every sports governing body be fair and impartial if it were immune to judicial scrutiny? Would courts in every country (or state) be fair and impartial, as well as sufficiently uniform and consistent, in overseeing sports governing bodies? How would Americans have reacted to a court order in the former East Germany that overturned the International Amateur Swimming Federation's disqualification of an East German swimmer for steroid use?

3. The IOC is considering requiring every prospective competitor in the upcoming 1996 Games in Atlanta to sign a written agreement that they will accept the decisions of international federations and their arbitration procedures, and not challenge these rulings in court? Would such agreements be effective in excluding judicial review?

In grappling with these dilemmas, the care and integrity of a sport's governing body are crucial. Consider a story told in *The Lords of the Rings*.[12] Apparently, IAAF president Primo Nebiolo and his assistant Luciano Barra, both Italians, arranged with Italian field judges to add almost one-half meter to the long jump of Italy's Giovanni Evangelisti in the 1987 world track and field championships in Rome so

11. In the drug testing context, however, courts have upheld the application of state constitutional restrictions to NCAA drug testing procedures. *See* Hill v. NCAA, 7 Cal.App.4th 1738, 273 Cal.Rptr. 402 (1990) (review granted 276 Cal.Rptr. 319, 801 P.2d 1070 (1990)).

12. See Simson & Jennings, *The Lords of the Rings*, note 9 above, at 164–83.

that he could win the bronze medal ahead of Larry Myricks of the United States—all in retaliation for what the Italians regarded as a bad foot-fault call made against Evangelisti at the world indoor championships the previous year in Indianapolis. Eventually the IAAF, over great resistance by Nebiolo, stripped Evangelisti of the bronze medal after the Italian Olympic Committee had exposed the cheating with the help of a video tape that had inadvertently been left running while an official tampered with the long jump measuring device.

This incident is part of a larger rift between Nebiolo and economically powerful United States track officials—in particular, long-time TAC (now USTAF) executive director and IAAF vice-president Ollan Cassell, whom Nebiolo regards as the greatest political threat to his presidency of the IAAF. Some have privately suggested that the IAAF's intransigence in the *Reynolds* case is merely part of an overall effort by Nebiolo to embarrass TAC at every opportunity in the international track community. If this story is true, does it affect your opinion on whether domestic courts should intervene in the decisions of international sports federations?

The IAAF has notified USTAF that it should make every effort to have *Reynolds* reversed, because if American courts exercise jurisdiction over international sports governing bodies, this may jeopardize holding the 1996 Olympics in Atlanta, where international officials might be subject to court sanctions for contempt. How should American courts respond to a "threat" that, unless they refuse to interfere in the affairs of international sports federations, the United States may not be allowed to host international athletic competitions? How should USTAF or the USOC respond? How should Congress and the President respond? Are such threats real or merely posturing?

As recently as 1984, Article 26 of the IOC's Olympic Charter declared that "[t]o be eligible for participation in the Olympic Games, a competitor must . . . not have received any financial rewards or material benefit in connection with his or her sports participation." Cynics have attributed the origin of this "amateurism" rule to the desire of the English upper classes (who were responsible for reviving the Olympic games in 1896) to exclude working class people, who could not afford to devote all of their time to unremunerated sporting competition.[13] In recent years, however, faced with the reality that governments in many countries heavily subsidize athletes and training programs, the Charter was changed to drop this prohibition, and under Article 45 eligibility standards for the Olympics are now left entirely to the international federation that governs each sport. (Hence the IAAF had the power to declare Reynolds ineligible for the 1992 Games in Barcelona.)

13. See Guttman, *The Olympics*, note 9 above.

Most federations, whose sports do not offer opportunities for large income or endorsements, still cling to a strict amateurism requirement (which does not bar government subsidies). Others, such as the IAAF, still formally require amateurism, but allow athletes to circumvent that principle by creating, through an athlete's national federation, a "trust fund" into which all money earned by the athlete is deposited and then distributed as "a subvention to an athlete to assist him in the expenses incurred in training for or participation in any competition" (IAAF Rule 16; TAC Regulation 9). Training "expenses" are liberally construed to include all transportation, food, housing, insurance, and other normal living expenses. When athletes retire, the balance in their trust funds become theirs to spend as they wish.[14]

Still other federations (for example, those in tennis and basketball) have completely abandoned any pretense of amateurism—Magic Johnson and Steffi Graf can now participate in the Olympics. Should the concept of amateurism required for Olympic eligibility be defined by individual federations, or should there be a uniform standard in all sports? What is the policy behind excluding some of the world's best athletes because they earn money from their athletic prowess? If there is some value to this policy, should it apply to governmental subsidies of athletes or to college athletic scholarships (a uniquely American phenomenon)?

———

Another challenge to an IAAF/TAC suspension for a positive drug test involved Delisa Walton–Floyd, one of the United State's top track stars. Before taking a medicine, Walton–Floyd called the USOC "Drug Hot–Line" to find out whether the drug was on the list of banned substances. After being told that it was not, Walter–Floyd took the medicine, and at a subsequent meet tested positive for sydnocarbi, a banned amphetamine found in the medicine she had taken. The IAAF and TAC suspended her, stating that it was irrelevant whether a banned substance was ingested unknowingly. Walton–Floyd sued the USOC and TAC in federal court in Colorado to enjoin her suspension. The trial judge refused to grant a preliminary injunction on the ground that he did not think it likely that she would win on the merits, although he acknowledged that a jury might return a verdict of negligence against the USOC for giving faulty information over its hot line. If the IAAF and TAC had properly followed their own rules and procedures, is this the correct result?

One of the most controversial of the IAAF's rules is its "contamination" policy, under which an athlete becomes ineligible simply by participating in a meet "in which any of the competitors were, to his knowledge, ineligible to compete under IAAF rules" (IAAF Handbook,

14. For insights into how this new system affects the life of America's most famous Olympic athlete, see Carl Lewis with Jeffrey Marx, *Inside Track: My Professional Life in Amateur Track and Field* (New York: Simon and Schuster, 1990).

Rule 53(ii)). As the court stated in *Reynolds*, the IAAF threatened to use this rule to ban the entire U.S. 400–meter team from the Barcelona Olympics if Reynolds ran in the trials. This threat caused the Sixth Circuit judge to lift the preliminary injunction the day after it was issued, although Justice Stevens refused to consider this factor in reinstating the injunction the following morning. Is it appropriate for a judge to consider, as a basis for denying an injunction, injuries to third parties that will be inflicted by the defendant if the injunction is granted?

What is the purpose of the "contamination rule"? Does the IAAF have a rational basis for it? If so, is the rule more restrictive than necessary to achieve that purpose? If the IAAF had declared the U.S. 400–meter team ineligible for the Olympics because Reynolds ran in the trials, on what legal grounds might the ineligible athletes have challenged that decision? How should a court have ruled in such a case?

———

Finally, a recurring issue in Olympic sports has been whether all the participants in women's events are really women. We alluded to this issue earlier in this chapter, in connection with the case of *Richards v. USTA*, 93 Misc.2d 713, 400 N.Y.S.2d 267 (1977), in which a New York judge held that the USTA could not rely solely on the Barr sex-chromatin test to exclude a recently operated-on transsexual from the Women's Division of the U.S. Tennis Open. Since the 1960s, both the USOC and most international federations have used the Barr test to try to detect competitors who are not actually female—in response to charges and controversies especially about athletes from behind the old Iron Curtain. In connection with the 1996 Summer Olympics which will take place in Atlanta, should an American court feel authorized to decide whether the Barr test may exclude athletes who otherwise appear to be female? For the benefit of non-American as well as American athletes?

Chapter Eleven

PERSONAL INJURY
FROM SPORTS

Participants in sporting events experience not only the thrill of victory and the agony of defeat—occasionally a tragic injury befalls one of the athletes. Highly publicized recent examples include the permanent crippling of Detroit Lions' tackle, Mike Utley, in an NFL game in the fall of 1991, and the collapse and death of Loyola Marymount star, Hank Gathers, in a college basketball game in the winter of 1990. Indeed, even a fan may fall victim, as occurred to a spectator struck by a fatal bolt of lightning while out on the golf course watching the 1991 U.S. Open.

Unsurprisingly, many serious athletic injuries find their way into the legal system.[1] At the heart of the legal system is society's concern about violent contact and personal injury. In the last quarter century there has been a sharp increase in the number of victims seeking legal redress for their injuries, sending liability insurance premiums spiralling.[2] That same phenomenon has been visible in the area of sports injuries.

Sports, however, pose a unique problem to the law of personal injury. The aim of a sporting event is to produce spirited athletic competition on the field or floor. In sports such as boxing, football and hockey, a central feature of the contest is the infliction of violent contact on the opponent. In other sports, such as basketball and baseball, such contact is an expected risk, if not a desired outcome, of intense competition.[3] Even sports such as golf that are intrinsically

---

1. Useful overviews of this topic can be found in two chapters of Gary Uberstine ed., *Law of Professional and Amateur Sports* (Deerfield, Ill.: Clark, Boardman, and Callaghan, 1991): Chapter 14 by Raymond L. Yasser, Liability for Sports Injuries, and Chapter 15 by Chris J. Carlsen, Violence in Professional Sports.

2. For a comprehensive analysis of the tort "crisis," see the two volume report done for the American Law Institute, Reporters' Study, *Enterprise Responsibility for Personal Injury* (Philadelphia: ALI, 1991), for which one of the editors of this book, Weiler, served as Chief Reporter.

3. Recall from Chapter 1 the case of the Cleveland Indians' Ray Chapman who was

non-violent to their participants may produce harmful contacts to spectators. This characteristic feature of sports requires the law to undertake a delicate balancing act when it tailors for use in sports litigation the standards of liability developed to govern relationships in very different walks of life.

A. TORTS AND SPORTS

The special problems sports pose to tort litigation are displayed most vividly in cases in which an injured athlete files suit against another athlete whose actions allegedly caused the injury. The cases in this section exemplify the current judicial response to such cases.[4]

HACKBART v. CINCINNATI BENGALS & CHARLES CLARK

United States District Court, District of Colorado, 1977.

435 F.Supp. 352.

[In the first exhibition game of the 1973 NFL football season, Dale Hackbart, a veteran free safety for the Denver Broncos, attempted on a pass interception to block Charles "Booby" Clark, a rookie running back for the Cincinnati Bengals. As the play continued upfield, Clark, "acting out of anger and frustration, but without a specific intent to injure," hit Hackbart on the back of the head with his forearm. No official observed the blow and no penalty was called.

Although Hackbart experienced soreness, he continued to play in that game and the rest of the exhibition season before being released by the Broncos. Hackbart then sought medical assistance and was diagnosed as having a neck injury. When that medical information was provided to the Broncos, the team paid Hackbart his full 1973 salary, pursuant to the injury clause in the NFL standard player contract. Hackbart then filed a tort suit against both Clark and the Bengals. At issue was whether these facts could support a viable tort claim. For the following reasons, the trial judge ruled for the defendants.]

Matsch, District Judge.

Football is a recognized game which is widely played as a sport. Commonly teams are organized by high schools and colleges and games are played according to rules provided by associations of such schools.

The basic design of the game is the same at the high school, college and professional levels. The differences are largely reflective of the

---

killed when struck on the head by a pitch thrown by the Yankees' Carl Mays. For an insightful philosophical analysis of the ethics of bodily contact sports, see Robert Simon, *Fair Play: Sports, Values, and Society* 53–70 (Boulder, Col.: Westview Press, 1991).

4. The best scholarly treatment of the legal issues posed by these cases is Daniel E. Lazaroff, *Torts and Sports: Participant Liability to Co-Participants for Injuries Sustained During Competition,* 7 Univ. of Miami Ent. & Sports L. Rev. 191 (1990).

fact that at each level the players have increased physical abilities, improved skills and differing motivations.

Football is a contest for territory. The objective of the offensive team is to move the ball through the defending team's area and across the vertical plane of the goal line. The defensive players seek to prevent that movement with their bodies. Each attempted movement involves collisions between the bodies of offensive and defensive players with considerable force and with differing areas of contact. The most obvious characteristic of the game is that all of the players engage in violent physical behavior.

The rules of play which govern the method and style by which the NFL teams compete include limitations on the manner in which players may strike or otherwise physically contact opposing players. During 1973, the rules were enforced by six officials on the playing field. The primary sanction for a violation was territorial with the amounts of yardage lost being dependent upon the particular infraction. Players were also subject to expulsion from the game and to monetary penalties imposed by the league commissioner.

The written rules are difficult to understand and, because of the speed and violence of the game, their application is often a matter of subjective evaluation of the circumstances. Officials differ with each other in their rulings. The players are not specifically instructed in the interpretation of the rules, and they acquire their working knowledge of them only from the actual experience of enforcement by the game officials during contests.

Many violations of the rules do occur during each game. Ordinarily each team receives several yardage penalties, but many fouls go undetected or undeclared by the officials.

Disabling injuries are also common occurrences in each contest. Hospitalization and surgery are frequently required for repairs. Protective clothing is worn by all players, but it is often inadequate to prevent bodily damage. Professional football players are conditioned to "play with pain" and they are expected to perform even though they are hurt. The standard player contract imposes an obligation to play when the club physician determines that an injured player has the requisite physical ability.

The violence of professional football is carefully orchestrated. Both offensive and defensive players must be extremely aggressive in their actions and they must play with a reckless abandonment of self-protective instincts. The coaches make studied and deliberate efforts to build the emotional levels of their players to what some call a "controlled rage."

John Ralston, the 1973 Broncos coach, testified that the pre-game psychological preparation should be designed to generate an emotion equivalent to that which would be experienced by a father whose family had been endangered by another driver who had attempted to force the family car off the edge of a mountain road. The precise pitch of motivation for the players at the beginning of the game should be the feeling of that father when, after overtaking and stopping the offending vehicle, he is about to open the door to take revenge upon the person of the other driver.

The large and noisy crowds in attendance at the games contribute to the emotional levels of the players. Quick changes in the fortunes of the teams, the shock of violent collisions and the intensity of the competition make behavioral control extremely difficult, and it is not uncommon for players to "flare up" and begin fighting. The record made at this trial indicates that such incidents as that which gave rise to this action are not so unusual as to be unexpected in any NFL game.

The end product of all of the organization and effort involved in the professional football industry is an exhibition of highly developed individual skills in coordinated team competition for the benefit of large numbers of paying spectators, together with radio and television audiences. It is appropriate to infer that while some of those persons are attracted by the individual skills and precision performances of the teams, the appeal to others is the spectacle of savagery.

PLAINTIFF'S THEORIES OF LIABILITY

This case is controlled by the law of Colorado. While a theory of intentional misconduct is barred by the applicable statute of limitations, the plaintiff contends that Charles Clark's foul was so far outside of the rules of play and accepted practices of professional football that it should be characterized as reckless misconduct within the principles of Section 500 of the Restatement of Torts, 2d.

Alternatively, the plaintiff claims that his injury was at least the result of a negligent act by the defendant. The difference in these contentions is but a difference in degree. Both theories are dependent upon a definition of a duty to the plaintiff and an objective standard of conduct based upon the hypothetical reasonably prudent person. Thus, the question is what would a reasonably prudent professional football player be expected to do under the circumstances confronting Charles Clark in this incident?

* * *

It is wholly incongruous to talk about a professional football player's duty of care for the safety of opposing players when he has been trained and motivated to be heedless of injury to himself. The character of NFL competition negates any notion that the playing conduct can be circumscribed by any standard of reasonableness.

Both theories of liability are also subject to the recognized defenses of consent and assumption of the risk. Here the question is what would a professional football player in the plaintiff's circumstances reasonably expect to encounter in a professional contest?

All of the witnesses with playing or coaching experience in the NFL agreed that players are urged to avoid penalties. The emphasis, however, is on the unfavorable effects of the loss of yardage, not the safety of the players. It is undisputed that no game is without penalties and that players frequently lose control in surges of emotion.

The conflict in the testimony is the difference in the witnesses' opinions as to whether Mr. Clark's act of striking the plaintiff on the back of the head in reaction to anger and frustration can be considered as "a part of the game." Several former players denounced this incident and said that Mr. Clark's conduct could not be considered customary or acceptable.

It is noteworthy that while this incident was clearly shown on the Denver Broncos' defensive game films, which were routinely reviewed by the defensive players and coaching staff, none of them made it a matter of special attention or concern.

Upon all of the evidence, my finding is that the level of violence and the frequency of emotional outbursts in NFL football games are such that Dale Hackbart must have recognized and accepted the risk that he would be injured by such an act as that committed by the defendant Clark on September 16, 1973. Accordingly, the plaintiff must be held to have assumed the risk of such an occurrence. Therefore, even if the defendant breached a duty which he owed to the plaintiff, there can be no recovery because of assumption of the risk.

* * *

The Application of Tort Principles to Professional Football. A Question of Social Policy

The business of the law of torts is to fix the dividing line between those cases in which a man is liable for harm which he has done, and those in which he is not. Justice O. W. Holmes, The Common Law (1881).

While the foregoing findings of fact and conclusions of law are determinative of the claim made by Dale Hackbart against Charles Clark and his employer, this case raises the larger question of whether playing field action in the business of professional football should become a subject for the business of the courts.

To compensate the injured at the expense of the wrongdoer, the courts have been compelled to construct principles of social policy. Through the processes of trial and error the judicial branch of government has historically evolved the common law principles which necessarily affect behavior in many contexts. The potential threat of liability for damages can have a significant deterrent effect and private civil actions are an important mechanism for societal control of human conduct. In recent years the pace of technical progress has accelerated and human conflicts have intensified. The resulting need to expand the body of governing law with greater rapidity and certainty than can be achieved through the litigation process has been met by legislation and administrative regulation. That is particularly true of industrial injuries. The coal mines became subject to the Federal Coal Mine Safety Act. The railroads have long been governed by the Federal Employers Liability Act and the Safety Appliance Act. The Occupational Health and Safety Act has broad application.

To this time professional football has been a self-regulated industry. The only protection which NFL contract players have beyond self-defense and real or threatened retaliation is that which is provided by the league rules and sanctions. It may well be true that what has been provided is inadequate and that these young athletes have been exploited and subjected to risks which should be unacceptable in our social order. In this respect, it is interesting to compare football with boxing. Because of the essential brutality of the contest, prize fighting has been held to be unlawful unless conducted under the sanction and authority of a governmental commission.

Football has been presumed to be lawful and, indeed, professional football has received the implicit approval of government because these contests take place in arenas owned by local governments and the revenues are subject to taxation. Like coal mining and railroading, professional football is hazardous to the health and welfare of those who are employed as players.

What is the interest of the larger community in limiting the violence of professional football? That question concerns not only the protection of the participants, but also the effects of such violence on those who observe it. Can the courts answer this question? I think not. An ordinary citizen is entitled to protection according to the usages of the society in which he lives, and in the context of common community standards there can be no question but that Mr. Clark's blow here would generate civil liability. It would involve a criminal sanction if the requisite intent were present. The difference here is that this blow was delivered on the field of play during the course of action in a regularly scheduled professional football game. The Illinois court was concerned with the safety of high school athletes in Nabozny v. Barnhill, 334 N.E.2d 258 (Ill.1975), and said (at 260):

> This court believes that the law should not place unreasonable burdens on the free and vigorous participation in sports by our youth. However, we also believe that organized, athletic competition does not exist in a vacuum. Rather, some of the restraints of civilization must accompany every athlete onto the playing field. One of the educational benefits of organized athletic competition to our youth is the development of discipline and self control.

The difficulty with that view as applied to professional football is that to decide which restraints should be made applicable is a task for which the courts are not well suited. There is no discernible code of conduct for NFL players. The dictionary definition of a sportsman is one who abides by the rules of a contest and accepts victory or defeat graciously. That is not the prevalent attitude in professional football.

There are no Athenian virtues in this form of athletics. The NFL has substituted the morality of the battlefield for that of the playing field, and the "restraints of civilization" have been left on the sidelines.

Mr. Justice Holmes' simple statement of the function of tort law and the evidentiary record now before me clearly reveal the density of the thicket in which the courts would become entangled if they undertook the task of allocation of fault in professional football games. The NFL rules of play are so legalistic in their statement and so difficult of application because of the speed and violence of the play that the differences between violations which could fairly be called deliberate, reckless or outrageous and those which are "fair play" would be so small and subjective as to be incapable of articulation. The question of causation would be extremely difficult in view of the frequency of forceful collisions. The volume of such litigation would be enormous and it is reasonable to expect that the court systems of the many states in which NFL games are played would develop differing and conflicting principles of law. It is highly unlikely that the NFL could continue to produce anything like the present games under such multiple systems of overview by judges and juries. If there is to be any governmental involvement in this industry, it is a matter which can be best considered by the legislative branch.

My conclusion that the civil courts cannot be expected to control the violence in professional football is limited by the facts of the case before me. I have considered only a claim for an injury resulting from a blow, without weaponry, delivered emotionally without a specific intent to injure, in the course of regular play in a league-approved game involving adult, contract players. Football as a commercial enterprise is something quite different from athletics as an extension of the academic experience and what I have said here may have no applicability in other areas of physical competition.

Judgment for defendants.

[On appeal, the Tenth Circuit Court of Appeals reversed. While the court appeared to concede that negligence actions based on "unreasonable risks of harm" were inapplicable to a game like football, its decision took a different view of intentional torts.]

HACKBART v. CINCINNATI BENGALS, INC.

United States Court of Appeals, 1979.

601 F.2d 516.

DOYLE, CIRCUIT JUDGE.

* * *

[T]he evidence shows that there are rules of the game which prohibit the intentional striking of blows. Thus, Article 1, Item 1, Subsection C, provides that:

All players are prohibited from striking on the head, face or neck with the heel, back or side of the hand, wrist, forearm, elbow or clasped hands.

Thus the very conduct which was present here is expressly prohibited by the rule which is quoted above.

The general customs of football do not approve the intentional punching or striking of others. That this is prohibited was supported by the testimony of all of the witnesses. They testified that the intentional striking of a player in the face or from the rear is prohibited by the playing rules as well as the general customs of the game. Punching or hitting with the arms is prohibited. Undoubtedly these restraints are intended to establish reasonable boundaries so that one football player cannot intentionally inflict a serious injury on another. Therefore, the notion is not correct that all reason has been abandoned, whereby the only possible remedy for the person who has been the victim of an unlawful blow is retaliation.

* * *

Is the Standard of Reckless Disregard of the Rights of Others Applicable to the Present Situation?

The Restatement of Torts Second, § 500, distinguishes between reckless and negligent misconduct. Reckless misconduct differs from negligence, according to the authors, in that negligence consists of mere inadvertence, lack of skillfulness or failure to take precautions; reckless misconduct, on the other hand, involves a choice or adoption of a course of action either with knowledge of the danger or with knowledge of facts which would disclose this danger to a reasonable man. Recklessness also differs in that it consists of intentionally doing an act with knowledge not only that it contains a risk of harm to others as does negligence, but that it actually involves a risk substantially greater in magnitude than is necessary in the case of negligence. The authors explain the difference, therefore, in the degree of risk by saying that the difference is so significant as to amount to a difference in kind.

Subsection (f) also distinguishes between reckless misconduct and intentional wrongdoing. To be reckless the act must have been intended by the actor. At the same time, the actor does not intend to cause the harm which results from it. It is enough that he realized, or from the facts should have realized, that there was a strong probability that harm would result even though he may hope or expect that this conduct will prove harmless. Nevertheless, existence of probability is different from substantial certainty which is an ingredient of intent to cause the harm which results from the act.

Therefore, recklessness exists where a person knows that the act is harmful but fails to realize that it will produce the extreme harm which it did produce. It is in this respect that recklessness and intentional conduct differ in degree.

In the case at bar the defendant Clark admittedly acted impulsively and in the heat of anger, and even though it could be said from the admitted facts that he intended the act, it could also be said that he did not intend to inflict serious injury which resulted from the blow which he struck.

In ruling that recklessness is the appropriate standard and that assault and battery is not the exclusive one, we are saying that these two liability concepts are not necessarily opposed one to the other. Rather, recklessness under § 500 of the Restatement might be regarded, for the purpose of analysis at least, as a lesser included act.

Assault and battery, having originated in a common law writ, is narrower than recklessness in its scope. In essence, two definitions enter into it. The assault is an attempt coupled with the present ability to commit a violent harm against another. Battery is the unprivileged or unlawful touching of another. Assault and battery then call for an intent, as does recklessness. But in recklessness the intent is to do the act, but without an intent to cause the particular harm. It is enough if the actor knows that there is a strong probability that harm will result. Thus, the definition fits perfectly the fact situation here.

Reversed.

After the appellate court remanded the case for trial, the case was settled with payment of $200,000 to Hackbart.

Questions for Discussion

1. Look closely at the legal standards used in both the trial and the appellate opinions. In what situations would the trial judge *permit* a tort suit by the injured athlete against another participant? In what situations would the appeals court specifically *exclude* such suits? What does "reckless misconduct" mean and how does this concept differ from either intentional or negligent misconduct? How would one illustrate the difference in examples drawn not just from football, but from boxing, baseball, or other sports?

* * *

As the next case shows, the courts have had to struggle to utilize the policy of assumption of risk in the sports arena, because this legal concept has fallen from favor in tort law generally.

ORDWAY v. CASELLA

Court of Appeals of California, Fourth District, 1988.

198 Cal.App.3d 98, 243 Cal.Rptr. 536.

CROSBY, ASSOCIATE JUSTICE.

Does reasonable implied assumption of risk remain a viable defense after the adoption of comparative fault? We hold it does.

I

Judy Casella, a veteran jockey who had ridden in 500 professional horse races without incident, was thrown from her mount and further injured when the equine fell and rolled over her during a quarterhorse race at Los Alamitos Race Course on January 3, 1983. The tragic chain of events began when Over Shadow, owned by petitioner Homer Ordway, tangled with another steed, Speedy Ball, who then stumbled in front of Casella's horse. The California Horse Racing Board determined the jockey riding Over Shadow violated a board rule by "crossing over without sufficient clearance, causing interference," and he was suspended for five racing days. Alleging "negligence, carelessness and unlawful conduct," Casella sued the riders, trainers, and owners of Over Shadow and Speedy Ball.

II

The initial question is whether the doctrine of reasonable implied assumption of risk survives in the era of comparative fault. We had occasion to touch on the subject once before, but a resolution of the matter was not essential to that decision. It is now, however; and the answer is, "Yes."

Courts and legal scholars have traditionally recognized three forms of assumption of risk. Express assumption of risk is exactly what the term describes: Where "the potential plaintiff agrees not to expect the potential defendant to act carefully, thus eliminating the potential defendant's duty of care, and acknowledging the possibility of negligent wrongdoing," the potential plaintiff has expressly assumed the risk of injury.

Reasonable implied assumption of risk is the inferred agreement to relieve a potential defendant of a duty of care based on the potential plaintiff's reasonable conduct in encountering a known danger. A second variety of implied assumption of risk is labeled unreasonable. After a brief prefatory digression, we will explain the importance of the distinction between them in determining the rights of the parties.

The relationship between the concepts of implied assumption of risk and contributory negligence has been the source of some confusion. The two doctrines are quite separate in one sense, but overlap in another. More than thirty years ago, our Supreme Court explained the basic differences between them as follows:

> The defenses of assumption of risk and contributory negligence are based on different theories. Contributory negligence arises from a [plaintiff's] lack of due care. The defense of assumption of risk, on the other hand, will negative liability regardless of the fact that

plaintiff may have acted with due care. It is available when there has been a voluntary acceptance of a risk and such acceptance, whether express or implied, has been made with knowledge and appreciation of the risk.

In Li v. Yellow Cab Co. (Cal.1975) 532 P.2d 1226, the court "recognized [that the doctrine of assumption of risk] in fact is made up of at least two distinct defenses. 'To simplify greatly, it has been observed . . . that in one kind of situation, to wit, where a plaintiff unreasonably undertakes to encounter a specific known risk imposed by a defendant's negligence, plaintiff's conduct, although he may encounter that risk in a prudent manner, is in reality a form of contributory negligence. . . . Other kinds of situations within the doctrine of assumption of risk are those, for example, where plaintiff is held to agree to relieve defendant of an obligation of reasonable conduct toward him. Such a situation would not involve contributory negligence, but rather a reduction of defendant's duty of care." The court determined that unreasonable assumption of risk should be merged with the theory of contributory negligence under comparative fault principles; i.e., while an injured party who unreasonably assumed a risk may recover, the damages will nonetheless be reduced by the percentage of fault attributed to him or her.

Li did not specifically determine whether a defense based on reasonable implied assumption of risk should survive the adoption of comparative fault, and the court has not had occasion to confront the issue since. Several other divisions of the Court of Appeal have, however.

In Segoviano v. Housing Authority (1983) 191 Cal.Rptr. 578, a player was injured during an amateur flag football game when an opponent, in violation of the rules, pushed him out of bounds. Ruling on an in limine motion, the trial court precluded the defendant, the institutional sponsor of the game, from relying on assumption of risk to defeat the plaintiff's claim. The plaintiff prevailed, but the jury discounted his award by 30 percent under comparative fault instructions.

Rejecting the notion "that a plaintiff who has reasonably assumed a risk may not recover damages because that form of assumption of risk negates defendant's duty of care to the plaintiff," *Segoviano* held that only express assumption of risk remained a viable defense after *Li*. The appellate panel conceded *Li* explicitly merged only unreasonable assumption of risk into the concept of contributory negligence; but it concluded that where "the plaintiff's conduct [is] entirely reasonable under all of the circumstances, we find no basis in reason or equity for barring his recovery. Elimination of [reasonable implied assumption of risk] as a separate defense avoids punishing reasonable conduct." Accordingly, the court not only reversed the judgment but also held the plaintiff's recovery could not be reduced under comparative fault principles because his implied assumption of the risk of injury in a flag football game was reasonable and, as a matter of law, provided no basis for apportionment of the damages.

Having studied the problem anew, we remain unpersuaded by *Segoviano's* holding. In our view, that opinion turned the law on its head. If plaintiff reasonably consented to participate in a touch football game, how could defendant's sponsorship of the contest be any less reasonable? Plaintiff and defendant had an equal opportunity to anticipate the over-exuberance of one of the participants and the potential for injury. There is no principled basis upon which any responsibility should be assigned to the defendant under those circumstances. The defendant merely provided plaintiff with the chance to play; he was the one who chose to risk an injury. There is also a strong policy basis for absolving the defendant in such circumstances: encouragement of persons and entities to provide opportunities to engage in sports and recreational activities without fear of suits by the participating beneficiaries.

The correct analysis is this: The doctrine of reasonable implied assumption of risk is only another way of stating that the defendant's duty of care has been reduced in proportion to the hazards attendant to the event. Where no duty of care is owed with respect to a particular mishap, there can be no breach; consequently, as a matter of law, a personal injury plaintiff who has voluntarily—and reasonably—assumed the risk cannot prevail. Or stated another way, the individual who knowingly and voluntarily assumes a risk, whether for recreational enjoyment, economic reward, or some similar purpose, is deemed to have agreed to reduce the defendant's duty of care.

The *Segoviano* court may have been misled because the distinction between the "reasonable" and "unreasonable" plaintiff is superficially anomalous: The former's civil action is barred while the latter's is allowed to go to judgment, reduced only in proportion to fault. But the explanation has nothing to do with rewarding or punishing a plaintiff, as *Segoviano* suggests. Rather, it is found in the expectation of the defendant. He or she is permitted to ignore reasonably assumed risks and is not required to take extraordinary precautions with respect to them. The defendant must, however, anticipate that some risks will be unreasonably undertaken, and a failure to guard against those may result in liability.

For example, borrowing from an old legal saw, "[Because a] drunken man is as much entitled to a safe street, as a sober one, and much more in need of it" (Robinson v. Pioche (1855) 5 Cal.460, 461), sidewalks should be constructed with safety in mind. If they are negligently built, inebriety will not bar a pedestrian's lawsuit for injury, although it may reduce his recovery.

Those who have taken a remunerative or recreational risk with a conscious awareness of all it entails, however, are on their own. A circus need not provide a net for an aerialist who does not want one. The owner of a dangerous piece of property, Niagara Falls for example, will have a complete defense to an action by a Hollywood stuntperson who, encased in a barrel, elects to enter the river above the falls. But the garden-variety inattentive member of the public who passes through a gate negligently left open, in the misguided belief that the water above the falls is safe for swimming, will only suffer a proportionate reduction in damages. A defendant must, under appropriate circumstances, anticipate the fool (which is merely another way of describing the careless and negligent).

The conduct of the stuntperson is "reasonable" in the eyes of the law, but not that of the negligent bather. Concededly, it does sound strange to decree that unreasonable plaintiffs may recover and reasonable ones may not; but the problem is not of law but semantics. If the "reasonable-unreasonable" labels were simply changed to "knowing and intelligent" versus "negligent or careless," the concepts would be more easily understood.

* * *

III

Having concluded that the doctrine of reasonable implied assumption of risk is alive and well, we discuss in this section its preclusive impact on Casella's lawsuit, specifically whether her action could be maintained on a theory of recklessness....

Historically, the doctrine of assumption of risk has provided a defense only to actions for negligence. It has little or no application in the case of intentional or reckless conduct. The reason is this: While a potential plaintiff who engages in dangerous activity is "held to have consented to the injury-causing events which are known, apparent or reasonably foreseeable consequences of the participation ... participants do not consent to acts [by others] which are reckless or intentional." While the line between negligent and intentional conduct is frequently obscured in sports injury litigation, we are satisfied it was not crossed here.

First, Casella's complaint alleged only that her injuries were caused by "the negligent, careless and unlawful manner in which the Defendants ... rode, ... owned and trained the horses, Over Shadow and Speedy Ball." She never used the words "reckless" or "intentional"; and neither expression would accurately characterize the defendant jockeys' conduct, as she herself described it. Her declaration in opposition to Ordway's motion for summary judgment explained, "[Over Shadow's jockey] severely guided his horse inside and in doing so crossed over and in front of other horses without looking to see whether he could safely do so. His horse crossed in front of Speedy Ball [whose jockey] did not take evasive action and the horses' legs tangled resulting in Speedy Ball tripping and falling onto the track ... directly [in front of my mount]." Casella's own assessment of the accident presents a classic case of negligence, i.e., a failure to exercise due care. But by participating in the horse race, she relieved others of any duty to conform their conduct to a standard that would exempt her from the risks inherent in a sport where large and swift animals bearing human cargo are locked in close proximity under great stress and excitement.

Casella seeks to avoid the negligence hurdle by equating suspension of one of the defendant jockeys for violation of California Horse Racing Board Rule No. 1699 (the equine equivalent of an unsafe lane change) with intentional conduct. We are not persuaded. Mens rea plays no part in the board rule. The penalty is levied when an infraction occurs; no evidence was presented to the trial court which suggested a jockey is suspended only where the conduct is determined to have been intentional.

Casella's allegations are legally indistinguishable from those found insufficient in *Turcotte v. Fell*, [502 N.E.2d 964]. There, a jockey was injured in an accident very similar to Casella's. He sued his fellow competitor, who had been sanctioned for violating New York's foul riding rule, and the owner of the horse he rode. The trial court dismissed the complaint because there were "no allegations of [the defendant jockey's] wanton, reckless, or intentional conduct." The high court of New York unanimously affirmed the dismissal, noting that the plaintiff's failure to allege intentional conduct by the defendant rider was fatal to his cause of action:

> As the [foul riding] rule recognizes, bumping and jostling are normal incidents of the sport. They are not ... flagrant infractions unrelated to the normal method of playing the game and done without any competitive purpose. Plaintiff does not claim that [the other jockey] intentionally or recklessly bumped him, he claims only that as a result of carelessness, [the defendant] failed to control his mount.... [A] professional clearly understands the usual incidents of competition resulting from carelessness, particularly those which result from the customarily accepted method of playing the sport, and accepts them. They are within the known, apparent and foreseeable dangers of the sport and not actionable....

Casella's allegations also stand in sharp contrast to the facts in two other recent professional sports injury actions, Hackbart v. Cincinnati Bengals, Inc. (10th Cir.1979) 601 F.2d 516, and Tomjanovich v. California Sports, Inc. (S.D. Tex., Oct. 10, 1979, No. 78–243). In *Tomjanovich*, a professional basketball player was severely injured when an opposing player deliberately struck a vicious blow to his face. Tomjanovich sued in federal district court in Texas, and the law of California was applied. The verdict in his favor was in excess of $2 million. The matter settled pending appeal.

A verdict for Tomjanovich was clearly proper. He did assume the risk of being hit in the face by a flying elbow in the course of defending against an opponent's jump shot, suffering a painful insult to his instep by a size–16 foot descending with a rebound, or even being knocked to the court by the sheer momentum of a seven-footer driving home a slam dunk. But the scope of his consent did not extend to an intentional blow considerably beyond the expected risks inherent in basketball. Intentional fouls are part of that game. But where the intent is to injure and the force used is far greater than necessary to accomplish a legitimate objective within the scope of play, a defendant may not prevail on an assumption of risk defense.

* * *

Despite Casella's disingenuous assertion that "I did not consider at the time of this race that I was participating in a dangerous activity," professional riders must realize that accidents are always possible and not uncommon. The degree of the risk anticipated varies, of course, from sport to sport. In prize fighting bodily harm is to be expected, but pugilists do not consent to be stabbed or shot in the ring. At the other extreme, in bridge or table tennis bodily harm is not contemplated at all. The correct rule is this: If the defendant's actions, even those which might cause incidental physical damage in some sports, are within the ordinary expectations of the participants—such as blocking in football, checking in hockey, knock-out punches in boxing, and aggressive riding in horse racing—no cause of action can succeed based on a resulting injury.[8]

It is of no moment that the participants may be penalized for these actions by the officials. Routine rule violations, such as clipping in football, low blows in boxing, and fouls in horse races are common occurrences and within the parameters of the athletes' expectations.

Here defendant jockeys were attempting to win a horse race. There has never been any suggestion that they, much less the owners of their horses, were motivated by a desire to injure plaintiff. Defendants' conduct, while perhaps negligent, was within the range to be anticipated by the other riders, or should have been. As a professional rider, Casella reasonably assumed the risk of her tragic injury. As with other persons who reasonably assume similar risks, her remedy was to purchase insurance from her athletic income beforehand, not to pursue a lawsuit against her counterparts in the sport afterward. The action, accordingly, is barred as a matter of law.

Summary dismissal granted.

———

American courts generally have adopted the rule that tort liability in an athletic contest must rest on reckless disregard of safety. As the Supreme Judicial Court of Massachusetts put it in *Gauvin v. Clark*, 404 Mass. 450, 537 N.E.2d 94 (1989) (a case involving severe abdominal

---

8. A borderline situation is presented by knock-out punches in hockey. They are quite common, but not officially condoned as part of the game. Reasonable minds might differ as to them. Tossing one's opponent out of the ring in professional wrestling is also a gray area. These sorts of cases are jury material.

injuries inflicted by a "butt-end" with the stick in a college hockey game):

> Allowing the imposition of liability in cases of reckless disregard of safety diminishes the need for players to seek retaliation during the game or future games. Precluding the imposition of liability in cases of negligence without reckless misconduct furthers the policy that "[v]igorous and active participation in sporting events should not be chilled by the threat of litigation."

Some courts, however, do permit suits predicated on negligence, although the standard of legal negligence is greatly modified to accommodate the normal risks of the game. This doctrinal position was expressed by the Missouri Court of Appeals in *Niemczyk v. Burleson*, 538 S.W.2d 737, 741–42 (Mo.App.1976) (a case involving a collision on the basepaths in a women's softball game):

> Material factors include the specific game involved, the ages and physical attributes of the participants, their respective skills at the game and their knowledge of its rules and customs, their status as amateurs or professionals, the type of risks which inhere in the game and those which are outside the realm of reasonable anticipation, the presence or absence of protective uniforms or equipment, the degree of zest with which the game is being played, and doubtless others.

Cases do take place of violent acts clearly beyond the pale of the game and the law. A notable example occurred in 1965 when Juan Marichal of the San Francisco Giants, upset at having been deliberately grazed by Los Angeles Dodgers' catcher John Roseboro's throw back to the mound, turned and struck Roseboro with his bat. After Marichal was suspended and fined by the league, Roseboro sued Marichal and collected $7,500 out of court. But what is the appropriate legal treatment of the following much "closer calls"?

1. A pitcher throws a ball far inside the plate and strikes the batter who has come up to the plate after the previous batter hit a three-run home run.

2. A runner from first base slides, spikes up, into the second baseman some distance away from the base, to break up a double play in a close late-inning game. (See *Bourque v. Duplechin*, 331 So.2d 40 (La.App.1976).)

3. A hard-hitting football free safety "blind sides" a wide receiver running a post pattern across the middle of the field, just after the ball has passed over both their heads.[5]

---

5. The most notorious such hit was inflicted by Oakland Raiders' Jack Tatum on New England Patriots' wide receiver Darryl Stingley. Stingley suffered a broken neck as a result of the hit. See John Underwood, *The Death of an American Game: The Crisis in Football* 45–46 (Boston: Little Brown, 1979); see also Jack Tatum with William Kushner, *They Call Me Assassin* (New York: Everest House, 1979).

In *Ordway*, the court alluded to a notorious 1977 incident involving the Los Angeles Lakers' Kermit Washington and the Houston Rockets' Rudy Tomjanovich.[6] Tomjanovich, who was trying to act as a peace-maker in a set-to between Washington and the Rockets' Kevin Kunnert, was punched in the face by Washington, fell, and struck his head on the court. Kareem Abdul Jabbar testified that the sound was "like a watermelon being dropped on a cement floor." The resulting skull fracture, concussion, and facial injuries effectively ended Tomjanovich's playing career. Washington was clearly liable in tort to Tomjanovich. But can Tomjanovich sue and collect from the Lakers—the "deep pocket" able to pay substantial monetary damages (including damages to the Rockets for the loss of Tomjanovich's services)? The legal criterion for imposing such "vicarious liability" on an employer is whether the harmful action on the part of Washington was "within the scope of his employment" with the Lakers. Precisely the same issue was posed about the San Francisco Giants' liability to John Roseboro or the Cincinnati Bengals' liability to Dale Hackbart. What additional facts might be relevant to that judgment? (An earlier decision on this issue is *Averill v. Luttrell*, 44 Tenn.App. 56, 311 S.W.2d 812 (1957), in which a catcher slugged a batter from behind after the batter, irate at several "brush-back" pitches, had thrown his bat at the pitcher.)

Courts have applied essentially the same doctrines immunizing clubs from liability for spectator injuries that flow from the normal risks of the game: for example, being hit by a foul ball, see *Schentzel v. Philadelphia National League Club*, 173 Pa.Super. 179, 96 A.2d 181 (1953), or by a hockey puck, see *Pestalozzi v. Philadephia Flyers*, 394 Pa.Super. 420, 576 A.2d 72 (1990). Consider, though, what factors would be relevant in determining the liability of the U.S. Golf Association for the death of the spectator killed by lightning when on the course during the 1991 U.S. Open.

An interesting variant on liability for spectator's injuries is *Manning v. Grimsley*, 643 F.2d 20 (1st Cir.1981). Baltimore Orioles' pitcher Ross Grimsley, while warming up during a game against the Boston Red Sox at Fenway Park, was being heckled by fans in the right field bleachers who were separated from the visitors' bullpen by a wire mesh fence. At the end of his warmup, Grimsley threw a ball hard at the fence, aimed at the hecklers. Unfortunately the ball passed through the mesh and struck and injured Manning, a fan who was not one of the hecklers. Is Grimsley liable to Manning? For the tort of battery or for negligence? Are the Orioles vicariously liable for either tort?

Return now to the more fundamental question posed by all these cases. Why, for example, does the plaintiff in *Ordway* assume the risk of negligent riding by another jockey on the racetrack, but not the risk of careless driving on the highway (perhaps by the same jockey on the

---

6. For a detailed account see David Halberstam, *The Breaks of the Game* 199–216 (New York: Alfred Knopf, 1981). The Jabbar quote in the text comes from a Note on the *Tomjanovich* case at 23 *American Trial Lawyer's Assoc. L. Rep.* 107 (1980).

way to the track)? For the last several decades the objectives of the general tort regime have been undergoing a major reevaluation. Until World War Two, most judges and commentators tacitly assumed that the role of tort law was to mete out corrective justice between the individual parties involved in a particular case. Presently, however, the intellectual consensus seems to be that our complex and expensive system of tort litigation and liability insurance constitutes a form of enterprise responsibility for personal injury. (Sharp disagreement remains about whether the law's priority should be compensation or prevention of injury.) Which of these visions suits the special case of torts in sports? Should the answers be the same for professional sports and for playground sports?

B. CRIMINAL LAW AND SPORTS VIOLENCE

Hockey has generated the most serious concern and extensive litigation about injuries inflicted by participants. The reason is that in hockey, while "roughing" and "fighting" are considered violations of the rules of the game that call for penalties of two and five minutes respectively, they do not evoke the ejections, suspensions, and fines meted out in other sports. Hockey owners believe that a certain amount of fighting helps win games and fans—recall the "Broad Street Bullies" reputation of the Stanley Cup-winning Philadelphia Flyers in the mid–1970s. The problem is that when fights break out between two players, especially when one combatant is bigger and tougher than the other, there is always a danger the fight will escalate, especially through the use of sticks. Sometimes stick swinging inflicts injuries that precipitate tort litigation. See *Babych v. McRae & Quebec Nordiques*, 41 Conn.Sup. 280, 567 A.2d 1269 (1989). Occasionally, the scene is bloody enough to yield criminal prosecutions.[7]

Perhaps the most highly-publicized such event took place in a 1969 exhibition game in Ottawa between the Boston Bruins and the St. Louis Blues. Ted Green, a star defenceman and "enforcer" for the Bruins, swung and hit the Blues' Wayne Maki on the head, drawing a delayed penalty signal from the referee. Maki then turned and speared Green in the abdomen with his stick. Green retaliated by swinging his stick at Maki's shoulder. Maki ended the fray by hitting Green on the head with his stick, which fractured Green's skull and required the insertion of a steel plate in his head. Although Green returned to play with the Bruins the next season, he was never the star player he was before the incident (though he is now head coach of the Edmonton Oilers).

---

7. The best treatment of this topic is Richard Horrow, *Sports Violence: The Interaction Between Private Law–Making and the Criminal Law* (Westport Conn: Greenwood Pub., 1980). See also Carlsen, note 1 above; Note, *Sports Violence as Criminal Assault: Development of The* *Doctrine by Canadian Courts*, 1986 Duke L. J. 1030; Gilles Letourneau & Antoine Monganas, *Violence in Sports: Evidentiary Problems in Criminal Prosecution*, 16 Osgoode Hall L.J. 577 (1978); and Note, *Consent in Criminal Law: Violence in Sports*, 75 Mich. L. Rev. 148 (1975).

Ontario authorities were so upset about this incident that they filed criminal charges against both Maki and Green. In separate decisions, the provincial court judges who tried the cases acquitted both players. In *Regina v. Green*, 16 D.L.R. 3d 137 (Ont. 1971), the judge commented as follows about Green's "consent" defense to the charge of simple assault:

> There is no doubt that the players who enter the hockey arena consent to a great number of assaults on their person, because the game of hockey as it is played in the National Hockey League, which is the league I am dealing with, could not possibly be played at the speed at which it is played and with the force and vigour with which it is played, and with the competition that enters into it, unless there were a great number of what would in normal circumstances be called assaults, but which are not heard of. No hockey player enters onto the ice of the National Hockey League without consenting to and without knowledge of the possibility that he is going to be hit in one of many ways once he is on that ice.

> I think it is notable that Mr. Maki in his evidence, when he was questioned about the fact that he was struck in the face by Mr. Green's glove, said this had happened to him hundreds of times. I think within our experience we can come to the conclusion that this is an extremely ordinary happening in a hockey game and the players really think nothing of it. If you go in behind the net with a defenceman, particularly one who is trying to defend his zone, and you are struck in the face by that player's glove, a penalty might be called against him, but you do not really think anything of it; it is one of the types of risk one assumes.

> One now gets the most difficult problem of all, in my opinion: since it is assumed and understood that there are numerous what would normally be called assaults in the course of a hockey game, but which are really not assaults because of the consent of the players in the type of game being played, where do you draw the line? It is very difficult in my opinion for a player who is playing hockey with all the force, vigour and strength at his command, who is engaged in the rough and tumble of the game, very often in a rough situation in the corner of the rink, suddenly to stop and say, "I must not do that. I must not follow up on this because maybe it is an assault; maybe I am committing an assault." I do not think that any of the actions that would normally be considered assaults in ordinary walks of life can possibly be, within the context that I am considering, considered assaults at all.

In *Regina v. Maki*, 14 D.L.R.3d 164 (Ont. 1970), the trial judge expressed a somewhat different view regarding the charge of assault causing bodily harm:

> If the fact situation in this case had been such that no doubt was raised in my mind regarding self-defence, I would not have hesitate[d] to convict the accused. The defense of consent would in my

opinion have failed. Although no criminal charges have been laid in the past pertaining to athletic events in this country, I can see no reason why they could not be in the future where the circumstances warrant and the relevant authorities deem it advisable to do so. No sports league, no matter how well organized or self-policed it may be, should thereby render the players in that league immune from criminal prosecution....

Thus all players, when they step onto a playing field or ice surface, assume certain risks and hazards of the sport, and in most cases the defense of consent as set out in § 230 of the *Criminal Code* would be applicable. But as stated above there is a question of degree involved, and no athlete should be presumed to accept malicious, unprovoked or overly violent attack. Bastin, J., states it this way in Agar v. Canning, 54 W.W.R. 302 at p. 305; affirmed 55 W.W.R. 384:

> But a little reflection will establish that some limit must be placed on a player's immunity from liability. Each case must be decided on its own facts so it is difficult, if not impossible, to decide how the line is to be drawn in every circumstance. But injuries inflicted in circumstances which show a definite resolve to cause serious injury to another, even when there is provocation and in the heat of the game, should not fall within the scope of the implied consent.

> The adoption of such principles in the future, would, I feel certain, be a benefit to the players, of course, to the general public peace and, in particular, to young aspiring athletes who look to the professionals for guidance and example.

The result in the second case, however, was the same: Maki was acquitted on the ground that there was at least "reasonable doubt" about whether he had used more than proportionate force in self defense.

Other courts have been unwilling to convict hockey players of criminal offenses, both in Ontario, see *Regina v. Maloney*, 28 C.C.C. 323 (Ont. 1976), and in the United States, see *State v. Forbes* (unreported), which produced a hung jury. But in 1988 Dino Ciccarelli, then of the Minnesota North Stars, spent one day in a Toronto jail for having clubbed the Maple Leafs' Luke Richardson twice on the head (fortunately, at this time the NHL required players to wear helmets).

The policy question posed by these cases was brought to the floor of the U.S. Congress in 1980 when Representative Ronald Mottl of Ohio proposed a *Sports Violence Act*, which would have created a new federal criminal offense of "Excessive violence during professional sporting events:"

> (a) Whoever, as a player in a professional sports event, knowingly uses excessive physical force and thereby causes a risk of significant bodily injury to another person involved in that event shall be

fined not more than $5,000 or imprisoned not more than one year, or both.

(b) As used in this section, the term—

(1) "excessive physical force" means physical force that—

(A) has no reasonable relationship to the competitive goals of the sport;

(B) is unreasonably violent; and

(C) could not be reasonably foreseen, or was not consented to, by the injured person, as a normal hazard to such person's involvement in such sports events; and

(2) "professional sports event" means a paid admission contest, in or affecting interstate or foreign commerce, of players paid for their participation."

This bill, vigorously opposed by the commissioners of all the major sports leagues, died in committee.

Questions for Discussion

1. Did the acquittal of Maki on self-defence grounds mean that Green did inflict a battery on Maki? Or vice versa? Did the judge in *Green* imply that we are not always expected to control ourselves—so long as we are playing sports?

2. Would the factual issues such as consent raised by these incidents be more easily resolvable if the Sports Violence Act had passed? Would a Sports Violence Act serve as a criminal court test run, at taxpayers' expense, for potential tort claims by injured athletes?

3. Why did the major sports commissioners oppose the Sports Violence Act? Does this imply that federal intervention to deal with sports violence is or is not in the best interests of the game? [8]

C. WORKERS' COMPENSATION FOR ATHLETES [9]

Workers' compensation is yet another legal instrument for dealing with sports injuries, designed not to punish an offender but to compensate the victim. Workers' compensation programs, which exist in every

---

8. See Horrow, *Sports Violence*, note 7 above, the book which was actually the source of this policy idea. For variations on this proposal, see Chris J. Carlsen & Matthew Shane Walker, *The Sports Court: A Private System to Deter Violence in Professional Sports*, 55 Southern Cal. L. Rev. 399 (1982), and Ronald A. DeNicola & Scott Mendeloff, *Controlling Violence in Professional Sports: Rule Reform and the Federal Professional Sports Violence Commission*, 21 Duquesne L. Rev. 843 (1983).

9. See Gerald Herz & Robert C. Baker, Professional Athletes and the Law of Workers' Compensation, Chapter 16 of Uberstine ed., *Law of Professional and Amateur Sports*, note 1 above, for a synopsis of this topic. The multi-volume treatise by Arthur Larson, *The Law of Workers' Compensation* (Desk Edition) (New York: Matthew Bender, 1992), is the authoritative and comprehensive statement of the law in this area, including the application of workers' compensation to injured athletes.

state (and in every province in Canada), pay defined benefits to employees who suffer "accidental injury arising out of and in the course of employment" (the standard statutory phrase) regardless of whether anyone was at fault in the incident. These statutory benefits, financed by the employer, typically cover medical treatment, physical and vocational rehabilitation, and earnings replacement pegged to the average wage in the state. For employment relationships and injuries covered by workers' compensation, this program is the exclusive legal remedy against the employer who is insulated by statute from tort suit by the injured employee. In the sports setting, the potential availability of workers' compensation generates an ambivalent attitude among the parties. In some cases the athlete seeks coverage and the club resists; in others, the tactical positions are reversed. The following cases provide a sample of the legal arguments regularly advanced on both sides.

1. COLLEGE ATHLETES [10]

The next case, involving an injury in intercollegiate football, recalls themes we explored earlier regarding the status of college athletes, the nature of their relationship with their schools, and the true character of big-time college sports.

RENSING v. INDIANA STATE UNIV.

Court of Appeals of Indiana, Fourth District, 1982.

437 N.E.2d 78.

[Fred Rensing, a varsity football player at Indiana State University, was rendered quadriplegic by a tragic injury in spring practice in 1976. At the time Rensing was on full scholarship—the standard NCAA "grant-in-aid" providing free tuition, fees, room and board, books, tutoring, and a limited number of game tickets. This scholarship was renewable by the university each year, for up to four years, as long as Rensing "actively participated in football competition." After his injury, Rensing sought and was denied workers' compensation benefits from Indiana's Industrial Board. This appeal to the courts followed.]

MILLER, PRESIDING JUDGE.

* * *

Thus, in the instant case the central question is not whether our Legislature has specifically excluded college sports participants from the coverage of the Act, since it is apparent the Legislature has not

---

10. Mark R. Whitmore, *Denying Scholarship Athletes Workers' Compensation: Do Courts Punt Away a Statutory Right?*, 6 Iowa L. Rev. 763 (1991), is the most recent and comprehensive analysis of this issue. An earlier treatment is Mark Alan Atkinson, *Workers' Compensation and College Athletics: Should Universities Be Responsible for Athletes Who Incur Serious Injuries?*, 10 J. of Coll. & Univ. Law 197 (1983–84).

expressed such an intention, but rather whether there was a "written or implied" employment contract within the meaning of the Act which obligated Rensing to play football in return for the scholarship he received.

Viewing the facts adduced in the case at bar, the conclusion is inescapable the Trustees did contract with Rensing to play football, regardless of whether one views the various documents submitted to Rensing and signed by him as constituting an express contract, or merely as evidence of the parties' understanding in support of an implied contractual relationship. In this regard, we note the settled law that "[a]ny benefit, commonly the subject of pecuniary compensation, which one, not intending it as a gift, confers on another, who accepts it, is adequate foundation for a legally implied or created promise to render back its value." The parties' financial aid "agreement," noted above, clearly anticipated not only that Rensing would play football in return for his scholarship, but also provided that in the event Rensing suffered an injury during supervised play that would make him "unable to continue to participate" in the opinion of the University doctor, the Trustees would ask him to assist in other tasks to the extent of his ability. The benefits would continue so long as Rensing was "otherwise eligible to compete." In light of such uncontradicted evidence, we can find no merit in the Trustees' suggestion Rensing's benefits were only a gift or "grant" intended to further the young man's education, particularly in light of the fact our Legislature has expressly recognized that scholarships or similar benefits may be viewed as pay pursuant to a "contract of hire" in the analogous context of unemployment benefits.

Additionally, the Trustees also retained their right to terminate their agreement for Rensing's services under certain prescribed conditions, a factor tending to distinguish his grant from an outright gift and which has previously been noted by this Court as a significant indicia of an employer-employee or master-servant relationship.

* * *

From these facts, the conclusion is compelling that Rensing and the Trustees bargained for an exchange in the manner of employer and employee of Rensing's football talents for certain scholarship benefits. Admittedly, the issue we resolve herein is novel to Indiana. In fact, our research of the appropriate law throughout the country reveals only three cases which are particularly relevant. In Van Horn v. Industrial Accident Commission, 33 Cal.Rptr. 169 (1963), the California Court of Appeals held that the widow and minor children of a college football team member, who was killed in a plane crash while returning with squad members from a game, were entitled to his death benefits since he had received an athletic scholarship plus a job and, therefore, was rendering services within the meaning of the California Workmen's Compensation Act. The sole question before the Court was whether the decedent was an employee of the college within the meaning of the

California's Workmen's Compensation Act so as to render the college liable thereunder for the death benefits to his dependents. In ruling affirmatively for the widow and her children the Court noted that "[t]he only inference to be drawn from the evidence is that the decedent received the 'scholarship' because of his athletic prowess and participation. The form of remuneration is immaterial. A court will look through form to determine whether consideration has been paid for services."

* * *

The Colorado Supreme Court has addressed the issue considered herein on two separate occasions reaching different results (with the same analysis) on these occasions. In State Compensation Insurance Fund v. Industrial Comm., 314 P.2d 288 (Colo. 1957), a college student who had received an athletic scholarship for his tuition plus a part-time job was fatally injured while playing in a college football game. The Colorado Supreme Court denied his beneficiaries' claims for death benefits under the Colorado Workmen's Compensation Act, holding that the evidence failed to establish that at the time of injury he was under a contract of hire to play football. Rather, his scholarship and part-time job were not based upon his athletic ability or participation on the football team. Lacking such a contract, the Colorado Supreme Court held there was no basis for a compensation claim. "Since the evidence does not disclose any contractual obligation to play football, then the employer-employee relationship does not exist and there is no contract which supports a claim for compensation under the [Colorado Workmen's Compensation Act]."

The Colorado Supreme Court used the same analysis to find in favor of the student-athlete in University of Denver v. Nemeth, 257 P.2d 423 (Colo. 1953). In *Nemeth*, the Court held a college student could be compensated under Colorado's Workmen's Compensation Act for injuries sustained during the spring football practice because in that case the student's employment by the University of Denver as the manager of its tennis courts was contingent upon his participation on the football team. In reaching this result, the Court emphasized that a contract existed requiring the University of Denver to employ Nemeth as long as he was on the football team and further noted the testimony of one witness who stated that "the man who produced in football would get the meals and a job." Since Nemeth's employment by the University was dependent on his playing football and he could not retain his job without playing football, the Court held Nemeth was an employee of the University. Thus, his injury during spring practice was an incident of his employment, and therefore, was compensable under the Colorado Workmen's Compensation Act.

While the facts of *Van Horn* and *Nemeth* are distinguishable from the case at bar to the degree that Rensing did not receive a non-athletic job in return for his football prowess, we feel such a distinction is not significant in view of the language of our statute discussed supra. The evidence presented in those two cases is comparable to that introduced before the Industrial Board in the case at bar in that in all three cases the "student-athlete" received benefits from a university solely because of his athletic ability and participation on a football team. If that ability declined and he did not make the team or if he quit the team for some other reason, the benefits he received would be terminated. As noted above, the evidence in the case at bar clearly demonstrates that the benefits received by Rensing were conditioned upon his athletic ability and team participation. Consequently, the scholarship constituted a contract for hire within IC 22–3–6–1(b) and created an employer-employee relationship between the Trustees and Rensing.

* * *

[Turning then to the issue of whether Rensing's employment was simply casual, the judge found that] for the team members football is a daily routine for 16 weeks each year. Additionally, during the "off-season" the "student-athlete" must daily work out to maintain his physical skills and attributes, thereby enhancing his eligibility for the team which is the basis for his scholarship. The University fields a major college football team and participates in a major college conference, the Missouri Valley Conference. In addition, the Trustees employ a large athletic department to administer the University's intercollegiate athletic program (in addition to physical education classes) and a sizable football coaching staff whose primary responsibility is to produce the best possible team so as to generate the largest possible income and whose teaching responsibilities to the general student body are, at best, of secondary importance. With regard to Rensing specifically, Coach Harp actively recruited him—his appearance at the University was not happenstance, liable to chance or an accident. In light of these facts Rensing's employment by the University was not "casual."

* * *

Decision reversed.

[The University appealed to the Supreme Court of Indiana, which took quite a different view of the situation.]

RENSING v. INDIANA STATE UNIV.

Supreme Court of Indiana, 1983.

444 N.E.2d 1170.

HUNTER, JUSTICE.

It is clear that while a determination of the existence of an employee-employer relationship is a complex matter involving many factors, the primary consideration is that there was an intent that a contract of employment, either express or implied, did exist. In other words, there must be a mutual belief that an employer-employee relationship did exist. It is evident from the documents which formed the agreement in this case that there was no intent to enter into an employee-employer relationship at the time the parties entered into the agreement.

In this case, the National Collegiate Athletic Association's (NCAA) constitution and bylaws were incorporated by reference into the agreements. A fundamental policy of the NCAA, which is stated in its constitution, is that intercollegiate sports are viewed as part of the educational system and are clearly distinguished from the professional sports business. The NCAA has strict rules against "taking pay" for sports or sporting activities. Any student who does accept pay is ineligible for further play at an NCAA member school in the sport for which he takes pay. Furthermore, an institution cannot, in any way, condition financial aid on a student's ability as an athlete. The fundamental concerns behind the policies of the NCAA are that intercollegiate athletics must be maintained as a part of the educational program and student-athletes are integral parts of the institution's student body. An athlete receiving financial aid is still first and foremost a student. All of these NCAA requirements designed to prohibit student-athletes from receiving pay for participation in their sport were incorporated into the financial aid agreements Rensing and his parents signed.

Furthermore, there is evidence that the financial aid which Rensing received was not considered by the parties involved to be pay or income. Rensing was given free tuition, room, board, laboratory fees and a book allowance. These benefits were not considered to be "pay" by the University or by the NCAA since they did not affect Rensing's or the University's eligibility status under NCAA rules. Rensing did not consider the benefits as income as he did not report them for income tax purposes. The Internal Revenue Service has ruled that scholarship recipients are not taxed on their scholarship proceeds and there is no distinction made between athletic and academic scholarships.

As far as scholarships are concerned, we find that our Indiana General Assembly clearly has recognized a distinction between the power to award financial aid to students and the power to hire employees since the former power was specifically granted to the Boards of Trustees of state educational institutions with the specific limitation that the award be reasonably related to the educational purposes and objectives of the institution and in the best interests of the institution and the state.

Furthermore, we find that Ind.Code § 22–4–6–2 is not applicable to scholarship benefits. In that statute, which deals with contributions by employers to unemployment insurance, employers are directed to include "all individuals attending an established school ... who, in lieu of remuneration for such services, receive either meals, lodging, books, tuition or other education facilities." Here, Rensing was not working at a regular job for the University. The scholarship benefits he received were not given him in lieu of pay for remuneration for his services in playing football any more than academic scholarship benefits were given to other students for their high scores on tests or class assignments. Rather, in both cases, the students received benefits based upon their past demonstrated ability in various areas to enable them to pursue opportunities for higher education as well as to further progress in their own fields of endeavor.

Scholarships are given to students in a wide range of artistic, academic and athletic areas. None of these recipients is covered under Ind.Code § 22–4–6–2, supra, unless the student holds a regular job for the institution in addition to the scholarship. The statute would apply to students who work for the University and perform services not integrally connected with the institution's educational program and for which, if the student were not available, the University would have to hire outsiders, e.g., workers in the laundry, bookstore, etc. Scholarship recipients are considered to be students seeking advanced educational opportunities and are not considered to be professional athletes, musicians or artists employed by the University for their skills in their respective areas.

* * *

All of the above facts show that in this case, Rensing did not receive "pay" for playing football at the University within the meaning of the Workmen's Compensation Act; therefore, an essential element of the employer-employee relationship was missing in addition to the lack of intent. Furthermore, under the applicable rules of the NCAA, Rensing's benefits could not be reduced or withdrawn because of his athletic ability or his contribution to the team's success. Thus, the ordinary employer's right to discharge on the basis of performance was also missing. While there was an agreement between Rensing and the Trustees which established certain obligations for both parties, the agreement was not a contract of employment. Since at least three important factors indicative of an employee-employer relationship are absent in this case, we find it is not necessary to consider other factors which may or may not be present.

We find that the evidence here shows that Rensing enrolled at Indiana State University as a full time student seeking advanced educational opportunities. He was not considered to be a professional athlete who was being paid for his athletic ability. In fact, the benefits Rensing received were subject to strict regulations by the NCAA which were designed to protect his amateur status. Rensing held no other job with the University and therefore cannot be considered an "employee" of the University within the meaning of the Workmen's Compensation Act.

It is our conclusion of law, under the facts here, including all rules and regulations of the University and the NCAA governing student athletes, that the appellant shall be considered only as a student athlete and not as an employee within the meaning of the Workmen's Compensation Act.

Vacated.

————

In a subsequent case, *Coleman v. Western Michigan University*, 125 Mich.App. 35, 336 N.W.2d 224 (1983), which also involved an injured college football player on full scholarship, the Michigan Court of Appeals listed what it considered the relevant factors for determining whether an employment relationship existed as a matter of "economic reality":

> (1) the proposed employer's right to control or dictate the activities of the proposed employees; (2) the proposed employer's right to discipline or fire the proposed employee; (3) the payment of "wages" and, particularly, the extent to which the proposed employee is dependent upon the payment of wages or other benefits for his daily living expenses; and (4) whether the task performed by the proposed employee was "an integral part" of the proposed employer's business. None of the foregoing factors is by itself dispositive. Each factor must be considered in turn, and all of them then taken into account in determining the existence of an employment relationship.

How would you assess the status of a scholarship athlete in light of these factors? Does your answer depend on whether the athlete is injured in a revenue-producing sport such as football or basketball, or a non-revenue producing sport such as lacrosse or gymnastics?[11]

Note on NCAA Insurance

Some states, such as California and Florida, have specifically excluded college athletes from workers' compensation coverage. Nevada, in contrast, has included injured athletes at least for purposes of medical benefits, and in Nebraska a bill has been proposed to provide full workers compensation coverage to the state's college athletes. And in early 1993, the Texas Workers' Compensation Commission ruled in a landmark decision (one that is certain to be appealed) that Kent Waldrep, a former football player at Texas Christian University who was paralyzed during a game in 1974, was an employee of the university for purposes of workers' compensation law and entitled to reimbursement of his medical expenses and a portion of his lost earnings—an award estimated to total well over a half-million dollars. One's judgment about the most sensible and equitable policy in this area depends to some extent on the availability of alternative avenues of redress for injured athletes. In response to initiatives taking place in state courts and legislatures, in the early 1980s the NCAA developed a Catastrophic

---

11. For contrasting views on this issue, see (besides the articles cited in note 10 above) Ray Yasser, *Are Scholarship Athletes At Big–Time Programs Really University Employees?—You Bet They Are!*, 9 Black L. J. 65 (1984), and Harry M. Cross, *The College Athlete and the Institution*, 38 Law & Contemp. Probs. 151 (Winter-Spring, 1973).

Insurance Plan for NCAA member-institutions.[12] The policy covered players, coaches, managers and cheerleaders who were injured while participating in intercollegiate sports and required at least $25,000 worth of medical care or suffered permanent loss of speech, hearing, sight, or use of hands or feet. The policy compensated actual economic loss—medical and rehabilitation expenses and lost earnings (up to $1,500 per month), less amounts received by the victim from other sources of insurance. The insurer was entitled to a lien for its payments against fifty percent of tort damages (less legal expenses) collected by the athlete from third-party wrongdoers.

This insurance policy had a remarkably low premium rate: coverage for all of its athletes cost a school between $2,000 and $8,000, depending on the number and type of intercollegiate sports at the school. However, the NCAA Manual left the decision whether to purchase coverage up to each institution, and many schools elected not to pay the premium.

The disastrous consequences of this NCAA deference to member autonomy soon became visible. In the fall of 1985, Marc Buoniconti, a sophomore linebacker at Citadel University (and son of former Miami Dolphins All–Pro linebacker Nick Buoniconti), suffered a broken neck, crushed spinal cord, and permanent paralysis when he tackled a runner in a game against East Tennessee State. The Citadel had opted not to pay the $5,000 premium required for its coverage against such a devastating injury. Buoniconti sued the school, its trainer, and its team physician for negligently allowing him to play that day: Buoniconti had been injured the week before, had been held out of practice with a sore neck, and had a special elastic strap attached to the front of his helmet and his shoulder pad. A week before trial, the Citadel (and its employee-trainer) settled for $800,-000. At trial, the jury rejected a medical malpractice claim against the doctor. After similar incidents at other schools—in particular, a paralyzing injury inflicted on Roy Lee (Chucky) Mullins at Mississippi State in a 1989 game against Vanderbilt (Mullins died two years later)—the NCAA finally decided in 1991 (against some heated objections) to spend part of its $1 billion television bonanza from the men's basketball tournament to guarantee such catastrophic injury coverage at all member-institutions.

Unlike workers' compensation, the NCAA insurance plan is not the legally exclusive remedy for college athletes (although if an injured player such as Buoniconti wants to avail himself of these benefits, he must agree to forego the right to sue). The value of the right to sue was vividly

---

12. See National Sports Underwriters, Ltd., *NCAA Athletics Insurance Programs Pamphlet* (Overland Park, Kansas: NCAA, 1991). Ironically, as we noted at the outset of Chapter 8, the reason why the NCAA was created in 1906 was national concern—in particular, by President Theodore Roosevelt—about high fatality and injury rates in college football (averaging 20 fatalities and 150 serious permanent disabilities a year). See Ronald Smith, *Sports and Freedom: The Rise of Big–Time College Athletics*, 191, 208 (New York: Oxford University Press, 1988). The initial role of this new governing body for college sports was to develop playing rules that would make football less dangerous for students to play. Not for eighty years did the NCAA finally address the question whether some of the revenues from the increasingly lucrative world of college sports should be spent to look after the needs of the victims of fatal or paralyzing athletic injuries—now only three or four per year in all college sports.

illustrated by the highly-publicized tragedy involving Hank Gathers, basketball star at Loyola Marymount.[13]

Gathers, who was voted to some 1989 All–American teams in his junior year (as the nation's leading scorer and rebounder), decided to forego the NBA draft and return to college for a final year, both to help his team reach the Final Four and to help himself become a "lottery" pick in the next draft. In an early season game in December, however, Gathers collapsed on the court, and tests indicated that he had an abnormal heart rhythm. The team physician, Dr. Vernon Hattori, a cardiologist, prescribed the drug Inderal to control Gathers's heart rhythm, and Gathers missed only two games. The school purchased a defibrillator, an instrument for restoring the heart beat, and kept it at courtside.

In his early games, Gathers experienced sluggishness and fatigue—normal side effects of Inderal. Following conversations with Gathers and Loyola coach Paul Westhead, Dr. Hattori gradually reduced the Inderal dosage from 240 to 40 milligrams per day. Gathers's play sharply improved towards All–American caliber, and Loyola became one of the top-ranked teams in the country. However, in the conference championship game in March 1990, Gathers, after making a slam dunk, collapsed on court and died two hours later of heart failure. For some reason, the defibrillator was not used immediately.

Gathers left behind him in the ghetto of north Philadelphia a mother, brothers and sisters, and a young son. They would not receive any of the benefits of the NCAA catastrophic injury policy nor would they get anything from the $1 million disability policy Gathers purchased to cover himself during his senior year: Gathers did not pay the extra $800 premium for a death rider. Instead, the family launched a $32 million wrongful death action against Loyola, Westhead, Hattori, and others. The litigation was settled in 1992 for a total of $2.6 million—$1 million from Dr. Hattori (the dollar limit on his malpractice liability insurance) and $1.6 million from Loyola on behalf of its employees.

Several months after the Gathers tragedy, the NCAA introduced a new disability insurance policy for "exceptional athletes" who have demonstrated their potential to play professional football, basketball, and baseball (but not hockey, at least yet).[14] This policy is designed to protect athletes against the loss of expected future earnings in these sports should they suffer an injury or illness while still in college. The policy does not require death or total disability: any disability will suffice if it prevents professional play for up to three seasons after the end of the athlete's college eligibility.

The maximum coverages (and maximum premiums) per player are $2.7 million ($24,750) for basketball, $1.8 million ($25,000) for football, and $900,000 ($12,000) for baseball. To help players pay these premiums, the NCAA has arranged a loan program with a Missouri bank. The loans can

---

13. The Gathers case inspired a fine scholarly article by Cathy J. Jones, *College Athletes: Illness or Injury and the Decision to Return to Play*, 40 Buffalo L. Rev. 113 (1992).

14. See National Sports Underwriters, Ltd., *NCAA Exceptional Student–Athlete Disability Insurance Program* (Overland Park, Kansas: NCAA, 1991).

be repaid either when the athlete signs a professional contract or when the athlete is injured. Eligibility for this policy is limited to athletes projected by the NCAA and its underwriter as potential first round picks in the basketball or baseball drafts, and first or second round picks in football.

What motivated the NCAA to provide this kind of disability coverage? How does it fit with the NCAA's objective of maintaining a clear demarcation between college and professional sports?

2. PROFESSIONAL ATHLETES [15]

While hockey has contributed the vast majority of sports cases to the criminal courts, football has been the prime sports contributor to workers' compensation claims. An interesting case surfaced in 1991 when Doug Williams, the quarterback for the 1987 Super Bowl champion Washington Redskins, won an estimated $1 million compensation award for a back injury suffered in 1989 while he was working out on a treadmill machine. The Redskins contested the claim on the ground that the injury, which occurred during the off-season in Williams's Louisiana home, did not "arise out of and in the course of employment." The D.C. hearing examiner disagreed, however, because the Redskins had asked Williams to undertake this conditioning program and had helped him get the treadmill. The size of the examiner's award was due to the fact that Williams, now a high school athletic director and coach, would receive the statutory maximum of $513 per week for this permanent disability for as long as his earnings in his new job did not exceed the $1.1 million salary level of his 1989 Redskins contract. The Redskins are now appealing that last feature of the compensation decision.

Football produces so many workers' compensation cases because the players absorb continuous bodily pounding in games and scrimmages, inflicting permanent physical impairments on a large percentage of the participants. The following decision illustrates a club trying to use this very feature of football life to argue that its former player's condition was not due to an "accident" within the meaning of the legislation.

PALMER v. KANSAS CITY CHIEFS

Court of Appeals of Missouri, Western District, 1981.

621 S.W.2d 350.

Shangler, Judge.

The employer Kansas City Chiefs Football Club appeals from a judgment which affirms the award of compensation by the Industrial Commission to claimant Palmer. The claimant, an offensive guard on the employer professional football team, was injured in the execution of a play in the course of a scheduled game. The administrative law judge

---

15. See Herz & Baker, *Professional Athletes and Workers' Compensation*, note 9 above.

found against Palmer, but the Industrial Commission on review of the transcript reversed that decision and entered an award for Palmer for injury to the back. The award of the Industrial Commission rests on the determination that the injury was from an abnormal strain in the course of the employment duty, and so the result of accident within the sense of § 287.020.2.

The normal function of an offensive guard according to Palmer is to block on runs and pass plays. The injury resulted during the execution of a run. The play called was a left trap. The assignment of the offensive guard in such a play is to drive the oncoming defensive tackle—in this instance, one Larry Hand—out of position so as to create a hole for the ballcarrier. The offensive guard executes the play by an opening step and then a position behind the center to apply a block to the defensive tackle as he comes through. The success of the maneuver depends upon the ability of the offensive guard to remain lower than the defensive player. The team had run that play with apparent success several times during the game, but on this occasion the defensive player diagnosed the play as it developed and stunted its effect. In the course of that defensive tactic, the claimant Palmer was injured. The claimant described that sequence:

> Larry [Hand] saw the play coming, stepped down inside ... to close the play, which is a defensive procedure to keep the offensive lineman from moving him out. "It was a situation where he got considerably lower than I did, and as I said, closed down the gap, and before I had the opportunity to get low enough again to block him, I was right on top of him, and he came up through me, and he was underneath my pads. I just was actually off balance and had not had the opportunity to make the play work right for me, and he drove up through me, you know, stopping me completely, and created, I felt a numbing sensation all through my upper body which would attribute to the position I was in and him coming up through my body underneath my pads.

* * *

The claimant disclosed on cross-examination that professional play was the culmination of football experience which began in junior high school and extended through the university. He acknowledged he had become an accomplished professional football blocker, that when the task was done proficiently, he succeeded in the assignment against the defensive player, but sometimes the opponent bested him.

* * *

The award of the Industrial Commission for compensation rests on the determination that the injury was the result of an abnormal strain. The law treats an abnormal strain as an accident and the resultant violence to the physical structure of the body as an injury within

§ 287.020.[2] The abnormal strain, the unforeseen event (the accident), by this analysis of workers compensation liability, amounts to the performance of the work in an abnormal manner or in a manner not routine. Work done in an awkward or unbalanced posture, albeit in the performance of a normal duty which subjects the worker to an excessive stress and produces an unexpected strain, results in a compensable injury under this principle. The right to compensation, nevertheless, rests on accident, an element of recovery not proved either by the fact of injury or from stresses usually incident to the work performance. The burden remains on the claimant to prove both the accident and injury, the occupational cause and effect, the unexpected event and the resultant trauma.

The appeal presents a question of law: whether the evidence shows an accident within the terms of the compensation law. In that assessment we are bound by the determinations of fact by the Industrial Commission drawn reasonably from the evidence and accord the employee favored with the award their full intendment.

The award of the Industrial Commission rests expressly on the excerpt of the Palmer testimony that the injury resulted when defensive lineman Hand diagnosed the trap and took countermeasure to nullify the play. . . .

The majority of the Industrial Commission applied the abnormal strain analysis to find an accidental injury:

> The Commission finds that in this particular instance the claimant's injury was caused by his unusual and abnormal position due to being thrown off balance, rather than the result of the actual play or assignment he was attempting to complete. As the employee testified, this instance was different and distinct from all others he had made before because he "just was actually off balance and had not the opportunity to make the play work right for me."

To invoke the abnormal strain doctrine the claimant must show that the usual occupation was done in an unusual manner or that the work was not the usual occupational task or that some other unexpected source of strain produced the injury. Thus, the critical component of the finding of fact on which the Industrial Commission rests award is: "As the employee testified, this instance was different and distinct from all others he had made before because he 'just was actually off balance and had not the opportunity to make the play work right for me.' "

* * *

The testimony by claimant Palmer stated, iterated and then reiterated was that the trap block assignment on the event of injury was "a block similar to the blocks that [he had] done many times against

2. Section 287.020.2: The word "accident" as used in this chapter shall . . . be construed to mean an unexpected or unforseen event happening suddenly and violently, with or without human fault, and producing at the time objective symptoms of an injury.

defensive people," that a block was "a normal assignment that was made in practice, after practice, after practice, after practice, and game, after game, after game, after game," that the block "was something which [he] had done on many occasions in [his] professional as well as [his] college career." These variants [among the others] on that theme of testimony, all straightforward and uncontradicted, simply do not allow the inference of fact found by the Industrial Commission majority as a predicate for liability that "this instance was different and distinct from all others he had made before." An inference inconsistent with the facts from which it is drawn fails as probative evidence.

The Industrial Commission majority also found as fact that the injury of the claimant was caused by a loss of balance in the execution of the block assignment—the other corollary of accident by abnormal strain.[6] . . .

The claimant acknowledged that an assignment to block was, in each instance, a test of proficiency between the offensive lineman and the defensive lineman which Palmer would sometimes win and sometimes lose. In the course of the schedule, Palmer came up against "equally proficient, tough, defensive men." The technique he employed varied "according to the type and quality and caliber" of the opponent. When he performed the assignment with skill, he "[blew] that defensive man out of the way." In a trap block, "the object of the offensive guard is to get underneath the defensive lineman's pads and drive him out of the hole." The critical tactic on the trap play in question was "to stay lower than him [defensive lineman Hand], but the opponent sensed the trap, got underneath the pads of the claimant, "drove up through [him]," and Palmer felt an injury. Palmer acknowledged repeatedly that he had executed that assignment many times, only this was one of the occasions the defensive man bested him "got to [Palmer] before [Palmer] could get to him." The only distinction between this occasion and the others, he acknowledged, was the injury Palmer "just had a bad result."

The record as a whole conclusively shows, therefore, that the function of a professional football lineman in a trap play is to maneuver the other player, to exploit his vulnerable posture. The lineman who establishes the lower stance succeeds. The unsuccessful lineman

---

6. There is doubt that by off balance Palmer meant (as the Industrial Commission majority assumes) the term in the usual sense of an awkward posture for the intended bodily function. The context in which Palmer used that term . . . and his testimony, insistently repeated, that "the object of an offensive guard in a trap block is to get underneath the defensive lineman's pads," "I should have been able to stay lower than him," and that on that account, "the defensive man got to [me] before [I] could get to [him]," all suggest an irresistible conclusion that Palmer used "off balance," not in the usual sense, but as a term of football art. The more reasonable import of that testimony (as our fuller discussion shows) is that the witness used "off balance" to describe a position of disadvantage of one lineman vis-a-vis the opponent lineman; in this case, a position not sufficiently low to strike the opponent beneath the protective shoulder pads and so dislodge him. We assume nevertheless for purpose of opinion that the evidence was probative of the finding of fact made by the majority that Palmer meant, and was, off balance in the usual sense.

Palmer in this instance can be jostled off balance. The method and purpose of that perfected skill are to find the opponent in an unexpected posture. The most accomplished among them, as Palmer concedes, will prevail only some of the times. The off balance position the claimant describes (and the Industrial Commission majority adopt as a premise for liability), therefore, was as usual an incident of the block assignment as not. This instance of play execution was no different than the many others, except for a bad result this time, Palmer was injured. The off balance posture, therefore, was not an unexpected occupational event, but rather as customary as not. Whatever strain resulted was an expected incident of the usual work task done in the usual way.

The original decision entered by the hearing judicial officer (and overruled by the Industrial Commission majority) denied the claim on the separate ground that injury was a normal incident of a professional football game.[8] That is a fact acknowledged by claimant Palmer. That is also a fact of judicial notice. Despite the advances in the design of protective equipment under the tutelage of sports medicine, football remains a dangerous pastime fraught with expectation of injury. The compensation law protects against injury the result of accident, that is: trauma from an unexpected or unforeseen event in the usual course of occupation, § 287.020.2. That enactment simply does not contemplate that the deliberate collision between human bodies constitutes an accident or that injury in the usual course of such an occupation is caused by an unexpected event.

* * *

Compensation denied.

Questions for Discussion

1. Is this decision (as well as *Rowe v. Baltimore Colts*, 53 Md.App. 526, 454 A.2d. 872 (1983)) an unwarranted effort by the court to introduce into workers' compensation, supposedly an accessible source of guaranteed benefits for occupational injuries, the same kinds of consensual limitations we saw earlier in tort cases such as *Hackbart*? Would Judge Shangler's reasoning exclude payment of compensation benefits to construction laborers with lower back problems or jackhammer operators with wrist and arm conditions? On the other hand, would extension to sports of the "cumulative trauma" basis for workers' compensation entitlement (see *Sielicki v. New York Yankees*, 388 So.2d 25 (Fla. Dist. Ct.App.1980)) mean that virtually every football player could collect benefits on retirement from the sport?

---

8. Administrative Law Judge Kaut concluded: "The testimony indicated being hurt was part and parcel of the game of football." That finding of fact, employed to deny the claim, was tantamount to a determination of law that an injury in the course of a professional football encounter is not a result of accident and so is outside the intendment of the compensation law. We agree with that insight.

Most reported judicial decisions regarding professional athletes and workers' compensation have actually involved the athletes' efforts, resisted by their clubs, to be *excluded* from coverage. The reason is that while workers' compensation benefits are guaranteed, they are also modest—geared to earnings levels of ordinary workers. At the same time as it mandates these specified benefits, the legislation ordains that this program will be the *exclusive* remedy for occupational injuries, at least to the extent of taking away the employee's right to sue the employer (or fellow employees). Although some states (e.g., Massachusetts) specifically exclude certain categories of athletes, there is no blanket exclusion of professional athletes:

> Finally, plaintiff argues that the Workmen's Compensation Act was not intended to apply to "high priced athletes." But the Act makes no such distinction. It applies to all employees regardless of their earnings. If professional athletes were excluded from coverage, then hundreds and possibly thousands of low as well as high priced athletes on Major and Minor League Teams would be deprived of the humanitarian benefits and protection the Act affords. My research has failed to disclose any cases excluding professional sports or players from Workmen's Compensation coverage. "A professional baseball league is a 'business operated for gain or profit' within the meaning of a compensation act, so as to entitle one employed as a player on one of the constituent clubs to compensation for injuries sustained in the course of employment."

Bayless v. Philadelphia Phillies,
472 F.Supp. 625, 631 (E.D.Pa. 1979).

However, a number of doctrines have evolved to limit the scope of workers' compensation exclusivity and to permit certain kinds of tort claims to proceed. The following case is illustrative.

GAMBRELL v. KANSAS CITY CHIEFS

Court of Appeals of Missouri, Kansas City District, 1978.

562 S.W.2d 163.

[Gambrell was a 1974 draft pick of the Kansas City Chiefs. When he reported to training camp, he was examined by team doctors and found fit to play. However, in an early exhibition game against the Rams, Gambrell suffered a permanently disabling injury to his back and neck. He filed for workers' compensation benefits and was awarded $5,250, which the Chiefs paid. Shortly thereafter Gambrell filed a multimillion dollar lawsuit charging fraud and deceit by the Chiefs and the team doctors. He alleged that the doctors knew or should have known of a pre-existing, physical disability, but that they deliberately concealed the disability from Gambrell to induce him to play for the

Chiefs. This decision dealt with the Chiefs' motion for summary dismissal on the ground that this was an accidental injury covered by workers' compensation.]

WASSERSTROM, JUDGE.

An appropriate starting point for a discussion of plaintiff's first and major proposition is the underlying philosophy of Workmen's Compensation legislation. This legislation rests on the foundation concept of the social desirability of giving employees a sure and speedy means of compensation for injuries suffered in the course of employment without the necessity of proving fault on the part of the employer. By way of exchange consideration to the employer, these Acts provide compensation in only a relatively modest amount and protect the employer by making that compensation exclusive of all other remedies. This latter consideration is reflected in Section 287.120 of the Missouri Act, which provides that the employer shall furnish compensation under the Act "and shall be released from all other liability therefore whatsoever" and that "[t]he rights and remedies herein granted to an employee, shall exclude all other rights and remedies. . . ."

This exclusivity, however, is qualified by a rule accepted in most jurisdictions that the Act bars common law suits for only those damages covered by the Act and for which compensation is made available under its provisions. This rule is followed in Missouri. Thus, under this rule the employee is still free despite the Act to bring suit at common law for wrongs not comprehended within the Workmen's Compensation Act, such as false imprisonment and defamation.

Most of the cases relied upon by plaintiff fall in this category. Thus, Skelton v. W. T. Grant Company, 331 F.2d 593 (5th Cir.1964) was an action for false arrest where the employee claimed damages for embarrassment and humiliation. Braman v. Walthall, 215 Ark.582, 225 S.W.2d 342 (1949), was a suit for slander in which the employee alleged damages for mental anguish, humiliation and damage to reputation. In each of those cases cited by plaintiff, and others like them, the damages for which the employee sought recovery were other than (or at least only to a very slight extent) physical injuries to the body of the type intended to be compensated by the pattern of the Workmen's Compensation Act.

The application of the rule just mentioned becomes much more difficult in a case by an employee for fraud and deceit where the plaintiff employee alleges that some fraud on the part of the employer interrelated with a bodily injury suffered by the employee in the course of his employment. Larson, a leading authority on the subject of Workmen's Compensation, discusses this problem at Section 68.32, p. 13–22, of his work where he cites and discusses decisions on this question from many jurisdictions and summarizes as follows: "The cases involving allegations of deceit, fraud, and false representation can best be sorted out by distinguishing those in which the deceit precedes and helps produce the injury, and those in which the deceit follows the

injury and produces a second injury or loss." Representative of the
latter class of cases, which are not precluded by the Workmen's Compensation Act, is Ramey v. General Petroleum Corporation, 343 P.2d
787 (Cal.1959), a case cited and relied upon by plaintiff in this case. In
Ramey, the plaintiff employee was caused by misrepresentations to wait
beyond the period of limitations before bringing suit against a third
party defendant, and he sued both his employer and the third party for
conspiracy to defraud him. The employer's defense of exclusivity of the
Workmen's Compensation Act was held not effective in its favor "under
the peculiar circumstances alleged." As pointed out by Larson, the
court in *Ramey* "sharply distinguished between the two injuries involved; first, the personal and physical injury compensated by the act;
and second, the fraud injury destroying a valuable right of action
against the third party by causing it to lapse because of the running of
the statute of limitations." Larson explains that cases falling within
this group are not precluded by the Workmen's Compensation Act
because "the alleged deceit has acted, not upon plaintiff's physical
condition, but upon his legal rights under the compensation act."

The case at bar does not fall within the category just discussed but
rather within Larson's first category "in which the deceit precedes and
helps produce the injury." As to this category, which represents the
situation with which we are dealing here, Larson states at page 13–22:
"In the first category, a tort action has usually been found barred, since
the deceit, so to speak, merges into the injury for which a compensation
remedy is provided." Larson's conclusion is persuasive and is supported by his analysis of the cases on the subject. A repetition of that
full analysis in this opinion would be redundant.

The conclusion that plaintiff's present common law action is precluded by the Workmen's Compensation Act remains valid despite the
fact that plaintiff in Counts II and IV prays for punitive damages.
True enough, the Act makes no provision for punitive damages, but
that omission was intentional and does not prevent the compensation
remedy from being exclusive. This point is well treated in Roof v.
Velsicol Chemical Corporation, 380 F.Supp. 1373, 1374 (D.C. Ohio 1974)
where the court held:

> The Ohio courts have apparently recognized no exception for ac-
> tions demanding punitive damages only. Nor would such an excep-
> tion be consistent with Ohio Workmen's Compensation Act. This
> Act provides statutory rights to relatively speedy and moderate
> reimbursement to workmen for injury sustained in work related
> activities. These rights were substituted for all previously avail-
> able remedies, on the theory that partial reimbursement is more
> socially desirable than the uncertainty of litigation for full compen-
> sation in such cases. To allow both compensation under the
> Workmen's Compensation Act and an action for punitive damages
> would clearly frustrate Ohio's policy of partial reimbursement.

* * *

Nor does plaintiff's allegation of conspiracy require any different result. No matter how his cause of action be framed, his claim ultimately reduces to one for bodily injuries for which compensation can be and actually has been had by plaintiff under the Workmen's Compensation Act.

Summary dismissal granted.

———

The Doug Williams case referred to earlier has sparked concern among football owners about application of the standard workers' compensation benefit structure to football players with high salaries and short careers. The NFL has pressed some state legislatures to revise their laws and place special limits on the financial benefits payable to players with permanent physical disabilities. Should states be receptive to the NFL argument? Should they tell the league that if it wants relief from the normal operation of workers compensation, it must accept exemption of the game from any feature of these laws. Would that step be in the best interests of owners or players?

D.   BACK TO TORTS

1.   Medical Malpractice

A number of jurisdictions have recently permitted tort suits against the employer for intentional infliction of physical injury, including deliberate concealment of medical information. In the sports context, a California appeals court upheld the player's tort claim in *Krueger v. San Francisco Forty Niners*, 234 Cal.Rptr. 579 (1987). The 49ers team doctor had consistently refrained from telling Krueger, the team's All–Pro tackle, of the serious long-term risks Krueger faced from continuing to play despite a series of knee injuries and operations. The court stated that deliberate failure by a team to disclose foreseeable risks to injured players, at least if done to induce him to keep playing, amounted to the tort of fraudulent concealment, and was actionable despite the exclusivity provision in the workers' compensation statute. A year later Krueger settled the litigation for more than $1 million from the 49ers.

Another potential escape valve from workers' compensation exclusivity is the "dual capacity" doctrine. This doctrine was first articulated in *Duprey v. Shane*, 39 Cal.2d 781, 249 P.2d 8 (1952), in which medical malpractice was alleged against the plaintiff's employer. In permitting the tort suit, the California Supreme Court reasoned that the workers' compensation statute barred employee suits against the employer only in its capacity as employer; the statute would not preclude suits against the employer in a different capacity—as provider

of medical services. This doctrine has subsequently been extended to several other contexts (for example, the employer as product manufacturer, see *Bell v. Industrial Vangas, Inc.*, 30 Cal.3d 268, 179 Cal.Rptr. 30, 637 P.2d 266 (1981)), and has been adopted in other states. However, in 1982 in its parent jurisdiction, California, the dual capacity doctrine was repealed by legislation. Thus, in *Hendy v. Losse*, 54 Cal.3d 723, 1 Cal.Rptr.2d 543, 819 P.2d 1 (1991), the California Supreme Court held that Hendy—who was injured in 1976 while playing for the San Diego Chargers and later reinjured and permanently disabled when the Chargers' team physician, Dr. Losse, sent him back to play too early— could not maintain a tort action against the Chargers or Dr. Losse.

Because the employer bears workers' compensation liability and pays for this insurance coverage, the employer (and its employees, such as Dr. Losse) gets the benefit of statutory protection from tort suits. In many athletic situations the team doctor is an "independent contractor" and thus is potentially exposed to suit, such as in the following case brought by two Chicago Bears players.

BRYANT v. FOX & CHICAGO BEARS

Court of Appeals of Illinois, First District, 1987.

162 Ill.App.3d 46, 113 Ill.Dec. 790, 515 N.E.2d 775.

JIGNATI, JUSTICE.

* * *

The documents before the trial court established the following facts concerning the relationship between the Bears and Dr. Fox. Dr. Fox was retained by the Bears in 1947 to render medical care to injured Bears' players. He was required to treat all injured players upon request, both during the regular season and the off season, and to report the treatment to the Bears' management. All anticipated treatment and surgery were discussed with the player and the Bears, either of whom could veto the proposed action. Dr. Fox did not bill the individual players for treatment. The record further shows that the agreement between the Bears and Dr. Fox required him to perform preseason physicals, which took place at Illinois Masonic Hospital. He was to attend all regular season games but could send a substitute subject to the Bears' approval. Dr. Fox was not obligated to attend preseason games or practices, but could do so at his convenience.

With respect to compensation and benefits, the record shows that Dr. Fox was paid an annual retainer of $12,000 which covered the preseason physicals and all treatment other than surgery. If surgery was required, Dr. Fox received fees for each surgery based upon the nature of the injury, the time involved and the complexity of the procedure. According to his discovery deposition, Dr. Fox had a very busy practice aside from the Bears and the compensation paid to him by the Bears represented "very much less" than 10% of his income.

Unlike employees of the Bears, Dr. Fox was not offered group medical insurance, life insurance or paid vacations, and was not invited to participate in the pension and profit-sharing plan. He was not provided with W–2 forms and the Bears never made Social Security deductions from his compensation. Dr. Fox stated that he considered himself to be an employee of Lakeview Orthopedic Associates, Ltd., and received W–2 forms from that corporation.

As previously stated, the exclusive-remedy provision bars an employee from bringing a common-law negligence action against a co-employee. It has been recognized that there is no clear line of demarcation between the status of employee and independent contractor. Illinois Appellate Court in Lister v. Industrial Commission stated a number of relevant factors in determining such status including the following: "[The] right to control the manner in which work is done; method of payment; right to discharge; skill required in the work to be done; who provides tools, materials, or equipment; whether the workmen's occupation is related to that of the alleged employer; and whether the alleged employer deducted for withholding tax." The single most important factor in determining the parties' relationship is the right to control the manner in which the work is done. An independent contractor has been defined as one who undertakes to produce a given result, without being controlled as to the method by which he attains that result.

* * *

In our view, the facts before the trial court on the Bears' motion to dismiss were insufficient to establish as a matter of law that Dr. Fox was an employee rather than an independent contractor. Although Dr. Fox was to treat injured players upon request, the evidence presented by the plaintiffs shows that the Bears were given little control over Dr. Fox's actions in accomplishing this result. He could send a substitute to regular season games if his attendance was not possible and was not obligated to attend practices or preseason games. Preseason physicals took place at Illinois Masonic Hospital using equipment belonging to the hospital. Although Dr. Fox was paid a relatively small retainer covering routine medical services, he would bill the Bears separately for each surgery he performed. Significantly, the plaintiffs presented evidence showing that the Bears did not withhold Social Security from Dr. Fox's compensation and did not provide him with W–2 forms. Dr. Fox stated that he received W–2 forms from Lakeview Orthopedic Associates, Ltd., and considered himself to be an employee of that corporation. A very small percentage of his practice was devoted to treating Bears' players. Finally, unlike employees of the Bears, Dr. Fox was not provided with benefits such as medical or life insurance, or a pension and profit-sharing plan.

Motion for dismissal denied.

————

Though the legal focus of the last several cases was on different techniques through which athletes could mount viable tort suits in the face of workers' compensation exclusivity, a common denominator in the actual litigation in *Bryant*, *Krueger*, *Buoniconti* and *Gathers* is that a principal target of the suit is the team physician. Several other notable athletes have successfully sued the team doctor for medical malpractice in the treatment (or non-treatment) of their injuries:

1. Dick Butkus, the Chicago Bears All–Pro linebacker, collected a $600,000 settlement for harm caused by cortisone injections into his injured knee.

2. Bill Walton, the Portland Trail Blazers All–Pro center, collected a substantial amount from the team doctor (not the Blazers) for the use of painkillers that aggravated his injured foot in 1977 and severely limited his subsequent career.[16]

3. Kenny Easley, the Seattle Seahawks' All–Pro safety, sued and collected from both the team doctor and the drug manufacturer after the drug he took for an injured ankle caused severe kidney damage and cut short his career.

4. Mike Robitaille, a defenseman for the Vancouver Canucks, won a substantial court award because the team and its doctor dismissed his complaints about an injury as purely mental, and subsequent play had permanently damaged his spinal cord. See *Robitaille v. Vancouver Hockey Club*, 3 W.W.R. 481 (B.C. C.A. 1981).

5. In *Classen v. Izquierdo*, 137 Misc.2d 489, 520 N.Y.S.2d 999 (1987), the court denied summary dismissal (based on assumption of risk) in a suit brought by the widow of a boxer who died in the tenth round of a 1979 boxing match at Madison Square Garden, after the ringside physician (appointed by the State Athletic Commission, not the Garden) examined the fighter at the end of the ninth round and let the match continue.

Why are so many medical malpractice suits brought by athletes against team doctors? Is this merely symptomatic of a broader explosion in malpractice claims? Or do special features of sports aggravate this problem? If the latter, are there any available cures?[17]

2. DEFECTIVE PRODUCTS AND HAZARDOUS FACILITIES

Besides the team physician, an attractive third-party target for a tort suit by an injured player is the manufacturer of a product used in

---

16. See Halberstam, *The Breaks of the Game*, note 6 above, 242–262, for a detailed account of the relationship between Walton and Dr. Bob Cook, the Blazers' team physician.

17. For the general issues posed by medical injuries and medical malpractice, see Paul C. Weiler, *Medical Malpractice on Trial* (Cambridge, Mass: Harvard University Press, 1991). For the distinctive issues posed by medical treatment of athletes and their injuries, see Jones, *College Athletes*, note 13, above; Joseph H. King, Jr., *The Duty and Standard of Care for Team Physicians*, 18 Houston L. Rev. 657 (1981); and Charles V. Russell, *Legal and Ethical Conflicts Arising from the Team Physician's Dual Obligations to the Athlete and Management*, 10 Seton Hall Legis. J. 299 (1987).

the game. Indeed, much of the "crisis" in products liability litigation and insurance costs generally has been fueled by suits brought by employees entitled to workers' compensation benefits.[18] Such litigation was facilitated by judicial adoption in the 1960s of strict liability for defective products, and by judicial expansion in the 1970s of what is considered a legally "defective" design or warning of product hazards. No sports product has been affected more by such suits than the helmets used in football, hockey, and elsewhere. The following case is illustrative.

BYRNS v. RIDDELL, INC.

Supreme Court of Arizona, 1976.

113 Ariz. 264, 550 P.2d 1065.

[After being injured by a blow to the head during a football game, the appellant, Byrns, sued the manufacturer of his football helmet. After extended testimony from witnesses about the nature of the impact and the design of the helmet, the defendant was granted a directed verdict, and Byrns appealed.]

HAYS, JUSTICE.

* * *

The law of strict liability in tort has followed a steady course of development since its early foundations in the case of Greenman v. Yuba Power Products, Inc., 377 P.2d 897 (1963). This court, in its decision in O.S. Stapley Co. v. Miller, 447 P.2d 248 (1968), adopted the theory of strict liability set forth in Restatement (Second) of Torts § 402A (1965). In view of the steady growth in this area of the law, coupled with the singularity of the facts in this case, a further review and analysis of the law of strict liability in tort is necessary. It is to this analysis that we first turn our attention.

The California Supreme Court in a recent decision in the case of Cronin v. J.B.E. Olson Corp., 501 P.2d 1153 (1972), rejected the "requirement that a plaintiff also prove that the defect made the product 'unreasonably dangerous' ..." a standard set forth in Restatement (Second) of Torts § 402A (1965). In O.S. Stapley, supra, we specifically adopted Restatement (Second) of Torts § 402A and its concept of an "unreasonably dangerous" defect, and as such rejected the California approach.

The term "unreasonably dangerous" has been considered by many courts in the jurisdictions that have adopted § 402A. A recent survey of cases which considered the concept of an "unreasonably dangerous" defect states that this concept is especially effective as a means of limiting the strict tort liability doctrine "in cases in which the issue is

18. See W. Kip Viscusi, *Reforming Products Liability* 182–86 (Cambridge, Mass: Harvard University Press, 1991); and Paul C. Weiler, *Workers' Compensation* and Product Liability: The Interaction of a Tort and a Non–Tort Regime, 50 Ohio St. L. J. 825 (1989).

the nature of the duty of a manufacturer with respect to safe design, or in situations in which injury does not follow as a matter of course from the defect, and in which there are serious questions as to the effect to be given harm producing conduct or misuse on the part of the injured person."

The United States District Court, Eastern District of Pennsylvania, adopted the following test of "unreasonable danger": "whether a reasonable manufacturer would continue to market his product in the same condition as he sold it to the plaintiff With knowledge of the potential dangerous consequences the trial just revealed." The court went on to state: "And in measuring the likelihood of harm one may consider the obviousness of the defect since it is reasonable to assume that the user of an obviously defective product will exercise special care in its operation, and consequently the likelihood of harm diminishes." Comment (i) Restatement (Second) of Torts § 402A further defines the element of an unreasonably dangerous defect from the viewpoint of the consumer in the following language:

> The article sold must be dangerous to an extent beyond that which would be contemplated by the ordinary consumer who purchases it, with the ordinary knowledge common to the community as to its characteristics.

* * *

The court in *Dorsey* subscribed to the following factor analysis prepared by Dean Wade to determine if a defect is unreasonably dangerous:

> (1) the usefulness and desirability of the product, (2) the availability of other and safer products to meet the same need, (3) the likelihood of injury and its probable seriousness, (4) the obviousness of the danger, (5) common knowledge and normal public expectation of the danger (particularly for established products), (6) the avoidability of injury by care in use of the product (including the effect of instructions or warnings), and (7) the ability to eliminate the danger without seriously impairing the usefulness of the product or making it unduly expensive.

We must add a note of caution at this point. No all-encompassing rule can be stated with respect to the applicability of strict liability in tort to a given set of facts. Each case must be decided on its own merits. The foregoing analysis is offered as an approach to the question of whether a defect is unreasonably dangerous.

* * *

The facts in this case as presented by appellant establish the possibility of a defect in the sling design of the TK—2 suspension system. This defect is established by the testimony of [witnesses] Irving and Rappaleayea regarding a series of tests conducted by them and measured by a standard known as the Z90.1 impact test. Rappleayea further established the defect based on his experience in testing the TK—2 while employed by appellee. This evidence is sufficient to raise the likelihood that reasonable men may reach different conclusions on the issue of an unreasonably dangerous defect in the sling design of the TK—2 helmet. The "bottoming out" defect might be of a type that a reasonable consumer would not contemplate.

There is a question of fact as to the place of impact, with a resulting question of causation in terms of the relationship between the impact and the injury. There is also a question as to the possibility of a substantial change in condition caused by the addition of a face mask manufactured and installed by someone other than appellee.

* * *

We hold that appellant established the presence of a defect in the helmet at the time it left the hands of the seller to the extent that reasonable minds could reach different conclusions as to that question of fact. Furthermore, we hold that appellant provided sufficient proof that a defect caused appellant's injury. The issue of causation is one of fact for the jury to decide.

The trial court concluded that the film, as a matter of law, left no reasonable doubt as to the place of impact, thus ruling that the appellant failed to show causation between the impact and the injury. We have carefully reviewed the portion of the moving picture film which contains the "onside" kick and cannot arrive at the same conclusion. The film is at best inconclusive on the question of the point of impact and in fact shows possible contact by two opposing players. We also note that Coach Hakes' testimony was similarly inconclusive in that he merely stated that appellant and an opposing player hit "head-to-head." The jury must be permitted to determine the issue of causation since there is a likelihood that reasonable minds could differ on the interpretation of the game film.

Appeal granted.

Questions for Discussion

1. In *Everett v. Warren*, 376 Mass. 280, 380 N.E.2d 653 (1978), the court listed several factors to be considered in determining whether the design of a hockey helmet was defective: "the gravity of the danger posed by the challenged design, the likelihood that such danger would occur, the mechanical feasibility of a safer alternative design, the cost of an improved design, and the adverse consequences to the product and to the consumer that would result from an alternative design." *Bryns* and *Everett* purport to use the Restatement (Second) of Tort's new mandate for *strict* products liability. How, if at all, does this doctrinal standard differ in practice from traditional negligence analysis? Is the threat of product litigation responsible for the sharp drop in the number of U.S. helmet manufacturers during the 1970s and 1980s?

2. In the summer of 1992, the National Hockey League changed its rules to make it no longer mandatory for players to wear helmets during the game. The NHL's objective was to encourage fan recognition of star players and thereby promote popular identification with the league's product. In Chapter 4 we asked whether the fact that the NHL took this step unilaterally, without first bargaining with the NHLPA, made this change illegal under federal labor law. Here we ask whether there might be a possible tort action if a young player, tempted by the prospect of a lucrative marketing deal, decided to play without a helmet and suffered severe brain damage when struck by a blow to the head. (In a number of jurisdictions, its NHL team is not subject to state or provincial workers' compensation law. But even if the local team is covered, does this statutory bar against suing the player's "employer" preclude a suit against the NHL itself?)

Still another potential third party target of liability for player injuries is the owner of the facility in which the game was played and whose hazardous condition may have contributed to the injury. The following case involved the Yankees' Elliot Maddox, who was injured on a wet Shea Stadium surface. The legal issue posed was whether the doctrine of "assumption of risk," which traditionally applied to sports but not to employment, should be a defense to a suit by a professional athlete.

MADDOX v. CITY OF NEW YORK

Supreme Court of New York, Appellate Division, 1985.

108 A.D.2d 42, 487 N.Y.S.2d 354.

PER CURIAM.

* * *

At an examination before trial, plaintiff Elliot Maddox (Maddox) said that after he chased and caught up with the ball in right centerfield and while he was in the process of throwing the ball back into the infield, his "left foot hit I guess it was a wet spot and took off" and his "right foot was stuck in the water, a mud puddle and wouldn't move and therefore, my right knee buckled." Maddox admitted that a game scheduled for the night before the accident had been canceled because of the weather and poor field conditions. He further admitted that earlier in the game in question he had observed the centerfield to be "awfully wet" with "some mud" and had even noticed "some standing water" above the grass line when he "went over after a fly ball once into right center." Maddox also stated that he had previously played on a wet field. Although Maddox claimed to have informed an unidentified grounds crew member of the aforementioned condition, he did not contend that he had requested not to play or to send in a replacement.

* * *

It has long been established in this State that participants in athletic events assume the risk of injury normally associated with the sport. Although, as Special Term noted, these cases essentially deal with amateur sports, we find no reason in the case at bar to depart from the stated rule.

In his examination before trial, Maddox admitted that he knew centerfield and right centerfield to be wet, that he continued to play ball in spite of this awareness and that he sustained injury after falling on a wet spot in right centerfield. Here, where the danger of falling on the wet playing field was obvious, it makes no sense to relieve plaintiffs from the effects of the doctrine of assumption of risk merely because Maddox was a professional, and not an amateur, player. To do so would be to hold a seasoned professional who is handsomely paid for his endeavors to a lower standard of care and place him in a more advantageous position than a less-seasoned amateur who receives no remuneration whatsoever. Simply stated, as long as there are, as here, open stadiums, natural grass fields, and rain, playing on an open wet field is part of the game of baseball, both for an amateur and a professional athlete. As much as one may sympathize with Maddox, the fact is that there is no cogent reason for holding assumption of risk inapplicable at bar and since the action accrued prior to September 1, 1975, as Special Term noted, that doctrine completely bars recovery.[1]

In an effort to avoid being called out at first base, however, Maddox argues that the assumption of risk doctrine is inapplicable at bar since his employer violated a "non-delegable duty with respect to the furnishing of a safe place to work," and in any event, his superiors forced him "to either work under unsafe conditions or abandon his work." We find these arguments unpersuasive.

It is quite true that a defense of assumption of risk (or contributory negligence) is unavailable to an employer who violates his statutory duty to supply an employee with a safe place to work. Nevertheless, to avail himself of a statute's protection, a plaintiff must demonstrate that he is within the class of persons the statute was designed to protect.

The applicable statutory provision at bar, Labor Law § 200, has its genesis in the Labor Law of 1909.... Clearly the purpose of these provisions was to protect a worker engaged in industry, and there is nothing in the subsequent amendments to these provisions or the legislative history that evinces an intent on the part of the Legislature to expand the class of protected individuals to include baseball players. Indeed, the language of present-day section 200 would suggest precisely the opposite.

---

1. When the Legislature enacted the comparative negligence statute (CPLR 1411), effective September 1, 1975, it abolished the doctrine of assumption of risk and contributory negligence as absolute bars to a plaintiff's recovery. Currently, assumption of risk and contributory negligence are termed "culpable conduct" and, if proven, operate only to proportionately reduce a plaintiff's recovery.

Initially, it bears noting that Labor Law § 200(1) does not expand coverage to workplaces beyond those enumerated in the predecessor section 20–b, cited above, but simply continues coverage to "[a]ll places to which this chapter applies." Furthermore, language added to subdivision 1 in 1962 ... suggests a continuing legislative concern for manual workers. Finally, the heading of section 200, a factor to be considered when interpreting the meaning of a statute entitled "General duty to protect the health and safety of employees; enforcement," and the statute defines an "[e]mployee" as "a mechanic, workingman or laborer working for another for hire" (Labor Law § 2[5]). Engaged as he was in the "national pastime" (see *Flood v. Kuhn*), Maddox can hardly be characterized as a mechanic, working person or laborer. Accordingly, from all indications, Maddox does not fall within the protected class of individuals, and the remedy, if any is indicated, is for legislative, not judicial action.

Even assuming, arguendo, that Maddox was within the class of protected individuals, he still could not invoke the protection of the statute. Although plaintiffs' complaints (each verified by an attorney) refer to defendants' failure, inter alia, to provide a safe workplace and properly construct, design and maintain the stadium, their motion papers fail to substantiate any fault on the part of Maddox's employer—a requisite to the invocation of section 200—which resulted in the wet condition of the playing field. We point out that defendants' motions were motions for summary judgment and it was incumbent upon Maddox to come forward with evidence that the accident resulted from defendants' breach of a duty to provide a workplace that was "so constructed, equipped, arranged, operated and conducted as to provide reasonable and adequate protection to the lives, health and safety of all persons employed therein" and not simply from the elements or other risks normally associated with the sport. This, plaintiffs failed to do.

Plaintiffs' second argument must also fail for lack of proof. It is indeed true, as Special Term noted, that continuation on a job after being directed by a superior to proceed under circumstances recognized as dangerous does not constitute assumption of the risk as a matter of law. Had Maddox been ordered to continue playing ball after informing his superiors of a dangerous condition, the results at bar might well have been different. The fact is, however, that there is not a scintilla of evidence in the record that Maddox was directed by a superior to continue playing after making known the field conditions or that he even requested to be relieved from playing. In fact, he merely contended in papers submitted at nisi prius that he informed an unidentified grounds crew member (or members) of the condition, and that he had previously commented to the team manager "a couple of times ... if the field was wet." Hence, on these motions for summary judgment, the proof offered by plaintiffs was insufficient to create a genuine issue of fact as to Maddox's assumption of the risk and Special Term erred in denying the motions, incorrectly inferring that Maddox "was acting within the confines of a superior's instructions.

Summary dismissal granted.

––––––

Another case, *Heldman v. Uniroyal Inc.*, 53 Ohio App.2d 21, 371 N.E.2d 57 (1977), framed as a suit about an allegedly defective product rather than a hazardous facility, yielded a similar result. Julie Heldman, while playing Virginia Wade in the Weightman Cup tennis competition between the United States and Great Britain, fell and severely injured her knee on Uniroyal's patented Roll–a–Way court surface. Heldman and other players had noted and complained about blistering and bubbling of the court surface, a problem that had been aggravated by rainfall collected in the seams. The court of appeals reversed a jury verdict in Heldman's favor, apparently on the ground that as a professional athlete she had a greater obligation than the recreational player to learn of hazardous conditions: professionals cannot simply follow the adage that "the show must go on." Is the judicial response to the *Maddox* and *Heldman* suits appropriate? What is the object of tort law in such cases?

Another unsuccessful tort action was launched by Hall–of–Famer Bubba Smith, who sued the Tampa Bay Sports Authority and the NFL after he suffered a career-ending knee injury when he crashed into and became entangled with the sideline downs marker. A jury rejected Smith's claim of defective equipment and negligent supervision of the markers.

E. DISABILITY AND THE RIGHT TO PLAY

Up to now we have examined the legal remedies available to players who have been hurt. Besides providing compensation after the fact, the law also seeks to provide incentives for the adoption of measures that will avoid injury before the fact. Suppose one measure adopted by a league is to screen out players with conditions that might make the player more susceptible to injury. Can these players obtain legal relief?

Illustrative of the legal dilemma is a case involving Mark Seay, another athlete playing for a Los Angeles college at the same time as Hank Gathers. Seay, the star wide receiver for the Long Beach State College football team, was struck by a stray bullet meant for a street gang member. Seay lost a kidney, and the bullet remained lodged near his heart. The school refused to allow Seay to return to the football team because of the risk of aggravating his injury. Seay sued, and on the eve of trial in March 1990, the school relented and allowed him to play football again—but only in return for a signed waiver of liability.[19]

19. The combination of the Gathers and the Seay cases inspired the article by Jones, *College Athletes,* note 13 above. Another insightful analysis of this legal di-

Precisely what source of legal relief might be available to someone such as Seay? One possibility is antitrust law. In the mid–1970s Greg Neeld starred in Canadian Junior A hockey even though he had sight in only one eye. Anticipating Neeld's wish to play professional hockey, the National Hockey League adopted a rule that rendered ineligible "any player with only one eye, or one of whose eyes has a vision of only 3–60ths or under." Neeld sued the NHL under the Sherman Antitrust Act and alleged that this rule amounted to an illegal concerted boycott of his services by the clubs. The Ninth Circuit Court of Appeals summarily dismissed the claim:

> Here, however, the record amply supports the reasonableness of the by-law. We agree with the District Court's conclusion that the primary purpose and direct effect of the League's by-law was not anticompetitive but rather safety.

> Neeld argues that if the rule of reason is applied then summary judgment was inappropriate because of alleged material issues of fact. Specifically, he contends the affidavits establish a disputed issue of fact whether a certain "safety mask" (designed especially for Neeld) would adequately protect Neeld from further injury.... Even assuming for purposes of argument that the adequacy of the "safety mask" for Neeld's protection is disputed, summary judgment was still appropriate since that fact alone would not affect the outcome of this case.

> The by-law is not motivated by anticompetitiveness and Neeld does not actually contend that it is. Further, any anticompetitive effect is at most *de minimis*, and incidental to the primary purpose of promoting safety, both for Neeld, who lost his eye in a hockey game, and for all players who play with or against him. We take judicial notice that ice hockey is a very rough physical contact sport, and that there is bound to be danger to players who happen to be on Neeld's blind side, no matter how well his mask may protect his one good eye. Also of some importance and legitimate concern to the League and its members is the possibility of being sued for personal injuries to Neeld himself or to others, if Neeld is permitted to play.

Neeld v. NHL, 594 F.2d 1297, 1300 (9th Cir.1979).

The next case illustrates a more precisely-tailored and more promising avenue of legal attack, using federal legislation that bars discrimination against the disabled.

lemma is Steven K. Derian, *Of Hank Gathers and Mark Seay: Who Decides Which* *Risks an Athlete Is Allowed to Undertake?* 5 UCLA J. of Ed. (1991).

WRIGHT v. COLUMBIA UNIVERSITY

United States District Court, Eastern District of Pennsylvania, 1981.

520 F.Supp. 789.

[Deprived since infancy of sight in one eye, John Wright became a star running back in high school football. However, when Wright enrolled at Columbia, the school barred him from its varsity football team. Wright sued, seeking a temporary restraining order on the ground that Columbia's action violated section 504 of the *Rehabilitation Act of 1973*, which stated that "no otherwise qualified handicapped individual ... shall, solely by reason of his handicap, be excluded from participation in, be denied benefits of, or be subject to discrimination under any program or activity receiving federal financial assistance."]

TROUTMAN, DISTRICT JUDGE.

* * *

Plaintiff has shown that irreparable harm will occur if the requested relief is not granted. Due to Columbia's freshman ineligibility rule, plaintiff may participate in the varsity football program for only a three-year period. Columbia's schedule includes a maximum of ten games per year commencing in early September and continuing through November. Team tryouts and practice will begin in mid-August and are a prerequisite to participation in the program for the remainder of the season. Hence, should plaintiff not be permitted to participate in the upcoming workout and tryouts, he will be deprived of the one opportunity which he has to participate fully in an intercollegiate football program. That deprivation may ultimately preclude a career in professional football.

Whether plaintiff has demonstrated a reasonable probability of success on the merits does not require him to show that a final decision after trial is wholly without doubt; rather, plaintiff must garner a *"prima facie* case of showing a reasonable probability." In the case at bar, plaintiff, who is handicapped within the meaning of the Act, must show at this stage of the proceedings that he is "otherwise qualified" to participate in a "program of activity receiving federal financial assistance" and that he is barred from participation therein "solely" by reason of his handicap.

Apparently, the parties here do not dispute that a private cause of action exists in plaintiff's favor and that, absent his handicap, he is "otherwise qualified" to participate in the intercollegiate football program. Defendant has not asserted that it would be forced to "lower or ... effect substantial modifications of standards" in order to accommodate plaintiff. Moreover, courts have enjoined high schools from preventing students with various handicaps from participating in sports programs.

* * *

In the case at bar, plaintiff has offered proof through a highly qualified ophthalmologist that no substantial risk of serious eye injury related to football exists. Moreover, plaintiff has testified that he seriously considered and appreciates the risks incident to playing football with impaired vision and willingly accepts them. As such, this case differs from Kampmeier v. Nyquist, 553 F.2d 296 (2d Cir.1977), where the court expressly pointed out that the plaintiffs had "presented little evidence, medical, statistical or otherwise" and accordingly denied the request of plaintiff's partially sighted students, for injunctive relief against public school authorities who denied their request to play contact sports. The court there also deferred to the defendant's exercise of discretion where the public school system acted pursuant to its "in loco parentis" powers to protect the well-being of the students who were not old enough to weigh the risks involved and to make a mature, informed decision.

In contrast, in the case at bar, plaintiff is obviously mature enough to make this important decision, and witnesses have so testified. Upon completion of one year at Columbia, plaintiff has attained a B grade point average and, as noted previously, has received many high school scholastic and athletic awards. In short, plaintiff is indeed an intelligent, motivated young man who is capable of making this decision which affects his health and well-being. Accordingly, defendant's reliance upon the *Kampmeier* case is, we believe, misplaced.

Neither Columbia University nor the public in general will be harmed by issuance of an injunction; in this case, a temporary restraining order. Columbia has never asserted that it would be harmed by plaintiff's intercollegiate football career; rather, it has premised its decision to exclude him on the understandable belief that plaintiff should avoid contact sports which might render him sightless and that he should properly concentrate on obtaining an education while at Columbia. Such motives, while laudably evidencing Columbia's concern for its students' well-being, derogate from the rights secured to plaintiff under Section 504, which prohibits "paternalistic authorities" from deciding that certain activities are "too risky" for a handicapped person. Here the defendant is acting "in a manner contrary to the express wishes of his parents who, together with their son, have reached a rational decision concerning the risk involved." ... Moreover, the public interest is enhanced by plaintiff's "dramatic example" that "hard work and dedication to purpose can overcome enormous odds."

Order granted.

In contrast, in *Colombo v. Sewanhaka Central High School,* 87 Misc.2d 48, 383 N.Y.S.2d 518 (1976), the court dismissed a challenge based on state educational law to a school board's ruling that a high school student with a hearing deficit in one ear could not play interscholastic sports.

Questions for Discussion

1. The Rehabilitation Act of 1973 applied to Columbia and its football program because the university received federal financial aid for a variety

of its programs. The Americans With Disabilities Act of 1990 now applies essentially the same substantive standards to a broad spectrum of private industry, irrespective of this connection with the government.[20] Assuming this antidiscrimination law applies to the National Hockey League, should the statute render illegal the rule that was upheld in *Neeld* under antitrust law? Could the NHL adopt measures that would reasonably accommodate Neeld's disability?

2. In the fall of 1990, Stephen Larkin (younger brother of the Cincinnati Reds' Barry Larkin) sought an order compelling Moeller High School to permit him to play football, despite medical evidence of a heart condition of the type that killed Hank Gathers. Should Larkin be allowed to play? Should the school be legally required to allow Larkin to play? Is it relevant that Larkin's older brother, Byron, starred at Xavier University and later played professional basketball in South America, despite having the same condition? Or that Terry Cumming of the San Antonio Spurs continues to play basketball despite an arrhythmic heart condition that requires regular medication?

3. An issue arose in the spring of 1992 about whether the pitcher for a women's college softball team should be permitted to play after she had become pregnant. Do schools have legitimate concerns, legal and nonlegal, about the athlete's decision? Could the school (or the NCAA) adopt a rule barring pregnant athletes from continuing to play? In what sports and at what stage of pregnancy? Is any such restriction precluded by the *Disabilities Act?* By Title IX which, as we saw in Chapter 9, bars gender discrimination in college sports?

4. In the fall of 1992, Magic Johnson abruptly ended his comeback to the NBA, reportedly because of adverse comments made by players and executives around the league about the risk of having an HIV-infected player on the court. Neither the NBA nor its Players Association had subscribed to that view and placed any obstacles in the way of Johnson's return to the game. Suppose, however, that the governing body in another sport sought to bar HIV-infected players. Would that action be permissible under the *Disabilities Act?* Does this depend on the nature and extent of the risk (and precisely what is the risk of HIV transmission)? On the nature of the sport (should boxers be treated differently than basketball players)? On whether less restrictive safeguards are available (and what might these be)?

5. In *Wright,* both Wright and his parents made it clear that they were "willing to release Columbia from potential liability it might incur by virtue of [Wright's] participation in the football program." (So also did Stephen Larkin and his parents.) Is this fact relevant to a legal judgment about whether the school's policy is discriminatory under federal law? Should a league be entitled to insist on such waivers of liability as a condition for eligibility of players who have a handicap disability? Consider the reasoning in the next case.[21]

20. See Long, note 13 above, at 189–97.

21. For academic commentary, see Andrew Manno, *A High Price to Compete: The Feasibility and Effect of Waivers Used* *to Protect Schools from Liability for Injuries to Athletes with High Medical Risks,* 79 Kentucky L.J. 867 (1991).

WAGENBLAST v. ODESSA SCHOOL DISTRICT

Supreme Court of Washington, 1988.

110 Wash.2d 845, 758 P.2d 968.

[Several school districts in the state of Washington, including Odessa and Seattle, adopted a policy that any student who wanted to participate in intercollegiate athletics (as well as their parents or guardians) must sign a standard form that purported to release the school district from "liability resulting from ordinary negligence that may arise in connection with the school district's interscholastic activities programs." Several students filed suit asking the state courts to declare these releases invalid. This was the response of the Washington Supreme Court.]

ANDERSON, JUSTICE.

* * *

We hold that the exculpatory releases from any future school district negligence are invalid because they violate public policy.

The courts have generally recognized that, subject to certain exceptions, parties may contract that one shall not be liable for his or her own negligence to another. As Prosser and Keeton explain:

> It is quite possible for the parties expressly to agree in advance that the defendant is under no obligation of care for the benefit of the plaintiff, and shall not be liable for the consequences of conduct which would otherwise be negligent. There is in the ordinary case no public policy which prevents the parties from contracting as they see fit, as to whether the plaintiff will undertake the responsibility of looking out for himself.

In accordance with the foregoing general rule, appellate decisions in this state have upheld exculpatory agreements where the subject was a toboggan slide, a scuba diving class, mountain climbing instruction, an automobile demolition derby, and ski jumping.

As Prosser and Keeton further observe, however, there are instances where public policy reasons for preserving an obligation of care owed by one person to another outweigh our traditional regard for the freedom to contract. Courts in this century are generally agreed on several such categories of cases.

Courts, for example, are usually reluctant to allow those charged with a public duty, which includes the obligation to use reasonable care, to rid themselves of that obligation by contract. Thus, where the defendant is a common carrier, an innkeeper, a professional bailee, a public utility, or the like, an agreement discharging the defendant's performance will not ordinarily be given effect. Implicit in such decisions is the notion that the service performed is one of importance to the public, and that a certain standard of performance is therefore required.

Courts generally also hold that an employer cannot require an employee to sign a contract releasing the employer from liability for job-related injuries caused by the employer's negligence. Such decisions are grounded on the recognition that the disparity of bargaining power between employer and employee forces the employee to accept such agreements.

Consistent with these general views, this court has held that a bank which rents out safety deposit boxes cannot, by contract, exempt itself from liability for its own negligence, and that if the circumstances of a particular case suggest that a gas company has a duty to inspect the pipes and fittings belonging to the owner of the building, any contractual limitation on that duty would be against public policy.

This court has also gone beyond these usually accepted categories to hold future releases invalid in other circumstances as well. It has struck down a lease provision exculpating a public housing authority from liability for injuries caused by the authority's negligence and has also struck down a landlord's exculpatory clause relating to common areas in a multi-family dwelling complex.

In reaching these decisions, this court has focused at times on disparity of bargaining power, at times on the importance of the service provided, and at other times on other factors. In reviewing these decisions, it is apparent that the court has not always been particularly clear on what rationale it used to decide what type of release was and was not violative of "public policy." Undoubtedly, it has been much easier for courts to simply declare releases violative of public policy in a given situation than to state a principled basis for so holding.

Probably the best exposition of the test to be applied in determining whether exculpatory agreements violate public policy is that stated by the California Supreme Court. In writing for a unanimous court, the late Justice Tobriner outlined the factors in Tunkl v. Regents of Univ. of Cal., 383 P.2d 441 (1963):

> Thus the attempted but invalid exemption involves a transaction which exhibits some or all of the following characteristics. It concerns a business of a type generally thought suitable for public regulation. The party seeking exculpation is engaged in performing a service of great importance to the public, which is often a matter of practical necessity for some members of the public. The party holds himself out as willing to perform this service for any member of the public who seeks it, or at least for any member coming within certain established standards. As a result of the essential nature of the service, in the economic setting of the transaction, the party invoking exculpation possesses a decisive advantage of bargaining strength against any member of the public who seeks his services. In exercising a superior bargaining power the party confronts the public with a standardized adhesion con-

tract of exculpation, and makes no provision whereby a purchaser may pay additional reasonable fees and obtain protection against negligence. Finally, as a result of the transaction, the person or property of the purchaser is placed under the control of the seller, subject to the risk of carelessness by the seller or his agents.

Obviously, the more of the foregoing six characteristics that appear in a given exculpatory agreement case, the more likely the agreement is to be declared invalid on public policy grounds. In the consolidated cases before us, all of the characteristics are present in each case. We separately, then, examine each of these six characteristics as applied to the cases before us.

1. The agreement concerns an endeavor of a type generally thought suitable for public regulation.

Regulation of governmental entities usually means self-regulation. Thus, the Legislature has by statute granted to each school board the authority to control, supervise, and regulate the conduct of interscholastic athletics. In some situations, a school board is permitted, in turn, to delegate this authority to the Washington Interscholastic Activities Association (WIAA) or to another voluntary nonprofit entity. In the cases before us, both school boards look to the WIAA for regulation of interscholastic sports. The WIAA handbook contains an extensive constitution with rules for such athletic endeavors. These rules cover numerous topics, including student eligibility standards, athletic awards, insurance, coaches, officials, tournaments and state championships. Special regulations for each sport cover such topics as turnout schedules, regular season game or meet limitations, and various areas of regulation peculiar to the sport, including the rule book governing the sport.

Clearly then, interscholastic sports in Washington are extensively regulated, and are a fit subject for such regulation.

2. The party seeking exculpation is engaged in performing a service of great importance to the public, which is often a matter of practical necessity for some members of the public.

This court has held that public school students have no fundamental right to participate in interscholastic athletics. Nonetheless, the court also has observed that the justification advanced for interscholastic athletics is their educational and cultural value. As the testimony of then Seattle School Superintendent Robert Nelson and others amply demonstrate, interscholastic athletics is part and parcel of the overall educational scheme in Washington. The total expenditure of time, effort and money on these endeavors makes this clear. The importance of these programs to the public is substantive; they represent a significant tie of the public at large to our system of public education. Nor can the importance of these programs to certain students be denied; as Superintendent Nelson agreed, some students undoubtedly remain in school and maintain their academic standing only because they can participate in these programs. Given this emphasis on sports by the public and the school system, it would be unrealistic to expect students to view athletics as an activity entirely separate and apart from the remainder of their schooling.[1]

This court observed in McCutcheon v. United Homes Corp., 486 P.2d 1093 (1971), that it makes little sense to insist that a worker have a safe place to work but at the same time to deny that worker a safe place to live. There is likewise little logic in insisting that one who entrusts personal property to a bank for safekeeping in a deposit box must be protected from the bank's negligence while denying such protection to a student who entrusts his or her person to the coaches, trainers, bus drivers and other agents of a school sports program.

In sum, under any rational view of the subject, interscholastic sports in public schools are a matter of public importance in this jurisdiction.

3. Such party holds itself out as willing to perform this service for any member of the public who seeks it, or at least for any member coming within certain established standards.

Implicit in the nature of interscholastic sports is the notion that such programs are open to all students who meet certain skill and eligibility standards. This conclusion finds direct support in the testimony of former Superintendent Nelson and the WIAA eligibility and nondiscrimination policies set forth in the WIAA handbook.

4. Because of the essential nature of the service, in the economic setting of the transaction, the party invoking exculpation possesses a decisive advantage of bargaining strength against any member of the public who seeks the services.

Not only have interscholastic sports become of considerable importance to students and the general public alike, but in most instances there exists no alternative program of organized competition. For instance, former Superintendent Nelson knew of no alternative to the Seattle School District's wrestling program. While outside alternatives exist for some activities, they possess little of the inherent allure of interscholastic competition. Many students cannot afford private programs or the private schools where such releases might not be employed. In this regard, school districts have near-monopoly power. And, because such programs have become important to student participants, school districts possess a clear and disparate bargaining strength when they insist that students and their parents sign these releases.

5. In exercising a superior bargaining power, the party confronts the public with a standardized adhesion contract of exculpation, and makes no provision whereby a purchaser may pay additional reasonable fees and obtain protection against negligence.

---

1. This intimate relationship between interscholastic sports and other aspects of public education serves to distinguish this case from those involving private adult education for hazardous activities, e.g., skydiving and mountain climbing.

Both school districts admit to an unwavering policy regarding these releases; no student athlete will be allowed to participate in any program without first signing the release form as written by the school district. In both of these cases, students and their parents unsuccessfully attempted to modify the forms by deleting the release language. In both cases, the school district rejected the attempted modifications. Student-athletes and their parents or guardians have no alternative but to sign the standard release forms provided to them or have the student barred from the program.

6. The person or property of members of the public seeking such services must be placed under the control of the furnisher of the services, subject to the risk of carelessness on the part of the furnisher, its employees or agents.

A school district owes a duty to its students to employ ordinary care and to anticipate reasonably foreseeable dangers so as to take precautions for protecting the children in its custody from such dangers. This duty extends to students engaged in interscholastic sports. As a natural incident to the relationship of a student athlete and his or her coach, the student athlete is usually placed under the coach's considerable degree of control. The student is thus subject to the risk that the school district or its agent will breach this duty of care.

In sum, the attempted releases in the cases before us exhibit all six of the characteristics denominated in Tunkl v. Regents of Univ. of Cal. Because of this, and for the aforesaid reasons, we hold that the releases in these consolidated cases are invalid as against public policy.

Declaration granted.

Questions for Discussion

1. In light of what you have read earlier in the chapter, precisely how much legal significance is there to an explicit release by players of a team's or league's liability for "ordinary negligence" for injury during a sporting event?

2. Do you agree with the Washington court's view of what is sensible public policy towards such contractual releases by high school athletes? Is the same view appropriate for releases by college athletes? Professional athletes? Consider the following waiver NFL teams sometimes demand from their players:

NFL

Waiver and Release

1. I have been informed by the Club physician that I have the following physical condition(s).

2. The physical condition(s) set forth above existed prior to the date of the physical examination for the current season.

3. I have received a full explanation from the Club physician that to continue to play professional football may result in deterioration of such pre-existing physical condition(s) rendering me physically unable

to perform the services required of me by my NFL Player Contract executed this date.

4. I fully understand the possible consequences of playing professional football with the physical condition(s) set forth in paragraph 1 above. Nevertheless, I desire to continue to play professional football and hereby assume the risk of the matters set forth in paragraph 3 above.

5. Because I desire to play professional football for the Club, I hereby waive and release the Club, the Club physician, its trainers and the National Football League from any and all liability and responsibility in the event I become physically unable to perform the services required of me by my NFL Player Contract executed this date because of a deterioration or aggravation of the physical condition(s) set forth in paragraph 1 above.

How would the *Odessa* court treat this release form?

3. Would your verdict differ if the school district (or college or professional team) provided and paid for catastrophic injury insurance (such as the NCAA policy described earlier) in return for *mandatory* waiver of tort liability? As an inducement for a *voluntary* waiver of liablity? [22]

---

22. For a broader discussion of these questions, see Jeffrey O'Connell, *A "Neo No-Fault" Contract in Lieu of Tort: Preaccident Guarantees of Postaccident Settlement Offers,* 73 California L.Rev. 898 (1985).

Bibliographic Index

Bork, Robert, Ancillary Restraints and the Sherman Act, 15 Antitrust L.J. 211 (1959), 372

Bork, Robert, The Antitrust Paradox: A Policy at War with Itself (New York: Basic Books, 1978), 128, n. 3, 590

Brody, Burton F., NCAA Rules and Their Enforcement: Not Spare the Rod and Spoil the Child; Rather Switch the Values and Spare the Sport, 1982 Arizona St.L.J. 109, p. 513, n. 9

Brown, Lori J., The Battle: From the Playing Field to the Courtroom— *United States Football League v National Football League,* 18 Toledo U.L.Rev. 871 (1987), 478, n. 10

Browning, Robert, A History of Golf: The Royal and Ancient Game (London: J.M. Dent & Sons, Ltd., 1955), 658, n. 2

Burgess, Paul C. and Daniel L. Marburger, Bargaining Power and Major League Baseball, in Paul M. Sommers, Diamonds Are Forever: The Business of Baseball (Washington, D.C.: Brookings, 1992), 273, n. 20

Byrne, Jim, The $1 League: The Rise and Fall of the USFL (New York: Simon and Schuster, 1986), 444, n. 3, 478, n. 10

Calabresi, Guido and A. Douglas Melamed, Property Rules, Liability Rules, and Inalienability: One View of the Cathedral, 85 Harvard L.Rev. 1089 (1972), 99, n. 15

Carlsen, Chris, Violence in Professional Sports, in Gary Uberstine, ed., Law of Professional and Amateur Sport (Deerfield, Ill.: Clark, Boardman, and Callaghan, 1991), 710, n. 1, 727, n. 7

Carlsen, Chris & Matthew Shane Walker, The Sports Court: A Private System to Deter Violence in Professional Sports, 55 Southern Cal.L.Rev. 399 (1982), 730, n. 8

Carpenter, R. Vivian & Linda Jean Acosta, Back to the Future: Reform with a Woman's Voice, Academe 23 (January–February 1991), 648, n. 28

Carter, Steven, Reflections of An Affirmative Action Baby (New York: Basic Books, 1991), 42, n. 18

Celler Report, *see* Committee of the Judiciary

Chaffee, Zechariah, Jr., The Internal Affairs of Associations Not for Profit, 43 Harv.L.Rev. 993 (1930), 28, n. 9

Chamallas, Martha, Evolving Conceptions of Equality Under Title XII; Disparate Impact and the Demise of the Bottom Line Principle, 31 UCLA Law Rev. 305 (1983), 542, n. 29

Chandler, Joan M., Sport as TV Product: A Case Study of "Monday Night Football," in Paul Staudohar and James A. Mangan, eds., The Business of Professional Sports (Urbana, Ill.: University of Illinois Press, 1991), 415, n. 16

Cirace, John, An Economic Analysis of Antitrust Law's Natural Monopoly Cases, 88 West Virginia L.Rev. 677 (1986), 493, n. 13

Closius, Philip J., Not at the Behest of Non Labor Groups: A Revised Prognosis for a Maturing Sports Industry, 24 Boston College L.Rev. 341 (1983), 165, n. 6

Collins, Bud, My Life with the Pros (New York: E.P. Dutton, 1989), 671, n. 6

Committee of the Judiciary, Report of the Subcommittee on Study of Monopoly Power of the Committee of the Judiciary, 82nd Congress, Organized Baseball (Washington, D.C., 1952) (Celler Report), 1, n. 1, 12, n. 7, 64, n. 1, 100, n. 16

Cox, Archibald, Labor and the Antitrust Laws—A Preliminary Analysis, 104 U. of Pa.L.Rev. 252 (1955), 167, n. 7

Cox, Archibald, The Duty to Bargain in Good Faith, 71 Harvard L.Rev. 1401 (1958), 245, n. 11

Cox, Landis, Targeting Sports Agents with the Mail Fraud Statute: *United States v Norby Walters & Lloyd Bloom,* 41 Duke L.J. 1157 (1992), 343, n. 23

Cozzillio, Michael J., The Athletic Scholarship and the College National Letter of Intent: A Contract by Any Other Name, 35 Wayne L.Rev. 1275 (1989), 551, n. 35, 583, n. 6

Crain, Marion, Expanded Employee Drug Testing Programs and the Public Good: Big Brother at the Bargaining Table, 64 New York U.L.Rev. 1286 (1989), 42, n. 20

Cross, Harry M., The College Athlete and the Institution, 38 Law & Contemp. Probs. 151 (Winter–Spring 1973), 737, n. 11

Cruise, David and Alison Griffiths, New Worth: Exploding the Myths of Pro Hockey (New York: Viking Penguin, 1991), 64, n. 1, 96, n. 12, 180, n. 10, 444, n. 3

Culhane, John G., Reinvigorating Educational Malpractice Claims: A Representational Focus, 67 Washington L.Rev. 349 (1992), 566, n. 37

Daly, George G., The Baseball Player's Labor Market Revisited, in Paul M. Sommers, ed., Diamonds Are Forever: The Business of Baseball (Washington, D.C.: Brookings, 1992), 352, n. 2

Dau–Schmidt, Kenneth G., Union Security Agreements Under the NLRA: The Statute, the Constitution and the Court's Opinion in Beck, 27 Harvard J. on Legis. 51 (1990), 275, n. 22.

Davis, Lance E., Self–Regulation in Baseball: 1909–71 in Roger Noll, ed., Government and the Sports Business (Washington, D.C.: Brookings, 1974), 472, n. 8

Davis, Robert N., Athletic Reform: Missing the Bases in University Athletics, 20 Capital Univ.L.Rev. 597 (1991), 649, n. 29

Davis, Timothy, Examining Educational Malpractice Jurisprudence: Should a Cause of Action Be Created for Student Athletes, 69 Denver U.L.Rev. 57 (1992), 566, n. 38

Dealy, Francis X., Jr., Win At Any Cost: The Sellout of College Athletics (New York, Birch Lane Press, 1990), 495, n. 1, 531, n. 21, 622, n. 19

Dell, Donald, Minding Other People's Business (New York: Villard, 1989), 290, n. 4

Demmert, Henry G., The Economics of Professional Team Sports (Lexington, Mass.: D.C. Heath, 1973), 352, n. 2

DeNicola, Ronald A. & Scott Mendeloff, Controlling Violence in Professional Sports: Rule Reform and the Federal Professional Sports Violence Commission, 21 Duquesne L.Rev. 843 (1983), 730, n. 8

Derian, Steven K., Of Hank Gathers and Mark Seay: Who Decides Which Risks an Athlete Is Allowed to Undertake?, 5 UCLA J. of Ed. ___ (1991), 759, n. 19

Dubin, Hon. Charles L., Commission of Inquiry Into the Use of Drugs and Banned Practices Intended to Increase Athletic Performance (Ottawa: Government of Canada, 1990), 699, n. 10

Durland, Dan, Jr. and Paul M. Sommers, Collusion in Major League Baseball: An Empirical Test, 14 J. of Sport Behavior 19 (1991), 277, n. 24

Dworkin, James B., Owners Versus Players: Baseball and Collective Bargaining (Dover, Mass.: Auburn House, 1981), 272, n. 19

Eagleson, Alan (with Scott Young), Power Play: The Memoirs of A Hockey Czar (Toronto, Canada: McClelland and Stewart, 1991), 180, n. 10

Earle, Peter G., The Impasse Doctrine, 66 Chicago–Kent L.Rev. 407 (1988), 246, n. 13

Easterbrook, Frank A., The Limits of Antitrust, 63 Tex.L.Rev. 1 (1984), 436, n. 17

Edwards, Harry, The Collegiate Athletic Arms Race: Origins and Implications of the "Rule 48" Controversy, in Richard Lapchick, ed., Fractured Focus: Sport as a Reflection of Society (Lexington, Mass.: D.C. Heath, 1986), 538, n. 25

Ehrhardt, Charles W. and J. Mark Rodgers, Tightening the Defense Against Offensive Sports Agents, 16 Florida State U.L.Rev. 633 (1988), 341, n. 20

Ensor, Richard J., Comparison and Arbitration Decisions Involving

Termination in Major League Baseball, the National Basketball Association, and the National Football League, 32 Saint Louis U.L.J. 135 (1987), 67, n. 4

Evans, Richard, Open Tennis: 1968–1989 (New York: Viking, 1990), 671, n. 6

Faurot, David J. and Stephen McAllister, Salary Arbitration and Pre–Arbitration Negotiation in Major League Baseball, 45 Ind. and Labor Rel.Rev. 697 (1992), 274, n. 21

Feinstein, John, Hard Courts: Real Life on the Professional Tennis Tours (New York: Villard Books, 1992), 671, n. 6

Feller, David B., A General Theory of the Collective Bargaining Agreement, 61 California L.Rev. 663 (1973), 259, n. 16

Finkin, Matthew W., The Limits of Majority Rule in Collective Bargaining, 64 Minn.L.Rev. 183 (1980), 266, n. 17

Fleischer, Arthur A., III, Brian L. Goff & Robert D. Tollison, The National Collegiate Athletic Association: A Study in Cartel Behaviour (Chicago: Univ. of Chicago Press, 1992), 569, n. 1, 570, n. 3

Fort, Rodney, Pay and Performance: Is the Field of Dreams Barren?, in Paul M. Sommers, Diamonds Are Forever: The Business of Baseball (Washington, D.C.: Brookings, 1992), 243, n. 9

Fraley, Robert E. and Fred Russell Harwell, The Sport's Lawyer's Duty to Avoid Differing Interests: A Practical Guide to Responsible Representation, 11 Hastings Comm. and Ent.L.J. 165 (1989), 311, n. 12

Frederick, David M., William H. Kaempfer and Richard L. Wobbekind, Salary Arbitration as a Market Substitute, in Paul M. Sommers, Diamonds Are Forever: The Business of Baseball (Washington, D.C.: Brookings, 1992), 272, n. 19

Freeman, Richard B. and James L. Medoff, What Do Unions Do? (New York: Basic Books, 1984), 243, n. 10

Friedman, Milton and Rose Friedman, Free to Choose: A Personal Statement (New York: Harcourt Brace Jovanovich, 1979), 65, n. 2

Funk, Gary, Major Violation: The Unbalanced Priorities in Athletics and Academics (Champaign, Ill.: Leisure Press, 1991), 495, n. 1

Garrett, Robert Alan & Philip R. Hochberg, Sports Broadcasting, in Gary Uberstine, ed., Law of Professional and Amateur Sport (Deerfield, Ill.: Clark, Boardman, and Callaghan, 1991), 415, n. 16

Goldman, Lee, Sports, Antitrust and the Single Entity Theory, 63 Tulane L.Rev. 751 (1989), 353, n. 3, 385, n. 7, 620, n. 16

Goldman, Lee, The Labor Exemption to the Antitrust Laws as Applied to Employers' Labor Market Restraints in Sports and Non–Sports Markets, 1989 Utah L.Rev. 617, pp. 165, n. 6, 199, n. 15

Gould, William B., Judicial Review of Labor Arbitration Awards: The Aftermath of AT & T and Misco, 64 Notre Dame L.Rev. 464 (1989), 259, n. 16

Grauer, Myron C., Recognition of the National Football League as a Single Entity Under Section 1 of the Sherman Act: Implications of the Consumer Welfare Model, 82 Michigan L.Rev. 1 (1983), 353, n. 3, 385, n. 7

Grauer, Myron C., The Use and Misuse of the Term "Consumer Welfare:" Once More to the Mat on the Issues of Single Entity Status for Professional Sports Leagues Under Section 1 of the Sherman Act, 64 Tulane L.Rev. 71 (1989), 353, n. 3, 385, n. 7

Gray, Charles, Keeping the Home Team at Home, 74 California L.Rev. 1329 (1986), 400, n. 11, 407, n. 13

Gray, John A., Section 1 of the Sherman Act and Control Over NFL Franchise Locations: The Problem of Opportunistic Behavior, 25 Amer.Bus.L.J. 123 (1987), 410, n. 14

Greene, Linda, The New NCAA Rules of the Game: Academic Integrity or Racism?, 28 St. Louis Univ. L.J. 101 (1984), 538, n. 25

Greenspan, David, College Football's Biggest Fumble: The Economic Impact of the Supreme Court's Decision in *National Collegiate Athletic Association v Board of Regents of the University of Oklahoma*, 33 Antitrust Bulletin 1 (1988), 603, n. 9

Guttman, Alan, The Olympics: A History of the Modern Games (Urbana, Ill.: University of Illinois Press, 1992) 690, n. 9, 707, n. 13

Halberstam, David, The Breaks of the Game (New York: Alfred Knopf, 1981), 726, n. 6, 751, n. 17

Harper, Michael C., Leveling the Road from *Borg–Warner* to *First–National Maintenance:* The Scope of Mandatory Bargaining, 68 Virginia L.Rev. 1447 (1982), 246, n. 14

Harper, Michael C. and Ira C. Lupu, Fair Representation as Equal Protection, 98 Harvard L.Rev. 1211 (1985), 266, n. 17

Harris, David, The League: The Rise and Decline of the NFL (New York: Bantam Books, 1988), 1, n. 1, 64, n. 1, 87, n. 10, 91, n. 11, 174, n. 8, 206, n. 1, 314, n. 13, 351, n. 1, 354, n. 4, 364, 399, n. 10, 444, n. 3

Hart–Nibbing, Nand & Clement Cottingham, The Political Economy of College Sports (Lexington, Mass.: D.C. Heath, 1986), 569, n. 1

Hauser, Thomas, Muhammad Ali: His Life and Times (New York: Simon and Schuster, 1991), 669, n. 5

Heckman, Diane, Women & Athletics: A Twenty Year Retrospective on Title IX, 9 Univ. of Miami Enter. & Sports L.Rev. 2 (1992), 622, n. 18

Heidt, Robert H., "Don't Talk of Fairness": The Chicago School's Approach Toward Disciplining Professional Athletes, 61 Indiana L.J. 53 (1985), 665, n. 4

Herz, Gerard & Robert C. Baker, Professional Athletes and the Law of Workers' Compensation, in Gary Uberstine, ed., Law of Professional and Amateur Sport (Deerfield, Ill.: Clark, Boardman, and Callaghan, 1991), 730, n. 9, 740, n. 15

Holmes, Oliver Wendell, Jr., The Path of the Law, 10 Harvard L.Rev. 457 (1887), 120, n. 21

Hoosie, Philip M., Necessities: Racial Bias in American Sports (New York: Random House, 1989), 41, n. 17

Horowitz, Ira, Sports Broadcasting, in Roger Noll, ed., Government and the Sports Business (Washington, D.C.: Brookings, 1974), 415, n. 16

Horrow, Richard, Sports Violence: The Interaction Between Private Law–Making and the Criminal Law (Westport, Conn.: Greenwood Pub., 1980), 727, n. 7, 730, n. 8

Hovenkamp, Hebert, Economics and Federal Antitrust Law (St. Paul, Minn.: West Publishing, 1985), 445, n. 4, 446, n. 5

Jacobs, Michael S., Professional Sports Leagues, Antitrust and the Single Entity Theory: A Defense of the Status Quo, 67 Indiana L.J. 25 (1991), 353, n. 3, 385, n. 7

Jacobs, Michael S. and Ralph Winter, Antitrust Principles and Collective Bargaining: Of Superstars in Peonage, 81 Yale L.J. 1 (1971), 165, n. 6

Jennings, Marianne M. and Lynn Ziioko, Student Athletes, Athlete Agents and Five Year Eligibility; An Environment of Contractual Interference, Trade Restraint and High Stake Payments, 66 U. of Detroit L.Rev. 179 (1989), 342, n. 21, 583, n. 5

Jerry, Robert H. and Donald E. Knebel, Antitrust and Employer Restraints in Labor Markets, 6 Indus.Rel.L.J. 173 (1984), 165, n. 6

Johnson, Arthur T. and James Frey, eds., Government and Sports (Totawa, N.J.: Rownen & Allenheld, 1985), 406, n. 12

Johnson, Arthur T., The Sports Franchise Relocations Issue and Public Policy Response, in Arthur T. Johnson and James Frey, eds., Government and Sports (Totawa, N.J.: Rownen & Allenheld, 1985), 406, n. 12

Johnson, Constance, Defense Against the NCAA, U.S. News & World Report, Jan. 13, 1992, pp. 25, 615

versity Press, 1971), 64, n. 1, 72, n. 6, 100, n. 16, 108, n. 19, 444, n. 3

Seymour, Harold, Baseball: The Golden Age, (New York: Oxford University Press, 1971), 1, n. 1, 7, n. 6, 64, n. 1, 100, n. 16, 107, n. 17, 113, n. 10, 444, n. 3

Shedlin, Leslie K., Regulation of Disclosure of Economic and Financial Data and the Impact on the American System of Labor–Management Relations, 41 Ohio State L.J. 441 (1980), 246, n. 12

Shriver, Pam, Frank DeFord & Susan Adams, Passing Shots (New York: McGraw-Hill, 1987), 671, n. 6

Shropshire, Kenneth L., Agents of Opportunity: Sports Agents and Corruption in Collegiate Sports (Philadelphia: University of Pennsylvania Press, 1990), 289, n. 1, 316, n. 14, 341, n. 20

Shropshire, Kenneth L., Opportunistic Sports Franchise Relocations: Can Punitive Damages in Actions Based Upon Contract Strike a Balance?, 22 Loyola of LA L.Rev. 569 (1989), 391-2, n. 9

Sifford, Charlie with James Gullo, "Just Let Me Play": The Story of Charlie Sifford, the First Black PGA Golfer (Latham, N.Y.: British American Publishing Co., 1992), 663, n. 3.

Silberstein, Eileen, Union Decisions on Collective Bargaining Goals: A Proposal for Interest Group Participation, 77 Michigan L.Rev. 1485 (1979), 239, n. 8

Simon, Robert L., Fair Play: Sport, Values, and Society (Boulder, Col.: Westview Press, 1991), 46, n. 21, 547, n. 33, 622, n. 18, 711, n. 3

Simson, Vyv & Andrew Jennings, The Lords of the Rings (Simon & Schuster, 1992), 691, n. 9, 706, n. 12

Smith, Rodney K., An Academic Game Plan for Reforming Big-Time Intercollegiate Athletics, Denver U.L.Rev. 213 (1990), 495, n. 1, 606, n. 11, 620, n. 16

Smith, Rodney K., The National Collegiate Athletic Association's Death Penalty: How Educators Punish Themselves and Others, 62 Indiana L.J. 985 (1985), 529, n. 19

Smith, Ronald, Sports and Freedom: The Rise of Big–Time College Athletics (New York: Oxford University Press, 1988), 496, n. 3, 525, n. 18, 554, n. 36, 738, n. 12

Sobel, Lionel S., The Regulation of Player Agents and Lawyers, 39 Baylor L.Rev. 701 (1987), 289, n. 1

Sobel, Lionel S., The Regulation of Player Agents and Lawyers, in Gary Uberstine, ed., Law of Professional and Amateur Sports (Deerfield, Ill: Clark, Boardman, and Callaghan, 1991), 289, n. 1, 325, n. 17

Sokolove, Michael Y., Hustle: The Myth, Life and Lies of Pete Rose (New York: Simon and Schuster, 2d ed., 1992), 2, n. 3

Sommers, Paul, ed., Diamonds Are Forever: The Business of Baseball (Washington, D.C.: Brookings, 1992), passim

Sperber, Murray, College Sports, Inc., The Athletic Department versus the University (New York: Henery Holt, 1990), 495, n. 1, 524, n. 16, 551, n. 34

Spink, J.G. Taylor, Judge Landis and 25 Years of Baseball (St. Louis, Mo.: Sporting News Press, 1974), 1, n. 1

Staudohar, Paul, The Sports Industry and Collective Bargaining (Ithaca, NY: ILR Press, 1989), 127, n. 1, 181, n. 12, 206, n. 1

Staudohar, Paul and James A. Mangan, eds., The Business of Professional Sports (Urbana, Ill.: University of Illinois Press, 1991), 127, n. 1

Steinberg, Leigh, National Football League, in Gary Uberstine, ed., Law of Professional and Amateur Sport (Deerfield, Ill.: Clark, Boardman, and Callaghan, 1991), 292, n. 6

Steinberg, Ted, in Gary Uberstine, ed., Law of Professional and Amateur Sport (Deerfield, Ill.: Clark, Boardman, and Callaghan, 1991), 292, n. 6

Stiglitz, Jan, NCAA Based Agent Regulation: Who Are We Protecting?, 67 North Dakota L.Rev. 215 (1991), 349, n. 24

Sullivan, Louis A., Antitrust (1977), 476, n. 36

Sullivan, Neil J., The Dodgers Move West, (New York: Oxford University Press, 1987), 399, n. 10

Summers, Clyde W., Legal Limitations on Union Discipline, 64 Harvard L.Rev. 1049 (1951), 28, n. 9

Summers, Clyde W., The Individual Employee's Rights Under the Collective Bargaining Agreement: What Constitutes Fair Representation?, 127 U.Pennsylvania L.Rev. 251 (1977), 266, n. 17

Summers, Clyde W., The Law of Union Discipline: What the Courts Do In Fact, 70 Yale L.J. 175 (1960), 28, n. 9

The Supreme Court, 1988 Term— Leading Cases, 103 Harvard L.Rev. 137 (1989), 506, n. 5

Symposium, Drug Testing in the Workplace, 33 William and Mary L.Rev. 1 (1991), 55, n. 23

Symposium, The Reform of Big-Time Intercollegiate Athletics, 20 Capital L.Rev. 541 (1991), 495, n. 1

Tatum, Jack with William Kushner, They Call Me Assassin (New York: Everest House, 1979), 725, n. 5

Tobin–Rubio, Lisa J., Eminent Domain and the Commerce Clause Defense, 41 U. of Miami L.Rev. 1185 (1987), 407, n. 13

Tokarz, Karen L., Separate But Unequal Educational Sports Programs: The Need for a New Theory of Equality, 1 Berkeley Women's L.J. 201 (1985), 639, n. 23

Tokarz, Karen L., Sex Discrimination in Amateur and Professional Sports, in Gary Uberstine, ed., Law of Professional and Amateur Sport (Deerfield, Ill.: Clark, Boardman, and Callaghan, 1991), 622, n. 18

Travalio, Gregory M., Values and Schizophrenia in University Athletics, 20 Capital Univ.L.Rev. 587 (1991), 547, n. 33

Tribe, Laurence, American Constitutional Law (Mineola, N.Y.: Foundation Press, 2d ed., 1988), 506, n. 7

Trope, Mike, Necessary Roughness (Chicago: Contemporary Books, 1987), 343, n. 22

Tygiel, Jules, Baseball's Great Experiment: Jackie Robinson and His Legacy (New York: Random House, 1983), 39, n. 13

Uberstine, Gary, ed., Law of Professional and Amateur Sport (Deerfield, Ill.: Clark, Boardman, and Callaghan, 1991), passim

Underwood, John, The Death of an American Game: The Crisis in Football (Boston: Little Brown, 1979), 725, n. 5

Uhlir, Ann, Athletics and the University: The Post–Woman's Era, Academe 25 (July–August, 1987), 648, n. 28

Vandervelde, Lea S., The Gendered Origins of the Lumley Doctrine: Binding Men's Consciences and Women's Fidelity, 101 Yale L.J. 775 (1992), 72, n. 7

Veeck, Bill, Hustler's Handbook (New York: Putnam, 1965), 412, n. 15

Vetter, Jan, Commentary on Multiemployer Bargaining Rules: Searching for the Right Questions, 75 Virginia L.Rev. 285 (1989), 238, n. 6

Viscusi, W. Kip, Reforming Products Liability (Cambridge, Mass.: Harvard University Press, 1991), 752, n. 18

Voy, Robert, Drugs, Sports and Politics (Champaign, Ill.: Leisure Press, 1991), 42, n. 19, 699, n. 10

Waicukauski, Ron, The Regulation of Academic Standards in Intercollegiate Athletics, 1982 Arizona L.J. 79, p. 532, n. 22

Wartman, William, Playing Through: Behind the Scenes on the PGA Tour (New York: William Morrow and Company, Inc., 1990), 658, n. 2

Weiler, Joseph M., Legal Analysis of NHL Players' Contracts, 3 Marquette Sports L.J. 59 (1992), 180, n. 10

Weiler, Paul C., Governing the Workplace: The Future of Labor and Employment Law (Cambridge, Mass.: Harvard University Press, 1990), 65, n. 2, 227, n. 3

Weiler, Paul, C., Medical Malpractice on Trial (Cambridge, Mass.: Harvard University Press, 1991), 751, n. 17

Woolf, Bob, Behind Closed Doors (New York: Atheneum, 1976), 289, n. 2

Yaeger, Don, Shark Attack: Jerry Tarkanian and His Battle With the NCAA and UNLV (New York: Harper Collins, 1992), 498, n. 4

Yaeger, Don, The NCAA's Injustice For All (Champaign, Ill.: Sagamore Publishing, 1991), 513, n. 9

Yasser, Raymond L., Are Scholarship Athletes At Big–Time Programs Really University Employees?—You Bet They Are!, 9 Black L.J. 65 (1984), 737, n. 11

Yasser, Raymond L., Liability for Sports Injuries, in Gary Uberstine, ed., Law of Professional and Amateur Sport (Deerfield, Ill.: Clark, Boardman, and Callaghan, 1991), 710, n. 1

York, Daniel S., The Professional Sports Community Protection Act: Congress' Best Response to Raiders, 38 Hastings L.J. 345 (1987), 410, n. 14

Zimbalist, Andrew, Baseball and Billions, (New York: Basic Books, 1992), 206, n. 1, 351, n. 1, 412, n. 15

Zimbalist, Andrew, Salaries and Performance: Beyond the Scully Model, in Paul M. Sommers, Diamonds Are Forever: The Business of Baseball (Washington, D.C: Brookings, 1992), 277, n. 24.

Index

Professional sports leagues, teams, and athletes are listed under their respective sports. All other individuals are listed according to their professions.

†